T0137012

IFIP Advances in Information and Communication Technology

504

IFIP – The International Federation for Information Processing

IFIP was founded in 1960 under the auspices of UNESCO, following the first World Computer Congress held in Paris the previous year. A federation for societies working in information processing, IFIP's aim is two-fold: to support information processing in the countries of its members and to encourage technology transfer to developing nations. As its mission statement clearly states:

IFIP is the global non-profit federation of societies of ICT professionals that aims at achieving a worldwide professional and socially responsible development and application of information and communication technologies.

IFIP is a non-profit-making organization, run almost solely by 2500 volunteers. It operates through a number of technical committees and working groups, which organize events and publications. IFIP's events range from large international open conferences to working conferences and local seminars.

The flagship event is the IFIP World Computer Congress, at which both invited and contributed papers are presented. Contributed papers are rigorously refereed and the rejection rate is high.

As with the Congress, participation in the open conferences is open to all and papers may be invited or submitted. Again, submitted papers are stringently refereed.

The working conferences are structured differently. They are usually run by a working group and attendance is generally smaller and occasionally by invitation only. Their purpose is to create an atmosphere conducive to innovation and development. Refereeing is also rigorous and papers are subjected to extensive group discussion.

Publications arising from IFIP events vary. The papers presented at the IFIP World Computer Congress and at open conferences are published as conference proceedings, while the results of the working conferences are often published as collections of selected and edited papers.

IFIP distinguishes three types of institutional membership: Country Representative Members, Members at Large, and Associate Members. The type of organization that can apply for membership is a wide variety and includes national or international societies of individual computer scientists/ICT professionals, associations or federations of such societies, government institutions/government related organizations, national or international research institutes or consortia, universities, academies of sciences, companies, national or international associations or federations of companies.

More information about this series at http://www.springer.com/series/6102

Jyoti Choudrie · M. Sirajul Islam
Fathul Wahid · Julian M. Bass
Johanes Eka Priyatma (Eds.)

Information
and Communication
Technologies
for Development

14th IFIP WG 9.4 International Conference
on Social Implications of Computers
in Developing Countries, ICT4D 2017
Yogyakarta, Indonesia, May 22–24, 2017
Proceedings

 Springer

Editors
Jyoti Choudrie
University of Hertfordshire
Hatfield
UK

M. Sirajul Islam
Örebro University
Örebro
Sweden

Fathul Wahid
Universitas Islam Indonesia
Yogyakarta
Indonesia

Julian M. Bass
University of Salford
Salford
UK

Johanes Eka Priyatma
Sanata Dharma University
Yogyakarta
Indonesia

ISSN 1868-4238   ISSN 1868-422X   (electronic)
IFIP Advances in Information and Communication Technology
ISBN 978-3-030-09639-7   ISBN 978-3-319-59111-7   (eBook)
DOI 10.1007/978-3-319-59111-7

Preface

This book comprises the papers presented at the 14th International Conference on Social Implications of Computers in Developing Countries (IFIP WG 9.4 2017 Conference) held in Yogyakarta, Indonesia, May 22–24, 2017. The theme of the conference was "ICTs for Promoting Social Harmony: Towards a Sustainable Information Society." A harmonious society is viewed as a peaceful and balanced "connected whole" in a transformed social dynamic, where there is a sustainable exchange of resources and development taking place through mutual agreement. As "all problems of existence are essentially problems of harmony," the goal of development is apparently not only to ensure social harmony, but also to minimize the elements that undermine or disrupt the connected whole. Ideally, the information society is seen as a "classless and conflictless" inclusive community, which strives to use technologies to diminish structural barriers, democratize information, balance power with dependency, and transform human values. However, in reality, a harmonious society faces several challenges including political and religious extremism, infringement of privacy and security, as well as disparity of wealth and social disconnection. As we are unavoidably intermingling toward a complex environment of the information society, we need to critically investigate the social construction role of information technology especially in the contexts of peace and conflict, cooperation, and development of human capital for creating a sustainable world.

Within this spirit, a call for tracks was distributed and 17 track proposals were submitted, of which 13 were finally selected:

1. Large-Scale and Complex Information Systems for Development
2. Women Empowerment and Gender Justice
3. Social Mechanisms of ICT-Enabled Development
4. The Data Revolution and Sustainable Development Goals
5. Critical Perspectives on ICT and Open Innovation for Development
6. The Contribution of Practice Theories to ICT for Development
7. Agile Development
8. Indigenous and Local Community-Grounded ICT Developments
9. Global Sourcing and Development
10. Sustainability in ICT4D
11. Information Systems Development and Implementation in Southeast Asia
12. IPID and Graduate Student Track
13. General

The IFIP WG 9.4 2017 Conference began a novel tradition of published proceedings in collaboration with Springer in the IFIP *Advances in Information and Communication Technology* (IFIP AICT) series. The main purpose for this novelty is to sustain and preserve the papers and offer a digital space that is accessible and visible to a larger audience. This book consisting of 71 papers offers three keynote submissions, with the remaining 68 being selected from 118 submissions, following a blind, rigorous review process assisted by over 150 peers from more than 40 countries. We thank Springer for their service in publishing the proceedings of this conference.

For a large event like this conference to happen, a considerable effort by numerous individuals is required. For this, we begin by thanking the 71 members of the Program Committee, the local arrangements chairs, and 123 additional reviewers for their enormous efforts in reviewing the submitted papers. We also express gratitude to all the sponsors: the IFIP WG 9.4 (ifipwg94.org), the Swedish Program for ICT in Developing Regions (SPIDER, spidercenter.org), International Network for Postgraduate Students in the area of ICT4D (IPID, ipid.se), UIINet (uii.net.id), and Cisco Indonesia (cisco. com/c/en_id/).

Special thanks go to the hosts of this conference, Universitas Islam Indonesia (UII, uii.ac.id) and Sanata Dharma University (USD, usd.ac.id). Both these private universities are among the pioneers of higher learning in Indonesia and are located in Yogyakarta, one of the most livable cities in Indonesia. Yogyakarta has more than 100 higher education institutions and is the city of tolerance. Yogyakarta is a melting pot of various cultures from all corners of Indonesia and is perhaps the pre-eminent city of culture in Indonesia. It was a great pleasure to hold the IFIP WG 9.4 2017 Conference in this special place.

May 2017

Jyoti Choudrie
M. Sirajul Islam
Fathul Wahid
Julian M. Bass
Johanes Eka Priyatma

Organization

Conference Chairs

Fathul Wahid	Universitas Islam Indonesia, Indonesia
Julian M. Bass	University of Salford, UK
Johanes Eka Priyatma	Sanata Dharma University, Indonesia

Program Chairs

Jyoti Choudrie	University of Hertfordshire, UK
M. Sirajul Islam	Örebro University, Sweden

Local Arrangements Chairs

Mukhamad Andri Setiawan	Universitas Islam Indonesia, Indonesia
Paulina Heruningsih Prima Rosa	Sanata Dharma University, Indonesia
Ari Sujarwo	Universitas Islam Indonesia, Indonesia
Agnes Maria Polina	Sanata Dharma University, Indonesia

Program Committee

Rose Alinda Alias	Universiti Teknologi Malaysia, Malaysia
David Allen	University of Leeds, UK
Ian Allison	University of West of Scotland, UK
Gary Cifuentes Alvarez	University of Los Andes, Colombia
Antonio Díaz Andrade	Auckland University of Technology, New Zealand
Ime Asangansi	eHealth4everyone.com
Arlene Bailey	The University of the West Indies at Mona, Jamaica
Julian M. Bass	University of Salford, UK
Caitlin Bentley	Nanyang Technological University, Singapore
David F. Birks	University of Winchester, UK
Stephen Burgess	Victoria University, Australia
Gary Burnett	Florida State University, USA
Ineke Buskens	UNU Computing and Society, Macau, SAR China
Wallace Chigona	University of Cape Town, South Africa
Brian Corbitt	RMIT University, Australia
Abubakar A. Dahiru	Robert Gordon University, UK
Robert Davison	City University of Hong Kong, Hong Kong, SAR China
Andy Dearden	Sheffield Hallam University, UK
Teduh Dirgahayu	Universitas Islam Indonesia, Indonesia

Mega Subramaniam	University of Maryland, USA
Felix Tan	Auckland University of Technology, New Zealand
Angsana A. Techatassanasoontorn	Auckland University of Technology, New Zealand
Devendra Thapa	University of Agder, Norway
Alvin Yeo Wee	Universiti Malaysia Sarawak, Malaysia
Chris Westrup	Manchester Business School, UK
Heike Winschiers-Theophilus	Namibia University of Science and Technology, Namibia
Tariq Zaman	Universiti Malaysia Sarawak, Malaysia
Pär-Ola Zander	Aalborg University, Denmark
Aljona Zorina	University of Leeds, UK

Additional Reviewers

Nor Zairah Ab.Rahim
Pamela Abbott
Noor Hazana Abdullah
Norris Syed Abdullah
Eric Adu-Gyamfi
Noor Hazlina Ahmad
Adel Alfalah
Samer Alkhouli
Annika Andersson
Gugulethu Baduza
Rehema Baguma
Ahmad Suhaimi Baharudin
Pierre Bakunzibake
Peter Bednar
Zakariya Belkhamza
David F. Birks
Adele Botha
Irwin Brown
Ann Bygholm
Maria Castro
Francis Chuah
Stephanie Hui Wen Chuan
Carina de Villiers
Eduardo Diniz
Sifiso Dlamini
Bill Doolin
Mohammad Dalvi Esfahani
Haemiwan Z. Fathony
Schubert Foo
Merryl Ford

Ellen Fruijtier
Mikael Gebre-Mariam
Leila Goosen
Farzana Quoquab Habib
Hasliza Abdul Halim
Mohd. Rizal Abdul Hamid
Nor Aziati Abdul Hamid
Xiong Han
Haniruzila Hanifah
Mathias Hatakka
Niall Hayes
Marlien Herselman
Roshan Hewapathirana
Janet Ho
Cheah Jun Hwa
Joshua Ignatius
Osama Isaac
Jens Kaasbøll
Normalini Md Kassim
Saifuddin Khalid
Hanna Krasnova
Kirstin Krauss
Caroline Wamala Larsson
Jasmine Yeap Ai Leen
Han-Teng Liao
Gan Pei Ling
May Chiun Lo
Saravanan Nathan Lurudusamy
Imran Mahmud
Sreeja Manghat

Machdel Matthee
Christine Mburu
Mumtaz Memon
Shegaw Anagaw Mengiste
Jyoti Mishra
Suraya Miskon
Abang Azlan Mohamad
Christina Mörtberg
Emilio Mosse
Brown Msiska
Hafeni Mthoko
Solange Mukamurenzi
Nadia Musa
Ahmed Mutahar
Maha Lecumy Narayanansamy
Kogilah Narayanasamy
Patrick Nathan
Saravanan Nathan
Simon Pettersen Nguyen
José Nhavoto
Amaka Nwanekezie
Uchenna Nwanekezie
Jacki O'Neill
Basil Okontah
Carol Ou
Egil Øvrelid
Caroline Pade-Khene
Xin Pei
Jackie Phahlamohlaka
Maryam Rabiee
Syed Abidur Rahman
Elham Rostami

Nor Hasliza Md Saad
Khalid Saifuddin
Devi Sakti
Katja Sarajeva
Sharidatul Akma Abu Seman
Sharmini Sharmini
Mira Slavova
Ronel Smith
Constantino Sotomane
Larry Stillman
Seyedeh Khadijeh Taghizadeh
Sayyen Teoh
Lei Mee Thien
Santhamery Thominathan
Hiram Ting
Antonios Tsertsidis
Gaki Tshering
Pitso Tsibolane
Hossana Twinomurinzi
Damascene Twizeyimana
Derval Usher
Ali Vafa
Ranjan Vaidya
Judy van Biljon
Christine Wanjiru
Lee Heng Wei
Siew Fan Wong
Maryati Mohd. Yusof
Xue Zhang
Yingqin Zheng
Aljona Zorina

Contents

Women Empowerment and Gender Justice

Social Mechanisms of ICT-Enabled Development

The Data Revolution and Sustainable Development Goals

Critical Perspectives on ICT and Open Innovation for Development

The Contribution of Practice Theories to ICT for Development

Agile Development

Information Systems Development and Implementation in Southeast Asia

Graduate Student Track (IPID)

Keynotes

Facilitating Social Harmony Through ICTs

Robert M. Davison[(⊠)] ⓘ

City University of Hong Kong, Kowloon Tong, Hong Kong
isrobert@cityu.edu.hk

Abstract. Social Harmony involves the peaceful interaction of people in a social setting. In this keynote address I briefly examine the historical antecedents of social harmony and identify some of the salient barriers to its realisations, before selecting examples of ways in which ICT can contribute to social harmony, with particular attention to the Asian region. I conclude by looking ahead to future research opportunities.

1 Introduction

Normatively, I would hope that social harmony is the kind of concept that we can easily understand. For me, social harmony refers to the peaceful interaction of people in a social group, and thus conveys a very positive message. However, social harmony has been misappropriated in contemporary China, where the government has co-opted it into the "Socialist Harmonious Society" slogan used as a form of propaganda that promotes social stability, yet is also associated with the crack down on protests and the arrests of journalists and opinion leaders on social media. In Chinese Internet slang, "to harmonize" now means "to censor", as occurs when social media content or news content is removed if it touches on sensitive topics. Unfortunately, even social harmony has been co-opted to the dark side.

Indeed, notwithstanding the Chinese context, the positive sense of social harmony does not get much attention in the news and media these days. Quite the opposite as most news media revel in gory depictions of violence, accidents, unhappiness, victimisation, fake news, malicious rumours and gossip, indeed anything but social harmony. As a species, we have a huge capacity for mutual intolerance, hate and a litany of inhumane behaviours that we seem to take delight in wreaking on each other. While the underlying motives for this behaviour lie in the realm of psychology, ICT applications often play an instrumental role in the conveyance of this intolerance, as encountered in the nauseous behaviour of online trolls and the 'shock jocks' of extreme opinion, very often through social media channels. It is tempting to imagine that this tendency for intolerance and hate is genetically hardwired in a survival mechanism of which we are entirely unaware (cf. [1]). But this seems to be too easy an excuse and diminishes any claim we have to being a higher species, equipped with wisdom (*homo sapiens*), if we unthinkingly use that wisdom in such unpleasant ways.

Nevertheless, I was delighted when I learned that the IFIP WG 9.4 conference chairs had selected as a theme 'Facilitating Social Harmony through ICTs'. I felt that this would be an opportunity for us to celebrate the social positives of ICT, to demonstrate

J. Choudrie et al. (Eds.): ICT4D 2017, IFIP AICT 504, pp. 3–9, 2017.
DOI: 10.1007/978-3-319-59111-7_1

that ICT can indeed facilitate social harmony in different ways. I greatly look forward to listening to the presentations in the conference theme track. I felt even more honoured to be invited as a keynote speaker, for this provided me with the opportunity to select this important conference theme as my topic.

However, my initial enthusiasm for the topic waned a little when I started to collect my thoughts and write this paper. It is one thing to agree that ICT-facilitated social harmony is a good thing, but quite another to talk about it for an hour with wit and erudition. There are certainly many inspiring examples of ICT-driven community development (as well as digital enablement at the bottom of the pyramid) that undoubtedly bring significant benefits at the bottom of the pyramid, alleviating the worst cases of poverty. For instance, the Free Lunch for Children project in China [2] and the Ceibal project to bring laptops to children in Uruguay [3]. Another example is the www.colab.re project in Brazil, designed to bring citizens and local governments closer together by locating common interests and solving problems. However, these examples are not quite the same thing as ICT-facilitated social harmony, even though they are closely related and social harmony may be an unintended consequence.

Let me reassure you that I have found good examples of ICTs facilitating social harmony. Indeed, one example that I hope to visit when I am in Yogyakarta is just a few kilometres from our conference site and I have found several others in the South East Asian region, as well as around the world, but before I get to the examples, I need to delve into the historical and cultural context of social harmony.

2 Historical and Cultural Context

In order to position social harmony in its historical context, I would like to consider some ancient traditions. In China, the origins of social harmony are often attributed to the teachings of Confucius (551–479 BC), who encouraged discussions of qin, one of the earliest forms of music in China. Qin music embodied the concept of harmony as it sought to balance the yin and yang associated with different aspects of the music, as well as the different weather conditions associated with the four seasons when the music might be played. This qin music was not written solely to please the ears, but instead to encourage people to moderate their likes and dislikes and help them achieve a 'correct direction' in life, achieving a balance between humans, society and the natural environment. Thus, in Confucian terms, just as qin music combining different instruments, tones, notes, speeds, keys, etc. could combine harmoniously, so human society could also, with its blend of different temperaments, personalities, preferences and tastes, combine in a harmonious social fashion with the peaceful interactions of multiple individuals who are transformed and civilised.

Harmony remains a key component of many musical traditions, where consonance and dissonance are resolved. For instance, the traditional Javanese musical instrument known as the *Angklung* also explains the philosophy of harmony. In order to play the angklung effectively, a number of players must cooperate and coordinate their movements. This is believed to enhance teamwork, mutual respect and social harmony, since each member of the team has a specific role to play. The overall message is that to ensure social harmony, people must be patient and work together with others.

A second historical tradition I wish to bring in to this discussion is Greek, whence the English word harmony is derived (via French and Latin) from ἁρμονία (*harmonía*), meaning "agreement or concord", which in turn is cognate with the verb ἁρμόζω (*harmozo*), "to fit together, to join". This brief etymological analysis indicates how harmony is associated with joining things (people, music, nature) together in a smooth fashion. I will return to nature later, but when we are dealing with people, clearly social harmony is a collective notion, involving multiple people or other objects. It is bound up with ideas of togetherness, relationships and a shared sense of belonging. A related concept is social capital, which is associated with social networks and the transactions between people that are characterised by reciprocity, trust and cooperation, all hallmarks of social harmony. Hanifan [4] notes that when there is "goodwill, fellowship, mutual sympathy and social intercourse among a group of individuals and families … there will be an accumulation of social capital, … which may bear a social potentiality sufficient to the substantial improvement of living conditions in the whole community". Social capital is thus something to be encouraged as it can lead to a social state where social harmony is more likely to emerge.

I suggest that a harmonious society will be one that is governed by mutual respect between members and a sense of reciprocity, with people altruistically helping one another. For social harmony in a real or virtual society to be effective, collective efficacy is important, for all the members of the society must work well together with tolerance and respect if that state of harmony is to be achieved and sustained.

Social harmony is a state that is not only peaceful but also founded on cooperation and collaboration, not conflict and dissonance. This does not exclude an economic element, but economic drivers often favour the bold, risk takers with a 'who dares, wins' mentality. As the Greek soldier and historian Thucydides (460–400 BC) is supposed to have remarked "τοῖς τολμῶσιν ἡ τύχη ξύμφορος", i.e. "fortune favours the bold". Such an attitude can induce individualistic competitiveness and exclusiveness, with a slippery slope that leads to conflict and a diminishment of harmony if inequalities emerge. Collective economic benefits can be realised in a socially harmonious way if it is the entire community that benefits, not the individual. I will explore this in more detail below.

In the Chinese context, key cultural elements in the traditional social harmony pantheon are guānxi (關係), héxié (和諧), rénqing (人情) and miànzi (面子). Guanxi, broadly, refers to situation where two or more individuals enjoy a "close and pervasive interpersonal relationship [that] is based on high quality social interactions and the reciprocal exchange of mutual benefits (renqing)" [5]. People who share guanxi target the formation of a state of harmony (héxié) between each other and also protect each other's face (miànzi). Guanxi is ubiquitous in China and is often seen as an essential survival mechanism: without guanxi, it is very hard to do anything related to work or social interaction. The social harmony that is a key component of guanxi is not only a face-to-face phenomenon, but also one that is firmly rooted in online communications. Social media technologies like WeChat and QQ are often used to build and maintain online relationships (guanxi) where interlocutors aim to achieve a state of harmony (hexie) as they interact. Although the desire for a harmonious interaction is a cultural one, the technology effectively supports this interaction by embedding tools central to such communication, as well as more special functions, such as WeChat's 'donating to charity' app.

3 Barriers to the Adoption of ICT

While social media technology may seem ubiquitous, there are in fact many barriers to the access and use of ICTs that may impede the development of ICT-facilitated social harmony. The research unit of the Chinese global telecommunications equipment manufacturer Huawei [6] suggested four key barriers, viz.: availability, affordability, appetite and ability, to digital enablement in developing countries. These barriers equally apply to ICT-driven social harmony.

Availability has two key components. Firstly it relates to the access to the technology, including networks and devices, electrical power supply and high speed infrastructure. Secondly, it relates to the need for local content that meets local needs in local languages. Affordability is a very familiar problem. It not only refers to the purchasing power of the intended users, but also to the value that can be obtained through the use of the technology. Appetite and Ability tap into a different set of issues. Appetite refers to the motivation to use the technology, prompted by questions like "Why do I need it?" and "How will it benefit me?" Appetite can also be related to technophobia: the fear of technology. Finally, and very critically, ability refers to computer literacy and the whole issue of "How can I use the technology?". This is premised on the need for appropriate education.

4 Examples of ICT-Facilitated Social Harmony

In the northern highlands of the island of Borneo, straddling the border between Indonesian Kalimantan and Malaysian Sabah/Sarawak, there are a number of communities that illustrate ideas central to ICT-facilitated social harmony. Two key projects are the eBario village and the eBorneo knowledge fair.

eBario (www.ebario.org) is a project that, starting in 1998, has brought the Internet to remote Kelabit communities in the highlands of northern Sarawak [7, 8]. The project has from the start been premised on close interaction between members of the community in their natural environment and the various researchers and agencies who have supported the project. These interactions give priority to the problems and opportunities that the community itself identifies. Thus the eBario community radio station, which broadcasts in the rapidly disappearing Kelabit language, is operated by the community for the community and features information of relevance to the community. The project includes a telecentre, established to provide access for the community to resources on the Internet including e-health and telemedicine, but also enabling the community to attract tourists who can supplement village income in their community-based tourism project. In these projects, it is the community as a whole which benefits, hence the link to social harmony. The community sells its indigenous Bario rice over the Internet and hopes to attract tourists keen to trek in the surrounding jungle, activities that ensure economic benefits for a disparate range of Bario villagers. The eBario project is donor funded and addresses all four barriers identified by Huawei. The technology itself was provided by donors, who also installed solar panels and a diesel generator to provide a reliable electricity supply. The content is generated locally, in the local Kelabit language. While the initial costs of the project were covered, locals need to generate income from use of the technology. In the Bario school, computers were provided to ensure that school children would learn how to use them as part of the curriculum, thereby addressing the issue of appetite and ability. The views of the Bario villagers who have benefitted from the eBario development are recorded by Tarawe and Harris [9].

Closely linked to eBario is the eBorneo knowledge fair (www.ebkf.org). The knowledge fair is designed to showcase how the use of ICTs can benefit the development of isolated rural communities. Such fairs are designed to allow all participants to learn from and interact with each other in an innovative and dynamic way in order to facilitate the transfer of knowledge. The knowledge fair is designed as a non-hierarchical community event that champions social harmony across the communities.

A few kilometres from our conference location, there is a very local example of a socially harmonious community: Kampung Cyber. http://www.rt36kampoengcyber.com/. As the website mentions: "Sebuah kampung yang penuh potensi dan ingin selalu berkembang. Utamanya berkembang melalui teknologi informasi.", which I loosely translate as "This is a village that always wants to develop, which it will do primarily through IT". Although the village is old, the cyberification of the village, which led to Kampung Cyber, was started in 2008 by Mas Koko, a village resident and graduate from the local Universitas Gadjah Mada. As he explained to me by email, Mas Koko had the objective of bringing not only free Internet to each house in the village, but also, and more importantly, educational programmes that help citizens to build their capacity to leverage the Internet effectively. The project started with just five villagers, who drew on their own savings to buy the necessary equipment but who also shared that equipment with their neighbours, who subsequently became interested in the project. Atmajaya University provided basic computer training for free. In early 2015, they received their first outside funding from a private company which has enabled them to improve the speed of their connections. Currently, many of the villagers are informally employed, seeking to sell their various products, e.g. batik, fishing equipment, T-shirt painting, food, snacks and traditional crafts via the Internet. As a result, the standards of living in the village have improved for the individuals as well as the village as a whole. Facebook is used as a village communication channel for sharing ideas, invitations and meeting minutes. The overall effect is for Kampung Cyber to be a harmonious location for the villagers who live there.

In southern Mexico, Ricardo Gomez is working with an indigenous Tzeltal community in Chiapas state [10] on a multi-year initiative that will involve an indigenous community library, indigenous community radio and what he terms fotohistorias [11], the use of photography to capture the salient elements of the culture. The common thread for the various activities is the local, indigenous notion of "likil cuxlejalil" which translates roughly as "The Good Life". In the Tzeltal indigenous tradition, The Good Life is defined by harmony. Harmony between heart, stomach, and spirit, harmony between individual, family, and community, and harmony in relation to Mother Earth or the environment. This project is therefore very much about social and community harmony and the way it can be enhanced through development programmes.

In Central Kalimantan, Indonesia, Raihani [12] draws on the indigenous Dayak *rumah betang* or long house as "a cultural symbol of harmony amongst different religions and ethnicities". The whole extended family or community would live in a rumah betang, with little privacy and the need for much respect of differences. In similar vein,

Raihani [12] documents how school children are brought up and educated to respect religious differences, just as they would have to in the rumah betang, in line with Indonesia's Pancasila philosophy. As "another feature of the harmonious inter-religious relations" these children described how they sent "short messages via mobile phones" and wrote "on friends' Facebook walls to express greetings" during religious celebrations and festivities such as Eid al-Fitr and Christmas.

In Liberia, Smyth et al. [13] developed a mobile information kiosk as part of the country's post-civil war truth and reconciliation process. The kiosk is called Moses and consists of "an interactive computer system which allows users to browse, watch, create and share video messages". It is thus a means for sharing of stories across the country with the objective of enhancing social harmony, despite very poor levels of Internet infrastructure, power supply and information or computer literacy. Smyth et al. [13] report that the over 900 people who recorded videos with Moses and the several thousand more who watched these videos across the country from 2008–2009 "saw Moses as giving them a voice and connecting them to other Liberians throughout the country". The system itself was often associated with group usage, with a throng of people gathered excitedly around the kiosk, helping each other to use the system, sharing their stories and looking towards a brighter future. Here, social harmony is being achieved as part of the reconciliation process.

5   Closing Thoughts and Future Directions

Social harmony needs intensive maintenance if it is to persist. From an ICT perspective, this means that there is an intensive need for the sharing of ideas, knowledge and best practices; thus communication is critical. Such communication, if online, is likely to involve some form of social media, assuming that Internet access is available. Facebook is very popular is many of these communities, but others include WeChat and Twitter. Email is also reported as being popular for more formal communications. In less well resourced communities, such as parts of West Africa where Internet accessibility is very weak and literacy is low, reliance on more indigenous applications is likely. All stakeholders, especially those in the local community, need to participate in a culture that nurtures the interests of the community as a whole. While ICT-facilitated community development projects are common, these seldom report on any social harmony that results. One might conclude that the lack of evidence suggests the absence of the phenomenon but I am more optimistic: I am certain that social harmony does exist, indeed it is abundant, but we need to find and report on it, sharing our stories. Gomez's use of fotohistorias provides us with a unique new tool that is well adapted to recording social harmony in practice.

Acknowledgements. I very much appreciate reflections and suggestions from Julian Bass, Ricardo Gomez, Alexandre Graeml, Roger Harris, Safirotu Khoir, Shirin Madon, Antonius Sasongko WK (Koko Mas) and Yingqin Zheng.

References

1. Eres, R., Louis, W.R., Molenberghs, P.: Why do people pirate? A neuroimaging investigation. Soc. Neurosci. (2016). http://dx.doi.org/10.1080/17470919.2016.1179671
2. Zheng, Y.Q., Yu, A.: Affordances of social media in collective action: the case for free lunch for children in China. Inf. Syst. J. **26**(3), 289–313 (2016)
3. Winocur, R., Aguerre, C.: Scope and limitations in the evaluation of programs for digital teaching in Latin America: a paradigmatic case: the 'Plan Ceibal'. Iberoamerican Commun. Rev. **5**(1), 59–68 (2011). http://www.infoamerica.org/icr/n05/winocur_aguerre.pdf
4. Hanifan, L.J.: The rural school community center. Ann. Am. Acad. Polit. Soc. Sci. **67**, 130–138 (1916)
5. Ou, C.X.J., Pavlou, P.A., Davison, R.M.: Swift Guanxi in online marketplaces: the role of computer-mediated-communication technologies. Manag. Inf. Syst. Q. **38**(1), 209–230 (2014)
6. Huawei: Connecting the Future: Digital Enablement: Bridging the Digital Divide to Connect People and Society. White Paper, 43 pages (2015). http://www.huawei.com/minisite/digital-enablement/download/Digital+Enablement_ENGLISH+online.pdf
7. Harris, R.W.: Tourism in Bario, Sarawak, Malaysia: a case study of pro-poor community based tourism integrated into community development. Asia Pac. J. Tourism Res.: Spec. Issue Pro-Poor Tourism: Linking Tourism Dev. Poverty Reduction **14**(2), 125–135 (2009)
8. Harris, C.A., Harris, R.W.: Information and communication technologies for cultural transmission among indigenous peoples. Electron. J. Inf. Syst. Dev. Countries **45**(2), 1–19 (2011)
9. Tarawe, J., Harris, R.W.: Stories from eBario. In: Living the Information Society Conference, Makati, Philippines, 23–24 April 2007
10. Gomez, R., Lefthand-Begay, C., Berwick, J., Zubair, C., Iribe, Y., Mora, S.: Indigenous information system in Chiapas, Mexico: integrating community radio, library and impact assessment for community development. In: Proceedings of iConference, Wuhan, China, March 2017
11. Gomez, R., Vannini, S.: Notions of home and sense of belonging in the context of migration in a journey through participatory photography. Electron. J. Inf. Syst. Dev. Countries **78**(1), 1–46 (2017)
12. Raihani, R.: Creating a culture of religious tolerance in an Indonesian school. SE Asia Res. **22**(4), 541–560 (2014)
13. Smyth, T.N., Etherton, J., Best, M.L.: Moses: exploring new ground in media and post-conflict reconciliation. In: CHI: Crisis Informatics, pp. 1059–1068 (2010). http://dl.acm.org/citation.cfm?id=1753484

Theoretical Framing of ICT4D Research

Chrisanthi Avgerou[(⊠)]

London School of Economics, London, UK
c.avgerou@lse.ac.uk

Abstract. Research on information and communication technologies for development (ICT4D) requires the combination of multiple theoretical strands. Central among them are the foundational theories on technology, on context, and on socio-economic development. In addition, ICT4D research draws from middle range theories, which shed light on specific topics of ICT related phenomena in the context of a developing world. In this paper, I explain what each of the three foundational theories is about and indicate the need for middle range theories. I suggest that the challenge for ICT4D research is to draw creatively from existing theoretical debates and to construct analytical routes and theoretical propositions suitable for the complex phenomena of ICT and development.

Keywords: ICT4D · Theory of technology · Contextual research · Socio-economic development · Middle range theory

1 Introduction

Research on ICT in developing countries emerged in the 1980s, with studies of computer diffusion in various countries and studies of government policy about the use of computers in various sectors [1–3]. At that time, governments in developing countries with pressing socio-economic needs used to tax computers as luxuries. Since in the then global economy the competitive advantage of many developing countries was cheap labour, government economists did not see computerization as a prudent policy. They feared that automating factories and offices would deprive their economies of much needed jobs in industrial and service sectors. However, early researchers of what came to be known as 'ICT for development' (ICT4D) shared the belief that computers can solve many of the severe problems confronting developing economies and societies, such as grossly inefficient government administration, inadequate provision of health care and education and inability to compete in a global economy. If only poor countries could acquire computers and engineering know-how to put them in effective use!

In the 1990s, concern about the slow diffusion of computers was compounded with concern about limited telecommunications infrastructures, which severely restricted access to the internet. It was about that time that international development organizations (the World Bank, various UN agencies, ITU, national development aid organizations such as Canada's IDRC) and multiple NGOs started promoting ICT and access to the web. The discourse on the digital divide/digital inclusion has been anchored on the argument that ICT is necessary for development. Numerous publications of international development agencies produced tables correlating country development and internet

J. Choudrie et al. (Eds.): ICT4D 2017, IFIP AICT 504, pp. 10–23, 2017.
DOI: 10.1007/978-3-319-59111-7_2

accessibility indexes [4–8], projecting a cause and effect relationship of ICT and development. At the top of the tables are countries that achieved high ICT diffusion with dynamic privatized telecommunication service providers; they are rich and have well educated and healthy population and democratic regimes. At the bottom of the tables are countries with pitifully little computing and telecommunication capacity; they are the poorest of the poor with low human development indicators and failed states. The causality between ICT diffusion and economic growth is supported with basic arguments about ICT and economic performance from neo-classical and institutional economic theories [9]. Moreover, as good government, fundamental democratic principles of freedom, equality, liberal education and health assume central importance in the debates of international development [4, 10], it is suggested that ICT is indispensable means for achieving such developmental objectives too.

Anecdotal evidence of transformative effects of ICT helped to popularise the causal claims about ICT and development. Women of a remote village on the Andes were selling handicrafts over the internet to American customers without ever having to leave their village or change their traditional lifestyle. Fishermen in Kerala started getting better prices for their catch as they received information on their mobiles about fish prices in the markets of different towns while they were still at sea. Indian villagers also made online requests and received government certificates in information telecentres without having to travel to towns and queue for hours in government offices. More than that, e-government software empowered them to keep government officials accountable by allowing them to file electronically grievances if they were not satisfied with government services.

Research on the implementation and use of computers and the internet in various types of organizations and in communities of developing countries, showed a more complex relationship of ICT and development. At close examination, the anecdotal stories of transformational ICT uses were shown to be more complex than initially reported. The e-commerce activities of the women on the Andes village depended on the facilitatory business skills of a Dutch visitor to the village, who set up their web page for orders, sales and payments. Other women's cooperatives that set up an online presence for their handicrafts could not that easily succeed in selling to international markets [11]. Keralite fishermen's optimal pricing on their catch had various other important conditions at play in addition to the use of mobiles [12]. And telecentres in Indian villages did not quite transform the relationship of Indian villagers with the Indian government [13]. Many of them struggled to be sustained and with time disappeared [14].

This is not to conclude that ICT diffusion has not been contributing developmental effects. In many developing countries, socio-economic conditions have been improving the last three decades; as millions of families have been lifted out of extreme poverty, ICT has been increasingly used in all sectors and all countries. Although not as ordinarily present as in the global North, computers, internet connectivity and mobile phones are found almost everywhere and are visible in the practices of all development policies. It is reasonable to assume that ICT plays an enabling role in socio-economic improvements. But a simple cause and effect relationship between ICT diffusion and development outcomes is misleading because it hides other conditions at play, and the challenge for ICT4D research is to understand and explain the complex processes of ICT-mediated socio-economic change.

For this, a lot can be learnt from the general theoretical debates on the relationship of ICT and organizational change in the Information Systems (IS) field. We need to add theoretical capacity to address two salient aspects of ICT4D research: the developing countries context and socio-economic development [15–17]. In this paper, I discuss the theoretical framing of ICT4D research as a combination of foundational theories on technology, context and development, with middle range theories, that is, theories of a less abstract nature, which are relevant for the specific research questions under investigation.

2 Theories of Technology

IS research has produced valuable insights on the theoretical relationship of ICT and organizational change by focusing on the interaction of individuals with ICT artefacts in the performance of organizational tasks. Seminal contributions to that end include Markus's [18] explanation of resistance to change, Markus and Robey's [19] essay on the causal structure of IT and organizational change, and Orlikowski and Iacono's [20] theorization of the ICT artefact. These contributions set foundations about the causal relationship between ICT artefacts and social change, which avoid technology deterministic and social deterministic theses. The former locates causal agency solely at the properties of technology and forms propositions of universal impact of specific technologies, irrespective of social context, while the latter locates causal agency at the social alone, positing that the material properties of technology do not matter as far as human societies are concerned [21]. Rejecting both technology and social determinism as inadequate to explain IS phenomena, IS research developed perspectives that locate causality at the interaction of people with technology and consider IS phenomena as being formed by the engagement of indiviual actors with IT artefacts in their social context.

Several research streams have elaborated on the IT/human actor relationship as the fundamental causal explanation of IS phenomena. They include the sociotechnical systems approach [22, 23] and various approaches taken from the interdisciplinary field of Science and Technology Studies (STS) [24–26] that articulate propositions about the way IS innovation happens. Particularly influential from among the STS theories has been actor network theory (ANT), which overcomes the lurking risk of social determinism by recognising technology itself as 'actor' and by seeing reality as formed by the actions of hybrid sociotechnical entities [27–30]. More recently, the theorization of the relationship between IT and human action has focused on the notion of 'socio-materiality' [31–37]. A major stream of arguments in this debate reaffirms the idea that IS phenomena result from the dynamic relation of the material properties of ICT with the socially derived ability of their human participants to act. It elaborates on the way ICT artefacts and people interact to bring about IS phenomena, using concepts such as 'affordances' [32, 35, 38], 'imbrications' [39], or 'functions' [40]. According to these views, both the ICT artefact and the human actor possess causal capacity in the formation of IS phenomena. They are ontologically independent (i.e. one may disappear and the other may still exist) and epistemologically separable (i.e. each of them can be studied and understood without studying the other).

An alternative perspective takes its departure from an assumption of ontological primacy of actions rather than entities – whether artefacts of human beings. It considers IS phenomena as mutually re-configuring 'ensembles' of human and technology entities that are constantly producing/reproducing or changing each other [33, 36, 41]. This view implies that IS phenomena are constituted by a dynamic human and technology entanglement (intra-actions). Neither technologies nor people have an independent, self-contained existence and they are epistemologically inseparable – that is, impossible to understand by studying them as independent entities.

Both versions of sociomateriality theory focus on micro-settings of situated practice where intra-actions and interactions of ICT artefacts and human beings occur. They both allude to broader contexts of IS phenomena [36, 38, 42], but neither elaborates on the way contexts beyond situated practice are implicated in IS phenomena. Context remains elusive in the IS theories of sociomateriality and this limits their explanatory capacity in ICT4D research.

3   Contextualizing the Study of ICT

A distinguishing feature of ICT4D research is that it includes national, regional or community conditions and processes in the explanation of IS phenomena. But such contextual research is confronted with the question of what, out of the infinite number of conditions and processes amidst which IS phenomena are formed, need to be accounted for [17, 43]. In other words, what is relevant context for ICT4D phenomena?

I define context as the processes and conditions, other than the constituent causal sociomaterial interactions (or intra-actions) of IS phenomena, that affect their formation and are effected by them. In other words, context refers to conditions and processes in the environment of an observed IS phenomenon. For example, an information system of a doctor's surgery consultation involves the interaction of a knowledgeable actor (the doctor) and a complex set of software/hardware/telecommunications artefacts. A description of the doctor's interaction with the system's functionality provides a rudimentary explanation of the ICT-mediated medical consultation, diagnosis and treatment decision. But we need to consider much more than the clinician/IT interaction to find answers to questions of interest in ICT4D research. For example, to understand whether and how a computerised clinician consultation system may help doctors to treat more effectively the population of a village, a city, or a country and improve population health outcomes or to explain why such systems may result in variation of health service delivery we may need to examine the organizational structures and processes of the wider health care system and the life conditions and health vulnerabilities of the population [44]. The theoretical challenge for contextual research is to identify what else, beyond the constituent parts of an information system (i.e. the functionality of the technology, the behavioural characteristics of the doctor, and their interaction), needs to be taken into account to construct convincing explanation of IS phenomena and to assess their developmental impact.

Contextualization is the research design concerned with the identification of relevant context. It involves two decisions: (a) the choice of conditions and processes of the environment of a focal IS phenomenon to be studied by the research and (b) the choice of domains to be researched as the phenomenon's environment.

3.1   Identifying Relevant Contextual Conditions and Processes

ICT4D research has studied a large variety of contextual aspects related with culture, power structures, history, etc. Increasingly, these are not ad hoc findings of empirical studies but derived from middle range theories adopted to address specific research questions. For example, in our research of entrepreneurial opportunities created by the internet in developing countries [45], my co-author and I first agreed that, in order to understand why the diffusion of the internet is having widespread entrepreneurial effects in some regions in the world and almost no such effects in others, we should consider entrepreneurial activity as a socially embedded process. There are other ways to explain entrepreneurial activity, for example by studying the behavioural characteristics of the individual entrepreneur, but our interest was in understanding why individuals come to start doing business online is some regions and not others. From preliminary research in China we understood that 'net-preneurs' in that country were clustered in some villages and towns and they all relied at the time of our research on the services of the giant IT services company Taobao. Existing knowledge couldn't explain why starting business on the internet was clustered in communities. We thought it a paradox that, while the internet overcomes information asymmetries, shrinks physical distance, and enables business collaboration and economic exchange from any place, entrepreneurship was not occurring randomly but was clustered.

We read a lot about clustering and entrepreneurship, ICT innovation, competition and collaboration and e-commerce. We found that there had been research that paid attention to the social embeddedness of internet-based activities in IS research and organizational studies, mostly drawing from the importance of networked social relations [46–49]. Relational embeddedness was therefore a promising theory to explain our puzzling observation of entrepreneurial clustering. But we thought that there were also other conditions enabling the formation of the Chinese clusters, which were not considered in the theories of relational embeddedness. We needed, for example, a conceptual language to address the role of the ICT services provider, on whom the net-preneurs so heavily relied. We thought that the institutional structure of the Chinese economy had also something to do with the emergence of small-scale online new business ventures by large numbers of people without prior business experience. This led us to complement the relational embeddedness approach for the study of the conduct of online business with a version of institutional embeddedness proposed by the economic historian Karl Polanyi and his followers [50]. These middle range theories of social embeddedness led us to construct an explanation of the emergence of entrepreneurial clusters in Chinese communities in terms of some specific institutional conditions of the Chinese political economy, the ICT services sector and aspects of culture in contemporary China.

Unlike the very abstract theories about the fundamental nature of social phenomena, such as the theories of technology I outlined in the previous section, middle range theories are relevant for specific topics [51]. The grounding of contextual explanation in middle range theory guides attention to contextual factors that may contribute to bringing about an observed phenomenon and the mechanisms through which they do so. It strengthens the ICT4D field by allowing us to trace the variation of research findings produced in different empirical studies [52]. But the choice of middle range theory limits research attention to the constructs of the theories we use. In ICT4D research we tend to use theories from social science fields, most frequently organizational theory, behavioural or social psychology, sociology and economics. This has resulted in studies that consider only social aspects of context, as in the example of our research of Chinese net-preneurship. Notable for their rarity are explanations that account for material/technological aspects of the environment of ICT4D phenomena, including temporal and spatial characteristics and material life conditions. It is odd that most IS research adopts a sociomaterial perspective of IS phenomena but a purely social perspective of their context. This is a weakness that I hope future ICT4D research will overcome by developing sociomaterial theoretical perspectives of the broader setting of IS phenomena.

3.2 Identifying Relevant Domains of Context

While in most IS research the assumed context of IS phenomena has been the organization in which ICT systems are implemented and used, ICT4D research tends to extend the research to domains of enquiry such as communities, countries, or global institutions. As I noted above, our research tends to consider context as a social domain, and we usually seek to unravel influences on the shaping of IS phenomena from social collectives that are assumed to be layered, typically organizations, regions, countries and the world at large. Our research design often involves cross-level or multi-level research strategies [53–55]. The layered view of social collectives is underpinned by a systems theory perspective, according to which social collectives emerge from the interaction of their sub-systems and, subsequently, they influence the interactions among their constituent subsystems. A good example of this is research that adopted Pettigrew's 'contextualist' ideas [56] and studied IS development and impact as a process of change that unfolds through time under organizational and national influences [57, 58]. Walsham's [58] case studies of IS development explained key decisions and actions of IS development with reference to the changing culture and politics of the organization, both linked to national socio-economic and political changes. Similarly, Madon's [57] case study of the introduction of computer based information systems in local administration offices in India explained their limited impact by showing how officers made sense of and used that innovation in the context of the layered Indian administration as well as the broader culture and social stratification of India.

The layered contextualization approach is compatible with and can be supported by middle range theories in established social sciences, such as political economy and sociology. But it has been criticised for reifying conventional notions of social structures. An alternative approach is achieved by tracing relations of the constituent parts of an IS phenomenon with other artefacts, individuals, and social groups contributing to its formation [59, 60]. In such relational approaches the study of IS phenomena may include influences from generally recognizable categories of social collectives, such as organizations and national states, but not necessarily in a layered order. Without levels of analysis that associate a phenomenon with assumed enduring social structures, this relational contextualization approach is open ended and the identification of contextual entities that create conditions of possibility of a phenomenon is a matter of empirical investigation in specific cases. The tracing of relevant context by examining relations of the constituent entities and processes of a focal phenomenon with a more extended range of entities or processes is a research design with the potential to develop powerful new explanatory theory.

4 Drawing from Theories of Socio-Economic Development

Socio-economic development is a multidisciplinary academic field in its own right. What do we seek to gain from its theories and how can we find our way in this complex area of academic research and policy practice? So far, ICT4D research has derived from development theories mostly definitions of desirable ends that ICT innovation should aspire to serve and to a lesser extent an understanding of the processes for achieving them.

Two means/ends relationships between ICT and development are discernible in ICT4D research. The first adopts the notion of development as economic growth [61] underpinned by the assumption of neo-classical economics that technology increases productivity in organizations and, in an aggregate form, the economy at large. It thus gives rise to cause and effects projections of ICT impact in developing countries that I mentioned in the introduction. In its crudest - yet widespread – form, the economic growth approach to development associates measures of the diffusion of computers, internet connections or mobile phones with increases of Gross Domestic Product (GDP) and employment. For example, the 2015 Human Development Report, quotes a study which estimates that 'if Internet access in developing countries were the same as in developed countries, an estimated $2.2 trillion in GDP and more than 140 million new jobs − 44 million of them in Africa and 65 million in India – could be generated' [62, p 89]. Similarly, Chavoula [63] derives the following estimate from an econometric analysis: 'on average, a 1% increase in mobile telephony users for every 100 people would increase per capita GDP by 0.39%, 0.26% and 0.15% for the upper-middle-, low-middle- and low-income countries, respectively'.

IS research has elaborated nuanced variants of ICT and economic performance, according to which productivity and economic growth are not just accrued from investment in ICTs but require management and policy interventions for organizational and institutional change [64, 65]. Socio-economic analyses of ICT and economic growth have also drawn from alternative economic approaches, which shift attention to other indicators of economic change, such as transaction costs [66] and competitiveness [6], and emphasise the importance of social institutions [67, Chap. 17]. In promoting ICT diffusion, international development agencies too explain that the way ICT innovation contributes to economic performance of organizations, sectors and countries is multifaceted and marred with uncertainty [5]. In short, economic developmental outcomes do not result from the diffusion of ICT alone, and policy makers have to muddle through models that associate economic growth benefits of ICT with government interventions for regulation, structural reforms, education and social welfare [68]. This is clearly an area where ICT4D research can make important contributions. We should endeavour to answer the question: what does it take for ICT innovation to contribute to economic effects such as business creation, employment, elimination of poverty, government revenue generation to fund social services programmes?

The second perspective of development that has been influential in ICT4D research, centres on the notion of 'human development', which underpins the UNDP's Human Development reports, and the UN's initiatives known as Millennium Development Goals and Agenda for Sustainable Development (Millenium Project 2006; United Nations Development Programme (UNDP) 2016). The notion of human development draws from Amartya Sen's ideas of development as people's freedom to 'lead lives that they value', known also as the 'capabilities approach' [69]. Key concepts in Sen's theory are wellbeing, which refers to a person's 'functionings' (what he/she can do or be) and agency, defined in this theory as the pursuance of what a person values or regards as important. Policies aiming to enhance human development adopt indicators for health, education, work, and political freedom. Income indicators are also included but they are understood as means for enlarging people's choices rather than as an end condition of development.

Sen's contribution to the critique of development as economic growth created awareness that development goals involve a moral choice. His capabilities theory has become the espoused theory of development for many ICT4D researchers. It serves as a normative intellectual device, from which ICT4D research derives objectives of ICT innovation. For example, from the perspective of the capabilities theory, conventional topics of IS research, such as entrepreneurial ICT activities or e-government, are examined for their potential and actual empowering effects for disadvantaged citizen groups (Jimenez and Zheng 2016; Madon 2005). More importantly, by invoking the capabilities approach, ICT for development researchers have broadened the research agenda of the field to study questions that rarely feature in IS research, but are crucial for human development, such as addressing gender inequalities [70] and education gaps [71].

In addition to defining development goals, ICT4D research can draw from the debates on socio-economic development valuable lessons about the nature of the processes of action for the realization of development goals. For example, the operationalization of development theory in policy action involves conflicts of interests and strategies for domination at the local and global level. A thought provoking study that considers multiple aspects of the political economy of ICT-driven development is Carmody's [72] critical study of the developmental role of mobile phones in Africa.

It is important to engage that ICT4D research engages with the debate on the definition of the general notion of 'development' and the processes it entails. But I would argue that the theoretical challenge of ICT4D regarding development is not the choice between economic growth or human development approaches, but the grounding of our research on theories that problematise desirable socio-economic objectives with adequate specificity for the domains of ICT-enabled activities we study.

For example, recently in my research I needed theoretical bearings to assess the contribution of ICT to the conduct of elections in Brazil and India, the formation of entrepreneurial activity in Chinese communities, or government administration reform in various countries. I deduced relevant developmental goals from theories that elaborated on desirable change, relevant contestations, and required enablers and impediments that are likely to frustrate the developmental contribution of ICT innovation specifically for each of these research areas.

I therefore suggest that the engagement of ICT4D research with socio-economic development discourse is not confined to the debates on the general definitions and approaches to 'development'. It is dispersed in a much broader theoretical literature that addresses transformative options in a range of domains of human activity. Again, such theoretical choice comprises middle range theories that conceptually describe problem situations and puzzling conditions of human institutions and offer models and analyses that help us identify the potential transformative role of ICTs.

5 Putting Together Multiple Theories in the Framing of Empirical ICT4D Research

The crafting of ICT4D research involves the framing of each of our studies by combining multiple theories. In this essay, I suggested three foundational theoretical perspectives that underpin all ICT4D research: ways of thinking about ICT and organizational or socio-economic change, ways of identifying relevant context, ways of thinking about transformations that make a positive difference in people's life conditions. These are present in all ICT4D research, but they are not always made explicit or argued about. In addition, ICT4D research involves conceptual vocabularies and assumptions of mechanisms of change that are specific to a topic under study – that is, middle range theories.

A comparison of two PhD studies in my university can exemplify choices in the theoretical framing I suggest for ICT4D research. Both studies concern the implementation of consecutive ICT systems for international trade management: one in Mexico, by Carla Bonina[1], the other in Ghana, by Atta Addo[2]. They both adopted a sociotechnical perspective of ICT, assuming a recursive dynamic relationship between ICT and organizational change, according to which IT is implemented to bring about organizational arrangements deemed desirable by some stakeholders, but is likely to be contested by others. Neither Bonina's nor Addo's research takes an explicit position regarding the definition of development – economic growth or human development. Instead, they both engage with specific questions about desirable transformation of public administration in relation to the development discourses in the countries they study and international influences.

In Bonina's study, the focal potential transformation is the mix of 'public values' at the core of public administration. She examines whether ICT implementation amidst

---

[1] http://etheses.lse.ac.uk/584/1/Bonina_public_values_information_2012.pdf.

[2] Forthcoming.

organizational reforms triggered by policies of economic liberalization altered core values of public bureaucracies, such as fair service by following the rule of law. She complements the theoretical analysis of public values with a theory on discourse (critical discourse analysis) to trace ideological influences that shaped the orientation if ICT implementation towards supporting specific public value combinations. In Addo's study, the focal transformation is the 'modernization' of public sector services, that is, the reduction of red tape that has historically been formed in Ghana's patrimonial tradition of government administration. He develops an analytical basis by combining a typology of government administration historically formed in developing countries with the institutional logics theory of organizational sociology [73]. Bonina's contextualization approach spans two layers of context. Her analysis associates ICT implementation and its effects on the values underpinning practice in international trade administration with Mexico's political economy – specifically the policies of successive governments for opening up the economy and pursuing economic development through strengthening the competitiveness of Mexican firms. Addo's contextual analysis associates the situated practice of civil servants with organizational reform interventions of the public sector. It is thus contained at the level of the inter-organizational domain of Ghana's public administration.

I hope the two examples show the kind of combinations of foundational and middle range theories required in ICT4D research. Both these studies address questions about the developmental effects of the same techno/organizational innovation – ICT platforms for the administration of international trade - and contribute insights on the way ICTs come to make a difference in the public sector of developing countries. They adopt the same foundational theory of technology, but they contextualise their research differently. Importantly, they both draw also from middle range theories - on public values, institutional logics, critical discourse analysis, ideal types of administration. A clear theoretical framing is necessary for the articulation of research questions in conceptual terms, for the construction of an analytical route for an empirical study, and for delineating the theoretical contribution of the research as propositions that extend or refute existing knowledge on ICT4D phenomena.

6 Conclusions

My argument in this paper is that ICT4D research requires the combination of two types of theories: foundational and middle range. Foundational theories are very general and highly abstract – they tend to elaborate on the nature of social phenomena and the processes through which they are formed. Invariably, ICT4D research requires theories about technology, about context, and about development. Middle range theories are more limited in their abstraction and relevance and their aim is to explain specific kinds of phenomena.

Students often ask me what theory they should use for the research of so-and-so a topic. This is an impossible question to answer: it is not one theory that is needed in ICT4D research, but many; and nobody can prescribe the theories for the study of a topic. Research framing is the informed choice of theories in relation to which questions for investigation are expressed and contributions to knowledge are made. I believe it is the most challenging part of academic ICT4D research.

References

1. Bhatnagar, S.C., Bjørn-Andersen, N. (eds.): Information Technology in Developing Cuntries. Amsterdam, North-Holland (1990)
2. Odedra, M., et al.: Sub-Saharan Africa: a technological desert. Commun. ACM **35**(2), 25–29 (1993)
3. Odedra-Straub, M. (ed.): Global Information Technology and Socio-Economic Development. Ivy League, Nashua (1996)
4. UNDP: Human Development Report 2001. Oxford University Press, New York (2001)
5. Kirkman, G.S., et al.: The Global Information Technology Report 2001–2002: Readiness for the Networked World. Oxford University Press, New York (2002)
6. Porter, M.E., et al.: The Global Competitiveness Report 2001–2002. Oxford University Press, New York (2002)
7. World Bank: The Networking Revolution: Opportunities and Challenges for Developing Countries. Global Information and Communication Technologies Department. World Bank, Washington (2000)
8. World Bank: Building Institutions for Markets. New York (2002)
9. Avgerou, C.: The link between ICT and economic growth in the discourse of development. In: Korpela, M., Montealegro, R., Poulymenakou, A. (eds.) Organizational Information Systems in the Context of Globalization, pp. 373–386. Kluwer, Dordrecht (2003)
10. UNDP: Human Development Report 1999. United Nations Development Programme, New York (1999)
11. Hassanin, L.: Egyptian women artisans: ICTs are not the entry to modern markets. In: Avgerou, C., Smith, M.L., Van den Besselaar, P. (eds.) Social Dimensions of Information and Communication Technology Policy. Springer, New York (2008)
12. Srinivasan, J., Burrell, J.: On the importance of price information to fishers and to economists: revisiting mobile phone use among fishers in Kerala. Inf. Technol. Int. Dev. **11** (1), 57–70 (2015)
13. Madon, S.: E-Governance for Development: A Focus on Rural India. Palgrave Macmillan, Basingstoke (2009)
14. Madon, S., et al.: Digital Inclusion projects in developing countries: processes of institutionalisation. In: IFIP WG9.4 9th International Conference 'Taking Stock of E-Development'. Sao Paulo (2007)
15. Heeks, R.: Theorizing ICT4D research. Inf. Technol. Int. Dev. **3**(3), 1–4 (2006)
16. Walsham, G.: Development informatics in a changing world: reflections from ICTD2010/2012. Inf. Technol. Int. Dev. **9**(1), 49–54 (2013)
17. Avgerou, C.: Discourses on ICT and development. Inf. Technol. Int. Dev. **6**(3), 1–18 (2010)
18. Markus, M.L.: Power, politics and MIS implementation. Commun. ACM **26**(6), 430–445 (1983)
19. Markus, M.L., Robey, D.: Information technology and organizational change: causal structure in theory and research. Manag. Sci. **34**(5), 583–598 (1988)
20. Orlikowski, W., Iacono, S.C.: Desperately seeking the 'IT' in IT research - a call to theorizing the IT artifact. Inf. Syst. Res. **12**(2), 121–134 (2001)

21. Grint, K., Woolgar, S.: The Machine at Work: Technology, Work and Organization. Polity Press, Cambridge (1997)
22. Griffith, T.L., Dougherty, D.J.: Beyond socio-technical systems: introduction to the special issue. Eng. Technol. Manag. **18**, 207–218 (2001)
23. Trist, E.L., Bamforth, K.W.: Some social and psychological consequences of the long-wall method of coal-getting. Hum. Relat. **4**, 3–38 (1951)
24. Bijker, W.E., Law, J. (eds.): Shaping Technology/Building Society. The MIT Press, Cambridge (1992)
25. Law, J. (ed.): A Sociology of Monsters: Essays on Power. Technology and Domination. Routledge, London (1991)
26. Howcroft, D., Mitev, N., Wilson, M.: What we may learn from the social shaping of technology approach. In: Mingers, J., Willcocks, L. (eds.) Social Theory and Philosophy for Information Systems, pp. 329–371. John Wiley, Chichester (2004)
27. Monteiro, E.: Actor-network theory and information infrastructure. In: Ciborra, C. (ed.) From Control to Drift, pp. 71–83. Oxford University Press, Oxford (2000)
28. Walsham, G.: Actor-network theory and IS research: current status and future prospects. In: Lee, A.S., Liebenau, J., DeGross, J. (eds.) Information Systems and Qualitative Research, pp. 466–480. Chapman & Hall, London (1997)
29. Latour, B.: Reassembling the Social: An Introduction to Actor-Network-Theory. Oxford University Press, Oxford (2005)
30. Akrich, M.: The de-scription of technical objects. In: Bijker, W.E., Law, J. (eds.) Shaping Technology/Building Society, pp. 205–224. MIT Press, Cambridge (1992)
31. Leonardi, P.M., Nardi, B.A., Kallinikos, J.: Materiality and Organizing. Oxford University Press, Oxford (2012)
32. Markus, M.L., Silver, M.S.: A foundation for the study of IT effects: a new look at DeSanctis and Pooles's concepts of structural features and spirit. J. Assoc. Inf. Syst. **9**(10) (2008). Article 5
33. Orlikowski, W.J.: Sociomaterial practices: exploring technology at work. Organ. Stud. **28**(9), 1435–1448 (2007)
34. Wagner, E., Newell, S., Piccoli, G.: Understanding project survival in an ES environment: a sociomaterial practice perspective. J. Assoc. Inf. Syst. **11**(5), 276–297 (2010)
35. Zammuto, R.F., et al.: Information technology and the changing fabric of organization. Organ. Sci. **18**(5), 749–762 (2007)
36. Orlikowski, W., Scott, S.V.: Sociomateriality: challenging the separation of technology, work and organization. Acad. Manag. Ann. **2**(1), 433–474 (2008)
37. Leonardi, P.M.: Theoretical foundations for the study of sociomateriality. Inf. Organ. **23**, 59–76 (2013)
38. Faraj, S., Azad, B.: The materiality of technology: an affordance perspective. In: Leonardi, P. M., Nardi, B.A., Kallimikos, J. (eds.) Materiality and Organizing, pp. 237–259. Oxford University Press, Oxford (2012)
39. Leonardi, P.M.: When flexible routines meet flexible technologies: affordance, constraint, and the imbrication of human and material agencies. MIS Q. **35**(1), 147–167 (2011)
40. Kallinikos, J.: Form, function, and matter: crossing the border of materiality. In: Leonardi, P. M., Nardi, B.A., Kallinikos, J. (eds.) Materiality and Organizing, pp. 67–87. Oxford University Press, Oxrford (2012)
41. Pentland, B.T., Singh, H.: Materiality: what are the consequences? In: Leonardi, P.M., Nardi, B.A., Kallinikos, J. (eds.) Materiality and Organizing, pp. 288–295. Oxford University Press, Oxford (2012)

42. Leonardi, P.M.: Materiality, sociomateriality, and socio-technical systems: what do these terms mean? How are they different? In: Leonardi, P.M., Nardi, B.A., Kallinikos, J. (eds.) Materiality and Organizing: Social Interaction in a Technological World. Oxford University Press, Oxford (2012)

43. Hayes, N., Westrup, C.: Context and the processes of ICT for development. Inf. Organ. **22**(1), 23–36 (2012)

44. Findikoglu, M., Watson-Manheim, M.B.: Linking macro-level goals to micro-level routines: EHR-enabled transformation of primary care services. J. Inf. Technol. **31**(4), 382–400 (2016)

45. Avgerou, C., Li, B.: Relational and institutional embeddedness of web enabled entrepreneurial networks: case studies of ntrepreneurs in China. Inf. Syst. J. (2012, forthcoming)

46. Granovetter, M.: Economic action and social structure: the problem of embeddedness. Am. J. Soc. **91**(3), 481–510 (1985)

47. Schultze, U., Orlikowski, W.J.: A practice perspective on technology-mediated network relations: the use of internet-based self-serve technologies. Inf. Syst. Res. **15**(1), 87–106 (2004)

48. Uzzi, B.: Social structure and competition in interfirm networks: the paradox of embeddedness. Adm. Sci. Q. **42**(1), 35–67 (1997)

49. Wasko, M.M., Faraj, S.: Why should I share? Examining social capital and knowledge contribution in electronic networks of practice. MIS Q. **29**(1), 35–57 (2005)

50. Polanyi, K.: The economy as instituted process. In: Polanyi, K., Arensberg, C.A., Pearson, H.W. (eds.) Trade and Markets in the Early Empires, pp. 243–269. Regnery, Chicago (1957)

51. Merton, R.K.: On sociological theories of the middle range. In: Merton, R.K. (ed.) On Sociological Theory: Five Essays, old and New, pp. 39–72. Free Press, New York (1967)

52. Robey, D., Boudreau, M.C.: Accounting for the contradictory organizational consequences of information technology: theoretical directions and methodological implications. Inf. Syst. Res. **10**(2), 167–185 (1999)

53. Braa, J., et al.: Developing health information systems in developing countries: the flexible standards strategy. MIS Q. **31**(2), 381–402 (2007)

54. Kambayashi, N., Scarbrough, H.: Cultural influences on IT use amongst factory managers: a UK–Japanese comparison. J. Inf. Technol. **16**(4), 221–236 (2001)

55. Nicholson, B., Sahay, S.: Some political and cultural issues in the globalisation of software development: case experience from Britain and India. Inf. Organ. **11**(1), 25–43 (2001)

56. Pettigrew, A.M.: Contextualist research and the study of organisational change processes. In: Mumford, E., et al. (eds.) Research Methods in Information Systems, pp. 53–78. North-Holland, Amsterdam (1985)

57. Madon, S.: Computer based information systems for development planning. In: Bhatnagar, S.C., Odedra, M. (eds.) Social Implications of Computers in Developing Countries, pp. 209–217. Tata McGraw-Hill, New Delhi (1992)

58. Walsham, G.: Interpreting Information Systems in Organizations. John Wiley, Chichester (1993)

59. Hayes, N., Westrup, C.: Context and the processes of ICT for development. Inf. Organ. **22**, 23–36 (2011)

60. Faik, I., Walsham, G.: Modernisation through ICTs: towards a network ontology of technological change. Inf. Syst. J. **23**(4), 351–370 (2012)

61. Mann, C.L.: Information technologies and international development: conceptual clarity in the search for commonality and diversity. Inf. Technol. Int. Dev. **1**(2), 67–79 (2004)

62. UNDP: Human Development Report 2015. United Nations Development Programme, New York (2015)

63. Chavula, H.K.: Telecommunications development and economic growth in Africa. Inf. Technol. Dev. **19**(1), 5–23 (2013)
64. Brynjolfsson, E., Hitt, L.M.: Beyond computation: information technology, organizational transformation and business performance. J. Econ. Perspect. **14**(4), 23–48 (2000)
65. Dedrick, J., Gurbaxani, V., Kraemer, K.L.: Information technology and economic performance: a critical review of the empirical evidence. ACM Comput. Surv. **35**(1), 1–28 (2003)
66. Jensen, R.: The digital provide: information (technology), market performance, and welfare in the south Indian fisheries sector. Q. J. Econ. **122**(3), 879–924 (2007)
67. Ros, J.: Rethinking Economic Development, Growth, and Institutions. Oxford University Press, Oxford (2013)
68. World Bank: World Development Report 2016: Digital Dividents. World Bank, Washington (2016)
69. Sen, A.: Development as freedom. Oxford University Press, Oxford (1999)
70. Buskens, I.: Agency and reflexivity in ICT4D research: questioning women's options, poverty, and human development. Inf. Technol. Int. Dev. **6**, 19–24 (2010)
71. Bass, J., Nicholson, B., Subrahmanian, E.: A framework using institutional analysis and the capability approach in ICT4D. Inf. Techn. Int. Dev. **9**(1), 19–35 (2013)
72. Carmody, P.: The informationalization of poverty in Africa? Mobile phones and economic structure. Inf. Technol. Int. Dev. **8**(3), 1–17 (2012)
73. Thornton, P.H., Ocasio, W., Lounsbury, M.: The Institutional Logics Perspective: A New Approach to Culture, Structure, and Process. Oxford University Press, Oxford (2012)

Design, Needs, and Aspirations in International Development

Kentaro Toyama[✉]

University of Michigan, Ann Arbor, MI 48109, USA
toyama@umich.edu

Abstract. As with other forms of social change, international development requires deep changes in human attitudes, skills, and values. Traditional design, however, stresses convenience and accommodation of users. Thus, while development requires human change, designers seek to avoid any need for people to change. This mismatch between the demands of social change and the mainstream attitude of design is at the heart of a range of persistent challenges in ICT for development. I propose that the problem can be addressed in part by shifting from an approach based on needs to an approach based on aspirations.

Keywords: ICT4D · ICTD · Design · Aspiration-based development

1 Introduction

In honor of our host country, I begin with a brief overview of the modern history of Indonesia [22, 23]. Indonesia gained independence in 1945 or 1949, depending on which of two events you count: It first declared independence immediately after the end of Japanese military occupation in 1945; but formal recognition of independence by its Dutch colonizers came only in 1949. Indonesia's first president, Sukarno, ruled as an autocrat, and he presided over a politically motivated mass murder that left half a million people dead. His successor was Suharto, who ruled from 1967 until 1998. Though Suharto was eventually undone by his authoritarianism, corruption, and nepotism, he nevertheless oversaw a period of rapid socio-economic growth. Suharto transitioned the country to a capitalist economy under which per capita GDP went from only US$56 (2016 US dollars) in 1967 when Suharto took power, to $1,137 in 1996, two years before the Asian financial crisis led to his resignation [25]. Suharto also fostered government institutions as well as a range of corporatist civil society organizations. Partly as a result, the period of his reign saw a 20-year increase in life expectancy, a 60% decline in infant mortality, and widespread improvement in education, with primary school enrollments that grew to above 90% with little gender disparity. Since Suharto, there has been significant democratization, with election reforms in 1999, direct elections for president since 2004, and several peaceful transfers of power to leaders that increasingly stress the value of democratic governance. Meanwhile, economic growth has continued: Indonesia's per capita GDP was $3,500 in 2014 [25].

J. Choudrie et al. (Eds.): ICT4D 2017, IFIP AICT 504, pp. 24–32, 2017.
DOI: 10.1007/978-3-319-59111-7_3

In just this brief history, we see a multifaceted story of socio-economic development. There was economic growth. Education improved. Democracy appears to have strengthened. But, what I want to highlight in each of these changes is the human element. Economic growth requires improvements in citizen skill and good regulation. Democracy requires strong institutions of governance and popular belief in self-determination. Gender equality requires education for women and maturity among men. Thus, the underlying causes of the country's transformation were significant changes within the people of Indonesia – from rural farmers to military generals, from NGOs to political parties. Indonesia thus provides an excellent example of the idea that the socio-economic benefits of international development are clearly and crucially dependent on human development, both for individuals and for society as a whole. There is no social change without a change in people.

The importance of human development may seem an obvious, unremarkable point for all of us, a community that concerns itself with international development. What I would like to suggest, however, is that the need for people to change runs completely counter to another community that we are also concerned with – the community of design.

Designers tend to see their goal as the creation of goods and services that are pleasant to use and convenient for people – that is to say, design explicitly avoids asking people to change. In his best-selling book, *The Design of Everyday Things*, Don Norman begins with a rant against badly designed doors: "I push doors that are meant to be pulled, pull doors that should be pushed, and walk into doors that neither pull nor push, but slide... I see others having the same troubles—unnecessary troubles" [13]. A well-designed door, he continues, should be so obvious in its use that people do not need to learn anything new or change their normal habits. The good designer's goal is to design things so that people can remain as they are. Norman writes that good design "puts human needs, capabilities, and behavior first, then designs to accommodate those needs, capabilities, and ways of behaving... *We have to accept human behavior the way it is, not the way we would wish it to be*" (emphasis mine).

Norman is one of design's most influential spokespersons, particularly among designers of computer systems. His book is frequently assigned in classes about human-computer interaction. At the school where I teach, students absorb the principles he espouses and strive for "ease of use" that gives users what they want. This stance makes perfect sense if the problem is the design of doors, radios, cars, mobile phone apps, and other things whose goals are to deliver efficiency, convenience, and pleasure. But how appropriate is an ethic of accommodating people as they are, when the goal itself is to change people?

2 Accommodating Non-literate Users

In 2005, I began working with a colleague, Indrani Medhi, to see how we could use technology to support the women residents of a slum community in the Jayanagar neighborhood of Bangalore, India. Applying the principles of human-centered design, we immersed ourselves in their daily lives, interviewed them about their day-to-day needs, and looked for problems that we might address with technology. It quickly emerged that the women wanted a reliable way to find informal work as domestic servants. However, because many of the women were non-literate, they could not read classified ads in the newspaper. They relied on word of mouth to hear about jobs.

This seemed like an opportunity for design: We imagined a computer kiosk housed in the office of a local non-profit organization that we partnered with. The kiosk would provide access to a database of jobs, which the women could browse. The critical element was the interface. Since most of the women could not read at all, the system would require what we dubbed a *text-free user interface,* designed specifically to be navigable by non-literate users.

Again, following good human-centered design practice, we prototyped various designs, asked potential users for feedback, and iterated over several months. We found, for example, that line drawings were more effective than photographs in conveying ideas, because they were understood to represent a class of things (or actions), rather than a specific instance [10]. We found that there was a spectrum of illiteracy and that many otherwise non-literate women were nevertheless familiar with numbers [11]. We found that the women had no mental model of how relevant information wound up in a computer, and so it helped to show a video that demystified how the whole system worked [12]. In a formal evaluation, the final system worked just as we had hoped, with 100% of a group of non-literate participants being able to navigate the user interface to find jobs of their choosing.

When it came to implementing the system and matching women with actual jobs, however, we ran into a host of unanticipated challenges [9]: The women often lacked skills – cooking specific dishes, or using a vacuum cleaner – that employers sought. They also needed to learn basic standards of professionalism, such as providing advance notice if they had to cancel. We also faced challenges with employers, mostly middle-class urban families. They could be stingy with pay or had degrading requirements, such as prohibitions on toilet use. Meanwhile, we – a partnership of researchers and the non-profit organization we worked with – needed to develop the institutional capacity to recruit employers, train employees, and negotiate terms between them. For two years, we worked to pull these elements together, but the total non-technical effort vastly outweighed what was required to design, build, and maintain a computer kiosk. Ultimately, I came to the conclusion that, at least for the problem of job placement with this particular community, text-free user interfaces were not solving any of the key issues. Had we instead focused entirely on the human infrastructure for job-matching and job performance, we would have provided something more meaningful for the women.

So, though we had designed a good technology that served its purpose, a host of additional human changes were more critical for the ultimate impact we sought. The employees required training; social norms among employers had to shift; and we needed to build an institution that could support the many moving parts of job-matching in the informal sector. Text-free user interfaces failed to affect those issues one way or another, but not only that, the real challenges did not even come up during the human-centered design process.

Furthermore, it could be argued that the underlying project itself was limited in its conception. To be sure, there is some value in helping non-literate people gain information that is otherwise only accessible to the literate. But, if the larger goal is socio-economic development, helping people to become literate might be a worthier goal. In searching for a technology solution that would accommodate users, we neglected to consider the ways in which people might need to change to achieve their larger objectives.

3 Not Enough

The story of text-free user interfaces is just one example, but it exemplifies many of the challenges of computing for international development. First, it reconfirms one of technological determinism's commonly noted flaws, that *technology* is not enough for meaningful social change. Text-free user interfaces by themselves are not enough to solve the original problem of women finding informal work [9]. SMS messages by themselves are not enough to raise community health worker performance [3]. Some individual capacity is needed. Some oversight and management is required. Some institutional support is essential.

Second, *design* is not enough, even when the design is human-centered, culturally appropriate, and participatory. Every design innovation that went into text-free user interfaces was based on the wishes of, feedback from, and evaluations with potential users, but as long as the designed output was a physical artifact or a process, no effort was put toward changing people. With changes limited to the external environment; the internal world of human attitudes, skills, and values remained unchanged and therefore, none the better. The same could be said for well-designed laptops which still fail to educate children [2], mobile phones which divert family funds away from school and nutrition [4], or any of a range of ICT-for-development projects where a technology is designed to meet immediate needs.

Third, *agency* is not enough. Individual agency is made much of in international development [19], but as important as it is, naïve conceptions of it also leave people as they are, no better able to take advantage of "opportunities" made available to them. Text-free user interfaces may present non-literate women with more job options, but the set of jobs they qualify for is no greater. Social media affords more people the option to "friend" national leaders, but whether those requests are reciprocated depends on prior relationships [21]. Massive open online courses offer free learning to anyone with Internet access, but completion rates are dramatically skewed toward college-educated professionals – i.e., those who have the educational foundation and the leisure time to learn on their own [18]. In other words, the ability to choose – even among good options – is not a guarantee of positive social change.

4 Problem-Solving, Neoliberalism, and Needs

Given the wide gap between the accommodationist ethic of design and the human change underlying international development, it is a wonder at all that we should expect the former to impact the latter. But, design and development share common tendencies, and these apparent similarities bring the two fields together.

The convergence begins with *needs*, something that both development and design have an interest in – an interest that arguably borders on fetishism. "Needs assessments," for example, are a beloved activity of both technology designers and development specialists. Much of the rhetoric of both development and design builds on the higher moral ground that comes from addressing human needs.

Then, a focus on needs leads to problem-solving as the high-level approach. International development, of course, seeks to solve some of the greatest problems of human civilization – poverty, oppression, and injustice. Meanwhile, design makes explicit claims that it has unique methodologies for problem-solving. So, it is not surprising that development should turn to design for new approaches, or that design would see its methodology as applicable to development. The well-known design firm IDEO, for example, published "a step-by-step guide that will get you solving problems like a designer," with the following opening sentence: "Embracing human-centered design means believing that all problems, even the seemingly intractable ones like poverty, gender equality, and clean water, are solvable" [7].

Finally, in their solutions, both design and development tend toward neoliberalism. International development, at least as practiced by Western multilateral organizations, is widely known for pushing the "Washington Consensus," a set of principles that emphasizes economic growth via open trade and capitalism [24]. The idea is that needs such as food, shelter, health, and income are best met by the invisible hand of Adam Smith, a hand which moves according to individual choice acting on selfish impulses. Design, to the degree that it thrives on consumerism, often adopts these values implicitly. This is not to say that design cannot exist outside of a capitalist framework, but design has a natural affinity for individualistic solutions. The affinity becomes clearer when development itself is unabashedly neoliberal. For example, the rhetoric around "bottom of the pyramid" social enterprises espouses the free market as a solution to poverty *and* puts an emphasis on customer-centric design [17]. Not surprisingly, IDEO's design guidebook makes frequent references to social enterprises [7].

To summarize, despite what seems like a mismatch between design's desire to accommodate people and development's objective of social change, there are natural alliances between the two fields. Long before any explicit interest in design, international development was already focused on needs, on problem-solving, and on neoliberal systems; design in many ways compounds these biases.

Of course, it would be folly to suggest that good things have not come from addressing needs, solving problems, or unleashing economic growth. Yet, it is also true that these approaches are not enough and that they can have harmful side effects. Whatever its benefits, the needs-based market-driven problem-solving paradigm leaves much to be desired.

5   From Needs...

The pathologies of the free market are well-known, so I will not belabor them here except to note that many of the challenges of design for development are inherited from the larger context of globalized capitalism: To the extent that solutions remain within the bounds of goods and services that individuals freely choose or not, approaches that involve collective action or that push people to change (other than through consumption) are largely neglected.

What remains to be considered are the challenges of needs-based problem-solving. As above, the focus on needs and the problem-solving mentality go hand in hand. Every unmet human need presents a problem to be solved. The core issues of international development – hunger, illness, ignorance, oppression, unemployment, and so on – seem to call for well-designed solutions.

Without impugning problem-solving altogether, however, we can nevertheless acknowledge that the language of needs and solutions comes with biases, which when amplified by the global machinery of international development, can lead to systematic difficulties.

The *Oxford English Dictionary* defines "need" in many ways, but one of them is "violence, force, constraint, or compulsion, exercised upon a person" [14]. This definition is consistent with the kind of needs that international development is concerned with, and it has two key characteristics: First, it evokes strong negative emotions such as fear or anger as a response. Second, needs are urgent and episodic by definition. Dire needs cannot be indefinitely sustained – they are either extinguished through satisfaction, or if long unmet, they kill their hosts.

The fear and urgency of needs pushes us toward packaged solutions. Hunger demands food. Illness demands treatment. Ignorance demands information. And if we view international development as one long succession of needs, it is tempting to respond with a succession of quick solutions – solutions that are easy to replicate and deploy. It is no wonder that so much of international development seems to be about providing rations, dispensing pills, or in the case of ICT, developing apps for smartphones. We allow the urgency of needs to dictate the timeframes in which our solutions must fit.

6   To Aspirations

Are there alternatives to needs-based problem-solving? I would like to propose an approach based on nurturing aspirations [21]. Turning again to the *Oxford English Dictionary*, an aspiration is "steadfast desire or longing for something above one" [14]. This concise definition captures the three elements that make aspirations what they are: they are a kind of *desire*; they are *persistent*; and they aim for something *higher*. Human beings have many other desires – some are fleeting, some are mundane, some are undesirable – but aspirations differ because of their long-term, growth-focused nature.

The strengths of an aspiration focus can best be seen when contrasted with needs-based approaches [20]. Compared with the negative associations of needs, aspirations have positive valence. Compared with the fleeting urgency of needs, aspirations are long-term. Aspirations are thus a stronger basis on which to build sustained effort and action. Needs tend toward quick problem-solving as an approach, but aspirations are more given to long-term engagement and people-nurturing as a response. And where needs are met with goods and services – often, physical goods that ultimately perish; aspirations nurture abilities and shift attitudes, which endure within individuals and are often propagated to future generations.

At one level, an aspiration-based approach is not that different from what thoughtful theorists and practitioners have asked of development for many decades. As the popular saying goes, "Give a man a fish, he eats for a day; teach a man to fish, he eats for a lifetime." Focusing on aspirations is very much in line with this popular dictum, except perhaps that instead of necessarily teaching fishing, one would mentor people toward their own aspirations.

But, aspiration-based development also has additional connotations. For example, instead of needs assessments, why not perform *aspiration assessments*? Over the past several years, I have asked people from all over the world in a range of socio-economic strata a single question, crafted carefully to elicit aspirations [20]: "Of those things that you have some control over, what would you most like to change about yourself or your life over the next five years?" Respondents mention desires such as, "to get a better job and be financially stable," or "to continue with my education in college," or "to help and educate kids and the poor." These are all descriptions of positive, long-term desires, and therefore expressions of aspiration. If one simple question can reveal this much, it bodes well for what more in-depth investigations could yield. Much more work could be done to develop and formalize aspiration assessments.

An aspiration focus also keeps the spotlight on the social forces that might be brought to bear on a problem. Healthcare, for example, is a frequent concern of international development. Needs-based approaches tend to focus on specific illnesses, their treatments, and technologies and processes to improve treatment delivery. It is all too easy to ignore the human stakeholders. An aspiration-based approach, however, would begin with people – with the dreams that patients have for themselves, the aspirations of patient families, and the ambitions of healthcare workers, any or all of which might furnish the necessary motivation for healthful action. Social scientists might find a focus on people obvious, but by explicitly focusing on aspirations, it would also help guide the attention of any technology-minded collaborators.

Additionally, a methodology guided by aspirations reconciles the great conundrum of aid versus agency, of paternalism versus participation, of top-down versus bottom-up development. At the heart of this issue is the difficult fact that communities that need help need help. Try as we might pretend otherwise with the language of "cooperation" and "participation," those of us coming in with the advantages of wealth, education, and political influence have something that beneficiary communities do not – that is the very premise of our engagement. The question, then, is not whether there is a power differential – there cannot but be – but whose desires ultimately guide the application of that power. With a needs-based approach, it is easy to sideline the aspirations of beneficiaries for the sake of needs abstracted from the people who have them. It is more difficult – though not impossible – to claim to follow an aspiration-based approach without respecting the long-term desires that people have for themselves.

In any case, aspiration-based approaches remain neglected both as theory and as practice. Most of the literature on aspirations focuses narrowly on career aspirations [5, 8]. Arjun Appadurai's conception of the "capacity to aspire" [1] is salient in development, but it deserves to be further developed and operationalized. In ICT and development, Joyojeet Pal and his colleagues have examined the aspirational symbolism of digital technology [15, 16], but not as a framework for causing development. Practitioners, meanwhile, continue to conduct needs assessments and roll out solutions based on user needs.

Overall, an aspiration-focus would tilt development efforts toward programs that help build people's own ability to achieve their aspirations. Arguably, such an approach makes traditional forms of design less applicable, but that is part of the point. Designed artifacts may serve as tools, but are less likely to cause personal or societal growth on their own. At the same time, much of the methodology of design could be repurposed for aspirations. Techniques for understanding people remain just as relevant, though they may require refocusing. Design practices around brainstorming different options and remaining detached from any one option, can be helpful once an aspiration has been articulated. And, methods of evaluation, both to analyze competing "designs" and to trial with actual people remain applicable. What aspirations ask of designers is to be committed for the longer time spans that social change requires, and to develop and learn a new design vocabulary for social change – one that remains focused on meaningful human change from beginning to end.

7   Conclusion

Traditional design works hard to accommodate people, to accept their attitudes, skills, and values as they are. International development, however, typically requires people to learn, grow, and evolve. In this paper, I have argued that this difference is among the deeper causes of the routine failures of ICT for development. A methodology that seeks to avoid changing people is unlikely to succeed at outcomes that require human change.

Design and international development nevertheless have an affinity based in part on their focus on needs. But while needs-focused approaches are appropriate for dire situations such as disaster relief, their tendency toward quick, replicable solutions is less appropriate for the sustained efforts required of international development. To counter this, I propose that development practice shift to a focus on human aspirations, one that moves attention from problem-solving to people-nurturing. The persistent, upward nature of aspirations is better suited for building the individual and institutional capacities that are required for long-term, large-scale international development.

References

1. Appadurai, A.: The capacity to aspire. In: Rao, V., Walton, M. (eds.) Culture and Public Action. Orient Blackswan, Delhi (2004)
2. Cristia, J.P., Ibarraran, P., Cueto, S., Santiago, A., Severin, E.: Technology and child development: evidence from the One Laptop per Child program. IDB Working Paper Series, No. IDB-WP-304. Inter-American Development Bank (2012)

3. DeRenzi, B., Findlater, L., Payne, J., Birnbaum, B., Mangilima, J., Parikh, T., Borriello, G., Lesh, N.: Improving community health worker performance through automated SMS. In: Proceedings of the Fifth International Conference on Information and Communication Technologies and Development, pp. 25–34. ACM (2012)
4. Diga, K.: Mobile cell phones and poverty reduction. Diss. Masters Dissertation. Durban, South Africa: School of Development Studies, University of KwaZuluNatal (2007)
5. Haller, A.O., Miller, I.W.: The occupational aspiration scale–theory, structure, and correlates. Report Number AES-TB-268, Michigan State University (1963)
6. Hayek, F.A.: The Road to Serfdom. Routledge, London (1944)
7. IDEO. The Field Guide to Human-Centered Design. IDEO.org (2015). http://www. designkit.org/resources/1. Accessed 24 Mar 2017
8. MacLeod, J.: Ain't No Makin' It: Aspirations and Attainment in a Low-Income Neighborhood. Westview Press (2009)
9. Medhi, I., Menon, G., Toyama, K.: Challenges in computerized job search for the developing world. In: CHI 2008 Extended Abstracts on Human Factors in Computing Systems, pp. 2079–2094. ACM (2008)
10. Medhi, I., Prasad, A., Toyama, K.: Optimal audio-visual representations for illiterate users of computers. In: Proceedings of the 16th International Conference on World Wide Web, pp. 873–882. ACM (2007)
11. Medhi, I., Sagar, A., Toyama, K.: Text-free user interfaces for illiterate and semi-literate users. In: Proceedings of the International Conference on Information and Communication Technologies and Development, ICTD 2006, pp. 72–82. IEEE (2006)
12. Medhi, I., Toyama, K.: Full-context videos for first-time, non-literate PC users. In: IEEE/ACM International Conference on Information and Communication Technologies and Development (ICTD 2007), Doha, Qatar (2007)
13. Norman, D.A.: The Design of Everyday Things. Basic Books, New York (2002)
14. Oxford English Dictionary: 2nd Edition. OED Online version, December 2013. http://www. oed.com/. Accessed 25 Mar 2017
15. Pal, J., Chandra, P., Vydiswaran, V.V.: Twitter and the rebranding of NarendraModi. Econ. Polit. Wkly. 51(8), 53 (2016)
16. Pal, J., Lakshmanan, M., Toyama, K.: My child will be respected: parental perspectives on computers in rural India. In: International Conference on Information and Communication Technologies and Development, 2007 (ICTD 2007), pp. 1–9. IEEE (2007)
17. Prahalad, C.K.: The Fortune at the Bottom of the Pyramid: Eradicating Poverty Through Profits. Wharton School Publishing, New Delhi (2004)
18. Selingo, J.J.: Demystifying the MOOC. New York Times, 29 October 2014
19. Sen, A.: Development as Freedom. Oxford University Press, Oxford (1999)
20. Toyama, K.: From needs to aspirations in information technology for development. Inf. Technol. Dev. (2017)
21. Toyama, K. Geek Heresy: Rescuing Social Change from the Cult of Technology. Public-Affairs (2015)
22. Vickers, A.: A History of Modern Indonesia. Cambridge University Press, Cambridge (2013)
23. Wikipedia: History of Indonesia. https://en.wikipedia.org/wiki/History_of_Indonesia. Accessed 23 Mar 2017
24. Williamson, J.: Democracy and the "Washington consensus". World Dev. 21(8), 1329–1336 (1993)
25. World Bank: World Bank Open Data. http://data.worldbank.org/. Accessed 23 Mar 2017

Large Scale and Complex Information Systems for Development

Leveraging Software Platform Capabilities to Support HIV (ART) Treatment Adherence Management: A Case from Sierra Leone

Eric Adu-Gyamfi[(✉)] and Petter Nielsen

Department of Informatics, University of Oslo, Oslo, Norway
{ericad,pnielsen}@ifi.uio.no

Abstract. Research on antiretroviral therapy (ART) programs reveal that HIV positive patients who adhere to treatment substantially improve their life expectancy and lower the risk of progression to full-blown AIDS. While there is a significant body of research in the medical and social science fields on ART adherence, Information Systems (IS) research has paid little attention to this subject. Especially lacking is research on how Information and Communication Technology (ICT) based solutions can be developed to better support ART adherence programs. We argue in this paper that software platforms offer capabilities that can be leveraged to address more effectively the information management challenges associated with ART adherence programs. The motivation for this paper is taken from a broader action research project planned to be carried out to support an ART adherence program in Sierra Leone.

Keywords: HIV · Software platforms · ART adherence · Health information systems · Ecosystems · Integration · DHIS2

1 Introduction

Studies reveal that higher ART adherence levels in HIV-positive patients lead to improved patient survival outcomes [1–6]. Still, research also shows that many intervention programs only manage to achieve very modest improvements in patient adherence [6]. Factors identified to contribute to this are broadly categorized as socio-cultural, technological, attitudinal, and economic in nature [7–12]. But also a major concern in the literature is that the *"inability to monitor adherence may ultimately undermine efforts to treat HIV/AIDS in high-burden areas"* ([13], p. 78). Addressed in this paper then is how we can tackle this problem from an Information Systems (IS) research point of view by exploring solutions which can effectively support ART adherence programs particularly in developing countries.

According to clinicians the effectiveness of antiretroviral (ARV) drugs for treating HIV[1] disease depends on strict adherence to stipulated usage guidelines. The World

---

[1] HIV/AIDS: Human Immunodeficiency Virus/Acquired Immunodeficiency Syndrome. Retrieved October 22, 2016 from http://www.who.int/mediacentre/factsheets/fs360/en/.

© IFIP International Federation for Information Processing 2017
Published by Springer International Publishing AG 2017. All Rights Reserved
J. Choudrie et al. (Eds.): ICT4D 2017, IFIP AICT 504, pp. 35–46, 2017.
DOI: 10.1007/978-3-319-59111-7_4

Health Organization's (WHO) guideline documentation[2] for example outlines a three-level program for administering ARV drugs to HIV positive patients, described briefly as follows: a new patient starts on first-level treatment regimen, is monitored for at least 6 to 12 months, and then switched to second and third-level regimen respectively when treatment failure is detected. Differences in patient demographics including age groupings, pregnancy status in women, and the prevalence of other co-morbidities such as tuberculosis (TB) also introduce variations into the ARV drug administration protocols. These guidelines and other information requirements (e.g. for managing HIV opportunistic infections) increase the complexities of patient monitoring hence the need for appropriate information systems. Therefore, this paper proposes information systems solutions that can support effectively the management of HIV treatment and related activities. The aim is towards enhancing health worker ability to monitor patient adherence to HIV (ART) treatment. The expectation is that the appropriate information system is able to support individual patient management activities. For instance including the ability to schedule patient hospital appointments, send automatic reminders to patient on upcoming events like drug refill, notify caregivers when necessary and enhance their capacity to carry out patient follow-up activities. Developing such solutions requires the integration of software systems, technological devices, data from health programs, and alignment of local information management practices around HIV treatment. Such system once developed will give a more holistic view of patient treatment data as well as improve caregivers' visibility of the treatment process. In pursuit of the proposed system we argue that software platforms provide capabilities which can be leveraged. The advantages offered include their ability to support the development of relatively cheaper, quicker and highly customizable solutions to meet adherence management needs especially in resource-constrained settings.

This paper introduces a broader research project motivated by an urgent need to restore and improve survival outcomes in HIV positive patients. These are patients enrolled into ART treatment programs within a challenged health context of Sierra Leone, still recovering from the Ebola disease outbreak. It was reported that the pandemic nature of the Ebola outbreak diverted attention and resources from HIV treatment activities resulting in increased deaths among HIV-positive patients. With attention shifted back to HIV as the Ebola subsides, areas identified as requiring immediate attention include; expanding patient access to antiretroviral (ARV) drugs, providing adequate clinical care, and improving ART adherence monitoring. In this paper we attempt to contribute to the efforts aimed at improving ART adherence monitoring. We approach this by investigating the development of appropriate information systems solutions to support adherence monitoring. The study draws extensively from HIS integration work within an international action research program known as Health Information Systems Program (HISP) [19]. Field intervention work is currently at an advanced stage of planning waiting for commencement in Sierra Leone. This paper contributes to HIS integration research by highlighting the capabilities of emerging software platforms, and how they can enable the development of ICT-based

---

[2] WHO | Consolidated guidelines on the use of antiretroviral drugs for treating and preventing HIV infection, 2016. Retrieved October 22, 2016, from http://www.who.int/hiv/pub/arv/arv-2016/en/.

solutions to help improve the management of ART adherence in resource-constrained settings. The emergence of District Health Information Systems 2 (DHIS2) as a software platform within the HIS field is discussed as an example of the opportunity presented to pursue the development of such solutions. The remainder of the paper is organized as follows: First, background literature review of concepts informing the study is presented. After this the research approach is described with a brief description of the problem diagnosis and the proposed solution. This is then followed with discussion and conclusion.

2 Background Literature

2.1 ART Adherence Monitoring

According to Amico et al. [6] ART adherence has gained wider recognition as a critical health promotion behavior for HIV- positive patients undergoing treatment. However there are still uncertainties about how higher levels of treatment adherence may be initiated and sustained especially in larger populations over longer periods [13, 33]. Because many of these studies are conducted on short-term basis with few patients, the long-term viability of adherence monitoring strategies are still unclear. Reported average study duration is about 20 weeks with an average sample size of about 56.7 participants [13, 34]. The ability to monitor large scale ART adherence programs especially within public health sectors of developing countries still require further exploration. This need is clearly articulated by Amico et al.: *the demanding nature of ART regimens underscores the need for more strategic and multifaceted interventions that extend beyond the typical patient-provider interaction or ad hoc clinic discussions* ([6], p. 285). Furthermore, research indicates that the scaling up of ART adherence programs to cover larger populations increases the complexities of monitoring the adherence - health outcome dynamics [35]. It is also stated that currently there is no established "gold standard" for measuring or reporting adherence outcomes [13]. The various methods used in monitoring ART adherence such as patient self-reporting, patient attendance at scheduled visits, pill counts, electronic bottle monitors, pharmacy records, and others are also identified as not effective for all conditions [6, 13]. Moreover, as the treatment of HIV transitions from acute to chronic disease [5] the long-term use of ART will require more strategic solutions that are responsive to the changing dynamics of adherence management in different settings [38].

2.2 ICT in ART Adherence Management

The potential for ICT-based tools to support ART adherence activities has been examined in intervention studies and systematic literature reviews [14–18, 39]. The advantages of ICTs are identified as their potential for interaction, collaboration, low cost, and use in areas with limited human and material resources [14]. Technological devices like mobile phones can facilitate the ability of health workers for example to track and follow-up patients to provide them with the necessary care. Some specific functions performed with ICT tools in managing ART adherence include reminding patients to take their drugs through phone calls, SMS messages, and pager devices [15–18]. Other devices such as medication events monitoring systems (MEMS) are used to remotely monitor patient-pillbox interactions to help determine medication adherence [38].

Despite these benefits there are challenges that need to be addressed if the full potential of ICT in the area of ART adherence management can be realized. For example the medication events monitoring systems (MEMS), which although efficient at monitoring pillbox events is regarded to be expensive technology [38], and as such may not scale in financially constrained settings. Other web-based solutions used for encouraging medication adherence through the use of social media and similar resource intensive technologies [39] may also not be suitable in some resource-limited conditions. Another dimension also worthy of consideration is the socio-economic and demographic differences in patients which could impact usability of certain technological solutions. But more importantly there are calls to look beyond current solutions which seem to be narrowly focused on the use of single technologies for more comprehensive approaches [6, 13, 14, 39]. Such standalone and mostly ad-hoc solutions may not for instance suit public health contexts for the long-term use. Due to information and process overlaps that often exist between different health programs, more integrative and sustainable solutions will be required to reduce information systems fragmentation typical in such contexts [22].

2.3   HIS Integration Strategies

Information systems integration is identified as a socio-technical process involving different actors [24]. Within healthcare, integration strategies must take *"the users' needs of the HIS, the purpose of the systems, and the wider organizational perspectives [...] and relate those to goals of better efficiency, effectiveness, and co-ordination in organizations"* ([20], p. 59). This has also been described as a negotiation process [23] involving technological systems, people, organizations, and cultural practices working toward achieving a more integrated view of information to facilitate decision-making and care delivery. Integration strategies should therefore be able to accommodate changes to the system implementation process [22]. Examples of these include *modular implementation strategies* [28] and *loose coupling integration* strategies [29]. These are also important for preserving evolutionary independence and modular maintainability of the systems involved.

Also depending on the information needs dictating the integration or *interoperability*[3] of a set of systems and actors, the underlying integration processes could be pursued either at the *horizontal* or *vertical* levels of the organization [20]. Vertical level integration supports bottom-up flow of usually aggregate data between levels of the administrative hierarchies for higher-level management decision-making. Horizontal level integration on the other hand supports lower-level routine care delivery activities

---

[3] In healthcare, **interoperability** is the ability of different information technology systems and software applications to communicate, exchange data, and use the information that has been exchanged. Retrieved November 29, 2016, from http://www.himss.org/library/interoperability-standards/what-is-interoperability.

enabled by a single point of access to more granular data from multiple sources. These can include patient data from wards, specialties, and data from other sources like pharmacies and logistics. The horizontal integration approach is therefore suitable for achieving integration objectives proposed in this paper. This could be enabled by ICT platforms capable of supporting the integration of software systems, technological devices, different health programs data and local practices.

2.4   Software Platforms and HIS Integration

Platforms are foundation technologies upon which complementary products, technologies, or services can be developed [26]. Functionalities provided by platforms allow multiple parties to work together to address common problems [26]. Potential benefits offered by platforms include cost and time savings on product development, which can be achieved through half-ready solutions and platform components reusability. They also facilitate the development of highly varied derivative products and services and enable higher levels of products and services customization to meet diverse user requirements [25]. Platforms, by enabling interactions among different sets of actors often result in ecosystems of solutions comprising of human actors, software systems and services working together towards common goals [26]. Examples of software platforms which have contributed to the development of many useful derivative software products and services include Google Android, Apple iOS, Microsoft Windows, and many more (see [26]). The capabilities offered by software platforms can therefore be seen as an avenue through which new healthcare related information systems solutions could be explored.

In the HIS field, the District Health Information Systems 2 (DHIS2) is presented as an example of an emerging software platform (see: www.dhis2.org/technology). Nielsen and Sæbø [30] conceptualize aspects of the platform evolution of DHIS2 as *functional architecting*. Following a number of user adoptions involving the DHIS2 tracker (a software module which runs on top of the DHIS2 platform), they describe three architectural strategies involved in extending DHIS2's platform functionality into different use domains. These are elaborated as *charting*, *encroaching*, and *connecting*. Charting extends a system's platform capability into another domain to fulfil unmet functional needs, encroaching offers alternatives to existing solutions in the domain, and connecting integrates with systems where each has clearly defined roles in the domain. With this conceptualization they demonstrate that software platforms emergence offer opportunities for advancing HIS integration work.

3   Research Approach

This paper introduces a longitudinal action research project planned to span several years. Using a canonical action research methodology [31] several cycles of research iterations involving *problem diagnosis*, *action planning*, *intervention* (action taking), *evaluation* (assessment), and *reflection* (learning) are planned to be executed. The research work done so far covers the first iteration of problem diagnosis and action planning. This is informed by an ongoing conversation between HISP UiO team and project partners in Sierra Leone. From this the research objectives have been identified and the initial requirements for the proposed solution have been analyzed. Additional data about the problem context has been gathered from sources like the *National AIDS Progress Response Report*[4] for 2014 and other relevant documentations. DHIS2 platform documentation including the implementers guide (see: www.dhis2.org/documentation) have been instrumental in planning the solution implementation roadmap. Also experiences have been drawn from similar HISP projects including a recent DHIS2 tracker implementation for a national malaria control program in Zimbabwe [40], in which one of the authors of this paper participated. In Sierra Leone, HISP UiO's involvement in health information system strengthening through the implementation of DHIS2 since 2008 [21] have also served as the groundwork in the build up to this current research. The next phase of this research process will focus on initiating planned field intervention activities at the research site.

3.1   Problem Diagnosis and Solution Description

The research problem is diagnosed as high fragmentation of information systems currently used for managing the HIV treatment program. The fragmentation is identified as: (1) the information systems used in managing the ART programs have been deployed as standalone systems and spread across localities in HIV clinics. And the lack of a common information platform makes patients monitoring challenging across localities, and (2) the information systems for managing HIV related health programs such as prevention of mother-to-child-transmission (PMTCT) for HIV pregnant women have been implemented as 'silo' systems. This lack of communication between systems also affect efficient delivery of care to patients who may be enrolled into other health programs which need to be managed together with HIV treatment. These problems have contributed to making adherence monitoring challenging, and impacting negatively on the effectiveness of the ART program.

A solution based on a software module on the DHIS2 platform known as tracker capture, is hereby proposed to address the identified challenges. The tracker capture module utilizes the DHIS2 platform's data warehousing functionalities to enable enrollment, management, and tracking of patients in specific health programs (see: www.dhis2.org/individual-data-records). With this approach the currently fragmented systems will be absorbed onto one instance of the tracker capture hosted on the DHIS2 platform. End users at the health facility level will then be able to access the centralized system via web-enabled devices such as computers and smartphones through the internet. Allied health programs like malaria and TB can also be deployed as separate instances on the same platform and configured to share data into the HIV system. Data sharing is also possible between third party systems through interoperable interfaces supported by the DHIS2 platform. With this, a more holistic view of patient data can be achieved for effective monitoring and treatment adherence promotion. It will also

---

[4] Sierra Leone National AIDS Response Progress Report 2014. Retrieved October 8, 2016, from http://www.unaids.org/sites/default/files/country/documents/SLE_narrative_report_2015.pdf.

improve health worker mobility through the DHIS2 tracker capture App available for deployment on Android-based devices.

3.2   Challenges with Managing ART Adherence and Why DHIS2

Complexities of ART treatment regimen and guidelines pose major information management challenges for care providers [6]. To manage patient adherence effectively requires continuous monitoring of multiplicity of events associated with the treatment process. These include for example the ability to access the right information to determine what ART regimen a patient is eligible for. While undergoing treatment a patient's progress have to be monitored continuously to inform subsequent actions. Other events such as viral load and CD4 count measurements, diet restrictions, drug resistance and side effects, and many other HIV associated complications also have to be monitored. This puts a huge information management burden on care providers instead of having more time for patient care. With current unavailability of more efficient information management tools the effects of ART adherence programs have been reported as generally weak, and underpowered [6, 34]. Also in adherence promotion, activities like patient education, treatment tracking and provision of follow-up services by health workers require the support of ICT tools. And lacking these tools can hamper their ability to effectively conduct adherence monitoring. In the contexts of developing countries under consideration, the viability of the needed supporting ICT tools will depend on factors such as systems availability, accessibility, and flexibility. This is where the DHIS2 platform is seen as a more viable solution. It is currently available and being used at various levels of health information management in 47 developing countries including the one under study (see: www.dhis2.org/inaction). The main strength of DHIS2 is its strong support base of researchers, system developers, system implementers, and users. This international support network is actively engaged in the continuous development of the DHIS2 platform and modules to meet the changing needs of health information management [19]. The platform has generic functionalities that can readily be customized to suit the requirements of the particular context. In the particular case of ART adherence management, platform modules such as the tracker capture and event capture can be used to manage patient information and related treatment events. DHIS2 also integrates internet technologies, SMS services, and Geographical Information Systems (GIS) which can support patient follow-up activities in the communities for adherence promotion purposes. One caution though, is that because DHIS2 was traditionally developed for aggregate data its security regime is currently less developed. Hence extra measures should be taken to safeguard data privacy when dealing with patient level data.

4   Discussion

Looking at the literature, the majority of the available studies are conducted as clinical trials with the primary aim of promoting ART adherence in HIV-positive patients. These studies do not necessarily focus on the ICT tools themselves involved in the intervention activities. Where ICT tools are the focus of analysis it is mostly about what activities they were used to perform [e.g. in 14–18] or assessing their effectiveness in systematic literature reviews such as in de Lima et al. [14] and Muessig et al. [39]. But generally speaking, studies on how more appropriate technological tools may be developed are still lacking. There is a need to take into account particular contextual needs, including resource limitation concerns such as lack of local expertise and financial resources and relatively poor state of technological infrastructures to support such activities. In recent times however, access to ICT services has improved considerably in many developing countries due to the proliferation of mobile telecommunication networks. This together with emerging technologies like software platforms and associated services in the health domain, now makes it more feasible to implement more effective ICT solutions to address information management challenges identified with ART adherence programs.

In this paper we emphasize leveraging the capabilities of software platforms due to several potential benefits that can be gained. The most fundamental capabilities software platforms offer are based on their architectural design principles The *platform* aspect which is *the extensible codebase that provides core functionality shared by the modules that interoperate with it and the interfaces through which they interoperate* ([25], p. 675) is designed to be stable. The other aspect, a complementary set of *modules* is designed to vary. A module is *an add-on software subsystem that connects to the platform to add functionality to it (ibid)*. Benefits that can be gained from this include providing a foundation on which information system solutions can be grounded in the context of adoption. This can contribute to local institutionalization and participation in the systems development processes. The current ad-hoc and off-the-shelf use of technologies do not provide the mechanisms necessary for enabling local participation. Implementing a platform upon which solutions can be developed and or tailored [36] can help generate local knowledge bases around such tools to ensure their long-term sustainability. Also important to long-term sustainability is the ability of platforms to interface with other systems to enable interoperability. In the context of HIV treatment this ability to share data across different systems is critical for treatment effectiveness due to complexities associated with ART regimens [6]. Platforms can enable different technological solutions to be pooled together for rapid innovations and experimentation to address the changing dynamics and information needs involved in ART treatment. This can also contribute to research by encouraging ART adherence studies to examine the effectiveness of combining different technological tools rather focusing on single technologies as is common currently.

With free and open-source software platforms like DHIS2, an added benefit in the context of developing countries is the lower economic barrier to entry. Liberal licensing regimes such as *Berkeley Source Distribution* (BSD)[5] license for DHIS2 for example, contribute to expanding access to platform services. Under such arrangements users have the freedom to use, share, change, or improve the platform and complementary services without the licensing overheads often associated with proprietary systems. Additionally

---

[5] BSD license definition. (2005). Retrieved November 25, 2016, from http://www.linfo.org/bsdlicense.html.

platforms enable integration of services such as SMS, email, internet, maps, etc. to support development of innovative solutions, for example to support geo-spatial disease surveillance activities. Platforms like the DHIS2 also provide data warehousing and data analytic functionalities which can be helpful in addressing difficulties with monitoring and measuring adherence programs efficacy [38]. Also designed into platforms are security mechanisms for safeguarding data privacy. This is particularly important because loss of patient privacy, confidentiality, or secrecy can lead to HIV patient stigmatization with negative consequence on ART adherence [14, 37].

Finally, concerning lack of local capacity or expertise for platform or module development and maintenance in developing countries, platform governance mechanisms [27] provide strategies to address such challenges. This is done through global community collaborations where responsibilities for development and maintenance are shared among platform owners, module developers, and users. This collaborative approach is especially characteristic of open-source software projects like the DHIS2 (see for example: www.dhis2.org/contact). Within such global communities, different types of expertise are available to provide assistance when needed [32].

5   Conclusion

The main idea explored in this paper is that the software platform phenomenon emerging in the health information systems domain presents new opportunities to develop ICT-based solutions to better support healthcare management. The specific area within healthcare management focused on in this paper is HIV treatment and ART adherence monitoring for HIV-positive patients. Current research studies involving the use of ICT in ART adherence programs tend to focus narrowly on the use of specific technologies such as mobile phones. There also seem to be a lack of studies exploring how to design or develop ICT solutions specifically for supporting ART adherence programs. We therefore call for more studies to focus on the technological solutions themselves involved in ART adherence management and monitoring. This means more IS research practitioners have to recognize the need to adequately engage in addressing this research problem. This can be pursued through the development of new ICT based solutions or innovative use of existing technologies. Proposed in this paper is a more integrated solution based on DHIS2 platform to integrate technological and non-technological actors, and processes to support ART adherence monitoring activities for the case of Sierra Leone. To improve chances of success the paper proposes the use of suitable IS integration strategies in the problem context. These are flexible implementation processes that are adaptable to role negotiations among the actors involved. Through the use of concepts and strategies discussed, this paper argues for the opportunities software platforms offer and how their capabilities can be leveraged to develop more effective and locally relevant solutions. Going forward we hope to begin work on planned field intervention activities to investigate further the viability of the solution proposed.

References

1. Fatti, G., Meintjes, G., Shea, J., Eley, B., Grimwood, A.: Improved survival and antiretroviral treatment outcomes in adults receiving community-based adherence support: 5-year results from a multicentre cohort study in South Africa. JAIDS J. Acquir. Immune Defic. Syndr. **61**(4), e50–e58 (2012)
2. Abaasa, A.M., Todd, J., Ekoru, K., Kalyango, J.N., Levin, J., Odeke, E., Karamagi, C.A.: Good adherence to HAART and improved survival in a community HIV/AIDS treatment and care programme: the experience of The AIDS Support Organization (TASO), Kampala, Uganda. BMC Health Serv. Res. **8**(1), 1 (2008)
3. Palella, F.J., Deloria-Knoll, M., Chmiel, J.S., Moorman, A.C., Wood, K.C., Greenberg, A.E., Holmberg, S.D.: Survival benefit of initiating antiretroviral therapy in HIV-infected persons in different CD4+ cell strata. Ann. Intern. Med. **138**(8), 620–626 (2003)
4. García, D.O.P., Knobel, H., Carmona, A., Guelar, A., López-Colomés, J.L., Caylà, J.A.: Impact of adherence and highly active antiretroviral therapy on survival in HIV-infected patients. J. Acquir. Immune Defic. Syndr. (1999) **30**(1), 105–110 (2002)
5. Deeks, S.G., Lewin, S.R., Havlir, D.V.: The end of AIDS: HIV infection as a chronic disease. Lancet **382**(9903), 1525–1533 (2013)
6. Amico, K.R., Harman, J.J., Johnson, B.T.: Efficacy of antiretroviral therapy adherence interventions: a research synthesis of trials, 1996 to 2004. JAIDS J. Acquir. Immune Defic. Syndr. **41**(3), 285–297 (2006)
7. Gonzalez, J.S., Penedo, F.J., Antoni, M.H., Durán, R.E., McPherson-Baker, S., Ironson, G., Isabel-Fernandez, M., Klimas, N.G., Fletcher, M.A., Schneiderman, N.: Social support, positive states of mind, and HIV treatment adherence in men and women living with HIV/AIDS. Health Psychol. **23**(4), 413 (2004)
8. Arrivillaga, M., Ross, M., Useche, B., Alzate, M.L., Correa, D.: Social position, gender role, and treatment adherence among Colombian women living with HIV/AIDS: social determinants of health approach. Rev. Panam. Salud Pública **26**(6), 502–510 (2009)
9. Sayles, J.N., Wong, M.D., Kinsler, J.J., Martins, D., Cunningham, W.E.: The association of stigma with self-reported access to medical care and antiretroviral therapy adherence in persons living with HIV/AIDS. J. Gen. Intern. Med. **24**(10), 1101–1108 (2009)
10. Kalichman, S.C., Grebler, T.: Stress and poverty predictors of treatment adherence among people with low-literacy living with HIV/AIDS. Psychosom. Med. **72**(8), 810 (2010)
11. Mills, E.J., Nachega, J.B., Buchan, I., Orbinski, J., Attaran, A., Singh, S., Rachlis, B., Wu, P., Cooper, C., Thabane, L., Wilson, K.: Adherence to antiretroviral therapy in sub-Saharan Africa and North America: a meta-analysis. JAMA **296**(6), 679–690 (2006)
12. Kalichman, S.C., Cherry, C., Kalichman, M.O., Amaral, C.M., White, D., Pope, H., Swetzes, C., Eaton, L., Macy, R., Cain, D.: Integrated behavioral intervention to improve HIV/AIDS treatment adherence and reduce HIV transmission. Am. J. Pub. Health **101**(3), 531–538 (2011)
13. Nachega, J.B., Hislop, M., Dowdy, D.W., Lo, M., Omer, S.B., Regensberg, L., Chaisson, R.E., Maartens, G.: Adherence to highly active antiretroviral therapy assessed by pharmacy claims predicts survival in HIV-infected South African adults. JAIDS J. Acquir. Immune Defic. Syndr. **43**(1), 78–84 (2006)
14. de Lima, I.C.V., Galvão, M.T.G., de Oliveira Alexandre, H., Lima, F.E.T., de Araújo, T.L.: Information and communication technologies for adherence to antiretroviral treatment in adults with HIV/AIDS. Int. J. Med. Informatics **92**, 54–61 (2016)

15. Reynolds, N.R., Testa, M.A., Su, M., Chesney, M.A., Neidig, J.L., Frank, I., Smith, S., Ickovics, J., Robbins, G.K.: Telephone support to improve antiretroviral medication adherence: a multisite, randomized controlled trial. JAIDS J. Acquir. Immune Defic. Syndr. **47**(1), 62–68 (2008)

16. Belzer, M.E., Naar-King, S., Olson, J., Sarr, M., Thornton, S., Kahana, S.Y., Gaur, A.H., Clark, L.F.: Adolescent Medicine Trials Network for HIV/AIDS Interventions: The use of cell phone support for non-adherent HIV-infected youth and young adults: an initial randomized and controlled intervention trial. AIDS Behav. **18**(4), 686–696 (2014)

17. Lester, R.T., Ritvo, P., Mills, E.J., Kariri, A., Karanja, S., Chung, M.H., Jack, W., Habyarimana, J., Sadatsafavi, M., Najafzadeh, M., Marra, C.A.: Effects of a mobile phone short message service on antiretroviral treatment adherence in Kenya (WelTel Kenya1): a randomised trial. Lancet **376**(9755), 1838–1845 (2010)

18. Hardy, H., Kumar, V., Doros, G., Farmer, E., Drainoni, M.L., Rybin, D., Myung, D., Jackson, J., Backman, E., Stanic, A., Skolnik, P.R.: Randomized controlled trial of a personalized cellular phone reminder system to enhance adherence to antiretroviral therapy. AIDS Patient Care STDs **25**(3), 153–161 (2011)

19. Braa, J., Monteiro, E., Sahay, S.: Networks of action: sustainable health information systems across developing countries. MIS Q. **28**(3), 337–362 (2004)

20. Braa, J., Sahay, S.: Integrated health information architecture. In: Power to the Users: Design, Development and Use, pp. 148–149. Matrix Publishers, New Delhi (2012)

21. Braa, J., Kanter, A.S., Lesh, N., Crichton, R., Jolliffe, B., Sæbø, J., Kossi, E., Seebregts, C.J.: Comprehensive yet scalable health information systems for low resource settings: a collaborative effort in Sierra Leone. In: AMIA Annual Symposium Proceedings, vol. 2010, pp. 372–376, November 2010

22. Braa, J., Hanseth, O., Heywood, A., Mohammed, W., Shaw, V.: Developing health information systems in developing countries: the flexible standards strategy. MIS Q. **31**(2), 381–402 (2007)

23. Chilundo, B., Aanestad, M.: Integrating the information systems of disease-specific health programmes: negotiating multiple rationalities. Electron. J. Inf. Syst. Developing Countries **20**(2), 1–28 (2004)

24. Berg, M.: Patient care information systems and health care work: a sociotechnical approach. Int. J. Med. Inform. **55**(2), 87–101 (1999)

25. Tiwana, A., Konsynski, B., Bush, A.A.: Research commentary-platform evolution: coevolution of platform architecture, governance, and environmental dynamics. Inf. Syst. Res. **21**(4), 675–687 (2010)

26. Jansen, S., Cusumano, M.A.: Defining software ecosystems: a survey of software platforms and business network governance. In: Software Ecosystems: Analyzing and Managing Business Networks in the Software Industry, p. 13 (2013)

27. Baars, A., Jansen, S.: A framework for software ecosystem governance. In: International Conference of Software Business, pp. 168–180. Springer, Berlin Heidelberg, June 2012

28. Aanestad, M., Jensen, T.B.: Building nation-wide information infrastructures in healthcare through modular implementation strategies. J. Strat. Inf. Syst. **20**(2), 161–176 (2011)

29. Henfridsson, O., Bygstad, B.: The generative mechanisms of digital infrastructure evolution. MIS Q. **37**(3), 907–931 (2013)

30. Nielsen, P., Sæbø, J.I.: Three strategies for functional architecting: cases from the health systems of developing countries. Inf. Technol. Dev. **22**(1), 134–151 (2016)

31. Davison, R., Martinsons, M.G., Kock, N.: Principles of canonical action research. Inf. Syst. J. **14**(1), 65–86 (2004)

32. Msiska, B., Nielsen, P.: Innovation in the fringes of software ecosystems: the role of socio-technical generativity. Under review (2016)

33. Simoni, J.M., Frick, P.A., Pantalone, D.W., Turner, B.J.: Antiretroviral adherence interventions: a review of current literature and ongoing studies. Topics HIV Med. Publ. Int. AIDS Soc. USA **11**(6), 185–198 (2002)
34. Fogarty, L., Roter, D., Larson, S., Burke, J., Gillespie, J., Levy, R.: Patient adherence to HIV medication regimens: a review of published and abstract reports. Patient Educ. Couns. **46**(2), 93–108 (2002)
35. Mihalko, S.L., Brenes, G.A., Farmer, D.F., Katula, J.A., Balkrishnan, R., Bowen, D.J.: Challenges and innovations in enhancing adherence. Control. Clin. Trials **25**(5), 447–457 (2004)
36. Davis, G.B.: Commentary on information systems: to buy, build, or customize. Account. Horiz. **2**(1), 101–103 (1988)
37. Rintamaki, L.S., Davis, T.C., Skripkauskas, S., Bennett, C.L., Wolf, M.S.: Social stigma concerns and HIV medication adherence. AIDS Patient Care STDs **20**(5), 359–368 (2006)
38. Samet, J.H., Sullivan, L.M., Traphagen, E.T., Ickovics, J.R.: Measuring adherence among HIV-infected persons: is MEMS consummate technology? AIDS Behav. **5**(1), 21–30 (2001)
39. Muessig, K.E., Nekkanti, M., Bauermeister, J., Bull, S., Hightow-Weidman, L.B.: A systematic review of recent smartphone, internet and web 2.0 interventions to address the HIV continuum of care. Curr. HIV/AIDS Rep. **12**(1), 173–190 (2015)
40. Matavire, R.: Health information systems development: producing a new agora in Zimbabwe. Inf. Technol. Int. Dev. **12**(1), 35–51 (2016)

Patchworks of Logistics Management Information Systems: Challenges or Solutions for Developing Countries?

Bjørn-Ingar Bergum, Petter Nielsen, and Johan Ivar Sæbø[✉]

University of Oslo, Oslo, Norway
johansa@ifi.uio.no

Abstract. Uninterrupted supply of health commodities is a prerequisite for a well-functioning healthcare system. Establishing and maintaining effective supply chains is at the same time challenging in developing countries. A key part of this chain and the focus of this paper are the information systems supporting the communication and distribution of commodities between national warehouses and health facilities. Such systems supporting storage, transportation, wastage reduction, forecasting, planning and avoiding commodity stock-outs are invariably called Logistics Management Information Systems (LMIS). However, the blurred boundaries between the various parts of the supply chain and the numerous information systems involved is reflected in the lack of a clear definition of LMIS. The main aim of this paper is to provide a better understanding of what an LMIS is, and how it interacts with other information systems. By presenting two case studies, from Tanzania and Uganda, we show that the landscape of LMIS consists of a patchwork of information systems, which often have tighter coupling with systems of other domains (such as patient management) than with the supply chain. This leads us to ask the following research question; what are appropriate information systems architectures for LMIS? Our response, main argument and contribution is that the nature of these supply chains favours the emergence of several independent information systems. This is particularly due to the variation in resources and capacities on the different levels of the health system and thus the supply chain. Interoperability between the different levels and other related information systems should then be considered, necessitating a scrutinous evaluation of what data needs to be shared with whom.

Keywords: Logistics management information systems · LMIS · Tanzania · Uganda

1 Introduction

To provide effective public health services, the right health commodities, such as medicines and equipment, must get to the right people at the right time [24]. To manage the distribution of commodities, relevant information is needed at all steps of the supply chain – from the point-of-origin to the point-of-consumption. Who needs how much of a certain commodity? Where can it be found, and at what price? How can we

© IFIP International Federation for Information Processing 2017
Published by Springer International Publishing AG 2017. All Rights Reserved
J. Choudrie et al. (Eds.): ICT4D 2017, IFIP AICT 504, pp. 47–58, 2017.
DOI: 10.1007/978-3-319-59111-7_5

get it to where it is needed? In addition to the direct need of logistics information for supply chain management, commodity data and indicators are also important for the routine monitoring and evaluation of health services in general. Are our immunization rates influenced by stock-outs? Do the facilities have the right staff to administer these commodities? Information systems are clearly essential for the proper management of the supply chain and the evaluation of it in the health sector.

Despite the apparent need for well-functioning information systems to support the supply chain across the different levels of the health system, such systems continue to be challenged [13, 17], including weak sharing of data amongst stakeholders, fragmentation of logistics data, a plethora of paper and electronic forms used in different locations, incomplete data on dispensing to patients and competing software for supply chain at the various levels [9, 10]. There have been many initiatives to improve supply chains and corresponding information systems in developing countries, but they have been limited in scope and do only in a limited way address the linkages to other relevant information systems [17]. A broader approach seems necessary. At the same time, a good understanding of the various parts of the supply chain information systems in developing countries is absent from the existing literature. The international organizations supporting many developing countries in this regard tend to focus only on limited parts of the system, and their definitions of such systems vary.

The health commodity supply chain is a multi-level system, that include producers of commodities at the global level; procurement, finance, and quality assurance mechanisms between national ministries and the producers; warehouses and distribution mechanisms in-country; and finally mechanisms around dispensing commodities to relevant beneficiaries, such as patients requiring medicines. The information needed for each of these tasks vary in their level of detail, and should also support the correct forecasting and replenishment of commodities. Given the above, it is not surprising that a range of different information systems are in use within a single country [10]. But questions remain related to the architecture these systems form and how they are integrated (or not) and interoperate (or not).

To get a better understanding of information systems for health commodity supply management, we take as a point of departure several international efforts to strengthen supply chains in developing countries. Examining their use of LMIS, we see that this can be understood as one out of many information systems involved in the supply chain. One of the aims of this paper is thus to explore what an LMIS is, and how it interacts or not with other systems. We do this by presenting two cases of LMIS, from Uganda and Tanzania. We further discuss and draw lessons learnt related to the information systems from these cases that can be generally applicable to strengthen health commodity supply chains. To guide our research on LMIS, we have sought to answer the following research question: What are appropriate information systems architectures for public health supply chain management in developing countries?

While integration is a common prescription for health information systems architectures [2], we argue for a critical perspective on the needs for integrating logistics management information systems across the different levels of the health system and with information systems from other domains. By architecture, we mean how various information systems work together, offer complementary and/or overlapping functionality and the related structures supporting their integration, interoperability and evolution over time. For us, architecture is not "theoretical" drawings or blueprints, but the actual and operative information systems on the ground, how they are interrelated and how they share functional responsibilities.

The rest of the paper is organized as follows. First, we look at common under-standings of LMIS as a concept to establish an understanding of its scope. Then we present the methods applied in our study of LIMS in Tanzania and Uganda, followed by the empirical findings. This is followed by a discussion related to the current understanding of LMIS, before we conclude with a more detailed view on LMIS architectures and draw lessons learned for their design.

2 Relevant Literature on LMIS

As countries are making efforts at strengthening their LMIS, they move toward digi-tizing previously paper-based systems. Currently there is not a lot of academic liter-ature on the subject of LMIS, what little there is does not have an IS focus, but is mostly concerned with assessing the supply chain as a whole, challenges in general related to supply chains in developing countries [1, 6, 16]. There has also been work done to improve the understanding of the different roles within health logistics [15]. Over the last decade, some large international organizations have led this work on a normative level, spearheaded by inter-agency initiatives such as the USAID sponsored Deliver project[1] and SIAPS program[2], and the United National Commission on Life Saving Commodities[3]. We start by examining these and related organizations' understanding of LMIS, before presenting our own definition of it.

Despite the frequent references to LMIS among the international organizations, which fund and lead supply chain projects in developing countries, a clear definition of LMIS is lacking. It is often treated as everything related to information that supports the supply chain, and also as an off-the-shelf product with seemingly little, if any, com-plexity. Such a broad understanding hides the various aspects of the health commodity supply chain and the variety of informational needs and can translate into poorly designed information systems.

The broadness of the existing definition is well illustrated by USAID: "A logistics management information system (LMIS) collects, processes, and reports logistics data. A well-functioning LMIS provides decision makers throughout a supply chain with accurate, timely, and appropriate data" [18]. Given a view of the supply chain as everything from raw material supply for medicines, to the individual patients [13], this definition includes users at local, national, and international levels. Little difference is made between the supply chain at large and LMIS, but a narrowing of scope is provided by more recent documents from USAID. Defining both supply chain and logistics management, they state that "the supply chain includes global manufacturers and supply and demand dynamics, but logistics tends to focus more on specific tasks

---

[1] http://deliver.jsi.com.

[2] http://siapsprogram.org.

[3] http://lifesavingcommodities.org/about/about-the-un-commision.

within a particular program health system" [19]. An LMIS then, supports planning and execution of flows and storage of commodities, primarily within the individual national health systems, i.e. all that is required to meet patient demand [13]. However, it is still broad in that it includes functions like procurement, finances, transportation and fleet management. A more narrow understanding is provided by the World Bank, who defines LMIS by emphasizing information on stock status and day-to-day management of commodities and forecasting [23]. In the latter, LMIS is seen as a more restricted system. Stock-out data and forecasts, outputs of the LMIS, are seen as informing procurement which will take place through other mechanisms and systems.

The different definitions open up for seeing the supply chain as being supported by a diverse set of information systems, of which the LMIS is only one. One distinction can be made between the LMIS and Warehouse Management Systems (WMS). A WMS is used to manage the flow of materials into, through, and out of storage facilities by processing the transactions associated with each movement, from receiving and put-away to picking, packing, and shipping [14]. Yet another, newer, USAID document engage in breaking up the domain further, where the supply chain is supported by warehouse systems and billing and accounting systems, in addition to the LMIS [20].

Based on our empirical work and these definitions, we argue for the following clarifications of the LMIS concept. First, we suggest defining LMIS as a system of records and reports on routine administration, dispensing, consumption, and loss and adjustments data, to support forecasting and distribution of health commodities from central national storage to point of health service delivery. Second, we argue for understanding LMIS as one of several information systems that supports the supply chain at large, where the different systems provide specialized functionality yet are linked together by sharing key data related to the overall supply chain. The second point is thus related directly to our research question. Given that LMIS potentially interacts with a range of other supply chain information systems, what is its functional role in relation to them? We now turn to relevant literature on health information systems architectures.

We define information systems architectures as the roles of system components and the relationships between them. Our focus is not on the individual software applications' inner workings, but how different constellations of information systems offer different functionality and interact with each other. Related to health supply chains, the architecture is composed of multiple information systems, such as LMIS, WMS, billing and accounting systems, etc.

Based on an understanding of information systems as open-ended and shared among a multitude of different actors, as articulated by research on information infrastructures [5], it follows that information system architectures are not centrally designed and controlled. Instead they tend to evolve, blurring the justification of how certain architecture emerged [3]. This evolutionary view downplays the role any actor has to impose architectural principles like service-orientation and modularity [4] that aim to add coherence throughout all parts of the information systems. As a result, national health information systems in developing countries seldom experience high degrees of reusability and interoperability [8].

Nielsen and Sæbø [11] examine architectures from a functional perspective, and note that in situations where functional needs are unmet, it is not uncommon for existing software to expand to meet these needs. In more limited markets, such as developing countries' public sector, the different components of the overall architecture can thus cover more ground than if there were many alternatives to choose from. Touching specifically on LMIS, they show how related health information systems expand to cover some aspects of the LMIS when there is no other viable solution in place.

3 Methods

The data presented in this paper is based on an interpretive case study [22] of the health sector supply chain information systems in Uganda and Tanzania. The primary data collection was conducted during a joint visit to both countries over the period of a month in January 2016. Secondary data collection was based on discussions with other participants in a larger research project on LMIS, as well as a document review of relevant international organizations who support developing countries with health system strengthening. An initial document search was carried out to identify those who either define or discuss logistics management information systems (LMIS) or supply chain information systems. We looked at documents from large international agencies such as World Health Organization (WHO) and UNICEF, relevant international projects they are part of, and technical partners of said organizations.

This fieldwork consisted of visits by the authors to different levels of the medical supply chain in the two countries. Data was collected through interviews and observations, with the aim of understanding the flow of information and commodities, and supporting technologies and information systems, summarized in Table 1.

Table 1. Data collection

Place	Primary data collection	Secondary data collection
Uganda	Interviewed two pharmacy clerks and the head of pharmacy at hospital	Report from interviews of three logistics managers, a warehouse manager, a warehouse officer, a doctor and a hospital manager
Tanzania	Report from interviews of three logistics managers, a warehouse manager, a warehouse officer, a doctor and a hospital manager	Report from other researchers spending two months in Tanzania examining various aspects of the health supply chain
International organisation documents	Reviewed 13 documents on supply chain information systems (examples: JSI, UNCoLSC, VillageReach)	

Data analysis was carried out jointly by the authors. For Uganda and Tanzania, the focus was on identifying software or paper systems used in the supply chain, what functionality the software had, how it was used, and what data the different systems contained. This was done by drawing illustrations, or "maps" of the health sector, where the scope and scale of the systems were outlined, as well as their integration or not. The document analysis focused on identifying definitions of LMIS, and secondary on related concepts such as supply chain, supply chain information system, warehouse information system, etc. These definitions were then compared, and similarities and differences outlined. Lastly, these definitions were compared with the functional "maps" from Tanzania and Uganda.

4   Cases - Tanzania and Uganda

In Tanzania, most health facilities report on consumption and order new commodities through paper forms (Report and Requisition, R&R), brought to district offices where this information is entered in an online system, eLMIS. In the capital some health facilities can enter their R&R reports directly into eLMIS, due to the more widespread availability of computers and Internet connection. The system handles the flow of this information between districts, regional and national warehouses. At the warehouses, a proprietary Electronic Resource Planning (ERP) system, Epicor9, is supporting their needs of warehouse management, distribution planning, and finances. There was at the time of research a partial integration between eLMIS and Epicor9, where eLMIS send data to Epicor9, but not the other way around.

eLMIS is used by the district pharmacist, who enters orders from the paper forms into eLMIS. This R&R contains each commodity's starting balance, commodities received, loss/adjustments and a closing balance, as well as orders for replenishment of stocks. The district pharmacist can call the reporting facility to confirm the data, and can make adjustments in cases where errors are detected. The district pharmacist also adjusts orders based on the facilities budget. The costs of the commodities appear in eLMIS, but the facility budget does not. The district pharmacist therefore receives the budgets for each facility, printed from Epicor9, from the higher levels. When an adjustment is made, the facilities are not notified.

There are in addition a multitude of other systems at the lower levels which also engage with logistics data. One such system is the ILS Gateway, a mobile reporting system used to report stock on hand and adjustments by facilities on a limited set of tracer commodities. It also sends SMS reminders to the facilities to submit reports and notifies them of upcoming supervision visits. The data collected via the ILS Gateway can be accessed in a website by the district pharmacist. Some reporting is done by sending SMS with mobile phones. Other logistics data is generated by electronic patient systems, which is then printed out and entered into eLMIS manually. An example is the CTC2, a patient record system used for HIV/AIDS patients used at large facilities, which keeps track of the patients' adherence to antiretroviral therapy (ART). A patient's current and previous ART regimens are registered in the system, and the system also tracks the stock balance of the ART medicines. When orders are to be placed, the order forms are printed and manually entered into eLMIS. Lastly, some data on commodities is entered into the national health management information system (HMIS), which runs on the DHIS2 software. This data is entered into DHIS2 by HMIS workers at district level, and the data is used by health managers. The primary use of logistics data for general management is to analyze stock-out data with service delivery data, and the HMIS is not used for ordering purposes. Interoperability between DHIS2 and eLMIS or ILS Gateway is not established and there is some duplication of data among the systems. A project to send statistics from eLMIS to DHIS2 in order to utilize the analysis tool in the latter was ongoing at the time of writing [21].

In addition to the official system, facility staff also uses other means to replenish their stocks. For example, we found that facility staff had WhatsApp groups where facilities helped each other out when they were low on stocks. They would then redistribute among themselves, and report these transactions in the R&R forms.

The situation in Tanzania is illustrated below, where at the national level there exists one ERP as WMS. At the district and national level there exist two LMIS systems, where only one is actually used as the system handling orders. At the facility and district level an LMIS system exists that is only used for reporting. While at the facility level there are smaller systems used for patient records and inventory management. Most information subsystems at lower level are completely paper-based due to lack of reliable electricity and internet support (Fig. 1).

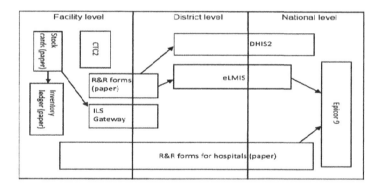

Fig. 1. Different systems used in the Tanzanian LMIS

The situation in Uganda is quite similar to that in Tanzania, with proprietary ERPs used at the national and regional warehouses. Two different systems are in fact used, SageLine 500 and the MACS Warehouse Management System. SageLine 500 is used for finances, account supervision, as well as a general ledger. The MACS WMS is used for order processing, facility budgets, picking and packing, and journey planning. In addition, public health facilities get some commodities from a large private supplier, The Joint Medical Stores (JMS), which also use an ERP (IFS) for their national and regional warehouses.

Most reporting and ordering in Uganda is done through paper forms from facilities to the warehouses. Of the computer-supported systems identified, they either had limited scope, such as related to one health program only, or used in only hospitals and not smaller facilities. A stand-alone system, Rx Solution, is used for inventory management at most hospitals, but reporting and ordering is done through reports printed from this system, which can also be sent as an email attachment. Other specific logistics streams, like that for ART, are supported by different software. Where such software exists, data is often stored on paper in addition. The DHIS2 software (which is also used for the national HMIS) is used for ordering ART commodities, where the paper orders are entered manually at the facility or the district office. Before an order is shipped, the facility is contacted in order to confirm the order. The order data is entered manually into MACS, as there is no integration between DHIS2 and MACS (Fig. 2).

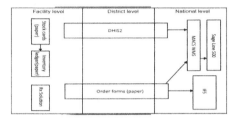

Fig. 2. Different systems used in Ugandan LMIS

In both Uganda and Tanzania there is a gap between the public and the private health sector and additional streams of information and commodities related to international agencies. Where electronic systems exist, they are not interoperable and unable to share data with the public health sector.

A pattern of how the field of LMIS is organized can be seen across the two cases. Large, complex proprietary ERP packages are used to support the national warehouses, with modules for inventory, finances, procurement and the like. The flow of commodities from the warehouses out to districts and health facilities is supported by smaller, less complex systems which focus on ordering and reporting. At the facilities, there is a group of specialized software, typically originating from needs around patient management, that also have small modules for local inventory and order management. Taken together, the field of logistics management is supported by a patchwork of systems, varying greatly in their complexity, origin, cost, and reach.

5   Discussion

The cases from Tanzania and Uganda show architectures consisting of fragmented and heterogeneous systems. While there are certainly systems that are used for supporting logistics, such as eLMIS in Tanzania and DHIS2 for ART medicines in Uganda, there are also other systems that contain data on health commodities.

Given our definition of LMIS, understood as a system of records and reports on routine administration, dispensing, consumption, and loss and adjustments data, to support forecasting and distribution of health commodities from central national storage to point of health service delivery, one finding is that there are several information systems which may qualify as playing the role of an LMIS. In both countries, LMIS functionality is spread out among different paper-based and electronic information systems. While in both countries there are systems that deal with both reporting and ordering between facilities and national warehouses, there are also several systems that focus on more local logistics, such as patient management systems or local inventory systems. In addition there are systems which contain some of the same data, but not for ordering purposes but rather as one of many data sources for general health management.

Looking at the different levels of the health system, there are strong similarities between Uganda and Tanzania. In general there are differences in infrastructure as well as the understanding of logistics at the different levels [15]. At the national level there is a logical, rational and mathematical approach to logistics. Their focus is getting commodities to the clinics and their area of operation is the broadest. Here both countries have large, proprietary ERP solutions that handle both warehouse management and finances and other related functional areas. At the facility level there is more of a pragmatic approach to logistics. The main facility level focus is on delivering health services to those who need it. They still have information systems that cover some logistics support, such as systems primarily for patient management (CTC2 in Tanzania), local facility inventory systems (Rx Solution in Uganda), and "shadow IT" that go beyond the official systems (use of WhatsApp for inter-facility redistribution in Tanzania). National and facility levels have very different infrastructure, needs and scope of operation which is reflected in the systems they use.

The district level resembles characteristics from both levels, where the management of health services is a primary focus. Technologically they are more advanced than the facility level, yet their needs differ from the national level as they are more of a middle-man between the facility and national level, adjusting the facility orders, and to a limited degree, partaking in the distribution of commodities.

The difference in technology used on the different levels is not only connected to the primary goals, but also its infrastructure and maturity. On a general level the district and national level has a more robust infrastructure than the facility level. This doesn't just concern Internet connectivity and electricity, but also the ability for on-site support. Together these factors results in the fragmentation of information systems, which both cases show. It is important to point out that even if different, the information systems in place are suited to their local needs.

When the need for a system has emerged in both Tanzania and Uganda, it has been developed and implemented in isolation, with little regard to other systems. This is at least partially due to different actors developing the systems, but more importantly a lack of an architectural vision from the national level guiding how systems should be developed and implemented. This has created systems working independently of each other, sometimes within the same functional area. The functional overlap is quite as expected given the tight integration of the various aspects of health service provision. For example, the CTC2 system in Tanzania is a patient-management system that also contains relevant data on health commodities, in this case on ART medicines for HIV patients. When treating HIV patients, a large part of that is to administer medicines and make sure you have enough of those medicines and forecast what you will need over the next few months. Developing a system to support patient management, it is thus natural to extend the functionality to also cover inventory management in the absence of any unified LMIS and inventory system that you can connect to. The same logic is behind the inclusion of stock-out data in the national HMIS.

Both countries show the same architecture of systems existing as separate entities in the supply chain, even though some of them share the same data. One way to interpret this is that this works and is suited to the context, but it may need optimization related to functional duplication. Another interpretation is that this doesn't work and that this patchwork of information systems should be replaced by one big system that can handle everything. However, such a strategy would easily face challenges related to the very different needs at the different levels. The third way could be to argue that this doesn't work as effectively as it could, but there is no need to start again from scratch. Integrating existing systems is a more feasible solution to the fragmented information systems. Integration will help circumvent some of the issues persisting today in the LMIS. The question then becomes, where do we integrate? There aren't necessarily any correct answers to this question. It depends on the systems already in place, the availability of supported, appropriate, technology, and the priorities of the health system as a whole. Integration should also be driven by informational needs. Today such integration is already working, though in a manual way. The important thing when opting for integration is having a full architectural vision [8]. This architectural vision should be based on the principles of service orientation [4].

Approaching the LMIS architecture with basic software design principles such as encapsulation, loose coupling, composability and normalization in mind will help make the LMIS more flexible. Encapsulation will ensure that the existing LMIS systems can be utilized when the new architectural vision is implemented. Systems developed under the new vision should emphasize loose coupling where dependency on other services should be minimized. Composability as well as normalization will help ensure less of a functional overlap between the systems in place, such as the case is today. Another important factor is data standards. When the same data exists on paper, as well as in different systems, data standards can help in creating a bridge between the software applications. Examples of challenges when integrating these systems can be found from the experiences when Tanzania wanted to create an integrated HMIS/LMIS dashboard [21]. Issues such as different facility names in the different system, different reporting periods and different naming conventions for drugs created issues that could have partly been solved with a more service oriented approach to the LMIS architecture. It is also important to mention that service oriented architectures empowers reuse which can help in reducing the number of systems in the LMIS, but it also increases the complexity.

In summary, both countries show that the functionality of an LMIS is spread out across many different systems, which may or may not have been developed with the aim of actually being an LMIS. When for instance a health management information system or an patient management system comes to include data and functionality around logistics, it is consistent with a situation where an LMIS has already been established but does not yet cover the needs of general management or patient management, respectively [11]. Given the different information needs and infrastructural situation at the various levels, this "patchwork" of logistics-related systems is not only expected, but also to a certain degree beneficial. Both countries have some systems that support horizontal reporting and ordering, but there are still needs for logistics data beyond these that has come to be supported by other systems. The crucial question then becomes if, and how, and where, they should be integrated.

Some answers to these questions are coming from the countries already. In Tanzania, there is a need for the eLMIS to be integrated with the ERP warehouse system, so that orders can be shared automatically to the higher level system and financial data can be shared down to district pharmacists. Such integration has already been established, but only allowing one-way data sharing. Likewise, there is a need to share financial data downwards, so that district pharmacists or others who enter ordering data can do this within the frame of the facilities' budgets. Since some logistics data is also relevant for health service management, there is also an initiative to integrate eLMIS and DHIS2. This is certainly an area where we would call for more research, and to document the learnings from the above mentioned initiatives.

6 Conclusion

Our research question in this paper is: *What are appropriate information systems architectures for public health supply chain management in developing countries?*

Our short answer is that this depends on the existing systems in place, and the needs they cover at the various levels. We caution against thinking that one system may cover all supply chain related needs, given the big differences in scope and technical infrastructure. Though we have only looked at two countries, a pattern emerges where a larger ERP-like system is needed at national warehouses, a "slimmer" transactional system that focus on reporting and ordering connects the warehouses with the facilities, and a range of other systems that primarily support other functions also cover some supply chain data. The transactional system between the levels is what most resembles the definitions of LMIS we have identified among the international organizations who support supply chain systems in developing countries, though there are many other systems who could be said to have limited LMIS functionality also.

References

1. Bossert, T.J., Bowser, D.M., Amenyah, J.K.: Is decentralization good for logistics systems? Evidence on essential medicine logistics in Ghana and Guatemala. Health Policy Plann. **33**(2), 73–82 (2007)
2. Braa, J., Sahay, S.: Integrated Health Information Architecture: Power to the Users: Design, Development, and Use. Matrix Publishers, New Delhi (2012)
3. Chen, D., Doumeingts, G., Vernadat, F.: Architectures for enterprise integration and interoperability: past, present and future. Comput. Ind. **59**(7), 647–659 (2008). doi:10.1016/j.compind.2007.12.016
4. Draheim, D.: Service-oriented architecture. In: Business Process Technology, pp. 221–241. Springer, Berlin Heidelberg (2010)

5. Hanseth, O., Kalle, L.: Design theory for dynamic complexity in information infrastructures: the case of building the internet. J. Inf. Technol. **25**(1), 1–19 (2010)
6. Jahre, M., Dumoulin, L., Greenhalgh, L.B., Hudspeth, C., Limlim, P., Spindler, A.: Improving health in developing countries: reducing complexity of drug supply chains. J. Humanitarian Logistics Supply Chain Manag. **2**(1), 54–84 (2012)
7. JSI: Guidelines for Managing the HIV/AIDS Supply Chain. John Snow, Inc./DELIVER, for the U.S. Agency for International Development, Arlington, VA (2005)
8. Moodley, D., Pillay, A.W., Seebregts, C.J.: Position paper: researching and developing open architectures for national health information systems in developing african countries. In: Foundations of Health Informatics Engineering and Systems, pp. 129–139. Springer (2012)
9. Management Sciences for Health/Health Commodities Services Management Program, Kenya, Work Plan: 1 October 2013–30 September 2014. Submitted to the U.S. Agency for International Development/Kenya by the MSH/HCSM Program. Nairobi, Kenya
10. Management Sciences for Health: Promising practices: quantification: forecasting and supply planning. In: Systems for Improved Access to Pharmaceuticals and Services (SIAPS) Program. Management Sciences for Health, Arlington, VA (2014)
11. Nielsen, P., Sæbø, J.I.: Three strategies for functional architecting: cases from the health systems of developing countries. Inf. Technol. Dev. 1, 1 April 2015
12. SIAPS: Report on Strengthening the Warehouse Management System for the Pharmacie Populaire du Mali. Submitted to the US Agency for International Development by the Systems for Improved Access to Pharmaceuticals and Services (SIAPS) Program. Management Sciences for Health, Arlington, VA (2016)
13. PATH: Common Requirements for Logistics Management Information Systems. PATH, Seattle (2010)
14. SIAPS: Report on Strengthening the Warehouse Management System for the Pharmacie Populaire du Mali, Submitted to the US Agency for International Development by the Systems for Improved Access to Pharmaceuticals and Services (SIAPS) Program (2016)
15. Silve, B.: Health logistics is a profession: improving performance of health in developing countries. Field Actions Sci. Rep. **1**(1) (2008)
16. Sohrabpour, V., Hellström, D., Jahre, M.: Packaging in developing countries: identifying supply chain needs. J. Humanitarian Logistics Supply Chain Manag. **2**(2), 183–205 (2012)
17. UNCoLSC: UN Commission on Life-Saving Commodities for Women and Children - Commissioners' Report September 2012 (2012)
18. USAID: Guidelines for Implementing Computerized Logistics Management Information Systems (LMIS). DELIVER, for the U.S. Agency for International Development, Arlington, VA (2006)
19. USAID: The Logistics Handbook A Practical Guide for the Supply Chain Management of Health Commodities. USAID | DELIVER PROJECT, Arlington, VA (2011)
20. USAID: Computerizing Logistics Management Information Systems. USAID | DELIVER PROJECT, Arlington, VA (2012)
21. VillageReach 2016: Supply Chain Technical Resource Team, UN Commission on Life-Saving Commodities. Technology, People & Processes: Enabling Successful HMIS/LMIS Integrations. Seattle: VillageReach (2016)
22. Walsham, G.: Interpretive case studies in is research: nature and method. Eur. J. Inf. Syst. **4**(2), 74–81 (1995)
23. World Bank: A handbook on supply chain management for HIV/AIDS medical commodities. The World Bank, Washington DC (2005)
24. Yadav, P.: Health product supply chains in developing countries: diagnosis of the root causes of underperformance and an agenda for reform. Health Syst. Reform **1**(2), 142–154 (2015)

Health Information Systems in Indonesia: Understanding and Addressing Complexity

Jorn Braa$^{(\boxtimes)}$, Sundeep Sahay, John Lewis, and Wilfred Senyoni

Department of Informatics, University of Oslo, Oslo, Norway
{jbraa,sundeeps}@ifi.uio.no, johnlewis.hisp@gmail.com,
senyoni@gmail.com

Abstract. The article is addressing the problem posed by fragmented and poorly coordinated Health Information Systems (HIS) in developing countries within the framework of complexity. HISs that can provide quality data for monitoring, management and health services provision are important for countries, which requires a sensitive understanding of complexity and how they can be managed. Using a case from Indonesia, we discuss the challenges of integrating HIS using the concept of attractor for change from the field of Complex Adaptive Systems (CAS). The dashboard is positioned as such an attractor as a means to get different stakeholders to discuss and reach a consensus on how to integrate and share data without disturbing the underlying systems too much. A more generic model to manage complexity is proposed.

Keywords: Complexity · HIS · Adaptive · Dashboard · Integration

1 Introduction

In this article, we use the concept of Complex Adaptive Systems (CAS) to understand the problems of fragmentation and poor coordination in the national Health Information Systems (HIS) in Indonesia. We specifically draw upon the CAS concept of 'attractor for change' illustrated through the use of dashboard both as a convincing metaphor and as a practical strategy for integration, which does not disturb underlying systems and political structures, and creating a 'win without losing' situation.

Complexity is an important concept in information systems research, to highlight the indeterminate nature of how they evolve and have impact, and the non-linear nature of change. Often the use of the term complexity hides more than what it reveals, and provides limited analytical leverage to describe or make sense of a phenomenon. For example, saying the "context is complex" does not help explain its particular characteristics and influences, and on the contrary, goes to obscuring its relevance. Analysis of complexity thus needs to be operationalized with specific concepts, such as of attractor for change which we employ.

We build upon Kling and Scacchi's theoretical framework [1] to understand why and how large information systems tend to be tied to the social context, and are best viewed as social systems. Applying a social system perspective helps to understand the mutual interconnections between technical and social systems and their underlying characteristics of complexity. For example, a specification of interoperability between

Published by Springer International Publishing AG 2017. All Rights Reserved
J. Choudrie et al. (Eds.): ICT4D 2017, IFIP AICT 504, pp. 59–70, 2017.
DOI: 10.1007/978-3-319-59111-7_6

systems in different organisations will be worthless if one of the organisations decides not to take part in the interoperability. By including organisational politics, culture and social behavior in the framework of analysis, the understanding of complexity becomes richer.

A networked perspective provides richer insights into complexity [2] as interconnections such as through the Internet can both shape and be shaped by each other. This contrasts with the 'classic' information system view based on a structural definition of systems in terms of boundaries, interconnected but discrete components. Networked structures are difficult to represent in a modular and structured way, as the boundaries between the system and environment are difficult to delineate, and are always changing. Concepts from CAS are better equipped to understand these dynamics. CAS pays particular attention on the study of how order emerges rather than it being created through design. In our case, we discuss the creation of "attractors for change" [3] as a strategy to bring about changes in areas with limited agreement, standards and stability [4].

As is typical in most countries [4, 5], health data in Indonesia is managed in vertical health program specific systems with minimal horizontal sharing, making overall monitoring of health system problematic. HIS for Tuberculosis and HIV/AIDS, for example, are managed as separate 'silos' with no data sharing, despite the fact that co-infection of TB and HIV/AIDS is a widespread critical health problem, requiring shared information. The project reported was to develop an integrated data warehouse and dashboard for health data in Indonesia. With this background, the paper seeks to address the research questions of "How can the understanding of complexity be sensitively applied to design and implement integrated HIS?"

This analysis is grounded within the empirical work of the Health Information Systems Programme (HISP), from the University of Oslo (UiO), which has over the last two decades been engaged with strengthening HIS in multiple countries. We draw upon examples from Indonesia to analyse the nature of complexity in multi-organisational contexts, and how concepts from CAS helps to understand both the complexity involved and how to address it.

2   Relevant Theoretical Concepts

2.1   Fragmentation of HIS in LMICs

Fragmentation and complexity of systems are terms that may be used interchangeably to describe particular contexts of HIS, but we emphasise an important difference. While fragmentation may be understood to be destructive representing systems being broken into small or separate and uncoordinated parts, complexity denotes that systems consisting of many different interconnected parts in multiple ways such that the whole system seems to be evolving on its own. While fragmentation refers to a lack of interaction and coordination, complexity may focus on the potential and actual interaction, both intended and unintended, between the different parts of an overall system. Both these concepts emphasize interactions and inter-dependencies between different elements of the whole, thus complexity becomes a useful lens for analysis of such HIS.

Looking at the history of HIS in Lower Middle Income Countries (LMICs), increasing fragmentation, lack of shared standards, and poor coordination are key challenges. In particular, since the advent of the large HIV/AIDS programmes around 2000, there have been increased numbers of NGOs and donors initiating projects with their own parallel reporting structures greatly magnifying fragmentation. A focus on HIV/AIDS patients and expensive ARV drugs made the ability to track patients and manage clinical pathways increasingly important, which led to a proliferation of patient record systems alongside an increasing number of typically overlapping aggregate reporting systems at the facility level. Good quality data is essential for effective monitoring, which is not easily forthcoming.

A key quest of HIS research and practice on integration, not only of the health services and population-based 'HMIS' and 'M&E'-like systems, but also of patient-based and population-based health data and systems. Such systems have historically evolved independently of each other, based on different logics, and promoted by different communities with different cultures of action [5]. In order to provide integrated information support to health systems across multiple levels of management, these systems and communities need to interoperate and speak with each other.

While integration of HIS has been on the global agenda for a long time, in recent years this interest has significantly heightened as WHO and other big donor organisations are increasingly demanding the integration of data and systems. These changes in attitudes of these organizations are welcome and are being expressed at a time when the rapid spread of the Internet has in fact made integration relatively easier than before. We can say we are moving from the challenge of handling fragmentation to handling complexity of systems.

2.2   CAS, Complexity and Social Systems

Complexity refers to a situation, or an overall system, where many different parts are interacting in multiple ways, so that the whole system appears to be evolving on its own. It can be a big city, a beehive, or the Internet. CAS is a field within complexity science which studies the adaptation dynamics of complex systems: how different parts of the system and their interaction adapt and evolve to changing conditions, and how order emerges rather than it being designed. Central to the emergence of orders is the notion of attractors which represents a shared standard that is followed by many. For example, MS Windows, for good or for bad, created order in the personal computing area representing an "attractor for change" [3]. This becomes a strategy to bring change in areas with limited agreement, standards and stability, such as fragmented HIS. Scaling is another central and related concept to understand how this emerging order can expand.

"Complex, adaptive systems exhibit coherence through scaling and self-similarity. Scaling is the property of complex systems in which one part of the system reproduces the same structure and patterns that appear in other parts of the system" [7].

The example of broccoli is a metaphor to understand scaling in a natural system, where branches and sub-branches replicate the structure of the whole plant. However, information systems are inherently social systems, and cannot be represented through the broccoli metaphor as people and organizations are always context specific. Kling and Scacchi's [1] web model provides insights to understand the challenges to scaling since information systems tend to be tied to the social context through a complex web of associations, as contrasted with the discrete-entity model that are viewed as relatively context neutral [1].

Another relevant concept we'll use is cultivation which denotes a way of shaping technology based on resources and potential already present, which is fundamentally different from construction as an engineering method based on structured planning which assumes a starting point of a clean slate [8]. As the metaphor indicates, cultivation is about interfering with, supporting and controlling natural processes already existing, like nurturing and watering a plant to nurture an "organism" with a life of their own [9]. Cultivation is seen in opposition to structured methods and consisting of incremental and evolutionary approaches, and "piecemeal engineering" [10]. While cultivation represents an approach within the social system model, structured engineering methods are linked to the discrete-entity model.

3   Research Methods

The project is to develop an integrated dashboard system for health data for the national ministry of health in Indonesia. This project was initiated and developed within the global HISP network by the University in Oslo (UiO), HISP India and the GadjaMadha University (UGM) in Yogyakarta. Action research was the key methodology used based on a prototyping approach which was both used as a tool for enhancing communication and cooperation on design approaches between the HISP team and ministry staff, as well as a practical way to actually implement solutions that are 'low hanging fruits' in terms of being both useful and easy to achieve. Action research, generally, aims at generating new knowledge through taking part in the full cycle of planning, design, implementation and evaluating the results from concrete interventions [11]. Action research in HISP is linked to the practices of system development. Engaging users in participatory prototyping through cycles of learning, refinement and further development of information systems are typical 'actions' in the HISP action research. The DHIS2 open source software platform (DHIS2.org) is developed within the HISP network and is used as a platform for the IS related parts of the action research.

In our action research, it has not been possible to follow the rigid cycles envisaged in the more formal versions of action research [12]. Our approach was for the research team, HISP, to become 'trusted' participants in the various processes of organisational change and negotiations in which the HIS project is embedded. The nature of engagement ranges from developing 'small' concrete solutions with local users, to the linking of these solutions together in a larger national level data warehouse and dashboard solutions for the Ministry of Health. This process has involved conducting negotiations at inter-organisational levels regarding design strategies, plans and funding. Such organisational processes are larger than what is possible to control, or fit into formal action research cycles. Rather, therefore, the action research applied consists of working to influence the development of the HIS in the planned direction through improvisations and opportunity based approaches, as in 'navigating the river' of continuous changes. Or as Heraclitus famously said, "You cannot step into the same river twice, for other waters are continually flowing on."[1] Meaning that change is constant; even things that appear constant, as the river, is undergoing change. The organisational context of the health systems may seem constant, but organisational politics, inter-personal matters, reshuffling of staff, changing health needs and global influences, leads to a constant changing context for the research.

The project was initiated in 2012–13 when HISP India was invited by the Ministry of Health (MoH) to start a pilot on system integration at district level in Yogyakarta province using the open source software platform DHIS2 which is a product of the HISP network. The following is the chronological sequence of events, which occurred during the project implementation.

3.1   Chronology of the Action Research Events

2012–2013: HISP India starts working with the MoH in Indonesia and key technical people take part in DHIS2 training in India. A pilot project aiming to integrate data from the Health Centres (called Puskesmas) at the district level was started in Yogyakarta province in collaboration with the UGM. Two people from HISP India worked with the UGM and the Yogyakarta health departments over two months and trained staff in the DHIS2 and created awareness which the follow up project benefited from. The pilot project 'dried up' because there were no funds and the central support ceased because the supportive director of the MoH department responsible for HIS was replaced (end of 2013).

2013: UiO established an agreement with the Global Fund (GF) for the support of DHIS2 implementation in countries, including Indonesia. The UiO team requested Global Funds for funds to conduct a scoping mission in the country. Following a successful regional meeting in Manila, where the DHIS2 dashboards were demonstrated, the new Indonesia MoH leadership agreed to this scoping mission to help develop a plan for the dashboard system.

Three of the authors went for a 3 weeks mission to Indonesia and worked with the MoH counterparts and the partners from UGM to develop this plan which was submitted to Global Fund, which was subsequently approved as a two years project to start in September 2015. The project consisted of two parts; (1) work with the national information and IT department team (called Pusdatin), to develop a national integrated dashboard; and, (2) work with the provincial health department in Yogyakarta province to develop an integrated dashboard in the province. Together with UGM, the UiO, HISP India and HISP Vietnam conducted a first round of training in Jakarta for the central level and Yogyakarta for the province level in September, 2015. Prior to the training sessions, the team, together with the MoH partners, visited and worked with different health programs at the national level (TB, HIV/AIDS) to learn about their systems and to export data for a first prototype dashboard. This prototype was then used and developed further in a participatory way during the training workshops.

---

[1] https://www.enotes.com/homework-help/heraclitus-said-you-cannot-step-into-same-river-377647.

Later in the year, during a new mission of the HISP India and UiO teams, more focused training of the technical staff from different health programs in Yogyakarta was conducted and the prototype was developed further. This was demonstrated during another regional meeting in Bali November 2015. The Pusdatin director and other MoH staff found it interesting, and during a side meeting it was decided that the dashboards should be implemented in selected provinces early 2016, and a plan was made to invite key people from these provinces for introduction and training in January 2016. However, in December 2015, a new reshuffle of staff happened and all plans had to be redeveloped and the future of the project was in flux. However, the objective of developing a shared integrated dashboard turned out to be relatively well entrenched, and the project was kept alive during the turbulent period. Training of province people was planned and cancelled twice before it eventually took place in March, 2016. But the implementation activities planned in the provinces were cancelled due to budget cuts.

The work continued in a different mode with the HISP team working with each of the health programs at central level, as well as with one selected district and the province department in Yogyakarta. This made up a sub-project within the overall project. The Malaria program is one example; they had developed a system for reporting data from the health facilities and all the way to the national level based on Excel. In a database perspective, Excel is suboptimal, and data from health facilities are sent to the district in Excel sheets. In the district the data is aggregated by district and sent to the province, which again send the data to the national level. Only in the districts, therefore, are the data from the health facilities are available, while at the central level, only the district aggregates are available. In order for this system to be able to share and include data from the reporting units (health facilities) and to export data by the level of the health centers, these data first needed to be imported to a database system. Consequently, a system for uploading the excel sheets in DHIS2 was developed for the malaria program, which at the same time provided a comprehensive system application for the malaria program using the DHIS2 platform.

In October 2016, the new 'Health Systems Strengthening' Global Fund project was initiated to strengthen HIS and establish 'dashboards' in 10 selected districts and the 5 provinces where these districts are located. A taskforce was established with members from Pusdatin, three universities selected as 'centres of excellence' in health informatics, UiO, UGM and eleven HSS hired consultants; one for each districts and one national. An online DHIS2 system was established with data from HIV, TB and Malaria and used to train the national pusdatin core technical team (super users), consultants hired by HSS, and selected provincial level members. The rollout of the DHIS2 and dashboard project started in February 2017 following a sequential approach selected as an adaptation of the cycles in action research, where the learning from each cycle is used to inform and improve the next cycle, with each province represent one cycle. At the time of finalising this paper, the rollout was in its first cycle and the authors were engaged in assessing systems at province, district and facility levels, in Lombok.

While the case study is focusing on the main project and the period November 2014–February 2017, without the preparatory project phase the main project would not have been initiated. This longitudinal aspect of action research in large 'as the river flows' contexts is a key component of the research methodology, and a key message of this article.

4   Case Study: DHIS2 Dashboard as an "Attractor for Change"

Indonesia is a large country with the fourth largest population globally, with well-developed infrastructure with regional variations. The HIS is fairly typical with multiple vertical health program-specific systems with own platforms working in 'silos' with little data sharing. The case study involved building a national level dashboard cross-cutting these programs, which was a non-trivial challenge given the multiplicity of systems, platforms and the absence of shared standards. For example, all systems used different codes for health facilities.

Indonesia has a federal structure where provinces and districts are relatively independent from the national MoH. There are stark contrasts between the developed western part of the country (Java, Bali, Sumatra) and the much less developed eastern parts (Papua). In Java island, all puskesmas have electronic patient record systems, very often locally developed, and often of different types even within the same district. At the national level, health programmes have their own systems, many of them web-based (e.g. TB, HIV/AIDS), but also Excel-based (e.g. malaria). Data from the puskesmas are reported to the districts, from where data is compiled and captured in national systems. All programs have officers at the district level who send data to province and national, with minimum horizontal sharing.

The national level is running a system called KOMDAT which collects data for about 130 national health indicators, based on data aggregated by district. The design limited the district data managers to enter data until they have received a complete set of data from all reporting puskesmas in their districts. The national health insurance agency (BPJS) has established a patient-based system for insurance claims in all hospitals and puskesmas. The BPJS system is not integrated with the other systems. For example, in Lombok Timur district all data had to be re-entered in another system that produced the actual claim as a printout. Also in our visit to Malang district, we saw that the only way to get an overview of data was to meet the officer in charge of each program. While KOMDAT was trying to address this need, it was limited to data aggregated by district, making it impossible to check quality of facility data or to see completeness of reporting from the facilities. Figure 1 illustrates the HIS complexity.

The situation differs between districts. For example in Surabaya City they have developed a comprehensive patient-based system covering all programs and health facilities. In all districts in Yogyakarta province, every health centre has its own electronic patient record system to report patient data to the district, where aggregated district reports are generated. In contrast, in Malang district, there is a plethora of systems in use at the facility level and limited integration at the district level.

The MoH and other actors have for a long time acknowledged the need for integration and data sharing, but have believed – due to the complexity arising from the independence given to districts and provinces under the federal structure – it would not be possible. With the dashboard approach, it was believed relevant data could be moved from different systems to a central repository, without disturbing the underlying structures too much. Seeing this potential, the MoH, HSS, UiO and UGM formed a joint project, funded by Global Fund, to develop an integrated dashboard using the

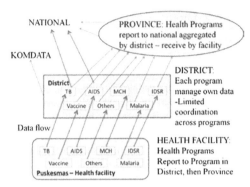

Fig. 1. Complexity as seen in the HIS in Indonesia before the HIS reform intervention

DHIS2 platform (see Fig. 2 for the proposed model). A major problem in sharing data across the vertical systems is that they are all using different codes or names for the health facilities. A first step for this integration was therefore to develop a facility register where facility IDs used by the different systems could be mapped to a common reference.

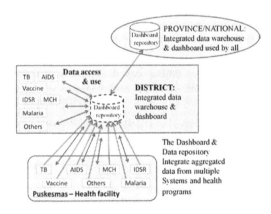

Fig. 2. Proposed dashboard and data warehouse integration model

For each of systems that will share data with the DHIS2, database and data models were studied and procedures for data extraction, transformation and loading into the DHIS2 were developed and one off transfer of data was conducted. Data from the HIV and the TB systems were the first systems to be incorporated. Apart from these two systems, most of the health program specific systems are only reporting data aggregated by district to the national level, and are therefore not really useful. Facility based data are typically reported by the systems from health facility and districts to the province level, where the data is aggregated by district and reported onwards to the national level. The rollout of DHIS2 to the 5 provinces therefore has as key tasks in the districts and provinces to identify data sources and establish procedures for data extraction and loading into the DHIS2. The study of data flows in West Nusa Tenggara, the first province in the rollout, showed that several systems, such as for nutrition, mother and child health, immunization and malaria, are reporting facility based data to the province. Meaning that data extraction to DHIS2 at the province level will provide data for all health facilities in all districts in the province. If this pattern is repeated in other provinces it will make scaling easier than if each district would have had to be handled one by one. The challenge, however, will be to establish and maintain routines for extracting data from the identified systems in each province and in some cases also districts and load them in the national DHIS2. Many of the local systems are based on Excel. As long as these systems are based on fixed templates it is technically easy develop systems for uploading the data. Local capacity and ownership will be the key to success. Technical people from the districts and provinces have been trained and take part in all aspects of the work during the rollout. Experience from West Nusa Tenggara shows that technical capacity is available and that managers at district and province level are supporting the initiative because good integrated information is currently not easily available and the 'dashboard' appears to be able to fill this gap.

5   Discussion

As a general rule we say that the higher the complexity, and the more embedded in the social context the systems are, the less easy it is to handle complexity. In the following model, we analyse complexity along two dimensions: more or less context-sensitive, and more or less networked or interdependent of other systems.

5.1   The Context-Sensitive vs. Context-Free Dichotomy

Complexity is a function of the nature of interaction of the system with local business processes, their levels of formalization, or standardisation, and the rate of change of the different components. The stronger the interaction and lower the levels of formalisation, the more unique features the system will need to include, making it more context-sensitive. This links with the web model [1] presented earlier, where the social systems model represents the context-sensitive end of the continuum and the discrete entity model the context-free end.

In the HIS domain, level of formalisation is referring to the level of standardization of data and routines and work processes for handling data. In our case, for example, most systems are using their own different codes and names for facilities, making data sharing difficult and illustrating a low level of standardization of meta-data in this area. Overlap of data being reported in different systems and reporting tools resulting in same data being captured and reported multiple times, is a common feature and is illustrating low level of standardisation of data handling routines.

The more networked a system and the more dependent it is on other systems and organisational structures, the higher is the level of complexity, and the less possible it is to apply a linear model of systems development. It is easier to develop a standalone system with no or few dependencies than an integrated system, or a system with multiple dependencies. This is the reason why HIS in countries tend to be fragmented into multiple 'silos' as each disease-specific programme makes its own system with little sharing of data. Such complexity can be described into two dimensions. That is, complexity is low when the systems in question are relatively context-free and have low dependencies with other systems. In contrast, complexity is 'very' high when systems are both context-sensitive and have multiple connections and dependencies, and in between there is a continuum of more or less complexity. The case study illustrates a system of high complexity, both in terms of the numerous connections and interdependencies with specific health programmes institutional structures, identifiers and others.

Systems development, whether it is about strengthening existing systems or developing a new one, such as the integrated solution in Indonesia, is, at a basic level, about identifying what needs to be done and then doing it, or to define tasks and then carrying them out. The less complex the situation, the more the system can be pre-defined and development done in a pre-planned manner. The opposite is also true – the more complexity and higher the level of uncertainty, the less of the development can be planned in advance. Of course, roadmaps and general directions of work can always be prepared, but the concrete medium to longer term plans will need to be developed and revised as part of the building process. The aim of the action research in our case is to generate knowledge on a wide range of issues in a participative process together with stakeholders and users, linked to, but not limited to the system development process. One aim of the action research is to explore and generate learning about how data can be used to improve health services. Systems development is used as a vehicle for generating knowledge, but the aims of the action research is wider than the development of systems and system components. In terms of methodology, however, action research in the IS domain have the same challenges as system development in managing uncertainty in complex contexts. The action research field may learn about handling complexity and uncertainty from the rich IS literature.

When uncertainty related to the context and goals of system development is high, experimental approaches, user participation and learning by doing are generally recommended [13, 14]. These are approaches within the concept of cultivation where development may not be controlled totally, but proceeds through user participation, tinkering, improvisation, and gradual development over time is an important approach to managing uncertainty. Attractors may be used as a strategy to enable cultivation over the two following components;

i. User participation, experiments around practical prototypes and shared learning-by-doing among users and developers as part of the day-to-day development. Seeking to develop and strengthen attractors for change through prototyping activities.
ii. An evolutionary and process oriented approach. Accepting that development will take time and that piecemeal development and learning are needed to help guide further work.

Robust, flexible and scalable system architectures are essential for systems development in contexts of high complexity and uncertainty as it must always be possible to add components. It is therefore important to delay decisions that can close future choices as much as possible. User participation and continuous interactions between the technical team and the users have been an important part of the strategy in the development of the dashboards in our case [15]. This contributed to mutual learning where users learn to what extent and how their information needs could be implemented using the technology, and the technical team learns about the context of use and users' needs. This created an evolutionary step-by-step approach as new modules and sub-systems were included.

Also in the early phases of the process of the Indonesia project, practical prototypes for demonstrating what can be done with integrated data was an important part of the interaction with the multitude of user groups and health programmes. Working towards integrated solutions in the highly complex context needs to be gradual and with a long-time horizon. The data warehouse and dashboard served as other effective attractors for change, and helped to navigate through high degrees of complexity. This approach was relatively successful because the dashboard was not closely embedded in complicated business processes, and could stand "above" it. Further, its flexible and scalable architecture allowed for adding new data sets and components as new actors joined. Such scalability would not have been possible in more complicated business models. Data input and outputs are relatively simple processes and not restricted to any place in a particular business process. The dashboard was loaded with data behind the scene; the user can access the data through the Internet, from any physical position, and, important in this context, from any place or stage in any business or work process.

6 Conclusion

Quality health data and good HIS are needed for countries to provide quality health services to the population [16, 17]. Poor coordination and fragmented HIS, which we have analysed within the framework of complexity, represent important challenges for developing countries in their endeavors to develop appropriate HIS that can provide quality health data. Better understanding and approaches to handle complexity, the topic and aim of the article, are therefore important research questions. We have presented and discussed the case of Indonesia using the concept of attractor for change to analyse the process to integrate several fragmented HIS using a dashboard approach. The process gained momentum because health programs came to understand that integration was feasible and that they could gain from it without having to give up their systems or independence. The process of integrating provincial HIS within a national framework in South Africa followed a similar pattern; the attractor for change in that case was a combination of the DHIS v1 software and a principle of hierarchies of standards making it possible for provincial systems to integrate with the national system while at the same time being able to independently add their own requirements to the system [4]. Another important learning from the case of Indonesia is that processes driven by the attractor for change and providing a way to handle complexity are basically social processes. Thus emphasising that complexity cannot be handled in a one-to-one specification of e.g. new integrated systems.

References

1. Kling, R., Scacchi, W.: The web of computing: computer technology as social organisation. Adv. Comput. **21**, 1–90 (1982)
2. Merali, Y.: Complexity and information systems: the emergent domain. J. Inf. Technol. **21** (4), 216–228 (2006)
3. Plsek, P.E., Wilson, T.: Complexity science: complexity, leadership, and management in healthcare organisations. Br. Med. J. **323**(7315), 746–749 (2001)
4. Braa, J., Hanseth, O., Mohammed, W., Heywood, A., Shaw, V.: Developing health information systems in developing countries: the flexible standards approach. MIS Q. **31**(2), 381–402 (2007)
5. Nielsen, P., Sæbø, J.I.: Three strategies for functional architecting: cases from the health systems of developing countries. Inf. Technol. Dev. **22**(1), 134–151 (2016)
6. Sahay, S., Sundararaman, T., Braa, J.: Public Health Informatics: Designing for Change - A Developing Country Perspective. Oxford University Press, Oxford (2017)
7. Eoyang, G.H.: Complex? Yes! Adaptive? Well, maybe.... Interactions **3**(1), 31–37 (1996)
8. Walsham, G., Sahay, S.: Research on information systems in developing countries: current landscape and future prospects. Inf. Technol. Dev. **12**(1), 7–24 (2006)
9. Ciborra, C.U.: De profundis? Deconstructing the concept of strategic alignment. Scand. J. Inf. Syst. **9**(1), 67–82 (1997)
10. Popper, K.: The Poverty of Historicism. Routledge & Kegan Paul, England (1957)
11. Baskerville, R.: Investigating information systems with action research. J. Assoc. Inf. Syst. **2** (19) (1999)
12. Susman, G., Evered, R.: An assessment of the scientific merits of action research. Adm. Sci. Q. **23**(4), 582–603 (1978)
13. Andersen, N.E., Kensing, F., Lundin, J.: Professional System Development. TekniskForlag, Copenhagen (1986)
14. Davis, G.B.: Strategies for information requirements. IBM Syst. J. **21**, 4–30 (1982)
15. Braa, J., Hedberg, C.: The struggle for district based health information systems in South Africa. Inf. Soc. **18**, 113–127 (2002)
16. AbouZahr, C., Boerma, T.: Health information systems: the foundations of public health. Bull. World Health Organ. **83**(8), 578–583 (2005)
17. Health Data Collaborative. http://www.healthdatacollaborative.org

Open Source Software Ecosystems in Health Sector: A Case Study from Sri Lanka

Roshan Hewapathirana[1(✉)], Pamod Amarakoon[2], and Jørn Braa[1]

[1] University of Oslo, Oslo, Norway
roshan.hewapathirana@gmail.com, jbraa@ifi.uio.no
[2] Nutrition Coordination Division, Ministry of Health, Colombo, Sri Lanka
pamod@pamod.net

Abstract. A software ecosystem consists of a software platform, a set of internal and external developers and domain experts in service to a community of users that compose relevant solution elements to satisfy their needs. Open source is well-known for its potential to frame software ecosystems with its networking tendency and provision for further customization with access to software source code. Open source is increasingly becoming the choice for health information system implementations in low resource settings.

This longitudinal case study was designed to study the research question, how a software ecosystem is being built around an open source health information system implementation. Empirically the study was positioned in a multi-sector initiative identifying and support nutritionally at-risk households to eliminating malnutrition. The discussion reveals how new dependencies between health and non-health sector actors were created with the emerging software ecosystem based on an open source framework and supplementary custom-built web and mobile components.

Keywords: Software ecosystem · Free and open source software · Health information system

1 Introduction

Compared to the traditional software project perspective, software ecosystem (SE) is an emerging trend within the software industry [1]. A SE typically consists of a software framework, internal and external developers, domain experts and a community of users that compose the relevant solution elements [2]. The SE is the choice to construct large software system on top of a software framework by composing components developed by actors both internal and external [3]. Hence, Free and Open Source Software (FOSS) provides a viable framework for growing a SE from the angles of implementation technology, development methodology and governance [4]. Being a relatively new concept, SE has not been discussed adequately in the IS discourse [5]. Hence, SE literature needs more empirical studies from various domains, such as open source and health [6].

Sri Lanka possesses a well-established health care delivery model, with most of the health indicators are at a comparable level to those of the developed world. However,

© IFIP International Federation for Information Processing 2017
Published by Springer International Publishing AG 2017. All Rights Reserved
J. Choudrie et al. (Eds.): ICT4D 2017, IFIP AICT 504, pp. 71–80, 2017.
DOI: 10.1007/978-3-319-59111-7_7

the nutritional indicators were lagging behind compared to other health indicators. Malnutrition has a multi factor contribution including both health and non-health denominators. Thus, the revised National Nutrition Policy (NNP) of Sri Lanka [7] suggested inviting non-health sector stakeholders to the nutrition management tasks giving them active roles in eliminating malnutrition. This demanded an integrated information system to monitor nutritional status and to track health and non-health intervention to coordination across different sectors. An open source HIS with supplementary custom developed web and mobile components was introduced to overcome the challenge of integrated information need across different sectors. This FOSS HIS implementation around multi-sector participation was an ideal empirical setting to study a domain specific SE. Hence, a longitudinal case study was aimed at understanding how a SE is being built around an open source HIS implementation, expecting to contribute to the growing body of knowledge on SE.

The organization of the rest of the paper is as follows. The second section reviews the current literature on the theoretical underpinning of the study while the third section elaborates the research approach and methodology. The next section reveals the findings of this longitudinal case study. Followed by which, the fifth section presents the analysis and the discussion leading to the conclusion of the study which is presented in the section six.

2   Theoretical Background

2.1   Software Ecosystems

A SE is a means to construct a large software system on top of a software framework by composing components developed by actors both internal and external. For the purpose of this study the SE was defined as to "*consists of a software platform, a set of internal and external developers and community of domain experts in service to a community of users that compose relevant solution elements to satisfy their needs*" [2]. This perspective differs from traditional software project approach in several important aspects. In a SE, the initiating actors (the client organisation) don't necessarily own the software produced by the contributing actors and may not hire the contributing actors [3]. In comparing traditional software projects to SE, it was shown that the scope of a traditional software project typically is intra-organizational. Whereas the scope of a SE is much broader and is including external developers and the further extensions that they provide as well as contributions from other parties [8]. SE are mainly categorised in three broad categories as being operating system-centric, application-centric and end-user programming centric SEs [9]. The application-centric software ecosystems, such as the empirical setting of this research, is organised around a domain specific application.

The general composition of a SE is the software firm (framework developer), (3rd party) software suppliers, client firm, intermediaries and client firm's customers. According to Dittrich [1] framework developers and 3rd party application developers are both important in a SE. This is particularly the case in the FOSS domain, where the core FOSS firm plays the role of framework developers. In this context 3rd party developers and FOSS implementers play the role of application developers working on extending the generic functionalities of the open source framework by aligning it with the needs of the implementation domain.

2.2 Open Source

FOSS is a well-established practice to manage both software development and distribution. It permits access to the software source code, together with the permission to modify the source code as well as to redistribute the derived works[1]. Given this kind of end-to-end control, FOSS is generally a good a framework for building SEs [4]. Open source software provides the capability to develop complex systems on freely available source code and enables constructing a SE without large initial investment [10]. FOSS reduces system implementation costs by eliminating vendor monopoly. Furthermore, it promotes indigenous technology development by allowing access to the source code which facilitates the global to local transfer of knowledge [11]. Additional benefits of FOSS include vendor neutral technology through free access to the source code and reduced total cost of ownership with no licence fee [12].

The open source phenomenon has undergone a significant transformation from its free software origin to a more mainstream, commercially viable form which is referred to as *Open Source 2.0* [13]. Clients are willing to pay for customizing Open Source Software for organizational business needs because customization related services are critical factors influencing the OSS adoption in many organizations [14]. Hence, FOSS firm also look to 3rd party software service providers to add specific functionalities to the core framework, which is beyond the capacity of FOSS firm alone. Several FOSS governance models are suggested to describe this 3rd party contribution in open source adoption, such as the Third Party Service Provider model proposed by Krishnamurthy [15]. This FOSS business models can be regarded as a stakeholder participation model in SE around open source adoption.

3 Research Approach and Methodology

This longitudinal interpretive case study was conducted in the State health sector of Sri Lanka over a period of two years from 2014 to 2016. It was empirically situated within a large scale FOSS HIS implementation effort, which is aimed at establishing a multi-sector stakeholder network consisting of health and non-health sectors around the implementation of a nutrition information system. We positioned ourselves within the qualitative research practice [16] with a case study approach [17]. The empirical work was guided by the research question, how a SE is being built around an open source HIS implementation. The reflection of the findings followed the interpretive tradition.

---

[1] Open Source definition, https://opensource.org/osd.

3.1 Data Collection

The data collection was done focusing on stakeholder behaviour of the SE around the open source HIS implementation for the Nutrition Monitoring and Intervention Tracking project. The empirical setting included the State health sector institutions in three districts, two public administrative settings and a central coordinating unit. The multi-method approach included participant observation, interviews, focus group discussions and document analysis [18].

Participant observation was a main approach of gathering data providing an overview of the stakeholder behaviour and the evolution of the SE. The observation were done during the project steering meetings, HIS and non-health IS design and implementation meetings and web and mobile application training sessions. The settings for the participant observation sessions included the central coordination unit, three regional and 17 peripheral health units and two peripheral administrative units. In-situ interviews were conducted during the participant observations to clarify the decisions taken on the SE trajectory and the stakeholder participation.

When interviewing the multi-sector organizational actors, semi-structured interviews and focus group discussions were used. Health managers and non-heath sector administrators were the key informants in the semi-structured interviews. They provided rich insights to the process of decision-making during the HIS implementation. This study used data from eight interviews with health managers, 11 interviews with the administrative sector managers, five interviews with the representatives of the funding agency and 12 interviews with FOSS implementers and 3rd party developers. Medical Officer of Health (MOH), Medical Officer – Maternal and Child Health and Public Health Midwives (PHM) were the participants in focus group discussions on mobile app and FOSS HIS back-end at peripheral level. The health sector group discussions included 17 MOH areas. Five group discussions were conducted with participation from the health and public administrative sector actors, funding agency and FOSS implementers. Participant observation and interviews were supplemented by the document reviews for a deeper understanding. The documents analysed comprised of email communications, project steering meeting and evaluation meeting minutes, official letters and policy documents related to the HIS ecosystem.

3.2 Data Analysis

During this study the raw data was recorded as manual field notes at the time of interviews and participant observation sessions, which were later transcribed into complete manuscripts. Interview data was compared and triangulated with other evidence such as participant observations and document analysis. The data analysis follows the interpretive tradition [19]. A basically inductive approach [20] was followed when interpreting field notes to understand the FOSS HIS ecosystem trajectory.

4   Research Findings

In Sri Lanka a nutrition policy was first introduced in 1986. However, the nutritional status of children were not satisfactory although a wide range of programmes from growth monitoring to nutrient supplements had been ongoing for many years.

4.1   Multi-sector Stakeholder Network

Hence, in August 2008, Department of Health appointed a task force to revise the NNP [7]. The committee apprehended the fact that the nutritional well-being of a population is influenced by determinants that cut across the areas of responsibilities of different sectors which extends beyond the scope of the Department of Health. The revised NNP was expected to provide a framework for inter-sectoral coordination in order to accelerate efforts to achieve optimum nutritional status. However, Department of Health alone could not achieve the multi-sector coordination. In this regard, the conventional paper based reporting system was not sufficient to facilitate the required multi-sector coordination to achieve the objectives laid down by the NNP.

In 2013, NNP was revised again and the National Nutrition Secretariat of Sri Lanka (NNS) was established to achieve a better coordination of multi-sector activities prescribed by NNP. The NNS was positioned directly under the Presidential Secretariat of Sri Lanka giving it the capability of inter-departmental coordination. A major task of the NNS was to develop the Nutrition Action Plan targeting the priority areas for action. NNS was entrusted to monitor and evaluate the progress of activities under the Nutrition Action Plan at National, Provincial, District and Divisional levels. Three districts, where malnutrition was prevalent, were selected to launch the pilot project. Under this project, MOH and Divisional Secretariat were the main coordination points for the health and non-health sectors respectively at the lowest administrative level. Field level multi-sector coordination was assigned to the Village Committees, which has the PHM as the focal person to identify nutritionally at-risk households. 'Grama Niladhari' (government officer to the village), 'Samurdhi Niyamaka' (government appointed social service officer), Agricultural Extension Worker and Development Assistant helped PHM to identify root causes for malnutrition during Village Committee meetings.

4.2   Implementation of the IS

NNS facilitated the implementation of an information system to realize the multi-sector coordination. Initial meetings were coordinated by the NNS and attended by health and non-health sector stakeholders, funding partners and HIS implementers. The open source public health information system framework, District Health Information System[2] (DHIS2) was used as the HIS back-end. Selection of FOSS was due to several reasons including the encouragement from funding agency for its potential sustainability with

---

[2] https://www.dhis2.org.

global contribution, satisfying the guidelines of national eHealth policy on software source code ownership and not having a recurrent licensing cost. DHIS2 was customized as per the requirements of the Nutrition Action Plan under the supervision of the NNS and the Department of Health. A significant customization was needed to adapt DHIS2 to cater the specific requirements laid down by Nutrition Action Plan. Sub-components of the IS were shaped by the functionalities prescribed by the Nutrition Action Plan.

Initially the system architecture was designed as a single component. However, there were some concerns among health sector stakeholders, such as, "Health information is too sensitive to be seen by 'Grama Niladhari' or 'Samurdhi' officer. So, the two systems cannot be a single integrated solution". Hence, later it was decided to keep the health and non-health components of the information systems separated due to the sensitive nature of health information and the information system was then designed as two separate sub-systems within a single SE. The selected information of the families with malnourished children supposed to be entered to the system by PHMs, who were appointed as the field level data collection operatives. It was agreed to share the data gathered to the HIS component with the non-health sector component only after removing the socially sensitive information. To assure the privacy and confidentiality of health data, only the minimum essential data set required for nutrition interventions were shared with the Village Committee and other non-health sector stakeholders.

The proposed HIS design demanded PHMs to enter data during home visits. This required a portable solution for PHMs instead of the standard web interface of DHIS2. Hence, NNS suggested PHMs to be given a mobile device for field level data collection. However, due to several unique requirements Nutrition Action Plan laid down, the native DHIS2 mobile app was not adequate for this purpose. Further, the DHIS2 mobile app was not fully developed to the potential of its web counterpart at the time of implementing this multi-sector nutrition IS. After several rounds of discussions, it was decided to develop a custom smart phone based mobile app as the field level data collection tool. The mobile app development was an iterative process where prototypes were created and feedback was received for the interfaces from NNS, Department of Health and the funding agency. The DHIS2 web Application Programming Interface (API) was used to communicate between the mobile app and the central server. The mobile app design was shaped by the inputs from the PHMs as well. The coding of the mobile app was outsourced to a third party software development firm by the HIS implementers. 600 smart phones and 70 laptops were provided by United Nations Children's Fund to pilot the system in the three selected districts. In-service, on-site training programme was conducted in each MOH area for MOHs and PHMs on mobile application and the DHIS2 based data analysis back-end. The pilot was supervised by NNS and the Department of Health. The development of the non-health components was negotiated in parallel to the piloting of HIS component. The non-health sector system was designed to track interventions done by the multi-sector stakeholders. A custom web app for the DHIS2 back end was developed to facilitate easy visualization of the intervention taken by the Village Committee and Divisional Secretariat level coordinators.

We observed that the implementers used to express their concerns about the weak technical documentation during custom component development. "We need support on integrating the custom modules/apps through web API. If support is available, we can speed up the development. Otherwise, it is a very time-consuming to study the API calls, especially when the API changes rapidly with frequent release cycles [of DHIS2]" was a such concern. We noted that client organization and the funding partners were also questioning about the support implementers get from the FOSS firm. "What would be the support you [implementers] are getting from DHIS2 community? If their support is readily available, we believe that this implementation would be more sustainable" was such a quote made by the funding partner.

5 Analysis and Discussion

In this section we discuss how a SE is being built around an open source HIS implementation. In this study the software framework is the DHIS2 open source HIS framework and the solution element it built was the nutrition monitoring and intervention tracking system. The internal developers are the HIS implementers employed by the NNS and the external developers included core DHIS2 team and the 3rd party software firm who developed the mobile and web components. Domain experts were the MOH and Divisional Secretariats who supervised the nutrition assessment and interventions. The community of users mainly included PHM from health sector and Village Committee members representing non-health sectors.

5.1 Emergence of the SE and Its Composition

Software implementation exercises need to consider the end user requirements as well as the needs of client organization commissioning the software customization [1]. In this study, the most important requirements leading to the inception of the SE were the need for the field level nutrition surveillance and the tracking of the multi-sector nutrition interventions enabling a collaboration across domains. This stakeholder integration in the SE emerged on top of the IS. Otherwise, these actors would have operated with fragmented information flows. According to Hanssen [5], SE emerges through the use of a technology focus, which in this case study was the open source framework, DHIS2. The selection of FOSS as the candidate technology was decided not only by the ability to align with the business requirements, but also the ability to comply with the policy and financial considerations. The scope of the SE is much broader than a single IS project, through the software extensions (e.g. web and mobile apps) provided by the external contributors [2]. The integration of 3rd party components with the core software framework makes the SE to expand beyond the conventional organizational boundaries. In the empirical setting this was evident from the use of custom components, which were integrating multi-sector stakeholders to a single SE.

In application-centric SEs, the aligning of software architecture to the organizational structure also plays a crucial role [2]. This was the case for DHIS2 and the multi-sector nutrition intervention tracking effort as well. FOSS doesn't incorporate special features that are catering only for minor sub-sets of users. Instead, FOSS framework such as DHIS2 aims at generic solution that can be accessed through APIs, on which custom component development may be used to develop special features by customising and extending generic functionalities. In this context, it was important to simplify the contribution of 3rd party developers. Not having a sufficiently detailed API documentation was a major drawback which delayed FOSS implementers developing 3rd party components.

In additions to its particular technical characteristics, the evolvement and behaviour of the stakeholder network is also a unique feature of the SE [5]. In general, a FOSS SE would comprise core FOSS developers providing a framework for 3rd party developers together with several layers of actors customizing and configuring the software product [5]. Similar features have been demonstrated in this paper, where behaviour and perspectives representing multiple organisations have been interacting and forming the SE. In a SE there will, at any time, typically be a leading or central organizational actor, which is referred to as the central referent organization [5]. The NNS emerged as the central referent organization in this case study. However, towards the later phase of the study, the HIS implementer played this role.

The network organization in this case comprised health sector and non-health sector organizational actors as domain experts and end users. The global DHIS2 implementer community and 3rd party mobile/software developer teams were indirectly involved in the implementation effort through the HIS implementers. As Bosch and Bosch-Sijtsema [2] mentioned, software ecosystems build new dependencies between components and their associated organizations that did not exist earlier. In this case study, the health and the non-health components of the system formed new links and dependencies between health and non-health actors, which were not there before. The overall objective of the project is to deliver coordinated nutritional services. For this objective to be achieved, the 'new' interdependent cooperation between different sectors that have evolved within the SE will need to be further strengthened and sustained.

FOSS implementers and 3rd party solution developers are important players in the FOSS SE [5]. The 3rd party developers are key actors as they are aligning and adapting the generic FOSS solutions to the specific domain needs by developing custom components. However, encouraging the 3rd party developers to contribute back to the FOSS code base is also important. The HISSL implementation team have contributed back to the code base by providing feedback and new requirements, which is as important as 'code' in a literal sense. DHIS2 core developers and developer community have supported 3rd party developers in Sri Lanka to understand the API, which is a key technology enabling integration of 3rd party contribution to the FOSS framework. However, active support is needed from the FOSS firm towards 3rd party developers and implementers in this regard. Evidence of the FOSS firm providing active support to the implementers improved the client organization's trust on the FOSS product as well as on FOSS implementers.

IS projects are in constant negotiation of boundaries within a SE [21]. In a software project, the technical negotiation happens on the boundary between local and global software development networks. For the domain specific negotiations in this case, the inside is the health domain and the outside is the non-health domain. Domain specific negotiations take place at the boundary between health and non-health through the PHM in this case. Over time, the stakeholders experienced the SE and its components were influenced by such negotiations. As a result, new spaces for negotiation, such as the Village Committees, emerge as the organizational structure of the SE is stabilizing.

PHM functions as a domain specific boundary spanning agent [22] in the nutrition intervention domain, freely moving between the health sector and the non-health sector. In the technical space of the SE, another boundary spanning role was noted for the role played by the local DHIS2 implementers. They bridge the gap between FOSS developer community and the 3rd party component developers to whom they out-sourced custom component development.

In the long run, uncertainty about whether the 3rd party components will be inte-grated with the FOSS code repository will also be an important factor in motivating external developers. Third party components with sufficiently generic use cases are potential candidate components to be merged with the FOSS code repository.

6   Conclusion

SE is a new business model which needs the contribution from new empirical domains to be further developed to include domain specific behaviours. Hence, we expect the lessons presented in this paper to help FOSS firms, implementers and clients to better understand the ecosystem building processes and how a sustainable ecosystem in the FOSS HIS domain may be developed. Some findings may be applied to custom software development ecosystems in the health domain and others may be applied to FOSS ecosystem development in general.

In LMIC context, multi-sector SE can be developed to enhance local technical capacity, which would otherwise be impossible to maintain in the State sector. Application-centric FOSS SEs contributes to this aim by providing access to the code repository and developer community. However, the presence of FOSS implementers and 3rd party component developers are essential for a viable FOSS ecosystem to emerge in LMIC contexts. The FOSS firm and domain experts (client organization) alone are not sufficient.

A SE has internal and external stakeholder networks which could be either domain specific or technical. In particular an open source SE need to have a central FOSS framework and custom components developed that are extending generic open source software functions. It is important to apprehend the role of the FOSS implementers, which a client firm can employ to customize an open source software. Whether internal or external to the client organization, the FOSS implementer has a boundary spanning role bridging the FOSS firm and the 3rd party component developers. Identifying the 'central referent organization' [5], who manage the participation of different stake-holders, was an important step in governing the stakeholder interactions in the SE in our case. However, the role of the central referent organization may be played by different organizations during SE evolution.

The role of 3rd party developers is also noteworthy for a viable SE around an open source implementation. The FOSS SE should maintain a good support for 3rd party developers. These include rich API documentations and a clear path for 3rd party components in the FOSS road map. Similarly, the FOSS firm needs to expose 3rd party FOSS development and implementation channels to prospective FOSS customers.

References

1. Dittrich, Y.: Software engineering beyond the project–sustaining software ecosystems. Inf. Softw. Technol. **56**(11), 1436–1456 (2014)
2. Bosch, J., Bosch-Sijtsema, P.: From integration to composition: on the impact of software product lines, global development and ecosystems. J. Syst. Softw. **83**(1), 67–76 (2010)
3. Manikas, K., Hansen, K.M.: Software ecosystems–a systematic literature review. J. Syst. Softw. **86**(5), 1294–1306 (2013)
4. Kilamo, T., Hammouda, I., Mikkonen, T., Aaltonen, T.: From proprietary to open source—growing an open source ecosystem. J. Syst. Softw. **85**(7), 1467–1478 (2012)
5. Hanssen, G.K.: A longitudinal case study of an emerging software ecosystem: implications for practice and theory. J. Syst. Softw. **85**(7), 1455–1466 (2012)
6. Pettersson, O., Svensson, M., Gil, D., Andersson, J., Milrad, M.: On the role of software process modeling in software ecosystem design. In: Proceedings of the Fourth European Conference on Software Architecture: Companion Volume, pp. 103–110 (2010)
7. Ministry of Healthcare and Nutrition. National Nutrition Policy of Sri Lanka (2010). https://extranet.who.int/nutrition/gina/en/node/7974
8. Scacchi, W., Alspaugh, T.A.: Understanding the role of licenses and evolution in open architecture software ecosystems. J. Syst. Softw. **85**(7), 1479–1494 (2012)
9. Bosch, J.: From software product lines to software ecosystems. In: Proceedings of the 13th International Software Product Line Conference, pp. 111–119. Carnegie Mellon University (2009)
10. Walton, C.: The open source software ecosystem. In: Sierra, C., Augusti, J. (eds.) IIIA Communications. Institut d'Investigacion en Intel. ligencia Artificial, IIIA, Barcelona (2002)
11. Câmara, G., Fonseca, F.: Information policies and open source software in developing countries. J. Am. Soc. Inform. Sci. Technol. **58**(1), 121–132 (2007)
12. Subramanyam, R., Xia, M.: Free/Libre open source software development in developing and developed countries: a conceptual framework with an exploratory study. Decis. Support Syst. **46**(1), 173–186 (2008)
13. Marsan, J., Paré, G., Wybo, M.D.: Has open source software been institutionalized in organizations or not? Inf. Softw. Technol. **54**(12), 1308–1316 (2012)
14. Nagy, D., Yassin, A.M., Bhattacherjee, A.: Organizational adoption of open source software: barriers and remedies. Commun. ACM **53**(3), 148–151 (2010)
15. Krishnamurthy, S.: An analysis of open source business models (2005). http://141.2.2.194/downloads/teaching/e-bmw/bazaar.pdf
16. Creswell, J.W.: Research Design: Qualitative, Quantitative, and Mixed Methods Approaches. Sage, Los Angeles (2013)
17. Yin, R.K.: Case Study Research: Design and Methods. Sage, Thousand Oaks (2003)
18. Flick, U.: An Introduction to Qualitative Research. Sage, London (2012)
19. Walsham, G.: Doing interpretive research. Eur. J. Inf. Syst. **15**(3), 320–330 (2006)
20. Thorne, S., Kirkham, S.R., MacDonald-Emes, J.: Focus on qualitative methods. Interpretive description: a noncategorical qualitative alternative for developing nursing knowledge. Res. Nurs. Health **20**(2), 169–177 (1997)
21. Elbanna, A.: Rethinking IS project boundaries in practice: a multiple-projects perspective. J. Strateg. Inf. Syst. **19**(1), 39–51 (2010)
22. Perrone, V., Zaheer, A., McEvily, B.: Free to be trusted? Organizational constraints on trust in boundary spanners. Organ. Sci. **14**(4), 422–439 (2003)

A Framework to Assess and Address Human Capacities Needed to Leverage Open Source Software Platforms in Developing Countries

Brown Msiska$^{(\boxtimes)}$ and Petter Nielsen

Department of Informatics, University of Oslo, Oslo, Norway
bmsiska@gmail.com, pnielsen@ifi.uio.no

Abstract. While open source health information software platforms provide developing countries a low-cost, quick and less risky way to build health information systems as compared to in-house solutions, human resource capacity challenges can limit their ability to leverage such platforms. Drawing from a case study focusing on the deployment and operation phases of the DHIS2 platform in Malawi, we observe open source software platforms require a range of human resource capacities that go beyond capacity to use the platform. To fully leverage open source health information software platforms entails the availability of platform usage capacity, platform deployment capacity, platform customisation capacity and platform module development capacity. Most capacity building initiatives for information systems in developing countries have been short-term efforts focused on initial end user capacity to use such systems. However, to cope with rapid innovations and evolution associated with open source software platforms, capacity building ought to be a continuous process encompassing a range of human resource capacities not only use of the platform.

Keywords: Health information systems · Open source software · Software platforms · Software ecosystems · Developing countries

1 Introduction

Health Information System (HIS) integrates data collection, processing, reporting, and use of the information necessary for improving health service effectiveness and efficiency through better management at all levels of the health services [1]. In most developing countries, there are major problems with the quality of health information which is often incomplete, inaccurate and not available at the right time for the right people. Consequently, strengthening HIS is recognised as one of the key activities required to improve the effectiveness and efficiency of health services in developing countries [2].

Resource constraints that characterise most developing countries form a key barrier to global HIS strengthening efforts. Due to high budget deficits, there is underinvestment towards HIS strengthening efforts which limits their ability to acquire appropriate software to drive their HIS operations [2, 3]. To mitigate this, a common strategy in developing countries is to adopt and adapt a generic health information system for use

J. Choudrie et al. (Eds.): ICT4D 2017, IFIP AICT 504, pp. 81–92, 2017.
DOI: 10.1007/978-3-319-59111-7_8

in the local context. This is different than starting from scratch. Adopting generic systems is cheaper, quicker and less risky compared to in-house software development [4]. By adopting generic health information systems, developing countries reduce the cost and more importantly the development time of the systems. Generic systems contain a standardised core made up of common components that remain stable across different contexts and customisable components that vary across contexts and over time [5]. Developing countries leverage these customizable components of generic health information systems to make them fit for use in the local context.

The extent of customisation afforded by generic systems varies. Some generic systems provide resources for developing third party applications (or components) which allow the end user community to extend the functionality of the systems in order to meet specific needs within context use. Such generic systems act as software platforms on which other applications required within context of use can be built by local developers or other third parties. A software platform is a software-based system with an extensible codebase that provides shared core functionality and resources with which derivative application can be created [6, 7]. In this paper, the term health information software platform is used to refer to an extensible generic health information system that provides resources with which derivative applications can be built. This is typical of some contemporary generic health information systems being used in developing countries; such as Open Medical Record System (OpenMRS), District Health Information Software (DHIS2), and Open Logistics Information System (OpenLMIS) to mention a few.

Traditionally, software is distributed under a proprietary license which requires clients to pay annual license fees for using the software and prevents them from modifying and redistributing the software [8]. With the prevailing resource constraints, the cost of ownership and freedom to modify software to fit local settings are major concerns for developing countries [3]. Open-source software provides an opportunity to build low-cost health information systems allowing countries with modest resources access to modern data analysis and visualization tools [9]. Open-source software, abbreviated as OSS, is software that is made available with source code and is provided under a software license that permits users to study, change, and improve the software [10]. By granting the user community access to the source code, open source software allows them to create and extend the software with local innovations that fit the local context. Furthermore, open source software is viewed as a tool for technical self-sufficiency as it eliminates the need for outside consultants and reduces costs of ownership of software [11]. Consequently, the use of generic open source health information systems in developing countries is common [2, 3]. The convergence of open source software and software platform approaches in the design and development of health information systems has given rise to open source health information software platforms with DHIS and OpenMRS as popular examples.

HIS strengthening initiatives in developing countries have a history of failure and unsustainability resulting from a number of factors. One important contributing factor is the lack of human resource capacity to use, develop and maintain the systems [12]. Furthermore, finding skilled developers in developing countries is a struggle due to lack of training and brain drain [13]. Other studies also show that developers participating in and contributing to open source projects are predominantly from developed countries [14, 15]. However, HIS cannot deliver expected benefits unless they are supported by appropriate human resource capacity locally [12]. Thus, to fully leverage open source health information software platforms appropriate human resource capacity must exist.

Software platforms are to some extent "half products" which have to be customised and/or extended before they can be fit for use in a particular context [16]. They constitute a departure from an era where end-users got a fully-fledged solution from a software vendor to an era where software vendors deliver solutions that must be completed by the end-user community within the context of use. Because of this, the capacity requirements for leveraging open source health information platforms vary from those of traditional HIS software. Platforms do not only allow for, support and encourage, but mandates local initiatives and innovations. The purpose of this paper is therefore to empirically address the question: what human resource capacities are required to leverage open source health information software platforms within context of use? By addressing this question the paper aims to strengthen our understanding of the implications open source health information software platforms have on HIS capacity building initiatives in developing countries. Beyond identifying concrete capacities in the case of HIS in Malawi, we also contribute with a general framework to assess and address human capacities needed to leverage open source software platforms in developing countries.

2 Software Platforms and Ecosystems

A software platform is an extensible codebase of a software based system that provides core functionality as well as an interface shared by the modules that interoperate with it [17]. Building on this definition others have gone further to describe a software platform as a software based system with extensible codebase that provides shared core functionality and resources from which derivative applications are generated [6, 7]. A software ecosystem is the software platform and the collection of modules specific to that platform [17]. Thus, the software platform is just one among other parts that make up a software ecosystem. Within the ecosystem, the software platform is complemented by modules (or applications). Modules are add-on software subsystems that connect and add new functionality to the software platform [17]. Associated with software platforms and software ecosystems is a shift from a closed software product-line based development approach to an ecosystem based development approach [16].

With the ecosystem based development approach, the software platform is rarely a solution itself; its functionality is exposed to end users through applications running on top of it. This shift in development approach comes with its own challenges. A key challenge emerges from the separation between the platform developer and platform's context of use, as well as the diversity of user requirements. Challenges faced by platform developers include making an informed decision on what applications or services to develop [18] and how to effectively respond to turbulent information processing requirements within context of use [7]. These challenges make the involvement of third party application developers close to context of use increasingly attractive for software platform developers [19, 20] as it allows them to focus on the core extensible base of the platform and defer satisfying specific user needs to third party developers. The proximity of third party developers to context of use enables them to make informed decisions on add-on modules and to develop them in response to particular needs. At the same time, deferring development to third parties creates new local capacity requirements within contexts of use. This makes the human resources capacity challenge prominent in initiatives aimed at assuring sustainability of health information system platforms in developing countries. This is the key challenge addressed in this paper.

3   Software Platforms and Human Resource Capacity Requirements

Once commissioned, a software system undergoes a number of phases within its context of use. For the purpose of this paper, distinction is made between two major phases: deployment phase, and operation phase. Software deployment is a process comprising all activities carried out in order to make a software system available for use [21]. This includes among other things setting up the required hardware and software environment; installing the software system in question; piloting and adapting it for local use; and testing it against functional and nonfunctional requirements to determine its readiness for use. Once deemed ready for use, the software system is rolled out into operation; ushering it into the operation (or productive use) phase (Fig. 1).

Fig. 1. Software system timeline within context of use

Once the software system is put into operation, anomalies are discovered, operating environments change, and new user requirements emerge and the software system must change accordingly [22]. The process of changing a software system or its component to correct faults, improve performance or other attributes, or adapt to a changed environment after it has been put into operation is called software maintenance [23, 24]. Software maintenance activities span a system's productive life cycle and 70% of all effort on a software system is estimated to be expended on maintenance alone [25]. A range of human resource capacities are therefore required during both the deployment and operation phases of a software system. For software platforms, in particular, the lack of appropriate human resource capacities in the deployment and operation phases can constrain their implementation, maintenance and hence sustainability within context of use. Understanding what human resource capacities are required for open source software platforms within each of these phases can therefore be instrumental in ensuring their success and sustainability in developing countries.

4 Methodology

This paper is based on a qualitative case study carried out in Malawi with DHIS2 as the focal software platform under study. DHIS2 is a web based, free, generic and open source health information software platform. It is currently the leading solution for aggregate health data and is being used in more than 50 developing countries by government ministries, donor agencies and NGOs [26]. DHIS2 is a flexible metadata-driven software that affords implementers the flexibility to customize its data model to fit the data needs of particular end-users. Besides the flexible data model, DHIS2 also allows customisation of data entry forms and reports. In addition, DHIS2 comes with a RESTful Web API that allows extension of its functionality through third party innovations built using common web technologies such as JavaScript, CSS and HTML5. In addition to applications running on top of it through the Web API, DHIS2 also allows development of custom software modules that sit side by side with its core modules. The introduction of such extensibility features into DHIS2 has seen it evolve from a traditional health information system to a software platform supporting open innovation through extensions by other developers within its ecosystem other than the core software development team at the University of Oslo [26, 27].

DHIS2, in Malawi, falls under the custody of the Central Monitoring and Evaluation Division (CMED) in the Ministry of Health (MoH). CMED is in charge of collecting and analyzing aggregate data used to monitor and evaluate various health programmes run by MoH. The DHIS2 platform is used by CMED and other stakeholders to collect, store, analyse and visualize aggregated data for decision making purposes. Therefore, the case study largely focused on CMED and key stakeholders involved in the deployment and operation of DHIS2 in Malawi. The aim of the case study was to address the question what human resource capacities are required to leverage open source health information software platforms within context of use. To address this question, we started by purposively sampling [28] key personnel from CMED and other stakeholders involved in the deployment and operation phases of DHIS2 as respondents for the study. The respondents were drawn from Ministry of Health and CMED, HISP Malawi, University of Malawi (UNIMA) and Baobab Health Trust. We then conducted semi-structured interviews with the selected respondents in order to establish prevailing human resource capacity requirements and challenges during the deployment phase and the subsequent operation phase of DHIS2 (Table 1).

Table 1. Respondents

Organisation	No. respondents	Designation
Ministry of Health/CMED	5	Director, CMED Chief Technical Assistant, HMIS DHIS2 Technical Assistants (3)
HISP Malawi	3	Board Members (3)
Baobab Health Trust (BHT)	4	Executive Director Software Development Manager DHIS2 Integration Team Members (2)
UNIMA	1	HISP Malawi Representative

Further data was collected through participatory observation which involved attending stakeholder meetings, training workshops, and working with the DHIS2 implementation team in Malawi comprising of staff from CMED/HISP Malawi and other strategic local partners. As part of these observations, one of the researchers worked as part of the DHIS2 implementation team in Malawi in addition to being a member of the team of trainers in a DHIS2 Application Development Workshop that took place in March 2016. In addition, data was also collected through document reviews comprising of reports on DHIS2 in Malawi by practitioners and other researchers.

The data yielded from the interviews, participatory observations and document reviews was thematically analysed [28] resulting in grouping of human resource capacities and challenges identified according to the two phases: deployment and operation. The capacities and challenges were further analysed with respect to the kind of human resource capacity; resulting in a framework which we present in our discussion. In the next section, we describe the human resource capacity requirements and challenges during the deployment and operation of DHIS2 in Malawi identified during the case study. This is followed by the discussion and later on, concluding remarks.

5 DHIS2 Software Platform in Malawi

A case study was carried out in Malawi focusing on the deployment and operation phases on the DHIS2 software platform. The aim of the case study was to establish prevailing human resource requirements and challenges in each of the phases. The results of the case study are presented in Sects. 5.1 and 5.2.

5.1 Human Resource Capacity Requirements in the Deployment Phase of the DHIS2 Platform in Malawi

DHIS2 deployment in Malawi commenced in 2009 as a pilot involving three districts; Blantyre, Zomba and Lilongwe. The pilot project ran for a period of three years and resulted in DHIS2 being rolled out to all districts and all health programmes in Malawi in 2012. The deployment of DHIS2 in Malawi involved: setting up a web server on which to run the platform; installing the DHIS2 platform on the web server; defining metadata for the platform in terms organizational units, users and user roles, data elements and indicators for data sets selected for the pilot. The deployment of DHIS2 therefore required appropriate human resources capacity to set up the web server, installing DHIS2, and define required metadata for selected data sets. Once the platform was deployed the default data entry forms and reports generated by DHIS2 turned out significantly different from the paper based forms and reports that were currently in use by end users. To preserve familiarity and ease the transition towards using DHIS2, custom reports and forms had to be designed and implemented. Implementing such custom forms and reports required the availability of human resource capacity to create custom forms and reports in DHIS2.

The human resource capacity requirements mentioned above came with a challenge: the lack of ICT personnel in CMED to carry out the deployment and customization tasks required for the deployment of DHIS2. To make ICT human resources available to CMED for the deployment of DHIS2 a local HISP node, HISP Malawi, was established. With funding acquired through the University of Oslo, HISP Malawi recruited two programmers on contract and placed them on secondment to CMED. These were joined by ICT staff from the University of Malawi constituent colleges: Chancellor College, College of Medicine and the Malawi Polytechnic. The pool of ICT personnel from HISP Malawi and University of Malawi underwent training on DHIS2 to enable them implement the deployment and customization tasks related to the pilot. In addition to the technical human resource capacities, there was a need for end users participating in the pilot study to be able to use DHIS2. Therefore, end users participating in the pilot study underwent training to enable them use DHIS2.

5.2   Human Resource Capacity Requirements in the Operation Phase of the DHIS2 in Malawi

Once a decision was made to roll out DHIS2 to all districts in Malawi, the demand for human resource capacity to use the software platform grew. As a result, a series of training workshops have been conducted targeting end-users of the software platform. Such trainings included, among others, a training of trainers workshop in August 2012 and a series of DHIS2 mobile trainings [29]. "The end user training employed a cascade approach" (Director, CMED). Trainer of Trainers (TOTs) at national level were identified and trained and the TOTs in turn trained district trainers who undertook training of health workers in their respective districts. However, we found out during the case study that end-user training has not been done regularly. As a result, there is still a backlog on untrained staff. Furthermore, changes in newer versions of DHIS2 have left a number of end-users requiring re-training.

At the same time, rolling out DHIS2 to all health programmes under the ministry of health required further deployment and customisation tasks in terms of metadata and implementation of custom forms and reports for the programmes that were not part of the pilot. Furthermore, frequent releases of newer versions of DHIS2 necessitated deploying and transitioning to newer versions of DHIS2. As a result, the demand for human resource capacity to deploy and customize the software platform grew as well. To catch up with advances in DHIS2 that came with each release members of the DHIS2 technical team have attended a number of regional DHIS2 Academies. Through the academies they acquired a range of knowledge required to install and customize DHIS2.

During the period DHIS2 has been in operation there have been a number human resource capacity challenges. First of all, staff turnover involving technical staff at HISP Malawi has threatened the day to day operations of DHIS2. All technical assistants recruited by HISP Malawi and placed on secondment to CMED between 2012 and 2015 have left for various reasons including funding for their retention. Currently, HISP Malawi has two technical assistants recruited towards the end of 2015. These were fresh graduates from the University of Malawi and have had to attend a series of DHIS2 academies to bring them up to speed with DHIS2.

In addition, the lack of ICT staff in CMED has left it dependent on external expertise, both local and foreign, to keep DHIS2 in operation. The MoH, like all other ministries in the Malawi Government, has an ICT department which has an allocation of ICT staff from the Department of e-Government in the Office of the President and Cabinet. However, until recently none of the ICT staff in the ICT department have been working with CMED on DHIS2. CMED has therefore relied on HISP Malawi and other external expertise to keep DHIS2 in operation. CMED sees the continued reliance on external expertise as a threat to the sustainability of DHIS2 and has been lobbying government to adjust its staff establishment to include ICT personnel. "We came up with a position paper requesting for ICT personnel under CMED … but things take time in government so we are not sure when that will happen" (Chief Technical Assistant, CMED). The decision to adjust CMED's staff establishment is however still outstanding.

Furthermore, some problems and requirements CMED has had with respect to DHIS2 required changing or developing new DHIS2 modules. Handling such requirements and problems required human resource capacity to develop or modify DHIS2 modules. These have usually been reported to DHIS2 core developers in Norway because of lack of necessary human resource capacity locally. As part of efforts to address this gap, In March 2016, a DHIS2 Application Development workshop took place at University of Malawi, Chancellor College from 7th March to 16th March 2016 [30]. The training introduced participants to the DHIS2 API and how to develop DHIS2 applications using the API. The training was funded by University of Oslo with support from UNICEF. It attracted participants from Kenya, Ethiopia, Zambia and Malawi including the two technical assistants at CMED.

6   Discussion

Analysing the deployment and operation phases of DHIS2 in Malawi reveals four categories of human resource capacity needed to leverage open source software platforms. Before a software platform can be put into operation it must be deployed first and this requires the availability of platform deployment capacity which includes ability to setup the platform operating environment and install the software platform. Once the software platform is installed, its customisable components have to be customised to fit local needs. This entails platform customisation capacity. Historically, donor driven HIS projects in developing have used foreign experts to mitigate the gap in deployment and customisation capacity in the deployment phase.

Once the system is put into operation it requires human capacity for its maintenance, including the development of new platform modules. This entails platform module development capacity. Such capacity is instrumental to third party innovations which respond to specific needs within context of use. Maintenance often happens at a time when donor and external support is no longer available leading to sustainability challenges where local capacity is lacking. Both during deployment and maintenance the software system is subject to use by end users. In the deployment phase this happens as a result of piloting and testing of the system against end user requirements. Therefore in both phases there is a requirement for human capacity to use the software platform, hereby referred to as platform usage capacity. Furthermore, during the

Table 2. Human capacity requirement for software platforms within context of use

Phase	Key activities	Human capacities required
Deployment	– Setting up hardware and software environment – Installation of the software platform – Customisation – Testing/Piloting system	– Platform deployment capacity – Platform customisation capacity – Platform usage capacity
Operation	– Correcting system faults – Upgrading to newer software versions – Customising new versions – Develop platform modules – Test implemented changes	– Platform deployment capacity – Platform customisation capacity – Platform module development capacity – Platform usage capacity

maintenance phase there are episodes of deployment where the software system is upgraded to a newer version. These capacity needs are summarized in Table 2.

The extent to which developing countries are able to leverage open source software platforms is, therefore, subject to the availability of human capacities to deploy, customize and use the platforms; complemented by capacity to develop platform modules is response to new requirements or those not adequately addressed by platform developers. This we summarise in the model in Fig. 2, showing a ladder of human resource capacities required to leverage software platforms within context of use. The model can act as a framework informing stakeholders implementing of open source health information software platforms in developing countries what human resource capacities to put in place in order to fully leverage the software platforms. At the same time, it could be used to inform efforts to assess and address gaps in human resource capacities needed to leverage open source platforms where they have been implemented.

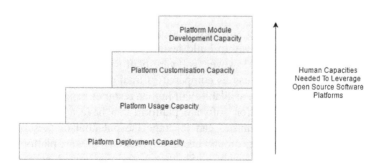

Fig. 2. A model for human capacities needed to leverage open source software platforms

Many of donor-driven HIS in developing countries have ended up as unsustainable and/or failures due to a lack of local human resource capacity left behind after implementation [31]. During implementation, donors and their agents have traditionally filled the human resources gap by engaging foreign experts at the expense of building local expertise [12]. While this works well in the short term it creates long term challenges with maintenance and sustainability. Without requisite capacity, locals fail to support and maintain the solutions leading to gradual decay and obsolescence of the solutions as they fail to respond to emerging needs within context of use. As shown in the model above, open source software platforms come with an implicit demand for local capacity not only in terms of use but also in terms of customizing and extending the platform to meet local needs. This supports the argument made by Sahay and Walsham [32] who state that health information systems need to be accompanied by the scaling of local human resources capacity at least two levels: level of end users and level of the implementation team.

The introduction of health information systems in developing countries is often accompanied by short-term training aimed at building the capacity of end-users to use the systems. This is important, but not enough to address long-term learning needs of end users and the implementation and maintenance team to stay up to date as the health information system evolves overtime. Capacity building is a continuous process [12]. To cope with rapid innovations and evolution associated with health information software platforms and open source software platforms in general, capacity building ought to be a continuous process and include more than the platform usage capacity. Associated with increasing complexity of health information systems is the need to scale the technical competence of users and that of the implementation team responsible for providing technical support to the users and the user organization [32]. With the shift towards health information software platforms, the issue of human resources capacity building in developing countries involves not only building capacity of local end-users and local implementation team but also ensuring that there is continuous learning to enable them cope with the rapid evolution and innovations that characterise software platforms.

7 Conclusion

Open source health information software platforms provide developing countries a low-cost, quick and less risky way to build health information systems compared to developing in-house solutions. However, software platforms also place new capacity requirements within context of use as compared to traditional off-the-selves or commissioned software systems. The availability of human resource capacity to deploy, use and maintain a health information software platform can have an influence on the extent to which developing countries can leverage the potential of these platforms. Thus, capacity building initiatives around health information software platforms should strive to build this range of capacities. Short-term training aimed at building the capacity of end-users to use the systems is important, but not enough to address long-term learning needs of end users and the implementation and maintenance team to stay up to date as the health information system evolves overtime. To cope with rapid innovations and evolution associated with open source software platforms, capacity building ought to be a continuous process covering a range of human resource capacities not only use of the platform.

References

1. WHO: Developing Health Management Information Systems: A Practical Guide For Developing Countries. World Health Organisation, Geneva (2004)
2. Karuri, J., Waiganjo, P., Orwa, D., Manya, A.: DHIS2: the tool to improve health data demand and use in Kenya. J. Health Inform. Dev. Countries **8** (2014)
3. Sheikh, Y.H., Bakar, A.D.: Open source software solution for healthcare: the case of health information system in Zanzibar. In: Popescu-Zeletin, R., Jonas, K., Rai, Idris A., Glitho, R., Villafiorita, A. (eds.) AFRICOMM 2011. LNICSSITE, vol. 92, pp. 146–155. Springer, Heidelberg (2012). doi:10.1007/978-3-642-29093-0_14
4. Bansler, J.P., Havn, E.C.: Information systems development with generic systems. In: ECIS 1994, pp. 707–718 (1994)
5. Silsand, L., Ellingsen, G.: Generification by translation: designing generic systems in context of the local. J. Assoc. Inf. Syst. **15**, 177–196 (2014)
6. Eck, A., Uebernickel, F., Brenner, W.: The generative capacity of digital artifacts: a mapping of the field. In: Proceedings of PACIS 2015 (2015)
7. Ghazawneh, A., Henfridsson, O.: Balancing platform control and external contribution in third-party development: the boundary resources model. Inf. Syst. J. **23**, 173–192 (2013)
8. Fogel, K.: Producing Open Source Software, 1st edn. O'Reilly, Sebastopol (2005)
9. Yi, Q., Hoskins, R.E., Hillringhouse, E.A., Sorensen, S.S., Oberle, M.W., Fuller, S.S., et al.: Integrating open-source technologies to build low-cost information systems for improved access to public health data. Int. J. Health Geogr. **7**, 29 (2008)
10. Kandar, S., Mondal, S., Ray, P.: A review of open source software and open source movement in developing countries. Int. J. Comput. Sci. Inform. **1**, 89–93 (2011)
11. Vital Wave Consulting: mHealth for Development: The Opportunity of Mobile Technology for Healthcare in the Developing World, Washington, D.C. (2009)
12. Kimaro, H.C.: Strategies for developing human resource capacity to support sustainability of ICT based health information systems: a case study from Tanzania. Electron. J. Inf. Syst. Dev. Countries **26**, 1–23 (2006)
13. Roets, R., Minnaar, M., Wright, K.: Open source: towards successful systems development projects in developing countries. In: Proceedings of the 9th International Conference on Social Implications of Computers in Developing Countries, Sao Paulo, Brazil (2007)
14. Paudel, B., Harlalka, J., Shrestha, J.: Open technologies and developing economies. In: Proceedings of CAN InfoTech (IT) Conference (2010)
15. Weerawarana, S., Weeratunge, J.: Open Source in Developing Countries. Sida, Stockholm (2004)
16. Dittrich, Y.: Software engineering beyond the project – sustaining software ecosystems. Inf. Softw. Technol. **56**, 1436–1456 (2014)
17. Tiwana, A., Konsynski, B., Bush, A.A.: Research commentary—platform evolution: coevolution of platform architecture, governance, and environmental dynamics. Inf. Syst. Res. **21**, 675–687 (2010)
18. Henfridsson, O., Lindgren, R.: User involvement in developing mobile and temporarily interconnected systems. Inf. Syst. J. **20**, 119–135 (2010)
19. Bosch, J.: From software product lines to software ecosystems. In: Proceedings of the 13th International Software Product Line Conference, pp. 111–119. Carnegie Mellon University (2009)
20. Boudreau, K.J., Lakhani, K.R.: How to manage outside innovation. MIT Sloan Manag. Rev. **50**, 69–75 (2009)

21. Carzaniga, A., Fuggetta, A., Hall, R.S., Heimbigner, D., Van Der Hoek, A., Wolf, A.L.: A characterization framework for software deployment technologies. DTIC Document (1998)

22. Pigoski, T.M.: Practical Software Maintenance: Best Practices for Managing Your Software Investment. Wiley, New York (1997)

23. Sommerville, I.: Software Engineering, 9th edn. Pearson Education, Boston (2011)

24. Van Vliet, H.: Software Engineering: Principles and Practice. Wiley, New York (2007)

25. Ogheneovo, E.E.: On the relationship between software complexity and maintenance costs. J. Comput. Commun. **02**, 1–16 (2014)

26. PATH: An Interim Review of the Health Information Systems Programme - University of Oslo - with Recommendations for Future Action, Seattle, September 2016

27. Polak, M.: Platformisation of an Open Source Software Product: Growing up to be a Generative Software Platform. University of Oslo, Oslo (2015)

28. Creswell, J.W.: Research Design: Qualitative, Quantitative, and Mixed Methods Approaches. Sage, Los Angeles (2009)

29. HISP Malawi: DHIS2 TOT Training [Internet]. DHIS2 TOT Training. http://hispmalawi.org. mw/index.php?page=pages&pid=39. Accessed 7 Nov 2016

30. University of Malawi: Computer Science Department holds DHIS2 Workshop - University of Malawi|Chancellor College [Internet]. Computer Science Department holds DHIS2 Workshop (2016). http://cc.ac.mw/news/computer-science-department-holds-dhis2-workshop-17-03-2016

31. Kimaro, H.C., Nhampossa, J.L.: Analyzing the problem of unsustainable health information systems in less-developed economies: case studies from Tanzania and Mozambique. Inf. Technol. Dev. **11**, 273–298 (2005)

32. Sahay, S., Walsham, G.: Scaling of health information systems in India: challenges and approaches. Inf. Technol. Dev. **12**, 185–200 (2006)

The Role of Global Standardization Communities in Shaping National Health Information Architectures

Simon Pettersen Nguyen[(✉)], Petter Nielsen, and Johan Ivar Sæbø

Department of Informatics, University of Oslo, Oslo, Norway
simonpn@ifi.uio.no

Abstract. Health sectors in developing countries are commonly struggling with disarrayed health information architectures, where multiple vertical, disease-specific programmes have implemented their isolated information systems. A consequence is parallel and overlapping systems where information is stored at different locations and in different formats. To address this, multiple global standardization efforts to harmonize health information architectures have been initiated. Still, there is only limited knowledge about the role of these global standardization communities in shaping national health information architectures. This article is based on a case study of the global Open Health Information Exchange (OpenHIE) standardization community. With an Information and Communications Technologies (ICT) ecosystem perspective, we aim to improve our understanding of the relationships between global standardization communities and national ICT ecosystems. Theoretically, we contribute with our conceptualization of national ICT ecosystems.

Keywords: Architecture · Health information systems · ICT ecosystem · Standardization

1 Introduction

Health systems in developing countries are commonly struggling with disarrayed health information architectures. Information systems (IS) are often implemented independently and in isolation by different health programmes, ministries of health and donors across different health domains such as health management, logistics, laboratory, and facility registers. As a consequence, information is often disaggregated and stored at different locations and in different formats, making it a difficult task to get access and a pressing need to integrate them [1, 2]. The lack of harmonized national health information systems makes collaboration and sharing of data, information and knowledge among different healthcare personnel and programmes an arduous affair. It is often almost impossible to obtain a clear overview of all the routine health data. At the same time, health systems in developing countries frequently suffer from parallel reporting of routine health indicators. Consequently, there is an urgent need for strengthening the coordination of information collection to support information sharing and strengthen health information architectures [3]. In response to this need, several

J. Choudrie et al. (Eds.): ICT4D 2017, IFIP AICT 504, pp. 93–103, 2017.
DOI: 10.1007/978-3-319-59111-7_9

global communities work towards standardizing health information architectures, addressing the challenges of fragmentation. In this paper, we try to understand how these global standardization communities influence what we refer to as national ICT ecosystems. National ICT ecosystems encompasses the people, policies, strategies, processes, information and other ICTs that together make up the socio-technical environment surrounding an ICT embedded within a country. Examples of global standardization communities trying to influence national ICT ecosystems are Integrating the Healthcare Enterprise (IHE), the Health Data Collaborative, and the Open Health Information Exchange (OpenHIE). This article is derived from a case study of the latter. OpenHIE intends to address the previously mentioned challenges by facilitating interoperability through the creation of a reusable architectural framework leveraging on standards.

The concept of architecture has been used inconsistently in IS research. It was for example described by Zachman as a logical construct for creating a structured set of descriptive representations of the future state of an undeveloped system [4]. Later, it has been extended to include social as well as the technical aspects [3]. Common to these definitions is a view of architecture as abstract images and blueprints of something to be. They further share a perceptive on architecting as a top down process, implying that there is a single architect in control of the process of implementing the architecture. The IS architecture literature also focus their discussion on interoperability. Arguably, OpenHIE share this view on architecture, as they are abstractly working on a global architectural blueprint. Nielsen and Sæbø [5] focused on another dimension of architecture and conceptualize functional architecting as the process of distributing, allocating or configuring of functional roles of the different components in architectures. As vendors of the different software components seek to retain and strengthen their position, there are strong incentives for extending their software components across (previously) logical boundaries for organizational units, work practices and professions. As a result, functional overlap is not an uncommon phenomenon in health information architectures. The functional architecting perspective can be used to describe what unfolds in terms of implementation and integration of independent software components in health information architectures.

Global standardization is an extremely challenging and complex task, and it is unclear what potential role global standardization communities have on national level information systems architectures. In this paper, we try to understand these communities by asking the following question: *What is the role of global standardization communities working towards harmonizing national health ICT ecosystems in developing countries?* By using a national ICT ecosystems perspective, we make an attempt to address this question by using a case study of the standardization community OpenHIE. Based on the case study, we contribute by improving our understanding of the relationship between global standardization initiatives and national health information architectures. Theoretically, we contribute with our conceptualization of national ICT ecosystems.

The remainder of this paper is organized as follows. In Sect. 2, we introduce the concept of the ICT ecosystem. In Sect. 3, we describe our method, followed by a presentation of our empirical case in Sect. 4. Then we discuss the empirical case from a national ICT ecosystem perspective. Finally, we present our conclusions and describe potential future work.

2 ICT Ecosystems

In this paper, we argue for taking an ecosystem perspective to understand the role of global standardization communities. The concept of ecosystem is borrowed from biology and is used to describe networks of diverse actors influencing each other's and being mutually dependent within a specific (eco)system [6]. Fransman [7] proposed using ecosystem as a metaphor for understanding the cause of changes in the socio-economy, as *"... the idea of interacting organisms in a constant process of change is more appealing than that of a mechanical system settling into equilibrium, if the aim is to understand living force and movement"* [7].

The ecosystems metaphor has lately been adopted for understanding the ICT sector. The first definition of ICT ecosystems is found in a "Roadmap for Open ICT Ecosystems" from 2005 developed by the Open ePolicy Group [8], where the following definition is provided: *"An ICT ecosystem encompasses the policies, strategies, processes, information, technologies, applications and stakeholders that together make up a technology environment for a country, government or an enterprise. Most importantly, an ICT ecosystem includes people—diverse individuals who create, buy, sell, regulate, manage and use technology"* [8]. However, the focus in their roadmap is on understanding how ICT ecosystem enable efficiency, innovation and growth, and they do not further elaborate on the concepts of the ICT ecosystem. Fransman [7] has conceptualized ICT ecosystems based on several key concepts. He argued that the term should be used to describe the interaction between four key groups of *players* interacting in a layered and hierarchical fashion: Network element providers; network operators; content and applications providers; and final consumers. These players interact within the same environment. The environment is formed by institutions that define the 'rules of the game' by which the players interact and are influenced by. The principal institutions in an ICT ecosystem include financial institutions, regulators, competition authorities, standardization bodies and universities. These institutions can in turn be changed by organizations which have the powers to do so, such as governments, political parties, cooperate interests and trade unions.

The ICT ecosystem is conceptualized by Fransman [7] as a set of *functionalities*, and the hierarchical nature of the model symbolizes the functional interdependencies required by the system. Each layer is dependent on its bordering layer (or layers). For the ecosystem to function as a whole, each and every layer is required to perform its functional job. The model is an engineering-architectural model and at the same time an economic-institutional model. As an engineering-architectural model, it defines and determines the technical interactions, and as an economic-institutional model, it describes how markets and other institutions shape the evolutions of the system. The purpose of the model is to serve as a tool for analysis of the ICT sector for making informed corporate strategies and government policies [7].

2.1   The Process of Change in the ICT Ecosystem

As a part of evolutionary theory, Darwin conceptualized the evolving ecosystem constituting of communities of organisms, or species interacting in a natural environment. Darwin viewed change as an evolutionary process propelled by the interaction between the generation of variety and the selection from that variety. Fransman [7] adopted this evolutionary thinking for analysing change in the ICT ecosystem. To understand the first part of the evolutionary process, generation of variety, Fransman referred to Schumpeter. Schumpeter [9] asserted that change in the capitalist system (in which the ICT sector is a part of) is driven by four different types of innovation: New or improved products or services; new or improved processes or methods of production; new or improved forms of organisation; and new markets.

According to Fransman [7], the generation of variety in the ICT ecosystem is caused by innovation in one or more of these four areas. How does this innovation come about? Fransman [7] argues that the innovations mainly emerge from six symbiotic relationships that transpire within the ICT ecosystem. A symbiotic relationship, or symbiosis, exists when two different species live together in a close and often long-term interaction which may or may not be mutually beneficial. The six symbiotic relationships which take place between the different players at the different layers are [7]:

1. Relationship between network element providers and network operators.
2. Relationship between network operators and content and applications providers.
3. Relationship between content and applications providers and final consumers.
4. Relationship between network element providers and final consumers.
5. Relationship between network element providers and content and applications providers.
6. Relationship between network operators and final consumers.

2.2   The Context of the Symbiotic Relationships

Fransman [7] argues that the symbiotic relationships of the players in the ICT ecosystem take place within distinguished context which influences the disposition of the relationships. More specifically, he identified that the context is made up by four different influential factors including competition, financial institutions, regulation and competition law and other institutions. The first influence is *competition*. For example, the relationship between a network element provider and a network operator is affected by the degree of competition which the network element provider faces from competing providers. This in turn influences the types of innovation that the network operator makes. The second influence is *financial institutions*. An illustration of the impact of this influence is the telecoms crash where the unrealistic expectations of the telecom sector caused inexpedient investments which ultimately crashed the stock market in 2001. This event had a significant impact on the function of the entire ICT ecosystem. The third influence is *regulation and competition law*, which are the institutions that define the 'rules of the game' which the symbiotic relationships are governed by. These institutions affect the innovation process and subsequent outcomes of the symbiotic relationships. The fourth and final influence is *other institutions*, such as legal institutions, standardization bodies and universities. Legal institutions include intellectual property laws and antitrust laws. Standardization has significant influence on the operation of the module producers of the ICT ecosystem and therefore also the interoperability of the system. Universities as institutions conducts research which generates new knowledge which through symbiotic relationships stimulate change in the system [7].

2.3 A National ICT Perspective

The ICT ecosystem concept has lately received substantial attention IS research in developing countries, as made evident by a special issue of The Journal of Information Technology for Development named *"The ICT Ecosystem: The Application, Usefulness, and Future of an Evolving Concept"* [10]. Diga and May [10] argue that ICT is to be viewed as embedded in the global, national, and local socio-economic context in which it is utilized. ICTs should not be viewed as technical systems in a vacuum, but rather as a part of a wider network that takes into account non-technical dynamics, being socio-economic, political, spatial, and such. The way in which the technical system is developed and operates is: *"... an aspect of emerging paradigms that consider the interplay between ICT multi-level usage by various players within systems of governance, citizenship, communication, knowledge, and innovation"* [10].

Inspired by Diga and May [10], we have developed a working definition of what we call the national ICT ecosystem based on the definition of ICT ecosystems provided by the Open ePolicy Group [8]:

> *"A national ICT ecosystem encompasses the people, policies, strategies, processes, information and other ICTs that together make up the socio-technical environment surrounding an ICT embedded within a country."*

Applying this perspective, an ICT is not viewed in isolation, but as part of a wider national ICT ecosystem made up by people, policies, strategies, processes, information and other ICTs. Outside the national ICT ecosystems there are several global actors trying to influence them, such as OpenHIE through standardization of national health information architectures. It is this relationship between the global standardization communities and the national ICT ecosystems we are trying to improve our understanding of. In Fig. 1, the national ICT ecosystem perspective is illustrated.

Fig. 1. Illustration of the national ICT ecosystem perspective. Here a few common health-related technologies are included: HMIS: Health Information System; SCM: Supply Chain Management System; LMIS: Logistics Management Information System; EHR: Electronic Health Record.

3   Method

This article reports from an interpretative case study [11] using an exploratory approach [12], offering the researchers an opportunity to access multiple data sources to study the phenomenon of interest. The empirical setting of this research is the global standardization community OpenHIE. The authors of this article are involved in the Health Information Systems Programme project at the University of Oslo (HISP UiO), a project which for several years has been a part of the OpenHIE community. The primary data collected for the case study is based on interviews conducted with four individuals who have all been a part of the OpenHIE community for several years. Three of them are project members at HISP UiO, and one of them is an independent consultant who has been involved with OpenHIE since its initiation. As HISPUiO is deeply involved in OpenHIE, access to these discussions and their accumulated data is granted. Hence, secondary data used for this case study consist of related documents such as articles from the encyclopedias of the OpenHIE and their partners contributing to the understanding of them.

4   Empirical Case: OpenHIE

This research is derived from a case study of OpenHIE, a global standardization community working towards harmonizing national health ICT ecosystems in developing countries. In order to understand the potential role of OpenHIE in doing so, we will in this section present its history and its work.

4.1 The History of OpenHIE

In 2010, the President's Emergency Plan for AIDS Relief (PEPFAR) in conjunction with the Innovative Support to Emergencies Diseases and Disasters (InSTEDD) initiative, Regenstrief Institute and Jembi Health Systems formed the Health Informatics Public Private Partnership (HIPPP) in response to the growing problem of fragmented Health Information Systems (HIS). The purpose of the HIPPP was to scale up and advance country ownership and leadership of the implementation of interoperable HIS in low-resource settings with the ultimate goal of improved health access and quality of care and increased productivity.

Over the years, HIPPP has provided different countries with technical support related to health information architecture. The first calls for support came from the Ministries of Health in Rwanda and Cambodia, and during 2011, HIPPP devoted substantial resources on establishing the health information architecture in Rwanda. The Ministry of Health in Rwanda saw an operationalized health information architecture as a crucial means for achieving the Millennium Development Goal of improving maternal health outcomes (MDG 5). They wanted to improve the coordination of care and cut down the number of key indicators by aggregating data from various actors providing care to maternal health patients, including hospitals, health clinics and community health workers. In parallel, the Rwanda Health Enterprise Architecture (RHEA) project was founded by an international project team consisting of the International Development Research Centre (IDRC) and the Rockefeller Foundation. The mission of RHEA was to scale up and advance ownership of an enterprise health architecture at country level. Having common interests, HIPPP partnered up with RHEA to support and deliver a health information exchange in Rwanda, which later became known as the Rwanda Health Information Exchange (RHIE).

According to OpenHIE [13], RHIE demonstrated the potentials of health information architecture, and it was used as a reference example by other actors in the global health community for understanding how to implement interoperability with technical, sociopolitical and capacity development challenges in mind. They further claim that after the launch of RHIE in 2012, there was a need for a more generalized approach as multiple countries requested assistance on health information architecture. In response to this need, the OpenHIE "community of communities" was established in 2013 by HIPPP based on the alleged potentials of RHIE. However, assessments carried out in 2014 of RHIE have quite unambiguously described it as a non-successful initiative [14]. According to the respondents of the assessments, the governance challenges were underestimated, the overall coordination was seen as weak, and an insufficient amount of time was dedicated to capacity building. In addition, there was a lengthy and challenging process of developing an infrastructure of networks and computers for facilitating RHIE. This was seen as a barrier to system scalability, as it was argued that 3G networks could have been leveraged for the same purpose. Measuring the actual use of RHIE, it was found that about half of the users were satisfied with the system, and most users felt that they had less time to spend with their patients. In terms of scalability, the system was only operational in about half of the initial implantation sites as of 2014. Most interestingly, the assessments found that no significant health impact has emerged from the RHIE initiative.

4.2   The Work of OpenHIE

The core activity of OpenHIE, as a global standardization community, is the development of a reusable architectural framework which leverages on health information standards, facilitates flexible implementation on country level, and supports interchangeability of individual components. In terms of standards, they seek to evaluate and implement already existing consensus-based, international interoperability specifications, and to be a driving force in the development of future specifications. They further aim to create an architectural framework where the components are interchangeable by clearly defining standardized interfaces for each component. Each component provides well-described core functionality for core health data management and interoperates with other components making sure that health information from the different components are used to support person-centric and population-based healthcare needs.

The blueprint of OpenHIE's architectural framework contains six open-source software components: terminology service, enterprise master patient index or client registry, shared health record, health management information system (HMIS), health facility registry and health worker registry, and optionally external systems, such as the OpenMRS electronic medical records system. All the systems interoperate via a health interoperability layer, which receives all communications from the different systems and orchestrates message processing among them using a unified person-centric medical record.

OpenHIE describes themselves as a community of communities committed to open collaboration and knowledge sharing. Each community corresponds to one of the components in their proposed architecture framework. In addition, there are three more communities: OpenHIE Implementers Network, a forum dedicated to bringing countries and implementers together for sharing knowledge; Architecture community, an assembly discussing cross-cutting technical issues, and; PEPFAR Data Exchange Implementer Community, a community for DATIM stakeholders. DATIM (Data for Accountability, Transparency, and Impact) is a PEPFAR-specific version of the open source HMIS DHIS2. It was created for PEPFAR's Country Operational Plan and the Site Improvement through Monitoring Systems. All the aforementioned communities are working on implementation processes, standards and at least one reference implementation related to their community.

OpenHIE being organized as a community of communities, was in fact identified as one of its key challenges by an interviewee. He argued that consensus building and community building is a difficult and lengthy process, but that the benefit is a community where competent people are well represented. In terms of competency, he claimed that there is an extensive amount of competency represented in OpenHIE in the form of "on the ground experience" (in relation to country implementations).

One of the main purposes of OpenHIE, an interviewee argued, is to advocate for the underserved regions in other standardization communities, like IHE and HL7, where their voices are not well represented from before. However, based on the interviews, it was evident that the involvement of the underserved regions in OpenHIE community itself is limited. The countries are typically only relating to OpenHIE as an advisory service. However, several of the interview subjects believe that OpenHIE has changed the narrative in the developing countries. It is believed that OpenHIE is giving an approachable way to help articulate interoperability. Therefore, it is also believed that it has changed the way in which countries think about investments that will lead to interoperability at scale.

5   Discussion

In this paper, we provide the following working definition of national ICT ecosystems: *"A national ICT ecosystem encompasses the people, policies, strategies, processes, information and other ICTs that together make up the socio-technical environment surrounding an ICT embedded within a country"*. Further, we argue that OpenHIE is a global actor influencing national health ICT ecosystems. In this section, we try to improve our understanding of the relationship between OpenHIE and national health ICT ecosystems by discussing the research question of this paper: *What is the role of global standardization communities working towards harmonizing national health ICT ecosystems in developing countries?*

Arguably, OpenHIE have made an architectural blueprint which would exist in a perfectly harmonized national health ICT ecosystem, where different ICTs have well-defined functional requirements. In reality, the constitution of ICTs within the health sectors of developing countries looks nothing like the architectural blueprint of OpenHIE. The health sector in developing countries is largely a fragmented sector due to the high level of professional specialization it holds, and the fragmentation is also apparent within HIS. In addition, ministries of health, global donors and aid organizations in developing countries are commonly arranged around programmes (such as HIV/ADIS or malaria), for which they have established various segregated IS. While these IS serve the need of their respective health programmes, they also often lead to the presence of overlaps in functionality and data [1, 2]. Therefore, a depiction of the national ICT ecosystem of the health sector in a developing country would most likely contain several redundant and missing actors (or players, put in the terms of Fransman [7]) in terms of the requirements of the OpenHIE architectural blueprint. Implementing the blueprint in real world national health ICT ecosystems will most likely involve extensive introduction and removal of ICTs. National ICT ecosystems as an analogy to natural ecosystem are extremely complex and sensitive to change. Therefore, it can be very difficult to understand the implications of the changes in the national health ICT ecosystems required by the OpenHIE architectural blueprint. Such changes could cause disturbance and substantial shifts (for better or worse) to the existing national ICT ecosystem. The changes would presumably affect not only the ICTs embedded within a country, but also the people, policies, strategies, processes and information tied to them.

Fransman [7] argued that there are symbiotic relationships between content and applications providers and final consumers in an ICT ecosystem. In the current national health ICT ecosystems in developing countries, some of these symbiotic relationships maybe missing, redundant or unnecessarily fragmented. Arguably, this is the issue which OpenHIE is trying to address through standardization. Fransman argued that standardization is a part of the context of the symbiotic relationships which *"... crucially affects the way in which the ICT Ecosystem's module producers operate, and in turn the interoperability of the system"* [15]. Smith and Elder [16] asserted that interoperability is the key to establish an open ICT ecosystem. By "open", Smith and Elder (2010) point to universal access, universal participation in informal and formal groups/institutions and collaborative production. In addition, Gasser and Palfrey [17] argued that innovation made possible by interoperability comes with extensive benefits for the people that come to cultivate it. More specifically, they state that the final consumer benefit as "...*interoperability leads to innovation that results in technology systems that work together more easily, with less hassle, and ensures that they have more choice when they are making a decision about what to buy or to use*" [17]. It can be said that OpenHIE is trying to achieve this by bringing harmony to the national health ICT ecosystems through defining both the players and 'the rules of the game', where the rules of the game are the standards which ensures interoperability. Arguably, their main goal is to ensure that the symbiotic relationships between content and applications providers and final consumers cater to the person-centric and population-based healthcare needs. In other words, OpenHIE can be viewed as an organization trying to change the institutions in the national ICT ecosystems of the health sector in developing countries.

Whether or not OpenHIE is actually contributing to the harmonization of national health ICT ecosystems in developing countries is discussable. OpenHIE was formed on basis of RHIE, which they refer to as a successful demonstration of the potentials of a health information architecture. However, according to assessments of RHIE, the project was quite unambiguously described as a non-successful initiative in terms of actual use, scaling and measurable health impact [14]. Hence, using RHIE as an example of harmonization of national health ICT ecosystems is unsubstantiated. Another remarkable observation is that there is little involvement of the developing countries in the OpenHIE community, even though they are the ones who are encouraged to adopt the architectural framework. At the same time, it is important to acknowledge two positive outcomes of OpenHIE: (1) The community is well-represented in terms of competency, and knowledge drawn from this competency is injected into the national heath ICT ecosystems through advisory service; and, (2) it is changing the narrative of the health ICT national ecosystem in terms of what investments that will lead to interoperability at scale.

6   Conclusions and Future Work

In this article, we contribute by improving our understanding of the relationship between global standardization communities and national health information architectures. This case study is only the beginning of a longitudinally and multilevel research project studying the phenomena of global standardization communities working towards strengthening HIS in developing countries. Future work therefore includes accumulating more empirical data, including at country level where the implementations are. It will also include studying more than one global standardization community. One candidate is IHE, in which OpenHIE is involved. IHE is working on the issues of interoperability and information sharing between various healthcare systems and medical devices.

This research contributes to the conceptualization of national ICT ecosystems through the development of a working definition and the utilization of this perspective. Hence, future work should continue to strengthen this concept by using it and evaluating its usefulness for understanding the phenomena at hand.

References

1. Sæbø, J., et al.: Integrating health information systems in Sierra Leone. In: 2009 International Conference on Information and Communication Technologies and Development (ICTD). IEEE (2009)
2. Heeks, R.: ICT4D 2.0: the next phase of applying ICT for international development. Computer **41**(6), 26–33 (2008)
3. Braa, J., Sahay, S.: Integrated Health Information Architecture: Power to the Users: Design, Development and Use. Matrix Publishers, New Delhi (2012)
4. Zachman, J.A.: A framework for information systems architecture. IBM Syst. J. **26**(3), 276–292 (1987)
5. Nielsen, P., Sæbø, J.I.: Three strategies for functional architecting: cases from the health systems of developing countries. Inf. Technol. Dev. **22**(1), 134–151 (2016)
6. Tansley, A.G.: The use and abuse of vegetational concepts and terms. Ecology **16**(3), 284–307 (1935)
7. Fransman, M.: The New ICT Ecosystem: Implications for Policy and Regulation. Cambridge University Press, New York (2010)
8. Open ePolicy Group: Roadmap for Open ICT Ecosystems. Havard Law School (2005)
9. Schumpeter, J.A.: The Theory of Economic Development: An Inquiry into Profits, Capital, Credit, Interest, and the Business Cycle, vol. 55. Transaction Publishers (1934)
10. Diga, K., May, J.: The ICT Ecosystem: The Application, Usefulness, and Future of an Evolving Concept. Taylor & Francis, New York (2016)
11. Walsham, G.: Interpretive case studies in IS research: nature and method. Eur. J. Inf. Syst. **4**(2), 74–81 (1995)
12. Yin, R.K.: Case Study Research: Design and Methods. Sage Publications, Thousand Oaks (2013)
13. OpenHIE: History (2017). https://ohie.org/about/-history. Accessed 23 Feb 2017
14. Sahay, S.: Data revolution in health: nature, challenges and implications (2014)
15. Fransman, M.: Innovation in the new ICT ecosystem (2009)
16. Smith, M., Elder, L.: Open ICT ecosystems transforming the developing world. Inf. Technol. Int. Dev. **6**(1), 65–71 (2010)
17. Gasser, U., Palfrey, J.G.: Breaking Down Digital Barriers: When and How ICT Interoperability Drives Innovation. Berkman Center Research Publication (2007–8) (2007)

From Abstraction to Implementation: Can Computational Thinking Improve Complex Real-World Problem Solving? A Computational Thinking-Based Approach to the SDGs

Maryam Rabiee[✉] and A Min Tjoa

Vienna University of Technology (TU Wien), Vienna, Austria
maryam.rabiee@tuwien.ac.at, amin@ifs.tuwien.ac.at

Abstract. Utilizing concepts derived from computational thinking—a method of thinking coined by Jeanette Wing—a problem-solving paradigm is presented to demonstrate the applicability of thinking computationally beyond the realm of computer science. The 17 Sustainable Development Goals (SDGs) are used as a set of real world problems to elaborate the function of the proposed four-stage paradigm. The paradigm seeks to provide a method of approaching problems with the aim of finding local and contextualized solutions that reach all members of different societies. This paper also serves as the foundation of further research in the development of computational thinking as a fundamental tool for finding solutions in a broad scope of disciplines and real-world situations.

Keywords: Computational thinking · SDGs · Problem solving · Global network

1 Introduction

The once 'imagined communities' of the twentieth century are now transforming into a global network of communities. Anderson believed that nations were a social construction of a group's imagined connection to other members that was enabled by print press [1]. Today, digital technologies, the internet in particular, have created a global network where the production and consumption of information transcends languages, nationalities, and borders creating a network of communities that is growing in its real-world connectivity. Our ever more connected world has developed a global network where our problems are becoming more complex and more intertwined. As a result, the world faces an acute problem: how can we devise solutions for our multi-layered and interconnected problems while ensuring that the solutions will benefit and reach everyone.

In 2006 Wing suggested that computational thinking, a method of thinking that derives from concepts fundamental to computer science, is a universally applicable attitude and skill set for everyone and all disciplines to solve problems and design systems that no one could accomplish alone [2]. Thereafter, the notion of computation thinking has received attention from scholars in various fields. This paper seeks to

J. Choudrie et al. (Eds.): ICT4D 2017, IFIP AICT 504, pp. 104–116, 2017.
DOI: 10.1007/978-3-319-59111-7_10

explore how computational thinking can serve as a tool, method, or approach to solving complex real-world problems and how can it be utilized. The goal is to conceptualize a method as an approach that would lead to universal efforts resulting in the increase of social, economic, political, and environmental harmony on a local and global level. The paper also suggests general solutions that serve as opportunities for further case studies and research.

2 Methodology

In this paper, the concept of computational thinking will be utilized to propose a four-stage problem-solving paradigm that tackles shared global problems in their localities. The 17 Sustainable Development Goals (SDGs) [3] set by the United Nations in 2015 identify current global problems that are shared across the globe and require immediate solutions. In effect, we have chosen to discuss the paradigm in relation to the SDGs. However, in spite of its broad scope and ambitious targets, we have chosen to address only one of the SDGs, Goal 4: Quality Education, in each stage of the paradigm in order to demonstrate the applicability of the proposed process.

3 What Does Computational Thinking Entail?

In 1950 Turing postulated the universality of the computing process, in that digital computers could mimic any other machine and therefore, possess the ability to function with the same program [4]. The universality of the computation process is also the basis of Wing's grand vision for computational thinking. She believes that it is a universally compatible method that can help solve complex problems by thinking with many levels of abstraction [2]. In her later work, Wing defines computational thinking as "an approach to solving problems, designing systems, and understanding human behavior that draws on concepts fundamental to computing" [5]. Wing does not suggest to "think" like a computer but to adapt the structural thinking process used by computer scientist to instruct computers to complete a task or solve a problem. Riley and Hunt reiterate Wing's statement in that computational thinking is characterized by the manner in which computer scientists think and reason [6].

Denning argues that computational thinking has its roots in what was referred to as algorithmic thinking in the 1950s and 1960s, which he describes as "a mental orientation to formulating problems as conversions of some input to an output and looking for algorithms to perform the conversions" [7]. For Denning, computational thinking is not a principle but a practice that develops various levels of skills [7]. Computational thinking has also been defined as "the thought processes involved in formulating problems so their solutions can be represented as computational steps and algorithms" by Aho [8] The suggested thought process is an applicable model in various discourses and establishes the foundation of a plan of action to tackle a problem. Algorithms alone may not be able to solve complex real-world problems, however, computational thinking can induce strategic objectives and models of action that enhance the development of solutions. A fundamental step towards understanding and solving complex real-world problems may rest on the ability to apply Wing's approach to computational thinking on comprehensive and (big) data sets.

Gouws et al. [9] attribute three elements to computational thinking: "exploring all aspects of the problem, considering the complexity of the problem, and finding an optimal solution that can be achieved with available sources" [9]. In their efforts to incorporate computational thinking in educational activities, they designed a computational thinking framework (CTF) to serve as foundation for computational thinking materials. The CTF is a two-dimensional grid: one dimension is the skill sets that make up computational thinking and the second dimension is the different levels in which the skill sets may be practiced. This approach, demonstrates the applicability of implementing computational thinking in real-world problem solving practices. García-Peñalvo's definition of computational thinking "as the application of high level abstractions and an algorithmic approach to solve any kind of problems" [10] also affirms the applicability of computational thinking in various domains. These definitions emphasize the applicability of computational thinking to problems from different disciplines as an active problem-solving approach.

The generalization of computational thinking to a universal discourse has been subject to criticism as well. Blackwell et al. argue that computer scientists use a literalistic approach to definitions because computers reason literally. This approach undermines the complexities and contexts of real-world problems and creates an illusion of universality. Their second argument suggests that abstraction compromises the end-goal by focusing on how the problem is structured. The third point argues that computational thinking can be a misleading foundation, as it is not rooted in a real-world problems or human phenomenon [11]. While authors raise valid points, the principle argument is that computational thinking is not *the solution* to our complex problems; it is *a tool* to aid the process of developing solutions.

Wing believes that computational thinking benefits our societies by enhancing intellectual skills to not only find solutions but also formulate problems in any domain [12]. The question for us now is how can computational thinking assist in consolidating the development of solutions for real-world problems that are subject to different and changing circumstances, diverse thought processes, and contain the element of unpredictability?

4 Real-World Problem: The SDGs

Sustainable development emerged as a concept in the report published by the World Commission for Environment and Development (WCED) in 1987, when the General Assembly of the United Nations called for "a global agenda for change" [13]. Section 3 Article 27 of the report—also known as the Brundtland report—states that sustainable development is development that "meets the needs of the present without compromising the ability of future generations to meet their own needs" [13]. Chapter 2 of the report expands the definition of sustainable development to: "It contains within it two key concepts: (1) the concept of 'needs', in particular the essential needs of the world's poor, to which overriding priority should be given; and (2) the idea of limitations imposed by the state of technology and social organization on the environment's ability to meet present and future needs. Thus the goals of economic and social development must be defined in terms of sustainability in all countries - developed or developing, market-oriented or centrally planned. Interpretations will vary, but must share certain general features and must flow from a consensus on the basic concept of sustainable development and on a broad strategic framework for achieving it" [13].

In 2015, 193 members of the UN General Assembly adopted 17 SDGs, which aim to achieve economic development, social inclusion, and environmental protection by 2030 [3]. The SDGs central position is to ensure that no one is left behind. The universal agenda featured in the SDGs are driven by problems that are shared globally, however, each of the outlined problems are caused under different circumstances in each of the target populations. The implementation of such goals requires a local-to-global framework that would provide a global yet localizable plan of action. This paper proposes that the conceptual elements of computational thinking can contribute to providing a universal framework and collective structure for problem-solving thought processes that is suitable for each local population.

5   A Local-to-Global Problem-Solving Approach

In practice, computational thinking stimulates a process of thinking in which the multiplicity of the problem is understood and deconstructed it to its core and periphery components, so that the development of solutions propel an effective and efficient implementation process. Given the fundamental concepts of computing, our proposed method approaches real-world problems with four core stages of abstraction, decomposition, solution development, and validation. Each stage of the process is attainable through the following steps (Fig. 1):

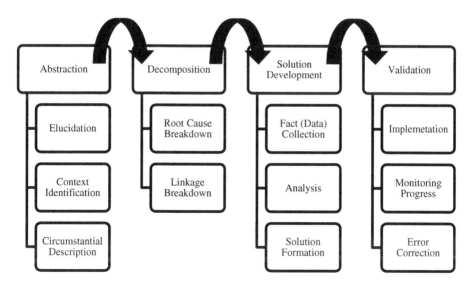

Fig. 1. Four-stage problem-solving approach

5.1 Abstraction

Abstraction, according to Wing, is the "mental tool" of computing; it identifies details that are crucial for solving a problem and extracts the knowledge embedded in the data [5]. The process of abstraction focuses on the relevant details required to solve a problem [14]. Wing's "thinking with multiple layers of abstraction" leads to defining different elements of a problem and how they relate to one another. Kramer points out two vital features of abstraction: simplification, by removing details, and generalization, to identify the common core [15]. Therefore, the central focus of abstraction is the process of extracting fundamental concepts of a complex problem that affect the outcome of the solution. In a real-world problem setting, generalizations do not eliminate the contextual factors that dictate the local circumstances. On the contrary, the generalization process identifies problems shared in local contexts and takes the "big picture" into consideration. The SDGs are a great example of how issues such as economic vulnerability, gender inequality, climate change, etc. are generalizable problems to all societies that need to be locally interpreted. The process of abstraction undergoes three steps of elucidation, context identification, and circumstantial description.

5.1.1 Elucidation

The outcome of this stage of the process is to define the core problems that need to be solved. Priami states that "computational thinking is a different way of approaching a problem by producing descriptions that are inherently executable" and understanding the problem at different layers of abstraction is "building a virtual hierarchy of inter-pretations" [16]. The first layer of abstraction provides a clear definition of the core of the problem. This step undertakes an important task as it generalizes the definition of the problem to the extent that it is clear and pertinent to all other layers so that the essential factors are extracted.

   In order to identify the underlying problems stated in the SDGs it is necessary to provide a clear definition of all the goals. In spite of the SDGs' vague language, a *re-formulation* of the goals will provide a more detailed definition, contextualize them in such a manner that is applicable to a broader variation of social constructs, and identify the underlying problem each goal seeks to overcome. Goal 4 of the SDGs, as stated in *Transforming Our World: The 2030 Agenda for Sustainable Development* [3], is: "Ensure inclusive and equitable quality education and promote lifelong learning opportunities for all." The re-formulation of Goal 4 provides a more inclusive and cohesive understanding of its purpose and function with the following description: *Facilitate all means—including educational material, facilities, and educators—that would build a diverse foundation of quality education, as both the process and outcome of learning, and equal access for all. Promote the benefits of education for individuals and their societies at large.* The elucidation process allows us to identify the general scope of the goal to its core problem of *inaccessibility of education*, in a way that is relevant to all layers of the problem.

5.1.2 Context Identification

To highlight the relevant details related to a problem is part of Wing's abstraction procedure [5]. Context identification contextualizes the general problem in its local context. The purpose of this layer of abstraction is to eliminate generalized details that are not applicable to that particular setting and simplify our understanding of the complex situation by highlighting local and relevant interpretations of a problem. The lack of contextualized information will result in the misinterpretation of that problem and exhaust efforts that are not beneficial to the solution development process.

Given the complexity and multiplicity of socio-cultural factors present in real-world problems, designing a model that is accommodating to everyone is as ambitious as the SDGs themselves. Nevertheless, including cultural factors in the problem definition will provide the means of designing solutions that will reach a wider range of populations. Now that the core underlying problem has been defined, the next step is to define each problem in their local and cultural setting: Does the local population perceive Goal 4 as a problem in their community? How does the local population define the problems derived from Goal 4? How does the local population define the relationship between local and global factors of the problem?

5.1.3   Circumstantial Description

Problems do not emerge independent from their circumstantial settings, which are vital details to examine in the problem-solving process. Zachman characterizes people (who), time (when), and motivation (why) as a necessary descriptive type in the field of information systems architecture [17]. In this layer of abstraction, Zachman's motivation factor has been substituted with the location factor in order to determine *who* is involved in the problems, *where* the problems take place, and *when* do the problems occur. Each of the circumstantial factors affects the composition of the problem and its susceptibility to change. In the case of the SDGs, the actors, location, and timeline vary and must be identified locally:

Who: The actors involved in the SDGs are networks of designs makers, contributors, recipients, and implementers. These interconnected networks of people who will design solutions, implement solutions, and collectively participate in the development process are: UN system and stakeholders, local governments, private sector, educational institutions, citizens and community organizers, local experts.

Where: The Sustainable Development Solutions Network published in a report that the SDGs will depend on a bottom-up approach that will connect local authorities and communities to national-level decision-making [18]. Therefore, the SDGs require a local-to-global approach. The SDGs have declared to "take into account different national realities, capacities and levels of development and respect national policies and priorities" [3]. Ensuring the inclusion of populations at a local level will lead to the foundation of national, regional, and global partnerships. For Goal 4, the local to global approach would start with local schools and education centers to form a cohesive community that take educational concerns to a national and global level.

When: There is a 15-year timeframe with 2030 as the deadline. The timeframe vary for each problem and location. The attainment of equitable and quality education is a long-term goal, however, it is plausible to believe that the foundations of Goal 4 are attainable in the remaining years of the SDGs timeline.

Outlining the circumstantial settings of the problem will provide insight on the following questions: Who are the influential local authorities? Who will the local populations accept as the solution implementer? In what time frame can the problems be resolved? What can citizens do to help solve the problem?

5.2   Decomposition

Breaking problems down by functionality is an important element of computational thinking, according to Wing [5]. In this stage, the complex set of problems is divided into simpler forms that are easier to solve. Simplifying the problem does not equate to dehumanizing its complexities in computer-identifiable codes, on the contrary, it serves to simplify the means of implementing the solutions. Solving each of the sub-problems will compose a solution to the original problem that was decomposed. The objective is to find a way to solve complex problems, which requires solving problems in parallel to one another, as they contain inter-component connections. After all, computational thinking also encompasses thinking recursively [2].

5.2.1   Root Cause Breakdown

The first phase of decomposition can be achieved by identifying the root causes, where each cause becomes a sub-problem that needs to be solved. Identifying the root causes will analyze the contextual constraints that exist in each location and recognize the connection between each of the sub-problems. The local-to-global approach will identify of root causes in their local and global contexts. The lack of education infrastructures, high cost of education, insufficient number of educators, far distances to nearest education facilities, cultural gender norms, conflict and war, and lack of services available for students with special needs are but a few barriers to education that concern the achievement of Goal 4. The following questions assist in identifying why the problem is occurring in its current circumstances: What do experts identify as the causes of inaccessibility to inclusive and quality education? What does the local population identify as the causes of inaccessibility to inclusive and quality education? What efforts have been made to eradicate the root cases? Why have they been unsuccessful in overcoming obstacles related to education in the past? Which of the underlying causes can be changed or eliminated?

5.2.2   Linkage Breakdown

Understanding the relationship among different layers is one of the essential components of computational thinking. The second phase of decomposition answers the question: how are the root causes related to one another? The interconnectivity of sub-problems requires the understanding of links within and between problems. The SDGs have emerged from a network of interdependent problems; not only do the goals address a broad scope of issues, but many of them overlap and generate the causality of one another. Meaning that the reduction of the root causes of problem 1 will result in the reduction of problem 2, problem 3, and so on, or understanding the root causes of problem 4 will help solve problem 5, problem 6, and so forth. Once the links between the root causes are identified in each context, the set of problems will be narrowed to manageable sub-problems. The assessment of the links between each of the underlying problems of the SDGs requires local information for a contextualized result. However, Table 1 provides a few examples of how some of the other SDGs are directly linked to Goal 4:

5.3   Solution Development

The end goal of computational thinking is to devise a solution for complex problems. The previous stages of the paradigm collect preliminary data in the process of defining, contextualizing, and decomposing the problem. In this next stage of the process, data pertaining to problems and solutions are collected, processed, and translated into solution strategies.

5.3.1   Fact (Data) Collection

This step gathers all the data that has been collected and combines it with data that is gathered by two groups; (i) the authorities, scientists, academics, and experts; and (ii) citizens and members of different communities. According to Hilgers and Ihl "the resulting input from an open call to a community to solve a given problem results in higher quality of the input (compared to solving the problem internally)" [27]. Citizenscience and citizensourcing are two methods that will propel the accumulation of detailed and solution-oriented data.

Irwin first introduced citizenscience to point out the expertise present among everyday citizens [28]. The term refers to a research technique of obtaining data from various locations provided by the public. By involving the public in providing scientific data, global projects can benefit from "global data-gathering networks" [29]. The public collaborates with scientists by "contributing data according to an established protocol, or completing structured recognition, classification, or problem-solving tasks that depend on human competencies" [30]. *Project BudBurst* (http://www.budburst.org/) for example, encourages citizens to observe how plants change with the seasons in different communities. The project also provides resources to integrate citizen science into various educational levels and settings.

Torres introduces the concept of citizensourcing to shift the function of citizens as consumers to actively partaking in government policies and programs [31]. Citizensourcing is an interactive relationship between citizens and decision makers by communicating information, concerns, and new ideas. Hilgers and Ihl note that citizensourcing is outsourcing the tasks that were formerly performed by a public agent to a large group of citizens. Linders defines this procedure as "online citizen consultation," a "powerful new problem-solving mechanism," and "government data mining" [32]. *UClass* (http://www.uclass.io/) enables teachers, schools, and organization personnel to store, share, search, and view curricula. The website provides teachers with access to a global education network and explore a variety of educational material and sources uploaded by their colleagues worldwide.

5.3.2   Analysis

Analyzing large quantities of data is an element of computational thinking that eventually finds the knowledge embedded in the data that has been collected [5]. In this step the collected data is analyzed with the aim to recommend potential solutions to the

Table 1. Demonstration of direct links (cause and/or effect) between the SDGs and Goal 4

SDG	Problem	Link to Goal 4
1	Economic poverty and vulnerability	The lack of education exacerbates the risk of poverty [19]. An increase in educational attainment can reduce the risk of poverty by increasing the possibility of employment [20]
2	Food insecurity	Educated individuals are more likely to meet their nutrition needs, which makes education an essential element to eliminate malnutrition in the long term [21]
3	Poor health and lack of healthcare	There is a strong correlation between level of education and awareness about diseases, preventative measures, and available health care services [22]
5	Gender inequality	Attainment of education available for women at a higher level would decrease the wage gap between men and women [23], postpones the age of childbearing, and decreases health risks [24]
6	Lack of clean water sources	Access to clean water would provide women who spend time collecting water and fuel with more time for education and employment [23]
7	Inaccessibility of energy	Educational programs can promote sustainable energy consumption while informing citizens about accessible and renewable energy sources [20]
8	Lack of economic growth and impacts	Employment raises the standard of living in terms of income and access to health and education [23]
9	Lack of effective infrastructures	The advancement of industrial economies is directly related to the populations' education. Education systems can develop technological capabilities and innovation at a higher rate [25]
10	Inequality on multiple levels	Inequality in opportunities to education and health has a negative impact on poverty and income levels [26]
11	Unsustainable human settlements	Urbanization can improve access to education, health, and better living conditions, where cities have the potential to improve those circumstances [23]
12	Lack of sustainable consumption and production (SCP)	Enhancing the quality and accessibility of education can influence behavioral and industrial patterns [26] and shift SCP patterns towards a more sustainable lifestyle
13	Climate change and its impacts	Education plays a vital role in informing populations about the causes and effects of climate change, and how to combat the impacts of climate change [20]
14/15	Destruction of oceans/Destruction of ecosystems	Education attainment can increase concerns for the environment and teach citizens how to protect the environment and reduce environmental impact [20]
16/17	Promotion of peace/Global partnership	These goals can be deemed as the means of implementation and/or the outcome of the SGDs. Therefore, education and its impacts on the first 15 goals will untimely effect these two goals

problem. This stage of data analysis will determine: (i) aspects of the sub-problems, and therefore the original problem, that are solvable; (ii) the limitation and barriers to solving the problems; and (iii) how to prevent the problem from reoccurring in the future. In regards to Goal 4 of the SDGs, the analysis will provide insight on the aforementioned points on social, institutional, and pedagogical level by collecting data about the significance of education in different communities, teaching and learning structures and practices, the nature of courses and subjects incorporated in the curricula, student interests, and financial recourses.

5.3.3   Solution Formation

The end goal of computational thinking is to design a solution to overcome the outlined problem. Evidently, each of the problems will require a solution that is contextualized for each population. For example, Massive Open Online Courses (MOOCs) are tools that can address specific educational needs worldwide and not only serve as a solution to Goal 4 of the SDGs. George Siemens and Stephen Downes established the first large online course in 2008 [33] which then developed into Massive Open Online Courses (MOOCs) as free and accessible courses available online to a large audience across the globe. Prominent MOOCs providers such as edX, Coursera, Khan Academy, and Udacity have emerged in association with top universities with a wide variety of open courses since 2012. MOOCs are not restricted to specific locations, operate on flexible schedules, and in some cases are free of charge. These characteristics increase the accessibility of education to wider range of individuals.

Kiron (https://kiron.ngo/) is an online platform that allows refugees to obtain a graduate degree worldwide and it is free of charge. *Kiron's* goal is to make education more accessible and utilize innovative methods in creating a global network of educational, entrepreneurial, and research initiatives with a focus on migration and pedagogy. Kiron highlights its five advantageous characteristics as: flexibility in location, flexibility in time, open to all despite the student's temporary or permanent status in a country, internationally accepted degree, and affordability. The website also outlines the benefits of such platforms in that a internationally accredited degree will increase the employment rate and economic growth among refugees and their country of residence while encouraging peaceful coexistence across different nationalities and religions. The characteristics of this platform indicate that MOOCs have a direct impact on reducing poverty risks (Goal 1), allowing more women attain education (Goal 5), increase employment opportunities (Goal 8), and provide more equal access to educational programs (Goal 10).

5.4   Validation

This stage of the process focuses on the implementation of contextualized solutions; the solutions are applied to the target population or location, monitored, and modified in order to perform with maximum effectiveness. This stage is accomplished through three steps of: implementation, monitoring progress, and error correction.

5.4.1   Implementation

The local-to-global approach has prepared the application of contextualized means of implementation and localized solutions—in addition to identifying local actors—and the circumstantial setting of each sub-problem and subsequently the problem in its entirety. However, this is not the final stage of the process, as the solutions are subject to the variability of human conditions affecting the problem.

5.4.2 Monitoring Progress

Solutions designed for real-world problems are not only aiming to resolve the problem but to produce productive outcomes. Monitoring the progress of an implemented solution will discover the errors and deficiencies the solutions may pose and allow for improving the means of implementation in each situation. In the case of the SDGs, local governments, the United Nations and their partners, education ministries and institutions, and educators play an important role in monitoring the local and global progress of each of the goals and targets.

5.4.3 Error Correction

In her description of computational thinking, Wing states that error correction is an important attribute of the process [2]. In the context of real-world problems the reception of solutions in various populations are not predictable and would have to be adjustable to the population's needs and interests. Therefore, this stage modifies any errors that arise in the previous step.

6 Conclusion

Universal goals require global initiatives that close the gap between developed, developing, and under-developed countries. A local-to-global approach promulgates universal respect for diverse thought processes and generates cooperative means to raise awareness about sustainable development and its implications, in addition to innovative solutions and productive outcomes. Forming a localizable model for shared global problems is to serve as a means to include all populations in the process of creating a more sustainable culture on a global level.

This paper intended to propose a paradigm to approach complex real-world problem solving that would promote a communal effort towards the global concerns that we face today. For that reason, further research should be pursued in order to investigate the applicability of computational thinking as a universal concept and real-world problem-solving tool in practice. Future case studies can identify the shared and local-specific factors of the thinking processes, investigate the universality of computational thinking across cultures and disciplines, and develop a method of approach that not only provides solutions but also compatible with future developments.

References

1. Anderson, B.: Imagined Communities: Reflection on the Origin and Spread of Nationalism. Verso, London (1983)
2. Wing, J.: Computational thinking. Commun. ACM **49**, 33–35 (2006)

3. UN: Transforming our world: the 2030 agenda for sustainable development (2015)
4. Turing, A.M.: Computing machinery and intelligence. Mind **59**(236), 441–442 (1950). Oxford University Press
5. Wing, J.: Computational thinking and thinking about computing. Philos. Trans. R. Soc. Math. Phys. Eng. Sci. **366**(1881), 3717–3725 (2008)
6. Riley, D.D., Hunt, K.A.: Computational Thinking for the Modern Problem Solver. CRC Press, Boca Raton (2014)
7. Denning, P.J.: The profession of IT: beyond computational thinking. Commun. ACM **52**, 28–30 (2009)
8. Aho, A.V.: Computation and computational thinking. Comput. J. **55**(7), 832–835 (2012)
9. Gouws, L.A., Bradshaw, K., Wentworth, P.: Computational thinking in educational activities: an evaluation of the educational game light-bot. In: Proceedings of the 18th ACM Conference on Innovation and Technology in Computer Science Education, ITiCSE, pp. 10–15 (2013)
10. García-Peñalvo, F.J.: What computational thinking is. J. Inf. Technol. Res. **l9**(3), v–viii (2016)
11. Blackwell, A.F., Church, L., Green, T.: The abstract is an enemy: alternative perspectives to computational thinking. Psychology of Programming Interest Group 20th Annual Workshop, pp. 34–43. Lancaster, UK (2008)
12. Wing, J.: Computational thinking benefits society. In: 40th Anniversary Blog, Social Issues in Computing. University of Toronto (2014)
13. UN General Assembly: Report of the world commission on environment and development: our common future. Annex to A/42/427 (1987)
14. Grover, S., Pea, R.: Computational thinking in k-12: a review of the state of the field. Educ. Researcher **42**(1), 38–43 (2013)
15. Kramer, J.: Is abstraction the key to computing? Commun. ACM **50**, 37–42 (2007)
16. Priami, C.: Computational thinking in biology. In: Priami, C. (ed.) Transactions on Computational Systems Biology VIII. LNCS, vol. 4780, pp. 63–76. Springer, Heidelberg (2007). doi:10.1007/978-3-540-76639-1_4
17. Zachman, J.: A framework for information systems architecture. IBM Syst. J. **26**(3), 276–295 (1987)
18. Sustainable Development Solutions Network: Getting started with the sustainable development goals: a guide for stakeholders (2015)
19. UNDP: Sustaining human progress: reducing vulnerabilities and building resilience. Human development report (2014)
20. Global Education Monitoring Report: Education for people and planet: creating sustainable futures for all. UNESCO Publishing (2016)
21. Education Transforms Lives Report. UNESCO Publishing (2013)
22. WHO: Research for universal health coverage. The world health report (2013)
23. UNDP: Work for human development. Human development report (2015)
24. UN: The world's women: trends and statistics. UN Publications (2015)
25. UNIDO: The role of technology and innovation in inclusive and sustainable industrial development. Industrial development report (2016)
26. World Bank Group and the IMF: Development goals in an era of demographic change. Global monitoring report (2015/2016)
27. Hilgers, D., Ihl, C.: Citizensourcing: applying the concept of open innovation to the public sector. Int. J. Public Participation (IJP2) **4**(1), 67–88 (2010)
28. Irwin, A.: Citizen Science: A Study of People, Expertise and Sustainable Development. Routledge, Oxon (1995)

29. Bonney, R., Cooper, C.B., Dickinson, J., Kelling, S., Phillips, T., Rosenberg, K.V., Shirk, J.: Citizen science: a developing tool for expanding science knowledge and scientific literacy. Bioscience **59**(11), 977–984 (2009)
30. Wiggins, A., Crowston, K.: From conservation to crowdsourcing: a typology of citizen science. In: 44th HICSS, pp. 1–10 (2011)
31. Torres, L.H.: Citizen sourcing in the public interest. Knowl. Manag. Dev. J. **3**(1), 134–145 (2007)
32. Linders, D.: From e-government to we-government: defining a typology for citizen coproduction in the age of social media. Gov. Inf. **29**(4), 446–454 (2012)
33. Cormier, D., Siemens, G.: Through the open door: open courses as research, learning, and engagement. Educause Rev. **45**(4), 30–39 (2010)

Women Empowerment and Gender Justice

Telecentres Use in Rural Communities and Women Empowerment: Case of Western Cape

Abiodun Alao[1](✉), Tandi Edda Lwoga[2](✉), and Wallace Chigona[1](✉)

[1] University of Cape Town, Cape Town, South Africa
alxabi001@myuct.ac.za
[2] Muhimbili University of Health and Allied Science, Dar es Salaam, Tanzania

Abstract. Women are still facing exclusion in the use of telecentres, largely because of cultural perceptions that they are responsible for the home; telecentres are also widely perceived appropriate for men to find employment. This paper presents an analysis of the benefits women derive from using telecentres. This study explores how telecentres empower women in the rural communities by analysing three telecentres in the rural setting of Western Cape, South Africa. A qualitative approach involving semi-structured interviews was used to gather in-depth details on individual empowerment of the rural women. The results obtained show that some rural women used the telecentres to enhance economic standards, which resulted in individual empowerment in social, psychological, information and economic dimensions. This study highlights the potential of telecentres in empowering women and proposes that the government and NGOs consider the telecentre as a means of addressing gender digital divide issues.

Keywords: Telecentres · Women empowerment · Gender · Rural communities · ICT use · Western cape

1 Introduction

The purpose of the study was to assess the contribution of Information and Communication Technologies (ICTs) for women empowerment and human development in South Africa. In particular, the study seeks to establish the current status of the ICT sector development in selected rural areas; secondly, to determine the pattern of ICTs use and impact of ICT use on women empowerment and development; and, thirdly, to identify factors affecting effective utilisation of ICTs. Access to ICT continues to be unequally distributed and, in most cases, segregated along income, education, age, gender and geographical location [1]. Although South Africa has made substantial efforts to make ICT infrastructures available in rural areas by providing access to the internet and other ICT facilities through telecentres, the problem of internet access persists. Women are faced with the problem of ICT access due to a host of socioeconomic factors [1]. Nevertheless, most telecentres do not focus on gender and how women can be empowered by the use of the telecentre [1]. Empowerment is the process of gaining substantial, new capability to perform some specific action [2]. The process

J. Choudrie et al. (Eds.): ICT4D 2017, IFIP AICT 504, pp. 119–134, 2017.
DOI: 10.1007/978-3-319-59111-7_11

of empowerment enables the transformation of individual lives to achieve goals and reach targets, which they had thought impossible [3]. This study investigates the impact of telecentres on woman empowerment in the Western Cape Province of South Africa. Previous literature shows the telecentres as a valuable ICT initiative that can be used to empower women in rural South Africa through the receiving and disseminating of information [4].

More studies demonstrate the personal characteristics of respondents in the rural areas; the extent of their effect on the diffusion and adoption of telecentres; and challenges women encounter in the use [5, 6]. The gap in research illustrates that enhancing people's informational capabilities is the most critical factor that determines the impact of ICTs on women's well-being. Although a number of studies have looked at the effects of the use of telecentres on the well-being of communities in South Africa [7] insights on the benefits derived from the telecentre and how they are expected to empower women are still lacking [8]. While most telecentre research addresses the benefits women derive from using telecentres, gender implications for the use of telecentres are not being addressed [9] Women, especially those in rural communities, carry a huge responsibility of looking after their families. Women are saddled with the responsibility of managing their homes, while the men work and engage in other economic activities [4]. In addition, it is assumed that in rural communities men are better positioned to benefit from ICTs than women and this contributes to gender inequality and digital divide [1]. Furthermore, ICTs can play an important role in this process of enhancing informational capabilities to achieve individual empowerment [9]. The failure to address the specific ICT needs of women in rural areas continues to contribute to the barriers women face in accessing ICTs. Therefore, this study was guided by the research question: How are telecentres empowering women in rural communities? Specific focus is on the Western Cape Province of South Africa. An investigation into the dimension of empowerment, the socio-cultural perception of the gender (male) computer culture, and how these reflects on women in rural communities was carried out. This paper adopted the empowerment framework as a theoretical foundation. The framework was considered appropriate because it explains the different dimension of empowerment in relation to individual capabilities and issues of gender (male) bias of computer culture are addressed.

2   Literature Review

2.1   Telecentres: An Overview

Telecentres are non-profit centres that offer access to computers. Furthermore, telecentres are established to solve the problem of digital divide, i.e., the gap between the 'information haves and have-nots'. Telecentres can be private enterprise, government-supported, and public-private partnership [10]. Private-owned telecentres such as the internet cybercafés are mainly for profit and are usually more financially sustainable. Moreover, telecentres are sometimes non-government organisations (NGOs) and government-owned and exist in almost every country [11]. Although they sometimes go by different name such as e-centre, computer centre, kiosk, e-chopper, information centre, cyber-café or public internet access points (PIAP) [12]. Access to telecentres is perceived as part of a process that can provide support to individuals for personal needs and goals [13].

2.2 ICT for Development

Over the years, a proponent of ICTs for development agenda claims technology creates opportunities for social and economic development of poor communities in developing nations [14]. [15] claims that, if information is critical to development, then ICTs, as a means of sharing information, are not simply a connection between people, but a link in the chain of the development process itself. ICT is perceived to not reach the under-privileged but, rather, the privileged in the society, which widens the socio-economic gap within developing countries [16]. ICTs enhance inequalities and potentially lead to social exclusion [17]. Scholars like [18] suggest that women are likely to select actions that are approved by their families and friends, as opposed to following rules or principles that are separated from their relationships. This indicates that women are somewhat reluctant to being introduced to technology or its utilisation in their everyday life. Technological empowerment is achieved by supporting the individual use of technology for personal needs and goals [13].

Individuals who have the opportunity to be empowered using technology usually have the confidence; high self-esteem; feelings of self-efficacy; control over their life; increased critical awareness; and increased civic participation [19]. According to [20], technologies contribute to the multiplier effects across income levels and innovative capacity. Modern technologies can support the empowerment of individuals and contribute to community development. However, lack of ICT skills in remote areas is one of the reasons telecentres are established in rural communities [21]. ICT skills development has been integrated as part of the service of telecentres to overcome the challenges of learning computer skills. Thus, the aim was to support the community to access ICT facilities and information via the internet or computer training skills offered at the telecentre to improve the livelihood and self-development of users [13]. Access to ICT initiatives, such as telecentres in themselves, cannot be a solution to poverty but can be adopted as a tool in poverty reduction initiatives. [22] claim "ICT for development" agenda examines the link between ICT and development, and empowerment of marginalised communities is under-researched whilst the "ICT in developing countries" agenda, comprising of cultural implications and local adaptation, is over-researched. Scholars such as [23] also questioned the potential of telecentres in empowering individuals and communities.

2.3 Rural Communities in South Africa

A rural community can be defined as a geographic area that is located outside towns and cities, with a generally not large population [24]. There are 1.4 billion people living on less than US$1. 25 a day and at least 70% of them live in rural areas [25]. The South African poor mainly live in rural communities, and a large number of South Africans live in poverty [26]. Statistics show that 52% of the South African population are women and 47% of these women live in rural communities [27]. A rural location is described as residents in settlements above or below a certain size where agriculture is presumed to be the principal activity of its populations [28]. A large number of rural South Africans live in poverty [27]. The make-up of the rural communities of South Africa consists of Blacks and the Coloured race who live in settlements in diverse locations outside of the cities in different provinces of the country.

2.4   Telecentre Implementation for Gender Empowerment

Telecentres are established to transform rural communities into a computer-skilled labour force which can support innovation [29]. Although telecentres are created in rural communities, the gender aspects are not put into consideration in the design-planning phase [30]. Furthermore, the approach to universal services and ICT policies in general neglect gender issues which may affect women's socio-economic and social conditions when the policies are implemented [31]. This is demonstrated in some government-sponsored telecentres in South Africa, where gender issues are not considered [32]. There is need to understand the actual use of telecentres in rural communities, how gender equality can be promoted and can also avoid exclusion of women [33]. This is because there are often limited resources available in the rural communities; men have the prospect to be exposed to possible job opportunities outside their environment, while women are expected to take up the responsibility of managing their homes [4]. There are also issues beyond access that need to be taken into account when implementing telecentres in rural communities; for example, skills development, local content, social capital and cultural issues [5, 21].

2.5   Impact of Telecentres on Women

The objective of the study is to understand how rural women can use the telecentres to improve their economic standard. The purpose of implementing telecentres in poor communities is to provide access to ICTs; inform; train; and provide economic opportunities to rural people on computer skills. The establishment of telecentres in rural communities has not really focused on how it can be used to benefit women in the rural areas. Therefore, the failure to address the challenges women encounter in using telecentres continues to contribute to the factors women face in accessing ICTs [34]. The use of telecentre services may support women in the process of self-reflection and problem solving to deal with their day to-day life challenges. These may assist women to strengthen their human capital in areas of knowledge, skills and ability to work and attain good health from the information obtained from using the telecentre. Women may benefit from the use of telecentre services if countries with existing telecentres create gender awareness programmes on the actual benefits from using telecentre facilities, and provide an encouraging environment for women's participation. This is most important in poor communities where women have limited access to information and minimum access to computer-training opportunities.

3   Conceptual Framework: Empowerment

This paper adopts the empowerment framework as a theoretical lens. The framework illustrates the different dimension of individual empowerment. Also how this relates to women empowerment [9]. The choice of this framework was to present the perception of women respondents. [35] views empowerment in the context of addressing women's "strategic gender needs", that is to say transforming structures, institutions and beliefs that embody "women's subordinate position to men in the society". She argues that meeting these needs helps women to achieve greater equality. Strategic gender needs include broader social, political and economic issues such as gender division of labour, legal rights, domestic violence, etc. which would be discussed in the dimension of empowerment. Past scholars such as [36] claims, if African women do not take the opportunity offered by ICTs initiatives such as telecentres to "catch up" technologically, they will find themselves further marginalised. Technologies including ICTs are not gender-neutral; rather, the use of ICTs and other technologies by women and men reflects to a large extent the wider socio-cultural and economic context within which the technologies are produced or used.

Furthermore, there have been studies based on the analysis of women and their relationship with ICTs that say women consider the word "technology" to have male connotations, even though "information" seems more feminine. It is assumed that some women even believed that working with ICTs would drive women mad. These examples indicate a high level of women's discomfort with information technologies [37]. Women empowerment refers to women having a right to develop their potential and improve on their self-development. The paper is focused on the individual empowerment of women through the use of the telecentre. Individual empowerment refers to the transformation of individuals' lives in achieving goals and reaching targets which they had previously thought impossible (i.e., to gain authority, skills, status, self-belief and image, progressing to greater things and increasing rewards) [38, 39]. Individual empowerment is also referred to as psychological empowerment because it involves an individual's participation in shared actions and has a greater control over his or her livelihood, a phenomenon referred to as "human agency" [9, 13]. Empowerment can be classified into different dimensions: Information, Economic, Social, Political and Cultural empowerment. Table 1 summarises the different dimension of individual empowerment [9].

Social empowerment refers to all members of the society being treated fairly and equally [40]. It is a multi-dimensional social process that helps people gain control over their own lives. Individuals can have the ability to enhance their technology and ICT literacy skills, enhance leadership skills and improve programme management skills through the services provided in the telecentre. This process fosters power (that is, the capacity to implement) in people, for use in their own lives, their communities and society, by being able to act on issues that they define as important [41]. Women using the telecentre can access social media platforms to communicate with friends and family and access information that addresses their personal needs.

Economic empowerment ensures that people have the appropriate skills, capabilities, resources and access to secure and sustain incomes and livelihoods, through the

Table 1. Dimensions of individual empowerment (Gigler, 2014)

Dimension	Output indicator
Information	• Improved capital to use different forms of ICT • Enhanced information literacy • Enhanced capacity to produce and publish local content • Improved ability to communicate with family members and friends outside immediate location
Psychological	• Stronger self-esteem • Improved ability to analyse one's own situation and solve problems • Stronger ability to influence strategic life choices • Sense of inclusion in the digital world
Social	• Enhanced ICT literacy and technology skills • Enhanced leadership skills • Improved programme management skills
Economic	• Improved access to markets • Enhanced entrepreneurial skills • Alternative sources of income • Stronger productive sources • Improved employment opportunities • Improved income through (a) lower transaction costs, (b) reduced transport need, (c) improved timeliness
Political	• Increased access to information or services • Improved capabilities to interact with local government and party politics
Cultural	• Improved social-cultural context that prevents gender (male) bias of computer culture and expectations

use of the telecentre, to seek for employment and other opportunities [42]. Through telecentre use, women can be empowered to gain computer skills that can equip them to be employable and improve on their economic standards.

Political empowerment is when individuals acquire the capacity to analyse, organise and mobilise in their respective communities. It can also be recognised as individuals having a say in how things are organised and how decisions are made in their environments [43]. Women living in poor communities are usually not involved in decision-making and political activities in their communities, because of the socio-cultural perception of only being expected to manage their homes [1].

Cultural empowerment is individuals having the freedom from socio-cultural norms to use the computer. Many feminist critics have argued that computer culture and the internet were inherently gendered; predominantly androcentric; therefore reproduced existing power structures and gender differences of the offline world in virtual reality [44]. According to this argument, many women non-users of the tele-centre were not using the telecentre due to lack of computer skills and the gender (male) bias of computer culture. Women are usually limited by their cultural belief's, which sometimes hinders empowerment. Some cultures do not allow women to expose themselves to opportunities that can empower them, but rather they are expected to be committed to the management of their homes and families.

4 Methodology

A qualitative research design method was used for this study. The aim of the study was to gain more insights into how telecentres empower women in rural communities. We selected a qualitative research due to its ability to provide insights into the interactions within a particular context [45]. To understand the potential benefits rural women derive from using the telecentre, the study was rooted in the interpretive paradigm [46]. An explanatory study was employed in the study to add a description and explain why certain outcomes occurred.

4.1 Case Description

The settlements used for this study were situated in the Western Cape Province of South Africa. The study selected three (3) telecentres from three (3) different districts in the province. The communities used for the study were mainly rural communities. The criteria for selecting the telecentres were: (1) to be situated in the rural communities; (2) to have been in operation for more than one year and (3) to offer a variety of services such as the internet, information services, computer-training and free services to the community.

Cape Access. The participants for this study were drawn from the three (3) selected telecentres with a view to ensure that the study was homogeneous. The telecentres were selected from the Cape Access project which is an ICT initiative of the Western Cape Government. This project provides ICT infrastructure such as e-centres (telecentre) for community development in rural communities. There are fifty-four (54) telecentres established in six (6) districts of the Western Cape Province. ICT facilities such as computers, printers, fax machines and internet facilities are made available in the e-centres for community members to access at no charge. The telecentres provide forty-five (45) minutes' free internet access to respective community users who have signed up to use the services provided at the e-centre/telecentre daily. Training sessions are offered on the International Computer Driving Licence (ICDL) and e-learning and basic computer training are offered to community members at no charge, while certificates are issued to successful participants who have completed the training services. To operate and manage the Cape Access e-centres (telecentres), telecentre managers, assistant managers and development managers are employed for the project.

4.2 Locations

Elim Community. Bredasdorp/Elim region is a small rural community situated in the Southern Overberg of the Western Cape Province of South Africa. It is a community with farming as the main source of livelihood and has a high rate of unemployment. It consists of 2,500 people who are mainly Afrikaans-speaking and Coloured [47]. Elim community consists of 91.6% Coloureds, 7.4% Black Africans and 1.0% Whites.

Klawer Community. Klawer Community is a rural town lying in the emerald green, tranquil Olifants River Valley just off the road to Namibia. There is a high rate of unemployment and the main source of livelihood in Klawer community is agriculture. The community is mostly occupied by an unemployed Afrikaans-speaking Coloured population. Klawer community is situated amongst the Matzikamma Mountains and on the Olifants River; the town is mainly into grape farming for wine production [48]. The community is 281 km from Cape Town; 24 km west-south-west of Vanrhynsdorp and 283 km north of Cape Town [49]. Klawer community is a small town, which consist of 6,234 inhabitants, of whom 9.42% are Black Africans, 75.25% are Coloureds, 0.98% are Indian/Asian, 0.72% are other and 13.62% are Whites [50].

Mbekweni Community. Mbekweni is an urban black township near Paarl in the Western Cape Province [47]. It is a community occupied by Afrikaans and Xhosa-speaking people who had migrated from the Eastern Cape Province in search of job opportunities. Mbekweni is situated in the Drakenstein Municipality (the municipality located within the Cape Winelands District Municipality), and is situated between the towns of Paarl and Wellington in the Berg River Valley region of the Western Cape. Mbekweni has a growing population estimated to be 50,000 [51] The wine and fruit industries are the main source of informal job creation in the Paarl/Wellington area, having 80% of vines in the country located in the Wellington region [51]. Though the wine and grape industries situated in the community serve as the backbone of the agricultural industry in the region, there is still a high rate of unemployment in the community because very few workers can be employed. The town population consist of 124, 878 residents [49].

4.3   Population and Sample

Three communities were used as study sites of the research. Elim, Klawer and Mbekweni are relatively small towns in the Western Cape. The women were categorised into users (women who used or accessed the telecentre) and non-users (women who did not use or access the telecentre). The non-users were used as a control sample for the study; these non-users were selected from women living in the surrounding environment of the telecentre. Twenty-eight (28) women within the age of fifteen (15) and above participated in the interview session from the communities. We studied the perceptions of a sample of women who are users and non-users of the telecentre. We investigated the reasoning structures of twenty-eight (28) rural women. Purposive sampling was used for selecting the respondents. The users were identified with the assistance of the telecentre managers. Women living within the surrounding environment of the telecentre were selected; women who were present during the time of the interview sessions were selected; and telecentre managers were also interviewed.

Sampling. The sampling strategy used to select the target population and provide the information used in the study was purposive sampling. Purposive sampling is used when the population is too small for a random sample [52]. The purposive sampling technique is used when the researcher selects samples because they have particular features and characteristics to enable detailed exploration and understanding of central themes and puzzles which the researcher wishes to study [53]. The sample used a qualitative research that allows interviewing until the redundancy of concepts; this is a situation where no new concepts are any longer emerging [54]. The samples used in the study were the telecentre managers, assistant managers, women users (women who use the telecentre), and non-users (women who do not use the telecentre) who were interviewed in different selected communities. Furthermore, focus group discussions were held with women telecentre users.

4.4   Data Collection

The data collected for this study was obtained from twenty eight (28) semi-structured in-depth interviews from women users across three villages. The factors considered in the purposive sampling included usage, gender and age, thereby allowing the researcher to gain a more robust insight into the data by purposely selecting a sample from which most can be learned [45]. Interviews lasted between eighteen (18) and sixty (60) minutes each and were audio-recorded. The interviews were conducted in the languages of English, Afrikaans and IsiXhosa, with the assistance of IsiXhosa and Afrikaans research translators. The study limitation identified was the limited number of women non-users available for the interview sessions. We explained and studied the cognitive representations that these individual women made. Due to ethical reasons, the identities of the participants have not been disclosed.

4.5   Data Analysis

Data was analysed using statistical techniques such as descriptive statistics to analyse the data, while content analysis was used to analyse qualitative data. Thematic analysis from field notes was performed to analyse the data. A descriptive analysis of all study variables and demographic variables examined in the survey interviews was carried out. Data collected from the interviews was recorded, transcribed and translated. Data was collected using a Dictaphone to record the interviews. The data was transcribed word for word into a textual format and digital copies of the data were retained for future reference. In addition, pictures were taken on the study site and used to further give a visual explanation of the activities of the study. Furthermore, data was analysed using statistical techniques. A descriptive analysis of all study variables and demographic variables examined in the survey interviews was conducted. We used codes to represent the identities of the respondents. For example codes K, E and M represent Klawer, Elim and Mbekweni locations respectively. Therefore, codes K2 and E1 were used to identify the participant 2 of Klawer and participant 1 of Elim. Table 2 below shows the profile of the participants.

Table 2. Profile of participants (N = 28)

		Users	Non-users	Total
Ages	15–19	5	2	7
	20–29	9	1	10
	30–39	5	0	5
	40–Above	6	0	6
Qualification	Degree	1	0	1
	Professional certificate	5	0	5
	Matric	9	1	10
	Grade 9 to 11	10	2	12
Location	Elim	6	2	8
	Klawer	7	3	9
	Mbekweni	8	3	11
Employment	Employed	9	0	9
	Unemployed	16	3	19

5   Result

The significant contribution of the research to existing literature is that ICTs are believed to be key drivers for rural development; therefore telecentres are established in rural areas. However, women are usually not specifically considered to be main beneficiaries of the telecentre but rather there has been significant male dominance of the telecentres. Thus there is limited literature on women empowerment and telecentres; therefore there is need for more literature to be provided. Findings show that the use of the telecentre by rural women has been actualised. Some women benefited from using the telecentre despite the socio-cultural perception and gender (male) bias of computer culture.

5.1   Uses

The purpose of the creation of the telecentre is to provide services to communities at a subsidised rate and to empower various communities where they are situated. Government-sponsored telecentres constitute a common non-profit mode of delivery that provides free services to the different communities. The computers in the telecentre have been used to create CVs for job-seeking applicants. Some women also had success stories of getting employment after using CVs created at the telecentre to apply for work. Furthermore, some women entrepreneurs used the computers at the telecentre to source and apply for grants for their personal businesses via the internet. Additionally, the telecentre offered free computer-training to users who signed up to be trained. Other free services such as faxing, scanning, printing, email and internet browsing were also used by women-users. Finally, this study shows the different outcomes from the use of the telecentre in relation to the empowerment dimension.

Information Empowerment. The outcomes from women's use of the telecentre to information empowerment were ICT literacy, access to information and public services amongst some women. Most women-users only visited the telecentre to access social media platforms such as Facebook and Instagram, and to play games and browse other websites. Very few women visited the telecentre to access their emails and to research. However, women who made use of the telecentre were empowered as a result of having better access to information and knowing what was happening within their communities. Some of the women-users claim women non-users of the telecentre were missing out and not informationally empowered. Women non-users of the telecentre were assumed to have been deprived of the benefits of using computers. Therefore, it is suggested that women should utilise the telecentre to access information that may assist them to deal with issues in their life. A respondent claims:

> "I think the telecentre adds value to the people of Elim because they can learn more. You can read there, visit other sites and you can even buy stuff and shop online" (User-E2).

Psychological Empowerment. Women users were able to use the services provided at the telecentre to overcome difficult social situations through self-reflection. Furthermore, the women non-users did not visit the telecentre due to their insecurities and lack of confidence. One of the challenges also confronting these women was the lack of self-esteem to use computers. The assumption was that telecentres are mainly for those with previous computer or personal experience and people who can relate to the use of computers effectively. Most women non-users believed they would be mocked if they visited the telecentre without having the knowledge of using a computer. In addition, some participants lack basic education and do not have the confidence to use the ICT facilities at the telecentre, as in this claim:

> "Women's lack education and some are afraid to come and sit here to learn from the training. They lack confidence and they don't want to come here" (Non-User-E1).

Social Empowerment. Due to socio-cultural perception, some women did not perceive the telecentre as a public space that could improve their economic standards. Some claim, however, that the telecentre empowered them to strengthen their social relations, knowledge sharing and computer skills. Some women users also claim to use the telecentre to communicate with friends and family via social media platforms such as Facebook, despite having internet-enabled smart phones, as the following participant claims:

> "I think the women use the e-centre for social networking because you don't see a lot of men using the internet for social media but for only if it is business related. I think it is the women that use it mostly for social media not men (lol!)" (User-M1).

Economic Empowerment. Results from this study show that the aim of the telecentre for improving the economic standard was actualised. One of the reasons women used the telecentre was due to the free services provided. This allowed these women to save money to buy other things such as food. However, some women rarely use the telecentre because of the responsibility of managing their families and because of the perception that telecentres were mainly used by men to look for employment opportunities. Services in the telecentre include ICT skills development, support with job seeking and other assistance such as typing of CVs and application letters, job advertisements that are posted at the telecentres and free printing services. The free training courses offered at the telecentres supported the women in using the ICT services with confidence and improving their employability. Furthermore, some women users claim to have success stories from the frequent use of the telecentre. Finally, women were using the telecentre to obtain information on how to apply for funds and loans. The women were able to get a job and increase their income using the telecentre services, resulting in improved economic empowerment. A telecentre manager says women were able to get employment after completing the computer skills training programs as in this claim:

"Yes, there is this woman whom we helped at the e-centre to get a job, she is a chef and we helped with her CV and she got a job at the children school" (Telecentre manager-K5).

Political Empowerment. There was limited political participation by women in the communities. Despite this, some women use the telecentre to communicate with the authorities through the assistance of the telecentre managers. The telecentre managers attested to the fact that they constituted a link to the government by assisting women to get their complaints across to the government sub-departments such as the parliament, through emails. However, some women users claim they were facing challenges such as unemployment and gender issues, which required support from the government. In addition, women in the rural communities did not know the procedure to initiate contacts with higher authorities. The telecentre managers supported the women to contact NGOs working in the communities to address women's challenges that were beyond the services of the telecentre, as in this claim:

"The telecentre helps the community to plug in with other community-based organisations and non-governmental organisations" (User-E5).

Cultural Empowerment. The socio-cultural reason that non-users were not using the telecentre was due to their cultural beliefs about the role women play in the responsibility of caring for their family, as in this claim:

"Yes it can because we are poor people and we don't have computers for our services and many of the women were stranded and many of them have men and because of culture the men would say no to the women and these are not be able to come to the e-centre because she must respect the man" (User-K4).

6 Discussion and Conclusion

6.1 Benefits Women Derive from the Telecentre

The study analysed how the telecentre empowered women in rural communities. Based on empirical evidence from rural communities' uses of ICTs in the Western Cape Province, the study concludes that enhancing women's information capabilities is the most critical factor in determining the impact of ICTs on their well-being [9]. Findings derived from the psychological and information empowerment show few women utilised the telecentre to search for information for improving their economic standards. Furthermore, it was shown that, economically, most of the women were unemployed because they were not frequent users of the telecentre and did not partake in the computer skills training programme. In addition, politically, the telecentre added limited value to women. Results further show some women benefited socially from the use of the telecentre through interaction with friends and family. Some women benefit from the services provided in the telecentres. These include ICT skills development, improved communication, access to information, employment opportunities, access to government information and strengthening of social capital. The findings from the study were consistent with similar studies on telecentres in other rural communities [5]. However, this study did not differentiate the usage of telecentres in terms of gender. This study joins the past debate about the benefits of using the telecentres not being the same between men and women users [1]. However, it is indicated that gender-(male-) biased computer culture did influence the behaviour of some women in the communities who were considering using the telecentres. Subsequently, not all women benefited from the use of the telecentre.

7 Recommendation

The study recommends for future research that telecentres should be used to accommodate programs that can enhance women's capabilities. Moreover, telecentres should also be consciously created as a space that can embrace the information needs of women, thereby empowering women. The limitation of the study was caused by insufficient funds, which was a major limitation in carrying out this research. An additional limitation of the study was the language barrier, which was due to some women lack of spoken English. In addition, some of the respondents had difficulty in reading the interview questions, which was written in English. Based on the analysis of the study, for policy, telecentre design, or future research, the study would suggest to government and NGOs using the telecentre as an intervention mechanism for empowering women in the rural communities of South Africa. This study suggests recommendations to policy makers and NGOs to consider the difference in ICT access and socio-cultural issues that may affect the implementation of the telecentres in empowering rural women. In addition, this study informs the national policy makers on the contribution of the telecentres for women empowerment, rural livelihoods and poverty reduction. The study will also make practical contributions and allow the South African Government and NGOs to use telecentres for socio-economic development. Finally, Cape Access should focus more on the creation of campaigns and awareness programmes for promoting the telecentre in the rural areas to increase women's output of the telecentre.

References

1. Hilbert, M.: Digital gender divide or technologically empowered women in developing countries? A typical case of lies, damned lies, and statistics. In: Women's Studies International Forum, vol. 34, no. 6, pp. 479–489. Pergamon (2011)
2. Dasuki, S., Quaye, A.: An Evaluation of Information Systems Students Internship Programs in Developing Countries: A Capability Perspective (2016)

3. Wilson, P.A.: Empowerment: Commun. economic development from the inside out. Urban Stud. **33**(4–5), 617–630 (1996)
4. Ngumbuke, F.: Gender Impact and Mobile Phone Solutions in Rural Development: A Case Study in Rural Iringa, Tanzania (2010)
5. Mbatha, B.: Pushing the agenda of the information society ICT diffusion in selected multipurpose community telecentres in South Africa. Information Development (2015). 0266666915575544
6. Chigona, W., Mudavanhu, S.L., Lwoga, T.: Framing telecentres: accounts of women in rural communities in South Africa and Tanzania (2016)
7. Attwood, H., Diga, K., Braathen, E., May, J: Telecentre functionality in South Africa: re-enabling the community ICT access environment. J. Commun. Inf. **9**(4) (2013)
8. Uys, C., Pather, S.: Government Public Access Centres (PACs): a beacon of hope for marginalised communities. J. Commun. Inf. **12**(1), 21–52 (2016)
9. Gigler, B.-S.: Informational capabilities: the missing link for understanding the impact of ICT on development. Closing the Feedback Loop, p. 17 (2014)
10. Gomez, R.: When you do not have a computer: public-access computing in developing countries. Inf. Technol. Dev. **20**(3), 274–291 (2014)
11. Bell, T.: Village computing: a state of the field. reflections on the village computing consultation, Grameen Foundation, Telecentre.org. Center for Internet Studies and USC. Information and Communication Technologies for Women's Socioeconomic Empowerment, p. 41 (2006)
12. Maitrayee, M.: Telecentres in rural India: emergence and a typology. EJISDC: Electron. J. Inf. Syst. Dev. Countries **35**, 5 (2008)
13. Aji, Z.M., Yusof, S.A.M., Osman, W.R.S., Yusop, N.I.: A conceptual model for psychological empowerment of telecentre users. Comput. Inf. Sci. **3**(3), 71 (2010)
14. Mukerji, M.: Introduction. In: ICTs and Development, pp. 1–11. Palgrave Macmillan, Basingstoke (2013)
15. Hudson, H.E.: Access to the digital economy: issues in rural and developing regions. In: Understanding the Digital Economy: Data, Tools and Research, 25–26 May. Department of Commerce, Washington, DC (1999)
16. Heeks, R.: Where next for ICTs and international development. In: ICTs for development, pp. 29–74 (2010)
17. Adera, E.O., Waema, T.M., May, J.: ICT pathways to poverty reduction: empirical evidence from East and Southern Africa. In: IDRC (2014)
18. Adeya, C.N.: ICTs and poverty: a literature review. In: IDRC, Ottawa (2002)
19. Clark, H., Barry, J.: Business ethics and the changing gender balance. Bus. Ethics: Crit. Perspect. Bus. Manag. **2**, 273 (2001)
20. Röger, U., Rütten, A., Frahsa, A., Abu-Omar, K., Morgan, A.: Differences in individual empowerment outcomes of socially disadvantaged women: effects of mode of participation and structural changes in a physical activity promotion program. Int. J. Pub. Health **56**(5), 465–473 (2011)
21. Hettiarachchi, C.: Role of Information and Communication Technologies (ICTs) in Human Development in South Asia. Department of Management of Technology, University of Moratuwa, Sri Lanka (2006)
22. Brown, A.E., Grant, G.G.: Highlighting the duality of the ICT and development research agenda. Inf. Technol. Dev. **16**(2), 96–111 (2010)
23. Bailey, A., Ngwenyama, O.: Community mediation and violence prevention through telecentre usage: ICTs mediating the 'Border Line'. In: Proceedings of SIG GlobDev Third Annual Workshop, Saint Louis, USA, 12 December 2010

24. Munyua, H.: Application of ICTs in Africa's agricultural sector: a gender perspective. In: Gender and the information revolution in Africa, pp. 85–124 (2000)
25. Hafkin, N.J., Nancy, T.: Gender, information technology, and developing countries: an analytic study. In: Office of Women in Development, Bureau for Global Programs, Field Support and Research, United States Agency for International Development (2001)
26. Carter, M.R., May, J.: Poverty, livelihood and class in rural South Africa. World Dev. **27**(1), 1–20 (1999)
27. Bobo, T.: Challenges of rural women. East London. Masimanyane Women's Support Centre, South Africa (2011)
28. Tacoli, C.: Rural-urban interactions: a guide to the literature. Environ. Urban. **10**(1), 147–166 (1998)
29. Sey, A.: Public access to ICTs: a review of the literature. Center for Information and Society, University of Washington (2008)
30. Sey, A., Bar, F., Coward, C., Koepke, L., Rothschild, C., Sciadas, G.: There when you need it: the multiple dimensions of public access ict uses and impacts. Inf. Technol. Int. Dev. **11**(1), 71 (2015)
31. Nath, V.: Empowerment and governance through information and communication technologies: women's perspective. Int. Inf. Libr. Rev. **33**(4), 317–339 (2001)
32. Jorge, N.S.: Engendering ICT policy and regulation: prioritising universal access for women's empowerment. In: Cinderella or Cyberella: Empowering Women in the Knowledge Society, pp. 15–47 (2006)
33. Asiedu, C.: Information communication technologies for gender and development in Africa: the case for radio and technological blending. Int. Commun. Gaz. **74**(3), 240–257 (2012)
34. Potnis, D.: Beyond access to information: understanding the use of information by poor female mobile users in rural India. Inf. Soc. **31**(1), 83–93 (2015)
35. Moser, C.O.N.: Gender Planning and Development: Theory, Practice and Training. Routledge, London, New York (1993)
36. Knight, P., Boostrom, E., Brajovic, V., Baranshamaje, E., Cader, M., Clement-Jones, R., Hawkins, R., Schware, R., Slaon, H.: Increasing internet connectivity in sub-Saharan Africa: issues, options, and World Bank Group Role. Online World Bank Publications (1995)
37. Obayelu, A., Ogunlade, I.: Analysis of the uses of information communication technology (ICT) for gender empowerment and sustainable poverty alleviation in Nigeria. Int. J. Educ. Develop. using ICT **2**(3) (2006)
38. Barnard, Y., Bradley, M.D., Hodgson, F., Lloyd, A.D.: Learning to use new technologies by older adults: perceived difficulties, experimentation behaviour and usability. Comput. Hum. Behav. **29**(4), 1715–1724 (2013)
39. Wilson, P.A.: Empowerment: community economic development from the inside out. Urban Stud. **33**(4–5), 617–630 (1996)
40. Ahmad, A.L.: The social reality of the Malaysian blogosphere. Int. J. Arts Sci. **4**(3), 239–252 (2011)
41. Macdonald, D., Hedge, N.: Enabling voices, making choices: explorations of gender, power and technologically enabled learning cultures. In: CATaC 2006 Proceedings, Cultural Attitudes towards Technology and Communication, Tartu, Estonia, Murdoch University, Murdoch, Australia, pp. 435–452 (2006)
42. Suresh, L.B.: Impact of information and communication technologies on women empowerment in India. Syst. Cybern. Inf. **9**, 17–23 (2011)
43. Geetha, G.S., Indira, R.: Women, income generation, and political capital in the silk industry in Karnataka. Gender Technol. Develop. **14**(3), 423–440 (2010)

44. Bruestle, P., Haubner, D., Schinzel, B., Holthaus, M., Remmele, B., Schirmer, D., Reips, U.-D.: Doing e-learning/doing gender? Examining the relationship between students' gender concepts and e-learning technology. In: 5th European Symposium on Gender and ICT Digital Cultures: Participation-Empowerment–Diversity, pp. 5–7 (2009)

45. Merriam, S.B.: Qualitative research and case study applications in education. Revised and Expanded from "Case Study Research in Education." Jossey-Bass Publishers, San Francisco (1998)

46. Walsham, G.: The emergence of interpretivism in IS research. Inf. Syst. Res. **6**(4), 376–394 (1995)

47. Schoeman, S., Visagie, C.: Local history teaching in the Overberg region of the Western Cape: the case of the Elim primary school. Yesterday Today **11**, 118–132 (2014)

48. du Plessis, M.: The role of knowledge management in innovation. J. Knowl. Manag. **11**(4), 20–29 (2007)

49. Census 2011: Community data profile. https://census2011.adrianfrith.com/place/160012

50. Ladley, A.: A guide to legal aid-some issues arising from the refusal of legal aid in the Mbekweni community council case. S. African Law J. **99**, 237 (1982)

51. Municipality, Drakenstein: Annual report 2011/2012 (2013)

52. Tran, V.M., Perry, J.A.: Challenges to using neem (Azadirachtaindica var. sianensisValenton) in Thailand. Econ. Bot. **57**(1), 93–102 (2003)

53. Chigona, W.: Should communal computing facilities cohabit with public facilities. J. Commun. Inf. **2**(3) (2006)

54. Trotter, R.T.: Qualitative research sample design and sample size: resolving and unresolved issues and inferential imperatives. Prev. Med. **55**(5), 398–400 (2012)

Young Women in South African Call Centres: A Case of Women's Empowerment or a Repackaging of the Conventional Global Factory?

Sisa Ngabaza[✉]

University of the Western Cape, Cape Town, South Africa
sngabaza@uwc.ac.za

Abstract. ICT4D is slowly making inroads into various communities in developing contexts globally, and this slow pace is equally noticeable within the field of gender and development. This paper draws from an ongoing research project that uses a qualitative feminist framework to investigate young women's participation in the call centre industry in Cape Town, South Africa. The paper further draws on intersectionality to tap into lived experiences of young women working in different call centres to critically explore the "value" for call centres as a project empowering young women economically in the South African context. Drawing from descriptive data collected from young women working as call centre agents, the paper argues that call centres may indeed be a huge ICT4D empowerment project for young women in the South African context, but also cautions that call centres continue to parade the hallmarks of 'traditional female employment ghettos'.

Keywords: Young women · Employment · Call centres · Cape town · South Africa

1 Introduction

Call centre business, largely mediated by computer and telephone technologies has become a popular ICT4D phenomenon and viable mode of employment for young people in numerous countries across the globe. Key global players in the field include India and the Philippines, and of late South Africa has joined this bandwagon. In South Africa the industry has increasingly grown in the last two decades, placing the country in the lead on the continent [1]. The government of South Africa is totally commitment to the call centre project and this commitment seemingly assures this growth. There is an increased interest in call centres as a viable project for employment creation, which has put call centres in the spotlight [2]. This visibility has equally attracted offshore multinational companies, which find South Africa an ideal destination, with compatible time zones, proficient English language speakers, and competitive attrition rates. In essence, South Africa prides itself in delivering worldwide service at highly competitive rates [3]. This paper draws on a study that focuses on the experiences of young women who work as agents in different call centres in Cape Town. The paper questions

J. Choudrie et al. (Eds.): ICT4D 2017, IFIP AICT 504, pp. 135–143, 2017.
DOI: 10.1007/978-3-319-59111-7_12

the value of call centres as economic empowerment spaces for young women in a South African context.

The current global economic environment promotes trade regimes that encourage the rapid growth of the service industry. Feminist scholars attribute this fast growth to the availability of women as cheap labour [4], in an employment model that foregrounds low wage labour. This model of employment has been largely criticized for diverging from the traditional model of male employment, which emphasized permanent employment [5], to that which centralizes part-time work such as call centre work. It is therefore not surprising that call centres are particularly pivotal in the service industry, with female employees constituting more than 75% of call centre agents [6, 7]. This feminization of labour is a current global concern for feminist scholars who are critical of the division of labour which differentiates what women do from what men do in wage work [5]. Call centres indeed promote a shift from male dominated wage labour to that dominated by females, and it is within the context of labour differentiation that I question if call centres are in essence a space where young South African women can be economically empowered, or whether they are just a version of the global economic 'factory' that capitalizes on women as "a cheap, submissive ... secondary workforce" [5] (p. 171).

Call centres are highly monitored environments, with call centre agents under constant surveillance from their managers. Monitoring includes activities such as tracking the number of calls, speed at which the calls are taken, time when the agent is on or off the phone, abandoned calls etc. [2, 8–11]. This surveillance renders call centres as spaces highly charged with power dynamics, as agents are pushed to meet numerous targets through multiple incentives. The Global Call Centre Report [12] explored 2500 call centres in 17 countries and found call centres in South Africa ranked amongst those with the highest degree of call centre monitoring [6], which is a matter of concern.

There is a huge body of work on call centres globally and this work seems to be focused largely on labour operations, processes, and agents [13, 14]. In South Africa such work is slowly emerging and seemingly in line with global trends. There are very few studies focusing on gender in call centre work and I have not come across any empirical work using intersectionality or a gender justice lens, to understand the nature of women's work in South African call centres. Yet it is necessary to disaggregate the 'call centre agent' as a worker, for a nuanced understanding of young women's work in South African call centres. A feminist intersectional analysis necessitates sensitivity to multiple categories of difference [15, 16] that constitute woman and worker, and this exploration is sensitive to the multiple intersecting categories that could possible shape young women's experiences as call centre agents.

Studies that raise the significance of gender in call centres have been conducted elsewhere. What is worrying though is that most of this global literature on women's participation in the call centre industry is more than a decade old [7, 17, 18]. ICT4D are rapidly changing, as are the work environments; it is indeed concerning that empirical evidence is not reflective of this process. This paper will contribute towards this scarce literature and particularly, towards understanding the lived experiences of call centre agents in a South African context. Belt [7] conducted a similar study in the UK and Ireland and was of the impression that call centres seem "to bear many of the old hallmarks of those traditional female employment ghettos", spaces mainly occupied by women, specialising in low skilled undemanding jobs, which most women would find it difficult to leave (p. 52). In this paper I question the value of call centres as economic empowerment zones for young women in this rapidly growing industry in a developing context.

2   The Study

This paper draws from a large ongoing research project, informed by qualitative feminist principles. The large project employs multiple data collection methods such as surveys, focus group discussions, and in-depth individual interviews, to explore young women's lived experiences in the call centre industry in Cape Town and Johannesburg in South Africa. This paper reports findings from 15 semi-structured interviews conducted with call centre agents in and around Cape Town. Interviews were conducted with female call centre agents from an array of call centres which offer different services. Interviews were held in spaces where the agents were comfortable to do so. All participation was voluntary, and informed consent was obtained from all participants before commencement of the interviews. Ages of participants ranged from 19 to 35 years. Pseudonyms have been used throughout for anonymity purposes. Most interviews were conducted in English and some in the language preferred by the participant. These were transcribed verbatim and translated accordingly. This data was analysed through a qualitative thematic approach [19] and the following section presents themes emerging from this analysis.

3   Findings and Discussion

3.1   Call Centres as Spaces of Women's Economic Empowerment

In Cape Town, as is the trend in South Africa and probably in other global spaces, call centres recruit young people of school leaving age with a school leaving certificate or university students [6]. These are people with absolutely no tangible qualifications for any kind of job, untapped cheap labour [11]. Rob Davies of the Department of Trade and Industry in South Africa, cited in [20], sees South African call centres providing an opportunity for employment and exposure, specifically for young people who fall in the 15 to 34 year age group. This means that call centres provide mostly entry-level job opportunities where young people are excited by the prospect of wage labour. It was therefore not surprising from this study that some young women found participating in the call centre as agents a financially empowering process:

Let me first explain why I say it (call centre work) is empowering: many call centre workers are women, single parents who fell pregnant when they were teenagers just like me, and never got a chance to finish studies because fathers of children ran away or are absent. Some call centres have flexi hours like this one, meaning you can work and take care of your children. (Noku-lunga, 29 years)

This participant who had been working in this inbound customer care centre for nine years found the place a welcome source of income for her child and her own welfare. This optimistic view of the call centre was further emphasised by other participants who did not only see call centres as worthwhile employment ventures but were confident that they also promoted upward mobility within the industry for mostly female workers who might not have been open to such mobility in other sectors:

I believe that call centre work is empowering to females, because they are more likely to be employed than males because of their characteristics. Call centre work is empowering to women because they feel that they can get into management positions much easier than males. While males feel that it is disempowering because, uhm ...They aren't acknowledged the way that women are in call centres. (Buhle, 25 years)

Other participants further supported this sentiment:

The positive aspect is that the call centre promotes women, most of the call centres prefer to hire women because women meet targets and the call centre is about talking, and women like talking... (Nokulunga, 29 years)

Uhm ... well ... females are more likely to get promotion opportunities ... But from, like my previous experiences in the call centre, females got the permanent posts and management jobs before males. The challenge for females though is to get further up the ladder. Uhm ... in other words I would say that it is harder for women to get beyond the lower management and to get into positions of higher management (Nonhle, 27 years)

My personal experience is that women are able to get the lower leadership positions because call centre companies see it as a way of empowering women. But in a way it does not fully empower women because they struggle to break the barrier of obtaining those superior leadership jobs, which are generally filled by males (Tarin, 25 years)

These extracts raise a number of issues about the participation of young women in the call centre industry in Cape Town. Optimistically, call centres are sources of employment opportunities, a safe haven for those with almost no job qualification, offering financial independence for students, single mothers, and above all a worthwhile opportunity for women's overall participation in the economy. Further positive sentiments regarding call centre employment have been raised in those studies conducted particularly in high areas of unemployment [21]. It should be noted that South Africa has very high unemployment levels and it remains a welcome initiative that call centres offer some kind of economic independence for those who would otherwise not have been employed.

Although these young women find call centres largely a source of economic empowerment, it should be noted that early global empirical work on call centres sees the cluster of women in the bottom rung as agents and in the managerial positions as, "ghettoising themselves" [7] p. 11. The main reason for such positioning of women is premised on the capability of women, particularly older women [22], to provide stability in the organisations. In such cases the expectation is that they will seldom move anywhere. This is the general feeling, particularly for those studies conducted elsewhere [23]. Findings in this study seem to pick up continuities on the positioning of women in the lower rung. What seems to be different though is that the majority of women on this rung in South African call centres are young, when compared to Skene's [22] observation that call centres were an employment source for older women.

Call centres are indeed an empowerment project for young women in this context but the concentration of women in the industry as call centre agents as well as frontline managers also continues to draw parallels with the industrial factory. Perhaps we should be asking if call centres are a repackaging of the industrial manufacturing factory, with "large scale and continuous production, extensive monitoring and control of the workplace…repetitive of work tasks". Are call centre agents the new face of the "industrial proletariat", and the advent of call centres largely a "continuous large-scale industrial production process?" [9], (p. 3). It is of concern and equally ironical that an industry hugely driven by ICT4D, such as the call centre continues to exhibit the same characteristics of work organisation that were prevalent in the conventional global factory [24] as shown in some responses from the participants above. Perhaps further exploration is needed for a deeper, more nuanced understanding of these questions on women's employment in the call centre industry.

Participants further reported finding call centres empowering in terms of skills:

You also learn to communicate better and that also improves your communication skills and it also improves your negotiation skills. You learn a lot from working with a diverse range of people and you learn how to handle different personalities such as rude customers and nice customers. (Marceline, 32 years)

It does expose you to various people and personality types, I guess you can become confident and learn valuable technical and human relation skills. (Nolwazi, 23 years)

Such positive notions on use of ICTs as potentially empowering in terms of skills in this industry have been noted elsewhere [17]. Writing from New Zealand, the author cautions though that most call centres in this particular context are extremely small government ventures and this may be different in other settings. Although the participants in this study emphasised positive notions about skills they acquired from call centres, empirical evidence on other global work in call centres seems to foreground the use of ICTs in call centres as rather deskilling, repetitive, and monotonous. ICT use in the call centre industry has been critiqued for lacking intensive skilling, as agents are exposed to basic keyboard skills [25]. Perhaps agents would benefit more if technologies in call centres were harnessed and utilized for intensive skilling and further potential growth for young women.

3.2   Pessimism in Use of ICT4D in Call Centres for Young Women Agents

A number of young women found call centres indeed a powerful economic empowerment venture for unskilled young people and students in tertiary institutions. However, juxtaposed to these views was a powerful pessimistic voice that was quick to dismiss the use of ICTs in the call centre by young women as empowering in any way:

As women we always have to prove that we are good enough to the clients, male employees and our bosses. So even though we are pressured, we are the hardest working because we try to show everyone that we know what we are doing. (Candice, 25 years)

Some spoke ambiguously about the remuneration process, which in most cases was also shaped by other intersectional factors in their lives. Feminist scholars are always conscious of the non-homogeneity of women as social players in different contexts, arguing instead that women's lived experiences are largely unique to other constraints in their lives [15, 16]. Although this paper generally refers to participants' age groups it should be noted that issues like race, language, class, and level of education were taken into consideration in the broad study. The study does not only acknowledge intersectionality for this group of workers, but also foregrounds the significance of how women's working experiences are mediated by other multiple factors in their lives. Whilst some participants expressed general gendered notions of participation, some were careful not to homogenise their experiences. Experiences were therefore diverse:

...I am telling you if I could go back to school I would! There is no money there especially for someone like me who is not married with three children. (Noma 32 years)

It is of course empowering because its quick and easy money ... Most students of X university work at the xxx Call Centre in xxx. They go to college all day and then the shift starts from 5 pm until 10 pm. It's an easy way of getting money and studying at the same time, especially for students who don't get enough money at home ... It was the same for me. If I got enough money at home, I wouldn't have had to work 6 months in the call centre xxx. But I didn't have that money and my parents didn't have it, I was forced to go and work at the call centre ... It's not conducive as a work environment. But I needed to do it to pay college registration money ... You know, most of the people who work there are...people with no aspiration, they choose the easy way out, it's not empowering at all. (Fatima, 23 years)

No! I am not well paid; in fact I am barely coping. If I had a family of my own, or still, rented a place I would not be able to survive. I don't know how the other people in the call centre make ends surviving on Rxxx per month. How can this be any form of empowerment? (Nolwazi, 23 years)

As evident in the above extracts, multiple intersecting factors seem to underlie young women's pessimism about call centres as an empowerment venture for young people. Both class and level of education are raised as challenges pinning down participants to call centre work. Further, another participant raises the challenge of single motherhood and an extremely troubling parenting dynamic for her and her child as shown here:

My early shift begins at 7am in the morning until 2 pm in the evening, which means I have to wake up early and prepare myself and my child early ... since I am a single mother I have to leave my child alone to wait for school transport which arrives at 7.30 to pick her up. Therefore I am constantly stressing because I am worried about my child's safety and my safety as well. I work a late shift, which normally happens for two weeks in a month ... I work from 12 noon until 8 pm and get home around 9 pm in the evening. This means I have to leave my child alone for the whole evening without taking care of her. Therefore if you are a woman in the call centre industry it is not easy because you cannot care for your family as much as you would like to do. (Akhona, 32 years)

Moreover, others continued to challenge the idea of call centre participation as a form of empowerment at all:

I met people who have worked for 10 years in the same call centre at the same space and they were fine with their position as agents. There was this one girl, she was 21 years old at the time and she was permanent. She has no aspiration of studying. When we asked why she didn't work part time to have the opportunity to study, she said that she was used to the money. This work is not empowering; I could never do it for more than a year. It's not a comfortable environment. I don't understand people who are comfortable with this work. Working 10 h a day for 10 years is not empowering at all! (Fatima, 23 years)

More participants raised further pessimistic sentiments challenging the proposition of call centres as a space for women's economic empowerment:

Okay, so some of the challenges obviously the hours, we had to work 12 h shifts, we had to work night shifts ...; you are always sitting down which is also quite unhealthy. There is also a language barrier between the clients and us because they don't really understand our type of English, ja language barriers are frustrating. Sometimes clients even ask to be transferred to an American based associate. (Charne, 25 years)

Disempowering, 'cause I feel like I'm losing my IQ every f... single day, honestly speaking ... in a call centre once you're in that position you can't climb. That's how it is in a call centre (Marceline 32 years).

Numerous studies seem to attest to the challenges of ICT4D within the call centre industry [7, 18, 26]; with scholars citing multiple challenges particularly for women workers. Shift work has been raised as interfering with women's distinctive cultures, particularly in developing contexts [18]. Further some scholars are largely dismissive of the empowerment discourse, instead seeing the use of ICTs in the call centres deepening women's exploitation on an international scale [15, 23, 24]. Evidence from this study shows that more than 75% of call centre employees are women, and that the use of ICT4D in this context remains contested as both an empowerment but also an exploitative venture for young women in Cape Town.

4 Discussion

A number of participants emphasise the gendered nature of call centre work, indicating that it is ideal and supportive to female employment because of their 'productivity and characteristics'. Call centre work is about 'talking and women like talking' as raised by some participants above. Is this a version of a 'female docility and nimble fingers' discourse [5, 27] that has been central to feminist critique of women's work in the traditional global factories, or is it a 'recomposition' of a new exploitative form of labour for young women through ICT4D? Feminist scholars have criticised labour differentiation based on gender ascriptive notions between men and women, arguing instead for a labour force undifferentiated by gender, a labour force that can 'dispose' women's labour power as their 'own commodity ... free of all the objects needed for the realisation of this labour-power' (Marx, 1976, cited in [27] (p. 197). Feminist scholars continue to challenge the disingenuous nature of women's work in global contexts, arguing that although women's wage work is an essential tool to fight patriarchal subordination, such work usually exposes women to the vulnerability of exploitation in low wage employment [4]. Participants in this study were equally quick to underline the low wages characteristic of most call centres in South Africa and the challenges of making a living out of these wages. Here multiple intersectional factors mediating their experiences as young women in call centres emerged. These factors strongly accentuated the necessity to disaggregate the call centre 'agent' for a more nuanced understanding of their subjective experiences as female workers in call centre employment in Cape Town.

5 Conclusion

This paper raises a dichotomous response to how young female call centre agents from a variety of call centres in and around Cape Town experience participation in the ICT employing call centre industry. Evidence given in this paper shows that young people find the call centre industry empowering as an employment venture in a place characterised by high rates of unemployment that are even higher for women. Within this broad context of empowerment, we are reminded of the challenges of call centre work as limiting in providing solid ICT skills with the potential to ensure women's growth in the economic sphere. Moreover we need to be mindful of the call centre industry continuing to exhibit the same qualities as those evidenced in the global factories popularly associated with women's exploitation.

Acknowledgement. This paper acknowledges support from the National Research Foundation (grant no. 99220) in South Africa.

References

1. Thompson, G.: Call centre special Africa fights for its share of a global market (2013). http://www.balancingact-africa.com/news/telecoms-en/9576/call-centre-special-africa-fights-for-its-share-of-a-global-market
2. Banks, D., Roodt, G.: The efficiency and quality dilemma: what drives South African call centre management performance indicators. SA J. Hum. Resour. Manag. **9**(1), 17 (2011). https://doi.org/10.4102/sajhrm.v27i4.331
3. Fieberg, M.: The efficient management of a call centre. Doctoral dissertation, University of the Free State (2014). http://hdl.handle.net/11660/713
4. Eisenstein, H.: Feminism seduced. How global elites use women's labor and ideas to exploit the world. USA Paradigm publishers (2009). https://doi.org/10.4324/9781315634623
5. Irving, Z.: Gender and work. In: Richardson, D., Robinson, V. (eds.) Introducing Gender and Women's Studies, pp. 161–183. Palgrave Macmillan, New York (2008)
6. Benner, C., Lewis, C., Omar, R.: The South African call centre industry: a study of strategy, human resource practices and performance. The global Centre Industry Project (2007). http://digitalcommons.ilr.cornell.edu/cgi/viewcontent.cgi?article=1012&context=reports
7. Belt, V.: A female Ghetto? women's careers in telephone call centres. HRM J. **12**, 56–66 (2002). https://doi.org/10.1111/j.1748-8583.2002.tb00077.x
8. Bain, P., Watson, A., Mulvey, G., Taylor, P., Gall, G.: Taylorism, targets and the pursuit of quantity and quality by call centre management. New Technol. Work Employ. **17**(3), 170–185 (2002). https://doi.org/10.1111/1468-005x.00103
9. Burgess, J., Connell, J.: Emerging developments in call centre research. Labour Ind. **14**(3), 1–13 (2004). https://doi.org/10.1080/10301763.2004.10669291

10. Taylor, P., Bain, P.: 'An assembly line in the head': work and employee relations in the call centre. Ind. Relat. J. **30**(2), 101–117 (1999). https://doi.org/10.1111/1468-2338.00113

11. Taylor, P., Bain, P.: 'India calling to the far away towns' the call centre labour process and globalization. Work Employ. Soc. **19**(2), 261–282 (2005). https://doi.org/10.1177/0950017005053170

12. Holman, D., Batt, R., Holtgrewe, U.: The global call centre report: international perspectives on management and employment, Ithaca, NY (2007). http://digitalcommons.ilr.cornell.edu/cgi/viewcontent.cgi?article=1012&context=reports

13. Russell, B.: Call centres: a decade of research. Int. J. Manag. Rev. **10**(11), 1468–2370 (2008). https://doi.org/10.1111/j.1468-2370.2008.00241.x

14. Robinson, G., Morley, C.: Running the electronic sweatshop: call centre managers' views on call centres. J. Manag. Organ. **13**(03), 249–263 (2007). https://doi.org/10.1017/S1833367200003722

15. Cole, R.E.: Intersectionality and research in psychology. Am. Psychol. **64**(3), 170–180 (2009). https://doi.org/10.1037/a0014564

16. Yuval-Davis, N.: Intersectionality and feminist politics. Eur. J. Women's Stud. **13**(3), 193–209 (2006). https://doi.org/10.1177/1350506806065752

17. Hunt, V.: Call centre work for women: career or stopgap? Labour Ind. J. Soc. Econ. Relat. Work **14**(3), 139–153 (2004). https://doi.org/10.1080/10301763.2004.10669299

18. Singh, P., Pandey, A.: Women in call centres. Econ. Pol. Wkly., 684–688 (2005). http://www.jstor.org/stable/4416207

19. Clarke, V., Braun, V.: Thematic analysis. Encycl. Crit. Psychol. 1947–1952 (2014). https://doi.org/10.1007/978-1-4614-5583-7_311

20. Cohen, M.: South Africa ideal for call centres, accent "sounds British" (2013). http://mg.co.za/print/2013-12-02-south-africa-ripe-for-call-centre-expansion. Accessed 30 Jan 2013

21. Richardson, R., Marshall, J.N.: Teleservices, call centres and urban and regional development. Serv. Ind. J. **19**(1), 96–116 (1999). https://doi.org/10.1080/02642069900000006

22. Skene, J.: Teaching old dogs new tricks: accessing employment opportunities for mature workers in the call centre industry. In: AIRAANZ Conference, Monash University, Melbourne (2003)

23. Coyle, A.: Women and organisational change. EOC research discussion series no. 14. Equal Opportunities Commission, Manchester (1995)

24. Russell, B.: The talk shop and shop talk: employment and work in a call centre. J. Ind. Relat. **44**(4), 467–490 (2002). https://doi.org/10.1111/1472-9296.00060

25. Buchanan, R., Koch-Schulte, S.: Gender on the line: technology, restructuring and the reorganisation of work in the call centre industry, status of women, p. 106. Canada's Policy Research Fund, Ontario (2000). https://pdfs.semanticscholar.org/625b/6699901d9a32dafe335865e1ecce21148658.pdf

26. van den Broek, D.: Monitoring and surveillance in call centres: some responses from Australian workers. Labour Ind. **12**(3), 43–58 (2002). https://doi.org/10.1080/10301763.2002.10722023

27. Elson, D., Pearson, R.: The subordination of women and the internationalization of factory production. In: Visvanathan, N., Duggan, L., Wiesgersma, N., Nisonoff, L. (eds.) The Women Gender and Development Reader, pp. 212–224. Zed Books, New York (2011)

Social Mechanisms of ICT-Enabled Development

Living in the Limits: Migration and Information Practices of Undocumented Latino Migrants

Luis Fernando Baron[1](✉) and Ricardo Gomez[2]

[1] Icesi University, Cali, Colombia
lfbaron@icesi.edu.co
[2] iSchool, University of Washington, Seattle, USA
rgomez@uw.edu

Abstract. Information practices, whether mediated by technologies or not, have critical roles on the experience leading up to and resulting from migration. This paper analyzes the relationships between information practices (information seeking, use, and sharing [1]) and Latino migration in and towards the US. The paper is based on findings from two convergent studies of Latin American migrants in the US [2, 3]. The two studies are based on the qualitative collection of stories by undocumented Latino migrants in different contexts. Based on our findings, we contend that migration is not a process that follows a linear progression of stages, as some scholars indicate, and that information practices can not only help expand migrants' perceptions of their place of origin and of destination, but they also help them reaffirm their notions of wellbeing, or what a good life means to them. In addition, we show that information and communication technologies (ICT) are affording migrant lives a stronger sense of 'in-betweenness', generating new experiences of nationhood, sense of belonging and citizenship, as well as forming new national-transnational identities. Methodologically, our convergent studies evidence the power of using stories as a research method to gain deeper understanding of the intricate dynamics and experiences of migration, a central phenomenon of our time.

Keywords: Migration · Information practice · Information behavior · Undocumented · Latino · Liminality

1 Introduction

International migration occupies one of the most important places in the media, academic and political agendas since last decade, with growing emphasis over the last five years, in which we have witnessed especially salient migration crises in the US and in Europe. The US has seen growing waves of undocumented migrants from Mexico, Central and South America at the US-Mexico border, including a spike of unaccompanied minors from Central America, seeking a new life in the US; immigration policy is vastly inadequate to deal with the problem, and congress inaction has left the country with no viable immigration reform in sight.

J. Choudrie et al. (Eds.): ICT4D 2017, IFIP AICT 504, pp. 147–158, 2017.
DOI: 10.1007/978-3-319-59111-7_13

According to the Pew Research Center (PRC) in 2014 there were 11.3 million unauthorized immigrants in the United States, about 3.5% of the nation's population. The number of unauthorized immigrants had peaked in 2007 at 12.2 million (4% of the U.S. population, and 5.1% of the U.S. labor force). The majority of unauthorized immigrants come from Latin America and the Caribbean, with **Mexi**cans making up about half of the total (49%). Mexico is followed by El Salvador (6.1% in 2012); Guatemala (4.7%); India (4.0%); Honduras (3.1%); China (2.7%); \ Philippines (1.8%); Korea (1.6%),\ Dominican Republic (1.5%) and Colombia (1.5%). In 2014, California, Texas, Florida, New York, New Jersey and Illinois were home to about 60% of unauthorized immigrants in the US.

Migration has also given rise to new types of social mobilization, as when migrants in the US demonstrate for their rights and for comprehensive immigration reform, or when people protest against international migrants, as we saw among Trump supporters in the US, or in the anti-immigration protests in European countries. Such anti-immigrant sentiments fueled political results such as "Brexit", the exit of the UK from the European Union early in 2016; according to The Economist, anger at immigration as well as globalization and liberalism were considered the most important factors that moved voters to decide [4].

While numerous scholars have studied communication and information practices of migrants for a good overview of recent research see [6], very few have focused on the "excluded" end of Nail's [5] continuum: asylum seekers, migrant workers, *sans papiers* (French for "without papers") and irregular, unauthorized, or undocumented migrants, among others, all of whom live at the margins of political life and in the extreme marginalization and exclusion from mainstream society. The communication and information practices of these extremely marginalized and excluded groups of migrants have received little attention by the studies handle the interactions among migration, communication and information. Notable exceptions include the studies of [3, 10–13].

The global dimension of migrations, the rising numbers of both immigrants and countries affected by migration, and the changes in technologies, especially ICT, called for a reexamination of migration and for an incorporation of new dimensions and academic approaches [14]. For these reasons our comparative study seeks to better understand the communication and information practices, whether mediated or not by information and communication technologies, of undocumented immigrants from Central and Latin America, and how these practices are impacting their migrations trajectories and cycles. In order to accomplish these goals, we first present the methodological common ground that supports our studies, offering information about their singularities as well. Then we present common and particular findings of our studies and finally we discuss our findings with the aim of documenting how family and friends are critical to the experience and information practices of migrants, particularly as they live in a state of "in-betweenness" that relies ever so strongly on information to strengthen the economic, social and cultural capital of migrants.

2   Migration, Communication and Information: Literature Review and Conceptual Stances

The field of studies analyzing information and immigration relationships shows very different theoretic and methodological approaches, where case studies are prevalent. Scholars in communications, linguistics, anthropology, sociology and, more recently, information sciences and other integrated and cross-disciplinary programs have contributed widely to this field. Many of the communication studies have a research tradition coming from media studies, emphasizing the effects of media discourses and the roles and uses of media among immigrants. Numerous cultural studies, which have a significant trajectory analyzing issues related to race, gender and power, have made important contributions on issues related to globalization and identities. The studies analyzing the relationships among information, communication, migration and ICT could be organized around 4 overlapping topics: The first one show the conditions and factors that influence perceptions, access and uses of ICT, emphasizing studies on digital divide and comparative studies between native and non-native groups [15–18]. They sustain the significant influence of ICT access and skills on employment, educational opportunities and civic engagement, and the advantages/disadvantages between immigrants and natives of the US. These studies also point out that ICT skills are crucial to success in the workplace and at school, and they play a vital role in civic and political engagement.

The second topic deal with the processes of embeddedness of media and ICT in daily life, emphasizing relationships and networks in local and transnational spaces [19–24]. This group of studies explores the use of ICT as a contextualizing tool for societal integration and inclusion amongst migrant populations, either in conjunction with ICT use for homeland connection, or as a distinct phenomenon.

The third topic focuses on the uses and appropriation of ICT and immigrants' information behavior [25–30]; This studies portray multiple, simultaneous, and complementary, practices and uses of different forms of information and communication, which implicates different social spaces, times, and technologies (from interpersonal communication to the use of sophisticated information technologies and platforms).

The last topic emphasizes the relationships between ICT and empowerment, social capital and civic engagement [8, 18, 31–35]. The studies show that both alternative media (e.g. radio and cartoons), and emerging Internet-based technologies, including social media (e.g. Facebook, Twitter or YouTube), have played significant roles in facilitating immigrants' navigation of and integration into society. However ICT have also enabled social and political participation of immigrants in different countries, helping them to become actors of the co-constructions of their new communities and cultures[1].

These topics provide significant evidence on how important information and communication are in different life aspects of migrants and migration. However we underline the following contributions of these studies: (1) they brought a valuable set of

---

[1] Fortunati, Pertierra, and Vincent suggest the concept of co-construction, which assumes that each society is a dynamic system which meets and maybe clashes with other cultures, but in so doing enriches itself and consequently changes (Fortunati et al. 2012).

theories and concepts that challenge and provide analytical tools for further research, including different approaches to globalization(s) and their links with both the roles of imagination [36], as well as the notions of information environment as well as in-betweenness (as a concept related to space; time and perceptions/representations); (2) they show the impact or potential impact of ICT in different activities of migrants (both as individuals as well as collectively) such as: the ways they imagine and represent reality; inform and get informed; communicate; build and share knowledge; create, strengthen and weaken social networks; forge and express identities and senses of belonging; and (3) they portray multiple, simultaneous, and in several ways complementary, practices and uses of different forms of information and communication, which implicates different social spaces, times, and technologies [37].

Particularly, for our comparative endeavor we follow Savolainen [1] and use the constructivist notion of "information practices," which allows for a more nuanced, less reductionist understanding than the behavioristic label given to information seeking, use and sharing. Additionally, we build on Caidi and colleagues idea of the overlapping settlement stages that helps situate the information and communication practices of migrants [6]; as well as the varying information practices of undocumented migrants that change between *places of departure, places of transition and places of destination*, where there are constant negotiations between "here" and "there" and information practices that help to broaden the world view of migrants [23].

3 Research Methods: Two Convergent Studies that Harness the Power of Stories

Within social sciences there is a resurgence of interest in narrative as social act and form of explanation, on storytelling as a social process, on life histories and accounts as social objects for research, and on the narrative construction of identity [38]. This author argues the contemporary narrative turn is part of a renewed emphasis on human agency, on context and the embeddedness of human experience, as well as the importance of language to the negotiation of meanings and the construction of identity in everyday life. However, from his perspective, stories are fundamentally transactional (we prefer to call them interactional), and this, in addition to their organizing operations, accounts for their discursive power. "The storytelling process, as a social transaction, engages people in communicative relationship. Through identification and "co-creation" of a story, the storyteller and reader/listener create a "we" involving some degree of affective bond and a sense of solidarity" [41, p. 19].

The studies that support this paper uses different forms of interviews and observations in order to develop migration stories that also provided us with other data such as demographics, gender issues, migrants networks and legal status. Building stories them offer us, at least, three important contributions to this endeavor: (1) elicit richer and complex understanding of individual experiences, opinions and feelings (2) address sensitive topics, and (3) empower participants with multiple and diverse perspectives. Stories, data and analysis also offer the opportunity to create vivid and clearer versions no just open for experts and academics but also more comprehensible for other social sectors, such as, policy makers, activists and social and cultural organizations.

After collecting information and stories both studies use a content analysis method, that includes the following steps: (a) transcription of material collected from audio and visual sources; (b) unitization, dividing textual material into units for further analysis; (c) categorization, in which categories relevant to the research questions were developed and revised through an iterative process of analysis; and (d) coding, in which the units were assigned to categories related to research questions (see Nastase, Koeszegi and Szpakowicz [39]). Finally, we weaved our own stories, giving visibility and importance to the main trends we found in our data. In the majority of the cases, we returned our versions and analysis to the people that participated in our research, and after that we adjusted our findings and conclusions with their feedback.

Historias de Migración, uses in-depth interviews as a technique designed to produce a vivid pictures of the participant's trajectories of migration, and to establish a human-to-human relation with the participants and the desire to understand rather than to explain [40]. The interviews are also the basis for the development of trajectories (short stories type) that provide both qualitative and quantitative information. For this particular endeavor we selected 28 stories, from more than 100 stories that we have collected with Colombian migrants. The 28 we selected represent migration stories of Colombians going to, or staying in, the United States.

Fotohistorias uses participatory photography and in-person interviews to elicit life experiences with a migrants in order to help surface the richness, diversity and depth of their roots, experiences and aspirations [3, 41]. The participatory photography process involves inviting participants to take pictures, them taking and/or bringing in their own photographs, and holding a conversational interview to talk about the pictures. In 2014–15 we conducted 39 interviews using Fotohistorias participatory photography and interviews in Seattle, WA (15), in Nogales, Mexico (8) and around Cali, Colombia (16). Interviews were transcribed, translated, and coded for emerging themes using qualitative analysis software.

4   Findings: Migration Stories, the Life "in-between"

In Historias de Migración and Fotohistorias, we find four main emerging themes related to information behaviors of migrants: (1) perceiving social networks of family and friends as the most important spaces and sources of information; (2) acknowledging transience and vulnerability of status; (3) viewing traditional media and interactive ICT portraying the images and models of progress; and (4) experiencing a deepened sense of 'in-betweenness' character of migration. In addition to the emerging themes, we note that the significant role of economic, cultural and information capitals in deciding the forms, destinations and results of migration.

4.1   Trustworthy Spaces and Sources of Information

Our two studies show that close social networks of family and friends are the most important spaces of communication and the sources of information that people used for making decisions to migrate and during their migration trajectories, especially when they were crossing national borders (legally and illegally). For instance, *Historias de Migración*, pointed out that the information and stories of relatives, friends, and loved ones are the primary sources in both processes to decide to migrate and the destinations to take. They are also the main bases to decide and to take the routes and forms of migration. The processes of adaptation and integration of new migrants in their destinations are mediated by their social networks. Issues such as achieving food and housing, finding work or study, or a school for the children, are definitive in the experiences of immigrants. Regular communication with family, friends and relatives in their hometowns are crucial for adaptation, integration and *co-construction*[2] of migrants. The use of ICT, especially mobile phones, text messages (like WhatsApp) and Skype are highlighted in the daily lives of migrants, which set well-defined routines communication and information with their original places.

4.2   Transience and Vulnerability

Fotohistorias found that at the border migrants prefer word of mouth information above any other source, in order to negotiate the extreme vulnerability of their transient existence. Word of mouth referrals come from family and friends, from other migrants, and from humanitarian service providers, and they are the preferred source to identify trustworthy guides and help in the border crossing. The information practices of migrants at the border are reminiscent of "life in the round" and other small-world information-poverty behaviors [42], but these behaviors are bound in time and place by the *transience and vulnerability* of the migrants' temporary lives at the border. Their information poverty can be life threatening, as they risk it all to cross the border; but their information poverty as "insiders" is only temporary, for they will soon be somewhere else, no longer at the border, and their friends of today will only be a memory of one of the most difficult moments in their journey of migration.

"You see all the latest news and see people who get a lot of money with simple jobs and sending remittances to their countries of origin, does influence the decision. But half the things they say are far from reality. People do not realize how hard it is to get what you have here, because we work so hard in the US, and many Latino immigrants undervalue their work." Migrant woman, 37 years old.

4.3   Images and Models of Progress

In the two studies, traditional media (press, radio and television) as well as more contemporary and interactive ICT (particularly Facebook, Instagram and Blogs), had a strong impact on the images and models of progress, freedom and wellbeing that migrants had before, during and after their migratory trajectories. Those images, which contrast the countries (origin and destination) poverty, security, equality and democracy,

---

[2] Fortunati, Pertierra and Vincent concept of co-construction assumes that each society is a dynamic system which meets and maybe clashes with other cultures, but in so doing enriches itself and consequently changes [9].

seem to be the main *engines* that stimulate, move and keep migrants looking for a better life. Particularly, *Historias de Migración*, portrays the articulation of national and international migration dynamics, especially when people express the main causes of their migration. In this sense, their stories show a mixture between the search of better living conditions (better jobs, better income, better professional development, and wellbeing) and the effects of the armed political conflict (more security and peacefulness). Local and transnational dynamics are triggered and maintained by building process of social networks, facilitated by ICT, that encourage and make more effective migration experiences of the group of Colombians of this study.

4.4   Deepening 'in-betweenness'

The two studies also confirm that communication and information practices supported by technologies have favored and deepened the 'in-betweenness' character of the whole dynamic of migration, which in words of [43] means that migrants are constantly negotiating cultural forms and identities at the crossroads of the nation-state and global diasporas. Accordingly, *Fotohistorias* show how migrants at the border experience the transience and vulnerability of their life in between "here" and "there". Migrants rarely fit the mold of the progressive stages, and undocumented migrants maybe least of all, given the sustained impermanence brought about by economic, social and political exclusion, and the constant fear of detention and deportation. (Undocumented) migrants tend to live in the in-between space of "moderately transient" to "moderately enduring" existence, where they have to balance their information practices between the careful seekers of information from trusted sources and the generous providers of information to others.

Meanwhile, *Historias de Migration* also show that United States is the preferred destination of transnational migrants from Colombia, but the US is also used as a transit place to go to Canada or some European countries, in their intent to conquest a better life. The communication and information practices through ICT (particularly Facebook, WhatsApp, Skype and Instagram), were considered as emotional and cultural supports that allow migrants to remain "connected" with their families, their neighborhoods and their countries, as well as with the socio-political situation of the nation and cultural traditions and practices of their hometowns, while enriching their daily lives elsewhere in the world. Moreover, ICT were understood as a definitive tool to link space, time, cycles and experiences between places of origin and those places where the people migrated. In this sense ICT support a *liminal*[3] experience of migration: this is a permanent transit and connection between different worlds.

"I do not feel only Colombian anymore; on the contrary I feel I belong to the world. Three years ago this would haven't been my answer, because I was not even thought of leaving the country." Migrant man, 43 years old.

---

[3] According to the Oxford English Dictionary, the word "liminal" comes from the Latin word limens, meaning literally, "threshold." In anthropology this term was traditionally used to describe ritual stages of transition. More recently, use of the term has broadened to describe political and cultural change as well [44]. Discussion: migration and information practices.

4.5 Role of Economic, Cultural and Information Capitals

Our studies also show that economic, cultural and information *capitals*[4] are decisive for the forms, destinations and results of migration. *Historias de Migración* show that Colombian migrants with higher capitals (middle-high class, professional and bilingual) are looking for settle in other countries or use their migration experience as a springboard to go to another country, mainly North America or Europe. Migrants with lower capitals tend to go to South American countries or they tend to move inside of the country. The younger, more educated and childless, they migrate in search of better education and better working conditions and practice to ensure them a good life, quiet, with good income and facilities to stay and enjoy the levels of development of countries, cities or regions they are staying. Previous access and use of ICT were essential for migrants in order to decide the places to go, the routes to take, the people to ask for supporting. Moreover, access and use to ICT were crucial during their trajectories, especially, to be connected with family and friends, as well as to communicate with national and international organizations that bring them support and protection. Meanwhile *Fotohistorias* show a relation between access and use of information and the integration and settlement of migrants. The information practices of migrants in Seattle reveal a clear progression between using cell phones to place and receive calls, and a growing use of smart phones, tablets and computers as tools for information, communication, and entertainment. The public library is frequently perceived as a gateway to a larger information universe, which complemented with English language lessons and other skills training, help to consolidate the information practices of the migrants as they settle and integrate, though they are rarely truly integrated given the generally irremediable exclusion of their undocumented status. And yet, their information practices help move them away from transience and toward endurance: from careful seekers of information by word of mouth, to savvy users of information from different sources, and to generous providers of information for others [46].

5 Discussion and Conclusions

Kymlicka [7] reminds us that categories of "immigrant" or "foreigner" are not brute facts, but are socially constructed, and these concepts reflect the forms societies and researchers define the "others". This author also points out that immigration and multiculturalism policies are confronting contemporary nations with a dilemma between solidarity and diversity. However, taking into account that immigrants are contributing with different forms of belonging, civic friendship, reciprocity and solidarity, he suggests the need to develop a form of multiculturalism that enables immigrants to express their culture and identity as modes of participating and contributing to the national societies. Boaventura de Sousa Santos [47] also recalls that modern societies had lived with the contradiction between the principles of emancipation, which continued pointing towards equality and social integration, and the

---

[4] We are using Bourdieu and Johnson, for whom capital is an actor's accumulation and uses of different forms of material and symbolic powers [45, p. 4].

principles of regulation, which went into effect the processes of inequality and exclusion produced by capitalist development. He also sustains that emancipatory politics and the development of new forms of citizenship are confronted within the tensions between equality and difference, that is, the need for redistribution and the demand for recognition.

In a similar vein Agamben [48], sustains that the dichotomy of being inside/outside the law constitutes the "state of exception": the legitimation of sovereign violence that reduces the other to a "bare life" with no political rights. Nonetheless, the work of the undocumented migrants reduced to "bare life" is a central component of the US economy, as they do work that others won't do, for less money, and in more dangerous or precarious conditions. This all helps to keep prices down and profits up. The work of the undocumented migrants "is essential to the functioning of the economy and to the comfort of citizens. The system is also, however, fundamentally unjust. By creating a necessarily subordinate workforce without legal status, we maintain a system of legalized inequality" [49, p. 14].

In our studies we focus on Latino migrants from South and Central America and Mexico, most of whom migrate to the US. Nonetheless, some head for Europe, and there is also in-region migration, as with Colombians going to Peru, Chile or Argentina and Central Americans going to Mexico, as well as in-country migration, especially internally displaced people given political and drug violence in Colombia and Honduras. Among these migrants we find there are (1) those who want to leave but can't, (2) those who can't stay and are forced to leave, and (3) those who stay and build a future for themselves and for others at home. At the same time, there are (4) those who long to return but can't, (5) those who can return but won't, and (6) those who are forced to return (deported), even if it is to a place where they no longer have any roots or ties. Six different experiences of migration, tumbling together like dice on a gambling table: where does society place its bets? Our combined studies shed some novel insight into these varied experiences of migration of Latinos in the US, and some of their related information practices.

Through two separate but convergent studies with migrants, we found a variety of information practices that change in relation the particular moment and motivations in the migration journey of each one (departing, staying or returning, willingly or unwillingly), and on their particular social, economic and legal situation. In all cases, the experience of migration involves a dynamic relation with their surroundings that invokes different information practices and uses of information technologies. There is no clear, linear progression between migration "stages" as suggested by Caidi et al. (2010) [6], but a complex and iterative web of interactions in the "liminal" space of migration where information is the glue that connects migrants to each other and to their original, transitional or new place of destination and belonging. As vulnerability and uncertainty increase, so does the reliance on word of mouth and interpersonal relations, but as the sense of safety and permanence increase, so does the use of broader and more diffuse networks, and of information technologies for self-expression and affirmation.

Both studies find that transnational migrant experiences are in a permanent cycle of transition and connection between different social, political and economic worlds. This implies a daily experience of different times, places and languages (codes), as well as differential, but connected cultural, institutional and technological rules and practices. The two studies also found similarities in the strong sense of vulnerability and strangeness legal and undocumented migrants experienced during their migratory journeys, and how technologies such as mobile phones or social media can have ambiguous uses and meanings. In some cases, they endanger the lives and freedom of migrants, while in other cases they offer the possibility of connection with family and friends as well as important forms of social expression and participation. Moreover, the combination of old and new communication and information technologies have a strong power in weaving and enabling the creation and consolidation of social memories and models that impact emotions, reasons and actions of many people who decide to move from their original territories.

The ICT in the hands of migrants are making viable their opportunities to express their own identities and their political, cultural and economic representations and practices. ICT are also providing them with material resources to be connected and informed faster as well as to share different times and spaces, both in their original and destination countries. Migrants, particularly undocumented migrants, represent a huge challenge as well as an enormous opportunity for new forms of nationhood, identity, justice and social inclusion. However, migrants, especially undocumented migrants, are the expression of deprivation of basic human rights for a whole group of society. By excluding them from legality, the state places undocumented migrants outside the boundaries of law, while selectively applying laws to systematically exclude them.

In such a context, this paper seeks to contribute to the small but growing body of work on information practices of undocumented migrants, and to contribute a small step to help them regain their full sense of humanity and bios, the qualified life that is the opposite of the bare life of homo sacer.

References

1. Savolainen, R.: Everyday Information Practices: A Social Phenomenological Perspective. Scarecrow Press, Lanham (2008)
2. Barón, L.F.: Imagination, networks and liminality: migration paths in the Latin American Pacific. In: Rouvinski, V. (ed.) Pacific Alliance. Palgrave MacMillan and Woodrow Wilson Center (2016)
3. Gomez, R., Vannini, S.: Fotohistorias: Participatory Photography and the Experience of Migration. CreateSpace, Charleston (2015)
4. The politics of anger. The Economist, 2 July 2016
5. Nail, T.: The Figure of the Migrant. Stanford University Press, Stanford (2015)
6. Caidi, N., Allard, D., Quirke, L.: Information practices of immigrants. Annu. Rev. Inf. Sci. Technol. 44(1), 491–531 (2010)
7. Kymlicka, W.: The three lives of multiculturalism. In: Guo, S., Wong, L. (eds.) Revisiting Multiculturalism in Canada, pp. 17–35. Springer, Heidelberg (2015)
8. Dekker, R., Engbersen, G.: How social media transform migrant networks and facilitate migration. Glob. Netw. 14(4), 401–418 (2014)

9. Fortunati, L., Pertierra, R., Vincent, J.: Migrations and diasporas: making their world elsewhere. In: Migration, Diaspora and Information Technology in Global Societies, pp. 1–20 (2012)
10. Jensen, B.: Service to day laborers: a job libraries have left undone. Ref. User Serv. Q. Ref. User Serv. Q. **41**, 228–233 (2002)
11. Fisher, K., Marcoux, E., Miller, L., Sanchez, A., Cunningham, E.R.: Information behavior of migrant Hispanic farm workers and their families in the Pacific Northwest. Inf. Res. **10** (2004)
12. Baron, L.F., Neils, M., Gomez, R.: Crossing new borders: computers, mobile phones, transportation and English language among Hispanic day laborers in Seattle. J. Am. Soc. Inf. Sci. Technol. JASIST **64**(5) (2013)
13. Newell, B., Gomez, R., Guajardo, V.: Information seeking, technology use, and vulnerability among migrants at the US-Mexico border. Inf. Soc. **32**(3), 176–191 (2016)
14. Gumpert, G., Drucker, S.J.: The Huddled Masses: Communication and Immigration. Hampton Press, Cresskill (1998)
15. Fairlie, R.: Academic achievement, technology and race: experimental evidence. Econ. Educ. Rev. **31**, 663–679 (2012)
16. Ono, H., Zavodny, M.: Immnigrants, English ability and the digital divide. Soc. Forces **86**(4), 1455–1479 (2008)
17. Landry, C.F., Kuglitsch, R.: La Casa Hogar–Bringing Families into the Community Digital Inclusion: Measuring the Impact of Information and Community Technology, pp. 43–52. Information Today Inc., Medford New Jersey (2009)
18. Garcia, O.P.M.: Gender digital divide: the role of mobile phones among Latina farm workers in Southeast Ohio. Gend. Technol. Dev. **15**(1), 53–74 (2011)
19. Burrell, J., Anderson, K.: 'I have great desires to look beyond my world': trajectories of information and communication technology use among Ghanaians living abroad. New Media Soc. **10**(2), 203–224 (2008)
20. Gonzalez, V.M., Castro, L.A., Rodríguez, M.D.: Technology and connections Mexican immigrants in the U.S. IEEE Technol. Soc. Mag. **28**(2), 42–48 (2009)
21. Panagakos, A.N., Horst, H.A.: Return to cyberia: technology and the social worlds of transnational migrants. Global Netw. **6**(2), 109–124 (2006)
22. Chib, A., Malik, S., Aricat, R.G., Kadir, S.Z.: Migrant mothering and mobile phones: negotiations of transnational identity. Mob. Media Commun. **2**(1), 73–93 (2014)
23. Hunter, A.: Empowering or impeding return migration? ICT, mobile phones, and older migrants' communications with home. Glob. Netw. **15**(4), 485–502 (2015)
24. Walker, R., Koh, L., Wollersheim, D., Liamputtong, P.: Social connectedness and mobile phone use among refugee women in Australia. Health Soc. Care Commun. **23**(3), 325–336 (2015)
25. Baron, L.F., Neils, M., Gomez, R.: Crossing new borders: computers, mobile phones, transportation and English language among Hispanic day laborers in Seattle. J. Am. Soc. Inf. Sci. Technol. JASIST **65**(1), 98–108 (2013)
26. Fisher, K., Marcoux, E., Miller, L.S., Sanchez, A., Cunningham, E.R.: Information behavior of migrant Hispanic farm workers and their families in the Pacific Northwest. Inf. Res. **10**(1) (2004)
27. Holmes, P., Janson, A.: Migrants' communication practices with ICTs: tools for facilitating migration and adaptation? Int. J. Technol. Knowl. Soc. (2008). http://ijt.cgpublisher.com/product/pub.42/prod.530
28. Srinivasan, R., Pyati, A.: Diasporic information environments: reframing immigrant-focused information research. J. Am. Soc. Inf. Sci. Technol. **58**(12), 1734–1744 (2007)

29. Benítez, J.L.: Salvadoran transnational families: ICT and communication practices in the network society. J. Ethn. Migr. Stud. **38**(9), 1439–1449 (2012)
30. Peile, C.G., Híjar, A.R.: Immigrants and mobile phone uses: Spanish-speaking young adults recently arrived in London. Mob. Media Commun. **4**(3), 405–423 (2016)
31. Costanza-Chock, S.: Digital popular communication: lessons on information and communication technologies for social change from the immigrant rights movement. Nat. Civic Rev. **100**(3), 29–35 (2011)
32. Ramirez, R.: Mobilization en Español: Spanish-language radio and the activation of political identities. In: Voss, K., Bloemraad, I. (eds.) Rallying for Immigrant Rights: The Fight for Inclusion in 21st Century America, pp. 63–81. University of California Press, Berkeley (2011)
33. Vårheim, A.: Gracious space: Library programming strategies towards immigrants as tools in the creation of social capital. Libr. Inf. Sci. Res. **33**(1), 12–18 (2011). Article No. 0266666915615645
34. Yong-Chan, K., Ball-Rokeach, S.: New immigrants, the internet, and civic society. In: Chadwick, A., Howard, P.N. (eds.) Routledge Handbook of Internet Politics. Routledge, London, London (2009)
35. Andrade, A.D., Doolin, B.: Information and communication technology and the social inclusion of refugees. MIS Q. **40**(2), 405–416 (2016)
36. Appadurai, A.: Modernity at Large: Cultural Dimensions of Globalization. University of Minnesota Press, Minneapolis (1996)
37. Baron, L.F.: The power of associations. social media and social movements: Facebook in the interactions of social movement organizations. Doctoral dissertation, University of Washington (2013)
38. Davis, J.E.: Stories of Change: Narrative and Social Movements. SUNY Press, Albany (2012)
39. Nastase, V., Koeszegi, S., Szpakowicz, S.: Content analysis through the machine learning mill. Group Decis. Negot. **16**(4), 335–346 (2007)
40. Spradley, J.P.: The Ethnographic Interview. Holt, Rinehart and Winston, New York (1979)
41. Yefimova, K., Neils, M., Newell, B.C., Gomez, R.: Fotohistorias: participatory photography as a methodology to elicit the life experiences of migrants. In: Proceedings of HICSS, Hawaii, vol. 48 (2015)
42. Chatman, E.A.: A theory of life in the round. J. Assoc. Inf. Sci. Technol. **50**(3), 207 (1999)
43. Srinivasan, R., Pyati, A.: Diasporic information environments: reframing immigrant-focused information research. J. Am. Soc. Inf. Sci. Technol. **58**(12), 1734–1744 (2007)
44. Thomassen, B.: Anthropology, multiple modernities and the axial age debate. Anthropol. Theor. **10**(4), 321–342 (2010)
45. Bourdieu, P., Johnson, R.: The Field of Cultural Production: Essays on Art and Literature. Columbia University Press, New York (1993)
46. Vannini, S., Gomez, R., Guajardo, V.: Security and activism: using participatory photography to elicit perceptions of information and authority among Hispanic migrants in the U.S. In: Proceedings of iConference 2016, Philadelphia, PA (2016)
47. de Sousa Santos, B.: Another Knowledge is Possible: Beyond Northern Epistemologies. Verso, London (2008)
48. Agamben, G.: Homo Sacer: Sovereign Power and Bare Life, 1st edn. Stanford University Press, Stanford (1998)
49. Chomsky, A.: Undocumented: How Immigration Became Illegal. Beacon Press, Boston (2014)

Critical Realism and ICT4D Research

Richard Heeks[1(✉)] and P.J. Wall[2]

[1] Centre for Development Informatics, University of Manchester, Manchester, UK
richard.heeks@manchester.ac.uk
[2] School of Computer Science, Trinity College Dublin, Dublin, Ireland
wallp2@tcd.ie

Abstract. There is little overt engagement with research paradigms in ICT4D research but what there is shows a dominance of positivism and interpretivism. In this paper we explore the value of a "third way" research paradigm: critical realism. We concisely review the main features of critical realism: its ontological realism combined with epistemological relativism; its iterative, pluralist and reflexive methodology; and its emancipatory values. Alongside the general value of explicit use of any research paradigm, we argue two particular types of value of critical realism for ICT4D research. First, generic values including exposure of context, a contingent causality that reflects real-world ICT4D experiences, legitimisation of different stakeholder views and reduction of research bias, and support for ICT4D's interventionist approach and its goal of delivering international development. Second, specific value in addressing current trends in ICT4D research: the growing search for causal links between "ICT" and "D", and the political and ethical turns in ICT4D that are spurring researchers to engage more with issues of power, rights and justice. We conclude that delivery of critical realism's utility will require the ICT4D research community to take actions that enable this emergent research paradigm to flourish.

Keywords: ICT4D · Critical realism · Philosophy · Methodology

1 Introduction

From the turn of the 21st century, there has been an ever-growing body of research and publication examining the role of information and communication technologies in socio-economic development (ICT4D).[1] Within this body of work, explicit consideration of research philosophy generally and of specific research paradigms is rare (Gomez and Day 2013). However, analysis has been undertaken to infer the paradigms being used which finds that interpretivist and positivist approaches dominate the current body of

---

[1] 299 publications during 2001–2005; 1,840 during 2006–2010; and 4,150 during 2011–2015 (Google Scholar: English language only; excluding patents and citations).

© IFIP International Federation for Information Processing 2017
Published by Springer International Publishing AG 2017. All Rights Reserved
J. Choudrie et al. (Eds.): ICT4D 2017, IFIP AICT 504, pp. 159–170, 2017.
DOI: 10.1007/978-3-319-59111-7_14

ICT4D research (Walsham and Sahay 2006, Gomez and Day 2013)[2]. Alongside generic concerns about the limitations imposed by this philosophical duopoly, each of these two paradigms individually has a number of limitations which constrain ICT4D (and other) research. Recognition of these limitations many years ago within social science overall resulted in a revisiting of the realist paradigm, and its development into a particular body of philosophical thought that has come to be known as "critical realism" (e.g. Bhaskar 1975, 1979). From these philosophical origins, critical realism has spread into use in a number of academic disciplines including one of ICT4D's main cognate disciplines, information systems (e.g. Mingers 2004a, b).[3]

Given the relative absence of explicit critical realism in ICT4D research, and the lack of discussion about research philosophy, we perceived a knowledge gap. In this paper our aim is therefore to explore the relevance of critical realism as a philosophical paradigm for ICT4D research. In Sect. 2 of the paper, we outline the main features of critical realism. We then compare these to features of ICT4D research looking for both the generic, enduring value of critical realism in ICT4D research, and also for specific fit with current trends in the field. After noting challenges of applying critical realism, we draw final conclusions and thoughts about possible actions.

2   The Features of Critical Realism

It is possible to trace a historical trajectory within social science that is dominated first by positivism which is then joined by interpretivism. Both paradigms have been subject to various criticisms (e.g. Kanellis and Papadopoulos 2009; Bevir and Rhodes 2005; Smith 2005). These criticisms of interpretivist and positivist approaches have led a number of scholars to search for a "third way" (Allen et al. 2013: 835). Critical realism has been put forward as one such, and in the following sections we will give a very brief overview based on the four main differentiators of research paradigms (Cresswell 2013):

- Ontology: what the paradigm understands to be the nature of reality.
- Epistemology: what the paradigm understands about how we construct and evaluate knowledge about that reality.
- Methodology: what research strategy, methods and techniques the paradigm uses in order to gather and analyse data.
- Axiology: what the paradigm does and does not value in research.

2.1   The Ontology of Critical Realism

Critical realism adopts a three-level "stratified ontology", as summarised in Fig. 1 (Mingers 2004a).

---

[2] With some sub-domain differences: e.g. IFIP WG9.4 conferences tend more towards interpretive work; ICTD conferences tend more towards positivist work (Gallivan and Tao 2013; Gomez and Day 2013).

[3] There is much less discussion of research philosophy in the other main cognate discipline – development studies –and little or no explicit discussion of critical realism.

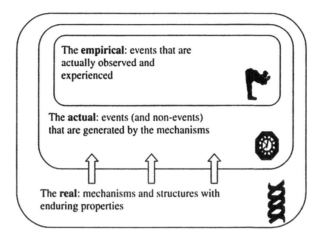

Fig. 1. Stratified ontology of critical realism

Within the domain of the real lie generative mechanisms: "causal structures that generate observable events" (Henfridsson and Bygstad 2013: 911). These mechanisms have an "intransitive" objective reality independent of human thought or belief: they are not merely social constructions. An example of an ICT4D-related mechanism would be an information infrastructure of technology and people in a country that attracts digital service providers, who create new services and thus attract more users, thereby strengthening the information infrastructure and creating a virtuous circle (Bygstad and Munkvold 2011).

Within the domain of the actual lie events: "specific happenings resulting from causal mechanisms being enacted in some social and physical structure within a particular... context" (Williams and Karahanna 2013: 939). An example of ICT4D-related events might be appointment of an ICT4D champion, formation of an ICT4D strategy group, or design of an ICT4D app. However, critical realism rejects linear notions of causality between mechanisms and events. It takes an open systems view of the world in which multiple mechanisms intersect, thus creating a "contingent causality" that is context-dependent (Smith 2010).

Social structures underlie and create the mechanisms within the domain of the real. There is therefore a danger that critical realism might be seen as structuralist: focusing on social structures as explanations and ignoring or downplaying the role of human agency. But this is inherently not so (Njihia and Merali 2013). One of the most explicit explanations has come from Archer (e.g. 1995) and the notion of morphogenesis; a cycle of three phases: "(a) the existing structure that shapes but does not determine actions that are about to take place; (b) social interaction, which in turn leads to; (c) structural elaboration that either changes ["morphogenesis"] or reproduces ["morphostasis"] the social structure" (Ram et al. 2014: 465). We can understand this as a rolling iteration between structure and agency; between the real and the actual.

2.2   The Epistemology of Critical Realism

Within the domain of the empirical lie human experiences and observations of the events generated within the actual. The underlying, intransitive structures and mechanisms of the real domain cannot therefore be directly experienced; hence they cannot be directly measured by research (Danermark et al. 2002). But, as Fig. 1 indicates, the empirical is contained within the actual and the real. Thus, any experience is shaped by the context of that experience: it is not objective but is contingent and transient. Different observers will give different accounts of events depending on, for example, their own historical experiences and their own position within social structures (Dobson 2001).

2.3   The Methodology of Critical Realism

Three methodological features of critical realism will be identified here: iterative retroduction, pluralism, and reflexivity. Retroduction – literally meaning leading backwards – is a "…mode of inference in which events are explained by postulating (and identifying) mechanisms which are capable of producing them…" (Sayer 1992: 107). It therefore means moving back across the domains from the empirical via the actual to the real, and represents the way by which the domains are connected within active research. Though potentially a one-time movement, in practice, retroduction is more generally understood as part of an iterative cycle in which mechanisms are postulated from existing data, evidenced or otherwise through gathering of new data, and supported or revised or rejected iteratively during the analysis of that data (Easton 2010).

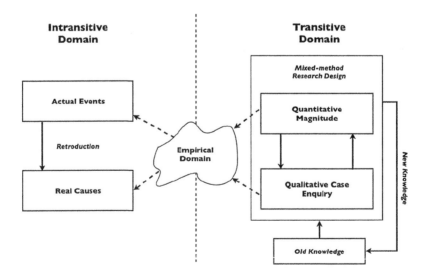

Fig. 2. Methodology of critical realism

Given the transitive relation between the empirical and the actual, critical realism requires pluralism of methods in order to improve the validity of insights into events (and, hence, into underlying mechanisms) (Downward and Mearman 2007). This is typically understood in terms of two types of triangulation. Data triangulation is most often operationalised by gathering data from different stakeholders, thus allowing for multiple perspectives and inter-subjective insights into the events of the actual. Method triangulation means critical realism is associated with mixed-methods research: combining qualitative and quantitative methods (Zachariadis et al. 2013: see Fig. 2).

Because the empirical is subject to the influence of context then data gathered will be value-laden. And this will also be true of the research process itself. Critical realism therefore asks of its researchers that they and their research participants be reflexive: "a dynamic process of interaction within and between ourselves and our participants, and the data that inform decisions, actions and interpretations at all stages of research" (Etherington 2004: 36). This process can also be retroductive: seeking to expose the underlying mechanisms that can explain the events of the research process.

2.4   The Axiology of Critical Realism

So far our explanation has been more realist than critical. The extent and nature of the critical within critical realism is debated (Klein 2004): for example, it could just mean critique of prior research paradigms. But there is a central thread within many writings on critical realism that associate it with critical theory (Bhaskar 1989). From this outlook, critical realism contrasts itself to positivism's notions of value-free research in two ways. Like interpretivism its epistemology recognises observation and research to be value-laden: shaped by experience and context. But additionally, it seeks research to be values-driven: specifically driven by the values of emancipation. This means recognising the way in which the social structures and mechanisms of the real domain can sometimes serve to generate events and processes that are oppressive and outcomes that are unequal. But beyond merely understanding the world, the critical of critical realism inspires changing the world through engagement with practice: "developing ways of working with practitioners to help them understand their situation, identify barriers and opportunities for change and implement solutions" (Ram et al. 2014: 465).

3   Critical Realism and ICT4D Research

In this section, we will look at the potential value that critical realism can bring to ICT4D research. We will also acknowledge some challenges.

3.1   Generic Value of Research Paradigms in ICT4D Research

We have previously noted that explicit consideration of research paradigms is rare in ICT4D publications. Is this a problem? There are certainly arguments, beyond use of any specific approach, about the general value of such consideration. Beyond the direct contribution to a particular ICT4D research project or publication, "explicit recognition of research philosophies can help researchers' self-development, their capacity to analyze the work of themselves and others, and the academic credibility of a research field" (Heeks and Bailur 2007: 252). There is also a current value to ICT4D as a research sub-discipline. If it is to achieve greater maturity and academic recognition then there will need to be greater attention to, and use of, research paradigms.

3.2 Ontological Value of Critical Realism in ICT4D Research

There is widespread agreement in ICT4D research on the importance of context; for instance, the way in which the outcome of ICT4D projects is influenced by the interests of stakeholder groups (Bailur 2006), by developmental goals (Prakash and De 2007), by local language and culture (Sinha and Hyma 2013), etc. Conversely, lack of engagement with context is a criticism of some ICT4D research and practice (Dodson et al. 2013, Turpin and Alexander 2013). Critical realism can help address these contextual issues: it requires an investigation of context because context is represented by the domain of the real. Other research paradigms can encompass context but only within critical realism is it an integral and required component (Ram et al. 2014). It forces that involvement with ICT4D context to focus on what is present – relations, systems, ideas, resources – rather than conceiving development contexts solely in terms of lack or absence (Njihia and Merali 2013).

We can identify two further values that the contextualist ontology of critical realism brings to the current state of ICT4D research. The first is its incorporation of causality. The open systems view taken by critical realism is one that does not provide for causal mechanisms that operate in the same way at all times and in all contexts; but it does develop an understanding of causality. As Njihia and Merali (2013: 866) explain, critical realism "should tell us with good reason why things are as they are now and where they could be heading, based on the causal tendencies of identified generative mechanisms". This is especially relevant in ICT4D today. The focus of ICT4D research has been shifting over time from issues of readiness and availability through adoption to development impact (Heeks 2014b). But the current interest in development impact has been hampered by lack of research that investigates or demonstrates a causal connection between technology and development (Andersson and Hatakka 2013). Critical realism helps engage with that causal connection.

The second timely value of critical realism is its relevance to what we might call the "political turn" in ICT4D. This has arisen to reflect the growing role of ICTs in politics in developing countries (e.g. Breuer and Welp 2014), the length and depth of diffusion of ICTs such that they are starting to impact structures of power in developing countries (Heeks 2016), and the greater salience of politics within international development and development studies (Hickey 2013). It is reflected in conference tracks and journal special issues dealing with political perspectives on ICT4D (Andrade and Urquhart 2012a; Heeks et al. 2016) and by calls for more political analysis in ICT4D research and practice (Andrade and Urquhart 2012b, Roberts 2015).

Critical realism, unlike other research paradigms, has particular features that facilitate political research. Political theory often conceives power in terms of underlying structures and mechanisms that shape but do not determine (e.g. Hearn 2012). This is, of course, precisely the ontological perspective of critical realism. It contrasts with the determinism of positivism (and its logical impossibility of denying the politics of research and observation while researching politics) and interpretivism's struggles to recognise social structure or the way in which power constitutes beliefs (Torgerson 1986; Bevir and Rhodes 2005). In addition, the critical aspect of critical realism means it has a central concern with the ways in which power structures society. Hence we find examples of explicitly critical realist research on issues of power and politics (e.g. Patomaki 2002).

3.3 Epistemological Value of Critical Realism in ICT4D Research

Critical realism's understanding of the empirical domain allows for different perceptions of common events within an ICT4D project. This legitimises an observed reality of such projects: that different individuals and groups will express different views (Chib et al. 2012); something which positivism at least can labour to encompass. Further, of course, through reference to the mechanisms of the real domain, critical realism allows for an explanation of why those differences occur. Alongside the methodological requirement for triangulation of multiple perspectives, critical realism therefore facilitates use of stakeholder theory in ICT4D research (and use of stakeholder analysis in ICT4D practice); something which has been advocated as a means to provide greater insights into the trajectories of ICT4D projects (Bailur 2006).

3.4 Methodological Value of Critical Realism in ICT4D Research

Concerns about lack of rigour in research can be found in every academic discipline. As already discussed, ICT4D research is seen to suffer from a lack of credible investigation into causality (May and Diga 2015), something which undermines internal research validity. Both positivism and critical realism address this but critical realism has an arguable additional value because its iterative retroduction forces ongoing contemplation and critique of the relation between causes and effects. And, as again noted, its contingent approach to causality provides a better reflection of the varied cause-effect patterns seen in ICT4D in practice.

There are also frequent concerns about bias in ICT4D research and the way in which it can undermine both reliability and validity. These include biases of case and respondent selection (Burrell and Toyama 2009), biases of the researchers themselves (Krauss 2012), and biases of individual research methods (Dearden 2013). Interpretivism seeks to address respondent and researcher bias by embracing them as integral to its worldview, but it struggles to deal with the other biases. By contrast, critical realism's methodological pluralism and triangulation force multiple viewpoints and data sources and methods to be incorporated. More generally, critical realism's mandated reflexivity forces ongoing introspection about the nature of the research process and its overall rigour including biases of context, respondents and researcher. In so-doing, it may be able to improve rigour and mitigate biases. Critical realism also forces reflection on the value of ICT4D research; something, again, that is a concern from those seeking to develop the field (*ibid.*, Krauss and Turpin 2013).

3.5 Axiological Value of Critical Realism in ICT4D Research

Some academic disciplines lend themselves to theorisation and abstraction. ICT4D is not such a field: from its very definition it is oriented to practice and it centres around ICT-based interventions in developing countries (Marathe et al. 2016). In a general way, critical realism's concern with engagement and change is supportive of practice-oriented disciplines.

But the role of ICT4D goes beyond the unspecific notion of practice. As the "4D" element directly indicates, it is seeking to achieve progressive social change; seeking to deliver specific development goals. While individual goals vary, foundational orientations of the Sustainable Development Goals are towards transformation: changing underlying systems of development; and towards inclusion: addressing both symptoms and causes of inequality (Heeks 2014a). The congruence of critical realism can therefore be argued given its fit with at least these main goals of development. As discussed above, critical realism is values-driven and orients not only towards understanding how structures and mechanisms constrain development, but also towards interventions that bring about emancipatory change. Dodson et al. (2013: 27) argue that the additional concerns of ICT4D, relating to both practice and change, create a problem: "the [ICT4D] research community is not unified on how to harmonize the difficult and sometimes competing goals of conducting experiments, producing social change, and studying the phenomena of ICT use in developing countries". Critical realism emerges as a basis for this harmonisation given that it encompasses research, practice, and developmental social change.

This is particularly timely because of its relevance to what we might call the "ethical turn" in ICT4D. This has been advanced by the growing use of Amartya Sen's work – with its focus on justice (Sen 2009) – within ICT4D, and by the growing interest in ethics and social justice within wider development (Oosterlaken 2015). It is reflected by literature on ethics in ICT4D research and practice (Traxler 2012; Mthoko and Pade-Khene 2013). The exact relation of critical realism to ethics and justice is debated (Norrie 2010). At a basic level, the emancipatory impulses of critical realism resonate with the ideas of ethics, and critical realism would thus be supportive of work on ICT4D and ethics. But at a deeper level, one might argue that the foundations of rights, ethics and justice in the ICT4D field lie within the structures of society: that these all derive from and are largely determined by social structures (Heeks and Renken 2016). If that argument is accepted, then critical realism becomes uniquely appropriate for work on ICT4D and ethics given its combined desire to both understand and progressively change the social structures that envelop ICT4D.

3.6 Challenges of Using Critical Realism in ICT4D Research

Critical realism faces challenges:

- Philosophical challenges: from a positivist perspective, critical realism is criticised due to its lack of objectivity; the limitations it places on the generalisation of findings; and the "provisional, fallible, incomplete, and extendable" nature of its explanations (Dobson 2009: 808). From an interpretive perspective, it is the realism of critical realism that is misguided.

- Practical challenges: critical realism has been criticised as hard to understand and "difficult, time-consuming and resource-intensive" to operationalise (Reed 2009: 436).

Well-supported ICT4D doctoral researchers may have the time and training to develop the knowledge and skills necessary to address these challenges, but for most ICT4D researchers, they will present important barriers.

These are issues facing any user of critical realism but we can also reflect on challenges specific to the ICT4D research domain: the lack of ICT4D academic culture and capabilities around critical realism means a lack of both drivers and enablers to greater use of critical realism. In practical terms, for example, there are few supervisors and reviewers who demand use of critical realism, and few supervisors and reviewers who are able to guide and comment on critical realism. This in turn perpetuates the lack of culture and capabilities. It will require express intervention, say of ICT4D journal editors, to encourage greater engagement with research paradigms; developing a more fertile ground for critical realism – among other paradigms – to flourish.

4   Conclusions

There is general value of direct engagement with any research paradigm in enhancing ICT4D researchers' analytical capacity and the overall credibility of themselves and our sub-discipline. But our specific interest was one particular paradigm – critical realism – and its potential value in ICT4D.

There is a generic ability of critical realism to address issues seen as concerns for ICT4D research. It engages with underlying structure: helping to expose causal mechanisms and, for example, facilitating use of theoretical frames that connect ICTs to development impact. It encompasses difference: reflecting the contingent and contextualised link between cause and effect seen in ICT4D practice, and legitimising the views of different stakeholders on ICT4D phenomena. It triangulates: reducing the bias of individual ICT4D respondents, researchers or methods. It asks for reflexivity: pressing the ICT4D researcher for deeper insights into their work. And it seeks progressive social change: supporting ICT4D's intervention-orientation and its goal of delivering international development.

We also identified particular value of critical realism to current trends in ICT4D research. It supports the recent and growing search for causality within ICT4D. It supports the "political turn" in ICT4D: exposing the structures and mechanisms of power that underpin application of ICTs in development contexts, but still allowing space for consideration of human agency. And it supports the "ethical turn" in ICT4D: seeking the outcome of a more just and equitable society, and necessitating investigation of the social structures that underpin rights, ethics and justice.

There are both general and domain-specific challenges to further use of critical realism within ICT4D research; not least the orientation of many ICT4D researchers towards alternative paradigms. But for those who share recognition of critical realism's value there can be a number of enabling actions. These could be critical realism-specific or relate more generally to research paradigms with specific incorporation of critical realism. Examples include: commissioning of special issues and conference tracks;

training and development activities for researchers such as workshops; and pressure from conference chairs, editors and reviewers for more explicit incorporation of research paradigms within the methodology sections of papers.

References

Allen, D.K., Brown, A., Karanasios, S., Norman, A.: How should technology-mediated organizational change be explained? MIS Q. **37**(3), 835–854 (2013)

Andersson, A., Hatakka, M.: What are we doing? In: Hayes, N., La Rovere, R.L. (eds.) Into the Future, IFIP WG9.4, Ocho Rios, Jamaica, pp. 282–300 (2013)

Andrade, A.D., Urquhart, C.: Special issue on the politics of ICT for development. Int. J. E-Politics **3**(3), i–iii (2012a)

Andrade, A.D., Urquhart, C.: Unveiling the modernity bias: a critical examination of the politics of ICT4D. Inf. Technol. Dev. **18**(4), 281–292 (2012b)

Archer, M.S.: Realist Social Theory. Cambridge University Press, Cambridge, UK (1995)

Bailur, S.: Using stakeholder theory to analyze telecenter projects. Inf. Technol. Int. Dev. **3**(3), 61–80 (2006)

Bevir, M., Rhodes, R.A.: Interpretation and its others. Aust. J. Polit. Sci. **40**(2), 169–187 (2005)

Bhaskar, R.: A Realist Theory of Science. Harvester Press, Brighton (1975)

Bhaskar, R.: The Possibility of Naturalism. Harvester Press, Brighton (1979)

Bhaskar, R.: Reclaiming Reality. Verso, London (1989)

Breuer, A., Welp, Y. (eds.): Digital Technologies for Democratic Governance in Latin America. Routledge, Abingdon (2014)

Burrell, J., Toyama, K.: What constitutes good ICTD research? Inf. Technol. Int. Dev. **5**(3), 82–94 (2009)

Bygstad, B., Munkvold, B.E.: In search of mechanisms, paper presented at ICIS2011, Shanghai, 4–7 December 2011

Chib, A., Ale, K., Lim., M.-A.: Multi-stakeholder perspectives influencing policy-research-practice. In: Chib, A., Harris, R. (eds.) Linking Research to Practice, pp. 95–106. IDRC, Ottawa (2012)

Cresswell, J.W.: Qualitative inquiry and research design. Sage Publications, Thousand Oaks (2013)

Danermark, B., Ekstrom, M., Jakobsen, L., Karlsson, J.C.: Explaining Society: Critical Realism in the Social Sciences. Routledge, London (2002)

Dearden, A.: See no evil? Ethics in an interventionist ICTD. Inf. Technol. Int. Dev. **9**(2), 1–17 (2013)

Dobson, P.J.: The philosophy of critical realism: an opportunity for information systems research. Inf. Syst. Front. **3**(2), 199–210 (2001)

Dobson, P.J.: Critical realism as an underlying philosophy for IS research. In: Khosrowpour, M. (ed.) Encyclopedia of Information Science and Technology, 2nd edn., pp. 805–810. IGI Global, Hershey (2009)

Dodson, L.L., Sterling, S., Bennett, J.K.: Considering failure: eight years of ITID research. Inf. Technol. Int. Dev. **9**(2), 19–34 (2013)

Downward, P., Mearman, A.: Retroduction as mixed-methods triangulation in economic research. Cambridge J. Econ. **31**(1), 77–99 (2007)

Easton, G.: Critical realism in case study research. Ind. Mark. Manag. **39**(1), 118–128 (2010)

Etherington, K.: Becoming a Reflexive Researcher. Jessica Kingsley, London (2004)

Gallivan, M., Tao, Y.: A scientometric analysis of research appearing in post-millennial IFIP 9.4 conferences. In: Hayes, N., La Rovere, R.L. (eds.) Into the Future, IFIP WG9.4, Ocho Rios, Jamaica, pp. 144–165 (2013)

Gomez, R., Day, S.A.: Research questions, paradigms and methods in ICT for development. In: Hayes, N., La Rovere, R.L. (eds.) Into the Future, IFIP WG9.4, Ocho Rios, Jamaica, pp. 301–317 (2013)

Hearn, J.: Theorizing Power. Palgrave Macmillan, Basingstoke (2012)

Heeks, R.: From the MDGs to the Post-2015 Agenda. IDPM Development Informatics Working Paper no. 56, University of Manchester, UK (2014a)

Heeks, R.: Future Priorities for Development Informatics Research from the Post-2015 Development Agenda. IDPM Development Informatics Working Paper no. 57, University of Manchester, UK (2014b)

Heeks, R.: Examining "Digital Development": the shape of things to come? GDI Development Informatics Working Paper no. 64, University of Manchester, UK (2016)

Heeks, R., Graham, M., Ramalingam, B.: "Power, Politics and Digital Development" track. UK Development Studies Association, Oxford, UK, pp. 12–14, September 2016

Heeks, R., Bailur, S.: Analyzing e-government research: perspectives, philosophies, theories, methods, and practice. Gov. Inf. Q. **24**(2), 243–265 (2007)

Heeks, R., Renken, J.: Data justice for development: what would it mean? Information Development, prepublished, 8 November 2016

Henfridsson, O., Bygstad, B.: The generative mechanisms of digital infrastructure evolution. MIS Q. **37**(3), 907–931 (2013)

Hickey, S.: Thinking about the Politics of Inclusive Development. ESID Working Paper no. 1, SEED, University of Manchester, UK (2013)

Kanellis, P., Papadopoulos, P.: Conducting information systems research: an epistemological journey. In: Cater-Steel, A., Al-Hakim, L. (eds.) Information Systems Research Methods, Epistemology, and Applications, pp. 1–34. Information Science Reference, Hershey (2009)

Klein, H.K.: Seeking the new and the critical in critical realism: déjà vu? Inf. Organ. **14**(2), 123–144 (2004)

Krauss, K.: Towards self-emancipation in ICT for development research. Afr. J. Inf. Syst. **4**(2), 1 (2012)

Krauss, K., Turpin, M.: The emancipation of the researcher as part of information and communication technology for development work in deep rural South Africa. Electron. J. Inf. Syst. Dev. Countries **59**(2), 1–21 (2013)

Marathe, M., Chandra, P., Kameswaran, V., Kano, T., Ahmed, S.I.: In search of missing pieces: a re-examination of trends in ICTD research. In: Wyche, S., Srinivasan, J. (eds.) Proceedings of the 8th International Conference on ICTD. ACM, New York (2016)

May, J., Diga, K.: Progress towards resolving the measurement link between ICT and poverty reduction. In: Chib, A., May, J., Barrantes, R. (eds.) Impact of Information Society Research in the Global South, pp. 83–104. Springer, Singapore (2015)

Mingers, J.: Re-establishing the real: critical realism and information systems. In: Mingers, J., Willcocks, L. (eds.) Social Theory and Philosophy for Information Systems, pp. 372–406. John Wiley, Chichester (2004a)

Mingers, J.: Realizing information systems: critical realism as an underpinning philosophy for information systems. Inf. Organ. **14**(2), 87–103 (2004b)

Mthoko, H.L., Pade-Khene, C.: Towards a theoretical framework on ethical practice in ICT4D programmes. Inf. Dev. **29**(1), 36–53 (2013)

Njihia, J.M., Merali, Y.: The broader context for ICT4D projects: a morphogenetic analysis. MIS Q. **37**(3), 881–905 (2013)

Norrie, A.: Dialectic and Difference. Routledge, Abingdon (2010)

Oosterlaken, I.: ICT4D and ethics. In: Mansell, R., Ang, P.H. (eds.) The International Encyclopedia of Digital Communication and Society, vol. 1, pp. 353–361. Wiley Blackwell, Chichester (2015)

Patomaki, H.: After International Relations. Routledge, London (2002)

Prakash, A., De, R.: Importance of development context in ICT4D projects. Inf. Technol. People **20**(3), 262–281 (2007)

Ram, M., Edwards, P., Jones, T., Kiselinchev, A., Muchenje, L.: Getting your hands dirty. Work Employ Soc. **29**(3), 462–478 (2014)

Reed, M.I.: Critical realism. In: Buchanan, D.A., Bryman, A. (eds.) The Sage Handbook of Organizational Research, pp. 430–448. Sage, London (2009)

Roberts, T.: Critical intent & practice in ICT4D. In: Nielsen, P. (ed.) Openness in ICT4D, pp. 622–633. Department of Informatics, University of Oslo, Norway (2015)

Sayer, A.: Method in Social Science, 2nd edn. Routledge, London (1992)

Sen, A.: The Idea of Justice. Penguin, London (2009)

Sinha, C., Hyma, R.: ICTs and social inclusion. In: Elder, L., Emdon, H., Fuchs, R., Petrazzini, B. (eds.) Connecting ICTs to Development, pp. 91–116. Anthem Press, London (2013)

Smith, M.L.: Reconsidering ICT for development research: critical realism, empowerment, and the limitations of current research. In: Bada, A.O., Okunoye, A. (eds.) Enhancing Human Resource Development through ICT, IFIP WG9.4, Abuja, Nigeria, pp. 30–40 (2005)

Smith, M.L.: Testable theory development for small-n studies. Int. J. Inf. Technol. Syst. Approach **3**(1), 41–56 (2010)

Torgerson, D.: Between knowledge and politics. Policy Sci. **19**(1), 33–59 (1986)

Traxler, J.: Ethics and ICTD research. In: Chib, A., Harris, R. (eds.) Linking Research to Practice, pp. 68–81. IDRC, Ottawa (2012)

Turpin, M., Alexander, T.: Desperately seeking systems thinking in ICT4D. In: Hayes, N., La Rovere, R.L. (eds.), Into the Future, IFIP WG9.4, Ocho Rios, Jamaica, pp. 166–178 (2013)

Walsham, G., Sahay, S.: Research on information systems in developing countries. Inf. Technol. Dev. **12**(1), 7–24 (2006)

Williams, C.K., Karahanna, E.: Causal explanation in the coordinating process. MIS Q. **37**(3), 933–964 (2013)

Zachariadis, M., Scott, S.V., Barrett, M.I.: Methodological implications of critical realism for mixed-methods research. MIS Q. **37**(3), 855–879 (2013)

A Spatial Perspective of Innovation and Development: Innovation Hubs in Zambia and the UK

Andrea Jiménez$^{(\boxtimes)}$ and Yingqin Zheng

Royal Holloway, University of London, Egham, UK
Andrea.JimenezCisneros.2011@live.rhul.ac.uk,
yingqin.zheng@rhul.ac.uk

Abstract. The rapid expansion of hundreds of innovation hubs across Africa and Europe raises compelling questions about the relevance of this dynamic sector for development. To address this, our paper presents findings of how the social and economic context of hubs influences its members' construction of concepts of community, collaboration and development. The paper argues that what counts as innovation is often constructed in Western discourse and projected onto African realities. Doreen Massey's theory of space-making is used as a lens to analyse how different hubs produce distinct forms of collaboration and innovation for development. The aim of this paper is to explore alternative narratives of innovation hubs through a spatial perspective with the aim of revealing a multiplicity of forms for these hubs. It draws on findings from two innovation hubs in London and Lusaka respectively, using the methodology of multiple case studies. This article thus contributes firstly to the so far very limited empirical data on innovation hubs, and second, strengthens the theoretical framings of innovation for development which have so far emanated from a Western- centric empirical evidence base.

Keywords: Innovation · Entrepreneurship · Development · ICT4D · Collaboration

1 Introduction

Over the last decade or so, innovation hubs have been spreading widely around the globe, but without the accompaniment of an official or institutional definition. In some cases, the "hub" label is used interchangeably with other names, such as innovation labs [1], incubators [2] and co-working spaces [3]. These hubs claim to encourage collaboration between its members and support serendipitous knowledge necessary for the stimulation and strengthening of businesses and projects. For some, innovation hubs build collaborative communities with entrepreneurial individuals at the centre [4].

Nonetheless, despite the conceptual clarity, there are common values that make hubs unique and different from other entrepreneurial organisations: hubs host a community of individuals that can collaborate to achieve innovations. This implies a flexible and dynamic type of organisation that can be taken up and adapted globally. In the Global North, hubs have been supported by government initiatives. In the Global

Published by Springer International Publishing AG 2017. All Rights Reserved
J. Choudrie et al. (Eds.): ICT4D 2017, IFIP AICT 504, pp. 171–181, 2017.
DOI: 10.1007/978-3-319-59111-7_15

South, hubs have also been supported by the government, but also by international organisations [5].

In the context of development, innovation labs and hubs have been framed as part of a digital and mobile boom in the African continent, "filling a gap in the community of academic and private sector players that technology innovation needs to spur economic growth" [6]. And even though the outcomes of innovation hubs are not clear yet, there are high expectations that these represent a model to promote entrepreneurship, innovation and economic growth [7]. This view is adopted from the experiences in economically advanced areas and is characteristic of the broader discourse of innovation for development. For the past 8 years, international organisations have been promoting an innovation for development agenda in Africa that is in response to a "[…] need for bold leadership by developing country leaders, including heads of state, supported by developed countries, to move subsistence agriculture to a knowledge-intensive sector" [8].

In 2015, we conducted fieldwork research of an innovation hub in Lusaka, Zambia. Around that same time, an innovation hub that was founded in London was looking to expand its franchise into the African continent. By the premise of being "globally connected, locally rooted", African hubs would have the same name and logo, be part of the same global network and apply the same business model. Members of the innovation hub in Lusaka applied to be part of the hub, attended workshops and seminars where they would learn all about the hub's strategy and how it could be applied in the Zambian context. After members conducted market research, this proved not to be a sustainable model for the Zambian context and the members did not continue with the process.

This seems to be an example of attempts to transfer Western models of innovation into the African context. Even though innovation hubs are championed for their flexible and hybrid nature that can fit and adapt to any context, some "[…] pursue a classic Silicon Valley type incubator model" [9]. In line with this, the already widespread label of "Silicon Savannah" is used to characterise the technology and innovation ecosystem in Kenya. This initiative has received significant support from the government and a number of development organisations. However, for some Kenyan entrepreneurs and technologists, the use of a label that stems from a pre-existing western model brings a lot of challenges. Jimmy Gitonga, a technology expert summarizes this view by saying that "words like Silicon Savannah—and you can see that not a lot of thought was put into the connotation, as if the perception of the American Silicon Valley had been taken wholesale and simply plastered onto an African scenario" [10, p. 18].

We argue that hubs have the potential to be mechanisms for development, but that there are multiple perspectives of development that are framing the way hubs work. Instead of considering that all hubs collaborate and host communities the same way, we perceive that these are shaped by local aspects and contexts. We propose a way in which this can be theorised, by applying a spatial perspective to see how a hub is embedded in its social economic context, and furthermore, is performed through various temporal-spatial configurations. The aim of this paper is employ a spatial perspective to explore how innovation hubs have a multiplicity of forms and interactions.

In light of this, in this paper we ask "How are innovation hubs constructed by spatial relations and practices?" and "How does understanding Tech Hubs as multiple spaces shed light on development discourses, policy and practice?"

The paper presents two innovation hubs in London and Lusaka respectively, using the methodology of multiple case study. Theoretically, we draw upon Doreen Massey's conceptualisation of space which focuses on the multiplicity of different time-spaces and the co-existing heterogeneity of narratives [11, 12]. In the rest of the paper, we start by presenting aspects of Massey's conceptualisation of space. These ideas will be incorporated in the analysis of the two case studies.

2   Space and Development

Throughout the years, various theories of development have been used to frame the impact of technology and innovation. The 1950's, for instance, were characterised by the theory of modernization, from which development was equated with growth and was considered the result of imitation and adaptation of strategies and ideologies rooted in developed countries. The less "powerful" countries were encouraged to mimic these "modernity" strategies of more "powerful" countries, and as such, these were seen as if they were situated in a different time and space but moving along the same trajectory. "Developing" countries are expected to reach the same destination of so-called "developed" countries.

Then dependency theory highlights the issue in this model that economic and political power are heavily concentrated and centralised in the industrialised countries, creating a dependence of poorer countries on the advanced economies for domestic accumulation and economic growth. Such a dependency dominates the path of development and presents only one direction for progression [13]. Therefore, development is seen as a single path for all countries and the difference between rich and poor countries is only temporal.

The Human Development Approach offers a different perspective. Based on a multidimensional view of development as the expansion of freedoms that people value, Amartya Sen's capability approach steps away from the limited view grounded on economic growth [14]. By understanding development from the capability approach lenses it criticises the "developed-developing countries" dichotomy. Even though this still may be considered for some a mainstream terminology, we understand that there are several dimensions by which the so-called "developed" countries are still in the process of developing.

Similarly, Massey's notion of space and place, which draws upon various streams of discourses in human geography provides a theoretical perspective of development that departs from the linear trajectory model to emphasise multiplicity, heterogeneity and coexistence of differences [11, 12].

Space is first of all the product of interrelations, namely, space does not exist before identities/entities; rather it stresses upon the relational construction of things [12]. For example, a university building is only a university when students, teachers, books, departments are in it, relating, discussing and studying. Space consists of not just physical dimensions, but aspects of the social, cultural, political and economic life of space (and the enacting of space) need to be studied as well [15].

Massey [12] writes about a "global sense of place" to address issues of development and inequality in the world. She refers to the "time-space compression" as the possibility of movement and communication across space, the flows and interconnections and our experience of all this. For Massey, the economic forces that concentrate most of the power construct what is understood to be good or desirable, creating hegemonic stories that seem to be the norm. The possibility to create these hegemonic narratives is not something that is available to all and thus is structurally differentiated. This reveals issues of inequality – some having the power and freedom to benefit from all the potentials of a "globalized economy" and some not – and contains an inherent view of development as modernisation.

Thus Massey argues that spatial distribution is not of autonomous existence, and is actually produced and reproduced in response to political issues. Massey's spatial perspective thus recognises "the existence in the lived world of a simultaneous multiplicity of spaces: cross-cutting, intersecting, aligning with one another, or existing in relations of paradox or antagonism" [15, p. 3]. Multiple interpretations of reality, narratives and discourses are not only possible but are necessary if different realities coexist in the same world. This spatial perspective allows us to understand the broader context in which a hub is embedded, the implications of this for development, as well as the ways in which forms of social differentiation influence practices of collaboration and community within the hub [14]. Hubs are shaped by structural and contextual dimensions and are not just "containers in which other entities or processes happen" [16].

3 Methodology

Our research questions are: "How are innovation hubs constructed by spatial relations and practices?" and "How does understanding Tech Hubs as multiple spaces shed lights on development discourses, policy and practice?"

This research draws from a study that explored two innovation hubs, selected as multiple case study approach [17]. Given that we want to see the framing of innovation and the impact of context in the day-to-day practices and dynamics, we selected two innovation hubs located in two very different contexts of the Global North and the Global South. Even though this is not a comparative study, we sought to what extent context shaped practices and how. The selection of these particular hubs is due to their similarities in relation to how they self-define and their objectives. Both hubs have "collaboration" and "community" as their core values. As such we wanted to see how these practices looked in situ.

Empirical data was gathered based on participant observation and semi-structured interviews [18, 19] between 2014 to 2016. Throughout the observations, detailed descriptions of visits to the hub were registered, in particular regarding member's use of the space and forms of interaction. Observation was conducted every day for a period of six months in one setting, and four months at two different times in the other setting. 30 semi-structured interviews were conducted with members and the management team. This provided us with a better understanding of the organisation's own framing, as well as members' perception of the hub.

Participant observation was used to cross-reference, provide some triangulation and to understand the context and observe people's behaviour within the space. A research diary was kept to clarify the topics and identify new ones. This allowed the researcher to see what people perceived and said about the space and its impact, and also observe interactions and dynamics within the space that allowed the construction of a more complete analysis. Of special interest was to be able to describe what happened inside a hub on a daily basis, what were the common dynamics and practices observed and how these compared with participant responses during the interviews. So, for example, if members were seen working together on specific projects, the researcher would follow up to see how frequently this occurred, between who and for what purposes.

Interviews were transcribed verbatim [20], transcripts were read several times and notes were taken on emerging topics. The research diaries had data from participant observation, as well as thoughts that were appearing in relation to the findings and potential streams to interpret them. Two research diaries were reviewed and digitally transcribed. Some quotations from the interview transcripts were selected to help illustrate the emerging themes. In the following case analysis, names have been changed to pseudonyms to protect participants' identities.

4   London Innovation Hub

This London Innovation Hub is one of many in London, and was founded in 2005. As of today, it has transformed into a franchise, with over 80 hubs with over 13,000 members worldwide, with headquarters in Vienna. The idea of this hub emerged in the wake of the anti-globalisation movement that arose at the turn of the millennium [21]. It looked to create a space for people with alternative models for systems change.

For Massey [12], London is located at the epicentre of the global power structure, a capital of neoliberal governance, as a centre of global appropriation, and as "a crucial node in the production of an increasingly unequal world" [22, p. 8]. In fact, the world often looks at London, and what happens in London, as the model.

In London, social entrepreneurship has been expanding rapidly in the past decade because it has been largely supported by the state [23]. This has important implications in the practice as there are formal support systems (i.e. reports, grants, discourses) that support this particular kind of entrepreneurship. An example of this form of support is the UK Conservative Party's "Big Society not Big Government Policy", launched in 2010. Furthermore, social entrepreneurship in the UK is inherently linked to revenue generating. This combination - "promoting the social" and "being a successful business" - requires for strong efforts, organisation and structure.

The main objective of this hub is to create local collaborative communities that are bringing about social change. It constitutes a cross between an "incubator, a learning lab and a professional membership community" [27, p. 23]. The hub places strong emphasis on hosting a "collaborative community" of individuals who want to work on social enterprises. Their website claims that they "are part of a global network of connected communities that enable collaborative ventures [...] Each community is a wealth of innovative programs, events, and cutting-edge content. [...]". Thus both the organisation's structure and the physical space have been designed with these values in mind. For example, the workspace contains open space areas, with leaf-shape tables, high ceilings, glass doors, relaxed social areas and an open kitchen, and designated meeting rooms for hire.

Interestingly, interviews revealed mixed findings with regards to aspects of "community" and "collaboration". Although some participants mentioned the importance of being part of the hub community and enjoying the "collaborative ethos", the majority of our respondents did not consider themselves part of a community, nor have they collaborated with anyone from the hub. This was an interesting finding, considering that some of these respondents used the space on a daily basis, and some for a significant period of time (e.g. two years). What resulted as more valuable for them were the aesthetics of the place and location, because clients got a sense of professionalism, portraying a positive image for members.

Our observation also confirmed that very little collaboration was happening at the hub. Even though there were a series of social events organised, there were very few instances where members were working together, or decided to partner with other members to advance their own projects. Furthermore, what was most visible on a day-to-day basis was that members spent most of their time working alone, on their laptops, wearing headphones.

With regard to aspects of "community" and "collaboration", one member said: "For shared workspace I think it's a great place. Apart from the intention of trying to get people to collaborate which I don't think it happens that much .... We haven't really become part of the network (Henry, 32)."

When asked why collaboration was not perceived as a valuable practice, some mentioned their nature of their work, the stage their business of project was at and a perceived lack of privacy members found at the hub. With regards to privacy, one respondent said: "So I think of the main problems is there's no private space, no room where people can just go into and have private chats. If you want to chat with a bunch of people, you have to do it out in the open (Pat, 28)."

5   Lusaka Innovation Hub

The Zambian innovation hub was founded in 2011 and is the only hub of its nature in the country. It started by a group of 3 male computer scientists who were concerned with the lack of knowledge that computer science students had after finishing their studies. It began as an informal group of young people wanting to improve their skills and learn coding languages. Soon, their community got bigger and with that, they had to move from a small room within an NGO to their own space. With this change, they also adapted their organisation model to include organisational values and a vision strategy. This led to changing the hub from just a community of technologists and programmers to including entrepreneurs. The hub is now a space for entrepreneurs and innovators to connect, collaborate and work on their projects to turn them into viable business models [24].

The hub presents itself as an organisation that fosters a "community" and holds values of "collaboration". On their website, the hub establishes itself "a social enterprise that contributes to local social and economic development." Furthermore, the objectives of the hub are to "aid creatives and technologists by enhancing skills, strengthening networks, increasing collaboration, providing a forum for ideas exchange and reducing the barriers to entrepreneurship."

Social entrepreneurship in Zambia has not received much attention from academia, and there is limited support for social entrepreneurs from the government. Characterised by a long history of precolonial, colonial and then democratic governance, Zambia is currently conceived as a developing, emerging market. Zambia's main forms of economic activity are mining, pastoralism and agriculture. These sectors continue to be the main attraction for foreign and local investment.

Despite these macro indicators, some studies have indicated great potential for entrepreneurship in the country. Frese [25] presented relatively high levels of entrepreneurship and innovation in Zambian entrepreneurs. The study suggests there is great potential for entrepreneurship in Zambia, yet there is lack a supportive structure and an organised market.

This is visible in the Zambian context, in particular with regards to their technology and entrepreneurship ecosystem. An InfoDev report states that there is great potential in Zambia towards high-growth entrepreneurship, particularly in technology [26]. The technology community, even though relatively emerging, is mainly characterised by business associations, international organisations and one technology and innovation hub. Most of these are supported mainly by government and donor-funded entities. At the time of the research, the government did not have any particular strategy to promote social entrepreneurship nationwide.

Overall, the relatively limited information we have on social entrepreneurship in Zambia leads us to consider the somewhat unstructured settings in which entrepreneurs are embedded, yet with a strong sense of "collectiveness". Given this, it is not surprising to see that much of the work entrepreneurs do is part of an experimentation process, rather than fitting into existing patterns supported by policies. Therefore, they mostly have to rely on "learning by doing together".

In the interviews, managers described the hub as a very flexible organisation structure; they started very small and eventually started growing but without a clear, formal plan. They decided to have a strategy of "experimentation", which meant that every year or so they would reassess their plan and change if needed. It was never in their plans to scale up to a big organisation, but to continue supporting their members in the best way possible.

The hub organisation is relatively unstructured. For instance, a group of members were interested in fashion, and felt that the fashion industry in Zambia had great potential but lacked a platform to expand it. The hub then took the initiative and organised a fashion event, inviting all relevant actors and organisations as well as young people interested in fashion. This inclusion of a range of sectors and event types was possible due to the hub's open-ended philosophy and their willingness to experiment with different issues and member proposals.

During our fieldwork we observed that the flow of movement and fluid enactment of the space was very common. One day, a group of members who work on robotics (Rasberry Pi, OLPC) gathered one day and placed all their devices on the floor, they moved the chairs and tables to the sides and started working in the middle of the room. When other members arrived, they grabbed tables and chairs and sat in the other rooms, or in the corridors. On warm days, members were observed bringing their individual desks and chairs onto the balcony and sitting there. At other times they would work to loud music. A respondent described the dynamics of the hub:

"When I see people going into these places [co-working places], I don't know why they bother doing it because they're just wearing headphones the whole time. There's just silence, is like a library. Whereas here is like is different, there are no barriers. Is very personal. You walk in and you're popping your head and saying hi to a bunch of people. Whereas in a co-working space you don't know all the people. They talk about the benefits of collaboration and all that stuff [in other co-working spaces], but I don't see that happening" (Mickey 29).

Practices of collaboration were also observed on several occasions, where we would find members brainstorming to help an individual develop further ideas for a website she was trying to develop. She would invite anyone who wanted to participate and they would work on one computer and add ideas regarding colour, form and text. Moreover, through the same process members were able to help clarify wider business objectives through questions regarding target audience and objectives of the website, which she did not previously have clear.

The expectation of a space provided for entrepreneurs is that revenue is considered as an important aspect for successful business model. Instead, what we found at the Zambia hub is a different narrative of doing business where the starting point is focusing on the community.

When asked how collaboration was enabled within the hub, an interviewee responded: "I think that's part of the culture they've created here and I think that's because of the motive and what you are doing. These guys started it because they wanted a community. They didn't start it because they thought it was a good sell model that would make lots of money. They never thought about money. They just thought about supporting the community, that was it (Vincent, 32)."

6   Analysis

Massey's conceptualization of space offers us the possibility to understand the multiplicity of trajectories, merging through global narratives of entrepreneurship and innovation combined with local sense-making of entrepreneurs from London and Lusaka respectively. Our study presents two innovation hubs located in two different contexts, both promoting core values of collaboration and community. The practices of both hubs arise from their own social meaning, rules regarding use and its physical properties.

6.1   Embeddedness of Hubs in Institutional Contexts

Our findings show how institutional support systems shape spatial relations and practices of both hubs. In the UK, there is a well-developed policy discourse that is actively supported by institutions of government and civil society. There is a policy framework, university support, voluntary sector funders, venture capital and a media and political narrative to frame the work of innovation hubs. Consequently, organisations supporting entrepreneurial work (like hubs) are legitimised, and thus, find structures that they can fit into to do their work.

Despite the strong institutional support, our findings show that there is little sense of community and collaboration and that the hub is mostly valued by the design of the space, the resources it provides and its effect in building positive relations with clients or potential clients. In this sense, even though the hub proposes values of collaboration and community, the wider institutional context has an impact in the way these take place.

The innovation hub in Zambia received very little support from the formal ecosystem. This hub is embedded in an unclear environment for social entrepreneurs, with little or no support for the work that they do. In this sense, member's dynamics at this hub were shaped by trial and experimentation. Despite constraints of a relatively structured and ordered physical space, people to act in a collaborative way and use of the space in a much more fluid way, demonstrating little structure and control in the day-to-day practices. In other words, the way the hub's space is enacted in ways that are strongly driven the values of community and collaboration, and also reflecting a lack of formalisation of institutions and practices of entrepreneurship.

Therefore innovation hubs need to be understood as constituted by local practices and conditioned by structural and institutional arrangements. Government bodies and international organisations seeking to promote innovation hubs should pay closer attention to the existing institutional support in the specific environment in which a hub is embedded.

6.2   Coexisting Narratives of Hubs

As mentioned previously, given the current lack of understanding of what hubs are and what they do, hub managers and enthusiasts may inevitably choose to identify one successful model and seek to replicate it. Here we see the power-geometry that shapes not only the way hubs are perceived, but how members of innovation hubs perceive their own work.

As mentioned previously, the success of the London innovation hub leads to its attempt to expand its franchise to other parts of the world, including some African countries. The London hub is not looking to be replicated in exactly the same way in Africa as it does transform and adapt according to contextual needs. It is still too soon to see whether this project proves successful, but the notion of diffusing a "successful" model to the global south echoes the "diffusion of innovation" theory with similar assumptions made about technology transfer in the 20th century that has often been found futile and inappropriate. Moreover, a fee is charged to use the hub's logo and model to generate revenue for the Global North which reinforces the hegemony of development models.

Conceptual frames are never neutral abstractions - they are deeply embedded in social and political structures. For authors like Rodgers [27], embracing the notion of multiplicity implies that there should not be a priory assignment of statuses and authorities, nor privileging certain stories over others. Through this, we can imagine a fuller recognition of the simultaneous coexistence of others, with their own trajectories and narratives, and thus understandings of the world.

Our empirical evidence reflects how the Zambian hub faces significant challenges and yet they are more successful at achieving an ethos of collaboration and community that the UK case. Perhaps it is because of the lack of support system that they rely on these components, but it becomes relevant to register this not in the hopes that the Zambian case will eventually one day achieve the same level of the UK case. Instead it speaks of the contemporaneous heterogeneity of the world [12]. The hub in Zambia, as located in the Global South would benefit from finding ways to increase resources without losing those components. Massey illustrates this when she explains that "we want them always to recognise that what is said about Samarkand may not apply to, say, New York" [21, p. 139].

Consequently, the more attention that hubs receive from governments and development organisations for their potential to development, the more risk there is of trying to fit into the model of innovation hubs under advanced economies in the West. This can have some implications in the narratives and identities of the entrepreneurs, and can impact the work they carry out. Instead of letting them be "local", there may be a risk of wanting to be "global" and fit into existing Western models of innovation, contributing to a phenomenon of reinforcing geographical uneven development. Furthermore, this process may lead to the failure of innovation hubs in the South, if measured by the standards set by advanced economies, as they are embedded in different contexts, with different resources and support systems.

7   Conclusion

Innovation hubs, as mechanisms for development, can hold underlying views of what development means. Mainstream development thinking and policy often promote the imitation and adaptation of strategies and ideologies of the Global North, which often result in a dependence of poorer countries on the advanced economies for domestic accumulation and economic growth. The global discourse around entrepreneurship and innovation has triggered the innovation hub phenomenon, which are spaces constructed in particular local contexts. It is thus possible to frame the innovation hubs as heterogeneous spaces of "global" processes and flows [28] interacting with local narratives and grounded practices.

What is considered "best practices" often stems from the perspective of those who hold the power, thus stifling alternative narratives of development. It is thus important to recognise the power hierarchy in global development and its effects, and embrace development as multiple co-existing narratives, including those coming from places that have been historically understood as less developed. In this respect, local governments and international organisations should seek to understand and evaluate the multiple narratives and practices of innovation embedded in different social institutional conditions on their own merits.

References

1. Schmidt, S., Erkner, V.B., Brinkhoff, S.: Innovation and creativity labs in Berlin. Zeitschrift Fur Wirtschaftsgeographie **58**(4), 232–247 (2015)
2. Nicolopoulou, K., Karatas-Ozkan, M., Vas, C., Nouman, M.: An incubation perspective on social innovation: the London Hub – a social incubator, pp. 1–24. R&D Management (2015)

3. Parrino, L.: Coworking: assessing the role of proximity in knowledge exchange. Knowl. Manage. Res. Pract. **13**(3), 261–271 (2015)
4. Toivonen, T., Friederici, N.: Time to define what a "hub" really is. Stanford Soc. Innov. Rev., 1–37 (2015)
5. InfoDev: The Business Models of mLabs and mHubs - An Evaluation of InfoDev's Mobile Innovation Support Pilots, Washington, D.C. (2014)
6. GIZ: Technology Hubs: Creating Space for Change: Africa's Technology Innovation Hubs. Deutsche-Gesellschaftfür Internationale Zusammenarbeit, Bonn, Germany (2013)
7. Jimenez, A., Zheng Y.: Tech hubs, innovation and development. Inf. Technol. Dev. (2013, forth-coming)
8. Gault, F.: The role of innovation in the area of development. In: Kraemer-Mbula, E., Wamae, W. (eds.) Innovation and the Development Agenda. OECD Publishing, Paris (2010)
9. Kelly, T., Firestone, R.: How Tech Hubs are helping to Drive Economic Growth in Africa. World Development Report 2016 Digital Dividends. World Bank (2016)
10. Gitonga, J.: The past, present, and future of the 'Digital Nyika': how to fix an aircraft in flight. In: Ndemo, B., Weiss, T. (eds.) Digital Kenya: An Entrepreneurial Revolution in the Making, pp. 13–23. Palgrave Macmillan, London (2017)
11. Massey, D.: Space, Place and Gender. (U. of M. Press, Ed.). Polity Press in association with Blackwell Publishers (1994)
12. Massey, D.: For Space. SAGE Publications Inc., London (2005)
13. Makki, F.: Reframing development theory: the significance of the idea of uneven and combined development. TheorSoc **44**, 471–497 (2015)
14. Sen, A.: Common Knowledge. In: Development as Freedom, vol. 9. Oxford University Press, Oxford (1999)
15. Bondi, L.: Troubling space, making space, doing space. Group Anal. **38**(1), 137–149 (2005)
16. Massey, D.: Understanding cities. City **4**(1), 135–144 (2000)
17. Yin, R.: Case study research: design and methods. Appl. Soc. Res. Meth. Ser. **5**(3), 1–17 (2004)
18. Becker, H.S., Geer, B.: Participant observation and interviewing: a comparison. Hum. Organ. **16**, 28–32 (1957)
19. Guest, G., Namey, E.E., Mitchell, M.L.L.: Collecting Qualitative Data: A Field Manual for Applied Research. Sage Publications, Thousand Oaks (2013)
20. Miles, M.B., Huberman, A.M.: Qualitative Data Analysis, 2nd edn. Sage Publications, Thousand Oaks (1994)
21. Bachmann, M.: . Case study: how the hub found its centre. Stanford Soc. Innov. Rev. (2014)
22. Massey, D.: World City. Polity Press, London (2007)
23. Grimes, M.: Strategic sensemaking within funding relationships: the effects of performance measurement on organizational identity in the social sector. Entrepreneurship Theor. Pract. **34**(4), 763–783 (2010)
24. Gathege, D., Moraa, H.: ICT Hubs model: Understanding Factors that make up Bongo Hive, Lusaka Zambia (2013)
25. Frese, M.: Success and Failure of Microbusiness Owners in Africa: A Psychological Approach. Greenwood Publishers, Westport (2000)
26. InfoDev: Enhancing Access to Finance: for Technology Entrepreneurs in Southern Africa, Washington, D.C. (2014)
27. Rodgers, J.: Doreen Massey. Inf. Commun. Soc. **7**(2), 273–291 (2004)
28. Massey, D.: A global sense of place. Marxism Today **35**, 315–323 (1991)

Methodological Approach for Identifying Mechanisms in ICT4D: A Critical Realism Perspective

Hans Olav Omland$^{(\boxtimes)}$ and Devinder Thapa

Department of Information Systems, University of Agder, Kristiansand, Norway
{Hans.O.Omland,Devinder.Thapa}@uia.no

Abstract. The ontological questions 'What is ICT?' and 'What is development?' are described and documented in literature. Similarly, methodological approaches for understanding how ICT leads to development or for measuring the impact of ICT are described. However, explaining 'why' ICT works or not in the contexts of developing countries needs further investigation. We propose a critical realism based methodological approach for answering the above mentioned 'why'-question. The core of a critical realism based approach is to identify the underlying mechanism(s) that may explain a phenomenon of why ICT leads to development. We demonstrate the proposed methodology through applying it on a case in an ICT4D context from Nepal.

Keywords: ICT4D · Development · Critical realism · Methodology · Mechanisms

1 Introduction

Over the years development has been viewed from different perspectives [1] depending on class, culture, historic context, politics, relationship to power and technology [1]. Along with changing perspectives on development the understanding of the role of technology in development has changed [1]. In their literature review Thapa and Sæbø [2] identified six research gaps for understanding the link between ICT and D [2, p. 11]. Most of the research gaps relate to a lack of understanding the link while some also relate to scope and context. However, no identifications or suggestions of research gaps was found for explaining why deploying ICT leads to development.

Scholars in ICT4D advocate for human oriented approach [4–6], particularly Sen's [3] idea of capability approach (CA) [7, 8]. According to Sen [3] development should be seen as the freedom for people to live the lives that they value and have a reason to value. Sen [3] argues that poverty should be viewed as capability deprivation, not only as an economic factor. This is an encouraging trend, since Sen's CA is seen as a suitable and appropriate lens for investigating how ICT may foster development [9]. However, a major challenge remains on explaining why development happens when pairing ICT and CA [10].

Information and communication technology is developed in an accelerating speed and has come to be regarded as more than a just tool. Through a more holistic

© IFIP International Federation for Information Processing 2017
Published by Springer International Publishing AG 2017. All Rights Reserved
J. Choudrie et al. (Eds.): ICT4D 2017, IFIP AICT 504, pp. 182–193, 2017.
DOI: 10.1007/978-3-319-59111-7_16

understanding of ICT, it can act as an enabler of capability enhancement [6]. Especially the emergence of Internet allowed "the small and new to compete on equal terms with the large and the well-established, and permit leapfrogging to an 'information economy'" [11]. With their "Desperately seeking 'IT' in IT Research" Orlikowski and Iacono [12] opened new strands of research on IT artifact that has benefitted many researchers in their quest for understanding IT artifacts. Using the conceptualization of IT suggested by Orlikowski and Iacono [12], Sein and Harindranath [6] focused on understanding the role of ICT in national development. They conceptualized ICT artifacts from five different views described as follows:

In the Nominal view of ICT, ICT is not distinguished from any other objects of study. In the Tools view ICT is conceptualized as a technical entity as means to achieve some objective like substitute ICT for manual labor to increase productivity. ICT may further ease communication and be an instrument for changing relationships thus supporting development activities. In the Computational view the conceptualization of ICT focuses solely on the technology as such, the machine itself and its algorithms. In the Proxy view ICT is conceptualized as a surrogate for other concepts. "We interpret this view as 'what ICT represent'... as a knowledge enabler" [6, p. 19]. In the Ensemble view ICT is conceptualized as going beyond the technology i.e. beyond the Computational view and into a view of ICT as part of the actual use of ICT in a social and development oriented context. "In this view, the social and contextual aspects determine how ICT is conceived" [6, p. 19].

ICT used in development will supposedly have some "impacts" compared to not using ICT. However, "How does ICT actually lead to development?" is a challenging question to answer [6, p. 19]. In their quest for answering this how-question Sein and Harindranath [6] suggests that new technology impact society through three effects (referring a framework proposed by Malone and Rockart [13], adopted by Sein and Ahmad [14]).

The first-order or primary effect is that old technology is substituted by new. Primary effects may not in itself indicate development, but are essential for higher-order effects to take place. The second-order or secondary effect leads to an increase in phenomenon enabled by using the new technology. The third-order or tertiary effect is that new technology-related businesses are established and societal change may take place. Based on the three conceptualizations (i.e. ICT use, ICT views, and ICT impacts) Sein and Harindranath [6] propose an integrated framework for studying ICT in development (p. 20) suggesting that ICT view and ICT use influences ICT impacts that in turn influence human development. However, they do not suggest any causal mechanism that can explain why ICT leads to these different impacts.

Kleine's [8] question "ICT4WHAT?" and the Choice framework to operationalize the capability approach to development give some direction for answering the why-question. The Choice framework of Kleine [8, p. 680] suggests that Structure and Agency influences each other and these two elements influences the degree, primarily as choice (including choice in ICTs), secondarily as easier communication, increasing knowledge, greener environment, increased income, increased mobility, more personal time, more voice, more autonomy, etc. The development outcomes then in turn influences Structure and Agency thus having a possible strengthening of these two elements leading to a greater degree of empowerment that in turn leads to more development outcomes in a positive spiral movement.

However, the question about the 'causal mechanism' by which agency interacts with ICT, and that enhance the individual capabilities still remain unanswered. We fully acknowledge the existing research; however, at the same time, argue that the existing research limits their methodological application to describing the phenomena. The causal explanation to the 'why' question still needs further investigation. To complement this research strand, we propose a methodology that is derived from the philosophy of critical realism. In the following sub sections, we discuss critical realism and methodology. We then present an exemplary case that is used to illustrate the methodology before we conclude the paper.

2   Critical Realism and Methodology

This section describes critical realism in brief, and, subsequently the proposed methodology.

2.1   Critical Realism

Seeking to answer our research question searching for mechanisms that may explain why ICT works for "D" we will discuss underlying philosophies used for researching information systems. "Historically, most IS research and systems development, particularly in the US, has been underpinned by a positivist (more generally empiricist) philosophy" [15, p. 87]. Initially, the ICT4D domain followed a similar tradition [16]. The challenge with the empiricist philosophic view on researching ICT4D is threefold: (i) perceptions of reality was mainly based on observations i.e. the reality is what you see and perceive, (ii) the observations made of the actual events did not provide opportunities for proving underlying mechanisms, i.e. what cause the event, and (iii) that universal laws could be derived from a set of particular observations, i.e. same cause-and-effect works in various situations [17]. However, it is difficult to ascribe universal laws to the success/failure of ICT4D. The nature of ICT4D research is highly contextual [18]. For example, positivist models and frameworks that claims that ICT deployment in particular ways will lead to development and does not consider the socio-political contexts in which they are deployed [19].

Other philosophical underpinnings in IS research, as interpretivism or conventionalism [15], according to the Kuhnian view, "highlights the constructed, conventional nature of scientific theorizing, and truth is that which is accepted by a scientific community rather than correspondence to some external reality" [15, p. 90]. The challenge with these approaches is that truth is contextual and based on the perceiver's perspective. A majority of the recent ICT4D research follows interpretive tradition, however the interpretive approaches are more interested in understanding context rather than explaining the phenomena. The interpretive tradition reject the idea of discerning causality through interpretive case study. To find the middle way of universal law vs mere understanding critical realists argue that the world is socially constructed but not entirely so. Sometimes we, as researchers, can transcend interpretation and explain the situations we research [20]. We therefore suggest turning to Critical Realism that we describe in the following.

Roy Bhaskar developed a general philosophy of science that he labeled transcendental realism and a special philosophy of the human sciences that he called critical naturalism. The two terms were combined by other authors to form the umbrella term critical realism [21]. The main idea behind Bhasker's critical realism is a stratification of reality in three domains: the real, the actual and the empirical [22].

According to critical realism, the real domain consists of structures of objects, both physical and social, with capacities for behavior through mechanisms [20]. The mechanisms may trigger events in the actual domain and the events may be observed empirically. Thus, structures are not deterministic, but have the potential to enable and constrain events through inherent mechanisms [20]. Therefore, from a critical realism perspective, understanding the societal effects/outcomes associated with introducing new structures (e.g. new ICT systems in ICT4D context) and how they occur can be viewed as understanding the generative mechanism associated with those structures [23]. However, critical realism does not aim to uncover general laws that predict outcomes, but to identify the underlying mechanism that have generated the phenomena of interest and could do so again. We therefore argue that critical realism is a methodology we can apply for seeking to answer our research question.

2.2   A Proposed Methodology

The layered ontology structures, mechanisms and events "is the key to the critical realist methodology" [24, p. 3]. Critical realism as a methodology (cf. Fig. 1) seeks to describe mechanisms and structures theoretically for hypothesize how the events observed or experiences may be explained [24]. The researcher in a critical realist research design will therefore systematically analyze the interplay between the three layers: structures, mechanisms and events. "The methodical question is; how do we identify mechanisms, since they are not observable?" [24, p. 3].

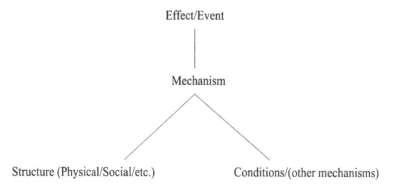

Fig. 1. Critical realist view of mechanisms (adopted from Sayer [27, p. 15])

Mechanisms are central in critical realist methodology, therefore, what are mechanisms? This question may be answered from different perspectives. Mechanisms are the casual powers that causes the events that we may observe [22, 24]. Mechanisms may also be called generative mechanisms [24]. For example, we may observe developers of information systems for ICT4D and buyer/users of the information systems agree on functions of such information system. However, the underlying mechanisms in the negotiations, the communication or the power differences prior to the signing of the contract may not be observable. Some other perspectives on mechanisms are "… a causal structure that can trigger events" [24, p. 3], being a causal relationship between objects [25], contingent causality [26], or causation [27 referred in 20] meaning that the same mechanism may produce different outcome in different situations and contexts depending on structures and conditions (other mechanisms) [27 referred in 20]. Mechanisms may therefore not be used for prediction, but may be useful for explaining why a given outcome was produced in a given context in an actual situation with actual structures and conditions.

The challenges in identifying mechanisms in a critical realism methodology are many in that there are no direct and stable links between structures, mechanisms andevents. However, the idea is to identify the mechanisms, not the empirical data. "The mechanisms are associated with the nature of the object of study, not with the attributes of the data" [24, p. 5]. These mechanisms can be uncovered through retroduction, a process of working backward from the empirical events, searching for the underlying mechanisms that could logically have produced the events. The retroduction may include interviews asking the question "what produces change?" [20, p. 123]. Through an iterative process, we may improve our understanding of the mechanisms that produce the change.

In addition to the real-actual-empirical stratification and the temporal separation of structure and action, structures themselves can be stratified. The structures may consist of various components. Rather than being a simple aggregation of parts, they combine into 'assemblages', whose causal properties emerge from the interactions between parts and are not just an additive combination of the properties of the components. Since the relations between parts matter the mechanisms that arise from these nested structures are a complex web of interpenetrating effects that can leads to evolution of new structures and mechanisms [15].

Critical realist methodology must have a research question of the form "What caused the events associated with the phenomenon to occur?" [20, p. 123]. Bygstad and Munkvold [24] suggests six steps in a stepwise framework for critical realist data analysis. The first step is describing the events observed [24]. A description may include a decision to start a project that may give internet connection to a remote village. Often such descriptions will include many different observations that are connected to the decision. The second step is to identify the entities/objects that characterize the phenomenon being studied [20] and collect data about these entities. The key components are for example persons, organizations and systems, i.e. the real objects of the case, forming networks with casual power. Then follows the third step, interpreting the data [20] also called theoretical re-description (abduction) [24]. Preparing for step four, retroduction, we need, in step three to abstract the case, searching for different theoretical perspectives and different explanations [24]. Theories for use in the abduction step of the process may be theories for ICT4D that may help us to increase the theoretical understanding of the case giving a deeper understanding of the events in the case. The fourth step, the key epistemological process, retroduction, "is a meta-process the outcome of which is the identification of mechanisms that explain what caused the events to occur" [20, p. 124]. According to Bygstad and Munkvold [24] this step is the most crucial. They have therefore divided the step in to two sub-steps, the interplay of objects and looking for micro-macro mechanisms [24, p. 6]. In the ICT4D field the interplay between objects will often be between social and technical objects. Since ICT4D may include cross cultural activities using technology that is developed in one culture for development in other cultures the interplay between the objects are important to identify. Bygstad & Munkvold [24] exemplify the micro-macro mechanisms as follows: the micro-macro mechanisms explain the emergent behavior, that is the interaction of different objects that produce some outcome at a macro level, and the macro-micro mechanisms that can explain how the wholes enables and constrains the various parts [19, 24]. In step five the results of the retroduction process, the mechanisms are then analyzed [24] to find what mechanisms may explain the outcomes. We may analyze the outcomes using forward chaining to understand intentions, or backward chaining to understand results [24]. For instance, studying ICT4D we may find some cases where the intended goals were reached, we should look for the mechanisms that led to the success. The results from Step five then prepare for the sixth and last step in the process, deciding if the explanations found are "good" or not [20]. The different explanations, i.e. mechanisms that caused the events may then be ranked and argued for as the last part of step six.

In the following section, we illustrate how this stepwise framework may be used in searching for underlying mechanisms that can explain ICT4D phenomena in the Nepal Wireless Networking Project (NWNP). The case relates to 10 villages and to Kathmandu, the capital of Nepal. The case description is an excerpt of around 60 interviews conducted in the period of 2009 to 2011.

3   An Exemplary Case

NWNP was initiated by educationist and social activist Mahabir Pun (team leader of the project). He wanted, initially, to solve the communication problem in a village called Nangi located 2000 m above sea level. There was no transportation facilities leading to the village and the villagers had to walk 8 or 9 h just to post their letter. It was a huge problem for the villagers because most of the people from this village had jobs in foreign countries, like India, Middle East, and UK. Letter from their relatives living abroad could take 2–3 months to reach the village. As late as 1997, the village had no telephone or Internet connection to the outside world. Realizing the pressing need of the Nangi people, Pun started to search for the possibilities of using ICT in solving this problem. In 2001, Pun wrote an email to the British Broadcasting Corporation (BBC) asking for ideas to connect this remote village to the outside world through the Internet. After the BBC broadcasted his email, the response was overwhelming. Within a year, volunteers from Europe and the United States began to pour into Nangi and helped him in setting up a wireless connection between Nangi and other neighboring villages using desktop and laptop computers, internet telephony equipment, network cameras, and TV dish antennas mounted in trees. Gradually, the story of NWNP spread across Nepal and to the outside world leading to Mr. Pun's social network expanding across Nepal and to other parts of the world. Volunteers from several countries started donating computers, parts, Wi-Fi equipment and their time to the related mountain villages in Nepal. The project initially started for solving the villagers' communication problem, but opened new possibilities for education, healthcare and income generating activities. For example, NWNP collaborated with OLE, for education, Kathmandu Model Hospital, for telemedicine services and Thamel.com, for e-commerce opportunities.

Since 2003, this project has been in full-fledged operation. Despite difficult circumstances, as lack of government support, lack of funding, lack of technical knowledge, and an unstable political system like the civil war between the government and the Maoists when the project started, the project succeeded in providing Internet services to villages in the Myagdi district. Currently, the NWNP has assisted in setting up networks in around 200 villages providing various services in education, healthcare, and income generating activities in the mountain regions.

4 Illustration of the Proposed Methodology

In this section, we describe how the methodology based on critical realism can be used to identify the mechanisms and structures that lead to development or capability enhancement in the NWNP case and provide a discussion of the literature related to the analysis of the steps.

4.1 Step 1: Description of Events

Since the purpose of this ICT4D research is to find out why ICT leads to some sort of capability development we needed to identify events that are related to enhancement of capabilities (freedom of choice) in the case we have described. We identified four events/effects of NWNP in the mountain region: communication through VOIP, telemedicine, online education, and online business activities. The identification of the events was done through discussing with key interviewee such as Mr. Pun, Dr. Dhital, Mr. Karmacharya, teachers, district officers and community people. Furthermore, one of the authors did field visits observing what happened in different situations and everyday activities related to the case.

4.2 Step 2: Identification of Entities

The process in step 2 revealed how various technologies, PCs, software, antennas, batteries etc., actors, internal from the village, from neighboring villages, from Kathmandu, and international actors, social structures formed by the actors mention and in addition some key social groups like 'mothers group' known locally as 'aama samoh', interacted and formed the 'assemblage'. The links to external stakeholders included actors such as Kathmandu model hospital, OLE, and thamel.com were also identified. As stated, "Entities only attain meaning if they are embedded in a theoretical framework ... entities can be tangible or intangible, social or physical, dormant or active" [20, p. 125]. In the next step, we therefore relate the entities to relevant theoretical framework.

4.3 Step 3: Theoretical Re-description (Abduction)

The abstraction and generalization of the events identified in Step 1 were performed over a 2-year's period being the data for identifying the entities in step 2. In step 2 we identified that the entities in the case interacted and formed an 'assemblage'. The assemblage includes enrolled network partners and local communities, and installation of internet connection. The process of forming assemblage can be theorized and explained with the ANT's (Actor-Network Theory) translation moments of problematization, interessement, enrolment, and mobilization [28]. The translation moments describe the key strategy factor of NWNP [28]. The results of this strategy led to a gradual establishment of NWNP' main infrastructural hub for telemedicine and distance education services. The popularity of the project after Pun received the Magsaysay award led to enrolling an increasing number of national and international partners to provide resources to extend NWNP services.

In the beginning of our theoretical re-description, we interpreted the enrolling of key actors and the mobilizing of them as a means of enhancing capabilities. However, later we found that people first form trust and norms in the network, thereafter they take collective actions as essential elements in the network in the formed assemblage.

ANT could therefore be used to describe the process of the formation of assemblage. However, to understand why and how people form trust and norm in the network, and why they take collective action, we furthered the theorizing process by introducing social capital theory [9] in step 3. The emergence of trust and norms in the network can be described more precisely in terms of mechanisms, which produce the outcomes described. Social capital explains why and how the participation of the actors in the NWNP case in turn lead to collective action [9]. The core element of social capital exercised in networks of social relations are characterized by norms of trust and reciprocity [29, 30]. By combining the perspectives from Actor-Network Theory and social capital theory, we can provide an explanatory lens to understand why and how different actors interacts and build social capitals in the above mentioned assemblage. A major focus of these theories in this particular context is to try to explore the processes whereby relatively stable networks of aligned interests are created and maintained successfully, or alternatively to understand why such networks fail to establish themselves [31]. ANT suggests that successful social networks of aligned interests are created through the enrolment of actors and translation of their interest so that they are willing to participate in particular ways of thinking and acting that will maintain the network.

4.4   Step 4: Retroduction: Identification of Candidate Mechanisms

Based on the description and analysis in steps 3 three interconnected mechanisms were identified as candidates for mechanisms. They were identified through applying ANT and social capital theories described in Step 3. The mechanisms can be described in this particular case as follows: (i) ICT provide possibilities to enhance capabilities, but the possibilities provided byICT need to be perceived by actors or mediators informed by ANT. Then (ii) to actualize these perceived possibilities, we need collective action. The source to collective action is social capital, informed by social capital theory. Furthermore, (iii) if the collective action is taken and the possibilities are actualized then it can enhance individual capabilities, informed by social capital theories. In summary, the first mechanism explains the roles of focal actor(s) in identifying the social problems and the possibilities of ICT that can solve the problems, thereafter enroll other actors who can facilitate in actualizing the ICT possibilities. The second mechanism explains the role of social capital in building trust and norms among the actors. The third mechanism explains the mobilization of actors-network through collective action. To make it more representational we coined the three interconnected term as 'Actor-Network in Action' mechanism (Ref. Fig. 2).

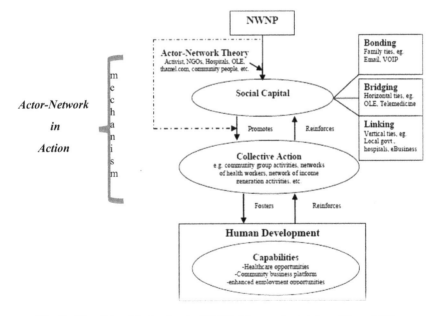

Fig. 2. Identifying Mechanism in ICT4D (Figure adapted from Thapa [32])

4.5   Step 5/6: Selection of Mechanism and Ranking of the Selected Mechanisms

Step 4 results in multiple interconnected mechanisms as candidates for explaining why events occur arising the question of selecting mechanisms. What mechanism is best or the most acceptable mechanism in the given situation [20]. Easton [20] suggested the idea of, ".. judgmental rationality. It means that we can publicly discuss our claim about reality as we think is, and marshal better or worse arguments on behalf of those claims" [20, p. 124].

The results of a critical realism based methodological analysis shows that the three interconnected mechanisms 'Actor-Network in Action' explain the process by which ICT enhance the capabilities leading to D in the NWNP case (cf. Fig. 2).

5   Conclusion

In this paper we started with defining ICT and Development, then related the two. We identified that when relating ICT to Development, the main focus of existing studies is on HOW questions, such as how does ICT leads to development, or how to measure the impact of ICT. However, explaining underlying mechanism like 'WHY' ICT leads to development remained unanswered and was therefore a matter of further enquiry. Therefore, to contribute to this knowledge gap we proposed a methodology based on critical realism. We also argued that critical realism reconcile the realism stand with the interpretivism stand by taking the middle ground of realist ontology and relative epistemology.

The proposed methodology was illustrated using a case from Nepal, the Nepal wireless networking project. We presented the case analysis using a step-by-step approach in identifying the mechanism 'actor-network in action' as an explanation of why ICT succeeded to create various opportunities in this case, for instance, because there was a goal oriented actor, who build trust in the vertical and horizontal network of various actors. The network finally took collective action to realize the affordances of ICT.

The methodology however is not without caveat. For instance, the critical realist still cannot claim that the mechanism identified is the best one. However, as we mentioned earlier, in a given situation the retroduction process can identify the best possible explanation that is consistent with the data. It may be questioned if results from using the methodology may be generalized per se. However, as for generalizability, Easton [20] suggests four supportive reasons that can be helpful in theory development: first, identification of the entities, structures and their relation, second, understanding of affordances and constraints of various tangible and intangible structures, third, identification of contingent relations among entities and structures, and finally, provide evidence through judgmental rationality. These are some avenues for further research.

Another avenue for further research is the relationships between the micro-macro mechanisms, morphogenesis, explaining the emergent behavior that produce an outcome at a macro level, and the macro-micro mechanisms, explaining how the whole enables and constrains the various parts [24]. Implicitly we touched upon these two sub-steps in step 4, but these sub-steps need more elaboration.

References

1. Pieterse, J.N.: Development Theory: Deconstruction/Reconstruction: TCS. SAGE Publications, Thousand Oaks (2001)
2. Thapa, D., Sæbø, Ø.: Exploring the link between ICT and development in the context of developing countries a literature review. Electron. J. Inf. Syst. Dev. Cries. **64**, 15 (2014). http://aisel.aisnet.org/cais/vol34/iss1/11/
3. Sen, A.: Development as Freedom. Oxford University Press, Oxford (2000)
4. Avgerou, C.: The link between ICT and economic growth in the discourse of development. In: Korpela, M., Montealegre, R., Poulymenakou, A. (eds.) Oraganizational Information Systems in the Context of Globalization, pp. 373–386. Kluwer Academic, Dordrecht (2003)
5. Heeks, R.: ICT4D 2.0: the next phase of applying ICT for international development. Computer **41**(6), 26–33 (2008)
6. Sein, M.K., Harindranath, G.: Conceptualizing the ICT artifact: toward understanding the role of ICT in national development. Inf. Soc. **20**(1), 15–24 (2004)
7. Hatakka, M., Lagsten, J.: The capability approach as a tool for development evaluation - analyzing students' use of internet resources. Inf. Technol. Dev. iFirst 1–19 (2011). doi:10.1080/02681102.2011.617722
8. Kleine, D.: ICT4WHAT?—using the choice framework to operationalise the capability approach to development. J. Int. Dev. **22**(5), 674–692 (2010)
9. Thapa, D., Sein, M.K., Sæbø, Ø.: Building collective capabilities through ICT in a mountain region of Nepal: where social capital leads to collective action. Inf. Technol. Dev. **18**(1), 5–22 (2012)
10. Andersson, A., Grönlund, Å., Wicander, G.: Development as freedom–how the capability approach can be used in ICT4D research and practice (2012)
11. Heeks, R.: i-development not e-development: special issue on ICTs and development. J. Int. Dev. **14**(1), 1–11 (2002)
12. Orlikowski, W.J., Iacono, S.C.: Resaerch commentry: desperately seeking the 'IT' in IT research - a call to theorizing the IT artifact. Inf. Syst. Res. **12**(2), 121–134 (2001)
13. Malone, T.W., Rockart, J.F.: Computers, networks and the corporation. Sci. Am. **265**(3), 128–136 (1991)
14. Sein, M., Ahmad, I.: A framework to study the impact of information and communication technologies on developing countries: the case of cellular phones in Bangladesh. Paper presented at the proceedings of the BITWorld international conference (2001)
15. Mingers, J.: Realizing information systems: critical realism as an underpinning philosophy for information systems. Inf. Organ. **14**(2), 87–103 (2004)
16. Sutinen, E., Tedre, M.: ICT4D: a computer science perspective. In: Elomaa, T., Mannila, H., Orponen, P. (eds.) Algorithms and Applications. LNCS, vol. 6060, pp. 221–231. Springer, Heidelberg (2010). doi:10.1007/978-3-642-12476-1_16
17. Mingers, J., Mutch, A., Willcocks, L.: Critical realism in information systems research. MIS Q. **37**(3), 795–802 (2013)
18. Prakash, A., De', R.: Importance of development context in ICT4D projects: a study of computerization of land records in India. Inf. Technol. People **20**(3), 262–281 (2007)
19. Njihia, J.M., Merali, Y.: The broader context for ICT4D projects: a morphogenetic analysis. MIS Q. **37**(3), 881–905 (2013)
20. Easton, G.: Critical realism in case study research. Ind. Mark. Manage. **39**(1), 118–128 (2010)
21. Dobson, P.J.: The philosophy of critical realism—an opportunity for information systems research. Inf. Syst. Front. **3**(2), 199–210 (2001)

22. Archer, M., Bhaskar, R., Collier, A., Lawson, T., Norrie, A.: Critical Realism Essential Readings. Routledge, Abingdon (2013)
23. Volkoff, O., Strong, D.M.: Critical realism and affordances: theorizing IT-associated organizational change processes. MIS Q. **37**(3), 819–834 (2013)
24. Bygstad, B., Munkvold, B.E.: In search of mechanisms. Conducting a critical realist data analysis (2011)
25. Bunge, M.: How does it work? The search for explanatory mechanisms. Philos. Soc. Sci. **34** (2), 182–210 (2004)
26. Smith, M.L.: Testable theory development for small-N studies: critical realism and middle-range theory. Int. J. Inf. Technol. Syst. Approach **3**(1), 41–56 (2010)
27. Sayer, A.: Realism and Social Science. Sage Publications, Thousand Oaks (2000)
28. Thapa, D.: The role of ICT actors and networks in development: the case study of a wireless project in Nepal. Electron. J. Inf. Syst. Dev. Countries **49**, 1–16 (2011)
29. Adler, P.S., Kwon, S.-W.: Social capital: prospects for a new concept. Acad. Manage. Rev. **27**(1), 17–40 (2002). http://www.jstor.org/stable/4134367
30. Yang, S., Lee, H., Kurnia, S.: Social capital in information and communications technology research: past, present, and future. Commun. Assoc. Inf. Syst. **25**(1), 183–220 (2009)
31. Callon, M.: Some elements of a sociology of translation: domestication of the scallops and fisherman of St. Brieuc Bay. In: Law, J. (ed.) Power, Action and Belief: A New Sociology of Knowledge, pp. 196–233. Routledge, London (1986)
32. Thapa, D.: Exploring the link between ICT intervention and human development through a social capital lens: the case study of a wireless project in the mountain region of Nepal. Universitet i Agder/University of Agder (2012)

Participatory Technologies: Affordances for Development

Tony Roberts[(✉)] (iD)

Institute for Development Studies, University of Sussex, Brighton, UK
t.roberts@ids.ac.uk

Abstract. This work-in-progress paper presents a line of research analysing the affordances of a range of participatory technologies for development. Affordances are the 'actionable possibilities' that are made possible (but not determined) by a technology. Participatory technologies are a range of technology-mediated practices used in participatory development initiatives, such as participatory video and participatory digital mapping. This research examines the relationship between technological artefacts, participatory processes and development outcomes and asks to what extent one contributes to another. As this is work-in-progress it is too early to draw firm conclusions however this paper identifies the need to distinguish between a participatory technology's technical features, its functional affordances and the affordances of participatory video practices. Affordances seem to provide a potential conceptual means to bridge the relatively technocentric and realist approaches of some IS, HCI and ICT4D with the relatively anthrocentric and constructivist approaches of some STS and development studies.

Keywords: Affordances · Participation · Development · HCI · IS · Informatics · ICT4D

1 Introduction

The rapid proliferation, new functionalities and falling costs of mobile phones, laptops and other information and communication technologies (ICTs) has facilitated their increasing incorporation within development initiatives and has prompted the study of the application of ICTs for development (ICTD) [1]. The accelerating adoption of digital tools by practitioners of 'participatory development' has given rise to a range of new tools and practices that Robert Chambers has called 'participatory technologies' [2]. In this research the term participatory technologies refers to the use of digital information and communication technologies in participatory development processes. The main aim is to better understand the relationship between technological artefacts, participatory processes and development outcomes.

That technology is increasingly important in development is generally accepted. However the precise ways in which technology inhibits or contributes to development outcomes remains the subject of much debate and research. In the existing literature on the use of information and communications technology for development (ICT4D) it has been argued that the technology itself is generally under-theorised [3], that the

J. Choudrie et al. (Eds.): ICT4D 2017, IFIP AICT 504, pp. 194–205, 2017.
DOI: 10.1007/978-3-319-59111-7_17

particular conceptualisation of development being used is rarely explicit [4, 5], and that the specific relationship of ICT to development is often uncritically assumed [6]. This research addresses these issues by making theoretical contributions in relation to the technology itself, making explicit the conceptualisation of development being used, and by presenting a critical analysis of the relationship between the technology, participatory processes and development outcomes. It achieves this without falling into technological determinism by grounding its analysis a critical realist ontology [7] and by using the concept of affordances in a way that takes seriously the role of technology in shaping society without ever losing sight of the way that technology is itself social shaped [8].

1.1   Matter Matters

Since the 1980s much Science Technology and Society research was part of a project to correct what it considered to be a technological determinism in the existing literature [9]. This body of work sought to theorise technology as social shaped and located in mutually constituted socio-technical assemblages of human and non-human actants [10]. So successful was this push back that Orlikowski argued convincingly that technology was the 'missing mass' in much Information Systems (IS) research [3]. From Orlikowski's perspective a failure to take seriously technology's materiality necessarily limits a comprehensive understanding of the relationship between information systems and social change. Following Orlikowski I argue that 'matter matters' in ICT4D research; that design and materiality have consequences for users. However any researcher that takes seriously technology's materiality is compelled to mount a defense against the accusation of technological determinism. Following MacKensie and Wajcman [8] I argue that it is perfectly consistent to recognize both that technology is shaped by society and that technology shapes society; that they are mutually constitutive. The ontological position of critical realism [7] is helpful in this regard as it recognizes that the physical world is Real at the same time as accepting that all human experience of the Real is necessarily partial, subjective and socially constructed. This ontological position effectively collapses the realism vs constructivism dichotomy. Critical realism allows us to recognize the Real without falling into technological determinism. This research is grounded in such an ontology.

1.2   Participatory Development

Participatory development practices derive their logic from a particular agency-based conceptualisation of human development [11, 12]. Orthodox development economics often reduces the evaluation of development success to econometric quantitative indicators such as GDP per person. Southern activists proposed a radically different 'bottom-up' normative approach in which disadvantaged people themselves determine the priorities of development [13]. This agency-based participatory approach to human development is the main heterodox approach to development. Distinctive features of this approach include its emphasis on the participation of disadvantaged people in epistemological processes that enable them to define, articulate and voice their own development concerns and priorities. This research is informed by this conceptualization of development in which disadvantaged people themselves are the authors, architects and arbiters of their own projects of development.

1.3 Affordances

This research is concerned to disentangle and better understand the complex interrelationship between the social and technical elements of participatory technology use in human development. The concept of affordances has some distinct advantages in this regard.

Affordances are the 'actionable possibilities' invited, enabled or allowed by a technology [14]. A cup for example has the actionable possibility of conveying tea for drinking. The material properties of a cup, its handle, its waterproof material and handy size matter; they invite and enable the action tea holding and conveyance. It is important to note that whilst affordances both enable and constrain the range of action possibilities they never determine; agency and choice remain. A person could use their agency to appropriate the cup for the action of pen and pencil storage. Costall [15] would distinguish tea holdabilty as the 'canonical affordance' of a cup i.e. the conventional and normative actionable possibility which socialisation has normalised for cups. The concept of affordances has not previously been systematically applied to participatory video. Participatory video is a social process in which non-experts co-produce and film about an issue that concerns them [16]. The existing literature often notes that participatory video is efficacious in stimulating increasing participant, agency and voice [17] all of which are considered valued human development outcomes [12].

The next section will review the existing literature and establish the theoretical framework adopted in this research. Although affordance theories are relatively well developed in the fields of Human Computer Interface (HCI), Information Systems (IS) and informatics, the application of affordance theory is relatively scarce in the development studies literature. Conversely, participation theories are well established in development studies literature but are relatively under-represented in the ICT4D literature. This research anticipates that a better understanding of the affordances of participatory technologies for development will act as one bridge between these research communities.

Section 3 considers the research methodology adopted in this research. By conducting desk research, interviewing leading practitioners, convening a one day conference, and by commissioning new research on existing and emerging participatory technologies this research will produce new knowledge and analysis and make new theoretical contributions on the specific affordances of technologies and practices of participatory development.

Although this is work in progress paper Sect. 4 presents some preliminary and tentative findings, using participatory video as an explanatory example. The affordances of the video technology itself gives rise to functional affordances but the research finds that it is only when these affordances are mediated through the social mechanisms of participatory practices that development outcomes are evidenced. The research also suggests that the nature of the development outcomes are contingent on other contextual factors not least the capacity and intent of the process facilitator(s).

2 Existing Literature

2.1 Development

Dominant models of development emphasise 'economic development' evaluated by means of proxy measures such as GDP income per head. Challenging this approach as reductionist heterodox models emphasise 'human development' [12]. Advocates of human development often argue that a person has reason to value things that cannot be reduced to economic indicators such as political freedom, well-being and personal agency. From this perspective a person's agency as a protagonist in their own development projects and their ability to 'voice' their own preferences and priorities is axiomatic elements of the kind of development that people have reason to value [12]. Post-colonial independence leaders such as President Nyerere of Tanzania argued that, "people can't be developed, they can only develop themselves" [18]. For this reason adherents of participatory development often argue normatively that individuals have reason to value participation in the design, implementation and evaluation of any development initiatives that affect them. This heterodox 'bottom-up' process of enabling people to determine and to attain their own self-defined objectives [13] was at the heart of Freire's [11] work in Brazil, as well as that of Orlando Fals-Borda in Colombia [19], Rajesh Tandon in India [20] and Swantz in East Africa [21]. Freire provided practical guidance on the group process of conscientisation by which disadvantaged people can better understand their circumstances, identify the root causes of the problems that they experience and act together to transform the situation [22]. Such participatory development processes constituted what Tandon [23] claimed represented a distinctly Southern approach to development practice and research. Participatory development approaches and methods were popularised in Anglophone development studies and practice by, among others, Robert Chambers [24] and form part of the conceptual framework for most of the canonical texts on participatory video [16, 17]. These ideas were later extended by the Nobel-prize winning economist and philosopher Amartya Sen as part of his agency-based conception of human development. Sen [12] wrote,

> *"With adequate social opportunities, individuals can effectively shape their own destiny and help each other. They need not be seen primarily as the passive recipients of cunning development programs. There is indeed a strong rationale for recognizing the positive role of free and sustained agency"*

This agency-based model of participatory development in which disadvantaged people are the authors, architects and arbiters of their own development priorities and projects, is the conceptualisation of development adopted in this research. This raises the question of what counts as participation in this research?

2.2   Participation

In the 1990s participatory development approaches were widely adopted by main-stream development institutions and funders like UNDP and the World Bank. Some scholars argued that this resulted in a dilution and corruption of the original radical intent of participation. Critiques of tokenistic and sham forms of participation were a feature of the contributions to the edited volume *The Tyranny of Participation* [25]. Whilst not seeking to negate this valuable critique, in *From Tyranny to Transformation*, Hickey and Mohan [26] attempted to recover and re-politicise participation and to clarify the ways and circumstances in which participation could again be emancipatory and transformational. It was argued persuasively that this could be accomplished by strategies such as embedding participation within wider political processes [27], and by returning to a focus on building critical consciousness and agency into participatory development through Freirian practices such as conscientisation where participants critique the social conditions that oppress them and use their collective agency to challenge the situation [28]. This research draws on these later approaches whilst recognising that participatory technologies have potential both to reproduce existing unequal social relationships as well as to transform them. This research therefore seeks to unravel the particular circumstances in which digital technologies and participatory practices can be emancipatory and transformative.

Participation is not a binary concept. Various scholars have argued for different scales of participation along a range from relatively weak to relatively strong forms of participation. Arnstein's [29] ladder of participation is the archetype and ranges from 'non-participation' through degrees of tokenistic participation up to degrees of real power through which citizens can take effective control of the participatory development process. White [30] uses a variant range extending from nominal participation to transformative participation.

For this research I have developed a range of 'Elements of Participation' to reflect the constituent elements of the agency-based conception of participatory development adopted in this research. At the 'weak' end of the range of participation is 'taking part in an activity' which most participatory technologies can be expected to involve. At the 'strong' end of the scale is 'achieving power reversals' which few participatory technologies may be expected to achieve. It is not proposed that technologies are considered to be participatory technologies only if all elements are maximally present; maximal presence is not necessarily expected in any case. It is only proposed that the elements provide a relevant reference point for tracing the relationship of a technology's affordances to the elements of participatory development.

2.3   Participatory Technologies

In this research the term participatory technologies refers to the use of digital ICTs in participatory development practices. However the use of participatory methodologies in development practices pre-date the introduction of digital technologies by several decades. Participatory video practice dates back to at least 1967 [31], participatory mapping to the 1980s and participatory monitoring and evaluation to the 1990s [32].

The existing literature on (pre-digital) participatory methodologies is a rich source of learning for practitioners and researchers of participatory ICT4D. It is important that ICT4D research and practice is mindful of the continuities between participatory methodologies and participatory technologies as well as the discontinuities.

Participatory video has a long history as an analogue participatory technology using celluloid film before it was later digitised and, even more recently, became possible entirely on mobile phones [33]. Participatory mapping was previously practiced by drawing on the earth, and later on paper (and these continue to be appropriate practices in many settings) but now also makes use of mobile phones, GPS, satellites, GIS software and unmanned aerial vehicles or 'drones' [34]. Previously analogue participatory methodologies that are now migrating to digital technologies are 'digital immigrants' whereas some are 'digital natives' [35] meaning that they were originated as digital methods without clear analogue precedents. Examples of this later group include online platforms for citizen participation in satellite-based environmental monitoring and 'crisis mapping' or the real time crowdsourcing of humanitarian data from the public using mobile phones and social media.

The types of participatory technologies considered by this research include participatory video, participatory photography, participatory digital storytelling, participatory digital community radio, participatory digital mapping, participatory digital monitoring and evaluation, participatory civic engagement technologies, participatory budgeting, participatory software development, and participatory political mobilisation. Whilst 'The Arab Spring' is often offered as an example of social media's role in stimulating political participation, the 2009 Obama, and 2016 Trump campaigns can also be considered to be examples of participatory online building of communities of political agency for radical social change. If it is argued that some technologies have advantages when it comes to stimulating participation then the questions arises as to what exactly are the technical features or participatory practices that contribute toward (or inhibit) human development. The next section explores the concept of affordances as a means to do so.

2.4 Affordances

The concept of affordances can be traced to its use by the visual psychologist James Gibson [14] to refer to the actionable possibilities suggested when viewing an object. Donald Norman [36] later applied the term to technology design using it to signify the particular aspects of a technology that *invite, allow or enable* a user to act in a particular way [37]. The design of a cup can be understood as inviting or enabling us to make use of its actionable properties as a drinking vessel. A fork does not invite the same use; we perceive the two technologies as having different actionable properties. Affordances are not however determinate; we can choose to interpret a cup as a pen holder. Hutchby's defines affordances as having both *"functional and relational aspects which frame, while not determining, the possibilities for agentic action in relation to an object"* [38]. Hutchby's definition requires us to pay attention to both the *functional* aspect of affordances that are based in the object's material form as well as the conventional boundaries of acceptable use that we learn as part of socialisation, which are situated. Zheng and Yu [39] use the example of chopsticks as artefacts whose affordances can be expected to be self-evident to most Chinese adults. However members of another society who have not learned that 'canonical' affordance may (mis) interpret chopsticks as a plaything; they would not however interpret them as a drinking vessel. The point here is that artifacts are always open to interpretive flexibility [9] but that their materiality places limits on that interpretation. There is always a thing being interpreted, and its 'matter matters'. Hutchby argues convincingly that "Ignoring the different affordances which constrain both the possible meanings and the possible uses of technologies denies us the opportunity of empirically analysing precisely what the 'effects' and 'constraints' associated with technological forms are" [38]. My intention in employing the concept of affordances is to allow such an empirical investigation. Faynard and Weeks [40] use the concept of affordances to integrate these appreciations of both the real materially-situated properties of an object and the scope for interpretative flexibility in relational use. This critical realist understanding of affordances is the one that informs this research.

In the context of agency-based conceptions of human development adopted in this research it is useful to understand a technology's affordances as those properties that invite or enable aspects of a user's agency; the way a person uses the technology to act in the world. The affordances of a technology can be either positive or negative in relation to a person's agency; features of a technology can either constrain or enable action on the part of a user. The viewability of text messages may be advantageous to a deaf person but disadvantageous to person who is print disabled. With respect to participatory video the multi-mediality of video mediated processes can enable print-disabled people to participate in social discourse, to voice their perspective and to retain editorial control over the way that they are represented. This is an example of the use of technology in participatory practices to produce development outcomes that individuals have reason to value. The next section outlines the methodology used in this research.

This research anticipated being able to trace the affordances of a particular technology (in the left-hand column in Table 1), via the particular Elements of Participation that they afforded (in the central column), to named development outcomes (in the right-hand column). Two examples are illustrated in the table. In the first example it could be argued that as video technology affords users the ability to project their self-authored films to audiences it contributes to amplifying their voice. In the second example, as has already been mentioned, the rewind and re-edit affordances of video afford participants the opportunity to reflect on their experiences and to co-produce new knowledge and learning.

3   Methodology

This research uses a mixture of qualitative methods including semi-structured interviews and three research phases. The first phase was desk research to review the existing literature on participation, participatory development, participatory technologies and affordances. Phase one also includes 16 semi-structured interviews with global scholars of participation, participatory technologies and affordances. Phase two

Table 1. Elements of participation

Elements of participation	Scale
Achieving power reversals	Relatively strong
Acting together for transformation	
Naming injustice and root causes	
Planning action for transformation	
Identification of power interests	
Group analysis of causes of inequality	
Voicing of experience & opinion	
Reflection about social circumstances and self	
Taking part in an activity	Relatively weak

involves the convening of a one day workshop of participatory technology specialists to inform the key research questions. New research will be commissioned for a special issue on the affordances of participatory technologies for development.

In phases one and two contributors will be asked to answer 'the technology question' i.e. what are the functional affordances of the technology that inhibit, invite, allow or enable participatory practices? They will also be asked the 'participation question' i.e. what 'Elements of Participation' are evident in their participatory processes and to which practice affordances are they attributable?

The third research phase will involve analysis of the above data to disentangle the social and material inter-connections. By interrogating each participatory practice it is intended to shed new light on the nature of the relationships between technologies, affordances and participatory development. By doing so the research will provide new empirical and theoretical resources for the application of digital technologies in development. Although this paper uses the example of participatory video the research will analyse the affordances of a broad range of participatory technologies to derive theoretically generalizable findings. Given the rapid proliferation and combination of participatory technologies any such lessons will be potentially valuable.

4 Findings and Discussion

Preliminary findings of this work-in-progress suggest that it is possible to map technology and affordances to development outcomes. The relationships however are more complicated than originally anticipated in a number of respects. Whilst the re-edit and project functions of the video camera do give rise to particular affordances they do not contribute directly to development outcomes; they appear to do so only through multiple social mechanisms. On one level the reasons for this are evident; other social forces are entangled. As Gibson himself emphasized, affordances do not determine; they do not make us do things in and of themselves [14]. Affordances are only action *possibilities* not sufficient causes. For this reason we can expect different people to use the same video camera in different ways and with different outcomes. Development outcomes cannot be read off technology in a deterministic way. The research has begun to shed light on the complex ways in which technologies' affordances are mediated not only by the social mechanisms of participatory video but also by the capacity and intent of the process facilitator and participants [41].

4.1   Functional Affordances vs. Practice Affordances

One way to begin to capture these differences is to make a conceptual distinction between the functional affordances arising from technological artifact itself (in this case the video camera) and the practice affordances arising from the social processes being employed (the participatory video practices). Figure 1 illustrates this division set within the wider context of this research. It should be emphasized that this is work-in-progress and this diagram is not presented as indicative of final research findings but rather as a schematic representation of research thus far using the example of participatory video [42]. Importantly the diagram illustrates that technologies are themselves socially shaped [8]. These processes do take place not in a social vacuum but rather in a social context that dynamically co-constructs the technological artefacts, affordances and development outcomes (as indicated by the six arrows).

The left hand column in Fig. 1 shows some of the technical features of a video camcorder. This is not intended to be a comprehensive list but rather illustrative examples. These technical features matter. Technical functions of the video camera such as edit and project give rise to the perception of actionable possibilities such as viewability and editability in the second column of the diagram. These functional

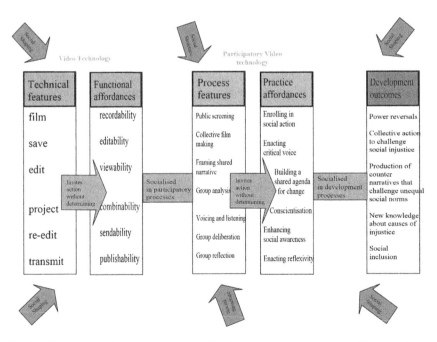

Fig. 1. Affordances of participatory video for development (adapted from Zheng and Yu).

affordances enable (and limit) the range of action possible with the technology (without determining or removing the scope for agency). Functional affordances do not themselves constitute development outcomes. They can however be drawn upon in participatory video processes in ways that may subsequently contribute to development outcomes.

Figure 1 shows that the functional affordances of video are socialized in the collective processes of participatory video film-making. Participatory video process typically involve a group of socially disadvantaged people in the collective process of making a film about issues of concern to them. The film maybe intended as advocacy to raise awareness on a neglected issue or to be viewed by distant decision makers to change policy on a subject of concern.

The third column illustrate some process features of participatory video. These are also significant as they give rise to the perception of the actionable possibilities for participatory video illustrated in column four. Participatory processes such as group deliberation and reflection enable actionable possibilities of participatory video such as enacting social awareness and formation of shared intent for social action. This is not a claim that participatory video causes or determines such outcomes. The only claim being made is that participatory video practices allow these action possibilities without determining them.

The affordances of participatory video practices are necessary but insufficient to determine wider development outcomes. The making of a single film may be meaningful to the individuals involved; it may increase their sense of self-efficacy and social awareness but in and of themselves they are unlikely to generate wider social change. To co-constitute social change participatory video practices will generally need to be embedded in wider social change processes [27, 28].

In summary Fig. 1 illustrates how the technical features of video make possible (without determining) its functional affordances, which are then socialised in the collective processes of participatory video. This relationship is then mirrored in the way that the process features of participatory video make possible (without determining) its practice affordances, which may then be socialised in wider development processes to co-generate development outcomes.

5   Conclusion

Based on this initial research it is argued that the concept of affordances offers a viable means to better understand the complex relationship between technologies, affordances, social mechanism and development outcomes. By continuing to pursue this research-in-progress across a range of established and newly emerging participatory technologies this research intends to shed new light on the relationships between technologies, affordances, social mechanisms and development outcomes. As Hutchby [38, p. 442] argues academics must examine the ways in which "social processes and the 'properties' of technological affordances are inter-related and inter-twined and need to analyse the ways in which they are".

References

1. Unwin, T.: ICT4D: Information and Communications for Development. Cambridge University Press, Cambridge (2009)
2. Chambers, R.: To Know Better: Reflection for Development. Practical Action Press, Rugby (2017, forthcoming)
3. Orlikowski, W., Icono, C.: Desperately seeking the IT in IT research: a call to theorize the IT artifact. Inf. Syst. Res. **12**(2), 121–134 (2001)
4. Walsham, G., Sahay, S.: Research on information systems in developing countries: current landscapes and future prospects. Inf. Technol. Dev. **12**(1), 7–24 (2006)
5. Walsham, G.: Development informatics in a changing world: reflections from ICTD 2010/2012. Inf. Technol. Int. Dev. **9**(1), 49–54 (2013)
6. Avgerou, C.: Discourses on ICT and development. Inf. Technol. Int. Dev. **6**(3), 1–18 (2010)
7. Baskar, R.: A Realist Theory of Science. Verso, London (1975, 1997)
8. Mackenzie, D., Wajcman, J. (eds.): The Social Shaping of Technology. Open University Press, Milton Keynes (1987)
9. Pinch, T., Bijker, W.: The social construction of facts and artefacts. Soc. Stud. Sci. **14**(3), 388–441 (1984)
10. Latour, B.: Reassembling the Social: An Introduction to Actor Network Theory. Oxford University Press, Oxford (2005)
11. Freire, P.: Education the Practice of Freedom. Writers and Readers, London (1973)
12. Sen, A.: Development as Freedom, p. 11. Oxford University Press, Oxford (1999)
13. Esteva, G.: Development. In: Sachs, W. (ed.) The Development Dictionary. Zed Books, London (1992)
14. Gibson, J.: The theory of affordances in perceiving, acting, and knowing. In: Shaw, R., Bransford, J. (eds.). OUP, London (1977)
15. Costall, A.: Socialising affordances. Theory Psychol. **5**(4), 467–481 (2012)
16. Lunch, N., Lunch, C.: Insights into Participatory Video, Insightshare (2006)
17. Shaw, J., Robertson, C.: Participatory Video: A Practical Guide to Using Video Creatively in Group Development Work. Routledge, London (1997)
18. Nyerere, J.: Freedom and Development, p. 7. Oxford University Press, Oxford (1973)
19. Fals-Borda, O.: Investigating reality in order to transform it: the colombian experience. Dialect. Anthropol. **4**, 33–35 (1979). Amsterdam
20. Tandon, R.: Participatory research and the empowerment of people. Convergence Int. J. Adult Educ. **14**(3), 20–24 (1981)
21. Swantz, M.L.: Research as education for development, a Tanzanian case. In: Hall, B. (ed.) Creating Knowledge: A Monopoly? Participatory Research in Development, New Delhi, SPRIA (1982)
22. Freire, P.: Pedagogy of Hope. Continuum, New York (1998)
23. Tandon, R.: Participation, citizenship and democracy: reflections on 25 years of PRIA. Community Dev. J. **43**(3), 284–296 (2008)
24. Chambers, R.: Whose Reality Counts? Putting the First Last. Practical Action Publishing, Rugby (1997)
25. Cooke, B., Kothari, U. (eds.): Participation: The New Tyranny. Zed Books, London (2001)
26. Hickey, S., Mohan, G.: Participation: From Tyranny to Transformation? Zed Books, London (2004)
27. Kelley, U.: Confrontation with power: moving beyond the tyranny of safety in participation. In: Hickey, S., Mohan, G. (eds.) Participation: From Tyranny to Transformation (2004)

28. Waddington, M., Mohan, G.: Falling forward: going beyond PRA and imposed forms of participation. In: Hickey, S., Mohan, G. (eds.) Participation: From Tyranny to Transformation. Zed Books, London (2004)
29. Arnstein, S.R.: A ladder of citizen participation. J. Am. Inst. Planners **35**(4), 216–224 (1969)
30. White, S.: Depoliticising development: the uses and abuses of participation. Dev. Pract. **6**(1), 6–15 (1996)
31. Snowden, D.: Eyes See, Ears Hear: supplement to a film under the same title, St. John's Memorial University of Newfoundland (1984)
32. Guijt, I., Gaventa, J.: Participatory Monitoring and Evaluation: Learning From Change. IDS Policy Briefing Issue 12, Brighton: IDS (1998)
33. MacEntee, K., Burkholder, C., Schwab-Cartas, J. (eds.): What is Cellfilm: Integrating Mobile Phone Technology into Participatory Visual Research and Activism. Sense, Rotterdam (2016)
34. Tushev, N.: Documenting illegal land occupancy using drones (2016). http://participatorygis.blogspot.co.uk/2016/05/documenting-illegal-land-occupancy.html. Accessed 23 Feb 2017
35. Prensky, M.: Digital natives digital immigrants. Horizon **9**(5), 1–6 (2001). MCB University Press
36. Norman, D.: The Design of Everyday Things. Basic Books, New York (1988)
37. Lidwell, W., Holden, K., Butler, J.: Universal Principles of Design. Massachusetts, Rockport (2003)
38. Hutchby, I.: Technologies, texts and affordances. Sociology **35**, 444 (2001)
39. Zheng, Y., Yu, A.: Affordances of social media in collective action: the case of free lunch for children in China. Inf. Syst. J. **26**(3), 289–313 (2016)
40. Fayard, A., Weeks, J.: Affordances for practice. Inf. Organ. **24**, 236–249 (2014). doi:10.1016/j.infoandorg.2014.10.001
41. Roberts, T.: Women's use of participatory video technology to tackle gender inequality in Zambia's ICT sector. In: Proceedings of the 8th International Conference on Information and Communication Technology and Development, 4–6 June 2016, Ann Arbor, USA (2016)
42. Roberts, T.: Critical Agency in ICT4D, Unpublished Ph.D., Royal Holloway, University of London (2015)

Amplifying Positive Deviance with ICT

Enabling Community Development and Interdependence

William D. Tucker[(✉)]

University of the Western Cape, Bellville, South Africa
btucker@uwc.ac.za

Abstract. Positive deviance is a social mechanism whereby a beneficial practice that is not considered as normal gets taken up and spread within a community. This enables a community to solve its own problems aided by mentorship and facilitation. Through two long term case studies, we have identified positive deviants and are now learning how to leverage the ICT inherent in our interventions to cultivate and amplify positive change. We find both ourselves and beneficiary communities developing through various stages of dependence, independence and interdependence. We consider the latter a strong form of development. We now look at ICT4D projects as opportunities to identify positive deviants, and to amplify positive deviance with ICT. We posit that affordable, accessible and generic ICTs offer a way to do so, and that explicitly aiming to mentor and facilitate positive deviance with such ICT offers a path toward community development and interdependence.

Keywords: ICT-enabled development · Social mechanisms · Theory of amplification · Computing and society · Mixed methods

1 Introduction

In the ICT for development (ICT4D) space, e.g. IFIP WG 9.4, we generally aim to empower a community to look out for its own best interests, leveraging ICT that we develop, often in collaboration with beneficiaries. Herein lies the tension of applying ICT for development with indigent and/or disadvantaged communities: power relations rise to the surface all too often. For example, technical researchers design and develop code for a given project based on their technical expertise, often employing a participatory design method. How do we deal with this? Obviously, there are many strategies. Tucker [28] describes a continuum of participatory design from weak to strong, because in reality, participation, engagement and indeed empowerment varies. As with partial success and failures described by Heeks [11], ICT4D efforts can be viewed along a continuum of 'weak' to 'strong'. This paper contends that we can also do this by understanding the stages of community dependence, independence and interdependence as described by Kaplan [14]. As often noted, ICT4D community members are also beneficiaries, and our 'community' goes through those same development stages.

© IFIP International Federation for Information Processing 2017
Published by Springer International Publishing AG 2017. All Rights Reserved
J. Choudrie et al. (Eds.): ICT4D 2017, IFIP AICT 504, pp. 206–217, 2017.
DOI: 10.1007/978-3-319-59111-7_18

Amongst many failures, examples of successful ICT4D projects exist. For example, Toyama [27] contends that Digital Green, a project meant to improve food production in India, was successful largely because local farmers featured in movies that conveyed best practise farming information to farmers. This low-tech intervention worked because movies, rather than mobile apps or web-based information, fit within the communities' cultural milieu. The Digital Green process was bottom-up: farmers informing farmers; not experts instructing locals. For Toyama [27], the practitioner/researcher takes the role of mentor/facilitator. Thus, technology is seen as an amplifier of personal and social will, and a facilitator's role becomes that of encouraging people to change their behaviour while bettering oneself, and others, through that process. We believe what happened with Digital Green was that the project encouraged positive deviance, by showcasing the knowledge and experience of local farmers who learned to improve crop yield, and the medium of movies encouraged wider adoption of those practices.

We can agree that helping people, and ourselves, to change their/our own behaviour is preferable to being told what and how to change by outsiders. The first person to make a positive change may be the bravest, yet it is the second, third and so on, that can move a given community toward a 'tipping point' as termed by Gladwell [9]; where innovative, or deviant, becomes the new norm. This paper contends that 'positive deviance', a social mechanism described by Pascale *et al.* [18] and Spreitzer and Sonenshein [25], can be innovatively applied in the ICT4D space. We have identified unintentional vestiges of 'positive deviance' in two long running ICT4D case studies that we have conducted. We believe when done intentionally, ICT can amplify [27] this social mechanism; and further, that Kaplan's [14] stages of community dependence to independence to interdependence offer an intriguing way to view the process. The paper posits that for research problems such as bringing ICTs to bear on the socio-economic challenges faced by indigent and disadvantaged communities, represented by the two case studies presented herein, the "power of positive deviance" [18] can be amplified by ICT and help realise mutual community development and interdependence.

2   Key Concepts

The narrative follows Walsham [29], and this IFIP WG 9.4 conference's call for papers, and first defines what we mean by 'development', and then we clarify what we mean by positive deviance and ICT amplification.

2.1   Community Development

Community development as offered by Kaplan [14] resonates with Toyama's [27] advocacy of mentorship and facilitation in that a dynamic process between facilitator(s) and beneficiaries moves interrelationships, in a non-linear fashion, amongst stages of dependence, independence and interdependence. In our view, many ICT interventions also plot, again non-linearly, amongst a continuum of canonical action research stages: diagnosis, planning, implementation, evaluation and reflection (see Davison *et al.* [7]) whereby stakeholders move toward mutually defined goals to tackle mutually identified problems in a mutually beneficial way [16]. Ideal outcomes of action research can result in what we would call a 'stronger' stage of community development –interdependence– where the practitioner/researcher community is in some way invited *to* and/or integrated *in* the beneficiary community. This could even happen after one party or the other was possibly side-lined during a stage of independence. Such independence may have followed on a dependent stage where locals may have thought they needed outsider expertise/intervention or the intervening practitioner/researcher tacitly felt that s/he knew better than the recipients. The challenge is to overcome such power relations that come about during these various stages, and manifest changes within communities of both beneficiaries and facilitators. This view of development is ostensibly compatible with the sentiment of Toyama [27] in that behavioural change can be mentored and facilitated. An attractive way to achieve this is with the "power of positive deviance".

2.2   Positive Deviance

Positive deviance is a social mechanism whereby a beneficial practice that is not considered normal gets taken up by a community [18, 25]. In other words, it is a mechanism for encouraging and enabling an abnormal behaviour, one that is positive and good, to spread within a community, effectively towards Gladwell's 'tipping point' [9]. Positive deviance is inherently bottom-up as community members take responsibility for their own solution to problems, guided by an invited mentor/facilitator. Pascale *et al.* [18] believe positive deviance is useful in situations where traditional top-down mechanisms, such as random control trials and the like, fail.

Pascale *et al.* [18] describe case studies with practical guidelines on how to perform the method and also how to measure its impact (see http://positivedeviance.org). A well-known case study involved child health in Cambodia. Local authorities were facing the problem of childhood malnutrition and invited the Sternins (a husband and wife team, co-authors with Pascale) based on their work with UNICEF. Most children in an area identified by authorities were consuming the same diet, and exhibited low body mass index (BMI) scores. The Sternins framed the problem differently, by asking 'reverse' questions, e.g. asking are there children with healthy BMI scores, as opposed to why do so many people exhibit low BMI? It emerged that some children did in fact have healthy BMI scores because it became revealed that some parents in the community were supplementing the 'normal' diet with tiny crustaceans that lived amongst the rice paddies. These 'positive deviants' were improving the nutrition of their offspring by breaking the norm and providing their children with additional protein. Once this positive deviance was identified, the challenge morphed to spreading this behavioural change throughout the community. Again, the Sternins turned to the community for answers, and the community itself devised hands-on methods for encouraging more parents to behave like the positive deviants. Subsequent measurement of BMI across the community showed that this process was indeed beneficial. Interestingly, Pascale *et al.* [18] included a sidebar on ICT and bottom-up open source software development as espoused by Raymond [19] that they feel is corollary to bottom-up positive deviance, in that an open source community provides itself with answers. However, Pascale *et al.* [18] did not go so far as to suggest using ICT to amplify positive deviance.

2.3 ICT Amplification

ICT amplification is a view about the role of ICT in society. According to Toyama [27] this is the notion that ICT amplifies whatever human will is already present in a given scenario, e.g. if gender dynamics in a given community are balanced and equitable, ICT can only but help amplify this situation, and males and females alike are encouraged to participate in digital spaces. Conversely, if there are negative power relations, such as poor gender dynamics, the introduction of ICT can only but amplify those negative aspects such as keeping digital devices away from females. Thus, we can understand why in many situations where we intend ICT to be beneficial, it can lead to negative consequences. When positive, the view of amplification resonates with emancipatory ICT research associated with Buskens [4].

3 Case Studies

Now we apply these key concepts to two case studies. Both are long term ICT-oriented action research projects led by this paper's author. Each case description below has a brief overview of the project's current thrust, and explores it in terms of positive deviance, ICT amplification and community interdependence. Additional low level details of both projects can be found via citations. It should be noted that positive deviance was not explicitly pursued from the start for either project. In fact, the idea of employing positive deviance, and then leveraging ICT to amplify positive deviance, came about by viewing our ongoing projects with these lenses. Methodological concerns for each case study are provided in Sect. 4.

3.1 Case Study: Zenzeleni, A Rural Community-Owned and Run ISP

Many rural areas of South Africa experience the unfortunate situation of having almost ubiquitous mobile phone coverage where the majority of residents struggle to afford even basic ICT services [24]. Since 2003, we have explored various forms of rural wireless networks in the remote Eastern Cape province of South Africa. Since 2012, we have concentrated on Zenzeleni, a not-for-profit cooperative who have installed and now maintain a rural mesh network (see zenzeleni.net). Their solar powered wireless network provides free internal calls and 'breakout' calls to land-lines and mobile phones at a fraction of incumbent costs. Zenzeleni Mankosi currently covers 30 km^2 with 'mesh potato' stations, each with its own handset. We are busy installing broadband backhaul from a nearby university approximately 60 km away, and intend to share the connectivity to numerous secondary schools in the area. Zenzeleni generates income by charging mobile phone batteries, and offers prepaid 'breakout' calls and internet connectivity via low cost WiFi hotspots. In 2014, Zenzeleni obtained license exemption from ICASA, the national regulatory authority, to operate telecommunications infrastructure, setting a precedent for other South African communities to do so, too [23].

   Positive deviance can be identified amongst people associated with Zenzeleni. Following on an earlier project that used solar power to charge phone batteries [1], many more people are now charging phones at a dozen charging stations located around the community. The people who have the mesh potato stations in their homes are transparently providing the revenue back to the community, and that money is being used for loans within the community (and the interest ploughed back into the cooperative). There is also a local team providing technical support instead of relying on external technical skills. For example, the team replaced mesh potato antennae without our help, and also sorts out wiring and fuse issues on a regular basis. It is clear that the project is creating jobs in the midst of massive unemployment, and also imparts the opportunity to acquire financial and technical skills. The presence of accessible and affordable ICT has enabled almost a dozen female high school students to find scholarships online, and all of them are currently studying at tertiary colleges. The reality on the ground is a mix of positives and negatives. The cooperative earns revenue primarily from charging mobile phone batteries and not from (breakout) phone calls as originally envisaged. We believe the latter is largely due to people resisting change, all the while paying double the price of a Zenzeleni 'breakout' call. We also recognise that in order to make a Zenzeleni call, inhabitants must use a 'public' call station. While we feel that supporting WiFi-based calls from personal handsets will address the 'public phone' issue, we must keep in mind the "geek heresy" that a purely technical solution cannot solve this problem [27]. Enabling positive deviance with respect to call behaviour will entail the identification of people who are already using the Zenzeleni network to make calls, to figure out with them how it may be possible to get other people to change their call behaviour, too; saving money on telecommunications that could otherwise be used for food. We also must devise ways to get more women more involved because women can also be excluded from Zenzeleni processes [12]. We are hopeful that connecting secondary schools will offer more women the opportunity to participate in digital spaces and that the use of technology will spread through the youth, both male and female.

ICT amplification has occurred in various ways. Many community residents appear to think that the network 'belongs' to the tribal authority; that only its headman and sub-headmen, or members of the Zenzeleni cooperative, are allowed to use the 'public' phones [22]. Thus, Zenzeleni acts as yet another conduit for existing power relations within the community to continue. Another view is that many inhabitants may simply not understand that the stations in the community are more than just phone charging points, because the community had earlier been exposed to the aforementioned charging efforts and this may be how people view the Zenzeleni infrastructure [12, 22]. On a more positive note, recall the dozen female high school students that are now busy with tertiary studies. Clearly, the ICT provided by Zenzeleni has amplified those girls' abilities to pursue their own aspirations.

Community interdependence can be viewed on several levels. Within the Mankosi community itself, inhabitants already enjoy financial benefits of supporting their community-owned and run business because its revenues are ploughed back into the community in the form of micro-lending. However, it must be noted that the cooperative is not installing more solar mesh stations or paying for network maintenance. Those costs are still handled by the research team, and thus a form of financial dependence still exists. We are more interested, though, in the interdependence that has emerged between Mankosi community and the researcher community. Dearden and Tucker [8] would contend that this beneficial inter-relationship exists due to the continued series of ICT projects, in spite of many of them having failed, partially or fully. Relationships have been forged, maintained and strengthened over time. The project appears to have thus far avoided a catastrophic independence phase, e.g. the researchers were never asked to leave. One sign of independence includes the revenues being transparently utilised according to the cooperative's wishes. Some of the research team have lived in the community for an extended period and others have continually 'bungee researched' for almost 15 years. Over time, some of us have become accepted as part of an 'expanded' sense of community. In a reciprocal fashion, a community research assistant has co-authored research with us and even travelled internationally (a first for him) twice to report on the project and network with an international community. Through these exchanges, we move towards a more interdependent relationship.

3.2   Case Study: SignSupport, Assistive Technology for Deaf People

Many Deaf people in South Africa primarily communicate in sign language and communication with hearing people who cannot sign is a daily struggle. This problem is compounded when Deaf people require information and communication regarding health. Such priorities led to the development of SignSupport (www.signsupport.org), a mobile assistive technology for Deaf people. Since 2001, we have designed a variety assistive technologies with and for a marginalized and under-employed Deaf people in the Cape Town area. These people are proficient and fluent in sign language, yet due to poverty and under-education exhibit limited functional literacy with written and spoken language when interacting with a hearing majority. A multi-disciplinary and trans-university team, together with a collection of Deaf People's Organisations (DPOs) is currently busy with iterative and incremental design and evaluation of a mobile tool suite that bridges information and communication gaps between Deaf and hearing people, in the language that these Deaf people understand: South African Sign Language (SASL). We are generalizing this tool to handle multiple limited interaction scenarios [3]. There are several scenarios in prototype: a visit to a pharmacy [5], international computer driver license (ICDL) training [17], and a diabetes information scenario [6].

Positive deviance is easy to spot within one DPO in particular, called Deaf Community of Cape Town (DCCT). Its entire staff has come to embrace technology due largely to a continuous ICT research presence. Several DCCT staff are certified with International Computer Driving License (ICDL), one of them manages the network and another helps to maintain the computer lab. These positive deviants are now role models for the thousands of Deaf people served by the DPO. Due to a spate of independence (see below), the research team only recently began to establish ties with other Deaf organisations in the area, with the hope of identifying and mentoring more positive deviants, especially amongst the youth. As we interact with more Deaf communities, we continually learn about new apps that Deaf people use to communicate. In other words, ICT literacy is 'catchy', and spreads, thus paving the way for positive deviance to spread.

ICT amplification is clearly enabled by SignSupport, a mobile app meant to increase the reach of official healthcare information to Deaf people in SASL, e.g. for diabetes [6]. It must be noted that the initial idea for SignSupport came from Deaf people who had participated with us after years of ICT research projects. We believe it was their increased familiarity with ICT in general that empowered them to frame their community's priority for understandable healthcare information via an app like SignSupport through drawings [5]. Positive deviants at DCCT also utilise ICT to amplify their own tasks, e.g. several staff members are trained HIV/AIDS community health workers and they leverage ICT to do that job better. However, their main dissemination of health information is via enacted dramas. The SignSupport project aims to incorporate videos of such info-dramas conducted on a stage, into the mobile app in yet another form of amplification. We are hoping that SignSupport provides a vehicle for positive deviance to spread by featuring well-known members of the community in those videos, a la Digital Green.

Community interdependence is emerging by learning how to better use the community-based co-design model [2]. It has not always gone easily. We are entirely dependent on sign language interpreters to conduct almost all aspects of the research. Of course, our students take sign language courses, but then they graduate and leave! And there are not only linguistic challenges; they can be cultural and interpersonal as well. Via reading between the lines of personal communication, it emerged that beneath the relatively benign suggestion by one Deaf community who asked researchers to include other Deaf communities, there was actually a 'push' indicating that they themselves felt 'pushed'; perhaps research fatigue or perhaps they felt they were not benefiting enough from the intervention? Kaplan [14] would say this is natural, and subsequent re-engagement with the 'pushing' community appears to be on track. Now, several more DPOs are now part of the universities' research programme, gifting us more perspectives on our work. One especially promising development is that we learned of a small group of Deaf students involved in a mobile programming course in another province. At some point, it would be wonderful to get Deaf programmers involved in the SignSupport project, and develop an even deeper sense of interdependence in the technical space.

4   Methodology

Both case studies operate under an action research umbrella [7, 10, 15, 16]. We view action research more as a paradigm than a specific methodology, and are most interested in generating new knowledge and ways to address social challenges. Given our background in experimental computer science, we produce computing artefacts, and aim to intervene with communities in such a way that their priorities drive our technology development agenda. This is one way to ensure that the technology we produce can help them drive their own social agenda. Then, together, we can reflect on the experience of using such a system. Overall methods for each project are explained below.

4.1   Zenzeleni Methodology

The data collection for the Zenzeleni project comprises a mix of quantitative and qualitative methods. In the Mankosi community, we work closely with the community's tribal authority (traditional leadership), a team of local research assistants (whose leader assumes the role of local champion) and also a co-located NGO. The thrust of a particular research project operates under a collective action research umbrella where we mutually define goals and mechanisms to achieve and evaluate them. Residents often collect data with us and also on our behalf; and at least one resident (most often the champion) helps to analyse and contextualise the results. Occasionally, we have a student from the area who speaks the local language and has a deeper personal experience of the local culture that can help interpret results beyond mere language translation.

An example of quantitative data collection on the project is a baseline study conducted to understand how residents use and spend on telecommunications. We used stratified sampling to survey households in the dozen villages that comprise Mankosi [24]. We used ODK (see opendatakit.org) on low end mobile phones to collect this data with the help of local research assistants who could translate the questionnaire questions and its answers. ODK also allowed us to record open-ended questions for subsequent translation. The questionnaire was adapted from the Household survey obtained from Research ICT Africa (RIA) (see [26] and www.researchictafrica.net). The tribal authority calculated the number of people in each village, and from there we determined how to sample. We conducted two surveys in 2012 and 2013 [24]. With baseline data in place, we can repeat this form of data collection in order to analyse changes in line with ICT interventions over time. We can also anonymously access call record details and network usage statistics to get fully instrumented usage metrics on the network.

In order to achieve a deeper understanding of the context, we also collect ethnographic data based on long-term presence in the community. For example, we have had academic team members resident in the community from 6–15 months at a time. Long-term presence enables rich engagement via a variety of formal and informal conversations with community members. More often, however, we conduct 2–3 week visits for a given purpose. Many of the younger generation speak basic English, yet the older generation prefers isiXhosa. We therefore employ local research assistants to conduct both structured interviews and focus group sessions. We use such techniques to enquire about a range of issues surrounding the project, e.g. designing the billing system [21], gender roles in the project [12] and the role of ICT in local schools (yet to be published).

4.2 SignSupport Methodology

Our take on action research with the SignSupport project has led us to what we call community-based co-design [2], with aspects of participatory action research [15] and co-design [13, 20]. 'Community-based' conveys the fact that we deal with groups of people rather than individuals, aligned with the African concept of 'ubuntu'. A group approach can be very different from engineering toward individual requirements, e.g. in Africa, phones are often shared devices and we must design accordingly. We must constantly remain sensitive to cultural differences and develop ways of entering into design conversations with people who may not have strong technical skills yet who are knowledgeable on their own needs, and especially how their own communities operate.

We collaborate with industrial design engineers who work with Deaf people as co-designers, and together identify the problems that needs to be addressed, the means of tackling the issues and then together decide on measures of success. We employ techniques such as cultural probes and generative sessions. Then we provide mock-up designs, conduct training with Deaf participants and provide exercises for end-users who then get together afterwards for a focus group discussion. This is very similar to early stage co-design [20]. From a practical standpoint, it is important to hold follow up feedback sessions to keep the community in the loop after we take the data back to the lab, e.g. to develop a mock-up into a proper mobile app. Then we return to the community with the app in a series of incremental feedback and iterative development cycles. We also conduct workshops to brainstorm how to move these research-driven apps out of the lab and into Deaf people's hands. We also take a wider view of community, and also involve, in the case of SignSupport for diabetes, health professionals in all phases of the action research. This is because the health professionals, who cannot sign, are just as interested in providing health care information to Deaf people as Deaf people are interested in gaining access to health information in sign language.

During the sessions described above, it is also critical that experts keep their own design decisions in abeyance, albeit temporarily, in order to allow for co-designers to find their own voice and participate meaningfully. With Deaf participants, we rely on sign language interpreters, and herein lie a subtle aspect of data collection with Deaf people. Sign language is an incredibly descriptive language and interpreters are tasked with explaining and describing concepts that may or may not have direct translation, in either direction. For example, finger spelling the name of a browser or a medical condition is often not enough. The interpreter often creates a story in order to characterise a technical term. Therefore, it helps to have an interpreter that has been immersed in the ICT research programme for an extended amount of time, to be better at explaining such terms that dominate our discourse during semi-structured interviews, surveys, and focus groups. Note that we have also conducted a baseline survey on telecommunications use of Deaf people, also with ODK. We instrumented ODK to have a sign language interface, and also record sign language video for subsequent interpretation.

5 Discussion

Both case studies show that there is a difference between identifying a positive deviant, and then applying or leveraging ICT to achieve more positive deviance. The former has been realised by introducing the ICT research project to the community; and attaching it to the community to enable their input. However, the next stage is more important. Our goal has been to provide generic ICTs, primed for appropriation using the local language (SASL for SignSupport and isiXhosa for Zenzeleni voice communications). What happens is that communities at first discover such ICTs dependently, and that then acts as a springboard for subsequent discovery *without* (independence) or *with* (interdependent) 'us'. For example, perhaps a DPO wants to start its own video relay service. They could seek our advice for the underlying technical platform, even ask us to develop it, or co-develop it with Deaf programmers and technical support. However, once in place, the Deaf communities themselves can leverage that video relay service for their own purposes; again, with or without us. This is very similar to the voice and internet services provided to rural inhabitants by Zenzeleni. If a given cooperative decides they want to sell WiFi-enabled mobile phones to establish another revenue stream, there is no reason why the coop cannot do this independently, with or without our help and/or advice. Furthermore, they can leverage the voice calling and internet connectivity to put that, or any other community effort, into practice.

Positive deviance is therefore a social mechanism that can operate within and between communities; and can indeed by amplified by ICT. We can further this agenda by designing and providing generic ICTs that allow for adoption and appropriation by communities. This is attainable when the technologies are affordable and accessible, and especially when content is provided in the local language. Thus, as ICT4D researchers and practitioners, we can turn our attention to a) developing ICTs that fit these characteristics and b) figure out ways to use those ICTs to amplify positive deviance. In the process of doing so, the development aspects apply to these communities as well as to ourselves. As we mentor and facilitate positive deviance in marginalised communities, we also develop and grow ourselves.

6   Conclusion and Moving Forward

The two case studies have afforded us the opportunity to identify positive deviants in very different ICT scenarios, and contemplate how ICT can leverage positive deviance [18, 25]. We note that originally, our projects were not conceived with positive deviance in mind. Yet that does not stop us from explicitly pursuing it now. Affordable, accessible and generic ICT in a local language, such as SignSupport's scenario-independent mobile app and Zenzeleni's voice calling and internet connectivity, provide a platform on which communities can amplify their own community-oriented priorities and aspirations. Reflecting on the social mechanism of positive deviance in connection with the principle of ICT amplification has led us to rethink what we mean by community development. We have found that the views of Toyama [27] and Kaplan [14] intertwine and resonate with how we have come to perceive relationships with our so-called 'beneficiary' communities. A key takeaway is that we are also beneficiaries, developing ourselves and our own capacities in ways that can be fed back to the communities with whom we work. From this, we learn our primary role is to be mentor and facilitator. As our case studies have evolved over the long-term, we have come to see positive deviance as a social mechanism that we should embrace and encourage mindfully, leveraging ICT to amplify this mechanism. We believe this can lead to community development, especially in terms of interdependence between the academic/practitioner community together with the communities we seek to assist. In our opinion, this serves to develop 'their' community as much as 'ours', and in many ways, as the communities overlap, we can realise a mutually beneficial interdependence.

Acknowledgements.   Various aspects of this work have been supported by the Telkom Centre of Excellence Programme (including contributions from Telkom, Cisco and Aria Technologies), South Africa's National Research Foundation (NRF) and the Department of Trade and Industry's Technology and Human Resources for Industry Partnership (THRIP) programme, the European Commission's CONFINE project, and the University of the Western Cape. Thanks also to Ineke for the idea origin spark.

References

1. Bidwell, N.J., Siya, M.B., Marsden, G., Tucker, W.D., Tshemese, M., Gaven, N., Ntlangano, S., Robinson, S., Eglinton, K.A.: Walking and the social life of solar charging in Rural Africa. ACM Trans. Comput. Hum. Interact. (TOCHI) **20**(4), 22 (2013). doi:10.1145/2493524. Article 22
2. Blake, E.H., Tucker, W.D., Glaser, M., Freudenthal, A.: Deaf telephony: community-based co-design. In: Rogers, Y., Sharp, H., Preece, J. (eds.) Interaction Design: Beyond Human-Computer Interaction, 3rd edn, pp. 412–413. Wiley, Chichester (2011)
3. Blake, E., Tucker, W.D., Glaser, M.: Towards communication and information access for Deaf people. S. Afr. Comp. J. (SACJ) **54**(2), 10–19 (2014)
4. Buskens, I.: Research methodology for personal and social transformation: purpose-aligned action research, intentional agency and dialogue. In: Buskens, I., Webb, A. (eds.) Women and ICT in Africa and the Middle East: Changing Selves, Changing Societies, pp. 291–310. Zed Books, London (2014). Chap. 22
5. Chininthorn, P., Glaser, M., Freudenthal, A., Tucker, W.D.: Mobile communication tools for a South African deaf patient in a pharmacy context. In: Proceedings of the IST-Africa. IIMC, Dar es Salaam (2016)
6. Chininthorn, P., Glaser, M., Tucker, W.D., Diehl, J.C.: Exploration of Deaf people's health information sources and techniques for information delivery in Cape Town: a qualitative study for the design and development of a mobile health application. JMIR Hum. Fact. **3**(2), e28 (2016). doi:10.2196/humanfactors.6653
7. Davison, R.M., Martinsons, M.G., Kock, N.: Principles of canonical action research. Inf. Syst. J. **14**, 65–86 (2004)
8. Dearden, A., Tucker, W.D.: Moving ICTD research beyond bungee jumping: practical case studies and recommendations. IEEE Technol. Soc. Mag. **35**(3), 36–43 (2016). doi:10.1109/MTS.2016.2593267
9. Gladwell, M.: The Tipping Point: How Little Things can Make a Big Difference. Abacus, London (2000)
10. Hayes, G.R.: The relationship of action research to human-computer interaction. ACM Trans. on Comp. Hum. Int. (TOCHI) **18**(3) (2011). Article 15
11. Heeks, R.: Information systems and developing countries: failure, success, and local improvisations. Inf. Soc. **18**(2), 101–112 (2002). doi:10.1080/01972240290075039
12. Hussen, T.S., Bidwell, N.J., Rey-Moreno, C., Tucker, W.D.: Gender and participation: critical reflection on Zenzeleni networks in Mankosi, South Africa. In: Proceedings of the AfriCHI, pp. 12–23. ACM Press, New York (2016). doi:10.1145/2998581.2998585
13. Kam, M., Ramachandran, D., Raghavan, A., Chiu, J., Sahni, U., Canny, J.: Practical considerations for participatory design with rural school children in underdeveloped regions: early reflections from the field. In: Proceedings of the Interaction Design and Children, pp. 25–32. ACM Press, New York (2006). doi:10.1145/1139073.1139085
14. Kaplan, A.: The Development Practitioners' Handbook. Pluto Press, London (1996)
15. Kemmis, S., McTaggart, R.: Participatory action research. In: Denzin, N.K., Lincoln, Y.S. (eds.) Handbook of Qualitative Research, 2nd edn, pp. 567–606. Sage, Thousand Oaks (2000)
16. McKay, J., Marshall, P.: The dual imperatives of action research. Inf. Technol. People **14**, 146–159 (2001)
17. Ng'ethe, G., Blake, E., Glaser, M.: SignSupport: a mobile aid for Deaf people learning computer literacy skills. In: Proceedings of the 7th International Conference on Computer Supported Education (CSEDU), vol. 2, pp. 501–511. SCITEPRESS (2015). doi: 10.5220/0005442305010511

18. Pascale, R.T., Sternin, J., Sternin, M.: The Power of Positive Deviance: How Unlikely Innovators Solve the World's Toughest Problems, vol. 1. Harvard Business Press, Brighton (2010)

19. Raymond, E.: The cathedral and the bazaar. Knowl. Technol. Policy **12**(3), 23–49 (1999). doi: 10.1007/s12130-999-1026-0

20. Ramachandran, D., Kam, M., Chiu, J., Canny, J., Frankel, J.L.: Social dynamics of early stage co-design in developing regions. In: Proceedings of the Human Factors in Computing Systems (CHI), pp. 1087–1096. ACM Press, New York (2007). doi:10.1145/1240624.1240790

21. Rey-Moreno, C., Ufitamahoro, M.J., Venter, I., Tucker, W.D.: Co-designing a billing system for voice services in rural South Africa: lessons learned. In: Proceedings of the 5th International Symposium on Computing for Development (ACM DEV-5), pp. 83–92. ACM Press, New York (2014). doi:10.1145/2674377.2674389

22. Rey-Moreno, C., Sabiescu, A.G., Siya, M.J., Tucker, W.D.: Local ownership, exercise of ownership and moving from passive to active entitlement: a practice-led inquiry on a rural community network. J. Commun. Inf. (JOCI) **11**(2) (2015)

23. Rey-Moreno, C., Tucker, W. D., Cull, D., Blom, R.: Making a community network legal within the South African regulatory framework. In: Proceedings of the 7th International Conference on Information and Communication Technologies and Development (ICTD). ACM Press, New York (2015). Article 57. doi:10.1145/2737856.2737867

24. Rey-Moreno, C., Blignaut, R., May, J., Tucker, W.D.: An in-depth study of the ICT ecosystem in a South African rural community: unveiling expenditure and communication patterns. Inf. Technol. Dev. (ITD) **22**, 1–20 (2016). doi:10.1080/02681102.2016.1155145

25. Spreitzer, G.M., Sonenshein, S.: Positive deviance and extraordinary organizing. In: Positive Organizational Scholarship, pp. 207–224. Sage Publications (2003). Chap. 14

26. Stork, C., Stork, M.: ICT household survey methodology and fieldwork, volume one. Policy Paper 1. Research ICT Africa (2008)

27. Toyama, K.: Geek Heresy: Rescuing Social Change from the Cult of Technology. PublicAffairs, New York (2015)

28. Tucker, William D.: Beyond traditional ethics when developing assistive technology for and with Deaf people in developing regions. In: Hersh, M. (ed.) Ethical Engineering for International Development and Environmental Sustainability, pp. 293–323. Springer, London (2015). doi:10.1007/978-1-4471-6618-4_10

29. Walsham, G.: Development informatics in a changing world: reflections from ICTD 2010/2012. Inf. Technol. Int. Dev. (ITID) **9**(1), 49–54 (2013)

The Data Revolution and Sustainable Development Goals

Open Data Reuse, Recycling and Sharing as Potential Solution to Data and Information Resource Inadequacies

Kyla Matias[1(✉)], Tetsuo Kidokoro[1], Scira Menoni[2], Ouejdane Mejri[3],
and Negar Aminoltaheri[4]

[1] Department of Urban Engineering, The University of Tokyo, Bunkyō, Japan
k.matias@urban.t.u-tokyo.ac.jp
[2] Department of Architecture and Urban Studies (DASTU),
Politecnico di Milano, Milan, Italy
[3] Department of Electronics, Information and Bioengineering,
Politecnico di Milano, Milan, Italy
[4] Faculty of Civil, Environmental and Territorial Engineering,
Politecnico di Milano, Milan, Italy

Abstract. This paper explores the reuse, recycling and sharing of open data (OD) as a potential solution to bridge gaps in existing baseline data and information in areas with scarce data resources. It focuses on open data generated during disasters, and analyses how these voluminous 'free disaster data,' such as social media posts, images, damage assessment reports, etc., could be reused and recycled to serve purposes other than emergency response and relief. To illustrate this, the paper makes use of a previous research that analysed how the open data of Super Typhoon Haiyan, the hydrometeorological disaster which affected several nations, and gained both local and global attention, could be reused and recycled as inputs for development planning, especially in post-disaster recovery and rehabilitation, and pre-disaster mitigation and prevention planning.

Keywords: Open data · Data reuse · Data recycling · Data sharing · Pre-disaster · Mitigation · Prevention · Post-disaster · Recovery · Development · Land use planning

1 Introduction

Information and communications technologies (ICT) are the impetus of this information age (Masuda 1981) wherein data and information are the new raw materials (Maeng and Nedovic-Budic 2007). Given this crucial role in the development and growth of societies, it may be said that data and information are the most valuable commodities of planning (Lord 2012).

As an inherently knowledge-intensive exercise (Goodspeed 2011), planning requires a steady stock of readily available and reliable data and information that could provide causal knowledge (Wildavsky 1973) that is needed to support strategy development and inform decision-making.

© IFIP International Federation for Information Processing 2017
Published by Springer International Publishing AG 2017. All Rights Reserved
J. Choudrie et al. (Eds.): ICT4D 2017, IFIP AICT 504, pp. 221–231, 2017.
DOI: 10.1007/978-3-319-59111-7_19

Fortunately, current ICT advancements are able to fulfill this demand through new and innovative data collection technologies and techniques, and wider data distribution channels (Sustainable Development Solutions Network (SDSN) 2015), which has made data generation and exchanges easier and faster. However, this is a privilege that is not enjoyed by all due to disparate development conditions and unequal distribution of resources (Graham 2002). These conditions pose limitations and create tensions, especially in developing regions (Maxwell and Reuveny 2000), where varying issues and interests abound and compete for the allocation of scarce resources. These areas struggle to sustain and boost growth and development while also trying to address other pressing issues, such as climate change, environmental hazards or disasters (UNISDR and ESCAP 2012). As a result, the obvious and perceptible problems get prioritised, while other "trifling" issues, such as the need to improve one's baseline data and information or geospatial data infrastructures, end up filed away and forgotten until the moment of necessity presents itself again.

Although data and information only form a part of the requirements for promoting and boosting one's growth and development, it plays an important part in accurately identifying vital concerns that must be put on top of the agenda. It is also required for monitoring and evaluating the performance and effectiveness of implemented programs and strategies so that adjustments could be made accordingly in order to avoid further resource wastage, which is crucial for disadvantaged communities. As such, greater attention must be accorded to these data and information gaps if we were to plan effectively and efficiently towards promoting sustainable development, and safeguarding achievements and gains.

In response to the issue, the paper offers an insight on how present ICT trends and developments could help deal with the problem, and explores potential alternatives that could ease data and information resource inadequacies, such as harnessing the potential of open data (OD). The next section discusses factors contributing to the problem, including conceivable hindrances to its resolution. It is followed by a case study that presents a practical application of OD reuse, recycling, and sharing, and concludes by discussing the perceived benefits and challenges that could be the subject of future investigation.

2 Data and Information Resource Inadequacy Issues

Data and information gaps come in various forms such as being unavailable, inaccessible or having questionable integrity and quality (World Bank 2014). While it is obvious that the absence of data and information can pose serious consequences, the utilisation of poor quality data and information may also lead to undesirable outcomes. Both were witnessed in past disaster events, such as the 2010 Haiti Earthquake where unmapped areas and roads had to be traced to aid emergency response, and the 2013 Typhoon Haiyan in the Philippines, wherein storm surge hazard maps underestimated the maximum inundation levels, which led to a false sense of security and complacency. The aforementioned examples showed that the lack of information slowed down emergency response and relief efforts, while the use of imprecise data aggravated the disaster's ill effects. Both of these unfortunate situations have contributed to the larger number of casualties, and could have been averted if better information had been available and accessible.

This problem is not only evident in disaster management, its crucial effects also extend to other components of development: social services, economy, etc., and could translate to poorer services, imbalanced growth and development trends, and although indirectly, lesser investment opportunities.

In everyday life it may seem that data and information issues do not pose grave immediate threats nor evoke a "real" sense of urgency, but the examples illustrate that leaving it unaddressed could impact future events. It also stresses the importance of having and sharing reliable data and information in order to fully understand various issues, and avoid making erroneous choices.

This problem is usually more critical in underdeveloped and developing regions where baseline datasets and information are scarce and often outdated. Understandably, there is a cost in addressing these issues, and it would require upfront investments being made. This cost becomes a major inhibiting factor for those that are typically plagued by this problem. For in most cases, the creation and access to data and information comes at a price tag that these lower and middle-income economies could hardly afford.

These are great challenges that could discourage and hinder willingness to genuinely address the issue, but the need to protect development gains and societies' well-being, as well as ensure the sustainability of progress, should be accorded with much greater significance, and this can only be attained when there's a full understanding of issues and situations so that the appropriate decisions and actions are made with sound judgment.

3   Reduce, Reuse, Recycle: The Potential of Open Data as Solution to Data and Information Inadequacies

There is no skirting around the fact that resources must be allotted to resolve data and information inadequacies. Fortunately, recent ICT developments could be utilised to devise more affordable and innovative solutions to this problem (Urbancic 2006).

With the proliferation of the internet and the World Wide Web, data and information creation, access, and sharing have become convenient for all, especially the public (Stauffacher et al. 2012). These incessant technological advancements have also led to the breaking down of physical boundaries. Previously, data and information sharing have been confined within common spaces, but now it is possible to access and share data and information even when you are in a different geographical region. This has been observed in the recent disaster events where in people from all over the globe actively participated in disaster information exchanges, as well as "remote disaster response efforts." The ease of access and sharing is a great feat made possible by modern technology, and it has allowed greater civic engagement and unrestricted information exchanges that has further led to an exponential growth of freely accessible information (Stauffacher et al. 2012) such as ODs.

In order to demonstrate how ODs can be reused and recycled for purposes other than its original intent, the case of Tacloban City in the Philippines was selected.

The reasons for this are (1) its involvement in a recent event that attracted immense attention and efforts to the area, (2) the availability of widespread materials generated by various volunteers and organisations around the globe, and (3) access to official maps and information supplied by the local authorities.

3.1 Typhoon Haiyan Quick Facts and Figures

In the early weeks of November 2013, Typhoon Haiyan, a Saffir-Simpson Category 5 typhoon, struck the Asia-Pacific region. It affected several countries including the Federated States of Micronesia (FSM), Philippines, Vietnam and China. Nonetheless, the massive destruction was concentrated in the Philippines where 9 out of 17 administrative regions of the country were disturbed. It was later reported that Haiyan claimed approximately 6,300 lives and caused immense damage amounting to an estimated $2B US dollars (National Disaster Risk Reduction and Management Council (NDRRMC) 2014).

Tacloban City in the Province of Leyte, Philippines suffered the most due to the unexpectedly high inundation from the storm surge, which was further aggravated by the robust winds. Despite carrying out pre-emptive evacuation, the number of casualties still soared as some of the evacuation centres were also submerged (ABS-CBN News 2013). As shown in Table 1, in Tacloban City alone, there were 2,678 casualties, which accounts for the 42.5% of the total number of fatalities in the country, and nearly 60,000 homes were destroyed and damaged causing the displacement of families, and leaving many parents and children bereaved.

Table 1. Data on affected households and population in Tacloban and the Philippines

Haiyan affected statistics	TotalCount (Tacloban City)	TotalCount (Leyte Province)	% Share of Tacloban vs. Leyte Province	TotalCount (Philippines)	% Share of Tacloban vs. PH
Damaged houses	58,823	381,810	15%	1,140,332	5.15%
Household (HH)	58,823	441,588	13%	3,424,593	1.7%
Persons	552,836	2,364,023	23.4%	16,078,181	3.4%
Fatalities	2,678	5,402	49.6%	6,300	42.5%
Injured persons	–	15,672	–	28,688	–
Missing persons	701	931	75.3%	1,062	66%

Source: National Disaster Risk Reduction and Management Council (NDRRMC) (2014)

3.2 Data Deluge: Mining Haiyan's Voluminous Open Data

Recent technological advancements have allowed both the authorities and the public to forecast imminent disasters, and prepare for it. The case of Typhoon Haiyan was no exception. Despite the soaring number of casualties brought about by the disaster's overwhelming destruction, it was a well-anticipated event whose enormous magnitude piqued various interests, and captured both local and global attention and concern.

Countless contributors from all over the globe, and all walks of life took advantage of the world wide web to collect and share data and information regarding the super typhoon, which eventually led to the generation of innumerable ODs. These ODs came in various formats and from different platforms such as text-based or image-based social media posts, interactive disaster simulation models, satellite images as well as dynamic maps.

These various data and information became useful during the course of the disaster as it aided preparedness, and response and relief efforts. However, after the catastrophe, many of these ODs and information will not be utilised, but will still remain in the wild. Given that many of these contain significant information that were once outdated or inaccessible, especially to those with scarce data and information resources, it may be worth considering to recycle and reuse these, and harness their potential.

With the primary objective of identifying how ODs generated during disaster events could be applied for other purposes other than the original intent, Typhoon Haiyan's case was used and its ODs were later collected manually using search engines, RSS feeds, social media, etc.

The resulting collection had diverse characteristics, which offered a wealth of information, but required tedious work to organise, and analyse prior to application and use. These were simplified through tabulation as shown in Table 2, which contains a partial list of the collected ODs. These were later grouped into different typologies using taxonomy and ontology, such as Fig. 1, which provided a visual representation of the collected data's typologies and relationships. This process of grouping and reorganising of the data helped uncover similarities in the nature of the collected data, and its potential usage. Most of the collected ODs were spatially-enabled, and had similar characteristics to the data requirements of local development planning (Table 3). As such, reusing ODs as alternative inputs for local development planning of the typhoon

Table 2. Haiyan data sorting table

Document Name	Document Type	Area of Interest (Location of Incident or Event)	Source / Origin (Name of generator, producer, owner)	OD Prod.		Context — Exposure / Resource	Crisis — Hazard / Disaster Consequence	Remarks / Other Details	Link to Document Location (if any)
Phils. Typhoon Haiyan/ Yolanda Map (Aggregated)	Text		Harvard / World Map	Volunteered x	Traditional x	Population x, Building x, Manpower x	Incident x, Indirect Loss x	Dynamic / Interactive Map	http://worldmap.harvard.edu/maps/typhoon_haiyan
Crisis Map		PH	GISCorps / Micromappers	x		Infrastructure —	Incident x, Direct Loss x, Direct Damage x	Urgent need Tweets/ Info about needed resources not available resources.	http://giscorps.maps.arcgis.com
Tacloban Damage Assessment Report	Vector Files	PH	Copernicus	x		Population x	Direct Damage x	Scale 1:12,500	http://emergency.copernicus.eu/mapping/list-of-components/EMSR058
Various Land Use Maps		Tacloban	Tacloban LGU	x		Population x, Building x, Critical Facility x		Scale 1:25,000	
Flood Susceptibility Map		Tacloban	MGB	x		Critical Facility x	Incident x	Official map for validation use / Scale 1:50,000	
Tacloban Storm Surge Hazard Map		Tacloban	Tacloban LGU	x			Incident x	Official map for validation use / Scale 1:17,000	
Landslide Hazard Map		Tacloban	Tacloban LGU	x			Incident x	Official map for validation use / Scale 1:17,000	
Comprehensive Land Use Plan	Table/ Graph	Tacloban	Tacloban LGU	x	x x x x	Population x	Incident x		
Tacloban Infrastructure		Tacloban/ PH	Tacloban LGU	x		Critical Facility x			

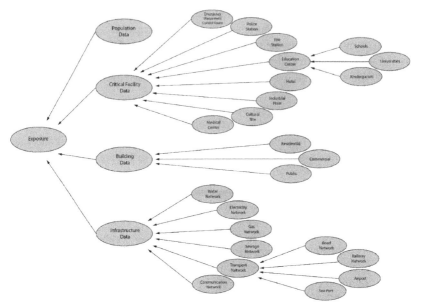

Fig. 1. The taxonomy of exposure data

afflicted area could be one of the practical applications of disaster-related ODs, and a suitable model for OD reuse and recycling.

3.3 Haiyan's Open Data Reuse and Recycling

In the Philippines, land use planning is commonly used by local authorities to guide area development. Coincidentally, there is also a prevalence of gaps in the existing planning datasets and information stock. Bearing this in mind, Haiyan's ODs were tested as alternative inputs for planning. This would also determine whether the retrieved open data may be reused and recycled to serve another purpose, and if it could help bridge existing data and information gaps.

Given the huge variety of the ODs, only those data that were spatially-enabled, and specific to the study area were chosen to be used. These data are listed in Table 2, and were applied as inputs in a land use planning exercise that is used to evaluate land suitability, commonly known as sieve mapping (Serote 2008). It is done by placing maps over another to produce new images that would reveal potential opportunities and threats for the area that is proposed to be developed.

In order to carry this out, the collected ODs need to be combined with other relevant data from the study area, such as administrative and hazard maps. These were obtained from the local and national authorities. (See Figs. 2 and 3.)

By combining these official maps and the open data collected, new maps were generated. (See Figs. 4 and 5.) Unfortunately, the collected ODs and the information supplied by the authorities came in varying formats and scales, which restricted its

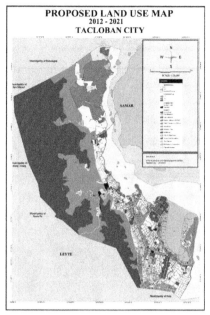

Source: Tacloban LGU, 2012

Fig. 2. Tacloban City's proposed land use map

Source: Tacloban LGU, 2012

Fig. 3. Official storm surge hazard map before Haiyan's occurrence

manipulation. As a consequence, scale has been sacrificed during the sieve mapping. Thus, the resulting overlays are more of approximations for illustrative purposes. Nevertheless, the resulting overlays fairly give us an idea how an area might have changed due to the recent disaster. It is also useful to highlight issues and problems that might have been previously overlooked during plan creation or review. Any finding from the new overlays could be later verified and further studied prior to making the necessary amendments in existing plans.

In the case of the generated maps using Haiyan's OD, it highlighted the weakness of the previous storm surge hazard map that have only illustrated modest levels of inundation as depicted in Fig. 3. Comparing this with Fig. 4, the overlay of the administrative map and the storm surge simulation map from Harvard's World Map site clearly shows that inundation could, and actually extended beyond the identified areas in the official storm surge hazard map. The OD map depicted a scenario that was closer to the actual flooding that happened during the typhoon.

Additionally, Fig. 5, the overlay of the storm surge model, crisis information and Tacloban's proposed land use, highlights other potentially hazardous areas, such as areas designated as future residential zones, that could be further evaluated during future amendments.

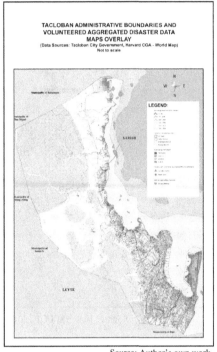

Source: Author's own work

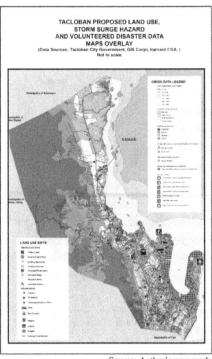

Source: Author's own work

Fig. 4. Overlay of administrative boundaries and storm surge model map

Fig. 5. Overlay of land use map and storm surge model map

Table 3. Charting the overlapping of emergency management and spatial planning data requirements based on the Disaster/Emergency Management (D/E)M data taxonomy and ontology

Disaster/Emergency Management (D/EM) data ontology		D/EM cycle phase use			Plan use	Remarks
		M/P	P	R	R	
Context data						
1 Exposure	Population	x	x	x	x	May be useful for future planning
	Building	x	x	x	x	
	Critical Facility (CF)	x	x	x	x	CF damage and consequence required in recovery phase
	Infrastructure	x	x	x	x	May be useful for future planning

(continued)

Table 3. (*continued*)

Disaster/Emergency Management (D/EM) data ontology			D/EM cycle phase use				Plan use	Remarks
			M/P	P	R	R		
2	Resource	Human	x	x	x		x	May be useful in recovery phase and future planning
		Monetary	x	x	x		x	Necessary for resource allocation and prioritisation decisions
		Vehicles		x	x		x	May be useful in future planning (esp. considering response)
		Vital Lines		x	x		x	May be useful in recovery phase and future planning
		Shelter		x	x		x	Proper location identification during SP
		Equipment	x	x	x		x	Specific equipment considered in SP
Crisis Data								
3	Hazard	Monitoring	x	x	x	x	x	Regular monitoring including historical data is useful for SP
		Alerts		x	x			May be useful in recovery phase with secondary effects
		Incidents			x		x	Past incidents can be used as basis for future mitigation through SP
4	Consequences	Direct	Loss	x	x	x	x	x	May be used as references in
			Damage	x	x	x	x	x	M/P, P, R to cut down future
		Indirect	Loss	x	x		x	x	losses
			Damage	x	x		x	x	

Source: Author's own work

4 Conclusion

Scarcity of resources has been the classic excuse for incompetence, slow growth or stunted development. Though it may be true that the availability of resources such as data, information and intellectual capacities influence one's own ability to be comprehensive (Lindblom 1959) when tackling problems, there are novel ways to deal with these inadequacies.

In response to these insufficiencies in data and information, the example cited in this paper investigated how open data can be reused and recycled to fill in these gaps. It analysed the case of Typhoon Haiyan in Tacloban, Philippines to show how freely available and publicly accessible data that were generated during disaster events could be retooled for local development planning, especially in pre-disaster mitigation and prevention, and post-disaster recovery and rehabilitation scenarios. It could be useful in aiding planners to craft more risk-sensitive development plans that would integrate appropriate disaster management strategies for their respective areas.

Various ODs of Typhoon Haiyan were collected, but priority was given to those with spatial references. These were utilised as inputs in a mock sieve mapping, an exercise that was commonly utilised for land use planning within the study area. The resulting overlay maps have highlighted some inconsistencies in the proposed land use plan and existing hazard maps, which might have been overlooked during plan creation and review, or could have been altered by the recent event, and may be investigated further in future planning exercises and research. Even though it was a test case, it demonstrated the possibility of reusing and recycling open data as an alternative input, specifically in situations where data and information resources are limited.

However, reusing and recycling ODs is not without challenges. Despite its potential, various concerns may arise, such as the need for data validation, source credibility check, the addition of requirements for technical capacity building for data manipulation, interpretation and utilisation, and for ensuring interoperability among different datasets. These concerns underline the problem's complexity, and underscores the fact that while scarcity of resources poses limitations, its abundance does not necessarily translate to more effective plans and strategies.

Such complex problems will always be difficult to solve using traditional methods and policy-making as more often than not, existing resources are not as unbounded as it assumes it to be. This is not just true for money and time, but also for knowledge and intellectual capacities (Lindblom 1959). Innovation and education can help overcome these. Teaching communities about the significance of data and information in decision-making, and promoting a culture of data appreciation, literacy and sharing will enable communities with minimal to no technological resources to still benefit from modern ICT advancements, and adapt using local means to create and retrieve pertinent information required to wield sound judgment, and take appropriate courses of action until such time that better data and information infrastructures could be afforded.

References

ABS-CBN News: Children, elderly drown as flood waters swallow Tacloban evac center, 11 November 2013. ABS-CBN News.com: www.abs-cbnnews.com/focus/11/09/13/children-elderly-drown-waters-swallow-tacloban-evac-center. Accessed 11 Nov 2013

Goodspeed, R.: Knowledge management for planning organizations, 14 February 2011. Planetizen: http://www.planetizen.com/node/48125

Graham, S.: Bridging urban digital divides? urban polarisation and Information and Communications Technologies (ICTs). Urban Stud. **39**(1), 33–56 (2002)

Lindblom, C.: The science of "muddling through". Public Adm. Rev. **19**(2), 79–88 (1959)

Lord, A.: The Planning Game: An information Economics Approach to Understanding Urban and Environmental Management. Routledge, Oxon (2012)

Maeng, D.-M., Nedovic-Budic, Z.: Urban form and planning in the information age: lessons from literature. Spatium **17–18**, 1–12 (2007)

Masuda, Y.: The Information Society as Post-Industrial Society. World Future Society, Bethesda (1981)

Maxwell, J., Reuveny, R.: Resource scarcity and conflict in developing countries. J. Peace Res. **37**(3), 301–322 (2000)

National Disaster Risk Reduction and Management Council (NDRRMC): Final Report re Effects of Typhoon "Yolanda" (Haiyan). NDRRMC, Quezon City. National Disaster Risk Reduction and Management Council (NDRRMC) (2014)

Serote, E.: Rationalized local planning system in the Philippines. Bureau of Local Government Development - Department of Interior and Local Government (DILG) (2008)

Stauffacher, D., Hattotuwa, S., Weekes, B.: The potential and challenges of open data for crisis information management and aid efficiency: a preliminary assessment, 23 March 2012. ICT4Peace Foundation: http://ict4peace.org/?p=2334

Sustainable Development Solutions Network (SDSN): Data for development: a needs assessment for SDG monitoring and statistical capacity development, 17 April 2015. Sustainable Development Solutions Network (SDSN): http://unsdsn.org/wp-content/uploads/2015/04/Data-for-Development-Full-Report.pdf

UNISDR and ESCAP: The Asia-Pacific Disaster Report 2012: Reducing Vulnerability and Exposure to Disasters. United Nations, Bangkok (2012)

Urbancic, T., Stepankova, O., Lavrac, N.: enhancing human choice by information technologies. In: Berleur, J., Numinen, M.I., Impagliazzo, J. (ed.) Social Informatics: An Information Society for All? In remembrance of Rob Kling. IFIP International Federation for Information Processing, vol. 223, pp. 255–264. Springer, Boston (2006)

Wildavsky, A.: If planning is everything, maybe it's nothing. Policy Sci. **4**, 127–153 (1973)

World Bank: Open Data for Resilience Initiative: Field Guide. The World Bank, Washington, DC (2014)

A Critical and Systemic Consideration of Data for Sustainable Development in Africa

Nyalleng Moorosi[1(✉)], Mamello Thinyane[2], and Vukosi Marivate[1]

[1] Council for Scientific and Industrial Research, Pretoria, South Africa
{nmoorosi,vmarivate}@csir.co.za
[2] United Nations University Institute of Computing and Society, Macau, China
mamello@unu.edu

Abstract. The "data revolution for development" pundits tout data as representing an undeniable opportunity for transforming and improving societies through the deployment of data-centric development approaches. The critics on the other hand question the legitimacy of these claims made on the role to data to transform society and development work, in particular considering the numerous systemic and structural challenges faced by some of the least developed countries. In this paper we consider the real positioning and role of the data, and in particular Big Data, for sustainable development in Africa. We highlight three perspectives and dynamics associated with the data revolution for development and suggest that the real utilization of data for development in Africa can only be realized when other ecosystem factors are considered in tandem.

Keywords: Data science · Internet participation · Open data · Big data · Data for development

1 Introduction

The resolution 70/1 of the United Nations general assembly, which articulates the 2030 Agenda for Sustainable Development, galvanized global action towards the achievement of the 17 development goals and the 169 specific targets (United Nations 2016). Effective development action towards these goals is dependent on an accurate understanding of the social well-being and environmental phenomena under consideration, and this in turn is dependent on the effectiveness of the indicators framework, and the quality of the observed metrics data. While countries have relied on and utilized data, typically collated by the National Statistics Offices (NSOs) for social indicators monitoring to inform their development policies and action, the twenty-first century presents an opportunity for the transformation of the social indicators monitoring domain through the developments in Internet technologies and also through the recent advent of Big Data.

© IFIP International Federation for Information Processing 2017
Published by Springer International Publishing AG 2017. All Rights Reserved
J. Choudrie et al. (Eds.): ICT4D 2017, IFIP AICT 504, pp. 232–241, 2017.
DOI: 10.1007/978-3-319-59111-7_20

Notwithstanding the discussions (Letouz 2012; WEF 2012) of the potential role of Big Data for sustainable development, it is not only necessary to critically interrogate the underlying developmental mechanisms and pathways of data for development, but also to consider the systemic positioning of Big Data within national data ecosystems, taking into account the country-specific factors and conditions. In this paper we consider these aspects of the data revolution for sustainable development from the context of countries in Africa. In Sect. 2, we present the theoretical framing of data for development and also discuss the related domain of social indicators monitoring. The diffusion of innovation model as well as the critical theory of technology are adopted to highlight inherent dynamics in the utilization of data for development. Section 3 adopts an ecosystem perspective to discuss the factors, contextualized for Africa, that support and enhance effective utilization of data for development. Section 4 then considers the opportunities and potential for the use of data for sustainable development in Africa. A conclusion that wraps the discussion on the importance of the ecosystem perspective and critical engagement in data for development is presented in Sect. 5.

2   Data for Development

The formal conceptualization of Data for Development (D4D) shares theoretical framing with the broader concepts of Knowledge for Development (K4D) and the Information and Communication Technologies for Development (ICT4D). In these frameworks information and technologies are viewed as indispensable resources and tools that are at the disposal of individuals, communities and governments towards their development. The utilization of these resources towards development can further be enunciated through the more nuanced theories such as the Capabilities Approach, which recognizes the potential of resources as inputs towards individuals capabilities (Sen 1999). The consideration of data for development is largely undertaken from two distinct yet related perspectives: the social indicators monitoring perspective, and the development perspective. The former, and perhaps the most prominent, recognizes the role of data to revolutionize the work of monitoring development phenomena and of collating development statistics (Letouz 2012; SDSN 2015). The latter sees opportunities for data to directly impact individuals and communities developmental imperatives. This latter perspective does not represent a new thinking or a revolution to the human development discourse but rather highlights an emphasis on a specific resource (i.e. data) and its consideration within developmental contexts. The former perspective holds potential to revolutionize social indicators monitoring through the introduction of new actors, new data sources and new tools.

The collation of social indicators needs to be understood as an enabler and a step towards better decision-making, policy and developmental action. The failure of better scientific evidence, insights, and knowledge, to translate into better decision-making and better policy making is bemoaned across the board, from researchers in public administration and policy, to stakeholders in social indicators monitoring. Cloete notes the lack of, usually assumed, definitive causal link between availability of better information and the resultant quality of the decisions and outcomes taken (Cloete 2009). Similarly, Cobb and Rixford note that having relevant data about a phenomenon does not directly induce the resultant appropriate action (Cobb and Rixford 1998). In order for data to be effective, it must be part of larger plan of action wherein evidence-basing approach is widely adopted as the core of policy development and analysis. This gap between evidence and action is a challenge in both developing and developed countries, and it is not a factor of the availability of quality data (Segone 2008; GAO 1995). The reasons for this failure, which is also termed the "utilization problem", include: failure to create ownership among the stakeholders, ineffective strategies regarding communicating the evaluation findings and data, lack of understanding of the political context and ecosystem factors, and failure to link the findings and data to a definite follow up plan (Segone 2008). The effectiveness of data, applied to social indicators data, has been shown to be improved when the indicators and the data are clearly associated with a policy outcome or a definite plan of action (Innes and Booher 2000). It remains therefore that far from the challenges of effective policy and development action being about the lack of social indicators data, in actual fact systemic and structural factors play a larger role in affecting the effective translation of evidence and insights into policy and action.

2.1   Critical Perspectives on Data for Development

The critical theory of technology recognizes technology solutions as being socially shaped and constructed and therefore of being able to be used for rationalizing power structures as well as for empowerment (Zheng and Stahl 2011; Feenberg 1991). Critical consideration of data for development therefore necessarily dismisses both the technology determinism and the instrumental rationality that typically accompanies the discussions on the potential for data to revolutionize development (Cecez-Kecmanovic 2005). Three perspectives emanating from the theory of diffusion of innovation and critical theory of technology are hereafter highlighted to suggest further issues that should remain within the locus of considerations of data for development.

Diffusion of Hype. This perspective is informed from the hype phase within Roger's Diffusion of Innovations which is typically accompanied by over-inflation of the potential of technology and therefore the associated expectations (Everett 1995). In the data for development literature and related work this is seen through the fetishization of data wherein data, and in particular Big data, is purported as the missing factor in development work. Best engages with this aspect by highlighting the engagement with statistics "as though they are magical, as though they are more than mere number as though they distill the complexity and confusion of reality into simple facts as facts we discover, not the numbers we create" (Best 2022). The over-emphasis on the role of data and the presumed data revolution that should transform development work and the implementation of SDGs is not only a naive proposition, it is also a risky one that shifts the focus away for the ecosystem factors that need to be taken into consideration for effective development work. Data and social indicators as tools that help understand the social well-being phenomena should remain ancillary to the core development agenda (Cobb and Rixford 1998).

The Tyranny of Benevolent Technocrats. From the perspective of critical theory, social indicators evaluation exists in a political landscape where values, beliefs, norms and power are contested. Thus, social indicators monitoring carries the overtones wherein the ruling class, or corollary in the case of SDGs the developed world, imposes certain values on the rest of the society (Cobb and Rixford 1998). This phenomenon and its numerous implications for the global power dynamics has been well articulated and enunciated by Thompson in his critical study of the role of Information and Communication Technologies (ICT) in not only advancing the interest of specific technocratic stakeholders, but also in normalizing a certain socio-political worldview (Thompson 2003). Further, the top down emphasis on the role of data (and Big Data) for development by the international development funding agencies necessarily imposes an agenda on the developing countries (those receiving international funding) that is not informed and driven bottom-up by the country specific considerations. The outcome of this tyranny of data dynamic is that the obligation-side of social indicators monitoring becomes the more emphasized, at the expense of leveraging the interplay between the enjoyment-side and the obligation-side towards informing holistic development policy and action (Green 2001).

Plateau of Empowered Productivity. Roger identifies the final stage in the diffusion of innovations as the productive utilization of the technological innovations (Everett 1995). This would represents the use of data in development activities, which is characterized by: a clear understanding of the role and positioning of data within development activities; a context-sensitive use of data within a holistic and systemic development framework; accurate and transparent data analytics and statistics; and accessible reporting and dissemination of data for the various development actors and stakeholders. It is critical that the use of data in development serves the primary role and agenda of development. When the characteristics identified above as well as other country-specific factors are taken into consideration, the potential for effective utilization of data for development is increased.

3   Data Ecosystem Considered

The use of data for development exists within complex multifaceted systems comprising multiple stakeholders, processes, frameworks, standards and protocols, as well as platforms and systems. Effective operationalization of data for development is dependent on mature and optimized data ecosystems. This section considers some of the ecosystem factors, considered from the context of Africa, that have an impact of the use of data for development.

3.1 Connectivity and Data Availability

Data and information have always been utilized to support economic and societal development, however the Internet revolution and the recent developments around Big Data and social media data have elevated the role and potential of data for transforming social indicators monitoring and development work (SDSN 2015). We consider the availability of social media data and indirectly the availability of the supporting connectivity, in the context of Africa to explore this potential. This preliminary exploration is undertaken for twenty African countries, made up of four clusters of five countries each from: the high Human Development Index (HDI), medium HDI, low HDI, and the lowest HDI. One of the critical factors that affects the availability of relevant digital data for social indicators monitoring is the extent of connectivity and participation of individuals on the Internet. In Africa there are increasingly more people who are connected through mobile devices, however this connectivity does not directly imply connectivity to the Internet, which could be affected by affordability, bandwidth availability and individuals capability; nor does it imply active "prosumption" (i.e. production and consumption facilitated by Web 2.0 tools) of data online. The "Active Internet Users" metric gives an indication of the potential generation of digital data from the different countries. From the ITU world telecommunication/ICT indicators database of 2016, out of the twenty countries under consideration in this study, the highest active Internet users (as a percentage of the population) is 69$ and the lowest is 2%, for Kenya and Niger respectively (ITU 2016). As expected and shown in Fig. 1, the more developed countries have higher numbers of active users compared to the least developed countries, at the mean of 46% (s2 = 10%) and 2% (s2 = 4%) respectively.

The above metric highlights a phenomenon and a trend which is observable across various other metrics (e.g. International bandwidth per Internet user, percentage of adults accessing electronic services) and which has implications for

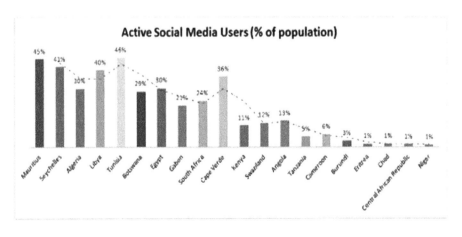

Fig. 1. Social media participation

development not only in Africa but across the world. The paradox of the assumed "Data revolution for development" is that the countries most in need (according to the widely accepted HDI model) of development are the same countries with minimal data repositories and relevant data sources, and in general those with data ecosystems that are not very mature.

Despite these challenges and limitations, it remains that the increasing real connectedness of individuals to the Internet, their greater participation in socio-economic activities, and the growing deployment of sensors and IoT devices, all represent a new opportunity in a form of new data sources that can contribute to informing the understanding of various social and environmental phenomena.

3.2 Privacy and Governance

The second factor we consider is data security and privacy infrastructure. Unlike more advanced data markets such as the European Union and the Northern America, African countries are only starting to build policies and processes to regulate the use of data by entities within the data ecosystem (Borena et al. 2015). The 2014 African Union (AU) Convention Cyber Security and Personal Data Protection act is the first comprehensive attempt at developing an all-Africa cyber protection guideline (AU 2014). However, this AU convention is yet to be rectified by member states. Thus practically, only a subset of African countries (i.e., Benin, Ghana, Tunisia, South Africa, Madagascar, and Gabon) have put into place legal frameworks that guide researchers and innovators in the Data Science space (Rick 2015). Therefore for African states, the use of extensive datasets and especially those containing personal data may be difficult to justify.

3.3 Empowered and Engaged Citizenry

In the space of privacy and information ownership, most laws are designed to protect the use of personal data (e.g. name, demographics, and health data). However, in data mining and data science studies, publicly available information can be combined and processed in ways that reveal of the identity of the owner of that information. For instance users may choose to have anonymous identities on social media and may not be aware that the individuals in their network, their posts and their geographic location can reveal their identities. Thus, it is imperative that the individuals whose data is used in developing systems be educated about what can happen to their 'harmless' data such as their social media network. Citizens should be aware of the dangers of disclosing information as well as their rights in cases where their data is misused. Figure 2 provides a guide on the openness of information based on the visibility levels that users choose.

3.4 Other Considerations

The following are other factors within the data ecosystem that are important for consideration.

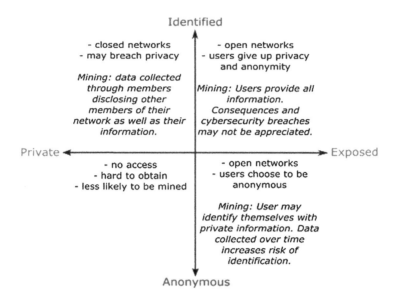

Fig. 2. Privacy in social media (Moorosi and Marivate 2015)

1. **Big Data Skills:** There is currently a global shortage of individuals with Big Data skills. With competition from leading international technology companies such as Google and Facebook, all institutions are finding it difficult to recruit/retain enough stuff to solve the problems pertinent to them.

2. **Computing Infrastructure:** Technologically, deploying large scale Big Data infrastructure can be prohibitively expensive for small enterprises in developing countries. To meet the minimal demands, techniques in distributed computing and the use of open source software can be deployed to a very effective scale. That said, for institutions running at smaller data sizes, he simple use of old standard computers connected together as a cluster can provide enough power to run complex machine learning and Big Data storage platforms. Additionally deploying technologies such as Hadoop, and Spark can make those same old machines sufficiently efficient while allowing for scaling and future upgrades to meet increasing demand and complexity.

3. **Transparency and Data Availability:** Data is not only a resource, it is also a commodity. In Big Data analytics, beyond personal data, governments and companies may not have the inclination to share data with other stakeholders within the data ecosystem. Initiatives such as the Open Data Forum work to improve this access.

4   Leveraging Big Data Opportunities for Africa

Big Data, when effectively utilized, stands to supplement the current social indicators monitoring systems with actionable knowledge and insights that have largely been derived from electronic source streams. This can be data that is collected passively from users as they undertake everyday activities online (data exhaust), information that is generated directly by the users online (online information), data that is collected from sensors and IoT devices (physical sensors), and data that is collected from the public (crowd-sourced data) (Letouz 2012). While the availability of the underlying data is an important and a necessary factor towards effective utilization of big data in sustainable development, it is also important that there is sufficient will and intent from the stakeholders, as well as the capacity and resources to process the data (Letouz 2012). The opportunity for utilization of Big Data for sustainable development is manifested when each of these factors: availability, intent and capacity, are in place within country.

Other opportunities can be observed where the Big Data stands to provide solutions to some of the long standing challenges in Africa. Due to the unstructured nature of African cities: high growth rate and a high number of informal settlements (Arku 2009), the problem of quantifying populations and understanding the built environment of the cities can be a challenge. It is commonly the most deprived members of the society that are the least known by the state and therefore the least heard and served. Without a proper understanding of demographics, African leaders cannot optimally plan and distribute resources such as health, education, and energy. Additionally they are at a disadvantage when they try to respond to matters of disease breakouts and natural disasters. Economically, not understanding the population means not fully understanding the state of several economic indicators such as employment, productivity and purchasing power parity and thus an impairment in designing optimal solutions for the citizenry. It is because of the above-mentioned that we see the use of citizens as contributors to geo-spatial annotation as one of key opportunities. The associated technologies and methods have already been used successfully in systems ranging from earthquake sensing to urban management (Laituri and Kodrich 2008; Song and Sun 2010) in developed and developing countries.

Furthermore, to achieve the goals of annotating and counting using citizen as sensor methods, African data scientists can piggy-back on already existing applications such as NextDrop[1], a system that alerts residents when public water taps are open, health apps such as Mom Connect[2], Find-a-Med a[3] and Smart-Health-App[4], which is deployed in several Eastern and Southern African countries. In most of these apps, there is a core GIS or mapping technology that is built in so as to provide relevant and reliable recommendations to its users. The use of this combination of demographic and spatial data can easily be adopted into machine learning tools that can decipher further information through more statistical and analytical methodologies.

---

[1] https://nextdrop.co/contact.html.

[2] http://www.health.gov.za/index.php/about-mom-connect.

[3] http://telecoms.com/interview/find-a-med-how-mobile-tech-is-changing-nigerian-healthcare/.

[4] http://www.itnewsafrica.com/2014/03/smart-app-to-help-fight-malaria/.

5   Conclusion

The Data Revolution for Sustainable Development represent a potential opportunity for countries to transform their indicators data ecosystem towards supporting the realization of the SDG goals and targets. Beyond the allure of fetishization of data, the tyrannical influence of the technocratic stakeholders, and the naive misuse of data analytics tools and instruments, lies a domain of effective utilization of data not only to drive national policy on development, but also to support development action at the micro, meso and macro levels of society. This effective utilization of data is only realizable when the full ecosystem factors and dynamics, which are specific and unique to individuals countries, are earnestly considered. These factors include: the overall ecosystem readiness and capacity, frameworks for ethical processing of data, measures for data security and privacy preservation, as well as data governance models.

While recognizing the potential for the Data Revolution for sustainable development, we similarly note the inherent paradox that the countries that would stand to benefit the most from this data revolution (through being the least developed) are the same countries that lack the data ecosystem maturity to effect and maximize this opportunity. In Africa the benefits of data to transform development monitoring will accrue to different countries at different levels, however overall, we have noted the positive impact and role that data can play in advancing the 2030 agenda for sustainable development on the continent.

References

Arku, G.: Rapidly growing african cities need to adopt smart growth policies to solve urban development concerns. Urban Forum **20**(3), 253–270 (2009). http://dx.doi.org/10.1007/s12132-009-9047-z

AU: African Union convention on cyber security and personal data protection. African Union, Addis Ababa, Ethiopia (2014)

Best, J.: Damned Lies and Statistics: Untangling Numbers from the Media, Politicians, and Activists. University of California Press, Berkeley (2012)

Borena, B., Belanger, F., Egigu, D.: Information privacy protection practices in Africa: A review through the lens of critical social theory. In: 2015 48th Hawaii International Conference on System Sciences (HICSS), pp. 3490–3497. IEEE (2015)

Cecez-Kecmanovic, D.: Basic assumptions of the critical research perspectives in information systems. In: Handbook of Critical Information Systems Research: Theory and Application, pp. 19–46 (2005)

Cloete, F.: Evidence-based policy analysis in South Africa: Critical assessment of the emerging government-wide monitoring and evaluation system. J. Public Adm. **44**(2), 293–311 (2009)

Cobb, C.W., Rixford, C.: Lessons Learned from the History of Social Indicators, vol. 1. Redefining Progress, San Francisco (1998)

Innes, J.E., Booher, D.E.: Indicators for sustainable communities: A strategy building on complexity theory and distributed intelligence. Plann. Theory Pract. **1**(2), 173–186 (2000)

Everett, M.R.: Diffusion of Innovations. Free Press, New York (1995). http://www.nehudlit.ru/books/detail8765.html

Feenberg, A.: Critical Theory of Technology. Oxford University Press, New York (1991)

GAO: Programme evaluation Improving the flow of information to the congress. General Accounting Office, Washington, DC (1995)

Green, M.: What we talk about when we talk about indicators: Current approaches to human rights measurement. Hum. Rights Q. **23**(4), 1062–1097 (2001)

ITU: World telecommunication/ICT indicators database. International Telecommunication Union, Geneva, Switzerland (2016)

Laituri, M., Kodrich, K.: On line disaster response community: People as sensors of high magnitude disasters using internet GIS. Sensors **8**(5), 3037–3055 (2008)

Letouz, E.: Thoughts on Big Data and the SDGs. United Nations Sustainable Development (2012)

Moorosi, N., Marivate, V.: Privacy in mining crime data from social media: A South African perspective. In: 2015 Second International Conference on Information Security and Cyber Forensics (InfoSec), pp. 171–175. IEEE (2015)

Rick, S.: Privacy & security law report. PVLR 1065 (2015)

SDSN: Data for Development: A Needs Assessment for SDG Monitoring and Statistical Capacity Development. Sustainable Development Solutions Network, New York, USA (2015)

Segone, M.: Bridging the gap: The role of monitoring and evaluation in evidence-based policy making (2008)

Sen, A.: Development as Freedom. Oxford University Press, Oxford (1999)

Song, W., Sun, G.: The role of mobile volunteered geographic information in urban management. In: 2010 18th International Conference on Geoinformatics, pp. 1–5. IEEE (2010)

Thompson, M.: ICT, power, and developmental discourse: A critical analysis. In: Wynn, E.H., Whitley, E.A., Myers, M.D., DeGross, J.I. (eds.) Global and Organizational Discourse about Information Technology. IFIP, vol. 110, pp. 347–373. Springer, Boston, MA (2003). doi:10.1007/978-0-387-35634-1_17

United Nations: The Sustainable Development Goals Report 2016. Technical report, United Nations, New York (2016). http://www.un.org/publications

WEF: Big Data, Big Impact: New Possibilities for International Development. World Economic Forum, Geneva, Switzerland (2012)

Zheng, Y., Stahl, B.C.: Technology, capabilities and critical perspectives: What can critical theory contribute to sens capability approach? Ethics Inf. Technol. **13**(2), 69–80 (2011)

Data Governance: A Challenge for Merged and Collaborating Institutions in Developing Countries

Thandi Charmaine Mlangeni[1] and Ephias Ruhode[2(✉)]

[1] Information Technology Department,
Cape Peninsula University of Technology, Cape Town, South Africa
charmza22@gmail.com
[2] Research, Innovations and Partnerships Department,
Cape Peninsula University of Technology, Cape Town, South Africa
RuhodeE@cput.ac.za

Abstract. Organisations now invest in ICT solutions to drive business activities and to provide the agility sought within changing environments. Owing to many reasons including inadequate financial resources, organisations in developing countries are characterised by mergers of two or more institutions. It means therefore that disparate systems with different data management schemes are merged or made to collaborate making access to quality data almost impossible. In turn, a level of inefficiency finds its way with potential to generate inaccurate, missing, misinterpreted and poorly defined information. This research is motivated by the need to investigate data governance challenges in institutions within developing countries that are characterised by complex dynamics rooted in merged and collaborating environments. The study has been empirically scoped to explore data governance challenges in a large university of technology in the Western Cape Region of South Africa as a developing country. The challenges with regards to ICT and data governance are equally applicable in higher education institutions as they do in business organisations. Higher education institutions have a growing ICT infrastructure used in everyday activities and online functionality, making them prone to data problems. Challenges related to data management in universities are a lot more pronounced in universities which were established through the merging of independent institutions and also those that exchange data through collaborations. Thematic analysis has been employed within the theoretical lens of two models, contingency model (Wende and Otto 2007) and the data governance decision domain model (Khatri and Brown 2010). Analysis of data through the two models led to the development of a data governance framework applicable to the case under study and deemed to apply to any organisation in the same context. Challenges related to data principles, data access, data quality, data integration, metadata, data lifecycle, and design parameters emerged as the main findings from the study. Since the institution under study was established through a merger of independent technikons, the findings were deemed to be applicable to many other institutions where mergers and collaborations characterise their environment.

© IFIP International Federation for Information Processing 2017
Published by Springer International Publishing AG 2017. All Rights Reserved
J. Choudrie et al. (Eds.): ICT4D 2017, IFIP AICT 504, pp. 242–253, 2017.
DOI: 10.1007/978-3-319-59111-7_21

Keywords: Data governance · Data quality management · Higher education · Higher education institution · ICT · Cape Peninsula University of Technology · South Africa

1 Introduction

Organisations, both private and public, are attempting to construct a paradigm for data quality management in the backdrop of ubiquity of information and data. Godfrey et al. (1997) portray information as an asset with economic value. This infers that looking after data has the potential to bring efficiency in the running of the organisation. To this effect, many studies have identified data governance as a discipline that can address data quality issues (Korhonen et al. 2013). The pervasive use of IT in organisations mandates IT governance as a corporate imperative (IoD 2009: 14). IT governance, under which data governance falls, is defined by Van Grembergen (2004: 1) as:

"... an integral part of corporate governance and consists of the leadership, organisational structures and processes that ensure that the organisation's IT sustains and extends the organisation's strategy and objectives"

This paper recognises that organisations in many sectors in developing countries face challenges in implementing data governance principles. An organisation in South Africa is examined to empirically identify the data governance challenges from a merger environment. Owing to many reasons including inadequate financial resources, organisations, especially public institutions in developing countries are characterised by mergers of two or three institutions. Merging of organisations, as has been witnessed in the South African higher education landscape since 2003, results in data governance challenges. Just like business organisations, universities are concerned about brand perceptions, business processes and human presence in the IT ecosystems (people, process and technology). Data repeatedly used across various business processes in universities mostly originate from these entities: students, classes, faculty, campus, facilities, location and employees. This data is often dispersed among units, departments or divisions (Drucker 2005: 102) and, therefore, a level of inefficiency finds its way with potential to generate inaccurate, missing, misinterpreted and poorly defined information (Redman 2004: 1).

This paper seeks to investigate the challenging obstacles faced by merged and collaborating institutions in obtaining clean, reliable, relevant data from their IT systems and how such electronic systems can be managed. These challenges are framed within the broader data governance paradigm. Under this background, the two critical questions which then emerge are:

What are the data governance challenges faced by organisations as a result of mergers and collaborations?

Which data governance framework can be adopted for merged and collaborating institutions?

The paper is organised as follows: the next section presents the literature review followed by the methodology adopted in the study. Data collection and analysis methods are explained in the methodology which is followed by a section on presentation of findings and implications to policy and practice before the paper ends with a summary and conclusion.

2 Literature Review

The literature review section presents the data governance concept followed by a presentation of the theories which underpinned the study.

2.1 Data Governance Concept

Organisations seek to break down the silos of data that result in poor quality of information which, in turn, lead to organisational costs, risks and wrong decisions (Korhonen et al. 2013: 11). Most of them realise that their strategic initiatives depend on the quality of data and their ability to manage fast-growing volume of information. Bryant (2014) asserts that this can be achieved through data governance. Data governance can be defined as an organisational approach to data management that formalises a set of policies and procedures to encompass the full life cycle of data (Korhonen et al. 2013: 11). It transforms an organisation's data, its management technology, who owns it and how it should be used (Russom 2008: 4). According to Russom (2012), a well-designed data governance programme should consist of both business and IT people. They must ensure information strategy and business strategy are aligned with the organisation's overall mission and strategy (Korhonen et al. 2013: 14).

Most organisations deal with data quality problems emerging from both systematic and structural perspective. In seeking for solutions they develop new systems to replace old ones and, as a result, neglect to address the issue inherited from the old systems (Lee et al. 2006). Some authors agree that if organisations have poor data quality that is inappropriately integrated, business operations will continue to be afflicted with data deficiencies that will make it hard to use data (Fisher 2009; Lee et al. 2006). According to Olson (2003), poor data management is said to cost many organisations some billions of dollars each year and a large portion of that cost is due to data quality inaccuracies. Redman (2001: 45) suggests that 10% of organisations revenue is impacted by poor data quality. Both authors recognise the impact data quality can have on the organisation's profit. According to Redman (2008), data quality issues experienced by most organisations include the following:

- People cannot find the data they need
- Incorrect data
- Poor data definition
- Data privacy/data security
- Data inconsistency across sources
- Too much data and
- Organisational confusion.

It is the contention of researchers in this study, that data quality issues that are experienced by organisations in developing countries are at a far wider scale than organisations in developed countries. Reasons for this lie in limited resources that range from financial to skills. An empirical case in a developing country was therefore selected to identify the data governance challenges.

2.2 Theoretical Lens

Two models have been identified and considered relevant in this study, namely the contingency model (Wende and Otto 2007) and the data governance decision domain model by Khatri and Brown (2010). Firstly, the relevance of the contingency theory (Wende and Otto 2007) lies in its design parameters which form the basis of a data governance framework. The two design parameters are organisational placement of decision-making authority and coordination of decision-making style. According to ibid, these two design parameters affect the configuration of data governance model as their value influences the assignment of responsibilities (Fig. 1).

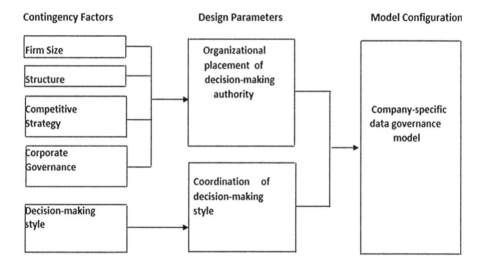

Fig. 1. Contingency model for data governance (source: Wende and Otto 2007)

Secondly, Khatri and Brown (2010) used data governance decision domains to structure their data governance decision domains. They identified the following data governance components:

- Data Principles – establish the linkage with the business, by describing the business uses of data and ensuring data is treated as an enterprise wide asset.
- Data Quality – involves ensuring accuracy and integrity data that is always available for an enterprise.
- Metadata – describes what the data is about and provides a mechanism for a concise and consistent description of the representation of data.

- Data Access/Data authorisation – involves data security and explaining variety of ways in which a dataset can be accessed.
- Data life cycle – involves understanding how data is used, and how long it must be retained to minimise the total cost of storing over its life cycle

The data governance domain model was coalesced with the design parameters of the contingency model and used as one framework to guide data collection from the empirical case. These components from the data governance decision domains model need to be assigned to roles that will be accountable for them (from the design parameters of the contingency model), also referred as locus of accountability (Fig. 2).

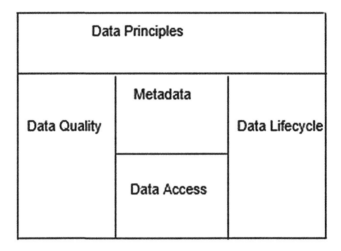

Fig. 2. Data governance decision domains (source: Khatri and Brown 2010)

3   Methodology

The study was conducted at the Cape Peninsula University of Technology in South Africa. Considering the case rationale provided in the case description section, the researchers contend that findings from CPUT will be applicable to all other organisations which exist as a result of mergers and collaborations in developing countries. In the next section, the empirical case is presented, as well as the context of mergers within which the case is located.

3.1   Case Description

In South Africa, the first decade of the 21st century was characterised by a massive transformation of the higher education landscape. Technikons were collapsed and merged with each other and in some cases with already existing universities. This transformation of higher education occurred "within the context of a formidable overall challenge of pursuing economic development (including restructuring economic relations to address inequitable historical patterns of ownership, wealth and income distribution), social equity and the extension and deepening of democracy simultaneously" (Moses 2014). Post-1994 (the democratic dispensation), the new South African government sought to redress a myriad of economic and social challenges which had been created by the apartheid government. The South African society under apartheid government had been characterised by social, political and economic discrimination and inequalities of class, race, gender, institutional and spatial nature (Badat 2010). Like all other sectors of the economy, the higher education landscape underwent a major restructuring and reconfiguration in the first decade of the 21st century. Merging of institutions of higher learning became a common phenomenon. After the new dispensation that saw mergers of institutions in higher education in South Africa, universities are divided into three broad categories, namely:

- Universities of Technology that focus on vocationally-oriented education;
- Comprehensive universities that offer a combination of academic and vocational diplomas and degrees;
- Traditional universities offering theoretically oriented university degrees.

The development of UoTs was regarded as the core in mergers between two or multiple technikons where one institution was always being historically disadvantaged and the other historically advantaged (UoT 2008).

Within the above landscape, the Cape Peninsula University of Technology (CPUT) was selected as a case under study. CPUT was formed on the 1st of January 2005 with the merger of the previously Peninsula and Cape Technikons and started operating as a new merged institution on the 1st of February 2006. The university is currently located in six campuses in the Western Cape Province of South Africa. The campuses are dispersed within Western Cape of which the farthest is around seventy kilometres from the central campus. Both former institutions had their own institutionalised systems which through the merger, were compelled to integrate and bring together both their IT departments and systems. As in all other mergers in the country, the integration process has been very slow such that Bellville campus, previously the main campus of the Peninsula Technikon, and the Cape Town campus, previously the main campus of the Cape Technikon, are still regarded as two different infrastructures. The computing services of the university are divided into three domains – Computer and Telecommunications Services (CTS), Management Information Systems (MIS) and E-learning. The CTS department is responsible for IT infrastructure, network, facilities, desktop support, printing and helpdesk support. MIS is responsible for institutional data which uses the Integrated Tertiary Software (ITS) integrator to capture both staff and student data. E-learning manages the university's learning management system (LMS).

The rationale for selecting CPUT as a case in this study is two-fold. Firstly, CPUT is one of the biggest merger universities with over 33,000 thousand students. Secondly, many merger related challenges are still experienced by CPUT. The challenges are both social and technological. Social challenges which are evident at CPUT relate to cultural and racial diversity as the two merged institutions had been defined by race. Technological challenges, which are the focus of this study range from difficulties to retrieve, manipulate and analyse aggregate data for metrics and planning, difficulties to manage unstructured data, and general data integration challenges. These data management challenges arise from institutions not thoroughly dealing with data content, records management, quality, stewardship, governance and research data management (Albrecht and Pirani 2009: 3).

3.2 Data Collection

This study followed a deductive approach, which is theory-driven, using both the contingency theory's design parameters (Wende and Otto 2007) and the data governance decision domains (Khatri and Brown 2010). Both models were used as guideline to test empirical data with the aim of analysing the impact of data governance at CPUT. A questionnaire and interviews were used to collect data. The questionnaire was structured using the data governance decision domains (Khatri and Brown 2010) and interviews followed the contingency theory's design parameters (Wende and Otto 2007). Data collected from the questionnaire allowed the researcher to determine and understand the impact of data governance in higher institutions of higher learning, in this case, CPUT as an institution. The interviews allowed the participants to express their opinions on experiences and challenges related to data, and their understanding of the issues related to data responsibilities and decision making by the business users.

This research employed purposive non-probability sampling to select the sample mainly from business users and IT technical personnel. Business people in this context included executive-level board members (for example, Vice Chancellors, Deputy Vice Chancellors and others). The following explain selected participants or unit of analysis for this study. Participants chosen to represent executive-level members included:

- Deputy Vice Chancellor of knowledge and information services: this individual was selected because he oversee the whole ICT function in the entire institution.
- Registrar: this individual was selected because he is liable for student data and he is a custodian for the institution policies.

    Participants chosen to represent ICT technical personnel included:

- IT manager: this individual is responsible for the integration of systems,
- IT Risk and Compliance officer: is responsible for the development and compliant of policies in the IT department, and lastly and
- IT coordinator: this individual focus more on IT projects involving student data. These are the participants that were used as unit of analysis.

3.3 Data Analysis

Thematic analysis is used to analyse both questionnaire and interviews data. It is used to analyse classifications and present themes that are related to data and further illustrates data in great detail, while dealing with diverse subjects via interpretations (Alhojailan 2012; Boyatzis 1998). It also provides description and understanding of answers through discovering patterns and developing themes. Themes come from both data itself (an inductive approach) and from the investigator's prior theoretical understanding of the phenomenon under study (Ruhode 2016). In this case, themes from the questionnaire emerged from the components within the Data governance decision domains (Khatri and Brown 2010). Burnard, Gill, Stewart, Treasure and Chadwick (2008) highlight that in deductive thematic analysis, a predetermined framework is used to analyse data. (ibid) contend that this approach is useful when one has specific research questions that already identify the main themes. Interview themes emerged from the data itself and the actual data was used to derive the structure of analysis.

4   Findings

As presented in the data analysis section, themes were derived from the data governance decision domains (Khatri and Brown 2010). An important phenomenon which evolved from the data is the emergence of one more theme – data integration. The findings per theme and related data challenges are discussed in the subsections which follow.

Data Principles. The responses from the questionnaire revealed that the institution recognises data as an asset and it is considered to have value at both strategic and operational levels in relation to analytics which, in turn, can help the institution with decision-making. The results also reveal that even though there is process in place, most business users do not take ownership of their data because they think IT people are responsible for it. From the interviews, it was identified that this challenge is exacerbated by poor communication among data users and technical people, a problem which mainly results from social aspects of merging culturally diverse groups.

Data Quality. Khatri and Brown (2010: 150) state that Data Quality involves ensuring accuracy and integrity of data that is always available for an enterprise. While the data quality committee has been established, the existence of too many systems whose origin is the different technikons makes it difficult for the team to work coherently. The university has, since the merger, been producing erroneous student examination results and this has cost the university huge amounts of money.

Metadata. Metadata describes what the data is about and provides a mechanism for a concise and consistent description of the representation of data (Khatri and Brown 2010: 150). The findings suggest that there are mechanisms that provide clear description of data representation and authorised users have access to it. The findings also indicate that data is documented and passed on to new employees through documentation. However, the interface between the ITS and the LMS is not as effective as anticipated. The schematic structure of data varies in these two systems and this has posed challenges in data integration.

Data Access. According to Khatri and Brown (2010: 151), Data Access involves data security and specifying access requirements of data. The findings reveal that the institution does recognise the importance of data security and access. CPUT has established an IT risk and compliance office that is responsible for data security and developing policies that guard data security and data access. The challenge to data access lies in users who rarely adhere to policies that focus on data security.

Data Lifecycle. Data Lifecycle involves understanding how data is used and how long it must be retained to minimise the total cost of storing over its life cycle (Khatri and Brown 2010: 151). The findings reveal that electronic data is stored for longer than required and there are no policies that focus on how long data can be used, retained and archived. The findings also show that the lifecycle of paper-based data is actively and properly managed in the institution by an established Records and Archive department, which determines the use of data, how long it should be retained and its archival value.

Data Integration. The MIS is not properly integrated with the sub-systems, which leads to data flow challenges that cause unsynchronised data which, in turn, affects data quality. Managing data that come in different forms is quite problematic and incorrect data capturing and the way data is received in the institution is an issue that contributes to data integration challenges. The institution is not entirely aware that data integration challenges caused by the lack of properly integrating the main system with sub-systems or the merger of the previous institutions are the reasons it is currently experiencing data quality and data management challenges.

Design Parameters. The study analysed data using the contingency theoretical framework and a theme was also generated from the framework. It was found that the institution is using both centralised and decentralised models for decision-making, meaning some decisions are made by the IT department in terms of the infrastructure and other decisions related to data are made by business. The findings also show that the decision-making structure incorporates both hierarchical and cooperative models, which mean there are instances where people coordinate and work together to ensure that the university is sustainable and cases where direct control is used where subordinates report to their superiors.

5 The Emergent Model for Data Governance in Organisations

The contingency theory's design parameters (Wende and Otto 2007) and the Data governance decision domains model (Khatri and Brown 2010) were coalesced to construct the emergent model for data governance (Fig. 3). The concept and constructs of the emergent model for data governance were discussed in the preceding section on findings. This new model forms a baseline for institutions to developing their own data governance strategies.

The Emergent Data Governance model places attention on design parameters and model configuration. Decision-making authority in CPUT uses a hybrid approach where some decisions are made by individual departments and others by the IT department. Any organisation which adopts the Emergent Data Governance model can however employ centralised, decentralised or hybrid. The same observation can be made on the coordination of decision-making authority which could be a hierarchical or cooperative approach. It is in this context that the Emergent Data Governance model is

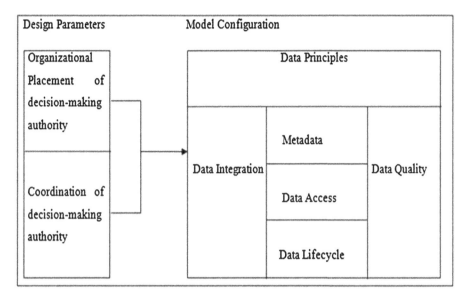

Fig. 3. Emergent data governance model

proposed to be used as a framework by organisations which intend to implement a data governance strategy.

6 Implications for Theory and Practice

While there is limited scholarly research on data governance, the concept is gaining traction in both public and private entities as data increasingly get recognition as an organisational asset. We contribute to data governance research by proposing an emergent data governance model for merged and collaborating institutions. The model has been constructed after a thematic analysis of data collected from one of the leading universities of technology through coalesced models. The use of thematic analysis as a theoretical foundation and a methodological approach for analysing data contributed to a better understanding of the institution's data. The main finding reported in this study is that access to quality data is not possible without an elaborate approach to data management.

7 Summary and Conclusion

This study identified data-related challenges in the institution that are the results of poor data management. Challenges were categorised in themes: data principles, data access, data quality, data integration, metadata, data lifecycle, and design parameters. The emergent data government framework was developed and its constructs are the themes that emerged from the two models which guided data collection and analysis. Since the institution under study was established through a merger of independent technikons, the findings were deemed to be applicable to many other institutions within a merger or a collaborating environment.

References

Albrecht, B., Pirani, J.A.: Revitalizing data stewardship through risk reduction: managing sensitive data at the University of Virginia. EDUCAUSE Center for Applied Research, Case study (2009). http://www.educause.edu/ecar. Accessed 15 Nov 2015

Alhojailan, M.I.: Thematic analysis: a critical review of its process and evaluation. W. East J. Soc. Sci. **1**(1), 39–47 (2012)

Badat, S.; The challenges of transformation in higher education and training institutions in South Africa. Development Bank of Southern Africa (DBSA) Report (2010)

Boyatzis, R.E.: Transforming Qualitative Information: Thematic Analysis and Code Development. Sage Publications, New York (1998)

Burnard, P., Gill, P., Stewart, K., Treasure, E., Chadwick, B.: Analysing and presenting qualitative data. Br. Dent. J. **204**(8), 429–432 (2008)

Bryant, W.: Data governance simplified. Point B management consultants (2014). http://www.pointb.com/documents/latest-insights/BTS_Data_Governance_Simplified.pdf. Accessed 15 Feb 2015

Drucker, P.: Academic analytics in the future of higher education. EDUCAUSE Center for Applied Research (2005). https://net.educause.edu/ir/library/pdf/ers0508/rs/ers05089.pdf. Accessed 2 Aug 2015

Fisher, T.: The Data Asset: How Smart Companies Govern Their Data for Business Success. Wiley, Hoboken (2009)

Gillard, E., Saunders, S., Terblanche, J., Sukel, M.: A review of four case studies in restructuring the South African higher education system. African Higher Education (2012)

Godfrey, J., Hodgson, A., Holmes, S., Kam, V.: Financial Accounting Theory, 3rd edn. Wiley, New York (1997)

Institute of Directors (IoD): King report on governance for South Africa. Institute of Directors Southern Africa, Johannesburg (2009)

Jansen, J., Taylor, N.: Educational Change in South Africa 1994–2003: Case Studies in Large-Scale Education Reform. Country Studies – Education Reform and Management Publication Series, vol. 11, no. 1. World Bank, Geneva (2003)

Khatri, V., Brown, C.V.: Designing data governance. Commun. ACM **53**(1), 148–152 (2010)

Korhonen, J.J., Melleri, I., Hiekkanen, K., Helenius, M.: Designing data governance structure: an organisational perspective. GSTF J. Comput. **2**(4), 11 (2013)

Lee, Y.W., Pipino, L.L., Funk, J.D., Wang, R.Y.: Journey to Data Quality. Massachusetts Institute of Technology (MIT) Press, Cambridge (2006)

Moses, A.: The strategic role of the Chief Information Officer during post-merger at institutions of higher learning: a case study. MTech thesis, Cape Peninsula University of Technology (2014)

Olson, J.: Data Quality: The Accuracy Dimension. Morgan Kaufmann Publishers, San Francisco (2003)

Poor, M.: Applying aspects of data governance from the private sector to public higher education. Mount Wachusett Community College (2011)

Redman, T.C.: Data Quality: The Field Guide. Digital Press, Boston (2001)

Redman, T.C.: Data quality: should universities worry? EDUCAUSE Rev. **39**(5), 12–13 (2004). http://net.educause.edu/ir/library/pdf/ERM0457.pdf. Accessed 11 Aug 2014

Redman, T.C.: Data Driven: Profiting from Your Most Important Business Asset. Harvard Business Press, Boston (2008)

Ruhode, E.: E-government for development: a thematic analysis of Zimbabwe's information and communication technology policy documents. Electron. J. Inf. Syst. Dev. Countries (EJISDC) **73**(7), 1–15 (2016)

Russom, P.: Data governance strategies: helping your organisation comply, transform, and integrate. The Data Warehouse Institute Best Practices Report, pp. 1–30 (2008)

Russom, P.: Seven reasons why master data management needs data governance. TDWI Checklist Report, TDWI Research (2012)

Universities of Technology (UoT): Position, role and function of Universities of Technology in South Africa. South African Technology Network, March 2008. http://www.satn.co.za

Van Grembergen, W.: Strategies for Information Technology Governance. IDEA Group Publishing, Hershey (2004)

Wende, K.: A model for data governance – organizing accountabilities for data quality management. In: Proceedings of 18th Australasian Conference on Information Systems, Toowoomba, Australia, 5–7 December 2007

Wende, K., Otto, B.: A contingency approach to data governance. In: Proceedings of the 12th International Conference on Information Quality, Cambridge, MA, USA (2007)

Critical Perspectives on ICT and Open Innovation for Development

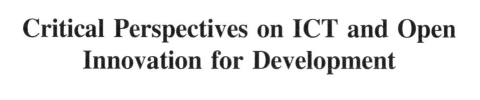

Collaborative Social Innovation in the Hybrid Domain

Organization and Rationality

Yuko Aoyama[1(✉)] and Balaji Parthasarathy[2]

[1] Clark University, Worcester, MA, USA
yaoyama@clarku.edu
[2] International Institute of Information Technology, Bangalore, India
pbalaji@iiitb.ac.in

Abstract. What are the institutional attributes that support the use of ICTs for social innovation? Based on the concept of the 'hybrid domain', we seek to better understand how various stakeholders with different priorities collaborate, combine economic and social objectives, and reconceptualize multi-stakeholder collaborative governance in the Global South. Using insights from behavioral economics and social psychology, we focus on two institutional aspects of social innovation - organizational arrangements and rationality. On the one hand, it is well recognized that social innovation stakeholders include not just states and commercial enterprises, but also NGOs, social enterprises, and for-profit/non-profit hybrid organizations. On the other hand, the rationality that brings together these stakeholders is not well articulated. While scholarship has emphasized utilitarian rationality, we highlight the importance of pro-social behavior in collaboration. We argue that scholarship in the past century has focused on utilitarian rationality while neglecting the role of prosocial behavior in collaboration. Further research on prosocial behavior and its incorporation in organizational theory would contribute to understanding the dynamics of collaboration for social innovation.

Keywords: Social innovation · Collaborative governance · Pro-social behavior · Global South

1 Introduction

How do social innovation stakeholders work together to develop norms and procedures, and what rationality do they adopt to overcome different priorities? In this paper, we explore the emerging organizational characteristics and rationality observed in case studies of social innovation stakeholders in India. We will unpack the concept of social innovation and the significance of ICTs, followed by the debate over governance, and in particular, the concept of the hybrid domain [1], which serves as an arena of collaboration among social innovation stakeholders. Based on our field research in India, we discuss three demonstrative cases in the areas of health, renewable energy and banking, explore organizational arrangements of collaborations, and theorize

© IFIP International Federation for Information Processing 2017
Published by Springer International Publishing AG 2017. All Rights Reserved
J. Choudrie et al. (Eds.): ICT4D 2017, IFIP AICT 504, pp. 257–268, 2017.
DOI: 10.1007/978-3-319-59111-7_22

the changing norms and emerging rationality of the hybrid domain. With the growing prominence of social innovation, and recent attention turning to systems and policies oriented toward more socially inclusive and pro-poor designs [2–4], the timing is ripe to develop a synthetic approach to institutional governance that involves the state, markets and civil society, and goes beyond the conventional state-market divide.

2 The Rise of the Hybrid Domain

Few theoretical frameworks explicitly incorporate multi-sectoral collaborations as an organizational dimension of innovation, whether technological, economic, or social. On the one hand, literature on governance seldom engages with innovation (see, for example, [5–7]) On the other hand, information systems theory is primarily concerned with intra-organizational transformations along with information system introduction (see, for example, [8, 9]).

The hybrid domain is conceptualized as a newly emerging domain that overlaps public and private interests [1]. Although the modern state has largely been the guardian of the public domain, and markets serve as the purveyors of the private domain, the distinction between the public and private domains does not correspond perfectly with the distinction between the public and private sectors (states-markets). The hybrid domain arises out of the blurring of the boundaries between public and private interests, and the blending of social and economic missions observed in various organizational forms today. The public interest may be represented by non-governmental entities (e.g., NGOs) or even by market actors (e.g., renewable energy providers). Widespread evidence suggests that, an increasingly important role of non-governmental, non-profit organizations as representatives of civil society, combined with technological innovation, particularly in ICTs, is having a profound effect on the lives of people around the world [1, 10–12]. The blurring and blending is intertwined and proceeds alongside the growing transnationalization of various interests and stakeholders. The hybrid domain sits on the boundary of, and overlaps with, the public and private domains. The hybrid domain demonstrates the 'swelling of the middle' and critiques the dominant analytical framework in understanding economic governance – one of state versus markets.

We observe a gradual transition from bilateral negotiations between the state and the markets to hybrid missions and heterarchical complexity. In some cases, this can be observed in subtle shifts in objectives or in articulations of multiple objectives in existing institutions. In other cases, this can be observed in cross-sector collaborations between existing institutions, or the rise of new hybrid institutions that straddle the public and private domains. The increasing popularity of various instruments such as corporate social responsibility (CSR) initiatives, corporate foundations, cross-sectoral collaborations involving corporations and NGOs, and the growth of entities such as strategic and leveraged-NGOs and social enterprises, point to the growth of the hybrid domain.[1]

---

[1] In the case of India, CSR was projected at USD2.5 billion in 2015 as the Companies Act of 2013 began requiring corporations to spend at least 2% of their net profits on CSR and articulate a CSR policy.

The reasons for the rise of the hybrid domain are many and complex. In the Global South, the rise of the hybrid domain is an outcome of both state and market failures that result in underserved populations. In the Global North, it emerges from a quest for economic sustainability. In both cases, the failure or retreat of the state, and growing inequality, has placed the state under scrutiny, whereas corporate scandals have rendered the private sector increasingly suspect. These trends have all contributed to the shift in societal legitimacy and the division of labor in balancing economic and social objectives.

3 Social Innovation and ICTs

The hybrid domain is a necessary organizational framework to produce social innovation. The use of the term "social innovation" grew more than 67 times between the years 2000 and 2014 – from 24 to 1,614 – in the legal and journalistic database compiled by LexisNexus. Despite its appeal and potential, a precise definition of social innovation remains elusive, and its current usage varies widely in the literature. Simply put, social innovation refers to innovation for social change [13], designed to satisfy unmet social needs [14]. Moulaert et al. [15] define social innovation as "the creation of new products, services, organizational structures or activities that are "better" or "more effective" than traditional public sector, philanthropic or market-reliant approaches in responding to social exclusion" (p. 1). As social innovation is both an outcome and a process of social change, and requires institutional change, formally and/or informally. A key feature of hybrid domain is cross-domain multi-stakeholder involvement that is distinct from earlier conceptualizations of multi-stake holder collaborations.

Social innovation emerged out of globalization aided by ICT revolution. Contemporary globalization represents an "epochal transformation" [16] driven by ICTs to produce an "informational, global and networked"[2] economy capable of applying "its progress in technology, knowledge, and management to technology, knowledge, and management themselves. Such a virtuous circle should lead to greater productivity efficiency, given the right conditions of equally dramatic organisational and institutional changes" [17]. However, the impacts of ICTs have been social inequalities and uneven geographies that very selectively connects "localities throughout the planet, according to criteria of valuation and devaluation enforced by social interests that are dominant in these networks" [18]. Social innovation also emerged out of ICT revolution that allowed inter-organizational, 'open' innovation [19]. Open innovation, however, has not been explicitly considered in understanding social innovation, perhaps due to the original geographic bias that favored strong intellectual protection typically available in the Global North [20].

---

[2] It is informational as the productivity and competitiveness of its units is dependent upon their capacity to "generate, process and apply efficient knowledge-based information." It is global as "its core activities of production, consumption and circulation are organized and generated on a global scale either directly or through a network of linkages between economic agents." It is networked as "its productivity is generated through and competition is played out in a global network of interaction between business networks."

Contemporary examples of social innovation include, but are not limited to, micro-credit financing, micro-franchising, clean/alternative sources of energy, and new modes of healthcare delivery using the Internet. Social innovation emerges from the juxtaposition of social mission with market logic, along with changing state–market relations, institutional design, and technological innovation. Among are many technologies that catalyze social innovation by enabling access to otherwise infrastructure-deficient, difficult to service areas and populations, ranging from the rural poor, the disabled, and the elderly, it is argued that ICTs have had the most significant impact on social change [6, 16, 17]. Although technological advances have promised to tackle poverty, illiteracy and poor physical infrastructure, the impacts on the poor have thus far been limited[3] because of significant challenges, including weak institutional support, the need for value-addition and finance, and ambiguous intellectual property rights [21].

4   Collaborations in the Hybrid Domain: Prosocial Rationality

How do collaborations take place across the hybrid domain, which involves competing objectives and institutional heterogeneity? Developing shared norms among heterogeneous organizations across domains is a formidable challenge, both conceptually and pragmatically. Few studies develop a conceptual framework involving heterogeneous stakeholder collaborations. Swanson and Ramiller [22] conceptualized 'organizing vision' that emerges along with an adoption of information systems, but their reference to 'inter-organizational community' appears to be limited to stakeholders in the private sector, and to instances of cross-organizational implementation of IT networks.

Rationality has been a crucial conceptual vehicle to understand human behavior in the social sciences, and various types of rationality have been examined [23–27]. Yet, as Genov [28] observes, collective rationality that governs social innovation is seldom elaborated. In particular, how stakeholders develop collective rationality based on the need to collaborate for mutual gains is poorly understood. Instrumental rationality, for example, cannot explain why organizations engage in innovation [29]. Similarly, motivations and behaviors involving philanthropy or charity have been understood quite separately from rationality that explains innovative behavior.

In distinguishing between substantive and procedural rationality [24], Simon characterized substantive rationality, typically adopted by economists, as being "viewed in terms of the choices it produces", whereas procedural rationality adopted by psychologists is viewed "in terms of the processes it employs" [25]. Simon critiques substantive rationality that constantly seek optimization as, in his view, it ultimately becomes unresponsive to decision contexts. This tendency has led to what some have

---

[3] Social innovation has long been attempted under various guises – for example – the "appropriate" technologies movement of decades past. More recently, grassroots innovation, such as *jugaad* (Hindi for local improvisation) in India's informal sector, has come to be celebrated as a reflection of ingenuity in meeting needs in conditions of scarcity. However, all of them have suffered from the high transaction costs for scouting and documentation, limited transferability and a perception that the technologies deployed were inferior.

called the 'norms of self-interest' [30], which justifies self-interested behavior in many Western societies. For example, research on charity suggests that people are more likely to donate a small amount if they receive a small token gift in return. This allows people to rationalize charity not simply as a self-less act but also as one that does not contradict self-interest [30]. Thus, a concept that was initially intended to be purely descriptive gradually adopts a prescriptive tone in shaping both individual behavior and social norms. Despite its deficiencies, substantive rationality with optimization of self-interest is still implicitly and explicitly assumed as the dominant paradigm of rationality.

The expectations of self-interested behavior as the norm is also reflected in scholarship; research that focuses on behaviors that cannot be described by utilitarian rationality are often characterized as irrational or emotional [31–35]. In such context, fundamentally prosocial behaviors, such as routine acts of kindness, altruism, and co-operation, are either unexplainable or interpreted as being motivated by self-interest. Methodologically, the dominance of game theory in analyzing socio-economic behavior functions to reinforce the norms of self-interest, as the assumptions inevitably involve reciprocity or some kind of quid-pro-quo as the motivational basis of prosocial behavior. For example, Axelrod [36] developed 'cooperation theory' based on substantive rationality, as reflected in his identifications of four properties of cooperation "in a world of egoists without central authority." (p. 20). Alternatively, Jensen [37] used the term 'enlightened value maximization' to explain behavior that involves not simply economic value maximization, but also social value maximization. The methodological constraint therefore precludes a possibility that social behavior may not be calculable.

Interest in prosocial behavior have risen in part along with the expansion of sympathy in contemporary Western society [see, for example, 38]. Drawing on scholarship in psychology, Lindenberg [39] defines prosocial behavior as those that are "intentionally beneficial to others (not necessarily without self-interest) and involving some sacrifice" (p. 24). Instead of focusing on "research toward explaining self-interested sources of cooperation [40]," research in psychology has "moved on to the question of when and how the same individual is governed by very different sets of motives, and under what conditions these different sets of motives lead to prosocial behavior." (p. 24). In fact, a form of hybrid rationality – a combination of strategy and charity – is perhaps far more accurately reflect reality than conventional substantive rationality.

Recent research in biology shows that prosocial behaviors are observed among chimpanzees without obvious quid-pro-quo [41–44], suggesting that such behaviors are neither learnt as previously assumed, nor unique to humans. Instead prosocial behavior is widespread and biologically programmed in other species, contradicting the Darwinian view of survival-of-the-fittest as the key to evolution. Thus, exploring how we conceptualize prosocial behaviors would help better understand collaborative impetus in the hybrid domain; why various stakeholders today seek to develop common agenda, how they develop norms that make cross-domain collaborations possible.

DiMaggio [45] argues that rationality needs to be 'constructed' to allow collaborations to take place. Whereas rationality of the commons has been conceptualized based on individual rationality [see, for example, 46], the concept of collective rationality, as it is used today, typically refers to political decision making [see, for example, 34, 47]. The 'communities of practice' would by default require a community, and while the concept parallels scholarship in information systems theory, cross-domain collaborations goes beyond professional communities in the private sector. Perhaps a better avenue is to adopt Searle's term, 'collective intentionality' [48], which can be developed through collaborative processes among organizations such as MNEs, NGOs, social entrepreneurs and the state. Collective intentionality can be framed as a starting point of collaboration for social innovation wherein divergent organizational rationales and the division of labor are gradually altered and ultimately produce discourse convergence fusing social and economic missions. Discourse convergence as an outcome of collaboration can, in turn, produce a new prosocial collective intentionality for yet another kind of social innovation.

5   Case Studies of Cross-Domain Discourse Convergence

In this section, we discuss three case studies of discourse convergence as a process of collaborative efforts in inducing and implementing social innovation. We conducted 115 semi-structured interviews of various stakeholders in major Indian cities (Bangalore, Chennai, Delhi, Hyderabad, Mumbai) in 2011–2014.[4] Stakeholders ranged from business units and CSR sections of multinational enterprises (MNEs), social enterprises, private foundations, and global and grassroots NGOs. The following three examples serve as paradigmatic cases which, in our view, best represented discourse convergence through cross-domain collaborations. Since our research was qualitative that aimed at uncovering new insights, our sample size does not allow us to demonstrate representativeness, and claim generalizability based on our findings. However, we believe these cases generate useful insights from which to generate hypothesis.

All three cases involve using ICTs. Also, they demonstrate how stakeholders, with varying norms and objectives, ultimately develop a common agenda, and in the process, alter their organizational discourse to develop shared, prosocial objectives. While developing shared objectives, discourse convergence occurs among stakeholders. We chose one case study each from the health, renewable energy, and retail banking sectors. These collaborations were initiated and led by different stakeholders, one was led by an MNE, another a social entrepreneur, and the third an NGO-turned social enterprise.

Traditionally, the interests of MNEs, NGOs and social entrepreneurship are understood to conflict with one another [49–51]. For instance, as MNEs seek to maximize profitability through volume sales, NGOs seek to achieve their social mission by providing health services, and SEs seek to develop niche products with social impacts, while the state attempts to give access to universal basic healthcare for the poor. Each stakeholder encounters constraints, however, arising out of one-dimensional intervention to complex and multidimensional 'wicked problems' [52, 53]. The MNE faces low profitability (and therefore exits from the market segment all together), the

---

[4] This research was supported by the National Science Foundation Grant (BCS-1127329), *The Global Shift in R&D Alliances: Multinational Enterprises (MNEs) and the Quest for the 'Base of the Pyramid' (BOP) markets*. Geography and Spatial Science Program, 2011–16.

NGO is mired by lack of funds, the SE lacks scale and therefore makes little social impact, and the state is unable to reach political agreement to divert resources to single-handedly develop healthcare infrastructure. In the cases we observed, these stakeholders entered into a collaborative arrangement in which each of their priorities was modified in the process of discourse convergence.

In Table 1, we summarized the similarities and differences of the case studies through the process of discourse convergence; the initial organizational priorities for the stakeholders involved and their constraints; organizational learning that leads to collaboration seeking; emergence of prosocial rationality; and the development of inter-organizational solutions.

Table 1. Examples of discourse convergence: health, energy, banking

	Common features	MNE	NGO	Social enterprise	State
Priorities	Divergent	Number of devices sold	Provide access to services for the poor	Sustainable revenue generation for social mission	Providing access to services for the poor
Constraints	One dimensional knowledge; fragmented solution-seeking	Profitability; weak agility; absence of trust; inadequate training (operators)	Unsustainable, under-resourced (personnel, technology)	Limited scale and constrained manufacturing and distribution networks	Under-resourced; political conflicts; limited state capacity; principal-agent problem
Learning	Complementarity seeking	Devices will not sell unless they are effective and actually deployed	Absence of solutions	Impacts are limited without scaling	State cannot solve the problem alone
Prosocial Rationality	Convergence of objectives	To reduce infant mortality rates; to develop an energy solution; to improve access to banking for the poor			
Inter-organizational solutions	Collaborations	Partner with SE for innovation, eco-system development; with NGO for contextual knowledge and training	Partner with MNE for device manufacturing and technological platforms	Partner with MNE for brand recognition and global distribution networks	Modify regulations, state contract bidding process, provide subsidy to encourage adoption

5.1   Case #1: Medical Devices

In the first case, a US MNE in medical devices partnered with an NGO and a social enterprise to develop an affordable incubator for use in an infrastructure deficient (i.e., inconsistent power supply) and knowledge deficient (i.e., lack of licensed medical professionals) environment. Collaborations emerged with a single objective of lowering infant mortality rates (IMR). The MNE described the new discourse as follows.

We need to have partnerships, because the equipment will go there and it won't get used ... as I have seen, not just India, in Vietnam, in Ghana. You need to monitor use, train people, tweak products... The company needs to have vision. Ours is to make a significant impact to infant mortality rate globally, the 4th goal of the Millennium Development Goals (MDG). Whatever we do feed into that vision. You can't just develop products, sell them and see what happens. Even if you go down the road of defeaturing and making a device affordable, at some point, it's important to loop back to the vision. Is the vision affordability or is the vision IMR reduction? Business is a side effect of the vision.[5]

What is notable is the shift of discourse within the for-profit sector from an economic ("number of units sold") to a of social ("number of babies saved") objective. Social motivations function as powerful incentives in the contemporary corporate environment, because economic objectives cannot be met in the long run if social objectives remain unmet. In doing so, the discourse within the corporation demonstrates an explicit engagement with social good which, in turn, encourages cross-domain collaborations.

5.2 Case #2: Renewal Energy

Similar processes were observed for collaborations in renewable energy and retail banking. For the former, social entrepreneurs led the development of business eco-systems involving micro-franchising, transnational financing and private foundations, and simultaneously realigning stakeholder discourse over providing access to solar lanterns. Generally, the discourse shifts from conflicting priorities to solutions seeking collaborations. Through this process, a new set of shared norms emerge and stakeholders, particularly in the private sector, begin to seek social value maximization instead of exclusively focusing on economic value maximization. Conversely, social mission alone does not guarantee sustainability. In particular, one-off charitable gifts (e.g., a MNE giving away solar lanterns through CSR initiative in collaboration with a NGO) not only fail to generate sustained use of renewable energy, but also could wipe out the local entrepreneurial eco-system. According to the social entrepreneur:

One CSR division of a company came [to us] and said, "can you do 1,000 houses for us ... by March 31st, I have to show this [to my superiors], and the money has to [be spent] ... And I might not remain in this position." They would have been happy doing 1,000 houses for free, [but] that would have destroyed the renewable energy market there ... [They have] not thought about the sustainability.[6]

By developing a revenue-driven business model that supports micro-franchises to offer hourly leases of solar lanterns, it becomes possible for street vendors and farmers to increase operating hours and generate higher revenues. This not only supports local entrepreneurs, but it also provides renewable energy solutions which, in some instances, reduces energy costs for the poor and those in the informal sector. This model requires coordination among social entrepreneurs and manufacturers of solar lanterns (e.g., MNEs). Operating costs of social entrepreneurs may also be subsidized by foundation and state grants.

---

[5] Interview by authors, June 22, 2012.
[6] Interview by authors, July 12, 2013.

5.3   Case #3: Rural Banking

A NGO-turned social entrepreneur led an effort to bring affordable and secure remittance transfer service to migrant construction workers. This required a combination of regulatory changes (i.e., the state), software platform development (i.e., MNEs), the participation of a bank and informal retailers. *"We benefitted indirectly from an MNE – who alerted us about an existing technological platform developed for a foundation and supported by another MNE. We developed a whole new transaction platform on it along with a telecommunication layer... Also, an endorsement by the MNE was beyond financial... a critical intervention for credibility. So, external help did matter."*[7] As was the case with the medical device collaboration, discourse convergence took place when the social entrepreneur's complex mission was understood to be unachievable without partnering across sectors. The social entrepreneur's role was to involve the MNEs, financial sector and the informal retailers, and develop a solution to a complex problem that can only be devised through collaborations. In the process, the MNE acquired context specific knowledge on the livelihood challenges faced by the poor, such as the difficulties faced by migrant construction workers without bank accounts to access affordable and secure remittance transfer services.

6   Summary Reflections

The new de-specialization trend is observed in corporations blending social and economic missions, through various forms of collaborations. These trends toward de-specialization and shifting boundaries of organizations culminate into hybridized missions that blend public and private interests simultaneously, and achieve societal goals by taking the best of both worlds, avoiding both the social neglect of the private sector and the inefficiency of the public sector.

Historically we have moved from a low (basic) to high (more sophisticated) division of labor and accordingly specialization of tasks and functions in the economy. Today, efforts are underway to avoid the disadvantages from over-specialization which outweigh advantages of specialization. Firms are getting rid of the 'silos' and developing R&D that brings together multidisciplinary teams of scholars and disciplines. The specialization has also resulted in a separation of social and economic missions within corporations, with corporate charitable foundations to fulfill social missions, and economic missions fulfilled by maximizing profit accumulation.

There remains a question of accountability in cross-domain collaborations. Since the main objective of this paper is to show how collaboration in the hybrid domain can lead to a convergence of economic and social objectives of stakeholders with different priorities, and thus point to how solutions can be found for wicked problems, it does not explicitly address the issue of accountability. However, we hypothesize that accountability can be fortified through collaboration. For instance, the movement of people from the corporate sector to NGOs makes it easier to share and develop norms

---

[7] Interview by authors, July 23, 2012.

for collaboration. The verification of this hypothesis offers a significant future direction for research on the role of collaboration in social innovation.

References

1. Aoyama, Y., Parthasarathy, B.: The Rise of the Hybrid Domain: Collaborative Governance for Social Innovation. Edward Elgar, New York, London (2016)
2. Altenburg, T., Lundvall, B.-A.: Building inclusive innovation systems in developing countries: challenges for IS research. In: Lundvall, B.-A., Joseph, K.J., Chaminade, C., Vang, J. (eds.) Handbook of Innovation Systems and Developing Countries: Building Domestic Capabilities in a Global Setting, pp. 33–56. Edward Elgar, Cheltenham (2009)
3. Foster, C., Heeks, R.: Conceptualising inclusive innovation: modifying systems of innovation frameworks to understand diffusion of new technology to low-income consumers. Europ. J. Devel. Res. **25**, 333–355 (2013)
4. Sonne, L.: Innovative initiatives supporting inclusive innovation in India: social business incubation and micro venture capital. Technol. Forecast. Soc. Chang. **79**, 638–647 (2012)
5. Ostrom, E.: Beyond markets and states: polycentric governance of complex economic systems. Am. Econ. Rev. **100**(3), 641–672 (2010)
6. Jessop, B.: The rise of governance and the risks of failure: the case of economic development. Int. Soc. Sci. J. **50**, 29–45 (1998)
7. Mittelman, J.H.: Global bricolage: emerging market powers and polycentric governance. Third World Q. **34**, 23–37 (2013)
8. Swanson, E.B.: Information systems innovation among organizations. Manag. Sci. **40**, 1069–1092 (1994)
9. Swanson, E.B., Ramiller, N.C.: Innovating mindfully with information technology. MIS Q. **28**, 553–583 (2004)
10. Pfeiffer, J.: International NGOs and primary health care in Mozambique: the need for a new model of collaboration. Soc. Sci. Med. **56**, 725–738 (2003)
11. Boddewyn, J., Doh, J.: Global strategy and the collaboration of MNEs NGOs and the government for the provisioning of collective goods in emerging markets. Glob. Strategy J. **1**, 345–361 (2011)
12. den Hond, F., de Bakker, F.G.A., Doh, J.: What prompts companies to collaboration with NGOs? Recent evidence from the Netherlands. Bus. Soc. **54**, 187–228 (2015)
13. Michelini, L.: Social Innovation and New Business Models: Creating Shared Value in Low-Income Markets. Springer, Heidelberg (2012)
14. Van Dyck, B., Van den Broeck, P.: Social innovation: a territorial process. In: Moulaert, F., MacCallum, D., Mehmood, A., Hamdouch, A. (eds.) The International Handbook of Social Innovation: Colelctive Action, Social Learning and Transdisciplinary Research. Edward Elgar, Cheltenham (2013)
15. Moulaert, F., MacCallum, D., Hillier, J.: Social innovaton: intuition, percept, concept, theory and practice. In: Moulaert, F., MacCallum, D., Mehmood, A., Hamdouch, A. (eds.) The International Handbook on Social Innovation, pp. 13–24. Edward Elgar, Cheltenham (2013)
16. Sassen, S.: Territory, Authority, Rights: From Medieval to Global Assemblages. Cambridge University Press, Cambridge (2006)
17. Castells, M.: The Rise of the Network Society. The Information Age: Economy, Society and Culture, vol. 1. Blackwell, Oxford (2000)

18. Castells, M.: Preface. In: Evans, P.B. (ed.) Livable Cities? Urban Struggles for Livelihood and Sustainability, pp. ix–xi. University of California Press, Berkeley (2002)
19. Chesbrough, H.: Open Innovation: The New Imperative for Creating and Profiting from Technology. Harvard Business School Press, Boston (2003)
20. Quan, X., Chesbrough, H.: Hierarchical segmentation of R&D process and intellectual property protection: evidence from multinational R&D laboratories in China. IEEE Trans. Eng. Manag. **57**, 9–21 (2010)
21. The World Bank: Unleashing India's Innovation: Toward Sustainable and Inclusive Growth. The World Bank, Washington, D.C. (2007)
22. Swanson, E.B., Ramiller, N.C.: The organizing vision in information systems innovation. Organ. Sci. **8**, 458–474 (1997)
23. March, J.G.: Bounded rationality, ambiguity, and the engineering of choice. Bell J. Econ. **9**, 587–608 (1978)
24. Simon, H.A.: From substantive to procedural rationality. In: Kastelein, T.J., Kuipers, S.K., Nijenhuis, W.A., Wagenaar, G.R. (eds.) 25 Years of Economic Theory: Retrospect and Prospect, pp. 65–86. Springer, Boston (1976)
25. Simon, H.A.: Rationality in psychology and economics. J. Bus. **59**, S209–S224 (1986)
26. Hirschman, A.O.: Rival interpretations of market society: civilizing, destructive, or feeble? J. Econ. Lit. **20**, 1463–1484 (1982)
27. Hirschman, A.O.: Shifting Involvements: Private Interest and Public Action. Princeton University Press, Princeton (1982)
28. Genov, N.: Towards a multidimensional concept of rationality: the sociological perspective. Sociol. Theory **9**, 206–211 (1991)
29. Lockyer, J., McCabe, D.: Leading through fear: emotion, rationality and innovation in a UK manufacturing company. Eur. J. Int. Manag. **5**, 48–61 (2010)
30. Miller, D.T.: The norm of self-interest. Am. Psychol. **54**, 1053 (1999)
31. Avgerou, C., McGrath, K.: Power, rationality, and the art of living through socio-technical change. MIS Q. **31**, 295–315 (2007)
32. DiMaggio, P., Powell, W.W.: The iron cage revisited: collective rationality and institutional isomorphism in organizational fields. Am. Sociol. Rev. **48**, 147–160 (1983)
33. Li, Y., Ashkanasy, N.M., Ahlstrom, D.: The rationality of emotions: a hybrid process model of decision-making under uncertainty. Asia Pac. J. Manag. **31**, 293–308 (2014)
34. Moshman, D., Geil, M.: Collaborative reasoning: evidence for collective rationality. Think. Reason. **4**, 231–248 (1998)
35. Ostrom, E.: A behavioral approach to the rational choice theory of collective action: presidential address, American political science association, 1997. Amer. Polit. Sci. Rev. **92**, 1–22 (1998)
36. Axelrod, R.M.: The Evolution of Cooperation. Basic Books, New York (2006)
37. Jensen, M.C.: Value maximization, stakeholder theory, and the corporate objective function. Bus. Ethics Q. **12**, 235–256 (2002)
38. Pinker, S.: The Better Angels of Our Nature: The Decline of Violence in History and its Causes. Penguin, London (2011)
39. Lindenberg, S.: Prosocial behavior, solidarity, and framing processes. In: Fetchenhauer, D., Flache, A., Buunk, B., Lindenberg, S. (eds.) Solidarity and Prosocial Behavior. Critical Issues in Social Justice, pp. 23–44. Springer, New York (2006)
40. Yamagishi, T.: Social dilemmas. In: Sociological Perspectives on Social Psychology, pp. 311–335 (1995)
41. Horner, V., Carter, J.D., Suchak, M., de Waal, F.B.: Spontaneous prosocial choice by chimpanzees. Proc. Natl. Acad. Sci. **108**, 13847–13851 (2011)

42. Warneken, F., Tomasello, M.: Altruistic helping in human infants and young chimpanzees. Science **311**, 1301–1303 (2006)
43. Silk, J.B., House, B.R.: Evolutionary foundations of human prosocial sentiments. Proc. Natl. Acad. Sci. **108**, 10910–10917 (2011)
44. de Waal, F.B., Suchak, M.: Prosocial primates: selfish and unselfish motivations. Philos. Trans. R. Soc. Lond. B: Biol. Sci. **365**, 2711–2722 (2010)
45. DiMaggio, P.: The new institutionalisms: avenues of collaboration. J. Inst. Theor. Econ. (JITE)/Zeitschrift für die gesamte Staatswissenschaft **154**, 696–705 (1998)
46. Ostrom, V., Ostrom, E.: Public goods and public choices. In: Savas, E.S. (ed.) Alternatives to Delivering Public Services: Toward Improved Performance, pp. 7–49. Westview Press, Boulder (1977)
47. Blair, D.H., Pollak, R.A.: Collective rationality and dictatorship: the scope of the arrow theorem. J. Econ. Theory **21**, 186–194 (1979)
48. Searle, J.R.: The Construction of Social Reality. Penguin Books, London (1995)
49. Burchell, J., Cook, J.: Sleeping with the enemy? Strategic transformations in business–NGO relationships through stakeholder dialogue. J. Bus. Ethics **113**, 505–518 (2013)
50. Arts, B.: 'Green alliances' of business and NGOs. New styles of self-regulation or 'dead-end roads'? Corp. Soc. Responsib. Environ. Manag. **9**, 26–36 (2002)
51. Yaziji, M., Doh, J.: NGOs and Corporations: Conflict and Collaboration. Cambridge University Press, Cambridge (2009)
52. Churchman, W.: Wicked problems. Manag. Sci. **4**, 141–142 (1967)
53. Buchanan, R.: Wicked problems in design thinking. Des. Issues **8**, 5–21 (1992)

Digital Innovation: A Research Agenda for Information Systems Research in Developing Countries

Petter Nielsen[(⊠)]

University of Oslo, Oslo, Norway
pnielsen@ifi.uio.no

Abstract. This paper is based on a survey of the current landscape of information systems research concerned with developing countries and development. Significant gaps are identified representing a lack of focus on digital technologies and the impact and significance of digital innovation for developing countries and development. We need to expand our focus from primarily addressing the challenges of access to and the ability to use ICTs, to also include how developing countries can participate in and take relevant roles in digital innovation. We are witnessing a wide-spread digitization of organizations and societies at large, and these significant changes warrant a new research agenda for information systems in developing countries. This paper proposes three new directions for research to support this shift; empirical research on digital innovation by developing countries; theorizing digital innovation by developing countries; and participation in digital innovation as freedom.

Keywords: Digital innovation · Information systems · Development · Research agenda

1 Introduction

There is significant interest in and a growing body of literature on digital innovation in information systems research [see e.g. 1]. Digital innovation is about the breaking up of vertical industry silos and the creation of networks where different actors come together and innovate by combining and recombining their digital technology components. With technologies such as platforms, new venues for innovation are opened up and participation in innovation potentially attracts a broader audience. Digital innovation is by many argued as a deep change in ways in which innovation is organized, influencing industrial structures and competitive landscapes. Digital innovation is also self-referential in the sense that it requires the use of digital technologies [1]. The widespread diffusion of digital innovations has created a virtuous circle that furthers the development and accessibility of digital devices, networks, services and contents [2, 3]. While there is a significant debate in research on the impacts of digital technologies and digital innovation, these discussions have still to reach the information systems literature engaged with developing countries and development. Instead of exploring the potential and impacts of digital innovation, research seems to be stuck in a perspective

© IFIP International Federation for Information Processing 2017
Published by Springer International Publishing AG 2017. All Rights Reserved
J. Choudrie et al. (Eds.): ICT4D 2017, IFIP AICT 504, pp. 269–279, 2017.
DOI: 10.1007/978-3-319-59111-7_23

on developing countries as passive, and often reluctant, receivers of innovations and new ICTs. The aim of this paper is to support a shift in this respect and bring digital innovation on the agenda of information systems research in developing countries.

While the potential of ICTs for developing countries and development is well established, the question of *how* to make ICTs relevant is still under scrutiny. Research has approached this how question from different angles. For example, by exemplifying a range of different ICT failures, Avgerou and Walsham [4] focus on the importance of taking into account the *contexts* in which ICTs are implemented and used. These context discussions include a broad array of influential factors such as for example information infrastructures [5], institutions [5] and local practices [6]. Other researchers have focused more particularly on understanding the *processes* of introducing, implementing and maintaining relevant ICTs in developing countries, related to integration [7], scaling [8] and sustainability [9]. These discussions are based on the 'classical' North-South digital divide [10, 11] where the prime challenge to be addressed is bridging the design-actuality gaps between the developed countries where the ICTs are designed and the actuality of the periphery where they are used (developing countries).

Reviewing the literature on ICTs in developing countries, Walsham and Sahay [12] identified four broad categories of information systems topics addressed. These include cross-cultural working, local adaptation of global technologies, particular marginalized groups, and the meaning of development in itself. These topics are still relevant, and of particular interest here, the definition and nature of development and how it relates to innovation has remained as an important concern. For example, Qureshi [13] discusses how innovations in the use of ICTs can transform development by enabling people to use ICTs in ways that benefits them and help them to establish the power to determine their own life. Along the same line of argument, Foster and Heeks [14] argue for *inclusive innovation* as a means to make innovation relevant for low income groups, defined as addressing problems relevant for the poor; involving the poor in the development; enabling the poor to adopt the innovations; and focus on innovations improving the livelihoods of the poor. But innovation is not limited to the relevance of, the access to and the ability to use ICTs effectively as discussed by for example Walsham and Sahay [12]. In this paper I argue that innovation is also about how individuals and organizations in developing countries are involved in and ultimately take a lead in innovation as a process.

The method adopted in this paper was as follows. I first made a literature review on digital technologies in developing countries, focusing on the main information systems journals and conferences concerned with ICT4D. It quickly became apparent that while 'electronic', 'online' and 'digital technologies' are popular terms, discussions related to how digital technologies and digital innovation represents something new and different for developing countries are more or less absent. Based on this, the review strategy was changed to also include more general ICT related innovation for development. This review was contextualized in the broader information systems discourse on digital innovation. Finally, this was used as a basis to develop new research directions to bring digital innovation to the research agenda for information systems in developing countries.

Digital innovation remains as more or less a void in information systems research on ICTs in developing countries. My aim and hope is that pointing out this gap and suggesting research directions will encourage future studies addressing this topic and stimulate research on how to approach digital innovation in developing countries and if possible how to make it relevant for development.

In the next section, digital innovation is introduced. In the following section a review is done of existing research on ICTs and digital innovation in developing countries. This is followed by a section outlining a research agenda for information systems in developing countries including digital innovation. The concluding section five summarizes the paper and discusses future research.

2 Digital Innovation

Digital innovation is on the agenda in information systems research [see e.g. 15–17]. In their research commentary, Yoo et al. [1] put forward that digital technologies and their modular architectures will have profound implications on how firms organize innovation. They describe digital technologies as different from analogue technologies on three levels: they are reprogrammable, enabling them to perform a variety of different tasks; data is homogenized enabling the same digital device the ability to store, transmit, process and display a variety of different digital contents and content becomes separated from the media; and finally digital innovation requires digital technologies creating a drive towards further digital innovation. These changes in technology are drivers towards radical changes in the way innovation unfolds [16]. The rapid drop in the cost of digital technologies including PC's and smartphones combined with the explosive diffusion of Internet have radically lowered the barriers of access to the digital tools for digital innovation: "Digital technology, therefore, has democratized innovation and almost anyone can now participate" [1].

Digital innovations are based on layered architectures comprised of core components, complementary components and interfaces between these components. With digital innovation, there is a separation between devices and services and networks and contents. While the core components are stable and with low variability, the complementary products are rapidly changing [18]. This layered and modular architecture enables innovation distributed among different and different kinds of actors. Yoo et al. [1] characterizes these architectures as doubly distributed, in terms of how they offer opportunities in combining a variety of resources on different levels as well as the control over and the knowledge about the different components being distributed among actors. Digital innovation activities require the ability to mobilize other actors to release the potential of platforms, to combine and recombine components, rapidly respond to changes in constellations of components and attribute new meanings and usages to existing technologies [19]. Technical attributes of platforms play key roles in concert with human relationships in shaping the socio-technical generativity of digital technologies [20]. Examples of digital innovations range from open source software projects, Google's shared platform and new mobile services.

Digital innovation is about the breaking up of silo systems and creation of networks where different actors comes together and interlink complementary digital components.

While user involvement in innovation is not something new [21], the pervasiveness and accessibility of digital technologies are. Even if the user is offered a more significant role and have the potential to make their own modifications of technologies, user driven innovation is based on a user – innovator relationship. Digital innovation is a deeper change in the ways in which firms organize innovation, influencing industrial structures and competitive landscapes. Old vertically integrated industries and models are broken down and new complex technical, organizational and social networks are emerging based on heterogeneous actors with control over and knowledge about different components. Instead of being based on a user – innovator relationship, digital innovation offers multiple venues for multiple different actors to participate in innovation. It opens up for different actors to take new roles, but participation will also require new knowledge, competencies and social relationships. The opportunities digital innovation offers and what it takes for individuals and organizations from developing countries to participate is by large unknown and yet to be explored.

3 A Review of Research on ICTs and Innovation in Developing Countries

3.1 Innovation *for* Developing Countries

There is a common concern that the context of developing countries poses certain challenges to ICTs and requires different technologies and implementation approaches. For example, resource constraints in terms of weak ICT infrastructure and electricity outages will inevitably result in expensive and fluctuation Internet connections. This mandates solutions using as little bandwidth as possible and providing offline capabilities [e.g. 22]. Discussing the design of hospital systems for resource constrained context, Sahay and Walsham [23] describe technical innovation as intrinsically related to social and institutional innovation, and argue that ICT based innovation in developing countries requires these different types of innovation to happen at the same time. They introduce the concept of *frugal innovation* to ICT4D research by arguing that innovation in resource constrained context must achieve doing more with less. In their concrete case, frugal innovation included amongst other factors saving money based on using open source software, reaching out to rural populations and reducing external dependencies. The focus on the particularities of the context in developing countries also includes research on the broader social context. For example, Khalid et al. [24] discuss and suggest a particular design of a partograph for real-time clinical decisions in India based on addressing key cultural barriers. These barriers include; the human capacity to absorb the complexities of a graphical format; the capacity of the health providers to give training to their staff; insufficient resources to assure accountability and usage in decision making; and linking the solution to the wider health system.

There is also a body of research on ICTs in developing countries that does not focus on the design of technology for a particular context, but the processes in which innovations are introduced and used. This is for example related to discussions on digital divides between the developed and developing countries and how marginalized groups and regions can achieve access to the 'network society' [25]. While research on digital divides have focused on who have access to technology (first order effects), there are also arguments for focusing on second order effects in terms of the ability for those who have access to use the technology in a meaningful way [26]. Dijk and Hacker [11] argue that while the lack of access to hardware that existed in the 1980s and 1990s in developing countries is less a challenge today, the lack of access to skills required for meaningful use is different and likely to increase. In a similar fashion, Kibere [27] in her study of the use and appropriation of mobile phones in the Kiberia slum in Kenya problematizes how social, cultural and political structures influences the processes of technology adoption, diffusion and use. More broadly, Diga and May [28] in their introduction to a special issue on ICT Ecosystems in the Information Technology for Development Journal, discuss how ICT usage is always framed in a context where for example socio-economic and political forces are at play. In sum, this body of literature focuses on different facets of the context in developing countries, and contributes by suggesting how technologies and implementation processes can be designed accordingly.

The digital divide is recognized as not only the lack of access to ICTs but also the social and institutional context shaping access and the capacity of people to use ICTs [29]. There is a stream of research on innovation and ICT4D, motivated by the challenges emerging when ICTs designed and developed for and by the developed countries are implemented in developing countries. Addressing technology production in general, Suchman [30] pointed out the different social worlds of users and developers, and the challenges emerging when technologies are crossing these boundaries. To address these challenges, she calls for developers to cross over to where technology is used. Heeks [6] have made a similar argument particularly for ICT4D research with his discussion of design-actuality gaps. Heeks describe these gaps, between the designers' approach to design and the local actuality of the users, along dimensions of; information; technology; processes; objectives and values; staffing and skills; management systems and structures; and other resources. Heeks argues for designing applications that comes with fewer assumptions related to these different dimensions. Instead, they should be enabling and put as little as possible constraints on local improvisations. There is, at the same time, the need to balance between the room for improvisation and what the design requires of local implementation capacity on the ground.

3.2 Innovation *by* Developing Countries

Bridging design-actuality gaps and drawing the balance between initial design and room for improvisation assumes a situation where developed countries are producers of innovations and developing countries form the implementation and use context. This perspective is reflected in for example the work of Nicholson and Sahay [31], discussing how political and cultural issues challenges the management of software development projects across developed and developing countries. While Nicholson and Sahay focus on outsourcing as motivated by manpower shortages and needs to cut costs by companies in developed countries, outsourcing can also have a development aim. Discussing impact sourcing, Nicholson et al. [32] describe how outsourcing can target the poorest people with a particular aim of poverty alleviation. The role of developing countries in impact sourcing is at the same time limited to data entry and digitization of documents.

There are attempts to explore and discuss developing countries as having a more active role in innovation. George et al. [33] define inclusive innovation as "innovation that benefits the disenfranchised" (p. 661). Inclusive innovation entails making the poor not only customers and employees, but also owners, suppliers and community members in innovation. Heeks [34] also seeks to expand existing innovation models by distinguishing between pro-poor, para-poor and per-poor innovation. Where pro-poor is innovation for the poor by the non-poor and para-poor is innovation by the non-poor alongside the poor, per-poor innovation is by poor communities themselves. This promising body of literature on per-poor innovation in developing countries is at the same time limited and not particularly addressing digital technologies.

To summarize this literature review, we can see that the research on ICTs and innovation in developing countries primarily focuses on the challenges emerging when innovation is driven by developed countries. There are a few initiatives to explore how developing countries can take a more active role in these innovation processes, but these are limited and not addressing digital technologies in particular.

4   A Digital Innovation Research Agenda for Information Systems in Developing Countries

In 2008, Thompson [35] introduced Web 2.0 to information systems research in developing countries and discussed its implications for development in terms of openness, collaborative logic and how it supports networked social behavior. He described Web 2.0 as reflecting a different social life, comprised of diversity, collaboration and multiple truths, enabled by technology. When Walsham and Sahay [12] suggested an agenda for research on information systems in developing countries, they also emphasized the role of technology and the need of detailed studies of particular technologies. These calls to study particular technologies in the developing country contexts; a global call to study digital innovation through theorizing and empirical research [1]; and the identified gap in research on digital innovation in this paper have shaped the first two research directions suggested below in this section. Linked to the two first, the third research direction suggested concerns how digital innovation can improve the livelihoods and the quality of life for individuals in developing countries. Inspired by Amartya Sen in the way he define development as human capabilities and the freedoms of individuals to participate in the activities they want [36], the third direction is based on appreciating the opportunity for individuals to participate in digital innovation as a freedom.

4.1   Empirical Research on Digital Innovation by Developing Countries

The implications of and what roles organizations and individuals from developing countries will take in digital innovation are unknowns. The scant, but growing body of empirical research on digital innovation involving developing countries have included studies of open source software projects and the participation of developing countries in software generification processes [37] and crowdsourcing platforms emerging from developing countries [38]. While unveiling new opportunities for developing countries, these studies also reveal the persistence of old and the emergence of new barriers and divides.

The very nature of digital technologies leaves a potential for developing countries participating in digital innovation. We should also appreciate participation in innovation as a potential venue to bridge design-actuality gaps. At the same time, while ICTs now are available and affordable for large populations in developing countries, the argument that digital technology: "… has democratized innovation and almost anyone can now participate …" [1] paints a too simple and rather naïve picture of the context in developing countries. Such an argument can only be based on the assumption that digital innovation is open for all and incentives, knowledge and human capacity are equally distributed on a global scale.

There is a need for more empirical research in this area. Will digital innovation be a democratization of innovation where innovation will be *by* developing countries, will developing countries only be users of digital platforms, or will digital innovation become the source of yet another digital divide? These questions could be approached by for example case studies in various domains on how platforms for digital innovation is shaped, influenced and developed by developing countries, how developing countries is taking part in innovation on top of platforms or more broadly on the role of developing countries in networks and ecosystems generating digital innovations. While these studies should focus and appreciate how organizations and individuals from developing countries can take active roles in digital innovation and how this can promote development, they should also critically scrutinize the real impact of digital innovation in this context.

4.2   Theorizing Digital Innovation by Developing Countries

Digital divides can be explained by economic, socio-cultural and infrastructural factors [39]. Infrastructural factors includes ICT penetration, Internet penetration and digital wireless penetration [26]. But access to ICTs does not equate effective use and participation in digital innovation. Further, digital technologies should be taken seriously and properly theorized as any other technology [40]. Research should find inspiration from existing theorizations not particularly focusing on the developing country context. For example, Ghazawneh and Henfridsson [41] argue that digital technologies are not only about platforms, their owners, applications and developers, and conceptualize boundary resources as a necessity to keep these different dimensions together. These resources, including for example software tools and regulations, are also tools that afford certain actors control over others. Another example is Dittrich [42] and her discussion of platforms as "half products", and how they *have to* be configured, customized and extended to fit a specific context. Other examples include the discussion of Diga and May [28] on how ecosystems can both facilitate and hinder the participation of certain communities in digital innovation, the discussion of different types of digital innovation networks by Lyytinen et al. [16] and the conceptualization of socio-technical generativity and role of human capacities in digital innovation in developing countries by Msiska and Nielsen [20].

To understand who stands to gain from digital innovation related to the developing country context, we need to further theorize digital technologies and the processes of digital innovation in the developing country context, including dimensions such as; boundary resources in terms of e.g. intermediaries; platform technologies and human capacity needs for implementation and use; and inclusion/exclusion and the openness of ecosystems.

4.3 Participation in Digital Innovation as Freedom

The question "... will the digital revolution revolutionize development?" [10] is not entirely new, but it remains by large unanswered. What should be a concern is that so little current research is engaged in answering this question. If we continue along this path, we will remain with only a weak understanding of what digital innovation is, the opportunities it may bring, the challenges it may pose and the actual and potential impacts on developing countries and development. I find it striking that the contribution from developing countries in digital innovation still is discussed as a simple source of 'insights' to developed countries engaged in digital innovation [43]. This is about the impact of digital innovation on development, but also about the impact of human development on digital innovation. It is also about bridging the often disconnected discussions on understanding ICTs *for* development and studies focusing on understanding ICTs *in* developing countries [44].

Sahay and Walsham discuss whether ICT-based innovation contributes to human development, using the capability approach of Sen by describing ICT as having the potential to offer increased freedoms [23]. Their discussion is focused on how access to innovation and particular kinds of innovation can enable a growing range of freedoms including political rights and economic choices and protection in developing countries. But at the same time, the focus of their research agenda is on how to best introduce and use innovations in developing countries which are developed elsewhere (the developed world). There is a need to push information systems research further by also include research on how developing countries can be enabled to participate and take relevant roles in digital innovation. To do this, we need to understand what relevant roles can be; how participation in digital innovation by individuals and organizations from developing countries can contribute to development; what are the additional barriers for participation; and what extra support is needed in developing country contexts. This is partly about exploring digital innovation and how it can open up for the engagement of a wider audience from developing countries. It is also about exploring the relevance of digital innovation for the development agenda and understanding how participation in digital innovation relates to the freedoms of individuals. Building a deeper understanding of digital innovation as development should inspire and influence information systems research on digital innovation as well as ICT4D research in general.

5   Conclusion

My goal in this paper is to support a shift in research on information systems in developing countries by bringing digital innovation on the agenda. Based on reviewing the existing literature and identifying a gap in research on digital innovation and developing countries, I have suggested and discussed three new directions for research; empirical research on digital innovation by developing countries; theorizing digital innovation by developing countries; and participation in digital innovation as freedom. My hope is that this discussion and the directions can act as an inspiration and guidance for further research. While research on information systems in developing countries has matured both methodologically and theoretically, there is still a need to focus on the relationship between ICTs and development [12]. This paper argues for a stronger focus on digital technologies and the particular relationship between digital innovation and development. With this agenda, I believe that information systems research can make an important contribution by exploring the opportunities and challenges of digital innovation in developing countries and avoid digital innovation becoming the source of yet another digital divide.

References

1. Yoo, Y., Henfridsson, O., Lyytinen, K.: The new organizing logic of digital innovation: an agenda for information systems research. Inf. Syst. Res. **21**(4), 724–735 (2010)
2. Hanseth, O., Lyytinen, K.: Design theory for dynamic complexity in information infrastructures: the case of building internet. J. Inf. Technol. **25**, 1–19 (2010)
3. Benkler, Y.: The Wealth of Networks: How Social Production Transforms Markets and Freedom. Yale University Press, New Haven (2006)
4. Avgerou, C., Walsham, G. (eds.): Information Technology in Context: Implementing Systems in the Developing World. Ashgate Publishing, Brookfield (2000)
5. Aanestad, M., Monteiro, E., Nielsen, P.: Information infrastructures and public goods: analytical and practical implications for SDI. Inf. Technol. Dev. **13**(1), 7–25 (2007)
6. Heeks, R.: Information systems and developing countries: failure, success, and local improvisations. Inf. Soc. **18**(2), 101–112 (2002)
7. Sahay, S., Monteiro, E., Aanestad, M.: Configurable politics and asymmetric integration: health e-infrastructures in India. J. Assoc. Inf. Syst. **10**(5), 399–414 (2009)
8. Sahay, S., Walsham, G.: Scaling of health information systems in India: challenges and approaches. Inf. Technol. Dev. **12**(3), 185–200 (2006)
9. Braa, J., Monteiro, E., Sahay, S.: Networks of action: sustainable health information systems across developing countries. MIS Q. **28**(3), 337–362 (2004)
10. Boas, T., Dunning, T., Bussell, J.: Will the digital revolution revolutionize development? Drawing together the debate. Stud. Comp. Int. Dev. **40**(2), 95–110 (2005)
11. Dijk, J.V., Hacker, K.: The digital divide as a complex and dynamic phenomenon. Inf. Soc. **19**(4), 315–326 (2003)
12. Walsham, G., Sahay, S.: Research on information systems in developing countries: current landscape and future prospects. Inf. Technol. Dev. **12**(1), 7–24 (2006)
13. Qureshi, S.: Networks of change, shifting power from institutions to people: how are innovations in the use of information and communication technology transforming development? Inf. Technol. Dev. **19**(2), 97–99 (2013)

14. Foster, C., Heeks, R.: Conceptualising inclusive innovation: modifying systems of innovation frameworks to understand diffusion of new technology to low-income consumers. Eur. J. Dev. Res. **25**(3), 333–355 (2013)

15. Yoo, Y., et al.: Organizing for innovation in the digitized world. Organ. Sci. **23**(5), 1398–1408 (2016)

16. Lyytinen, K., Yoo, Y., Boland, R.: Digital production innovation within four classes of innovation networks. Inf. Syst. J. **26**, 47–75 (2016)

17. Nambisan, S., et al.: Digital innovation management: reinventing innovation management research in a digital world. MIS Q. **41**, 223–238 (2016)

18. Baldwin, C.Y., Woodard, C.J.: The Architecture of Platforms: A Unified View. Harvard Business School Finance Working Paper No. 09-034 (2008)

19. Lane, D.A.: Complexity and innovation dynamics. In: Antonelli, C. (ed.) Handbook on the Economic Complexity of Technological Change. Edward Elgar Publishing Limited, Cheltenham (2011)

20. Msiska, B., Nielsen, P.: Innovation in the Fringes of Software Ecosystems: The role of Socio-Technical Generativity (2016, in review)

21. Hippel, E.V.: Lead users: a source of novel product concepts. Manag. Sci. **32**(7), 791–805 (1986)

22. Braa, K., Nielsen, P.: Leveraging the potential of mobiles in developing country health initiatives: from ICT4D to information infrastructures 4D. In: Proceedings of the 12th International Conference on Social Implications of Computers in Developing Countries, Ocho Rios, Jamaica. Faculty of Social Sciences, University of West Indies, Mona, Jamaica (2013)

23. Sahay, S., Walsham, G.: Information technology, innovation and human development: hospital information systems in an Indian state. J. Hum. Dev. Capabilities, 1–18 (2017). doi:10.1080/19452829.2016.1270913

24. Khalid, M., et al.: Designing a mobile partograph for real-time decision support for safer deliveries in India. In: Proceedings of the 13th International Conference on Social Implications of Computers in Developing Countries, Negombo, Sri Lanka. University of Oslo, Norway (2015)

25. Mosse, E.L., Sahay, S.: The role of communication practices in the strengthening of counter networks: case experiences from the health care sector of Mozambique. Inf. Technol. Dev. **11**(3), 207–225 (2005)

26. Riggins, F.J., Dewan, S.: The digital divide: current and future research directions. J. Assoc. Inf. Syst. **6**(12), 298–336 (2005)

27. Kibere, F.N.: The Paradox of Mobility in the Kenyan ICT Ecosystem: An Ethnographic Case of How the Youth in Kibera Slum Use and Appropriate the Mobile Phone and the Mobile Internet, pp. 47–67. Information Technology for Development (2016)

28. Diga, K., May, J.: The ICT ecosystem: the application, usefulness, and future of an evolving concept. Inf. Technol. Dev. **22**(Suppl. 1), 1–6 (2016)

29. Madon, S., et al.: Digital inclusion projects in developing countries: processes of institutionalization. Inf. Technol. Dev. **15**(2), 95–107 (2009)

30. Suchman, L.: Located accountabilities in technology production. Scand. J. Inf. Syst. **14**(2), 91–105 (2002)

31. Nicholson, B., Sahay, S.: Some political and cultural issues in the globalisation of software development: case experience from Britain and India. Inf. Organ. **11**, 25–43 (2001)

32. Nicholson, B., et al.: Evaluating impact sourcing: a capabilities perspective from a case study in Pakistan. In: Proceedings of the 13th International Conference on Social Implications of Computers in Developing Countries, Negombo, Sri Lanka. University of Oslo, Norway (2015)

33. George, G., McGahan, A.M., Prabhu, J.: Innovation for inclusive growth: towards a theoretical framework and a research agenda. J. Manag. Stud. **49**(4), 661–683 (2012)
34. Heeks, R.: ICT4D 2.0: the next phase of applying ICT for international development. Computer **41**(6), 26–33 (2008)
35. Thompson, M.: ICT and development studies: towards development 2.0. J. Int. Dev. **20**(6), 821–835 (2008)
36. Sen, A.: Development as Freedom. Oxford University Press, Oxford (1999)
37. Gizaw, A.A., Bygstad, B., Nielsen, P.: Open generification. Inf. Syst. J. (2016). doi:10.1111/isj.12112
38. Marsden, J.: Stigmergic self-organization and the improvisation of Ushahidi. Cogn. Syst. Res. **21**, 52–64 (2013)
39. Skaletsky, M., Soremekun, O., Galliers, R.D.: The changing - and unchanging - face of the digital divide: an application of kohonen self-organizing maps. Inf. Technol. Dev. **20**(3), 218–250 (2014)
40. Orlikowski, W.J., Iacono, C.S.: Research commentary: desperately seeking the "IT" in IT research - a call to theorizing the IT artifact. Inf. Syst. J. **12**(2), 121–134 (2001)
41. Ghazawneh, A., Henfridsson, O.: Balancing platform control and external contribution in third-party development: the boundary resources model. Inf. Syst. J. **23**(2), 173–192 (2013)
42. Dittrich, Y.: Software engineering beyond the project – sustaining software ecosystems. Inf. Softw. Technol. **56**, 1436–1456 (2014)
43. Barrett, M., et al.: Service innovation in the digital age: key contributions and future directions. MIS Q. **39**(1), 135–154 (2015)
44. Brown, A.E., Grant, G.G.: Highlighting the duality of the ICT and development research agenda. Inf. Technol. Dev. **16**(2), 96–111 (2010)

Social Mapping for Communal Sensemaking: The Case of Development Informatics Researchers in South Africa

Judy van Biljon[1]([⊠]) and Mario Marais[2]

[1] University of South Africa, Johannesburg, South Africa
vbiljja@unisa.ac.za
[2] CSIR Meraka Institute, Pretoria, South Africa
mmarais@csir.co.za

Abstract. The community dynamics revolve around shared interests, norms, and identities. The sustainable exchange of resources for development is only possible if the members of the community are connected and the collaboration opportunities and practices are well-understood. This work in progress paper proposes social mapping as an innovative way of making sense of the connections between Development Informatics researchers towards understanding the research landscape and behavioural collaboration patterns. The data set includes the associations, collaborations and publication connections of at least 50 South African researchers. The maps were constructed using the Kumu social mapping tool. The results show that social mapping has the potential for presenting research connections visually in a way that supports sensemaking of the social dynamics within the society by considering the structural and behavioural patterns. The findings are limited by the fact that any attempt at representing the members of a dynamic community is seldom up to date and never complete. That limitation is managed by rigorously specifying the data capturing process and period. Furthermore, sensemaking theory informs that human sensemaking implicitly involves the unmaking of sense to adjust to time-space gaps. The contribution is a description and demonstration of how social mapping technology can be used to display information towards making sense of a research community.

Keywords: Communal sense-making · Social mapping · Social dynamics · Development informatics

1 Introduction

Participatory Community mapping as a sociotechnical innovation integrates the oldest social institution of human kind with the newest frontiers of material society through the joining and convergence of community with information sciences and technologies [1]. Research communities co-exist in a complex context of relations and interactions with other communities, supported by a multi-layered technical infrastructure. To improve their collaboration, community members and network stakeholders need to continually make sense of it [2]. The Development Informatics (DI) community experience

© IFIP International Federation for Information Processing 2017
Published by Springer International Publishing AG 2017. All Rights Reserved
J. Choudrie et al. (Eds.): ICT4D 2017, IFIP AICT 504, pp. 280–291, 2017.
DOI: 10.1007/978-3-319-59111-7_24

collaboration challenges due to the multi- and transdisciplinary nature which necessitates sharing knowledge from dissimilar disciplines [3]. The diversity in the stakeholders, which include researchers, funding agencies, government departments, participants and practitioners from the developing, emerging and developed economies introduce further complexities in knowledge management and knowledge sharing [4].

This knowledge management complexity underlie the challenge of building on existing knowledge towards research standards, methodologies and theories [3, 5] and agreement on how research quality can be ensured [6–8]. Community building can also aim at building social capital. Research on the social capital of rural ICT entrepreneurs has shown that the very fact of seeing oneself as part of a network has a positive effect [9].

Community-building is an iterative process in which community members increasingly become aware of what binds them, the increased level of awareness can inform and trigger new community building activities [10]. According to Rey-Moreno, Miliza, Mweetwa, van Stam and Johnson [11] the main opportunities of wireless Community Networks lie in the engagement of community members and the provisioning of a space for their development, in the community, for the community.

In the multi-, inter- and transdisciplinary research areas such as DI research, there are researchers from related fields as well as stakeholders interested in getting a quick overview of the research landscape of the DI community. The need involves basic information in response to questions like, who are the DI researchers, which institutions are they affiliated with and what are their fields of specialisation? In addition, tacit knowledge is required to answer questions such as how do DI researchers disseminate their research (considering conferences and journals), who do they collaborate with and why? This tacit knowledge is not available to novice researchers or international researchers without access to a South African DI champion.

Tacit knowledge poses a major challenge to KM as expertise and reasoning processes are difficult for individuals to articulate [4]. Communities of practice [12] play an important role as tacit knowledge is used and shared by the participants in social learning processes to identify appropriate actions to deal with shared challenges. Formalization of sensemaking efforts help to reduce ambiguity and to create common foundations for collaborative action [13]. A core communal sensemaking activity is community mapping. Originally started as a cartographic exercise to map the geographical connections and common ground that local communities share, community mapping is also being used for providing visualizations of argumentation and conversations [14]. Communal sensemaking aids technology enabled development. For example, the use of communication and mapping technology to connect individuals in geographical communities that live in the same area, but live separate lives and have individual experiences of the various and often uncoordinated development interventions. In the DI field it can break down the boundaries between the disciplines of researchers (e.g. computer science, geography, development studies, community development) and the boundaries between researchers and implementing bodies such as non-governmental organizations (NGOs) to create a space to support sensemaking. Going beyond the academic community it can drive coordination of development and other investments in a community from the bottom-up. In SA this is a major need of the Department of Rural Development and Land Reform [15] as evidenced at the five week strategy session in Sept/Oct 2016.

The purpose of this paper is to explore the use of social mapping towards representing collaboration in a research area by considering the case of South African Development Informatics research. Abiding by the programming mantra: "Eat your own dogfood", we as DI researchers aim to investigate social community mapping technology for mapping the South African DI community. Geographical community mapping methods stress strong community participation in the map making process. Therefore we continually document the social mapping process and engage the community for consent, peer-review and feed-back. We outline the approach being developed; present initial results of applying social mapping in the case of the South African DI community, and reflect on the lessons learned in this community mapping exploration.

2 Knowledge Management and Sensemaking for Participatory Community Mapping

The literature review covers knowledge management, the design of knowledge repositories in ICT4D and the use of social mapping in supporting knowledge management and sensemaking.

2.1 Knowledge Management and Sensemaking

The objective of a Knowledge Management (KM) is to support the construction, sharing and application of knowledge in organizations [16]. This means that the KM activities consists of the administration of knowledge assets of an organization and the sharing and enlargement of those assets [17]. The terms *knowledge transfer* and *knowledge sharing* have not been well-distinguished. According to Paulin and Suneson [18] authors who use the term knowledge transfer tend towards the objectivist perspective of knowledge while knowledge sharing is used with a more subjective perspective i.e. sharing via synchronous or asynchronous conversations and communications between people. The effectiveness of IT artefacts can be demonstrated through knowledge sharing activities [19]; conversely these activities can generate valuable insight in improving knowledge sharing towards supporting communication and ensuring a solid foundation for collaboration.

The human need to make sense of their experience in the world underlies much of this activity which has been defined as sensemaking [20]. The sense-making approach to studying and understanding users and designing systems to serve their needs has been developed in the fields of communication, library and information science but it has wider implication also for knowledge management [21]. Sensemaking and unmaking is a mandate of the human condition. The theoretical assumptions of the theory are based on the metaphor of situation-gap-uses that has been validated in numerous empirical studies [22]. Sense making departs from the premise that humans live in a world of gaps: a reality that changes across time and space which involves, at least in part a gap in any given time-space. Primary emphasis is placed on moving conceptualizations of users, information and reality from the noun-based knowledge-as-map frameworks of the past to verb based frameworks emphasizing diversity, complexity and sense-making potentials. The core sense making assumptions is the idea that knowledge made today is rarely perfectly suited to application tomorrow and in some cases becomes tomorrow's gap. In this view, attending to the unmaking of sense is as important as attending to its making. Fundamental to this study is sensemaking as a mechanism towards turning circumstances into a situation that is comprehended explicitly in words and that serves as a springboard for action [23]. The concepts of making and unmaking sense are critical in defending the usefulness of an incomplete and even incorrect knowledge representation (considering the time-space domain). Knowledge management in the ICT4D space will now be considered.

2.2   ICT4D Knowledge Repositories

Knowledge management systems used in the ICT4D context are known by different names including e-portals, online knowledge repositories and knowledge sharing platforms (KSPs). All of these systems are essentially Web based collections of information providing varying degrees of access and interaction but there are critical differences between what knowledge is made available, the target audience, the access and the interactions [24]. KM is recommended as part of any DI project to optimize its probability of success specifically by sustaining and growing a user community of practice [4, 25]. The provision of a social map also makes a practical contribution to development by creating an awareness of the social infrastructure that accompanies the technological infrastructure and the need to adopt a socio-technical systems (STS) view [26]. In this research the social mapping is part of a bigger goal, namely to create an open knowledge repository which supports identification of relevant research and possible collaborations, discussions and the formation of communities of practice to share information such as: research agendas, funding opportunities, publication opportunities, methodologies, theories, models and frameworks with the wider DI community including practitioners, government and NGOs. KM requirements need to continually adapt to fit the needs of the intervention. In the context of ICT4D the nature of the intervention has changed over time and Heeks [27] refers to phase ICT4D 0.0 (use of computers in the economy), 1.0 (ICT as development tool – telecentres) and 2.0 (ICT as the transformative platform for development). Participation to foster innovation is key and Heeks (ibid.) refers to innovation strategies as being pro-poor (for the poor), para-poor (working with the poor) and per-poor (innovation by the poor in their communities). In an ICT4D 1.0 approach, KM can be applied to sustain technology support and maintenance without the aid of the original development team [4] or remote experts [28]. An example of ICT4D 2.0 para-poor innovation is the development of a pharmacy system for antiretroviral drug dispensing in South African public health clinics [29]. The research and development team adopted the concept of Open Development [30] which emphasizes universal access to information, collaborative participation in knowledge creation and diversity of knowledge systems. In this approach Louden and Rivett [29] contend that communities of practice may be the route to "actionable knowledge" [31] that is developed and sustained after the end of research processes and projects. In the broad DI context there are multiple stakeholder communities including beneficiaries, practitioners, academia, government, civil society (e.g. NGOs) and private sector organisations. The diversity of the target audience for a knowledge management endeavour is challenging if an open access environment is planned. For example, academics may seek examiners, reviewers and collaborators, while funding agencies and NGOs may seek research experts in a specific field. Students and novice researchers may seek links to reputable sites and research opportunities. The community context influences the nature of the formal and informal knowledge production processes and the tools that need to be supported. Wenger, White and Smith [12] advocate for the use a range of tools and platforms to support communities of practice. Considering the dimensions in Fig. 1, participatory community social mapping can be described as *informal* sharing *with* each other and hence fits in the upper right hand quadrant. Social mapping is an example of what Wenger calls "Building shared understanding (3)" and also provides a means of "Producing assets (4)".

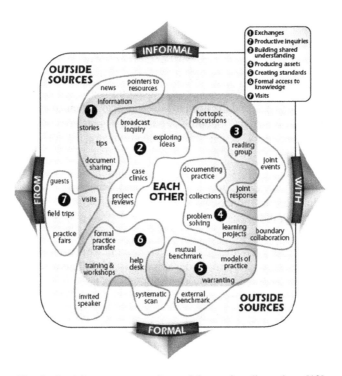

Fig. 1. Participatory community social mapping dimensions [12]

3   Research Design

The community was defined as Development Informatics or ICT4D researchers in South Africa. They were identified by doing a Google Scholar search using the terms "Development Informatics" or "ICT4D" and 'South Africa'. The search was carried out during September 2016. The search returned 66 names and those were contacted for consent to use their research profile information. Consequently 52 replied, 51 positively and one declined. The following information categories were then added to a spreadsheet for the researchers who consented: their affiliations (institution where they were employed), the conference proceedings published in, the journals published in and the domains sub-field(s) of DI or related field that they were involved in. A total of 16 institutions were added which include universities and other research institutions such as the Council for Industrial and Scientific Research (CSIR). The researchers had published in 24 conferences' proceedings and in 38 different journals.

We acknowledge the limitations on correctness (in terms of being up-to date) and completeness of the data. Despite our best efforts and intentions of diligently capturing all the ICT4D and Development Informatics researchers the process described is prone to human error with the result that not all the researchers have been included. The next step would be to periodically present the map to the community for feedback and then update it to improve the accuracy.

3.1   The Mapping Language

The mapping language needs to distinguish between elements (depicting socio-technical concepts of the community network) and connections (representing relations and interactions between those elements). Informed by the participatory community mapping knowledge structure proposed by De Moor [10] the following was constructed in terms of elements and connections. The following *elements* have been identified:

- Participants including *Persons; Institutions; Conferences; Journals* and *Domains*
- Activities (Activities are outcomes as well, but being processes, they can also generate other processes and results and are a direct source of community building). These include *events, funding proposals* and *calls for papers*.
- Results (tangible static results like publications)
- Tools that can be used to support activities like physical Meetings (e.g. "Annual Meetings", "Network Meetings", "Presentations", "Conferences") or online tools (e.g. participant websites, social media such as project apps, Twitter, Facebook).

Regarding *connections*, communities are networks of relationships and interactions for mutual benefit. A conceptual model of community consists of collective identity, local participation, and diverse support networks [10]. Carrol [32] mentions four composite variables for community membership and participation, namely: Belonging (identity), Informedness (passive participation), Activism (active participation), and Associations (support networks). De Moor [10] built on this approach to identify four types of connections, ordered in increasing degree of participant involvement:

- Informedness (being informed about activities of the community, but not being part of it).
- Associations (being an explicit member of the community in the sense of having made a commitment to participate)
- Participation (actual participation in the activities of the community)
- Producing (producing visible, measurable results as outcomes of the activities). This is the most involved kind of participation).

Given our approach to data capturing (as explained above) all the researchers had published papers which places them on the fourth level, namely that of *producing*. Extending the data set to reflect the member *participating* (without having published) may be advisable but there lies the challenge of balancing completeness with focus - a challenge to be explored in further research. The map making has been done by the authors with the help of three research assistants to capture and validate the data and manage the researchers. Ideally, community managers or members should be involved and be trained to become map makers but given the complexity of the mapping language, tool, and process that may not be feasible, also in terms of the time and effort required. De Moor [10] also distinguished various levels of map making literacy including the overall structure, layout, and functionality of a community map which could be created by a "master map maker". Selected community managers or members could be trained to expand the partial "domain maps". A map of a dynamically evolving community is never complete and there is always a trade-off between completeness and feasibility. For researchers as community members, the main reason to contribute to and use the map is to improve the bigger picture in terms of correctness and completeness and to ensure that their participation as researchers is represented accurately. In summary, the researchers were abstracted as the object type *person*, together with *institution*, *conference*; *journal* and *research domain* as object types. The connections affiliation (between *person* and *institution*), publish (between *person* and *conference* and also between *person* and *journal*), as well as research domain between (*domain* and *person*) were then added to the connections table. The findings are limited by the incomplete nature of any map of a dynamic community. Furthermore the publication data was captured from the Internet using Google Scholar; using another search engine may provide different information. The next step will be to present the map to the researchers to give feedback on the map and update their information, thereby creating an updated map which will be shared with the wider DI community.

4   Results

Figures 2 and 3 are examples of how the information about the community can be depicted to support sensemaking of the elements and connections. Figure 2 focuses on the institutions and provide some indication of the number of researchers affiliated to the institutions. The data capturing procedure is limited by the visibility and discoverability of the individual researcher's so it does not claim to provide a complete picture merely the starting point of a map that needs to be completed.

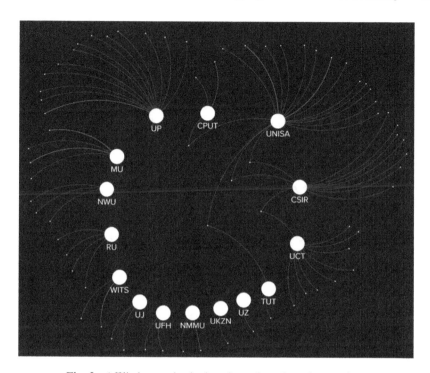

Fig. 2. Affiliations to institution show clustering of researchers

The following abbreviations were used: University of Pretoria (UP). Council for Scientific and Industrial Research (CSIR), Cape Peninsula University of Technology (CPUT), University of South Africa (Unisa), University of KwaZulu Natal (UKZN), University of Cape Town (UCT), University of Pretoria (UP), University of Johannesburg (UJ), University of Zululand (UZ), Tshwane University of Technology (TUT), Rhodes University (RU), Monash University (MU), North-West University (NWU), Nelson Mandela Metropolitan University (NMMU), University of Fort Hare (UFH) and the University of Witwatersrand (WITS).

Considering Fig. 2, the results highlight that four institutions dominate in terms of the number of researchers (UP, UCT, CSIR and Unisa) with a cluster of eight or more researchers, followed by four institutions with three or more researchers (CPUT, RU, NWU and MU). There are only five researchers with formal relationships with more than one university and all but one of these relationships is with Unisa. The data is based on institutional affiliations reported in publications so it would show an affiliation even when the researcher had left the institution. The advantages of having an up-to-date map has to weighed against building a history of how the community evolved; at this stage the creation of a history seems more helpful towards sensemaking. Figure 3 depicts the conferences attended by South African researchers in this sample.

South African and African conferences have the most attendees but an international conference like CONF_IRM features prominently since it was recently hosted in

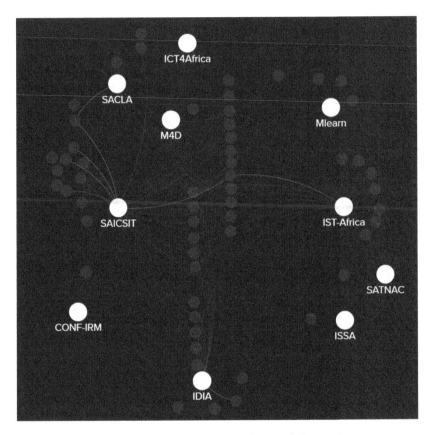

Fig. 3. Popular conferences among the sampled researchers

Cape Town, South Africa. The SAICSIT (62), IST-Africa (31) and IDIA (21) conferences had the most attendees and many attendees attended both or all three of these
conferences. Six had attended all three conferences. Twelve researchers had attended
SAICSIT and IST-Africa which are conferences that are hosted in Africa. Five had
attended SAICSIT and the IDIA, which is an international conference that is held
mostly in the Global South. IDIA is organised by Monash University South Africa
(MU) and hence has a strong South African link. The importance of research regarding
mobile device use is reflected in the attendance of the M4D and the Mlearn conferences
and indicates the size of this particular research community. This overview of the
conferences that researchers had attended could be valuable to novice researchers when
planning submissions. Due to space limitations the connection between researchers and
research domains had to be omitted but that is important in determining the active
research fields, the researchers working in these fields, the relationships between the
researchers and their relationships with researchers in related fields.

5 Discussion

Despite the acknowledged limitations and the reduced scope of the mapping, the community maps representing researchers' links to institutions and conferences respectively proved useful in identifying behaviours that would be more difficult to observe from textual information. The information was displayed as noun-based knowledge-as-map frameworks but once these have been presented to the community for feedback and refinement, future research will look into verb based frameworks for improving diversity, complexity and sense-making potential. Qualitative research involving interviews and focus groups with different stakeholder is necessary to improve the quality and depth of the representation and to extend this to stakeholders beyond the academic research community.

The selection decisions, including the point of departure and selection criteria for researchers, how to filter the data and how to disseminate the results to the community without inadvertently disadvantaging a person or entity by omission or inaccuracy resonate with the sensemaking challenges of conceptualizing knowledge making. Furthermore, as Dervin [21]:45 advises, sensemaking "mandates attentions to ways of bracketing or taming at least in part the impacts of power which constrain human willingness to share and problem solve collaboratively". Presenting this study for peer-review and scrutiny through continuous publication is one of the initiatives in the drive for accountability and transparency towards a fair, unbiased representation of the South African Development Informatics community. Besides the theoretical contributing towards highlighting the knowledge management challenges, the community mapping artefact of a specific community also has practical use. An example is the use by local communities of participatory social mapping to provide comprehensive information to government departments regarding the coordination, alignment and duplication of development initiatives [20].

6 Conclusion

This paper outlined preliminary work on a participatory, community mapping project piloted for South African DI researchers. Initial findings show potential for mapping the evolution of the community towards creating some history of involvements as well as the status quo. A moral challenge for community mapping is ensuring that everyone can participate in and benefit from the innovation. This raises questions about how much the communities can realistically be involved and finding a balance between making the information accessible and as accurate as possible on the one hand and not inconveniencing the community with constant requests on the other. More research is required to extend the scope to include the other stakeholders in ICT4D and also to optimise the selection criteria for data capturing towards presenting the dynamics of benefit to the community. The mapping component will be integrated into the *South African Development Informatics & ICT4D Platform* (SADIIP) which will increase the visibility and usefulness for the wider community.

Acknowledgement. This work is based on the research supported by the South African Research Chairs Initiative of the Department of Science and Technology and National Research Foundation of South Africa (Grant No. 98564). We also acknowledge all the South African researchers who responded to our communication.

References

1. Carroll, J.M., Shih, P.C., Kropczynski, J.: Community informatics as innovation in sociotechnical infrastructures. J. Commun. Inf. **11**(2) (2015)
2. De Moor, A.: Communities in context: towards taking control of their tools in common(s). J. Commun. Inform. **11**(2), 4–9 (2015)
3. Walsham, G.: Development informatics in a changing world: reflections from ICTD2010/2012. Inf. Technol. Int. Dev. **9**(1), 49–54 (2013)
4. Conger, S.: Knowledge management for information and communications technologies for development programs in South Africa. Inf. Technol. Dev. **1102**, 1–22 (2014)
5. Burrell, J., Toyama, K.: What constitutes good ICTD research? Inf. Technol. Int. Dev. **5**(3), 82–94 (2009)
6. Walsham, G.: Are we making a better world with ICTs? Reflections on a future agenda for the IS field. J. Inf. Technol. **27**(2), 87–93 (2012)
7. Weber, R.: Research on ICT for development: some reflections. In: Proceedings of the 3rd International Development Informatics Conference, Kruger National Park, South Africa, pp. 2–27 (2009)
8. Tibben, W.J.: Theory building for ICT4D: systemizing case study research using theory triangulation. Inf. Technol. Dev. **21**(4), 628–652 (2015)
9. Marais, M.A.: Social capital in the Village Operator model for rural broadband internet access and use. Unpubl. Dr. Diss. Univ. Pretoria, Pretoria, South Africa (2016)
10. De Moor, A.: Towards a participatory community mapping method: the Tilburg urban farming community case. In: Adjunct Proceedings of Communities Technologies Conference, vol. 12, p. 11 (2015)
11. Rey-Moreno, C., Miliza, J., Mweetwa, F., van Stam, G., Johnson, D.L.: Community networks in the African context: opportunities and barriers. In: AfriCHI, pp. 237–241 (2016)
12. Wenger, J.D., White, E., Smith, N.: Digital Habitats: Stewarding Technology for Communities. CPsquare, Portland (2009)
13. Vlaar, P.W.L., Van den Bosch, F.A.J., Volberda, H.W.: Coping with problems of understanding in interorganizational relationships: using formalization as a means to make sense. Organ. Stud. **27**(11), 1617–1638 (2006)
14. Okada, A., Buckingham, S., Sherborne, T.: Knowledge Cartography: Software Tools and Mapping Techniques. Springer, London (2008)
15. Marais, M.A.: Researcher notes. Phakisa workshop of the Department of Agriculture, Forestry and Fisheries with the Department of Rural Development and Land Reform, Kemptonpark, Johannesburg (2016)
16. Leidner, D.: Knowledge management and knowledge management systems. J. Strateg. Inf. Syst. **9**(2–3), 101–105 (2000)
17. Ben Chouikha, M., Dakhli, S.: The dimensions of knowledge sharing. In: MCIS 2012 Proceedings (2012)
18. Paulin, D., Suneson, K.: Knowledge transfer, knowledge sharing and knowledge barriers – three blurry terms in KM. Electron. J. Knowl. Manag. **10**(1), 81–91 (2012)

19. Li, T.: The interplay between knowledge sharing and IT artifacts in the working contexts. In: Twenty-Second Americas Conference on Information Systems, San Diego (2016)
20. Klein, G., Moon, B., Hoffman, R.F.: Making sense of sensemaking: alternative perspectives. IEEE Intell. Syst. **21**(4), 70–73 (2006)
21. Dervin, B.: Sense-making theory and practice: an overview of user interests in knowledge seeking and use. J. Knowl. Manag. **2**(2), 36–46 (1998)
22. Savolainen, R.: The sense-making theory: reviewing the interests of a user-centered approach to information seeking and use. Inf. Process. Manag. **29**(1), 13–28 (1993)
23. Weick, K.E., Sutcliffe, K.M., Obstfeld, D.: Organizing and the process of sensemaking. Organ. Sci. **16**(4), 409–421 (2005)
24. Mosweunyane, G., Carr, L.A.: Direct desktop-repository deposits with SWORD. In: 2014 IST-Africa Conference Proceedings (2014)
25. Singh, J.P., Flyverbom, M.: Representing participation in ICT4D projects. Telecomm. Policy **40**(7), 692–703 (2016)
26. Whitworth, B., De Moor, A.: Handbook of Research on Socio-Technical Design and Social Networking Systems. IGI Global, New York (2009)
27. Heeks, R.: ICT4D 2.0: the next phase of applying ICT for international development. Comput. IEEE **41**(6), 26–31 (2008)
28. Geldof, M., Grimshaw, D.J., Kleine, D., Unwin, T.: What are the key lessons of ICT4D partnerships for poverty reduction? (2011)
29. Loudon, M., Rivett, U.: Enacting openness in ICT4D research. Inf. Technol. Int. Dev. **7**(1), 33–46 (2011)
30. Smith, M.L., Elder, L.: Open ICT ecosystems transforming the developing world. Inf. Technol. Int. Dev. **6**(1), 65–71 (2010)
31. Hearn, G., Foth, M.: Action research in the design of new media and ICT systems. In: Topical Issues in Communications and Media Research, pp. 79–94. Nova Science, New York (2005)
32. Carroll, J.M.: The Neighborhood in the Internet: Design Research Projects in Community Informatics, 1st edn. Routledge, New York (2012)

The Contribution of Practice Theories to ICT for Development

Affordance and Habitus: Understanding Land Records E-services in Bangladesh

Laurence Brooks[1(✉)] and Muhammad Shahanoor Alam[2]

[1] Centre for Computing and Social Responsibility (CCSR),
De Montfort University, Leicester LE1 9BH, UK
Laurence.Brooks@dmu.ac.uk
[2] Ministry of Public Administration, Dhaka, Bangladesh
shahanoor79@gmail.com

Abstract. Technology is ubiquitous, including in some public sector organisations in developing countries. This paper explores the introduction and use of e-services into the land records service in Bangladesh and how the role and position of 'middlemen' has re-asserted itself. The concept of affordance, both dispositional and relational, together with social affordance (habitus) offers an opportunity to better understand why this has happened and potentially to look at how to approach this in the future.

Keywords: Affordance · Habitus · Land records management · Bangladesh

1 Introduction

Information Technology (IT) is seen as important in land records service because it provides insights into significant opportunities for public service through reducing cost and time of service delivery, enabling citizens' easy access to these services and ensuring transparency and accountability [1]. Since the late 1980s, development partners and governments in developing countries (DC) have been experimenting with a number of projects on IT in land records service delivery [7]. However, a significant number of projects and initiatives on IT in land related services have drastically failed in both developed and developing countries [5]. Thus, until now using IT in land records services remains a complex field for both practitioners and academics [2]. The land records service in Bangladesh has been identified as a problematic, outdated, corrupted and litigated matter by the government itself, the development partners, practitioners and the civil society [3]. Rampant corruption in this sector is seen as a barrier to economic growth of such an agrarian country. Further, the World Bank finds that most of the crimes and corruption involved with land records matters in Bangladesh. There are four core components of land records service delivery in Bangladesh: registering deeds of land ownership transfer known as land *registration*; updating records for changing ownership known as *mutation*; updating the cadaster (or survey) and receiving officially attested exact duplicate copies of land ownership records (Records of Rights). An attested copy of land records is widely used and it is the basis of all other land related services and a requisite for many public and private services in

© IFIP International Federation for Information Processing 2017
Published by Springer International Publishing AG 2017. All Rights Reserved
J. Choudrie et al. (Eds.): ICT4D 2017, IFIP AICT 504, pp. 295–306, 2017.
DOI: 10.1007/978-3-319-59111-7_25

the country. This service is known locally as: *Khatiyan, Nokol, Porcha, Soi Muhuri Nokol* etc. This study uses the common term 'land records service'. On average, per day 20 to 30 thousand applications are received from citizens for this service in Bangladesh. There is no other public service that receives this volume of applications from citizens. Consequently, the government has designed electronic or 'E-services' for the land records service. Two main concepts are involved in this study: 'attested copy of land ownership records' and 'service delivery of attested copy of land ownership records'. They will be referred to as 'land records' and 'land records service' respectively. Land records and land records service are inextricably connected with the life and livelihoods of people in Bangladesh. Land records is the key document for receiving loans from banks and financial institutions; buying, selling and donating of land; determining ownership and size of land; managing land litigations and civil suits of land; applying for basic services including electricity, gas, water; receiving subsidized rate of fertilizers, pesticides, fuels and other agricultural services [1]. Aiming to ensure citizens' easy access, the government and development partners across of the world have taken a number of initiatives. However, few projects have succeeded, and the key question here is why? Orlikowski and Baroudi [5] argue that interpretive studies assume that people create and associate their own subjective and inter-subjective meanings according to their interaction with participants. Thus, interpretive researchers aim to understand phenomena through meanings constructed by participants. Consequently, it provides a deeper insight to analyze the complex world from experience and interaction of its living being [6].

2 Affordance and Habitus

Development of human society and technology is mutually dependent. However, there is lack of agreement on how technology and organizations interact with one another [7]. Previous studies have shown that there are ambiguous and conflicting relations between organizations and technology [8]. A socio-technical view on technology shows it is both rooted in organizational processes, and organizations are seen as integral to the technology [9–11]. Orlikowski and Iacono [12], conceptualize technology as an ensemble artifact that includes software and hardware and activities and interactions performed in a specific social and cultural context. Thus, IS research has identified that mutual interaction in organizational contexts and technological processes plays a pivotal role in enhancing service delivery. Technology cannot be seen as a discrete entity beyond organizations, either by domain or logic; rather, it is interwoven with human work and organizational contexts [13]. Evidently, dynamic relations in technology and organization develop intended and unintended consequences [14].

Technology can be seen as affordance [15] that refers to possibilities of an object to perform an action and these possibilities belong to the varied context in which they sit [16]. For example, a rock can be used as a shelter for a lizard but it also can be used as a weapon by a human. Technology is neither an independent actor nor capable of determining human actions [16]. Further, Zammuto et al. [17] assert that affordance is the result of intertwined relations between technology, organizational contexts and intents of human actors. With this notion, Barley [18] sees technology as a social object with its meaning defined by social context; as such, technology is always interpreted by human beings in this social context [19]. It can also be interpreted and reshaped by the need of situated agents [20]. If it fails to meet the expectation of its agents, it can be ignored, resisted or reshaped to achieve the goals of its users and agents [20]. Consequently, it can be seen as complex interdependent systems that rely on social, technical and organizational aspects [20]. This concept of affordance has begun to be used more commonly in IS research, as a way to better understand technology and individuals conjointly, mirroring the tight relationship of the material and social worlds in which they sit (see also Ciborro's ideas on imbrication [21]). Fayard and Weeks [22] conceptualize affordance as a dualistic concept, "affordance is both dispositional and relational, which we believe is a more difficult, yet potentially more useful interpretation". This allows for insights into how contexts might shape practices and use of technology by people, but the physical and social aspects of the context do not completely determine those practices. Affordances are 'dispositional', which is they are visible and physical, and linked to practice, as in what can be done with an artifact (and often what is expected of it). However, affordances are also 'relational', linked to a person's objectives (what they want to achieve), the technologies' material properties and also the organisational context, as a situation for use. Fayard and Weeks [23] use the example of informal interactions in photocopier rooms in three different organisations, identifying that these were shaped by "what was physically possible and socially appropriate". By accepting that there is a social meaning of space which constrains what might happen there, the physical environment is shown to be more than just a passive container.

There is also room for a third complimentary concept, that of 'social' affordance, which can be seen as "how the social construction of a technology impacts the practices afforded by that environment" [22]. The concept of 'habitus' [24, 25] can be seen as complimentary to affordance here, as it shows how practice is influenced by social structures, but without reifying those structures. Habitus, unlike affordance, is seen as something which is acquired by individuals over time, through lived experience and the conditions of their existence. While two people, living in the same environments and experiencing the same things, are very similar they are never actually the same. The result is that for a full understanding of practice, we need analysis of the affordances of the environment as well as social and cultural factors, plus insights from the habitus, the social significance of the space and what is acceptable (the norms) for what might happen there for any given group of people.

3 Methodology

This paper is derived from a two year interventional and longitudinal study of land records E-service in Bangladesh. One of the authors is a former practitioner who served in a similar organization for about five years and has gathered empirical evidence of the context where the study has been conducted. The study applied a number of methods, tools and techniques for data collection and analysis. They are mainly participant observation, interviews, focus group discussions, open ended discussions, workshops and organizational process and documents analysis. For the last two years, the E-service of land records has been observed in a district namely Khulna by the researchers and they intervened in designing and redesigning of this E-service delivery process with the collaboration of the organizational managers. This study has been conducted in a public sector organization – the District Record Room (DRR) – involved in delivering E-service of land records with the help of technological networks and telecentres. A total of 20 interviews were conducted among service recipients, service providers, middlemen and telecentre operators. Two focus group discussions were conducted; one with telecentre operators and the other with middlemen. One consultation workshop and open ended discussion were made with organizational managers, staff, telecentre operators and citizens, the service delivery recipients.

In addition, the initial findings have been presented and discussed with the practitioners at a national level workshop. Further, the research findings have been gathered and presented in five monthly review meetings and also five consultative and evaluative workshops with organizational staff. Data has been gathered and analysed thematically with a combination of top down and bottom up approaches. Although the theoretical lens provides themes, field findings generated themes in different ways than theoretical themes. Thus, thematic codes are derived both from top down and bottom up levels. The following sections present the findings from the study, followed by a discussion of how these can be interpreted in the context of affordances.

4 Using IT in the Land Records Service

4.1 A Cross Cultural Scenario

IS research in developing countries focuses on development, implementation and usage of IT artefacts. It also traces underlying political, economic and cultural and behaviour contexts and processes that are obstacles in IT implementation [26–28]. IT in service delivery in developing country is challenging due to the complex interrelationships with socioeconomic factors. Moreover, land records services are strongly influenced by social, cultural and bureaucratic processes. Thus, ignoring existing practices, capacity and socio-cultural contexts resulted in the failure of IT in land records services [29]. Sahay and Avgerou [30] identified that domination of existing organizational networks hindered IT in land records services in developing countries. Consequently, IT in land records service is challenging due to various forms of interests, networks and actors involved in land records service. Thus, the success of IT in land records service rests on organizational contexts, designing and redesigning of the IT alongside the organizational context. Heeks [31] asserts that IT in public sector organizations needs to be aligned with data resources, economic resources, social resources and action resources [31]. Consequently, successful integration of IT in organizational contexts relies on data capturing, storing, updating, manipulating, mining, analysing and displaying [31]. Thus, IT in public sector organizations are intermediated, interconnected, indigenized intelligently with organizational contexts instead of technical ones [31]. Nowadays, governments, no matter how big or small, are embarking on IT leveraging to improve their performance. Evidently, there is significant investment in IT in land information systems to enhance citizens' easy access, reduce cost and improve process of service delivery, reduce corruption and achieve good governance. However, while about 85% of IT projects have been failed in developing countries [32], surprisingly, most of the IT projects failed due to technology driven designs [33].

4.2   Current State of IT in Bangladesh

Since 1996, Bangladesh has connected with Internet Service through VSAT. However, the rate of internet penetration is very low i.e., 0.35%. Even lower than the neighbouring countries, such as: Bhutan (5.8%), Maldives (18.1%), India (7.0%), Sri Lanka (5.4%), and Pakistan (10.6%) [24]. Bangladesh has been striving to implement IT in public sector organizations to enhance the capacity of the government and to ensure better service delivery since its independence in 1971. Along the line, in 2009 the government launched the manifesto 'Vision 2021 – Digital Bangladesh'.

5   Problems in the Land Records System in Bangladesh

Land records are popularly known as 'Porcha' which clearly indicates the description of a piece of land, easily understandable to land owners. However, from the legal perspective, land records in Bangladesh is known as Record of Rights (RoR), and contains geographic, legal and revenue information for every plot of land. Thus, it includes the name and details of land owner(s) along with ratio of ownership in the case of multiple owners, plot(s) size and total number of plots, type of land, taxes and geographic boundary of land plot(s) and the name of the jurisdiction where land plots are located. Thereafter, land plots information is aggregated into a holding according to family based ownership. In addition, for every plot there are three to four versions of the land record. Consistent with these, the researcher and the managers of the organization have identified three main problems in the land record system: problems with complex land information, problems with multiple versions of land records and problems with aggregated land holding systems. Each of these are now discussed.

5.1   Complex Land Information Systems

Although the cadastral survey system collects land information through a plot to plot survey; the Bangladeshi land records system follows a top down and complex process. The country is divided into 64 districts. Every district, an administrative unit, is again divided into a number of cadastral survey blocks called jurisdictions. The jurisdiction has a certain geographic and cadastral survey boundary. Each jurisdiction has a name and ID number called Jurisdiction List number (J.L. No). For example, the district under study, Khulna, comprises a total of 796 jurisdictions. A jurisdiction comprises of many thousands of land holdings (land records) or RoR. A land record comprises information about several of land plots within a jurisdiction. In order to trace the land record for a land plot requires knowing its plot ID numbers, holding ID number or RoR number, J.L. number (name) or name of the owner and name of the district.

Land plots owned by family members within a jurisdiction are recorded in a land holding. So, a land record comprises land information of several plots of land in a jurisdiction and land records are prepared as a family based aggregated land holding system. In order to access the land record of a plot requires information on its jurisdiction number or name, holding number and plot number. Thus, if someone needs a land record for a plot only; s/he needs to apply for the whole holding because the attested copy of the land record is issued as a whole holding. Further, within a holding there are a number of owners and the ratio of ownership also varies from plot to plot of the holding. Consequently, it is difficult for the citizens to understand both the land records system and its service delivery too.

5.2 Problems with the Different Versions of Land Records

Bangladesh was governed under British India (1757–1947), Pakistan (1947–1971) and gained independence as Bangladesh in 1971. With these three political regimes, three distinct versions of land records have evolved in the country. Surprisingly, all the three versions of land records are treated as active records. The first version, known as the Cadaster Survey Record (CS) was developed by the British Colonial government during 1888–1920. The second version, called the State Acquisition survey (in short SA) was prepared in 1955. The final version, called Bangladesh Revised Survey record (BRS or RS) was started in 1972 and is ongoing. Therefore, every plot of land has two to three versions of land records. In some cases, there were four versions land records for a plot of land. The multiple versions of active land record have made the system more complex. Since all versions of land records are active, citizens need attested copies of land records for all versions, for example, for purchase or sale. Equally, every plot has three to four ID numbers for a land plot and holding (record) numbers. Thus, it is difficult to remember and maintain three types of holding ID numbers and plot ID numbers by the land owners who are mostly illiterate people. Consequently, citizens need to rely on middlemen to collect accurate land holding IDs and land plot IDs for filing applications for land record services. In addition, many citizens do not know jurisdiction list (J.L.) numbers or name too. Evidently, three different versions of land records along with three types of land plots and holding ID numbers have become a confusing matter and vexatious problem for citizens to access the land records E-service. To avoid these complications citizens rely on the middlemen to access this service. Consequently, the E-service hardly made any difference to citizens' access to this service.

5.3 Family Based Aggregated Land Record System

As discussed above, the land record system follows an aggregated top down method. Several land plots in a jurisdiction are grouped into a holding called a land record or Record of Rights (RoR). Thus, a RoR comprises a number of plots owned by family or clan members. A cadastral jurisdiction consists of approximately 2000 to 5000 family based land plots and on the basis of family based ownership, land plots are grouped into a land record and a jurisdiction contains approximately 200 to 500 land records. An average land record contains 10–50 land plots. Since a land record is an aggregated system, it contains name(s) of land owners against each of the land plots along with different ratio of ownership. So, land owners need to know ID numbers of their land records and plots along with versions of land records. As a result, if any citizen needs an attested copy of a land record for a land plot from a holding which contains 30 plots and names of many owners, it is not possible to issue an attested copy of land record for the particular plot of land, instead an attested copy of the whole land record (holding) is needed. Due to this aggregated system, over time, various middleman networks have been developed for mediating this service to the citizens. Citizens would rarely have the full information to submit an application for their land records. Thus, the complicated land record system is an obstacle to citizens' access to this E-service and pushed the citizens towards the middlemen. Consequently, even after the introduction of the E-service, citizens' continued to access to this service through middlemen who submit applications and mediate this service efficiently.

6   Problems in the Application Submission Process

Access to land record service requires submission of an application to the DRR. However, the forms and the application process remained complicated. The prescribed paper based application forms as well as fees and folios were full of jargon and so tricky for citizens to understand. Further submission of an application required a complete set of documents: a completed application form or a written application paper with necessary information of required record, certain amount of stamps pasted on application as fees for this service and appropriate number of folio papers for copying land records. None of the elements were available to the DRR; rather they were available to the middlemen. So citizens requiring this service first needed to go to a middleman (see Fig. 1).

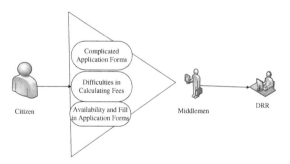

Fig. 1. Problems in application submission for land records service

Thus, various types of middlemen have evolved to mediate this service namely, Stamp Vendors, Lawyers' Assistants (*Muhuri*), Lawyers, Mobile Middlemen, staff of land related sections and offices and staff of other offices.

7   Problems in the E-service of Land Record in Bangladesh

With the inherent nature of an agro-based, post-colonial and developing country, Bangladesh's land record service is inextricably connected with organizational processes, structure, statutes, practice, staff, technology and intermediaries. Moreover, this service was complicated, centralized, middlemen oriented, vested interest driven and bribable. To address these problems, E-service of land record has been developed in 2011. The E-service network has been designed with three online access points for citizens' easy access to land record service. They are: Union Digital Center (UDC) - a telecentre at every rural union council; E-Service Center (ESC) a front desk in each district headquarters and a District Web Portal (DWP) – a website for each district. They are electronically connected to the DRR, the service provider of land records. This E-service of land records aimed to ensure citizens' easy and direct access to this service through the E-service networks (UDCs, DWP and ESC), and without middlemen networks. However, various forms of middlemen networks have been strongly rooted in this service over many years. Thus, after introducing the E-service of land records, the IT networks and the middlemen networks intra-act dynamically and continuously with organizational processes, staff and citizens.

8   Vested Interest of the Staff and Officers

The empirical data revealed that a range of officers had vested interest in land records services. They are: the RRDC - the section officer of the DRR, Additional Deputy Commissioner Revenue (ADCR) - involved in overseeing the DRR staff and the RRDC, Additional Commissioner General (ADCG) - involved in posting and transfers of the DRR staff, the Deputy Commissioner - involved in overall management and control of the DRR and the Divisional Commissioner - involved in inspection of the DRR (see Fig. 2). The flow of the vested interest moved vertically from the DRR staff to the Divisional Commissioner in the organizational process. Since the DRR staff are

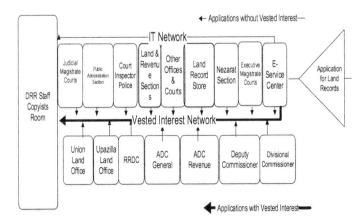

Fig. 2. Vested interest network in the land record service

involved in receiving vested interests from this service and it goes upper level officers; thus, either the officers discipline them or the staff pushed the officers to also receive benefits from the vested interests from this service. So, every staff of the Deputy Commissioner office has a keen desire to have a posting at the DRR.

As the organizational processes and actors continued with their vested interests; it was not possible to remove the flow of vested interest overnight from this service, i.e. through setting-up some E-service access points.

Better service delivery largely depends on the leadership and management capacity of a DC, because the DC approves the work distribution among the Additional Deputy Commissioners and the section officers. A senior official commented that a few DCs also have vested interests in this service. In the case of the district under study, during the research period, two DCs have been found. However, both of them have reputation for honesty. One was disinterested in executing or improving this service with a view to passing his tenure without any risks. This is another kind of vested interest. His preference was to keep things as stable as possible in order to have a quiet tenure there, even if some of his staff were acting corruptly.

9 Discussion

The E-service networks have been designed with a view to creating multiple access points for citizens' easy access to this service and to remove middlemen. However, the E-service networks have merely focused on the underlying contexts, processes and practices and their interactions. Consequently, the E-service has failed to remove the middlemen. Rather, the middlemen networks intra-act with the E-service access points through existing organizational processes and contexts. Thus, the middlemen networks entangled with this service to expedite citizens' service delivery. They provided 'speed money' to the DRR staff to expedite their clients' service quickly. Where the DRR staff declined to receive speed money from citizens they received speed money from the middlemen instead. Consequently, applications submitted by middlemen through the ESC received quicker service delivery than the applications submitted by the UDCs and the DWP. In terms of the affordance concept (see Table 1), what can be seen is the complex interplay of dispositional (i.e. linked to the norms and practices of how things are done using the existing pathways and blocking the citizens' direct access to the land records service), relational (achieving the best outcome for access to land records with the new technology still involved the middlemen and paying the 'speed money') and social/habitus (acceptance by most parties involved that middlemen and extra payments were legitimate, from the citizens perspective of getting things done, from the middlemen of subverting the avowed purpose of the computer-based technologies so that their role was still relevant and from the DRR staff that this extra income continued, especially as sometimes that was essential for their livelihood).

What was not appreciated by most of the parties involved was that the overall effects of these 3 affordances were reinforcing the legitimacy of the revised functioning of the system, post-introduction of the computer-based technologies; but in so doing were preventing those same technologies from properly bedding in and being allowed to take shape and create the new norms that would enable greater citizen direct access

Table 1. Using affordances to analyse role of technology in land records e-services

Name	Role	Dispositional affordance	Relational affordance	Social affordance	Habitus
Citizen	End user	Option to use technology blocked through lack of knowledge	Trying to access land records, in as easy fashion as possible	Technology becomes another obstacle to be overcome	Resigned return to use of middlemen
Middlemen	Bridge between citizens and land records officials	Knowledge of processes, and literacy enables engagement with technology	Maintain usefulness and value in the process; use of bribes to speed up processes with DRR	Subvert E-service Center as best way to be re-introduced into the process; provide extra income to DRR staff	Without fundamental shift in citizens knowledge and understanding, middlemen return to bridging role
RRDC (District Record Room - DRR)	The section of the DRR	Grudging engagement with the technology	Concerns over lack of extra income	Ensure middlemen can still access, but now through the technology;	Alternative routes maintained; regain extra income
Deputy Commissioner (DC)	Involved in overall management and control of the DRR	Little change to practices	Maintain status quo	Try to avoid any impact of the technology	Re-insertion of the middlemen, keeping things as before

to these services, i.e. autonomy. In this way, the concept of affordance and habitus allows greater insight into the systems, and potentially offers suggestions for how they might be developed in the future, for example, what might happen if the middlemen were brought inside the system and made a legitimate part of it, but without the option for speed money/bribes. While not yet seen as a failure, the IT systems in the land records e-service in Bangladesh do come close [26]. Reflecting on the use of affordance in this type of context [16], the paper shows that it provides insights which may not be seen other ways, and the challenge for the future is to identify these habitus-grounded solutions and then to implement them.

References

1. Thomas, P.: Bhoomi, Gyan Ganga, e-governance and the right to information: ICTs and development in India. Telematics Inform. **26**(1), 20–31 (2009). doi:10.1016/j.tele.2007.12.004
2. Holstein, L.: Review of Bank Experience with Land Titling and Registration. World Bank, Washington, D.C. (1993)

3. Imran, A., Gregor, S.: Vested interests obstructing information systems use: land administration in a least developed country. Paper presented at the SIG GlobDev fourth annual workshop, Shanghai, China, 03 December 2011 (2011)
4. Kulkarni, M.N.: Beyond computerisation of land records. Econ. Political Weekly **38**(24), 2338 (2003)
5. Orlikowski, W., Baroudi, J.: Studying information technology in organizations: research approaches and assumptions. Inf. Syst. Res. **2**(1), 1–28 (1991)
6. Schwandt, T.A.: Constructivist, interpretivist approaches to human inquiry. In: Denzin, N.K., Lincoln, Y.S. (eds.) Handbook of Qualitative Research, pp. 118–137. Sage, Thousand Oaks (1994)
7. Orlikowski, W.: The duality of technology: rethinking the concept of technology in organizations. Organ. Sci. **3**, 398–427 (1992)
8. Barley, S.R.: The alignment of technology and structure through roles and networks. Adm. Sci. Q. **35**(1), 61–103 (1990)
9. Davis, L.E., Taylor, J.C.: Technology, organisation and job structure. In: Dubin, R. (ed.) Handbook of Work Organisation and Society, pp. 379–419. Rand McNally, Chicago (1986)
10. Barua, A., Brooks, L., Gillon, K., Hodgkinson, R., Kohli, R., Worthington, S., Zukis, B.: Creating, capturing and measuring value from IT investments: could we do better? Commun. Assoc. Inf. Syst. (CAIS) **27**(2), 13–26 (2010)
11. Wanyama, I., Zheng, Q.: Organizational culture and information systems implementation: a structuration theory perspective. In: 2nd IEEE International Conference on Information and Financial Engineering (ICIFE), pp. 507–511 (2010)
12. Orlikowski, W.J., Iacono, C.S.: Research commentary: desperately seeking the "IT" in IT research—a call to theorizing the IT artifact. Inf. Syst. Res. **12**(2), 121–134 (2001). doi:10. 1287/isre.12.2.121.9700
13. Kling, R., Iacono, S.: The institutional character of computerized information systems. Office Technol. People **5**(1), 7–28 (1989)
14. Markus, M.L., Lee, A.S.: Special issue on intensive research in information systems: using qualitative, interpretive, and case methods to study information technology – second installment; foreword. MIS Q. **24**(1), 1–2 (2000)
15. Gibson, J.: The Ecological Approach to Perception. Houghton Mifflin, London (1979)
16. Lâm, D.P.: Sociomaterial entanglement in virtual spaces: knowledge creation practice in online platforms. In: de Vaujany, F., Mitev, N. (eds.) 2nd Organizations, Artifacts and Practices Workshop: Materiality and Space in Management and Organization Studies, p 14. DRM UMR CNRS, LSE Department of Management, Université Paris Dauphine (2012)
17. Zammuto, R.F., Griffith, T.L., Majchrzak, A., Dougherty, D.J., Faraj, S.: Information technology and the changing fabric of organization. Organ. Sci. **18**(5), 749–762 (2007). doi:10.1287/orsc.1070.0307
18. Barley, S.: Technology as an occasion for structuring: evidence from observation of CT Scanners and the social order of radiology departments. Admin. Sci. Q. **31**, 78–108 (1986)
19. Fulk, J.: Social construction of communication technology. Acad. Manag. J. **36**(5), 921–950 (1993). doi:10.2307/256641
20. Kallinikos, J.: Farewell to constructivism: technology and context-embedded action. In: Avgerou, C., Ciborra, C., Land, F. (eds.) The Social Study of Information and Communication Technology: Innovation, Actors and Contexts, pp. 141–161. London School of Economics and Political Sciences, London (2004)
21. Ciborra, C.: Imbrication of representations: risk and digital technologies. J. Manag. Stud. **43**(6), 1339–1356 (2006)
22. Fayard, A.L., Weeks, J.: Affordances for practice. Inf. Organ. **24**(4), 236–249 (2014)

23. Fayard, A.L., Weeks, J.: Photocopiers and water-coolers: the affordances of informal interactions. Organ. Stud. **28**(5), 605–634 (2007)
24. Bourdieu, P.: Outline of a Theory of Practice. Cambridge University Press, Cambridge (1977)
25. Bourdieu, P.: The Logic of Practice. Stanford University Press, Stanford (1990)
26. Avgerou, C., Madon, S.: Framing IS studies: understanding the social context of IS innovation. In: Avgerou, C., Ciborra, C., Land, F. (eds.) The Social Study of Information and Communication Technology: Innovation, Actors and Contexts, pp. 162–182. London School of Economics and Political Sciences, London (2004)
27. Avgerou, C., Walsham, G.: Information Technology in Context: Studies from the Perspective of Developing Countries. Ashgate, London (2000)
28. Walsham, G.: Making a World of Difference: IT in a Global Context. Wiley, Chichester (2001)
29. Acharya, R.B.: Adopting Geo-ICT for land administration: problems and solutions. In: 7th FIG Conference, 'Spatial Data Serving People: Land Governance and the Environment – Building the Capacity', Hanoi, Vietnam, 19–22 October 2009 (2009)
30. Sahay, S., Avgerou, C.: Introducing the special issue on information and communication technologies in developing countries. Inf. Soc. **18**(2), 73–76 (2002). doi:10.1080/01972240290075002
31. Heeks, R.: Information system in developing countries: failure, success and local improvisations. Inf. Soc. **18**(2), 101–112 (2002)
32. Heeks, R.: Most E-government for Development Project Fail: how can risk be reduced?, iGovernment Working Paper Series, Paper No. 14. Institute for Development Policy and Management, University of Manchester, UK (2003)
33. McGrath, K., Maiye, A.: The role of institutions in ICT innovation: learning from interventions in a Nigerian e-government initiative. Inf. Technol. Dev. **16**(4), 260–278 (2010). doi:10.1080/02681102.2010.498408
34. International Telecommunication Union: Measuring the Information Society: The ICT Development Index. International Telecommunication Union, Geneva (2009)

Socializing Accountability for Improving Primary Healthcare: An Action Research Program in Rural Karnataka

Shirin Madon[1(✉)] and S. Krishna[2]

[1] London School of Economics and Political Science, London, UK
s.madon@lse.ac.uk
[2] GSM Academy and Indian Institute of Management Bangalore,
Bengaluru, India

Abstract. The Alma Ata Declaration of 1978 invoked a socialising form of accountability through which communities and health workers participated in and were jointly accountable for primary healthcare. Aside from a few experiments, by the 1990s these ideals were quickly replaced by policy prescriptions based on increasing efficiency in data quality and reporting through the introduction of health information systems. More recently, there has been a revival of interest in community participation as a mechanism for improving the poor status of primary healthcare in developing countries through the constitution of village health committees. This paper documents and reflects on nine years of research on interventions aimed at improving primary healthcare accountability in rural Karnataka. Over this period, our focus has shifted from studying how computerised health information systems can strengthen conventional accountability systems to a period of extended participatory action research aimed at socialising accountability practices at village level. The findings from this study constitute vital knowledge for reforming the primary healthcare sector through different policy measures including the design of appropriate technology-based solutions.

Keywords: Health information systems · Socializing accountability · Participatory action research · Karnataka

1 Introduction

From the time of the Alma Ata Declaration of 1978 with its focus on community participation and inter-sectoral engagement, the issue of improving accountability of primary healthcare has been of key concern. Over the years, however, there have been different ideas about how to achieve this. The Declaration placed much emphasis on decentralising health planning and implementation with the primary health centre (PHC) identified as a new focal local point for coordinating different programmes and for integrating healthcare delivery with other community development priorities such as education and livelihood generation. An important aspect of this approach was its focus on broadening the accountability agenda beyond economic and functional

© IFIP International Federation for Information Processing 2017
Published by Springer International Publishing AG 2017. All Rights Reserved
J. Choudrie et al. (Eds.): ICT4D 2017, IFIP AICT 504, pp. 307–320, 2017.
DOI: 10.1007/978-3-319-59111-7_26

explanations of health agencies to a socialising form of accountability which included informal spaces and local contexts (Lawn et al. 2008).

The focus on socialising forms of primary healthcare accountability, however, was short-lived. By the early 1990s, influenced by the growing dominance of neoliberal policies amongst donors, attention was placed on achieving cost-effectiveness through performance-based measures. This triggered a wave of studies aimed at measuring improvements in primary healthcare based on targets set for specific programmes under the MDGs[1], for example measuring the reduction in maternal mortality rates (Zere et al. 2011). An increasing importance was accorded to the use of data as evidence for improving the way health programmes were implemented However, while computer-based systems produced 'evidence' of efficient usage of funds and supported increased scrutiny of health workers for non-achievement of targets, they did little to improve local planning and analysis of primary healthcare at the community level (Heeks 2006; Sahay and Latifov 2009). More recent efforts made by governments and international development organisations to improve primary healthcare accountability through the deployment of mobile phones to health workers have led to similar conclusions (Madon et al. 2014).

In recent years, there has been a revival of policy interest in community participation through the establishment of health committees at village or ward level in many developing countries such as India, Tanzania, Bangladesh and South Africa (George et al. 2015). Village health committees can be considered part of a wider move to introduce institutionalized or 'invited' spaces for citizens to participate in the monitoring and directing of public service delivery (Cornwall 2004; Aiyar 2010). While remaining partially embedded within the institutional apparatus of the state, these spaces have a semi-autonomous existence offering an opportunity for local discretion in the use of government funds and increasing community participation. This paper focuses on the contribution of practice theories in the ICTD field of study with a specific emphasis on the relevance of participatory action research for studies on primary healthcare in developing countries. Drawing on the experiences we have gained over the past five years in rural Karnataka, we demonstrate how our research trajectory has been directed by the social situation in which our study was embedded which, in turn, has influenced the theories and methods we have adopted.

In the next section we commence by reviewing action research studies in the ICTD field drawing on literature from the health information systems field and extend our discussion to participatory action research in the primary healthcare domain. This is followed by a detailed description of our research trajectory in rural Karnataka first as health information systems researchers and later as participatory action researchers involved in improving village health and community development. Finally, we reflect on the role of practice theories in improving our understanding of the social situation in which ICT interventions are embedded leading to important implications for policy and practice.

---

[1] These are the 8 Millennium Development Goals set by the UN in 2000.

2 The Role of Practice Theories in Improving Primary Healthcare in Developing Countries

While all research ultimately aims to generate knowledge and influence practice, in action research this coupling has been identified to be much closer (Brydon-Miller 2003). At a philosophical level, scholars discern validity for action research in terms of perceived functionality of the chosen action to produce desirable consequences for an organization as against producing scientific explanation which motivates positivistic science (Sussman and Evered 1978). A key value shared by action researchers in a variety of disciplines is the respect for people's knowledge and their ability to understand and address the issues confronting them and their communities using a variety of approaches and methodologies (Elden and Chisholm 1993; Brydon-Miller 2003).

In the field of information systems, four broad interrelated premises are recognised as characterizing action research: a prior explication of the purpose of action, practical action in a problem setting, action informing theory, and reason and action to be socially-situated (Baskerville and Myers 2004). While recognised as useful for ICTD study, relatively few action research studies have been undertaken (Avgerou 2008). An exception to this are the studies on the HISP system. For example, action research has been used to improve understanding of health systems sustainability with researchers undertaking practical action to trace how local solutions are aligned with larger networks of national-level teams (Braa et al. 2004; Byrne 2005; Asangansi 2012). In the field of health policy and planning, there has been a concomitant recognition for moving away from conventional qualitative case studies towards practice-oriented research approaches (Walt et al. 2008; Lehman and Gilson 2014).

While action research studies have rendered important insights about health information systems implementation in developing countries, the fourth premise of action research, namely for reason and action to be socially-situated has so far been only partially explored. The focus of studies undertaken to date has been on the formal health planning apparatus and hierarchical systems of accountability typically involving the district health agency reporting to government, rather than on studying, reframing and reconstructing actual social practices through community participation. In an attempt to bridge this gap, in this paper we focus on studying the extent to which the Village Health Sanitation and Nutrition Committees (VHSNCs) established in India in 2008 provide scope for the emergence of an alternative socialising form of accountability to improve the status of primary healthcare which remains poor even in more progressive states like Karnataka with nearly 80% of the 635 maternal deaths reported in 2015–16 being due to preventable causes such as anaemia (The Hindu 2016).

By creating a space for participation by local government, political and civil society representatives, village health committees provide a semi-autonomous space for collaborative action and have provided the impetus for our participatory action research (PAR) study. PAR is distinct in that it aims to combine theory and practice in cycles of action and reflection by providing a space in which community partners can come together and critically examine issues they face, generate knowledge and take action to address their priorities (Brydon-Miller et al. 2011). Influenced by numerous social struggles and movements particularly in developing countries, PAR has been conceptualised as a participatory and collaborative research approach that aims to carry out more politically-informed and socially-engaged forms of knowledge creation for addressing real world issues (Kemmis and McTaggart 2005).

In the context of India's VHSNCs, the authors have been engaged in PAR together with field researchers and community partners in order to critically examine the issues they face and to generate knowledge and take action for improving village health. Following Kemmis and McTaggart (2005) we identify four key aspects of the social situation to guide our study. First, we are interested in the actual practices that the committee engages in. Second, we would like to understand what knowledge members hold about these practices. Third, of interest to us are the social structures that shape and constrain those practices. Finally, we are interested in the broader discourse within which the daily practices of the VHSNC are becoming institutionalised.

The rest of this paper describes the various activities we undertook as participatory action researchers and how they have contributed to improving our theoretical understanding of primary healthcare accountability.

3 Participatory Action Research on Village Health in Karnataka

Our first encounter with research on primary healthcare in Karnataka commenced in 2007 with a three-year project funded by the British Council in partnership with the Karuna Trust, a local NGO that had been involved with primary healthcare and community development work in Karnataka for many decades. The aim of the project was to improve primary healthcare accountability by building a computerised data management infrastructure at PHC level that could be used to account for monies spent to higher levels of administration and funding bodies. The study was undertaken in Gumballi PHC managed by the Karuna Trust and through our discussions with agency staff and upon scrutinising the data sets collected at the PHC we found serious concerns related to data quality. For example, monthly reports were routinely incomplete and data presented on similar items under different headings was often found to be inconsistent. This investigation enabled us to improve data management and usage by designing a computerised system to automatically correct for data anomalies as a routine practice although these efforts were directed towards improving conventional upward accountability structures for reporting. During the course of our project, a new policy was launched in India under the auspices of the National Rural Health Mission to introduce VHSNCs[2] across the country in order to make primary healthcare more accountable to the community it served. Each committee was mandated to include 15–20 members of the community comprising health workers, school teachers, local

---

[2] When established, these committees were called VHSNCs (Village Health and Sanitation Committees). Nutrition was added as an additional aspect of the committees' mandate resulting in the acronym VHSNC from 2014.

politicians, civil society representatives and ordinary members of the community for addressing health, sanitation and nutrition needs of the village and receiving an annual untied grant of Rs. 10,000 (approximately US$152) from the government. From 2008 until 2010, we observed that in most locations these new village-level structures were only just incipient committees that met infrequently with poor attendance as villagers were unclear about the purpose of the committee (Madon et al. 2010).

From 2011, there was a growing interest among Karuna Trust to investigating how community participation in the VHSNCs would affect primary healthcare. Hence, the participatory action research component of our research on socialising accountability in primary healthcare commenced in earnest in 2011 with a grant from the British Academy to study the VHSNCs in Gumballi PHC and is currently ongoing. Our close involvement with the villages was facilitated by the working relationship we had established earlier with the Karuna Trust NGO. Two observations about the conduct of action research have particularly influenced our approach. First, as proposed by Baskerville and Myers (2004), "social situatedness means that the action researchers must be participant observers". Our team members have assumed the role of participant observers during VHSNC meetings in 12 villages of Gumballi and have facilitated various activities related to improving village health over a period of years. There has been a steady increase in the frequency of meetings and in member attendance which has coincided with the emergence of five key activities, namely raising health awareness, deciding on untied grant usage, self-organisation of the committee, localised village health planning and monitoring, and cross-sector integration (Madon and Krishna, 2017). Over time we have observed three main phases in VHSNC functioning in the villages. The first phase was characterised by the initial identification and enrolment of VHSNC members and by putting in place basic procedures for the conduct of meetings. In the second phase, VHSNC members began to show a more active interest in conducting meetings and in raising awareness about health, sanitation and nutrition practices. This phase was also characterised by a diversification of spending which resulted in noticeable improvements in water cleanliness, sanitation and hygiene in the villages. The third phase represents the current stage of the VHSNCs in Gumballi where regular meetings take place in all the villages and where the five key activities mentioned above have become routinized with a growing confidence amongst members to tackle larger issues such as long-term planning and monitoring in the village, often in conjunction with the gram panchayat[3] and health authorities.

A second observation that has inspired our action research comes from Elden and Chisholm (1993), "if system self-improvement is a goal, then system members must learn how to make sense of their own data in terms of their own language and in relation to their own perception and values". Over the past four years, the Karuna Trust has supported activities that facilitate this learning experience and in which we have participated as action researchers. We describe these activities below.

---

[3] This is the village council.

3.1   VHSNC Capacity-Building Workshops

Capacity-building workshops have been an essential part of our action research strategy in Gumballi. These workshops were held between August to October 2014 in each of 15 villages in Gumballi organised by the PHC manager and by ASHA workers[4] from each village. Approximately 15–17 VHSNC members attended each workshop.

We invited members to make sense of and share their own understanding of the VHSNCs. Figure 1 illustrates the informal layout of the workshop with members sometimes accompanied by their children. In each village, a member of our team began the workshop with a welcome speech after which the first part of the workshop was devoted to an articulation of village problems by VHSNC members. Members referred to problems related to blocked drains, waste disposal, water sources that needed cleaning, the difficulty of accessing government funds for building an individual household toilet, and the non-receipt of assistance under a government scheme that enables low-income pregnant women to avail of benefits. About one-third of VHSNC members described a major health-related problem to be the lack of cleanliness in the anganwadi centre[5] and school buildings due to garbage disposal and lack of proper toilet facilities. A few villages identified other problems related to damaged roads in the village, irregular clearance of village dustbins and the incidence of malnourished children.

Fig. 1. A VHSNC capacity building workshop

---

[4] ASHA stands for Auxiliary Social Health Activist. These workers are local women trained by the health department to act as educators. They serve as an important interface between the community and the health system.

[5] Anganwadi centres offer basic nutrition and health education and well as pre-school activities for the village.

In the second part of the workshop we invited members to share with the other workshop participants what they saw as their role in promoting village health. In the majority of villages health workers volunteered for this exercise in which case the female health worker explained that her duties involved providing information about family planning and about government schemes for maternal and child health. In addition, she recognised her duties to involve promoting health and nutrition education, carrying out immunization of communicable diseases and maintaining birth and death register. Male health workers recognised their duties as providing early diagnosis and treatment for communicable diseases such as malaria, TB and leprosy, conducting health surveys, taking water sample from drinking water sources for testing in the PHC laboratory, and providing education in schools. In a small number of cases, the anganwadi worker described her role as treating malnourished children and for imparting education to women and lactating mothers about the importance of regular monitoring of child health as well as maintaining good nutrition and hygiene practices. Similarly, the local school teacher spoke of his responsibility to ensure good sanitation and hygiene within the school and in soliciting the support of the VHSNC in promoting child health.

A third theme in the workshop involved members sharing their ideas about what should be the key priorities for the VHSNC. In almost all villages, members felt that the focus of the committee should be to provide clean drinking water and basic medicines for the PHC, to ensure school children are routinely checked and to identify malnourished children, to create greater awareness of seasonal diseases and to monitor the workload of ASHA and ANM workers as well as provide additional health services. In all villages, VHSNC members found that households were reluctant to build individual toilets despite Government support due to the complexities of actually receiving the grant.

3.2   Community Monitoring

The need to involve the community in monitoring health services was expressed during the VHSNC capacity-building workshops and resulted in Karuna Trust working with us to develop a simple format for collecting responses on different aspects of maternal and child health including difficulties faced by health workers in achieving targets. The community monitoring exercise commenced in January 2015 and involved selecting for each village a 6-member team of VHSNC members: President, Secretary, an SC/ST female member, a self-help group member, a youth foundation member, and a villager concerned about maternal and child health. In each village, a member of the community monitoring team asked whether the respondent felt that service delivery was good, average or poor and we further probed the respondent to elaborate on their answer.

The first part of the exercise was about the provision of antenatal, postnatal and new-born care in the village and involved asking ASHA workers about the extent to which they had been able to register antenatal cases, administer tetanus injections for pregnant women, administer IFA tablets, organise institutional delivery, carry out PNC check-up, complete child immunization and prescribe family planning. Figure 2 provides an example of the format used to tabulate questions and answers collected by the

Sl.No	Descriptions	Month
		Jan-16
1	No of registered ANC	😊 This indicate Smiley face
2	Total no of women received TT	😊
3	Total no of women received the IFA	😊
4	Women have received the PNC service	😊
5	Institutional delivery	😊
6	ANC women received 6 times ANC check up	😊
7	Children to be immunized during the month	😊
8	Number of eligible couples adopted family planning (Permanent and temporary)	😊

Fig. 2. Excerpt from community monitoring format

team. One common issue raised by the ASHA worker in all villages was her inability to complete antenatal services because it was customary for pregnant women to relocate to their husband's house after the sixth month of pregnancy. In just under half the villages, the ASHA worker reported she was unable to administer IFA tablets because the stock had run out at the PHC.

The second part of the exercise involved asking the anganwadi worker[6] about how successfully she was able to provide nutrition services such as organising mothers meetings and the statutory Village Health and Nutrition Day, providing supplementary food to antenatal and postnatal women as well as to underweight children, and maintaining cleanliness at the anganwadi centre. In just under half the villages, the anganwadi workers reported that while she had identified malnourished children in the village for support through a government rehabilitation programme, parents were unwilling to send their children as the referral centre was around 20 km. away from the village. In a few cases, the anganwadi worker reported that she was unable to provide food supplements to antenatal and postnatal women during mothers' meetings because of the heavy workload of maintaining 10–12 registers.

The third aspect of the monitoring exercise involved asking VHSNC members about whether the committee was paying importance to ensuring that sanctioned posts were filled, that water sources in the village were periodically tested, that the Immunization Day programme organised every month by the health department was conducted, that adequate benefits were provided to ANC and malnourished children in the village, and that all low-income new mothers had received a free health kit. Responses were generally positive apart from a small number of villages in which antenatal and malnourished beneficiaries had not received benefit from the VHSNC and where water testing had not been carried out.

---

[6] The anganwadi worker is a female worker who specializes in providing basic healthcare and nutrition education to pre-school children under the Integrated Child Development Scheme run by the Ministry of Women and Child Development.

The final part of the community monitoring exercise was devoted to asking questions to villagers about infant/maternal deaths in the village, deaths due to communicable disease, and whether child marriages took place. In the majority of cases, the responses indicated a low prevalence of deaths although in some villages it was indicated informally that the practice of child marriages was rare but persistent.

3.3   Village Health Plan

As referred to earlier, the current stage of VHSNC functioning in Gumballi is characterised by a desire amongst members to tackle larger issues which connect village health with broader community development objectives. In partnership with staff from the Karuna Trust, we commenced the village health plan exercise in September 2015 to address these broader objectives. Three days were spent in each of the villages using participatory rural appraisal tools to involve VHSNC members in drawing maps to identify key resources, the effect of seasons on village life, and income and expenditure patterns in the village.

Using coloured chalk on concrete ground, VHSNC members from each village identified key resources such as drains, toilets, roads and health facilities as illustrated in Fig. 3. Often we commenced the exercise of drawing the map as a demonstration which was then continued by 2 or 3 VHSNC members with others contributing to the process. In all villages, members reported that they had access to a 24/7 subcentre, an anganwadi centre and good drinking water facilities. In contrast, the percentage of villages with proper concrete drains ranged from 15–90% but in all cases the problem of blocked drains was reported as a result of inadequate waste management provision. The percentage of households with individual toilets ranged from 2% in some villages to 50% in others signalling that in the majority of cases, villagers practiced open

Fig. 3. A village health plan mapping exercise

defecation. While in the majority of villages, people had health insurance, in some cases this was less than 30% of the population.

The effect of seasons on village life was captured by asking self-help group VHSNC members to draw a calendar on the concrete ground using coloured powder. A good farming season was identified twice a year around April and December which necessitated hard work on farms in the months preceding. Heavy rains were experienced between July and September with fever and cough occurring at the start of the summer season as well as during the rainy season. In all cases, villages held festivals three times a year in January, March/April, September/October and November. The mapping exercise enabled VHSNC members to reflect on the important role of seasonal activities on their health. They identified the need for the VHSNC to plan ahead to promote health awareness before the summer season through home visits, to ensure that testing of water quality and cleaning of drains had been carried out and that the PHC was well-stocked to supply seasonal medicines.

The final exercise involved VHSNC members drawing a pie chart to show income and expenditure patterns within the village. In the majority of villages, members estimated that approximately 20% of income was spent on food and nutrition and 20–30% was spent on agricultural purposes, for example to purchase seeds, fertilisers, equipment and for labour charges. On the other hand, in all villages, expenditure on festivals was common with the most marginalised of communities spending around 15% of their income on alcohol and tobacco. The exercise revealed that the rest of household income was spent on a combination of education and for a small amount of saving despite the fact that in all villages women belonged to self-help groups and could access credit. In all villages, the majority of villagers had health insurance but preferred not to spend on health and preferred to use government facilities.

4   Discussion

Our research efforts over the past nine years have been dedicated to improving our understanding of how the primary healthcare system in Gumballi PHC, Karnataka can be more accountable to the community. Table 1 show a timeline of the different phases of our study. We refer back to the four key aspect of the social situation that have helped frame our study. First, the VHSNCs were established in 2008 based on the assumption that community participation is needed for improving primary healthcare accountability. However, this theoretical premise went unquestioned almost as if the particulars of the

Table 1. Timeline showing the trajectory of our study

Dates	Research activity
2007–2010	Evaluating the impact of health information systems at primary healthcare level in Karnataka
2011	Participant observation at VHSNCs in Gumballi
Aug 2014	Participatory Action Research - VHSNC Capacity Building Workshops in 15 villages of Gumballi
Jan 2015	Participatory Action Research - Community Monitoring Exercise
Sep 2015	Participatory Action Research - Village Health Plan

practical situation were not important. For example, these committees were not looked upon seriously by higher echelons of the health administration or by PHC medical staff for the first few years of their formation with little interest in understanding how they were functioning. Our focus on the regular routines that take place at village level has presented the opportunity to take seriously these new committees as spaces for social-ising accountability in primary healthcare. Acting as PAR in the three support activities promoted by the Karuna Trust has enabled us to gain a deeper insight into the actual lived practices of village health and community development.

Second, a wealth of knowledge has accumulated amongst committee members which comes to live in the routine activities that are undertaken within the VHSNCs. For example, members have learnt to use discretion to raise awareness, purchase items members prioritise for maintaining village health, self-organise themselves and net-work with other village bodies. The three support activities promoted by the Karuna Trust have provided a mechanism for the community to make sense of their own realities in terms of their own language and values. For example, the capacity-building workshops enabled key health workers to articulate what they saw as the role of the VHSNC and their own role and responsibilities for maintaining village health. VHSNC members were seen to reflect on village problems to identifying priorities for the VHSNC. The community monitoring exercise provided an opportunity for health workers to account for their own performance in terms of the contingencies they face, for example related to excessive workload and customary practices. Collective development of a village health plan provided the opportunity to elicit knowledge from the VHSNC members about village resources and about how seasonality affected livelihoods, health and income.

Third, PAR has illuminated the enabling and constraining influence of social structures on practice. When the VHSNCs were first established, attendance was poor and meetings were infrequent and it has taken time for these committees to become accepted as part of the social structure within the village, for example in terms of gaining support of the village council in the conduct of its activities. Social structures have influenced almost all of the support activities that have been implemented. For example, during the community monitoring exercise, social norms have dictated the movement of pregnant women to their husband's house which in turn have impacted the achievement of antenatal check-up targets for the ASHA worker. Similarly, the social structure of the bureaucracy has resulted in a heavy workload for anganwadi workers to maintain registers thereby preventing them from providing food supple-ments to antenatal and postnatal women. Finally, social practice of child marriages although only informally reported during our study suggests a constrain for improving village health and promoting community development.

Fourth, there are signs to suggest a transformation of the broader discourse within which village-level practices are being institutionalised. Action on our part has involved several new dimensions that suggest that the VHSNC is gaining more voice. For example, over the past few months we have been asked by the VHSNC members to help in the writing of formal complaint letters addressed to the PHC about health workers who underperform. In another case, we were recently asked by VHSNC members to help formulate a letter to be sent to the gram panchayat to complain about the non-repair of water pipes. In August 2016 we held a public dialogue meeting at Gumballi PHC inviting members from VHSNCs and the wider community to raise concerns about any aspect of primary healthcare service delivery. Points highlighted by attendees included an inadequate provision of basic medicines and nutritious food for school children and complaints about non-performing health workers. Proposal were made to hold a regular gynaecological camp for rural women at the PHC, to improve the display of government and PHC services to the community as it was felt that many were unaware about services offered, and to establish a new VHSNC in villages with large populations.

Our action research approach in Gumballi PHC is currently part of a British Academy-sponsored study in which we have worked out an action plan with Karuna Trust for the next two years. During this time, we will continue to conduct PAR in the in the 15 villages of Gumballi with further rounds of community monitoring and village health planning and are in the process of identifying emergent village health issues such as the growing prevalence of non-communicable diseases, psychiatric problems, alcohol and tobacco consumption, and domestic violence in Gumballi. Our research has pointed to the fact that ICT used to gather data through numbers-oriented, centralized and top-down systems to monitor performance of field level workers has been insufficient and problematic in efforts to improve primary health care systems. The action research program we have reported has explored greater local participation through education and participation of community as an essential complement. This naturally leads to the question as to whether ICTs can be used to support more effective functioning of local institutions and organizations in the health care domain. This is indeed possible. Currently health data is aggregated at the PHC level for reports to be considered by higher level bureaucracy. It be would be a simple matter to aggregate at village level and make the information available to VHSNCs for consideration. This simple step, in addition to improving awareness of health parameters at the local level, will vastly improve data validity which has been a major concern in the present system in which ANMs have a dual and conflicting role as both caregivers as well as providers of data used to monitor their own performance. Further, the knowledge that is derived at monthly VHSNC meetings can be systematised and used for improved observation, comparison and learning at higher levels of the health administration. However, the main constraint at least in villages in Karnataka appears to be one of resources. The present VHSNC annual budget of around $150 utilized for multiple purposes as discussed earlier cannot, in addition, pay for tablet-based systems and internet connection. At a state level however additional funds to provide such ICT resources are not beyond reach. Hopefully, sustained effective functioning of VHSNCs will persuade state Government to provide required additional resources to move towards next level development of VHSNCs in which they have access to ICT support to help them grow further.

To conclude, one of the broader implications from our paper is that the focus of scholarship on ICTD topics should be not just be on ICTs but on the 'D' for development, a point that has repeatedly been raised by scholars in the field (Thompson and Walsham 2010; Toyama 2015). As stated by the founder of Karuna Trust at the start of our action research project, 'only after we have developed a shared understanding of what is involved in improving village health can we think about introducing ICT tools'. As our study has shown, penetrating the complexities of poverty and underdevelopment is a non-trivial exercise in which practice theories can play an indispensable role in improving primary healthcare accountability in resource-poor settings.

Acknowledgement. The authors acknowledge the assistance of Karuna Trust and our two field researchers Lakshmana and Rudresh in producing this study.

References

Aiyar, Y.: Invited spaces, invited participation: effects of greater participation on accountability in service delivery. India Rev. **9**(2), 204–229 (2010)

Asangansi, I.: Understanding HMI implementation in a developing country ministry of health context – an institutional logics perspective. Online J. Publ. Health Inf. **4**(3), e8 (2012)

Avgerou, C.: Information systems in developing countries: a critical research review. J. Inf. Technol. **23**, 133–146 (2008)

Baskerville, R., Myers, M.D.: Special issue on action research in information systems: making IS research relevant to practice-foreword. MIS Q. **28**(3), 329–335 (2004)

Braa, J., Monteiro, E., Sahay, S.: Networks of action: sustainable health information systems across developing countries. MIS Q. **28**(3), 337–362 (2004)

Brydon-Miller, M., Greenwood, D., Maguire, P.: Why action research? Action Res. **1**(1), 9–28 (2003)

Brydon-Miller, M., Kral, M., Maguire, P., Noffke, S., Sabhlok, A.: Jazz and the banyan tree: roots and riffs on participatory action research. In: Denzin, K., Lincoln, Y.S. (eds.) Handbook of Qualitative Research, pp. 387–400. Sage, Thousand Oaks (2011)

Byrne, E.: Using action research in information systems design to address change: a south african health information systems case study. In: Proceedings SAICSIT 2005 Proceedings of the 2005 Annual Research Conference of the South African Institute of Computer Scientists and Information Technologists on IT Research in Developing Countries, pp. 131–14 (2005)

Cornwall, A.: New democratic spaces? The politics and dynamics of institutionalised participation, IDS bulletin **35**(2), 1–10 (2004)

Elden, M., Chisholm, R.F.: Emerging varieties of action research: introduction to special issue. Hum. Relat. **46**(2), 121–142 (1993)

George, A., Scott, K., Garimella, S., Mondal, S., Ved, R., Sheikh, K.: Anchoring contextual analysis in health policy and systems research: a narrative of contextual factors influencing health committees in low and middle income countries. Soc. Sci. Med. **133**, 159–167 (2015)

Heeks, R.: Health information systems: failure, success and improvisation. Int. J. Med. Inf. **75**(2), 125–137 (2006)

The Hindu: Primary Health Centres Fail to check Avoidable Maternal Deaths in State, The Hindu, 23 June 2016

Kemmis, S., McTaggart, R.: Participatory action research: communicative action and the public sphere. In: Denzin, K., Lincoln, Y.S. (eds.) Handbook of Qualitative Research, pp. 556–604. Sage, Thousand Oaks (2005)

Lawn, J., Rohde, J., Rifkin, S., Were, M., Paul, V., Chopra, M.: Alma-Ata 30 years on: revolutionary, relevant, and time to revitalize. Lancet **372**, 917–927 (2008)

Lehmann, U., Gilson, L.: Action learning for health system governance: the reward and challenge of co-production. Health Policy Plann. **1**, 7 (2014)

Madon, S., Krishna, S.: Challenges of Accountability in Resource-Poor Contexts: Lessons about invited spaces from Karnataka's village health committees. Oxford Development Studies (2017)

Madon, S., Krishna, S., Michael, E.: Health information systems, decentralisation and accountability. Publ. Adm. Dev. **30**(4), 247–260 (2010)

Madon, S., Amaguru, J., Malecela, M., Michael, E.: Can mobile phones help control neglected tropical diseases: experiences from Tanzania. Soc. Sci. Med. **102**, 103–110 (2014)

Sahay, S., Latifov, M.: The data to indicator (Mis)match: experiences from trying to strengthen this link in the health information system in Tajikistan. In: Proceedings of the 10th International Conference on Social Implications of mpCouters in Developing Countries, Dubai School of Government, Dubai, May 2009 (2009)

Sussman, G.I., Evered, R.D.: An assessment of scientific merits of action research. Adm. Sci. Q. **23**(4), 582–603 (1978)

Thompson, M., Walsham, G.: ICT research in Africa: need for a strategic developmental focus. Inf. Technol. Dev. **16**(2), 112–127 (2010)

Toyama, K.: Geek Heresy: Rescuing Social Change from the Cult of Technology. Public Affairs, New York (2015)

Walsham, G., Sahay, S.: Research on information systems in developing countries: current landscape and future prospects. Inf. Technol. Dev. **12**(1), 7–24 (2006)

Walt, G., Shiffman, J., Schneider, H., Murray, S., Brugha, R., Gilson, L.: 'Doing' health policy analysis: methodological and conceptual reflections and challenges. Health Policy Plann. **23**, 308–317 (2008)

Zere, E., Oluwole, D., Kirigia, J., Mwikisa, C., Mbeeli, T.: Inequities in skilled attendance at birth in Namibia: a decomposition analysis. BMC Pregnancy Childbirth **11**, 34 (2011)

System Failure for Good Reasons? Understanding Aid Information Management Systems (AIMS) with Indonesia as State Actor in the Changing Field of Aid

Kyung Ryul Park[1]([⊠]) and Boyi Li[2]

[1] London School of Economics, London, UK
k.park5@lse.ac.uk
[2] University of Exeter, Exeter, UK
b.li@exeter.ac.uk

Abstract. Information systems (IS) failure in developing countries has been often understood as the failure of development practitioners to think and act in accordance with the local context. Such explanatory accounts mostly take contingency as the situation in the local context in which multiple stakeholders can coordinate and adapt to the local. There is a lack of understanding of contingency as the global context of the international development field, in particular how IS failure can be shaped by the state actor. In this paper, we trace the change of the global aid governance that influenced the context of aid information management systems (AIMS) in Indonesia. We argue that understanding the failure of AIMS in Indonesia needs to move from the project's local situation to the global-level, recursive relationship between the field of aid governance and the state actor. Interpreting AIMS failure as the result of Indonesia's strategic agency in the shifting landscape of global aid agenda allows information communication and technology and development (ICTD) researchers to reflect upon the macro political economy of development, in particular how the emerging powers can shape the development agenda in which future ICT innovations unfold.

Keywords: ICTD · Information systems failure · Aid information management systems (AIMS) · Indonesia · Recursive contingency

1 Introduction

Many studies have been conducted to explain the failures of information systems (IS) in developing countries [7, 27, 30]. One of the main challenges, according to Heeks [21], can be described as the problem of the "design-actuality" gap. In ICTD literature, this is associated with the theorizing efforts to understand the local context in its recursive relations with ICT interventions [3, 4], constituting a growing body of knowledge to address the gap between system design and local contingency [2, 8]. State actors, in this context, are widely seen as the indispensable intermediary in translating and coordinating multiple stakeholders' expectations and actions [1, 14]. System failure in the field of ICTD has been predominantly framed as a micro-situational struggle to bring together

J. Choudrie et al. (Eds.): ICT4D 2017, IFIP AICT 504, pp. 321–332, 2017.
DOI: 10.1007/978-3-319-59111-7_27

multiple stakeholders and to generate a contingent fit between local use and the dominant logic of the field of international development [21, 24]. Such explanatory accounts mostly take contingency as the local or domestic context in which a developing country coordinates multiple domestic interpretations and objectives on the recipient side. There is a lack of understanding of contingency in the macro context of international development, in particular how IS failure can be shaped by the state actor as an agency in the field of global aid. Indeed, foreign aid is such an established field where the relationship between donor and recipient countries is subject to historically evolved rules, governance, tensions, and cultural dispositions, which jointly define a distinctive organizational field [12]. The success or failure of IS has rarely been explained by examining state actor in the context of an organizational field. Moreover, understanding the role of state actor in global context bears the key to explaining those particular cases of failure where the major sources of contingency are to be found on the donor's side instead of the recipient's [31, 35]. This is often associated with what Heeks [21] referred to as "sustainability failure", in which IS initiatives were initially successful in developing countries but subsequently abandoned after a short period of time. Much of the disuse of IS needs to be explained by tracing the changes in relations, ideologies, and institutional arrangements among the donors and international organizations (IOs), which are normally beyond the influence of state actors in the context of developing countries. Contingency in the global field of aid has rarely been accounted for and theorised in ICTD literature to explain system failure.

In this paper, we aim to understand why a donor-funded information system, aid information management systems (AIMS) designed to institute aid principles outlined in the Paris Declaration on Aid Effectiveness (PD), was implemented, used, and then abandoned in Indonesia. It is theoretically significant because it illustrates a specific case of "sustainability failure" in a struggle with contingency as the change of relations, rules, and understandings in the global field of aid. By tracing the justifications for the failure of AIMS from its local context to the global context, we illustrate how an IS failure in Indonesia needs to be seen as the result of macro events occurring in the global field of aid and how the state of Indonesia has actively shaped this global-level contingency, which used to be dominated by the West. Through this case, we demonstrate an emerging situational gap in what is referred to as "recursive contingency" [11], in which the Indonesian state seizes opportunities to find an alternative legitimacy to justify the 'failure'. The state actor can be clearly seen in this recursive contingency as the dominant logic of institutions is challenged by the state. We suggest that this new understanding of contingency presents a unique opportunity for the use of new theoretical lens to examine system failure in developing country.

2 The Global Field of Aid: Governance and Institutional Power

2.1 Paris Declaration and Institutionalization of the Field

Based on a plethora of research and international calls for effective aid, a series of international forums in the 2000s shaped a new framework known as 'aid effectiveness'.

In particular, the OECD DAC built significant momentum to improve aid effectiveness and reached a major milestone, namely the endorsement of the PD in 2005 [32]. The Declaration was endorsed by 138 countries and 28 IOs in the Second High Level Forum (HLF) on Aid Effectiveness, and may be the most authoritative principle and practical roadmap to improve aid quality, imposing commitments to share aid information for enhanced transparency and coordination [32]. Based on the assumption of transaction cost theory and result-oriented approach, five principles are suggested: ownership, alignment, harmonization, results, and mutual accountability. The PD was often criticized for the challenges to achieving goals in practice [37], its technocratic orientation, and conflicting or misleading principles [20], and the lack of involvement of non-DAC emerging donors and CSOs. However, the PD was still influential in creating powerful political momentum to reorganize the way recipient countries and development partners cooperate. In addition, through the Accra Agenda for Action (AAA) endorsed at the third HLF in Ghana in 2008, the OECD tried to incorporate feedback and suggest a more recipient-focused action plan. Building on the PD, AAA highlights sharing aid information as the most fundamental action to be achieved as a prerequisite of better transparency, coordination and aid effectiveness.

2.2   Information Systems in Aid Management

The use of information systems in the public sector has been widely discussed as an innovative tool for the process of information rationalization. Envisioned by the new public management (NPM), ICT adoption in the public sector in developing countries was expected to enhance transparency [6], increase efficiency [41], improve service delivery [23], and improve interaction with citizens [40]. In the aid effectiveness debate, information systems are perceived as an innovative tool to enable stakeholders to enhance aid coordination and transparency [17], and help recipient governments plan and predict their budgets better, taking more ownership in aid coordination mechanism. With this backdrop, a number of ICT applications commonly referred to as AIMS have been implemented in developing countries over the past two decades. As a generic term, "AIMS includes websites or databases that store and process aid information on donors' activities, budgets, and development indicators" [34]. The PD may be the most significant momentum for the global adoption of AIMS which has been largely supported by major donors [34]. In spite of significant attention given to such systems and the heavy investment made, many cases have not achieved the expected outcomes that the rhetoric of AIMS promised, and even failed to reach sustainability [34].

3   Recursive Contingency and Institutional Change

If practice theories provide a broad avenue to make sense of the recursive relationship between structure and agency, current theoretical approaches prevalent in ICTD – structuration theory, actor network theory, activity theory, etc. – are mostly focused on the micro-situational actions of individual and organizational actors, and their unfolding relations with technological artefacts. This paper develops an understanding of practice theories by defining contingency as macro situations in which state actors are being governed by, and purposefully negotiating the global institutions; and state actors, have the practical, evaluative agency to interpret the "dilemmas, and ambiguities of presently evolving situations" [13]. We maintain that ICTD field can benefit from shedding light on the macro perspectives which view state as a constructive member of the international aid community with specific, strategic concerns about its status and prestige in power relations with other states, where the recursive relationship between state actor and global institutions are put into the central fora of enquiries. The agency of the Indonesian state can be seen in its efforts to negotiate with the institutions of aid, which frames the meanings and justification of implementing the AIMS ant its eventual shutdown. Such framings of ICTD projects as the practical, strategic agency of the state actor concerning its position and power on global stage of institutions constitutes the essential novelty of theoretical contributions that we are trying to make.

According to this school of practice theory, institutional structures are reproduced by the actors who accept the set of norms, rules, and cultural understandings as the dominant logic of institutions [38] while collectively changing the structures through actions [18, 36]. The theory of recursive contingency aims to address the situations where established institutional structures become unstable and the possibility of a de-institutionalisation process is real [11, 25]. It refers to the institutional change scenarios in which certain events take place and cannot be interpreted and categorized by applying existing dominant logic of institutional structures. The incapability of codifying these events usually leads to two divergent consequences: either the actors improvise a new set of codes that become recognized and accepted as the legitimate means of understanding, or the actors find alternative schemes of codification that potentially de-stabilize the dominant institutional logic. Events are defined as scenarios that are "not known, unexpected, and unwelcomed by the 'master planners' or the organizational manageables of dominant institutions" [9, 19]. When events take place and become knowable by actors, the flexibility of interpreting the meanings of events and the following rhetorical and discursive movements becomes the source of recursivity and contingency.

Once the corresponding relationship between the dominant institutional logic and the emerging practical scenarios becomes decoupled, the alternative possibility becomes open and accessible to actors' practical knowledge, which means the politics of competing for legitimacy of reasoning is unleashed. The legitimacy of the logic is challenged as actors possess alternative, competing means of interpretation to justify different logic of actions and relationship-building. Recursive contingency may not necessarily cause the dominance of the alternative, as the process of recursive constructions of understandings is subject to the process of a competitive game for gaining legitimacy [26]. Yet, it is directly conducive to the de-institutionalisation process in a field [11].

Recursive contingency in the field of aid and development is likely to happen when the leading donors attempt to design and implement information systems in recipient countries with the purpose of setting up a system (such as AIMS with its supporting institutions) to codify aid principles such as aid effectiveness, transparency, and coordination into the practice guidelines in recipient countries. As an institutional logic, these governance principles correspond to a system of codification schemes that enable actors to make sense of specific situations they encounter in their everyday work.

Ideally, the structures of dominant institutions are reproduced by the actors who skillfully and compliantly recognize their daily encounters as codes and translate the meanings into the AIMS that reduce the social complexity into computable forms of data, tables, and texts. In practice, however, users of AIMS may encounter context-specific situations, scenarios, or cultural phenomena that they find difficult to either translate or simply too complex to reduce to the computable forms of data and tables. Such difficulty leads to two divergent consequences: (a) users of AIMS improvise new codes that are consistent with the existing codification schemes and are accepted as part of aid governance structure, or (b) users might find alternative codification schemes and translation that belong to different, rival paradigms of interpreting the social reality; in other words, the possibility of a different aid governance structure. Based upon these theoretical propositions, the research question of this paper can framed as: *how does Indonesia, as a state actor, find alternative ways of justification and legitimacy to implement and then abandon the AIMS system in the changing field of global aid governance institutions?*

4 Methodology

This research adopts an interpretive single case study design. The purpose of the research is to explore why AIMS fails to achieve in sustainability, and the case study is appropriate strategy of inquiry when the main research questions are *'how'* or *'why'* to study a phenomenon in its natural setting [42]. Case study methodology has often been used in order to give rich narratives in the field of IS in past decades [39]. For the case selection, we focused on the AIMS category of 'implemented once but abandoned', a case of "sustainability failure" [34]. Among the countries, the Indonesian AIMS was the most interesting, unique and accessible case for the following reasons. First, Indonesia has had multiple experiences in IS implementation for aid management. In 2005, the government implemented the Recovery Aceh Nias (RAN) database with UNDP and ADB financial support in order to manage humanitarian assistance and enhance coordination for post-tsunami recovery. The RAN was used during the recovery period, and was arguably considered a success story by international development agencies [28]. However, the AIMS implemented in 2010, the subject of this study, seems not successful. Second, the IT developer of the case is not one of the major competitors in the global market that was identified [34], but a mix of local IT consultants. Third, as a member of the G20, Indonesia's position in the global field of aid is quite different from other recipient countries. It has been a recipient country, while taking a role of, leading South-South cooperation. This setting provides uniqueness to the case study.

The fieldwork in Indonesia took place of August 2015 to August 2016. From an interpretive epistemology, this study relies interviews, informal conversations, and archival research [15]. Semi-structured interviews were conducted with aid experts in donor agencies and IOs, as well as government officials and the IT experts who developed the AIMS. The interviews were generally 1 to 1.5 h long. During this time several secondary data sources were collected and reviewed that included official project documents, policy briefs, evaluation reports, government regulations, media articles, contracts with IT consultants and technical documents on the AIMS.

5 Case Study

5.1 Aid Governance in Indonesia

Foreign aid has been an important component of Indonesian domestic politics and economy, and is also considered to be a diplomatic tool for donor countries seeking military, political and economic advantages since the establishment of Indonesia as a nation state [22]. Indonesia's legacy in political and international relations continues to shape the current debate on the national development strategy and to have an influence on its perspective on aid in many ways. Before the 1997 Asian Financial Crisis, foreign aid played a big role in 'budget support' helping the country maintain fiscal stimulation, but making its economy unstable with a very high debt rate. This economic instability forced the authoritarian regime to finally step down and ushered in a new era of democracy. Susilo Bambang Yudhoyono's (SBY) inauguration in 2004 could be viewed as a turning point in terms of the country's development policy and aid management. He declared that Indonesia no longer regarded foreign aid as a financial supplement to domestic resources, but as a national catalyst for enhancing socio-economic development and improving institutional capacity. His administration sought to improve aid governance and to focus on building the capacity of government to effectively manage loans and grants in two ways: (1) the establishment of the National Medium-Term Development Plan (RPJMN) (2004–09 and 2009–14), (2) the issue of regulations including the Government Regulation No. 2/2006 that provides general guidance for decision makers to negotiate with multilateral and bilateral donors.

5.2 Aid Information Management Systems (AIMS)

Realizing the importance of an aid effectiveness agenda, the Indonesian government took leadership in establishing the roadmap of a country-specific action plan—the Jakarta Commitment—to bring the PD and the AAA to the national level. The Commitment was signed by 26 development partners in January, 2009, and defines the policy direction towards better aid management and enhanced coordination among stakeholders. Furthermore, the Aid Effectiveness Secretariat (A4DES) was established with the transitional multi-donor fund to provide support in facilitation and coordination of activities to achieve the Commitment. One of the key activities was the implementation of AIMS as a single-window system for monitoring and evaluating aid activities.

Even before 2009, the terms of reference for AIMS had already been developed by the National Development Planning Agency (BAPPENAS) through a series of interim meetings and the UNDP-led four-day workshop on 'Effective Aid Management' in October 2008. The BAPPENAS finally received a grant from the German Technical Cooperation Agency (GTZ) and entered into a contract in February, 2010. A series of AIMS coordination meeting was held with diverse stakeholders including BAPPENAS, the Ministry of Finance, the State Secretariat, A4DES, and GTZ. Soon after, the recruitment process was carried out, and four local IT professionals were hired for developing the system. The AIMS was launched in June, 2010 with a description as a national computerized system for long-term aid management. The web-based system was designed to give an overview of loans and grants by geomapping donors' activities and providing a visual presentation and analysis of aid data. However, the short term objective of the AIMS was a computerization of the Survey on Monitoring PD Phase 3 to be done before the Busan HLF in 2011. The national launch of the Survey Phase 3 was held with development partners in November. By late 2012, however, the AIMS was no longer being used, and was subsequently abandoned.

6 Analysis and Discussion

Now we analyse the process of AIMS implementation and failure in the narrative of Indonesian state striving for position and power in the reform of aid governance. There are three episodes of major change in the relations and common understanding of aid governance in the global context. As we briefly discussed, the PD of 2005 is a milestone event in the global field of aid that marks a new process of institutionalization, through the establishment of a set of norms and rules rationalizing the concept of aid effectiveness. The process prescribes a set of legitimate principles for governing aid activities, and provides protocols shared by all signatory to coordinate aid efforts. Through a series of meetings, agenda-setting, survey and monitor exercises, these legitimate principles and framework are sufficiently communicated between stakeholders. This communication ensures that the global community shares institutional structures. The institutional work can be clearly seen in the activities such as the Survey on Monitoring PD, and the AAA produced in the third HLF in 2008. The five PD principles and the Survey, are emerging institutional frameworks orchestrated and driven by powerful actors, particularly the OECD DAC countries and IOs. In this institutionalized context, recipient countries are generally expected to accept and practice these codes in managing aid.

6.1 Episode One: Reluctance (2005–2008)

In this scenario, the state agency of Indonesia in the context of global aid becomes rather peculiar. Indonesia signed the PD in 2005 but decided not to participate in the first round of the Survey in 2006. Instead, Indonesia established the new Government Regulation No. 2/2006 on Managing Foreign Aid in an effort to institutionalise aid governance and promote aid effectiveness, without being directly involved in and accountable for the PD institutions. In 2007, the Consultative Group on Indonesia (CGI), the long-established donor coordination body, was dissolved by President SBY. The move was, however, widely welcomed by domestic media and CSOs. It was viewed as a symbolic event marking the growing independence of Indonesia as a state actor taking full ownership of its own development agenda.

How did Indonesia justify its actions in the sense that it joined the PD in 2005 and yet distanced itself from the actual institutional work prescribed and expected by the PD community? To address this question, one needs to consider the particular "recursive contingency" that the Indonesian state was facing. Such contingency existed because Indonesia was embedded in a situation where two sets of codes were established, namely the PD and the domestic codes. These were created to help to understand the state's challenges with aid governance reform and to justify its actions. The SBY administration signed the PD in acknowledgement of the importance of participating in the global aid agenda. However, it was also evident that Indonesia did not submit to the new institutional regime of the PD in 2006 by resisting the first-round Survey, since the SBY administration opted for the utilization of domestic institutions in the reform of aid governance. In fact, the turn to domestic institutional capacity building to manage aid resonated well the notion of 'independence', which was a historically powerful discourse that generates political credit. Indonesia has been a fast-recovering economy since the Crisis in 1997, and on-track to be recognized as a middle-income country, which meant that 'ownership' of its development agenda was essential for SBY.

The recursivity of contingency can be seen in the efforts of both the Indonesian state and the leading international actors of the PD to understand each other's positions, actions and intentions; and to try to reach an agreement on how to regulate this situation by modifying their policies without undermining the essential principles. There was rising criticism from the international community on the non-participatory behaviour of Indonesia. From Indonesia's perspective, too much criticism risked drifting its commitment, as SBY's cabinet was trying to avoid being seen as submitting to international pressure. Such recursivity was dramatized by an event in 2008 in which Indonesia took the U-turn decision to fully participate in the PD, promising to take the Survey, and to maintain relations with donors under AAA, including the establishment of a new AIMS that had been recommended by the PD and AAA. Given Indonesia's historical preference for independence and ownership, how did this become possible?

6.2   Episode Two: Compliance and AIMS (2009–2011)

The AAA in 2008 concluded with a supplementary provision to the PD, on the roles of the recipient government in building domestic institutional capacity. Specifically, the principles of 'ownership' settled and emphasized in AAA highlighted "stronger leadership on aid coordination and more use of country systems for aid delivery" [33]. The implementation of AAA was followed by a full Indonesian endorsement in 2009, during which SBY was re-elected and commenced his second term. In this period of 2008 to 2009, it is evident that the Indonesian state was actively shaping the agenda of aid governance by finding common ground with the leading actors of the PD as well as other emerging economies while attempting to secure the legitimacy to justify its preference for the domestic reform agenda, which emphasizes the discourse of 'independence' and 'international leadership'. In January 2009, Indonesia commissioned the Jakarta Commitment in an effort to implement the AAA principles on a national level. The A4DES was established to support the commitment *"to ensure that the government of Indonesia's institutions have the capacity to take full ownership and to lead the aid coordination and aid management processes"* (Jakarta Commitment).

The Indonesian AIMS was designed according to AAA principles and Jakarta Commitment in the hopes of better aid coordination and effectiveness. With financial support from GTZ, the AIMS was implemented in BAPPENAS and launched in June, 2010. The BAPPENAS managed AIMS, and led a series of stakeholder meetings and training workshops for data collection from donors. The system was used by donors and the government for completing the Online Survey in 2011. In the establishment of AIMS, we find the convergence of two distinctive codes of sense-making, if possible, whose meanings become simultaneously inscribed into the design of technological systems. The design and use of AIMS, and its attendant, serve to justify the legitimacy of the global aid agenda towards better coordination and effectiveness at the local government level, while strengthening 'stronger leadership' of the government. From the SBY administration's view, the AIMS served to endorse its political campaign for 'independence', while keeping its commitment to the PD process intact. Stability is temporally achieved by the state actor negotiating with other international leading actors on a common code for interpreting the contingency created by the institutional aid agenda.

6.3   Episode Three: Reshuffle (2012 – Present)

The year 2011–12 marked a paradigmatic shift in the institutional logic of aid governance [29]. The Fourth HLF in Busan, a year-long process of consultations and negotiations involving not only state actors and IOs, but also diverse stakeholders, resulted in the conclusion of the Busan Partnership Document with two significant changes. The first is the shift of focus from 'aid effectiveness' to 'development effectiveness,' namely, aid is just one of many development initiatives, such as trade and investment, where convergence is needed to create synergy. Another shift is the growing emphasis on the role of 'emerging powers' including CSOs, private sectors, and most importantly emerging non-DAC donors. These new shared understandings have become the logic of a new institutional arrangement, Global Partnership for Effective Development Cooperation (GPEDC), to be officially launched in 2014.

As the Chair of ASEAN, and the host of the South-South Cooperation High Level Meeting (Bali 2012), Indonesia saw an opportunity to promote its leading role in the global field of aid. During the first GPEDC meeting (Mexico City 2014), Indonesia became the Co-Chair of GPEDC along with the UK and Nigeria. As Indonesia become the leading actor in aid governance reform after 2011, the Indonesian AIMS became increasingly irrelevant in the changing environment characterized by new codification schemes to justify the legitimacy of aid governance, which stressed alignment with new codes such as 'aid heterogeneity' and 'emerging power'. The system was shut down in late 2012 with a part of databases moving to another unit that attempted to recycle its value for internal bureaucratic purposes for the South-South cooperation. During the process in which the international community searched for new sources of legitimacy to justify the institutionalization of aid governance, the state agency of Indonesia can be clearly seen as shaping the understandings of contingent situations while simultaneously being shaped by the same international context in which it participates.

7 Conclusion

In this paper, we argue that understanding the failure of AIMS in Indonesia requires a shift in focus from the project's local context to the recursive relationship between the global field of aid governance and the state agency. By tracing the historical context of AIMS in Indonesia, we identify a new source of contingency, as the structure-agency relationship between the macro global aid governance and Indonesia as a state which characterized by the enduring, contesting, negotiating, and collaborative relationship between the state actor and the institutional structures of aid, effectively justifies both the implementation and abandonment of the information system. Despite the fact that there had been substantial investment and coordinative efforts on the AIMS project, the eventual disuse and abandonment of AIMS is not attributable to anyone in particular. No stakeholder may be held justifiably responsible for adapting the system to the contingency caused by institutional changes in the global field of aid. Instead, all stakeholders were working together to define and implement a shifting consensus of aid governance characterized by the emerging powers and heterogenous aid partners.

This paper contributes to ICTD literature in two ways. Firstly, we shift the theorizing focus from the local to the macro contingency, which is characterized by the evolution of global aid institutions and the rising power of emerging states. Such a shift can engage ICT4D researchers in a direct critique of development discourses and international political economy. Avgerou (2008) called upon the ICTD field to develop *"the epistemological capacity to associate the study of IS innovation with the particular socioeconomic and policy rationale that provides its underlying justification and targets"*. Future research needs to further develop in-depth critical understandings on the power struggles, particularly how those emerging economies shape the global development agenda by strategically planning, designing, and implementing IS innovations. Secondly, we highlight the "recursivity" of contingent relations and interpretations in the context of developing country. Recursive contingency is particularly useful when IS failure occurs as part of the (de-)institutionalization process, where state actors have the agency of the reflexivity to choose alternative ways of understanding, rationalizing their situations, and justifying decisions with strategic intentions. Future research in ICTD can benefit by focusing on the "recursive contingency" in which the holistic view of actions in a field and the strategic agency [10, 16] to challenge and change the field structure, offer new ways of understanding failure in developing country. We believe the recursivity of relations between developing states and the global power structure of development will be an important aspect shaping ICTD in the coming decades.

References

1. Al-Jaghoub, S., Westrup, C.: Jordan and ICT-led development: towards a competition state? Inf. Technol. People **16**(1), 93–110 (2003)
2. Avgerou, C.: Information Systems and Global Diversity. Oxford (2002)
3. Avgerou, C., Walsham, G.: Information Technology in Context: Implementing Systems in the Developing World. Ashgate Publishing, Brookfield (2000)

4. Avgerou, C.: The significance of context in information systems and organizational change. Inf. Syst. J. **11**, 43–63 (2001)
5. Avgerou, C.: Information systems in developing countries: a critical research review. Journal of Information Technology **23**(3), 133–146 (2008)
6. Avila, R., Chak, S., Gomicki, J., Victor, K., Presley, S., et al.: Technology for Transparency: The Role of Technology and Citizen Media in Promoting Transparency, Accountability, and Civic Participation (2010)
7. Baark, E., Heeks, R.: Donor-funded information technology transfer projects: evaluating the life-cycle approach in Chinese science and technology projects. Inf. Technol. Dev. **8**(4), 185–197 (1999)
8. Bada, A.O.: Local adaptations to global trends: a study of an IT-based organizational change program in a Nigerian Bank. Inf. Soc. **18**(2), 77–86 (2002)
9. Bartley, T., Schneiberg, M.: Rationality and institutional contingency: the varying politics of economic regulation in the fire insurance industry. Sociol. Perspect. **45**(1), 47–79 (2002)
10. Bourdieu, P.: The Social Structures of the Economy (2005)
11. Deroy, X., Clegg, S.: Back in the USSR: introducing recursive contingency into institutional theory. Organ. Stud. **36**(1), 73–90 (2015)
12. DiMaggio, P.J., Powell, W.W.: The iron cage revisited: institutional isomorphism and collective rationality in organizational fields Paul J. DiMaggio; Walter W. Powell. Am. Sociol. Rev. **48**(2), 147–160 (1983)
13. Emirbayer, M., Mische, A.: What is agency? Am. J. Sociol. **103**(4), 962–1023 (1998)
14. Evans, P.B.: Indian informatics in the 1980s: the changing character of state involvement. World Dev. **20**(1), 1–18 (1992)
15. Flick, U.: An Introduction to Qualitative Research. Sage, London (2009)
16. Fligstein, N., McAdam, D.: Toward a general theory of strategic action fields. Sociol. Theory **29**(1), 1–26 (2011)
17. Ghosh, A., Kharas, H.: The Money Trail: Ranking Donor Transparency in Foreign Aid (2011)
18. Greenwood, R., Diaz, A.M., Li, S.X., Lorente, J.C.: The multiplicity of institutional logics and the heterogeneity of organizational responses. Organ. Sci. **21**(2), 521–539 (2010)
19. Greenwood, R., Raynard, M., Kodeih, F., Micelotta, E., Lounsbury, M.: Institutional complexity and organizational responses. Acad. Manag. Ann. **5**(1), 317–371 (2011)
20. Hayman, R.: From Rome to Accra via Kigali: "Aid Effectiveness" in Rwanda. Dev. Policy Rev. **27**(5), 581–599 (2009)
21. Heeks, R.: Information systems and developing countries: failure, success, and local improvisations. Inf. Soc. **18**(2), 101–112 (2002)
22. Hindley, D.: Foreign aid to indonesia and its political implications. Pac. Aff. **36**, 2 (1963)
23. Jaeger, P.T., Thopmson, K.M.: E-government around the world. Gov. Inf. Q. **20**, 389–394 (2003)
24. Krishna, S., Sahay, S., Walsham, G.: Managing cross-cultural issues in global software outsourcing. In: Information Systems Outsourcing: Enduring Themes, New Perspectives and Global Challenges (2006)
25. Lawrence, T., Suddaby, R., Leca, B.: Institutional work: actors and agency in Institutional Studies of Organizations. In: ASQ, pp. 673–677 (2010)
26. Maguire, S., Hardy, C., Lawrence, T.: Institutional entrepreneurship in emerging fields: HIV/AIDS treatment advocacy in Canada. Acad. Manag. J. **47**(5), 657–679 (2004)
27. Masiero, S.: Redesigning the indian food security system through e-governance: the case of Kerala. World Dev. **67**, 126–137 (2015)
28. Masyrafah, H., Mckeon, J.: Post-Tsunami Aid Effectiveness in Aceh: proliferation and coordination in reconstruction. Washington DC (2008)

29. Mawdsley, E., Savage, L., Kim, S.M.: A "post-aid world"? Paradigm shift in foreign aid and development cooperation at the 2011 Busan high level forum. Geogr. J. **180**(1), 27–38 (2014)
30. Moussa, A., Schware, R.: Informatics in Africa: lessons from world bank experience. World Dev. **20**(12), 1737–1752 (1992)
31. Moyo, D.: Dead Aid: Why Aid is not Working and How There is Another Way for Africa. Penguin, London (2008)
32. OECD: Paris Declaration on the Aid Effectiveness. Paris (2005)
33. OECD: The Paris Declaration on Aid Effectiveness and the Accra Agenda for Action. Paris (2008)
34. Park, K.R.: An analysis of aid information management systems (AIMS) in developing countries: explaining the last two decades. In: Proceedings of the 50th Hawaii International Conference on System Sciences (2017)
35. Ramalingam, B.: Aid on the edge of chaos. J. Chem. Inf. Model. **53**(9), 1689–1699 (2013)
36. Scott, W.R.: Institutions and organizations: ideas and interests (2008)
37. Sjösted, M.: Aid effectiveness and the paris declaration: a mismatch between ownership and result-based management? Public Adm. Dev. **33**, 2 (2013)
38. Thornton, P.H., Ocasio, W.: Institutional Logics (2005)
39. Walsham, G.: Interpreting Information Systems in Organizations. Wiley, New York (1993)
40. Wittemyer, R., Bailur, S., Anand, N., Park, K.R., Gigler, S.: New routes to governance. In: Closing the Feedback Loop: Can Technology Bridge the Accountability Gap? World Bank, Washington DC (2014)
41. WorldBank and InfoDev: Information and Communications for Development 2012: Maximizing Mobile (2012)
42. Yin, R.: Case Study Research: Design and Methods (2009)

Practices of Disease Surveillance and Response in Burkina Faso

Stine Loft Rasmussen[(✉)]

University of Oslo, Oslo, Norway
stinelra@student.matnat.uio.no

Abstract. Efforts to fight communicable diseases in Africa have been harmonized through the Integrated Disease Surveillance and Response (IDSR) framework. Following recent large outbreaks of SARS and Ebola further calls to strengthen disease surveillance and response, for example through information technology, are being made. To avoid parallel systems, data for IDSR is sought to be integrated into countries' existing electronic health information systems (HIS). As experiences in this area are still limited, studying existing practices of disease surveillance and response could serve as a prerequisite for providing such electronic support for IDSR. The paper engages in this question by applying a knowing-in-practice perspective to a case of disease surveillance and response in Burkina Faso. The findings suggest that disease surveillance and response can be conceptualized as two interrelated yet distinct practices; that of surveillance and that of response. Surveillance is being both sustained and developed through everyday practices. It is also similar to routine HIS data collection, and thus seems fairly straightforward to integrate in existing HIS. Response, on the other hand, is both more complex and less sustained in everyday practice due to low frequency and unpredictability of outbreaks. Providing electronic support for IDSR should focus on maintaining a link between surveillance and response, but it would require an IS design flexible enough to also accommodate for situations that are yet unknown.

Keywords: Disease surveillance and response · IDSR · HIS · Practice theory

1   Introduction

Healthy populations are one of the prerequisites for development. If a population is not healthy, it does not have the capability to engage in work, politics, social issues and other activities that all together generate development in a society, in an economic sense as well as in a human sense [1]. Through delivery of health services by health systems countries ensure healthy populations. Disease surveillance and response is a corner stone of any health system. It is concerned with acquiring and sharing of up to date information about potential cases of communicable diseases to be able to take the necessary actions to fight these diseases. In an African context WHO-AFRO have developed the Integrated Disease Surveillance and Response (IDSR) framework, which unites these two purposes of monitoring and public health action [2].

© IFIP International Federation for Information Processing 2017
Published by Springer International Publishing AG 2017. All Rights Reserved
J. Choudrie et al. (Eds.): ICT4D 2017, IFIP AICT 504, pp. 333–344, 2017.
DOI: 10.1007/978-3-319-59111-7_28

Recent large scale outbreaks have highlighted the importance of information gathering and sharing both on the events leading to the outbreak as well as evaluation of the response [3]. However, experiences so far with electronic support for disease surveillance and response are sparse [4] and have been mixed [5, 6]. In many countries data that supports monitoring and improvement of health systems is collected on a routinely basis often through electronic health information systems (HIS). As the main storage for health information, a well-functioning HIS could potentially play a critical role in disease surveillance and response.

Providing electronic support for strengthening of disease surveillance could lead to increased sharing of, and use of information for action. However, sharing of health information is likely to involve more than the technology, for example communication, knowledge management, learning and taking action [7]. It can be argued that in order for this to happen the HIS will have to correspond with the social structures surrounding it. Research in information systems (IS) has shown that this is a general issue when it comes to IS. To better understand the interplay between an IS and the social world it is a part of scholars have applied and further developed various practice theories. Practice theory is an umbrella term for several theories used to explain social change through the manifestation of knowledge into action facilitated by practice [8, 9]. An advantage is that it is an approach that is not individually oriented; instead it conceptualizes action as an endeavor dependent on its location, the actors, tools and practices that are part of it. When it comes to understanding disease surveillance and response, which is a collective and distributed task involving multiple stakeholders at a variety of organizational levels, it is likely that there is something to gain from using such a perspective. The paper seeks to contribute to the design for integration of IDSR into HIS by using a practice lens to better understand the distributed practice of disease surveillance and response in a country.

Through a case of the national health system in Burkina Faso the paper presents an analysis of the practices of disease surveillance and response. The paper is organized in the following way; first disease surveillance and response is outlined, second a theoretical lens based on structuration theory is discussed, and third the theoretical lens is applied to the empirical case. The paper concludes with a discussion on the complexities involved in providing electronic support for disease surveillance and response as well as the benefits and limitations of using a practice theory to understand this type of work and inform future design.

2 Disease Surveillance and Response

Disease surveillance and response is the work that goes into monitoring communicable diseases in order to identify new cases and to control the transmission of these diseases before they spread and develop into epidemics. Surveillance can be done in different ways but it is important that the resulting information is used for public health action [10].

Following severe outbreaks of largely preventable diseases in Africa in the 1990's, the member states of WHO AFRO in 1998 adopted the resolution on integrated disease surveillance and response (IDSR) as an approach to strengthen disease surveillance in [2, 10]. IDSR has many objectives [10], which are all essential, but those that are of most interest when it comes to HIS are the objectives to integrate multiple surveillance systems, improve the use of information, and improve the flow of surveillance information. More than 45 diseases are included in IDSR, but as the burden of diseases vary from country to country, each country defines its own specific list of priority diseases.

Although the IDSR guidelines have been adopted in many African countries [4], recent epidemics in West Africa have shown that there's still a need to improve disease surveillance and response in the region. When it comes to information sharing and communication in outbreaks it has been difficult to diagnose fast enough, to provide up to date and accurate information to the highest levels, to coordinate among the many actors involved in the response, and to inform populations about the protective measurements to take [11–13]. Also data on the effectiveness of the response could be strengthened [3].

3   Practice Theories and Structuration Theory

The IDSR framework focus on the streamlining of practices of surveillance and response and the integration of those practices across organizational and sectorial levels. Providing technological support for IDSR for example through an electronic HIS needs to take into account the various dimensions of these practices.

Designing IS to support increased knowledge sharing has often been challenging as having knowledge at hand might not being the same as being able to act [14]. Much early IS research built on the rather positivistic assumption that an IS would lead to the change they were designed to bring along. This assumption was challenged by empirical research which argued that technology is not independent of the social world it is part of; instead it is used in a variety of unforeseen ways, which leads to unpredicted changes, sometimes completely different from the desired or expected changes [15, 16]. In ICTD this has also been the case, and it has been described as a design-reality gap [17]. A challenge to both IS and ICTD research has thus been to understand the relationship between technology and the social world it is being used in. In IS studies researchers have been engaged in developing theoretical frameworks that can span both the technical and social aspects of technology as well as the change technology brings about [18, 19]. Since the 1980's different practice theories have been explored as a lens to bridge this gap [20, 21]. Practice theories have also been used in ICTD [22], but much research has been more oriented towards design and less unifying in their use of theory [23].

3.1   Agency, Structure and Practice

Practice theories are characterized by their focus on uniting thought and action rather than separating them [8, 24]. Structure and agency and their relationship of mutual constitution are central aspects of Giddens' structuration theory, which is one of the most adopted in the IS field [20, 21]. According to Giddens too much emphasis is often put on the structures in society and their potential to shape human action. Instead he argues that structures and agency are mutually interrelated because they influence and are influenced by each other through time and space [25]. To illustrate this interdependent relationship Giddens introduces the concept of duality, which describes a mutually constituting relationship between structure and agency, or knowing and doing.

Structures are the rules and resources that human agents draw on in social actions. To Giddens it is the institutions in society or a social context. The rules – but also more than that; They are not to be understood strictly as rules in for example a game, instead they are defined quite broadly as both social norms or habits, and can therefore be more or less subtle or outspoken [25]. Agency, or human action, is the capability of a person, or an agent, to act in social situations. This capability is both dependent on the knowledge, experience and motivation of the agent as well as the situation where the action occurs [25]. According to Giddens human agents are always knowledgeable but their actions very often have unintended consequences, which can result in an unconscious reproduction of the social system or structural properties of it.

Practice and organizational change is closely linked to knowledge as one key idea of practice theory is that knowledge or theory is inherent in action and that it is manifested in action [24, 26]. An often used example is that of riding a bike; it is hard to explain how to do it in theory but easy to do once you have learned it. This idea is also sometimes referred to as "knowing in practice" [8, 9]. Orlikowski [9] further defines it as knowing rather than knowledge and stresses how knowledgeability that is built through every day practices is a central aspect of distributed work. She further argues that:

> "... paying attention to organizational knowing might complement our understanding of organizational effectiveness by highlighting the essential role of situated action in constituting knowing in practice. In particular, we might learn some useful insights about capabilities if we also focus on what people do, and how they do it, rather than focusing primarily on infrastructure, objects, skills, or dispositions" [9, p. 271]

Disease surveillance and response is carried out by many people over time and space, and is an example of a distributed practice. It is a practice that relies on knowledge of what to do and how to do it. In this paper a knowing-in-practice perspective will be applied to understand the distributed practice of disease surveillance and response.

4   Method

The empirical material for the paper is drawn from a larger on-going qualitative study of health information use from the national HIS in Burkina Faso. As the aim of the research is to better understand the social structures around the IS, the research approach has been interpretive [27]. The study was conducted over a one-year involvement with the Ministry of Health in Burkina Faso, where the researcher was affiliated with the IT-department in the Ministry of Health. Data for this paper was mainly collected through 22 structured and semi-structured interviews, which focused on health information use and practices of disease surveillance and response (Table 1). Additional material was gathered through observations, participant observation, as well as documents, such as the IDSR guidelines, reporting templates and surveillance reports.

Table 1. Overview of fieldwork

Level	Organizational unit	Observations	No. of interviews
National	Office for the fight against diseases		Data manager
	Office for statistics		Director Statistician
	Office for health informatics	Participant observation	Director Data base administrator
Regional	Region A: Urban		Director of health programs Data manager (2 times)
	Region B: Rural/semi urban		Director Data manager
District	District A.1: Urban	Observations of daily work	Director Data manager
	District A.2: Urban	Observations of data entry	Data manager (2 times) Data manager assistant
	District B.1: Rural/semi urban		Data manager
Facility	Clinic B.1.1: Semi urban	Observations of data entry	Managing nurse 2 nurses Mid-wife
Other	Academic		Epidemiologist Previous district director
			Total: 22

A weakness of the study, which will be returned to in the discussion, is that while data collection was going on, there were no epidemics taking place. Thus there are no observations from an epidemical situation to support the statements given by the participants. To compensate for this weakness, participants were asked to describe their work during response with reference to a recent epidemic.

All interviews were recorded and transcribed for closer analytical examination. Themes regarding disease surveillance and response, practices and knowledge where extracted from the transcripts and the notes. In addition, data collection and data dissemination flows were mapped out based on the empirical material, which showed a difference between surveillance and response. This difference was further explored in a matrix-mapping where different aspects of practices were related to the different phases of disease surveillance and response.

5 The Case

Burkina Faso shares borders with six other West African countries but was not directly affected by the 2014–2015 Ebola epidemic. However, during the epidemic the alert level was high in the country and procedures for identifying and handling an eventual case of Ebola were integrated into the country-wide system for disease surveillance. Apart from the apparent threats from the Ebola epidemic, Burkina Faso is prone to suffering from outbreaks of meningitis, measles and malaria. In total 14 diseases or conditions are monitored on a weekly basis and the information is collected and transmitted from facilities (CSPS from "Centre de santé et de promotion sociale") to the district, regional and national level. There are 13 regions, 63 districts and approximately 1,650 CSPS [28].

In Burkina Faso the IDSR guidelines have been adopted into its own country-specific technical guidelines [29]. These guidelines contain detailed information for each disease on how to handle disease surveillance and response at each level throughout the health system. The public health sector, which is responsible for the delivery of the majority of health services, is also responsible for the administration of the national IDSR-guidelines.

6 Analysis of IDSR Practices

Many of the interviewees distinguished between before, during, and after and epidemic. The work practices and information needs in each of these phases are somewhat different. For the purpose of this analysis focus will only be on the work that takes place before and during epidemics, including the transition between these two phases.

6.1 Surveillance

During the pre-epidemic phase surveillance takes place. All interviewees described a clear, consistent, and well-organized process for the weekly routine surveillance. The managing nurses from the 1,650 CSPS across the country report weekly data to the district health data manager. Once all CSPS have reported in, the data is compiled and aggregated and sent, via e mail or phone, to the regional level. Here, the regional level data manager repeats the process of compilation but also checks data quality, before forwarding to the national level. These initial steps must take place by 10 am every Tuesday. The national office for the fight against diseases produces a national bulletin that is used at the weekly ministerial meeting and also circulated back to the regional and district offices and other relevant partners. Observations confirmed the workload that this process generated on Monday, Tuesdays and Wednesday each week. Data managers were often unavailable for appointments on these days, and where observation was done, there were a stream of visitors coming in with reports or phone calls to report in with data. All of this information had to be taken down by the data manager. For surveillance, the IDSR guidelines seem to have provided a structure, which is both known and embedded in the work practices concerned with gathering and sharing information on surveillance.

There is one standardized template that is used for the collection of data at all levels. For each disease, aggregate numbers of suspected cases, confirmed cases and deaths are collected. Such standardized tool helps to reinforce the structure of the guidelines. However, small variations of daily practice also help to maintain the structure and keep it functioning. For example, facilities far away from their district can transmit data via phone instead of the form. Similarly, a phone call could be made from districts to regions in case the internet was down. In this way the structure is shaped by adaptations based on the environment within which the daily practice of surveillance is taking place.

The information flow described above is very similar to the information flow for collection of routine health information. The main difference is that the IDSR data are collected on a weekly basis where the routine data are collected on a monthly basis. But in both cases it is the data managers under the supervision of the facility, district or regional directors who are the key persons managing and transmitting the information. During interviews and observations with these two groups of people, they all explained how they worked with surveillance based on recent experiences. This similarity to routine data collection provides an additional structure that further strengthens the practice of surveillance.

6.2   Response

Surveillance is done to inform response. Turning to the possible outcomes of surveillance they can roughly be grouped into the following three; no alerts resulting in surveillance going on as usual, an alert resulting in further investigation and control of the situation, or an alert turning into an outbreak.

According to interviewees a level of alert is reached if the notified suspected cases reach a certain threshold. These thresholds are specified in detail in the national IDSR guidelines, but generally speaking it could be a single suspected case of one of the very contagious diseases or a certain amount of cases for other diseases. When this happens, contact is made immediately by phone to the higher level in order to ensure prompt notification of the potential risk. If a suspected case is reported two actions are taken; case confirmation and site investigation. A specimen sample is send to the closest laboratory for confirmation and further analysis. The documentation of this work is done with a line list, which there is a standardized template for. Furthermore, an investigative team can be formed at district level if necessary. The role of such a team is to go to the site of the case to analyze the nature of the case, how many have potentially been effected, and what protective measures should be taken? The documentation of this work does not follow a strict standard.

The main differences from the collection of routine health information collection is that much more information is being collected, there are differences in information needs between the diseases, and it is not done on a routinely basis but rather every other month. Many of the interviewees had experience with this type of work for diseases, such as meningitis or measles, which would most often be the ones with cases that needed investigation. Again the structure of the national IDSR guidelines would shape the work on case investigation.

During the epidemic phase surveillance must still be done to monitor the development of the outbreak, however the response takes priority. The type of response is very dependent on the disease, but it could for instance be vaccination campaigns targeting vulnerable populations, awareness campaigns in communities carried out in collaboration with community resource persons, or deployment of specialized treatment centers. A certain challenge here is that contextual factors also influence which actions can be taken. When it comes to known diseases, the national guidelines are very clear on how to respond on each specific disease at each organizational level. But the decision on which type of response to do is based both on the guidelines, the spread of the disease, and the analysis of the situation at the specific site. Some action is taken based on routine while other action is taken based on the actual characteristics of the epidemic. Agency, as in the capacity to take action, is thus not only dependent on the structure provided by the guidelines, but also on unknown structures specific to the nature of the disease. The guidelines recognize this by being specific about how to do the site investigations, but there are no daily routines to reinforce this structure into daily practice or vice versa.

In both the two regions where the study took place actual large scale outbreaks appeared to be quite rare. When asked to describe how response was carried out by taking a recent outbreak as an example, all participants would answer that it had been a long time since there actually were an outbreak.

"Well, luckily we've not had epidemics. For a good period of time, we've not had an epidemic. Since I've been in this office, there has not been any."

(Regional health manager)

Also during the time spent on site there were no investigative team missions done, nor were there epidemics taking place in the two regions. Response thus appears to be a task that is not routinely performed. This means that although the country specific IDSR guidelines are well known and well adopted there are not many possibilities to exercise them when it comes to response. Although everyone throughout the health system seems to be well aware of what to do and how to it, routine and experience has not been built or tested.

6.3   Knowing-in-Practice

Disease surveillance and response go hand-in-hand, which is logical as surveillance is supposed to trigger response. However, from the case it appears to be important to also recognize that it indeed covers two different practices. The national IDSR guidelines can be seen as a structure for how to do both surveillance and response. Health care workers can rely on this structure to seek knowledge on how to perform this type of work. However, following Orlikowski's argument that knowledge is not the same as knowing, this might have consequences for the capacity to act based on the guidelines. The table below summarizes how the practices of surveillance and response differ (Table 2).

Table 2. Summary of practices

	Surveillance	Alert	Response
Knowledge of tasks and procedures	Well-defined and adopted for all priority diseases	Well-defined and adopted for outbreak prone diseases	Well-defined and adopted for outbreak prone diseases
Frequency	High Done on a routine basis before, and during an outbreak	Low Done when an alert level is reached	Very low Done during an outbreak
Knowing-in-practice	Easily obtained due to weekly procedures	Obtained to some extent due to bi-monthly alerts	Difficult to obtain due to low frequency of outbreaks

The knowledge created through surveillance, response and evaluation it is not the same type of knowledge. The objective of surveillance is to spot a potential threat in order to be able to roll out the recommended treatment for this threat if it is detected. This is a routine task that becomes integrated in the daily work and where knowing in practice of how to do it is built through everyday activities. In a response phase the objective is to understand the development of a beginning or ongoing outbreak of one disease, the factors that nourish it as well as the effect of the action taken to counter it. When it comes to well-known diseases, where small-scale outbreaks occur more often, the response is to some extent done on a routine basis. But in large-scale outbreaks or outbreaks in a region previously unaffected, there are more unknowns and a higher chance that things may develop in unexpected ways. This can lead to ad-hoc decisions and new non-standardized procedures. Knowing-in-practice only becomes enacted as the outbreak unfolds.

From a practice-based perspective which recognizes a duality between knowing and doing, disease surveillance and response inherits a challenging paradox; that you need to be prepared (know what to do) for something that does not occur on a routinely basis or – as in cases such as Ebola in West Africa – have never occurred before. This is a phenomenon that applies to many aspects of medical practice, such as for instance treatment of life-threatening conditions. In many cases applied medical knowledge is obtained through practical hands-on experience. But there are critical situations, such as heart attacks where it would be unethical to ask a new doctor to practice on the patient [30]. In such cases techniques such as clinical simulation or emergency drills might be used in order for health workers to obtain the skills and experience need to act in an urgent situation. In Burkina Faso one simulation had been done as preparation for an eventual Ebola outbreak, but for other types of outbreaks it is not prioritized due to lack of resources. This might potentially also affect HIS design as it might be difficult to design a system for a practice that is mainly described in guidelines and where experience from real-life situations has yet to be gained.

7 Discussion

The case discusses how national IDSR guidelines provides a standard for how disease surveillance and response is done in Burkina Faso. It is argued that the guidelines can be seen as the structure that defines and dominate agency through both standardization and contextualization of practice. However, the mutual reinforcing relationship between structure, as knowledge, and agency, as action, is stronger for surveillance than response. This seems to be due to the low frequency of outbreaks and the effects this has on the opportunities to practice response and thereby obtain knowing-in-practice.

This difference also has a methodological implication. For the same reasons that it is difficult to exercise response, it also becomes more complicated to study it and to get solid information on how it is done. Consequently, a recommendation for future research is to consider paying more attention to this challenge both in the framing of the study and in the research design.

The analysis further highlights that the practice of surveillance is very similar to routine data collection in a HIS, while the practice of response is not. As a consequence, response might be overlooked when strengthening disease surveillance and response through existing electronic HIS. Attention should thus be given to keeping the connection between surveillance and response in such work.

The main focus of the paper has been to make an empirical contribution to the understanding of IDSR as a domain of international interest, and to use concepts from practice theory to unfold this understanding. The practice-based perspective, has served as a useful lens to analyze the interplay between the guidelines and the actions health workers need to take action based on both the guidelines and the situation on the ground. It has worked better for assessing the structures in this interplay than the agency itself. This might be due to agency being more a difficult concept to address empirically. As it is within the action the potential for change lies, it could be interesting to explore this part of practice further in future studies. This could also potentially support the calls made within ICTD for strengthening the link with theories of development in order to better assess the consequences of the technology [22]. Structuration theory, has been criticized for not focusing sufficiently on technology itself [21]. In this case the analysis did not provide many leads as to how to improve a technical solution for IDSR strengthening. It is likely that this is due to the practice-lens being less technology focused and thus less strong as a prescriptive tool.

In spite of the practices of surveillance and response being different they should not be separated. With action being an inherent part of IDSR, future research and design strategies should rather focus on reinforcing the link between collecting data and using data for public health action in order to provide electronic support for the whole IDSR concept. This would, however, require a stronger focus on the response part of IDSR. In addition, it would require strategies for doing IS design flexibly enough to accommodate for situations that are yet unknown – which is especially critical when it comes to countering epidemics in environments where a disease, or a new strain of a disease, occur for the first time. If this is not done, design-reality gaps might persist, and future IS to support IDSR might not hold the ability to support a change towards improving health for all.

References

1. Nussbaum, M., Sen, A. (eds.): The Quality of Life. Oxford University Press, New York (1993)
2. CDC: Integrated Disease Surveillance and Response: What Is Integrated Disease Surveillance and Response (IDSR)? http://www.cdc.gov/globalhealth/healthprotection/idsr/what/index.html
3. Cancedda, C., Davis, S.M., Dierberg, K.L., Lascher, J., Kelly, J.D., Barrie, M.B., Koroma, A.P., George, P., Kamara, A.A., Marsh, R., Sumbuya, M.S., Nutt, C.T., Scott, K.W., Thomas, E., Bollbach, K., Sesay, A., Barrie, A., Barrera, E., Barron, K., Welch, J., Bhadelia, N., Frankfurter, R.G., Dahl, O.M., Das, S., Rollins, R.E., Eustis, B., Schwartz, A., Pertile, P., Pavlopoulos, I., Mayfield, A., Marsh, R.H., Dibba, Y., Kloepper, D., Hall, A., Huster, K., Grady, M., Spray, K., Walton, D.A., Daboh, F., Nally, C., James, S., Warren, G.S., Chang, J., Drasher, M., Lamin, G., Bangura, S., Miller, A.C., Michaelis, A.P., McBain, R., Broadhurst, M.J., Murray, M., Richardson, E.T., Philip, T., Gottlieb, G.L., Mukherjee, J.S., Farmer, P.E.: Strengthening health systems while responding to a health crisis: lessons learned by a nongovernmental organization during the Ebola virus disease epidemic in Sierra Leone. J. Infect. Dis. **214**(suppl_3), 153–163 (2016). doi:10.1093/infdis/jiw345
4. Phalkey, R.K., Yamamoto, S., Awate, P., Marx, M.: Challenges with the implementation of an Integrated Disease Surveillance and Response (IDSR) system: systematic review of the lessons learned. Health Policy Plan. **30**, 131–143 (2015). doi:10.1093/heapol/czt097
5. Adokiya, M.N., Awoonor-Williams, J.K., Barau, I.Y., Beiersmann, C., Mueller, O.: Evaluation of the integrated disease surveillance and response system for infectious diseases control in northern Ghana. BMC Public Health **15**, 75 (2015). doi:10.1186/s12889-015-1397-y
6. Lenaway, D.D., Perry, H., Fagan, R.: A conceptual strategy for strengthening eSurveillance in the African Region. Online J. Public Health Inform. **6**, e117 (2014). doi:10.5210/ojphi.v6i1.5009
7. Kelly, S., Noonan, C., Sahay, S.: Re-framing evidence-based public health: from scientific decision-making to occasioning conversations that matter. In: Proceedings of the 12th International Conference on Social Implications of Computers in Developing Countries, Ocho Rios, Jamaica, pp. 76–91 (2013)
8. Nicolini, D.: Practice as the Site of Knowing: Insights from the field of telemedicine. Organ. Sci. **22**, 602–620 (2010). doi:10.1287/orsc.1100.0556
9. Orlikowski, W.J.: Knowing in practice: enacting a collective capability in distributed organizing. Organ. Sci. **13**, 249–273 (2002). doi:10.1287/orsc.13.3.249.2776
10. Kasolo, F., Roungou, J.B., Perry, H.: Technical guidelines for integrated disease surveillance and response in the African Region. In: World Health Organization Regional Office for Africa Disease Prevention and Control Cluster Brazzaville, Republic of Congo and Centers for Disease Control and Prevention Center for Global Health Division of Public Health Systems and Workforce Development Atlanta, Georgia, USA, Atlanta and Brazzaville (2010)
11. Dahl, B.A., Kinzer, M.H., Raghunathan, P.L., Christie, A., De Cock, K.M., Mahoney, F., Bennett, S.D., Hersey, S., Morgan, O.W.: CDC's response to the 2014–2016 Ebola epidemic - Guinea, Liberia, and Sierra Leone. MMWR Suppl. **65**, 12–20 (2016). doi:10.15585/mmwr.su6503a3

12. Gostin, L.O., Friedman, E.A.: A retrospective and prospective analysis of the west African Ebola virus disease epidemic: robust national health systems at the foundation and an empowered WHO at the apex. Lancet **385**, 1902–1909 (2015). doi:10.1016/S0140-6736(15) 60644-4
13. Moon, S., Sridhar, D., Pate, M.A., Jha, A.K., Clinton, C., Delaunay, S., Edwin, V., Fallah, M., Fidler, D.P., Garrett, L., Goosby, E., Gostin, L.O., Heymann, D.L., Lee, K., Leung, G. M., Morrison, J.S., Saavedra, J., Tanner, M., Leigh, J.A., Hawkins, B., Woskie, L.R., Piot, P.: Will Ebola change the game? Ten essential reforms before the next pandemic. The report of the Harvard-LSHTM Independent Panel on the Global Response to Ebola. Lancet **386**, 2204–2221 (2015). doi:10.1016/S0140-6736(15)00946-0
14. Walsham, G.: Knowledge management: the benefits and limitations of computer systems. Eur. Manag. J. **19**, 599–608 (2001). doi:10.1016/S0263-2373(01)00085-8
15. Orlikowski, W.J.: Using technology and constituting structures: a practice lens for studying technology in organizations. Organ. Sci. **11**, 404–428 (2000). doi:10.1287/orsc.11.4.404. 14600
16. Suchman, L., Blomberg, J., Orr, J.E., Trigg, R.: Reconstructing technologies as social practice. Am. Behav. Sci. **43**, 392–408 (1999). doi:10.1177/00027649921955335
17. Heeks, R.: Health information systems: Failure, success and improvisation. Int. J. Med. Inf. **75**, 125–137 (2005). doi:10.1016/j.ijmedinf.2005.07.024
18. Orlikowski, W.J., Iacono, C.S.: Research commentary: desperately seeking the "IT" in IT research—a call to theorizing the IT artifact. Inf. Syst. Res. **12**, 121–134 (2001)
19. Robey, D., Boudreau, M.-C.: Accounting for the contradictory organizational consequences of information technology: Theoretical directions and methodological implications. Inf. Syst. Res. **10**, 167–185 (1999)
20. Jones, M.R., Karsten, H.: Giddens's structuration theory and information systems research. MIS Q. **32**, 127–157 (2008)
21. Nicolini, D.: Practice Theory, Work, and Organization: An Introduction. Oxford University Press, Oxford (2012)
22. Avgerou, C.: Discourses on ICT and development. Inf. Technol. Int. Dev. **6**, 1–18 (2010)
23. Heeks, R.: Theorizing ICT4D research. Inf. Technol. Int. Dev. **3**, 1–4 (2006)
24. Schmidt, K.: The concept of "Practice": what's the Point? In: Rossitto, C., Ciolfi, L., Martin, D., and Conein, B. (eds.) COOP 2014 - Proceedings of the 11th International Conference on the Design of Cooperative Systems, 27–30 May 2014, Nice (France), pp. 427–444. Springer International Publishing (2014). doi:10.1007/978-3-319-06498-7_26
25. Giddens, A.: The Constitution of Society: Outline of the Theory of Structuration. Polity Press, Cambridge (1984)
26. Feldman, M.S., Orlikowski, W.J.: Theorizing practice and practicing theory. Organ. Sci. **22**, 1240–1253 (2011). doi:10.1287/orsc.1100.0612
27. Walsham, G.: Interpretive case studies in IS research: nature and method. Eur. J. Inf. Syst. **4**, 74–81 (1995). doi:10.1057/ejis.1995.9
28. Ministere de la Santé Burkina Faso: Annuaire Statistique 2013 (2013)
29. Ministère de la Santé Burkina Faso, Organisation Mondiale de la Santé: Guide Technique Pour la Surveillance Intégrée de la Maladie et la Riposte au Burkina Faso: 1 à 8 Etapes de la Surveillance (2012)
30. Ziv, A., Wolpe, P.R., Small, S.D., Glick, S.: Simulation-based medical education: an ethical imperative. Simul. Healthc. J. Soc. Simul. Healthc. **1**, 252–256 (2006). doi:10.1097/01.SIH. 0000242724.08501.63

Design Science Research and Activity Theory in ICT4D: Developing a Socially Relevant ICT Platform for Elderly Women in Remote Rural South Africa

Ronel Smith[1,2] and Marita Turpin[2(✉)]

[1] CSIR Meraka Institute, Pretoria, South Africa
rsmith2@csir.co.za
[2] Department of Informatics, University of Pretoria, Pretoria, South Africa
marita.turpin@up.ac.za

Abstract. ICT4D projects in rural communities face many challenges to successful execution. These include the development of an ICT artifact which is suited to the needs of a specific community, as well as a complex socio-cultural context which can have unexpected impacts on an ICT4D project. In Mafarafara, a remote rural community in South Africa's Limpopo province, researchers who were using a Design Science Research framework to guide the development of an ICT platform recognized the importance and potential impact of unvoiced social and political issues. Managing these dynamics are important for not only a better understanding of the community, but also for the success and sustainability of the project. Activity theory is used to complement the DSRM to make these social aspects visible, thus contributing to the success of the project. Two examples of the socio-political dynamics are described using the activity theory concepts of tension and hierarchical activity.

Keywords: Design science research · Activity theory · ICT4D · South africa · Rural women · Empowerment

1 Introduction

Despite wide-spread acceptance that ICT4D is a socio-technical discipline, theories focusing on the acceptance and resistance of technology, and understanding technology adoption, still predominate ICT4D research [1, 2]. In a comprehensive classification of the theories used in ICT4D, Andersson and Hatakka [2] highlight that very few ICT4D researchers apply theories from outside the domain. In response, Andersson and Hatakka [2], and Karanasios [3] argue that ICT4D researchers should use theories which allow the focus to be placed on the social context, poverty reduction, and development. More use should be made of theories from other domains such as gender studies and education [2]. This would allow for an investigation of the relationship between technology, human activity, and development, aspects that are particularly relevant for this research project, which is aimed at providing elderly women in a

© IFIP International Federation for Information Processing 2017
Published by Springer International Publishing AG 2017. All Rights Reserved
J. Choudrie et al. (Eds.): ICT4D 2017, IFIP AICT 504, pp. 345–356, 2017.
DOI: 10.1007/978-3-319-59111-7_29

remote rural community in South Africa's Limpopo province with access to an ICT platform designed to meet their stated needs.

Within a case study context, this paper presents the theoretical framework which underpins a research project. It discusses how, the social and political dynamics of a remote rural community can be made visible and taken into account by applying activity theory within a design science research framework.

The Design Science Research Methodology (DSRM) formulated by Peffers, Tuunanen, Rothenberger and Chatterjee [4] provides the overall framework for the research project. Activity theory is simultaneously applied during each phase of the DSRM. Activity theory is used to make visible the relationships between the women, the ICT platform and the researchers, and to describe the social and political dynamics in the community. Activity theory is hence used to complement the DSRM by surfacing and emphasizing social aspects that are important, not only for better understanding of the community but also for the success and sustainability of the project. This study contributes to the theoretical body of knowledge in ICT4D by demonstrating how the combination of Design Science Research (DSR) and activity theory can lead to a more appropriate practice theory for ICT4D.

The theoretical framework of the study is the main focus of the paper. It proceeds with a discussion of DSR in the ICT4D domain, followed by a presentation of the case study. The role of activity theory in this research project and ICT4D is then explored. Finally, the paper discusses the theoretical framework that incorporates activity theory in the Design Science Research Methodology.

2 Design Science Research in ICT4D

2.1 Overview of Design Science Research

DSR is a creative problem solving methodology that focuses on creation and innovation with the purpose of changing "existing situations into preferred ones" [5–7]. DSR therefore creates a new reality, rather than attempting an explanation of the existing reality [5, 7]. Through its focus on problem solving, DSR aims to "produce and apply knowledge of tasks or situations in order to create" new, innovative and effective artifacts, rather than the creation of general theoretical knowledge [8]. The production of innovative new knowledge to solve a specific problem differentiates DSR from routine design [9]. DSR researchers value relevance, making a visible impact, creative problem solving, and efficient ways to accomplish the desired end result. Key criteria for the assessment of a DSR project pertains to questions of pragmatic validity (does the artifact produce the intended result and is it effective: does it work as it is supposed to) and practical relevance (does the artifact make a valuable contribution to solving a significant real-life problem) [10].

Various DSR frameworks have been developed since Simon published The Sciences of the Artificial in 1996. Concepts central to these frameworks focus on problem identification, the design and build of a prototype solution, evaluation and testing of the solution, and analysis and reflection.

DSR produces both tangible and intangible artifacts which includes constructs, models, methods, instantiations, and better theories [4, 8, 9].

Changes in the Information Systems (IS) domain over the past two decades have led to DSR becoming an established research methodology in IS. Various authors including Drechsler and Hevner [11], Goldkuhl and Lind [12], and Iivari [13] argue that DSR is appropriate for the IS domain because it addresses the centrality of the IT artefact in IS, lends increased legitimacy to the discipline's creative aspects, and increases the relevance of IS research.

2.2 Design Science Research in ICT4D

The application of DSR in ICT4D is a more recent, but evolving phenomenon. The synergies between ICT4D and DSR are discussed below.

ICT4D has been described as a "complex socio-technical activity in which the social and the technical negotiate and evolve together", to address "ill-structured and wicked problems" [14]. Wicked problems result from, amongst others, ill-defined environmental contexts, complex relationships, and a reliance on teamwork to deliver relevant and effective solutions [15]. As argued by Rittel and Webber [16], DSR is particularly suited to managing wicked problems.

Although firmly rooted in engineering, DSR is applicable in the ICT4D domain because it focuses on phenomena which result from the interaction of a social system (the elderly women) and a technical system (the ICT platform) [11, 17]. Drechsler and Hevner [11] recently proposed the addition of the fourth "change and impact" cycle to Hevner's Three-cycle view of DSR to allow the latter to better deal with the dynamic contexts in which DSR projects are conducted, as well as the impact of the introduction of an artifact within a context.

Pragmatic validity and utility is key in DSR [10]. Towards achieving these aims, DSR allows for the identification of a specific problem that is important to the community in which a development project is being executed; and for the development of a relevant, innovative solution. Validity and utility of the ICT4D intervention can address failure as a result of irrelevant solutions which are enforced from outside. Dearden, Light, Kanagwa and Rai [18] define the term "Technical ICTD", and call for innovation and adaptation of technologies to ensure that technical ICT research makes a positive contribution to development. In this context, and with ICT4D being a practical discipline, DSR is a suitable research methodology in the ICT4D domain [17].

3 Case Study

The aim of the research project was threefold: (1) with the women as co-creators, design an ICT platform adapted to suit the specific requirements of elderly rural women with respect to physical design, content and applications; (2) develop a framework aimed at improving the adoption of an ICT platform which can empower elderly women in a rural community in South Africa; and (3) gain an improved understanding of the role that ICTs can play in rural development.

The research project was operationalized through a DSR process consisting of three phases. The various aspects of the project were investigated through the use of case study research. As depicted in Fig. 2, the study followed an iterative process of designing, developing, testing and evaluating an ICT platform in a rural community with the active participation of the elderly women. To date, the three phases of the DSR process indicated in Fig. 2 have been completed while the analysis of data that were collected as part of the case study is ongoing.

3.1   The Situation of Elderly Rural Women in South Africa

Elderly rural women form the most deprived population group in South Africa [19, 20]. Apartheid, enduring patriarchal prejudice, discriminatory customary laws, and a dearth of initiatives aimed at their empowerment have conspired to leave these women in a dire situation [19, 21]. They are marginalized, mostly illiterate, isolated in their communities, and have extremely limited access to resources [20, 22]. Despite the mentioned disadvantages that elderly rural women face, and as a result of men working away from their communities, the women frequently care for a multi-generational household, with their R1,520 (just over $100) monthly old age grant as the only household income [20].

Empowering and improving the economic condition of rural women has been shown to have a positive multiplier effect which results in improved nutrition and health, as well as access to education for their family members [21, 23]. The prevailing majority opinion is that Information and Communication Technologies (ICTs) have an important role to play as vehicle through which rural women in particular can empower themselves economically and socially [24].

3.2   Mafarafara

The research project was conducted in Mafarafara, a small very remote rural community in the Greater Tubatse local municipality in South Africa's Limpopo province (see Fig. 1). The community is surrounded by mountains, and can only be reached by a 4 × 4 vehicle due to the poor condition of the access road that passes through the Tubatse river. The community is completely isolated when the river is in flood. There is limited and unreliable cell phone coverage. According to Mma C (Mma is a respectful form of address for elderly women), the project champion, there are 280 households with a population ranging between 1700 and 2000 people in Mafarafara [25]. The majority of families in Mafarafara survive on government grants and subsistence agriculture. The lack of infrastructure development has a severely negative impact on the community's quality of life in general, and on the elderly women in particular. Although there are connections for running water, water is not available because the main water pump was stolen. Pre-paid electricity was installed in a section of the community in October 2013. However, many houses have electricity sockets installed without access to electricity, and many inhabitants cannot afford to pay for electricity. Mafarafara still resides under the tribal chieftaincy tradition.

Fig. 1. Community centre where ICT platform is installed, and Mafarafara village

4   Activity Theory in ICT4D

4.1   Social and Political Dynamics

The project has been executed by the Council for Scientific and Industrial Research (CSIR) in South Africa. Their research team all have significant experience in various aspects of ICT4D, ranging from designing ICTs for remote rural areas, deploying technology projects in rural areas, and conducting various types of research in these communities. Particular attention was therefore paid to honoring local customs and acting accordingly.

To this end, the site visits were conducted by Sepedi (local language) speaking researchers. All focus group sessions and one-on-one interviews were conducted in Sepedi. The project lead (one of the authors) is English speaking, necessitating the transcription and translation of the Sepedi audio and video recordings to English before the data could be processed. Although debriefs were conducted after each site visit, an in-depth analysis of the transcriptions revealed complex social and political dynamics in the community—between the elderly women themselves, and between the women and the research team—the extent of which was not evident during the debriefing sessions. These dynamics, as well as the agency of the women, directly impact on the success of this project, and must be made visible and taken into account to ensure that the final artifact meets the DSR criteria for a successful project, namely validity and relevance. However, given its roots in engineering, DSR neglects the social aspects of the complex environments in which ICT4D initiatives are executed.

The need to make sense of these human dynamics in an ICT4D project leads Karanasios [3] and Hashim and Jones [26], amongst others, to argue for the suitability of activity theory in ICT4D because it provides the researcher with "a well-developed model of the dynamics of human activity" in developmental contexts [3].

4.2   Activity Theory

Activity theory, which is defined by Kaptelinin and Nardi [27] as a "general theoretical framework for the analysis of human and communal action in the world", can provide the structure for articulating and studying the social aspects highlighted above. Using Gregor [28], activity theory can be described as a theory for analysis, and for describing and studying design rather than as a theory for prediction.

In this research study, Engeström's [29] third generation activity theory is applied in the Design & Development and Demonstration activities of the DSRM. The belief that the "human mind emerges, exists, and can only be understood within the context of meaningful, goal-oriented, and socially determined interaction between human beings and their material environment" is foundational in activity theory. This interaction (activity) is socially and culturally determined. By emphasizing socio-cultural factors, the interaction between human actors and their environments, and the concept of tool mediation, activity theory can provide a suitable foundation for the Design & Development and Demonstration activities of this research project [27, 30].

The concept of tool mediation allows for a specific focus on people's interaction with each other and with artifacts [27]. In the context of Mafarafara, activity theory therefore allows the researchers to explore the relationships between the women themselves, the women and the ICT platform, as well as the relationship between the women and the researchers.

Activity theory is well established in the ICT4D domain, where it serves to highlight and frame the importance of the social and development aspects of ICT implementation and use [3, 27]. Activity theory provides researchers with a tool to describe and gain an understanding of the cultural, inter-personal, and ethnographic dimensions involved with the introduction of an ICT artifact to a community [3].

Karanasios [3], highlighting that activity theory is not excessively prescriptive, states that it can easily draw on or be used with or within other theories to produce deeper knowledge than would otherwise be the case. Accordingly, in this study, activity theory is used to complement the DSRM by providing a means to describe and understand the social and political dimensions of the social context that became evident during the study.

Due to space limitations, which preclude an in-depth discussion of the project as a whole, two examples are given where the application of activity theory makes visible the social and political dynamics. The first example illustrates the activity theory notion of tensions between components and the second illustrates the structure of human activity.

5   Theoretical Framework in This Project

This section discusses the theoretical framework underpinning the research study, and provides a short overview of how it should be applied. The third iteration of phase 2 of the DSRM is then used to illustrate the application of the framework in the Mafarafara case study by means of example stories.

Figure 2 describes the three phases of the DSRM, positions activity theory in the design & development, demonstrates activities of the three phases, and shows how the outputs of each phase are integrated towards the final artifacts.

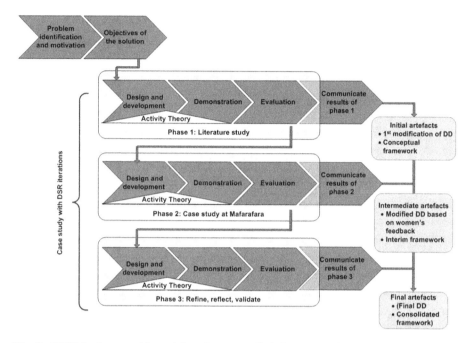

Fig. 2. DSRM phases with activity theory applied in the design & development and demonstration activities (adapted from Peffers, et al. [4] and Herselman and Botha [7])

5.1   Design Science Research Methodology

The six activities of the DSRM [4] in this project can be described as follows:

1. **Identify the problem and motivate why it should be addressed:** The problems that this research project seeks to address are the plight of elderly rural women and the low success rate of ICT4D initiatives.
2. **Define objectives of the solution**: The objective of the created artifacts are an improved success rate of ICT4D initiatives in rural areas; the design, development, testing and improvement of an ICT artifact for use by elderly rural women; and influencing government decision-making.
3. **Design and develop:** Design and develop various artifacts over three project phases, with three iterations in phase two. The learning from each iteration informs the following iteration towards finalization of the framework and ICT artifact.
4. **Demonstrate:** The created artifacts are demonstrated in the context of a case study. An iterative process is followed in Mafarafara.
5. **Evaluate**: Each iteration of the ICT artifact is evaluated by the elderly women participating in the research project. The final framework is evaluated by the women and by expert reviewers from the ICT4D and DSR domains. An internal review with members of the project team who conducted the site visits is further included.
6. **Communicate:** The results of this research project will be communicated through a PhD thesis, academic publications, project progress reports, and presentations to government departments.

5.2   Activity Theory: Making the Social and Political Dynamics Visible

Figure 3 is a graphical representation of the components of activity theory in this research project that will be used to make the social and political dynamics in the community visible after introduction of the ICT platform.

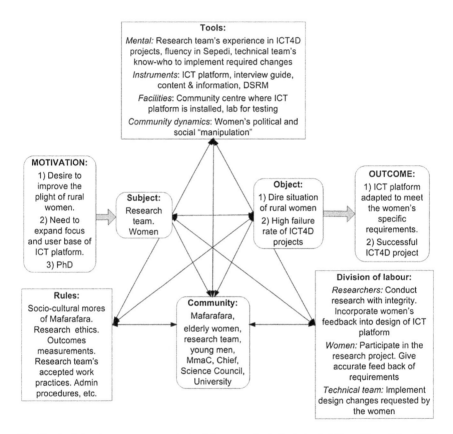

Fig. 3. Activity theory components in this research study (adapted from Engeström [31])

Example 1: Tensions between components of the activity systems
The purpose of the third site visit was to get feedback from the women about their experiences with the redesigned ICT platform. A number of the women stated that the CSIR should "reward" them for participating in the project. These comments highlight tensions between the tool of social dynamics that the women are utilizing to change their situation and the rules (ethics and good research practice) guiding the research process. Although the research team was not in a position to, for example, build a brick and mortar community centre for the women, they were able to ensure the women that their honest (even critical) feedback would not result in the project being cancelled and/or the ICT platform removed (Fig. 4).

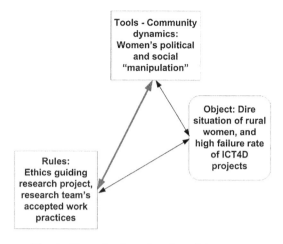

Fig. 4. Example of tensions in activity system

"Is there any other thing that CSIR is going to give us if we follow all the directions (sic) you gave us?"

"The CSIR should support us more because we have contributed our resources to this research. We've started our vegetable garden and have not been supported, and we have built our Centre (a mud room) and have not received any support to have a more concrete structure to secure the DD (Digital Doorway)."

Example 2: Hierarchical structure of human activity

Leontiev, recognizing that an activity can happen on several layers simultaneously, formulated the hierarchical structure of human activity, depicting how a subject can interact with a number of objects at the same time [3, 27]. In this hierarchy, activities are seen as being comprised of actions, which in turn are comprised of operations. These correspond to the concepts of motive, goals and conditions. Motives, the top level goal, can be equated to human needs and represent the objective of the whole activity [27]. Goals are the objects at which human activities are directed. A move down the hierarchy crosses the border between conscious and automatic processes. Operations do not have their own goals but rather provide an adjustment of actions to current situations. During the third site visit, Mma C told the research team the following:

"At this moment even if we know how to open the DD...we will not touch the machine because we were not given permission to open and close that machine...even if I can go to the centre as early as eight o-clock I do not open the machine, instead I just clean and continue with sewing or marking my register of the elderly women..."

This, and similar statements, reflect the feedback regarding usage provided to the research team. After several interviews during this and subsequent site visits, it became clear that the women want a big "handing over" ceremony where CSIR management

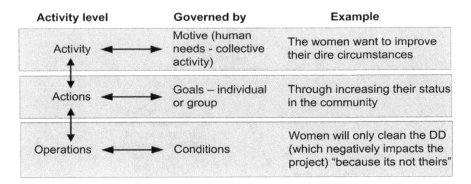

Fig. 5. Hierarchy of activities by women to improve their circumstances (adapted from Karanasios [3])

and representatives of government departments recognize them as "the owners" of the ICT platform, thereby conferring status on the women in front of the whole community. Figure 5 shows the hierarchy of activities with expected outcomes that the women employed.

6 Conclusion

Designing a fit-for-purpose ICT solution, which takes into account the unique socio-cultural context of a specific community is central to the success of ICT4D initiatives. DSR's requirements that an ICT artifact should have both utility and relevance, makes it an appropriate research methodology to inform the co-creation of the ICT platform with the elderly women of Mafarafara. However, as discussed DSR is not best suited to take cognizance of, and incorporate socio-political dynamics into the design process. The understanding of the unvoiced needs of the women, and their use of social and political 'manoeuvring' to meet these needs, gained through the use of activity theory, contribute to the success of the research project by decreasing the likelihood of failure.

This study contributes to the theoretical body of knowledge in ICT4D by demonstrating how Design Science Research (DSR) can be supplemented by the use of activity theory to lead to a more appropriate practice theory for ICT4D.

References

1. Zheng, Y.: ICT4D, overview of theories. In: Manswell, R., Ang, P.H. (eds.) The International Encyclopedia of Digital Communication and Society, pp. 1–10. Wiley, New Jersey (2015)
2. Andersson, A., Hatakka, M.: What are we doing? - Theories used in ICT4D research. In: IFIP Working Group 9.4 12th International Conference on Social Implications of Computers in Developing Countries, pp. 282–300, Ocho Rios, Jamaica, May 2013

3. Karanasios, S.: Framing ICT4D research using activity theory: a match between the ICT4D field and theory? [IFIP Special Issue] Inf. Technol. Int. Dev. **10**(2), 1–17 (2014)
4. Peffers, K., Tuunanen, T., Rothenberger, M.A., Chatterjee, S.: A design science research methodology for information systems research. J. Manag. Inf. Syst. **24**(3), 45–77 (2007)
5. Simon, H.A.: The Sciences of the Artificial. MIT press, Cambridge (1996)
6. Venable, J.R.: A framework for design science research activities. In: Khosrow-Pour, M. (ed.) Emerging Trends and Challenges in Information Technology Management, pp. 21–24. IDEA Group Publishing, Hersey PA (2006)
7. Herselman, M., Botha, A.: Designing and Implementing an Information Technology for Rural Education Development (ICT4RED) Initiative in a Resource Constrained Environment: Cofimvaba School District, Eastern Cape. South Africa. CSIR Meraka, Pretoria (2014)
8. March, S.T., Smith, G.F.: Design and natural science research on information technology. Decis. Support Syst. **15**(4), 251–266 (1995)
9. Vaishnavi, V.K., Kuechler, B.: Design Science Research in Information Systems (2015). http://desrist.org/desrist/content/design-science-research-in-information-systems.pdf. Accessed 30 April 2016
10. van Aken, J., Chandrasekaran, A., Halman, J.: Conducting and publishing design science research. J. Oper. Manag. **47**, 1–8 (2016)
11. Drechsler, A., Hevner, A.: A four-cycle model of is design science research: capturing the dynamic nature of IS artifact design. In: Parsons, J., Tuunanen, T., Venable, J.R., Helfert, M., Donnellan, B., Kenneally, J. (eds.) 11th International Conference on Design Science Research in Information Systems and Technology (DESRIST) 2016, St. John, Canada, 23–25 May, pp. 1–8 (2016)
12. Goldkuhl, G., Lind, M.: A multi-grounded design research process. In: Winter, R., Zhao, J. L., Aier, S. (eds.) Global Perspectives on Design Science Research. 5th International Conference, DESRIST 2010, pp. 45–60. Springer, St Gallen, Switzerland, June 2010
13. Iivari, J.: Twelve theses on design science research in information systems. In: Hevner, A., Chatterjee, S. (eds.) Design Research in Information Systems - Theory and Practice, vol. 22, pp. 43–62. Springer, New York (2010)
14. Dodson, L., Sterling, S.R., Bennett, J.K.: Considering failure: eight years of ITID research. In: Tongia, R., Subrahmanian, E. (eds.) Fifth International Conference on Information and Communication Technologies and Development (ICTD 2012), pp. 56–64. ACM, Atlanta, USA (2012), Tongia, R., Subrahmanian, E.: ICT for Development - a Design Challenge? IEEE/ACM International Conference on Information and Communication Technologies and Development, ICTD 2006, 25–26 May 2006, Berkeley, USA (2006)
15. Hevner, A., Chatterjee, S.: Design Research in Information Systems. Springer, New York (2010)
16. Rittel, H., Webber, M.: Planning problems are wicked problems. In: Cross, N. (ed.) Developments in Design Methodology, pp. 135–144. Wiley, New York (1984)
17. Iivari, J.: A paradigmatic analysis of information systems as a design science. Scandinavian J. Inf. Syst. **19**(2), 39–64 (2007)
18. Dearden, A., Light, A., Kanagwa, B., Rai, I.: Technical ICT research for development? Getting from Research to Practice. Mobile HCI 2010, 7–10 September 2010, Lisboa, Portugal (2010)
19. ANC Women's League: Women and Poverty - Discussion Document (2014). http://www.anc.org.za/docs/discus/2014/women_povertyj.pdf. Accessed 23 Aug 2016
20. Statistics South Africa: Social Profile of Vulnerable Groups 2002–2012. Statistics South Africa, Pretoria (2013)

21. Ozoemena, R.: Poverty Alleviation Strategies in South Africa: Creating Dignified Living for Women through Social Justice and Development (2010). http://www.consultancyafrica.com/index.php?option=com_content&view=article&id=526:poverty-alleviation-strategies-in-south-africa-creating-dignified-living-for-women-through-social-justice-and-development&catid=59:gender-issues-discussion-papers&Itemid=267. Accessed 7 April 2012

22. ILO: Global Employment Trends 2012. International Labour Organisation, Geneva (2012)

23. World Bank: World Development Report 2008 - Agriculture for Development. World Bank, Washington DC (2008)

24. Buskens, I.: Agency and reflexivity in ICT4D research: questioning women's options, poverty, and human development. Inf. Technol. Int. Dev. 6(Special Edition), 19–24 (2010)

25. Mma C.: Personal discussion RE: Demographics of Mafarafara (2014)

26. Hashim, N., Jones, M.L.: Activity theory: a framework for qualitative analysis. In: 4th International Qualitative Research Convention (QRC), 3–5 September, Malaysia (2007)

27. Kaptelinin, V., Nardi, B.A.: Acting with Technology: Activity Theory and Interaction Design. MIT Press, Cambridge (2006)

28. Gregor, S.: The nature of theory in information systems. MIS Q. 30(3), 611–642 (2006)

29. Engeström, Y.: Innovative learning in work teams: analysing cycles of knowledge creation in practice. In: Engeström, Y., Miettinen, R., Punamäki, R.L. (eds.) Perspectives on Activity Theory, pp. 377–406. Cambridge University Press, Cambridge (1999)

30. Ditsa, G.E.M., Davis, J.: Activity theory as a theoretical foundation for information systems research. In: Khosrowpour, M. (ed.) Information Resources Management Association International Conference, pp. 240–244. Idea Group Inc., Anchorage May 2000

31. Engeström, Y.: Activity theory as a framework for analyzing and redesigning work. Ergonomics 43(7), 960–974 (2000)

Agile Development

Building Capacity in Kenya's ICT Market Using Cross-Border Scrum Teams

Andy Haxby[1(✉)] and Rohit Lekhi[2]

[1] Competa IT bv, Rijswijk, The Netherlands
andy@competa.com
[2] University of Westminster, London, UK
http://www.competa.com

Abstract. This practitioner report outlines the nature of constraints to the development of ICT markets in Kenya, and identifies the cause of key market failures to grow domestic capacity. Results of an initiative to improve Kenyan ICT capacity though mentoring, international collaboration and the use of Agile project management methods are discussed. Based on findings from CodePamoja, a two-year collaboration between Dutch and Kenyan IT companies and the German government, the report explains how the use of cross-border Agile teams may align well to the objectives of those working in ICT4D.

Keywords: Agile · Scrum · Cross-border teams · ICT4D

1 Introduction

Kenya is at the forefront of the drive to harness ICTs to transform African economies and societies. Almost two-thirds of Kenya's population has access to the Internet; the country has a well-established network of incubators and start-up spaces as well as a legacy of high-profile successes such as mobile money platform M-Pesa. Much of what has been achieved to date is the result of a tertiary education system that produces graduates with good technical skills, and high-level commitment to the sector from within the Kenyan government, whose stated goal is to make Kenya "Africa's most globally-respected knowledge economy" by 2017. Despite these ambitions, a number of structural constraints limit the ability of Kenya's ICT sector to develop in line with international best practice. As a result, Kenya's capacity to grow its ICT market remains limited.

Constraints are largely the result of a market structure which fails to involve domestic capacity in fulfilling large-scale ICT projects, thereby preventing knowledge transfer especially Soft Skills such as team-work and Project Management. CodePamoja is a project to overcome these constraints and catalyse sector growth by providing the opportunities for knowledge transfer missing in the Kenyan market. The project has been demonstrably successful.

© IFIP International Federation for Information Processing 2017
Published by Springer International Publishing AG 2017. All Rights Reserved
J. Choudrie et al. (Eds.): ICT4D 2017, IFIP AICT 504, pp. 359–366, 2017.
DOI: 10.1007/978-3-319-59111-7_30

1.1 Scale in Kenya's ICT Market

The market for ICT services in Kenya is divided. One end of the market is driven by the needs of a small number of sizeable organisations requiring large-scale ICT services. Many ICT projects for organisations such as Safaricom and the Kenyan government have been too large and complex for local Kenyan companies to undertake. As a result these projects tend to be outsourced to partners typically in the USA or India [6]. This is at odds with the desire to award contracts to local Kenyan companies, and so an intermediate tier of Kenyan ICT companies has evolved to act as intermediaries between Kenyan customers and large international suppliers. Over time some of these companies have grown to be significant in terms of revenue and staff numbers, but still relatively weak in terms of the availability of technical skills. Effectively, the larger Kenyan ICT firms might be considered more as contract management firms and BPO facilitators than as pure-play ICT service providers. Outsourcing offers few opportunities for Kenyan staff to learn from more experienced peers, because work is undertaken overseas or by foreign staff working in Kenya for short periods and in isolation.

At the other end of the market are many small companies and "start-ups". In developed markets start-up companies are generally formed by people who have gained business experience in larger firms. This is not the case in Kenya where start-ups are typically formed by young graduates, often as a vehicle for freelancing. The people involved usually have exceptional technical skills but lack the management skills required to build successful businesses. Unsurprisingly many companies fail, usually blaming lack of seed funding whereas lack of management experience is often the real issue. Some small companies succeed in growing to employ tens of staff but further growth is constrained by failings in management structure and lack of project management skills, resulting in the inability to undertake more complex work. Attempts to perform larger projects results in failure, reinforcing the view that Kenya's domestic ICT market lacks the capacity to undertake larger-scale projects.

Between the large outsourced projects and the smaller service companies a capability and capacity gap exists, as shown in Fig. 1. Projects that fall in this gap are too small or low-budget to be outsourced, but too complex for local companies. As a result, many projects fail, or are not even contemplated. This is a critical problem for Kenya, especially given that many of the projects so constrained are in areas such as health and social improvement.

The outsourcing of large projects acts as a barrier to growth of the sector as a whole. Local firms lack contact with more experienced mentors and are unable to learn from involvement in larger projects. As a result a ceiling exists to their competence levels and they are effectively barred from participation in work at a higher level. This situation does not exist in developed markets where agile methods are used in large-scale development programmes [1]. For example, in the Netherlands a food-chain of subcontracting allows small companies and the staff who work for them to participate in larger projects alongside more experienced market actors, growing experience and capacity as they go.

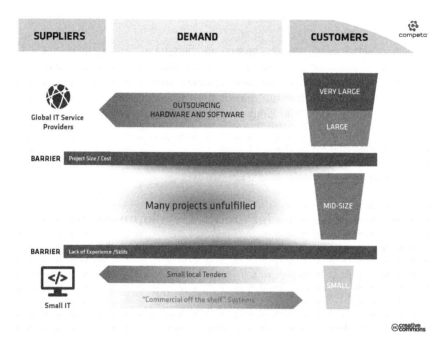

Fig. 1. IT market in Kenya

1.2 Capacity Building Strategies

Kenya needs to grow the ability of the local ICT companies in line with international best practice, in order that companies with locally-specific knowledge and pricing can support other sectors of the Kenyan economy with ICT services.

To date, efforts to grow local capacity have focused on the development of training facilities and tech hubs. Reputationally, hubs have proved to be important in raising Kenya's profile and have proved attractive to global ICT companies and aid donors looking for social venture focused projects (see, for example, Omidyar's support for iHub [2]). Nevertheless, despite the repetitional gains delivered by Kenya's tech hubs, growth of the sector is limited and the failure of the majority of ICT innovators to scale is a weakness in Kenya's ICT sector.

A Dutch/German/Kenyan initiative, CodePamoja ("CodeTogether" in Kiswahili) adopts an alternative approach, using international collaboration to provide the mentoring and knowledge transfer opportunities lacking in the Kenyan market. By giving Kenyan software developers the opportunity to work alongside Dutch professionals on real projects managed to international standards, CodePamoja provides the role-models and learning "food-chain" currently missing. Crucially, CodePamoja focuses on the use of Agile techniques such as Scrum to achieve results and deliver projects, rather than the purely technical aspects of ICT that have been the focus of many other training initiatives.

2   Methods

This is a practitioners report, based on first-hand experiences with the CodePamoja project over a two-year period from early 2015 to date. The report is substantiated with responses from more than 30 industry experts, policymakers and developers - in Kenya and internationally - who were interviewed and asked a range of questions about the Kenyan ICT market and how Kenya's potential in this key sector might be realised. These interviews were conducted as part of a study for the Dutch Government's Rijksdienst voor Ondernemend Nederland (Netherlands Enterprise Agency) internal report "Information & Communications Technologies in Kenya - A Market Study".

3   Evolution of the CodePamoja Development Model

3.1   Fair Trade Software

CodePamoja is a Fair Trade Software project. Fair Trade Software (FTS) is an economic model that aims to deliver high-quality and cost-effective software for corporate customers whilst simultaneously helping to grow knowledge economies in developing countries. By creating virtual teams with members in developing countries it is possible for software development services to meet Fair Trade criteria. Labelling software (such as corporate websites) produced in this manner with a Fair Trade label signals to end-users and consumers that societal needs are being addressed, adding value for all parties, as shown in Fig. 2.

Fig. 2. Fair trade software overview

A detailed explanation of FTS is outside the scope of this report but a key point to note is that the model focuses on capacity building and growth of local capability more than simply providing work to people in low income countries, as in the case of off-shore outsourcing. FTS is an example of Shared Value Creation, defined by Porter and Kramer [7] as creating economic value in a way that also creates value for society. The number of companies and organisations currently adopting the FTS model is small but growing. FTS is developed by non-profit organisation the Fair Trade Software Foundation, and the model is under continuous development.

3.2 CodePamoja

CodePamoja is an initiative to give graduates in the Netherlands and Kenya work experience which builds upon academic qualifications and prepares them for a career as an IT professional at an international standard. Working in small cross-border teams led by experienced professionals, participants get hands-on experience in Agile project management (Scrum). Skills and techniques learnt at CodePamoja increase employment prospects of attendees in both the Netherlands and Kenya, and also help seed and catalyse the adoption of international best working practices amongst the Kenyan firms that hire people from the CodePamoja programme. CodePamoja focuses on Scrum because this has been identified as the area where expertise in Kenya is lacking. An international software development working-environment is replicated as closely as possible, with projects for real customers in the EU or Kenya. There is no fixed course syllabus, agenda or duration, participants work in small teams with members of varying skills and experience, and team members join or leave at random times as in a real company. Team members may be physically located in Nairobi, Kenya or The Hague, Netherlands. The first successful project to be completed at Code-Pamoja was a portal for foreign exchange students at The Hague University of Applied Sciences, which is now in operation. In its second year CodePamoja has begun work on a larger project to develop the Enterprise Kenya portal for the Kenyan ICT Authority.

CodePamoja is jointly funded by Dutch firm Competa and the Federal German Government develoPPP.de program. The project is run by Competa in conjunction with Kenyan partners BTI Millman and DewCIS. CodePamoja's funding under current arrangements runs out in June 2017 and the aim is to make CodePamoja self-sufficient within this timeframe. The project demonstrates the viability of co-development in virtual teams both as a commercial proposition and also as a mechanism for ICT4D.

4   Key Findings and Implications

To date, CodePamoja has provided work experience for around 100 people. During this time the way teams have been organised has evolved from multiple Scrum teams split geographically, to virtual teams spanning different geographical locations. The reasons for this are described below.

4.1   Learning Scrum - Cross-Border Teams and Culture

Based on experiences in the Netherlands it was anticipated that developers participating in CodePamoja would quickly learn the Agile mindset. This proved more difficult than expected for two reasons. Firstly, was found to be almost impossible to teach Scrum academically and then build functioning teams from scratch - it is much easier for individuals to learn Scrum if they are immersed into existing fully-functioning teams. Secondly, there are cultural aspects that make Scrum difficult in Kenya. The Kenyan education system is highly competitive, with performance ranked individually. There are few team-based activities and people are encouraged to compete with other students. This culture of individual competition extends to society in general, making Scrum initially a rather alien way of working. It was observed that even when Agile ways of working were put in place, teams quickly fell back into Waterfall methods and non-Agile behaviour.

To overcome these problems CodePamoja implemented cross-border virtual teams, with at least one person from each location on every team. This proved highly effective in maintaining Agile behaviour, as more experienced Dutch team members acted as a check if Kenyan colleagues started to fall into Waterfall patterns of behaviour. Using Scrum in international projects is not unusual, but it is believed that cross-border virtual teams is a novel implementation as team members are usually in the same location.

Despite initial difficulties it was observed that once Kenyans become comfortable with team-based working they start to use Scrum to overcome cultural issues that can cause problems or barriers in the workplace. For example, it is culturally very difficult for Kenyan staff to ask management to address organisational problems such as lack of food facilities or non-performance of colleagues. However, within CodePamoja "the team" has been used as a way of separating complaint from individuals and presenting issues to management in a non-confrontational way, for example as an action point from a Scrum Retrospective.

4.2   Reputational Gains and Performance Enhancement

Companies involved in CodePamoja have leveraged the experience to win substantial new business and conduct socially important projects. BTI Millman beat established vendors from other countries including South Africa and the UK to win a contract to develop a CRM system for Barclays Bank Kenya. The ability to demonstrate knowledge of Agile project management to international standards played a crucial role in winning the contract. The system was deployed nationally with a user base of 900 members of staff in 120 branches. With the success of the Kenyan deployment, Barclays are planning to scale the application to the 9 other African markets. The impact of this project has been far-reaching for both Barclays and BTI Millman. Barclays are now able to provide a range of financial services to people who were previously unable to access such services. This results in a knock-on effect, benefitting other people and other economic sectors. Over the duration of the project BTI Millman has grown from 5 staff to 12 and tripled turnover. Thanks to improved reputation, the company has been invited to tender for other large projects and has attracted external investment.

DewCIS used experience gained through participation in CodePamoja to implement innovative and complex mobile health systems. Mobile implementation for Maternal, Newborn and Child Health (mPAMANECH) is a mobile app built for the African Population and Health Research Center. The app replaces numerous paper-based forms and allows integration of patient data from the community to health facilities for better referral and management of patients. The system has improved the reporting abilities of Community Health Volunteers (CHVs) and enhanced data quality with built-in data validation and verification. Following successful implementation the system was extended to include a decision support function, mobile Decision Support System (mDSS). Community Units are divisions for residents dwelling in the slum areas of Kamukunji Location, Nairobi County. Utilisation of the mDSS tool by the CHVs to screen expectant mothers and newborns improved the awareness of health danger signs by the CHVs, allowing them to provide advice or take action. The tool has also improved attendance of antenatal clinics by the mothers, leading to more deliveries in approved health facilities. The adoption of Scrum by DewCIS has resulted in a significant improvement in project delivery, and common problems with software development have been avoided. The company found that Scrum results in software that is properly tested and bug-fixed, giving projects a better chance of successful deployment and adoption. The company is now capable of executing more projects with significant local development impact.

4.3   Imitative Behaviour and Viral Improvement

More than a third of CodePamoja "graduates" found employment as a result of participation in the initiative, and many report using the techniques learned in their new jobs, and teaching others. Whilst it was expected that developers would learn Agile techniques and use these in work with other companies, it was not expected that this would spread into management layers or customer organisations. However, when CodePamoja started work on Enterprise Kenya it quickly became apparent that the customer did not have a clear view of project requirements and so were unable to create User Stories for the project. This led to a member of the government staff joining one of the Scrum teams, rapidly learning Scrum and adopting an Agile approach to dealing with stakeholders internally in the government. This has encouraged the Kenyan government to use Agile methods more widely.

5   Conclusion and Implications for ICT4D

People employed in software development in developing countries lack role models and opportunities to learn industry best practice. This is particularly true of skills such as project management which are difficult to learn in a academic setting and are typically acquired by imitating more experienced colleagues.

Lack of such opportunity seriously limits individuals personal ability, and the capacity of the organisations they work for.

There seem to be three conclusions to draw from CodePamoja. Firstly, whilst relocating experienced staff from locations such as the EU is neither practical nor cost-effective, significant advances can be made by creating virtual teams. This benefits people in developing countries who can build skills, and also those in developed countries who can be rewarded through cultural and social exchange.

Secondly, there is a good deal of agreement within the literature that what Haikin [4] refers to as the 'widespread failure of ICT4D projects' is the result of an over-reliance on top down, 'engineered' approaches to delivery (see also, [3,5,8]). It is demonstrably possible to adopt an Agile approach to the management of such projects which can potentially reduce the rates and impacts of failure.

Finally, the collaborative approach of cross-border Agile enables international best practice to be embedded within local structures of decision-making. This can greatly benefit ICT4D projects, where often the greatest challenge is to maintain the scalability and sustainability of a project after delivery. The successes of BTI Millman and DewCIS demonstrate that foreign involvement and knowledge sharing opportunities, particularly in the area of Agile project management, can trigger local improvements that achieve significant development goals.

References

1. Bass, J.M.: Artefacts and agile method tailoring in large-scale offshore software development programmes. Inf. Softw. Technol. **75**, 1–16. http://www.sciencedirect.com/science/article/pii/S0950584916300350
2. Colaço, J.: Nairobi: announcing funding from omidyar network. http://ihub.co.ke/blogs/5711
3. Dodson, L., Sterling, S.R., Bennett, J.K.: Considering failure: eight years of ITID research **9**(2), 19–34. http://itidjournal.org/index.php/itid/article/view/1050
4. Haikin, M.: Reflections on applying iterative and incremental software development methodologies (agile, RAD etc.) to aid and development work in developing countries. https://matthaikin.files.wordpress.com/2013/03/agile-blarticle-part-11.pdf
5. Hamel, J.-Y.: ICT4D and the human development and capability approach | human development reports. http://hdr.undp.org/en/content/ict4d-and-human-development-and-capability-approach
6. Herbsleb, J., Moitra, D.: Global software development. IEEE Softw. **18**(2), 16–20 (2001)
7. Porter, M.E., Kramer, M.R.: Creating shared value. https://hbr.org/2011/01/the-big-idea-creating-shared-value
8. Walton, M., Heeks, R.: Can a process approach improve ICT4d project success? http://www.gdi.manchester.ac.uk/research/publications/working-papers/di/di-wp47/

Agile Methods in Ethiopia: An Empirical Study

Zelalem Regassa[1], Julian M. Bass[2(✉)], and Dida Midekso[1]

[1] Addis Ababa University, Addis Ababa, Ethiopia
zelalem.regassa@aau.edu.et, mideksod@yahoo.com
[2] University of Salford, Salford, UK
j.bass@salford.ac.uk

Abstract. This paper provides empirical evidence of agile method adoption in smaller companies in Ethiopia. Agile methods are emerging as best practice for software development in the global north. So, is there evidence that agile methods are being used in Ethiopia? A Grounded Theory approach was adopted using face-to-face interviews with 17 software professionals from 7 software companies, which were selected by using a snowball sampling technique. The interviews were semi-structured and open-ended and have been audio-recorded and transcribed. Participants in the study identified the importance of agile principles, values and practices. Agile practices are used to address issues with requirements and to encourage user participation. However, it was discovered that the companies in the study were conducting software projects for government clients that mandate substantial documentation with elaborate staged approval procedures, using fixed price contracts with predefined delivery schedules.

1 Introduction

Software development has a key significance for developing countries to harness IT opportunities for their socio-economic growth [36]. In particular, the development of local software industry can provide a number of opportunities for developing countries of Africa [23]. By utilizing the relatively low cost base in Africa, it can create economic growth through export earnings and it can provide employment opportunities for the increasing number of skilled graduates. Moreover, locally developed software is a lot cheaper and can better address the unique contextual requirements of developing countries than software from external sources.

In recent years, agile methods have emerged as an alternative potential solution to problems of information system development [37]. The overall principles underpinning the agile approaches emphasizes individuals and interactions over processes and tools; working software over comprehensive documentation; customer collaboration over contract negotiation; and responding to change over following a plan. Agile methods belong to the latest class of iterative and evolutionary software processes [10]. Agile methods employ 'short iterative cycles,

© IFIP International Federation for Information Processing 2017
Published by Springer International Publishing AG 2017. All Rights Reserved
J. Choudrie et al. (Eds.): ICT4D 2017, IFIP AICT 504, pp. 367–378, 2017.
DOI: 10.1007/978-3-319-59111-7_31

actively involve users to establish, prioritize, and verify requirements, and rely on a team's tacit knowledge as opposed to documentation' [11]. The significance human and social factors for the success of information system development are at the centre of agile methodologies. As a consequence, agile methods increase flexibility in the face of evolving requirements, improve productivity, and enhance product quality [20].

There is a paucity of research literature on agile information system development in the global south and previous studies have been dominated by researchers from the global north. There is lack of empirical data on information system development practices by African software companies. Comparatively little is known about how African companies develop information systems and what challenges they face during software development. This paper contributes to filling this gap.

The structure of this paper has four sections. Section 1 presents the introduction. In Sect. 2, previous studies have been discussed. Sections 3 and 4 present the research method and research finding respectively. Sections 5 and 6 provide discussion and conclusion of the paper respectively.

2   Related Work

Agile methods have been proposed as a project management technique for minimising risk of project failure and enhancing flexibility prior to deployment [19]. There is evidence that agile methods can improve both product quality and development productivity [20].

Iterative and incremental development approaches emerged in the 1980s and in the 1990s evolved into agile methods [28], such as Extreme Programming [8] and Scrum [32]. There is a trend away from wholesale adoption of XP practices [18], towards adoption of scrum [4]. Scrum comprises a product owner [6], scrum master [5] and self-organising development team [25].

In general, software development project success can be defined in terms of Quality, Scope, Time, and Cost. Project success can be influences by organisational, people, process and technical factors. The three main critical success factors of agile software development projects are: delivery strategy, agile software engineering techniques, and team capability [16].

Agile methods are adopted by software development organisations in a series of assimilation stages [37]. Agile method tailoring, which involves selecting methods or practices depending on local context [13], has become well documented [21]. Smaller companies tend to 'cherry-pick' selected Scrum and XP practices from the full constellation of practices available [17].

Agile requirement engineering practices can be used to address challenges with customer involvement and cross-functional teams introducing new approaches to requirements management and requirements review sessions [26]. Scrum practices are used in conjunction with more conventional software development practices in large-scale business information system development [7].

For developing countries the importance of local context and involvement of local stakeholders during the implementation of systems has been stressed [29] and should consider the social, cultural and technical context [9]. Participatory involvement of end-users is a challenge in both global south [12] and for SMEs using agile methods in the north [24]. As introduction of technology to a new local context can involve cultural transfer and mutual learning, local practices need to be understood and valued [3].

Nigerian software companies, for example, typically have 11–50 staff with an average average work experience of one to five years [33]. Most customers are from domestic private service sector and companies had an average of 12 projects with a duration of six months. Companies commonly use in-house tailored software development methods. System developers need to employ development approaches that consider the resource constrained environment and matches local culture [27]. Further, there is a lack of awareness of agile methods [1].

In Sri Lanka, while there is growing interest in agile, team members find it difficult to take responsibility for their work [31]. Hierarchical management approaches are deeply entrenched, posing challenges for self-organising team creation.

3   Methods

The objective of this research was to explore the practice of information systems development by software firms in Ethiopia. To achieve this, the Grounded Theory methodology has been employed. The GT method is a qualitative research method that seeks to develop theory that is grounded in data systematically gathered and analyzed [22]. The use of the method was considered relevant for this research as it enables deep understanding of a phenomenon or process in a unique context [22]. There is lack of literature on information system development by software companies in Ethiopia. This makes the local context unique to information system research and the use of the GT method relevant.

3.1   Research Sites

This study investigated seven software companies from a population of IT service providers operating in Ethiopia's capital city Addis Ababa. Ethiopia was the world's fastest growing economy in 2014 (10.3%) [35]. The participating companies are small having less than 20 employees to work on development activities except one with around 30 development professionals. The companies' years of experience ranges from 5 to 20 years. Companies A and B have been in the industry for around 14 to 20 years.

The younger companies such as Company D, Company E and F were founded by former employees of the older ones like Companies A, B and C. There are also people who have worked in two or more of the companies in this study. The majority of the companies work on automation of external services and internal business process of different public sector organizations. They mainly involve development of payroll, accounting, finance and human resource information systems. Information systems developed for public services involve systems for tax payment, billing, court management and business licensing. Companies develop systems from scratch and/or customize previously developed systems to the requirements of a new client. Some of the companies are market driven; they develop, market and sell systems to selected private businesses.

3.2 Data Collection

The research used audio-recorded, open-ended semi structured interviews with 17 software practitioners, as shown in Table 1. The interviews were conducted in a combination of Amharic and English. The interviews were then translated, where necessary and transcribed in English. An interview guide was developed based on the software development lifecycle. The interview questions asked focused on the development process used and challenges faced, as shown in Appendix 1. The average length of interviews was one hour. During the interviews, probing questions were used to explore relevant topics raised by participants. The snowball sampling technique was used to recruit participants for interviews.

3.3 Data Analysis

To analyse the interview data, the grounded theory method has been employed [22]. The GT method enables the emergence of theory from data that can explain the study phenomenon in a particular situation. Data analysis in Straussian GT has three coding steps namely open, axial, and selective coding [34]. Open coding was performed to identify key points and concepts in the data. Axial coding was performed to identify the relationships among concepts. Finally, selective coding was conducted to discover the major categories of concepts. Memoing was used to collate information about each major category, bringing together quotations and concepts to form each element of the grounded theory.

Table 1. Software company and participant details

Company	Participant job title	No. of interviews	Contract type
A	Chief Technology Officer Manager	2	Bespoke Development
B	Chief Technology Manager Operations Manager Programmer	3	Bespoke Development
C	Manager Programmer	2	Bespoke Development
D	Manager Programmer	1	Bespoke Development
E	Senior Programmer/Manager Senior Programmer	2	Bespoke Development
F	CEO[a] Architect	2	Bespoke Development
G	Manager Scrum Master Programmer	5	Outsourcing

[a]CEO, Chief Executive Officer

4   Findings

The grounded theory analysis has resulted in the identification of conceptual categories that emerged from the data which describe the agile practices used, the context in which they are used, their use benefits and challenges of using them by small companies in this research.

4.1   Using Agile Methods

Most participants from different companies in this study claimed to use agile methods on projects. This has been described by using terms such as "we internally develop the software agile way" (Chief Technology Officer, Company A); "we do the work agile way" (Chief Technical Manager, Company B); "we use an agile process internally" (Developer and manager, Company D), "our process is the agile-Scrum method" (Manager and Programmer, Company C). In Company F we observed a full implementation of the Scrum method. Agile methods are used because of the perception that they provide solutions to challenges commonly experienced by the software development companies in the study. By using agile practices, the companies are able to improve requirements elicitation by involving users and quickly constructing product features. It is also perceived that following the waterfall approach cannot work in the existing development context where requirements are vague and user participation is limited. Documentation has little or no importance for the actual development of software due to frequent requirements changes resulting from lack of users knowledge and their limited participation during development.

Iterative and Incremental Processes. The majority of organizations in this study use iterative and incremental development practices as part of their agile processes. Multiple iterations are conducted during requirement elicitation for each module of the system and the modules are developed incrementally. Chief Technical Officer from Company B, for example, stated that "Each of our teams iteratively collect requirements for the assigned software modules and develop them incrementally". Chief Technology officer from Company A has pointed out, "Iteration is important as we can repeatedly develop prototypes and we use them to clarify requirements by involving users during our frequent visit." In Company D, the iterative and incremental approach has been used after software design has been completed:

> "after completing the design phase, we try as much as possible to make the development iterative and incremental which is release or build based. We conduct iteration release demonstration every month" (Manager and Programmer, Company D).

Release/Prototype Demonstration. During the iterative and incremental process, release demonstrations are provided to validate and enrich user requirements. The release demonstrations are performed weekly, monthly as in Company

C and D respectively or as required by the development team, which is the case in company B. Release demonstrations are used to enrich and complete requirements based on user feedbacks. They are used for internal purpose; otherwise, product delivery is done on the final release. A participant has pointed out

> "during the monthly project reports, we were also providing release demonstrations to the client representatives. They then tell us what new features to include and which ones to exclude" (Senior Programmer and Manager, Company E).

Face to Face Communication. The companies in this study organise frequent internal meetings of team members and external meetings with customers. In companies A, C and G, they have daily team meetings. The Chief Technology Officer from Company A stated that:

> "each of our development teams conduct a 10 to 15 min meeting as their first activity of the day. During this meeting, the team discusses their progress, problems and challenges faced, they also share experience and learn from each other this is a good practice we picked from the Scrum method we have also weekly meeting with all teams as our ISO standard process requirement."

However, in contrast, the Chief Technical Manager from Company B stated, "we do not need daily team meeting as each team is collocated but we have weekly meeting of all teams." The meetings are used as a platform to discuss progress and challenges. They are also used to enable learning from each other.

Working Software. Working software has a number of advantages for organizations. It enables early understanding of requirements, to monitor if the project is on the right track and meet schedule. By showing something functional to customers, it is possible to motivate them to participate and provide quick feedbacks. Manager and Programmer from Company E emphasized, "our milestone is producing a working module that is acceptable by our customer." Chief Technical Manager from Company B stressed, "we want a method that is product focused; provides the opportunity to start the actual development as quickly or early as possible."

User Involvement and Customer Management. Involving users is a common challenge for the companies working on government projects in this study. To address this challenge, the software companies in this research use frequent product feature demonstrations to involve users and collect requirements. Companies A, E and F also have dedicated teams working on client sites. The Manager and Programmer from Company E stated that "we have a customer relations management team which is a technical team working at our customer site with the user to identify variations we should accommodate in our system." There are also practices of setting up client representatives separately for technical and management people as in Company D for example.

4.2   Contract Challenges

Participants have identified bureaucracy in government organizations and the tender and contract nature as major barriers to companies use of agile methods and success of projects. Government contracts mandate formal documentation and milestone phase delivery. The contract award criteria are based on the least bid/tender cost and the project schedules are fixed and very short. (Chief Technical Manager, Company B; Manager and Programmer, Company C; Chief Technology Officer, Company A).

> "Our big challenges are [government] project tender/bid procedure and contract requirements. We are forced to follow the waterfall cycle, we should produce inception, analysis and design documents based on fixed schedule... project schedules are commonly four to six months" (Chief Technology Officer, Company A).

4.3   Issues of User Involvement, Requirement and the Waterfall Method

There is a common problem of shortage of user involvement particularly for government projects. Users are not interested in the project, they are not reachable and they believe software project is not their responsibility. Participants believe that following the waterfall process results in failure mainly due to the difficulty of getting clear and complete requirement during early stage of the project in one short phase. There is also limited or shortage of user involvement and they lack knowledge and understanding of software requirement and have difficulty of describing their requirements. Manager and Programmer from Company D has pointed out that "users understand their requirement at implementation." It has also been indicated, "if you follow the waterfall cycle only, you know you will fail... Users start to ask for new and different features at UAT [user acceptance test]. At the end of the day, no one will be willing to sign off the project" (Chief Technology Officer, Company A). On the importance of documentation, Chief Technical Manager from Company B has mentioned, "you should accommodate documentation for payment purpose." Participant indicated the problem of using agile methods stating, "if you purely follow agile you will get no money. So you try to mix them [agile with waterfall]..." (Chief Technology Officer, Company A).

In summary, this research has shown that small companies in the study are working on government projects; they are using agile practices with documentations; there are a number of situational issues affecting the use of agile practices by companies. The next section discussion on how the findings of this research can relate to previous studies.

5   Discussion

Our study participants largely agree with practitioners from the global north that 'frequent delivery of working software', 'daily interaction between business people and developers', and 'face-to-face communication' are the most important features of agile methods [15]. Most of our study participants stated that increment demonstrations have helped them to manage incomplete and evolving requirements, which they believe would have been difficult or impossible using the waterfall methodology.

Agile requirements engineering employs an iterative approach and intensive face to face communication with customers to improve requirement understandability and completeness [14,26]. In addition, prototyping and release demonstration have also been used by companies in our study to support requirement elicitation [16]. However, in our study, product delivery is done at the end while software construction or customization may begin at early development stage with frequent feature demonstration for user feedback.

Lack of user participation has been identified as the major barrier to organizations use of agile requirement engineering practices [14]. Participants in our research try to address a lack of user participation by using frequent product feature demonstrations and having teams work at the customer site.

It has been argued that formal documentation of requirements does not eliminate the need for frequent communication [14]. However, the stringent requirement for extensive documentation imposed by government projects in our study has been identified as a major challenge. Most participants in the current research believe that using agile with documentation is costly and time consuming as it creates repetition of work.

Tailored approaches that mix agile practices with plan-based approaches have been observed in many organizations [7,21]. Those studies provide evidence of pragmatic approaches to process tailoring. Paradoxically, participants in this research perceive that there are extreme differences between agile and waterfall approaches. Despite constraints placed on participating software companies, for example by bureaucratic government clients, participants tended to adopt a somewhat dogmatic view of the differences between agile and plan-based approaches.

Agile methods can be used to improve job satisfaction, productivity, and increased customer satisfaction while its success requires focusing on individual and social issues [19]. The findings of our research indicated that agile use enable companies to improve participation of customers and manage requirements through release demonstration. Cross functional teams also improve team motivation by providing team autonomy. This in turn can improve staff retention in a labour market with pronounced shortages of skilled people.

Though agile methods are believed to be particularly applicable to small software companies [19], our results indicate that they are finding adoption of the method difficult. Government demands for extensive documentation and reporting requirements impose a barrier to agile procurement adoption in the U.S. [30]. Participants in our study believe that agile conflicts with contracts that have milestone and extensive documentation requirements. Critical success factors for agile use [16] hold for the companies in our study too. For example, they do not have personnel to fill all agile roles. The findings of our research also suggest that there are gaps in practically using agile practices in the study organizations regardless of the widespread perception of the method importance.

Successful agile adoption for larger projects requires a disciplined approach [2]. However, scrum related roles, ceremonies and artefacts are missing from the methods adopted by companies in our study because of a lack of staff and finance as well as the lack of capacity more generally in the local context.

6 Conclusions

This research has investigated software development by smaller software companies in sub-Saharan Africa. The research has adopted the grounded theory method to analyse audio-recorded semi structured interview data collected from 17 participants from 7 software companies in Addis Ababa, Ethiopia, which were recruited using the snowball sampling technique.

Our findings focus on three main areas: agile practices used in small companies, the type of projects they use them on, the benefits and barriers of using agile. Software companies use agile methods to address development problems that can arise if they follow the waterfall process. Iterative methods, which provide the opportunity to work closely with users, enable vendors to get valid and complete requirements from clients. During each iteration, continuous tests and demonstrations of working software earn customers' trust, encouraging their participation in projects and managing their expectations.

By using agile methods companies are trying to create motivated and cohesive teams by allowing them to be self-managed and self-organized. Frequent team meetings create a platform to share experience, collaborate and reflect on the challenges they face. Companies in our study have strong focus on starting software construction earlier in the development process. Participants in our study do not give much attention and importance to documentation and yet are often obliged to produce extensive documentation to comply with government contract terms.

This study makes three main contributions to literature on information system development in sub-Saharan Africa. First, the research discovered that there is a widespread awareness and use of agile practices. Participants have stressed that the focus on working software enabled companies to motivate user involvement, improve requirement understanding, gain customer trust and get market to their product. Moreover, companies believe that agile use enables retention as a result of motivation from the autonomy it provides to the team; it also provides the opportunity to have cross-functional team. The barriers to companies use of agile practices on government projects have also been identified.

Second, it is interesting that companies in this study are working on government projects. Such projects have fixed price contracts with a pre-determined delivery schedule and formal document approvals.

Third, the study has shown the barriers to the practical use of agile method to the level required in companies. We have provided empirical evidence on how agile adoption by companies can be influenced by the nature of contract, nature of client, user involvement, shortage of finance and skill.

Further research is required on how agile methodologies can be tailored for use in a developing country context, for example investigating how agile practices are mixed with plan-based approaches in African and other developing countries.

Appendix 1 - Illustrative Interview Guide

1. Please tell me about yourself: your educational and professional background, years of experience and your role at your company.
2. Can you please tell me about your interesting development projects? What are your roles and responsibilities in those projects?
3. What are the team size and duration of the projects?
4. What software development processes and practices do you use in your company?
5. How do you collaborate/communicate with team members, managers and customers?
   (a) How frequently (weeks, months) do meetings take place between team members, customers and management?
6. What artefacts/project specifications and documents (for e.g. requirement, design, user) do you produce or use during software development?
7. What project guidelines or standards do you have or use at your company for: coding, communication, design, testing and documentation etc.
8. What difficulties do you face in carrying out your project responsibilities?
   (a) In relation to teamwork
   (b) In relation to software development process used at your organization
   (c) In relation to organizational management
   (d) In relation to customers
9. How do these difficulties or issues influence successful completion of software projects?
10. What improvements do you recommend on the areas of difficulties?
11. Is there anything that you think we should have discussed?

References

1. Akinnuwesi, B.A., Uzoka, F.M., Olabiyisi, S.O., Omidiora, E.O., Fiddi, P.: An empirical analysis of end-user participation in software development projects in a developing country context. Electron. J. Inf. Syst. Developing Countries (EJISDC) **58**(6), 1–25 (2013)
2. Ambler, S.W., Lines, M.: Disciplined Agile Delivery: A Practitioner's Guide to Agile Software Delivery in the Enterprise. IBM Press, New York (2012)
3. Bada, A.O.: Local adaptations to global trends: a study of an IT-based organizational change program in a Nigerian Bank. Inf. Soc. **18**(2), 77–86 (2002)
4. Bass, J.M.: Influences on agile practice tailoring in enterprise software development. In: Agile India, pp. 1–9. IEEE, Bangalore, February 2012
5. Bass, J.M.: Scrum master activities: process tailoring in large enterprise projects. In: 2014 IEEE 9th International Conference on Global Software Engineering (ICGSE), pp. 6–15, August 2014

6. Bass, J.M.: How product owner teams scale agile methods to large distributed enterprises. Empirical Software Eng. **20**(6), 1525–1557 (2015)
7. Bass, J.M.: Artefacts and agile method tailoring in large-scale offshore software development programmes. Inf. Softw. Technol. **75**, 1–16 (2016)
8. Beck, K.: Extreme Programming Explained: Embrace Change. Addison Wesley, Upper Saddle River (2004)
9. Blake, E., Tucker, W.: Socially Aware Software Engineering for the Developing World. In: Cunningham, P., Cunningham, M. (eds.) Proceedings IST-Africa 2006. Pretoria, South Africa (2006)
10. Boehm, B.: Some future trends and implications for systems and software engineering processes. Syst. Eng. **9**(1), 1–19 (2006)
11. Boehm, B., Turner, R.: Management challenges to implementing agile processes in traditional development organizations. IEEE Softw. **22**(5), 30–39 (2005)
12. Akinnuwesi, B.A., Uzoka, F.-M., Olabiyisi, S.O., Omidiora, E.O., Fiddi, P.: An empirical analysis of end-user participation in software development projects in a developing country context. Electron. J. Inf. Syst. Developing Countries (EJISDC) **58**(6), 1–25 (2013)
13. Campanelli, A.S., Parreiras, F.S.: Agile methods tailoring a systematic literature review. J. Syst. Softw. **110**, 85–100 (2015). http://www.sciencedirect.com/science/article/pii/S0164121215001843
14. Cao, L., Ramesh, B.: Agile requirements engineering practices: an empirical study. IEEE Softw. **25**(1), 60–67 (2008)
15. de Cesare, S., Lycett, M., Macredie, R.D., Patel, C., Paul, R.: Examining perceptions of agility in software development practice. Commun. ACM **53**(6), 126–130 (2010)
16. Chow, T., Cao, D.B.: A survey study of critical success factors in agile software projects. J. Syst. Softw. **81**(6), 961–971 (2008)
17. Clutterbuck, P., Rowlands, T., Seamons, O.: A case study of SME web application development effectiveness via agile methods. Electron. J. Inf. Syst. Eval. **12**(1), 13–26 (2009). www.ejise.com
18. Conboy, K., Fitzgerald, B.: Method and developer characteristics for effective agile method tailoring: a study of XP expert opinion. ACM Trans. Softw. Eng. Methodol. **20**(1), 1–30 (2010)
19. Dybå, T., Dingsøyr, T.: Empirical studies of agile software development: a systematic review. Inf. Softw. Technol. **50**(910), 833–859 (2008)
20. Dybå, T., Dingsøyr, T.: What do we know about agile software development? IEEE Softw. **26**(5), 6–9 (2009)
21. Fitzgerald, B., Hartnett, G., Conboy, K.: Customising agile methods to software practices at Intel Shannon. Eur. J. Inf. Syst. **15**(2), 200–213 (2006)
22. Glaser, B.G., Strauss, A.L.: Discovery of Grounded Theory: Strategies for Qualitative Research. Aldine, Chicago (1967)
23. Heeks, R.: Building software industries in africa. Inf. Technol. Developing Countries **6**(4), 5–7 (1996)
24. Hoda, R., Noble, J., Marshall, S.: The impact of inadequate customer involvement on self-organizing agile teams. Inf. Softw. Technol. **53**(5), 521–534 (2011)
25. Hoda, R., Noble, J., Marshall, S.: Self-organizing roles on agile software development teams. IEEE Trans. Software Eng. **39**(3), 422–444 (2013)
26. Inayat, I., Salim, S.S., Marczak, S., Daneva, M., Shamshirband, S.: A systematic literature review on agile requirements engineering practices and challenges. Comput. Hum. Behav. **51**(Part B), 915–929 (2015)

27. Korpela, M., Soriyan, H., Olufokunbi, K., Mursu, A.: Made-in-Nigeria systems development methodologies: an action research project in the health sector. In: Information Technology in Context: Studies from the Perspective of Developing Countries, pp. 134–152 (2000)
28. Larman, C., Basili, V.: Iterative and incremental development: a brief history. IEEE Comput. **36**(6), 47–56 (2003)
29. Macome, E.: On the implementation of an information system in the mozambican context. In: Korpela, M., Montealegre, R., Poulymenakou, A. (eds.) Organizational Information Systems in the Context of Globalization, pp. 169–184. No. 126 in IFIP The International Federation for Information Processing. Springer, New York (2003)
30. Mergel, I.: Agile innovation management in government: a research agenda. Gov. Inf. Q. **33**(3), 516–523 (2016)
31. Safwan, M., Thavarajah, G., Vijayarajah, N., Senduran, K., Manawadu, C.: An empirical study of agile software development methodologies: a Sri Lankan perspective. Int. J. Comput. Appl. **84**(8), 1–17 (2013)
32. Schwaber, K., Beedle, M.: Agile Software Development with Scrum. Prentice Hall, Upper Saddle River (2002)
33. Soriyan, H.A., Heeks, R.: A Profile of Nigeria's Software Industry. Technical Report 21, University of Manchester, Global Development Institute, Manchester (2004). http://www.gdi.manchester.ac.uk/research/publications/working-papers/di/di-wp.21/
34. Strauss, A., Corbin, J.: Basics of Qualitative Research: Techniques and Procedures for Developing Grounded Theory. SAGE Publications Inc., Thousand Oaks (1998). 2nd revised edition
35. United Nations Economic Commission for Africa: Greening Africa's Industrialization: Economic Report on Africa 2016. Technical report, Addis Ababa, Ethiopia (2016). http://www.uneca.org/publications/economic-report-africa-2016
36. UNTAD: Information Economy Report 2012. http://unctad.org/en/pages/PublicationWebflyer.aspx?publicationid=271. Accessed 30 Oct 2016
37. Wang, X., Conboy, K., Pikkarainen, M.: Assimilation of agile practices in use. Inf. Syst. J. **22**(6), 435–455 (2012)

Indigenous and Local Community Grounded ICT Developments

Deriving Engagement Protocols Within Community-Based Co-design Projects in Namibia

Gereon Koch Kapuire[1(✉)], Heike Winschiers-Theophilus[1],
and Margot Brereton[2]

[1] Namibia University of Science and Technology, Windhoek, Namibia
{gkapuire,hwinschiers}@nust.na
[2] Queensland University of Technology, Brisbane, Australia
m.brereton@qut.edu.au

Abstract. Indigenous Knowledge (IK) is used by community members for survival in the rural context and to sustain their way of living. The procedures on how community members share their knowledge amongst themselves and with others are unique. Cultural practices communication protocols differ from mainstream research and technology development procedures. Thus appropriate community engagement is instrumental towards the success of technology co-design with communities. Co-design endeavors should be framed in consistent and harmonized partnerships between community members and researchers for mutual learning and benefit. However, this has not been formulated as an objective of many ICT endeavors with communities in the past. With a raising number of interaction challenges reported we are reviewing our own community design experiences and promoting the development of an engagement protocol.

Keywords: Community engagement · Co-design · Mutual learning · Protocols · Participatory design · Reciprocity · Indigenous knowledge

1 Introduction

Engagements with rural communities have become a central theme in ICT4D, community technology design and related fields. It has been established that contributions from Communities is vital to develop relevant solutions and therefore researchers should partner and work cooperatively with community members [20, 27, 31]. However, researcher-community collaborations have reportedly faced numerous challenges which need urgent resolution at a conceptual and practical level, in order to ensure successful and sustainable co-operations.

Thus, the paper draws upon related work and our interaction efforts with rural communities to co-design technologies. The various projects with different communities throughout Namibia are clarified and challenges encountered described, as a starting point. We have further involved communities into focus group discussions to guide further steps in the development of engagement protocols. We argue that for a

J. Choudrie et al. (Eds.): ICT4D 2017, IFIP AICT 504, pp. 381–393, 2017.
DOI: 10.1007/978-3-319-59111-7_32

long-term collaboration, engagement protocols must be developed jointly and a commitment of engagement beyond singular projects should be strived for.

2 Background

We have embarked in ICT research with a number of different rural communities in Namibia. Various ICT projects have taken off to explore the co-design of technologies with community members as an attempt to preserve traditional and indigenous knowledge. We describe the successful collaboration work to the fact that we involve community members in all activities of the research and development process, including later dissemination of results.

2.1 Theoretical and Methodological Grounding

Our community collaborations in Namibia are theoretically framed in the concepts of Ubuntu and Afrocentricity [35]. Ubuntu stresses principles of humanness in interactions, while Afrocentricity frames research activities and ethics [16]. We have adopted a Community-Based Co-Design (CBCD) approach which is grounded in principles of participatory design and action research [1, 34]. CBCD takes place within a communal value system and opens up a new debate around the principles of participation and its benefits within HCI4D and ICTD projects [16]. The co-design methods allowed community members to be actively involved in design of tools and services. This promoted appropriate engagement and participation, creating trust between researchers and community members as a basis for a good continuous collaboration.

2.2 Engagement

Our research visits to the rural communities were overseen by engagement protocols. This is the way we enter the community, communicate, requesting for permission to conduct research, and participation by the communities. During every research trip, our first encounter was to get the community members interested in the research activities. It was important as community members leave their daily activities to partake in the research endeavors.

Rural communities are defined by many community members so the briefing for the purpose of the visit was handled in a focus group. The focus group encouraged community members explore ideas to create a common understanding amongst themselves, as well as with the researchers. This created harmony between the community members and the researchers. The introduction was way back when the project started. Even when the project matured, this process never changed. It has been an instrument to get proper engagement. It was crucial as there were different agendas at every technology intervention. Once community members were comfortable, only then technology and co-design sessions started. This was determined by the acceptance of the introduction.

This establishment allowed researchers and community members to create a partnership of trust. Part of the process to get engagement, was to explain to the communities about their duty as co-designers. Even though the concept of co-designing was difficult to understand at earlier stages of project interventions, with many engagements it became a term familiar to them later on.

Once a mutual understanding was met, a platform for interactions opened up. It was important to get community members interact by practically being engaged. This ensured the voice of communities to be heard when involved in technological interventions with researchers. Technology developments and research was based on reciprocity and consensus thereby enriching the outcomes.

Furthermore, the native and external researchers had appropriate structures to follow, which supported a fruitful and successful collaboration with the communities. The native researchers bridged the gap between the community and the external researchers [16]. The native researcher used familiar analogies to get the underlying ideas across [35], as the culture was familiar.

During years of project work, a number of researchers have been part of the projects. Some leave a project, with new members joining, and some were continuously part of the project. This allowed community members to engage with old and new researchers. At times, they asked about the members who are no more part of the project. At every occasion, a native researcher always explained to the community members about the whereabouts of the others researchers in case they are not present. This was done to keep community members value their previous engagement sessions.

2.3   Challenges in Engagements

Based on current community collaborations, we observed that many newly joining researchers first lack the skills and knowledge to be able to build, develop and maintain a good relationship with the communities [35]. Equally the community has not developed strong mechanisms of expressing their own set of rules and regulations of appropriate interactions. While on the one hand researchers often lacked an understanding of contextual factors such as culture, on the other hand communities have not expressed explicit codes of ethics. Moreover, current codes of ethics developed in the academic research context foster a researcher-community power relation which is unacceptable and undesirable in a co-design collaboration research project.

At one workshop, a teacher raised a concern during an IK content uploading session. Teachers pointed out that trust is one of their main worries when collecting knowledge from the community members, sometimes due to political reasons.

Furthermore, some international researchers visited the country and engaged community members without the awareness of a local researcher. During a research visit, they promised things to the rural communities, and then suddenly disappeared once they were done collecting their research data. This created frustration when the local team visited the communities, as there were unsolved expectations by the community members. It caused distrust in the engagement process.

2.4   Towards an Engagement Framework

As our main aim is to co-design technologies with the community members, we strived to promote reciprocity. Communities are well informed on how their IK will be joining an information sharing society. And as such, our endeavors were influenced on how the community members participate in the co-design sessions. Thus, we aimed to strengthen our collaboration through harmonized participation. This was important as it ensured the voice of the community members to be heard. The challenges allowed us to inquire solution on how best to integrate new researchers into a community, and how best the community members can win from the research being undertaken in the community. We seek to systematically analyze our lessons learnt over the years in order to formalize a community engagement framework to guide further technology co-design processes.

3   Literature on Related Work

3.1   Community Engagement

Community engagement is the process of involving rural community members in active ICT research being conducted in their communities by researchers. It is a core element for researchers seeking for research output, to place themselves properly in the rural communities. [29] adds that an effective collaborative design entails designers and communities co-creating their own applicable tools. Thus, in order for strong community engagement to be built, [20] urge that ways be found to ensure all voices of the community are heard when involved in a research project. [33] states that to make sure that community members understand how ICT is effective in their local context their voices must be found and heard. The use of ICTs for community development opens possibilities for voices to be exercised [30]. If your voice is heard, it evaluates to a democratic communication which creates openness and recognition [7]. [34] urges researchers and communities to jointly define and negotiate their situated approach to participation and interaction around the technology co-design process.

3.2   Community Values

In a local context, values and protocols frame participation [36, 37]. [16] added that user interactions are driven by communal values. We consider humanness as a set of values guiding community-based interactions [16]. In order to comply with local ethics, humanness is practiced by involving community members in research agendas in a respectful manner [17]. Other collaboration values that have reoccurred in the literature are trust, respect, and reciprocity.

Trust is crucial, as [19] advised, with a community based project they had, the designs were determined by the community. [27] mentioned an example about a research project with an Arctic community that they have a common consensus in the process which developed from a mutual trust. When mutual understanding is achieved in the community based research, [19] stress that community members accept researchers easily into their setup. To have proper community collaboration, the AIATSIS (Australian institute of Aboriginal and Torres Strait Islander studies) [11] elaborates that during a research commitment session, the community members and researchers are equal partners.

Furthermore, our relationship as researchers with any community is to strive for reciprocity [2]. [3] argue that the notion of reciprocity can lead to sustainable designs, valid research, and profound innovation (2014). This determination is based on respect as communities can decide to participate in research if they feel like it [4]. [3] added that reciprocity constructs joint trust, commitment and benefit. Even the AIATSIS [11] comment that research is significant when there is reciprocity between the community members and researchers. To nurture collaboration values, [23] mentioned reciprocity between the researchers and participants based on an Afrocentric paradigm. Thus, [14] state that a partnership between the researchers and community members must be formed, and that mutual learning gets ensured when strategies are developed with the community partners [8].

3.3   Challenges

Some researchers do not respect cultural norms due to the unknown rural community they are placed at. Even if it's intentional or not, the failure to respect cultural norms is a concern as it leads to conflict, and increases negativity in engagements [35]. Working with rural communities, challenges such as unmet expectation by the community members is visible especially when the agenda is not well explained at start of project.

In most cases researchers want to speak and think for community members especially new researchers embarking research in a community. [28] urge that community members should speak for themselves. If what they are expecting or thinking is not spoken, long term engagement will not be sustainable.

3.4   Formalizations of Collaboration

[20] suggest that researchers and the community can share decision making when they develop a code of research ethics. According to [27] there is an ethical obligation by researchers to engage with the community members as they are part of the research focus. An MOU approach is a strategy proposed by [14] which addresses rules of engagement between researchers and community members. It is not an easy task to engage communities due to cultural differences which increases fear of participation by community members [8]. Another ethical challenge comes when responsibilities are being shared when all research partners are gathered together [12]. [20] emphasizes that community members must be protected, as well as researchers having guidelines, thus, all research requires ethical guidelines. Vulnerable community members should not be oppressed, and should get a chance to receive benefits of the research outcomes [5]. So this makes it vital to identify ethical goals by involving the communities in the approval [6]. If consensus is not met new ethical goals and guidelines need to be developed [4].

Once their voice is heard, freedom for the community members to claim their own IK is created. This ensures that their ideas and opinions raised is shared and protected. [21] best described that community ownership of data prevents potential misuse of the results during the research journey, or even after the research is finished. To identify protections ensuring the safety of the community members, consultation efforts should be designed and conducted [6].

In most research projects data is collected and kept by the researchers, and returned to the community members for getting permission on how the data is disseminated [20]. Taking back the data is vital, as community members get informed about the status of the project, and can guarantee their results are correct [27]. [27] add that this creates a platform for feedback about the research by the community members. It also makes the community members share a common understanding about the aims of the research [11].

[19] founded an approach to facilitate the exchange of knowledge between rural communities and researchers using a participatory rural appraisal. [14] presented a structure for establishing effective community research partnerships which is useful when implemented prior to formulation of the research design. To test the relevance of the structures members facilitated the discussions [14]. [26] introduced a participatory poverty assessment method that they developed which showcased the participation of poor men and women. [14] conducted workshops for researchers and community as a tool for effectively establishing community research partnerships.

Hence, various attempts have been made to create frameworks which try to engage community members in research. For example, [9] developed a framework as a Canadian initiative, which allows decisions be made by communities involved in research partnership, in regards to what research will be conducted. Even though the framework allows for community engagement, [38] shared that the framework is limited to data and information governance. Therefore, [38] developed a structured Indigenous Knowledge Governance Framework (IKGF), which has a communication engagement layer. Indigenous people need to participate in decision making [13], and also influence policies and laws that support the safety of their knowledge [15], as such the part presented in the framework allows the process to establish collaboration between community members and researchers [38].

Academia has been identified to coordinate efforts between rural communities, governments and businesses to support ICT4D (research) projects [24]. [22] added that universities are in a position to solve community issues, and as such they endorse development of consistent university-community collaboration. The Academic Designer's point of reference with communities is made possible through continuous discussions and re-interpretations of engagements by the community themselves [16]. Therefore, strong university-community collaboration has been essential for fruitful community-based co-creations. While attempts were made to regulate the engagement much works still needs to be done and therefore we are investigating the derivation of engagement protocols alongside our projects.

4 Community Collaboration Approach

At this point of time we have no formal collaboration framework in which we operate. Much of the interactions are guided by best practices, lessons learned from the past experiences as well as individual researchers" knowledge about local protocols.

Research studies towards IK protection is a significant focus in the developing Namibia. The presentation for the need to preserve IK reached the ears of local funders, government and other tertiary institutions in Namibia. The stakeholders have shown the need to partake in this exciting journey to protect the country's rich cultural belongings.

One of the national objectives is to develop local communities. Cases have been presented for the collection of IK to promote an information society. Local IK is derived by community members being engaged in the projects. Our focus is to allow the voices of the community members to be heard as well as promote reciprocity. This creates harmony, as community members feel appreciated as they can raise their opinions which is taken as a design construct.

As such researchers have various outcomes when executing research. Thus, their visit to the communities is based on this outcome. It is important for the researchers to be aware that even though they have their own agenda and expectations from a specific community, engagement protocols still needs to be followed. This allows projects to have a partnership between communities and stakeholders.

5 Engagement Challenges Exemplified

In the following we first depict a number of various selected challenges that we have been facing in the different projects followed by community focus group sessions elaborating on community-researcher interactions.

5.1 Wikipedia and Motivation

Wikipedia has become one of the most popular repository [10]. As such, we aimed to show school teachers and community members how to use the platform to upload content. The idea was highly welcomed and teachers participated in uploading content sessions held. We motivated teachers to continue uploading content while we are not there. One researcher kept monitoring the platform to see any uploaded content. We noted that nothing was done. We than tried the sessions with different communities. The same process happened. We concluded that teachers are not motivated enough to upload content in our absence.

We opted for another attempt by identifying a champion. The champion was someone who will be a leader to motivate others to upload content. Yet again the champion was not motivated enough to monitor and lead others.

[25] suggested the usage of a persuasive technique based on motivational factors as a worthy tool to improve the upload of content on Wikipedia. To keep the teachers aware, we created a Facebook page to keep them tagged to the idea. The researcher

provided the teachers with reminders. Yet again teachers were not motivated enough. This has been our biggest challenge with our Wikipedia project.

5.2   Indigenous Communities Engaging with Teams of Local and International Researchers

The project involved local and international researchers from different countries having various research outcomes. The international researchers were not based in Namibia, so the agreement was for them to engage with the communities upon arrival. At one encounter, various researchers visited a community to establish a partnership and agreement with the traditional leaders to conduct research. Some international researchers did not understand the culture of the community members causing distrust and hindering the relationship to be established.

We established that the local team is the gatekeeper to the communities. Gatekeepers are researchers who have worked with rural communities for years and through that trust have been built [35]. Rules like how to behave and what to say was communicated to the international researchers, which was not well respected. Cases occurred where they raised insensitive questions. The local team had to constantly keep a close guard to the questions and replies by the international researchers. This also created conflict between local and international partners.

6   Discussions

We had regular discussions with the community members alongside the technology design sessions to ensure the community members can express concerns about processes. Recently we had a dedicated focus group session with community members from our two research sites namely Erindiroukambe and Otjisa. Community members who have been co-designers took part in the focus group discussions. Being involved in the project for a long time facilitated the conversation.

The elders from Erindiroukanbe reflected on how happy they are being part of the project. For them seeing researchers enter their community is a sign of learning something new. They learn about new technologies, how to co-design technology and services, understand the evolution of ICT and development. They also learn how to collect IK and preserve it. The community members repetitively insisted that researchers should come frequently. One of the native researchers is from the local research site making is easy for collaboration as community members felt comfortable. This resulted for the elders to welcome the researchers as being part of the community.

The elders from Otjisa mentioned that those who enter their community should humble themselves e.g. walking in a respectful manner. When the visitors approach the elders they should greet without stating their agenda. The elders will greet back which then the elder will ask what they are looking for and only then the visitors can proceed stating what brought them there. Once the elder feels comfortable and respected by the visitors, the elder warmly welcomed the visitors.

6.1 Ethical Questions

During one research trip in Otjisa, the researchers decided to accept a prior invitation by the elder to stay over for a couple of days. A focus group session was held to discuss how community members perceive researchers. The researchers asked a few questions (some listed in Table 1) to the community elders.

Table 1. Some ethical questions with elder in Otjisa

Researcher asked	Elder replies
"Don't you ever feel if there are researchers they are invading your space?"	"When you come to my homestead, we will find you a place to settle down. So none of us will have anything else to think about. It's a place where you can sleep and freely walk around. You can come to me anytime you want to talk"
"We came yesterday, and overnight at your homestead as you requested in an earlier trip. How do you feel about that?"	"I always say, if you overnight to teach each other, and spend the day together is the best as I can easily learn the things. It also becomes easy for me to come back in case there is something I didn't understand"
"How do you feel us calling your homestead also ours?"	"The person will be like your elder, or child, etc. So you do not have to make a difference from where you come from, and where you are. The only thing which will bring a difference is perhaps not able to do activities at the homestead"
"How does it place you with others when we are at your homestead?"	"It all depends on the hearts of the people. The community members have heard that you are here at my homestead. So any person who wants to know will come here. To come find out who are the people and what is the purpose of your visit"

6.2 Joint Engagement Protocol Development

Most literature suggests that engagement protocols should be settled before the project start, with elaborated informed consent. However, communities who have no experience with researchers would not be able to spell out those desirable rules. Also the process unfolds within the technology design space, so neither outcome nor negotiated methods are known at the beginning of the project only main agendas and underlying values are known. Thus, we suggest that it is an ongoing process of negotiation. In order to engage with the community members, it is best to develop the engagement protocol with them alongside the project. This elevates trust as they decide and agree on what is expected from them and are part of the outcome. Defining rules beforehand may result negatively depending on the take in by the community members. They do not want to sign anything as that gives the impression that we might have a bad intention.

It is also important to regularly inquire about dos' and don'ts. The process allows the researchers to know when to do anything. Even though researcher might think they know what is best, it is important to always re-confirm whether they are doing anything right or wrong. This is something we established to make sure new researchers do not fall short by doing something wrong.

In order to affirm engagement, a research day at the local tertiary institution was held whereby our co-designer was invited to attend. One of our co-designer from Otjisa gave a talk about the project. He talked about how happy he is being a co-designer. He demonstrated a tool he uses on a tablet which he co-designed. We also discussed a written paper with the elder. As academic papers are in English, we had the paper translated into the elder traditional language. He appreciated the effort of the elder, as he can read the work being published. This engagement protocol allowed the elder to affirm his position in the research team, and showed appreciation that he was chosen.

6.3   Engagement Beyond Projects

Our co-designers regularly request for the research team to come longer and more frequent. The elders mentioned that researchers must just come even if there is no research agenda.

Engagement is a relationship established with all its responsibilities. Even though there are no research outcomes needed by the research team, the project still runs. Elders commented that they want the research team to come frequently even if there are no co-design expectations. For the sites which are new, at first encounter we create a partnership. This opens up space for the research team to sustain engagement. During a normal visit by the native researchers, researchers and elders gathered just sit to talk about normal things.

7   Future Work

[14] urge that if a mutual understanding needs to be met by the researchers and communities, the aims and objectives should be clearly outlined. Therefore, we will analyze all engagements and technology sessions to initiate the co-design of the framework which will guide interactions between researchers and communities.

Acknowledgments. We would like to give our sincere gratitude to the two rural communities working with the research team. We acknowledge and appreciate the National Commission on Research, Science and Technology (NCRST) for funding this project.

References

1. Blake, E., Tucker, W., Glaser, M., Freudenthal, A.: Case study 11.1: deaf telephony: community-based co-design. In: Preece, J., Rogers, Y., Sharp, H. (eds.) Interaction Design: Beyond Human-Computer Interaction, 3rd edn, pp. 412–413. Wiley, Chichester (2011)
2. Blake, E., Glaser, M., Freudenthal, A.: Teaching design for development in computer science. Interactions **21**, 54–59 (2014)
3. Brereton, M., Roe, P., Schroeter, R., Lee Hong, A.: Beyond ethnography: engagement and reciprocity as foundations for design research out here. In: Proceedings of the CHI 2014, Presented at the CHI 2014. ACM Press, Toronto (2014)
4. Buchanan, D.R., Miller, F.G., Wallerstein, N.: Ethical Issues in Community-Based Participatory Research: Balancing Rigorous Research with Community Participation in Community Intervention Studies. The Johns Hopkins University Press, Baltimore (2007)
5. Dearden, A.: See no evil? Ethics in an interventionist ICTD. In: Proceedings of ICTD 2012, Atlanta, GA, USA (2012)
6. Dickert, N., Sugarman, J.: Ethical goals of community consultation in research. Afr. J. Public Health **95**(7), 1123–1127 (2005)
7. Dreher, T.: A partial promise of voice: digital storytelling and the limit of listening. Media Int. Aust. Incorporating Cult. Policy Q. J. Media Res. Res. **142**, 157–166 (2012)
8. Edwards, K., Lund, C., Gibson, N.: Ethical validity: expecting the unexpected in community-based research. Pimatisiwin J. Aborig. Indig. Community Health **6**(3), 17–30 (2008)
9. First National Centre: OCAP: Ownership, Control, Access and Possession. First Nations Information Governance Committee, Assembly of First Nationals Ottawa, Ottawa (2007)
10. Gallert, P., Winschiers-Theophilus, H., Kapuire, G.K., Stanley, C.: Clash of cultures, clash of values: Wikipedia and indigenous communities. In: van der Velden, M., Strano, M., Hrachvec, H., Abdelnour-Nocera, J., Ess. C. (eds.) Culture, Technology, Communication: Common Worlds, Different Futures? Proceedings of the Tenth International Conference on Culture, Technology, Communication, London, UK, pp. 200–213, 15–17 June 2016
11. Guidelines for Ethical Research in Australian Indigenous Studies: Australian Institute of Aboriginal and Torres Islander Studies (2012)
12. Green, L.W.: Ethics and community-based participatory research: commentary on minkler. Health Educ. Behav. **31**(6), 698–701 (2004)
13. Holland, M. P.: Digital Collectives in Indigenous Cultures and Communities Meeting: Meeting Reports. University of Michigan, Michigan (2002)
14. Hunter, J., Lounsbury, D., Rapkin, B., Remien, R.: A practical framework for navigating ethical challenges in collaborative community research. Glob. J. Commun. Psychol. Pract. **1**(2), 12–22 (2011)
15. Kamira, R.: Te Mata o Te Tai - the edge of the tide. In: Proceedings of the Information Technology in regional areas, Rockhampton (2002)
16. Kapuire, G.K., Winschiers-Theophilus, H., Blake, E.: An insider perspective on community gains: a subjective account of a Namibian rural communities' perception of a long-term participatory design project. Int. J. Hum. Comput. Stud. **74**, 124–143 (2014)
17. Kapuire, G.K., Cabrero, D.G., Winschiers-Theophilus, H., Stanley, C.: Framing technology design in Ubuntu: two locales in pastoral Namibia. In: Proceedings of OzCHI 2015, pp. 212–216. ACM Press (2015)
18. Le Dantec, C.A., Fox, S.: strangers at the gate: gaining access, building rapport, and co-constructing community-based research. In: CSCW 2015, Vancouver, Canada (2015)

19. Light, A., Egglestone, P., Wakeford, T., Rogers, J.: Research on an equal footing? A UK collaborative inquiry into community and academic knowledge. In: IKTC 2011, Windhoek, Namibia (2011)
20. Macaulay, A.C., Delormier, T., McComber, A.M., Cross, E.J., Potvin, L.P., Paradis, G., Kirby, R.L., Saad-Haddad, C., Desrosiers, S.: Participatory research with native community of kahnawake creates innovative code of research ethics. Can. J. Public Health (1998)
21. Martinez, D.F.C., Mora, H.G.C., Reyes, J.I.P.: ICT application from the perspective of university social responsibility in ICT4D projects. In: Proceedings of the 12th International Conference on Social Implications of Computers in Developing Countries, Ocho Rios, Jamaica (2013)
22. Mulemi, B.: Salvaging african perspectives of reality via afro-centric and intersubjective methodologies. In: Proceedings of the 4th European Conference on African studies ECAS4: Panel 111. The Nordic Africa Institute, Uppsala, Sweden (2011)
23. Mushiba, M., Winschiers-Theophilus, H., Du Preez, V., Molokwane, S., Kolhi, J.: Academia's responsibilities in community-based co-creation education – a critical review of two cases in South Africa and Botswana. In: Proceedings of the 13th International Conference on Social Implications of Computers in Developing Countries, Negombo, Sri Lanka (2015)
24. Mushiba, M.: Exploration of value sensitive–persuasive technology design for Wikipedia adoption in Namibian schools. Master mini-thesis, Polytechnic of Namibia (2014)
25. Narayan, D., Patel, R., Schafft, K., Rademacher, A., Koch-Schulte, S.: Can Anyone Hear Us? Voices from 47 Countries. Poverty Group, PREM, World Bank, Washington, DC (1999)
26. Pearce, T.D., Ford, J.D., Laidler, G.J., Smit, B., Duerden, F., Allarut, M., Andrachuk, M., Baryluk, S., Dialla, A., Elee, P., Goose, A., Ikummaq, T., Joamie, E., Kataoyak, F., Loring, E., Meakin, S., Nickels, S., Shappa, K., Shirley, J., Wandel, J.: Community collaboration and climate change research in the Canadian Arctic. Polar Res. **28**, 10–27 (2009)
27. Peters, A.N., Winschiers-Theophilus, H., Awori, K., Bidwell, N.J., Blake, E.H., Kumar, A., Chivuno-Kuria, S.: Collaborating with communities in Africa: a Hitchhikers guide. In: CHI Extended Abstracts, pp. 1969–1974 (2014)
28. Sabiescu, A.G., Salomao, D., Van Zyl, I., Cantoni, L.: Emerging spaces in community-based participatory design: reflections from two case studies. In: Proceedings. of the 13th Participatory Design Conference, Windhoek, Namibia, pp. 1–10. ACM Press (2014)
29. Sabiescu, A.G.: Empowering Minority Voices. Universita della Svizzera Italiana, Switzerland (2013)
30. Seifer, S.D.: Building and sustaining community-institutional partnerships for prevention research: findings from a national collaborative. J. Urban Health Bull. NY Acad. Med. **83**(6), 989–1003 (2006)
31. Stanley, C., Winschiers-Theophilus, H., Blake, E., Rodil, K., Kapuire, G.K., Maasz, D., Chamunorwa, M.: Formulating "the obvious" as a task request to the crowd: an interactive design experience across cultural and geographical boundaries. In: Proceedings of the 14th Participatory Design Conference, Aarhus, Denmark, pp. 87–89 (2016)
32. Tacchi, J.A.: Finding a voice: digital storytelling as participatory development in Southeast Asia. In: Hartley, J., McWilliam, K. (eds.) Story Circle: Digital Storytelling Around the World. Wiley-Blackwell, Malden (2009)
33. Winschiers-Theophilus, H., Chivuno-Kuria, S., Kapuire, G.K., Bidwell, N.J., Blake, E.: Being participated: a community approach. In: Proceedings of the 11th Biennial Participatory Design Conference, Sydney, Australia, pp. 1–10 (2010)
34. Winschiers-Theophilus, H., Zaman, T., Yeo, A.: Reducing "white elephant" ICT4D Projects: A Community-Researcher Engagement. ACM, Limerick (2014)

35. Winschiers-Theophilus, H., Bidwell, N.J.: Toward an Afro-Centric indigenous HCI paradigm. Int. J. Hum. Comput. Interact. **29**(4), 243–255 (2013)
36. Winschiers-Theophilus, H., Jensen, K., Rodil, K.: Locally situated digital representation of indigenous knowledge. In: CATAC 2012, Aarhus, Denmark (2012)
37. Winschiers-Theophilus, H., Bidwell, N.J., Blake, E.: Community consensus: design beyond participation. Des. Issues **28**(3), 99–100 (2012). Summer 2012, Masaachusetts Institute of Technology
38. Zaman, T.: Indigenous Knowledge Governance Framework: A Holistic Model for Indigenous Knowledge Management. University of Malaysia, UNIMAS. Malaysia (2013)

Continuing Medical Education on a Stick: Nepal as a Test Bed

Yan Li[1(✉)], Manoj A. Thomas[2], Sarbartha S.J.B. Rana[1], and Debra Stoner[3]

[1] Claremont Graduate University, Claremont, CA, USA
yan.li@cgu.edu, ranasarbartha@gmail.com
[2] Virginia Commonwealth University, Richmond, VA, USA
mthomas@vcu.edu
[3] Himanchal Education Foundation, Kearney, NE, USA
debra@himanchal.org

Abstract. The imbalance of health workforce between rural and urban has the most severe impact in low-income countries (LICs). One of the key elements in this disparity is the lack of professional development opportunities, such as Continuing Medical Education (CME), for rural medical practitioners. There exist few useful tools to effectively bridge the paucity of resources and access to CME for rural health care workers. Focusing on Nepal as a test-bed, we build, deploy, and evaluate an ICT-based platform called CMES (CME on a Stick), for the delivery and sharing of affordable and high-quality CME content for rural medical practitioners. We also refine the Citizen-centric Capacity Development (CCD) framework for ICT4D (Information and Communication Technology for Development). The CCD framework guided the development and evaluation of the CMES platform. The research contributes not only to the theoretical knowledge of linking ICT design and achievement of development goals, but also the practical knowledge of building ICT-based CME capacity for rural areas in LICs.

Keywords: ICT4D · Nepal · Continuing Medical Education · Citizen-centric Capacity building framework · CMES

1 Introduction

The world is steadily growing more urban than rural, yet the gulf between the quality and availability of medical care between the two remains wide. A major contributor is the difficulty in recruiting and retaining rural health workers. While the imbalance of health workforce is common to almost all countries, it has the most severe impact in low-income countries (LICs) [1]. For example, the urban to rural disparity of practicing physicians per capita in Nepal has been estimated at more than 40 to 1 [2]. There is no one single explanation towards this disparity, but one key element is the isolation and lack of professional development opportunities, such as Continuing Medical Education (CME) for rural physicians.

© IFIP International Federation for Information Processing 2017
Published by Springer International Publishing AG 2017. All Rights Reserved
J. Choudrie et al. (Eds.): ICT4D 2017, IFIP AICT 504, pp. 394–409, 2017.
DOI: 10.1007/978-3-319-59111-7_33

CME is defined as educational activities that serve to maintain, develop, or increase the knowledge, skills, and performance of medical practitioners in the medical field [3]. The ultimate goal of CME is to improve the health of individuals through services provided by the medical practitioners. CME is not only essential to improve physician performance and patient health outcomes, but also critical to maintaining a sense of professional pride, distinction, and identity [4]. Studies have shown effectiveness of CME in areas such as the acquisition and retention of medical knowledge, improving attitudes, skills, physician behaviors and clinical outcomes [5]. However, CME represents an overwhelming challenge in rural areas of LICs due to the complexity of socioeconomic and infrastructural problems, including limited access to context-relevant CME content from conferences, textbooks, journals and the internet, lack of mandated CME standards, as well as financial and technical challenges. There exist few useful tools to effectively bridge the paucity of resources and access to CME, and little knowledge about how CME might be used to improve rural medical care and population health.

This research serves two objectives. First, we build, deploy, and evaluate an ICT4D (Information and Communication Technology for Development) solution called CMES (CME on a Stick) for the delivery and sharing of affordable and high-quality CME content for rural medical practitioners, focusing on Nepal as a test-bed. We believe that a free and open platform for CME knowledge sharing and distribution in LICs can catalyze significant reductions in urban-rural health disparities. It is important to note that ICT solutions such as Internet-in-a-Box and Raspberry Pi have been used to deliver educational contents to offline communities. However, none addresses the unique characteristics of effective CME in LICs, such as providing interactive and multi-modal methods of learning, gaining administrative support, offering incentives for practice change, and conducting needs assessment of health professionals.

Second, in the process of building CME capacity among rural medical practitioners, we continue the application and refinement of the Citizen-centric Capacity Development (CCD) framework for ICT4D [6]. As an inter-disciplinary research domain, ICT4D integrates computer science, information systems, and development studies [7]. While ICT includes the full range of computer hardware, software, and telecommunication facilities, ICT4D research is envisioned as an enabling tool with the capability to improve quality of life, empowerment, and economic development for the communities where it is introduced. Despite the huge investment from government, non-government organizations and private sectors in ICT4D projects, the impact of ICT in LICs remains minimal [8]. The struggle of linking ICT deployment and achievement of development goals is usually a result of focusing more on technology and neglecting the complex social, economic, and political factors in LICs [9]. Although literature calls for exploring a broader context for ICT4D project [8, 10], existing research in ICT4D mostly focuses on either technical solutionsor impact evaluation. Because the broader development context often influences the design choices of the ICT solution within which it is set [11], we believe that it should be considered throughout the ICT solution design process rather than explored in isolation. The purpose of CCD framework is to assist the design, implementation, and evaluation of ICT4D project with the consideration of the unique and complex context for development in resource constrained communities (e.g. LICs, rural communities).

The rest of the paper is organized as follows. First, we review CME challenges in LICs Sect. 2, followed by a description of proposed CCD framework and project background in Sects. 3 and 4. Section 5 discusses the CMES design process for CME capacity development, and Sect. 6 concludes the paper by examining long term project goals and future research directions.

2   CME and Its Challenges in LICs

The instructional design of CME activities draws insights from different academic disciplines such as adult learning, practice-based learning, continuing professional education, organizational change, development and behavior, and health services research [12]. Most of the CME methods and activities are based on theories on adult learning, such as lifelong learning, theories of motivation, self-directed learning, reflection, and adult learning [13]. Different CME methods include conferences and workshops, printed or recorded materials, mentoring and opinion leaders, clinical practice guidelines, interactive education, case-based training, audit and peer group discussions, educational outreach visits, reminders, and online education [5, 14]. Among these, attending conferences and reading printed materials are CME activities most commonly undertaken by medical practitioners.

While CME is identified as a key element for maintaining good quality clinical care and a priority for health care providers in many countries [15], the effectiveness of CME remains debatable. A recent synthesis of systematic reviews [4] on CME effectiveness concluded positive impact on physician performance and patient health outcomes. In addition, literature identifies key attributes of successful CME: (1) use multiple media and methods of learning; (2) provide adequate time to digest and incorporate knowledge; (3) incorporate needs assessments to ensure that the activity is controlled by and meets the needs of health professionals; (4) be interactive; (5) administrative support, and (6) provide policy incentives for practice change [4, 16]. In our solution design, we take into consideration the first four attributes, while fully aware that attributes five and six represent social and political aspects of CME and may not be directly addressed by our ICT-enabled solutions.

Additionally, literature highlights many unique challenges to CME in LICs. First, in many developed countries such as in Europe and America, CME is mandatory and its quality and participation are often warranted by a national board. For example, the Accreditation Council for Continuing Medical Education (ACCME) enforces standards and quality of CME, and requires recertification of medical professionals to maintain their licenses. On the contrary, in many LICs, there is no external enforcement of CME activities. As a result, there is no incentive for CME, or sanction for non-participation, except self-motivation. Other challenges include lack of time to participate due to pressures of work, lack of funded study leaves, insufficient financial support for external CME activities, limited access to CME content especially for rural medical professionals, lack of basic ICT knowledge required for accessing information online, and shortage of CME activities tailored towards individual needs [17]. These challenges are even greater in rural areas. For example, most rural medical professionals do not have access to up-to-date CME content due to unavailable or unreliable internet access. Medical practitioners who work in rural hospital and clinics generally prefer local access to CME to reduce travel time and avoid absence from work. When many have access to computers, they would need support to use it for CME [2].

Considerable effort and research have focused on promoting CME content sharing in LICs. Research4life[1] provides free or low cost online access of scientific research content for LICs. One of the Research4life programs, the Health InterNetwork Access to Research Initiatives (HINARI)[2] offers free access to up-to-date biomedical and health literature for health and medical institutions in LICs. While it postulates a way of supporting online access to CME content, it does not address the issues of limited internet connectivity and lack of basic ICT knowledge among medical professionals in LICs. For example, there are often difficulties in logging into HINARI and many participating organizations experience problems of organizing password distributions [18] even when there is internet connectivity. Our CMES design not only presents a novel solution towards offline CME knowledge sharing and distribution, but also ensures CME content update when internet is available.

3   Citizen-centric Capacity Development (CCD) Framework

In this research, we adapt the initial citizen-centric framework for ICTE capacity development [6] to guide our solution design and evaluation. Two key strengths highlight the rationale for its adaptation: citizen-centric requirement engineering and a pluralist research design. The revised CCD framework for ICT4D (Fig. 1) involves two similar phases. Phase 1 adapts the citizen-centric approach [19] for ICT capacity development. Phase 2 is the evaluation and interpretation of the effective use and benefit of ICT. Below, we highlight and justify the main changes in the revised CCD framework, while interested readers can refer to the original framework (Thomas and Li 2015) for detailed definitions and steps.

First, we consider that the citizen-centric approach for capacity development from the original framework is essential for linking ICT with development. In the context of development literature, capacity development can be defined in a wider context as "…the process through which individuals, organizations and societies obtain, strengthen and maintain the capabilities to set and achieve their own development objectives over time" [20]. In ICT4D where many diverse and competing actors are involved in development, it is critical for an engaged outsider (i.e. ICT solution designers and developers) to understand and support local people to determine their own societal goals and challenges, build the capacity through ICT-enabled solution implementation that help the community achieve positive societal changes, and organize community members to act upon and sustain these changes [21]. Thus, it is desired to involve local people from the start of ICT solution development through citizen-centric requirement engineering (Phase 1 of Fig. 1). Second, we believe that innovative design and effective evaluation of ICT-based intervention are two integral parts of ICT4D research. The ICT-enabled development goal

---

[1] http://www.research4life.org/.

[2] http://www.who.int/hinari/en/.

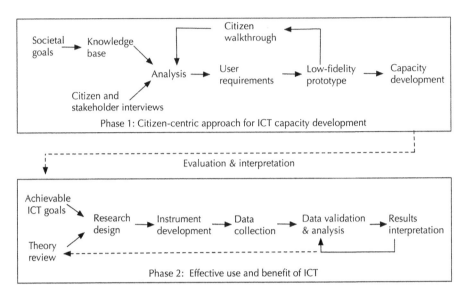

Fig. 1. Citizen-centric Capacity Development (CCD) framework

can only be achieved through dynamic integration of social, psychological, and technical mechanisms in the ICT-solution design and evaluation. Such integration requires different research methods to address different tasks and research problems. The initial framework provides a strong foundation by systematically combining qualitative, quantitative, and design science research methods.

We further revised the framework to address some of its limitations. First, it does not explicitly capture the ultimate goal of the ICT-based intervention in LICs, which is the social-economic development of local community. An ICT4D project should start with a clearly defined societal goal that can be potentially addressed by an ICT solution. Furthermore, while the complex socio-economic, political, cultural, and financial factors should be examined to achieve the potential benefit of the ICT-based intervention, an ambitious yet achievable ICT4D project goal needs to be described. An achievable project goal serves two purposes. One is to provide the basis for searching existing information and knowledge base that would inform the ICT solution design. The other purpose it to guide the research design towards evaluating the effective use of societally-beneficial ICT-based intervention. This goal-oriented design and evaluation process is incorporated in the improved CCD framework. Second, the original framework assumes the evaluation and interpretation of effective use and benefit of ICT (Phase 2 of Fig. 1) to be quantitative. Often, ICT4D projects present intangible outcomes that can be difficult to define and measure quantitatively. Further, even when a project has clearly defined short-term goals, it is hard to articulate well-defined metrics to measure its long-term benefits. Thus, a good project evaluation should be resilient to accommodate multiple methods, capture changes over time, and be scientifically sound [22]. The updated CCD framework reflects the multi-method approach towards evaluation and interpretation for ICT capacity building.

4   CMES Project Background

In this section, we describe the background of CMES[3] project. The project was initiated by a group of medical doctors in Nepal, who advocate improving rural health care by focusing on training rural health care workers, especially those in hard to reach villages in the Everest region. As an underdeveloped country (145th of 188 countries in the Human Development Index) [23], Nepal faces great challenges as medical resources are extremely limited and infrastructure for the delivery of health care is fragile. As a landlocked country between India and China, 83% of Nepal's terrain is mountainous and about 80% of the population lives in rural and remote areas. Despite years of efforts to expand Nepal's telecom market, infrastructure development in the rugged high altitudes of the Himalayas is extremely difficult. Furthermore, the political instability (25 prime ministers in just 26 years of democracy) has had an adverse effect on Nepal's already struggling economic situation.

In the context of health care, World Health Organization (WHO) identifies Nepal with a critical shortage of health care providers with only seven providers per 10,000 capita. There is also a huge gap between urban and rural health care, where rural population has very limited access to doctors and hospital services. Lack of professional development opportunities is one of the main reasons for reluctance among medical practitioners to serve in the rural areas of Nepal (Butterworth et al. 2008). Based on interviews with Nepal medical practitioners, one of main challenges to CME is that it is not mandated by the medical standards body (i.e., the Nepal Medical Council). This results in localized medical practices with great disparities between rural and urban areas.

The inception of the CMES project was inspired by the Computer-on-a-Stick (COS) solution that we developed for schools in Haiti [6]. One of the doctors who came across the COS said:

> *"The wisdom of the Haiti COS project is providing learning resources for students without the need for an Internet connection. In countries where Internet connection and electricity are unreliable...this leaps over the limiting step to access CME content. This is a common problem in Nepal where load shedding occurs daily for 12+ h and for days in the rural areas. I started thinking about using the same model for medical education."*

While CME covers many areas, CME in Emergency Medicine (EM) was identified as an immediate need because Nepal has a large ethnic population living in the mountainous regions and is a popular destination for adventure travelers. EM is one of the newest and fastest developing medical specialties in Nepal. Yet, national standards in EM training and certification have not been developed or mandated. While major urban hospitals start to adopt EM practices and training, the emergency care is entirely lacking in rural areas [24]. The excessive mortality in the recent 2015 earthquake is a direct testament to this dire situation. One of the doctors described the needs for EM training in Nepal as:

---

[3] www.cmesworld.org.

"From remote villages to larger cities, my experience has been a lack of quality and affordable EM CME for all health providers including nurses, rural community health workers (CHW), midwives, and physicians. I realized my EM training and wilderness medicine background provided pertinent topics for Nepal's austere environments...the villages and even the cities... Kathmandu is an austere environment considering strikes, earthquakes, the petro embargo and rush hour traffic."

Initial target participants were also identified, as described by one of the doctors:

"In Nepal, the target audience will be rural health providers, nurses, midwives, first-year interns, residents, or interns that are unable to secure one of the few residency spots in a specialty. The only EM residency program in Nepal that I am aware of is at Patan Hospital and it only has four positions open to GPs (General Practitioners) who have EM experience. Residency programs in all specialties are scarce in Nepal and residents pay tuition level fees during their training. Often, it is only the wealthy or well-connected that can afford to continue their studies. The city and town Emergency Departments are staffed by GPs and interns. The village health posts are staffed by nurses and CHW. These should be the target practitioners."

After obtaining the support from a world-class CME content provider, and multiple medical administrators at hospitals and clinics in Nepal, we assembled a project team to investigate potential ICT-enabled solutions for CME in LICs with the goal of using Nepal as a test bed. In the following section, we describe the CMES project that is guided by the first phase of the CCD framework. The project has gone through multiple iterations of ICT artifacts design and testing, and initial CMES-based capacity building. At the time of this paper submission, we have initiated the second phase of the CCD framework, which is the qualitative and quantitative evaluation of CMES use and benefit. The second release that includes an improved CMES software targets launch in nine rural and urban locations in January, 2017.

5   CMES Platform Development

5.1   CMES Project Goals (Phase I)

The CMES project started with a clear societal goal from local medical practitioners in Nepal, which is to improve the rural health care by providing affordable and quality CME content for rural health care workers. The local doctors also suggested a potential ICT solution that is similar to COS to solve the problem of accessing CME content with limited or no Internet connectivity. In order to translate this societal goal to an ambitious, achievable and measurable ICT goal, we first consulted the knowledge base related to offline content delivery and CME challenges in LICs and rural areas. Among existing offline content delivery solutions, Internet-in-a-Box and RACHEL-Pi[4] are two alternatives for the delivery of educational contents without the need for Internet. There is also E-Pustakalaya solution[5] that provides education-focused free and open digital library for rural schools and can be installed on low power servers with limited or no Internet connectivity requirements. However, none of these solutions include CME

---

[4] https://racheloffline.org/.

[5] http://www.olenepal.org/e-pustakalaya/.

content. Furthermore, all of them offer pre-loaded static content, and content update is quite cumbersome. The previous COS solution is also not desirable, as it requires the Linux computing environment and focuses on K-12 education rather than professionals in the medical field.

In addition to literature review as highlighted in Sect. 2, we also consulted stake-holders (e.g., medical administrators, NGO leaders who share similar interests, government officials, and medical policy makers) and citizens (e.g., medical doctors). Interviews with medical administrators (including senior medical doctors) and NGO leaders confirmed the literature findings. For example, the most common challenge for CME in Nepal is the lack of regulatory requirement for CME, as highlighted by the founder of a community-based, not-for-profit hospital:

> *"Like many developing countries, CME in Nepal is not mandated by the authorization body (Nepal Medical Council) and there is no CME standard. It becomes a voluntary effort of the director of each department to implement CME... The CME goal will be (even) different from department to department in the same hospital. This results in the localized medical practices (knowledge sharing usually happens at the individual department level) with great disparities between Urban and Rural areas."*

The interviewees also identified many social, political, and financial factors critical to the success of CME, such as administrative support, mentoring and encouragement, access to relevant and update-to-date CME content, policy incentives, and intrinsic motivation of medical practitioners. For example, a NGO Leader describes the issue of self-motivation as:

> *"The medical practitioners would be more encouraged to work in rural areas if they feel connected with the main/urban hospitals. The practitioners must be motivated from their heart to adopt and use CME. Otherwise it would be too difficult to implement it. We can encourage them for sure telling that it will help for their career but that is not good enough. If the practitioners are interested to work just for money, we can't motivate them."*

Although not all of these identified factors can be addressed by ICT-based intervention alone, they should nevertheless be considered in a broader context for CME capacity development. For example, we met with the Secretary of Health at Nepal Central Government and the Director of the Medical council as it is the government's responsibility and interest to improve the rural health. Keeping them aware and receiving their support are essential for the long-term development and sustenance of a project of this nature.

Our interviewees included not only initial targeted participants, but also doctors who work in the participating urban hospitals and medical clinics. All interviewees provided valuable input in shaping our project goals. For example, one western doctor who volunteers at an advanced travel clinic in Kathmandu mentioned that access to medical content was really not an issue there, as they had high speed internet and subscription to content services. However, she knew many different groups and people who are interested in promoting rural health services in Nepal. she suggested the need for a platform to brings those players together and distribute CME with various entities, groups, and organizations that share the same goal.

Informed by existing knowledge and voice of the local people, we defined our project goals as: "provide free and open access to CME content in LICs, and promote standardized CME knowledge sharing and distribution". Based on these goals, we targeted the development of a low-cost, adaptable CMES platform that include:

- A CME content storage solution that capitalizes on Internet-based modalities for provisioning CME content;
- A CMES software application that enables CME content dissemination and synchronization with minimal need for Internet connectivity;
- An offline CME content server based on raspberry-pi where content can be accessed when Internet connectivity is unavailable or insufficient for most practical purposes;
- and a LISTSERV for participants to discuss CME related topics.

The team also acknowledged that promoting standardized and localized CME content sharing requires a long-term commitment from multi-functional and multi-cultural teams. Many key stakeholders were identified and brought into the project as partners and advisers.

5.2   Citizen-Centric Requirement Engineering (Phase 1)

Once the project goals were articulated and a set of potential ICT solutions were identified, we started the citizen-centric requirement engineering for the CMES software application development. It included iterations of citizen and stakeholder interviews, analysis, user requirement, low-fidelity prototype development, and citizen walkthroughs (Phase 1 of the CCD framework). The citizen-centric approach ensured the design and construction of CMES application met the vocalized needs of local medical practitioners. Interviews with stakeholders identified three design principles for our application:

- Free: the CME content is delivered for free to the users;
- Adaptive: the CME application is adaptive to the user's device modality;
- Ease-of-use: the application should look and feel like something they already know how to use and require minimal training.

Citizen interviews provided insights into key features that were desired for the CMES application:

- Content on CMES should be updatable when internet is available (e.g. when a rural doctor goes to a location with internet connectivity);
- A search function that enables the quick identification of content by tags or keywords;
- Display storage information of the USB drive;
- A personalizable and customizable local CME library structure that enables the user to retain CME topics of interest and delete irrelevant or unused ones.

Because the CMES application was envisioned to require a computer to operate, it was critical to understand the types of computers (including hardware and software) that users might have. Having conducted a survey and visited the hospital sites in Nepal, we found out that 100% of targeted users were using Windows machines, among which 60% were older than 4 years and 20% were running Windows XP operating systems. This brought some system constraints in the application development, such as:

- How to ensure version management across different operating systems?
- How to ensure the application runs the same and effortlessly across different machine?
- How to make sure that the application will retain the same user experience in different types of operational systems?

Figure 2 depicts our CMES architectural design. The CMES application was written in Java. For content storage and management, we used Microsoft Azure, a scalable cloud-based computing platform with integrated tools and managed services. Our project takes advantage of its built-in server management, security, availability, and scalability features.

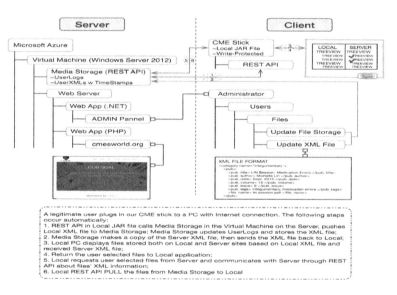

Fig. 2. Initial CMES architectural design

Soon after the initial architectural design was finalized, a low-fidelity prototype including initial application screen mock-ups was presented to the citizens for feedback. For example, three different content viewing structures were presented to the citizens and they all chose the tree-view (commonly seen in windows operating environment) which they felt most comfortable with. The citizen walkthrough also inspired additional design features for the CMES application:

- A launch screen with links to tutorials in pdf and video format;
- Focus on simplicity of use (e.g., a landing page following the launch screen with two options: Search and Sync);
- Sync feature activated only when Internet is available;

- USB write-protection to prevent accidental content deletion and safe guard intellectual property of CME content provider;
- Packaged Java Runtime Environment (JRE) within the application (during the low-fidelity prototype testing, it was found that many computers in Nepal hospitals did not have JRE).

Figure 3 presents a snippet of our application launch screen and interested readers can explore more about the CMES by viewing the video tutorial[6].

Fig. 3. Application launch screen

Based on the feedback from citizen walk through and analysis, many changes were made to the initial prototype. For example, the look and feel of the initial screen was refined and tailored as shown in Fig. 4, which was well received during the citizen walkthroughs. Some additional features were designed for software usability. For example, Nepal does not have reliable Internet connections, especially in rural areas. An Internet connectivity indicator was therefore added at the bottom of the screen.

As the CMES project continues to evolve, the citizen's needs and preferences have become more articulated, and the supporting software infrastructure and application design have expanded. For example, all screens automatically resize to match the display resolution of the viewing device and tooltips added to guide user interactions. Each CMES content type included a file type logo and a simple click of the file would invoke the default application registered with the computer's operating system. Because Internet speed is a challenge in Nepal, a status bar was added to indicate both percentage and number of files downloaded or deleted. In the event of Internet failure during download or delete, the application will roll back to the previous state.

---

[6] https://youtu.be/qyvZOC4c85I.

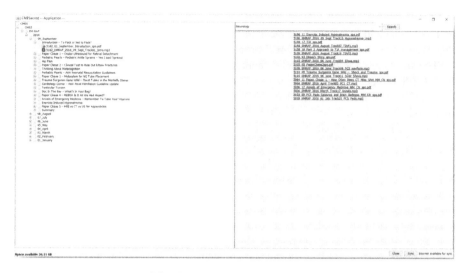

Fig. 4. Application landing screen

5.3   CME Capacity Development (Phase 1)

After multiple iterations of software development and two field visits (two weeks each) by the researchers and CMES developers to Nepal, the CMES program was officially launched during Fall 2016. A medical doctor dispensed USB drives to the participants and provided CMES training. The training of doctors was conducted at hospitals in Kathmandu. It consisted of either one to one training session or a Power Point group presentation, which included instructional documents and video, and hands-on demonstration of the CMES application. This was followed by a question and answer session, during which the participants were given time to practice using the software. For participants who were unable to attend training in Kathmandu, their organizational administrator was trained to demonstrate and train the medical staff on site. Troubleshooting and follow-ups were encouraged via phone, Skype and email. Six organizations participated in the initial launch with a total of 25 hospitals and/or clinics sites and 39 participating medical practitioners. All participants were physicians, among whom more than half were working in remote and rural areas of Nepal. Since the completion of onsite training, 80 additional medical practitioners have expressed interest in the CMES thumb drives. Two rural hospitals, one in Lukla and one in Chitwan, have submitted requests to participate in the CMES project. We anticipate approximately 100 thumb drives to be distributed among medical practitioners in Nepal by January 2017 to meet the demand.

As described preciously, ICT-enabled capacity building in LICs has to be deeply embedded in its social, economic, and political environment [21]. Successful ICT-enabled capacity building requires the balance of ambitious yet achievable ICT goals with the long term societal goals. Slower than expected pace of measurable outcomes is expected when developing ICT solutions for challenging environments [25]. The capacity development in Phase 1 (Fig. 1) of the CCD framework is not just about delivering the ICT solution to end users. Rather, it requires strategic consideration of social and psychological mechanisms that need to be addressed to achieve the effectiveness use of ICT. The CMES project is no exception.

The success of the initial CMES launch is attributable to a couple of factors. First, the CMES project is a multi-functional, multi-cultural collaboration effort that has engaged many different stakeholders from the start. This allowed us to identify voluntary participants and seek administrative support from partnering hospitals. Second, meetings with the Nepal Medical Council and several senior doctors confirm impending policy changes related to CME in the near future. According the director of Nepal Medical council, the council is committed to introducing CME mandate in Nepal, and has already created a committee to initiate the necessary steps. Although the CMES program will not directly influence such a policy change, the director viewed the proposed solution as a valuable asset to deliver customized, updatable and personalizable CME knowledge library. Third, the application design benefited greatly from involving citizens in the process. The functionality and simplicity of the software was very well received. All participants commented on the ease of use, navigation, and click-and-go features of the software. Fourth, we were able to engage several key stakeholders who are well respected senior doctors or NGO leaders in Nepal. They served as local champions for the project and helped us connect with many medical intuitions. For example, a chief medical doctor in a rural hospital sent the following email:

> "I am super excited to hear about your CMES program, exactly something that is greatly lacking in this remote part of the world. Thank you so much for your kind interest in including us in this program. I am sure it will give very useful medical information for our team up here and truly will be well used in this remote hospital."

Last but not least, long before the design and building of the CMES application, we opened dialog with various stakeholders regarding CME challenges and factors to be considered to ensure the success of CMES program. The level of commitment and belief in the potential societal benefits of CMES varied significantly among those stakeholders. One of the NGO leaders with enormous experience in training rural health workers noted "...mentors and administrative support are an important component of any training and CME program." As such, we carefully evaluated the needs of participating organizations, which include regional and district hospitals, medical clinics, and health centers. One of the hospitals initially expressed interest in participating in the CMES program, but later showed little engagement and administrative support. Subsequently, although keeping them in our participants list, we only provided one USB drive to their chief EM officer. On the other hand, the experience at another hospital was awe inspiring. The hospital's director is passionate about improving rural health and the hospital has an aggressive in-house CME program for their nurses, plastic surgery residents, staff doctors, and house officers (those who have graduated from medical schools but not completed residency). The lead doctor not only engaged all available staff in the initial CMES program launch, but also suggested co-developing CME content. We consider the capacity development at their site a success, as described by the medical doctor who provided CMES training at their site:

"...arranged a conference for all available staff so I presented the CMES program not only to ED [emergency department] doctors but the critical care, surgery and medical teams. They are all interested in CMES. They consider the thumb drives as property of the hospital and are treating them like a library book to be borrowed. The ED Director and the CEO will each have a thumb drive. Any other doctor is welcome to use one for a two-week period of time so they will circulate between the departments. Then they have to present one article at their CME conference."

5.4 Effectiveness and Benefit of CMES (Phase 2)

The evaluation of CMES program towards achieving its ICT4D goals has been initiated. We plan to include both qualitative and quantitative methods to evaluate the adoption, effective usage, and benefits of our CME platform. The CMES application includes extensive logging features to track usage patterns of each device, such as frequency of application launch, synchronization, content viewed, and search behaviors. The logs are uploaded to remote server any time the CMES sync operation is triggered, which will enable us to conduct varying levels of assessment related to the ICT usage. A follow-up questionnaire will be sent to each participant. They will be encouraged to provide comments and criticisms on how the program can be improved to meet their CME needs. Qualitative in-person interviews are planned in May 2017 to determine whether and how CME access has impacted practice patterns, physician identity, and professional networking. We expect a longer period of time for participants to see the societal-benefit of the CMES. We also plan to have post implementation meetings with stakeholders for future recommendations. Moreover, we are currently in the process of reviewing theoretical foundations of CME, such as experiential learning theory [26] and transformative learning theory [27], to help us better understand the CMES program adoption and usage.

6 Conclusion and Future Research

We developed a low-cost, adaptable platform for the delivery of CME content for medical practitioners in LICs. The initial implementation of CME content server and the USB-based CMES software application for capacity development was conducted in Nepal. While planning the second iteration of application release and continuing CME capacity building, the evaluation of capacity building effort has also started. This research contributes not only to the theoretical knowledge of linking ICT and development in ICT4D solution design and evaluation, but also the practical knowledge of building ICT-based CME capacity for rural areas in LICs.

For the future research, we have started prototyping two other components of the CMES platform: a CMES-pi offline CME content server based on raspberry pi and a LISTSERV. The CMES-pi solution will include a content server that can be updated remotely, and a mobile application that will allow medical practitioners view CME content on their mobile devices. A needs assessment is planned to identify CME content needs of the rural healthcare workers. It will provide us insights on how to expand CME to other medical specialty areas, such as nursing and pediatrics.

As suggested by the secretary of Nepal Health Services, we plan to engage Nepal Medical Association and Nepal Nursing Association for participation from those specialties. We also plan to provide a web-based, Internet dependent CMES version for urban doctors in LICs, who are also often constrained by limited CME resources. To encourage participation, we are in the process of designing feedback loops, such as certificates of completion when CME content is reviewed and related questions are answered. As described on our website, the long-term project goals include engaging a global community to contribute core CME content for free in many languages, and benefit the public health in a global context. We are currently reaching out to agencies in other LICs for CMES program participation.

Acknowledgements. We thank the Research Initiatives Fund and Fletcher Jones Foundation Faculty Research Fund at Claremont Graduate University (CGU), and Undergraduate Research Fellowship Fund at Virginia Commonwealth University (VCU) for funding this research, and the Microsoft Research Grant for providing the Azure Sponsorship to support our ICT infrastructure needs.

References

1. Chen, L., Evans, T., Anand, S., Boufford, J.I., Brown, H., Chowdhury, M., Cueto, M., Dare, L., Dussault, G., Elzinga, G.: Human resources for health: overcoming the crisis. The Lancet **364**, 1984–1990 (2004)
2. Butterworth, K., Hayes, B., Neupane, B.: Retention of general practitioners in rural Nepal: a qualitative study. Aust. J. Rural Health **16**, 201–206 (2008)
3. ACCME. http://www.accme.org/requirements/accreditation-requirements-cme-providers/policies-and-definitions/cme-content-definition-and-examples
4. Cervero, R.M., Gaines, J.: Effectiveness of continuing medical education: updated synthesis of systematic reviews. Report by Accreditation Council for Continuing Medical Education (ACCME), Chicago, IL (2014)
5. Marinopoulos, S.S., Dorman, T., Ratanawongsa, N., Wilson, L.M., Ashar, B.H., Magaziner, J.L., Miller, R.G., Thomas, P.A., Prokopowicz, G.P., Qayyum, R.: Effectiveness of continuing medical education. Evidence Report/Technology Assessment, Agency for Healthcare Research and Quality (2007)
6. Thomas, M.A., Li, Y.: A citizen-centric framework for ICTE capacity development in Haiti. In: 13th International Conference on Social Implications of Computers in Developing Countries (2015)
7. Unwin, P.T.H.: ICT4D: Information and Communication Technology for Development. Cambridge University Press, Cambridge (2009)
8. Thapa, D., Sabo, O.: Exploring the link between ICT and development in the context of developing countries: a literature review. Electron. J. Inf. Syst. Dev. Countries **64**, 1–15 (2014)
9. Brown, A.E., Grant, G.G.: Highlighting the duality of the ICT and development research agenda. Inf. Technol. Dev. **16**, 96–111 (2010)
10. Njihia, J.M., Merali, Y.: The broader context for ICT4D projects: a morphogenetic analysis. MIS Q. **37**, 881–905 (2013)
11. Prakash, A., De', R.: Importance of development context in ICT4D projects: a study of computerization of land records in India. Inf. Technol. People **20**, 262–281 (2007)

12. Bennett, N.L., Davis, D.A., Easterling Jr., W.E., Friedmann, P., Green, J.S., Koeppen, B.M., Mazmanian, P.E., Waxman, H.S.: Continuing medical education: a new vision of the professional development of physicians. Acad. Med. **75**, 1167–1172 (2000)
13. Merriam, S.B., Caffarella, R.S., Baumgartner, L.M.: Learning in Adulthood: A Comprehensive Guide. Wiley, San Francisco (2012)
14. Bloom, B.S.: Effects of continuing medical education on improving physician clinical care and patient health: a review of systematic reviews. Int. J. Technol. Assess. Health Care **21**, 380–385 (2005)
15. Peck, C., McCall, M., McLaren, B., Rotem, T.: Continuing medical education and continuing professional development: international comparisons. BMJ **320**, 432–435 (2000)
16. Institute of Medicine: Redesigning Continuing Education in the Health Professions. National Academies Press, Washington, DC (2010)
17. Ogbaini-Emovon, E.: Continuing medical education: closing the gap between medical research and practice. Benin J. Postgrad. Med. **11**, 43–49 (2009)
18. Smith, H., Bukirwa, H., Mukasa, O., Snell, P., Adeh-Nsoh, S., Mbuyita, S., Honorati, M., Orji, B., Garner, P.: Access to electronic health knowledge in five countries in Africa: a descriptive study. BMC Health Serv. Res. **7**, 1 (2007)
19. van Velsen, L., van der Geest, T., ter Hedde, M., Derks, W.: Requirements engineering for e-Government services: A citizen-centric approach and case study. Gov. Inf. Q. **26**, 477–486 (2009)
20. Wignaraja, K.: Capacity Development: A UNDP Primer. United Nations Development Programme, New York (2009)
21. Eade, D.: Capacity building: who builds whose capacity? Dev. Pract. **17**, 630–639 (2007)
22. Lannon, J.: An evaluation framework for ICT capacity building projects: action research in Armenia. Inf. Dev. **32**, 1585–1599 (2015). Article No. 0266666915615645
23. Jahan, S.: Human Development Report 2015 (2015)
24. Pandey, N.R.: Emergency medicine in Nepal: present practice and direction for future. Int. J. Emerg. Med. **9**, 1–6 (2016)
25. Agyemang, G., Awumbila, M., Unerman, J., O'Dwyer, B.: NGO accountability and aid delivery (2009)
26. Kolb, D.A., Boyatzis, R.E., Mainemelis, C.: Experiential learning theory: previous research and new directions. Perspect. Think. Learn. Cogn. Styles **1**, 227–247 (2001)
27. Mezirow, J.: Transformative learning: theory to practice. New Direct. Adult Continuing Educ. **1997**, 5–12 (1997)

Supporting Sustainability Through Collaborative Awareness Raising – A Case of Sri Lankan Telecentres

Sirkku Männikkö-Barbutiu[1(✉)], Harsha Perera[2], Upul Anuradha[2], Ranil Peiris[1], and Thomas Westin[1]

[1] Department of Computer and Systems Science,
Stockholm University, Kista, Sweden
{sirkku,ranil,thomasw}@dsv.su.se
[2] School of Computing, University of Colombo, Colombo, Sri Lanka
{hdp,uar}@ucsc.cmb.ac.lk

Abstract. For the development of sustainable ICT services, participation of the local communities is crucial. A meaningful involvement requires awareness and understanding of the various possibilities of the ICTs. In this paper, the processes of awareness raising among underprivileged population in the Sri Lankan tea estate district of Nuwara Eliya are examined, drawing on the findings from an empirical study conducted at two telecentres. A specific participatory methodology, where co-inspirational sessions and brainstorming constituted main activities of co-creation of knowledge was applied. Our empirical data confirms that the participatory methods can trigger curiosity and engagement among participants. Ideas and suggestions that emerged during brainstorming demonstrate relevance, realism as well as they are a proof of real needs and requirements of a population that lives under difficult conditions in remote locations. Participatory methods can initiate community engagement for a longstanding, sustainable transformation of the TCs, in collaboration with ICT developers, and TC staff.

Keywords: Workshops · Participatory methodology · Telecentres · ICT diffusion · Sustainability

1 Introduction

Telecentres (TCs) as access points and training facilities to ICTs and the Internet constitute an important strategy in many present day countries in Africa and Asia. In ICT4D research literature, the potential of TCs as central in providing education and other government services in rural areas is discussed [3, 15, 17, 21] recognising the role of TCs as central in endeavours of ICT diffusion and implementation in societies.

Even though there seems to exist a wide consensus among policy makers of the relevance of TCs [4, 6, 9, 18], sustainability of these establishments can be questioned, if their existence and operations are not well-grounded in the local community [14]. With well-grounded we mean both awareness of the possibilities of ICTs among the local population and awareness of the local needs and requirements among the

© IFIP International Federation for Information Processing 2017
Published by Springer International Publishing AG 2017. All Rights Reserved
J. Choudrie et al. (Eds.): ICT4D 2017, IFIP AICT 504, pp. 410–421, 2017.
DOI: 10.1007/978-3-319-59111-7_34

researchers and developers. By emphasizing the importance of social embeddedness and the context-specific meaning making and practices, we, the authors of this paper, position ourselves in the field of progressive transformation, where the aim is to create socioeconomic improvements with the help of ICTs through locally situated action [1, 7, 8]. As Hanna [7] points out, the centrally driven programs often lack strategies to promote local, bottom-up initiatives to build capacity at grass root level and to create innovative partnerships, which all are critical in supporting local knowledge and capabilities for achieving scalability and sustainability. Instead, a lot of initiatives have the characteristics of hierarchical orderings of a techno-state with top-down approach to development [24]. Heeks [11] outlines good practices for successful ICT in development projects, in three main categories: (1) Actors and Governance (stakeholders and open, competitive environment); (2) Sustainable projects (financial and social sustainability, local ownership); and (3) Design techniques (local participation, appropriate technologies, local development goals, and project risks).

Despite the criticism directed towards TCs as outdated in the modern era of smartphones, we believe that TCs still have an important role to play in the remote, disadvantaged areas, where the population lives with limited or no access to the ICTs and where the educational institutions fail to provide adequate training in the use of these technologies. Even if the population may have access to mobile phones, these are often of simple standard without functionalities needed for elaborate e-learning activities, for example. Our previous studies in Sri Lanka [20] confirm the existence of a wide digital divide between the urban and rural areas. The remote tea estate population distinguishes as particularly disadvantaged regarding computer literacy with only 9% of the population over ten years of age being computer literate. The corresponding figure for the rural population is 25.5% and for the urban one 39.2% [5].

The purpose of this paper is to discuss the issue of awareness raising through a case study conducted in two TCs at the tea estate district Nuwara Eliya in the central hill country of Sri Lanka. We draw on empirical data from a field study that employed a set of collaborative methods with the goal of engaging the local community in the development of their TC.

1.1 Problem and Research Questions

The government initiated nationwide e-Sri Lanka and the TC (Nenasala) projects [23] can be described as typical top-down endeavours of a techno-state, where the local involvement is limited. Inauguration of a TC with a big cultural celebration in the presence of political leadership being the only (official) awareness raising activity, many people have only a vague idea of the possibilities of TCs, which may partly explain the low engagement and use of TCs at present. Half of the government initiated TCs (over 500) are not operational today (private communication with ICTA representative).

We argue that the situation could be improved through collaboration between local stakeholders, TC staff and visitors, the government ICT agency (ICTA) and TC organizations, to achieve a sustainable project with local ownership [11] taking into consideration the specific local needs and requirements. Particularly, the underserved populations of tea estate areas might benefit more of the local TCs, if their voices were made stronger in the development process. Estate areas have developed their own particular socio-economic and cultural conditions with the imported/migrated Indian Tamil population as the workforce. They have remained isolated and marginalized with limited possibilities for social mobility and development. Due to their particular character, tea estate areas can benefit from a TC as a service provider.

Based on the idea of inclusion and with a specific focus on tea estate areas, an international team of five researchers from the universities of Colombo and Stockholm embarked a research and development initiative to explore the conditions of TC development now that a decade has passed since the commencement of the TC initiative by the Sri Lankan government.

Research questions addressed in this study are: (1) How can participatory methods inform development initiatives in the tea estate context? and (2) What are the particular needs and requirements of the tea estate populations regarding telecentres?

2 Methodology

The research and development project addressed in this paper, is framed theoretically and methodologically by participatory approach [13, 22] applying a specific methodology of *Future workshops* consisting of four separate parts: (1) co-inspirational activities; (2) brainstorming sessions; (3) applied photo voice sessions, and (4) a final appreciation session with refreshments and a photo show. Our notion of *Future workshop* is not to be mixed with the one Jungk and Mullert [12] have introduced in the MDI literature. Our *Future workshop* has been designed to meet the conditions of a specific setting where the researchers' aim is to maximise the limited resources (time and funding) for a best possible outcome. The design could be described as "quick and dirty" (informing the design process through short, focused study) gathering enough data to initiate a development process with the TC staff and users jointly.

The two-day *Future workshop* was commenced with co-inspirational sessions with targeted activities for different participant groups in the community. Research team introduced programming through gaming and English language learning sessions with a new mobile application developed at the University of Colombo for the school children and school leavers. We demonstrated the Internet for a group of women and we talked about the possibilities of Wikipedia and Wikiversity for teachers and library personnel.

During photo voice sessions [25, 26], participants took photos of their community using the tablets that we lent them. These photos give a vivid illustration of the community and the neighbourhood. Brainstorming sessions constituted the principal activity in the *Future workshops*. Participants were urged to come with ideas for further development of TCs. This paper is based mainly on the brainstorming data. Additional data collection was conducted through a questionnaire, participant observations and interviews during the *Future workshops*.

2.1   Setting of the Study – Sri Lankan TCs of Tea Estate Areas

Prior to the study reported in this paper, a reconnaissance trip was made in the tea estate district of Nuwara Eliya to explore the overall present day status of TCs in the area with the aim to identify good candidates for further collaboration. Our criteria were to find TCs that were operational in the sense that basic equipment would be in place and that the staff would be interested in collaborating with us.

Our choice fell on two different types of TCs; one government *initiated Nenasala* (TC1) and the other, Thondaman Foundation initiated, e-kiosk, called *Prajashakthi* (TC2), see Table 1. Our sampling approach followed the idea of purposefulness [19] identifying and selecting information-rich sites that would allow us to examine the situation of TCs in detail, and understand the present conditions of these establishments.

Table 1. TCs in Nuwara Eliya district chosen for the study.

	Location	Equipment	Activities	Users
TC 1 (Nenasala) government initiated	Small town Shared space with the local library	4 PCs Scanner Printer WiFi-router No functioning Internet connection	Basic computer courses, English language courses	Mainly school children A group of mothers/housewives
TC 2 (Prajashakti) Thondaman Foundation initiated	Next to a tea factory, own building with four rooms	4 PCs Scanner Printer Projector No functioning Internet connection	Basic computer courses, English language courses	Mainly school children and school leavers

TC1 manager is not paid for his work, but he is employed by the local governmental body *Pradesheeya Sabhaa*. He is a former teacher and dedicated to work for the community. He is assisted by the library personnel and the librarians also use the computers in their library work. The TC1 manager has got many ideas of how to develop the activities. His main concern is the lack of resources. He tries to collaborate with another TC in a near-by town but the lack of funds makes it difficult, as he cannot afford compensating any training engagements from the other TC. At present, he relies on collaboration with the library staff and on the voluntary efforts by the local community. For him, the research team and the idea of outside collaboration seems as an opportunity he cannot afford to miss as no other assistance is in sight.

The Prajashakthi type TC 2 receives funding from the "*Ministry of up country, new villages, estate infrastructure and community development*", for the salaries, and maintenance expenses. However, the Internet costs have not been covered for some time due to the political uncertainties and shift of government. Manager here would also like to offer a wider selection of courses. For example, school leavers would need preparatory courses and even vocational training that would help them widen the range of opportunities after finishing school.

Both TCs share the problems with insufficient resources and the lack of functioning Internet connection. Both TC managers recognize the need for further training for the TC staff as a first and crucial step in their development plans, and they both are eager to develop the services for their communities. Against this background, the international research team initiated a collaboration to plan for new activities that would engage both the TC staff and the local community for further development of their TCs.

2.2   Participants

For recruiting participants for the *Future workshops*, the research team relied on the TC managers who made the invitations in their communities. Table 2 provides a summary of the participants.

Table 2. Participants of the *Future workshops*.

	Gender		Age		Language	
	Female	Male	Children	Adults	Tamil	Sinhala
TC1	19	11	13	17	22	8
TC2	23	14	37		37	
Total	42	25	50	17	59	8

Majority of the children were those at school, another group consisted of school leavers who had just finished their O-levels and waiting for the results of the examination. In addition, small children not at school yet, were present during the days drawn by curiosity to the TC to see the visitors. The group of adults represented various vocational groups, such as teachers, librarians, office workers, and police as well as housewives. Our sample could thus be described as a combination of chain sampling and mixed purposeful sampling [19], not representative of the whole community, but fairly representative of the TC users as school children constituted the majority of the participants in the study. As the TC managers were our key informants and most likely used their own networks to invite participants, those who actually showed up during the *Future workshops* were either typical visitors to the TCs, or potential visitors, and interested ones with motivation for TC development.

2.3   Brainstorming Sessions and Questionnaire

For the purpose of defining a baseline understanding of the participants, a questionnaire with 10 questions was conducted among them by the research team during the first day of the *Future workshop*. In addition to basic background information about the participants (gender, age, occupation, first language), the questionnaire covered questions about the media ownership and use as well as TC use.

The main activity during the *Future workshops* was brainstorming sessions for collecting ideas and concrete suggestions for improvements of the TCs. The research team was also keen to learn more about the understandings of the participants in relation to the use of TCs. Third central aspect was the importance of drawing attention to active participation and ownership of the TCs.

Participants were asked to respond to two questions: (1) What can you do for the TC? and (2) What can the TC do for you? With these two questions we wished to capture the reciprocity in the relationship: a TC is not only a place where the community members can receive services. Equally important is to plan how the community members can contribute to their TC. The theme of reciprocity emerged during our conversations with the TC managers prior to the awareness raising activity. They complained that the community members saw the TC as a government service provider that should be free of charge.

Participants were divided into small groups of five and given a large sheet of paper and a pen for documentation of their thoughts and ideas. After half an hour of group work, the results of each group were presented and discussed in plenum. All the ideas were collected on a large sheet of paper for everyone to see the results. These papers were photographed and transcribed by the research team for later analysis.

Qualitative data from the *Future workshops* was analysed through a systematic, thematic analysis [2] applying MAXQDA. This analysis was conducted with focus on the specific research questions, with a data-driven approach where the coding was done without a pre-existing coding framework. Furthermore, the analysis focused not only on describing but also interpreting the data, resulting in latent rather than semantic themes (ibid.). The questionnaire has been quantitatively processed.

3   Findings

3.1   Questionnaire Results

Table 2 summarizes basic information about the participants. At TC 1, almost all of the children visit the TC at least once a week. At TC 2, half of the participants visit TC frequently and one third was there for the first time.

Most participants have a TV and radio at home. At TC 1, 60% have a computer at home, compared to 30% at TC 2; however, only half of all these possess Internet connection at home (excluding smartphone connection). Many young people at TC 2 share a mobile phone with their families, while adults at TC 1 have their own devices. 70% of all participants at TC 1 have a smartphone, versus 24% at TC 2. Phones are used mainly for making voice calls and for text messaging. Attending computer or English language classes are the main reasons for visiting TCs. Some of the young also come for entertainment like gaming. Adults rely on the TC for other services like scanning and copying documents. Social media, like Facebook, YouTube, and Twitter, are mostly known by the name without real understanding of what they represent. Results from the questionnaire confirm that access to ICTs and training digital literacy are needed as the ownership of mobiles is often a shared one and availability to computers and the Internet is limited.

3.2   Findings from the Brainstorming Sessions

Analysis of the brainstorming results shows two main themes: (1) 'Needs' of the participating community members; and their (2) 'Relations to the TC'. Under the category 'Needs' we found three main subcategories: 'ICT education'; 'ICT for education', and 'More Resources'. Under the category of 'Relations to the TC', following two themes emerged: partly the brainstorming participants were discussing their understanding of TC ('Notions of TC') and partly we could distinguish an emergent 'Sense of community' which was expressed in various ways.

3.2.1   Needs – What Is Lacking in the TCs?

TCs were mainly understood as places for educational activities. This understanding is based on the principal experience of these places, but reflects also the central need in the community: educational opportunities are scarce and thus there is a need to learn more about ICTs as such and as a vehicle for further studies, as well as there is a need to learn English language as a preparation for further education. Thus, it is understandable that needs explicated by participants focused on improvement of the educational facilities. In the same line of reasoning, another central aspect of improvement expressed during the brainstorming was human resources; the need for more qualified teachers and continuous service to the community (Fig. 1).

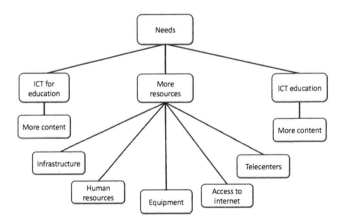

Fig. 1. Conceptual map of needs.

The need for more computers, more class room space and more teachers was expressed by all. The existing 4 stationary PCs and one laptop (for the instructors) are not sufficient for conducting classes for bigger groups. Children were also specific about the need for more in-depth and up-to-date knowledge about the technological development. They want to have good Internet connection and download games. Courses in web design, graphics, and game development are also in their wish list. The school leavers are also keen to receive more education and information about the possibilities that exist for them. They also note that it would be important to educate parents about the relevance of free services at the TC, in contrast to the private and expensive classes in the city.

Another important aspect that the participants brought up is the lack of materials in Tamil, the first language of these communities. Dictionaries (hardcopy) of computer vocabulary from English and software manuals (hardcopy) in Tamil, e.g. about image editing were listed as crucial educational material required in TCs. It may be noted that one of the TCs had received a translation device, but it was not in use due to lack of batteries.

For the participating women the offerings of the telecentre were not sufficient. *"TC should contribute with different services to the community"* and there should be *"more useful things to women"*. Employability and communication are major concerns:

"I have my sister working in the Middle East, I would have loved to learn how to Skype, so I can let her know her children are well cared." Woman 1

"I like to go there and learn how to use the Internet and improve my English so I can get a better job in the Middle East." Woman 2

"We have relatives in India they are well connected to the Internet we would like to look for possibilities to do business but I am reluctant to go there as the place is run mainly for young people. So I send my kids perhaps they can teach me one day." Woman 3

Women also point out that there should be several TCs in these remote areas as transportation is troublesome and time consuming in the winding, steep roads of the hill country.

3.2.2   TCs and the Sense of Community

Prior to the workshop activities, the TC managers had complained that the local community does not regard the TC as 'theirs' but rather as a government service. Against this background, it is interesting to note that all the workshop participants formulated expressions of social responsibility toward the TC. They stated a need to take care of their TC; they viewed it as their property to be protected and maintained. In addition, they claimed a new goal of making "the best TC in the world". The adults also proposed to create funding for the teachers as a community effort, a clear indication of the emergent sense of community involvement.

The mothers and other adults became quite enthusiastic about promoting TCs in their own community: *"We could go the schools here and talk about TCs and the services it provides"*. They also suggested a *"Nenasala club"* as a way of gathering members of the community around the TC to support it in various ways, even economically; today the TC1 instructors work for free. The Nenasala club can also be related to a *"mega-meeting"* envisioned at TC2, to gather users once a year with other

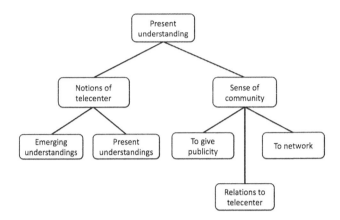

Fig. 2. Conceptual map of the notion of TC and community.

TCs to share knowledge and create a regional network of TCs and their users. Another suggestion was to build a social media community of TC users in order to strengthen the geographically isolated TCs (Fig. 2).

Children were also ready to "*Make their TC the best one in the world*" and "*Arrange competitions in ICT use to increase motivation among children to study harder*". There is a sense of pride and ownership in statements like: "*I will tell others about the TC and what is going on in the TC*"; "*We will do our best, listen carefully in order to learn, and use the resources wisely.*"; "*We will maintain the TC clean, tidy*".

We can record how the notion of TC was expanded by the participants from a sole ICT access and training centre into a place with multiple functions. The idea of using the TC as a place for knowledge sharing on issues relevant for the community suggests this. Expressions like "*a good place to spend time*" and "*communicate with people outside the area*" indicate that the participants are beginning to realise the potential of the TCs as social places where they can come to meet others and for example play games. Further, adults showed a great enthusiasm once they realized how ICTs could be used in various ways. For example, as women were taught about social media, they realised the potential of it in their own lives and came up with ideas of applying social media for their businesses. One of the teachers in the participant group wanted to develop an ICT curriculum for her nursery class when she realised she could receive support in the TC. Thus, the idea of TC as a resource centre was starting to take form.

4 Discussion

Our point of departure, based on action research tradition, has been the conviction that sustainability of a TC requires active participation of the local community, which has been lacking in much of ICT4D research [10, 14]. By engaging two TCs and their users in development activities, we have discovered that the present offerings of these TCs are inadequate and not meeting the specific needs of the community. The choice of two TCs with different financial arrangements, and different geographical locations (one in a small town, the other next to a tea factory) was deliberate to examine whether these differences play any role in the way TCs are functioning. It is evident that despite the differences, they share many issues regarding the TC operations: Lack of network and hardware resources, absence of well-trained instructors, and limited hours for training being the most crucial ones according to the brainstorming results. Also, the absence of community involvement is mutual.

The state of TCs in the tea estate areas demonstrate how digital divide cannot be erased by simply bringing in some technology. We believe that only through engaging the community in digital literacy projects that are intimately connected to the local context and the specific needs and requirements there, a real transformative change can be commenced. As Breitenbach [3] notes: "People need to and want to be informed in order to be able to take part in their own development – to become part of the information society". Raising awareness becomes an essential part in community ownership as people need to be aware of what they can do for the TC and what they can get from the TC by actively involving in TC activities. In the brainstorming session, several ideas of social engagement were presented, like creating a TC club; organising TC mega-meetings; supporting the TC financially; and taking care of the property in a responsible way so that the community could be proud of theTC. All these ideas reflect a budding sense of community awareness of possibilities related to TCs as instruments for local development [8, 11] and change. This shows that community ownership is a possible way of establishing sustainable TCs with focus on targeted community based services. Based on our findings, we believe that *Future workshops* may function as a catalyst to this participative process. However, development and transformation requires a longitudinal engagement as has been pointed out repeatedly in the development discussions [3].

The information and knowledge that was produced during the brainstorming are well grounded in the needs and requirements of the participants and their families giving expression to wishes that would provide the TC with the very basic resources for ICT and language training. Notable is the lack of ideas for economic development. Women expressed some ideas in this direction but as studies [3, 16] suggest, development should not be based exclusively on educational offerings but need to be combined with economic development initiatives that can enhance employability in the community. This is crucial in tea estate areas where economic opportunities are scarce, tea industry being the main source of income.

Even though this study was fairly small and limited in a specific context, it demonstrates how knowledge and awareness can be co-created through collaborative methods. During *Future workshops* the participants have shown their willingness to take ownership of their local TCs, but at present, mechanisms to initiate ownership are missing, which is why we suggest that *Future workshops* can function as such a mechanism. The method may be applied during a longer period of time in conjunction with a set of supportive activities. As the TC managers pointed out: several occasions and a longer period of time would be more suitable to attract different groups in the community to initiate more profound conversations about the development work.

5 Conclusions and Future Work

Our findings suggest that for a sustainable development of TCs following measures should be considered to meet the specific local needs and requirements:

- A substantial expansion of course offerings, equipment and human resources to meet the needs of the local population while creating a sufficient and functional study environment
- Targeted competence development activities (both digital literacy and vocational training) for women and school leavers to support employability
- Create a proper systematic approach to commence community ownership
- Consider economic development as an essential part of the TCs and raise awareness of the economic opportunities through TCs
- A locally operational supportive network for the TC staff for resource sharing and competence development
- Learning and technical instruction materials in Tamil language

It is evident that an active community around TCs is required and that different services and interactions for diverse groups of people in the society are needed in the TC for it to become attractive. A move from one purpose (ICT training) TC to multipurpose (innovations, entrepreneurship) TC is vital.

Even though the community might be willing to provide financial support to the TC and thus enhance the quality of the services, TCs need alternative means of income to ensure financial stability. Further, TCs need to develop strategies on how to eliminate infrastructure barriers of connectivity and ways to strengthen the competences of the TC instructors. These may be realized through private sector partnerships.

The continuation of our project contains of supporting activities. TC 1 is in the process of expanding the number of courses offered. The research team organises occasional training sessions through Skype-based communication. We have also sponsored the TC with an Internet subscription, and the TC is examining crowd funding options for financial support.

References

1. Avgerou, C.: Discourses on ICT and development. Inf. Technol. Int. Dev. **6**(3), 1–18 (2010)
2. Braun, V., Clarke, V.: Using thematic analysis in psychology. Qual. Res. Psychol. **3**(2), 77–101 (2006)
3. Breitenbach, M.C.: Telecentres for sustainable rural development: review and case study of a South African rural telecentre. Dev. South Africa **30**(2), 262–278 (2013)
4. Davison, R.M., et al.: Information Systems in Developing Countries: Theory and Practice. City University of Hong Kong Press, Hong Kong (2005)
5. Department of Census and Statistics: Sri Lanka Labour Force Survey Annual Report - 2015. (2015)
6. Gomez, R.: When you do not have a computer: public-access computing in developing countries. Inf. Technol. Dev. **20**(3), 274–291 (2014)

7. Hanna, N.K.: E-transformation as an integrating strategy. In: Hanna, N.K., Knight, P.T. (eds.) Seeking Transformation Through Information Technology, Innovation, Technology, and Knowledge Management, pp. 1–19. Springer, Heidelberg (2011)

8. Hanna, N.K.: Mastering Digital Transformation: Towards a Smarter Society, Economy, City and Nation. Emerald Group Publishing Limited, Cleveland (2016)

9. Harris, R.W.: Explaining the success of rural Asian telecentres. In: Information Systems in Developing Countries: Theory and Practice, pp. 83–100. University of HK Press, Hong Kong (2005)

10. Harris, R.W.: How ICT4D research fails the poor. Inf. Technol. Dev. **22**(1), 177–192 (2016)

11. Heeks, R.: The ICT4D 2.0 Manifesto: Where Next for ICTs and International Development? (2009)

12. Jungk, R., Mullert, N.: Future Workshops: How to Create Desirable Futures. Institute for Social Inventions, London (1987)

13. Kemmis, S., McTaggart, R.: Participatory action research: communicative action and the public sphere. In: The Sage Handbook of Qualitative Research, 3rd edn., pp. 559–603. Sage Publications (2005)

14. Loh, Y.A.: Approaches to ICT for development (ICT4D): vulnerabilities vs. capabilities. Inf. Dev. **31**(3), 229–238 (2013)

15. Malek, J.A., et al.: Symbiotic relationship between telecentre and lifelong learning for rural community development: a Malaysian experience. Turkish Online J. Educ. Technol. **13**(3), 148–155 (2014)

16. Mamba, M.S.N., Isabirye, N.: A framework to guide development through ICTs in rural areas in South Africa. Inf. Technol. Dev. **21**, 1 (2015)

17. Mbatha, B.: Pushing the agenda of the information society: ICT diffusion in selected multipurpose community telecentres in South Africa. Inf. Dev. **27**(4), 47–62 (2015)

18. Miller, P.B.: From the digital divide to digital inclusion and beyond: update on telecentres and Community Technology Centers (CTCs), 28 March 2013. http://dx.doi.org/10.2139/ssrn.224116

19. Patton, M.Q.: Qualitative Research & Evaluation Methods: Integrating Theory and Practice. Sage Publishing, Thousand Oaks (2015)

20. Peiris, R., et al.: Bridging the digital divide in Sri Lankan tea estate areas. In: Nielsen, P. (ed.) Proceedings of IFIP 9.4 13th International Conference on Social Implications of Computers in Developing Countries, pp. 773–784 (2015)

21. Rahman, T., Bhuiyan, S.H.: Multipurpose community telecenters in rural Bangladesh: a study of selected union information and service centers. Inf. Dev. **32**(1), 5–19 (2014)

22. Reason, P., Bradbury, H.: Handbook of Action Research. SAGE, Los Angeles (2006)

23. Shadrach, B.: Nenasala the Sri Lankan Telecentre Experience. Information and Communication Technology Agency, Colombo (2012)

24. Singh, J.P., Flyverbom, M.: Representing participation in ICT4D projects. Telecomm. Policy **40**(7), 692–703 (2016)

25. Wang, C.: Photovoice: a participatory action research strategy applied to women's health. J. Women's Health **8**(2), 185–192 (1999)

26. Wang, C., Burris, M.A.: Photovoice: concept, methodology, and use for participatory needs assessment. Heal. Educ. Behav. **24**(3), 369–387 (1997)

Global Sourcing and Development

Understanding the Development Implications
of Online Outsourcing

Fareesa Malik[1]([⊠]), Brian Nicholson[2], and Richard Heeks[3]

[1] NUST Business School, National University of Science and Technology,
Islamabad, Pakistan
fareesa.malik@nbs.nust.edu.pk
[2] Alliance Manchester Business School, University of Manchester,
Manchester, UK
brian.nicholson@manchester.ac.uk
[3] Centre for Development Informatics, University of Manchester,
Manchester, UK
richard.heeks@manchester.ac.uk

Abstract. Online outsourcing (OO) involves global outsourcing of tasks from clients to freelancers via platforms such as Upwork, Guru, Freelancer and Fiverr. Governments and donor agencies in several developing countries are currently starting OO training initiatives to enable access to digital livelihoods for marginalised groups such as youth and women. However, little is known about the impact of these initiatives and in response this paper reports on empirical research into OO projects in Pakistan. Supported by the sustainable livelihoods framework, the analysis shows a context of politico-economic vulnerability. Many freelancers do not succeed but some entrepreneurial individuals motivated by earnings potential are able to generate sufficient livelihoods. Contrary to an image of deinstitutionalised work, this form of digital labour involves a substantial institutional ecosystem. This implies a broad range of stakeholders including the platforms, formal interventions from policymakers and development agencies and the creation of informal support mechanisms.

Keywords: Online outsourcing · Digital development · Freelancing · Gig economy · Livelihoods

1 Introduction

Online outsourcing (OO) involves outsourcing of tasks from clients to workers all over the world via online platforms such as Upwork, Freelancer and Fiverr. Two of the largest platforms – Upwork and Freelancer – are estimated to have 4.5 and 7.5 million workers worldwide [9]. It is predicted that, by 2020, the OO sector overall will be worth US$15–25bn [15]. OO freelancers already provide services from several developing countries including India, Pakistan, the Philippines, South Africa and Kenya [15, 23]. Donor agencies such as the World Bank and national policy makers in developing countries, for instance, the Philippines, Malaysia and Pakistan have all seen potential for OO to create livelihoods for marginalised groups: women, youth and those on lowest incomes. OO initiatives involving government- and donor agency-funded training

© IFIP International Federation for Information Processing 2017
Published by Springer International Publishing AG 2017. All Rights Reserved
J. Choudrie et al. (Eds.): ICT4D 2017, IFIP AICT 504, pp. 425–436, 2017.
DOI: 10.1007/978-3-319-59111-7_35

programmes for economic empowerment of these groups are therefore already underway. However, the novelty of this model for economic growth has created significant knowledge gaps in relation to its development potential. The knowledge gaps include issues of incentives and motivation, infrastructural requirements, financial and non-financial impacts, and impact on longer-term career trajectories [23]. This paper attempts to fill these gaps based on preliminary fieldwork undertaken in 2016 in Pakistan. Specifically, using the sustainable livelihoods framework (SLF) [7] as a sensitising lens, it addresses three questions:

- What drives those in marginalised groups to engage in OO?
- What infrastructural and institutional ecosystems are required, particularly addressing barriers to OO for marginalised groups?
- What are the short- and longer-term impacts of OO?

Our aim is a three-fold contribution: reducing the knowledge gaps via our findings; demonstrating an SLF conceptualisation of OO to marginalised groups; and offering nascent guidance to practitioners and policy-makers in developing countries who wish to make more effective use of OO as a development tool. Following a review of literature on OO, the paper outlines the SLF conceptual framework that was used to shape fieldwork and analysis, details of which are discussed in the methodology section. Following presentation of the findings, some conclusions are drawn.

2 Literature Review

There are two main types of platforms: microwork such as Amazon Mechanical Turk and online freelancing such as Upwork, Freelancer, Guru, Fiverr etc. each targeting different segments of workers and employers. Estimates vary on the number of OO platforms and the marketplace is dynamic but we know there are hundreds of examples that incorporate a wide range of tasks including data entry and transcription; data analytics; web, mobile apps, and software development; legal and accounting services; engineering and architecture services; translation; administrative support; customer service; and sales and marketing. The World Bank estimated OO annual revenues of $4.8 billion in 2016 and between $15–$25 billion by 2020 [15].

The information systems (IS) and business literature on OO has, necessarily because of the global nature of the platforms, encompassed work undertaken in developing countries. However, despite a paucity of research that takes a development orientation two identifiable streams of literature have emerged. The first has tended to focus on organisational or sectoral-level issues, e.g. identifying OO as a new "human cloud" type of business model [13]. Others scholars examine the client end of the value chain: for example identifying the capacity of OO to reduce barriers to offshoring and thus enable a wider range of client organisations (e.g. smaller enterprises) to become involved [10]. Another set has focused more on the "mechanics" of OO platforms looking, for example, at IT-enabled work monitoring systems [17] or use of feedback and profile information [1] that underpin the functions of the platforms. There is also a significant discourse focussing at the worker end of the value chain adopting a critical lens pessimistically viewing OO as a "digital sweatshop" [25]. [5] and [9] emphasize the lack of typical employment benefits from OO: absence of holiday pay, sickness benefits, health insurance, minimum wage, retirement benefits and compensation in the event of injury. Workers are driven to accept these terms because of a background of economic austerity and uncertainty. Such outcomes are conditioned by the institutional context explained in terms of a de-institutionalisation of work: an absence of legislative oversight for a work process that is invisible, mobile and transcends national borders; and an absence of collective bargaining, collective wage agreements and unionisation [5]. Alternatively it can be explained in terms of the particular institutional rationalities imposed by digital platforms: decentralisation, precarisation and informalisation [9]. In either case, there has been a concern to re-institutionalise; particularly helping to develop fair labour-oriented institutions. Suggested actions include creation of platforms that seek to mitigate information asymmetries between clients and workers; providing reputational information on clients to match the reputational information on workers that main platforms provide [12] and creation of labour unions for OO workers [26]. Because of the novelty of OO, critical research is often based on secondary sources, and primary research has given a somewhat more nuanced view with a picture emerging of differentiation. Study of skill and employment impacts of OO found, that this enables workers "to renew existing skills through practice, to discover and utilise latent skills and to develop specialist skills" and to improve their employability [2, p. 28]. However, this was only for workers who could overcome skill and other barriers to entry, and who could employ "continuous marketing, good client management skills and self-promotion" and who operationalised "characteristics of self-efficacy, motivation, self-reliance and adaptability" [2].

Research on financial impact of OO shows most workers use this to supplement other sources of income but many use it as a main source of income [4]. Here also there is a differentiation, but geographic. First, those in developing countries are more likely to use OO as a main source of income: half of Indian workers on Amazon Mechanical Turk stated this [4]. Second, payments differ. OO workers in the global North tend to earn more in absolute terms but workers in the global South earn more in relative terms, i.e. relative to average wages in their country [2, 3]. This promise of relatively good wages and livelihoods has propelled significant interest in OO in developing countries, with particular aspirations that it could provide livelihoods to groups often excluded from the economic mainstream such as women and young people (it is estimated that two-thirds of young people in developing countries are either unemployed or trapped in low-quality, low-skill jobs [15]). As a result, there are a number of OO initiatives underway, e.g. the NaijaCloud initiative in Nigeria, sponsored by the World Bank and supported by the national government, which provides awareness workshops on OO; The Youth Employment Programme (http://www.youthemp.com) of Pakistan's Khyber Pakhtunkhwa (KPK) provincial government which aims to train 40,000 young people; and Malaysia's eRezeki initiative (https://erezeki.my/en/home) which has trained hundreds of freelancers and now uses a "walled garden" approach with US crowd-sourcing platform Massolutions: a managed portal for OO work such that the work process is controlled by government.

As stated there is a paucity of OO research taking an explicit development approach. But a related stream of academic and practitioner research focuses on global outsourcing practices of social enterprises and outsourcing service providers aiming to create social and economic value [6, 18, 20, 21]. This shows that global outsourcing work opportunities can positively contribute to development of marginalised individuals' capabilities and livelihoods [11, 16, 18, 19]. Other prior literature [3, 4] takes a perspective of OO workers in developing countries. However, to date there has been little if any academic research looking specifically at OO and its development impact that focuses on marginalised groups in developing countries.

3 Conceptual Framework

Work in OO represents a livelihood. Reflecting earlier work analysing outsourcing of IT-based work to marginalised groups [11], we thus decided that our conceptualisation of this activity would be shaped by the sustainable livelihood framework [7]. The SLF (see summary overview in Fig. 1 [8]) sees livelihoods as existing within a context of vulnerabilities which drive livelihood strategies, so we use this context to answer our first research question.

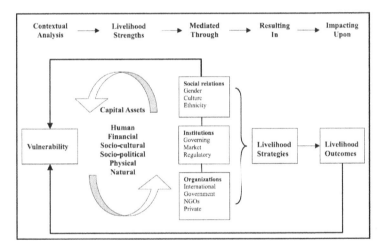

Fig. 1. Sustainable livelihoods framework

To create a strategy, individuals draw on a set of capital assets. Here, and following the earlier [11] study, we considered the four that were particularly relevant:

- Human capital: "the skills, knowledge, ability to labour and good health that together enable people to pursue different livelihood strategies" [7, p. 7].
- Social capital: "the social resources upon which people draw in pursuit of their livelihood objectives" [7, p. 9].
- Physical capital: "the basic infrastructure and producer goods needed to support livelihoods" [7, p. 13].
- Financial capital: "the financial resources that people use to achieve their livelihood objectives" [7, p. 15].

These assets are accessed and integrated into strategies within a broader environment of relations, institutions and organisations. In answering our second question, we therefore understand barriers and ecosystem in terms of the asset access that the institutional and organisational environment provides. Finally, we understand the impact of a livelihood in terms of the lower reverse arrow in the diagram: improvements or otherwise to the stock of assets that individuals can call upon [11]. We will use this approach to answer our third question.

4 Methodology

The empirical field study, undertaken in 2016, involved interviews with stakeholders at two World Bank-funded OO training organisations in Pakistan: the Karakoram Area Development Organization (KADO) and Empower Pakistan (EP). These organisations have designed and implemented training and support schemes aiming to enable women and unemployed youth in Pakistan to engage in OO. A qualitative exploratory field study method [22] was followed to investigate the context and impact of OO livelihoods, with fieldwork focused on the Northern Pakistan region of Gilgit-Baltistan (GB). A purposive sampling technique was followed to approach different stakeholders: project leads, OO freelancers, trainees who had received training from KADO and EP, trainers and project managers. Data was collected through 29 semi-structured interviews conducted through Skype (1 from Washington DC, 3 from Lahore and 1 from Karachi) or face-to-face during a Pakistan field visit to GB and Islamabad. SLF categories and concepts provided the structure to guide the interviews but allowed the interviewer flexibility to probe into unanticipated areas of interest. Interviews were recorded, translated, transcribed, and coded in computerised qualitative data management software (NVivo 10) using a template analysis approach [14].

5 Findings

In the sections to follow we present the results and analysis of our field data grouped in relation to the categories of the SLF.

5.1 Vulnerability Context

The starting point for any livelihood analysis is an understanding of the vulnerability context. As indicated, the field study was undertaken in GB, the northernmost administrative territory of Pakistan. Geographically, the region is home to the world's highest mountain ranges including Karakoram, Himalayas and Hindu Kush. The project coordinator related GB's geography to lack of industries and commented: "... *the problem here is that our job market is very poor. We do not have industries here*" (RE – Project Coordinator, KADO).

Alongside physical vulnerabilities to climate-related disasters, the area has been subject to a negatively reinforcing politico-economic vulnerability context that limits conventional employment routes. First, GB is located in the disputed region of Kashmir the result of which is that it is a separate state in Pakistan but without status of a province eligible for independent provincial government, legislation and budget. GB is not integrated with any of the other provinces of Pakistan. The result is a "no man's land" position that severely restricts private and public sector investment, infrastructural development and employment opportunities: *"The problem is that we live in GB; which is itself a conflicted area. That is why the government is not doing much investment for prosperity here"* (EJ – Project Manager, KADO).

EP targeted educated youth of middle and lower socio-economic status in Punjab province, which is a highly populated province of Pakistan; and also provided OO training to educated youth of Khyber Pakhtunkhwa (KPK) province, which is the most terrorism-effected province of Pakistan. Lack of investment, lack of opportunities and high unemployment create a fertile environment for growth of radical Islamic extremism which, in turn, serves to further discourage investment and employment: *"The reason is it's the front line of extremism. The next biggest issue is unemployment. Both of these issues are interrelated because when there is unemployment the chances of frustrated youth to be involved in terrorist activities would be higher."* (SK–Project Manager, EP).

The absence of alternative livelihoods is a core driver to involvement in OO: *"Everyone wants to get the government job but it is not available... Maybe the condition gets better in the future but currently, there is nothing better here than freelancing and working and earning at home"* (HA – Ex-trainee, KADO). The ability to work at home is an especial driver for women, *"who have to stay at home... who can't work in offices for various cultural and other reasons."* (AL– Project Lead, WB).

But alongside this generic socio-economic push are specific pulls into OO. For some of those involved, there is the attraction of a livelihood that offers more freedom than traditional jobs: *"You are your own boss. You don't have any boss. You can work of your choice at any time you like"* (YA – Trainer and Freelancer, KADO).

Another important pull has been the presence of attractive role models who demonstrate not just the viability but the significant benefits of an OO livelihood. Sometimes these role models are friends, but they can also be presented at formal events. One trainee shared his inspiration: *"...RA (a famous blogger in the region) tells once about his freelancing experience. He opened his account and showed it to us. At that time, his earning was twelve to fifteen lakh Pakistani rupees per month (c. US $12,000–15,000)"* (HU – Trainee, KADO).

Related to its relatively remote, troubled and under-invested context and notwithstanding a strong emphasis on education in the region Gilgit-Baltistan has important resource constraints that are barriers to engagement of marginalised groups with OO. Respondents mentioned three recurring barriers. First, the state of technological infrastructure: *"We don't have high speed Internet and full time electricity in this area. So we don't have basic things for freelancing"* (SA – Trainer, KADO). *"Sometimes there is some internet work of web research for which client demands to check your internet speed and asked to send its screenshot. So, when I sent them the screenshot of the low internet speed; they did not give work."* (RE – Project Coordinator, KADO).

Second, a lack of knowledge and skills: members of marginalised groups lacked an understanding of what OO was and how to link in to OO jobs. They lacked relevant skills: not just technical skills but broader interpersonal and business skills: *"The one-week freelancing training is sufficient for the people in cities who are experts and highly qualified with MCS, MBA, MBBS Degrees. .... However here, we have to engage the trainees with us for six months so that they can learn how to communicate with the clients"* (EJ – Project Manager, KADO).

Third, there are problems with finance and getting payments from overseas, though that has recently improved for some: *"...when you transfer the money locally, so there are no deductions. I have a Soneri Bank account, so when I received my freelancing payments recently, there was no charges that deducted"* (YA – Trainer, KADO).

More challenging to address are cultural barriers. Gender barriers were one: project managers who said male freelancers were "more serious" further explained the additional domestic workload expectations on women: *"...when the guests come, so being a girl, I have to serve, of course. Boys do not need to do this. They just sit on one side and work"* (SA – Trainer, KADO). Another was the cultural expectations of what constitutes a livelihood which reflected negatively on freelancing. Trainees and freelancers shared their personal experiences: *"My parents are uneducated. So, they won't understand freelancing. They just want that their son to go to the office, use a big car and work on some important government position, and people can praise them how successful is their son"* (HU – Trainee, KADO). *"My younger brother is a translator of Chinese language. The parents are very happy with him. He is three years younger to me but they have got him married first and in that way, they have given him the family responsibility. People around me don't think me right. They say that this person wakes up at 10 o'clock in the morning. He keeps awake the whole night. Overall, in the family, my image is bad as I do not do a proper job"* (MU – Trainee, KADO).

5.2 Mediation Effect of Institutions

Contrary to "de-institutionalisation" critiques, at least three observable institutional forces impinged on OO to marginalised groups in Pakistan. First, there are the OO platforms themselves. These constrain the relations between clients and freelancers, particularly the lack of human connection and trust sometimes leading to problems: *"I think the system of Freelancer and Upwork is very tough. ... I cannot work on that level. I made an account on Upwork but we have some difficulties there. We had some problem in creating a profile there. I cannot do work in English correctly. Sometimes, they cancel the jobs. We do not understand what they are talking about. Sometimes, they give us poor rating. That is also a dead block"* (WA – Trainee, KADO). *"It happened with me that I worked with some fake people. I anyhow completed their work, and they got their work, but I did not get any payments"* (YA – Trainer, KADO).

However, in a number of ways the digital platforms are seen as recently improving the institutional context for OO to the relative benefit of freelancers; particularly trying to reduce the moral hazard that arises due to the asymmetry of power and lack of trust between clients and freelancers, and the lack of social costs for "bad behaviour" by clients: *"The freelancing marketplaces are improving their processes. They are blocking accounts for any violation of their terms and conditions. They have introduced different matrix like job success rather than relying on customers' reviews"*

(SK – Project Manager, EP). "*Now Upwork holds advance payment from the clients and transfers it to the freelancer once the job has completed successfully. Which has reduced the fraud and exploitation. Upwork has also introduced easier payment methods*" (YA – Trainer, KADO). "*Upwork has changed its policy of minimum work wage. Previously, they had allowed working for US\$1 per hour. Later they fixed it to minimum US\$3 per hour*" (RE – Project Coordinator, KADO).

Second, there has been the intervention of development agencies, government and NGOs. As described, local NGOs supported by the World Bank have been providing training in a wide variety of skills, guidance, and access to ICTs, etc. Government bodies in Pakistan are also launching freelancing schemes. At the least, this re-institutionalisation is helping to overcome asset deficits that would otherwise exclude marginalised workers from participating in OO. In some cases, the re-institutionalisation goes further: for example the neighbouring government of KPK province will use a "walled garden" approach. This creates a protected area of the online platform into which tasks specifically suitable for the Pakistan freelancers are channelled, sheltering them from bidding activity and the full force of competition.

Third, among the freelancers themselves, there is a range of institutions formed; again to address barriers to OO. These may be individual and social to address knowledge deficits about OO: "*I completed my first online outsourcing project with the help of one or two of my friends*" (MU – Trainee, KADO) and "*I have recently guided my cousin about freelancing*" (NU – Trainee, KADO). And they range up to more formal and economic formations used to help balance workloads, and also to assist more junior freelancers. "*People are working in groups here. Some of the freelancers are getting local small projects and they are working on it for \$300 to \$400 together*" (YA – Trainer, KADO).

This does not mean that competition and asymmetries of power between clients and freelancers are not an issue, but these institutions do introduce some compensations and protections. Without these it is likely that few, if any, of the freelancers in this relatively remote and resource-constrained area of Pakistan would create successful OO livelihoods.

5.3   Capital Assets and Livelihood Outcomes

All interviewed freelancers who went through the formal training programmes developed their human capital in various ways. They develop ICT-related capabilities: "*the technical skills for freelancing such as e-marketing, blogging, search engine optimization, graphic and web-designing*" (EJ – Project Manager, KADO) but also broader skills including communication in English: "*They even teach us how to write cover letters. Also, they taught about proposal writing, means they told us everything about how to deal with the clients. I am getting a new skill, which I have not learnt before. There is growth on personal level as well. I won't be able to talk to you had I not been doing a job. I had very less confident.*" (MK – Trainee, EP).

However, in terms of conversion of this human capital into financial capital via a freelancing livelihood, the trainees divide into four trajectories: sinking, struggling, surviving and swimming. The majority fall into the first camp: one programme manager estimated c. 60% of trainees did not take up freelancing livelihoods. Of those that do, a number struggle to find work because of the highly competitive nature of the bidding process and the paradox that it is difficult to win work without a profile of work experience but building such a profile can only be done by obtaining work: *"There is a friend of mine … When he did not get any order for six months so his family members were also irritated. They said to him to leave this freelancing and work in a factory. He went to the factory as a data entry operator"* (AZ – Trainee, EP).

A number of respondents also echoed concerns in the literature about the lack of employment benefits that OO employment would bring (noting that care must be taken in choice of comparison point: those employed in government jobs in Pakistan have a number of rights and privileges; those employed in informal sector jobs do not). This was mainly framed in terms of illness: *"When a person is healthy, he can do this work. If he gets ill, so he will be unable to work and there would be no chances for any money"* (WA – Trainee, KADO).

Of those that do find work, some are just surviving at a low level of activity; again largely due to the high level of competition: *"I applied for around three to four hundred jobs, and then I got one job. It is not an easy task. On Upwork, there are millions of freelancers. We have to compete with them"* (NU – Trainee, KADO).

Finally, there are those in the "swimming" category who have been able to build up their experience, reputation and contacts to create reasonable earnings, bearing in mind monthly per capita income in Pakistan in 2015 was US$120 [24]: *"I am earning twenty five thousand to thirty thousand per month ($250 to $300). When I will become Level 2 seller and would get more orders in freelancing projects. The one which I did in the morning, it was of $30 and I did it in three hours. Now, one of $60 and two of $90 are left to deliver"* (MK – Trainee, EP). *"If you can check online, please see the profile of our graphics and web trainer, Aslam. He started from $1 per hour. Now, he is working on $27 per hour"* (RD – Trainer, KADO). These amounts are sufficient for reinvestment in other forms of capital. Some are seeking to invest in physical capital, for example, saving to buy a home. Others are studying and invest their earnings in development of their own human capital: *"My brother and two other cousins, who are studying Masters, meet their expenses through earning online by designing logos and websites. They also send money to their homes"* (TR – Trainee, KADO). *"My one semester fee is twenty thousand PKR (US$200) that I earn through freelancing in 15 to 20 days"* (WA – Trainee, KADO).

There is an observable chronology: those struggling and surviving are typically in the early days of freelancing, and they either give up or work their way up to better work and better rates of pay. There is some differentiation that was interpreted in terms of personality type or characteristics, echoing the findings of [2] reported earlier: *"Not everybody can be a freelancer and it takes some characteristics and some drives to do the kinds of jobs there would be through technology or leveraging the tech sector for people who are entrepreneurially freelancing"* (AL – Project Lead, World Bank).

For those that do persevere, progression often relates to the changing profile of work they undertake: where data entry jobs pay at most US$4 per hour, web/graphics/programming work can attract rates of US$30 per hour. All freelancers are at a relatively early stage as few of them have been involved in OO for more than a year. A number see it as a short-term livelihood e.g. to pay college fees: *"People do not make this as a career. You cannot go with this for the long term*" (KM– Trainee, KADO). Others recognised the longer-term potential: "*I have left everything else and choose to do this only because I know that its future is expanding further. Even I think that I bring people from my family, friends, relatives, siblings in this and convince them to work in this very field*" (MU – Trainee, KADO).

However, whether that long-term potential means continuing with freelancing work is unclear. Some were trying to trade the reputation and client contacts they had made via the platforms into direct, off-platform working which would pay more and potentially be less volatile: "*I have been working with different clients and we have communicated now and then so it happens that once your profile is built on Upwork so you can work outside it as well as clients and companies know you now. Even leaving from there, you can work directly with those companies or you can become their online employee*" (YA – Trainer, KADO). But it remains to be seen what the longer-term career trajectories will be in practice.

6   Conclusions

The answer to the first research question "What drives those in marginalised groups to engage in online outsourcing?" lies particularly in the context of significant vulnerability: physical, political, economic. It means the main driving force is necessity of earning a living and absence of other livelihood strategies. For a sub-set, this "push" driving force is set alongside a "pull" of opportunity: the perception that OO offers an entrepreneurial work- and life-style.

In addressing the second question – "What infrastructural and institutional ecosystems are required, particularly to address barriers to OO for marginalised groups?" – we found a number of important barriers relating to capital assets and institutions. Physical and human capitals were especially lacking and there were also institutional barriers, for example around payment systems, gender roles, and cultural constructions of what constituted meaningful work. The cultural barriers are deep-rooted and addressing them lies beyond the scope of main OO stakeholders. Overcoming asset-based barriers is more straightforward but still requires the creation of a broad-based ecosystem: an infrastructure of electricity, telecommunications and ICT; and a set of institutions that were helping to level the playing field – raising individuals and locations up from their asset-deficit status to a situation where they were able to participate in OO. The range of institutions involved was substantial and slightly confounds the negative portrayals of OO in one stream of the extant literature. There were instances in which the digital platforms made concessions and improvements that benefited the workers though of course done in order to maximise activity on the platform. There were also examples of re-institutionalisation: of interventions by donors, governments and NGOs that were mainly beneficial to the freelancers; and less-formal institution-formation by workers themselves, creating social networks of assistance.

Finally, in answering the third question – "What are the short- and longer-term impacts of OO for those involved?" – there were universal gains in human capital. This was entirely expected given we focused on those who had been trained. There was a differentiated financial impact: many trainees "failed to launch" while others struggled to make minor amounts. A significant number were able to generate earnings and build themselves up to earn a reasonable living from OO enabling them, for example, to invest in their own property or education. There was limited evidence on impacts on social and physical capital and, similarly, the relative novelty of OO makes it difficult to assess longer-term impacts such as those on career trajectories.

In practical terms, the research shows OO interventions can be successful in assisting those from marginalised groups into forms of digital employment. These interventions were also shown to be necessary: the barriers to entry into OO are too high for most individuals in resource-constrained environments. One concern could be the high drop-out rate though this may be countered by numbers who do move into OO work. Future work may identify if the psychological or other differences between those who succeed in OO and those who do not might have a practical value. In conceptual terms, we have shown the sustainable livelihoods framework to be viable and useful in structuring evidence and ideas relating to online outsourcing.

References

1. Assemi, B., Schlagwein, D.: Provider feedback information and customer choice decisions on crowdsourcing marketplaces. Decis. Support Syst. **82**, 1–11 (2016)
2. Barnes, S.A., Green, A., Hoyos, M.: Crowdsourcing and work: individual factors and circumstances influencing employability. New Technol. Work Employ. **30**, 16–31 (2015)
3. Beerepoot, N., Lambregts, B.: Competition in online job marketplaces: towards a global labour market for outsourcing services? Glob. Netw. **15**, 236–255 (2015)
4. Berg, J.: Income Security in the On-Demand Economy. ILO, Geneva (2016)
5. Bergvall-Kåreborn, B., Howcroft, D.: Amazon mechanical turk and the commodification of labour. New Technol. Work Employ. **29**, 213–223 (2014)
6. Carmel, E., Lacity, M.C., Doty, A.: The impact of impact sourcing: framing a research agenda. In: Hirschheim, R., Heinzl, A., Dibbern, J. (eds.) Information Systems Outsourcing. Towards Sustainable Business Value, pp. 397–429. Springer, Heidelberg (2014)
7. DFID: DFID Sustainable Livelihoods Guidance Sheet. DFID, London (1999)
8. Duncombe, R.: Using the livelihoods framework to analyze ICT applications for poverty reduction through microenterprise. Inf. Technol. Int. Dev. **3**(3), 81–100 (2007)
9. Ettlinger, N.: The governance of crowdsourcing: rationalities of the new exploitation. Environ. Plann. A **48**(11), 2162–2180 (2016)
10. Hanley, A., Ott, I.: What Happened to Foreign Outsourcing when Firms Went Online? Kiel Institute for the World Economy, Kiel (2012)
11. Heeks, R., Arun, S.: Social outsourcing as a development tool: the impact of outsourcing IT services to women's social enterprises in Kerala. J. Int. Dev. **22**, 441–454 (2010)
12. Irani, L., Silberman, M.: From critical design to critical infrastructure: lessons from turkopticon. Interactions **21**, 32–35 (2014)
13. Kaganer, E., Carmel, E., Hirschheim, R., Olsen, T.: Managing the human cloud. MIT Sloan Manag. Rev. **54**, 23–32 (2013)
14. King, N.: Doing template analysis. In: Symon, G., Cassell, C. (eds.) Qualitative Organizational Research, pp. 426–450. Sage Publications Ltd., London (2012)

15. Kuek, S.C., Paradi-Guilford, C., Toks Fayomi, S.I., Ipeirotis, P., Pina, P., Singh, M.: The Global Opportunity in Online Outsourcing. World Bank, Washington, D.C. (2015)
16. Lacity, M., Rottman, J.W., Carmel, E.: Impact sourcing: employing prison inmates to perform digitally-enabled business services. Commun. Assoc. Inf. Syst. **34**, 914–932 (2014)
17. Liang, C., Hong, Y., Gu, B.: Effects of IT-enabled monitoring systems in online labor markets. In: 37th International Conference on Information Systems, Dublin, Ireland (2016)
18. Madon, S., Sharanappa, S.: Social IT outsourcing and development: theorising the linkage. Inf. Syst. J. **23**, 381–399 (2013)
19. Malik, F., Nicholson, B., Morgan, S.: Evaluating impact sourcing: a capabilities perspectives from a case study in Pakistan. In: 13th International Conference on Social Implications of Computers in Developing Countries, Negombo, Sri Lanka (2015)
20. Malik, F., Nicholson, B., Morgan, S.: Assessing the social development potential of impact sourcing. In: Lacity, M.C., Nicholson, B., Babin, R. (eds.) Socially Responsible Outsourcing: Global Sourcing with Global Impact. Palgrave Macmillan, Basingstoke (2016)
21. Monitor: Job Creation Through Building the Field of Impact Sourcing. Monitor, New York (2011)
22. Palvia, P., Pinjani, P., Sibley, E.H.: A profile of information systems research published in information & management. Inf. Manag. **44**, 1–11 (2007)
23. Wood, A., Graham, M., Lehdonvirta, V., Barnard, H., Hjorth, I.: Virtual Production Networks: Fixing Commodification and Disembeddedness. UK Development Studies Association Conference, Oxford (2016)
24. World Bank: GDP per Capita. World Bank, Washington, D.C. (2016)
25. Zittrain, J.: The Internet Creates a New Kind of Sweatshop. Newsweek, 7 December 2009
26. Zuckerman, M., Kahlenberg, R.D., Marvit, M.: Virtual Labor Organizing. The Century Foundation, New York (2015)

Sustainability in ICT4D

The Impact of Stakeholder Management on the Sense of Ownership in Telecenter Projects: The Case of Malawi

Christopher Banda[1] and Wallace Chigona[2(✉)]

[1] University of Malawi, Zomba, Malawi
[2] University of Cape Town, Cape Town, South Africa
Wallace.Chigona@uct.ac.za

Abstract. Telecenters are meant to provide public access to information and communication technology (ICT) services to contribute to the development of the masses. The government of Malawi is implementing a telecenter project to provide ICT services to rural areas. However, most of the telecenters are not meeting the expected goals. The aim of this study was to explore how telecenter projects in rural areas are conceptualised and implemented. The study sought to understand who was involved in the project and how that influenced the sense of ownership of the telecenters. The research used the Stakeholder Theory as a theoretical framework. It was found that the telecenters faced challenges in the management of stakeholders. Although the projects identified stakeholders at the initiation of the project, they failed to keep the stakeholders engaged in the later phases of the project. This led to a low sense of ownership. Due to these occurrences, the telecenter projects have worked in isolation of the key stakeholders.

Keywords: Telecenter · Stakeholder analysis · Sense of ownership · Rural community · Malawi

1 Introduction

Despite the opportunities which Information Communication Technology (ICT) bring to communities, diffusion of ICTs in rural areas remains slow (ITU 2010). Different governments and organisations are using different approaches to connect rural villages and communities. One such approach is the establishments of telecenters. It is hoped that telecenters may improve the livelihood of the rural communities.

The government of Malawi is implementing the ICT for Sustainable Rural Development Project (ISRDP) which seeks to provide ICT services to the rural areas. By 2012, the government, through the Malawi Communications Regulatory Authority (MACRA), had established about 50 telecenters across the country (MACRA 2012). The performance of these telecenters has been poor and has not met expected goals. The telecenters are performing poorly due to various factors such as lack of awareness, location, staff competence and the model.

Telecenters continue to face challenges of sustainability. One of the factors which affects sustainability of telecenters is lack of meaningful stakeholder engagement and

© IFIP International Federation for Information Processing 2017
Published by Springer International Publishing AG 2017. All Rights Reserved
J. Choudrie et al. (Eds.): ICT4D 2017, IFIP AICT 504, pp. 439–450, 2017.
DOI: 10.1007/978-3-319-59111-7_36

relationship in formulating and running such projects (Bailur 2006; Perrini and Tencati 2006). There is, therefore, a need to explore factors which affect stakeholder engagement in telecenter projects. Many studies stress the need for participation of the local community to foster activities such as assessment of information needs, planning and operations (Bailur 2006; Roman and Colle 2002).

Using a case study approach, we explored how stakeholder management was conducted in a telecenter project in Malawi and how that affected the sense of ownership of the project. The study collected data through semi-structured interviews from various stakeholders, focus groups, documents analysis and observation. The results of the study would provide useful guidance both to telecenters project managersand ICT policy-makers on ways to improve the sustainability of telecenters.

2 Study Setting: Malawi

Malawi is a small country with a population of about 14.84 million. About 84.7% of the population live in the rural areas (NSO 2008). Malawi is divided into 29 local government administrative districts; a District Commissioner heads each local District Assembly. The district is divided into traditional chieftainships called Traditional Authorities, which are further divided into villages. The district development planning system for the government of Malawi provides guidelines on how the projects can be implemented in the districts. The guidelines emphasise the approach to be district-focused, people-centred, bottom-up and participatory by local people (Chiweza 2010). The guidelines specify committees at village, Traditional Authority and District level, through which development projects should be coordinated.

The government of Malawi through MACRA implemented ICT infrastructure development through the establishment of telecenters in several rural areas. The projects were implemented under government funding in partnership with development partners such as the World Bank and the International Telecommunication Union (MACRA 2011). The government adopted different models for implementing telecenter projects, (MACRA 2011). Of interest to this study is the ISRDP model. ISRDP sought to provide ICT services to rural and underserved areas through the establishment of Multipurpose Community telecenters. The project had the mandate to support the government's efforts to reduce poverty and isolation of the rural communities, making accessible ICT-enabled services through scalable and cost-effective communication infrastructures.

3 Theoretical Framework: Stakeholder Management Theory

3.1 Definition of Stakeholder

A stakeholder in an organisation is any group or individual who can affect or is affected by the achievement of the organisation's objectives (Freeman 2010). Stakeholders are vital to the survival and success of an organisation (Freeman et al. 2004). Stakeholders can be primary or secondary (Carrol and Buchholtzl 2012). Primary stakeholders have a direct stake or interest in the organisation and its success. Secondary stakeholders have a public or special interest stake in the organisation.

3.2 Stakeholder Theory – Overview

The Stakeholder Theory is intended both to explain and to guide the structure and operation of an organisation (Donaldson and Preston 1995). It views an organisation as an entity through which numerous and diverse participants accomplish multiple, and not always entirely congruent, purposes. The theory takes into consideration the interests of all legitimate stakeholders (Freeman 2010; Fontaine et al. 2006). The purpose of stakeholder management is to create methods to manage the different groups and relationships that result in a strategic action (Fontaine et al. 2006).

The researchadopted the framework from Bailur (2006) which has three stages: 1. Stakeholder Identification, Stakeholder Behaviour Explanation and Coalition Analysis 2. Stakeholder Management and 3. Concessions/Bargains.

Stakeholder analysis is a process of determining whose interests should be taken into account when developing and/or implementing a policy or project (Schmeer 1999). Stakeholder analysis helps to identify the key actors, their knowledge, behaviour, interests, positions, alliances and importance related to the project, while allowing policymakers and managers to interact more effectively with key stakeholders and increase support for a given policy or project (Schmeer 1999).

The main objective of stakeholder management is to ensure that the primary stakeholders achieve their objectives and that other stakeholders are dealt with ethically and are also relatively satisfied (Carroll and Buchholtz 2012). Stakeholder management for an organisation must address five major questions which are (Carroll and Buchholtz 2012): (a) Who are the stakeholders? (b) What are the stakeholders' stakes? (c) What opportunities and challenges do the stakeholders present? (d) What economic, legal, ethical and charitable responsibilities does the organisation have to the stakeholders? (e) What strategies or actions should be taken to best manage stakeholder challenges and opportunities?

Concessions and bargains are important aspects for developing projects, as they define how different stakeholders reach agreement and get assurance that threats or risks from complaints or lawsuits arising from unsound and unethical business practices have been minimised, if not totally eliminated (Freeman 2010).

4 Methodology

The research was a qualitative cross-sectional exploratory study. We adopted a case study approach for the study. The cases in the study were the telecenters and the communities where the telecenters are located. We targeted the key stakeholders within the 5 km catchment area for the telecenters; these included traditional leaders, surrounding communities, community-based organisations, Local Management Committee (LMC), telecenter staff and schools. We also targeted implementers such as MACRA and district councils.

The study targeted two telecenters. We sought telecenters which had been operating for at least two years, since these would have had enough data: these were Vikwa Telecenter in Kasungu and Khudze Telecenter in Mwanza. Purposive and snowball sampling was used to identify stakeholders who were involved in the projects, including officials from MACRA, district councils, traditional leaders, telecenter staff, LMC and the surrounding community of the 5 km catchment area.. These included community-based organisations, users of the telecenters, community extension workers and farmers. At Khudze, all the traditional leaders within the impact area of the telecenter were involved. Representation from the following community-based organisations were involved: Area Development Committee (ADC), Village Development Committee (VDC), dairy farmers, fruit farmers, teachers, students, wine groups and business people. The study involved MACRA as the regulator of the telecommunication sector in Malawi and also the implementer and financer of the project. Two MACRA members of staff who were involved in the initial setup of the project and one participant who was involved in the initial stage but had left for another institution, were interviewed. The sample also included (i) District Council – the highest policymaking body at the district level, responsible for promoting infrastructure and economy development in the local government; and (ii) Directors of Development Planning: one from Mwanza and one from Kasungu.

The main data collection tools for the study were semi-structured interviews and focus groups. These were supplemented by direct observations and document analysis. The focus groups provided an opportunity for participants to report their individual experiences, and also respond to the experiences of other group members. The data from LMC, village heads and students was collected through focus groups. The interviews and focus groups were audio-recorded and transcribed for analysis. Direct observation was mainly on telecenter activities and the community behaviour towards the telecenter. Secondary data was obtained from various sources such as reports on telecenters. The study used thematic analysis with the use of Weft QDA, a free and open-source software for the analysis of textual data.

5 Case Study Description

Vikwa Telecenter is located in Kasungu, 22 km from Kasungu Town. It is surrounded by trading centres and schools including the elite Kamuzu Academy High School. Khudze telecenter is located about 5 km from Mwanza town. Both telecenters were officially opened in 2010 (MACRA 2012). The telecenters are located in rural villages and are in the midst of the villages. The telecenters are housed in a building which cost MACRA over MK70 million.

The telecenters were managed by a ten-member Local Management Committee (LMC) which included two ex-official members from MACRA and District Council, and the telecenter staff (MACRA 2006). The committee acted as Board of Directors of the telecenter. The operational issues of the telecenter were managed by the telecenter staff; the staff was paid by MACRA. The committees were set up in 2007 and the staff was recruited in 2010, prior to the launch of the telecenters. LMC was tasked with the responsibilities of getting the telecenter operational, ensuring that the centers were used effectively and served as the link between the telecenters and MACRA (MACRA 2011). The telecenters were supposed to operate for one year under MACRA sponsorship and, thereafter, to start operating and sustaining themselves (MACRA 2011). At the time of the study, both telecenters had operated close to three years and were still fully sponsored by MACRA.

The telecenters offered basic ICT services at a fee. Each telecenter charged, depending on the market value of the service offered within the community. The aim of charging for services was for the telecenters to sustain themselves. Each telecenter had a bank account into which they deposited its revenue. The funds were kept for future use when the telecenters would be weaned off to sustain themselves. However, some funds were used at the telecenters when necessary. The committee and staff were also encouraged to use the funds to venture into other services which were needed at the telecenters.

6   Findings

6.1   Telecenter Stakeholders Identification

The stakeholders in this study were categorised at two levels: national and community. Records from MACRA show that 12 categories of stakeholders were identified at national level (MACRA 2006). At national level, stakeholders for the two telecenters were identified through brainstorming by MACRA, based on the national roles they played in the country that could relate to the project. Stakeholders at the community level were identified through various approaches such as through (i) the results of the preliminary research, (ii) a bidding process, election and recruitment, and (iii) based on the services or roles which they would provide to the project.

The members of the LMC were chosen through election from the surrounding communities. Traditional leaders from within telecenter catchment areas were asked to identify representatives who could be members of the LMC. The major criteria for selection were representation from villages and from different backgrounds such as churches, retired personnel and farmers.

The telecenter staff was identified through a formal recruitment process. The village headmen posted vacancy advertisements within their areas. The recruitment was done by the LMC with the help of MACRA. Some respondents were dissatisfied with the way the recruitment was managed, mainly when filling posts that subsequently fell vacant. Traditional leaders felt that the process was not transparent as the community was not informed of the vacancies. LMC recruited additional staff members without informing the community and the existing staff.

The committees which are responsible to monitor developmental projects at the district and traditional authority village levels were not included as part of the stakeholders for both telecenters.

6.2   Behaviour Towards the Telecenter

Some stakeholders believed that the telecenters were brought to the community by the government through MACRA and the community had not requested the project. Others were ignorant of who had requested them, while some thought the project had been requested by the community through the District Council. Nevertheless, the community accepted the project after MACRA had explained it to traditional leaders and the community. However, the community did not understand the concept and the services which could be offered.

The community felt the major benefit of the projects to the community were some non-ICT related services which came withthe telecenter. These included electricity which had enabled the instalment of the maize mill in the community, charging of phones, a venue for social activities such as parties and meetings for various institutions, and water for the surrounding villages.

> We used to struggle to go to the maize mill, ... now it is closer because of the electricity. Most people are connected to electricity and most of the functions that happen in this area are done there ... such as weddings, engagements, ... meetings. (Traditional leader, Khudze)

Respondents at Vikwa telecenter felt the most important benefit were the ICT services; although the telecenter was also used for other non-ICT related services. This could be due to levels of development at the time the telecenter was implemented. Due to the proximity of an established elite school, Kamuzu Academy; electricity was already available in the area. Furthermore, it was near a trading centre which provided basic needs to the community. The telecenter was used to access internet to do some online transactions by the communities.

The community from both telecenters expected the projects to provide more services, such as training the youth from the catchment area on computer use, at no charge. They also wanted additional services such as TV, tuckshop, and more books with relevant content. They also wished for involvement of other stakeholders such asADC, VDC and chiefs. At both telecenters, some villagers were scared to use the facilities and felt the building and services offered were not for their level. This was strong at Khudze telecenter where some villagers were even scared of entering the building since it looked too "*high class*" for them. At Vikwa, despite the feared to enter a computer room, villagers could enter the building to buy groceries:

> There are some who have never dared entering the offices; others consider the building to be too good for their levels by looking at aspects of dressing. They fear the computer, the furniture and look of the building. (Staff at Khudze)

Some stakeholders at Khudze telecenter felt the project was not owned by the community but, rather, by MACRA and the LMC. The community felt that the telecenters did not involve the community, but only those who were directly involved and had direct benefit such as staff, LMC and MACRA. They felt it was the business of MACRA and they did not see the benefit of the telecenters in terms of the revenue generated there. They felt the telecenter revenue would be used for constructing other developmental projects within the community.

That thing is a MACRA business, all workers at the centre are doing business on behalf of MACRA and not for the community. MACRA just wanted to be given free land for construction by the chief here for their business. If you ask anyone in the village here, you will be told that they are not aware how much is realised from that place and we are not updated on anything. (Traditional leader, Khudze)

Despite good relationships at Vikwa telecenter, traditional leaders had similar opinionsto traditional leaders as at Khudze telecenter on the use of the funds from the telecenter. The traditional leaders wanted the funds from the telecenter to be used for other projects within the community. The LMC, on the other hand, felt chiefs were not allowed to know financial issues, as guided by MACRA.

There was a strong relationship among LMC, traditional leaders and telecenter staff at Vikwa telecenter. This started during the site identification, construction and operation, as traditional leaders were continuously engaged in providing guidance when there were problems.

… I make sure that when there are problems we should solve them together and also I do have time to go there and see how other things are done. (Traditional leader, Vikwa)

The stakeholders at Khudze felt there was a proper approach to consultation during the initial stages of the project. However, as time went by, the key stakeholders such as chiefs were left out of the project. Some felt that the LMC had overstayed their welcome; the committees had been elected in 2007. Some of the stakeholders expressed the need forchange and to incorporate new members into the committee. They felt that since the committee hadstayed too long and they were prone to make mistakes and nobody would criticise them.

6.3 Behaviour Towards Telecenter Sustainability

There were leadership challenges at both telecenters. Some stakeholders felt that extension workers (e.g. Agricultural, Health) should be incorporate into the committee, so that they could provide knowledge on how to apply ICT in their sectors. Others misused the powers which they had in the community to the disadvantage of the telecenter. The committees for both telecenters lacked knowledge since they had not been adequately trained. Some of the committee members resisted change and hindered the normal operations of telecenter. This caused conflict, misunderstandings between staff and the community.

There could have been a committee comprising people working in government andNGOs, to develop a plan on how they can manage the telecenter, but those running lacksknowledge of how an institution like that one is supposed to operate as most droppedschool and cannot run that complicated modern facility. (Interviewee, Khudze)

The challenges are that the telecenter committee comprises majority members who arerelated… it is difficult to hold meetings because members already discuss the issuesoutside (Interviewee, Vikwa)

6.4 Stakeholder Interaction

During the formation stage of the telecenter project, some stakeholders such as the District Council felt that they were side-lined. They felt that they were supposed to be involved in all stages of the project and, even after the handover of project to the community, thecouncil felt that it could provide necessary advice to the community. District Council is mandated to monitor projects and provide leadership in the district; members were also ex-official members in the LMC. However, there was limited interaction with the telecenter for both projects.

Furthermore, although traditional leaders were consulted during the initial phase of the project, they were not updated on the activities of the telecenter and they felt side-lined about the operation of the telecentre.

There is no link between us as community leaders and MACRA... the project doesn't seem like the one we wanted and was explained to us initially. What if we turn it into something else like hospital so that we can claim ownership so that we don't say it belongs to MACRA? (Traditional leader at Khudze)

I could have loved if reports were being submitted. Everything that is happening, whether good or bad, we should not only be meeting when there are problems, but Ishould be following each and every step so that we should see how to progress. (Traditional leader at Vikwa)

At both telecenters, the staff and the LMC met once a month to report on progress; they then reported to MACRA at the beginning of each month. Although, previously, Khudze telecenter staff used to attend District Executive Committee meetings with the District Council and consequently update the council on the Telecenter, after the first telecenter manager left, the staff never again attended the meetings. On the other hand, members of staff from Vikwa telecenter never attended any District Executive Committee meetings at all. There were no documented clear roles for Khudze telecenter as LMC and staff did not have job descriptions. In contrast, at Vikwa telecenter, there were clearly documented roles for both staff and LMC.

Since telecenter was opened, we don't have job descriptions and even the LMC don't have as we just saw draft Memorandum of Understanding (MOU) documented which was presented by MACRA but it was no signed until now. (Staff member Khudze)

The MOU was signed with Telecenter and Assembly which has job descriptions for LMC while staff have job description and everyone knows what to do. (Staff member, Vikwa)

The major interaction among stakeholders was between the telecenter staff and MACRA, where they exchanged reports and other operational issues at the telecenter. There were no clearly documented reporting lines; there were no operational guidelines or any policy given to the staff or the LMC at the telecenter.

6.5 Stakeholder Management

At the formation phase of the project, the District Council and traditional leaders were briefed on the results of the research which had been conducted and the sites which had been selected for the telecenter. At the district level, the consultation was mainly a courtesy call to the District Assembly to introduce the project through the District

Commissioner by MACRA. The aim of meeting with the council was to inform, consult, create partnership and identify the area in which the telecenter could be built. MACRA also met traditional leaders to brief them of the telecenter projects. The meetings were to explain the aim and objectives of the project and what the local authorities were supposed to do on the project.

We found no formal documents such as policies or concept papers about the project presented to the District Council and there were no consultations with the District Executive Committee.

During the planning phase, a comprehensive market research was conducted at community level to identify the main components of the marketing mix and to estimate the social relevance of the telecenter to the community (MACRA 2006). The stakeholders identified the locations of the telecenter and its management model. The community chose the community-managed model rather than the privately-managed model (MACRA 2006). Further meetings were carried out with the local authorities and the open communities to validate the research findings (MACRA 2006).

During the execution phase, telecenter staff was recruited and the community was tasked to mould bricks for the construction of the telecenter. At Vikwa telecenter, the community moulded all the bricks for the telecenter. The process was coordinated by the LMC and the traditional leaders. In contrast, the community at Khudze telecenter did not complete the task. The community only managed to mould a few bricks; unfortunately the bricks were destroyed by the rain. The contractor had to buy all the bricks for the telecenter. Besides providing the piece of land, the community did not participate in other activities.

6.6 Concessions/Bargains

During the implementation of the telecenters project, there were conflict at both telecenters which were between staff and committee, between community and management and, finally, between management and political interference. At both telecenters there were different conflicts between staff and LMC. Some of the conflicts were over finance, superiority and power.

There was a recurring problem of transparency at the Khudze on management of funds. Initially, the telecenter manager was the only signatory to the bank account and there was misunderstanding between LMC and the manager. This led to mismanagement of funds and it was alleged that the telecenter manager had swindled the money. The police investigated the matter; it was taken to a court of law and the telecenter manager was eventually dismissed. Three members of LMC became signatories to the bank account. This, however, did not address the concerns over transparency of the funds. The staff complained that they generated the revenue but were not aware of how much was in the bank account.

At Vikwa, since the opening of the telecenter, the telecenter manager and two LMC members had been signatory to the bank account and things were working well. However, there were challenges in monitoring of revenue. It is evident that there is a general challenge in management of funds in rural developmental projects.

One of the problems faced at both telecenters was the relationship between staff and the LMC. The staff felt that the LMC had more power; the staff worked with fear and embarrassment due to the behaviour of members of the LMC. They felt the committee made decisions on recruitment without consulting the staff; in one instance, they even exceeded the number of positions available at the telecenter.

The way they speak to us, because they know our salaries, they even announce them at drinking joints. Right now everybody's salary is known in the villages. (Telecenter staff member)

Another major problem was the remuneration for staff. The salaries had not been revised for four years (since the opening of the telecenter in 2010). Since the project belonged to government, the staff perceived themselves as civil servants and expected their salaries increment to be aligned with the annual increment for civil servants. Due to salary problems, some staff quit the job for other better-paying jobs.

Conflicts between the community and the telecenter management mainly revolved around water and land issues. Each telecenter had a water supply; the water was utilised at the telecenter. The villages around the telecenters had no safe water. The community felt they owned the telecenter since they had contributed through the moulding of bricks and other activities; therefore, they expected to utilise the safe water at the telecenter. All the requests from the villagers and schools to utilise the safe water were turned down by MACRA through LMC. This brought dissatisfaction from the community.

Both telecenters experienced problems with the land. The land was initially donated to the project; however, there was lack of clarity and proper guidelines on land. At one of the telecenters, the person who had given free land later changed his mind as there was supposed to be some payment for the land. At another telecenter, the former owner of the land believed he could still come to do things like cutting some bamboos without authorisation from the chiefs. The land issues were resolved after consulting other stakeholders such as chiefs and also after obtaining information from other telecenters.

7   Discussion and Conclusions

The community sense of ownership at the telecenters was low. The traditional leaders, the LMC and the staff felt that the project was owned by MACRA and not the community. After two years of operations, the decision-making was still in the power of MACRA. The community at Khudze was involved only in the site identification and possible selection of committee, while other issues such as bricks and other building material were sourced by the contractors. The implementation of the telecenters project was monitored by MACRA through the committee and no updates were communicated to local leaders. This meant that the communities were not empowered to fully participate in the running of the telecenter project, which led to over-reliance on MACRA this led to LMC, staff and traditional leaders working in isolation, with no recognition of political culture in the areas. There was no coordination among LMC, staff and traditional leaders on any issues, as things were reported directly to MACRA.

Local leaders at Vikwa had a high sense of ownership of the telecenter and played a role at the telecenters, especially when there were problems which needed their intervention. There was coordination among staff, LMC and traditional leaders. However, there was no link with District Council. During the construction of the building, the communities, through the local leaders, moulded bricks for the telecenter which showed their participation and responsibility. Consequently, in comparison to Khudze, there were more services which were demanded by the community.

Communities at both telecenters expected that the telecenter would benefit the community. They expected that the funds from the telecenter could be used to construct a school block or a borehole so that those who did not use the telecenter could indirectly benefit. However, these expectations were not met, since MACRA advised the telecenters management against doing that. The foregoing suggests that MACRA should limit its roles in the management of telecenters and empower the local community to own the telecenters. The stakeholder participation needs to start from the beginning of any project, while external actors, who traditionally lead design and formulation phases, need to limit their direct roles and responsibilities and, as far as possible, encourage local stakeholders to participate and take the lead (Ballantyne 2003). MACRA's continued involvement in decision-making led to dissatisfaction of the communities.

Some local people were afraid of using the telecenters due to the 'class' of the building and furniture in the telecenters. Most locals were afraid to use, or even to touch, a computer. The building and the furniture was perceived to be of a high standard; even the District Councils wanted the structures to be in the town so they could change the face of the towns instead of putting the structures in the villages. This suggests that there were no consultations with the community on what type of the building could be constructed in terms of the standard and the furniture to put in place. Colle and Roman (2001) suggest research as a tool for finding out the needs of the community, their participation and a systematic, persistent effort toward community awareness about telecenters and ICT.

References

Bailur, S.: Using stakeholder theory to analyze telecenter projects. Inf. Technol. Int. Dev. **3**(3), 61–80 (2006)

Ballantyne, P.: Ownership and partnership: keys to sustaining ICT-enabled development activities. IICD Research Brief (2003). http://editor.iicd.org/files/Brief8.pdf. Accessed 31 May 2013

Carrol, A.B., Buchholtzl, A.K.: Business and Society, Ethics and Stakeholder Management. South-Western Centre for Learning, Cincinnati (2012)

Chiweza, A.: A review of the Malawi decentralisation process: lessons from selected districts. Ministry of Local Government and Rural Development-Malawi, Concern Universal, Zomba (2010). http://www.ndr.mw:8080/xmlui/handle/123456789/401. Accessed 13 Mar 2013

Colle, R.D., Roman, R.: The telecenter environment in 2002. J. Dev. Commun. **12** (2001). http://www.communicationforsocialchange.org/body-of-knowledge.php?id=2229

Donaldson, T., Preston, L.: The stakeholder theory of the corporation: concepts, evidence, and implications. Acad. Manage. Rev. **20**(1), 65–91 (1995)

Fontaine, C., Haarman, A., Schmid, S.: The stakeholder theory (2006). m/svn/trunk/pdfs/diazPace/Stakeholders%20theory.pdf. Accessed 16 Mar 2013

Freeman, E.R.: Strategic Management: A Stakeholder Approach. Cambridge University Press, New York (2010)

Freeman, R.E., Wicks, A.C., Parmar, B.: Stakeholder theory and "the corporate objective revisited". Organ. Sci. **15**(3), 364–369 (2004)

ITU: World telecommunication/ICT development report 2010 – monitoring the WSIS targets, Geneva (2010). http://www.itu.int/pub/D-IND-WTDR-2010. Accessed 27 June 2012

MACRA: ICT for Sustainable Rural Development (SRD) project - Malawi-field survey activity. In: Review of Research Findings Workshop, Blantyre (2006)

MACRA: Malawi government connect a constituency project concept paper (2011)

MACRA: ICT policy implementation overview - telecenters status in Malawi. In: Telecenter Managers Workshop, Blantyre (2012)

NSO: Spatial distribution and urbanisation in Malawi (2008). http://www.nsomalawi.mw/images/stories/data_on_line/demography/census_2008/Main%20Report/ThematicReports/Migration%20Report.pdf

Pade-Khene, C.: An investigation of ICT project management techniques for sustainable ICT projects in rural development. Rhodes University (2006). http://eprints.ru.ac.za/900/. Accessed 31 May 2013

Perrini, F., Tencati, A.: Sustainability and stakeholder management: the need for new corporate performance evaluation and reporting systems. Bus. Strat. Environ. **308**, 296–308 (2006)

Roman, R., Colle, R.: Themes and issues in telecentre sustainability (2002). Accessed 28 Oct 2012

Schmeer, K.: Guidelines for conducting a stakeholder analysis. Partnerships for Health Reform, Abt Associates Inc., Bethesda (1999). http://www.who.int/management/partnerships/overall/GuidelinesConductingStakeholderAnalysis.pdf. Accessed 7 Jan 2013

ICTs for Agroecology

Shifting Agricultural ICT4D from "I" to "C"

Linus Kendall[✉] and Andy Dearden

Sheffield Hallam University, Sheffield, UK
linus.e.kendall@student.shu.ac.uk, a.m.dearden@shu.ac.uk

Abstract. The urgent need for inclusive and sustainable agriculture has seen transition towards holistic, situated and participatory approaches to agricultural development such as agroecology. In this paper we use observations drawn from an action research project to examine the implications of such approaches on ICT design and implementation strategy. We suggest that ICTs designed for sustainable agriculture need to shift their emphasis from packaging and transmitting information toward facilitating communication and sharing of practice, adopting diverse collective, social and situated forms of knowing and learning.

Keywords: ICT4D · Agroecology · Social learning · Sustainable agriculture · Knowledge management · ICT for sustainability

Responding to the fact that a large number of the world's poor reside in rural areas and draw their livelihoods from agricultural activities there has been a wide variety of ICT interventions designed and implemented to support rural and agricultural development. These interventions have provided information services, advisory, education and training through various modalities such as text message (SMS), interactive voice response (IVR), smartphone applications and video.

Agricultural "ICTs for development" (ICT4D) regularly take as their starting point the challenges of extension services to adequately reach out to and support farmers. As Patel et al. [1] notes *"only 6% [of respondents in an IFPRI survey] reported having interacted with an extension officer"*, further highlighting how *"ICTs have the potential to increase the reach of agricultural extension"*. In their paper on Digital Green, Gandhi et al. [2] begins with the recognition that *"the scale of actual impact [of extension services]...is confounded by logistical and resource challenges that include the sheer number of households that are assigned to a single extension officer"* and suggests participatory video as one way of supporting extension officers. In a recent review, Aker et al. [3] suggests ICTs as a way to *"increase the scale and sustainability of extension services"* while also enabling greater accountability.

This starting point is one which addresses logistical and practical challenges of government extension programmes. However, increasing concerns for sustainable agricultural development have called extension programmes themselves into question. In response to this, we set out in this paper to elaborate some of the implications of sustainable agricultural approaches for technology strategy within ICT4D.

© IFIP International Federation for Information Processing 2017
Published by Springer International Publishing AG 2017. All Rights Reserved
J. Choudrie et al. (Eds.): ICT4D 2017, IFIP AICT 504, pp. 451–462, 2017.
DOI: 10.1007/978-3-319-59111-7_37

1   What Is "Sustainable Agricultural Development"?

The second half of the 20th century saw great increases in agricultural productivity through, most prominently, the Green Revolution (GR). The GR programme focused on crop genetic improvement–development of high yielding varieties (HYV)–as well as ensuring the availability to farmers of modern inputs such as fertilisers and pesticides. As a result, wheat, rice and maize saw yield increases of over 100% in developing countries, with the greatest impact in Asia [4]. While the GR as a programme was considered over by the 1980s, direct impacts were still seen into the 2000s and the varieties and practices developed as part of it are still in use [5].

Despite its success in intensifying agriculture, the outcomes of the GR programme have increasingly been critiqued from the perspective of sustainability. There is evidence that the improvements in crop yields–especially for wheat and rice–have stagnated and in some cases collapsed [6]. Furthermore, the adoption and intensive usage of inputs such as pesticides and fertilisers have caused negative ecological impacts, degrading both soil and water resources [4]. Adding to this, HYVs were designed to transition farmers from rain-fed seasonal agriculture towards year round irrigation, which has led to overuse and depletion of ground water resources with subsequent increases in fresh-water scarcity and soil salinity [7].

Evidence suggests that the "modernisation of agriculture" achieved through GR and post-GR agricultural development have not benefitted the most marginal farmers and in many cases been directly harmful to their food security and livelihoods [8, 9]. In part this is because GR practices and HYVs were never designed to be used in marginal agricultural areas, but were still promoted and spread widely through government subsidies, extension programmes and commercial interests [4].

A response to these challenges are approaches such as natural resource management (NRM) and agroecology [10]. Agroecology emphasise sustainable use of natural resources through locally situated agricultural practices developed in participatory ways with farmers [9]. The UN Rapporteur on the Right to Food, holds that agroecology is a means by which to achieve "a low-carbon, resource-preserving type of agriculture that benefits the poorest farmers" [10]. Evidence for this can be found in a survey of 286 projects in 57 countries [11] which suggests that agroecological and resource conserving practices could lead to considerable improvements in yields for smallholders while at the same time reducing water and pesticide use.

One of the hallmarks of these approaches is that they recognise a need to shift from a top-down research, extension and technology driven approach to one which is participatory and bottom-up focused on learning [9, 12]. Röling and Jiggins [13] suggests that sustainable agricultural development requires transition to a new "ecological knowledge system" built upon participatory, social and action based learning.

2   How Can ICTs Support Sustainable Agriculture?

As was highlighted in the introduction of this paper, ICT4D interventions in agricultural development often take as their starting point the current practice of extension and how to bridge the gaps caused by insufficient capacity to reach farmers. Many, if not most, of these interventions have been concerned with information and knowledge dissemination, training or education in one form or another. If sustainable agriculture requires a shift in the way extension and, more broadly, the agricultural knowledge system is organised, it follows that changes to strategies for ICT design and implementation will also be needed.

One way to view this change can be drawn from the field of knowledge management (KM) where there has been a longstanding debate of how to incorporate social and situated theories of learning [14, 15]. ICT designs, it is argued, need to transition away from a view of knowledge as an object which can be packaged, stored and transferred [16]. The alternative is a "knower-centered" approach, building on the idea that knowledge is, to a large degree, tacit and as such cannot be separated in a lossless manner from its knower and context [17]. Oreglia [18] highlights that when viewing farmers as a community of practice [15], it is clear that approaches which privileges disconnected information-sharing are inappropriate. In contrast, "knower-centered" view of agricultural knowledge is one which recognises that it is embedded in and transferred through participation in shared community practice.

In other words, while access to information may allow for learning *about* sustainable agriculture, in order to learn how *to be* a sustainable farmer more than information is required [19]. Consequently, overcoming obstacles to information access is a necessary but not sufficient condition for improved performance. To acquire "know how", participation in a community of practice is needed. We suggest this argument separates access to *information* from opportunity to *communicate*, the latter a concept encompassing not only access to necessary media but importantly also social relationships, shared language and iterative dialogue. This aligns with calls for an "ecological knowledge system" [13], suggesting an alternate approach to ICTs for agroecology.

In order to better explore these approaches and what they might mean in practice for the development of ICT4D interventions, we are working together with an NGO in an action research project. The NGO, Development Research Communication and Services Centre (DRCSC), is based in West Bengal in Eastern India and has worked for several decades supporting small-scale and marginal farmers in adopting agricultural practices which are "environment friendly, economically appropriate, socially just and developed by mutual cooperation" [20].

3   Methodology

The methodology we have adopted is action research [21]. Action research (AR) involves a specific set of epistemological, ontological and methodological choices which we perceive as being well aligned with working in the intersection of development, sustainability and technology [12, 21, 22]. As an AR programme, the project is organised around cycles of reflection, planning, action and observation, where action is intended to involve interventions into the knowledge system of the organisation and its stakeholders. In this paper, we report on the initial cycles of this work. For these we have decided to draw on Ethnographic Action Research (EAR) [23] a form of Participatory

Action Research (PAR) that combines PAR with ethnography. Accordingly, our initial focus has been supporting the establishment of a technology research culture, along with conducting ongoing ethnographic inquiry into work practices, values and challenges facing the organisation.

AR in general, and PAR approaches such as EAR in particular, demand engagement *with* those affected by research, adopting methods aimed at enabling participation. This project aims for active participation of the organisation in the planning and execution of the research program, achieved primarily through the engagement of an action learning set consisting of staff from the organisation. The action learning set was formed at the start of the project and meets regularly to discuss the progress and findings of the project, set goals and plan future activities.

The initial cycle was conducted between March and August of 2016 and consisted of an in-depth ethnographic study of the current knowledge system and work context of the organisation. Ten weeks were spent with the head office staff in Kolkata and six weeks spread between two field offices. A pragmatic, multi-method approach was taken involving participant observation, semi-structured and informal interviewing, and small workshops. Data was collected in the form of field journals kept by the researcher as well as photographs and audio-recordings of interviews. Interviews were later transcribed and translated. In-depth interviews lasting a minimum of an hour were conducted with eight staff members who hold roles of varying seniority in the head office as well as six staff members in the field offices. In addition to these longer interviews, shorter, informal interviews were held with both farmers as well as other staff from field and head offices. The collected data was analysed thematically using themes sourced from prior theory, literature and from the data itself.

Acknowledging that the training as well as, importantly, the time and funding to lead such work was primarily available to the researcher (first author), this work was mainly conducted by the researcher on behalf of the action learning set. The analytic approach taken placed ongoing findings and observations in the context of the work and mission of the organisation and involved continuous reporting back to, reflection upon and discussion of data and analytical notes with the action learning set. Ongoing engagement with the organisation in planning, conducting and analysing the research meant that it was not possible for the researcher to operate purely as a detached observer. Rather, we recognise a dual role for the researcher as observer and participant. In the role as an observer or "friendly outsider" [24], the researcher provides an external perspective of the organisation and its work context, facilitating discussions and analysis. Long-term embedding in the organisation enables this role through relationships, background knowledge and trust, but also results in a second role as an active participant in the research context. In order to retain the ability to provide an external perspective on the data under these conditions, we have employed external advisors as well as a process of continuously relating findings back to the broader literature.

This dual role requires an approach to research ethics adapted for interventionist research to ensure that trust and along with it informed consent is maintained between different actors in the research project. In this respect, we adopted an ongoing, mediated process of consent, risk and benefits analysis [25]. This process involved repeated explanations of and negotiations about research in general and the research project itself. This was combined with continuous inquiry into perceived risks and benefits.

4   Findings

From the initial research phase, several aspects and challenges of the work and context of the organisation that might impact technology strategy were identified. Below we review these through the lens of their relationship to the organisation's value of and commitment to sustainability.

4.1   Content for Sustainability

That sustainable agriculture requires a holistic approach was highlighted through several of the challenges faced by the organisation and the farmers, as well as in the design of some of the organisation's programmes.

One example of this is the intertwining of farmer food habits with the sustainability of their agricultural practices. Greater integration with agricultural supply chains have meant farmers are increasingly looking to consume produce which does not grow in the nearby area. In one of our discussions a field officer noted: *"Now people want to eat cabbage, cauliflower and apples"*. As a result, farmers opt for a narrower selection of crops and seed varieties optimised for sale or exchange value as opposed to nutrition or local ecological conditions. Micro-nutrient deficiencies is a recognised challenge which few mainstream agricultural development programmes have been able to address [4]. Reduced crop variety and dependence on market forms a challenge to sustainability and resilience of these agricultural communities especially as they experience greater climactic variability as a result of climate change. It is not only through the preference for newly available products that food habits impact the sustainability of farms in the area. The staple of crop of Bengal–rice–plays a significant role in livelihoods and for nutrition in the area. As part of the food culture, a belly full of rice is a significant measure of well-being, "bhat gum" ("rice sleep") being the desired result of a good meal. Since the green revolution, HYVs along with a package of practice including irrigation, pesticides and fertilisers have been introduced which allow for a second rice harvest during the summer months. However, in a meeting at one of the farmer's houses a trainer from the organisation worked with farmers to tally outcomes from different summer cropping patterns. Their results showed clearly that not only were alternative crops such as lentils ecologically more sustainable but they were also more economically profitable and provided better nutrition. In spite of having generated this evidence for themselves, several of the farmers knowledgeable of agroecology still choose the HYV rice crop.

These accounts highlight how promotion of agroecology needs to address the issue in a holistic way, taking into account both agricultural practice but also acknowledging sociocultural preferences. The organisation found these types of intertwining socio-agricultural concerns difficult to document and represent; speaking about the case studies they create from their programmes and for funders a staff member, A., shared:

A: "What we usually thought about is that income is only indicator. [Others think] if the income rises the farmer will be fine. But that is not the case... what we thought is that, in our case, in our like us organisation, where we focus on the ecological agriculture, yes, income is one of the indicator but there should be a ecological diversity also. [For example: Previously] there was not so much diversity but now there is a ecological diversity and maybe the food basket is diversified. And another one is the acceptance in society, maybe that farmer became a leader, that farmer became a trainer. That [is] what we need actually in the course of our implementation. Or maybe they are as an organisation, maybe as a group they formed, [in order for] the others [to] learn from them. The others meaning the outside villagers, they can learn from it. That should be the motto, but sometimes it is missed [...], that kind of data."

The inappropriateness of reductionist approaches suggested by the examples above was made explicit by T., one of the most senior trainers in the organisation. In discussing an attempt at providing advice over an IVR system, where most of the questions had been about pest problems, he highlights the incompatibility of the implicit reductionism in the questions asked with sustainable approaches to agriculture:

T: "Actually not only over telephone. When I go to give training with them, there also when we do question and answer session most of the questions is pest and disease. The problem is that they have no orientation about holistic agriculture. Pest is one component. But there are soil fertility, seed, design of the far [....] They think: now, now pest is come so what shall I do [...] The pest is coming because you are not maintaining proper your field. Ecological balance is not right so pest is coming. You should know what kind of [farm] management you need for protecting against pest."

4.2   Work Practices for Sustainability

One of the observations made of the field workers of the organisation was that their work was entirely dependent upon their social and community relationships. They lived in or near their work areas and there were often relatively weak distinctions between social and work oriented relationships and interactions. This relates both to interactions between field workers themselves as well as with the farmers.

As one of the field worker's described it: their real purpose went beyond supporting agricultural development, it was really about promoting *"social cohesion"*. As he saw it, their role was to bring together farmers from different communities around common concerns. In describing their attempts at engaging new groups of farmers, one of the trainers related that it was not so much about teaching new technical practices as about building relationships and trusts.

In another instance, it was observed that a group of farmers who were well acquainted with the organisation and its programmes were being given training on a topic which most of them were already very familiar with. When questioned about this D., the trainer, responded: *"these events are much more about creating a social meeting space [than training], this kind of discussion would have happened 30 years ago, but it is not happening any more"*. These meetings served a bigger role than simply a way to deliver agricultural knowledge. The researcher observed that more experienced farmers were given a forum in which they could reaffirm their knowledge in front of less experienced farmers by agreeing with, challenging or elaborating on what the trainer said. Events provided spaces for people who would have little opportunity to interact, for example the elderly farmer sharing the design of his vermicompost pit to a younger, female farmer from a completely different village.

Another example relates to the way field workers interact with each other. In looking at the technological tools they use, several instances of using WhatsApp were observed. Their uses of WhatsApp often moved beyond the basic functionality of keeping in touch with each other. Taking a few examples, one involved sharing images of documents and hardcopy materials between geographically dispersed staff. Another connecting with others within and outside of the organisation working on similar projects or programmes in order to share experiences, pictures and materials. A third involved using it for financial reporting by "scanning" bills and receipts and sharing them with the project manager. In a fourth case, they used it for scheduling events and meetings such as trainings. Several of these uses may appear inefficient. Taking a print-out of a digital document in order to send a photograph of it via WhatsApp is perhaps the most striking example. However, WhatsApp is a tool that fits with the social and informal nature of the field officers' work context where there is often little distinction between social and work oriented relationships.

4.3   Management for Sustainability

Early on, a team leader, C., suggested that the main sustainability challenge for the organisation was how to manage projects more efficiently & effectively and that a system should be designed to help them: "*I am managing multiple projects and if you ask me, I cannot tell you now what they did last month–I would need a few days to collect information to answer that. We need some way to better track what projects are doing*". In explaining her system of managing projects she said: "*I look at the financial record. How much has been spent? Then I look at the project budget, how much should we have spent. In this way, I can see if we are on track.*".

The emphasis on increasing efficiency inproject management as critical to the sustainability of the organisation was, however, challenged by other staff members. As one senior team leader explained: "*Actually project are not sustaining [our organisation]. How project is sustaining [us]? Project is a time*-bound, na? There are 2 years, 3 years, after that what do we do?" He continued to explain that any changes toward sustainable agricultural practices took many years to establish and involved continuous engagement. The type of transition they were advocating for therefore fit poorly with the 3–5 year timeframes and specific project objectives required by external funders. Another staff member, A., highlighted the potential conflict between an emphasis on accounting or budget utilisation and sustainability of their intervention:

A: "…from the [last] two to three years, the involvement of the funding agencies is much more… They are always thinking about budget utilisation, ok let us do that, utilise that gross budget. Whatever will be the impact. Let us utilise that money. What the ultimate work is [, is] not accepted actually. Yes, we have spent the money, we have do[ne] some more programmes. But ultimately it is not sustained."

This greater emphasis on projects, oriented towards specific targets was described as being implicated in multiple changes within the organisation. One of the founders of the organisation highlighted that it had re-oriented their recruitment towards people from educational backgrounds such as social work, who intended to do a career in the development field. Another senior staff member shared how he and others of the staff, when they joined, would spend months living and working in the field areas, something that staff members now recruited would be unwilling to do. Taking on new staff members as a result of external projects furthermore contributed to a continued and growing need for more funding diverting their attention towards donor objectives:

> T: "Sometime it is happening by pressure, because there is so many staff. Let's say […] project is completed they have so many staff, how we can provide salary to them? So agency is providing new project. So this is also pressure, for the new staff. Sometime we are doing for they are giving money and we are giving the project, sometime maybe that is not for our, thematic area, but we want to give salary to somebody. When we are taking project we are taking liabilities, so pressure is increasing. So we are so much busy so we have no time for learning."

As these quotes illustrate, contributing to greater project management efficacy would not adequately address sustainable development. As such alternatives to a project management system were sought. A staff member, R., suggested that what was really needed was a system that enabled greater sharing between teams, increased democracy in decision making and introduction of new staff to the values of the organisation. Interestingly, a version of such an information system had previously existed in the form of Saturday film shows:

> A: "We usually, earlier, [the organisation] earlier used to have on Saturdays a film show. Not every Saturdays but maybe once in a month, there are various films on the awareness generation…"

> Linus: "You say, before, we used to have?"

> A: "Yes, now, now it is not there. Maybe the time is very much short. As you know, that there are various projects right now. So that there is no one who can spend, maybe it is not mandatory, but you have to spend one hour or maybe half an hour…"

5   Discussion: Towards Collective Learning

As has been argued in the introduction to this paper, sustainable agroecological development and management of natural resources requires forms of learning which are social and collective in nature. Integral to these is the combination of multiple perspectives and engagement with multiple knowledges [26, 27].

In order to unpack these in our case we will adopt the five cultures or paradigms of knowledge, inquiry and content defined by Brown [27], namely: individual lived experience; local shared experience of people and places; specialised disciplinary knowledge; organisational and managerial knowledge and holistic understandings of value generated through aesthetic practices. Brown highlights how the prevailing power-hierarchy between these knowledge types can undermine our collective learning towards sustainable living. As in the case described by her, the organisation we studied have seen an increasing weight given to the "organisational knowledge culture", and technical/specialised knowledge forms. The strengthening of this culture has resulted in the decline of practices sourced from and embedded in other knowledge cultures, such as film screenings or extended individual experiences of field sites. This is most clearly seen in the head office, whereas in the field offices "community" and relational communication practices are still dominant. We can see this evidenced by the field officers work being a primarily "social activity" based in dialogue and shared experiences between themselves and the farmers they work with. This difference in dominant knowledge paradigms and interests between head and field offices can be identified as one source of conflict and communication gaps.

As described by multiple members of the organisation, the organisational knowledge culture is one which has accompanied a transition towards external funders along with a change in the type of staff members recruited. As is evidenced through the interviews reported above, this knowledge culture has evolved in response to both external pressures as well as internal enactment of what has been termed an increasingly prevalent "formalising, development work regime" [28, 29].

The dominance of this knowledge culture is detrimental to practicing sustainability, as is shown through both the ethnographic work described in this paper as well as through Brown's work [27]. While the language of the organisational knowledge culture needs to be one voice in a collective learning process, its reductionist approach and emphasis on accounting as a lens for understanding is insufficient to support the way sustainability is turned into practice by the organisation and their farmers.

Choices of technology for knowledge management can easily serve to strengthen the dominance of the organisational and specialist knowledge cultures, as exemplified by the impact assessment tools and spreadsheets described by Ramos and Hayes [28] and Hayes and Westrup [29]. The adoption of spreadsheets to monitor NGO work supports the creation of new definitions of what "really happens" and orients the working practices of NGOs towards "calculative practice" [29].

Likewise, agricultural information systems can orient both farmers and NGO workers towards certain paradigms of agricultural development, such as those amenable to "off the shelf" solutions delivered through questions & answers. As T. highlights above, this model is built on the modernist premise and the "specialist knowledge paradigm". In this paradigm the problem solving approach is to apply an increasingly specific solution to problems as they emerge. It is a model for knowledge management easily supported by ICT interventions and therefore readily adopted. However, we argue that in order to better support sustainable agricultural development, ICT strategies for sustainable agriculture need to move towards strengthening the voices of other knowledge cultures.

Another way in which agricultural advice systems strengthen organisational and specialist knowledge cultures concerns individual vs collective approaches to agricultural decision making. Designing information systems where advice is provided in interactions by individual farmers through SMS or IVR strengthens a shift away from the collective, social spaces that field workers of the organisation emphasise as critical, towards farmers as individuals and individual managers of their farms. As one ICTD evaluation states: "Farmers offered the service turn less often to other farmers and input sellers for agricultural advice" [30]. While this was perceived as a benefit of the ICT intervention, when seen through the lens of collaborative learning, we might take a different stance. Reduced reliance on local, social relationships is potentially detrimental to the resilience and long-term sustainability of the farming system. As Oreglia [18] recognises, ICTs designed around individual farmer use and decision making fit poorly in the context of community learning patterns among Chinese farmers. We suggest that this also applies to the context of sustainable agricultural development detailed here.

Our empirical findings reveal practices and concerns that move well beyond "information provision" suggesting need for a technology strategy built upon community relations and multiple forms of inquiry and knowledge. Returning to the difference between access to information and opportunity to communicate, it is clear that a system built on an information access paradigm will be unable to meet these demands. This implies a strategy whereby we seek to privilege supporting communication practices as opposed to disseminating information. This requires recognising that ICTs cannot, do not, and should not be approached as a neutral transmission channel that allows for efficient and (ideally) lossless communication. The "social life of information", i.e. the communicative practices in which information is embedded, is not "noise" to be filtered, but rather what our interventions should place their focus on. Critically, this includes engaging with knowledge cultures different from the organisational, institutional and specialist. We argue that this is a necessary step if ICTs are to be able to contribute to sustainable and agroecological agricultural development.

6   Conclusion: Shifting Agricultural ICT4D from I to C

The ability of ICTs to allow for dissemination of advice and practices across wide social, spatial and temporal distances, for which they are commonly lauded, is key to the separation of knowledge from knower [17]. Reliance on such attributes diminishes the tacit and situated knowledges deemed critical to sustainable, agroecological development. It builds on universalist assumptions "obscuring the role of the knower and of the knower's social system" [17]. It is premised on the "myth of information" as separated from the human practice within which it is embedded [19]. Systems built on these attributes commonly conceptualise "knowledge" as an object to be stored, indexed and transferred, designed to separate the outcomes of knowing from the context in which it is experienced or produced. In this view, learning is the successful access to and understanding of such knowledge objects. This form of learning and view of knowledge may not only be unsuitable to sustainable and resilient agricultural systems but may also serve to marginalise and perpetuate inequalities between different actors in the development system [16].

In this paper, we have argued that ICTD for sustainable agricultural development requires approaches that engage with multiple knowledges and collective learning. This entails placing the knowers and the knowers' context in focus, defining learning as part of, and facilitated through, engagement in communities of practice. When it comes to attributes of ICTs, the focus therefore should be on the ways in which they facilitate shared practice, communication and interaction within and between communities of practice. It also requires ICT strategies to engage with languages and forms of inquiry other than those of specialists or organisational managers, such as individual reflection, storytelling or aesthetic forms.

This holds implications for what we perceive as the purpose of and strategies employed for ICTs for agricultural development. For an organisation, such as the one discussed in this paper, rather than using ICTs as way to transmit knowledge this could translate into systems enabling field workers to better facilitate sharing through scheduling social spaces and face to face encounters. It could also mean, as suggested by one staff member, ICTs which allow the organisation to be better at promulgating values and motivating staff. For agricultural ICT4D interventions in general the broader implication, we argue, is a need to shift our focus from practices and designs related to "Information" towards those emphasising "Communication".

Acknowledgements. This work has been conducted with the active engagement and participation of DRCSC (www.drcsc.org.in) in Kolkata. It has been made possible through Linus' affiliation with the International Institute of Information Technology in Bangalore (IIIT-B) and the support provided by them.

References

1. Patel, N., Chittamuru, D., Jain, A., Dave, P., Parikh, T.S.: Avaaj Otalo: a field study of an interactive voice forum for small farmers in rural India. In: Proceedings of the 28th International Conference on Human Factors in Computing Systems – CHI 2010, pp. 733–742. ACM Press, New York (2010)
2. Gandhi, R., Veeraraghavan, R., Toyama, K., Ramprasad, V.: Digital green: participatory video for agricultural extension. In: International Conference on Information and Communication Technologies and Development (2007)
3. Aker, J.C., Ghosh, I., Burrell, J.: The promise (and pitfalls) of ICT for agriculture initiatives. Agric. Econ. **47**, 35–48 (2016)
4. Pingali, P.L.: Green revolution: impacts, limits, and the path ahead. Proc. Natl. Acad. Sci. **109**, 12302–12308 (2012)
5. Evenson, R.E., Gollin, D.: Assessing the impact of the green revolution, 1960 to 2000. Science **300**, 758–762 (2003)
6. Ray, D.K., Ramankutty, N., Mueller, N.D., West, P.C., Foley, J.: A: recent patterns of crop yield growth and stagnation. Nat. Commun. **3**, 1293 (2012)
7. Singh, R.B.: Environmental consequences of agricultural development: a case study from the green revolution state of Haryana, India. Agric. Ecosyst. Environ. **82**, 97–103 (2000)
8. Holt-Giménez, E., Altieri, M.A.: Agroecology, food sovereignty and the new green revolution. Agroecol. Sustain. Food Syst. **37**, 90–102 (2012)
9. Altieri, M.A.: Agroecology: the science of natural resource management for poor farmers in marginal environments. Agric. Ecosyst. Environ. **93**, 1–24 (2002)
10. De Schutter, O.: Report submitted by the Special Rapporteur on the right to food (2010)
11. Pretty, J.N., Noble, A.D., Bossio, D., Dixon, J., Hine, R.E., De Vries, F.W.T.P., Morison, J.I.L.: Resource-conserving agriculture increases yields in developing countries. Environ. Sci. Technol. **40**, 1114–1119 (2006)
12. Pretty, J.N.: Participatory learning for sustainable agriculture. World Dev. **23**, 1247–1263 (1995)
13. Röling, N.G., Jiggins, J.: The ecological knowledge system. In: Facilitating Sustainable Agriculture: Participatory Learning and Adaptive Management in Times of Environmental Uncertainty, pp. 281–311 (1998)

14. Lave, J., Wenger, E.: Situated Learning: Legitimate Peripheral Participation. Cambridge University Press, Cambridge (1991)
15. Wenger, E.: Communities of Practice: Learning, Meaning, and Identity. Cambridge University Press, Cambridge (1998)
16. Ferguson, J., Huysman, M., Soekijad, M.: Knowledge Management in Practice: Pitfalls and Potentials for Development. World Dev. **38**, 1797–1810 (2010)
17. van der Velden, M.: Knowledge facts, knowledge fiction: the role of ICTs in knowledge management for development. J. Int. Dev. **14**, 25–37 (2002)
18. Oreglia, E.: When technology doesn't fit: information sharing practices among farmers in rural China. In: Proceedings of the Sixth International Conference on Information and Communication Technologies and Development, ICTD 2013, pp. 165–176. ACM (2013)
19. Brown, J.S., Duguid, P.: The Social Life of Information. Harvard Business Press, Boston (2000)
20. DRCSC: DRCSC - About Us. http://www.drcsc.org/aboutus.html
21. Hearn, G., Foth, M.: Action research in the design of new media and ICT systems. In: Topical Issues in Communications and Media Research, pp. 79–94 (2005)
22. Dearden, A., Rizvi, H.: Participatory IT design and participatory development: a comparative review. In: Proceedings of the Tenth Anniversary Conference on Participatory Design, pp. 81–91 (2008)
23. Tacchi, J.: Ethnographic Action Research: Media, information and communicative ecologies for development initiatives. In: The SAGE Handbook of Action Research, 3rd edn. pp. 220–229 (2015)
24. Hayes, G.R.: The relationship of action research to human-computer interaction. ACM Trans. Comput. Interact. **18**, 1–20 (2011)
25. Sterling, S.R., Rangaswamy, N.: Constructing Informed Consent in ICT4D research. In: Proceedings of the 4th ACM/IEEE International Conference on Information and Communication Technologies and Development, p. 46 (2010)
26. Raymond, C.M., Fazey, I., Reed, M.S., Stringer, L.C., Robinson, G.M., Evely, A.C.: Integrating local and scientific knowledge for environmental management. J. Environ. Manag. **91**, 1766–1777 (2010)
27. Brown, V.A.: Multiple knowledges, multiple languages: are the limits of my language the limits of my world? Knowl. Manag. Dev. J. **6**, 120–131 (2010)
28. Ramos, R.R., Hayes, N.: The formalising regime and its formalising technology: the case of informal trade in Recife, Brazil. In: Proceedings of the 13th International Conference on Social Implications of Computers in Developing Countries (IFIP 9.4), pp. 643–653. Department of Informatics, University of Olso, Negombo (2015)
29. Hayes, N., Westrup, C.: Power/knowledge and impact assessment: creating new spaces for expertise in international development. New Technol. Work Employ. **27**, 9–22 (2012)
30. Cole, S.A., Fernando, A.N.: The value of advice: evidence from mobile phone-based agricultural extension. Harvard Business School - Finance Working Paper No. 13–047 (2012)

An Exploration of the Integration Challenges Inherent in the Adoption of ICT in an Education System

Isabel Meyer[1], Mario Marais[2(✉)], Merryl Ford[2], and Sifiso Dlamini[2]

[1] Impact Advantage, Pretoria, South Africa
isabelmeyer@mweb.co.za
[2] CSIR Meraka Institute, Pretoria, South Africa
{mmarais,mford,sdlamini}@csir.co.za

Abstract. The high failure rate of development interventions is well known. An approach to sustainable interventions is defined, based on a systems perspective that focuses on the ability of a system to integrate an intervention. The design of an intervention requires an understanding of the current state of the system from the perspective of being able to realise the intended benefit. This is called the readiness of the system, and is constituted by the level of maturity of the essential elements and the nature of the interrelationships that are required to realise and sustain the benefits. Interventions can be designed to match the current readiness of the system and to define the system changes toward the desired end state. These principles were developed during the implementation of an ICT for Rural Education (ICT4RED) project in the Eastern Cape province of South Africa. The practical implications for project design, execution and handover to the education system are illustrated.

Keywords: Sustainability · ICT in education · Systems thinking · System integration · ICT4D

1 Introduction

The high failure rate of development interventions bears testimony to the urgent need for new approaches. The use of technology in general and ICT in particular, has a poor track record, with quoted failure rates of as high as 80% [1]. The significant investment in ICT4D is characterised as being "limited" or "largely unsuccessful" [2]. While ICT4D is often seen as the "silver bullet" to development problems, its dual role of reducing the digital divide and fulfilling development objectives is seen as contributing to its failure [3]. In this context, we explore the *sustainability* of interventions, with specific focus on the integration of an ICT4D intervention into its intended environment.

Sustainability is an often-used, but also often ill-defined, concept. Heeks [4] emphasizes this when stating that "sustainable development is an empty slogan: continuously invoked but never examined." While seen as key to the future success of ICT4D [5], authors define the concept of sustainability from perspectives that range from classical views related to resource preservation [6] to the ability of a project or

J. Choudrie et al. (Eds.): ICT4D 2017, IFIP AICT 504, pp. 463–474, 2017.
DOI: 10.1007/978-3-319-59111-7_38

intervention to sustain itself without outside support [7, 8]. The research programme in which this work is embedded was developed out of the participation of the researchers since 2008 in the implementation of ICT4D initiatives. Projects, funded by South African national government departments, used a mainly top-down and technology-centric approach in the development contexts of rural broadband access [9, 10], the deployment of telecentres in rural areas [11], and the deployment of ICTs in rural schools [12]. Based on these experiences, we adopt a pragmatic perspective on sustainability, and focus on sustaining the *benefits* that are created by an ICT4D project within its context. We therefore define sustainability as *the ability to sustain the anticipated benefits of the project or programme, over an appropriate period of time, for pre-defined project participants.* Sustainability is viewed from a systems perspective, by considering the *elements* that are essential to make things work in the long run, as well as the *relationships* between them. From this perspective, the sustainability of an intervention relates to how well the system (the participating organisation or community) is able to absorb a project into normal operations.

This focus of this paper is a conceptual approach to integrate ICT4D projects into their implementation environment, by considering pathways and strategies towards systemic change, the use of a modular implementation framework, and the application of an implementation readiness framework. The final framework was developed to assess readiness of an environment before the implementation of an ICT4D project, with the aim of designing the project in such a manner that the intervention meets the readiness of the community to adopt the intervention. Section 2 takes a conceptual perspective on the integration problem, the project in the context of a system, and pathways toward systemic change. Section 3 describes the ICT for Rural Education (ICT4RED) project in the Eastern Cape province of South Africa [12] and the implementation framework used. Section 4 applies the implementation readiness framework to the ICT4RED project and reflects on the benefits of taking a systemic view on the sustainability of ICT4D implementations.

2 The Problem of Integration

2.1 Introduction

Through appropriate design, an ICT4D project (similar to any ICT project), aims to deliver technology to achieve specific objectives. As such, a linear approach from technology design through implementation and ultimately transfer to users is often followed, and projects or programmes are designed accordingly.

However, ICT4D projects are in many respects fundamentally different from commercial ICT projects, and failure is to some extent the result of the unique nature of IC4D projects and their implementation environment [2, 17]. Based on project experience, the authors have identified the following as differentiating characteristics of ICT4D projects [14].

Some of these differences are attributable to the divergence between resource-rich and resource-poor environments (such as differences in literacy, skills, technology base, and the ability to maintain technology). Others are rooted in the unfamiliarity of the implementation environment to the implementation team, and the inability to predict uptake and adoption, given these inherent differences. Such uncertainties render the path to progress unclear.

Given these differences, the *integration* of an ICT4D solution into the community or organisational system where it is intended to reside presents unique challenges. For example, limited budgets would prevent an organisational environment from meeting the technology support requirements. Similarly, over-ambitious technology designs could be difficult to integrate into environments that are unfamiliar with sophisticated solutions, from a user as well as a support perspective.

2.2   Methodology

A literature study was conducted to determine the current state of research into the transition of an ICT4D project into a functional part of a sustainable system. Systems thinking was adopted as the conceptual framework for analysis of the current research, and was augmented by the researchers' own practical expertise. This approach was used as basis for the development of a systems-based approach for the integration of ICT4D projects within implementation environments.

2.3   Approaches to the Design and Delivery of ICT4D Projects

Solutions to the unique ICT4D project challenges (see Table 1) have focused on various elements of the process of designing and delivering technology solutions. These include a focus on alternative approaches to solution design, such as addressing the design-reality gap [3, 15, 16], participatory design methods (e.g., [17, 18]), frugal technology design [19], or design for resource constraints [13]. Other remedies include alternative approaches to project transfer and scaling (e.g., [20, 21]). Project or process-wide approaches include project planning and design for sustainability [21], project roadmaps [1], and frameworks to guide development [22]. These solutions are all aimed at fixing a linear development process in such a manner that the inherent peculiarities of ICT4D projects are catered for.

Table 1. The differentiating characteristics of ICT4D projects

Project phase: Commercial ICT project	ICT4D project
Single proposal with budgets and timelines	Many proposals to many different funders; Unclear objectives
Conceptualisation	Ambitious concept; Unknown or unfamiliar project environment
Design	Design by learning
Solution development	Resource-rich solution for a resource-poor world
Implementation	Unexpected challenges
Training and maintenance	Limited literacy; Remote locations; Low skills and technology base

Participatory design is seen by many authors as a means of developing solutions that will integrate well. Not many approaches focus on developing the *capacity to integrate* the ICT4D solution into the environment where it should reside. The project or programme remains an external process in which community members may participate, but that ultimately needs to be transferred into the "foreign" environment where it will reside. While the extent of social embeddedness of a project has been described [23], the method of achieving embeddedness, as well as the dimensions in terms of which embeddedness is required, could benefit from further exploration.

2.4 A Project or Programme Enhances a System

In order to arrive at sustained systemic change, an approach is required in which a "project" or "programme" would alter the fundamental relationships between entities in the system. A flexible and responsive approach is required that would allow the intervention to be designed for, and progress in accordance with, the increasing readiness and maturity of the system. For example, an ICT4D solution that is aimed at enhancing teaching and learning should be delivered in line with the capacity of the education system as a whole to absorb and support the intervention (see Sect. 3).

To this end, we conceptualise the environment within which a project or programme will reside as a collection of entities and relationships. These could include organisational processes, structures, capabilities, culture, political influences, resources, social or community groups, etc. These elements and relationships would be modelled depending on the nature of the problem under consideration.

The project or programme would be seen as a means of affecting these entities and relationships in such a manner that change would be sustained. Here, the balance between entities needs to be considered, and interventions need to be mindful of the fact that *relevant* elements need to be affected in a *balanced* manner to achieve sustained change. For example, an over-focus on technology would be meaningless in an environment where basic computer literacy is lacking, and where the focus should rather be on the development of literacy (entity) and strengthening of the sharing of information (relationship) within communities of practice.

2.5 Pathways to Systemic Change

The concepts outlined above imply that the project or programme changes the *state of the system* from an initial to a changed reality that is capable of sustaining the benefits that are brought about by the project or programme. This changed reality is reflected in changed entities as well as in changed relationships between entities. The progression can be represented as a shift from a current state (*readiness*) to the *intended* state, based on the intended change that should be brought about, to the long-term *desired* state, associated with long-term desired outcomes. This can be represented as follows: (Fig. 1).

Fig. 1. A pathway to a system state that delivers desired outcomes (Source: researchers)

In the above representation, the initial state of readiness determines the initial approach that can be followed by the project. To this end, it is important to be clear about the *intended benefits* of the programme, the systemic *elements* and *relationships* that are required to sustain such benefits, and the *pathway* that needs to be followed to achieve the desired change. Instead of focusing on a linear progression from design through implementation and transfer, the focus is to develop an insider's perspective on the system, and to identify the key entities and relationships between them. These should be analysed to understand the readiness to absorb the benefits of the project or programme, after which existing or additional entities and relationships should be developed so as to mature the *systemic ability to absorb change*.

In this process, appropriate *pathways* to change should be identified. Given our formulation, the premise is that sustainability is inherent in the ability of the system to absorb change. This systemic approach to the development of an appropriate artefact incorporates Ali and Bailur's concepts of *unintended consequences, improvisation,* and *bricolage*, the latter of which means "tinkering through the combination of resources at hand" [24: 5].

The manner in which the pathway is constructed becomes critical to the extent of success that can be attained. Here, *modularity* becomes a key enabler of gradual change that is matched to the readiness of the system. By designing an artefact to have different modules, the flexibility that is called for in the design of ICT4D artefacts [25] is catered for. Modules can be delivered in accordance with the readiness of the system to engage with different levels of complexity, and modules can be used to strengthen different entities and relationships towards increased readiness to absorb more complex solutions. In addition, to allow for flexibility in the intervention, such an approach also allows for accommodation of resource constraints. In the education example outlined below, different modules (technology, professional development, community engagement, etc.) could be delivered depending on the readiness of the system to absorb and afford different parts of the intervention.

3   Integrating ICT4D in Education

The ICT for Rural Education (ICT4RED) project, undertaken by CSIR Meraka and sponsored by multiple government departments, was particularly successful in implementing technology in 26 deep rural pilot schools, and in empowering teachers to comfortably use tablets in their day-to-day teaching activities [25]. It was not as successful in institutionalising change within the Eastern Cape Department of Education (ECDoE) [25].

The project undertook a purposeful systems approach in its design, initially identifying 6 implementation modules that needed to be focused on [12] in order to ensure sustainability and integration of the schools into the education ecosystem.

This implementation model was tested, extended, and improved throughout the project, resulting in an eventual 12 modules [12], categorised under "Governance and Processes", "Technology" and "People and Practices" as indicated in Fig. 2.

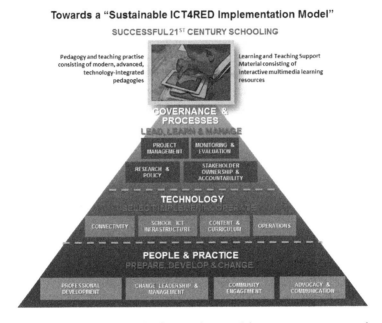

Fig. 2. ICT4RED 12 component implementation model - a systems approach towards sustainability of ICT in schools [12]

Unfortunately, despite the existence of a protocol document between the partner government departments, the project team underestimated the level of "unreadiness" of the district and provincial education entities [26], and did not afford them sufficient focus. This resulted in handover to the ECDoE being problematic. There was difficulty in obtaining commitment with regard to both budget and resources, as well as a general low prioritisation of the needs of the project. The problem was not an unwillingness to incorporate the project into the provincial educational environment, but reflected a lack of resources and a structural design problem regarding integration of ICT initiatives into the existing system. Without the support of the district and province, it becomes difficult for the schools to continue to sustain the change.

In reflecting how the learning from this project could be generalised for all ICT4D projects, the 12 modules were turned into a matrix. Each module can be shaded according to the intensity of effort needed to adequately make provision for weaknesses of various entities and their relationships. Thus the modules can be adjusted to fit the needs within a target environment. The aim is to have a balanced system in which modules do not overpower each other. In a balanced system, the intervention needs to adjust to the level of readiness of each focus area. For example, in the context of ICT4RED—where there was a general lack of skills ("People & Practice") and where there were challenges within the stakeholder environment ("Governance & Processes") required extra effort—investment and focus was needed in the darkly shaded modules as demonstrated in Fig. 3.

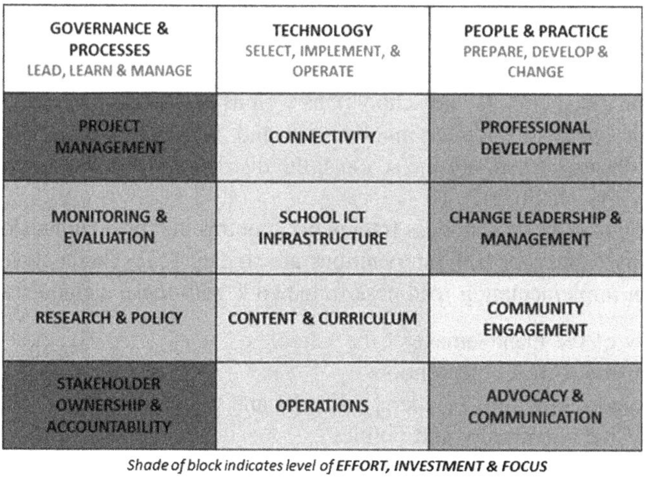

GOVERNANCE & PROCESSES LEAD, LEARN & MANAGE	TECHNOLOGY SELECT, IMPLEMENT, & OPERATE	PEOPLE & PRACTICE PREPARE, DEVELOP & CHANGE
PROJECT MANAGEMENT	CONNECTIVITY	PROFESSIONAL DEVELOPMENT
MONITORING & EVALUATION	SCHOOL ICT INFRASTRUCTURE	CHANGE LEADERSHIP & MANAGEMENT
RESEARCH & POLICY	CONTENT & CURRICULUM	COMMUNITY ENGAGEMENT
STAKEHOLDER OWNERSHIP & ACCOUNTABILITY	OPERATIONS	ADVOCACY & COMMUNICATION

Shade of block indicates level of EFFORT, INVESTMENT & FOCUS

Fig. 3. ICT4RED 12 component implementation model - customised focus according to the strengths and weaknesses in the target environment [26]

In order to adjust an intervention to make provision for the strengths and weaknesses within the target environment so that the change can be absorbed into the system, it is critical to evaluate the readiness of the system.

4 The Development and Implementation of the Readiness Framework

4.1 Methodology

On completion of ICT4RED, there was a need to understand the issues that had not worked well in the project. In order to develop a deep understanding of the dynamics at school and district levels, immersion into this system was required. An ethnographic approach was adopted and a researcher spent two periods of three and four weeks, respectively, at the schools and villages to conduct classroom observation and individual teacher interviews. In order to validate and supplement the researchers' experiences of the provincial system, the whole research team conducted two days of intensive individual interviews with senior provincial management and also held a focus group with teachers and district officials. Based on these inputs, the readiness framework was developed [28].

4.2   The Application of the Implementation Readiness Framework

4.2.1   Introduction

This section aims to provide a very brief overview of the implementation readiness framework. It illustrates how this framework helps with the analysis and understanding of the education system's readiness for ICT interventions in the ICT4RED context. It does so by listing the framework elements that were identified during the research (see below), an then describing how imbalances between elements affect the ability to sustain benefit. An application of the framework would highlight such imbalances, to be rectified through an appropriate intervention design.

The system comprises the provincial department of education with its structures (provincial, districts, circuits and schools), as well as all stakeholders (e.g. parents and funders) with direct or indirect involvement and interests in education [28]. The sub-systems discussed here are the schools, the district, and the provincial head office departments.

The development of a readiness framework requires that the elements of the system and their preparedness for ICT interventions are studied [28]. The analysis of the data resulted in an implementation readiness framework with these elements:

- the quality of the management of the school
- prior exposure to ICT interventions
- school support structures (funders, sponsors and grants)
- the role of the community and politics
- the geographical location of the school

The elements listed above may also be ranked in terms of their relative degree of influence on the readiness of the school. For example, school support structures may be less influential than the quality of the school management [28]. The framework was designed to guide the process of examining different elements of the education system for their readiness to ensure sustained benefit of ICT interventions. The framework can be used to understand the status of different modules of the system, and identify the modules to focus on.

4.2.2   Balance and Imbalance Between the Elements of a System

Balance refers to the configuration of the key elements that are required for everything to work coherently at a systems level. The necessary elements should be present and resourced to a sufficient level. As discussed above, this applies to the school and also to the specific ICT4D implementation (as discussed in the ICT4RED 12 Component implementation model). The generic view of the readiness framework considers how ready the school should manage the operations associated with an ICT system and to develop capacity for the use thereof [28]. The hypothesis is that a school that has a good management team to execute management processes is likely to manage the initiative at the school level to ensure sustained benefit. However, this does not mean that good management is the only factor that will ensure successful implementation and incorporation of the initiative into schools. There are balances and imbalances that need to be understood when deciding what implementation is relevant for a particular school. For example, if the results from the readiness assessment indicate that a school meets all the requirements for a large scale ICT intervention, then implementers can implement at the appropriate scale. The framework helps implementers to scale interventions to be manageable by the school and not to overwhelm them.

A school is a system in itself, but is also enclosed in the larger system of circuits of schools that form part of a district. These in turn constitute the province, which is managed by the provincial head office.

In the case of the ECDoE, as mentioned earlier in this section, a lack of resources and a silo-based organisational structure creates imbalances in the system. For example, the system would provide for only one IT technician per district (e.g. 350 schools in Cofimvaba). If each school has to accommodate 30 tablets in addition to a few PCs, it is obvious that the introduction of the ICT4D intervention makes an already impossible task even worse. A subject advisor maybe allocated to more than a hundred schools. Advisors are not necessarily computer literate, which means that they can are not able to use IT as a means to teach their subject and are unable to provide support and leadership to the schools to the required levels of competence.

Most interventions in schools in rural areas fail to be sustainable due to these systemic imbalances. Provincial departments have to institutionalise the initiatives that are implemented at school level to ensure that the benefits are sustained. On conclusion of the initiative, it has to be handed over to the provincial department or be sustained by the schools themselves. In general, departments may not have the relevant human or financial resources to provide support to the schools that are participating in a particular intervention.

The lack of resources at the province and district levels, and the inability of the national department to support the initiatives, leave the national system unprepared for ICT initiatives in the most impoverished schools, especially in rural areas. Even if the schools are equipped with the best technology and change management processes, and even if teacher professional development processes are executed, the unpreparedness of the system to incorporate these interventions makes it difficult to sustain the benefits from ICT4D interventions. These therefore need to be designed to address the balance required within the sub-systems of the provincial system.

The framework also considers the readiness and balance of the implementation team and the funders. A team may, for example, need to facilitate the management of change. Since many of the rural schools in South Africa have never received large scale ICT interventions, the soft, technical, and managerial skills required to incorporate the project into the school are not readily available [28]. This calls for the implementation team to facilitate a change management process to equip the teachers and school management to sustain the intervention at the school, as was done in the ICT4RED project.

Funders need to be ready to learn about the system and improve their strategy. Funders often focus on the improvement of marks through large-scale ICT interventions, but neglect the status of the system and the diversity of influences on learner achievement. It was evident from the ICT4RED project that there is often no direct relationship between an ICT intervention at schools and the improvement of learner's marks [29] in the short term. The readiness of the funders can be referred to as their ability to change their mindsets about the purpose of funding and the strategies to achieve desired outcomes.

5 Conclusions and Recommendations

The concept of sustainability has been defined in systems terms by describing the *elements* and the *interrelationships* that are required to sustain the benefits of an intervention. Analysis of the ICT4RED intervention showed that the modularity of a project is key to enabling gradual change from the current state of the system (the readiness), as defined from the perspective of being able to realise the desired benefits. A pathway from the current state to the end state of the system, based on the gradual increase of readiness via systemic change can be developed. An implementation readiness framework with five key elements was developed. The framework can be used to characterise the differences in readiness of schools, which can in turn be used to customise the implementation according to the initial configuration of weak and strong elements, and to scale the implementation appropriately.

The same concepts were applied to illustrate the readiness of the systems that support schools, namely the circuits of schools within a district that are managed within a provincial system by the provincial head office. Intervention design therefore has to take into account the nexus of the intervention (e.g. a school) and the supporting systems that would need to be ready to integrate the intervention into the system as a whole.

The work contributes to the ICT4D discourse in that it highlights the need for interventions to be designed in a manner that is cognisant of readiness (or not) of a community to adopt the intervention. It provides a tool that can be applied in practice to assess readiness, and to inform the appropriate pathway that needs to be followed to achieve incremental adoption of the intervention.

References

1. Kettani, D., Moulin, B.: E-government for Good Governance in Developing Countries: Empirical Evidence from the eFez Project. Anthem Press, London (2015)
2. Dodson, L., Sterling, S., Bennet, J.: Considering failure: eight years of ITID research. Int. J. Serv. Learn. Eng. **9**(2), 19–34 (2013)
3. Musiyandaka, D., Ranga, G., Kiwa, J.: An analysis of factors influencing success of ICT4D projects: a case study of the schools computerisation. J. Commun. Inf. **9**, 4 (2013)
4. Heeks, R.: ICT4D 2016: New Priorities for ICT4D Policy, Practice and WSIS in a Post-2015 World. Development Informatics Working Paper Series: Paper 59. Centre for Development Informatics, Institute for Development Policy and Management, SEED, University of Manchester, Manchester (2014)
5. Heeks, R.: ICT4D2.0: the next phase of applying ICT for international development. Computer **41**(6), 26–31 (2008)
6. World Commission on Environment and Development (WCED): Our Common Future. Oxford University Press, Oxford (1987)
7. Harris, R.W., Kumar, A., Balaji, V.: Sustainable telecentres? Two cases from India. In: Krishna, S., Madon, S. (eds.) The Digital Challenge: Information Technology in the Development Context, pp. 124–135. Ashgate Publishing, Aldershot (2003)

8. Bailey, A., Ngwenyama, O.: Toward entrepreneurial behavior in underserved communities: an ethnographic decision tree model of telecenter usage. Inf. Tech. Dev. (2013). doi:10.1080/02681102.2012.751571

9. Roux, K., Marais, M.: Design for Sustainability: rural connectivity with village operators. In: IEEE Global Humanitarian Technology Conference (GHTC): Technology for the Benefit of Humanity, Seattle, Washington, 30 Oct–1 Nov 2011, pp. 522–527 (2011). doi:10.1109/GHTC.2011.58

10. Marais, M.A.: Social capital in the village operator model for rural broadband internet access and use. Unpubl. Dr. Diss. Univ. Pretoria, Pretoria, South Africa (2016)

11. Smith, R., Cambridge, G., Gush, K.: Digital doorway computer literacy through unassisted learning in South Africa. In: CSIR Research and Innovation Conference: 1st CSIR Biennial Conference, CSIR International Convention Centre, Pretoria, 26–27 February 2006 (2006). http://hdl.handle.net/10204/2676

12. Ford, M., Botha, A., Herselman, M.: ICT4RED 12-component implementation framework: a conceptual framework for integrating mobile technology into resource-constrained rural schools. In: IST Africa, Mauritius (2014)

13. Chen, J.: Computing within limits in ICT4D. First Monday **20**, 8 (2015)

14. Meyer, I.A., Marais, M.A.: Design for sustainability: countering the drivers of unsustainability in development projects. J. Commun. Inf. **11**, 3 (2015)

15. Heeks, R.: Information Systems and developing countries: failure, success, and local improvisations. Inf. Soc. **18**, 101–112 (2002)

16. Barjis, J., Kolfschoten, G., Maritz, J.: A sustainable and affordable support system for rural healthcare delivery. Decis. Support Syst. **56**, 223–233 (2013)

17. Steyn, J., Rampa, M., Marais, M.: Participatory development of ICT entrepreneurship in an informal settlement in South Africa. J. Commun. Inf. **9**, 4 (2013)

18. Shiang, C., Halin, A., Lu, M., CheeWhye, G.: Long Lamai Community ICT4D e-commerce system modelling: an agent oriented role-based approach. Elec. J. Inf. Syst. Dev. Countries **75**(5), 1–22 (2016)

19. Watson, R., Kunene, K., Islam, M.: Frugal Information Systems (IS). Inf. Tech. Dev. **19**(2), 176–187 (2013). doi:10.1080/02681102.2012.714349

20. Foster, C., Heeks, R.: Innovation and scaling of ICT for the bottom-of-the-pyramid. J. Inf. Tech. **28**, 296–315 (2013)

21. Pade, C.I.: An investigation of ICT project management techniques for sustainable ICT projects in rural developments. Master's dissertation, Rhodes University, Grahamstown, South Africa (2006)

22. Mamba, M.S.N., Isabirye, N.: A framework to guide development through ICTs in rural areas in South Africa. University of Fort Hare, East London, South Africa (2014)

23. Breytenbach, J., De Villiers, C., Jordaan, M.: Communities in control of their own integrated technology development. Inf. Tech. Dev. **19**(2), 133–150 (2013)

24. Ali, M., Bailur, S.: The challenge of "sustainability" in ICT4D - Is bricolage the answer? In: Proceedings of the 9th International Conference on Social Implications of Computers in Developing Countries, Sao Paulo, Brazil (2007)

25. Herselman, M., Botha, A., Ford, M.: Designing and implementing an ICT4RED initiative. In: Designing and Implementing an Information Communication Technology for Rural Education Development (ICT4RED) Initiative in a Resource Constrained Environment, Cofimvaba School District, Eastern Cape, South Africa. Creative Commons, South Africa (2014)

26. Ford, M.: Discussion Document - ICT4RED Institutionalisation. Unpublished project report, CSIR Meraka Institute, Pretoria, South Africa (2016)

27. Blake, E., Tucker, W., Glaser, M.: Towards communication and information access for deaf people. South Afr. Comp. J. **54**, 10–19 (2013)
28. Meyer, I., Marais, M., Dlamini, S.: Framework for assessing implementation readiness in ICT4E projects. Unpublished framework document, CSIR Meraka Institute, Pretoria, South Africa (2016)
29. Human Science Research Council (HSRC): Report on Monitoring Evaluation and Learning of the TECH4RED initiative. Pretoria, South Africa (2016)

Learning to Be Sustainable in ICT for Development: A Citizen Engagement Initiative in South Africa

Caroline Pade-Khene[1(✉)] and John Lannon[2]

[1] Rhodes University, Grahamstown, South Africa
c.khene@ru.ac.za
[2] University of Limerick, Limerick, Ireland
John.lannon@ul.ie

Abstract. The uncertainty and complexity of ICT4D projects call into question the suitability of conventional approaches to project management that are imposed exogenously, particularly in relation to the challenge of supporting sustainability and resilience. Attempts to transfer knowledge or ownership to local stakeholders or other responsible bodies fail, and consequently many worthwhile initiatives become unsustainable. The problem is particularly acute in the case of citizen engagement projects, where diverse stakeholders are involved and perspectives need to merge when identifying and realising the benefits of the initiative. Borrowing from literature on project management, knowledge management and organisational learning, this paper draws on experiences from a citizen engagement initiative for basic service delivery in a local municipality in South Africa, by reflecting on the learning processes that can contribute to ongoing sustainability in such projects in the global South. The findings highlight the value of emergent learning and negotiation rather than rigid processes linked to pre-determined success factors that are typically adopted in project-based ICT4D initiatives.

Keywords: Sustainability · Organizational learning · Project management · e-Government · Citizen engagement

1 Introduction

While the value of ICT4D initiatives (usually donor-funded) has been confirmed over the past decade, projects are still plagued by failure and sustainability challenges. ICT4D projects are often more complex than expected [1, 2] and are not always conducted with adequate sensitivity and awareness of the environments and contexts they are targeting [3]. An ICT4D initiative, whether managed locally or not, is often driven by foreign funding agendas. The implementer, who may be an NGO or research institution, is often viewed as a proxy of the funder and has to meet specific objectives, typically with in a defined time, scope, cost and quality. These aspects are fundamental to project management, and are often used as an assessment of the effectiveness of an implemented ICT4D initiative. This view is problematic as ICT4D projects are often associated with immense uncertainty and complexity in terms of the factors and actors

© IFIP International Federation for Information Processing 2017
Published by Springer International Publishing AG 2017. All Rights Reserved
J. Choudrie et al. (Eds.): ICT4D 2017, IFIP AICT 504, pp. 475–486, 2017.
DOI: 10.1007/978-3-319-59111-7_39

that make them 'work'. The uncertainty has been a big contributor to the failure of projects, and to what Toyama [4] refers to as 'pilotitis'. Dodson, Sterling and Bennett [5] point out that while there is plenty of ICT4D literature on failures, researchers and practitioners still do not take full cognisance of the failures to *learn* from them, to apply the lessons learned in practice, or to develop mechanisms and theories to address the failures – above the constraints of time, scope, cost and quality. This paper aims to address this by proposing strategies for learning to be sustainable in ICT4D projects. In doing so it asks the following questions: (1) How does the complex nature of ICT4D projects affect sustainability, (2) How can project management, knowledge management, and organizational learning contribute to learning to be sustainable in complex ICT4D environments.

The paper begins with a review of literature on sustainability and project management in ICT4D. Subsequently, the case for 'learning' in ICT4D is discussed. A case study of a digital citizen engagement project called Mobile Social Accountability Monitoring (MobiSAM) is then reflected on using theory on organisational learning, knowledge management, and project management. Finally, the findings are summarised, and the conclusion is reached that learning strategies enable the untangling of uncertainties and complexities in environments that are typically associated with ICT4D projects and international development. Most importantly, learning allows donors and project implementers to realise the true contribution of 'taken-for-granted' perspectives of local beneficiaries.

2 Sustainability, Project Management, and Learning

2.1 Finding the Definition of Sustainability

The definition of sustainability has evolved overtime in ICT4D research and practice, and literature has played around with the term in an effort to understand what the concept really means in practice. Sustainability has been thought of as the ability of a project to continuously function in the context it has been operating in, without hindering the future opportunities of individuals from benefiting from the original initiative [6]. Sustainability has also been related to scalability, in an effort to replicate and maintain the initiative in other contexts [4]. Ali and Bailur [7] call for less emphasis on the term sustainability in ICT4D, as it will never be attained – but rather bricolage should be a focus. Pade-Khene *et al.* [6] proposed a set of critical success factors essential to supporting sustainability by drawing on existing ICT4D initiatives. However, the application of these factors are not clearly defined in relation to the strategies to allow a project to *learn to be sustainable*.

Marais and Meyer [8] talk about their experiences working in a donor-funded project in South Africa. They discuss the key systematic drivers for sustainability which include the question of 'who' defines changes among stakeholders (donors, project implementers, beneficiaries); whether the capacities and readiness of the beneficiary system are understood sufficiently from multiple perspectives; and the extent to which the project aligns change agents in the intervention with the 'natural' agents of change in the beneficiary system. All these speak to the need to shift the focus from the "donor system of innovating on behalf of the beneficiary, to innovation that is driven by the beneficiary system in response to its natural dynamics" [8: 3]. Project managers need to probe and understand the beneficiary system, and to then react appropriately in order to direct and design the project toward effective sustainable practices. Development should not be seen as a problem that should be fixed, but rather a complex system that needs to be *understood* and explored holistically over time [9].

2.2   Project Management Complexity in ICT4D

Project management in international development and ICT4D is often an 'offshoot' of conventional project management [10]. However, some authors [9–11] argue that structured rigid approaches associated with conventional project management result in failure, especially in complex environments. In fact, Mansell [12: 3] argues that conventional project management approaches are a typical example of exogenous models of development (i.e. external to the context) that are imposed on ICT4D initiatives. With these, the focus is invariably on what should be done (scope, time, budget, quality) rather than what happens (learning). Like all international development projects, ICT4D projects face a broad range of issues as outlined by Ika and Hodgson [10: 1185):

> *"...intangible and conflicting objectives and outcomes; changing scope of ambition levels, many layers of stakeholders with conflicting, if not contradictory, expectations; over-optimism and political interferences and manipulations including strategy misrepresentation or misinformation about costs,... media scrutiny; intolerance of failure;...corruption, capacity building setbacks, recurrent costs of projects, lack of political support, lack of implementation and institutional capacity and overemphasis on visible and rapid results from donors and political actors."*

Together, these add to the difficulties associated with the use of standard, exogeneous approaches to projects and project management in the ICT4D sphere.

Many ICT4D failures are more institutional than technical, and project management in such contexts needs to take cognisance of this. Walton and Heeks [9] propose that ICT4D projects should adopt a process approach, highlighting the factors that should be considered. These are beneficiary participation; flexible and phased implementation; learning from experience; local institutional support and capacity development; and sound project leadership. All these speak to the need for a process and learning perspective, where success emerges from *"a wider understanding of the systems that make a particular context, which can always be improved upon further"* [9: 19]. Here, success and failure are not associated with finality, but with an opportunity to incrementally learn and generate feedback for growth in an atmosphere of social experimentation and interaction [9, 10, 12].

Project managers that work in ICT4D initiatives have to deal with a range of issues relating to power and influence amongst the diverse group of stakeholders [13]. The projects have more to do with people engagement than technology, and as a result the project manager needs to shift from being the "economic man, objective arbiter of interest, or technocratic" to being more 'proactive' and 'engaged' with the actors that have the power and influence. In particular (s)he needs to engage key stakeholders that are local and benefit directly from the project in a process of realising/learning the operation and sustainability of the ICT4D initiative [13].

2.3 The Case for 'Locally' Learning to Be Sustainable

Mansell [12] argues that ICT4D initiatives need to move beyond exogenous models of development that justify their implementation as a stimulator of economic growth in the developing world. Toyama [4] agrees on the basis of having previously implemented ICT4D projects with that view. He argues that technology is not transformative in and of itself, but is primarily an amplifier of existing institutional forces like differential access to technology, capacity to use the technology and motivation to see the value in using the technology for its true purpose [14]. Mansell [12] proposes that *endogenous* models should thus be applied, where insight is provided on the factors that influence development. No single endogenous model exists that can explain a context, and therefore 'local' learning with key stakeholders is fundamental. Endogenous models also embrace the idea of engaging through participatory approaches with multiple perspectives. These allow "meanings of technology to emerge through an open, emergent process of dialogue which respects multiple sources of knowledge" [12: 13]. Knowledge transfer and development occur in the evolving incremental learning processes of project implementation, typically *between and with* implementers, donors, and most importantly local beneficiaries of the initiative. The knowledge ranges from expertise knowledge on technology implementation and integration, to knowledge on practice and operations in the local context. Consequently, participatory approaches move beyond being just a *consultative* process to considering redistributions of power and influence over constructive decision-making among local beneficiaries of the project [4, 10].

Resilience goes hand-in-hand with sustainability in ICT4D, as the project moves iteratively between failure, learning and success overtime while strengthening its ability to recover through knowledge transfer. Knowledge management is a key component in ICT4D as it allows an initiative to realise its full potential and resilience through strategic and tactical decision-making. Conger [15: 114] defines it as the "systematic process of acquisition, organisation, and communication of organisational member knowledge for reuse by others in the community", and indicates that there is limited work looking at this in ICT4D literature. Yet it is a fundamental component as initiatives need ongoing development and maintenance without the aid of the original implementation team. In order to acquire knowledge, a process of interaction between explicit and tacit knowledge needs to occur through processes of sharing [16]. This relates to organisational learning which is the "internal adaptation processes triggered by some kind of disjunction or unease in the relationship between the organisation and what lies external and challenging to it in its environment" [17: 160]. It is in the context of these processes that this paper explores strategies used for learning to be sustainable' in ICT4D using a case study on digital citizen engagement i.e. citizen engagement supported by digital technology [18].

3 Research Methodology

This study adopts a pragmatic research philosophy in which the experience of the researchers is based on reflective interaction between action and belief [19, 20]. By iteratively reflecting on existing theory and practice [19], it not only examines 'what works' but also 'why it works'. A qualitative approach is applied to reflect on the MobiSAM case study as it seeks to ask 'how' a learning strategy is used and 'why' it worked in a particular way. Data was collected through participant observation, as one of the researchers is part of the project team and has played a significant role in applying project management practice and learning in the project. Further qualitative data was collected overtime from project team meetings and engagements, from closed and public meetings with stakeholders (including citizens, municipal staff, civil society, and media), and from public forums held by the local municipality. Documents from a previous phase of the project were also analysed to identify lessons learned.

Data collection took place from February to December 2016 during the implementation of phase 2.0 of the MobiSAM project. The data was analysed using open thematic analysis to allow aspects to emerge from practice while reflecting on theory in project management, knowledge management, and organizational learning.

4 The Case of MobiSAM – a Digital Citizen Engagement Initiative

MobiSAM is a project that uses mobile technology to supports two-way communication between citizens and government about basic service delivery issues. It was founded in 2012 by local researchers who were frustrated by the growing issue of water service delivery in their municipality [21]. MobiSAM aims to support citizen engagement, through providing platforms (not only technology related) that citizens can use to engage in social accountability practices. It is widely promoted as a 'game changer' for development [22], as the voiceless become empowered to evoke change in society. For it to be effective, demonstrating results from engagement, designing multiple channels of participation, providing multi-tiered levels of engagement, reinforcing a sense of civic duty and collectiveness, and getting pre-commitment from citizens are all essential for increased participation [23].

When an individual citizen has a service delivery issue in South Africa they typically report it to the municipality at a front-desk (face-to-face), by telephone, or through a Ward Councillor or Community Development Worker. These reports often remain as individual *undisclosed* reports which the public may not be aware of. Civic (collective) action may also be used to draw attention to service delivery issues. However this is often isolated and may not reflect the true nature of the problem for the wider population. MobiSAM plays a strategic role as it brings together individual and collective action with real time access to mechanisms to report issues to all stakeholders. Figure 1 illustrates where MobiSAM sits in local municipal contexts.

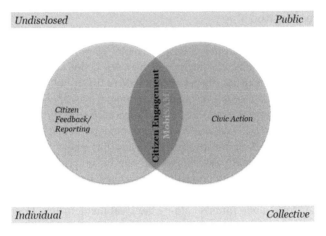

Fig. 1. Citizen engagement in MobiSAM (adapted from [18])

The MobiSAM technology incorporates both a reporting interface for citizens (via a mobile application, website, and SMS), and a ticketing function (mainly used by the municipality to address internal communication challenges). Initially, before system launch, Facebook and WhatsApp social media platforms were used to 'experience' the idea of reporting using technology. MobiSAM has a Facebook page for citizens to report and the municipality to make service delivery announcements.

4.1 The Stakeholders in MobiSAM

The MobiSAM stakeholders include the donor, the project implementation team, and the beneficiaries, and as with all citizen engagement projects the beneficiaries consist of citizens, government, civil society, and the media. The project manager needs to continuously engage with all these stakeholders as they interact in a web of complexity and uncertainty in an environment that is politically influenced and marginalised. Conflicting perspectives on what MobiSAM is expected to achieve exist between stakeholders and even within stakeholder groups. The project manager needs to devise strategies to engage all the stakeholders, either separately or together, in order to address the conflicting perspectives and to learn how the digital citizen engagement initiative can best function within its context.

4.2 Learning Strategies in the MobiSAM Project

This section reflects on strategies applied in the MobiSAM project to support learning. It draws on organisational learning theory, with knowledge management and project management literature providing additional insight. According to Easterby-Smith and Araujo [24], organizational learning can be viewed as a technical process [25] or a social process [26] that emphasizes situated learning and learning within communities of practice. The perspective of Argyris and Schön [25] on organisational learning presents two often conflicting modes of operation, namely espoused theory, which is the formalized part of the organization, and theory-in-use, which reflects the implicit mental models and theories people actually use to get things done. By questioning the theories in use of an organization this can help to adapt and to learn from an unexpected situation. This reflection provides insight into double-loop learning in the MobiSAM project, taking cognisance of the unique nature of ICT4D and digital citizen engagement projects in the global South. This is added to by drawing on social perspectives on the transfer of knowledge within the project. The section concludes with a look at the role of the project manager in creating a climate of learning in the MobiSAM project.

4.2.1 Double-Loop Learning

Phase 1.0 of the MobiSAM project experienced some challenges which mainly emanated from the contextual political influence of government stakeholders. It adopted a somewhat adversarial approach to implementing citizen engagement which was met with resistance from government. This led to despondency among citizens who felt that reporting service delivery via the platform would not result in a response from government. The lessons learned in Phase 1.0 [21] were reflected on, resulting in the development of a new approach for Phase 2.0. Thisdouble-loop learning focused on studying and learning from the contextual influences in order to build government responsiveness, civil society partnerships, and citizen capacity to become engaged citizens. In going from Phase 1.0 to Phase 2.0 the MobiSAM project had to reflect on 'why we do what we do'. The goals and values of Phase 1.0 had to be re-evaluated and reframed, not through a once-off process, but an incremental process to define the operational model of Phase 2.0.

The MobiSAM operational model involves activities that are more than just about the technology; they include mechanisms to manage the uncertainty and complexity of the context of digital citizen engagement initiatives. Five key aspects make-up the operational model: (1) citizen education and training, (2) building government responsiveness and citizen engagement capacity, (3) stakeholder engagement, (4) iterative technology development, and (5) comprehensive evaluation throughout the project and embedded in learning.

The MobiSAM operational model is not static, but evolves with changes in the environment that relate to both internal and external influences. There is no clear start and end to the project, but rather a model to allow for its evolution over time, as it becomes embedded in citizen engagement practice as well as government practice. Applying this approach has been instrumental in garnering beneficiary support and engagement in the project from both citizens and government.

4.2.2 Promoting Transfer of Internal Capabilities

Knowledge transfer is a fundamental component of organisational learning [27]. However, in ICT4D contexts knowledge transfer processes are usually formalised through communities of practice that include project team members and experts from other projects but usually exclude local beneficiaries. At times, the knowledge or expertise associated with implementing an ICT4D initiative resides with the 'temporary' implementer who leaves with this expertise when the project ends or funding runs out [4]. To promote sustainability these capabilities should be transferred to local beneficiaries (as well as other local project implementers), in order to support the continuity and progressive development of the initiative. Furthermore, knowledge on the local system in which the ICT4D initiative is implemented needs to be transferred to the project team and funding agencies. For knowledge transfer to be meaningful in the ICT4D context, where there is an interactive exchange of project *and* context knowledge, identifying the right source and recipient matters [27]. Both the project team and beneficiaries can play the interchangeable role of 'source' and 'recipient' depending on the knowledge shared. The MobiSAM project applies various strategies to support learning, which can be explored using Szulanski's four stage process [27]:

1. *Initiation:* This first step leads to a decision to transfer knowledge. It is an exploratory process resulting in the identification of a need for and feasibility of a transfer. In MobiSAM Phase 2.0 the project team had to devise ways in which knowledge could be shared within the team and with other key stakeholders as implementation still remained uncertain. Furthermore, new relationships and partnerships needed to be developed with local citizens, government, civil society and media, allowing a space to share perspectives that contribute to the direction of the project. The project managers needed to provide an environment to encourage and motivate people to communicate and share their knowledge with others [28]. The kind of knowledge that needed to be transferred related to government practice, protocols for working with various local stakeholders and citizens, communication designs and ecologies that work best in particular contexts, discipline specific expertise from the diverse project team, and how to collaborate with specific municipal wards, etc. In this context, knowledge from all stakeholders was essential, and needed to be shared and appreciated as essential.

2. *Implementation:* This stage is associated with establishing transfer-specific social ties between the source and recipient. Here, the transfer practice is adapted to suit the needs of the recipient – in this case, not only project team members, but also target beneficiaries of the project. The project manager of an ICT4D initiative is the one that lobbies for this transfer in the first place, as beneficiaries may not yet realise the true potential or benefit of the project. Therefore certain strategies have to be applied to ensure that a suitable environment is developed for transfer. For example, from the perspective of beneficiary transfer practices, the MobiSAM project had to run strategy formulation workshops. The first two workshops were held separately, with the first group being the government staff, and the second group being citizens, civil society and media. The aim was to provide an environment that allowed for transfer, avoiding conflict between stakeholders. Once commonalities were established, a joint workshop was held with all stakeholders, to provide a shared understanding on how best to implement the MobiSAM project.

3. *Ramp-up:* This stage occurs when the recipient begins to use the knowledge. In MobiSAM all stakeholders, including the project team, are recipients. New knowledge contributes to learning about how the project can function and operate among citizens and government. The MobiSAM project team proceeded with caution, now understanding the political dynamics and operations in the municipality. Municipal staff had also now begun to integrate MobiSAM in their communication policy and strategy documents in collaboration with the project team,

and had suggested that MobiSAM be part of a new citizen engagement initiative from government known as *Masiphathisane* meaning "let us help each other" (based on an integrated service delivery model). Civil society advised and committed to integrating MobiSAM in its existing activities, and local media has incorporated MobiSAM into its local broadcasts and publications.

4. *Integration:* This stage is reached when transferred knowledge becomes institutionalised. For beneficiaries this may still be early in the adoption process but within the project team shared knowledge has become embedded in routine practices. For example, the team has a shared understanding of how to reflect on citizen engagement and government practice based on discipline specific knowledge. Behaviours and events have become understandable, as types of actions are associated with types of actors. The project team learns to understand the project more holistically, not only from an information systems or computer science perspective, but also from a sociological and journalistic perspective.

Integration remains ongoing in MobiSAM, as engagement with additional stakeholders takes place.

In digital citizen engagement projects, engaging with diverse stakeholders' perspectives coupled with issues of power and political influence can result in the need for ad hoc solutions to knowledge transfer problems. It becomes difficult to apply a traditional approach to knowledge transfer in such a dynamic environment. Nonetheless Orlikowski [29] argues that sharing knowledge enables better understanding of practices relating to "know-how", and hence better understanding of the origins of knowledge stickiness [27] and how to work around it. Such ad hoc processes of learning have enabled the MobiSAM project to operate in the conditions that have emerged.

4.2.3 The Development of Trust Among Stakeholders

In creating a climate of learning the project manager needs to establish a climate of trust between stakeholders where "it is safe to make mistakes, sharing knowledge is the norm, and helping others is promoted" [30: 13]. Stakeholders need to feel they can trust the engagement process especially where unlearning or learning from mistakes can occur as failed aspects of a project are likely to yield more valuable knowledge than focusing on the successful aspects [16]. Knowledge sharing in digital citizen engagement can evoke feelings of conflict of interest among individuals or groups involved [31]. In the MobiSAM project, the project manager's role is to manage the knowledge bases of the project team and stakeholders so that they combine in the best possible way to learn from each other. As highlighted previously, conflict already exists between stakeholders, and an environment of trust is fundamental to project activities that enable learning. For example, MobiSAM had to hold workshops to engage stakeholders in a process of learning and work had to be done to ensure stakeholders felt comfortable to engage. Affective commitment by the project manager also influences knowledge sharing, as this plays a significant role in determining perseverance in the conflicting interactions and reactions among stakeholders. The project manager, and even the project team in MobiSAM, had to play a neutral role, open to understanding the conflicting perspectives of the main beneficiaries - that is, government and citizens – in order to establish a common ground for learning and engagement.

A project manager in this case has to be affectively committed, and highly motivated by a concern for the community and a desire to serve the interests and values of the public and government for the greater good [13]. This is one of the key lessons that the project managers had to learn in the MobiSAM project.

5   Limitations and Future Research

This research reflects on only one case study. Nonetheless, it highlights key aspects that can resonate with other ICT4D projects, based on the challenges experienced and the need for iterative incremental learning to occur [9]. This research also serves as a foundation for further exploration of the theories and concepts of project management, knowledge management and organizational learning in ICT4D practice. At this stage the research only provides a high-level view of what could be explored.

6   Concluding Remarks

ICT4D is a growing field that seeks to understand how sustainability can be realised in projects that have been proven to hold value in socio-economic development. These projects are characterized by complexity and uncertainty; as a result, rigid conventional approaches to project management, which are quite typical of project-based donor funded initiates, result in project failure. Previous research advises that ICT4D projects should be flexible, iterative and incremental overtime, providing an opportunity to incrementally learn and generate feedback for growth in an atmosphere of social experimentation and interaction. Reflecting on organisational learning, knowledge management, and project management, the MobiSAM project provides an example of a case in ICT4D of 'learning to be sustainable'. Three key strategies are fundamental in the learning approach applied; these are double-loop learning, promoting the transfer of internal capabilities, and development of trust among stakeholders. The MobiSAM project continues to function and grow based on this approach, with stakeholder buy-in. The strategies can be applied in general ICT4D practice in an effort to untangle the uncertainties and complexities of environments that are typically associated with such projects. Most importantly, learning allows donors and project implementers to respect and realise the true contribution of 'taken-for-granted' perspectives of local beneficiaries.

Acknowledgement. This research was funded by the National Research Foundation of South Africa and the 'Making All Voices Count' initiative. The researchers also thank the MobiSAM team for their continued support and participation in the project, and generation of practical experience to reflect on.

References

1. Loh, Y.: Approaches to ICT for Development (ICT4D): vulnerabilities vs. capabilities. Inf. Dev. **31**(3), 1–10 (2013)
2. Turpin, M., Alexander, P.M.: Desperately seeking systems thinking in ICT4D. Electron. J. Inf. Syst. Dev. Countries **61**(6), 1–15 (2014)

3. Avgerou, C.: The significance of context in information systems and organizational change. Inf. Syst. J. **11**, 43–63 (2001)
4. Toyama, K.: Geek Heresy. Public Affairs, New York (2015)
5. Dodson, L., Sterling, S., Bennett, J.K.: Considering failure: eight years of ITID research. J. Inf. Technol. Int. Dev. **9**(2), 19–34 (2013)
6. Pade-Khene, C., Mallinson, B., Sewry, D.: Sustainable rural ICT project management practice for developing countries: investigating the Dwesa and RUMEP projects. J. Inf. Technol. Dev. **17**(3), 187–212 (2011)
7. Ali, M., Bailur, S.: The challenge of "sustainability" in ICT4D - Is bricolage the answer? In: 9th International Conference on Social Implications of Computers in Developing Countries. São Paulo, Brazil (2007)
8. Marais, M., Meyer, I.: Design for sustainability: countering the drivers of unsustainability in development projects. J. Commun. Inf. **11**(3), 1–13 (2015)
9. Walton, M., Heeks, R.: Can a Process Approach Improve ICT4D Project Success. Development Informatics Group, Institute for Development Policy Management, Manchester (2011)
10. Ika, L., Hodgson, D.: Learning from international development projects: blending critical project studies and critical development studies. Int. J. Project Manag. **32**(2014), 1182–1196 (2014)
11. Shenkar, A.J., Dvir, D.: Reinventing Project Management: The Diamond Approach to Successful Growth and Innovation, 1st edn. Harvard Business Press, Brighton (2013)
12. Mansell, R.: Power and interests in information and communication and development: exogenous and endogenous discourses in contention. J. Int. Dev. **26**(1), 109–127 (2014)
13. Jałocha, B., Krane, H.P., Ekambaram, A., Prawelska-Skrzypek, G.: Key competencies of public sector project managers. Proced. Soc. Behav. Sci. **119**(2014), 247–256 (2014)
14. Toyama, K.: Technology as an amplifier in international development. In: Proceedings of the iConference, p. 75 (2011)
15. Conger, S.: Knowledge management for information and communication technologies for development programs in South Africa. J. Inf. Technol. Dev. **21**(1), 113–134 (2015)
16. Ajmal, M., Koskinen, K.: Knowledge transfer in project-based organisations an organisational culture perspective. Project Manag. J. **39**(1), 7–15 (2008)
17. Spender, J.C.: Organisational learning and knowledge management: whence and whither. Manag. Learn. **39**(2), 159–176 (2008)
18. Peixoto, T., Fox, J.: When does ICT-enabled citizen voice lead to government responsiveness? World Bank, Washington, D.C. (2016)
19. Morgan, D.: Pragmatism as a paradigm for social research. Qual. Inquiry **20**(8), 1045–1053 (2014)
20. Hall, J.: Pragmatism, evidence, and mixed methods evaluation. J. New Dir. Eval. **138**, 15–26 (2013)
21. Thinyane, H.: Stumbling at the start line: an analysis of factors affecting participation with local government in South Africa. In: Proceedings of SIG GlobDev 6th Annual Workshop, Milano, Italy (2013)
22. Gaventa, J., Barrett, G.: Mapping the outcomes of citizen engagement. J. World Dev. **40**(12), 2399–2410 (2012)
23. Spada, P., Mellon, J., Peixoto, T., Sjoberg, F.M.: Effects of the Internet on Participation: Study of a Public Forum Referendum in Brazil. World Bank, Washington, D.C. (2015)
24. Easterby-Smith, M.P.V., Araujo, L.M.: Organizational learning: current debates and opportunities. In: Easterby-Smith, M., Araujo, L., Burgoyne, J. (eds.) Organizational Learning and the Learning Organization: Developments in Theory and Practice, pp. 1–21. Sage, London (1999)

25. Argyris, C., Schön, D.A.: Organisational Learning II: Theory, Method and Practice. Addison-Wesley, Reading (1996)
26. Lave, J., Wenger, E.: Situated Learning: Legitimate Peripheral Participation. Cambridge University Press, Cambridge (1991)
27. Szulanski, G.: Exploring internal stickiness: impediments to the transfer of best practice within the firm. Strat. Manag. J. **17**(Winter Special Issue), 27–43 (1996)
28. Yeh, Y., Lai, S., Ho, C.: Knowledge management enablers: a case study. Ind. Manag. Data Syst. **106**(6), 793–810 (2006)
29. Orlikowski, W.J.: Knowing in practice: enacting a collective capability in distributed organising. Org. Sci. **13**(3), 249–273 (2002)
30. Reich, B.H.: Managing knowledge and learning in IT projects: a conceptual framework and guidelines for practice. Project Manag. J. **38**(2), 5–17 (2007)
31. Matzler, K., Renzl, B., Mooradian, T., von Krogh, G., Mueller, J.: Personality traits, affective commitment, documentation of knowledge, and knowledge learning. Int. J. Hum. Resour. Manag. **22**(2), 296–310 (2011)

Self-Reinforcing Linkages Between Value and Local Ownership: Rethinking Sustainability of ICT4D Project

Sundeep Sahay[✉] and Arunima Mukherjee

Department of Informatics, University of Oslo, Oslo, Norway
sundesundeeps@ifi.uio.no, arunimam@gmail.com

Abstract. The paper addresses the wicked problem of unsustainable health information systems in the context of low and middle income countries (LMICs), specifically using a case study from India in the public health sector. The paper makes the argument that current analysis of sustainability tends to be largely "supply-driven" focusing on the provision of external resources and technical assistance needed to sustain a project. But since these external injections are self-multiplying, requiring more and more over time, they tend to not lead to satisfactory and sustainable solutions. The paper argues for a more "demand-driven" approach, where the focus is on the user and the use context. Taken from this perspective, the paper identifies two sets of processes – evolving local ownership and enhancing use – as being key to establish sustainability. Further, these processes are seen to be mutually self-reinforcing, and supported by an enabling context of use.

Keywords: ICT4D · Low and middle income country · Sustainability

1 Introduction

This paper addresses the wicked problem of sustainability of ICT for Development (ICT4D) projects. The notion of sustainability gained prominence in the Rio Summit of 1992, and Agenda 21 which was adopted at the summit [1] described sustainability as "Meeting the needs of the present generation without compromising the ability of future generations to meet their needs."

In the field of ICT4D the issue of sustainability has remained a matter of great concern and has been discussed and analysed by various researchers. The common question of concern is "how systems can continue to exist after external assistance is withdrawn?" Many ICT4D projects fade away as pilots, getting discontinued after the external technical and financial assistance is withdrawn [2], leading to significant wastage of time and resources.

Despite this huge work on sustainability [3], there are limited explanations of how sustainability can be best achieved. The sustainability problem has proved to be wicked, as trying to find solutions in one domain, lead to the emergence of other problems. For example, in trying to address the problem of resource constraints, donor funds could be solicited, which creates further dependencies which challenge sustainability. In the

Published by Springer International Publishing AG 2017. All Rights Reserved
J. Choudrie et al. (Eds.): ICT4D 2017, IFIP AICT 504, pp. 487–497, 2017.
DOI: 10.1007/978-3-319-59111-7_40

public health sector of LMICs, this problem is especially acute [4]. Blaschke [2] coined the term "pilotitis" to describe the multiplicity of mHealth projects in Uganda which died as pilots. Braa et al. [5] argue that unsustainable projects to not scale, and if they don't scale they remain unsustainable.

The why of unsustainability remains inadequately understood. Braa et al. [5] have described the "networks of action" approach as a means to strengthen sustainability by promoting collective learning and sharing in the network. However, this approach is limited in explaining the micro level adoption and use processes within an organization. Solutions towards achieving sustainability are often superficially restricted towards providing advice on enhancing capacity through training, or the provision of organizational budgets. This supply side focus is limited, which this paper seeks to address by emphasizing two demand side inter-related processes of "building local ownership" and "leveraging use value from the system." This paper explores these dynamics within the context of a project around designing and implementing a hospital information system (HIS) for the public health sector in an Indian state.

In the next section, we discuss relevant literature on sustainability, following which the research methodology is described, and then the case study. The case analysis and discussions follow and then some brief conclusions.

2   Sustainability of HIS: Arguing for a More User Driven Perspective

In this section, we discuss some perspectives around sustainability of HIS initiatives, while emphasizing the need for strengthening use or supply side processes. Sustainability, in general terms implies that the system is unable to continue in the long run after external technical and financial assistance, typically from the World Bank and other donors, is withdrawn. This leads to project dying as pilots, a phenomenon termed as "pilotitis" [2]. Braa et al. [5] described lack of sustainability to be the largest problem facing HIS in LMICs, which limits also their scalability.

Identified reasons for unsustainability include lack of commitment from political leadership, poor coordination between donors, fragmented structures, and unrealistic ambitions around what ICTs can do [6]. Heeks [4] describes "design-reality" gaps to indicate the wide chasm that exists between systems designed in the West for organizational contexts in LMICs, leading to a total or partial failure of the system. Wahid [6] describes how different local governments in Indonesia worked with their own systems with poor coordination contributing to sustainability failures.

Naby researchers have described sustainability as an attribute of the IS [3, 6] such as of it being long term, scalable, adaptable, responsive to changing needs, and stable and robust. Such a view of IS inscribed agency disregards agency of people, organizations, and history which also shape sustainability. Wahid argues for sustainability to be better conceptualized as information infrastructures rather than isolated systems, and proposes a triple helix model. Kumar and Best's [7] conceptualization of sustainability covers five aspects of social, financial, technological, political/institutional and environmental. Furholt [8] analyzes sustainability with respect to supply and demand related dynamics.

Various conditions have been identified for both sustainable and unsustainable systems. Maruster et al. [9] describes sustainability to relate to the adaptability of the system to changes in the environment, the involvement of relevant stakeholders, and supporting the complete knowledge life cycle of the project. Jaccuci et al. [10] identified conditions under which systems are unsustainable, including the neglect of local use of information, narrowly driven interventions and a dominant technical bias in projects. In the context of HIS in Tanzania, Smith et al. [11], see the unsustainability of systems due to the very managerialist manner in which the problem of integration is tried to be addressed, which leads to technically biased short-term solutions which do not endure. Instead, they argue that guidance on the conceptualization of integration should be drawn from also the disciplines of Sociology and Development Studies.

Kimaro and Nhampossa [3] in their analysis of sustainability of HIS drawing upon case studies from Mozambique and Tanzania, point to the problem of financial dependencies of countries on donor funds. This dependency they argue is shaped by three key sets of relationships. The first concerns the relationship between the Ministry of Health (MoH) and the software development agency, the second between the MoH and the donors, and the third between the donors and the software development agency. All these relationships which are crucial for the establishment of the HIS, in practice tend to create dependencies of the host country on external assistance which cannot be sustained after the withdrawal of donor support.

2.1 Sustainability from a User-Perspective

The above brief review of IS/HIS in LMIC contexts points to two sets of issues. One, analysis of sustainability takes on a very supply driven perspective, putting the onus of unsustainability to external support withdrawal or the paucity of funds. Within such a perspective, proposed solutions tend to focus on how to augment the supply side resources, which more often than not may lead to continued and more complex dependencies – the nature of a wicked problem. Two, the onus of unsustainability is placed on the IS perse, as an attribute of the system. This perspective ignores the agency of users, the role of institutions, and many other conditions relevant to building a social systems understanding. For example, new technologies such as mobile phones may be positioned as being more sustainable, reinforcing the attribute view discussed above.

This paper argues to switch the analysis perspective of sustainability by building a demand side focus which places the user at the center of the analysis, and emphasizing two sets of processes. One, relates to the question of how the local ownership of a system can be cultivated over time. Two, concerns how the use of the system relevant to local needs can be made to evolve over time. These two sets of processes are argued to be inter-related, and mutually supporting processes can help develop more rounded insights on the sustainability problem. We analyze these processes in our case study. But first, the research methods adopted are briefly described.

3   Research Method

The research is based on an ongoing project since 2010 into the design, development, implementation and support of an integrated HIS for district hospitals in an Indian state (called NSTATE). Both the authors of this paper have been directly involved in the execution of the project from its initiation to now.

Broadly, an interpretive approach was adopted, where the focus was on understanding the multiple interpretations around sustainability, through discussions with various actors including the health care providers at the hospitals comprised of field nurses, medical doctors and technicians, and also the district and state administrators. Our research also involved a multi-level engagement, talking to the global developers responsible for the open source platform on which the HIS was developed, to the state authorities, and hospital staff. These different groups would view sustainability from varying frames of reference, for example, for INGO sustainability was understood in relation to the period of the contract agreement, while for the state it would involve building ownership beyond the contract period. For users, the meaning of sustainability is embedded in their everyday work context, and their understanding of how the system could ease and improve their work processes over time.

The research was longitudinal in nature with both authors engaged in it from its inception in 2010 to date. During this period they both engaged in the research in terms of its conceptualisation, building the proposal, understanding system requirements, system design, capacity strengthening, institutionalisation, feedback, trouble shooting, implementation support, and much more. Both authors have been both continuously visiting the implementation sites over the years, once in few months, meeting various actors to help understand their expectations, experiences and fears, and how these have changed or not over time. These interactions gave rich insights to different dynamics that shape sustainability. Being following this project for long, we also have had the privilege to see whether the project has actually sustained over time.

Interpretivism [12] was coupled with action research [5], where the aim was to make the system work, in the context of the hospitals, which spanned processes of design, development, implementation and support. The project activities were intensive involving everyday work of meetings, coordinating development tasks, making presentations, documentation, conducting trainings and various others. All these tasks created vast amounts of data which were compiled as meeting minutes, project documents, observations during meetings, and various others. Data collection thus involved diverse and multiple means. Lots of data was also collected through informal means, through casual interactions, phone calls, email exchanges and the like. The project management tool used in INGO served as the repository of all project related information which was available for this research.

Data analysis was complex, as it involved making sense of diverse data collected for varying purposes, and focusing on specific data related to the phenomenon under study. The analysis was largely inductive in nature and spirit, where we allowed ourselves to be guided by the field experiences. However, we took a "top-down" process of analysis, trying to develop holistic interpretations of our combined field experiences over time, rather than using reductionist methods of developing codes in the data and seeking inter-rater reliabilities. We believe our interpretive process provides for a rich and holistic understanding of the phenomenon. Given the analytical focus on sustainability, we focused on those actions and processes which we believed would contribute to the system continuing in the state after INGO, the technical support partner, had withdrawn. This made us focus understanding processes by which users tried to take control of the system or in defining the desired future trajectory of HIS.

4 Case Study Description

This section is divided over two main parts. In the first, we provide an extended discussion of the case study context, which is pertinent to understand conditions for sustainability. In the next part, we provide a narrative of the case.

4.1 Case Study Context

The case/project is based in a hilly north Indian state (anonymized as NSTATE) located in the foothills of the Himalayas. NSTATE has a population density of 123 persons per square km, with about 90% rural population, and much lower than the national average of 382 (2011 Census). This contributed to a high dependence of the population on the public health system, and provides the political impetus to the government to continually strengthen it, including through computerization. NSTATE has the reputation of being stable, inclusive, cohesive, and a well-governed, and was ranked third in the country on the Human Development Index [13].

NSTATE's commitment to strengthen public services delivery is seen in its efforts to decentralize its information systems, along with the financial and functional powers to the facility level. The state has made investments to use ICTs in overcoming the geographic challenges, such as through high profile tele-medicine initiatives. The state has deployed a fleet of over 200 hundred well equipped ambulances across the districts to ensure efficient referrals. The state has been pioneering in connecting all district and sub-district hospitals with a HIS, which is the focus of this paper.

4.2 Case Study Narrative

In 2008, NSTATE decided to introduce a HIS in 20 district and sub-district hospitals, and floated a request for proposal (RFP) to which 53 companies responded. The RFP specified a 'perfect and utopian' system with features including telemedicine, SMS based electronic appointment scheduling, and digitizing of medical images and videos. With no success on the selection of a vendor, the state approached INGO, an Indian NGO working in NSTATE since 2008 on other systems. In 2009, NSTATE signed an agreement for INGO to design, develop and implement the HIS project.

A District Hospital (DH) is typically a 100 to 300 bedded hospital with multiple specialties catering to a daily load of about 800–1000 outpatients and 40–50 inpatients. The systems in a DH are largely manual, thus making computerization a formidable challenge. INGO adopted an incremental approach where patient registration and billing were selected as the first modules to be implemented, followed by the more complex OPD and IPD modules. The plan was after the system was successfully piloted in the reference hospital, the same system would be taken to the other 19 hospitals.

Right from initiation, a participatory and incremental approach was adopted, including for modules prioritization, conducting requirements, design and implementation. An important design guideline was not to 'just' automate processes, but also to add value by 're-engineering' existing processes. This required the design process to be based on strong mutual collaboration and dialogue, where the users were not assumed to be passive providers of requirements, but as actively engaged in co-constructing them. The process followed included INGO understanding the work and information flows in a department, followed by discussions, returning with mock-up screens representing their understanding of the requirements, making revisions based on user feedback, presenting final design for signoff and then initiating module development. The proposed design was very context sensitive with strong user involvement.

Given that this was first experience of the hospital of using real-time electronic HIS for recording all patient transactions, the INGO team was intensively present in the hospital. In the first week after "go-live", the INGO team made a roster of its five member team to be in the hospital before start of work to ensure LAN, printers, systems were up and working. This process continued for a month before INGO started discussing with the hospital to try and create a local team, and two members were identified. The team started to be trained following an approach of "learning by doing", and slowly their skills expanded from doing routine support tasks for hardware, to operating the server and conducting internal capacity building tasks. Over the period, the hospital team with their responsibilities was formalized. More into the future, the team started to generate data on system use and circulate to hospital staff.

It took about one-and-a-half years for INGO to implement the integrated suite of 10 modules in the HIS and stabilize use processes. They could then initiate scaling processes to the other hospitals which were located in other cities of the state, typically involving a day's travel from where the reference hospital was located. As a result of these time and resource constraints, it was not possible to replicate the intensive process of support and capacity building carried out in the reference hospital in the other hospitals. An approach was improvised which involved INGO enrolling staff from the reference hospital like data entry operators and pharmacists to support training of counterpart staff from the other hospitals. In this way, some networks of learning and sharing were enabled, allowing for enhanced user ownership.

Processes of creating local teams in each hospital then ensued. Interestingly this was not something which was mandated by the state, rather a self-initiative which slowly spread as learning within the 'networked-hospitals'. These processes of transition spanned over five-years, still ongoing, starting from local teams doing basic hardware fixes to taking on complete system use and related processes.

As technical and capacity building processes stabilized, the focus shifted to the use of data and analysis of questions relating to what does the data mean, how can I start looking into my data, and what can we say about improvements in hospital performance. We take an example to explain this maturing process. In its second year of implementation the reference hospital initiated a system of routing every new patient to general OPD after registration, rather than directly sending them to specialised OPDs (as was the practice earlier). Only after the examination if the doctor in general OPD felt the need for specialist, could the patient be sent to specialist OPD. This change was triggered after the hospital management started looking into data of OPD queues, waiting time for patients at specialist OPDs, and identifying patients who came only for medical examinations for purposes of getting a drivers' license or to support a job application. By focussing on the critical patients requiring longitudinal care (such as Diabetes and Hypertensive), the load of creating electronic medical record for each patient was reduced.

Soon we saw requests from doctors for customising auto-generated reports showing patients seen in the OPD with diagnosis and patient profiles to help discern disease and demographic trends. Reports were demanded by doctors to see turn-around time for patients, which helped the hospital to re-visit work processes to make it efficient for the patient to complete all transactions in a day, thus reducing travel demands on patients. A repercussions of this process was extending the lab and pharmacy timings.

Later in the process, the first 'data use' workshop was organised by the state team which was attended by all hospital heads and the Secretary, Health. The initial discussions were around trying to understand why are there more new patients registered as compared to re-visit patients which was atypical. One of the reasons identified was the laziness of the registration clerks who did not make enough effort to search a patient, and rather registered the same patient each time as a new one. This led to further training for the data entry clerks. The questions of 'improvement in quality care', and how has the 'patient' gained from 'computerisation' became important topic of discussion in the data use workshops and review meetings. Each hospital shared experiences and suggestions to address patient quality care questions. This led to requests from staff for creating system enhancements such as adding a screen to prompt the registration clerk to ask patients if this was first or revisit; printing clinical summary for every patient, and giving laboratory results with reference ranges for the tests. Currently, the state has initiated discussions on integrating the HIS with a national identification system (Aadhar) at registration and also linking public utility portal for patients to pre-book appointments at respective hospitals. These enhancements, when materialized, would significantly help to improve the user friendliness of the HIS.

5   Case Analysis and Discussion

The case study has focused on describing two sets of processes, one relating to evolving local ownership, and the second on enhancing data use value.

5.1   Evolving Local Ownership

Important to enhancing local ownership was the manner of project initiation which helped frame future trajectory of ownership. After experiencing the failure of the initial tendering process, the state adopted a more "open" process where the definition of the requirements was a component of the agreement and was not pre-determined. It provided the space for user agency to be exercised, which set the stage for a user driven partici-patory process, which took place in an iterative and evolving manner. Such an approach, made allowances to the fact no one had absolute knowledge – INGO about the system, and the users about their requirements – and practical, useful knowledge about both needed to evolve through a mutual process of dialogue and co-learning. And most importantly, the state provided the time and the enabling environment for this process to evolve. An acknowledged constraint to this process was that during the initial stages, it was INGO who knew the system, which rang the danger of them framing requirements at the expense of the users. But this framing to a certain extent was inevitable, and was addressed by both sides being conscious of this issue, and secondly, by the users engaging in a process of "proactive participation."

Some examples of enhancing ownership are provided. Initially, printing paper was provisioned by the state, but slowly with time, the hospital started provisioning their own paper. Networking of the hospitals was initially planned for by the state office, but with time, the hospitals started to create their own contracts with third party vendors for the same. Similar processes were also seen in the development of Annual Maintenance Contracts for hardware repair, and the provision of capacity building, where internally people started to support each other. The local team of data entry operators employed for registration and billing, soon started to undertake other tasks such as hardware support and also training internally for other hospital users. The state took some policy measures by making training on the HIS a mandatory task for entering medical doctors. At the level of a department in the hospital, for example, in the Laboratory, some tech-nicians took immense pride in ensuring that the supporting systems like printers and papers are operational, so that they are able to give the printed lab results to the patients, who really liked that output and demanded it.

The open source platform (OpenMRS) on which the HIS was developed also enabled the possibilities for the users to enhance ownership. Given that there were no license restrictions to modify the system, INGO could speedily respond to user requests. As users saw their requests being responded to, they felt confident to ask for more and build their ownership of the system. Such developments were not uniform across and within hospitals, But a general trajectory could be discerned relating to evolving ownership at the three levels of the state, hospital facility and the individual.

5.2   Evolving Use of Data

The initial use of the system was largely a process of automation – where existing manual systems were computerized. However, this automation was not done as a "copy and paste" process from the paper to the computer, but was accompanied with a "judicious design" which involved making process changes, and a selective combining of paper and computer. For example, billing which was previously done at different points in the hospital was modified to a centralized one to enable automation of the billing process.

Similarly, the OPD slip was printed with a pre-defined format where the tests and procedures showed up on the slip, and the doctor would tick mark those required for a particular patient by hand. This hybrid automation was to help deal with the problem of high patient loads, and limited availability of computers.

Over time, there was an increasing level of HIS use at the departmental and hospital levels, enabled by the state convening workshops where managers emphasized the importance of using the HIS for improving patient care and overall hospital administration. The workshop attendees were told in no uncertain terms, that the use of the HIS was not voluntary, and needed to become an integral part of work. Users were shown statistics of HIS usage in the hospital, gaps and achievements were identified, and suggestions taken for improvements. INGO facilitated the process by generating the required statistics from the HIS. With hospital wide use becoming more widespread, the state authorities gained confidence in trying to also enable wider use outside the scope of only the hospitals. Examples included the decision to take a slimmed down version of the HIS to the primary health care (PHC) facilities, which currently work with aggregate and not patient based data. Other examples includes efforts to integrate with the Aadhar and the "Outpatient Registration System" discussed earlier.

5.3   Building Synergies: Process of Evolving Ownership and Enhancing Use

We conceptualize these two sets of processes described above to be mutually self-reinforcing, with one supporting the other, and each itself being also enhanced through this support. We depict this figure schematically and then discuss it (Fig. 1).

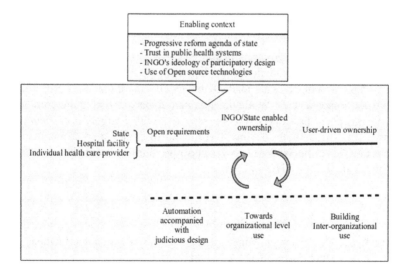

Fig. 1. Self-reinforcing mechanisms of sustainability

The two sets of processes can be seen to be mutually reinforcing. The more the hospital takes ownership of the various processes, the more they develop the capability to understand the possibilities offered by the system, and how it can help to support their everyday work. With this growing maturity, they are able to shape use processes including defining what is needed. The more they see their specific needs are catered to by the system, the more is their motivation to take increasing ownership. In this way, these two sets of processes can be seen as mutually self-reinforcing. The converse is also true, with limited ownership, the HIS is seen as an external implant without direct relevance and value, it will be seen as a burden and users will withdraw from it.

The important question is of how can these self-reinforcing mechanisms be designed? The case points to the need to not have detailed design specifications but to allow it to evolve through a collaborative process. Instead, the design or plan could be seen to be operating at a more meta-level, being rather open in nature, with the positive possibilities of the users being able to drive it forward in the way they considered relevant. A pertinent example in this regard was how specifications were not defined in the tender document, but were allowed to evolve with time and use.

Important, is also the role of the enabling context, which arguably was supportive towards encouraging these two sets of process. Two aspects of this enabling context were important. The first was a progressive state, committed to strengthening public health systems, and promoting decentralized and open forms of governance. The second was the role of INGO, the technical partner of the state, who were deeply rooted in an ideology of participatory design and the use of open source platforms. Taken together, these two sets of processes within the setting of an enabling context had positive implications on participation, providing the technical potential for evolution, with positive impacts on sustainability.

6   Conclusion

This paper has argued for more user-focused analysis of HIS sustainability in LMICs. This is argued to be a more realistic approach to try and achieve sustainability, as supply side approaches by themselves are inadequate. Seeking more funding from donors may only create new dependencies. While the dominant focus of existing literature is on the supply side, this paper has reversed this perspective with a largely user focused view. This adds to the discussions of Unwin [14] who discusses market and society led approaches in ICTD projects. We hope this paper provides an interesting path for future analysis of sustainability of HIS in LMICs.

References

1. Bruntland, G.: Our Common Future: The World Commission on Environment and Development. Oxford University Press, Oxford (1987)
2. Blaschke, S.: Scaling up mobile health: elements necessary for the successful scale up of mHealth in developing countries. White Paper (2011). www.slideshare.net/texttochange/pilotitis-the-biggest-disease-in-mhealth
3. Kimaro, H.C., Nhampossa, J.L.: The challenges of sustainability of health information systems in developing countries: comparative case studies of Mozambique and Tanzania. J. Health Inform. Dev. Countries **1**(1), 1–10 (2007)

4. Heeks, R.: Information systems and developing countries: failure, success and local improvisations. Inf. Soc. **18**, 101–112 (2002)
5. Braa, J., Monteiro, E., Sahay, S.: Networks of action: sustainable health information systems across developing countries. MIS Q. **28**(3), 337–362 (2004)
6. Wahid, F.: A triple helix model of sustainable information infrastructure: case study of the eProcurement system in the Indonesian public sector. In: Linger, H., Fisher, J., Barnden, A., Barry, C., Lang, M., Schneider, C. (eds.) Building Sustainable Information Systems, pp. 554–567. Springer, Boston (2013)
7. Kumar, R., Best, M.L.: Impact and sustainability of e-government services in developing countries: lessons learned from TN, India. Inf. Soc. **22**, 1–12 (2006)
8. Furuholt, B.: Bridging the digital divide: sustainable supply and demand of internet access in developing countries. Ph.D. thesis, Aalborg University, Denmark (2009)
9. Maruster, L., Fabers, N.R., Peters, K.: Sustainable information systems: a knowledge perspective. J. Syst. Inf. Technol. **10**, 218–231 (2008)
10. Jacucci, E., Shaw, V., Braa, J.: Standardization of HIS in South Africa: the challenge of local sustainability. Inf. Technol. Dev. **12**, 225–239 (2006)
11. Smith, M., Madon, S., Anifalaje, A., Lazzaro-Malecela, M., Michael, E.: Integrated health information systems in Tanzania: experience and challenges. Electron. J. Inf. Syst. Dev. Countries **33**(1), 1–21 (2008)
12. Walsham, G.: Interpreting Information Systems in Organizations. Wiley, Chichester (1993)
13. Dreze, J., Sen, A.: An Uncertain Glory: India and Its Contradictions. Princeton University Press, Princeton (2013)
14. Unwin, T.: States, markets and society. Institute for Development Studies (2016). https://www.ids.ac.uk/70D75510-E094-11E5-85B8005056AA4991

ICT4D Sustainability as Generativity

Terje Aksel Sanner[(✉)]

Department of Informatics, University of Oslo, Oslo, Norway
terjeasa@ifi.uio.no

Abstract. In the wake of "the mobile revolution", there has been an immense surge in mobile phone-based health innovations. Scholars and industry specialists have found a large portion of such innovations in less developed economies unsustainable beyond pilot projects. However, "sustainability" is a difficult aspiration to operationalize. Based on insights from recent literature on digital innovation, the paper suggests an alternative focus on *generativity* – a perspective on longevity that emphasizes the continuous facilitation of innovation over stewardship and control. To illustrate the relevance of generativity to ICT4D, the paper draws on examples from a mobile phone-based implementation to strengthen routine reporting of public health data in Malawi. By foregrounding generativity as an ICT4D aspiration, the paper begins to consider implications at the level of projects, national policy and international development collaboration.

Keywords: mHealth · ICT4D · Sustainability · Generativity · Digital innovation

1 Introduction

The rapid expansion of mobile networks and the proliferation of mobile phones have put digital information and communication technologies (ICTs) in the hands of people who lack access to proper roads, clean drinking water, basic health services, electricity and publicly relevant media such as television and newspapers. Market competition has fueled the penetration of mobile networks, while development agencies have been able to "focus on tools and services for the poor built atop these networks" [1, p. 100].

Mobile phone-based innovations have catered to information and communication needs at the periphery of national health systems [2–4]. However, with a recent surge in mHealth projects, it has become increasingly difficult for governments to consolidate disparate efforts into overarching health information system architectures [5, 6]. Ministries of health often lack the means and skills to develop appropriate policies and routines and to monitor, prioritize, and maintain numerous ICT initiatives [7, 8].

The high failure rate associated with donor funded mHealth projects has led researchers to diagnose the field with "pilotitis" [9–12]. Pilotitis can be articulated as "the unfettered proliferation of lightweight mHealth 'solutions' which fail to translate or scale into health systems" [11, p. 2]. The failure to sustain technology innovations, although symptomatic of ICT for development (ICT4D) [13–15] and health information systems in general [7, 16, 17], has been particularly pronounced when these domains have been conflated into mHealth ventures [9]. However, "sustainability" is

© IFIP International Federation for Information Processing 2017
Published by Springer International Publishing AG 2017. All Rights Reserved
J. Choudrie et al. (Eds.): ICT4D 2017, IFIP AICT 504, pp. 498–509, 2017.
DOI: 10.1007/978-3-319-59111-7_41

difficult to operationalize at the level of particular ICT4D projects and in relation to specific ICT capabilities. To address this challenge, the paper proposes generativity as an operational ICT4D aspiration. Generativity, as an ideal, aligns with the general sustainability ethos, but it is particularly sensitive to the "self-reinventing" characteristics of digital ICTs.

Zittrain [18, p. 1980] defines generativity as "a technology's overall capacity to produce unprompted change driven by large, varied, and uncoordinated audiences". Hence, the notion of generativity, reviewed in the next section, emphasizes the interplay between innovative ICT capabilities and available human capacities to leverage and extend those capabilities. Section 3 presents the methods of the empirical study. Section 4 describes an mHealth innovation for routine data collection and reporting from public health facilities in Malawi. The discussion, in Sect. 5 considers the generative potentials of mobile ICT capabilities in resource sparse settings, while Sect. 6 considers the implications of a generativity aspiration for ICT4D projects, national policy and international development collaboration.

2 The Problem of Sustainability

The global discourse on "sustainable development" gained momentum with the 1987 United Nations Brundtland report [19]. The report reconciles economic growth with an ecological rationale and defines *sustainability* as meeting "the needs of the present without compromising the ability of future generations to meet their own needs" [19, p. 43]. Since then, "sustainability", with strong connotations to resource management and stewardship, has become embedded in international development agendas, sometimes with perverse and contradictory consequences [20, 21]. Sustainability has emerged as a key aspiration in both ICT4D [22–25], and mHealth [12, 26–29].

ICT implementations in health in less developed economies have been deemed *unsustainable* due to factors such as short-term donor funding, lack of development of local capacity, and too much focus on technological rather than social and institutional issues [7, 8, 30]. ICT implementations often succumb when project money runs out or foreign experts resign from projects [31, 32]. In particular, the uncoordinated surge in health information system funding has "created a plethora of tools, methods and practices for data collection and analysis that have placed a counterproductive and unsustainable burden on front line health workers" [33, p. 7]. mHealth projects exacerbate this burden as they typically target the same cadre of peripheral health workers. To address sustainability challenges, researchers have called for new modes of stakeholder collaboration [34], business models [15, 35], and project and governance principles [36]. Yet, exactly what sustainability entails in the context of ICT4D often remains unclear.

Ali and Bailur [13] criticize the use of the term "sustainability" in ICT4D altogether. To them sustainability is an unrealistic concept. Instead, they point to Ciborra's [37] notion of *bricolage* and suggest that ICT4D needs to be more open to *local improvisation* and "accept the changing nature of the ICT artifact and the unintended consequences of technology" [13, p. 1]. Bricolage constitute locally apposite improvisation through the expedient combination of resources at hand [37]. However, [13, p. 1] also note that "since the majority of ICT for development projects still continue to be funded by donor agencies and multinationals, improvisation faces many practical challenges". This paper takes concerns with the operationalizability of sustainability in ICT4D as a starting point and proposes generativity as an operational amendment to the sustainability doctrine. Generativity foregrounds improvisation, while recognizing the importance of extant technologies and human capacities as foundations for innovation.

2.1   The Generative Potential of Digital Technology

Generativity describes a technology from which its users draw an ability to generate, or produce new capabilities without additional input from the original creators [38, 39]. The TCP/IP and http protocols of the Internet and the PC are exemplary generative technologies that have enabled "self-reinventing" ICT capabilities like the World Wide Web, emails and blogs.

Specifically, Zittrian [18, 40] identify five characteristics that constitute the generative potential of a technology, namely: capacity for leverage, adaptability, ease of mastery, accessibility and transferability. *Leverage*, describes the extent to which the technology assists in performing a task otherwise not possible or difficult. *Adaptability* refers to the breadth of a technology's use without change and its readiness to broaden use through modification. A technology's *ease of mastery* reflects how easy it is for broad audiences to adopt and adapt it, regardless of whether the technology was designed with those tasks in mind. *Accessibility* – the more readily people can come to use and control a technology, along with what information might be required to master it, the more accessible the technology is. Finally, *transferability* refers to how easily changes and improvements made to the technology, through skillful adaptation, can be conveyed to others, thus allowing for a community of development and use.

Smith et al. [41] specifically consider the generative potential of mobile phones in the context of ICT4D. They argue that mobiles embody four out of Zittrain's five characteristics: they provide significant *leverage* in communication tasks, they are easy to *access* and *master*, and mobile technology innovations are easily *shared* with others. However, they argue that "the relatively basic models of mobiles used in a majority of developing country contexts, and the often rather controlled nature of the infrastructure on which they run, limit the upper end of adaptability" [41, p. 83]. Although, generativity relates to a particular technology, it is essentially a socio-technical construct. Generativity does not emanate from the properties of a technology alone, but represent potential outcomes from creative interactions between technology, people and organizations. In particular, [42] found that digital innovation depends on a generative combination of a technology and an active community of skilled users and developers.

In general, digital technologies possess more generative potential than their analog counterparts do. Digital services, applications and content can be reused and recombined and they increase in breadth and value with the number of people involved in their production and consumption. This paper considers how generativity, as an ICT4D aspiration, may help us foreground ways to balance digital ICTs' potential for further appropriation and innovation with skills and capacities to leverage that potential in resource sparse settings.

3   Methods

This paper consider post-hoc the applicability of generativity to empirical observations from a mobile phone-based implementation in Malawi. The aim is to illustrate the relevance of generativity as an operational ICT4D aspiration. In accordance with the primary health care mantra of "health for all" [43], the implementation in Malawi focuses on routine reporting of public health data, such as confirmed malaria cases and number of pregnant women with HIV receiving antiretroviral therapy.

The implementation in Malawi uses the open source District Health Information Software (DHIS2). Countries in Africa, Latin America and Asia use DHIS2 for reporting, analysis, and presentation of routine health data. The Health Information System Programme (HISP), with the University of Oslo, coordinates DHIS2 development. Software development and participatory implementation research have gone hand in hand since the inception of the program in 1994 [44]. With the rapid uptake of mobile technologies in the Global South, HISP has embraced the opportunity to bring ICT capabilities to health workers where there are no computers and limited power supply. To this end, HISP Oslo has coordinated the development and implementation of DHIS Mobile – a suite of mobile phone-based functionalities that extend DHIS2. The author has been involved with DHIS Mobile implementation research since 2009.

The implementation in Malawi received initial financial and technical support from a grant funded research project coordinated by HISP Oslo. The ministry of health in Malawi, by the Central Monitoring and Evaluation Division (CMED), hosted the implementation. CMED envisioned that they could enhance their current use of the DHIS2 national data warehouses with mobile reporting, but lacked the technical capacity to manage the customization and implementation processes.

The author's filed notes from participant observation have been the primary source of data. The main body of data was collected during on-site fieldwork from September 2011 to December 2011 (three months) and from April 2012 to May 2012 (one month). This include observational visits, focus group discussions and interviews of staff at nine health facilities, two health area hospitals and one district health office. Furthermore, the author conducted ad-hoc interviews with medical officers, monitoring and evaluation officers, and health information managers at districts and national level. Additional empirical data stem from interaction with fellow DHIS Mobile implementers, DHIS2 and DHIS Mobile software developers, local DHIS2 software customizers and mobile network operators in Malawi. Participant observation centered on practical tasks such as facilitation of mobile trainings, configuration of mobile phones and server, pilot evaluation, and project management. The author has maintained longitudinal correspondence via teleconferences and emails with CMED concerning the continuation of the mobile phone-based reporting.

Sustainability challenges were a key theme throughout the study. The focus on sustainability was motivated both by the author's practical interest in the long-term value of mobile phone-based routine health data reporting and by the general problem of mHealth and ICT4D "pilotitis". However, sustainability proved difficult to operationalize in research and practice at the project level. During the implementation in Malawi, the author noted the important balance between malleable digital ICT capabilities and the capacity among local stakeholders to leverage that malleability along with the financial resources, mandate and responsibility to do so. Through engagement with literature on digital innovation [39, 40, 42, 45], generativity, as a socio-technical construct, was identified and employed in data analysis post-hoc to sort observations concerned with local adaptation of mobile reporting ICT capabilities. The next section describes how the implementation in Malawi facilitated local adaptation and innovation.

4 Mobile-Phone Based Routine Reporting in Malawi

During autumn 2011, the Ministry of Health in Malawi represented by CMED, the Lilongwe district health office (DHO), and HISP Oslo agreed on the scope of a pilot project for mobile reporting from health facilities. The solution, called DHIS Mobile, had been developed through previous iterations of HISP implementation research in India, Tanzania, Nigeria, the Gambia and Zambia.

At the time, health workers collected data during the provision of essential health services such as child immunization and antenatal care and recorded it in paper registers and tally sheets. Health service provision was coordinated from health facilities. Routine health data reports were collated monthly. However, the submission of reports to districts were done quarterly across the country due to transportation challenges and general resource constraints. Computers were available at districts and higher organizational levels, where data clerks entered data into the web-based DHIS2 national data warehouse. Unfortunately, health information system assessments found reported data to be incomplete, inconsistent and inaccurate [46].

At health facilities, lack of stationery was impeding health workers from collating information correctly and efficiently. Overshot district budgets for printing and distribution contributed to the lack of printed forms. At some health facilities, staffs were drawing columns and rows on paper to produce forms. This, however, led to inconsistencies between facilities and haphazard omissions of some data. Despite challenges that affected the accuracy and reliability of routine health data, the *timeliness* of data reporting was perhaps the greatest concern to health program managers in Malawi.

In order to submit reports, health facility staff would for instance hand them over to ambulance drivers or await personal trips to the district center. During rainy season, the transportation of paper forms from some health facilities was simply not feasible due to flooded roads. Reports that failed to reach decision makers on time did not help inform the distribution of limited resources and equitable prioritization of health care interventions. CMED envisioned that mobile phone-based reports could mitigate some of the challenges experienced with paper-based reports.

4.1   Pilot Implementation in Lilongwe

The DHIS Mobile solution allowed health facility staff to open a mobile web-form, enter data, and submit it to a DHIS2 server. The HTML5-based solution supported offline data entry and automated data integrity and form validation checks. Mobile data connectivity allowed for report submissions from mobile phones and form updates from the DHIS2 server whenever mobile network coverage was available.

The Lilongwe DHO initially targeted 17 health facilities in two health areas, called Kabudula and Area 25, for implementation. Each health facility in the two health areas received staff training and either one or two preconfigured Nokia feature phones. Each mobile phone was bundled with MK500 (USD 1) worth of airtime per month for three months. Facility staffs were informed that they would need to use their own money to buy airtime after three months due to the limited availability of project funding and the complicated logistics of reimbursement.

The implementation initially covered only two reports. One was a weekly report for communicable disease surveillance. The other report, called HMIS-15, constituted a monthly summary of essential data for key health programs in Malawi. Before training of end-users could commence, the two forms had to be set up for mobile reporting on the national DHIS2 server. Consequently, the DHIS Mobile implementers established contact with the local DHIS2 coordinators located at the Malawi College of Medicine in Blantyre, about 300 km from CMED's headquarters in Lilongwe. However, the DHIS2 coordinators in Blantyre did not immediately embark on form customization, as they were behind schedule with other DHIS2 related tasks.

As CMED did not have sufficient IT expertise to manage the national DHIS2 server and other mundane IT-tasks, the DHIS2 coordinators in Blantyre were responsible for all DHIS2 implementation and maintenance activities, including system customization and end-user training. In order to commence with mobile reporting the DHIS Mobile implementers received administration rights to configure the two forms for mobile reporting on another DHIS2 server instance, which had been set up for training purposes.

At the start of the pilot, the Lilongwe DHO and the health area offices at Kabudula and Area 25 did not have reliable Internet connectivity and were unable to monitor mobile reports. The offices received USB Internet modems and orientations on how to monitor reports and provide basic technical support to health facilities.

4.2   Further Adaptation and Innovation

Following the initial implementation, focus group discussions and interviews were conducted at health facilities over a period of one and a half years. These interactions revealed that health workers would prefer mobile reports to replace all paper-based reports. As the two health-area offices and the DHO in Lilongwe had noted improvements in timely availability of data, the DHO decided to embrace mobile reporting from all the 44 government health facilities in Lilongwe. At the time, the mobile reporting function was moved from the demonstration server to the national

DHIS2 production server and the team of local DHIS2 coordinators became more actively involved.

Steps towards long-term technical support and further customization of DHIS Mobile in Malawi were taken through the employment of a project-funded technical assistant working out of CMED's offices. The arrangement was seen as a step towards the creation of a new IT position within CMED, which for bureaucratic reasons could take several years. The technical assistant was to work closely with the aforementioned DHIS2 coordinators who were relocating from Blantyre to Lilongwe. Furthermore, DHIS Mobile implementers contributed to the development of terms of reference (TOR)for future engagement of CMED in-house IT positions. A key motivation with the TOR was to tie accountability for mobile phone-based reporting to organizational roles rather than specific project individuals.

By 2014, local customizers and the technical assistant with CMED had set up 14 additional health program reports for mobile reporting. Reports covered areas such as antenatal care, family planning, newborn health, sexual transmittable diseases, nutrition, disease surveillance and child immunization. The customization work commenced without support from the original DHIS Mobile implementers as project funding had expired. By 2016, mobile reporting had expanded to seven more of the 28 districts in Malawi with support from development partners. An organization called Support for Service Delivery Integration (SSDI) opted to replace the worn Nokia feature phones in Lilongwe district with Android Smartphones and retrained health facility staffs.

Some of the health facility staffs in Lilongwe, who were part of the original implementation, had not been informed about the 14 new reports that started to appear on their mobile phones due to server side updates. Despite this lack of sensitization, follow-up visits revealed that some staffs had taken it upon themselves to study the mobile forms and train their colleagues on filling them. A social media page, "RepotiMufoni", (Eng. mobile reporting) was created on Facebook to allow DHIS Mobile users in Malawi to share experiences and interact with the technical assistant at CMED.

5   Sustainability as Generativity

Sustainability is an often-touted aspiration with ICT4D. However, it often remains unclear *how* sustainability may be achieved and *what* exactly is to be sustained and for *whom*? Is it a mobile technology, a software product, the activities of a development partner, a new work routine or facets of a "Western centric and universalist model of economic growth and development" [47, p. 2]? As [48, p. 365] recognize, sustainability is primarily a problem with "externally situated ICT4D programmes, and in part reflect a desire by those who create them to guarantee their continued success after the initial period of investment is over". Sustainability challenges, which are endemic to mHealth and ICT4D, may be associated with the need to demonstrate impacts within the short duration of grant funded pilot projects [49], whereby immediate quantifiable deliverables receive priority over collaboration and harmonization with extant arrangements.

In this paper, the struggle for ICT4D longevity is seen in relation to *ICT capabilities*, which cannot easily be discerned from the human activities, skills and values they are infused and intertwined with. Generativity, as an operational ICT4D aspiration, highlights the interplay between available skills and innovative ICT capabilities. This interplay is enabled through a combination of stakeholder alliances, capacity building, legislations, policy revisions and technical configurations. In the following, empirical observations concerning the mobile reporting in Malawi is drawn on to exemplify the generative potential of mobile digital ICT capabilities along Zittrain's five dimensions: leverage, adaptability, ease of mastery, accessibility and transferability.

Leverage: *Describes the extent to which a technology helps in performing an otherwise difficult or impossible task.* Mobile phones excel as information sharing and communication technologies. In Malawi, mobile phone-based reports replaced vulnerable paper-based transmission of health data. As the solution relied on a web-based platform, people traditionally involved in the paper trail were brought on board by the provision of internet connectivity and login credentials to the online database. Mobile reporting supported the key task of making timely data available to public health managers.

Adaptability: Describes *the breath of a technology's use without change and its readiness to broaden use through modification.* In relation to ICT4D, [41] point out that the adaptability of basic mobile phones and the controlled nature of mobile networks restricts adaptability. However, in the context of primary health care alone, simple feature phones have been adapted to support areas such as treatment compliance, routine data collection and disease surveillance, point of care decision support, health promotion and disease prevention, and emergency medical response [9].

With the mobile phone based reporting in Malawi, the lack of relevant capacity within CMED to configure and maintain novel ICT acquisitions informed a minimalist approach to implementation. This involved implementation of only two forms across 17 health facilities and the initial use of a server instance originally set up for teaching purposes. These arrangements were made with the awareness that, if managed carefully, the solution could be adapted to accommodate more specialized health program reports, more reporting health facilities and be shifted to the production server. Indeed, local DHIS2 coordinators and the project funded technical assistant took such measures as health facility and district health staff started to express an interest in replacing other paper-based reports. To strengthen CMED's long-term capacity to maintain and further develop the mobile reporting solution, DHIS Mobile implementers participated in the development of relevant terms of reference for future in-house IT-positions.

Ease of Mastery: *A technology's ease of mastery reflects how easy it is for broad audiences to adopt and adapt it.* Mobile phones have become the user friendly and ubiquitous PCs of the Global South. ICT4D initiatives are able to leverage rapid growth in mobile literacy. With a mobile client-server infrastructure, the limited available technical capacity could be centralized with CMED and focus on supportive tasks such as server management and form customization, while end users could focus on the primary tasks of data collection, information consumption and decision-making. Vis-à-vis paper, digital technology offers a range of real time support such as automatic updates, hiding irrelevant data entry fields in forms and validation rules that prompts the user about potentially erroneous data. Recent advances in support for offline work such as the new HTML5 standards further strengthens this advantage over paper forms.

Accessibility: *The more readily people can come to use and control a technology, along with what information might be required to master it, the more accessible the technology is.* While only 11% of the population in Malawi have access to the national power grid, mobile network coverage soared at 93% already in 2011 [50]. Mobile ICT4D capabilities inherit accessibility from mobile networks and devices.

With the implementation in Malawi, a few health facility staffs who mastered the mobile reporting took it upon themselves to teach their colleagues how to report on new forms made available from the server. Furthermore, DHIS Mobile implementers ensured that the mobile phone-based reporting did not sideline the traditional custodians of routine health data at the Lilongwe DHO and the two health area offices. USB Internet modems were provided along with training on how to access and inspect the electronic reports submitted from mobile phones. The creation of a social media page called "RepotiMufoni" for peer interaction and technical support further exemplify the advantage of having digital access to the shared experiences of collaborative network.

Transferability: According to Zittrain [40], *transferability* refers to how easily changes and improvements made to a technology can be shared with others. The DHIS Mobile solution implemented in Malawi emanated from the transfer of technologies, open-source code and skilled people across settings in India, Tanzania, Nigeria, the Gambia and Zambia. This led to the development of an increasingly generic solution. However, as the generic qualities of digital technologies increase, so does the knowledge and practical work required to facilitate their appropriation [51, p. 139]. Unfortunately, in the context of less developed economies, the need for local adaptation often puts an unrealistic burden on local (government) organizations to maintain, integrate and innovate on top of interventionists' many uncoordinated ICT innovations. One way to mitigate some of these challenges may be to decide on a few national priority areas for mHealth and ICT4D intervention and develop *minimum requirements* to ensure that innovations can be harmonized and maintained through reuse and sharing of devices, physical networks, software and human capacities.

Overall, generativity is sensitive to how the characteristics of particular digital technologies interplay with human capacities to enable appropriation and innovation in the context of a rapidly changing landscape of mobile devices, networks, services, applications and content. Generativity constitute five interdependent socio-technical dimensions. If one of the five dimensions falters, it constrains the total generative capacity of an ICT capability or system. Most likely, tradeoffs will occur along the different dimensions to match digital ICT capabilities with available skills and resources. The problem of mHealth pilotitis is not that there is too little "unprompted change driven by large, varied, and uncoordinated" stakeholders, but that the available skills and technologies are not able to adapt those innovations, and hence generativity is limited.

6   Conclusion: Generativity in Policy and Practice

Generativity has been applied post-hoc to illustrate its applicability to an mHealth implementation in Malawi. How can generativity inform future implementation planning and policy? The surge of mHealth innovations in developing economies puts pressure on information system managers and policy makers to develop strategies that emphasize coordination and harmonization over short-term impacts. In particular, strategies need to identify ways to balance the innovative use of ICT capabilities at the fringes of national health systems with the governance of a robust foundation of skills and IT services such as an integrated national health data warehouse. This balance is necessary to facilitate the long-term and steady pursuit of national goals, without causing unnecessary disruptions to existing work practices, career trajectories and information flows.

Generativity may at once be both a useful framework and an aspiration informing the development of ICT strategies that are sensitive to this balance. In practice, international donors and NGOs can play an important role by providing much needed long-term financial, strategic and technical assistance, rather than brief bursts of external support. Not only is there a dire need for local capacity to maintain solutions, but also to leverage an extant ecology of ICT acquisitions, networks and databases for further innovation. One way to strengthen the local capacity to absorb ICT innovations may be to pool donor funding to finance local technical assistance beyond the scope of individual projects. This was the case, to some extent, with ad hoc partner arrangements to support the mobile reporting in Malawi. Generativity provides a perspective on how different stakeholders extend, replace and reproduce ICT capabilities over time.

At the level of ICT4D projects, stakeholders may try to balance the malleability of new ICT capabilities with the local capacity to alter those capabilities by applying generativity as a pilot evaluation framework. However, far from all challenges to the longevity of ICT4D and mHealth implementations can be resolved at the level of projects. Systemic challenges such as *pilotitis* require significant international collaboration where both donors and governments harmonize ICT-oriented development activities. This can for instance involve the development of international evaluation criteria that emphasize intra-project collaboration to develop generative ICT capabilities.

References

1. Zuckerman, E.: Decentralizing the mobile phone: a second ICT4D revolution? Inf. Technol. Int. Dev. **6**(8), 99–103 (2010)
2. Black, J. et al.: Mobile solutions for front-line health workers in developing countries. In: e-Health Networking, Applications and Services, pp. 89–93 (2009)
3. Haberer, J.E., Kiwanuka, J., Nansera, D., Wilson, I.B., Bangsberg, D.R.: Challenges in using mobile phones for collection of antiretroviral therapy adherence data in a resource-limited setting. AIDS Behav. **14**(6), 1294–1301 (2010)
4. Sanner, T.A., Roland, L.K., Braa, K.: From pilot to scale: towards an mHealth typology. Health Policy Technol. **1**(3), 155–164 (2012)
5. Estrin, D., Sim, I.: Open mHealth architecture an engine for health care innovation. Science (Washington) **330**(6005), 759–760 (2010)

6. Norris, A.C., Stockdale, R.S., Sharma, S.: A strategic approach to m-health. Health Inf. J. **15**(3), 244–253 (2009)
7. Kimaro, H.C., Nhampossa, J.L.: Analyzing the problem of unsustainable health information systems in less-developed economies: case studies from Tanzania and Mozambique. Inf. Technol. Dev. **11**(3), 273–298 (2005)
8. Lucas, H.: Information and communications technology for future health systems in developing countries. Soc. Sci. Med. **66**(10), 2122–2132 (2008)
9. Curioso, W.H., Mechael, P.N.: Enhancing 'M-health' with South-to-South collaborations. Health Aff. (Millwood) **29**(2), 264 (2010)
10. Germann, S., Jabry, A., Njogu, J., Osumba, R.: The Illness of "Pilotitis" in mHealth – Early Lessons from the KimMNCHip Partnerships in Kenya (2011)
11. Labrique, A., Vasudevan, L., Chang, L.W., Mehl, G.: H_pe for mHealth: more 'y' or 'o' on the horizon? Int. J. Med. Inf. **82**(5), 467–469 (2013)
12. Lemaire, J.: Scaling up mobile health: elements necessary for the successful scale up of mHealth in developing countries. In: Advanced Development for Africa, December 2011
13. Ali, M., Bailur, S.: The challenge of 'sustainability' in ICT4D–Is bricolage the answer? In: Proceedings of IFIP 9.4, São Paulo, Brazil (2007)
14. Best, M.L., Kumar, R.: Sustainability failures of rural telecenters: challenges from the sustainable access in rural India (SARI) project. Inf. Technol. Int. Dev. **4**(4), 31 (2008)
15. Kleine, D., Unwin, T.: Technological revolution, evolution and new dependencies: what's new about ICT4D? Third World Q. **30**(5), 1045–1067 (2009)
16. Heeks, R.: Health information systems: failure, success and improvisation. Int. J. Med. Inf. **75**(2), 125–137 (2006)
17. Kreps, D., Richardson, H.: IS success and failure—the problem of scale. Polit. Q. **78**(3), 439–446 (2007)
18. Zittrain, J.L.: The generative internet. Harvard Law Rev. **119**(7), 1974–2040 (2006)
19. WCED: Our Common Future, vol. 383. Oxford University Press, Oxford (1987)
20. Blaikie, P.: Is small really beautiful? Community-based natural resource management in Malawi and Botswana. World Dev. **34**(11), 1942–1957 (2006)
21. Swidler, A., Watkins, S.C.: 'Teach a man to fish': the sustainability doctrine and its social consequences. World Dev. **37**(7), 1182–1196 (2009)
22. Heeks, R.: ICT4D 2.0: the next phase of applying ICT for international development. Computer **41**(6), 26–33 (2008)
23. Mansell, R., Wehn, U.: Knowledge Societies Information Technology for Sustainable Development. United Nations Publications, New York (1998)
24. Pade-Khene, C., Mallinson, B., Sewry, D.: Sustainable rural ICT project management practice for developing countries: investigating the Dwesa and RUMEP projects. Inf. Technol. Dev. **17**(3), 187–212 (2011)
25. Tongia, R., Subrahmanian, E.: Information and Communications Technology for Development (ICT4D)-a design challenge? In: ITID 2006, pp. 243–255 (2006)
26. Akter, S., Ray, P.: mHealth-an ultimate platform to serve the unserved. In: Faculty of Commerce-Papers, pp. 94–100 (2010)
27. Hwabamungu, B., Williams, Q.: m-Health adoption and sustainability prognosis from a care givers' and patients' perspective. In: Proceedings of SAICSIT, pp. 123–131 (2010)
28. Källander, K., et al.: Mobile health (mHealth) approaches and lessons for increased performance and retention of community health workers in low-and middle-income countries: a review. J. Med. Internet Res. **15**(1), e17 (2013)
29. Tomlinson, M., Rotheram-Borus, M.J., Swartz, L., Tsai, A.C.: Scaling up mHealth: where is the evidence? PLoS Med. **10**(2), e1001382 (2013)

30. Avgerou, C.: Information systems in developing countries: a critical research review. J. Inf. Technol. **23**(3), 133–146 (2008)
31. Baark, E., Heeks, R.: Donor-funded information technology transfer projects: evaluating the life-cycle approach in four Chinese science and technology projects. Inf. Technol. Dev. **8**(4), 185–197 (1999)
32. Lewis, D.: The Management of Non-Governmental Development Organizations. Taylor & Francis, New York (2006)
33. Stansfield, S., Orobaton, N., Lubinski, D., Uggowitzer, S., Mwanyika, H.: The case for a national health information system architecture; a missing link to guiding national development and implementation. Mak. Ehealth Connect. Bellagio (2008)
34. Pfeiffer, J.: International NGOs and primary health care in Mozambique: the need for a new model of collaboration. Soc. Sci. Med. **56**(4), 725–738 (2003)
35. Kaplan, W.A.: Can the ubiquitous power of mobile phones be used to improve health outcomes in developing countries? Glob. Health **2**(1), 9 (2006)
36. Jensen, C.B., Winthereik, B.R.: Monitoring movements in development aid: recursive partnerships and infrastructures. MIT Press, Cambridge (2013)
37. Ciborra, C.: The Labyrinths of Information: Challenging the Wisdom of Systems. Oxford University Press, Oxford (2002)
38. Sørensen, C.: Digital platform and-infrastructure innovation. In: Higashikuni, H. (ed.) Mobile Strategy Challenges (In Japanese). Nikkan Kogyo Shimbun Ltd., Tokyo (2013)
39. Tilson, D., Lyytinen, K., Sørensen, C.: Research commentary-digital infrastructures: the missing IS research agenda. Inf. Syst. Res. **21**(4), 748–759 (2010)
40. Zittrain, J.L.: The Future of the Internet and How to Stop It. Yale University Press, New Haven (2009)
41. Smith, M.L., Spence, R., Rashid, A.T.: Mobile phones and expanding human capabilities. Inf. Technol. Int. Dev. **7**(3), 77 (2011)
42. Avital, M., Te'Eni, D.: From generative fit to generative capacity: exploring an emerging dimension of information systems design and task performance. Inf. Syst. J. **19**(4), 345–367 (2009)
43. UNICEF, World Health Organization and others: Primary health care: report of the International Conference on Primary Health Care, Alma-Ata, USSR, 6–12 September 1978
44. Braa, J., Hedberg, C.: The struggle for district-based health information systems in South Africa. Inf. Soc. **18**(2), 113–127 (2002)
45. Yoo, Y., Henfridsson, O., Lyytinen, K.: Research commentary-the new organizing logic of digital innovation: an agenda for information systems research. Inf. Syst. Res. **21**(4), 724–735 (2010)
46. Bhana, J.: Situation analysis of the Ministry of Health's Central Monitoring and Evaluation Department in Malawi. HMST (2013)
47. Mansell, R.: Power and interests in information and communication and development. J. Int. Dev. **26**(1), 109–127 (2014)
48. Unwin, P.T.H.: ICT4D Information and Communication Technology for Development. Cambridge University Press, Cambridge (2009)
49. Sanner, T.A., Sæbø, J.I.: Paying per diems for ICT4D project participation: a sustainability challenge. Inf. Technol. Int. Dev. **10**(2), 33 (2014)
50. Foster, V., Shkaratan, M.: Malawi's infrastructure: a continental perspective. In: World Bank Policy Research Working Paper Series (2011)
51. Suchman, L.A.: Practice-based design of information systems: notes from the hyperdeveloped world. Inf. Soc. **18**(2), 139–144 (2002)

Sustainability of the aAQUA e-Agriservice: A Case Study of Maharashtra, India

S.K. Wadkar[1]([✉]), K. Singh[2], A. Mohammad[2], K.S. Kadian[2],
and R. Malhotra[2]

[1] Tata Institute of Social Science, Mumbai, Maharashtra, India
sagarkwadkar@gmail.com
[2] ICAR - National Dairy Research Institute, Karnal, Haryana, India
khajansingh_singh@yahoo.co.in, mail.asif.m@gmail.com,
kskadian@rediffmail.com, rmall1962@rediffmail.com

Abstract. The present study aimed to determine the sustainability of the aAQUA (Almost All Questions Answered) e-Agriservice in Maharashtra state, western parts of India covering the four districts of the state. The study used the ex-post facto (cause to effect) research design in a quasi-intervention setting. The list of registered users was obtained from the service provider (presently Agrocom Software Technologies Pvt. Ltd.) and total of 120 users were selected randomly from four districts (30 users from each district). The sustainable-Agriservice Index (SeAGRSI) was computed based on the five dimensions viz. technological, economic, social, institutional, and political by using combinations of Multi-Criteria Analysis (MCA), Mixed Method Approach and Normalized Rank Order Method (NROM). The study revealed that the SeAGRSI for the social indicators was the highest among other dimensions of the sustainability (SeAGRSI = 0.77) followed by the technologically (0.73), economic (0.71) political (0.62) and institutional (0.58) sustainable. It was also found that the mean SeAGRSI was 0.70 as reported by one third (32.50%) of the users, which means 70% the aAQUA e-Agriservice was technologically, socially, economically, institutionally and politically sustainable. The indicators developed would be useful to develop strategy for sustainability of ICT efforts in many developing countries.

Keywords: Dimensions of sustainability · Rural ICT projects · Sustainable aAQUA e-Agriservice Index

1 Introduction

Information and Communication Technologies (ICTs) are constantly evolving as key tools that provide access to information and knowledge for rural development in developing countries. Over the last decade, India has emerged as a testing ground for innovations in ICTs (Dossani et al. 2005; Kuriyan et al. 2008; Rao 2008). They have the potential to enhance development activities in combating poverty, as an information, communication or knowledge component of virtually every development challenge can possibly be discerned (McNamara 2003). There are many efforts in India and other developing countries to demonstrate the economic benefits of ICT on productivity

© IFIP International Federation for Information Processing 2017
Published by Springer International Publishing AG 2017. All Rights Reserved
J. Choudrie et al. (Eds.): ICT4D 2017, IFIP AICT 504, pp. 510–521, 2017.
DOI: 10.1007/978-3-319-59111-7_42

and growth (Draca et al. 2006; Kretschmer 2012; Singh 2007). Many researchers have reported that these kinds of ICT projects helped in catering needs of the farming community and facilitated in enhancing knowledge level of users/beneficiaries of the services (Promilla 1994; Sah 1996; Wadkar et al. 2015). Lio and Liu (2006) reported that the use of ICTs helped to increase farmers' bargaining power, which help them to get remunerative prices to their produce. They have also found the strong correlation between the use of ICT and farmers' productivity.

However there are cases where the implementation of ICT projects has actually not made a difference, or the effects have been harmful in communities (Buré 2007; Gomez and Hunt 1999). Musa (2006) cites a number of authors who indicate that there is huge evidence of failure and wastage of resources linked to sudden massive implementations of ICT projects in developing countries, with the hope of promoting development and alleviating poverty. Consequently, debates have arisen with growing skepticism about the usefulness of funding or implementing ICT projects for development (Tacchi et al. 2003).

In this backdrop, there is much hope for sustainable impact arising from development oriented ICT interventions, especially in the field of agriculture (Mbarika et al. 2005; Meso et al. 2006). In the past, emphasis has been placed on the supply side (for example, infrastructure building) rather than the demand side (for example, users' willingness and capacity to acquire/use services) (Ashraf et al. 2007; Heeks 2002). Hence, the main focus of the interventions has been on implementation of the ICT4D project rather than understanding the impact on the micro (community) level. This lack of understanding has led to many failures of ICT4D projects reported in the literature (Heeks 2002). Several organizations have launched ICT based or e-Agriculture initiatives, which lacks the sustainability of services for long term period (Annamalai and Rao 2003; Raju 2004; Rao 2006, 2008; Upton and Fulle 2004).

Unwin (2009) states that sustainability is primarily a problem with "externally situated ICT4D programmes, and in part reflect a desire by those who create them to guarantee their continued success after the initial period of investment is over". Here little attention is paid on how initiatives can become self-supporting, and recommends that all ICT4D programmes that are introduced by external players have a framework for ensuring "continued viability beyond the initial period of funding" in order to not saddle the beneficiaries with the burden. This needs to include total-cost-of-implementation models. Finally, he has put forward a fairly simple recipe for the underlying basis of sustainability as, if people's needs are met in an appropriate, cost-effective way, then the ICT4D initiative will be sustainable.

Heeks (2002) attributed the high rates of failure of Information Systems (IS) projects in developing countries due to a "design-actuality gap" where, there is a mismatch between the desired systems state of the IS designers and the local actuality of the user needs and interest. According to Heeks (2010) identified the three issues, which need to be undertaken while planning for any ICT interventions viz design, governance and sustainability. Here sustainability is seen as wider than purely economic sustainability.

The term sustainability has grown increasingly popular in recent years as development experts and practitioners seek to measure the long-term impacts of their projects. The word is most often used to describe the desired goal of lasting change within institutions, communities, and projects. Sustainability in the context of sustainable development is defined by the World Commission on Environment and Development

(1987) as "forms of progress that meet the needs of the present without compromising the ability of future generations to meet their needs". This emphasizes the aspect of future orientation as a basic element of sustainability. In the context of ICT, it is defined as "Ensuring that the institutions supported through projects and the benefits realized are maintained and continue after the end of the project" (IFAD 2007). It talks in terms of the resource flows. It acknowledges that assessment of sustainability entails determining "whether the results of the project will be sustained in the medium or even longer term without continued external assistance".

This poses a challenge to all development strategies and calls for the multi-stakeholder involvement, when evaluating and improving the sustainability of development strategies and development initiatives at the project and enterprise level. A narrow focus on the project itself does not suffice to surface the reasons for failure, or to identify the route towards sustainability. The reasons for failure lie inside the scope of the project, within the community itself, and outside the community in the larger socio-economic system which includes the economy. Therefore, the socio-economic, socio-personal characteristics of the target clientele, resource available with the society (target area of the project) needs to be undertaken, while planning and implementation of ICT based intervention with due consideration of its long term sustainability.

Keeping above in view, there is need to understand the loopholes in the process of ICT efforts through its assessment, evaluation and determining long term sustainability which can then inform at the policy and strategic levels. Thus in present study attempt was made to assess the sustainability of aAQUA (Almost All Questions Answered) e-Agriservice.

1.1   aAQUA e-Agriservice www.aaqua.org

aAQUA e-Agriservice is ICT based project, launched by the Developmental Informatics Laboratory (DIL) at Indian Institute of Technology, Mumbai in collaboration with the Farm Science Centre (Krishi Vigyan Kendra, KVK), Baramati and Vigyan Ashram (NGO), Pabal, Maharashtra in 2003 as an information providing system to deliver technology options and tailored information for the problems and queries raised by Indian dairy farmers. It is capable of multi-lingual retrieval in three Languages spoken among Indian farmers – Marathi, Hindi and English, allowing the registered users (anybody can register freely) to search, ask, see and/or select agricultural keywords on the database. In addition to this, they get information on crop, livestock, government schemes and subsidies, weather and market information for proper planning and management of their farms. The field engineer prints the new queries, allocate these to the Farm Science Centre's (KVK-Baramati) extension personnel on the basis of their area of expertise, get the answers and upload these on aAQUA. It normally provides answers to farmers queries (agri-dairy-livestock and other related) within 24 to 48 h depending on its difficulty. After the queries are answered and uploaded on aAQUA, the kiosk operators or the users can check these. With this the farmers' query resolving process is completed (Ramamritham et al. 2011).

2 Materials and Methods

2.1 Research Design

The study used the ex-post facto (cause to effect) research design in a quasi-intervention setting. Since 2003 aAQUA e-Agriservice is continuing to deliver its services, hence it was used as the cause to change in the effectiveness of dairy farming. Further, user dairy farmers' responses were elicited to determine the sustainability of the e-Agriservice.

2.2 Sampling

The aAQUA e-Agriservice was initially launched in the eight pilot districts of Maharashtra in 2003 covering the four geographical regions of the state. The state has also covered a maximum number of registered users. The four districts viz. Pune, Nashik, Jalna and Amravati were selected randomly from four zones. The block wise list of registered users was obtained from the service provider (presently Agrocom Software Technologies Pvt. Ltd.) www.agrocom.co.in. The blocks were divided based on number of registered users for the further sampling of the respondents. Consequently, 30 users from each block, who are rearing at least five dairy animals and posed at least one query per season, especially about animal husbandry and dairying to aAQUA were selected randomly for the purpose were selected randomly. Thus, a total 120 users were studied in the present study.

2.3 Development of Sustainable aAQUA e-Agriservice Index (SeAGRSI)

In this study, Mendoza and Prabhu's (2003) Multi-Criteria Approach (MCA), mixed-method approach suggested by Parkins et al. (2001) and Normalised Rank Order Method (NROM) of Guilford (1954) is followed to analyze complex problems involving multiple criteria to develop sustainability index. An index is the number that is composite of two or more other numbers (Kerlinger 1983) and a composite index is an aggregation of sets of variables for the purpose of meaningfully condensing large amounts of information (Dash et al. 2007).

There are three advantages of this method viz. firstly; it can deal with mixed sets of data, quantitative or qualitative, including experts' opinions. In this case, qualitative information from existing researchers in area, experts groups, and experiential knowledge has distinct advantages for assessing sustainability indicators of rural ICT project (Mendoza and Prabhu 2003). Secondly, it enables a collaborative planning and decision-making, provides an opportunity to develop mechanism for the involvement and participation of stakeholders in the sustainability assessment process. Finally, these methodologies are intuitive, transparent, and have strong technical and theoretical support in its procedure. In present study sustainability was assessed under these five categories of sustainability viz. Technological, Economic, Social, institutional and political on the lines of Pade et al. (2006) categories of the sustainability.

Assessing the Importance of Sustainability Indicators. In the first part of analysis, the 25 indicators had been identified after reviewing the literature and discussion with experts in the field of agricultural extension, ICT, dairy science, etc. The expert driven indicators need to be assessed for its local acceptability (Parkins et al. 2001).

In the second part of analysis, we evaluated the appropriateness sustainability indicators in terms of their degree of importance by simply ranking each indicator ('Most Relevant', 'Relevant' and 'Not Relevant' and scored as 2, 1 and 0, respectively). For this purpose, indicators were sent by post, through e-mail and also handed over personally to a judge's panel of 40 in the field of ICT for development, extension education, and dairy economics, veterinary and animal science of state agricultural universities and selected ICAR institutes. Based on their responses, relevancy weight of an indicator estimated using the formula as follows:

$$RW = \frac{\text{Most Relevant X 2} + \text{Relevant X 1} + \text{Not Relevant X 0}}{\text{Maximum Possible Score}}$$

Finally, the items/statements were framed on each selected indicator based on review of literature and discussion with experts in the field of agricultural extension education. The statements were edited based on 14 criteria suggested by Edward (1969).

Determination of Scale Values. In the next analysis we examined each dimension using NROM of Guilford (1954) for judging their current condition relative to their perceived target or desired condition. It is used to assign specific weights (scale values) to each dimension of the based on their perceived significance. The method has got a unique advantage that it can be used with any number of variables and does not require a large number of judges. In the study, selected indicators under 5DS were ranked by the group of judges according to their perceived significance in determining the sustainability of the aAQUA e-Agriservice. Ranking (1 to 5) was obtained from 30 judges who involved experts in the field of social science, extension education, rural development and especially ICT experts. In the next step, the proportions were worked out for the ranks assigned by all the judges by using following formula.

$$p = \frac{(R_i - 0.5)100}{n}$$

Where,

p = centile value which indicated the area of the dimensions in the normal distribution

R_i = the rank value of the dimension i in the reverse order as five to one

n = the number of dimensions ranked by the judges

Computation of the Composite Index. Each dimension of SeAGRSI consists of a number of indicators and items/statements and hence, their range of total scores was different. Therefore, the total score of each dimension was converted into unit score by using simple range and variance as given below.

$$U_{ij} = \frac{Y_{ij} - \text{Min } Y_{ij}}{\text{Max } Y_j - \text{Min } Y_j}$$

Where,

U_{ij}	= unit score of the ith respondents on j^{th} dimension
Y_{ij}	= value of the ith respondent on the jth dimension
Max Y_j	= maximum score on the jth dimension
Min Y_j	= minimum score on the jth dimension

Thus, the score of each dimension ranged between zero to one, i.e. when Y_{ij} is minimum, the score is zero and when Y_{ij} is maximum the score is one. Then, the unit scores of each respondent were multiplied by the respective scale value of the each dimension and summed up. Thus, the score obtained was divided by the total scale values and multiplied by 100 to get the SeAGRSI for each user.

$$\text{SeAGRSI}_i = \frac{\sum U_{ij} * S_j}{\text{Sum of scale values}}$$

Where,

SeAGRSI$_i$	= sustainable e-Agriservice Index of ith respondent
U_{ij}	= unit score of the ith respondent on j^{th} dimension
S_j	= scale value of the jth dimension

The status of the aAQUA e-Agriservice was calculated based on the total index score of all the indicators. The classification of the users into the five categories (very low, low, medium, high and very high sustainable level) was done based on the composite sustainability index scores by using Cumulative Square Root Frequency (CSRF) method as suggested by Dalenius and Hodges (1959). The above categories were equated with the Adrianto et al. (2005) classification as, extremely weak performance, poor performance\ unfavourable, acceptable, very favourable performance, and sustainable for better interpretation of results.

3   Results and Discussion

As mentioned in the previous section, the first analysis for sustainability indicators was to generate a set of indicators under five dimensions (technological with 5 indicators; social – 6; economic – 5; institutional – 4; and political – 2) in terms of their importance judged by a group of stakeholders and experts. The next part of analysis was to estimate the "relative weightage" and "scale values" elaborated from the perceived targets or conditions judged by the stakeholders and experts. Finally, data were collected from the target users of the e-Agriservice on each indicator and computed sustainability index (SeAGRSI). The results are presented in Tables 1 and 2.

The importance of degree of indicators was judged using a 3-point scale by the expert group. It is clear from Table 1 that almost all the indicators are rated moderately

Table 1. The operational definition of sustainability indicators under 5DS with their scale values and relevancy weightage

Indicators	Operational definition
Technological Sustainability *(Scale Value = 7.37)*	
Appropriateness *(RW = 0.80)*	The degree to which aAQUA e-Agriservice was suitable for the farming communities' needs, interest and their social-cum-infrastructural situations.
System capability *(RW = 0.84)*	The ability of an aAQUA web-portal to provide the agro-advisory services to farmers effectively and efficiently. It undertakes the operational simplicity of portal and its availability to the users.
Information quality *(RW = 0.88)*	It refers to the value of the output produced by aAQUA e-Agriservice as perceived by the users.
Integrated performance *(RW = 0.78)*	The arrangement of different features to provide information regarding agriculture and allied sectors.
Usability *(RW = 0.80)*	The ease of use as well as degree of comfort and satisfaction users had with the aAQUA e-Agriservice.
Social Sustainability *(Scale Value = 6.23)*	
Local adaptability *(RW = 0.83)*	The extent to which the technology was adaptable to the existing local conditions of the farmers.
Societal acceptability *(RW = 0.83)*	The extent to which the technology was acceptable by the different sectors of the society.
Cultural desirability *(RW = 0.83)*	The extent to which the technology fits with the cultural patterns, ethos and values of the society.
Loyalty intention *(RW = 0.79)*	Perceived ways of technology experience and word-of-mouth publicity of the e-Agriservice used for fulfilling their farming needs.
Service provider commitment *(RW = 0.77)*	The extent to which the portal managers/experts and kiosk operators were loyal to respond and solve the query of farmers.
Self-reliance *(RW = 0.88)*	The extent to which the technology improves the capacity to execute decisions and making the individual farmers independent in farming practices.
Economic Sustainability *(Scale Value = 7.27)*	
Economic feasibility *(RW = 0.77)*	The capacity of farmers to afford and avail the e-Agriservice facility to solve problems of farming within his realm of financial status and position.
Economic viability *(RW = 0.78)*	The returns to investment of every rupee counts. It deals with the economic and financial profitability of project induced products and services.
Cost incurred to users *(RW = 0.80)*	The amount spent by the users in availing the e-Agriservice.
Potential monetary benefits *(RW = 0.85)*	The degree to which the users got benefited by utilizing the e-Agriservice.

(continued)

Table 1. (*continued*)

Indicators	Operational definition
Economic gain to the service provider *(RW = 0.80)*	The extent to which the service provider got profit by delivering timely services to the farming community.
Institutional Sustainability *(Scale Value = 5.83)*	
Institutional expansion *(RW = 0.77)*	The ability of the stakeholders in providing sustainable e-Agriservice to the farming community.
Lucrative linkages and partnership *(RW = 0.78)*	The degree to which the association of the stakeholders in maintaining the functioning of the aAQUA e-Agriservice in post project period.
Capacity building and training *(RW = 0.80)*	The degree to which the service providers undertaken the training programs and other related activities to update knowledge of the users.
Stakeholders' engagement *(RW = 0.81)*	The degree to which the stakeholders were committed to facilitate and share a better understanding in providing the e-Agriservice.
Political Sustainability *(Scale Value = 5.30)*	
Political determinism *(RW = 0.78)*	Ability to work together (both public and private) for agreed ends without obstructing the existing intricacies and implications of political set up.
Government commitment *(RW = 0.81)*	The degree to which the government functionaries were providing public facilities-cum-services and promoting private investment in a particular area for enhancing efficiency and effectiveness of the e-Agriservice activities.

Table 2. Sustainable e-Agriservice index (SeAGRSI) by the users (n = 120)

Sustainability level	Range	Frequency
Extremely weak performance	(< 0.60)	18 (15.00)
Poor performance	(0.61–0.66)	24 (20.00)
Acceptable performance	(0.67–0.74)	39 (32.50)
Very favourable performance	(0.75–0.79)	20 (16.67)
Sustainable	(> 0.80)	19 (15.83)

Note: Figures in parenthesis indicates percentage

to highly relevant. It can be seen from the relevancy weight value, ranging from 0.77 to 0.85, showing that all the developed indicators are important. The scale values based on the response of experts reveal that technological (7.37) and economic (7.27) dimensions were more important followed by social (6.23), institutional (5.83) and political (5.30) dimension (Table 1). In experts' perspectives, the study found that the technological and economic sustainability are more important than social, institutional and political dimension of rural ICT sustainability.

The composite Sustainable e-Agriservice Index (SeAGRSI) was worked out by taking into account all the five-dimensions of sustainability. The SeAGRSI by user group ranged from 0.53 to 0.84. It is evident from Table 2 that almost one third (32.50%) of users informed that the e-Agriservice performed at an acceptable level (0.67 to 0.74) of sustainability, followed by poor performance (0.61 to 0.66) and very favourable performance (0.75 to 0.79) level of sustainability categories, respectively. On the three point continuums viz. Poor performance (extremely weak performance +poor performance), Acceptable performance, and Sustainable (very favourable performance+sustainable) level of SeAGRSI, 65% of users reported that the aAQUA e-Agriservice had acceptable to a sustainable level of performance.

The possible reason might be, the e-Agriservice is technically realistic, user-friendly and accepted by the dairy farmers. Socially compatible and there was no any relation of this technology to the farmers dynamics (relationship within the community), which hampered use of the e-Agriservice. Farmers had to pay a meager amount to access this facility, and get the appropriate return on investment. Thus, the e-Agriservice is technologically sound, socially acceptable and economically viable. However, on institutional and political dimension, the technology is not able to provide the same level of service as like during the pilot project period, such as capacity building and training to the new users, kiosk accessibility etc. These are the reasons for the poor performance level of sustainability in the study area.

In target users' point of view, it was inferred that the social sustainability was more crucial than other dimensions of the sustainability to continue the services of aAQUA e-Agriservice in Maharashtra. The sustainability index for the social indicators was the highest among other dimensions of the sustainability (SeAGRSI = 0.77) followed by the technologically (0.73), economic (0.71) political (0.62) and institutional (0.58) sustainable.

The findings of the present research are in consonance with the findings of the Best and Kumar (2008) found that the lack of long term financial viability was a major reason for the closure of the telecentres. The telecentres that were owned by the individuals with prior training in computers or that had a separate trained operator, remained operational for a longer period. In the present research, after the project period, the rights of the web-portal handed over to the private company (Agrocom Software Technologies Pvt. Ltd.), which provided the technical support to the web-portal and KVK Baramati as project partner institute remained for providing information and solving the farmers' queries.

Thus, it can be concluded that the social sustainability was crucial for ICT based technology in the rural areas followed by the technological sustainability. The loyalty of the farmers towards the usage of the service and service provider's commitment were the vital factors which lead to the social acceptability of the technology. The information quality and usability of the e-Agriservice were found to be the important parameters for the suitability of the technology for the farming community. The farmers have to pay a meager amount to access the e-Agriservice. Better co-ordination and linkages among the different actors of the e-Agriservice and strong and positive-will make it institutionally and politically sustainable.

4   Conclusion

Information is a key ingredient for success of any individual and same is true in the case of farmers as well. Readily availability of information at the right time and in right form will enhance the success rate of farmers. In this background, during the last two decades, many organizations have undertaken knowledge interventions for promoting scientific dairy farming. In this process few organizations succeeded and others have failed in achieving the targeted outputs and their scaling up of delivery, monitoring and evaluation still remains at the pilot project stage. Among these interventions that have made significant progress in taking messages to the farming community the present study highlighted the sustainability of the aAQUA e-Agriservice. The study revealed that the SeAGRSI for the social indicators was the highest among other dimensions of the sustainability (SeAGRSI = 0.77) followed by the technologically (0.73), economic (0.71) political (0.62) and institutional (0.58) sustainable. It was found that 32.50% of users reported the acceptable level of performance and equal number of users reported very favourable to a sustainable level of performance of aAQUA e-Agriservice. Experts' opined that the technological and economic sustainability are more important than social, institutional and political dimension of rural ICT sustainability. However the target users' reported that the social sustainability was more crucial than other dimensions of the sustainability to continue the service of the e-Agriservice in Maharashtra.

Acknowledgement. The authors would like to thank the users of the e-Agriservice who participated in the evaluation study and special thanks to 'Agrocom Technologies Pvt Ltd.' for supporting the research study.

References

Adrianto, L., Matsuda, Y., Sakuma, Y.: Assessing local sustainability of fisheries system: a multi-criteria participatory approach with the case of Yoron Isaland, Kagoshima prefecture. Japan. Mar. Policy **29**(1), 9–23 (2005)

Annamalai, K., Rao, S.: What Works: ITC's e-Choupal and Profitable Rural Transformation: Web-based Information and Procurement Tools for Indian Farmers. World Resources Institute, Washington, D.C. (2003)

Ashraf, M.M., Hanisch, J., Swatman, P.: ICT intervention towards development. In: 3rd Conference on Computer and Information Technology (ICCIT). Developing Countries: Theory and Practice, Bangladesh, pp: 83–100. City University of Hong Kong Press (2007)

Best, M., Kumar, R.: Sustainability failures of rural telecentres: challenges from the Sustainable Access in Rural India (SARI) project. Inf. Technol. Int. Dev. **4**(4), 31–45 (2008)

Bure, C.: Grounding gender evaluation methodology for telecentres: the experiences of Ecuador and the Phillipines. In: International Development Research Centre (IDRC). Telecentre.Org, Ottawa (2007)

Dalenius, T., Hodges, J.L.: Minimum variance stratification. J. Am. Stat. Assoc. **54**, 88–101 (1959)

Dash, R., Chattopadhyay, P., Pahuja, N.: Environmental Sustainability Index for Indian States. Centre for Development Finance Institute for Financial Management and Research, Chennai (2007)

Dossani, R., Misra, D.C., Jhaveri, R.: Enabling ICT for rural India. Project Report, Asia-Pacific Research Center, Stanford University and National Informatics Centre, Government of India (2005)

Draca, M., Sadun, R., Reenen, J.V.: Productivity and ICT: a review of the evidence, Centre for Economic Performance (CEP) discussion paper No. 749. London school of economics and political science, London (2006)

Edward, A.L.: Techniques of Attitude Scale Construction. Vakils, Feffer and Simons Pvt. Ltd., Mumbai (1969)

Gomez, R., Hunt, P.: Telecentre Evaluation: A Global Perspective. International Development Research Centre (IDRC), Ottawa (1999)

Guilford, J.P.: Psychological Methods. Tata McGraw Hill Publishing Co., Ltd., Noida (1954)

Heeks, R.: Information systems and developing countries: failure, success and local improvisations. Inf. Soc. **18**(2), 101–112 (2002)

Heeks, R.: Do information and communication technologies contribute to development? J. Int. Dev. **22**, 625–640 (2010)

IFAD Strategic Framework: enabling the rural poor to overcome poverty. EB 2006/89/R.2/Rev.1. 89th Session, Rome (2007)

Kerlinger, F.N.: Foundation of Behavioural Research, pp. 151–153. S. S. Chabra Publishers, Delhi (1983)

Kretschmer, T.: Information and communication technologies and productivity growth: a survey of the literature, OECD Digital Economy Papers, No. 195. OECD Publishing (2012)

Kuriyan, R., Ray, I., Toyama, K.: Information and communication technologies for development: the bottom of the pyramid model in practice. Inf. Soc. **24**(2), 93–104 (2008)

Lio, M., Liu, M.: ICT and agricultural productivity: evidence from cross-country data. Agric. Econ. **34**, 221–228 (2006)

Mbarika, V.W.A., Okoli, C., Byrd, T.A., Datta, P.: The neglected continent of IS research: a research agenda for Sub-Saharan Africa. J. AIS **6**(5), 130–170 (2005)

McNamara, K.S.: Information and communication technologies, poverty and development: Learning from Experience. A Background Paper for the InfoDev Annual Symposium, Geneva (2003)

Mendoza, G.A., Prabhu, R.: Qualitative multi-criteria approaches to assessing indicators of sustainable forest resources management. Forest Ecol. Manage. **174**, 329–343 (2003)

Meso, P., Datta, P., Mbarika, V.: Moderating information and communication technologies influences on socioeconomic development with good governance: a study of the developing countries. J. Am. Soc. Inf. Sci. Technol. **57**(2), 186–197 (2006)

Musa, P.F.: Making a case for modifying the technology acceptance model to account for limited accessibility in developing countries. Inf. Technol. Dev. **12**(3), 213–224 (2006)

Pade, C. I., Brenda, M., Sewry, D.: An exploration of the categories associated with ICT project sustainability in rural areas of developing countries: a case study of the Dwesa project. In: Proceedings of the 2006 Annual Research Conference of the South African Institute of Computer Scientists and Information Technologists on IT Research in Developing Countries. South African Institute for Computer Scientists and Information Technologists (2006)

Parkins, J.R., Richard, C.S., Varghese, J.: Moving towards local-level indicators of sustainability of forest-based communities: a mixed-method approach. Soc. Ind. Res. **56**, 43–72 (2001)

Promila: Gender analysis in dairy and crop production in Kangra district, Himachal Pradesh. Ph. D. thesis, NDRI, Karnal, Haryana (1994)

Raju, K.A.: A case for harnessing information technology for rural development. Int. Inf. Library Review 36, 233–240 (2004)

Ramamritham, K., Bahuman, C. and Bahuman, A.: aAQUA: ICT-enabled knowledge services to farmers in India. In: Hazelman, M., Attaluri, S. (eds.) Success Stories on ICT/ICM in AR4D in Asia and the Pacific Region, FAO (2011)

Rao, N.H.: A framework for implementing information and communication technologies in agricultural development in India. Technol. Forecast. Soc. Change 74, 491–518 (2006)

Rao, S.S.: Social development in Indian rural communities: adoption of telecentres. Int. J. Inf. Manage. 28, 474–482 (2008)

Sah, A.K.: A descriptive study of existing dairy farming practices and constraints in adoption of improved dairy practices among dairy farmers in Banka district, Bihar. M.Sc. thesis, NDRI, Karnal, Haryana (1996)

Singh, N.: ICT and rural development in India, UCSC working paper (2007)

Tacchi, J., Slater, D., Lewis, P.: Evaluating community based media initiatives: an ethnographic action research approach. In: Paper Presented at the Meeting of the Information Technology for Development Conference, Oxford, UK (2003)

Unwin, T.: ICT4D: Information and Communication Technology for Development. Cambridge University Press, Cambridge (2009)

Upton, D.M., Fuller, V.A.: The ITC e-Choupal initiative (Case No. 9-604-016). Harvard Business School, Boston (2004)

Wadkar, S.K., Singh, K., Kadian, K.S., Malhotra, R., Garde, Y.A.: Comparative study on effectiveness of the aAQUA e-Agriservice among dairy farmers of Maharashtra. Indian J. Dairy Sci. 68(4), 408–411 (2015)

World Commission on Environment and Development: Our common future. Oxford University Press, Oxford (1987)

www.aaqua.org

www.agrocom.co.in

Information Systems Development and Implementation in Southeast Asia

Experience with the Mobile4D Disaster Reporting and Alerting System in Lao PDR

Ahmed Loai Ali[1]([✉]), Jasper van de Ven[1], Thatheva Saphangthong[2],
Christian Freksa[1], Thomas Barkowsky[1], Sithong Thongmanivong[3],
Houngphet Chanthavong[3], and Peter Haddawy[4]

[1] Capacity Lab, Bremen Spatial Cognition Center, University of Bremen,
Bremen, Germany
{loai,jasper,freksa,barkowsky}@capacitylab.org
[2] Lao Ministry of Agriculture and Forestry, Vientiane, Laos
thatheva@cst-maf.la
[3] Faculty of Forestry, National University of Laos, Vientiane, Laos
{sithong,houngphet}@nuol.edu.la
[4] Faculty of ICT, Mahidol University, Salaya, Thailand
peter.had@mahidol.ac.th

Abstract. Information and Communication Technology (ICT) is used
to support developing countries in many different ways, such as poverty
reduction, public services enhancement, and disaster management and
recovery. Mobile4D is a software framework that applies the crowdsourcing paradigm to facilitate information exchange between people during
disaster situations. It acts as a disaster reporting and alerting system
as well as an information sharing platform. Mobile4D facilitates rapid
communication between local citizens and administrative units. Moreover, it allows exchanging experience and knowledge between people to
reduce poverty and increase living standards. The Mobile4D framework
has been deployed in a pilot study in three provinces in the Lao People's Democratic Republic (Lao PDR). The study was limited to report
particular types of disasters, however, it revealed further use cases and
identified the required extension of Mobile4D to cover the entire country. This paper presents a report about Mobile4D: initiative, challenges,
status, and further extensions.

Keywords: ICT4D · Crowdsourcing · Volunteered geographic information · Disaster management · Location based services · Mobile technologies

1 Introduction

Evolution of Information and Communication Technology (ICT) played a major
role in various fields like disaster management and poverty reduction in developing countries [11,19]. In particular, ubiquity of Internet and broadband communication channels empowers ordinary people to voluntarily contribute information.

© IFIP International Federation for Information Processing 2017
Published by Springer International Publishing AG 2017. All Rights Reserved
J. Choudrie et al. (Eds.): ICT4D 2017, IFIP AICT 504, pp. 525–535, 2017.
DOI: 10.1007/978-3-319-59111-7_43

With the vast availability of location-sensing devices, advances in Web 2.0, and GeoWeb technologies people are enabled to contribute Volunteered Geographic Information (VGI), which has a significant role in disaster relief [9,10]. Natural and human-made disasters usually result in destruction and in the worst case in deaths. Although there is no possibility to eliminate the risk of a disaster, projects utilizing ICT demonstrated that the damage caused by disasters can be reduced by proactive planning, mitigation, and rapid response [19]. For example, Ushahidi[1] and Sahana[2] are the most common software frameworks that employ ICT to support disaster management activities [2,18]. Their functionalities focus mainly on post-activities of disaster management; they support decision makers and aids organizations to coordinate actions and to allocate resources during disaster relief. In contrast, this paper presents Mobile4D software framework that concerned with pre-activities of disaster management. Mobile4D provides location-based early stage reporting and alerting functionalities.

This paper shows research-in-progress of Mobile4D. The paper comprises the initiative, the development status, the pilot deployment in parts of the Lao People's Democratic Republic (Lao PDR), the encountered challenges, and the future plans. The system has been developed in the Capacity Lab[3] at the University of Bremen, Germany. The Capacity Lab was established to support development and to achieve poverty reduction in developing countries though applying advanced ICT. Lao PDR is a landlocked country located in Southeast Asia, bordered by Myanmar, China, Vietnam, Cambodia, and Thailand. About 80% of Lao's population are involved in agriculture activities. Such activities are directly influenced by natural disasters like floods, drought, and epidemic diseases. Therefore, Mobile4D is built upon the potential role of ICT to support such essential activities.

Mobile4D is a software framework that facilitates rapid communication between Lao district officers and administrative units in disaster situations. In case of disaster, such grass-root communication is required to provide insights into the real situation. The framework employs mobile technology to achieve broader and rapid utilization. Since 2015, Mobile4D is in use in three Lao provinces collecting early stage reports about disasters.

Development and deployment of Mobile4D encountered various challenges related to technical and non-technical issues. For instance, the system is mostly used in the early stage of disasters, when the situation requires rapid communication and easy-of-use. The reports should be delivered to users in rural and urban areas as well. Based on location, alerts should also be sent to the expected hazard locations. Moreover, the issued reports by non-authorities should be verified by a certain way to ensure their occurrences. Limited experiences of users might results in imprecise use of the system. Therefore, the development team considered all these challenges to develop a reliable system.

---

[1] https://www.ushahidi.com/.
[2] https://sahanafoundation.org/.
[3] http://capacitylab.org/.

The remainder of the paper is organized as follows: Related works are discussed in Sect. 2; The initiative of Mobile4D is presented in Sect. 3; Sect. 4 demonstrates Mobile4D use cases; A technical overview of the system is given in Sect. 5; The experience and lessons learned are presented in Sect. 6; whereas Sect. 7 discusses future work and further development of the system.

2   Related Work

Since the end of 1990s, the Internet and the Millennium Development Goals (MDGs) particularly inspired the evolution of ICT for development (ICT4D), when governmental and non-governmental organizations (NGOs) harnessed the ICT to achieve more development in various domains: education, agriculture, employment, health, ... etc. Several projects were successful executed to support poverty reduction, such as, e-choupal[4] and Katha[5] in India and the Expanded Public Works Programme[6] (EPWP) in South Africa. Whereas other projects encountered sustainability or scalability problems [1], such as, the Economic Transformation Programme[7] (ETP) in the Malaysian government [16].

The ubiquity of the Internet, wireless communication technologies, and location aware devices moved ICT4D to another era [12,13]. In this era, ICT empowered public citizens to collect and exchange information following the crowdsourcing paradigm. After the Haiti earthquake on 2010, the potential role of crowdsourcing to support disaster relief had been recognized [8]. Several crowdsourcing platforms were used to report about this catastrophic event [15,17]. Although social media and crowdsourcing can be utilized for reporting and information propagation in disaster situations, they do not support early warning capabilities or easily coordination of responses. Therefore, dedicated software platforms have been developed – utilizing advance of ICT – to support disaster management activities. So far, most of these platforms focuses on responses coordination and resources allocation (post-activities) in disaster situations, while limited ones consider early stage warning and alerting (pre-activities) toward proactive disaster management plans.

In the last decade, increase availability of Mobile devices fostered mobile-based ICT applications in various domains. The authors in [4] review various mobile-based health applications, while the research in [14] proposes SMS based disaster alert system in developing countries. Moreover, web and mobile applications of voluntary-based flood risk management approach are presented in [5]. Although utilizing mobile technologies allows implementation of low cost systems, development and deployment of these systems encounter various challenges particularly in developing countries; Low communication broadband, limited experience of users, and ensuring the data quality are among other challenges that encounter mobile-based ICT applications in developing countries.

---

[4] http://www.itcportal.com/businesses/agri-business/e-choupal.aspx.
[5] http://www.katha.org/.
[6] http://www.epwp.gov.za/.
[7] http://etp.pemandu.gov.my/.

Most of previous research focus on collaboration and coordination of rescue activities, while Mobile4D supports location-based early warning and alerting functionalities. Various applications have been developed addressing a particular disaster in a certain location (e.g., district), while Mobile4D aims to support various kinds of disasters and targets national coverage. It takes into account the information propagation and integration among different levels of decision makers.

3   The History of Mobile4D

In 2007, the Lao Ministry of Agriculture and Forestry (MAF) embarked on a program to strengthen the capacity of staff at the local level as part of the country's poverty reduction strategy. In collaboration with the Wetlands Alliance[8], the Ministry piloted an innovative professional Bachelors degree program in Poverty Reduction and Agriculture Management (PRAM)[9] to provide broad skills at the grass-root level. In contrast to the piecemeal short-term training that many development projects provide, the PRAM program provided students with a more complete spectrum of skills to form a broader base of competencies for poverty reduction. The success of the pilot led the Ministry of Agriculture and Forestry to ask how it could be scaled up to serve a larger proportion of the 6,000 extension workers throughout the country. But the unavailability of a sufficient number of qualified teachers and the fact that the poorest districts are also the most remote posed great challenges.

In 2011 the PRAM Knowledge Sharing Network (PRAM-KSN) was developed as a web-based platform to accelerate capacity building among extension workers [3]. The goal of PRAM-KSN was to facilitate peer-to-peer learning among agricultural extension workers. A key design element of the platform was allowing user-authored multimedia content to be uploaded and shared. Uptake of the system was rapid and as of February 2012 there were already active users in 18 districts over 8 southern provinces of Lao PDR.

One topic often addressed in PRAM-KSN was how to deal with reoccurring destructive events. For example, in severe weather conditions and disaster situations such as drought or flooding, people in rural and remote districts suffer from limited support. Hence, bi-directional and rapid communication channels between citizens and higher administrative officers was required to minimize disaster risk [6]. As a reaction to this, the project *Mobile for Development* (Mobile4D) [7] was established in 2012 within the activities of the Capacity Lab. About 15 students of the faculty of computer science at the University of Bremen worked in collaboration with MAF, the E-Government Centre in Laos, and the National University of Laos (NUOL) to develop the mobile disaster alerting and reporting system. To get a better understanding of the development context, the team adopted hybrid research methodologies including: interviews, questionnaires, prototype developments, field visits, and discussion workshops.

---

[8] http://www.wetlandsalliance.org/.
[9] http://www.pramlaos.org/.

Mobile4D was planned as real-time location-based reporting and alerting system. Moreover, it is integrated with PRAM-KSN to allow dual functionality in a single system. In 2013, Mobile4D was tested in Luang Prabang in Northern Laos. During this test, field studies and questioners had been conducted to collect feedback and to identify further development challenges and requirements.

As a result of active collaboration, it was decided to carry out an information/training session of Mobile4D. At the beginning of 2015, the 3-day session was held in Attapeu province for district officers from six districts. The session served as a pilot study of the system in 6 districts over three provinces: Phouvong and Xansay of Attapeu Province, Dakcheung and Kaleum in Xekong Province, and Ta'Oy and Samuay of Salavan Province. The training was collaboratively conducted by computer scientists from the University of Bremen and trainers from MAF and NUOL. During training, participants were provided with the developed system on smart-phones. The training included deploying the system and becoming familiar with its functionality. After the training, each participant was able to utilize the developed system to send reports and to receive alerts. Moreover, each participant could act as a tutor for other district officers.

Since 2015, Mobile4D has been used in these three south Lao provinces. District officers and local staff use the system to report on small disasters and incidents that happened in their districts such as floods, infrastructure damage, and diseases. Afterward, MAF conducted an additional training session for district officers from eleven districts over five provinces, as well as participants from surrounded districts. Currently, we are investigating possible expansions of the system to the entire country of Laos aiming to achieve better reporting possibilities and to be able to provide better support where it is required. Figure 1 provides an impression of the interface of the mobile client of the system; Fig. 1a shows a list of recently issued reports, while the map in Fig. 1b demonstrates various filters of the reports based on type of disasters (flood, fire, ...etc.) or the status of reports (active/inactive).

(a) report list   (b) report map   (c) disaster selector   (d) flood level

Fig. 1. Impression of the mobile interface of the Mobile4D system

Whereas Figs. 1c and d illustrate the easy-of-use requirements; Through interactive GUI users are able to interact with the system by easy ways.

4 Use Cases of Mobile4D

In this section, we introduce the primary use cases of the Mobile4D system and additional ones, which were identified during the pilot study in Laos. The use cases can be classified into three categories: reporting and alerting (Sect. 4.1), knowledge sharing (Sect. 4.2), and information distribution (Sect. 4.3). The first two scenarios (reporting and alerting and knowledge sharing) are the original scenarios of Mobile4D, while the last scenario is one of the upcoming extensions.

4.1 Reporting and Alerting

The main scenario during the development of the Mobile4D system was the crowdsourced disaster reporting and alerting. That is, if a disaster like flooding occurs, ordinary people act as sensors creating reports using a mobile phone. The reports are directly sent to all local people concerned as well as to all concerned authorities on all levels of administration. This reduces the reaction time as the information is directly available to everyone. And even more important, all other possibly affected individuals are informed and can immediately react, securing or rescuing livestock and tools.

At the moment, Mobile4D only addresses limited types of disasters: flooding, wildfires, animal disease, plant disease, human disease, and infrastructural damage. However, the pilot study in Laos showed that the possibility to add further types of disasters is required (e.g., drought or plagues like locusts).

4.2 Knowledge Sharing

Another use case of the Mobile4D system is the functionality of supporting direct information sharing between people. Specifically, to provide people in Laos with a possibility to communicate information regarding specific local problems. This resulted in the inclusion of information and material from the previously mentioned Poverty Reduction and Agricultural Management Knowledge Sharing Network (PRAM-KSN). Thus, the Mobile4D system allows its users to directly access especially the tutorials provided through the PRAM-KSN.

4.3 Information Distribution

A further result of the pilot study in Laos is the insight that people who do not use a system on a day-to-day basis may not be fully prepared to use it when they need to use it. To address this issue the additional scenario of distributing useful information on a daily basis was requested. This new extension aims to build trustworthiness between users and the proposed system.

One example of such daily information distribution are so-called *farm gate prices*. These are the prices a farmer can sell his goods for. However, farmers do not always know the day-to-day prices and it is difficult for them to communicate with other farmers in the area to determine the best current offer from companies. The idea is to extend Mobile4D to allow buyers to announce their offers through the system and provide this information directly to local farmers. This would allow farmers to easily determine where and to whom to sell their goods.

5   An Overview of the Mobile4D System

The Mobile4D framework consists of three systems: a disaster server (Sect. 4.1), a web service (Sect. 4.2), and a mobile client (Sect. 4.3) [7]. In this section, we address the technologies used to implement the Mobile4D system and its functionality as it is currently deployed in Laos.

5.1   The Disaster Server

The disaster server is one of the two key pieces of the Mobile4D system (the other one is the mobile client). It allows to centrally collect information regarding disasters provided by individuals observing them. In addition, the server allows to access this information and it proactively informs authorities and individuals that either requested this information or will be directly affected by the event. The software is implemented in Java[10], using the JPA/eclipselink/h2[11] libraries to provide a database, and mosquitto[12] as a push service.

5.2   The Web Service

The web service provides the possibility to access the disaster server and information provided by it through the Internet. Thus, this web service allows to report incidents or inspect reports. It is specifically designed to allow government authorities to receive and manage warnings and reports about current disaster events, and to send warnings and information material to affected people. It is implemented using HTML5[13] and JavaScript[14].

5.3   The Android Client

The mobile client is an application that allows to provide and receive information regarding disaster events from almost anywhere. It is implemented as an application for Android[15] smart phones. A main focus during the development was on

---

[10] http://www.java.com.
[11] http://www.eclipse.org/eclipselink/.
[12] http://mqtt.org/.
[13] https://www.w3.org/TR/2010/WD-html-markup-20100304/.
[14] http://www.ecma-international.org/ecma-262/5.1/#sec-12.13:.
[15] https://www.android.com/.

the graphical user interface, in order to ensure a simple usage, i.e., intuitive and text-free. Figure 1c shows the first page of the disaster report creation process. Figure 1d shows the first approach to a text-free interface for the selection of the water level of a flooding incident. This interface allows the use of a touchscreen and provides an intuitive design to slide the water level to the observed height.

5.4   The Mobile4D Framework

The Mobile4D framework combines all three systems to create an integrated mobile crowdsourcing-based disaster reporting and alerting system. The disaster server provides an REST[16] interface to manage information and supports JSON[17] and Common Alerting Protocol (CAP)[18] to formalize disaster events. The REST interface is used by the mobile client and the web service to create and retrieve disaster reports on or from the server. In addition, the server uses a push service to directly inform affected people and government authorities by sending reports and information to their respective mobile clients.

6   Experience with the System

This section summaries the learned lessons and describes our experience with the Mobile4D. During a field visit in February 2016 we interviewed end users of the Mobile4D system in three districts in three separate provinces of southern Laos. The interviews were conducted with various enduser groups: district and province officers. These users utilize the system to report incidents on provincial and district levels. The most common reports concerned infrastructure damage such as landslide blockage of a new road in Dakcheung district. Other use was not anticipated in the original design of Mobile4D. This included new types of incidents as well as new ways of making use of the reports. An example of the former was the reporting of locusts in northern Laos. An example of the latter was the use of foot and mouth disease reports to determine locations to which vaccine needed to be distributed.

We learned that sometimes other reporting channels (e.g., email) still are used, that do not have the communicative advantages of Mobile4D; therefore it will be important to further encourage users to make their reports through Mobile4D.

Typically incidence reports are issued on a monthly basis on the district level, but only in cases of major incidents. However, it appears desirable to also record minor incidents in order to get the full picture and to keep the users fully familiar with the use of the system. Therefore it seems sensible to encourage users of Mobile4D to use the system more regularly, also for minor incidents and

---

[16] http://www.ics.uci.edu/~fielding/pubs/dissertation/rest_arch_style.htm.
[17] http://www.json.org/.
[18] https://docs.oasis-open.org/emergency/cap/v1.2/CAP-v1.2-os.html.

immediately when they occur. A way to make it more common for end users to work with the system could be to support users to also report positive events over the system to make Mobile4D a continuously used communication channel.

Currently reports made on the district level must be approved on the provincial level. In order to get urgent information as quickly as possible to directly affected community members, it should be considered to warn these citizens directly, but with not yet approved information marked as preliminary.

7   Conclusion and Future Work

Experience with the pilot use of Mobile4D has resulted in identifying a range of desired new functionality. Users expressed a desire to have ready access to information concerning human and animal diseases. This could be retrieved using the information in the reports in order to suggest useful relevant information concerning a problem at hand. Reports of animal disease could also be supplemented by display of a buffer region for vaccine distribution purposes. This could be readily inferred from a map which can supply information about connectivity. Supplementary information would also be valuable for locust reporting, such as, wind speed and direction, which are highly relevant to spread of locusts. It would be useful to supplement each report with this information, which can be retrieved automatically from online services.

The pilot also raised implementation aspects that could be improved. For example, the feature to link photos to reports requires high bandwidth, which might be problematic in many parts of Laos. Therefore, a compression facility needs to be added to make it more usable. Finally, if Mobile4D can be linked to social media (e.g., Facebook) that could increase the day-to-day use of the system as well as the familiarity of the system among local people. In addition to new functionality, remote and personal training of users will be one of our priorities. The pilot study showed that this is absolutely essential for the success of the system.

We will also investigate possibilities to apply mobile crowdsourcing and artificial intelligence techniques (e.g., spatial reasoning and machine learning) to tackle issues related to vector-borne diseases like malaria and dengue. The idea is to generate and provide a prediction of the expected spatial and temporal pattern of transmission of the disease and its vector. The hypothesis is that the availability of this information will allow more timely and targeted intervention.

Last September 2016, we conducted a discussion workshop at the Capacity Lab with our partners. During this workshop, we discussed possible integration between Mobile4D and other services provided by the Lao E-government center. Furthermore, potential utilization of Mobile4D in other countries has been addressed.

Acknowledgements. We gratefully acknowledge valuable suggestions by Lutz Frommberger and Falko Schmid in numerous discussions.

This work was partially funded by the German Research Foundation (DFG) through the projects SOCIAL (FR 806/15) and Human-centered relational feature classification for VGI (FR 806/17) in the priority program VGIScience, as well as a Fellowship from the Hanse-Wissenschaftskolleg Institute for Advanced Study to Peter Haddawy. Moreover, we thank Lao DECIDE info phase III (CDE/SDC) and Food Nutrition Marketing Linkage (FNML/IFAD) for their support in the deployment of the test system and organizing training in Laos.

References

1. Ali, M., Bailur, S.: The challenge of "sustainability" in ICT4D? is bricolage the answer. In: Proceedings of the 9th International Conference on Social Implications of Computers in Developing Countries (2007)
2. Careem, M., De Silva, C., De Silva, R., Raschid, L., Weerawarana, S.: Sahana: Overview of a disaster management system. In: 2006 International Conference on Information and Automation, pp. 361–366. IEEE (2006)
3. Chew, H.E., Sort, B., Haddawy, P.: Building a crowdsourcing community: How online social learning helps in poverty reduction. In: Proceedings of the 3rd ACM Symposium on Computing for Development, p. 21. ACM (2013)
4. Déglise, C., Suggs, L.S., Odermatt, P.: SMS for disease control in developing countries: A systematic review of mobile health applications. J. Telemed. Telecare **18**(5), 273–281 (2012)
5. Degrossi, L.C., de Albuquerque, J.P., Fava, M.C., Mendiondo, E.M.: Flood citizen observatory: A crowdsourcing-based approach for flood risk management in Brazil. In: SEKE, pp. 570–575 (2014)
6. Frommberger, L., Schmid, F.: Crowdsourced bi-directional disaster reporting and alerting on smartphones in Lao PDR. CoRR abs/1312.6036 (2013)
7. Frommberger, L., Schmid, F.: Mobile4D: Crowdsourced disaster alerting and reporting. In: Proceedings of the Sixth International Conference on Information and Communications Technologies and Development: Notes, Vol. 2, pp. 29–32. ACM (2013)
8. Gao, H., Barbier, G., Goolsby, R.: Harnessing the crowdsourcing power of social media for disaster relief. IEEE Intell. Syst. **26**(3), 10–14 (2011)
9. Goodchild, M.F.: Citizens as sensors: The world of volunteered geography. Geo-Journal **69**(4), 211–221 (2007)
10. Goodchild, M.F., Glennon, J.A.: Crowdsourcing geographic information for disaster response: A research frontier. Int. J. Digit. Earth **3**(3), 231–241 (2010)
11. Haddawy, P., Sayakoummane, S.: ICT for poverty reduction in Lao PDR. UN Chronicle: The Digital Dividend **48**(4) (2011)
12. Heeks, R.: ICT4D 2.0: The next phase of applying ICT for international development. Computer **41**(6), 26–33 (2008)
13. Kleine, D., Unwin, T.: Technological revolution, evolution and new dependencies: What's new about ICT4D? Third World Q. **30**(5), 1045–1067 (2009)
14. Mahmud, I., Akter, J., Rawshon, S.: SMS based disaster alert system in developing countries: A usability analysis. Int. J. Multi. Manage. Stud. **2**(4), 1–15 (2012)
15. Muralidharan, S., Rasmussen, L., Patterson, D., Shin, J.H.: Hope for Haiti: An analysis of Facebook and Twitter usage during the earthquake relief efforts. Public Relat. Rev. **37**(2), 175–177 (2011)

16. Nawi, H.S.A., Rahman, A.A., Ibrahim, O., et al.: Government ICT project failure factors: Project stakeholders' views. J. Inf. Syst. Res. Innov. **2**(1), 69–77 (2012)
17. Oh, O., Kwon, K., Rao, H.: An exploration of social media in extreme events: Rumor theory and twitter during the haiti earthquake 2010. In: ICIS 2010 Proceedings - Thirty First International Conference on Information Systems (2010)
18. Okolloh, O.: Ushahidi, or 'testimony': Web 2.0 tools for crowdsourcing crisis information. Participatory Learn. Action **59**(1), 65–70 (2009)
19. Palen, L., Liu, S.B.: Citizen communications in crisis: Anticipating a future of ICT-supported public participation. In: Proceedings of the SIGCHI Conference on Human Factors in Computing Systems, CHI 2007, pp. 727–736. ACM, New York (2007)

Applying ICT to Health Information Systems (HIS) in Low Resource Settings: Implementing DHIS2 as an Integrated Health Information Platform in Lao PDR

Anh Chu[1(✉)], Chansaly Phommavong[2(✉)], John Lewis[3(✉)], Jørn Braa[3(✉)], and Wilfred Senyoni[3]

[1] WHO Country Office, Vientiane, Lao PDR
Chuhonganh2011@gmail.com
[2] Ministry of Health, Vientiane, Lao PDR
Hsipchansaly@etllao.com
[3] University of Oslo, Oslo, Norway
Johnlewis.hisp@gmail.com, jbraa@ifi.uio.no, senyoni@gmail.com

Abstract. In the 3 years since initial discussion on application of ICT for the Lao Health and Management Information System (HMIS) and initiation of the Lao Health Sector Reform process, DHIS2 has become the official national health information reporting platform for the HMIS including the major health programs, such as MNCH, TB, Malaria and HIV. The platform now provides a data warehouse that collects and manages routine data from all public health facilities nationwide and dashboards for dissemination and use of information. The system generates programme reports, national health system reports, statistics reports as well as other reports serving monitoring purposes for the Ministry of Health (MOH) and the Government of Lao (SDGs; UHC). This article describes the process of developing the integrated HIS in Lao People Democratic Republic (PDR) from 2013 to December 2016. Overcoming challenges of human resource capacity and infrastructure disadvantages; strengthening the utilisation of health information especially for planning and decision making have been and will be crucial for the strength and sustainability of the integrated HIS on DHIS2 platform similar to other setting in developing countries.

Keywords: DHIS2 · Integrated HIS · ICT for health

1 Introduction

This article documents the process to develop an integrated Health Information System (HIS) in Lao PDR. Fragmentation of HIS into different health program and disease specific systems, which was the situation in Lao PDR, has been a general problem in developing countries for a long time [1, 2]. Responding to the HIV pandemic and other public health problems in the developing world the first decade of the new century saw a drastic increase in funding and efforts in fighting killer diseases, such as HIV/AIDS, Tuberculosis (TB) and Malaria, as well as other poverty related health problems, such

© IFIP International Federation for Information Processing 2017
Published by Springer International Publishing AG 2017. All Rights Reserved
J. Choudrie et al. (Eds.): ICT4D 2017, IFIP AICT 504, pp. 536–547, 2017.
DOI: 10.1007/978-3-319-59111-7_44

as maternal and infant mortality. The UN Millennium Development Goals were formulated in 2000, the Global Fund to fight AIDS, TB and Malaria (GFATM) was established 2002 and the United States (US) Government PEPFAR program to fight HIV/AIDS commenced in 2008. One unintended consequence of this surge of funding for disease specific health programs was poor coordination and increased fragmentation of overall HISs in developing countries. Fit for purpose HIS was seen as critical for achieving the MDGs [3] and the World Health Organisation (WHO) established the Health Metrics Network (HMN) in 2005 as a global effort to support countries develop strong integrated national HIS, a measure to counteract the tendency of increased fragmentation of national HISs. The MDGs have now been replaced by the SDGs, but the international focus on strengthening country HISs as a key vehicle to achieve these goals remains pertinent. In 2016, WHO and other international agencies established the Health Data Collaborative as a forum, or 'low scale' agency for coordinating funding and support to countries for their efforts to strengthen their HISs and to pursue the SDGs [4]. Fragmentation and lack of coordination are still seen as key impediments for countries in developing their HIS.

We present the case of strengthening and integrating the HISs in Lao PDR, which has many challenges similar to other developing countries, such as fragmented and uncoordinated vertical disease specific programme HISs. While this case study starts with the efforts to strengthen the HIS in 2013, it is worth mentioning that in 2009–10 Lao PDR participated in the HMN process of (1) conducting a situation analysis of current systems, and (2) developing and implementing a strategic plan to harmonise and guide all HIS inputs. This HMN process, however, was not finalized due to lack of funding and a relatively abrupt termination of the HMN initiative in 2011, due to problems of funding and conflicts over strategies. It is important to note here that the integrated architecture promoted, called the HMN Framework [5], was largely accepted in the country and it has to a large extent been implemented during the process we present. The HMN architecture promotes a data warehouse approach to integration, where a central data repository integrates and manages aggregate data from multiple data sources, and uses various analytical tools, such as dashboards and GIS, for the output.

In Lao PDR, the DHIS2 open source platform has been utilised as the central data warehouse in line with the HMN architecture. It is employed first as a web-based data collection tool for the Health Management Information System (HMIS) in the Ministry of Health (MOH), then as data warehouse for other surveys, with legacy data supporting the analysis and development of national health statistics reports. Three years after it was implemented based on the HMIS reporting data sets, DHIS2 is an integrated HIS platform that hosts the reporting systems from 8 health programmes, which were previously uncoordinated separate HIS 'silos', one for each program. Given the current success, more health programs and reporting structures, such as reporting on financial data, are in the pipeline to be included

The development of the system was a participatory process with active involvement from both government sectors and development partners with coordinated support and use of the system under the national framework of the health sector reform, led by the MOH.

The remainder of this article has the following sections; (1) key concepts, (2) methodology, (3) the case study, (4) discussion, and (5) conclusion.

2 Key Concepts

Fragmented and poorly coordinated HIS, often to report to donor funded projects and programmes, are common problems in developing countries [1]. This situation creates both duplication and overlap of data collection and reporting and increased workload for health workers. Lack of coordination and integration also creates gaps in that essential data is not collected. In Lao PDR, such gaps are identified in the cross cutting areas of human resources, governance, finance and logistics, at all administrative levels. The HMN architecture promoted a data warehouse approach to integration, where aggregated data from different sources are managed in a central repository [5]. In a study of the efforts in countries to implement data warehouses to integrate national data, Sæbø et al. [6] identify three overall strategies:

1. The HMIS strategy; key data from different health programs are collected by the HMIS in order to have all data required to calculate essential indicators in 'one place', or in one data collection system. A consequence of this strategy is that data will be collected from multiple places. It might be seen as a legacy of the paper based systems, where sharing of data across (paper based) systems was difficult. This strategy has successfully been applied in South Africa.
2. All data in 'one bucket': All data collected are managed in one data warehouse. Data are not properly harmonised before being collected; due to different data collection procedures and sometimes also different definitions, the same data are collected by different health programs. This is an approach that needs to be part of a process to harmonise the data sets and to attain at a situation where all data are well defined and collected only once.
3. Aggregate data from all health programs are integrated within the data warehouse. Instead of running their own systems, all health programs use central data warehouse for their data. The advantages are; sharing of data, shared dashboards, and ease of coordination.

The first of these strategies, the HMIS strategy, was the typical strategy used by countries during the period of predominantly paper based systems. Today, many countries are applying a variation of the third option. A key challenge in being able to manage aggregate data from multiple programs is to be able to extract data from other transaction based systems, for example from HIV/AIDS electronic patient record systems.

The four cases studied by Sæbø et al. [6] all used various versions of the DHIS open source platform and they were all part of the so-called HISP action network. HISP is an international collaborative network where independent HISP groups, universities and health authorities in countries, all engaged in implementation focused projects, are sharing experiences and best practices [7]. The DHIS2 open source platform is a central part of the HISP action network. While the software development is being coordinated by the University of Oslo, participation and feedback from country implementations are the key components of the DHIS2 process.

With current technology development, especially the internet, ICT has become part of the health sector development, from supporting the networking and communication within health care facilities and administrative issues, to HIS, visualisation, sharing and disseminating of information. The establishment of the Asia eHealth Information Network (AeHIN) in 2010 has been important in bringing ICT solution into the core business of the health sector in the region. In Lao PDR, HIS is under the department of planning and international cooperation, it has the advantage of mobilising funding and the 'one shared plan' concept has been well supported by all involved development partners. Other partners such as JICA, Swiss Red Cross and Save the Children have provided additional support for training of MOH staff at central, province and district levels [8].

3 Methodology

The impetus behind this paper is to share learning from the process of applying DHIS2 for the health management information system as well as its expansion to become an integrated information platform in Lao PDR with the global health and ICT community, highlighting issues that are common to the process and describing how challenges were overcome.

The research methodology used has been based on action research approach [9], where three of the authors are part of global HISP network with experience in implementation of DHIS2 in different countries along with regional and global challenges facing HIS implementation. Implementation of DHIS2 in Lao PDR has followed a collaborative approach with team members from Ministry of Health, Development Partners both at country and regional/global level. The progress and challenges of implementation process and its output was shared and discussed in broader forums such as Asian eHealth Information Network conferences, regional DHIS2 Academies in Vietnam and conference and development partner meetings at country level.

The action research approach applied has not followed the prescribed cycles of design, development, implementation, use and evaluation [10] in a formal way. Rather, these concepts have been applied without following the sequence in the cycles in a strict way. Activities carried out during the project including the following:

- Repeated prototyping cycles of the DHIS2 application to incorporate the Lao PDR health administrative hierarchy and reporting structure and cycles of new requirements and the gradual incorporation of new health programs
- Standardization and harmonisation of the multiple data collection tools in use by engaging and negotiation with various national health programs
- Inclusion of key necessary data field in the routine HMIS to meet global standards and discussion with various stakeholders at country level
- Adaptation of standard data dictionary with its data source, frequency of reporting, common problems
- Creation of national core DHIS2 team including members from different health programs, departments and member of cabinet and linking them to global networks such as DHIS2 and AeHIN
- Restructuration of DHIS2 to enable integration of national health programs such as Malaria, TB, and HIV/AIDS
- Continuous discussions and updates of progress and challenges with Development Partners in Lao PDR and Global level

- Evaluation of the DHIS2 national implementation (June 2015 and Nov 2016)
- Routine update on progress and challenges to Cabinet of Lao PDR (2014 to 2016)
- Development of three dashboards highlighting the status of Lao PDR including Universal Health Coverage, MDG and Integrated HIS
- Presentation, meeting and discussion in regional form such as DHIS2 Regional Academy in Vietnam (2014, 2015, 2016) and AeHIN conference (2013 and 2015)

The implementation process of DHIS2 in Lao PDR began with joint appraisal missions with members from MOH, DHIS2 experts from the Oslo University and the private sector, development partners such as World Bank (WB), WHO and AeHIN members. The missions visited all administrative levels of the health system: from the community and health facility levels, to the district, province and national levels. The discussion engaged all potential stakeholders and users of health information to determine the country's situation, information usage and ICT landscape to support the reform of HIS. This process resulted in the joint decision of applying DHIS2 for HMIS as the first step toward an integrated health information system, as well as convincing new partners, such as WHO and the World Bank to support the process.

A team form HISP Vietnam (www.HISP.vn), experts on DHIS2, has provided technical assistance throughout the process. DHIS2 structure and operational procedures were designed with active participation from not only the software specialist, but also with public health staff from MOH at central level, and sub-national level HIS staff, together with some of the hospitals at central and provincial levels. This process ensured that the DHIS2-based HMIS reflected well the organisational structure of the Lao health system, yet retained flexibility and adaptability that are key features of the DHIS2, in order to meet the user's needs.

4   Implementing DHIS2 Application for Health Information System in Lao PDR

4.1   Background

Lao People's Democratic Republic is a landlocked country in South East Asia, bordering with China, Myanmar, Thailand, Cambodia and Vietnam. According to the Census of 2015 report, Lao PDR has a population of 6.5 million from 47 ethnic groups, 32% of them are between 10–24 years old and 67% live in rural areas. Despite the fact that the Lao HMIS has been set up with routine data collection since 2008 [11], the information was hardly generated and poorly used. Reasons for poor data quality and use are varied, but fragmentation of data collection and reporting systems that created burden for health facility staff to collect the data and to fill the required data collection forms represent a key problem. Delay in publication of National Health Statistic Report made it difficult for MOH and other stakeholders to use evidence for planning and decision making. As the information systems were organised in vertical 'silos' with limited data sharing across the program, using data from these systems to get an overview across program areas was difficult.

Furthermore, the health statistics division under the (former) planning and finance department in the MOH performed the only mandate of collect the HMIS data set. Other functions such as setting standards; developing policy and coordination with other reporting systems; database management etc. [11], despite having been stated in the HIS Strategy 2009–2015, was not effectively carried out, thus made HMIS another silo in the Lao HIS landscape. Non-wage domestic funding for the HIS implementation was not available, thus the implementation relied on the donor funding and supports.

As of October 2013, each health centre had to collect data into at least 17 different forms that were then reported upwards to the district. Many of the forms had overlapping data. The vaccination reports, for example, were submitted to both the EPI (Extended Programme on Immunisation) and the MCH (Mother and Child Health) programmes. Information sharing required issuance of lots of official documents yet standards and quality of information were uncertain. The HMIS reports were normally submitted very late to the central office, incomplete, and almost impossible to verify, for example, prior to the introduction of DHIS2, only half of the districts were recorded to have submitted their monthly reports to provincial level before these reports were consolidated to provincial quarterly reports for submission to central level [12]. The provinces did not see the need to follow up, and no national report would be published. During the period between 2005–2013, two national annual health statistics reports were produced, both by external consultants funded by donors through WHO Lao, indicating little local participation and ownership of the data and its utilisation.

The Ministry of Health of The Lao People's Democratic Republic developed a National Health Sector Reform (HSR) Strategy 2013–2025 [12], which highlights the twin goals of Millennium Development Goals (MDGs) by 2015 and Universal Health Coverage (UHC) by 2025. Key to this will be a creation of sufficient technological health infrastructure, to "establish and strengthen an effective health information system to monitor and evaluate the progress of achieving MDGs and UHC".

Under the HSR framework, the Ministry of Health (MOH) of Lao PDR decided to switch their health management information system (HMIS) from excel paper based to web-based DHIS2 at the end of 2013. After 3 years of further implementation, DHIS2 and the HMIS are now extended to include the reporting from the maternal and child health (MCH) programme; the immunisation programme (EPI), key intervention of the nutrition (NUT) programme; hospital in and out patient flows (OPD, IPD); and Malaria, TB and HIV programs [13].

4.2 Reforming the Lao HIS with DHIS2

The key components that Lao MOH considers as crucial for a successful implementation of any programme/project in the health sector, are the following:

- Leadership, legislation and coordination
- Internet connectivity and system configuration
- Technical capacity at all levels
- Financial sustainability

4.2.1   Leadership, Legislation and Coordination

In countries with centralised planning and governance structure like Lao PDR, ensuring the ownership and leadership of the government is critical. Informing and engaging with health sectors leaders have been the key to Lao DHIS2 integrated platform. The approval and support from MOH leaders have led to a number of legal documents that officially recognised DHIS2 and enabled the application to roll out smoothly. In addition, despite no domestic funding was invested in the DHIS application, leadership support have given a very strong signal to involve all development partners in health to support the system technically and financially. More importantly, it indirectly supports a single routine reporting system in the country, avoiding fragmentation and duplication. Legislation also plays a crucial role as an implementation framework for rolling out the DHIS2; a Ministerial decree stated that the country would implement DHIS2 country-wide and specified policy guidelines for unified data collection, data flow policy and implementation guidelines. This legal document also served as the foundation for the MOH statistics division, which, with support from HISP Vietnam, WHO, World Bank and other development agencies, could develop the national health information system policy and reporting guidelines [14].

Coordination and collaboration among partners in the support of the MOH to implement DHIS2 have played a crucial role in the process in Lao. The WHO country office has played the role of coordinating the other development partners and to ensure that the support to the MOH have kept the momentum, which is important in a country where most activities are funded by donors. At the strategic level, major donors like the WB, GF, Lux-Development, ADB and WHO, all have voiced their support on the integration of health information systems using the DHIS2 platform under the umbrella of the health sector reform. Given that donor driven systems are typically the main reason for the fragmentation of HIS in developing countries, this is an important shift for the health sector in the country. At implementation level, collaborated efforts made by other agencies have joined the support by using the reports generated by DHIS2, or build capacity for local staff on data use and analysis; supporting computer and internet connectivity, etc.

It's the collaboration between the complementary capacities of Lao MOH HIS unit, WHO HIS unit and HISP Vietnam that has ensured the day to day leadership of the project. These capacities have proven to be a good complementary blend:

- The MOH HIS unit represents the ownership, makes sure that legislation and regulations are in place, leading the standardisation process and coordinating within the MOH and with other ministries
- WHO takes the leading role of coordinator of the project, provide technical public health competence and they have the necessary authority to coordinate the partner community
- HISP Vietnam provides technical leadership and guidance on the DHIS2 system structure and configuration, server management and IT support

However, looking at how DHIS2 is implemented in other countries at the time of this paper being written such as Myanmar [15], Bangladesh [16], Mongolia, Indonesia where the government plays a strong leading roles in the implementation process, more balance is needed in Lao PDR between the needed leading role of the government and the support provided by partners.

4.2.2   Internet Connectivity and System Configuration

The big advantage of a web based system like DHIS2 is that no local software installation is needed; the disadvantage is the reliance on internet connectivity, albeit intermittently. Although the bandwidth required for users to enter data into the DHIS2 server is modest, computers, electricity, and some amount of connectivity are required. The DHIS2 server has been located to and managed by the eGovernment Centre, managed by the administration of Ministry of Telecommunication under a MOU between the two ministries. Server maintenance and connectivity are problematic due to the low internet speed and infrastructure set up, especially outside big cities.

The MOH (with support from WB and GF) has contracted internet providers to provide internet connection to all province and district health offices. 3G mobile network also covers >90% of the country geographically in 2015, according to the Ministry of Communication. By the end of 2016, Internet connectivity is available in all districts and most health facilities, but remains slow and unreliable many places. Computers and laptops are available in all health facilities, but appropriate use of them as shared tools for data entry and report generation are limited because they will typically be owned by particular projects and programs, making sharing difficult. Managerial instruction to share IT equipment is often required.

4.2.3   Capacity Development

Capacity development is the key to rendering the system sustainable and useful. National and provincial teams play a crucial role in ensuring data quality and that the data are being used and that the system is managed and adapted to the needs of the users. According to the appraisal assessment, capacity of the staff working in HIS across country is generally low. The job assignment to these staff prior to the DHIS2 application was to consolidate reports for submission to higher level. This historical legacy has made building capacity the most important part of the HIS strengthening process in Lao PDR. The role and function of HIS staff at all levels will need to change from only focus on data consolidation and reporting to have data analysis, monitoring and feedback as the major focus.

Building a national core team (NCT) is critical and essential to the effectiveness and sustainability of the DHIS2 based HIS. This was prioritised at the beginning of the implementation with focus on building a team with members from key related departments and partners. WHO, in collaboration with MOH and Global Fund have recruited and built capacity of a team of local young professionals working in the core team to support the country in the longer term. WHO has mobilized from other networks such as UNV to have additional staff working closely with the national team, building their capacity in system management and DHIS2.

Building subnational teams for provincial and district levels was the next step to sustain the new web based HIS. The provincial participants are trained to be able to manage DHIS2 at their level, support the district team and to provide reports, dashboards and enable managers to use data.

The biggest shift in the reporting system is that district information staff at district hospital and district health offices are now responsible for capturing data in a national system, while the roles of district and provincial health statistics teams are to ensure data quality and to approve data before submission, or publishing. The National Core Team functions changed from data consolidation to setting standards, coordinating with involved health programs and generating regular periodical reports to be disseminated countrywide within the health sector, government and other sectors. The provincial and district managers play a crucial role in improving the reporting system by regularly checking data quality, ensuring that reports are submitted on time and requesting for support when needed.

4.2.4   Funding and Financial Resources

The DHIS2 platform is free, but like any sophisticated software platforms, significant resources are required for customization and training – both initially and ongoing, as the Ministry wishes to introduce more functionality and extend the system to new categories of users. The implementation started in five southern provinces with World Bank funding. Then, under the flagship of health sector reform and WHO technical assistance, the MOH was able to mobilise support from other partners to cover the rest of the country with funding from Lux- Dev. UNFPA, UNICEF, KOICA, KOFHI. In this way, coordination of funding from multiple partners made it possible to roll out the DHIS2 countrywide. The Government also allocates a budget to the implementation.

The concept of one plan - one routine HIS system, and the Vientiane Declaration of Aid Effectiveness, which calls for harmonisation of donor funded plans and government plans, have enabled MOH to shift the ownership of DHIS2 to beyond a vertical programme and make it a crosscutting area of the health system. A main challenge is to be able to continue the domestic funding of the DHIS2 and HIS strengthening process so as to arrive at financial sustainability.

5   Discussion

The most significant advantage for the DHIS2 process in Lao PDR is that the process started when the health sector reform strategy and framework had just been approved and the existing HIS was of poor quality. The reform document provided a policy pathway and strategic framework on which the concept and design of the DHIS2 application were discussed and agreed upon. This was also an opportunity to strengthen the use of HIS in the sector for planning, M&E and budgeting, thus making HIS a more significant part of the national health system.

The Department of Planning and International Cooperation, who is in charge of HIS, has suggested that the best way to sustain the current DHIS2 based system is to institutionalise the integration of multiple sub-systems using the DHIS2 platform. This can be seen as a strategy to both (1) continue strengthening the current DHIS2 based system, and (2) be flexible and ready for further expansion and justification to meet additional needs of the MOH at different levels.

The case of Lao PDR shows that applying ICT such as DHIS2 to strengthen HIS in a country low on resources and human capacity and with a poorly functioning HIS, has certain advantages. The advantages have been the opportunity to setting up standards and norms for an IT foundation nearly from scratch, enable the government to use their authority to set the legislation for a systematic implementation of the project, and the request from donors and partners to use and support one single system have created a supportive environment for the implementation of the system. Particularly important has been the ability to establish shared standards for both the DHIS2 system and for data reporting and thereby being able to overcome the traditional fragmentation of reporting systems from different health programs and competing software systems. this conducive environment for setting standards have been an important enabler for the relatively rapid rollout and expansion of the reformed HIS in Lao PDR, as compared with other countries [6].

Funding of the HIS remains a challenge, as all activities and key staff are funded through donors. The HIS Centre have applied the concept of one single routine system – multiple partners, allowing partners to send their staff to work together with the MOH team and build their capacity. This is just a short term solution, for the longer term, securing domestic funding and capacity will be a key priority in order to ensure sustainability. Data use among managers and decision makers at all levels of the health system remains as another priority and goal of the system. Progress in this area will be crucial for the sustainability of the system.

Apart from TB, all health programmes now integrated in DHIS2, previously used a paper based system with Excel as their 'database', thus making the switch from Excel to DHIS both sensible and relatively easy. The paper based routine reporting systems, however, were not easy to change, as they represented well established systems and standards, or installed base [17]. At the early stage of developing the roadmap for integration, several of the vertical paper and Excel based reporting systems were found to be underperforming. After the successful roll out of the HMIS data collection forms using the DHIS2 platform, the various vertical programs and projects realized that a web based database system would be both possible and easier to use for managing their data than their current systems. They could see that the new HMIS using the DHIS2 had already laid the basic human and technical infrastructure that they also could use. It was therefore relatively easy to reach consensus on integration and to make use of the new online system, which also included dashboards, GIS and data visualisation features. The fact that the major health programs have all joined the DHIS2 process means that DHIS2 has become part of the installed base of pre-existing and long-time running reporting systems, which is promising in terms of being able to institutionalise and sustain the DHIS2. Challenges ahead will include building capacity and strengthening the infrastructure to support the expansion of the system, while at the same time maintaining the current operational and productive platform.

Comparing the Lao PDR process within the framework of 4 strategies for integration described in Sæbø et al. [6], we see that the Lao PDR process started out as pure HMIS system in 2013 (as South Africa), including the key data variables from several programs. During the following process of incorporating new health programs, data elements and data sets have been standardised in order to remove duplications and to be able to accommodate multiple data sets and data sources within one data warehouse, similar to the example from Zanzibar in Sæbø et al. [6].

6 Conclusion

Three years after the initial discussions on applying ICT for strengthening the Lao HMIS in September 2013, DHIS2 has been established as the official health information platform in Lao PDR, integrating an increasing number of sub-systems. Routine data reported from health facilities countrywide are collected and managed in the platform, which is now established as a national data warehouse and dashboards and statistical reports are used for dissemination of information and for monitoring key indicators by MOH and the Government of Lao.

As in many similar settings in developing countries, key challenges are related to insufficient human capacity, poor infrastructure and little or no systematic use of data for planning and decision making. Further strengthening and sustainability of the platform will depend on. Sustainability will depend on how well these challenges are being addressed. The current and planned expansion of the platform to other health programs and reporting systems will help pooling more human and other resources to the platform, as well as widen and strengthen the ownership at all levels of the health services.

References

1. Chilundo, B., Aanestad, M.: Negotiating multiple rationalities in the process of integrating the information systems of disease-specific health programmes. Electron. J. Inf. Syst. Dev. Ctries **20**(2), 1–28 (2004)
2. Jeppsson, A., Okuonzi, S.A.: Vertical or holistic decentralization of the health sector? experiences from Zambia and Uganda. Int. J. Health Plan. Manage. **15**, 273–289 (2000)
3. AbouZahr, C., Boerma, T.: Health information systems: the foundations of public health. Bull. World Health Organ. **83**(8), 578–583 (2005)
4. Health data collaborative (2016). http://www.healthdatacollaborative.org/
5. Health Metric Network. Framework and Standards for Country Health Information Systems (2008). http://who.int/healthmetrics/en/
6. Sæbø, J., Kossi, E., Titlestad, O., Tohouri, R., Braa, J.: Comparing strategies to integrate health information systems following a data warehouse approach in four countries. Inf. Technol. Dev. **17**(1), 42–60 (2011)
7. Braa, J., Monteiro, E., Sahay, S.: Networks of action: sustainable health information systems across developing countries. MIS Q. **28**(3), 337–362 (2004)
8. MOH. DHIS2 review report (2015)
9. Braa, K., Nilsen, P.: Sustainable action research: the network of action approach. In: IFIP.9.4, pp. 331–343 (2015)
10. Susman, G., Evered, R.: An assessment of the scientific merits of action research. Adm. Sci. Q. **23**(4), 582–603 (1978)
11. MOH, Lao PDR. Health Information System Strategy 2009–2015 (2008)
12. MOH, Lao PDR. Health Sector Reform Strategy 2013–2025 (2012)
13. MOH, Lao PDR. Roadmap to Integration of TB, HIV and Malaria to HMIS (2016)
14. MOH, Lao PDR. Health Information Policy and Guideline for DHIS2 (2014)

15. MOH, Myanmar. Review of DHIS2 implementation experience (2016)
16. USAID, Bangladesh. Bangladesh Health Information Mapping Analysis (2015)
17. Hanseth, O., Monteiro, E.: Inscribing behaviour in information infrastructure standards. Account. Manage. Inf. Technol. **7**(4), 183–211 (1997)

From Routine to Revolt: Improving Routine Health Data Quality and Relevance by Making Them Public

Thanh Ngoc Nguyen[✉] and Petter Nielsen

Department of Informatics, University of Oslo, Oslo, Norway
{thanhng,pnielsen}@ifi.uio.no

Abstract. Health Information Systems in developing countries struggle with vicious cycles of lack of information use. Substantial investment has been spent to improve the situation but results are still very limited. Adding to the body of research on strategies and solutions to break out of such cycles, this paper focuses on the effects of making routine data public through mass media and using data to fuel debates on critical health issues. Based on an action research project building a reporting system for accidents and emergencies during the Tet holiday in Vietnam, this paper discuss how making data public can have direct impact on the use and quality of health data in the health system. We discuss and draw implications related to tactics to improve the demand and use of routine health data.

Keywords: Information use · Data quality · Rapid scaling

1 Introduction

Health Information Systems (HISs) have long been recognized as an important component of public health systems because they provide vital data for effective planning and sound decision making [1]. Although HISs play an important role in improving healthcare service delivery, they often fail, especially in developing countries [2]. Many HISs end their life-cycle in the pilot stage because they do not scale and provide useful data for managers [3]. Together with the scaling challenge, developing countries are also challenged by health managers' limited use of data in decision making. Nutley, Gnassou [4] argue that turning data into action is critical for improving the health services delivery and outcomes. There are many reasons attributed to limited data use, including culture and capacity [5] as well as the information needs of decision makers [6]. Another complication is the poor quality of data. Braa, Hanseth [3] use the notion of a vicious cycle to refer to situations in which "national health data are used little because they are of poor quality, and their relative lack of use, in turn, makes their quality remain poor" (p. 379). This is a hard to break cycle. Several attempts have been made to break out of the vicious data use cycle (see for example Nutley and Reynolds [1], Braa, Heywood [2], Rhoads and Ferrara [3]). These attempts can broadly be classified into two streams. The first deals with problems related to the data supply side such as data quality, availability, and access. The second stream focuses on the demand side by encouraging data use based on changing social institutions such as information culture and human capacity.

J. Choudrie et al. (Eds.): ICT4D 2017, IFIP AICT 504, pp. 548–558, 2017.
DOI: 10.1007/978-3-319-59111-7_45

With a focus on understanding data use and approaches to generate data demand from decision makers, we conducted an action research which involved the design, customization, and implementation of an information system that supports the collection and analysis of various health indicators during the Lunar New Year in Vietnam between 2014 and 2016. Data reported from more than one thousand hospitals and health facilities (accounting for 95% hospitals in Vietnam) revealed a harsh reality of violence and traffic accidents during Lunar New Year holidays. And the general public was perplexed when figures of traffic accidents announced by MoH and Ministry of Public Security (MPS) contradicted each other significantly. It also sparked a big public debate on data quality, data collection and related processes.

In developing countries, routine health data and indicators are not usually high in demand. Those collecting it commonly collect it only for the purpose of upward reporting and receive little if any feedback. And those receiving it commonly do not trust the data nor use it for decision making. This paper presents a contrasting case to this where the mundane and neglected routine health data suddenly was in the spotlight.

The rest of this paper is organized as follows. In the next section, we review related research and debates on the problem of data use and offer our perspective. Research method and the case description are provided in Sects. 3 and 4 respectively. We discuss the findings and implications for theory and practice in Sect. 5 before conclude the paper in Sect. 6.

2   Related Research

The ultimate goal of any HISs intervention is to ensure quality data that informs decision making. Informed decisions will lead to better use of limited and often scarce resources where they are needed. If data are not used, HISs and efforts to collect, aggregate and distribute health data are meaningless. Unfortunately, despite investments in and improvements of HISs, lack of data use is common (Braa et al., 2012, Wyber et al., 2015). This section presents recent studies that discuss efforts to tackle the problem of little data use.

Lomas [7] in a study from the healthcare sector in Canada emphasizes the role of intermediaries in disseminating research results, thus facilitating the use of health data. He argues that there is a poor understanding of context where the research result is generated and realities facing policy makers. A solution to this problem is to improve the communication between the two sides. He discusses the approach that has been applied in Canada for many years, which involves the institutionalization of the knowledge brokering roles in disseminating the data. In particular, research results should be communicated effectively and succinctly through Mythbusters and Evidence Boost, which are a form of research summary, to other groups of users such as legislative, administrative, and industrial decision-makers.

Bowen, Erickson [8] identify 8 different barriers that constrain the use of data for decision making in a study that involves health staff from 11 Regional Health Authorities in Manitoba province of Canada in three years. They argue that efforts to improve data accessibility and data use competency are important but might not increase the level of data use if the key barriers to the issue are not properly lifted. Their findings include an interesting discovery of "politics trumps evidence" which refers to a phenomenon where data are sought to back a political decision rather than inform decision making process. Sometimes, decision makers could not make an evidence-informed decision because they lack of means and supporting structure to implement a decision. Nutley and Reynolds [9] synthesize previous works related to the issue of health data use including the World Health Organization's Health Metric Network tool [10], the Performance of Routine Information System Management (PRISM) framework [11, 12], Lomas [7], and Patton [13] to propose a comprehensively logical model that encompasses a set of eight processes and activities to strengthen data use.

In a developing country context, Braa, Heywood [14] conduct an action research with the aim to break the "vicious cycle" of data quality and data use. The underlying assumption of their intervention is that piecemeal increased data use can gradually improve the data quality and build up data use capacity. Quarterly workshops on data use are organized at both national and district levels. During the workshops, district staff will show data from their districts and present their own interpretation while other district staff will discuss and criticize. In three years between 2005 and 2008, there are noticeable changes in data use as a result of the intervention. Similarly, based on action research in Kenya with the aim to establish mutually agreed activities among key stakeholders to improve data use for action, Manya et al. (2015) argue that data quality audits must be organized at the same time with monthly data review meetings and training in data management in order to address the problem of little use of data. Moyo and Kaasbøll [15] also discusses the process of development and introduction of a League Table to compare the performance of different health districts in Malawi. They argue that the module is a useful tool to remedy the problem of information transparency. Also according to them, transparency of information should be treated as a totality of all aspects including disclosure, clarity, and accuracy rather than separately.

In the extant literature on the use of health data, the attention is central on how to provide health managers high quality data to support the decision making process. There is little discussion on how health data mean to the public and how the public can participate in the routine health system design and use. Presumably, most data from the routine health management information systems (HMIS) are supposed to serve managerial purposes. The public who is subject of all health policies is often ignored from such systems and they do not have access to their data. They neither know about how such systems operate, what data are collected nor raise their voice on how such systems should be designed to benefit them. The primary aim of this research is to contribute to that discussion and more specifically focus on finding appropriate approaches that could make boring routine health data become attractive to the public.

3   Method

This research follows an action research approach [16]. Action research is a method that aims to solve practical problems and at the same time generate theoretical knowledge [17]. Action researchers have dual responsibilities: to improve the situation and to report findings of their study. Action research is different from other methods in its ability to develop knowledge for both theory and practice. In studying technology in social context, action research is a strong candidate [18]. While there are many forms of action research, canonical action research is commonly used as it ensures the rigor of the research [19].

Data for this study mainly come from the daily interactions, participation and observations of the first author in the daily activities of the project. A research diary was used to capture important events, incidents, or other important discussions related to the system development and implementation. To improve the reliability, data from this source were regularly shared with the second author to independently verify. Other modes of data collection include interviews. A total of 15 interviews with different kinds of informants: MoH officials (2), the technical and support teams (6), provincial health administrators (2), and data clerks from hospitals (5) was conducted in early 2014 through face to face and phone. Each interview lasted between 30 and 45 min. Notes were taken during the interviews for subsequent use in the analysis step. Informants who were hospital users were selected from those who called the supporting team to get support. The purpose of these interviews was thus to understand better users' difficulties in using the system. Examples of interview questions for this type of informants were *"How do you find the design of that functionality? How should it be improved?"*. Archival records were another means utilized for collecting data. To understand the view of the public on various social issues such as traffic accidents and violence during Tet, mass media articles were also considered, mostly in the electronic form (e-newspapers) including statements of officials from the Government and Assembly.

After being collected, data was grouped into broad themes such as technical infrastructure and social infrastructure, the rapid process of development and implementation of the system, the inconsistency of reported data in comparison with other available sources, and the public's attitudes and the perspectives of different governmental agencies. Several concepts from the literature information transparency, development, and data use were used to guide the analytical process. Part of the analysis process is the narrative of the case, which is now presented.

4   The Case

In early 2014, the Department of Medical Services Administration (VAMS) of the Ministry of Health decided to build an online system to support collecting data related to accident and emergency during the Lunar New Year (Tet) in Vietnam. A medical doctor from VAMS, who is responsible for Information Technology (IT) and health data, consulted a technical team (here after called the DHIS2 Team) that had worked in previous health information systems projects at MoH. His aim was to explore the possibilities of using an open source platform especially developed for the health sector called DHIS2 (dhis2.org) to build an online system for Tet reporting. As the decision by VAMS was made very late, they only had one week to complete the system. After some considerations, the DHIS2 Team confirmed that they were able to build the system and immediately embarked on the mission. DHIS2 is a software platform developed by University of Oslo, Norway. It provides a flexible mechanism in handling data elements and forms, making it easy to define new datasets. However, the default data entry form in DHIS2 only allowed data entry for one period at a time. This was considered to be confusing for the users. The team thus decided to design a custom data-entry form that shows multiple periods in a single screen.

After building the data entry forms, the DHIS2 Team deployed the system on one of MoH servers. A few months before Tet, MoH had implemented a hospital quality and inventory system which was also based on the same DHIS2 software. User accounts for this system were generated using a script and forwarded in Excel files to each health province which subsequently forwarded to their subordinate hospitals. The DHIS2 Team decided to leverage this existing user base. Since they already had access and knew the system, this would shorten the implementation process and eliminate the need of training. An official letter requesting hospitals to use the Tet reporting system was distributed by the MoH.

As it was the first year using the Tet reporting system, many hospitals still viewed the system as a "pilot". As a consequence, lack of rigor in data entry was observed. Some users entered garbage numbers into important fields like injured cases by firecrackers, as if such figures would not be subsequently aggregated and reported to the government and visible to the public via mass media. It should be also noted that according to the law in Vietnam, the head of province will receive disciplinary action if there is illegal use of firecrackers in his/her province. To avoid such data entry incidents, the IT specialist from MoH who was assigned to work on this system had to frequently verify if there were any suspicious numbers entered. He also called the person who was responsible for reporting on that day in the hospital to confirm the reported numbers.

During the Tet 2014, data from more than one thousand hospitals were daily aggregated by MoH and subsequently reported to the Government Office. Many journalists approached MoH to acquire data to write articles because they believe accident and emergency during the Tet are matters of public concern. After articles were published, the public was shocked to know that nearly 7,000 people were hospitalized, out of which 15 people died, due to violence during the 9 days of the Tet holiday. The Deputy Chair of Social Committee, Vietnam Assembly said: "This figure was an alarm of the increasing violence in our society. It was very unusual because the Tet holidays were the time dedicated for joy and relax. The Committee welcomes MoH for its first time publication of the data which we did not have previously." [20]. The Prime Minister insisted that such figures were very serious and directed all concerned agencies to propose and implement effective measures to mitigate violence [21].

In addition, many scholars, educators, and psychologists proactively joined the debate, trying to locate the root causes of the issue. An economist from the Center of Economic Research in the South stated: "People solve their conflicts by using violence because they have lost their trust on justice and government" [22]. And a researcher from Research Center of Sino-Nom said: "It is a really crisis of the crowd, once its psychology is compressed throughout the year and it bursts on the Tet. It accumulates all conflicts with the root cause of unstable and insecure society. Culture, morality, and education in Vietnam have never been degraded like they are now" [20, 22]. There was a broad agreement that in combination with stricter punishment for violent crimes, schools should focus more on ethical and behavioral education for youngsters.

Regarding the reported figures of traffic accidents, the public was at the same time very puzzled by the gap [23] between the figures announced by Ministry of Public Security (MPS) and Ministry of Health (MoH). While the figures published by MPS showed a significant decrease in the number of injuries (−25%) and death (−5%), MoH announced an increase of traffic accidents during the Tet holiday. Quantitatively, MPS reported only 408 traffic accidents whereas MoH reported more than 40,000 hospitalized cases related traffic accidents. This triggered debates related to the trustworthiness of these two different information sources. For instance, the Head of Road Transportation Department (MPS) argued that the police could only collect data from traffic accidents that were reported to them while, in reality, most victims were transferred directly to hospitals. This argument was supported by a statement made by a representative of National Committee of Transportation Safety (NCTS): "NCTS will make a proposal to the Prime Minister to get permission to use data from MoH as an official source for traffic accident reporting, instead of exclusively using data from the police" [24].

5   Analysis and Discussion

The design and implementation of the Tet reporting system can be considered as a successful story because it rapidly achieved national coverage and generated data that triggered public debates on several social issues. We now provide analysis on how the system attracted the public's attention to what is commonly treated as boring and mundane routine data.

5.1   Collecting Data that Highly Concern the Public and Commodifying Health Data

Hospital users often see reporting duty as a burden rather than something useful for them or the healthcare sector (Krickeberg, 2007, Kuhn and Giuse, 2001, Littlejohns et al., 2003). In the case of the Tet reporting system, the number of data elements was minimal and only important data elements were included. The small dataset approach also helped reduce complexities of the system both at technical and social levels. The flat structure of dataset made the design and use of the system become easy and helped shrink "the time to market" (Smith, 2004). This small dataset approach has another implication. Data entry forms of HISs in developing countries tend to be overly complex (Sahay et al., 2010) and merely serve the need of health managers. The public, however, should have the right to know about data that directly concern their life. In other words, HISs should also be designed in a way that it collects kinds of data that are highly related to the lives of majority of citizens. This is not the case in Vietnam where figures on traffic accidents and violence are completely absent on the routine report.

Routine health data are often too complex to understand and use even for health professionals [15]. In order to attract attention of the public, the data need to be simplified and commodified. For example, the number of deaths related to traffic accidents and number of injuries related to violence are simple and easy enough for anyone to understand. The use of raw numbers to some extent gives better impression about the situation compared to the use of indicators. Regardless the size of the population, thousands of people injured by violence is something hard to believe and unacceptable.

Commodifying data also relates to the two aspects of information transparency which are disclosure and clarity [15, 25]. While disclosure only focuses on the availability and accessibility of data to interested parties which are very often governmental agencies and not-for-profits organizations, commodifying also involves making sense of data to the public. In the attempt to engage the public in the debate of critical health issues, clarity must be more focused to the level that it is understandable for the public who do not know anything about the healthcare domain.

5.2   Engaging Mass Media and Fueling Public Debates

Routine health data are often moved upward, i.e. from health facilities to higher level. Little if any feedback from higher level health managers are provided to health facilities after data are reported [26]. To attract the public's attention on critical health issues, novel channels of rapid and large-scaled data propagation must be sought. One such channel is mass media, i.e. newspapers and magazines. With large numbers of readers and hourly news posting, newspapers (both paper-based and online) can draw attentions from the public in a quick and effective way. Also, thanks to the rhetoric of journalists, titles of articles are often written in an impressive and attractive way which no doubt makes the boring and mundane data become lively and attract the attention of the public.

As a general practice, mass media often engage important and renowned figures to comment on emergent social issues. They can be professors from universities, experts in various domains, and incumbent officials or politicians. This approach is to bring the readers multiple perspectives on a particular issue. In the case of violence, the debate of data accuracy was sparked by MPS officials who expressed suspicion on the big number of hospitalized cases because of violence. There was a firm response from the Head of Medical Service Administration (VAMS, MoH) about that. The response included the unpacking of procedures and systems through which the number was aggregated. This was an important step to keep the dialog continue and remain constructive. Later, the IT specialist who was the key contact point of the project agreed to give an exclusive interview to an online newspaper on the history and backstage story of how the system was built and implemented.

5.3   Creating Feedbacks and Triangulating Data

Also through newspapers the public knew more about the work of hospitals during the holiday. This gave users the feeling of participation. Through the circulation process, data are extensively validated and flexibly interpreted by a large collection of human actors. We argue that data circulation processes are crucial for sustainable HISs as it blurs the boundaries between data collection and data use, creating the congeniality [27] between the ICT initiative and the environment. The findings of our case are slightly distinct from literature discussing the role of new social media such as Facebook, Twitter etc. on changing awareness of the public and creating new channel of two-way communication between public health experts and the public. Recent works on social media emphasize the significance and effectiveness of using social media to engage the public in public health issues [28–31]. However, we argue that depending on the situation, traditional media are still very powerful means in amplifying and visualizing health issues to the public which in turn would help to increase accountability and transparency.

We believe one factor that played an important role in the success of the Tet system was the feedback mechanism. The extant literature often reports cases of HISs in which data reported by data entry clerks do not receive adequate feedbacks to improve the quality of data [32]. In our case, there exist two types of feedback mechanisms: feedback from MoH to hospitals and from the public to hospitals. As the reporting process took place on a daily basis, hospitals received feedback from MoH within almost the same day. This instant feedback played a crucial role in not only improving data quality but also increasing the completeness of data. In order to have timely data to report to government and share with the public, the technical team had to play the role of designer and user at the same time. For example, they had to check data on an hourly basis to early discover any mistake in reported data. They had to call hospitals to verify the figures and sometimes directly modified them. In another flow of feedback, when a data entry clerk reported a figure through the system, the figure was aggregated at the national and subsequently shared with the public. As a member of the public, the clerk also received that aggregated figure and had her own interpretation thus she became a user of the system.

Many studies report the problem of fragmentation in HISs in developing countries (see for example Chilundo and Aanestad [33]). Fragmentation refers to the situation where multiple, duplicate and overlapping systems coexist but cannot provide data necessary for decision making. While we agree that overlap in data collection should be minimized to the best extent, in some special occasions, it is a chance for restructuring and improvement. For example, in the case of traffic accident reporting, MPS and MoH are the two agencies that have routine data collection systems. The contradiction in data reported by the two systems made the public suspicious about the veracity of the data. The number of traffic accidents reported by MPS system was unreasonably too small compared to what reported by MoH system. As a result of this triangulation, the Head of National Traffic Safety Committee agreed that data from MoH system would be incorporated into the report next year.

5.4 Getting Full-Coverage Data Ready and Publishing Data

One of the issue that face HISs practitioners and researchers is the dilemma of "all or nothing" (see Braa, Hanseth [3]). Incomplete data for a geographical area have little value in use. Complete and Full-coverage data is only attainable when a full scale implementation of HISs is achieved. Scaling, however, is a big challenge as it is not about mechanically replicating the same technical artefact to other contexts but also multiple sociotechnical rearrangements [34].

Research emphasizes the role of installed base in terms of existing technology and established use practices in shaping (and being shaped) the outcome of ICT interventions [35]. Taking advantage of what already exists to kick-start, or bootstrap [36], is an advisable strategy. The Tet reporting system was built on the existing DHIS2 software system already implemented in the hospitals. By leveraging the existing software, the team cut down the expensive and lengthy processes of full life cycle of software development. Since users at the hospital were knowledgeable of the DHIS2 system, expensive and time consuming training was not necessary. DHIS2 has a data entry module that is highly configurable to adapt to a wide range of requirements. However, this module is sometimes too complicated for beginners. The technical team was inspired by the design of social media tools such as Facebook where anyone can create an account and start to use Facebook without attending any training classes. Therefore, they designed the system in a way that minimal or no training was needed. For instance, the data entry form was customized to enable data entry for multiple days in a single screen. Also, a report printing button was integrated into the data entry form, making it easier for users to view and export data to other formats such as Microsoft Excel for further processing. This approach was also more responsive to changing requirements. For instance, the Tet reporting system required an additional dataset. This could be easily be made through the dataset management module of DHIS2. No line of code was required. As a result, the system became ready in a short time.

Many researchers emphasize the role of good data in improving the quality of health service delivery [37, 38]. Substantial efforts have been made in building reliable and sustainable HISs. However, having data does not automatically lead to data use. Noir and Walsham [39] discuss the ceremonial and mythical use of HISs in the public health sector in India where health centers entered data into local computers, exported them to flash drives and carried the flash drives to higher level to submit data. The authors challenge the simplistic view that ICTs adoption will directly generate efficiency and gains. In our case study, the collected data were processed by the MoH team and subsequently shared with other stakeholders and news agencies to trigger data use process. The decision of MoH to publish the data to mass media created a feedback loop that reinforced the data reporting activities at hospitals, motivating hospitals to collect and report accurate data.

Publishing data goes in hand with accountability and transparency because MoH must be responsible for data it published. Prior to the implementation of this system, MoH only used the data for internal management. It was not obliged to make the data public. This decision was thus an important step toward public transparency. And public transparency led to public accountability.

6   Conclusion

Making life better is a goal of any ICTs project. This research presents an empirical case where data collected by a software system were used to trigger public debates that could contribute to shape policy and the public's attitudes. The approach discussed in the paper emphasizes the significance of selecting matters of public concern (few critical data elements) and rapidly scaling the implementation to get full data coverage. Collected data are disseminated and amplified by mass media to attract public's attention and trigger debates. Through the mass media, public express their concerns on critical health issues. As a collective effect, voices of people are better heard by the government.

Lessons learnt from this research are hoped to provide public health administrators and IT practitioners design ideas and principles that help design sustainable HISs that empower people especially those who are marginalized. Time constraint did not allow us to venture deeply into the interpretations of collected data, i.e. geographical analysis of violent cases or traffic accidents. We believe the quantitative analysis in this area will be useful for the public and policy makers in preventing and reducing the cases related to traffic and violence. Our findings also contribute to the debates of how to improve the efficiency of HISs through the use of data for decision making.

References

1. AbouZahr, C., Boerma, T.: Health information systems: the foundations of public health. Bull. World Health Organ. **83**(8), 578–583 (2005)
2. Heeks, R.: Information systems and developing countries: failure, success, and local improvisations. Inf. Soc. **18**(2), 101–112 (2002)
3. Braa, J., et al.: Developing health information systems in developing countries: the flexible standards strategy. Manage. Inf. Syst. Q. **31**(2), 381–402 (2007)
4. Nutley, T., et al.: Moving data off the shelf and into action: an intervention to improve data-informed decision making in Cote d'Ivoire. Global Health Action **7** (2014)
5. Braa, J., Sahay, S.: Integrated Health Information Architecture: Power to the Users: Design, Development and Use. Matrix Publishers, New Delhi (2012)
6. Davies, P., et al.: Conceptualising the information needs of senior decision makers in health. Health Inform Syst Knowl Hub **18**, 1–20 (2011)
7. Lomas, J.: The in-between world of knowledge brokering. BMJ **334**(7585), 129–132 (2007)
8. Bowen, S., et al.: More than "using research": the real challenges in promoting evidence-informed decision-making. Healthc. Policy **4**(3), 87 (2009)
9. Nutley, T., Reynolds, H.W.: Improving the use of health data for health system strengthening. Global Health Action **6**, 20001 (2013)
10. Health Metrics Network and World Health Organization: Assessing the National Health Information System: An Assessment Tool. World Health Organization (2008)
11. Aqil, A.: PRISM case studies: strengthening and evaluating RHIS. MEASURE Evaluation, USAID (2008)
12. Aqil, A., Lippeveld, T., Hozumi, D.: PRISM framework: a paradigm shift for designing, strengthening and evaluating routine health information systems. Health Policy Plan. **24**(3), 217–228 (2009)
13. Patton, M.Q.: Utilization-Focused Evaluation. Sage publications, Thousand Oaks (2008)
14. Braa, J., Heywood, A., Sahay, S.: Improving quality and use of data through data-use workshops: Zanzibar, United Republic of Tanzania. Bull. World Health Organ. **90**(5), 379–384 (2012)
15. Moyo, C., et al.: The information transparency effects of introducing league tables in the health system in Malawi. Electron. J. Inf. Syst. Dev. Countries **75**, 1–16 (2016)
16. Avison, D.E., et al.: Action research. Commun. ACM **42**(1), 94–97 (1999)
17. Winter, R.: Learning from Experience: Principles and Practice in Action-Research. Falmer Press, London (1989)
18. Baskerville, R.L., Wood-Harper, A.T.: A critical perspective on action research as a method for information systems research. In: Willcocks, L.P., Sauer, C., Lacity, M.C. (eds.) Enacting Research Methods in Information Systems: Volume 2, pp. 169–190. Springer, Cham (2016). doi:10.1007/978-3-319-29269-4_7

19. Davison, R., Martinsons, M.G., Kock, N.: Principles of canonical action research. Inf. Syst. J. **14**(1), 65–86 (2004)
20. MoH_Portal. 6.200 cases hospitalized due to violence: usual or unsual? (2015). http://moh.gov.vn:8086/news/Pages/TinKhacV2.aspx?ItemID=569
21. Life&Law. Prime Minister: Violence during Tet is not minor. Life and Law (2015). http://www.doisongphapluat.com/xa-hoi/thu-tuong-khong-the-xem-thuong-chuyen-danh-nhau-dip-tet-a84907.html
22. Vu, A.: Why aggressive behavior is on the throne. RFA (2015)
23. Tuong, T.: Every institution reports a different number: the public can not trust (2016)
24. Ha, M.: Death by traffic accident: contradictory figures (2016). http://thanhnien.vn/thoi-su/chet-vi-tai-nan-giao-thong-moi-co-quan-bao-cao-mot-kieu-667572.html
25. Schnackenberg, A.K., Tomlinson, E.C.: Organizational transparency a new perspective on managing trust in organization-stakeholder relationships. J. Manage. **42**, 1784–1810 (2014). doi:10.1177/0149206314525202
26. Charles, N., Geoff, W.: The great legitimizer: ICT as myth and ceremony in the Indian healthcare sector. Inf. Technol. People **20**(4), 313–333 (2007)
27. Sanner, T.A., Manda, T.D., Nielsen, P.: Grafting: balancing control and cultivation in information infrastructure innovation. J. Assoc. Inf. Syst. **15**(4), 220–243 (2014)
28. Abroms, L.C., Schiavo, R., Lefebvre, C.: New media cases in Cases in Public Health Communication & Marketing: the promise and potential. Cases Public Health Commun. Market. **2**, 3–9 (2008)
29. Heldman, A.B., Schindelar, J., Weaver III, J.B.: Social media engagement and public health communication: implications for public health organizations being truly "social". Public Health Rev. **35**(1), 1 (2013)
30. Newbold, K.B., Campos, S.: Media and Social Media in Public Health Messages: A Systematic Review. McMaster Institue of Environment and Health, Hamilton (2011)
31. Willoughby, J.F., Smith, H.: Communication strategies and new media platforms exploring the synergistic potential of health and environmental communication. Sci. Commun. **38**, 535–545 (2016). doi:10.1177/1075547016648151
32. Braa, J., Hedberg, C.: The struggle for district-based health information systems in South Africa. Inf. Soc. **18**(2), 113–127 (2002)
33. Chilundo, B., Aanestad, M.: Negotiating multiple rationalities in the process of integrating the information systems of disease specific health programmes. EJISDC Electron. J. Inf. Syst. Dev. Ctries. **20**, 2 (2005)
34. Sahay, S., Walsham, G.: Scaling of health information systems in India: challenges and approaches. Inf. Technol. Dev. **12**(3), 185–200 (2006)
35. Grisot, M., Hanseth, O., Thorseng, A.A.: Innovation of, in, on infrastructures: articulating the role of architecture in information infrastructure evolution. J. Assoc. Inf. Syst. **15**(4), 197–219 (2014)
36. Hanseth, O., Aanestad, M.: Design as bootstrapping. on the evolution of ICT networks in health care. Methods Inf. Med. **42**(4), 384–391 (2003)
37. Donaldson, M.S., Lohr, K.N.: Health Data in the Information Age: Use, Disclosure, and Privacy. National Academies Press, Washington, D.C. (1994)
38. Rhoads, J., Ferrara, L.: Transforming healthcare through better use of data. Electron Healthc. **11**(1), 25–31 (2012)
39. Noir, C., Walsham, G.: The great legitimizer: ICT as myth and ceremony in the Indian healthcare sector. Inf. Technol. People **20**(4), 313–333 (2007)

Design and Build OLAP Business Intelligence for Village Sustainable Development Planning

Irya Wisnubhadra and Stephanie Pamela Adithama(⊠)

Informatics Engineering Department, Atma Jaya Yogyakarta University,
Yogyakarta, Indonesia
{irya,stephanie_pamela}@staff.uajy.ac.id

Abstract. The Indonesian government-year period 2014–2019, endorsed the National Medium Term Development Plan (RPJMN) with the concept of building Indonesia from the rural area. One of the RPJMN focus is the development of rural and border areas brings a new paradigm for the village development. This village development paradigm change requires the support of village information system. Village Information System and Rural Areas (SIDeKa) has developed and implemented in dozens of villages in the some district as a pilot project. The transaction data and information in the village have captured accurately using SIDeKa. These data and information becoming crucial sources for development planning in the next phase. This paper describe design and build OLAP Business Intelligence for development planning at village and supra village (district) that integrates SIDeKa's data from all villages and aligns the development planning with the vision, mission, and objectives of rural development. This paper presents model/architecture for ETL, star schema, and new measures that capture spatial and temporal dimensions. OLAP Business Intelligence will be useful for Village Sustainable Development Planning.

Keywords: OLAP Business Intelligence · Sustainable Development Planning · Village Information System and Rural Areas (SIDeKa)

1 Introduction

The Indonesian government year period 2014–2019, endorsed the National Medium Term Development Plan (RPJMN) with the concept of building Indonesia from the rural area. The government develops all sectors in order to get a better Indonesia, with the several objectives focus: (a) improve competitiveness, (b) improve the quality of human being, including mental development, (c) utilize and restore the lost potential in maritime and marine sectors, (d) improve the quality of economic growth, (e) reduce the inequality between regions, (f) restore environmental damage, and (g) advance social life. In the fifth focus that is the reduction of inequality between regions, government provides a large focus on the development of rural and border areas [1].

Village authority in the philosophy of "Village Builds" in the government of President Joko Widodo, change the village development paradigm from object becomes the subject of development. The development initially overlapping as an institution, financial and planning is now becoming more consolidated.

© IFIP International Federation for Information Processing 2017
Published by Springer International Publishing AG 2017. All Rights Reserved
J. Choudrie et al. (Eds.): ICT4D 2017, IFIP AICT 504, pp. 559–569, 2017.
DOI: 10.1007/978-3-319-59111-7_46

Changes in the development paradigm and village authority is the authority on village government administration, the implementation of rural development, rural community development, and community empowerment requires support from village information system. Village information system explicitly has appeared in the Village Law, in article 86 concerning Rural Development and Development of Rural Areas Information System, which contain (1) Village has right to access information through the village information system developed by the local district/city government, (2) The government and regional governments must develop a rural development and development of rural areas information system, (3) Village information system referred in paragraph 2 includes hardware and software facilities, network, and human resources, (4) Village information system referred in paragraph 2 includes the villages data, rural development data, rural areas data, and other information related to rural development and the development of rural areas, (5) village information system referred in paragraph 2 managed by village government and can be accessed by village communities and all stakeholders, (6) The local district/city government provide district/city information planning for the village. Village information system then becomes very important.

Rural development should also be aligned with the level of development in the above village level (Supra Desa), i.e. district/city and sub-district. Development plans at village level should be aligned with the policy and strategy of the district/city, Regional Development Plan (RPJMD), Strategic Plan Working Unit (SKPD), Spatial Planning and Regional Plan (RTRW) District/City, and the planned development of rural areas [2].

In the previous research, the authors have designed and build integrated Village Information System and Region (SIDeKa). The information system developed through strategic planning based on Enterprise Architecture, and priority-based information system development planning [3]. SIDeKa has implemented in several villages in districts in Indonesia, i.e. in Meranti, East Belitung, Boalemo Gorontalo, Pangkajene Islands, Raja Ampat, Gianyar, Pemalang, Tasikmalaya, and Kulon Progo. The transaction data and information in the village have captured accurately using SIDeKa. These data and information becoming crucial sources for development planning in the next phase.

The volume of data generated by the SIDeKa for daily operations of the different kinds of businesses has experienced an explosive growth. Data warehouses play an important role in helping decision makers obtain the maximum benefits of these large amounts of data. Data are extracted from several sources, cleansed, customized and inserted into the data warehouse. A data warehouse is defined as a subject oriented, integrated, time-variant and non-volatile collection of data in support of management decision making process. [7]. The most popular analysis mean is the Online Analytical Processing (OLAP) which enables users to examine, retrieve and summarize data within a multidimensional model.

This paper describe a design and implementation of OLAP Business Intelligence for development planning at village and supra village (district) that integrates SIDeKa's data from all villages and aligns the development planning with the vision, mission, and objectives of rural development in the Village Law No. 6 of 2014. OLAP Business Intelligence will be useful for Village Sustainable Development Planning for support the strategic and tactical decisions [4] as well as being a tool to monitor development progress in every villages which are connected as human neural network. In the end OLAP Business Intelligence is expected to improve organizational performance in sustainable development [5].

2 Related Work

Nowadays we are witnessing of explosion of transactional data transferred in the internet. 2 billion people from developing countries using the internet. The huge data need to be efficiently gathered, stored and analyze to support decision making not only for business institution but also for the government. One of the solution is Data warehouse and Online Analytical Processing (OLAP) Business Intelligence. Data warehouse is a collection of data that is subject oriented, integrated, time variant, and non-volatile designed for complex queries [11, 12].

Data warehouse is used to strengthen action ability of Health Information System, in Tajikistan [13]. This research proposed process of standardization using meta-data dictionary that would support data for action. Business Intelligence also useful for developing countries. Purkayastha et al. proposed Big Data Analytics for developing countries, using cloud computing for operational Business Intelligence in health [14]. This big data is resulting from integration of health data from multiple sources. Mohamed et al. show that KM is critical for innovation, prioritization and efficient use of resources. A significant linear association between IICTs and KM across time and geography is detected. IICTs improve the quality of shared decision making in inter- and intra-organizational settings [15].

Inspired by the usefulness of data warehouse and business intelligence as a tool for decision making in the government or in organization, authors design and build an OLAP Business Intelligence for sustainable development.

3 Research Methodology

This research comprehensively done by doing some related activities, can be viewed on a fishbone diagram in Fig. 1 below:

Activity 1, Villages and Rural Areas information system strategic planning implemented in phases: (1) Literature Study. A literature study by gathering information from books, articles, and scientific journals that discuss information system/information technology strategic planning related to Village Information System and Rural Areas. (2) Data Collection. Data collection related to information system strategic planning is done for several techniques, including: (a) direct observation, surveying the location, (b) interview, interviewing stakeholders related to village government organization, and business processes related to information system strategic planning, (c) survey, if interview with stakeholders not enough yield important information. (d) Business processes analysis in organization. The business processes are analyzed with analysis tools, i.e.: Porter's Value Chain [6] and Business Process Analysis [7]. (e) Enterprise Architecture modeling, using phases in TOGAF ADM methodology [8]. This approach is a complete and comprehensive approach that is suitable for strategic information system planning [9].

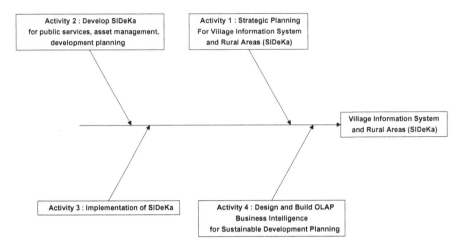

Fig. 1. SIDeKa research activity

Business process identified for village government services shown in Fig. 2 below:

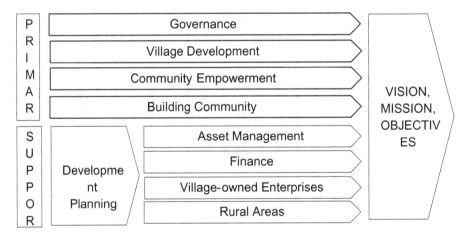

Fig. 2. Village value chain

Activity 2 and 3 is Design and Build Village Information System and Rural Area (SIDeKa) and its implementation. This system has been implemented in several pilot areas. The results are shown in Fig. 3 below:

Activity 4 is Design and Build OLAP Business Intelligence for sustainable development planning conducted in this study. The design process of OLAP Business Intelligence performed with the following steps: (1) Identify the sustainable development planning regulation and procedures, (2) Presenting a star schema based on dimensional model that captures information needs for sustainable development planning, (3) Introduction new measures that captures both the temporal and spatial dimensions, (4) Design

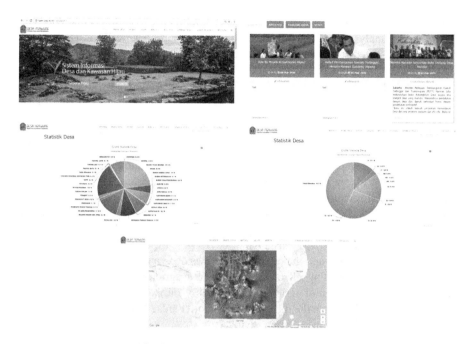

Fig. 3. Front end side screenshot SIDeKa

model/architecture for Extract, Transform and Loading, and (5) Implementing the OLAP Business Intelligence System.

4   OLAP Business Intelligence for Village and Rural Areas for Sustainable Development Planning

Indonesia is a big country that have at least 70 thousand villages. The new development paradigm turn village into new role as become the subject of the development instead of as an object. The new role implies the need for management information system of village development. Right now villages already have an open source information system that could support for village development planning, actuate, and monitoring that called SIDeKa.

The information system has been developed in the early stages (SIDeKa) is an application which is still in transactional scale and handle daily operations. The information needs in aggregation and reporting form are important for sustainable development planning at the village and supra village (district) level. The application is then called OLAP Business Intelligence. OLAP Business Intelligence is a decision making support applications that could satisfy organization needs to meet the efficiency of decision making using technology to rapidly extract useful information from very large data so that accelerate the decision-making [10].

The development of OLAP Business Intelligence Application develop in the following steps: (1) Identify the sustainable development planning regulation and procedures. This step is an OLAP Business Intelligence Requirements Analysis. Requirements analysis was conducted through Focus Group Discussion (FGD) with stakeholders at the district level such as Bappeda and SKPD and business processes analysis related to development planning. Several government regulations related to development planning are: (a) Law No. 25 of 2004 concerning National Development Planning, (b) Law No. 32 of 2004 concerning Regional Government, (c) PP 08 of 2008 concerning Stages, Preparation Procedures, Control and Implementation Evaluation, Regional Planning, (d) Regulation 54/2010 concerning the implementation of PP 08/2008, and (e) Law No. 11 of 2008 on Information and Electronic Transactions. One of the main business processes related to development planning is shown in block diagram in Fig. 4 below. The first block from the block diagram shows that the data processing and information is the first main issue. This first block is then filled by the Online Analytical Reporting (OLAP) application, which is one of the basic functionality of business intelligence application. Some important questions related to OLAP, which need to be answered for sustainable development planning such as: (a) How large and which land area, and the potential revenues that can be achieved for the entire area in the district, including all of the potential of agricultural, livestock, tourism? (b) How is the development of agricultural, livestock, tourism, etc. during the period of last five years? (c) How large the disaster-prone district area? (d) How many people that was born, died, migration in a certain district?

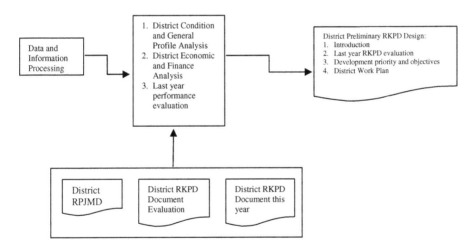

Fig. 4. Preliminary drafting RKPD regency/city diagram [2]

(2) OLAP Business Intelligence Design. This design phase comprises of: (a) presenting a star schema based on dimensional model that captures information needs for sustainable development planning. Create dimensionality model in information package and star schema design is conducted in this design phase. Information package explain the facts/measure, and dimension along with the attributes and hierarchies that will compose data warehouse. Data warehouse is a collection of data that is subject

oriented, integrated, time variant, and non-volatile designed for complex queries [11, 12]. (b) Introduction new measures that captures both the temporal and spatial dimensions, and (c) Design model/architecture for Extract, Transform and Loading

OLAP Business Intelligence application architecture is shown in Fig. 5 below:

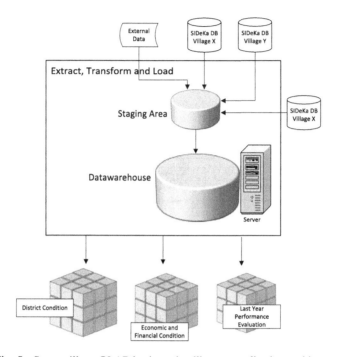

Fig. 5. Supra village OLAP business intelligence application architecture

Transactional Data for village development planning from SIDeKa integrated through a process of extraction, transformation, and loading into data warehouse. Furthermore, the data is accessed through an application in OLAP Business Intelligence web application.

Village conditions involving location and region characteristic information obtained from external data such as BMKG and other institutions. Extract, Transform, and Load process using two databases comprises Staging Area and Data Warehouse. Staging area is used for preliminary ETL and the star schema

Data warehouse/star schema design for district condition indicator shown in Fig. 6 below:

This star schema represents district condition fact, and dimensions that could be analyze from our OLAP Business Intelligence application. The continuous dimension also include in this design to accommodate continuous query. Besides district condition, this fact could be answered economics and finance condition.

Economics and finance condition fact also could be derived from Fact Demography in Fig. 7 below:

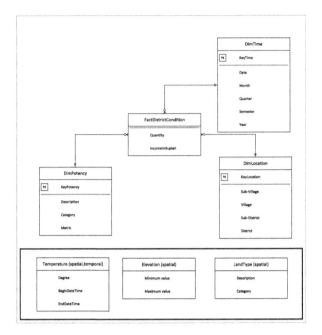

Fig. 6. Data warehouse design for district condition

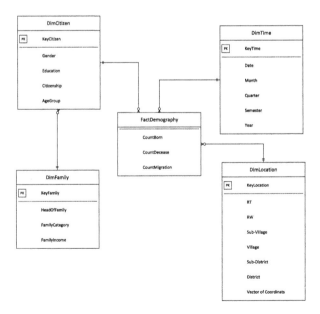

Fig. 7. Data warehouse design for demography

This Demography fact could answer economic and financial condition in the district/supra village level. These birth rate, death rate, and migration rate could be used to predict district population and district income.

District performance indicator star schema depicted in Fig. 8 below:

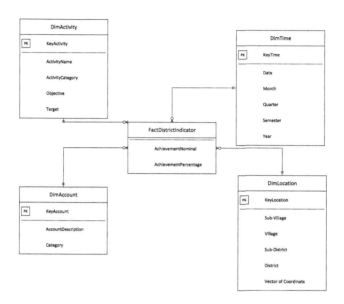

Fig. 8. Data warehouse design for district performance indicator

This District Indicator fact could answer how success the district development performance in term of planning and realization. This information could be drill down to detail villages/sub villages, time, activity planned, and development account.

5   The Result

The result of the development of OLAP Business Intelligence application shown in Fig. 9 below:

This screenshot depicts the dashboard of the OLAP Business Intelligence that could display the previously defined report. Report is based on OLAP Business Intelligence standard capabilities that could choose measures and dimension for reporting and display it in variety of reports like map, graph, and table. The OLAP Business Intelligence is an open source tool that embed with the SIDeKa (Village Information System and Rural Areas).

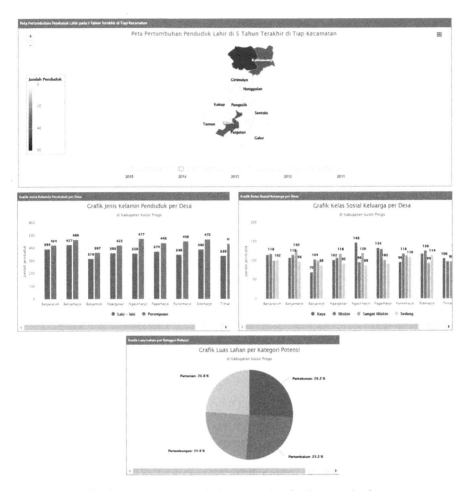

Fig. 9. Data warehouse design screenshot for demography fact

6   Conclusion and Future Works

The OLAP Business Intelligence Application and Information System at district/supra village have been built by integrating transactional data from SIDeKa that have been developed previously. This system be able to answer the important questions used for development planning at the district/supra village includes the district condition, economic and financial potency, and the timely development performance by district.

The application is open source in nature and could be used as tool for gathered, stored, and presented information of aggregate data to integrated district development planning. Reports are created custom and could be presented on map, table, or graph.

In the future, the challenge is how to extend OLAP Business Intelligence in the province and national level. There is so many data integration issues because of the variability of Village Information System that has already deployed. Analytical

Reporting presented in this study is only limited to development planning, which is very important for developing country like Indonesia. The research have opportunity to extend to covers the food fulfillment decision making for the community.

References

1. Kementerian Perencanaan Pembangunan Nasional/Badan Perencanaan Pembangunan Nasional. Rencana OpenPembangunan Jangka Menengah Nasional (RPJMN) 2015 – 2019 (2014)
2. Dirjen Bina Pembangunan Daerah. Peraturan Menteri Dalam Negeri Nomor 54 Tahun 2010 Tentang Pelaksanaan Peraturan Pemerintah Nomor 8 Tahun 2008 Tentang Tahapan, Tatacara Penyusunan, Pengendalian, Dan Evaluasi Pelaksanaan Rencana Pembangunan Daerah (2010)
3. Ward, J., Peppard, J.: Strategic Planning for Information Systems, 3rd edn. Wiley, West Sussex (2005)
4. Ranjan, J.: Business intelligence: concepts, components, techniques and benefits. J. Theor. Appl. Inf. Technol. 9(1), 060–070 (2009)
5. Nazier, M.M., Khedr, A., Haggag, M.: Business intelligence and its role to enhance corporate performance management. Int. J. Manage. Inf. Technol. 3(3), 8–15 (2013)
6. Porter, M.E.: Competitive Advantage Creating and Sustaining Superior Performance. The Free Press, New York (1985)
7. Al-Aboud, F.N.: Strategic information systems planning: a brief review. IJCSNS Int. J. Comput. Sci. Netw. 11, 179–183 (2011)
8. Open Group, 1999–2011. www.opengroup.org. http://pubs.opengroup.org/architecture/togaf9-doc/arch/
9. Alonso, I.A., Verdun, J.C., Caro, E.T.: The IT implicated within the enterprise architecture model: analysis of architecture models and focus IT architecture domain. In: 2010 IEEE International Conference on Service-Oriented Computing & Application (SOCA), Perth, WA (2010)
10. Farrokhi, V., Pokorádi, L.: The necessities for building a model to evaluate business intelligence projects. Int. J. Comput. Sci. Eng. Surv. (IJCSES) 3(2), 1–10 (2012)
11. Inmon, W.H.: Building the Data Warehouse, 4th edn. Wiley, New York (2005)
12. Ponniah, P.: Data Warehousing Fundamentals, 2nd edn. Wiley, New York (2010)
13. Latifov, M.A., Sahay, S.: Data warehouse approach to strengthen actionability of health information systems: experience from Tajikistan. Electron. J. Inf. Syst. Dev. Countries 53(4), 1–19 (2012)
14. Purkayastha, S., Braa, J.: Big data analytics for developing countries – using the cloud for operational BI in health. Electron. J. Inf. Syst. Dev. Countries 59(6), 1–17 (2013)
15. Mohamed, M., Stankosky, M., Mohamed, M.: An empirical assessment of knowledge management criticality for sustainable development. J. Knowl. Manage. 13(5), 271–286 (2009)

Graduate Student Track (IPID)

Subalternity in Information Systems in Developing Countries

A Critical Analysis of Ghana's TRADENET

Atta Addo[(⊠)]

London School of Economics & Political Science, London, UK
a.a.addo@lse.ac.uk

Abstract. In the search for explanations of contradictory effects and its disappointing outcomes in developing countries, Information Systems (IS) have been critiqued as pursuing techno-economic rationalities of western modernity with no recognition of alternatives. Development has also been critiqued as a western program promoted through discourses that do not admit local conditions and histories. Through critical discourse analysis (CDA) and a case study of Ghana's trade clearance system (TRADENET), we analyse how problematizations of IS in developing countries relate with local positions and contexts. We draw on the concepts of subalternity and hegemony to evaluate TRADENET's effects vis-à-vis its problematization by powerful actors. We find that TRADENET is contradicted by historically formed behaviors, culture and traditions that were unrecognized in technical problematizations of trade, development and IS. Despite importance of unrecognized, alternative or 'subaltern' positions in shaping IS in developing countries, they remain unrecognized in dominant or 'hegemonic' problematizations. Findings suggest that uncovering subaltern positions might illuminate 'blind spots' of IS in developing countries such as peculiar contradictory effects; and hence, inform better theory and practice.

Keywords: Information Systems in Developing Countries (ISDC) · Critical theory · Post-colonial theory · Hegemony · Subalternity · Public reform · Critical discourse analysis

1 Introduction

Information Systems (IS) transferred into developing countries have been noted as inconsistent with the local realities [1–3]. It has further been suggested that IS in developing countries (ISDC) is carried out under western universal positions with no recognition of alternative ways of perceiving it when deployed in historically formed contexts of developing countries [2]. Because of this, ISDC fail to make sense of alternative positions that might complicate or challenge its 'solutions', leading to observation that "the techno-economic rationality of western modernity is instrumental in defining a series of problems and determining their solutions [through IS] [but] is blatantly unsuccessful in streamlining people's behavior to the achievement of such solutions" [2, p. 2].

© IFIP International Federation for Information Processing 2017
Published by Springer International Publishing AG 2017. All Rights Reserved
J. Choudrie et al. (Eds.): ICT4D 2017, IFIP AICT 504, pp. 573–592, 2017.
DOI: 10.1007/978-3-319-59111-7_47

Development itself has long been critiqued for being western-centric and for promoting discourses that marginalize local cultures, histories and worldviews [4, 5]. In the development context, what is included or excluded as legitimate development "may depend on specific relations established in discourse; relations, for instance, between what experts say and what international politics allows as feasible" [5, p. 44]. E.g., problematizations of poverty in developing countries construct underdevelopment as a crisis that requires 'poverty-alleviating' western technical solutions [4, 5]. Escobar [5] shows how rather than advancing universal well-being, blanket application of western rationalities in the later parts of the twentieth century impeded capacity of the poor in developing countries to shape their own discourses and to sustainably better their lives.

Distinctiveness of ISDC lies in its attention to developing countries' context and problematization of the developmental role of IS [6, p. 140]. Yet, problematization of ISDC—the way 'development' is constructed through discourse and linked to technical IS solutions—rather than being objective or 'neutral', might be understood as an act of power that privileges some positions over others. Mobilization of resources and actors into networks that pursue particular technical solutions over others [7, 8] occurs through powerful development organizations, 'developed' country governments and elites in developing countries.

Against such backdrop, we explore how problematization of IS in developing countries relates with local positions and contexts. Through a critical discourse analysis (CDA) and case study, we examine how Ghana's TRADENET and its developmental effects were problematized through discourses; whether such discourses acknowledged local positions and contexts of development and administration; and the implications. We contribute by highlighting how unattended positions and contexts (subalternity) might help explain problems like contradictory effects of IS in developing countries. Recognizing subalternity can also sensitize extant approaches to ISDC that pay insufficient attention to local positions, contexts and worldviews. The paper proceeds as follows: we elaborate our theoretical framing of power in discourses of ISDC through the conjoint concepts of hegemony and subalternity. We then present our research approach, case and analysis. A discussion and conclusion follows.

2   Theoretical Background

2.1   ISDC Problematization as Hegemonic

IS are not neutral but have been shown to carry politics and ideology [9], context [10], policy [11] and to be shaped by specific rationalities [2, 12]. While a dominant rationality for IS draws from rational models e.g., technical economic rationalities, little is known of alternative positions and their implications in developing countries [2]. Gramsci's notion of hegemony helps explain the consenting, largely un-coerced acceptance within developing countries of dominant IS rationalities for development. Gramsci argued that a 'social group or class' ideas, interests or supremacy is exerted in two ways—coercion or 'domination' (*dominio*) and 'intellectual and moral leadership' (*direzioneintellettuale e morale*) or hegemony (Gramsci's Il Risorgimento [13, p. 25]). Hegemony may involve ideologies of different groups that collectively express a way of seeing the world and a belief system that radiates from an elite group then becomes generally accepted as superior. Hegemony is the success of dominant groups in presenting their understanding of reality in a way that makes it not only accepted but viewed as common sense, the only 'proper' way. Alternate intellectual, moral, cultural perspectives are marginalized.

We conceptualize ISDC as hegemonic because local actors often adopt its discourses as 'taken-for-granted' and common sense, thereby rejecting or de-emphasizing alternative realities. Although global institutions like the World Bank, International Monetary Fund (IMF), World Trade Organization (WTO), and multinationals that promote IS into developing countries exert power, ISDC phenomena are not sufficiently explained by theorizations of coercive power and politics in IS which assume control, authority, legitimization or pressure [14–16]. Granted that many development programs are tied up with binding conditionalities [17, 18], coercive institutional pressures alone do not explain willingness with which developing countries embrace western rationalities at the expense of alternatives.

2.2 Subalternity and ISDC

According to Gramsci, subalterns are outside hegemonic structures; groups without well-articulated historical narrative or ideology. Subaltern may be defined in juxtaposition to a power or economic 'elite' and subalternity created when the subaltern has "learnt to recognize himself not by properties and attributes of his own social being but by diminution, if not negation, of those of his superiors" [19, p. 8], much like Gramsci theorized that "the lower classes, historically on the defensive [against hegemony], can only achieve self-awareness via a series of negations" [20, p. 273]. But while subalterns view themselves in relation to the dominant, they "stand in an ambiguous relation to power; subordinate [...] but never fully consenting [...] never adopting the dominant point of view or vocabulary as expressive of its own identity" [21, p. 2194].

Being subaltern is equally about not having expression. To be subaltern is to be denied ability to speak directly for oneself without the re-presentation of others [22]. Hence without intervention of mediators like intellectuals and technical 'experts', subalterns, invariably, 'cannot speak' [22]. An implication is that subaltern positions remain 'shut out' and unable to contribute to discourses on development in developing countries. But if subalterns 'cannot speak', how are their positions expressed? Postcolonial studies document subaltern counter-discourses to hegemony. They include violent forms like armed resistance, terror and insurgency [23]; as well as nonviolent everyday means that are neither organized nor chronicled in "public transcript". These are "the ordinary weapons of relatively powerless groups: foot dragging, dissimulation, desertion, false compliance, pilfering, feigned ignorance, sabotage, and so on" [24]. Such "Everyday forms of resistance" often "make no headlines" and escape inquiry. Other means include constructing alternate narratives as well as informal relations and institutions [25]; constructing 'micro histories' [26]; deconstructing dominant narratives [27]; cohesion and communalism [28].

Subalternity manifests in different ways even if it "cannot speak" e.g., in the context of ISDC, it might manifest as conducive or subversive behaviors in relation to

IS. Subalterns either descript IS faithfully if consistent with their position or enact differently if contradicting. Example of conducive manifestation of subalternity might be when local workers use native knowledge for IS innovation. Subversive manifestations might include manipulation, tampering and sabotage; resistance, rejection or circumventing; reliance on informal networks, social clicks or parallel channels instead of formal IS mediated processes; using micro narratives to counter technology, e.g. 'we are more effective without IS; technology slows us down'; using IS differently from its capabilities. Subversive positions therefore produce a 'parallel work world' at—odds with ISDC.

In contrast to hegemonic positions of ISDC, subaltern positions may be situated (rather than planned), contextual (rather than universal), historically formed (rather than ahistorical), colloquial (rather than formalized), latent (rather than taken for granted), and often associated with less powerful, 'unrecognized' local actors (rather than powerful elites and organizations). Table 1 summarizes such hegemonic and subaltern relations in ISDC.

Table 1. Hegemonic versus subaltern positions of ISDC

Attribute in relation to ISDC	Hegemonic position	Subaltern position
Rationalityand action	Universal/a-contextual	Contextual
Mode of phenomena	Planned	Situated
Nature of change	Ahistorical	Historically formed
Social or material articulation	Formal	Colloquial
Relation to power	Centre/high	Periphery/low
Direction of phenomena	Top-down/center-periphery	Bottom-up/local
Typical manifestation	Taken for granted	Latent
Relevant actors	Powerful elites e.g. international organizations, experts	'Unrecognized' less powerful actors e.g. local bureaucrats who use IS

3 Research Approach

Our research combines two interrelated investigations. First, we uncovered dominant problematizations of Ghana's trade, development and TRADENET. Second, we conducted a case study of TRADENET to understand effects from point of view of users—local customs officers, declarants (freight forwarders, importers and exporters) and members of the trade community in Ghana. Our goal was to identify contradictions between problematizations and unrecognized local positions and contexts. Our case was purposively selected as typical of IS in developing countries that have unclear or contradictory developmental effects.

To unpack how trade and development were constructed through discourse as problems and linked to TRADENET as a solution, we employed critical discourse analysis (CDA). CDA enables investigation of how discourses relate to social change [29–31]. It examines use of language in speech and text to reveal assumptions and power dynamics [32] underlying social processes like organizing. Based on constructed corpus of key texts and text analogues, CDA links language of influential actors to claims and themes that materialize in specific change events. Data corpus consisted of World Bank project documents, reports by international organizations, government documents, audit reports, and documents from private technology and services providers (Table 2).

Table 2. Overview of data collection

Data corpus	Data collection site	Sources/contacts/location	Data coverage	Dates of collection	Methodology/analysis
World Bank documents covering GHATIG/TRADENET	Libraries, online websites, archives	Consultants and staff from World Bank, Accra/other	1998–2005	2014	CDA
World Bank reports on trade, development, TRADENET	Libraries, online websites, archives	Consultants and staff from World Bank, Accra/other (correspondence)	1990s–2015	2014	CDA
International organization documents on trade, trade facilitation e.g. WTO, WCO, OECD	Libraries, online websites, archives	Director, ministry of Trade and Industry, Accra; WCO officer, Geneva (correspondence)	1990s–2015	2014	CDA
Regional protocols on trade and TRADENET	Libraries, online websites, archives	Director, ministry of Trade and Industry, Accra	2004–2015	May-August, 2015	CDA
Customs guides, procedures and TRADENET documents	Libraries, online websites, archives	Customs officers, Tema	2004–2015	May-August, 2015	CDA/Case study/thematic analysis
GCNET documents and reports on TRADENET; notes from workshops on TRADENET	GCNET offices in Accra; other locations in Accra	GCNET officers, Accra	2004–2015	May-August, 2015	CDA/Case study/thematic analysis
Other trade documents e.g. ports; shippers' guides	Tema Harbor	Head of IT, Tema Harbor	2004–2015	May-August, 2015	CDA/Case study/thematic analysis
Ghana National Development Plan (Poverty Reduction Strategy (GPRS I&II) documents), Ghana Trade Policy	Government ministries and agencies, Accra	Officers of Ghana Development Planning Commission (GDPC), Accra	2003–2005; 2006–2009	May-August, 2015	CDA/Case study/thematic analysis
Ghana Export Promotion Authority (GEPA) reports	Government ministries and agencies, Accra	Directors, GEPA offices in Accra	2012–2014	May-August, 2015	CDA/Case study/thematic analysis

(continued)

Table 2. (*continued*)

Data corpus	Data collection site	Sources/contacts/location	Data coverage	Dates of collection	Methodology/analysis
Interview transcripts from interviews with 78 informants	Government ministries and agencies, Accra; Tema Harbor, offices and other locations in and around Accra and Tema	Customs officers, government officials, declarants (freight forwarders, importers, exporters), DICs, GCNET staff, trade and policy experts, etc., Accra, Tema	1990s–2015	May-August 2015; February-May, 2016	Case study/thematic analysis
Notes from 4 months of non-participant observations of TRADENET related activities	Tema Harbor	Customs officers, declarants, DIC inspectors and staff, Accra, Tema	2004–2015	May-August, 2015	Case study/thematic analysis
Expert reports and studies on TRADENET	Libraries, online websites, archives	Policy consultants, academics, IT consultants	2004–2015	2014–2016	Case study/thematic analysis

Our case study employed data collected during eight months of field work in Ghana between 2015 and 2016. Research site was primarily Ghana Customs Division (GCD)'s office at Tema, Ghana's main port. Open-ended formal and informal interviews were conducted with 78 informants comprising customs officers, senior officials, declarants (freight forwarders, importers, exporters) and experts on Ghana's trade and development. Other data included notes from direct observations of TRADENET related operations among exporters, importers, freight forwarders and clearing agents; transcripts from stakeholder workshops; system demos and observations of port operations; archival reports, web contents, project artefacts; news clippings and public records.

Interviews probed customs practices, uses or non-uses of TRADENET. We focused on capturing several "voices", particularly those typically unrecognized in dominant discourses e.g., local artisans and street level bureaucrats. Interviews concluded when new insights ceased i.e., theoretical saturation had occurred [33]. Informants were drawn purposively and by snow-balling [34] with sensitivity to their position relative to power. Interviews were audio recorded, transcribed and analyzed—during and after the data collection phase—for key themes.

4   Case

TRADENET, an electronic data interchange (EDI) was implemented to enable processing of trade clearance documents, duties, taxes and data. It was designed to automate processes and to support government of Ghana (GOG)'s revenue collections. As a business-to-government (B2G) platform, it was meant to integrate various public and private actors involved in trade. Prior to TRADENET, trade clearance and data flow was convoluted and involved replications and inefficiencies. Agencies required multiple documents that were not shared. Processes were paper-based, labor intensive, time consuming, costly and error-prone, requiring transcriptions and data entries. 13–30 stages were required, depending on the goods. This situation created opportunities for customs officers to demand bribes to 'speed up' for anxious declarants by e.g., allowing queue jumping, or manipulating processes. GoG suffered perennial revenue losses and customs, for several years, counted among Ghana's most corrupt organizations. TRADENET was intended to change this status quo with a 'single window' system whereby declarants had to submit one document—Import Declaration Form (IDF)—to fulfil all requirements.

4.1 Problematization of Ghana's Trade and Development

International trade has been juxtaposed as superior to aid in enabling developing countries overcome poverty; a view captured with the popular slogan 'trade not aid'. As such, international trade has been promoted by international organizations as a sure route to development. Ghana's trade and development prior to TRADENET was problematized within what could be described as neoliberal discourses.[1] Such discourses assumed discernible patterns of ideology, policies and programs, state form, and governmentality.

Ghana's neoliberal trade and development discourse has been dominated by an elite network of policymakers, government officials, and international technical experts. As an ideological position with coherent interpretations and worldview, such neoliberal positions are generally accepted, providing a kind of 'common sense'. 'Neoliberal common sense' governed not just ideas about international trade but also the role of the state, public administration and technology. E.g., neoliberal common sense drew from neoclassical economic theory to suggest that international trade based on competitive advantage is the best means to achieve economic growth, and with it, development. Developing countries like Ghana were to focus on advantages such as production of minerals and agricultural raw materials and to boost exports to international markets. Consequently, Ghana's developmental plans, as captured in plans and documents by government ministries and the Ghana National Development Planning Commission (GNDPC), focused on promoting traditional export commodities such as cocoa, bauxite, gold, timber as well as non-traditional exports such as cash crops like cashew, artisanal crafts etc.

Government of Ghana in conjunction with its development partners designed and pursued policies and programs aimed at strengthening Ghana's exports, improving international trade and enhancing revenue from trade-related activities. Neoliberal

---

[1] Neoliberalism has become a 'catch phrase' but remains contested [74]. Here, it suggests a collection of economic policies to reduce state intervention and promote laissez-faire capitalism or a 'free-market economy' as a means to economic efficiency, individual freedom and wellbeing. Such policies often aim to dismantle welfare or regulationist state interventions through means like privatization, deregulation, and lowered taxes for businesses and investors. There is also emphasis on free movement of capital, goods and services across state borders [75, 76].

discourses on policy and programs focused on reforming 'frontline' trade-related government organizations such as customs, and wholly or partially privatizing key functions. Such policies and programs endorsed a particular form of state; Ghana was required by its development partners e.g., World Bank and IMF to pursue structural transformations to become competitive among trading states as far-flung as in East Asia and as close as neighbors, Ivory Coast and Nigeria. Structural transformations involved 'rolling back' or reconfiguration of state capacities and functions and increased reliance on private actors. E.g., TRADENET was developed by a private provider (SGS) and implemented along with reforms at customs that outsourced functions such as destination inspection, classification and valuation to private destination inspection companies (DICs).

Despite such limits on the roles of GoG and its agents, neoliberal discourses championed a kind of governmentality where government decentered to allow effective "governance at a distance" through use of technology and innovative public administration.[2] Rather than coercive power, such governance at a distance relied on the state's "infrastructural power" [35] and was enabled by information and knowledge production.[3] Information and knowledge production, an intrinsic part of modern state administration enabled GoG to pursue its interests by control strategies such as quantification and revenue target setting, monitoring and management.

4.2   Problematization of Ghana's TRADENET

TRADENET was problematized as a technological solution to inefficient and ineffective trade processing in Ghana's trade administrations, especially customs, as part of broader global neoliberal push for increased international trade. Red tape, corruption and unlawful seizures of goods were deemed as great costs on businesses and governments. Thus, 'trade facilitation'—defined by the World Trade Organization (WTO) as "the simplification and harmonization of international trade procedures" [36] —took center stage since the mid-90s as a critical issue with development implications.

Administrative dysfunctions were said to put businesses at a competitive disadvantage, increasing costs of providing information and fulfilling compliance with authorities like customs, as well as indirect costs of delays and opportunity costs. According to United Nations Conference on Trade and Development (UNCTAD), trade facilitation was good for development because it increased transparency and trust, increased fiscal revenues for governments, made it easier for members of informal economies to enter the formal economy, improved effectiveness and efficiency e.g.

---

[2] Defining government as the 'conduct of conduct' [77], Foucault [78] develops the notion of governmentality to describe ways in which the state exercises control over, or governs the body of its populace.

[3] Mann (1984) develops a conception of the institutional aspects of state power. Mann conceptualizes two types of power the state and its elites have –despotic power and infrastructural power. Infrastructural power is "the capacity of the state to penetrate civil society, and to implement logistically political decisions" (p. 113). This is characteristic of the modern industrialized and capitalist state e.g., ability to tax incomes at source, without using physical coercion or getting consent.

automating simple tasks thereby freeing up customs officers to do value adding tasks. There were also pro-poor dimensions, it had been argued, which resulted from enabling small and medium-sized enterprises as well as informal cross-border traders to easily comply with regulations. Trade facilitation was also introduced to improve living standards through enhanced state revenues.[4] In principle, customs collections from trade was deemed important for developmental purposes such as infrastructure provision, providing public goods and services.

Discourses of problematization were produced through development 'consensus' by networks of technocrats who have similar western training e.g. in neoclassical economics and engineering; form a community of practice and often affiliated with powerful organizations such as World Bank, IMF, UN, WTO. Such discourses were further 'consumed' and reproduced by local government officials and elites in developing countries who might be western-trained or dependent on foreign expertise, aid and other support. Table 3 presents vignettes from our CDA.

Table 3. Illustrative findings from CDA

Discourse theme	Sub themes	Illustrative text
Trade and development		
Ideology of a powerful elites	– International trade key to development – Economic growth based on exports and comparative advantage – Globalization and external integration good for developing countries	– *The need for a radical transformation of Ghana's internal production and foreign trade is one of the most widely-shared beliefs among intelligent laymen, [...] as well as the professional and political lenders. In the face of widening development opportunities [...] this universal ideology informs the decision to re-focus policy* [37, p. ii] – *Attainment of [...] rapid growth rates require structural transformation of the productive sectors of the economy. Ghana needs to move away from a heavy dependence on exports of a limited number of primary commodities to create competitive advantage on a more diversified range of products with higher levels of value-addition. In international trade, competitive advantage is increasingly less a function of cost or price and more a function of quality, design and logistics management, leading to timely sales and after sales service* [38, p. 4]

(continued)

---

[4] African states, through their customs, collect 20 to 60% of revenues as international trade-related duties, levies and taxes [79, p. 1]. E.g., Ghana's 2011 figure was nearly 40%, roughly equal all direct domestic tax receipts [80, p. 3].

Table 3. (*continued*)

Discourse theme	Sub themes	Illustrative text
Policy and programs	– Developing countries must structurally adjust and reform e.g. Reform 'front line' trade related institutions – Private sector 'engine' of economic growth with government as enabler	– *When the capacity of the public sector to manage the economy and deliver public services is weak, the prospects for development are poor. The public sector in many developing countries has been characterized by uneven revenue collection, poor expenditure control and management, a bloated and underpaid civil service, a large parastatal sector that provides poor returns on the scarce public funds invested in it, and weakness in the capacity of core agencies to design and implement policies that would address these problems [...] [a situation that] progressively erodes the capacity of the state to provide economic and social services (World Bank 1992, p. 12)* – *It is imperative that both the private sector and supporting public sector institutions understand and are able to respond to the demands and requirements of the marketplace. This necessitates policy interventions geared towards complementing rather than supplanting the market, as elaborated in the Ghana Trade Policy* [38, p. 4]
State form	– Reduce/'roll back' state in key areas by privatizing functions	– *Few government activities are more prone to corruption than customs and procurement. Some countries try to correct the mismanagement of their customs service by contracting it out to a wholly independent private enterprise [...] private inspection and supervisory services can play a valuable role* [39, p. 44]
Governmentality	– Decentered government reliant on information, management controls	– *The basic strategy for modernizing customs...is straightforward: establish transparent and simple rules and procedures [] and foster voluntary compliance by building a system of self-assessment buttressed by well-designed audit policies. Implementing this, however, requires addressing a range of issues, involving links with trade policy, organizational reform, the use of new technologies, the appropriate nature and extent of private sector involvement, designing incentive systems to overcome*

(*continued*)

Table 3. (*continued*)

Discourse theme	Sub themes	Illustrative text
		governance issues—and many others [40]
TRADENET and customs		
Modernization	– IT modernizes public sector i.e., promotes efficiency and effectiveness when used properly – IT enables transformation of undesirable practices and shift to managerial rationalism – Enhance state revenues by reducing corruption and 'leakages'	– *"The challenges of the 21st Century are placing massive demands on Customs administrations. Now, more than ever before, there is a need for Customs administrations to be more responsive. An understanding is required of issues such as globalization, the dynamics of international trade, the technicalities of the trade supply chain, emerging policy directions and the complexities of the global landscape"* [41] – *"CEPS [later renamed GCD] is now ISO 9000 certified on its administrative procedures. The Gateway Project [TRADENET precursor] was able to reengineer the institution with a new mission and vision. As a result, the simplification of its procedures enabled Ghana to be recorded as one of the top ten reformers in the Africa in 2007 and 2008. The GCNet system for CEPS, it has enabled flow of information among institutions"* [42, p. 29]

4.3 Contradictory Local Positions on Trade and Development

There is uneasy tension between promises of international trade and realities of Ghana's economic development. Ghana's Poverty Reduction Strategy (GPRS) laments that, "in the forty years since the days of Nkrumah [Ghana's independence leader], economic policy-making in Ghana has had to contend with a popular sense of grievance over an arrested national development still blocked by an unfair international trading system" [37, p. ii].

The promise of export-led growth remains a mirage for Ghana. Ghana's exports, mostly low value-added raw materials and agricultural products which employ majority of the country's labor, face disfavorable terms of trade, cascading tariffs, stiff international markets and abnormally high quality requirements whose net effects deter exports. Ghana's trade balance as of 2014 was negative, with $4.62 billion in net imports, mostly high value-add goods from import sources like China, India and USA. During the five years prior to 2014, Ghana's imports outgrew its exports significantly, at an annualized rate of 13.7% compared to 9.8% [43].

Many exporters, importers and local manufacturers interviewed complained about worsening prospects in Ghana and the international economy that made their trade untenable. E.g., handicraft and garment exporters complained about cut-throat competition and counterfeiting from lower-cost countries like Vietnam and China;

increasingly prohibitive regulatory and technical restrictions from main markets like the EU; and lack of financing facilities. Importers complained about hidden costs, intransparency, and excessive rent seeking (high duties and taxes, fees, bribes etc.,) on the part of government and customs officers who viewed them as source of 'easy' revenues. Local manufacturers such as furniture makers also complained about lack of government and policy support, excessive rent seeking, competition from cheap Chinese imports, and rising production costs (as they had to internalize non-core costs like utilities and access roads given deficits in government provisioning).

4.4   Contradictory Effects of TRADENET

A decade after TRADENET was implemented, several administration dysfunctions it sought to transform persisted. Rent-seeking behaviors of customs officers such as bribery, extortion and corruption were reconfigured rather than eliminated [44]. While clearance practices improved, the system was not used as planned and was functioning below capability as a 'single window'. E.g., despite TRADENET's affordance to fully automate and integrate IDF processing, processes still involved redundant paper-based steps that required declarants to print out the electronic IDF and present to officers face-to-face. The face-to-face opportunities created by such paper submissions could be viewed as attempts by officers to re-intermediate the now automated and integrated process that had physically disintermediated them by design. Several officers interviewed complained about diminished influence of customs and 'loss of control' to outsourced private companies such as Destination Inspection Companies (DICs) that performed previously core customs functions like valuations and classification.

The resulting mode of IDF processing at GCD, rather than fully reflecting planned capabilities of TRADENET, maintained aspects of pre-TRADENET manual clearance procedures that took place in the 'long room'. Prior to IT automation at GCD, the 'long room' was where customs clearance occurred. It was a hallway where officers sat behind adjoining glass- partitions (multi-windows) to interact with declarants and process declarations. Long room process was tightly coupled with various interdependent steps and hence highly prone to errors and inefficiencies as well as officers' coercion and discretion. Furthermore, at various stages, the IDF was prone to tampering and falsification to evade taxes and duties.

Despite such known limitations of manual, paper-based steps, many officers preferred paper-based to full electronic IDF processing. This contradiction had no obvious justification and was puzzling to senior officials who unsuccessfully encouraged officers to use TRADENET fully. As one administrator lamented, "customs officers have so much confidence in paper [...] you don't need the physical receipt but they still want to see it."

The issue of corruption at customs was indirectly explored in our research through narratives of declarants and informal discussions with bureaucrats. Corruption was found to involve both formal, state-sanctioned practices and informal private practices such as bribery, extortion or pilfering. Corruption remained a topical issue in Ghana and most Ghanaians perceived the government and bureaucrats as corrupt [45].

In the formal sense, a consequence of several GoG agencies mandated in customs clearance by law was that such agencies charged rents like 'inspection fees' or 'levies' autonomously and without coordination. The Ghana Museums and Monuments Board (GMMB), for example, were to charge handicraft exporters 50 Ghana pesewas per item,[5] to issue supporting documents to an IDF.[6] Such practices caused tensions between traders who felt extorted from, and bureaucrats who failed to acknowledge that various 'small fees' created burdensome hidden costs (the author witnessed a verbal feud between traders and bureaucrats at a TRADENET workshop). GoG-sanctioned rent-seeking did not only have historical roots, but were also attributable to perennial budget deficits and poor public finance which meant that under-funded agencies were pressured to generate funds.

Aside such issues, various traditional and cultural behaviors undermined Ghana's TRADENET e.g., local lackadaisical attitudes towards time and time management naturally undermined western-assumptions underlying automation and efficient clearance. This was captured by a local pidgin phrase "go and come, go and come" that many declarants complained about as the typical perfunctory response from customs and other bureaucrats whenever declarants made critical enquiries. During fieldwork, it was common for customs officers and government officials to repeatedly miss or be extremely late for various pre-scheduled appointments and meetings; a fixture of life in Ghana that ordinary Ghanaians have come to take for granted (Table 4).

Table 4. Summary of findings

Area of discourse	CDA findings (on problematization)	Fieldwork findings (on local positions)	Implications
Trade and development	– International trade key to development – Economic growth based on exports and comparative advantage – Private sector 'engine' of economic growth	– Unfavorable international trade climate for developing countries – Many developing countries like Ghana are net importers given lack of industrial base for	– International trade-driven development questionable in practice. Net effects of international trade on Ghana's development debatable

(continued)

---

[5] 50 pesewas, or about 13 US cents as of October 2015. E.g., a cargo container with 1000 woodcarvings would cost an exporter 1000 * 0.13, or $130 for 'inspection fees' to one of several agencies in charge of regulating woodcarvings. These payments were not 'official', meaning while legal, they were not payments collected by GCD into national treasury.

[6] In the example of GMMB, the document was to confirm that export-bound items were not national relics. Handicraft exporters complained against such inspection because they dealt in new decorative artefacts.

Table 4. (*continued*)

Area of discourse	CDA findings (on problematization)	Fieldwork findings (on local positions)	Implications
	– Government as enabler of private sector	manufacturing, among other reasons. – Import substitution discredited in dominant discourses. Ghana is market/ 'dumping' ground for imports and international trade stifles domestic industrialization – Government rent seeking, lack of public infrastructure and favorable policy intervention stifles private sector development	– Alternative policy and practical options inhibited – 'Non-technical' 'solution' e.g. behavioral change; and long term fundamental transformations unexplored
IT and public administration rationalization	– IT modernizes public sector i.e., promotes efficiency and effectiveness – IT enables transformation of undesirable bureaucratic practices and shift to managerial rationalism	– Personalization of public office i.e. neopatrimonialism, means that formal rules are subject to negotiation – Historically formed behaviors such as rent-seeking and corruption materialized through paper processing – Cultural and traditional behaviors e.g. subjective notions of time and informal interactions inimical to goals of TRADENET	– Contradictory effects of IT e.g., persistence of paper use ("fetishization of paper") and historically formed behaviors

5   Discussion

5.1   Subaltern Positions on Ghana's Trade and Development

Our findings indicate that the neoliberal problematizations of trade and development as well as TRADENET were frequently at odds with local realities or ignored context and history. Indeed, political structures and institutional arrangements governing neoliberal international trade remain intransparent, disfavorable to developing countries, and often inimical to socioeconomic development [46–49]. It has been pointed out that the promise of neoliberal reforms to deliver developmental outcomes for developing countries remains dubious [48, 50, 51]. E.g., policies of powerful international trade actors like the WTO have been said to limit the options of developing country governments thereby shrinking not only their "development space" but also "self-determination space" [49].[7]

Based on observation that export is not a principal source of economic growth, it has been argued that developing country economies should follow "internal integration" rather than "external integration" [49, p. 635].[8] Developing countries like Ghana might be well of building up regional-level organizations and embedding their markets not only nationally but also in regionally distinct configurations that provide tailored policy solutions for vulnerabilities of different countries and regions [49, p. 638]. Nonetheless, neoliberal discourses of influential organizations like WTO, and contemporary development theory generally hold that comparative advantage and international trade are to be preferred to alternatives such as import substitution or regional trade, no matter how appropriate they might be in particular contexts.[9]

5.2 Subaltern Positions on TRADENET Enabled Administration Modernization

Contradictory outcome of TRADENET post implementation such as the 'fetishization of paper' as well as corruption, bribery and rent-seeking behaviors might be best understood through a historical and contextual lens that considers institutional peculiarities of customs administration. Considering these and their underlying power dynamics illuminates subaltern positions in relation to IS use and effects. E.g., contrary to principles of Weberian bureaucracy, in administrations around the world, particularly in developing countries such as Ghana, decision-making rarely emanates from rational-legal authority but is subject to negotiation [52, p. 5].

In Africa, neopatrimonialism has been widely used to describe public administration [53–55]. It is defined as organization in which "relationships of a broadly patrimonial type pervade an administrative system which is formally constructed on

---

[7] We take a relaxed view of subaltern positions that is limited within contemporary global structures like capitalism. A more radical interpretation might reject any 'western' structures and discourses as a starting point. E.g. scholars have investigated if developing countries like those in Africa had/have indigenous/non-western administrations or rationalities [81, 82].

[8] 'Integration' often implies integration into the world economy, with an assumption that more integration is always developmental. Wade [48, p. 635] argues an internally integrated economy has better developmental thrust since it has dense input–output linkages, and a structure such that a high proportion of domestic production is sold to domestic wage earners.

[9] It has been suggested that despite import substitution going awry in Latin America, Africa, South Asia etc., this no more discredits it as a principle than the failures of democracy discredits the principle of democracy [49, p. 234]. Policy response might be to do import replacement better, not less [83].

rational-legal lines" and where officers hold "powers which are formally defined, but exercise those powers [...] as a form [...] of private property" [56, p. 48]. It has been further claimed that neopatrimonialism distinguishes African institutions from others [57, 58], and the argument has been made that "the distinctive institutional hallmark of African regimes is neopatrimonialism" [59, p. 277].

In the African context, separation between private and public spheres—the basis of modern state and public administration—is said to be thin or non-existent [60]. Such blurring has deep cultural and historical roots. E.g., local ideas of administration and work are personalized in fundamental ways: from subjective notions of time, to modes of accountability, interaction and (in)formality. The term 'African time' has come to characterize a cultural tendency in African societies to keep a relaxed, slow-paced, nonchalant attitude toward time [61, 62].

Such historically and culturally formed behaviors further sustained rent-seeking. Rent seeking elaborates another important aspect of the political economy of Africa's underdevelopment [63–65]. Rents occur when non-market forces such as politics or corruption, distort mechanisms of a free market and arise from "politically mediated opportunities for obtaining wealth through non-productive economic activity" [66, p. 427]. Lewis [67, p. 438] similarly notes a "mutually reinforcing pattern of neopatrimonial governance and a rentier economy." Neopatrimonialism and rent seeking are underpinned by informal structures where formal ones might exist.

Rent-seeking and corruption at Ghana's customs could be viewed in broader historical context from the organization's inception over 150 years ago when the country was a colony of Britain [68, 69]. Early customs enforced collections of taxes and duties in line with Britain's doctrine of self-sufficiency of colonies, whereby Africans had to finance their own domination to lower the cost of imperialism to Britain's treasury [70, 71]. Given that direct taxation on colonial subjects was prone to rebellion and was extremely costly for overstretched colonial administrations, indirect trade rents were preferable [72]. Peculiar patterns established by colonial administrators were adopted by post-colonial countries after independence [70, 73]. Reliance on customs as a major and preferred channel for extractive rents outlasted the colonial period and continued into modern Ghana.

6 Conclusion

The dominant problematizations of Ghana's TRADENET— (1) international trade as solution to poverty and under-development (2) IS-enabled customs administration rationalization as a technical solution to dysfunctions of traditional administration that impede efficient international trade—do not consider historically shaped local positions and contexts that contradict their appropriateness. As a net importer, Ghana derives less direct benefit from the promise of export-led economic growth through international trade facilitated by TRADENET. The government rather views the primary benefit of TRADENET as the efficient collection of rents in the form of taxes, fines and fees. Similarly, administration modernization potential of TRADENET is impeded by neopatrimonial rent-seeking behaviors like bribery, extortion, corruption etc., and institutionalized practices like "African time" constituted through informal face-to-face negotiations and materiality of paper.

Historical and ongoing power relations and their manifestation through discourse are important for uncovering biases of development and its interventions [4, 5]. Such perspective is useful for critically assessing implications of IS in developing countries. E.g., by problematizing development in technical rational terms that require programmatic interventions, development discourse conveniently neglects history, politics, traditions and other 'messy' phenomena it has no obvious explanations for, nor ready 'solutions' to [4]. Furthermore, development discourse marginalizes local positions not only through political and economic power, but also through intellectual and moral leadership or hegemony. These clarify why alternative positions to IS remain unrecognized and under-explored while universalist positions dominate despite their inadequacy in situated contexts [1, 2].

Subalternity is not merely about marginalization but also the extent to which subalterns 'speak for themselves' or own their discourse without re-presentation of others [22]. Our contribution is to show how it provides a fresh window into understanding 'wicked' ISDC problems that sociotechnical accounts struggle against such as our 'fetishization of paper' example. Recognizing subalternity in ISDC offers emancipation by negotiating values and objectives of IS with positions and contexts of developing countries. A methodological implication is that ISDC should venture beyond typical case studies with technical rational assumptions. Ethnographic and anthropological methods might hold promise for uncovering subaltern perspectives in relation to ISDC.

References

1. Avgerou, C.: Information Systems and Global Diversity. Oxford University Press, Oxford (2002)
2. Avgerou, C.: Recognising alternative rationalities in the deployment of information systems. Electron. J. Inf. Syst. Dev. Ctries. 3(7), 1–15 (2000)
3. Heeks, R.: Most e-government for development projects fail: how can risks be reduced? Manchester, 14 (2003)
4. Ferguson, J.: The Anti-Politics Machine: Development, Depoliticization and Bureaucratic Power in Lesotho. Cambridge University Press, Cambridge (1990)
5. Escobar, A.: Encountering Development: The Making and Unmaking of the Third World. Princeton University Press, Princeton (1995)
6. Avgerou, C.: Information systems in developing countries: a critical research review. J. Inf. Technol. 23(3), 133–146 (2008)
7. Callon, M.: Some elements in the sociology of translation: domestication of the scallops and the fishermen of St. Brieuc Bay. In: Law, J. (ed.) Power, Action and Belief: A New Sociology of Knowledge, pp. 196–223. Routledge, London (1986)
8. Latour, B.: Technology is society made durable. In: Sociology of Monsters? Essays on Power, Technology and Domination, Sociological Review Monograph, pp. 103–131. Routledge, London (1991)

9. Gagliardone, I.: 'A country in order': technopolitics, nation building, and the development of ICT in Ethiopia. Inf. Technol. Int. Dev. **10**(1), 3–19 (2014)
10. Heeks, R.: E-Government as a carrier of context. J. Public Policy **25**(1), 51–74 (2005)
11. Cordella, A., Iannacci, F.: Information systems in the public sector: the e-Government enactment framework. J. Strateg. Inf. Syst. **19**(1), 52–66 (2010)
12. Avgerou, C., McGrath, K.: Power, rationality and the art of living through socio-technical change. MIS Q. **31**, 295–315 (2007)
13. Femia, J.: Gramsci's Political Thought: Hegemony, Consciousness and the Revolutionary Process. Clarendon, Oxford (1987)
14. Jasperson, J.S., Carte, T., Saunders, C.S., Butler, B.S., Croes, H.J.P., Zheng, W.: Review: power and information technology research: a metatriangulation review. MIS Q. **26**(4), 397 (2002)
15. Silva, L.: Power and politics in the adoption of information systems by organisations: the case of a research centre in Latin America (1997)
16. Markus, M.L.: Power, politics, and MIS implementation. Commun. ACM **26**(6), 430–444 (1983)
17. Santiso, C.: Good governance and aid effectiveness: the world bank and conditionality. Georg. Public Policy Rev. **7**(1), 1–22 (2001)
18. Kapur, D., Webb, R.: Governance-related conditionalities of the international financial institutions. In: G-24 Discussion Paper Series Research papers for the Intergovernmental Group of Twenty-Four, no. 6 (2000)
19. Guha, R.: On some aspects of the historiography of colonial India. In: Subaltern Studies. Oxford University Press, Oxford (1982)
20. Gramsci, A.: Selections from the Prison Notebooks. International Publishers, New York (1971)
21. Leitch, V.: Gayatri Chakravorty Spivak. In: Leitch, V. (ed.) Norton Anthology of Theory and Criticism (2010)
22. Spivak, G.: Can the subaltern speak? In: Nelso, C., Grossberg, L. (eds.) Marxism and the Interpretation of Culture, pp. 271–313. Macmillan, London (1988)
23. Scott, J.: Revolution in the revolution: peasants and commissars. Theory Soc. **7**(1), 97–134 (1979)
24. Scott, J.: Weapons of the Weak: Everyday Forms of Peasant Resistance. Yale University Press, New Haven (1985)
25. Guha, R.: Elementary Aspects of Peasant Insurgency in Colonial India. Oxford University Press, Oxford (1983)
26. Prakash, G.: Writing post-orientalist histories of the third world: perspectives from Indian historiography. Comp. Stud. Soc. Hist. **32**(2), 383 (1990)
27. Spivak, G.: Selected subaltern studies. In: Guha, R., Spivak, G. (eds.) Subaltern Studies: Deconstructing Historiography. Oxford University Press, Oxford (1988)
28. Pandey, G.: The Construction of Communalism in Colonial North India. Oxford University Press, Oxford (2006)
29. Chouliaraki, L., Fairclough, N.: Critical discourse analysis in organizational studies: towards an integrationist methodology. J. Manag. Stud. **47**(6), 1213–1218 (2010)
30. Fairclough, N.: Critical Discourse Analysis: The Critical Study of Language. Longman, Harlow (2010)
31. Fairclough, N.: Analysing Discourse: Textual Analysis for Social Research. Routledge, Abingdon (2003)
32. Fairclough, N.: Language and Power. Longman, London (1989)
33. Eisenhardt, K.: Building theories from case study research. Acad. Manag. Rev. **14**, 532–550 (1989)

34. Bryman, A.: Social Research Methods. New York University Press, New York (2001)
35. Mann, M.: The autonomous power of the state: its origins, mechanisms and results. Eur. J. Sociol. (1984)
36. WTO, WTO: A Training Package; What Is Trade Facilitation? Geneva (1998)
37. Ghana National Development Planning Commission: Growth and Poverty Reduction Strategy (GPRS I & II). Accra (2007)
38. Ministry of Trade and Industry: Ghana Trade Policy. Accra (2005)
39. World Bank Group: Governance and Development. The World Bank Group, Washington, DC (1992)
40. Ter-Minassian, T.: Changing customs: challenges and strategies for the reform of customs administration. In: Keen, M., Mansour, M. (eds.) International Monetary Fund (IMF), Washington, DC (2003)
41. Gordhan, P.: Customs in the 21st century. World Cust. J. 1(1), 49–54 (2007)
42. World Bank Group: Implementation, Completion and Results Report: Ghana Trade and Investment Gateway Project (GHATIG). Washington, DC (2010)
43. OEC: The Observations of Economic Complexity (OEC): Ghana (2016). http://atlas.media.mit.edu/en/profile/country/gha/. Accessed 24 Oct 2016
44. Addo, A.: Explaining 'irrationalities' of IT-enabled change in a developing country bureaucracy: the case of Ghana's TRADENET. Electron. J. Inf. Syst. Dev. Ctries. 77, 1–22 (2016)
45. Afrobarometer: "Ghana Report," Afrobarometer: An African-led series of national public attitude surveys on democracy and governance in Africa (2014). http://www.afrobarometer.org/countries/ghana-1. Accessed 17 Oct 2015
46. Easterly, W.: How the millennium development goals are unfair to Africa. World Dev. 37 (1), 26–35 (2009)
47. Gore, C.: The rise and fall of the Washington Consensus as a paradigm for developing countries. World Dev. 28(5), 789–804 (2000)
48. Wade, R.H.: Is globalization reducing poverty and inequality? World Dev. 32(4), 567–589 (2004)
49. Wade, R.H.: What strategies are viable for developing countries today? The World Trade Organization and the shrinking of 'development space'. Rev. Int. Polit. Econ. 10(4), 621–644 (2003)
50. Chang, H.-J.: Rethinking Development Economics. Anthem Press, London (2003)
51. Chang, H.-J.: 23 Things They Don't Tell You About Capitalism. Bloomsbury Press, London (2010)
52. Minogue, M.: The Internationalization of New Public Management. In: McCourt, W., Minogue, M. (eds.) The Internationalization of Public Management: Reinventing the Third World State, pp. 1–19. Edward Elgar Publishing Ltd., Cheltenham (2001)
53. Chabal, P., Daloz, J.: Africa Works. Disorder as Political Instrument. Indiana University Press, Bloomington (1999)
54. Bratton, M., Van de Walle, N.: Neopatrimonial regimes and political transitions in Africa. World Polit. 46(4), 453–489 (1994)
55. Van de Walle, N.: African Economies and the Politics of Permanent Crisis. Cambridge University Press, Cambridge (2001)
56. Clapham, C.: Third World Politics: An Introduction. University of Wisconsin Press, Madison (1985)
57. Medard, J.: The underdeveloped state in tropical Africa: political clientelism or neo-patrimonialism? In: Clapham, C. (ed.) Private Patronage and Public Power: Political Clientelism and the Modern State, pp. 162–192. St. Martin's Press, New York (1982)
58. Englebert, P.: State Legitimacy and Development in Africa. Lynne Rienner, Boulder (2000)

59. Bratton, M., Van de Walle, N.: Democratic Experiments in Africa: Regime Transitions in Comparative Perspective. Cambridge University Press, Cambridge (1997)
60. von Soest, C.: How Does Neopatrimonialism Affect the African State? The Case of Tax Collection in Zambia. Hamburg, 32 (2006)
61. Howes, A., Grimes, P., Lopez, A.L., Esteban, P.G., Shohel, M.M.C., Neff, D., Ramsden, A.: PhD fieldwork in developing countries – the issue of time. In: BAICE Conference 2006: Diversity and Inclusion (2006)
62. Rosaldo, R.: Culture & Truth: The Remaking of Social Analysis. Routledge, London (1993)
63. Mkandawire, T.: Neopatrimonialism and the political economy of economic performance in Africa: critical reflections (2013)
64. Mbaku, J.: Corruption and rent-seeking. In: Borner, S., Paldam, M. (eds.) The Political Dimension of Economic Growth, pp. 191–211. Macmillan, London (1998)
65. Herbst, J.: States and Power in Africa: Comparative Lessons in Authority and Control. Princeton University Press, Princeton (2000)
66. Boone, C.: The making of a rentier class: wealth accumulation and political control in Senegal. J. Dev. Stud. **26**, 425–449 (1990)
67. Lewis, P.: Role of government in the economy and the role of rent-seeking in african political economies: introduction. World Dev. **22**(3), 423–425 (1994)
68. Ghana Customs: Customs Excise and Preventive Services (2006). http://ghanadistricts.com/districts/?news&r=8&_=100. Accessed 5 Jan 2016
69. Chalfin, B.: Neoliberal Frontier. The University of Chicago Press, Chicago (2010)
70. Gardner, L.: Taxing Colonial Africa: The Political Economy of British Imperialism. Oxford University Press, Oxford (2012)
71. Young, C.: The African Colonial State in Comparative Perspective. Yale University Press, New Haven and London (1994)
72. Waijenburg, M.: Financing the African colonial state: the revenue imperative and forced labour (2015)
73. Acemoglu, D., Johnson, S., Robinson, J.A.: Institutions as a fundamental cause of long-run growth. In: Aghion, P., Durlauf, S.N. (eds.) Handbook of Economic Growth, vol. 1, no. 5. Elsevier B.V., Amsterdam (2005)
74. Boas, T.C., Gans-Morse, J.: Neoliberalism: from new liberal philosophy to anti-liberal slogan. Stud. Comp. Int. Dev. **44**(2), 137–161 (2009)
75. Harvey, D.: A Brief History of Neoliberalism. Oxford University Press, New York (2005)
76. Kotz, D.M.: Globalization and Neoliberalism. Rethink. Marx. **14**(2), 64–79 (2002)
77. Foucault, M.: The Subject and the Power. In: Dreyfus, H., Rabinow, P. (eds.) Michel Foucault: Beyond Structuralism and Hermeneutics, pp. 208–226. Harvester, Brighton (1982)
78. Foucault, M.: Governmentality. In: Burchell, G., Gordon, C., Miller, P. (eds.) The Foucault Effect: Studies in Governmentality, pp. 87–104. University of Chicago Press, Chicago (1991)
79. Cantens, T.: Is it possible to reform a customs administration? The role of the customs elite on the reform process in Cameroon (2012)
80. Bank of Ghana: Monetary Policy Report: Fiscal Developments. Financ. Stab. Rep., vol. 2, no. 1 (2012)
81. Stout, M., Amoah, L., Howe, L.: Public policy formation in Africa: toward a grounded ontology. Adm. Theory Prax. **32**(4), 606–609 (2010)
82. Amoah, L.: Constructing a new public administration in Africa. Adm. Theory Prax. **34**(3), 385–406 (2012)
83. Bruton, H.: A reconsideration of import substitution. J. Econ. Lit. **36**(2), 903–936 (1998)

Challenges for Health Indicators in Developing Countries: Misconceptions and Lack of Population Data

Flora Nah Asah[✉], Petter Nielsen, and Johan Ivar Sæbø

University of Oslo, Oslo, Norway
florana@ulrik.uio.no

Abstract. Indicators are foundational for planning, monitoring and evaluating of health services in developing countries. Most health indicators use population-based data, to enable comparison across geographical areas and over time. This paper is based on an interpretative case study on health indicators and how they are calculated and used at health facilities in Cameroon. We found that health managers at different levels of health systems do not share the same understanding of health indicators and we observed a wide-spread absence of population data. We further observed that health managers derive alternative ways of calculating indicators in the absence of population data. This paper contributes by discussing the implications of a lack of a common understanding of health indicators and the absence of population data to calculate health coverage indicators. Though this study was limited to data and program managers at district and regional levels, the findings raise issues that have wider applicability in the implementation of electronic health information system as well as how indicators such as UHC goals are calculated.

Keywords: Health indicators · Population-based data · Health management information system · Cameroon

1 Introduction

A key goal of a health system is to provide the necessary healthcare services to all those who are in need; thereby improving the health status of the population. International organisations such as WHO and United Nations, in partnership with governments of countries, have developed global initiatives to monitor performances of the health system. One concrete example is the United Nations' Sustainable Development Goals (SDGs) which target major health problems alongside other related problems alongside other related issues and constitutes a coordinating framework for these efforts (WHO 2010). Universal Health Coverage (UHC) is one of the goals of this initiative. UHC has been defined as the ability of all people who need health services to receive them without incurring financial hardship (WHO 2010; Kieny and Evans 2013). To monitor countries' health progress and performances towards supporting UHC, a range of health determinants' indicators have been developed. These indicators are measurable and time-bound.

J. Choudrie et al. (Eds.): ICT4D 2017, IFIP AICT 504, pp. 593–604, 2017.
DOI: 10.1007/978-3-319-59111-7_48

Examples of these health indicators include; *children under 5 sleeping under insecticide Treated Nets (ITNs)* and *births delivered in a birth facility*.

Health indicators are powerful tools used at all levels of the health system, for monitoring and evaluating and communicating information about the population's health (Mant 2001; Klazinga et al. 2001; Maniz 2003). They could be used to track how well (quality) and how far (quantity) countries' health system are performing (Klazinga et al. 2001; Maniz 2003).

An indicator has two parts; numerator and denominator that go into the formula for calculating them (Klazinga et al. 2001; Maniz 2003). Numerators are the things we count, i.e. *infants immunized* or *new cases of TB*. Denominators are the group with which the things we count are compared, i.e. *total population* or *all births in a year*. In the health system, indicators could also be used to measure a variety of dimensions concerning the health situation of the population; mortality, morbidity, health status.

There exist different types of indicators which could be used to monitor health progress, namely; health status, health systems, risk factors and health service coverage. Of important to this paper are health service coverage indicators.

These indicators reflect the extent to which people in need actually receive the health service they need (Tanahashi 1978; WHO 2009). This group of indicators measure the effectiveness of health programs. They help service providers to understand how effective an intervention is, and whether one target group is reached more effectively than another. They also help to identify underserved areas or regions which need more attention (Boerma et al. 2014). Most UHC indicators fall in this group.

Indicators in this group use population data as denominator, as it facilitates comparison of health status or health service provision over time and space. Coverage indicators are equally specific and valid for small and large geographic entities, and for any given time interval (WHO 2009). Examples of such indicators are; *immunization coverage, HIV testing coverage*, and *delivery in facility rate*. A common challenge is that there is lack of reliable population data to calculate them.

Population data is usually not accessible for smaller areas such as communities or districts (WHO 2009; Linard et al. 2012). Often, available population data is either outdated, not available for current administrative entities, not available for certain target populations (such as women of child-bearing age), or they may be duplicated sources of population data that do not necessarily provide the same figure (Linard et al. 2012; Leegwater et al. 2015; Bharti et al. 2016). The purpose of this paper is twofold. First, we are empirically exploring the understanding and use of health indicators by health program managers for decision-making. Second, we draw implications from this situation related to local practices and global initiatives such as UHC.

This study is derived from an ongoing implementation of an electronic system as a measure to strengthen Health Management Information system (HMIS) in Cameroon. This system is the main tool used for the management of health information nationwide. In this system, indicators are core element of data analysis, used to measure healthcare services.

2   Related Literature

In this section, we present relevant literature on health indicators to establish an understanding of what they are, what makes a good or poor indicator, and how they are used in health management.

Indicator(s) is developed by international organizations, reference groups and interagency groups, countries, academics, advocacy groups and others. From a performance management perspective, Flowers et al. (2005) describe indicator as a measure used to express the behavior of a system. In the public health context, indicators are specific tools for programme management, including the analysis and diagnosis of problems, and for taking correctives actions (Sahay et al. 2009).

Indicators are key statistical measure used to describe a situation, track progress and performance over time and to compare entities doing similar work. They could be used as a guide to decision making and set priorities (Donabedian 1966). They help to inform policy and policy-makers and can be used to improve quality of care and promote accountability (Donabedian 1966; Mainz 2003).

The literature explains that the process of selecting indicators should be systematic and based on facts rather than on feelings (Mant 2001). The process should involve all stakeholders and be based on "who wants the indicator", "how it is used" and "by whom" (Mant 2001; Klazinga et al. 2001). Heywood et al. (2001) explains that the process should employ understanding, discipline, teamwork and negotiation. Therefore, an ideal indicator should: (i) be based on agreed definitions; (ii) measure what it is intended to measure; (iii) give the same results if used by different people in different places; (iv) be simple to calculate using readily available data; (v) fit local needs, capacity and culture and the decisions to be made; (vi) be highly sensitive to changes in the situation concerned; (vii) permit useful comparison; (viii) be evidence-based (Heywood et al. 2001; Mainz 2003; Larson and Mercer 2004).

Indicators can be classified as: input, process, output, outcome and impact. Input indicators are the resources needed to implement work. Input indicators measure resources, both human and financial, allocated to a particular program. Process indicators measure whether planned activities did take place. For example, in antenatal care, process indicators can be *antenatal 1st visit before 20 weeks rate*, *antenatal client re-test rate*, and *post-natal visit with 2 weeks rate*. Output indicators measure first level results associated to an intervention. They are defined as what we produce. Some examples include; I*nfant 1st PCR test around 6 week uptake* or *delivery by caesarean section rate*. Outcome indicators measure what we have achieved and should be linked to concrete goals. Examples include; *delivery at facility for women under 18 years* and *live birth under 250 grams in facility rate*. Finally, impact indicators are the cumulative effect of the overall program (Mainz 2003; Heywood et al. 2001).

Indicators can be calculated in different ways; ratios, proportions, or rate (Worning et al. 1992; Mainz 2003). Ratios are numbers expressed in relation to another by dividing one number by the other. Here, the numerator is not part of the denominator. Proportion measures a part or amount that is part of a whole. The numerator is part of the denominator. Rate represents the frequency of an event in a specified period. In calculating a rate indicator, the numerator is the number of occurrences of an event during a period of time. The denominator is the number of person exposed to that event in the time period. These indicators are illustrated in Table 1 below.

Table 1. Different types of indicators

Indicator type	Description	Example
Ratio	Numerator is not included in the denominator	Ratio of male TB deaths to female TB deaths
Proportion	Numerator is contained in the denominator	Proportion of children one year old immunized against measles
Rate	Frequency of the event during a specific time in a given population	Deaths of children less than one year of age per 1000 live births

Population data is required as denominator to calculate these types of indicators. Since these are integral for health management, the lack of population data poses a challenge.

3   Research Context

The empirical setting within which the study was conducted is Cameroon. It is a low-income country, situated in the sub-Saharan Africa (SSA) region. It has an estimated population of 20.6 million (Chen et al. 2004). In Cameroon, basic public and social amenities for the vulnerable are either absent or inadequate. Nationally, 29.7% of the population does not have access to safe drinking water and 66.9% lack adequate sanitation, resulting in regular outbreaks of cholera and other water-related diseases (UNICEF 2015). The burden of healthcare financing is born largely by households through out-of-pocket payments (OOP). The government of Cameroon spends an average of USD 61 as per capita per person on health. Out of this amount, only USD 17 paid by the state, USD 8 comes from international donors, and USD 36 is OOP (Cameroon Economic Update 2013). Over the past two decades, health indicators have remained poor, and in some cases even worsened. Cameroon is struggling with high mortality and morbidity especially in rural communities. Mortality rate for children under 5 is 148 per 1000 live births, ranking Cameroon as 18th amongst 20 countries in the world with the highest mortality rate. Only 13% of children under the age of five sleep under insecticide-treated nets, in a country where malaria accounts for more than 40% of all deaths in this age group. Maternal mortality rate is alarmingly high, 670 per 100,000 births as compared to 546 per 100,000 live births in SSA. In addition, many women and girls have limited access to, and utilization of, prevention-of-mother-to-child transmission (PMTCT) services, resulting in HIV infection transfer to children (UNICEF 2015).

The healthcare system adheres to the district health approach, organised in three levels: the operational level, corresponding to district health care; hub of all health interventions; the intermediate level which is responsible for technical support, while the central level deals with the development of health policies. Different programmes operate at all three levels, engaged in the provision of specialised services such as maternal and child health, malaria,

HIV/AIDS, TB, and are supported by different donor agencies. The health system suffers from qualitative and quantitative shortage of human resources, and lack of technical and managerial expertise (Cameroon Economic Update 2013).

The health management information system (HMIS) in Cameroon is fragmented and characterised by vertical and fragmented information system and non-standardized data collection methods. DHIS2, the electronic tool used is housed at "Cellular National d'Informations Sanitaires" (CNIS), the department responsible for the management of health information in the country.

4   Research Design and Methods

The study is drawn from an interpretative strand (Walsham 1995). Interpretive research in Information Systems (IS) is useful as it helps researchers understand the problem in the contextual nature (Klein and Myers 1999).

Data was collected by the first author using qualitative methods. It included interviews, group discussion, and a document review. A total of 2 focus group discussions and 7 interviews were conducted in January and in July 2016, with Maternal and child health Programme Managers at district and national levels; data managers at district healthcare facilities, Matron in-charge of data management in wards, and Sister-in-charge of health facilities. 22 health and program managers participated in the study, of which 13 were females. Ten had no access to a computer and only 6 had Internet access. The document review included annual reports, strategy documents, and program reports.

Purposive sampling technique was used to select interviewees (Creswell 2007). This technique is used to achieve a homogeneous sample; that is sample of cases who share the same characteristics e.g. background or occupation. In this study, the interviewees shared a similar occupation; i.e. involved in data management at their respective facilities. An interview guide with broad themes around data management was used, focusing on understanding and use of health indicators. Permission to conduct the study was obtained from the Office of Regional Health delegate of each region and signed informed consent was obtained from each interviewee. The principle of data saturation was applied; i.e. interviews were ended when further probing were not adding new information. Permission to audio record interviews was obtained from interviewees at the start of every discussion and interviews were transcribed.

Data analysis was driven by the interpretive process and a descriptive approach with content analysis was used to analyse the data (Elo and Kyngas 2008). The interviews were transcribed verbatim. The interviews were read through several times to obtain a sense of the whole. The text was then divided into condensed meaning units. Open codes were used to group headings into categories to formulate a general description of the research questions. The interviews revealed themes which are interrelated. During this process, the data, themes and topics was discussed among the authors and based on these discussions the data was revisited.

5 Analysis

The analyses of the interviews and review of documents revealed the following:

A general observation in Cameroon is that population data is either outdated or not available. In the absence of reliable census data, the National Bureau of Statistics issues population figures per province and district to the Ministry of Public Health annually. However, for areas below the districts, it provides percentage per population group and annual projected growth rate per age group that has to be calculated by those who want to use population data. Usually, healthcare managers lack the necessary numeracy skills to perform such calculations. Also, these figures are not publicly available.

Data is collected at health facilities, and reported upward through health districts to the national level. At health facilities, daily registers are used to record activities from various units of the facility; outpatient, antenatal unit, labour and delivery, immunization and in-patient. At the end of each month, data from these registers are collated manually in to the Monthly Reporting Activity[1] (MRA) and also on Program Template forms. Thereafter, these forms are forwarded to the district office where data is captured electronically and their respective databases. MRA is captured into DHIS2 while program-specific data is captured on pre-designed Excel templates, hence forwarded to the regional level. At the regional level, data is also aggregated and synchronized to get the profile of the entire region before it is forwarded to the national level where analyses is done. We observed that the MRA is not comprehensive, as it does not contain all the data elements of health programs, as explained by one district manager:

> *"Previously, programs manage have their own reporting system but since the new CNIS director was appointed, he is trying to put some order in the system; starting by standardizing data collection tools. The data elements in MRA were selected based on the 100 indicator datasets as stipulated by WHO."*

Theme 1: Issues relating to Data Quality
Data Quality - Data review and giving feedback

It is essential to perform data quality checks. Exploring issues of data quality, we observed that data reviews and feedbacks are not standardized processes of data management. They are often done haphazardly and not frequently conducted at most facilities. District managers explain that due to lack of feedback, data clerks have cultivated the habit of falsifying data:

> *"When data clerks submit data and receive no feedback, they believe nobody checks the data submitted. Thus, they have cultivated the habit of cooking data and submitting."*

Despite being aware that neither data quality reviews are done nor feedbacks provided, district managers said they trust the quality of data: *"I only type and submit I do not use data. I cannot say anything about the quality of data. But I trust the data submitted by the matron in-charge"*

---

[1] The MRA does not have certain data elements which programs have to report on. Consequently, individual program have created their own data collection tools to collect program specific data.

Theme 2: Understanding of and use of health indicators
Understanding indicators: Nurse Managers at District & Regional Health facilities

We observed that health managers at operational levels seldom discuss about indicators and do not share the same level of understanding of indicators. In particular, facility level managers interviewed were not aware that there is a difference between an indicator and data element. They were neither able to understand what makes up an indicator nor how an indicator is calculated. They were also not able to differentiate a data element from an indicator. During the discussions, they would refer to "indicators" but when probing it became apparent that what they meant were "data elements". When asked to present a list of monthly priority indicators, a matron in-charge showed a list of monthly summary data element forms, noting: *"these are all our indicators that we report monthly. I write everything here on these forms and submit to them."* A similar situation was observed among district program managers. When asked to give example of some of the SDGs indicators in the program she manages she noted:

> *"Last week I went to the hospital for a visit. As I was walking out of the hospital, I caught sight of this beautiful picture with the following caption "breastfeeding is a sustainable development goal as will reduce infant mortality". That was the very first time I heard about sustainable development goals. I was so happy."*

While attending a monthly district meeting, Program managers were presenting monthly reports on facility visits conducted in their sub-districts. In the course of presenting these reports, they use phrases such as "low ANC coverage, low immunization coverage" as outcome of their visits. It was not clear from the presentations how they arrived at the decisions.

Use of indicators: Nurse Managers at Healthcare Facilities.

We also observed that health managers' use of indicators was minimal. A nurse manager explained that she uses indicators when preparing her performance-based business plan to help allocate targets (excerpt of plan presented on table below). A general complaint was the difficulties to do the calculations as illustrated in Table 2 below. For example, column 2 depicts how population data are presented to managers at health facilities.

A matron in-charge explains how she uses indicators:

> *"At the beginning of the year we have priority activities and also set which are reviewed annually. For example I know in this hospital, our consultation at the end of last year was 40,000. For this year, we should move up to about 45,000. If that is not achieved, we will know that we have not performed well and need to do something so that we can achieve more consultations. Two years ago, our consultations moved from 20,000 to 30,000. As a result of this increase, the director saw that the consultation area has become small. He expanded the waiting area, bought more chairs so that patients should sit down while waiting to be seen by a doctor."*

In the explanation above, the manager talked of "indicators" but what she is referring to are "data elements". She added that to calculate indicators, they would use the performance of the previous year or quarter to evaluate their facility's performance against set targets. To set indicator targets, it was observed that there are no clearly

Table 2. Level of achievement of the objectives of the last quarter business plan

Indicators	Monthly target calculation	Objective for the previous quarter (A)	Objective planned for the quarter (B)
Out Patient Consultations (new cases): Nurse	Total pop. of catchment area/ 12 × 80% × 90%	4025	4026 + 660
Referral received in the hospital	Pop × 1/12 × 1%	55	55 + 18
Cases of STIs treated	Total pop. of catchment area × 3%/ 12 × 80%	134	134 + 30
Children completely vaccinated	Total pop. of catchment area/ 12 × 4%	223	223 + 70
Normal Assisted Delivery	Total pop. of catchment area × 4%/ 12 × 80% × 70% × 90%	112	112 + 50

defined criteria to use. With reference to the Table 2 above, Columns 3 and 4, the nurse manager from another facility shared her experience:

> "As we prepare the business plan for PBF, we have working sessions with the PBF team. They will say for example, on the indicator: "Outpatient consultations (new cases): nurse", since we achieved 4025 in the last quarter, what do you think if we shift your objective for next quarter to 660 that is 4025 +660 = 4685. What do we do, we just have to accept? They do not take into consideration any other factor. It is our responsibility to ensure that the number cases are achieved at the end of the quarter. If we do not achieve it, we shall not benefit a single franc on this particular indicator."

Another facility manager added:

> "To set a target, we merely take the performance for the previous quarter, and add at least 5%. Five percentages is just an amount we decide to use. The idea is to encourage them to perform better than the previous quarter. However, there is a challenge because most often those targets sets are not achieved."

Use of Indicators at District Level

District managers use indicators to compile quarterly reports as explained by one of them:

> "Programs have specific indicator targets. Take for example, the indicator "immunization coverage." I am a statistician so when data arrives my office, after capturing, I do my calculation base on the targets and population projection I have. Hence, I compare the results (figures) with what was submitted for the previous months to know when I have achieved the target or not."

Another Program manager shared her experiences:

> "For example, as a HIV/AIDS program manager, this program is a priority program. I have monthly targets that were set and sent to me from Yaoundé [the capital in Cameroon] at the beginning of the year. Consider, for example, the indicator, "Treatment coverage among HIV/

AIDS positive pregnant women". Based on the data submitted, at the end of each month, I calculate the indicator and send the report to the national office in Yaoundé. "

Furthermore, the district program manager explains:

"If for examples the targets are not met, I will have to wait for instructions from Yaoundé before going out or planning for an intervention because Yaoundé makes all the decisions. "

Use of Indicators at the National Level

A director at the national explained that all decisions are made at the central level, the reason why data analyses are done there; at the national level. He added that indicators are used to evaluate program, but lamented on the quality of data. For example, he mentioned that most of the indicators routinely collected for his program are irrelevant. He also added that district managers are not involved in decision-making as this is the responsibility of those at the central level:

"Districts are not involved in decision-making. Except for the HIV/AIDS program, where program managers at district level have targets. Reasons being it is a priority program, with lots of international funding from PEPFAR. However, about which SDGs my program is reporting against, SDGs have not yet been made published. They are still waiting for the indicators and targets. "

Further, he added, indicators are often discussed only when preparing annual reports. This is the responsibility of the national program manager for monitoring and evaluation.

6   Discussion

The study provides tangible examples of health managers' understanding and use of indicators in healthcare settings. So how transferable are the findings? We found that these behavior were similar to other countries reported by Silvia et al. (2013), Thaizy et al. (2015).

The world's political agenda for the next 15 years (2016–2030) on health systems' strengthening is to reduce poverty through SDGs in general and UHC goals in particular. These are global initiative to monitor countries health performance. UHC are time-bound and measurable indicators to be monitored and reported against, annually by each country. Though internationally developed, most of the indicators are similar to those in a country's operational plans. Thus, decision and interventions made by policy makers and healthcare providers should be based on these indicators.

At the operational level, data to generate these indicators come from various health interventions done at district and communities levels. Therefore, it is important that healthcare professionals understand indicators and also know how they are calculated, as it might help them to monitor and evaluate their performances, and in the event of an outbreak, they intervene immediately.

While managers are should understand health indicators, it is important the government provides reliable population-based data. In Cameroon, population-data is available for the regions, and for administrative units below the district, projected population estimates are provided instead, and it is the responsibility of the district or facility managers to calculate these estimates, who in most cases lack the necessary numeracy skills.

A reliable source of population data is through census, but census is not frequently conducted. Data available is either outdated or does not exist in administrative unit below the district. However, there are other reliable sources of population-data. Citing an example from the developed countries, in Norway, the civil registration and vital statistics (CRVS) systems are reliable sources of population data. The government has introduced a method whereby these systems are maintained through incentives given to bother public and private entities and citizens to engage in proper and timely registration of vital events (Nielsen et al. 2015). Thus, the saying goes "population-data is the true denominator for development" (Purcell 2016).

Population-based provide an important piece of mosaic of evidence for decision-makers as well as healthcare providers. It can be used to assess the magnitude of health problems of which population are most vulnerable, such as to track and evaluate the effectiveness of health intervention for UHC.

Furthermore, health care providers dealing with indicators need to understand their meanings and what goes into calculating it (Sahay et al. 2009). In addition, indicators should be standardized as it improves data quality (Maniz 2003; Flower et al. 2005).

7   Conclusion

The study found that healthcare managers have difficulties understanding data elements and indicators. In the absence of population data, they use alternative method to calculate indicators. Although managers have priority indicators they report on monthly, coverage indicators are not calculated using population as denominator. This study extends research on how health information is used by healthcare providers based on a case study in Cameroon. Though this study was limited to data and program managers at district and regional levels of the health systems, the findings raise issues that have wider applicability in the implementation of electronic health information system as well as how health indicators such as UHC goals are calculated.

The primary concerns of case study research centers around validity and reliability (Merriam 1985). To address these concerns; for validity, we employed the process of triangulation, i.e. the use of a variety of data sources (interviews, focus group discussions and documents review) as opposed to relying solely upon one source. We have also included verbatim quotations (Johnson 1997) in the analysis section, consulted with senior directors at the ministry of health. To ensure reliability, the following measures were employed; interviews were recorded and transcribed, and during data analysis themes identified were discussed and agreed among the authors, before it was included in the paper (Roberts et al. 2006).

References

Bharti, N., Djibo, A., Tatem, A., Grenfell, B., Ferrari, M.: Measuring populations to improve vaccination coverage. Sci. Rep. **6**, 3454 (2016)

Boerma, T., AbouZahr, C., Evans, D., Evans, T.: Monitoring Intervention Coverage in the Context of Universal Health Coverage. PLoS Med. **11**(9) (2014)

Cameroon Economic Update: Towards greater equity. The World Bank, July 2013 (issue 6). http://www-wds.worldbank.org/external/default/WDSContentServer/WDSP/IB/2013/08/27/000333037_20130827110226/Rendered/PDF/806710WP0ENGLI0Box0379812B00PUBLIC0.pdf. Accessed Apr 2016

Chen, S., Ravallion, M.: How have the World's poorest fared since the early 1980s? World Bank, Development Research Group, Poverty Team, Washington, D.C. (2004)

Creswell, J.: Research Design: Qualitative, Quantitative, and Mixed Methods Approaches. Sage Publications, Thousand Oaks (2007)

Donabedian, A.: Evaluating the quality of medical care. Milbank Mem. Fund. Q. **44**, 166–206 (1966)

Elo, S., Kyngas, H.: The qualitative content analysis process. JAN **62**(1), 107–115 (2008)

Flowers, J., Hall, P., Pencheon, D.: Mini-symposium – Public health indicators. J. R. Inst. Publ. Health **119**, 239–245 (2005)

Heywood, A., Rohde, J.: Using Information for Action: A Manual for Health Workers at Facility Level. EQUITY Project, South Africa (2001)

Johnson, B.: Examining the validity structure of qualitative research. Education **118**(2), 282 (1997). Winter 1997, Research Library

Klein, K., Myers, D.: A set of principles for conducting and evaluating interpretive field studies in information systems. MIS Q. **23**, 67–94 (1999)

Kieny, M.-P., Evans, D.: Universal Health coverage. East Mediterr. Health J. **19**(4), 305 (2013)

Klazinga, N., Stronks, K., Delnoij, D., Verhoeff, A.: Indicators without a cause. Reflections on the development and use of indicators in health care from a public health perspective. Int. J. Q. Health Care **13**(6), 433–438 (2001)

Larson, C., Mercer, A.: Global health indicators: an overview. CMAJ **171**(10), 1199–1200 (2004)

Leegwater, A., Wong, W., Avila, C.: A concise, health service coverage index for monitoring progress towards universal health coverage. BMC Health Serv. Res. **15**, 230 (2015)

Linard, C., Gilbert, M., Snow, R., Noor, A., Tatem, A.: Population distribution, settlement patterns and accessibility across Africa in 2010. PLoS One **7**(2), e31743 (2012). Published online 21 Feb 2012

Mainz, J.: Developing Clinical indicators. Int. J. Qual. Health Care **15**(suppl 1), i5–i11 (2003)

Mant, J.: Process versus outcome indicators in the assessment of quality of healthcare. Int. J. Qual. Health Care **13**(6), 475–480 (2001)

Merriam, S.: The case study in educational research: a review of selected literature. J. Educ. Thought **19**(3), 204–217 (1985)

Nielsen, P., Sahay, S., Latifov, M.: Civil registration and vital statistics: a neglected area in information systems research. In: Proceedings of the 13th International Conference of Social Implications of Computers in Developing Countries, Negombo, Sri Lanka, May 2015

Purcell, W., Hall, I., Bernstein, L., Gift, L., McCray, E., Mermin, J.: The importance of population denominators for high-impact public health for marginalized populations. JMIR Publ. Health Surveill **2**(1), e26 (2016)

Roberts, P., Priest, H., Traynor, M.: Reliability and validity in research. Nurs. Stand. (through 2013) **20**(44), 41–45 (2006). Proquest

Sahay, S., Latifov, M.: The data indicator (Mis)Match: experiences from trying to strengthen this link in the Health Information System in Tajikistan. In: Proceedings of the 10th International Conference on Social Implications of Computers in Developing countries, Dubai, UAE, May 2009. Dubai School of Government (2009)

Silvia, G., Ramos, D., Boldrini, A., Silveira, K., Bernardes, A., Rocha, F.: Usage of quality indicators in hospital nursing in services in Brazil. J. Hosp. Adm. **2**(4), 2013 (2013)

Tanahashi, T.: Health service coverage and its evaluation. Bull. World Health Organ. **56**(2), 295–303 (1978)

Thaizy, S., Pedro, P., Andréia, G., de Oliveira, F.M.: The importance of using quality indicators in nursing care. Rev. Gaúcha Enferm. **36**(2), 82–88 (2015). Porto Alegre

UNICEF: Trends in Maternal Mortality 1990–2015. Estimates by WHO, UNICEF, UNPFA, World Bank Group and the United Nations Population Division (2015)

Walsham, G.: Interpretive case studies in IS research: nature and method. Eur. J. Inf. Syst. **4**(2), 74–81 (1995)

Worning, A., Mainz, J., Klanzinga, N., Gotrik, J.K., Johansen, S.: Policy on quality development for the medical profession in Danish. Ugesks Laeger **1992**(154), 3523–3533 (1992)

WHO 2009: World Health Statistics (2009). http://www.who.int/whosis/whostat/EN_WHS09_Table4.pdf. Accessed Apr 2016

WHO-World Health Report: Health Systems Financing: the path to Universal Health Coverage (2010). http://www.WHO.int/whr/2010/en. Accessed Apr 2016

Riding Waves of Change: A Review of Personas Research Landscape Based on the Three Waves of HCI

Chu Hiang Goh[1]([✉]), Narayanan Kulathuramaiyer[2], and Tariq Zaman[2]

[1] School of the Arts, Universiti Sains Malaysia, Gelugor, Penang, Malaysia
goh@usm.my
[2] Institute of Social Informatics and Technological Innovations,
Universiti Malaysia Sarawak, Kota Samarahan, Malaysia

Abstract. With the current growth of personas studies in HCI, we undertook the mapping out of the research approaches done for the past 18 years to provide an overall view on the landscape of personas research. Based on the narrative literature review of published work and paired with the three waves of HCI research development, we identified (1) the publication milestones of personas, (2) established genre of research approaches, and (3) the emerging issues and research trends. By looking at historical development of personas, the studies highlighted some key areas which might be the future trends of personas in the new wave of HCI. These will provide significant insight and direction for future research of personas.

Keywords: Personas · HCI · Participatory design · Cross-cultural design

1 Introduction

The field of HCI has evolved throughout the years; focus of research has progressed from human factors and usability to user experience and beyond. The use of computer devices shifted from office to the private and public spheres. Technology spreads from the workplace to our homes and everyday lives and has become part of our culture. Through the use of social media, the distinction of designer-user relationship becomes closer and the boundaries between professional designer and novice user are becoming fuzzy. The task of designer and developer as the sole creator for software and web application is no longer a paramount. Interaction between user and designer and the participation of user in the software and web application development process is crucial in the contemporary scene of HCI research and development. The in-depth understanding of the evolution of personas which has become the key user research instrument in User-Centred Design (UCD) is crucial to the HCI research.

This paper presents the literature review of an ongoing research that investigates the use of personas in sustaining local cultural identity. Drawn from the analysis of publications from ACM digital library and paired with Susanne Bødker's [1, 2] Three Waves HCI Challenge and Beyond, we mapped and visualised the landscape of personas studies throughout the years and foresee what lies beyond.

© IFIP International Federation for Information Processing 2017
Published by Springer International Publishing AG 2017. All Rights Reserved
J. Choudrie et al. (Eds.): ICT4D 2017, IFIP AICT 504, pp. 605–616, 2017.
DOI: 10.1007/978-3-319-59111-7_49

2   Etymology

The use of the term *persona* has an extraordinary shift if one were to trace it back to the classic origin in Greece [3]. The word is derived from Latin and its original meaning is very close to the idea of mask worn during drama performance and ritual activities. It was later described by the Roman philosopher, Cicero, as the peculiar relation of the individual to the society. In the early years of internet usage, it was referred to as the user's online identity which was distinct from the real-world identity. It was Allan Cooper [4] who gave the contemporary definition of persona which referred to as a creative way of constructing the type of person who would use a particular computer application. In a more precise approach, Putnam [5] defined it as an archetypal representation of a group of users with common goals, attitudes and behaviours when interacting with a product. Apparently, the wide spread use of persona in user experience design has overlooked the earlier definition of persona studies in representing one's online identity.

Personas are one of the most understandable deliverables in the user experience design. Three forms of terms were identified throughout the 315 publications. Namely: *persona* (in its singular form), *personas* (plural form) and *personae* which is the original form of the plural Latin word.

Most user experience designers adopted the plural form of *personas* due to the influence of the analytical work of Carl Jung [6]. The analysis of the 315 publications shows that 85.0% of the publications used the term personas to refer to the architype that referred to the collective character of users, 14.2% used the term *persona*, and 0.32% used *personae*. Nevertheless, the finding leaves room for further debate as the majority publications in ACM are User-Centric research focused.

3   Methodology

The literature review began with the construction of corpus of papers on personas in HCI by searching in ACM digital library's Full Text Collection. A total of 315 publications from ACM were retrieved as the result of an advanced search setting of keyword *Personas* in both titles and abstracts with the range of publication from year 1998 to 2016 (Fig. 1). 1998 was a significant year for the contemporary studies of personas as this was the year when Alan Cooper [4] published his ground-breaking book, *The Inmates Are Running The Asylum*. Publications in ACM's digital library were chosen because it is related to the ongoing research which focuses on the formulation of user-centric persona in the domain of HCI. Each publication was examined in the area of abstract, keywords and references. Inclusions and exclusions were made. The whole selection process was guided by four research questions:

RQ1: Which publications were cited in the reference?
RQ2: Which wave of the three waves of HCI does it belong to?
RQ3: What is the research approach carried out?
RQ4: What are the significant findings of the research?

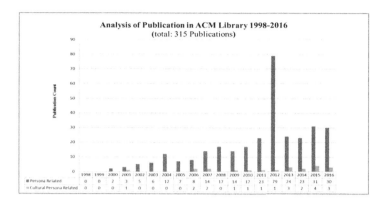

Fig. 1. Analysis of publications in ACM Digital Library 1998-2016

RQ1 led us to more publication findings for publications (such as books and book chapters) which are not in the collection of ACM digital library but have significant impact in the whole landscape development of personas. Publication milestones like Alan Cooper's [4] book *The Inmates Are Running The Asylum* scored the highest citation score amongst the 351 publications. The discovery of other review papers such as Marsden and Haag [7] *Stereotypes and Politics: Reflections on Personas* and Cabrero, Winschiers-Theophilus [8] *A Critique of Personas as representations of "the other" in Cross-Cultural Technology Design* provided resourceful references to reference findings of other related publications (Fig. 2). RQ2 and RQ3 helped us to analyse and classify the publications according to research approaches and pairing with the three waves of HCI development. This provided as information to visualise the landscape of the research approaches taken in the past years according to the research patterns that emerged.

Publication	ACM Citation	ACM Citation
Cooper (1998)	82	2592
Grudin & Pruitt (2002)	69	489
Grudin & Pruitt (2003)	110	608
Norman (2004)	27	39
Nielsen (2004)	41	PhD Thesis
Chapman (2006)	33	112
Adlin & Pruitt (2006)	61	719
Nielsen (2007)	42	16
Bodker (2012)	6	18
Friess (2012)	1	46
Bodker (2013)	1	4
Cabrero (2014)	0	5
Cabrero (2015)	0	8

Fig. 2. Citation Counts

RQ4 aimed to evaluate and exclude publications which are least significant. Citation counts were used as measurement for publications which are published for more than five years whilst new publications published for less than 5 years were selected based on the reputation of the authors in terms of publications in the field and the significance of the publications to the personas inferred in the three waves HCI development.

The analysis of the key publications indicates that there is a drastic increase in the publications of personas starting from 2007. This shows that the interest in gaining new knowledge in the studies of personas is growing. There was steep rise in 2012 with a record of 79 publications. This was due to a special conference on personas-*13th International Conference on Interacción Persona-Ordenador*. A total of 55 publications related to personas were yielded from that conference. The latest record in 2016 showed that there were 30 publications which is a 400% increase compared to 10 years ago. The research of personas has become a leading method in user experience design and it is gaining momentum every year.

A further filtered search in the existing 315 publications in ACM library with the keyword - *culture* and *cultural* resulted in the increase of cultural related studies of personas. This shows a new variant in personas which focused on local cultural approach and the awareness of the importance of ICT4D has increased.

4   Three Waves of HCI

Initiated by Bødker [1], the three waves of HCI captured and presented the challenges faced by HCI in the past three decades. Harrison, Tatar [9] postulated an almost similar idea in categorizing the development of HCI into 3 stages. Bødker [1] referred to it as three waves of HCI while Harrison (2007) referred to it as three paradigms of HCI development based on the phenomenological matrix they created. These prove that Bødker [1] was not alone in this effort and both studies capture an almost similar time-frame of the HCI development.

Referring to the history of HCI publications, Bødker [1] conjectured the challenges in HCI research which the HCI community has broadened intellectually from its root in engineering research to cognitive science, sociological studies, emotional design as well as social participatory research. It provides appropriate timeline for the quest of mapping the landscape development of personas in this research.

According to Bødker [2], we are currently 10 years beyond the third wave of HCI when she first introduced it in 2006. She established the three waves timeframe: first wave - from the early years of HCI to 1992, second wave – 1992 to 2006 and third wave – 2006 and beyond. The transition of first wave to second wave was discussed by Liam Bannon [10] in his milestone paper *From Human Factors to Human Actor*. The first wave was geared towards cognitive science and human factors. It was model driven and focused on the human being as a subject of rigid research with formal guidelines and systematic texting, and most of the studies were conducted in a closed scientific lab setting.

Bannon [10] observed there was a significant change in the second wave as there was a transition from *human factor to human actor* in the HCI research. User studies were carried out from the confined scientific labs to the real-life environment as anthropology ethnographic research approaches were adopted. Concept of context became important. This signified the beginning of UCD. Theories and research approaches from non-computer science disciplines were applied. Proactive methods, such as a variety of participatory design, prototyping and contextual inquiries, started to emerge in this wave [2, 11].

In the third wave, we observed the flourishing of consumer technology, integration of multiple devices such as desktop, laptop, iPad and mobile. Multiple user experience based situations become apparent when the devices were used in different environment. Ubiquitous computing (or "ubicomp") thrived whereby computing is made to appear anytime and everywhere [2]. Research in the third wave challenged the value related to the second wave and embraced experience and meaning-making [12]. User created content, common artifact and shared artifact coursed the boundary between user and designer becomes fuzzy in the realm of social network service (SNS). Scopes of proactive methods such as participatory design as well as the argument of the ability of such method from existing practices to the need of emergent use were broadened.

5   Four Research Approaches of Personas

In the investigation of the common personas research approach practice by researches, we discovered an additional approach which is popular among the researches other than the three which has been posited by Lene Nielsen in 2004. It is Donald Norman [13] Ad-Hoc Personas. The additional ad-hoc personas discovered in our finding showed a significant number of references due to its ad-hoc basis. The four research approaches in chronology are:

- Alan Cooper (1998)– Goal Oriented Personas
- Adlin and Pruitt (2002) – Role Based Personas
- Donald Norman (2004) – Ad-Hoc Personas
- Lene Nielsen (2007)– The Engaging Personas

The goal-oriented persona was the earliest method used by user experience designers and researches based on Cooper's book and his earlier practice in his user experience and strategy firm – Cooper. The approach was strictly goal oriented whereby goals were set in various personas and were differentiated from one another based on their different goals. The approach was popular in the 90's and early 2000.

Norman [13] ad-hoc personas were created in a simple and fast ad-hoc approach which was mainly used as a communication tool to assist quick design decision making. Persona methods comprised ad-hoc assumption to invent personas based on the designer's experience. Role plays and affinity diagramming were involved in the process. Non-data and non-real user involved. Even though the approach may lack scientific validation, it provided a useful agile solution to practicing designers who needed a quick design decision making. The approach was popular among designers from the non HCI domain.

Adlin and Pruitt [14] in their book *Persona Lifecycle: Keeping People in Mind Throughout Product Design* proposed another new approach which was based on the personas' life cycle. It was a role-based approach. Personas were defined by their roles. The similar approach was engaged in another two publications - Grudin and Pruitt [11],

Grudin and Pruitt [15]. There were five phases in the persona life cycle. Personas were able to be re-cycled and given new life by updating the user data.

Lene Nielsen [16, 17] posited a method which engaged both personas and scenarios in her PhD thesis. The method claimed to be more precise and effective in user personas studies as it was scenario oriented and each persona's differences were based on the task they performed at different time and occasion.

6   Mapping of the Landscape of Persona Studies

Based on the analysis from the popularity of citation references and crossed references in the collected ACM publications, 20 papers were identified and engaged in the mapping of the personas research landscape. Four highly cited papers were selected to signify the changes of waves in the landscape map. As discussed earlier in the three waves of HCI section, based on Bødker [1] Three Waves of HCI, the four publications by Bannon [10], Bødker [1], Harrison, Tatar [9], and Bødker [2] were positioned as publication milestones for each wave of HCI in the left column of the map. Themes were drawn based on the criteria of the three waves as posited by Bødker [2]. These are used as guidelines to identify and justify the personas in the right column of the map (please refer to Appendix). No theme nor papers were identified in the first wave as it was not significant in user personas studies.

These identified themes are:

Second wave:

- Transition from human factor to human actor
- Engagement of other disciplines in research.
- Proactive methods such as participatory design was engaged.

Third wave:

- Embracing user experience and meaning-making by the user.
- Re-examination of the scopes and effectiveness of participatory design.
- The use context and application type broadened and intermixed.

6.1   Second Wave

The emphasis on user centered design in the second wave of HCI provides opportunities in user personas development. Various key developments of personas took place during this period. A total of 7 papers were selected and positioned under the second wave of HCI. These papers were selected based on the popularity in reference citation and a crossed check in both google scholar citation and ACM citation have been carried out to verify the selection. All the publication milestones in the four leading research approaches of personas posited in earlier section were all found here in the second wave. Alan Cooper's [4] book, *The Inmates Are Running The Asylum,* is the leading paper in the area with a score of 2592 in google citation and 27 in ACM citation of the 315 paper analyzed. Cooper's definition of personas remains the most cited definition to date.

Adlin and Pruitt [14]'s book, *Persona Lifecycle: Keeping People in Mind Throughout Product Design,* is the second most cited publication with a score of 719 in google citation and 61 in ACM citation. Together with other two papers, Grudin and Pruitt [11], Grudin and Pruitt [15], it provides popular resource in persona creation methods. Norman (2004) and Nielsen (2004) are the other two publication milestones in defining the four research approaches of personas.

Adlin and Pruitt [14] and Grudin and Pruitt [15] posited the argument of the *personas vs scenario* proposition which seemed in line with the theme of the second wave - transition of human factor to human actor. The pursuit of ethnographical data collection method attempts to imitate human behaviour in the creation of personas. This is demonstrated in the second wave of research trend which attempts to engage other disciplines in persona research.

Grudin and Pruitt [15] showed the attempt to anticipate participatory design in personas and this was highly sorted by other researches with a high google citation count of 489 and ACM citation 69. These show a good acceptance of engaging participatory design in this era.

Chapman and Milham [18] is the sole paper that warned about the pitfall amidst the high popularity of the usage of personas. They argued about the validity of methods employed in personas which led to political conflicts and undermined the ability for researchers to resolve questions with data.

6.2 Third Wave

The third wave signified the awareness of user participatory design, and this has created a significant impact in the studies of personas whereby participatory design has become the focus in many major persona research papers. The third wave also indicated that some researchers have started to argue about the effectiveness of user personas in HCI research. This provided a counter-checking effect in the field and it helped in re-evaluating and refining the user study method and further improved the studies in the long run. These adhered to the formulated third theme as mentioned above.

The selection of the 8 publications in this era were merely based on inferring to the significant contribution of the publications adhered to the formulated theme of the third wave. Bødker, Christiansen [19] argued that personas do not support participatory design in her studies of e-government user studies. She warned about the overwhelming popularity of personas where researches overlooked the effective link of created personas and design decision-making in design process. Echoing her argument, Friess [20] conducted a discourse analysis of the decision-making of designers in a top tier design firm which revealed that although the designers dedicate much efforts in developing and refining personas, personas were relatively low in appearances in the designers' design decision-making. Personas merely served as an effective communication in both findings. Bødker and Nylandsted [21] further posited a new approach in the research of personas by connecting created personas with the underlying technology of an application. This was in line with the theme of the third wave of personas which embraced multiple devices and mixed complex engagements. Marsden and Haag [7] provided an in-depth reflection on personas regarding the benefits and downfalls of persona methods in most of the academic discourse. She warned of the potential stereotyping and the use of personas as political tool in design process which is different from the original motive of design.

In a nutshell, the third wave research highlighted certain pitfalls in the studies of personas as outlined below:

- There was a missing link between personas and designers. There was a tendency for designers not to design according to the personas and made design decision based on their own intuition. This problem occurred mostly due to time and financial constraint during design process.
- There was no direct link between data generated personas and the automated design application (persona vs techsona [21]).
- Data generated personas posted a threat in marginalizing minority user groups to fulfill the requirement of majority groups.
- Potential bias and stereotyping occurred during the creation of personas as well as design process by designers who had agenda in their design.

7   Cultural Personas in Beyond the Third Wave

Bødker described the HCI development of 10 years after the third wave as a chaos of multiplicity in terms of technology, use situations, methods and concepts [2]. We are in the era of the emergent of diversive communication devices which leads to intermixing of personal, work space, user experiences, common artifacts and meaning making and the fuzziness in professional designer and novice use boundaries. The development of personas and participitary design has no exception. Our analysis revealed that there are multiple dimensions of development in personas beyond the third wave. It is rather early to define it and map it in the research landscape, albeit demonstrating a potential trend of development in various dimensions. As the publications in cultural personas research per se, the development is encouraging.

The ACM digital library publication analysis shows the interest in cultural related personas research starting from 2006 and there is an increase since 2015. Research of the underrepresented cultural group and the micro-culture seems to be an interesting one. Daniel G. Cabrero published a total of five articles in ACM digital library from between 2014 and 2016. This demonstrated the highest publication of an individual author in the review. Cabrero, Winschiers-Theophilus [8], Cabrero [22], Cabrero [23] demonstrated a new dimension in the studies of personas in the third wave and beyond with rigorous participatory research involving realist emic engagement.

Cabrero [22, 23] conducted his research in rural folks in Namibian whereby participatory design approach was adopted with the involvement of the local in the creation of personas. Sharing his participatory design approach in cultural personas were Zaman and Winschiers-Theophilus [24] where they conducted a community-based co-design personas creation involving semi-nomadic Penan in Borneo Island, Malaysia. The studies focused on digitalizing the Penan sign language – Oroo which are only known by the older generations of the locals whereby co-design with the locals seemed to be the effective method in capturing the tacit indigenous knowledge. The personas formulated were hand-drawn and created by the locals themselves.

Conducting cultural design studies outside the real insider context could post a risk if culturally designs are flawed as posited by Goh [25]. Under justified and false *pseudo-etic* claims in cultural 'findings' represent common problems in cross-cultural design and realist emic engagement approaches carried out by both authors above seemed to be a virtuous solution in capturing and creating local cultural sensitive personas.

Decolonising research methodology has become one of the new agendas beyond the third HCI wave. This demonstrated how indigenous peoples and locals could be involved in research within their own communities and defining their own indigenous knowledge. This echoes with Raewyn Connell's [26] Southern Theory in decolonising local knowledge. She posited the key contemporary form of southern theory was the use of main stream institution and tools to break free from the Northern hegemony by defining intellectual agendas. The creation of local cultural sensitive personas and the participation of users in the process seem to be the emerging trend in personas studies. Further research in this area to fill the gap and the need to generate new knowledge in this area would be crucial.

8   Conclusion

The studies of personas are becoming a leading method in current user centred studies in information system design. Starting from 1998, there are various researches done and papers published to develop and improve the efficiency of the method and user studies approach. The fundamental methodology influences of leading researches namely - Alan Cooper, Tamar Adlin & John Pruitt, Lene Nielsen are significant insight in many researches. The emerging trend of personas in international users and local cultural contexts is becoming crucial at this present moment and fast becoming a significant method in sustaining local cultural identity and securing the future of ICT4D. Participation design and co-creation of personas seems to be a noble solution in the effort of sustaining local culture and identity.

Appendix- Personas Research Review Landscape

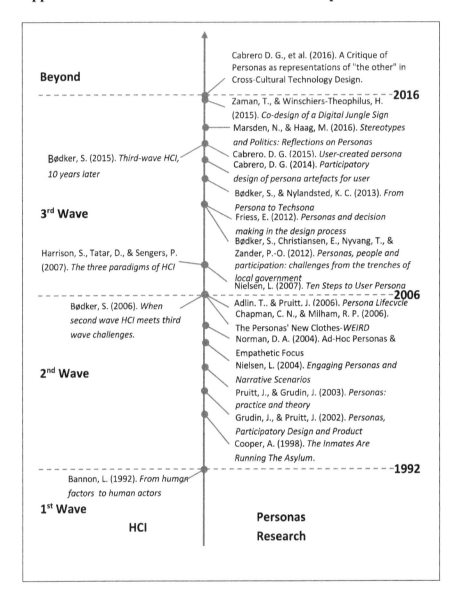

References

1. Bødker, S.: When second wave HCI meets third wave challenges. In: Proceedings of the 4th Nordic Conference on Human-Computer Interaction: Changing Roles, pp. 1–8. ACM, Oslo (2006)
2. Bødker, S.: Third-wave HCI, 10 years later—participation and sharing. Interactions **22**(5), 24–31 (2015)

3. Marshall, P.D., Barbour, K.: Making intellectual room for persona studies: a new consciousness and a shifted perspective. Pers. Stud. **1**(1), 1–12 (2015)
4. Cooper, A.: The Inmates are Running the Asylum. Sams Publication, Indianapolis (1998)
5. Putnam, C., Kolko, B., Wood, S.: Communicating about users in ICTD: leveraging HCI personas. In: Proceedings of the Fifth International Conference on Information and Communication Technologies and Development, pp. 338–349. ACM, Atlanta (2012)
6. Jung, C.: Psychological Types: The Collected Works of CG Jung, vol. 6. Routledge, London (1991)
7. Marsden, N., Haag, M.: Stereotypes and politics: reflections on personas. In: Proceedings of the 2016 CHI Conference on Human Factors in Computing Systems, pp. 4017–4031. ACM, Santa Clara (2016)
8. Cabrero, D.G., Winschiers-Theophilus, H., Abdelnour-Nocera, J.: A critique of personas as representations of "the other" in cross-cultural technology design. In: Proceedings of the First African Conference on Human Computer Interaction, pp. 149–154. ACM, Nairobi (2016)
9. Harrison, S., Tatar, D., Sengers, P.: The three paradigms of HCI. In: Alt. CHI (2007)
10. Bannon, L.: From human factors to human actors: the role of psychology and human-computer interaction studies in system design. In: Greenbaum, J., Kyng, M. (eds.) Design at Work, pp. 25–44. L. Erlbaum Associates Inc., Hillsdale (1992)
11. Grudin, J., Pruitt, J.: Personas, participatory design and product development: an infrastructure for engagement. In: Proceedings of the Participatory Design Conference, Malmo, Sweden (2002)
12. McCarthy, J., Wright, P.: Technology as Experience. MIT Press, Cambridge (2004)
13. Norman, D.A.: Ad-Hoc Personas & Empathetic Focus (2004). http://www.jnd.org/dn.mss/personas_empath.html. 28 October 2016
14. Adlin, T., Pruitt, J.: Persona Lifecycle: Keeping People in Mind Throughout Product Design. Morgan Kaufmann, Burlington (2006)
15. Grudin, J., Pruitt, J.: Personas: practice and theory. In: Proceedings of the 2003 Conference on Designing for User Experiences, pp. 1–15. ACM, San Francisco (2003). ISBN: 1-58113-728-1
16. Nielsen, L.: Ten Steps to User Persona By Dr. Lene Nielsen (2007)
17. Nielsen, L.: Engaging Personas and Narrative Scenarios. Ph.D. series, vol. 17, Copenhagen Samfundslitteratur (2004)
18. Chapman, C.N., Milham, R.P.: The personas' new clothes: methodological and practical arguments against a popular method. Proc. Hum. Factors Ergon. Soc. Ann. Meet. **50**(5), 634–636 (2006)
19. Bødker, S., et al.: Personas, people and participation: challenges from the trenches of local government. In: Proceedings of the 12th Participatory Design Conference: Research Papers - Volume 1, pp. 91–100. ACM, Roskilde (2012)
20. Friess, E.: Personas and decision making in the design process: an ethnographic case study. In: Proceedings of the SIGCHI Conference on Human Factors in Computing Systems, pp. 1209–1218. ACM, Austin (2012). ISBN: 978-1-4503-1015-4
21. Bødker, S., Klokmose, C.N.: From persona to techsona. In: Kotzé, P., Marsden, G., Lindgaard, G., Wesson, J., Winckler, M. (eds.) INTERACT 2013. LNCS, vol. 8120, pp. 342–349. Springer, Heidelberg (2013). doi:10.1007/978-3-642-40498-6_26
22. Cabrero, D.G.: Participatory design of persona artefacts for user eXperience in non-WEIRD cultures. In: Proceedings of the 13th Participatory Design Conference: Short Papers, Industry Cases, Workshop Descriptions, Doctoral Consortium Papers, and Keynote Abstracts - Volume 2, pp. 247–250. ACM, Windhoek (2014)

23. Cabrero, D.G.: User-created persona: Namibian rural Otjiherero speakers. In: Proceedings of the 33rd Annual International Conference on the Design of Communication, pp. 1–6. ACM, Limerick (2015). ISBN: 978-1-4503-3648-2
24. Zaman, T., Winschiers-Theophilus, H.: Co-design of a digital jungle sign language application. In: Proceedings of the 15th IFIP TC 13 International Conference (INTERACT 2015) (2015)
25. Goh, C.H.: Cross-cultural web design study: designers' challenging task in developing country. Asia Pac. J. Contemp. Educ. Commun. Technol. **2**(1), 190–199 (2016)
26. Connell, R.: Decolonising Knowledge, Democratising Curriculum (2016). (cited 2006 18 December 2016). http://www.raewynconnell.net/2016/10/decolonising-curriculum.html

A Model for Developing Usable Integrated Case Management Information Systems

Edgar Kuhimbisa[✉], Rehema Baguma, and Agnes Nakakawa

College of Computing and Information Sciences,
Makerere University, Kampala, Uganda
edgarkuhimbisa@gmail.com, rehema.baguma@gmail.com,
agnesnakakawa@gmail.com

Abstract. The increased adoption of technology in government-driven processes and services over the years has led to the use of information and communication technologies (ICTs) as mechanisms and platforms for citizens to
access justice services and participate in the judicial process. In Uganda, there are
current and ongoing efforts, through e-justice initiatives in the Justice, Law and
Order Sector, to integrate case management information systems in criminal
justice institutions as a means of improving worker productivity, facilitating
information sharing, collaboration, better information access by the general
public, citizen engagement and satisfaction with public services. The focus for
this study was to devise a model that provides guidance on how to develop
integrated information systems that are usable – by supporting improved
human-driven legal processes, increased citizen engagement and facilitation of
interaction between justice agencies and the general public. Based on the
requirements for usable integrated information systems obtained from the review
of literature and a survey, a model for guiding development of usable integrated
case management information systems known as the Architecture-driven
Usability Process Model (AdUPRO) was created.

Keywords: Usability · Integrated information systems · Case management ·
E-Justice

1 Introduction

Uganda's Justice, Law and Order Sector (JLOS) is a collection of government institutions with shared and closely linked mandates of administering justice, maintaining
law and order and human rights. Whereas JLOS program reforms are credited with
improved access to justice, there still exist systemic challenges in ensuring access to
justice for all Ugandans especially for the poor and marginalized persons [10]. The lack
of well designed, effective and efficient case management information systems has been
identified as one of the bottlenecks in the delivery of justice in Uganda characterized by
challenges in reporting crimes by the public, tracking cases, citizen participation in
court processes, management of suspects and allocation of human and financial
resources [10]. Where information systems exist in Uganda's criminal justice system,
these (systems) were originally designed to function within individual institutional

© IFIP International Federation for Information Processing 2017
Published by Springer International Publishing AG 2017. All Rights Reserved
J. Choudrie et al. (Eds.): ICT4D 2017, IFIP AICT 504, pp. 617–628, 2017.
DOI: 10.1007/978-3-319-59111-7_50

contexts with minimal or no interface with systems in other institutions. Furthermore, most of these systems were acquired off-the-shelf and they are mainly used for data capture with little or no support for dissemination of information and user interaction. This lack of effective mechanisms for interaction and engagement disempowers members of the public who are participants in the justice process as victims of crime, accused parties, court litigants, private counsel and members of the jury.

Systems integration in the justice sector can be viewed as a step towards "ICT4D 2.0" where new e-governance realities are created through more information intensive processes, information sharing, collaboration, increased user engagement and participation in the justice due process. This e-governance paradigm facilitated by integration of information spaces leads to "i-governance" – which according to Heeks [8] integrates people, processes, information and technology in the service of achieving governance objectives. However, the systems integration process results into a union of different processes, end users, corporate cultures and diverse information behaviors [3]. This environment of diversity presents a critical usability challenge that may ultimately contribute to the failure e-governance projects. The recommendation therefore, is that technology implementations should not undermine but rather accommodate this diversity [14].

ISO defines usability as "the extent to which a product can be used by specified users to achieve specified goals with effectiveness, efficiency, and satisfaction in a specified context of use" [11]. Therefore for the integrated information system for Uganda's Justice, Law and Order Sector to achieve its intended objectives, it must be usable – designed to consider various usability aspects such as users of the system (considering their behavioral characteristics, cognitive abilities and conative tendencies), tasks and roles, business processes, goals of the users and an understanding of the dynamic contexts in which the (integrated) information system will be used [6, 7].

However, there is still lack of an appropriate approach for analyzing and incorporating the dynamic and often complex usability aspects in the design of integrated information systems. Existing models do not provide adequate guidance on how to achieve usability in the development of integrated information systems. Hence, there is need for more research about how usability issues of integrated information systems can be addressed. This study examines how the usability aspects of integrated information systems can be addressed in the process of developing integrated information systems that are a must have in certain settings such as the Justice, Law and Order sector in Uganda. The next section presents the methodology that was used to address the objectives of this study.

2 Methodology

To achieve the objectives of this study i.e. to collect requirements for usable integrated information systems; and to design a model for developing usable integrated criminal case management information systems, the following methodology was followed: For the first objective, the study used review of related literature from journals, book chapters, conference proceedings and a survey to establish usability requirements for integrated information systems. The aim of literature review was to establish what related research studies have given as usability requirements for integrated information systems. On the other hand, the survey was aimed at establishing the usability needs for an integrated case management information system in Uganda and ways such needs can be met from public officials in the four JLOS institutions studied i.e. the Uganda Police, Directorate of Public Prosecutions (DPP), the Judiciary and the Uganda Prisons Services. These institutions are representative of the case management process in the criminal justice system in the country.

Other respondents in this survey were drawn from members of the general public and practicing private lawyers. Members of the general public that participated in the survey were those that regularly interact with the Police, DPP, Judiciary and the Uganda Prisons Services through requests for information and services.

Selection of respondents was based on participants' level of knowledge and insight into how the justice system operates based on previous verified experience. This sampling technique was vital in order to obtain first hand information about the usability needs, information collected, stored and used in the Justice, Law and Order Sector.

Eighty-five (85) officials from the Uganda Police, DPP, Judiciary and Uganda Prisons Service (state actors) participated in the survey. These included: Uganda Police (06 Criminal Intelligence and Investigation Department Officers, 05 Data Managers, 06 Records Clerks/Officers (02), Forensic Officers; 01 Public Relations Officer); Directorate of Public Prosecutions (08 State Attorneys, 01 Client Relations Officer, 05 Records Clerks, 04 Data/Information Managers; Judiciary (04 Judges, 07 Magistrates, 05 Data/Information Managers, 06 Records Clerks/Officers, 02 Public Relations Officers); Uganda Prisons (06 Prison Warders, 07 Facility administrators (Officers-in-Charge), 05 Records Clerks/Officers, 04 Data/Information Managers, 01 Public Relations Officer).

Fifteen (15) members of the public – seven males and eight females, with a history of interaction with the criminal justice system were selected to participate in the survey. Ten (10) private lawyers that interact with the criminal justice system through legal representation of members of the general public during the litigation process were selected to also participate in the study.

A self-administered questionnaire was chosen as an appropriate data collection tool for public officials because it facilitated gathering of a significant number of responses from a large sample of respondents in a relatively short period of time. An interview guide was deemed suitable for gathering responses from the general public and private legal practitioners due to its ability to gather detailed responses (opinions and perceptions).

Requirements gathered from the questionnaire, interviews and review of related literature were used to design a model known as the Architecture-driven Usability Process Model (AdUPRO) that provides guidance on how to design usable integrated information systems. The next section presents findings from the study.

3   Findings

This section presents usability requirements for integrated information systems gathered from the review of related literature, and the survey.

Information Presentation is Critical for Decision-Making

Information presentation is the use of computer-supported interactive visual representation of abstract data to amplify cognition [4]. According to Dykes et al. [5], information presentation aims at providing graphical presentations and user interfaces for interactively manipulating information items. Integrated information systems should therefore be able to provide a mechanism for providing appropriate presentation of processed data from the various institutions into well-aggregated facts for users to derive meaning and use as a basis for decision-making.

Early Focus on Users is a Critical Design Success Factor

Understanding user needs is a necessary condition for designing a system that users can integrate into their work and which reflects their worldview [14]. Participation of the public (citizens) in e-government processes is identified as a critical success factor where public decisions are responsive to citizen's views or needs [8]. Therefore, involving the public in the systems design process ensures that their views and perspectives on the usability of technology (integrated information systems in case management) are taken seriously and adhered to as critical.

Iterative Design

Iterative design relates to being able to continuously modify a system as per the testable behavioral goals and available user feedback till the system is deemed usable. However, iterations to design are often ignored because they make the entire process of systems development a long and expensive venture [12]. According to Gould and Lewis [7], iterative design should not be viewed as a luxury tuning method that puts finishing touches on a design but rather as a way of confronting the design actuality of unpredictable user needs and behaviors that can lead to sweeping and fundamental changes in the design.

Information Systems Currently Used by JLOS Institutions

The four (4) institutions surveyed use different types of information systems each tailored to the agency's mandate and information needs. The Crime Records Management System (CRMS) in the Uganda Police supports the day-to-day transactions of crime records management at police stations; the Prosecutions Case Management System (PROCAMS) in the office of the DPP provides overall management of case files management by the prosecutions offices; the Court Case Management System (CCAS) in the Judiciary is customized software for managing case records-with both civil and criminal case management modules; and the Prisons Information Management System (PIMS) manages prisons data on inmates and prison facilities across the country. Although all JLOS institutions currently have information systems in some form, they are still stand-alone. Therefore, there is a need for an integrated information system that the four (4) institutions can jointly use and leverage for collaboration, information sharing and engagement with the public in the provision of services.

Levels of Proficiency with Information Communication Technology

Respondents were asked about their level of proficiency in use of information and communication technologies (ICTs). Among state actors, 33% rated their ICT proficiency as sufficient; 57% as basic; and 10% insufficient. For private lawyers, 85% of private lawyers rated themselves as sufficiently IT proficient while 15% rated their proficiency with ICTs as basic. None of the private lawyers surveyed rated themselves insufficient in the use of ICTs. A big section of respondents from the public (85%) said their knowledge of ICTs was insufficient, 5% sufficient and 10% basic.

Information Management Practices
Ninety two (92%) of state actors; 80% of members of the general public; and 90% of private lawyers viewed information sharing between institutions involved in case management as vital. State actors viewed information sharing as vital to increasing the rate of case completion leading to better service delivery (through improved collaboration and coordination). Members of the general public and private lawyers viewed information sharing as critical in improving the quality of investigations (between the Police and DPP); and an avenue for resolving cases faster (in the Judiciary). Therefore, there is need for a uniform information organization scheme for the JLOS institutions that will form the basis for information integration and sharing.

The next section presents requirements for developing usable integrated case management information systems.

4 Requirements for Developing Usable Integrated Information Systems

This section presents requirements for developing usable integrated information systems based on the findings from the review of related literature and the survey.

4.1 Information Aggregation and Presentation Requirements

Integrated case management information systems should be able to provide a mechanism for providing appropriate presentation of processed data from various sources into well-aggregated facts for users to derive meaning and use as a basis for decision-making. Process managers and policy makers at the JLOS Secretariat (program coordination office) and in other management structures at institutional level require tools and interfaces to be able to access and manipulate the vast amounts of interconnected case data and visualize the outcome as a basis for decision making, formulation of policy direction, planning and strategy development.

4.2 User Diversity (Cognitive Ability, Physical Capacity and Technical Proficiency) Requirements

Unique characteristics of the diverse end-users in JLOS that impact on the overall usability of integrated information systems should be taken into account during the design process. These characteristics relate to user's cognitive ability (general appreciation and comprehension of subject matter, knowledge of the application domain and knowledge of the interface syntax/semantics); ICT proficiency; and physical state of the users. For example 33% of state actors rated their ICT proficiency as sufficient; 57% as basic; and 10% as insufficient. Eighty five (85) % of private lawyers rated themselves as sufficiently IT proficient while 15% rated their knowledge of ICTs as basic. Additionally, the majority of those surveyed (90%) viewed issues of physical disability as vital considerations during design and development of information systems (ergonomics).

4.3   Information Organization Requirements

Information organization is the process of providing structure to information and definition of relationships between information items and groups [13]. An average of 81% of respondents (65% in the Police; 85% in the DPP; 90% in the Judiciary; and 84% in the Prisons) said their institutions had some form of scheme for logically organizing information. However, only 18.5% of these respondents believed their in-house schemes for structuring information are satisfactory and aligned to case management business processes. Lack of a uniform case identification scheme used by all the four institutions for processing cases in the criminal justice system was identified as a major information organization challenge. Therefore, there is need to provide useful and creative ways of sorting and organizing (structuring) information through an enterprise information architecture.

4.4   Information Sharing Requirements

Information sharing is the process of exchanging of information assets between people and agencies. Ninety two (92%) of state actors, 80% of members of the general public, and 90% of private counsels viewed information sharing between institutions involved in case management as vital. State actors associated information sharing to increasing the rate of completion of the case management process leading to better service delivery (through improved collaboration and coordination). Members of the general public and private counsel viewed information sharing as critical in improving the quality of investigations (between the Police and DPP); and as an avenue for resolving cases faster (in the Judiciary). Therefore, the model should support the discovery of information and collaboration between users in the different JLOS institutions through information sharing.

4.5   Need to Cater for the Evolving Nature of Information Systems

Seventy-five (75%) of state actors surveyed during the survey identified the changing nature of information systems in the Sector as a major challenge to sustainable usability. Changes in user needs, introduction of new processes (and business rules), introduction of new technologies et cetera often call for re-engineering of the existing systems. This creates challenges of balancing usability and functionality – with the former being often sacrificed at the expense of the latter. The requirement to address this scenario is to ensure that usability of the systems is synchronized with the changing nature of the business environment and technology. That is there should be proper integration of usability aspects in the overall design process during changes in business vision and transitions.

4.6   Harmonize Technologies Used

The four (4) institutions surveyed operate and maintain different types of case management information systems each tailored to the agency's mandate and information needs. Additionally, this problem is also faced in some individual institutions such as judiciary that has different versions of the Court Case Management System running in different courts. The diverse nature of different (and in some instances legacy) technology platforms currently in use presents interoperability challenges in the integration effort. There is therefore need to harmonize hardware and software platforms across the JLOS institutions involved in criminal justice case management.

4.7   Process Efficiency Requirements

The primary interest of case management is how information on file is leveraged in solving the case at hand. State actors were asked to rate the service turn around for their respective case management systems. Process completion rates in the Uganda Police were rated at an average of two to three (2–3) days; two (2) days for the DPP; three (3) days for Judiciary, and one (1) day for the Uganda Prisons. Ninety (90%) of public officials attributed the slow case management process to poorly designed business processes; and 10% attributed this challenge to entrenched institutional bureaucratic tendencies. There is therefore need to reengineer case management processes in the criminal justice system through a comprehensive business process review that ensures that only relevant tasks and procedures are maintained and supported by technology.

In summary, the requirements for developing usable integrated information systems as established from the review of related literature and a survey are: Information aggregation and presentation requirements; User diversity (cognitive ability, physical capacity and technical proficiency) requirements; Information Organization Requirements; Information Sharing Requirements; Need to cater for the evolving nature of Information Systems; Standardizing technologies used; and Process efficiency requirements.

The next section, discusses a model for developing usable integrated case management information systems.

5   Design of the Model for Developing Usable Integrated Case Management Information Systems

5.1   Introduction

The model for developing usable integrated case management information systems is composed of a combination of design aspects derived from three (3) models that meet the requirements for the development of usable integrated information systems. The

Architecture Development Method (ADM) provides a step-by-step guideline for architecture development and is, to considerable extent designed to deal with most system and organizational requirements from a functionality and usability point of view [18]. LUCID/Star* Model provides the core building blocks for user centered design that are represented in four stages of analyze, design, implement and evaluate [9]. The Model-based Framework for the Integration of Usability and Software Engineering Lifecycles provides development infrastructure in which the usability engineering and software engineering life cycles co-exist in complimentary roles [15].

5.2   Description of the Model

This section discusses a model for the design of usable integrated information systems known as the Architecture-driven Usability Process Model (AdUPRO) based on the requirements for developing usable integrated information systems discussed in Section Four (4). AdUPRO is composed of three modules: the enterprise architecture module, the interaction module and the Module Alignment Process (MAPs).

The "enterprise architecture module" provides a shared and enterprise approach to design, a common language for the realization of the shared design, a framework for requirements gathering and creation of a mutual understanding between how users, business and technology should integrate and mutually evolve over the course of time.

The "interaction module" provides an approach to user-centered design and incorporation of various usability aspects in the systems design process. The interaction design module is based on the LUCID/Star* process model.

The Module Alignment Process (MAPs) links the architecture and interaction modules into mutually existent, complimentary and integrated (but independent) components.

Figure 1 is a detailed illustration of the three modules of the architecture-driven usability process model – the architecture module, the interaction module and the module alignment process – as well as the illustration of each module's components, sub-components and activities.

The **enterprise architecture module** (*components 1.1–1.4*) represents a systematic involvement of stakeholders in the design process of integrated case management information systems by providing a coordinated vision of the enterprise's strategic direction, business practices, information flows and structure, and technology resources. The "architecture" of a typical information system is further a blueprint for the business process (business architecture), data structures (data architecture), business applications (applications architecture) and the interrelationships between these layers [1]. Activities under the architecture module provide the basis for understanding the "big picture" of the integrated case management information system and fulfilling requirements related to information sharing, information discovery, information organization, process reengineering, standardization of technology platforms and data formats. These requirements are fulfilled through: a critical appreciation of the enterprise architecture scope and definition of the design roadmap (Foundations architecture); a comprehensive understanding of users and the information environment and business context that they operate in (business architecture); an understanding of the user applications for processing and

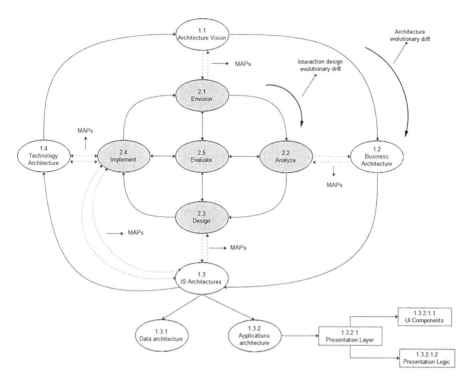

Fig. 1. Architecture-driven usability engineering process model

presenting business data (IS architecture) and proper alignment of technology to end user needs and requirements to enhance the user experience (technology architecture).

The goal of the **interaction module** (*components 2.1–2.5*) is to develop an inter-active integrated information system that is aligned to the user's unique environment, contexts and way of work [2] and responsive to how people (users) connect/interact with others to perform collaborative tasks and exchange (share) information [16, 17]. To enhance the user experience with the integrated information systems, the interaction module supports intuitive navigation and content search mechanisms at the user interface (UI) level thereby enhancing users' ability to find information. This attribute contributes to fulfillment of information sharing requirements that address challenges experienced by users to find information that spans organizational boundaries, as is the case in the Justice, Law and Order Sector.

The **Module Alignment Process** (MAPs) illustrates sharing/coordination of activities, iterations, timelines, techniques, artifacts and mappings between the enter-prise architecture and interaction modules. According to Pyla et al. [15], this referred to as "module activity awareness". MAPs, further illustrated in Fig. 2 supports coordi-nation of schedules and specification of activities and components in the interaction and enterprise architecture modules that have commonalities. For such activities, MAPs is able to indicate where and when those activities should be performed, who the involved stakeholders are, and communicates this information to both the architects and

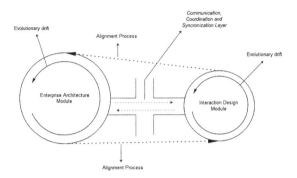

Fig. 2. Illustration of the Module Alignment Process (MAPs)

interaction designers. MAPs therefore provides a synchronized mapping of activities in the enterprise architecture and interaction modules through a link (alignment process) that ensures proper conceptualization of the integrated information environment and representation of usability aspects in integrated information systems.

The "evolution drifts" represent the evolving nature of the integrated information system. These changes to both the architecture and interaction modules are illustrated by the architecture and interaction evolution drifts respectively. During the design process, the architectural models tend to appear too high level and too simple to adequately be aligned with certain design realities such as new and emerging user requirements. Secondly, changes in the enterprise (business, technology and user environment) are likely to trigger changes in the overall architecture of the integrated information system. This implies that a dynamic organizational environment requires a dynamic architecture that evolves and aligns itself to new and emerging parameters of the users (usability requirements), business and technology. The Architecture Development Method (ADM) supports this required flexibility. Relatedly, the interaction design activities should be synchronized with the changes in the architecture to reflect the most current shared vision and concept of the integrated information system. A *communication, coordination and synchronization layer* provides connectivity between the modules to implement this "alignment" process.

6   Conclusion and Future Work

This study was an attempt to develop a model that significantly incorporates human factors in the development of integrated case management information systems. The study was further focused on addressing design-reality gaps represented by usability dimensions in integrated e-justice projects in Uganda's Justice, Law and Order Sector – specifically in criminal justice institutions. These design reality gaps relate to the usability dimensions of information, technology, processes, objectives and values, skills and knowledge, management systems and structures, and other resources. Review of literature and a research survey were conducted to provide information on the extent of the problem and other usability issues encountered in integrated information systems. Findings from this survey provided the basis for the development of requirements and design decisions to address the identified issues, problems and usability gaps. To fulfill these requirements and design decisions, an artifact known as AdUPRO (Architecture-driven Usability Process Model) was developed to guide the development of a usable integrated information system.

AdUPRO to a great extent addresses the core problem of this study – how to develop usable integrated case management information systems. The model shows how requirements for usable integrated case management information systems can be achieved in the development of integrated information systems through its three modules. However, the model is still at the theoretical stage. Our next steps will be to validate the extent the model can effectively guide development of usable integrated information systems through development of a prototype integrated case management information system used by the Police, DPP, Judiciary and Uganda Prisons Service.

For purposes of future research, the recommendation is that the model should systematically and specifically address psychodynamic factors (unconscious aspects of human behavior) and their implications on the usability of integrated information systems.

Acknowledgements. We are grateful to the Justice, Law and Order Sector (JLOS) Secretariat (Ministry of Justice and Constitutional Affairs, Government of Uganda) and all participants in the study from the general public, legal fraternity (Uganda Law Society), the Judiciary, Uganda Police, the Directorate of Public Prosecutions and the Uganda Prisons Service.

References

1. Arnold, B., Op't Land, M., Dietz, J.: Effects of an architecture approach to the implementation of shared service centres. In: Conference Paper for the Dutch National Architecture Congress in 2002 (2002)
2. Benyon, D., Turner, P., Turner, S.: Designing Interactive Systems: People, Activities, Contexts, Technologies (2005). ISBN-13: 978-0321116291
3. Bradley, R., Pridmore, J.L., Bryrd, T.A.: Information systems success in the context of different corporate cultural types: an empirical investigation. J. Manage. Inf. Syst. **33**(2), 267–294 (2006)
4. Card, K.S., Mackinlay, J.D., Shneiderman, B.: Readings in Information Visualization, Using Vision to Think. Morgan Kaufmann, San Francisco (1999)
5. Dykes, J.A., MacEachren, A.M., Kraak, M.-J. (eds.): Exploring Geovisualization, p. 710. Amsterdam, Elsevier (2005)
6. Gabbard, J.L., Hix, D., Swan, E., Livingston, M.A., Hollerer, T.H., Julier, S.J., Brown, D., Baillot, Y.: Usability engineering for complex interactive systems development. In: Proceedings of Human Systems Integration Symposium 2003, Engineering for Usability, Vienna, VA, 23–25 June 2003 (2003)
7. Gould, J.D., Lewis, C.: Designing for usability: key principles and what designers think. Commun. ACM **28**(3), 300–311 (1985)
8. Heeks, R.: Understanding e-Governance for Development, I-Government Working Paper Series, Paper No. 11, Institute for Development Policy and Management (2001)

9. Helms, J.W.: Developing and Evaluating the (LUCID/Star)*Usability Engineering Process Model, Thesis submitted to the Faculty of the Virginia Polytechnic Institute and State University (2001)

10. Integrated Justice Information Management Systems Project Plan: The Justice, Law and Order Sector. Government of the Republic of Uganda (2012)

11. International Standards Organization (ISO 9241-210:2010): Ergonomics of Human System Interaction – Part 210: Human-centered Design for Interactive Systems

12. Lederer, A.L., Prasad, J.: Nine management guidelines for better cost estimating. Commun. ACM **35**(2), 51–59 (1992)

13. Morville, P., Rosenfeld, L.: Information Architecture for the World Wide Web, 3rd edn. O'Reilly Media, Sebastopol (2006)

14. Pitula, K., Sinning, D., Radhakrishnan, T.: Making technology fit: designing an information management system for monitoring social protection programmes in St. Kitts (2015). http://sta.uwi.edu/conferences/09/salises/documents/D%20Dysart-Gale.pdf. Accessed 27 Feb 2017

15. Pyla, P.S., Pérez-Quiñones, M.A., Arthur, J.D., Hartson, H.R.: Towards a model-based framework for integrating usability and software engineering life cycles. In: Interact 2003 Workshop on Closing the Gaps: Software Engineering and Human Computer Interaction. 2003: Universite catholigue da Louvain, Institut d 'Administration et de Gestion (IAG) on behalf of the International Federation of Information Processing (IFIP), pp. 67–74 (2003)

16. Saffer, D.: Designing for Interaction: Creating Innovative Applications and Devices (Voices That Matter), 2nd edn. New Riders, Berkerly (2009)

17. Sharp, H., Rogers, Y., Preece, J.: Interaction Design: Beyond Human-Computer Interaction. Wiley, Chichester (2007)

18. The open Group Architecture Forum (TOGAF): The Open Group Architecture Framework. Van Haren Publishing, Zaltbommel (2009). Version 9

Bringing Visibility to Community Health Work with mHealth Systems: A Case of Malawi

Esther Namatovu[1(✉)] and Chipo Kanjo[2]

[1] University of Oslo, Oslo, Norway
estherna@ifi.uio.no
[2] University of Malawi, Zomba, Malawi
chipo.kanjo@gmail.com

Abstract. The paper explores how technology created visibility of work and its implications. Places create social meanings and significance in which work is situated. Community health work is mostly confined in places of physical settings for many mobile and distributed workers. As their work contexts stretch in place and far from other actors, the visibility of their work becomes blurry. An in-depth interpretive case study of a mobile health system designed to support decision-making for Community Health Workers in maternal and infant care in Malawi was used to unravel how mHealth systems make their work visible. We uncover work aspects like; work interactions, collaboration, coordination, surveillance among others that flow through place and space in our empirical findings. Each relates to work visibility/invisibility creating both theoretical and practical implications.

Keywords: Visibility · Place · mHealth systems · Community Health Workers

> *"...work has a tendency to disappear at a distance, such that the further removed we are from the work of others, the more simplified, often stereotyped, our view of their work becomes."*
>
> [1]

1 Introduction

Community health work has thrived for decades. The Alma Ata declaration backed this work to support primary healthcare in underserved communities with low human resource [2]. The term Community Health Worker (CHW) covers a generic type of community based workers known differently in various countries [3]. A widely accepted definition was proposed by the World Health Organization [4] as, *"Community health workers should be members of the communities where they work, should be selected by the communities, should be answerable to the communities for their activities, should be supported by the health system but not necessarily a part of its organization and have shorter training than professional workers"*

They are trained as health aides to conduct various tasks in communities. For example; sanitation inspections, home visits, treating simple illnesses, facilitating

© IFIP International Federation for Information Processing 2017
Published by Springer International Publishing AG 2017. All Rights Reserved
J. Choudrie et al. (Eds.): ICT4D 2017, IFIP AICT 504, pp. 629–639, 2017.
DOI: 10.1007/978-3-319-59111-7_51

maternal and child health, collecting data among others. The tasks are performed with varying degrees of breadth and depth across countries [4]. Notably, CHWs remain lowly recognized [5, 6] with their work backgrounded in communities. Yet, this work input backs formal health systems. This invisible work has important consequences for CHWs and others involved. Making CHWs' work visible creates community recognition, an incentive for CHWs [4]. It also motivates Ministries of Health to support and sustain CHWs. Visibility of work and actors has been implicated in influencing recognition, control, social identities and power relations according to social places and subjects [7, 8].

This paper does not cover the full range of services provided by CHWs. We study a group of CHWS in Malawi, referred to as Health Surveillance Assistants (HSAs). HSAs live with local communities, providing similar services in maternal and child healthcare. This work is currently supported by a mobile Health (mHealth) system developed to aid decision-making while attending to infants and expectant mothers.

HSAs' work is conducted in their catchment areas far from their supervisors and other actors at health facilities, the district and Ministry of Health. Supervisors often see finished work products through indicators in reports and changed community conditions. This work becomes invisible to differently placed individuals who only see it through some indicators [1, 9]. Work contexts, practices and categorizations from a distance are often narrowed and simplified. This can be consequential for system development and implementations. We seek to address the following question;

How does the introduction of technology influence the visibility of the work of community health workers?

We address this question by combining two bodies of theory based on the notions of 'visibility of work' and 'place'. With place, we take the two time-space configurations of place and space that characterize the temporal and spatial dimensions in which HSAs' work is constructed. With visibility, we learn how work situated in different places may become visible or invisible. The mHealth system we describe is part of an initiative to strengthen HSAs' work delivery in maternal and child health. We undertake an interpretive case analysis.

2   Theoretical Background

2.1   Place

Place elucidates how social meanings and existential significance are related to places-physical, social and electronic [10]. Places embody social and cultural milieus that shape and are shaped by recursive social actions [11–13]. Place and time are temporal and spatial environments in which individuals make sense of their interactions and work organization [14, 15].

Place and space should not be equated [13, 14, 16]. Space is an abstract and infinite expanse in which people and ideas freely move with potential for newness and growth [15]. Space is freedom [17] and a container for place, whose meanings are shaped by what one does in them [18]. Place on the other hand relates to a person's sense of boundedness, being and contented belonging where tradition prevails [14].

In place, social activities and interactions occur in physical settings situated geographically where time and space are intertwined [14]. In Giddens' account [14], modernity broke away from locality, tradition and cyclical time associated with place in what he describes as time-space distanciation. The social world is homogenized, interactions lifted out of the here and now and the ties that hold practices in their place are dissolved in space. Space takes on an image of a uniform and infinite expanse in which people and ideas move freely promising generalizability of knowledge, freedom of movement, social independence and growth [15].

Place and space are socially constructed configurations of the time-space continuum and are interrelated [17, 18]. We attempt to understand their difference in order to examine physical presence, an absence of it and work visibility without presence. Noteworthy, ICTs have disembedding mechanisms separating space and time, creating absent actors but simultaneously extending locally specific social relations to different space and time contexts. Interactions can thus occur in placeless spaces [19].

HSAs' work provides a subtle case in which work is predominantly contained in a physical world. Situated in their rural catchment areas, HSAs are mobile and distributed workers but seek work coherence. However as their work is predominantly bound in place, it may become invisible to others differently placed. Suchman [20] notes that, "the relation between our own social location and our views of others sustains boundaries among organizational actors, including boundaries between professional designers of technology and technology users". Implying that if a place of work is territorial, it can become blurry and black boxed by outsiders including technology designers who do not know the details of the territory but enter work contexts to build technology supporting systems. Place therefore creates a basis for our understanding of how work may be visible or invisible to those differently placed.

2.2   Visibility

Visibility denotes legitimacy and rescue from obscurity or exploitation [9]. Work invisible to formal requirements analysis, is crucial in representing effort levels and subtleties [9]. Making work visible is crucial in motivating and determining the significance of events [21]. But what exactly is work and whom should it be visible or invisible to? Star and Straus [9] describe how domestic work was for decades not considered work and invisible to family and workplaces. They stress the "contextual importance" of what work is and what may or may not be visible citing a scene from a film, "The Gods Must be Crazy". The scene is between a western ecologist studying elephant migration and a !Kung tribesman curious about what the ecologist does. "The !Kung man asks the ecologist what he does to which he replies, he is an ecologist. Seeing a puzzled look on the !Kung man's face, he narrows it down to the activity: "Well, actually, I walk around all day behind elephants and pick up their dung." The !Kung man's expression changes to pity mixed with amusement. Lacking a mutual context, only plain action is visible, which is of great importance in the scientific world, yet preposterous to the !Kung man. Suchman [20] describes it as work getting black boxed by those differently placed.

Work becomes invisible in three ways [9]. First, in work where the actor is seen as a non-person, the work product is visible to both employer and employee. The employee however is invisible due to power relations between employer and employee. For example domestic workers' legitimate work is defined by employers and employees are invisible. This creates complications especially that certain work processes may get excluded and misrepresented in system development and implementation.

Secondly, work becomes invisible when it is disembedded background work [9]. Hamson and Junor [22] also refer to this as "invisible, routine work". Workers are quite visible but their work is demoted to background expectations. For example, nurses are visible in healthcare but continue to struggle to make their work visible. Their work is expected but is backgrounded and invisible by virtue of routine and social status. Such work often supports others and CHWs in rural communities support formal health systems. Suchman [20] narrates the articulation work of air traffic controllers who improvised communication strategies outside standard procedures to maneuver the orderly arrival and departure of planes out of their sight blocked by buildings. This articulation work although relatively easy to uncover, is not registered yet it is necessary. Such background work is vulnerable in systems design especially because it is diffused through the working process, partly due to the social status of workers and also because it requires so much articulation work.

Thirdly, by abstracting and manipulating indicators, both work and people become invisible when; (1) formal and quantitative work indicators are abstracted from work settings and they become the basis for decision-making especially by those who do not see the work first hand. And (2) when work products are commodities purchased at a distance from the work setting making both work and workers invisible [9].

But should all work be visible? Much invisible work remains so for various reasons [9]. For instance, workers hide flaws. For technology design, the less of users' behavior systems encode, the less functionality they can provide. The more behavior they encode, the more they may prescribe human activities [1]. Therefore, for information systems, forced representations of work may antagonize work processes.

Technology is implicated with visibility. It enlarges the field of the socially visible, liberating visibility from the spatial-temporal properties of here and now [8]. We assess the mHealth system's implications on work visibility.

3   Research Approach

The research approach aimed at developing a detailed understanding of work processes among HSAs. We therefore undertook an interpretive case study [23] to achieve this. The case was selected because it represents the work of mobile and distributed workers in different physical settings currently using a mHealth system.

3.1   Research Context and Case

Malawi is a developing country in southeast Africa with over 17 million people [24]. This is one of the highest population densities in sub-Saharan Africa. It is among the poorest countries in the world with 85% of its population in rural areas [25]. Among its many challenges, is its poor health system laden with a heavy disease burden [26]. This is evidenced by a high disease prevalence of; malaria, HIV/AIDS, other tropical diseases, high childhood and adulthood mortality rates.

Maternal mortality in Malawi is still considered the highest in Africa [27] at 675 births per 100,000 and infant mortality at 66 per 1000 live births [25]. Universal health coverage is low and the country still has a struggling healthcare system. For example, human resource challenges cannot meet Malawi's health demands. The few medical personnel available are often distributed in urban areas.

In 2005, Malawi implemented an Emergency Human Resource Plan (2005–2010) to increase its health work force [27]. By 2011, Malawi had over 12,000 HSAs linking communities to the health system [28]. These become the largest health workforce for the country offering both preventive and curative health services [5]. For maternal and child health, HSAs perform activities such as; educating, treating, referring and following-up cases in communities. They are deployed in rural communities where professional health workforce is low and these under-recognized but important health workers endure most of the additional work pressure.

What and Where is HSA's Work?

HSAs core work involves disease prevention and extending primary healthcare services to local communities. The health facility acts as a focal point of healthcare to community members in a catchment area. In this study, the catchment area serves 34,325 people. This catchment area is further divided into smaller catchment areas each with a HSA serving up to 10 villages, and an average of 2,286 people. HSAs work significantly in communities where they provide primary healthcare and link community members to the formal health system. A locally constructed structure- a Village clinic (VC) - in a HSA's catchment area is a focal point for service provision. Community members come to the VC for immunization, treatment, education among others. A heavy workload requires collaboration with colleagues but HSAs also work with Village Health Committees in communities. Other activities like sanitation inspections, data collection, and follow-up exercises among others require HSAs to move around in catchment areas often walking or using bicycles.

HSAs are attached to a health facility, an average of 7.2 km away from their catchment areas. 12 HSAs are attached to the health facility we contacted. They make formal reports, get facilitation, training and organize their work at the health facility. Additionally, tasks like attending to patients, vaccinating women of reproductive age and children are assigned to HSAs by professional medical personnel in need of assistance. HSAs organize themselves in groups, often rotating their services in the community and at health facilities amongst these groups.

Their immediate supervisor is the HSA coordinator with similar duties. HSAs record daily activities in paper registers which they aggregate monthly. Monthly reports are physically delivered to the HSA coordinator at the health facility. The coordinator aggregates all HSAs' reports and submits them to the health facility In-charge. The In-charge makes a health facility report he delivers to the District Health Office and the Ministry of Health. However, daily work registers are stacked at the health facility. Apart from the HSA coordinator, all other superiors are differently placed in various physical and hierarchical places. They only receive aggregated reports on particular indicators from HSAs' work and often give no feedback.

The Mobile System
Organization mHealth (pseudonym) developed a decision-support system on smart phones. The system is designed to facilitate HSAs' decision-making. Existing paper protocols were integrated into the system to facilitate antenatal and postnatal care of expectant mothers and infants. The system goes through a step by step data capture of signs and symptoms which it analyses and gives a recommendation to either treat or refer patients. The data is simultaneously sent to the organization's database shared with the Ministry of Health. Patient follow-up after an initial visit is crucial, as moving forward to a new section in the system, requires completion of previous sections.

3.2   Data Collection

Empirical data was collected with semi-structured interviews, observations and a Focus Group Discussion for two months in Dowa district. We visited 12 HSAs, 3 health facility staff and 4 community members. 6 HSAs were interviewed for a group's perspective on their work. HSAs narrated their everyday work, where they conduct it, work interactions and experiences using the mobile system. Health personnel and community members also discussed their interactions with HSAs.

We also observed HSAs' work in health facilities and communities. We combined observations with informal discussions to understand what HSAs said they did and what they actually did. This was done for a full understanding of their work and its interaction with the mobile system. We made field notes and recorded interviews.

3.3   Data Analysis

We started our analysis by reading and discussing emerging themes from collected data. Recorded data was transcribed from field notes and audio recordings to proceed with analysis. We moved from raw data by giving similar data codes to organize it. Then, we analyzed the coded data to generate themes with similar descriptions grouped as; HSAs' work description, HSAs' work location, social interactions and experiences with the mHealth system. We moved back and forth through the themes and transcribed data, to make sense of the data. We then related the themes to our theoretical concepts of place and visibility for further assessment. From this comparison, we generated interpretations for the study.

4 Findings/Discussion

The mobile system has driven some work aspects like collaboration, mobilization, data reporting and work organization previously bound by temporal or spatial constraints of here and now to be conducted in spaces. This impacts on work visibility as the next discussion depicts.

4.1 Work Made Visible/ Invisible with the Mobile System Implementation

Visibility Among Colleagues

HSAs work activities are physically bound in communities and the health facility that shape their work interactions [13]. One's catchment area embodies locally specific activities and interactions in physical places of here and now. In communities, HSAs are highly mobile but seek sameness in work delivery across their distributed workplaces. Previously, the health facility was a common ground for HSAs to plan and seek assistance. The mobile phone has lifted these interactions out of the here and now of the health facility into space [15] affording work interactions, coordination and collaboration in space while sharing common interests and meanings [18]. An example is a 'WhatsApp group created by HSAs.

> "We have a WhatsApp group and we now coordinate some activities with each other there. We are very active in the group; we share interesting experiences and make inquiries amongst ourselves. We now do not have to wait until the weekly meeting or the monthly meeting at the health facility to do this because everyone is distributed in different geographical areas...we reach each other anytime on WhatsApp and if something is urgent, we call." (HSA in group discussion)

The mobile phone affords HSAs with spatial features where group collaborations and inquiries occur. It liberates work from the confines of place and translates it into spatial integrations where HSAs interact. This accommodates knowledge sharing and work coherence across distributed physical locales. Locally specific social relations are dissolved to occur in placeless spaces without physical presence of colleagues creating visibility for work interactions occurring in a virtual space.

Visibility to Supervisors

The mobile system instantly captures fieldwork activities into the organization's database. Work processes- the how, with whom and when- previously only in places of the community, become visible to supervisors. HSAs reported that data on how they attend to expectant mothers or infants in the community was immediately captured. Disembedded background work [9] formerly seen through monthly abstracted indicators become visible to contextually distanced supervisors at the District Health Office and Ministry of Health. Consequently HSAs focused on making their work visible due to increased control and surveillance. To HSAs, working more implied more registered work performance for supervisors to see, evaluate and appraise their efforts. Work processes were freed from places of the community and information entered by individual HSAs encompassed their work processes in electronic spaces (Fig. 1).

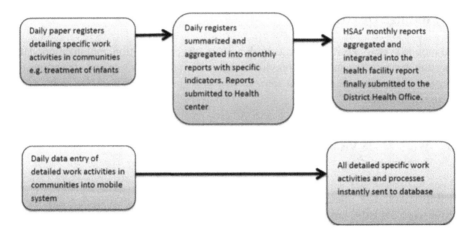

Fig. 1. Illustration of reporting formats before and after mobile system intervention

The HSA coordinator noted;

"Every field visit is accompanied with reporting whether we intend it or not. They (HSAs) are forced to do the work. Before, people were lazy but now they have improved. They can visit 10 expectant mothers in a day. That is good. If they do not, I can see that so and so is not registering any data in the system. I call them to ask what is going on. The phone has enabled me to monitor and follow up with what is happening in the field."

Space denotes to freedom, a uniform expanse where people and ideas move freely [15, 17]. However, as HSAs work is lifted into this infinite electronic expanse, it becomes visible to supervisors and they are forced to work more due to increased surveillance. This raises the question whether all work should be made visible [9]. Traditional monthly reports did not entirely illuminate HSAs' fieldwork processes as the mobile system does. Notably, HSA's laziness is thrown out. Schultze and Boland [15] argue that space creates social independence but this is diminishing as HSAs feel more control and seek approval for their efforts by working harder.

Besides supervisors, HSAs' fieldwork impacts in rural catchment areas also indirectly become visible to health personnel at the health facility. One noted,

"HSAs are the ones reaching out to expectant mothers in communities. The mothers tell us when they come here to the health facility, that they have been referred by so and so (a HSA). ...yes they do still refer patients but not as much because most times, cases are solved in the community. That mobile app is really supporting their decision-making which means more work is done in the field" (Community midwife Technician).

Health personnel reported having no access to the database or HSAs' work in electronic space but insisted that reduced cases at health facilities indicated more impact in communities.

Knowledge Visibility to the Community
HSAs reported infant and maternal healthcare to require efficient knowledge to foster diagnosis and treatment. Patients are seen in homes or the village clinic. HSAs

traditionally used paper forms to register signs and symptoms, make thorough analysis and develop diagnosis. However, some acknowledged forgetting to ask some questions which affected diagnosis. With the mobile system, it is impossible to skip questions as interactions are standardized and continuation to another section requires completion of previous sections.

> *"...with the paper forms, sometimes we forgot to ask some questions. But with the mobile system app, you cannot go to the next level without filling in responses to all the various sections...we are able to properly assess various conditions and also give a proper diagnosis"* (HSA)

With the system, HSAs' knowledge to effectively diagnose health conditions is made visible to community members who recognize them as knowledgeable village doctors. The HSAs' social status and recognition increased as one noted,

> *"Our value has increased. The number of pregnant women one week after we received the phones went up. Now husbands are coming up to us and request we go to their homes to visit their expectant wives with the mobile phone. They see us with the smart phones and presume we are knowledgeable because they see the phone as a computer...With the phone we display our knowledge. For example the phone helps me to calculate the gestation period of a woman so I don't come off like as if I do not know what I am doing."* (HSA)

Another HSA proudly added,

> *"...they [community members] do not even know the health center In-charge. They know me as the doctor because I am giving skilled health services..."*

And a community member added,

> *"...our names are in that computer [referring to the HSA's smart phone]. They enter our details so when I come back to the village clinic, they can trace my health information. They know what they are doing..."* (Community member)

As HSA's knowledge is displayed with the mobile system use, the health facility personnel's identities slowly fade. Simultaneously, HSAs' identity grows to a doctor-like level for the community. Community members sometimes consult HSAs physically distant, over the phone and are no longer limited to face to face interactions. HSAs' knowledge is shared in space making it visible to communities across time-space spans. However with standardized care provision on the mobile system, other potential forms of knowledge like tacit knowledge gained through practice in patient care are underplayed. Suchman [1] warns that when every aspect of human behavior is encoded in information systems, they prescribe human activity.

Work Needs Made Visible to Superiors

HSAs' traditionally made logistics demands from communities on monthly forms, delivered to the HSA coordinator who submitted them to the health facility In-charge and finally to the District Health Office. All interactions occurred in places of hierarchical structure. With the mobile system, it became possible to skip the hierarchies through instant messaging requests. This made visible HSAs' logistics needs in communities to the Ministry of Health, prompting immediate responses. One HSA noted,

> *"Government now knows our needs whenever they arise. We send out our logistics needs anytime instead of the monthly forms and having to wait."* (HSA)

5   Contribution/Conclusion

This analysis has implications for ICT4D, Giddens' agenda of place and visibility work. Place interacts dynamically with work, forming a sphere for shared meanings and interactions for HSAs. HSAs' work requiring mobilization, collaboration and organization was mostly confined in physical places and obscured. The mobile system created space [14, 19] where work continued without physical presence. Noteworthy, place remains relevant for constructing some work aspects like patient treatment. This refutes Giddens' [9] 'phantasmagoric places' logic where relations are between absent actors without face to face interactions. HSAs remained place-dependent and sought stability by situating patient treatment in places of the village clinic. Other activities like coordination and mobilization flowed into space. This implicated on visibility.

Practically, the movement of work from physical to technological spaces created more visibility in communities. This had implications like; facilitating work coherence, knowledge exhibition, work identity affirmation and increased work effort. However work interactions between HSAs and patients (expectant mothers and infants) were so standardized blocking the expression of other knowledge forms gained in practice. It raises questions for system design and implementation. How much work should be encoded in technology? How much work should be made visible? It is our view that approaches to system design and implementation understand work contexts and technology users to meet their objectives.

We have presented how HSAs' work flows through the logics of place and space implicating on work visibility with technology intervention. We also found that work does not simply become place free as HSAs simultaneously sought work situatedness in place. The study demonstrates the significance of understanding place for various work actors and the implications of making work categorizations visible to differently placed actors with technology intervention. Our theoretical basis presents opportunities for perspectives that seek to discuss technological work representations.

References

1. Suchman, L.: Making work visible. Commun. ACM **38**, 56–64 (1995)
2. World Health Organization. Community Health Workers: Challenges and Progress in Africa (2016). http://www.who.int/woman_child_accountability/ierg/news/usaid_chw_regional_meeting_ethiopia_19_21_june_2012/en/
3. Haines, A., Sanders, D., Lehmann, U., Rowe, K.A., Lawn, E.J., Jan, S., Walker, G.D., Bhutta, Z.: Achieving child survival goals: potential contribution of community health workers. Lancet **369**(9579), 2121–2131 (2007). http://dx.doi.org/10.1016/S0140-6736(07)60325-0
4. Lehmann, U., Sanders, D.: Community Health Workers: What do we know about them? The State of the Evidence on Programs, activities, costs and impact on health outcomes of using community health workers. World Health Organ., Geneva, Switzerland (2007)
5. Kok, C.M., Muula, S.A.: Motivation and job satisfaction of health surveillance assistants in Mwanza, Malawi: an explorative study. Malawi Med. J. **25**, 5–11 (2013)
6. Braun, R., Catalani, C., Wimbus, J., Isrealski, D.: Community health workers and mobile technology: a systematic review of literature. PLoS ONE **8**, e65772 (2013). doi:10.1371/journal.pone.0065772

7. Reicher, S., Levine, M.R., Gordijn, E.: More on deindividuation, power relations between groups and the expression of social identity: three studies on the effects of visibility to the in-group. Br. J. Soc. Psychol. **37**, 15–40 (1998)

8. Brighenti, A.: Visibility: a category for the social science. Curr. Sociol. **55**, 323–342 (2007). doi:10.1177/0011392107076079

9. Star, L.S., Strauss, A.: Layers of silence, arenas of voice: the ecology of visible and invisible work. Comput. Support. Coop. Work **8**, 9–30 (1999)

10. D'Mello, M., Sahay, S.: "I am kind of a nomad where I have to go places and place"… Understanding Mobility, Place and Identity in Global software Work from India. Inf. Organ. **17**, 162–192 (2007)

11. Harrison, S, Dourish, P.: Re-Place-ing space: the role of place and space in collaborative systems. In: CSCW 96 Proceedings of the 1996 ACM Conference on Computer Supported Cooperative Work, Boston, Massachusetts, USA, pp. 67–76 (1996). doi:10.1145/240080. 240193

12. Kakihara, M., Sørensen, C.: Mobility: an extended perspective. In: The Proceedings of the 35th Hawaii International Conference on Systems Science, Hawaii (2002)

13. Foley, Simon: Understanding a sense of place in collaborative environments. In: Smith, Michael J., Salvendy, Gavriel (eds.) Human Interface 2007. LNCS, vol. 4558, pp. 863–872. Springer, Heidelberg (2007). doi:10.1007/978-3-540-73354-6_94

14. Giddens, A.: The Consequences of Modernity. Polity Press, Cambridge (1990)

15. Schultze, U., Boland, J.R.: Place, space and knowledge work: a study of outsourced computer systems administrators. Acc. Manage. Inform. Technol. **10**, 187–219 (2000)

16. Casey, E.S.: Getting back into place: toward a renewed understanding a renewed understanding of the place-world, pp. 130–148. Indiana University Press (1993)

17. Harrison, S., Tatar, D.: Places: people, events, loci- the relation of semantic frames in the construction of place. Comput. Support. Coop. Work **17**, 97–133 (2007)

18. Saker, S., Sahay, S.: Implications of space and time for distributed work: an interpretive study of US-Norwegian systems development teams. Eur. J. Inform. Syst. **13**, 3–20 (2004)

19. Castells, M.: The Rise of the Network Society. Oxford & Malden, MA, Blackwell (1996)

20. Suchman, L.: Supporting Articulation Work. In: Kling, R. (ed.) Computerization and Controversy: Value Conflicts and Social Choices, pp. 407–423. Academic Press, USA (1996)

21. Hatuka, T., Toch, E.: Being visible in public space: the normalization of asymmetrical visibility. Urban Stud. J. (2016). doi:10.1177/0042098015624384

22. Hampson, I., Junor, A.: Invisible work, invisible skills: interactive customer service as articulation work. New Technol. Work Employ. **20**, 166–181 (2005). doi:10.1111/j.1468-005X.2005.00151.x

23. Walsham, G.: Doing interpretive research. Eur. J. Inform. Syst. **15**, 320–330 (2006)

24. World Bank. Population: Malawi (2016). http://data.worldbank.org/country/malawi

25. UNDP. About Malawi (2015). http://www.mw.undp.org/content/malawi/en/home/countryinfo.html (21.10.2016)

26. Ministry of Health Malawi and ICF International. Malawi Service Provision Assessment (MSPA) 2013-14. Lilongwe, Malawi, and Rockville, Maryland, USA: MoH and ICF International (2014). https://dhsprogram.com/pubs/pdf/SPA20/SPA20[Oct-7-2015].pdf

27. World Health Organization. Country Cooperation Strategy at a Glance: Malawi (2014). http://www.who.int/countryfocus/cooperation_strategy/ccsbrief_mwi_en.pdf

28. UNICEF. In Malawi, Health Surveillance Assistants provide a life-saving link between Communities and the healthcare system, 12 June 2012. http://www.unicef.org/health/malawi_62611.html

True Value of Telecentre Contribution to Bario Community Development

Ghazala Tabassum[1(✉)], Narayanan Kulathuramaiyer[1], Roger Harris[1],
and Alvin W. Yeo[2]

[1] Institute of Social Informatics and Technological Innovations (ISITI),
Universiti Malaysia Sarawak (UNIMAS), Kota Samarahan, Malaysia
ghazala.tabasum@gmail.com, nara@fit.unimas.my,
roger.harris@rogharris.org
[2] University of Waikato, Hamilton, New Zealand
awyeo@waikato.ac.nz

Abstract. Telecentres have been widely deployed worldwide particularly in the area of ICTD to bridge the gap between urban and rural development. This paper explores the value and impact of a telecentre on the community living in Bario, a small village in the highlands of Malaysia. The focus is mainly on the less studied tangible and intangible impacts of the telecentre on users and non-users. This topic is discussed based on stories collected through "Most Significant Change Technique (MSC)" providing facts from the insights of the local community. In nutshell, Bario community has greatly benefited from the use of the telecentre, whether directly or indirectly, particularly in the areas of connectedness, psychological empowerment, and financial improvement. Greater awareness and use of the telecentre shall continue to benefit this small rural community in their social and economic wellbeing.

Keywords: ICTD · Telecentre · ICTs · Users · Non-users · Intangible impact · Tangible impact · Socio-economic impact

1 Introduction

The emergence of ICTD interventions has played a crucial role in driving developing countries towards modernization particularly in the area of socio-economic development. The growing body of literature has further strengthens the impacts of ICTD interventions in measuring the tangible contributions of ICT, forgoing the intangible impact evaluation of ICTs especially on the non- user beneficiaries [23]. Thus, a question arises whether or not these unquantifiable intangible impacts such as self-esteem, sense of self-efficacy, self-confidence, enhanced capabilities, social cohesion, social capital etc. are important for community well-being and growth. Sey et al. [20] accentuate on the "impacts of public access to ICT" on users and non-users, stating that this issue needs to be put in focus to study the dynamics of public access impacts on non-users". The assessment of public access impacts often neglects to examine non-users, although they could consti- tute past and potential beneficiaries [19]. Confirmation is made by studying the numerous benefits that ICT's have given to both users and non-users beneficiaries in their respective socio-economic spheres. Grunfeld [11] claims that numerous ICT4D project appraisals frequently neglect to answer key inquiries concerning how these ICT activities can add to empowerment, capability and sustainability. According to [4], "by fostering a sense of belonging and connectedness to community and to a larger world, public access to computers often leads to feelings of empowerment and development of social capital, two intangible factors that are critical for community development". According to [10], "Measuring the development impacts of ICTD interventions continues to be an unresolved problem when trying to include non-traditional development measures beyond economic growth, particularly empowerment and social capital". According to [23], evaluating, the intangible impact of ICTs remains an unresolved issue, particularly when it comes to measuring intangible impact on non-user. Although these outcomes were mostly measured quantitatively in social sciences using self-efficacy and self-esteem scales, focus was less on its ICTD perspective [22]. This strengthens that the point of ICTs impact in non-traditional and intangible contexts remain unreciprocated [9, 10, 15] to an extent that it is not enough to place emphasis only on the tangible and quantifiable benefits of ICT that is easily measurable. According to researchers, intangible impact of ICTs is hard to measure on people's well-being [8, 9] but social impact can be measured and explained qualitatively [23]. Amartya Sen Development approach was adopted to understand the development experienced by the telecentre users and non-users. This Capability Approach (CA) sees development as "a process of expanding the real freedoms that people enjoy" and emphasizes the need for the "expansion of 'capabilities' of persons to lead the kinds of lives they value [18]. Empowerment is reflected in Sen's CA whereby human development is viewed as expanding people's capabilities and achievements [11]. Empowerment is an important dimension of human development [12] and the capacity to make and transform choices is influenced by two factors; namely, agency and opportunity structure [2].

2   Methodology

The MSC is a participatory monitoring and evaluation technique. It is used for collecting, discussing & selecting stories about the significant changes that people experience resulting from a program or initiatives [6, 24]. According to [6, 24], consider the importance of storytelling technique "as stories are one of the more participative forms of communication. Stories can deal with complexity and context; sometimes stories can carry hard messages. Stories told in casual conversation can harness another sort of information; they provide insights into how storytellers construct reality and to what they attach importance". However, various research studies documented around the world have used various methodologies to evaluate the telecentre impacts on the rural communities, which aimed to obtain sufficient information from the community. So far, researchers have succeeded to some extent in the impact evaluation but some part of impact remains concealed. Thus, with the intention to evaluate the intangible impact of the telecentre, we considered the MSC approach more suitable than other orthodox research approaches.

2.1 Four Steps and Procedures Used in the Main Study Data Collection Process (Interviews)

This study has adopted 4 out of 10 steps of MSC method [6] for the main empirical study: Step 1 identify "domains of change" by gathering relevant stories from users and non-users of the telecentre with the aim to evaluate direct and indirect impacts resulting in tangible and intangible benefits. 'Domains of change' are used to categorize changes reported through the monitoring system [14]. Step 2 collect stories in an informal way by keeping participants relaxed and interview questions were kept simple. A total of 22 "tape-recorded" interviews were collected and transcribed from audio to text into two pages with formatted layout. Step 3 involves reviewing and representing process of selection & validation for identifying and selecting the MSC stories within the set of collected stories. Step 4 involves the analysis of the stories. The first method uses "content analysis" data into valid categories through inductive inferences via tentative constant comparable examination [17]. The purpose is to identify the domains and sub-domains of change in collected stories, extracting the MSC to illustrate covering the variables of respondents' life experiences [13]. Second method uses "Leximancer 4.5" semantic analysis [27] technology to study the participants' linguistic research Douglas [7] converting textual documents into visually conceptualized mapping-context-extracted information. Leximancer functionalities employ two stages of information extraction: semantic and relational data, by calculating frequencies of each word for each stage using non-linear dynamics and machine learning algorithm. Results are displayed as hierarchical concept maps where relationship between individual concepts/themes can be explored [21].

3 Data Analysis

Data Analysis was categorized into three parts using three methods:

Method 1: Using Microsoft Excel to analyze charts/diagrams to interpret the demographic profile of respondents in the form of percentage of number people that obtained benefits from the telecentre.

Method 2: Involved two techniques, the first "Content Analysis" analyzes the collected stories and categorizing each significant stories (reviewed transcript) into information/themes, further ascertain for information validity and relevancy. The second technique used Leximancer 4.5 to provide results for the textual documents.

Method 3: In order to measure the extent of indirect intangible impact, percentages calculated method was adopted as it determines "the percentage of people experiencing a particular impact in a particular area, noting whether it was tangible, intangible, direct, indirect, positive or negative, or non-existent" [20].

3.1 Key Findings

Results are segregated into relevant parts: The first part illustrates the demographic profile of usage pattern. The second part describes the Content Analysis of the stories (see Table 1) and Leximancer analysis results. The demographic Profile illustrates that a total 22 participants of the semi-structured interview sessions were divided according to gender specification consisting 6 females and 16 males (refer Fig. 1). Respondents (users & non-users) age varied from 19yrs to 50+ yrs (refer Fig. 2). Interviewees were from all occupations representing male, female, young, old, users, and non-users (Refer Fig. 3: Fig. 4). Internet usage pattern for 11users varied from "Twice a week" to "Twice a year" and "Proxy help". Among 11 non-user respondents, only 3 obtained proxy help, whereas 6 benefited through friends and family help, and the remaining 2 have never experienced the telecentre facilities due to living outside. (Refer Fig. 5).

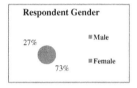

Fig. 1. Respondent gender

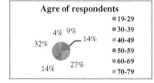

Fig. 2. Respondents age

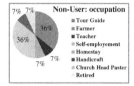

Fig. 3. Non-user occupation

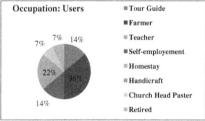

Fig. 4. Occupation: users

Fig. 5. Internet usage

3.2 Content Analysis

Table 1. Domains and sub-domains of change based on 11 Users & 11 Non Users

Domain of change	Sub-domain of change	Sub-domain of change	Sub-domain of change	Sub-domain of change	Sub-domain of change
Connectedness	**Feelings of belongingness:** being part of a stronger community of national or international	**Ease of better communication and information access:** Telecentre facilitates a faster communication and easy access to information	**Communication via Proxy help**	**Strengthen social ties b/w Friends & Families (F&F)**	**Mobile:** Basic call & WhatsA pp
Psychological empowerment	**Self-efficacy:** the belief in one's capabilities to organize and execute the courses of action required to manage prospective situations [3]	**Self-esteem:** Self-esteem refers to the totality of the individual's thoughts and feeling including a positive or negative attitude toward the self [16]			
Telecentre sustainability	**Internet connection:** e.g. poor internet connectivity	**Demand for services:** (Request to reopen Telecentre premises, ICT literacy Trainings, Staff member)			

(continued)

Table 1. (*continued*)

Domain of change	Sub-domain of change	Sub-domain of change	Sub-domain of change	Sub-domain of change	Sub-domain of change
Acknowledgement of Telecentre (TC) role in community development	**Business opportunities:** Telecentre provides various opportunities in the form of business solutions i.e. homestay and tour guides, handicrafts.	**Associated developments:** e.g. road, farming mechanization, new clinic, festival, road, tourism	**Community Exposure:** Experiencing the outside world	**Boosterism:** the enthusiastic promotion of a person, organization, or cause [26]	**Financial & Time savings**
Financial improvements	**Tourism:** e.g. Homestay, tour guide, handicrafts income	**Agriculture:** e.g. Farming			
Knowledge and skills	**Knowledge transformation:** knowledge sharing means an expertise, information, & skills are transferred from benefactor to beneficiaries	**Knowledge gained through Internet:** Learned new things: e.g. cooking recipes, dance, designing,	**Staying updated on news:** Keep updating oneself on local & global news		
Early communication issues	Communication via Postal Service & Radio Call				

3.2.1 Content Analysis: Domains and Sub Domains of Change

Figure 6 reflects responses received from both the telecentre users and non-users. The most common domains of change annotated by the respondents in the telecentre impact areas were early communication issues, connectedness, and the telecentre sustainability with a total percentage of 100%. This was followed by acknowledgement of TC role in community development (users: 100% & non-users: 91%), psychological empowerment (users: 100% & non-users: 82), financial improvements (users: 55% & non-users: 36%), and Knowledge and skills (users:45% & non-users: 27%). The findings indicate that all domains of change in the telecentre impact area showed greater improvements in the perception of both users and non-users about the telecentre role in community development.

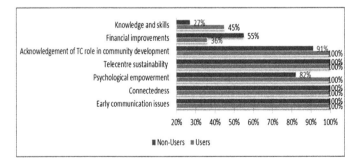

Fig. 6. Domains of change (Reported by Users & Non-users)

A closer look at key findings shows both users and non-users perceived positive tangible and intangible impact of telecentre. Unlike non-users, users benefited at large. However, most surprisingly, the percentage ratio of non-users in the area of intangible impact was phenomenal such as connectedness at 100%, and psychological empowerment at 82%. It is interesting to note that unlike users, non-users lack the ICT skills. But through indirect assistance those non-users who had alternative access to Internet exhibit feelings of connectedness and positive psychological empowerment. The study found that they have positive attitude towards themselves and the changes they have experienced both in tangible and intangible impacts. As illustrated, both respondent groups indicated communication as the major issue they faced earlier for the community inhabitants to be connected with their loved ones as well as keeping updated with the global & local events. But with the presence of the telecentre as a hub of easy internet access, the communication barrier is bridged and social ties with friends and families is strengthened. The business opportunities brought about by the telecentre have benefited both users and non-users. Baron, Gomez [4] stated, "This sense of connectedness is strengthened by the speed and ease with which people can now access multiple sources of information, and it results in a sense of empowerment and confidence building on the part of users of ICT".

Thus, these results indicate that the social connectedness and access to all variety of information without limit further led to sense of empowerment and confidence-building, stronger self-esteem of the respondents. User and non-user respondents stated that their ability to cope with new challenges have improved along with their decision-making power. These insights reaffirmed the presence of intangible impacts of the telecentre within the community.

3.2.2   Content Analysis of Stories by Sub-Domains (Users and Non-users)

Figure 7 below illustrates the elements that make up the domain "Connectedness" in accordance to the given percentages per elements. It is worth noting that non-users who are not able to access the telecentre services by themselves acquired proxy help while other non-users who gained access to information through external sources received benefits indirectly. Communication has been the main issue that was always in the limelight agenda of users and non-users through their collective stories. The telecentre brought positive changes encompassing "ease of better communication and information access", "access to the world at large" to a "sense of belongingness". This strengthens social bond among friends and family members living outside of the community. Putting further into focus is the use of mobile communications (smart phones, ordinary mobile phone) in particular the use of "WhatsApp" for digital interaction.

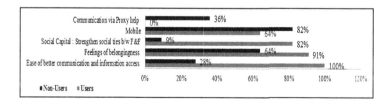

Fig. 7. Sub-domains of change within connectedness domains

Figure 8 illustrates the elements that make up the domain of 'the telecentre sustainability", which indicate that all respondents reflect their need for telecentre. Figure 9 illustrates the elements that make up the domain "Psychological Empowerment", which show the presence of the positive "Psychological Empowerment" pattern among users and non-users. Figure 10 illustrates the elements that make up the domain "Financial Improvements", which provides stronger evidence of the business opportunities brought by the telecentre for the tourism livelihood increase the household income of the community. Figure 11 illustrates the elements that make up the domain "Knowledge and skills" revealed the positive impacts of the telecentre towards the community addressed by users and non-users in terms of improved viability of information and communication providing a catalyst for the community to enrich their knowledge about the outside world. Figure 12 below illustrates the elements that make up the domain "Acknowledgement of TC role in community development", revealed the telecentre's positive attributes that contributes to positive opportunities such as in Eco-Tourism and other sectors of developments etc., resulting in financial improvements amongst users and non-users lifestyle.

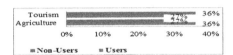

Fig. 8. Percentage of stories addressing sub domains of change within the telecentre Sustainability

Fig. 9. Percentage of stories addressing sub domains of change within Psychological empowerment

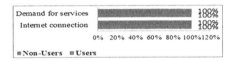

Fig. 10. Percentage of stories addressing sub domains of change within domain of financial improvements

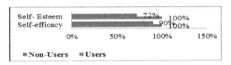

Fig. 11. Percentage of stories addressing sub domains of change within domain of knowledge and skills

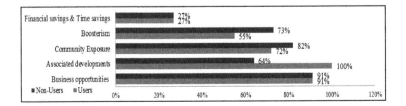

Fig. 12. Sub-domains of change within Acknowledgement of TC role in community development

3.3 Analysis of Collected Stories from Users and Non-users with Leximancer 4.5

At this stage, Leximancer 4.5 assisted in the analytical review by calculating, extracting and displaying the collected stories, providing visual interpretation of the actual data uploaded from the MS Word database aligned by two sentences per block prose threshold of 1. The results are shown in (Users: Table 2 and Fig. 13: Non-Users Table 4 and Fig. 14), which depict concepts/themes along with its connectivity measurement extracted from analysis of results in the form of visual concepts to present interactive connectivity. The map entails conceptual clusters as colored circles to summarize semantic point connection of particular groups of concepts (colored circles for themes and small grey dots for annotated concepts). Relational value between concepts is dependent upon range between concepts, which represents top-level classification of noted stories, the larger the circle the richer the content impact factor of concept/themes.

3.4 Users Theme Map and Concept Nodes Within Themes

These 7 themes highlight the users' perception of the telecentre's positive influence on beneficiaries, positive socio-economic change at individual level, and collective level. Dominant themes fall into the categories of "Internet", followed closely by "People", "Use", "Time", "Satisfied", and "Radio". Themes overlay depicts users' (individual and collective level) experience level in using the telecentre internet access to improve socio-economic status since these themes materialized larger conceptual semantic relationship, which exists within the threshold rate of 100%. Closer examination on these 7 major themes indicated the potential of expanding the telecentre's role towards improving rural development in terms of "Better Communication", "Information Access", connectivity to the outside world and financial improvement to further strengthen the sense of connectedness. Respondents were satisfied with their wellbeing

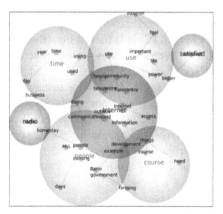

Fig. 13. Users theme map and concept

Table 2. Theme & concept coding classifications and explanation

Theme	Concepts	Hits
Internet	Internet, outside, world, telecentre, telecentre, information, communicate, things, doing, development, access	268
people	people, Bario, example, Miri, coming, government, days, homestay	182
use	use, community, important, feel, better, life, family, internet, power	166
time	time, used, using, day, year, business	132
course	course, need, farming	81
satisfied	satisfied	23
radio	radio	13

and the changes that came into their livelihood through either direct or indirect approach provided by the telecentre as stated below:

User1: *If the telecentre did not exist, we will have struggling to get access to the outside world; of course, it is a challenge to get something and a way to improve our life.*
Users2: *Telecentre improved my motivation for living better life. The telecentre did motivate me because with the telecentre I can communicate with the outside world.*

Table 3 indicates a summary of 10 high level concepts discovered in the collected stories represented as groups of parallel point connected text that is aligned to represent weighted themes/terms weighted, to present frequencies of influence that each text to determine the frequency of co-occurrence between concepts [25]. The percentage of relevance indicates relationship/linkage between frequently occurring concepts, represented in highly ranked concepts associated to indicate the path of travel of between texts [13].

Table 3. Count related concepts and relevance of the top identified concepts

Ranked Concept List		
Name-Like	**Count**	**Relevance**
Internet	151	100%
Bario	64	42%
Telecentre	50	33%
Miri	22	15%
Word-Like	**Count**	**Relevance**
people	79	52%
use	67	44%
time	56	37%
outside	53	35%
world	50	33%
telecentre	50	33%

3.4.1 Analysis of Non-user Stories with Leximance 4.5

Figure 14 depicts themes/concepts map from Leximancer analysis. Eight depicted themes represent non-users' evaluation of the telecentre. Closely interrelated concepts representing top-level classification of stories (gray dots) linked by solid lines, suggest how non-users perceived indirect benefits provided by the telecentre, improving their socio-economic status with proxy help. They also expressed satisfaction, which is another fact, that some non-users, even though lacking in IT skills benefit from the acts of others to help them use the telecentre facilities. According to non-users, Internet gave them seamless access to knowledge and social connectivity to, for example, exchange ideas to the outside world and improving farming techniques for sustainable livelihood. Telecentre contributed largely in domains such as "connectedness", "financial improvements" and "psychological empowerment" and enhanced technical skills. Following are the words of interviewees: **Non-User1**: *The presence of telecentre encouraged me and motivated to explore new opportunities homestays, hand phone.*

Non-User2: *I did not use it but I know the advantages of this telecentre because it is easy to get information. It has motivated me to live a better life. I am satisfied and proud what I have but I want to improve.*

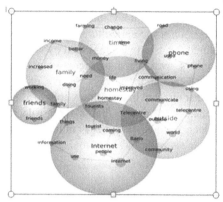

Fig. 14. Non user's themes/concepts map

Table 4. Presents a summary of 8 higher-level themes.

Themes	Concept	Hits
Internet	Internet, people, Bario, use, coming, things, tourist, information	205
outside	outside, world, telecentre, communicate, community, using	135
homestay	homestay, improved, tourists, life, communication	96
family	family, doing, need, better, income, increased	90
time	time, change, living, money, farming	70
phone	phone, used, road	47
friends	friends, working	35

Table 5. Count related concepts and relevance of the top identified concepts

Ranked Concept List		
Name-Like	**Count Relevance**	
Internet	115 100%	
Bario	48 42%	
Telecentre	29 25%	
Word-Like	**Count Relevance**	
people	62 54%	
outside	49 43%	
use	49 43%	
world	47 41%	
telecentre	43 37%	
communicate	30 26%	

3.5 Discussion

3.5.1 Succinct Reflection on Tangible Impact of Telecentre from Users and Non-users' Perspectives

The findings indicate that a domain of change addressed by participants in the area of the telecentre tangible impact was financial improvements at Users: 36%, Non-users: 55%. The percentages of non-users stories in the area of financial impact that addressed the domains of change were considerably higher even though they lack in ICT skills. This suggests that improvements experienced by non-users in this area involved indirect assistance from friends & family, proxy and those who had access to other Internet sources. The sub-domains of change indicate improvements in "Tourism" recorded at Users: 27% & Non-users: 36%: "Agriculture" at users: 36%, non-user:27%. This indicates that users with ICT skills obtained considerable higher impact in "Agriculture" whereas non-users obtained in Tourism. Moreover, financial savings users & non-users reported at 27%, business opportunities users & non-users at 91%. The results further indicate that community have experienced the modern way of farming which resulted in saving their time, labor cost, while some community people still practices the traditional farming method. But, due to the unavailability of required labor force, the modern way of farming takes its role in the agriculture society of the community. In contrast, non-user farmers benefitted from knowledge shared by tourists resulted in improving vegetables and fruits yields, which led to increase in their income. Both respondent groups indicated that Tour guides always receive clients directly from their associated homestays owners that resulted in their household income improvements. Both respondents' groups revealed that internet has a huge role in promoting community to the outside world, which resulted in tourists' influx, which further led to financial improvements in the business of homestays, tour guides and farming.

3.5.2   Succinct Reflection on Intangible Impact of the Telecentre from Users and Non-users Perspectives

Empirical evidence from Bario rural community indicates that the telecentre's benefits were not limited to direct users but also benefited the non-users, demonstrating the intangible impact area, all users & non-users (100%) experienced "Connectedness". This finding indicates that "Connectedness" was deemed as the most important value added benefit to the community with contribution towards bridging communication barrier between community and outside world, bringing closer family value ties and business opportunities. Whereas all 11 users (100%) and 9 in 11 non-users (82%) experienced psychological empowerment. Within the "Psychological Empowerment", the focus of change was on the sub-domains of change of "self-efficacy (Users: 100% Non-users: 90%) and "Self-esteem (Users: 100% Non-users: 72%), it is pertinent to mention that 3 non-users had access to other sources than the telecentre. This study found strong evidence that easy access to communication and information encouraged the users and non-users to explore new opportunities provided by telecentre for living better life. Chamberlain [5], who views empowerment more in the perspective of mental health rehabilitation, refers to empowerment as a process that has a number of qualities such as decision making power, access to information and resources, and having a range of options from which to make choices. These have been defined in this study through data analysis of facts taken for respondent's feedback. Empowerment through ICT means transforming skills into actions to produce a self-determined change [1] of which non-users who have not been able to use computer and the internet directly at the telecentre but obtained benefits in terms of communication with family and friends and also dealt with business clients' registration. In this context, the results of this study show digital opportunities offered by the telecentre empowered poor marginalized community people to achieve their desired goals.

Thus, the major finding of this study is that the sense of empowerment was noteworthy at an individual level among users, particularly non-users of the telecentre. The evidence showed the influential impact of Empowerment was not only apparent in users' beneficiaries group but also in non-users group such as being able to gain control over social economic conditions results in stronger sense of empowerment, and positive psychological empowerment (i.e. building confidence and efficacy level, strengthened sense of self-esteem, enhanced motivation level). From the CA perspective, respondents who were interviewed from different life style did their best to expand their capabilities and use their resources from the Eco-Tourism business, farming or knowledge/skills, which resulted in their tangible and intangible outcomes achievements. Thus, these are the most important intangible outcomes found within collected stories.

3.5.3 Leximancer 4.5

The comparative results obtained through Leximancer 4.5 has shown that the telecentre contributed to positive changes in community's wellbeing in terms of ease of communication and information access, promoting community to outside world which created/enhanced business opportunities. Analysis suggests the psychological empowerment experienced by users and non-users exhibit high self-esteem, self-efficacy, and positive level of confidence and motivation.

4 Conclusion

In conclusion, better communication with internet connectivity has enabled the community to strengthen social bonds among families, friends and business network, giving a sense of connectedness and sense of belonging, financial improvements, enhanced sense of empowerment, enhanced positive Psychological empowerment (building confidence, self-efficacy, strengthened sense of self-esteem, and motivation level). Thus, this study has shown a way to quantifying the intangible impact and shown at least as significant. The adopted theoretical lens provided a deeper understanding of how the telecentre expanded and extended the socio-economic opportunities for community people and how they utilized their abilities to achieve their desired goals. When this project was concluded in July 2016, the telecentre internet Wi-Fi facilities has ended, respondents then have started to make demand for the telecentre services to be re-operated. This study contributes a qualitative methodology approach to the analysis of collected data in the form of stories focused on the MSC within the context of the telecentre tangible/intangible impact on the users & non-users. Thus, the MSC approach was useful to chart stories based on the telecentre impact at individual and collective level.

References

1. Aji, Z.M., et al.: A conceptual model for psychological empowerment of telecentre users. Science **3**(3), 71–79 (2010)
2. Alsop, R., Bertelsen, M.F., Holland, J.: Empowerment in Practice: From Analysis to Implementation. World Bank Publications, Washington, D.C. (2006)
3. Bandura, A.: Self-Efficacy in Changing Societies. Cambridge University Press, NY (1995)
4. Baron, L.F., Gomez, R.: Relationships and connectedness: weak ties that help social inclusion through public access computing. Inform. Technol. Dev. **19**(4), 271–295 (2013)
5. Chamberlin, J.: A working definition of empowerment. Psychiatr. Rehabil. J. **20**(4), 43–46 (1997)

6. Davies, R., Dart, J.: The 'Most Significant Change'(MSC) Technique. A guide to its use (2005)
7. Douglas, H.: Building an analysis of new venture startup with Leximancer. In: Gurd, B. (ed.) Proceedings of the 24th Annual Australian and New Zealand Academy of Management Conference (ANZAM 2010), Adelaide, Australia, 8–10 December 2010, pp. 1–15 (2010)
8. Gomez, R.: The quest for intangibles: Understanding ICTs for digital inclusion beyond socio-economic impact. Paper presented at the Prato CIRN 2008 Community Informatics Conference: ICTs for Social Inclusion: What is the Reality (2008)
9. Gomez, R., Pather, S.: ICT Evaluation: Are we asking the right questions? Electron. J. Inform. Syst. Developing Countries **50**(5), 1–14 (2012)
10. Gomez, R., Reed, P., Chae, H.Y.: Assessment of community wellness outcomes to measure ICT impact. Paper presented at the Proceedings of the Sixth International Conference on Information and Communications Technologies and Development: Notes, vol. 2 (2013)
11. Grunfeld, H.: Framework for evaluating contributions of ICT to capabilities, empowerment and sustainability in disadvantaged communities. Indian Institute of Technology (IIT). Paper presented at the CPRSouth2 (Communication Policy Research) Conference, 'Empowering rural communities through ICT policy and research, 15–17 December, Madras, Chennai (2007)
12. Hamel, J.-Y.: ICT4D and the Human Development and Capabilities Approach. Technical report #37 (2010). http://hdr.undp.org/sites/default/files/hdrp_2010_37.pdf
13. Heck, D., Sweeney, T.: Using most significant change stories to document the impact of the teaching teachers for the future project: An Australian teacher education story. Aust. Educ. Comput. **27**(3), 36–47 (2013)
14. Keriger, R.: MSC Guide: Based on the Experience of ADRA Laos. A guide to implementing the Most Significant Changes (MSC) monitoring system in ADRA country offices (2004)
15. Kozma, R.B.: Monitoring and evaluation of ICT for education impact: a review. In: Wagner, D.A., Day, B., James, T., Kozma, R.B., Miller, J., Unwin, T. (eds.) Monitoring and Evaluation of ICT in Education Projects. A Handbook for Developing Countries, pp. 11–18. infoDev/World Bank, Washington, DC (2005). http://www.infodev.org/en/Publication.9. html. Accessed 24 Mar 2012
16. Rosenberg, M.: Society and the Adolescent Self-Image (rev. ed.), vol. xxxii. Wesleyan University Press, Middletown (1989)
17. Patton, M.Q.: Qualitative analysis and interpretation. Qual. Res. Eval. Methods **3**, 431–539 (2002)
18. Sen, A.: Development as Freedom. Oxford University Press, Oxford (1999)
19. Sey, A., Bar, F., Coward, C., Koepke, L., Rothschild, C., Sciadas, G.: There when you need it: the multiple dimensions of public access ICT uses and impacts. Inf. Technol. Int. Dev. **11**(1), 71 (2015)
20. Sey, A., Coward, C., Bar, F., Sciadas, G., Rothschild, C., Koepke, L.: Connecting people for development: Why public access ICTs matter (2013)
21. Smith, A.E., Humphreys, M.S.: Evaluation of unsupervsied semantic mapping of natural language with leximancer concept mapping. Behav. Res. Methods **38**(2), 262–279 (2006)
22. Ssozi-Mugarura, F., Rivett, U., Blake, E.: Using activity theory to understand technology use and perception among rural users in uganda. In: Proceedings of the Eighth International Conference on Information and Communication Technologies and Development, p. 13. ACM, June 2016
23. Tabassum, G., Yeo, A.W.: Measurement of tangible and intangible impacts of Telecentres on rural communities. In: Proceedings of the Seventh International Conference on Information and Communication Technologies and Development, p. 61. ACM, May 2015

24. Tarawe, J., Harris, R.W.: Stories from e-Bario. Living Inform. Soc. Asia **365**, 109 (2009)
25. http://info.leximancer.com/
26. https://www.google.com/search?q=Boosterism&oq=Boosterism&aqs=chrome..69i57j69i59l3 j0l2.1304j0j4&sourceid=chrome&ie=UTF-8
27. Zaitseva, E.: How to make sense of the Leximancer analysis. Liverpool John Moores University Academic Enhancement Unit, 5th Floor, Kingsway House, Hatton Garden, Liverpool, L3 2AJ (2012)

Linkage Between ICT and Agriculture Knowledge Management Process: A Case Study from Non-Government Organizations (NGOs), India

Ram Naresh Kumar Vangala$^{(\boxtimes)}$, Asim Banerjee, and B.N. Hiremath

DA-IICT, Gandhinagar 382007, Gujarat, India
{ram_kumar,asim_banerjee,bn_hiremath}@daiict.ac.in

Abstract. This paper addresses the linkage between information and communication technology (ICT) and agriculture knowledge management (AKM) process in non-government organizations (NGOs) in India. Sample of 145 respondents were collected using questionnaires in two NGOs. The analysis and hypothesis testing were implemented using structural equation modeling (SEM). The analysis shows that there is a significant ($\beta = 0.61$ at p = 0.001) and positive relationship between ICT and AKM process. The results obtained would help managers to better understand the linkage between ICT and AKM process in their organizations. They could use the results to improve their ICT infrastructure and tools for effectiveness of AKM process.

Keywords: Agriculture · Agriculture knowledge management (AKM) · Confirmatory factor analysis (CFA) · Information and communication technology (ICT) · Non-Government Organizations (NGOs) · Structural equation modeling (SEM)

1 Introduction

Agriculture is an important sector of Indian economy. Nearly 60–70% of the Indian population depend upon agriculture and allied fields. As much as 67% of India's farmland is held by the small and marginal farmers[1]. Many of these small and marginal farmers are illiterate and have meager resources to access modern technology in agriculture [1]. It has been widely recognized that transfer of relevant knowledge plays an important role in agricultural growth and productivity. Transfer of relevant knowledge to small and marginal farmers can help them to improve their yields and get better market prices [2].

---

[1] http://www.business-standard.com/article/news-ians/nearly-70-percent-of-indian-farms-are-very-small-census-shows-115120901080_1.html.

© IFIP International Federation for Information Processing 2017
Published by Springer International Publishing AG 2017. All Rights Reserved
J. Choudrie et al. (Eds.): ICT4D 2017, IFIP AICT 504, pp. 654–666, 2017.
DOI: 10.1007/978-3-319-59111-7_53

Management of agricultural knowledge takes place at different levels: individual, within communities, within organizations or institutions and networks of them [3]. The knowledge for agriculture development is often not created, documented or disseminated by one single source or organization [4]. Different organizations produce different kinds of knowledge and the lack of coordination or linkage between these organizations (public, private, agricultural research and extension institutions) [5] are often cited as a reason for ineffective transfer of knowledge to farmers. The interrelated activities of these organizations may or may not converge at the field level. In this context, the notion of an agriculture knowledge management (AKM) is often put forth. AKM refers to the process of creating knowledge repositories, improving knowledge access, sharing and transfer and enhancing the knowledge environment in the rural communities [2]. Exchange of knowledge and its bidirectional flow (i.e. from farmers to experts and vice versa) is beginning to be recognized in this domain [6].

In the Indian context, the main agencies engaged in creating agriculture knowledge resources can be broadly classified into three categories: Public, Private, and Non-Government Organizations (NGOs). NGOs is any non-profit, voluntary citizens' group which is organized at local, national or international level. NGOs, as a third sector institutional framework have been playing an important role in Indian agriculture. Their main activities are: to promote and develop weaker sections of the people, to create and establish the means of food security among the poor people, to promote sustainable agriculture, to mobilize, inspire and enable tribal through a participatory approach working towards their own rehabilitation using their own resources.

The term, information and communication technology (ICT) has been defined differently by many authors. UNDP[2] defined ICT as the combination of microelectronics, computer hardware and software, telecommunications, and storage of huge amounts of information, and its rapid dissemination through computer networks. ICT has a prominent role to play in knowledge management (KM) in an organization. It helps in achieving organizational effectiveness and

Table 1. List of ICT initiatives projects in Indian agriculture

Categorize	Name of the projects
Web-based technology	Agropedia, Rice Knowledge Management Portal (RKMP), AgriTech, KISSAN Kerala, AGRISNET, AGMARKNET, eKirshi, iKisan, Almost all questions answered (aAQUA), Electronic solution against agriculturepest (e-SAP) SasyaSree
Human intermediaries (between ICT and user)	e-Sagu, Arik, e-Choupal, Digital Green Tata Kisan Sansar, MSSRF-VKC
Mobile technology or telecommunication	Kissan Call Center, IFFCO-IKSL, RML, mKrishi Nokia Life Tool, Spoken Web, Fisher Friend Project, Lifelines

---

[2] http://hdr.undp.org/en/content/human-development-report-2001.

is considered as an essential tool to manage organizations' knowledge assets. ICT can make Indian AKM more competitive by providing affordable, relevant, searchable and up-to-date agriculture information services to the farm communities [2]. Table 1 summarizes some of the ICT project initiatives in Indian agriculture which have been broadly categorized into three categories viz. web-based technology, human intermediaries (between ICT and users), and mobile technology or telecommunication.

ICT tools deployed for agriculture knowledge management in India includes organizational web pages and special portals created for specific commodities, sectors, and enterprises and for e-commerce activities [7]. These ICT projects in Indian AKM revealed that they primarily focused on the transfer of knowledge to the farm communities, following a one-way flow of knowledge i.e. from experts to farmers without many opportunities for interaction. Many ICT projects are pushing external content towards local people based on what experts think the community needs [8]. Hence there is a need to focus on knowledge acquiring, creating, storing, organizing, and sharing or disseminating at the organization level for effective AKM in the agricultural organizations taking into account the need for bidirectional flow of knowledge.

Studies so far focused on the importance or impact of ICT in Indian agriculture. For example, Gummagolmath et al., discussed ICT initiatives in Indian agriculture [9]. Xiaolan Fu and Shaheen Akter, examined the impact of a mobile phone technology-enhanced service delivery systems on agricultural extension service delivery in India [10]. There have been very limited studies on knowledge management process at the organizational level and still fewer on the relationship between ICT and knowledge management process at agricultural organization level in the Indian context. It is not clear how the ICT competency and agriculture knowledge management process works are influence each other. Empirical work in this area is required. Our studies focuses on establishing a relationship between ICT and agriculture knowledge management process in NGOs working in Indian agricultural organizations.

2   Research Framework and Hypotheses

The main objective of this study is to understand the relationship between knowledge enablers like ICT and the knowledge management process in Indian agricultural organization specifically in NGOs. Figure 1 is proposed research model depicting a relationship between ICT and KM process.

2.1   Knowledge Management Process (KM Process)

KM process includes activities of acquiring, creating, storing, sharing, diffusing, developing and deploying knowledge by individuals and groups [11]. According to Davenport and Prusak, KM has three processes that have received most consensus viz. knowledge generation, sharing and utilization [12]. On other hand,

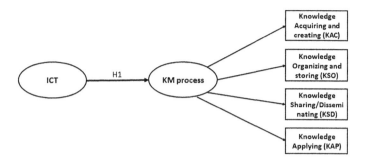

Fig. 1. Research framework

Alavi and Leidner proposed four processes of knowledge management viz. creation, storage, transfer and application [13]. The present study examines the following four processes: acquiring and creating, organizing and storing, sharing or disseminating and applying as proposed by in early studies for agricultural organization [14].

Knowledge Acquiring and Creating (KAC): Knowledge acquiring and creating is a process where members in the organization gain, collect, create and obtain required and useful knowledge to perform their job functions. It involves updating existing content or developing new content by using organization's tacit and explicit knowledge [15]. KAC is about obtaining knowledge from external and/or internal sources or capturing of the knowledge (explicit or tacit) that resides inside the people working in the organization [16].

Knowledge Organizing and Storing (KOS): This process involves structuring, indexing, evaluating and storing the knowledge in organization's repository. Knowledge is validated, codified (to represent a useful format) before it can be used [17]. Once knowledge is evaluated, it is categorized and represented in a structured manner with indexing or mapping to enable efficient storage in the organizations repository and for effective usage at a later point [18].

Knowledge Sharing and Disseminating (KSD): It is the process in which sharing of knowledge take place among individuals and/or groups within and outside the organization. Knowledge sharing is considered as a core process of knowledge management because one of the main goals and objectives of knowledge management is to promote sharing of knowledge among individuals, groups and organizations [19,20]. Knowledge in organization is transferred through social networks, collaboration, and daily interaction like chatting, face-to-face, formal (meetings) and informal (over a cup of tea) conversations [12].

Knowledge Applying (KAP): Knowledge applying is to put the knowledge to good use. The members or employees of the organizations can apply and adopt the best practices in their daily work [21]. According to Davenport and Klahr, the effective application of knowledge can assist the organization to improve efficiency and reduce cost [22]. This process also implies putting knowledge into practice, where the employee should use lessons learnt from previous experience or mistakes made in the past [23].

2.2 Information and Communication Technology (ICT)

ICT plays an important role in facilitating communication between different parts of the organization that often inhibits through normal channels of communication [24]. Many researchers have found that ICT plays a crucial element for knowledge management process [12,13]. ICT tools help in capturing the knowledge created by knowledge worker and making it available to the large community [25]. Information technology has been widely used in organizations, and thus qualifies as a natural medium for the flow of KM process in the organization [24]. Thus, we hypothesize:

H1: ICT has significant and direct effect on Knowledge Management process.

3 Research Methodology and Data Collection

The quantitative research approach was used to empirically test the research hypothesis. A survey questionnaire was designed to determine and understand the linkage between ICT and KM process. The critical metrics for measuring ICT and KM process (acquiring and creating, organizing and storing, sharing/disseminating and applying) that were derived from the literature were used [26–28]. Respondents were asked to rate the extent to which these metric were practiced in their organization using a Likert scale (five-point scale from 1 = strongly disagree to 5 = strongly agree). For the details of items used to measure research constructs refer [29].

Two non-government organizations (NGOs) were selected for this study. Unit of analysis in this study were middle-level managers, veterinary doctors, agriculture extension officers, project coordinators, cluster in-charge or supervisor and field workers/operators. These people were surveyed as they played a key role in managing knowledge. These people were positioned at the intersection of both vertical and horizontal flow of knowledge. Therefore they could synthesize the tacit knowledge of both top (scientist group) and bottom (farmer group) level, convert them into explicit knowledge, and incorporate the same into the organizational knowledge repository.

There is no prior personal or formal relationship between researchers and interviewees or the organization as a whole. This allowed for triangulation and also helped to validate data interpretation and findings [30]. The questions were well-structured, understandable and were developed in four languages namely English, Hindi, Gujarati and Telugu keeping in the mind there geographical location and the composition of people working in NGOs that were the part of the study.

Responses from 148 respondents were collected from these two organizations. Data was collected during their weekly and monthly meetings in the organization. During these meetings, questionnaires were distributed to participants and they were asked to fill the form. Before filling the form, the objectives of the research and questionnaire were well explained to them.

4 Data Analysis and Results

Data analysis was most crucial as it helped us to establish the relationship between ICT and KM process in Indian agricultural organizations Data analysis data was performed by using Statistical Package for the Social Sciences (SPSS version 20.0). Further analysis was conducted by using structural equation modeling (SEM) via the Analysis of Moment Structures (AMOS version 20.0) software. SEM is a multivariate statistical analysis technique that is used to analyze structural relationships.

4.1 Demography of the Respondents

Out of 148 responses, 0 were discarded from our study due to insufficient information. Thus our study consider of 139 respondents. Table 2 summarizes the profile of the respondents.

4.2 Analysis and Results

After analyzing the descriptive statistics, further analysis was conducted by using SEM via the AMOS. Confirmatory factor analysis (CFA) provides an appropriate means of assessing the efficacy of measurement among the items [28]. In this study, the analysis was divided into three parts, viz. the first-order CFA and second-order CFA for the measurement models, and third, the structural model analysis and overall model fit.

First, the measurement models have been assessed for reliability, validity, and unidimensionality. The term reliability refers to the consistency of a research study or the degree to which an assessment tool produces stable and consistent results. Cronbach's alpha, has been one of the most commonly used methods to assess the reliability [31]. To satisfy the reliability criterion, a Cronbachs alpha value of more than or equal to 0.7 is required [32,33]. Referring to Table 3, this condition has been satisfied by all the constructs.

Validity is defined as the degree to which a measurement assesses what it is supposed to measure. Convergent validity and discriminant validity have been checked for each construct. Convergent validity refers to the degree to which the items that should be related are in actual reality related [17]. For convergent validity, the composite reliability (CR) value must be more than or equal to 0.7 and the average variance extracted (AVE) value must be greater than or

Table 2. Demography of the respondents

Sample characteristics	Frequency (n = 139)	Percent (%)
Gender		
Male	102	73.4
Female	37	26.6
Education		
High school	47	33.8
Bachelor degree	62	44.6
Master degree	30	21.6
Working position		
Regional managers	3	2.2
Project managers/program managers	20	14.4
Project officer/supervisor	24	23.0
Field in-charge/cluster assistant	92	60.4
Work experience		
0–5 years	56	40.3
6–10 years	49	35.3
11–15 years	18	12.9
Above 15 years	16	11.5

equal to 0.5 [32]. As shown in Table 3, all the constructs have satisfied these two requirements.

Unidimensionality is achieved when the items have acceptable factor loadings that are greater than or equal to 0.5 [17,32]. During the process, ICT2, KAC5, KAC6, KOS1, KOS2, KSD2, KSD8, KSD9 were dropped due to poor factor loading of less than 0.5. The results of unidimensionality for all the constructs have been showed in Table 3

Next, the second-order CFA was conducted for the first-order constructs of the study. It was used to confirm that the underlying measurement constructs loaded into their respective theorized construct (KM process) [17]. In this respect, the factor loadings between first-order constructs and second-order constructs must be greater than or equal to 0.5 [32]. The result of second-order CFA are displayed in Table 4 and the finalized model of second-order CFA of KM process construct are illustrated in Fig. 2.

The final stage was structural model analysis. In this, the structural equation modeling (SEM) was tested using the maximum likelihood method. It has been designed to judge how good a proposed conceptual model can fit the data collected and also to find the structural relationships between the sets of latent variable [34]. The final model of the study is illustrated in Fig. 3.

Table 3. Results of unidimensionality, reliability and convergent validity

First order constructs	No. of items	Indicators	Factor loadings	CR (≥ 0.7)	AVE (≥ 0.5)	Cronbach's alpha
Information Communication Technology (ICT)	5	ICT6	0.849	0.836	0.561	0.791
		ICT3	0.749			
		ICT1	0.755			
		ICT5	0.691			
		ICT4	0.640			
Knowledge acquiring and creating (KAC)	4	KAC1	0.789	0.854	0.532	0.723
		KAC2	0.759			
		KAC3	0.723			
		KAC4	0.637			
Knowledge organizing and storing (KOS)	4	KOS3	0.823	0.845	0.610	0.771
		KOS4	0.790			
		KOS5	0.772			
		KOS6	0.694			
Knowledge sharing/disseminating (KSD)	6	KSD7	0.779	0.914	0.628	0.78
		KSD1	0.728			
		KSD4	0.721			
		KSD3	0.720			
		KSD5	0.696			
		KSD6	0.694			
Knowledge Applying (KAP)	3	KAP2	0.779	0.888	0.594	0.703
		KAP3	0.777			
		KAP1	0.756			

Note: Items with low factor loading (<0.5) have been dropped

To ensure the fitness of the structural model, i.e. how well the data set fits the research model, there are several indicators which are computed by using AMOS. The most fundamental measure of overall fit in a structural equation model is the likelihood-ratio chi-square statistics. As suggested by Bagozzi and Yi, a p-value exceeding 0.05 and a normed chi-square value (χ^2/df) that is below 3, are normally considered as acceptable [35]. Along with this, the fitness of the structural model can be studied by using the Comparative Fit Index (CFI). This must be greater than or equal to 0.9 [36], Root Mean Squared Error of Approximation (RMSEA) must be less than or equal to 0.08 [37], Goodness-of-Fit Index (GFI) must be greater than or equal to 0.9 [32], and Adjust Goodness-of-Fit Index (AGFI) must be greater than or equal to 0.9 [32]. The developed model has been proven to meet all the requirements and the results are shown in Table 5. Therefore, the model was utilized to test the hypothesis relationships among the constructs.

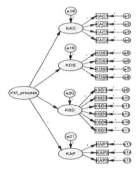

Fig. 2. Second-order CFA

Table 4. Results of Second-order CFA

Second order construct	First order construct	Factor loading ($\geq$0.5)
KM process	KAC	0.93
	KOS	0.895
	KSD	0.945
	KAP	0.768

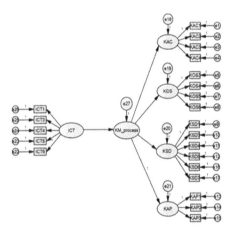

Fig. 3. Final model for the study

Table 5. The Fitness of the model

Name of the index	Value obtained	Accepted fit	Results
chi-square (χ^2/df)	1.849	Below 3	Satisfied
CFI	0.902	>=0.90	Satisfied
RMSEA	0.08	=<0.08	Satisfied
GFI	0.931	>=0.90	Satisfied
AGFI	0.911	>=0.90	Satisfied

Table 6 presents the hypothesis testing result for the causal effect of ICT on KM process. The results revealed that ICT has a significant ($\beta = 0.61$ at p = 0.001) and positive effect on KM process. Therefore H1 was supported and accepted.

Table 6. Results of hypothesis

Hypothesis	β value	p-value	Comment
H1:ICT KM process	0.61	***	Significant

Note *** significant at 0.001

5   Discussions

This study has applied SEM approach to examine and prove the existence of significant impact of ICT on KM process. Our analysis showed that ICT had a significant effect on KM process in the organizations that were part of our study. The result is also consistent with the findings from past studies. For instance, Chadha et al. found that ICT enhances the visibility of knowledge and facilitate the process of acquiring, creating, storing and disseminating [25]. Allahawiah et al. also verified that there is the positive impact of information technology on knowledge management processes [38].

In case of the two organizations, there were clear indications that the staff at various levels and experts has been using Internet, emails, mobile technology for acquiring, storing and sharing knowledge among individuals, groups and organizations. The majority of the respondents were field in-charges and supervisors, who are actively involved in agriculture knowledge management process. Most of the respondents in the sample of the study owned a cell phone and used it to access agriculture knowledge from neighbors, friends, families and subject experts in the organizations. In Digital Green, digital videos were created on local relevant agriculture and livelihood practices by using ICT tools like video cameras. Then these videos were screened for farm communities using battery-operated Pico projectors. All these videos were organized and stored in organization repository, for accesses in both off-line and on-line mode.

From the observations and discussions with members and employees, we that understand that there is a limit of using ICT in organizations. For an instant, we observed that only top and senior management in DHRUVA had access to laptops and Internet facilities. The field supervisors used a mobile phone to communicate with peer and farm communities. Most of the time in DHRUVA, face-to-face, group meetings and personal visits were used for disseminating agriculture knowledge to farm communities because of low bandwidth of the Internet, ICT infrastructure.

6   Conclusion

The availability of ICT has had a significant ($\beta = 0.61$ at p $= 0.001$) effect on AKM process in the two organizations that were part of our study. ICT was found to assist in the process of getting required knowledge and enabling easy communication among and between the farm communities and organizations. The availability of ICT is seen to enhance dissemination of explicit and tacit knowledge and sharing of best practices effectively among the farm communities and expert groups in the organizations. For example, we found that Digital Green is using ICT tools like Picos to disseminate agriculture knowledge (videos) to farmers. These videos are downloaded or streamed online which are stored in organization repository. DHRUVA provides access to their materials (like best practices, success stories, annual reports) on their websites. They show audio and video clips on water resources development, sericulture, agroforestry, post-harvesting product development to farm communities using DVD and television.

The rapid development in the field of ICT, for example, mobile technology, availability of the internet, web technologies and mode of communications like emails, video conference etc. helps in faster creation, storing, sharing of knowledge within and outside the organization. In organizations where face-to-face meetings are used very frequently, ICT tools can play a supportive role in recording such meetings for future use.

We believe that our results will contribute in several ways to the knowledge management theory and practice specific to Indian agriculture. An attempt has been made to conduct this kind of research study in Indian agriculture organizations to establish the relationships between ICT and AKM process. The study will help managers at different levels in selecting tools and technologies that can be used to support AKM process in their organizations. The proposed set of metrics used in this study may also be used in future as basic tools to measuring the effectiveness of ICT on AKM process in agricultural organizations.

Acknowledgment. We would like to acknowledge the two organizations DIGITAL GREEN and DHRUVA for their cooperation and participation and in allowing us to conduct the study.

References

1. Yadav, K., Sulaiman, R.V., Yaduraju, N.T., Balaji, V., Prabhakar, T.V.: ICTs in knowledge management: the case of the Agropedia platform for Indian agriculture. Knowl. Manag. Dev. J. **11**(2), 5–22 (2015)
2. Hugar, L.B., Patil, V.C., Priya, P., Prabhuraj, A., Balaji, V., Yaduraju, N.T.: Information and communication technologies for agriculture knowledge management in India. World Appl. Sci. J. IDOSI Publ. **14**(5), 794–802 (2011)
3. Engel, P.G.H.: Knowledge management in agriculture: building upon diversity. Knowl. Technol. Policy **3**(3), 28–35 (1990)
4. Rafea, A.: Managing agriculture knowledge: role of information and communication technology. In: Think Piece for CGIAR Sci. Forum Workshop on ICTs Transforming Agricultural Science, Research and Technology Generation (2009)
5. Saravanan, R: ICTs for agricultural extension in India: policy implications for developing countries. In: Proceedings of the 8th Asian Conference for Information Technology in Agriculture, AFITA, pp. 1–11 (2012)
6. Vangala, R.N.K., Hiremath, B.N., Banerjee, A.: A theoretical framework for knowledge management in Indian agricultural organizations. In: Proceedings of the 2014 International Conference on Information and Communication Technology for Competitive Strategies, p. 6. ACM (2014)
7. Sulaiman, R.V., Hall, A., Kalaivani, N.J., Dorai, K., Vamsidhar Reddy, T.S.: Necessary, but not sufficient: critiquing the role of information and communication technology in putting knowledge into use. J. Agric. Educ. Ext. **18**(4), 331–346 (2012)
8. Glendenning, C.J., Ficarelli, P.P.: The relevance of content in ICT initiatives in Indian agriculture. Int. Food Policy Res. Inst. Discuss. Paper **1180**, 1–40 (2012)
9. Gummagolmath, K.C., Sharma, P.: ICT Initiatives in Indian agriculture-an overview. Indian J. Agric. Econ. **66**(3), 489–497 (2011)

10. Fu, X., Akter, S.: The impact of ICT on agricultural extension services delivery: evidence from the rural e-services project in India. TMD Working Paper 46, Department of International Development, University of Oxford (2045-5119) (2012)
11. Demarest, M.: Understanding knowledge management. Long Range Plan. **30**(3), 374–384 (1997)
12. Davenport, T.H., Prusak, L., Knowledge, W.: How Organization Manage What They Know, vol. 102. Harvard Business School Press, Boston (1998)
13. Alavi, M., Leidner, D.E.: Knowledge management systems: issues, challenges, and benefits. Commun. AIS **1**(2es), 1 (1999)
14. Vangala, R.N.K., Mukerji, M., Hiremath, B.N.: ICTs for agriculture knowledge management: insights from DHRUVA, India. In: Proceedings of the Seventh International Conference on Information and Communication Technologies and Development, p. 51. ACM (2015)
15. Pentland, B.T.: Information systems and organizational learning: the social epistemology of organizational knowledge systems. Account. Manag. Inf. Technol. **5**(1), 1–21 (1995)
16. Jackson, C.: Process to Product: Creating Tools for Knowledge Management. In: Knowledge Management for Business Model Innovation, pp. 402–413. Idea Group Publishing, Hershey (2001)
17. Tan, L.P., Wong, K.Y.: Linkage between knowledge management and manufacturing performance: a structural equation modeling approach. J. Knowl. Manag. **19**(4), 814–835 (2015)
18. Rollett, H.: Knowledge Management: Processes and Technologies. Springer, New York (2012)
19. Chua, A.: Knowledge management systems architecture: a bridge between KM consultants and technologies. Int. J. Inf. Manag. **24**, 87–98 (2004)
20. Karadsheh, L., Mansour, E., Alhawari, S., Azar, G., El-Bathy, N.: A theoretical framework for knowledge management process: towards improving knowledge performance. Commun. IBIMA **7**, 67–79 (2009)
21. O'Dell, C.S., Essaides, N.: If Only We Knew What We Know: The Transfer of Internal Knowledge and Best Practice. Simon and Schuster, London (1998)
22. Davenport, T.H., Klahr, P.: Managing customer support knowledge. Calif. Manag. Rev. **40**(3), 195 (1998)
23. Datta, P.: An agent-mediated knowledge-in-motion model. J. Assoc. Inf. Syst. **8**(5), 287–311 (2007)
24. Allameh, S.M., Zare, S.M.: Examining the impact of KM enablers on knowledge management processes. Procedia Comput. Sci. **3**, 1211–1223 (2011)
25. Chadha, S.K., Ritika, S.: Information technology support to knowledge management practices: a structural equation modeling approach. IUP J. Knowl. Manag. **12**(1), 39 (2014)
26. Choy, C.S., Yew, W.K., Lin, B.: Criteria for measuring KM performance outcomes in organisations. Ind. Manag. Data Syst. **106**(7), 917–936 (2006)
27. Lee, Y., Lee, S.: Capabilities, processes, and performance of knowledge management: a structural approach. Hum. Factors Ergon. Manuf. Serv. Ind. **17**(1), 21–41 (2007)
28. Andrew, H., Gold, A.H., Arvind Malhotra, A.H.S.: Knowledge management: an organizational capabilities perspective. J. Manag. Inf. Syst. **18**(1), 185–214 (2001)
29. Vangala, R.N.K., Banerjee, A., Hiremath, B.N.: An association between information and communication technology and agriculture knowledge management process in Indian milk co-operatives and non-profit organizations: an empirical analysis (2017). https://arxiv.org/abs/1702.03621v1

30. Venkitachalam, K., Bosua, R.: Roles enabling the mobilization of organizational knowledge. J. Knowl. Manag. **18**(2), 396–410 (2014)
31. Sekaran, U.: Research Methods for Business: A Skill Building Approach. Wiley, Singapore (2006)
32. Hair, J.F.: Multivariate Data Analysis, vol. 6. Pearson Prentice Hall, Upper Saddle River (2006)
33. Nunnally, J.C., Bernstein, I.H.: Psychometric Theory. McGraw-Hill, New York (1994)
34. Byrne, B.M.: Structural Equation Modeling With AMOS: Basic Concepts, Applications, and Programming. Routledge, New York (2013)
35. Bagozzi, R.P., Yi, Y.: On the evaluation of structural equation models. J. Acad. Mark. Sci. **16**(1), 74–94 (1988)
36. Bentler, P.M.: Comparative fit indexes in structural models. Psychol. Bull. **107**(2), 238 (1990)
37. Browne, W.M., Cudeck, R.: Alternative ways of assessing model fit. Sociol. Methods Res. **21**(2), 230–258 (1992)
38. Allahawiah, S., Al-Mobaideen, H., al Nawaiseh, K.: The impact of information technology on knowledge management processes: an empirical study in the Arab Potash Company. Int. Bus. Res. **6**(1), 235 (2013)

Current Issues

Are Online Social Networks, Leading to a 'Better World in the Omani Public Sector? A Qualitative Study

Jyoti Choudrie[1], Efpraxia Zamani[2], and Ali Al-Bulushi[1(✉)]

[1] Hertfordshire Business School, University of Hertfordshire, Hatfield, UK
j.choudrie@herts.ac.uk, ali.albulushi@yahoo.com
[2] Faculty of Technology, De Montfort University, Leicester, UK
efpraxia.zamani@dmu.ac.uk

Abstract. Information and Communications Technologies (ICT) penetration is growing at exponential rates and affecting societies, countries and organizations, which has led to a need for understanding whether they contribute to development. To ascertain whether ICT are contributing to development, the example of a current ICT, Twitter is used, along with the aim of this research: *To understand and explain how public sector organizations are adopting and using online social networks; namely twitter, for the delivery of e-government services that will provide a better world to live in the Omani public sector.* By considering this aim, we attempt to explain whether Twitter, contributes towards the creation of a 'better world' to live in, or leads to diverse outcomes in a developing country, Oman. To achieve the aim, we used two public sector organizations workforces' experiences and applied the Choice Framework (CF) developed by Kleine [1]. For the research approach, we employed a qualitative approach and the data collection techniques, reference to archival documents, interviews, photographic evidence and observations. The analysis was completed using the lens of interpretivism, socio-materiality along with grounded theory concepts. The study reveals that ICT4D is providing a better world for most of the citizens, but for the providers of the improved e-government services, it implies aligning local practices to the technology, which affects their home/work life balance. The contributions of this research lie in emphasising largely how the use of Twitter in Oman will lead to development. The Choice Framework selected for our understanding was adapted and led to diverse results to those mentioned in previous ICT4D studies; therefore, our research makes a contribution of understanding ICT4D in an e-government context, which was amiss in the previous frameworks. For businesses, our findings inform practitioners on the ICT Technologies areas that need attention while implementing them within an environment similar to Oman's public sector. For policymakers, this research informs of the areas that require policymakers' attention when placing their efforts where they are best served.

Keywords: Twitter · Online social networks · Public sector · Oman · The choice framework

© IFIP International Federation for Information Processing 2017
Published by Springer International Publishing AG 2017. All Rights Reserved
J. Choudrie et al. (Eds.): ICT4D 2017, IFIP AICT 504, pp. 669–680, 2017.
DOI: 10.1007/978-3-319-59111-7_54

1 Introduction

A recent phenomenon causing changes in public and private sector organizations and society alike, are Online Social Networks (OSN) which is witnessing major growth especially in developing countries. Within the Middle East region, including the Gulf countries, the use of OSN has grown by 47% in the last 12 months with mobile social media up by 40%, with Qatar and United Arab Emirates ranked no 1 and 2 respectively worldwide in social media penetration, while Saudi Arabia ranked no 1 in social media growth worldwide [2].

Twitter, an OSN tool is particularly growing in popularity especially in the middle east and there is a need to understand whether it can contribute to development, or, in the words of Walsham [3], whether "they are creating a better world in which we live?" Magro [4] provided a timeline of e-government research and OSN where recommendations were made for research in the areas of objectives and strategy, categorization of e-government applications, and policy-making. Twitter's growing use as online platforms and applications warrant further research into its adoption and use. Besides being a communication channel and voice for citizens that emphasises their political views and opinions. Twitter also aligns with the need for future research in e-government and OSN as recommended by Magro [4]. By considering this issue, we attempt to explain whether Twitter does contribute towards the creation of a 'better world' to live in, or otherwise. For readers, the concept of a 'better world is drawn from "IS scholars where practitioners should be concerned with how to use ICTs to help make a better world, and everybody has the opportunity and capability to use technologies to make better lives for themselves, their communities and the world in general" [3].

2 Theoretical Background

ICT4D: A Review. ICT4D is a contentious issue in research as the notion of development in ICT4D is one that has multiple facets. For instance, when considering ICT4D Sen [5] established that development is fundamentally about freedom. This makes participation and empowerment two essential components of contemporary theory and research about human development. Practically, ICT4D is essentially seen to be a framework for the application of tools and techniques to the practice of development. It is a multidisciplinary field within the practice of development that has benefited tremendously from the research, application and immense support from academia, the private sector and major development agencies [6]. It can be summarised as the use of ICT to reach development objectives with their potential impact lying in the uniqueness of these new tools, such as mobile phones and World Wide Web (3W), which have revolutionised the ease with which people are able to exchange and share information across vast distances. Their potential for accumulation of searchable knowledge and information are responsible for what many are now calling the advent of the Information Age [7]. Contrary to the physical objectives of ICT, which are fundamental to overcome limitations of existing techniques of information storing and sharing, ICT4D has a "profoundly moral agenda" that aims to empower people and communities by answering the difficult questions of not only "what should be done" in the practice of development but also "how we should do it" [6].

The Choice Framework. To evaluate development, a Choice framework (CF) was suggested (Fig. 1) that is based on Sen's capability approach, where 'development' is defined as 'a process of expanding the real freedoms that people enjoy' [5, 8]; Alsop and Heinsohn [9] empowerment framework where 'individual agency' (measured by an individual's asset endowment including, 'psychological, informational, organizational, material, social, financial or human assets). Alsop and Heinsohn [9] is connected with an opportunity structure' (shaped by the presence and operation of formal and informal institutions) that results in 'degrees of empowerment' (these are the existence of choice, use of choice, and achievement of choice), Alsop and Heinsohn [9] and the Sustainable Livelihood Framework used by the UK Department for International Development [10] drawing on its concepts of the capital portfolio and elements of its visual representation.

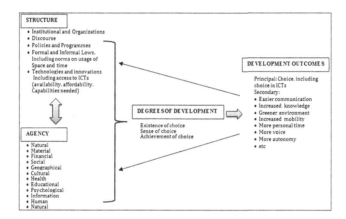

Fig. 1. The choice framework. Source: Kleine [1].

We recognize and apply the CF, a tool that has been identified as suitable for ICT4D understanding. A further reason for using it is that Kleine [1] identified a limitation of the framework being applicable to the micro-level of the individual, but a recommendation made is that consideration of its use should be made at the groups of individuals, communities or nations front.

2.1 ICT4D and E-Government Research

ICT are viewed to have tremendous administrative 'potential' for governments and generally for the public sector [11]. This 'potential' is considered to be a natural extension of the technological revolution that has accompanied the knowledge society, which is known as electronic (e-) government. E-government has many diverse definitions, with the majority agreeing that e-government is the government's use of different ICT to provide citizens and businesses the opportunity to interact with the government. This research considers a combination of Government 2 Government and Government 2 Citizen research where the provision of ICT and placing the citizen in a central position, whether as a participant or consumer.

In the context of e-government and Oman[1] research, Abanumy, Al-Badi and Mayhew [12] found that the government of Oman needs to develop a set of policies and regulations to enhance the development of accessible sites and encourage the use of ICT that facilitate citizens needs in the context of e-government. Ashrafi and Murtaza [13] then used a survey instrument to find that the use and impact of ICT on Small and Medium Sized Enterprises (SMEs) in Oman was still low compared to the expectations of the government. Albusaidy and Weerakkody [14] findings of Oman's e-government implementation efforts revealed that e-government is still in its initial stages, with the country facing a number of challenges such as, a lack of strategy, leadership, legal and regulatory frameworks and infrastructure related issues. These studies also support the earlier view that the application of an institutional perspective is provided, but they do not reveal how an ethical consideration to the provision of government products and services to the citizen is proffered. This is better informed by considering the outcomes of government products and services to citizens, which the next section explains.

2.2   E-Government and OSN/Social Media (SM) Research

In e-government e-services research, OSN have gained importance due to their enhancing of online citizens' participation and economic revitalization in austerity times due to the OSN revolutionary business innovations and business models [15]. Despite their penetration, OSN are still an enigma, which has led to varying existing definitions of the technologies with researchers utilising definitions according to the research scope. For this research, OSN are defined as "web-based services that allow individuals to (1) Construct a public or semi-public profile within a bounded system, (2) articulate a list of other users with whom they share a connection, and (3) view and traverse their list of connections and those made by others within the system" [16]. A term synonymous with OSN is Social Media (SM) that is defined as "a group of internet-based applications that build up on the ideological and technological foundation of Web 2.0, which allows the creation and exchange of user-generated content" [17]. Researchers interchangeably apply terms such as, SM, Web 2.0, Social Networks, Social Information Systems, Social Networking, Social Networking Sites when considering OSN, but upon closer examination they refer to OSN, which is the view that this research study follows [18].

With OSN/SM, the citizen's role has changed to that of a provider where citizen participation has become a key issue of consideration. In this instance, participation appears to be the key concept that explains the difference between 'old' and 'new' web technologies in the form of OSN/SM, although basic tools for interaction such as, chat

---

[1] Oman was mentioned and emphasized as it is the case study context used for this study.

and forum were also available in the early days of the 3W. What is also amiss in such studies is how the government agencies are transforming to cater to the citizens' needs, which our paper is revealing.

In e-government and OSN/SM research, an understanding of the 'global citizen' and whether this role can exist where a digital divide exists, examines citizen participation at a global level as OSN reach is global. The view is held that the 'global citizen's' role can be enhanced by reducing the digital divide using OSN/SM [19]. By participating in government focused debates, ICT in general have been viewed as applications that can be used as an effective means of reducing corruption, but social attitudes can decrease the effectiveness of ICTs as an anti-corruption tool [20], which subscribes to the ethical considerations and reveals a better world. Researchers have also attempted to understand whether citizen participation using OSN can be used to understand the transparency and corruption emerging due to e-government [21].

3 Research Methodology

For this research, the framing of our research question: 'How is Oman's public sector using Twitter for development and why?" suggests a qualitative case study method is most suitable for this purpose. We also employed the interpretive research approach that involves embracing [36]'s view that "our theories concerning reality are making sense of the world and shared meanings are a form of inter-subjectivity rather than objectivity" [22]. Finally, it should be noted that the understanding for this study was approached following Orlikowski [23] conceptualisation of the IT artefact.

Case Selection. For this research, two public sector organizations of Oman were used to compare the role of Twitter in Oman's e-government initiatives. One of the organizations is a high user of Twitter and the other, a medium-user. Further, one of the organizations is one that has more interaction with the citizens, which is Muscat Municipality (MM) and the other is the Public Authority for Investment Promotion and Export Development (Ithraa) of Oman that has less interaction with citizens. Both organizations were selected for theoretical reasons as both organizations use OSN; namely Twitter, interact with citizens and provide an opportunity to determine whether OSN do provide a 'better' world, but in diverse contexts. MM Services include, building permits, naming of roads, maintenance of roads and lighting, organizing local, community and religious events, or providing public sector employees with personal details such as, salary payments. Comparatively, Ithraa is a central government organization that deals more with the business and entrepreneurial aspects affecting citizens. Their services include, informing organizations interested in investing in Oman with vital information such as, required licenses for trading in Oman, or registering organizations seeking entrepreneurship in Oman. Ithraa, therefore, will provide a comparative basis for understanding ICT4D as the two cases will allow a comparison of a local and central government department's application of an OSN.

Data Collection. Participants were selected with a view that individuals employed in key organizational positions are best suited to answer the research questions [24], would ensure diversity and provide adequate experience of the e-government project of

OSN (either presently, or in the past). Specifically, snowball sampling was used that led to participants being invited informally rather than to be obtained using an organizational hierarchical system (i.e., a 'senior member of staff' command). In the latter case, there is a risk for bias; because it is typical for respondents to obey their seniors' command and provide answers aligned with the researchers' aims. The research team sought to ensure that no one was forced to participate and that individuals from all the organizational levels participated. We also ensured that there was theoretical saturation of the empirical material; i.e., that any additional interviews would be conducted only if they provided supplementary and substantial findings and perspectives; thus adding value to the study. Overall, this study used 19 participants of which 11 were female and 8 males. The numbers of participants was also essential to ensure that triangulation, which allowed verification and validation of the findings could be obtained. To acquire the data, semi-structured interviews that consisted of open ended questions were held.

Data Analysis. The analysis was conducted using a deductive approach, based on the Grounded Theory coding methodology, proposed by Glaser [25]. Further, as this research is focused on OSN and uses on interpretivism stance, we followed the analysis technique used by Choudrie and Zamani [26]. Specifically, the coding scheme derived from Walsham [3] on what constitutes a 'better world with ICT4D' and the Choice frameworks proposed by Kleine [1]. For the working practices analysis the socio materiality examples provided by Orlikowski [23] were applied. This led to the application of grounded theory approach, which was solely for the purpose of coding our material (rather than for developing our entire research design that is based on interpretivism). This allowed newly identified concepts to emerge and to be coded in terms of the extant (present in the literature) codes. This approach also allowed for the possible identification and analysis of newly emergent codes. It also facilitated the close examination of participants' opinions, perceptions and behaviours without imposing our own preconceptions onto our coding scheme.

4   Findings and Analysis

4.1   Development Outcomes

Since the main emphasis of this study is e-government, our questions and observations were focused on determining a government's provision of online products and services to citizens.

4.2   Primary Outcomes

Sen [5] identified 'choice' as both the aim and the principal means of development, where the primary development outcome is choice itself. For this, we identified the primary development choice being the choice of ICT to include the use of various government provided internet applications and services that established interaction between citizens, the government and public sector organizations.

From our interviews, the incumbent application for the workforce was a high reliance and use of e-mail, which is still within the remit of ICT. Additionally, the government was providing an infrastructure that provided choices to the workforce between using the classic form of ICT: e-mail and novel form of ICT: the various OSN. Participants were asked: *"What are the online social networks tools used in your organization?"* Participants from both MM and Ithraa cited using the various application choices offered by the internet.

4.3   Secondary Outcomes

Secondary development outcomes depend on an individual's choice as what lives they value [1]. Examples include easier communication with personal and professional contacts, increased knowledge, more income or time saved.

Easier Communication. For the analysis, unlike the CF, which was based on an individual and largely a household effort, our research employed a macro perspective and considered the individual perspective to using Twitter, which resulted in utilising Orlikowski [23] socio-material perspective. This assisted in understanding how there was easier communication within the organization and between the organization and citizens. Due to the networks, the servers functioned for 24 h/7 days a week. This led to the workforce working practices aligning with a feeling that they should 'be in the loop'. This led to a faster, transparent and effective communication process. However, the use of Twitter had also affected their personal lives and ultimately, the work/life balance (Table 1).

Table 1. A Socio-Materiality aspect to twitter's communication processes

Level 0	Citizen raises issue/s on Twitter-content mentions a department of MM and High Position Individual (HPI) associated with the department
Level 1	Feed is viewed by call center individual and HPI. Twitter service is socio-materially configured by MM Information Technology and Networks department to continually 'push' tweets' to devices
Level 2	Message is sent to a mobile device that has an internet connection as the push facility from servers have settings sending messages 24 h a day/7 days a week
Level 3	Tweet is relayed on the internet and visible to members of the public
Level 4	As message is 'open', it is relayed, and picked up by the department of HPI and HPI on mobile or desktop
Level 5	HPI and department of HPI Individual view tweet and become aware of issue
Level 6	Actions and measures to address the problem are undertaken. Socio-materiality occurs here as the team the HPI is responsible for has to lodge and complete the task using whatever means at whatever time
Level 7	Citizen issue is addressed
Level 8	New feed: Citizen thanks MM and HPI on Twitter

Cost Savings and an increase in income. Since Twitter is a web based service an organization does not have to endure complex, slow and expensive software integration and focus instead on the value of their offerings and mission critical tasks. In turn, this implies efficiency in terms of cost savings of the reusable, coupled software components and expensive integration. Effectiveness occurs in terms of savings in time as explained earlier, and work practices are being addressed by relevant individuals in a timely fashion. These savings should lead to an increase in the income of the government funds, which Kleine [1] referred to in the CF.

Increased Knowledge, Information and More Voice. From the interviews it was induced that citizens were happier with Twitter as it offered more knowledge of the processes that were involved in completing a particular issue that they raised. Therefore, in this respect Twitter was offering citizens a better world to live in, a world where clarity and transparency was provided. Increased knowledge was due to the workforces becoming more accountable to and aware of being under the scrutiny of citizens. The reflective nature of Twitter also meant that whereas previously citizens would e-mail the organizations, and there was no possibility of the citizens being aware of their concerns being addressed, or even attended to. With Twitter this was a possibility, which meant that citizens had become active stakeholders in the e-government initiatives, which was not there before.

Better Governance and Improved performance. Before using Twitter, senior managers would not be held responsible in front of public eye, which is the major difference identified by the use of Twitter. Due to Twitter, a senior management person holds a 'sense of responsibility' for an action. As there is an online mention, this leads to a government person being compelled to investigate and examine the issue. This leads to the senior manager identifying other people who can complete the task. These actions are all attributed to a citizen using Twitter, which in turn assures the citizen that the issue is being dealt with in an efficient, effective and transparent manner.

Twitter use led to an indirect and informal 'name and shame' policy, which is something that may be present before, or if it was present, it was in a hushed and silent manner. Now, with Twitter, everyone and everything is clearly identified, which shows a major development in improving the working practices of the public sector. A middle level, male manager of Ithraa confirmed this: *"Dealing with tweets does require a quick action and to reply back to the public...otherwise the organization image will be affected negatively if there is a delay"*. At a lower level, a female staff member could further identify and evaluate the impacts of OSN: *"OSN saves time and makes the organization's work easier; particularly, with the information provided by the public, which most of the time includes pictures. So, interaction with the public has increased and more transparency is now available by both the organization and the public. There is also clarification because many services that members of the public thought were associated with one organization only is clear, and now they can understand the coordination needed and the time it takes to do something"*. For the organization at a process level, the person noted: *"...work processes have become much easier and clear...but also some processes have been altered to include social media."*

Personal Time and Policies. A drawback of Twitter is the imbalance caused to the work/life balance. Several participants from the middle and lower levels of MM and Ithraa commented that they had to deal with tweets after work hours. This meant that time was being taken away from their personal lives. From a socio-material perspective, this is something that is a sign of the times.

We also found that most of the workers frequently viewed their handheld device, as they chose to 'stay in touch' or to be kept 'in the loop'. This was because workers formed expectations that others will be available via their devices, as they were which led to them replying to e-mail/s and in time this leads to collective socio-material enactments. These enactments are almost continual electronic communication within the organization. In the same way, many of the middle and lower level workforce were viewing their mobile devices continuously, which led them to form expectations that their colleagues, seniors were doing the same and felt the need to reply. This enactment was being completed at any time or day, which is leading to an enacted working practice that is delineating the work/life balance of individuals.

5   Discussion, Implications, Limitations and Future Directions

This paper provided a deeper understanding of ICT4D in Oman using findings of the use and development of Twitter in two of Oman's public sector organizations. Additionally, our paper has offered rich descriptions regarding issues of how choices are made in a country that can and will lead to development. We have also illustrated 'how' and 'why' development can and will occur in different settings, and considered the issues of gender, and ethics, which have been viewed as pertinent issues to be addressed when making choices for development utilizing ICT and if an answer is to be provided to whether a better world is being obtained in the world we live. For this, the CF proposed by Kleine [1] and shown in Fig. 1 was applied and addresses the question Walsham [3] posed on whether 'ICT4D are creating a better world in which we live'. The CF also assisted in identifying not only ethical, equality, management and infrastructure' issues being addressed as development occurs, but by supporting them with rich acquired data.

Discussing first the issues that require addressing when considering whether ICT4D do create a better world in which we live, our research showcases the choices that have to be made by citizens when a government provides online products and services; in this case, Twitter. From the development outcomes it was found that there is an equal and ethical perspective provided by Twitter. This was confirmed by CF and our findings. However, our study used a socio-materiality perspective provided by Orlikowski [27] to form an understanding of the ICT4D being provided by e-government, which is missing in CF. Our findings revealed that unlike the CF, that was based on an individual and largely a household effort, a macro and individual perspective to using Twitter in organizations, will result in the organizations' development that will lead to a better world to various individuals, but not all. A socio-material analysis explained that due to the networks settings, the servers functioned for 24 h and 7 days a week. This led to the workforce in the public sector organizations working practices to change and becoming aligned with the technology patterns due to; for instance, feeling that they should 'be in the loop'. Therefore, their working practices become synonymous with the technology. In turn, this affected their personal lives and ultimately, the work/life balance.

By applying an organizational context, this study explains how better governance and improved performance of public and private enterprises can occur for the secondary outcomes, which Unwin [6] recommends should be included in ICT4D studies. Due to Twitter features and functions, citizens could clarify and identify the departments that could manage and deal with their issues of concern, which was not possible before. Previously, individuals faced delays and confusion as information regarding correct departments would not be provided. This led to lags, confusion and in some instances, matters not being addressed. From the interviews, it was apparent that citizens were happier with Twitter as it offered more knowledge of the processes that were involved in completing a particular issue that the citizen raised. Therefore, in this respect Twitter was offering citizens a better world to live in.

Twitter also provides increased knowledge to the citizens about their concerns. Finally, in terms of the choices made between Twitter and other applications, mobility, which were identified using the three forms: spatial, temporal and contextual was explained and provided further impetus for Oman, its citizens and public sector organizations to select using Twitter. Next, when considering the agency element it was found that resources were required, which included the geographical and natural resources. In Oman, there are plentiful natural and geographical resources available that can, in turn, provide a financial base for supporting and encouraging the government's aims, visions and strategies. However, finances are not solely sufficient to ensure that all the citizens will utilize Twitter. For this, there has to be a willingness, tenacity and motivation to use the technology, which our findings showed was available. Also important for an agency was the role of support, which a network, whether, friends and family, or colleagues was pertinent as they supported, encouraged and informed each other of the benefits and drawbacks of the technologies. From the secondary data it was learnt that the Omani government has been providing measures and resources that offer one of the best health care systems in the region, which implies that healthy citizens can also utilize and improve their lives using Twitter. An important outcome that explains how ICT4D is leading to a better world is the outcome of social capital. In Kleine [1] study, social capital was high. However, from our findings, due to the transparency of Twitter, there was a reduction in personal network connections making an impact. This was also confirmed by our findings of the secondary data obtained from TLO.

In the CF, for an agency to be realized there has to be interaction with a structure, which is possible due to formal and informal laws, programmes and innovations. Our study explained how programmes are being implemented to diverse individuals, irrespective of age and gender. Women were offered education in higher education institutions and the devices to use Twitter were also being provided to various individuals, which again emphasizes equality in the emerging development occurring in Oman. Training and educational programmes and software due to agreements signed by the Omani government and large ASPs such as, Microsoft were also viewed pertinent for the structure of the CF. A final note that was made for the structure of the CF was the provision of policies that prevented the misuse of the internet and facilities proffering internet related products and services. Finally, the degrees of empowerment explained, how due to Twitter, there was an increase in available choices for the citizens when utilizing e-government and the citizens were also aware of the uses or non-uses of the choices, which revealed a sense and use of choice. Thereafter, the achievement of using the choices aligned with the earlier outcomes, showed how a better world was being provided in some instances, but not in others.

There are several emerging implications of our study. Overall, we explained and showed how ICT4D in Oman's e-government initiatives is leading to a better world, which is not about poverty and development, but has more of a moral agenda that ICT4D scholars have been seeking in ICT4D studies [6]. When addressing the moral aspect, ethical and equality issues became apparent, which were better understood using Kleine [1] CF. The CF framework can provide pillars and issues to consider, but the results of the original CF cannot apply in an e-government context as shown by our findings. There can be contradictory emerging results as our study showed. For instance, we revealed how social capital can be reduced due to the provision of an OSN, Twitter. We also utilized socio-materiality to understand how governance could, or not occur as well as address technology related issues. Heeks [28] suggested that ICT4D studies when emphasizing the ICT4D element in their studies have more of an emphasis on the social sciences where the technology artefact than disappears. We have attempted to address this issue by utilizing socio-materiality in ICT4D studies and shown that the context, process and technology can be explained and addressed. What was also shown, is that unlike in developed countries where Twitter is used more by celebrities and world leaders to emphasize their achievements, or personal pledges. Twitter in Oman is being used at a grassroots level. This shows that culturally, the OSN has been amended to local ways; thereby supporting the views of culture researchers such as, Walsham [29, 30], Robertson [31] and Appadurai [32].

References

1. Kleine, D.: ICT4WHAT? Using the choice framework to operationalise the capability approach to development. J. Int. Dev. **22**, 674–692 (2010)
2. Kemp, S.: Digital In 2017: global overview (2017). www.wearesocial.com/uk/blog/2017/digital-in-2017-global-overview. Accessed 1 Feb 2017
3. Walsham, G.: Are we making a better world with ICTs? Reflections on a future agenda for the IS field. J. Inf. Technol. **27**, 87–93 (2012)
4. Magro, M.J.: A review of social media use in e-government. Admin. Sci. **2**, 148–161 (2012)
5. Sen, A.: Personal utilities and public judgements: or what's wrong with welfare economics. Econ. J. **89**, 537–558 (1979)
6. Unwin, P.: ICT4D: Information and Communication Technology for Development. Cambridge University Press, New York (2009)
7. Castells, M.: Materials for an exploratory theory of the network society1. Br. J. Sociol. **51**, 5–24 (2000)
8. Sen, A.: Resources, Values and Development. Harvard University Press, Cambridge (1984)
9. Alsop, R., Heinsohn, N.: Measuring empowerment in practice: structuring analysis and framing indicators. World Bank policy research working paper (2005)

10. DFID: Sustainable Livelihoods Guidance Sheets. Department for International Development, London (1999)

11. Heeks, R.: Understanding e-governance for development. i-Government Working Paper Series. Paper No. 11 (2001). http://www.seed.manchester.ac.uk/medialibrary/IDPM/working_papers/igov/igov_wp11.pdf. Accessed 2 Dec 2015

12. Abanumy, A., Al-Badi, A., Mayhew, P.: E-government website accessibility: in-depth evaluation of Saudi Arabia and Oman. Electron. J. e Gov. **3**, 99–106 (2005)

13. Ashrafi, R., Murtaza, M.: Use and impact of ICT on SMEs in Oman. Electron. J. Inf. Syst. Eval. **11**, 125–138 (2008)

14. Albusaidy, M., Weerakkody, V.: Factors influencing e-government implementation progress in Oman: a discussion. In: Proceedings of the 2008 European and Mediterranean Conference on Information Systems. Citeseer (2008)

15. Williams, A., Macrowikinomics, T.D.: Rebooting Business and the World. Portfolio Hardcover, New York (2010)

16. Boyd, D., Ellison, N.: Social network sites: definition, history, and scholarship. IEEE Eng. Manage. Rev. **3**, 16–31 (2010)

17. Kaplan, A.M., Haenlein, M.: Users of the world, unite! The challenges and opportunities of Social Media. Bus. Horiz. **53**, 59–68 (2010)

18. Al-Badi, A.H.: The adoption of social media in government agencies: Gulf Cooperation Council case study. J. Technol. Res. **5**, 1–26 (2014)

19. Couldry, N.: New media for global citizens? The future of the digital divide debate. Brown J. World Affairs **14**, 249–261 (2007)

20. Shim, D.C., Eom, T.H.: Anticorruption effects of information communication and technology (ICT) and social capital. Int. Rev. Admin. Sci. **75**, 99–116 (2009)

21. Bertot, J.C., Jaeger, P.T., Grimes, J.M.: Using ICTs to create a culture of transparency: e-government and social media as openness and anti-corruption tools for societies. Gov. Inf. Q. **27**, 264–271 (2010)

22. Walsham, G., Sahay, S.: Research on information systems in developing countries: current landscape and future prospects. Inf. Technol. Dev. **12**, 7–24 (2006)

23. Orlikowski, W.J.: Using technology and constituting structures: a practice lens for studying technology in organizations. Organ. Sci. **11**, 404–428 (2000)

24. Elmendorf, W.F., Luloff, A.: Using key informant interviews to better understand open space conservation in a developing watershed. J. Arboric. **32**, 54 (2006)

25. Glaser, B.G., Strauss, A.L.: The discovery of grounded theory: strategies for qualitative research (1967)

26. Choudrie, J., Zamani, E.D.: Understanding individual user resistance and workarounds of enterprise social networks: the case of Service Ltd. J. Inf. Technol. **31**, 130–151 (2016)

27. Orlikowski, W.J.: The sociomateriality of organisational life: considering technology in management research. Camb. J. Econ. **34**, 125–141 (2010)

28. Heeks, R.: ICT4D 2.0: the next phase of applying ICT for international development. Computer (2008). http://research.microsoft.com/en-us/um/people/cutrell/papers/heeks-ictd%20two-point-zero.pdf. Accessed 2 Dec 2015

29. Walsham, G.: Making a World of Difference: IT in a Global Context. John Wiley & Sons Inc., Chichester (2001)

30. Walsham, G.: Cross-cultural software production and use: a structurational analysis. MIS Q. **26**(4), 359–380 (2002)

31. Robertson, R.: Globalization: Social Theory and Global Culture. Sage, London (1992)

32. Appadurai, A.: Modernity at Large: Cultural Aspects of Globalization. University of Minnesota Press, Minneapolis (1997)

Four Strategies of Social Media Use Among Indonesian Politicians

Alfatika Aunuriella Dini[1,2(✉)] and Fathul Wahid[1,3]

[1] Department of Information Systems, University of Agder,
Kristiansand, Norway
alfatika.a.dini@uia.no
[2] Faculty of Law, Universitas Gadjah Mada, Yogyakarta, Indonesia
[3] Department of Informatics, Universitas Islam Indonesia,
Yogyakarta, Indonesia
fathul.wahid@uii.ac.id

Abstract. This study aims at unveiling strategies based on the patterned use of social media by politicians. Using an interpretive case study involving Indonesian politicians from national, provincial, and district level parliaments, the study identifies four strategies: nominal, instrumental, manipulative, and genuine. The selected strategy is reflected by internal and external affordances of social media perceived by the politicians, and influenced by a variety of constraints. These include poor Internet connection, limited capabilities of politicians, low ICT literacy among constituents, security issues, personal attack, unsupportive regulation, and fake accounts.

Keywords: eParticipation · Social media · Affordance · Strategy · Politicians · Indonesia · Developing country

1 Introduction

In the last 15 years, social media as user-generated platforms have become rapidly gaining popularity on the Internet [1]. Social media manifest in various forms such as blogs, social networking sites, microblogging site, video sharing site and many other user-driven platforms [2]. As social media communication for eParticipation gets denser, more complex and more participatory, citizens are getting more access to information and even more opportunities to engage in political discourse [3]. eParticipation involves the use of information and communication technologies (ICT) to deepen political participation by enabling citizens to connect with one another and with their elected officials [4] as well as to better involve citizen in a decision-making process by the government [5, 6].

The use of social media in eParticipation may provide various "action possibilities" (i.e. affordances) that are perceived differently by users since one object can produce different outcomes [7]. Actualized affordances explain action taken by the actors as they take advantage of the use of ICT to achieve goals [8]. For instance, for politicians, social media may provide various affordances, such as value sharing, opinion gathering,

© IFIP International Federation for Information Processing 2017
Published by Springer International Publishing AG 2017. All Rights Reserved
J. Choudrie et al. (Eds.): ICT4D 2017, IFIP AICT 504, pp. 681–692, 2017.
DOI: 10.1007/978-3-319-59111-7_55

political networking, campaign funding, vote gathering, and promoting participation [9, 10]. From the constituent perspective, it may provide a means for political participation. Furthermore, previous studies on social media applied affordance concept to examine implication and relationship between these new technologies within organization [7, 11, 12], government and public bodies [13] and also political parties [10, 14].

The vast majority of studies on this topic focused on the functional affordances at the organizational level (such as government agencies), which are tightly coupled with features and functionalities of social media, and only few so far has been scrutinizing affordance for practice which *"sees affordances as both dispositional and relational and explore the affordances of social media as embedded in and emergent from social processes within organizational boundaries"* [15, p. 307]. Hence, there is a need to further explore social media affordances emerging from practice actualized by individuals (e.g. politicians). In this study, we attempt to fulfil this void by studying the affordances of social media perceived by politicians and unveiling the possible strategies they chose.

More specifically, we seek to answer: *What are strategies adopted by politicians in using social media for eParticipation initiative?* In doing so, we conducted an interpretive case study involving Indonesian parliament members from three levels of centrality: national, provincial, and district levels. We have identified both internal and external affordances of social media use [9]. However, we have not yet further analysed possible patterns that may emerge from the identified affordances, which lead to specified strategies. Further, to better understand and conceptualize the identified strategies, we borrow the concepts of eParticipation (i.e. information, consultation, and active participation) [16] to guide the discussion.

This study is important for several reasons. First, conceptually, it contributes to the rather neglected study of social media affordances in the political arena at the individual levels. Second, contextually, it provides a picture of social media use in eParticipation from less articulated context, which is Indonesia, reported in literature. Third, practically, the findings may be useful as references in formulating suitable strategies for a specific context.

2   Theoretical Premises

The increasing interest of social media adoption for eParticipation makes it relevant to look into what these new media afford in the context of encouraging more citizen participation in decision-making processes. The notion of affordance was first coined by Gibson [17] who explained that affordance emerged from the interaction of an actor related to the surrounding of the actor (the environment). Such view implies that multiple affordances of the same object may surface relating to different perspectives of the actor [8, 14, 17]. Information systems scholar argued that affordances exist as a relationship between an actor and an artefact reflecting possible actions on the artefact, dependent to the capabilities of the actor [18]. However affordances may also constrain an actor to perform an action. Indeed, affordances emerged from object features and dependent on the actor's capabilities, in result these potentials serves the dual concept of affordance, it can be enabling and constraining at the same time [18]. The constraints serve as the reference for both feedbacks from behavior and feed-forward to anticipate future behavior. The fourth dimension is the value constraints, which are necessary to differentiate the possibilities for behavior in terms of "good or ill" [19].

With the changing dynamic of affordance perspectives in the information systems field, scholars offered an alternative standpoint of affordance-for-practice where the analytical focus shifted from technology to practices [20]. Here affordance is always emerging from technology-involved practices associated to the experience, skills, cultural understanding and capabilities of the actors, which is most relevant to examine specific users with certain needs, goals, and practice in particular social, cultural, and historical context [15, 20, 21]. Previous study showed affordances approach was able to display multiple benefits of social media use by political parties in which revolutionizing political campaign by affording many different issues and interest to appear in a political discourse [14].

Our previous study identified affordance for practice by politicians, which includes internal and external social media affordances. Internal affordances refer to affordances arising from practices, which involve social media that are perceived between politicians at the parliament. External affordances are perceived capabilities of social media between politicians and constituents. We will use the concept of internal and external affordances to see whether it may or may not influence the chosen strategy of social media use in eParticipation among politicians.

In doing so, we want to see whether politicians in affording social media in practice are also motivated by perceived constraints of social media. By analysing the relationship between identified affordance for practice and perceived constraints from the perspective of politicians and citizens, we hope that it will help us in conceptualizing the identified strategies of social media use.

3 Research Context and Methods

3.1 Research Context

This empirical study is performed in Indonesia aiming at identifying different strategies of social media use by Indonesian politicians. Indonesia is a country where Internet users are reaching 100 million in 2016, almost half of the total population of 250 million. Different level of parliament in three distinct areas includes national parliament in Jakarta (DPR RI), provincial parliament in Special Region of Yogyakarta (DPRD DIY) and district parliament in Gunungkidul (DPRD Gunungkidul) may give different perspectives in promoting participation via social media by politicians. The parliament at any level is obliged to perform the function of legislation, budgeting, and supervision where the representatives shall give priority to the interest of the constituents.[1] Various insights from different geographical areas in Indonesia may enrich our understanding of the politicians' strategy in harnessing social media for eParticipation influenced by several different contextual issues such as ICT infrastructure, constituents' characteristic, customary, and cultural background in the electoral base. In addition, having considered the history of democracy in Indonesia, which experienced a government

---

[1] www.dpr.go.id.

transformation from authoritarian to democratic and open system in 1998; it is interesting to look into the development of citizen participation after the ICT, e.g. social media, is entering the scene.

3.2   Data Collection

By adopting interpretive case study approach [22], we conducted in-depth interviews, from January to September 2016, with key actors of eParticipation in three levels of parliament in Indonesia: five politicians in the national, five in the provincial, and four in district parliament. During the interviews, we emphasized on how politicians perceived social media affordance in relation to their choice of strategies for eParticipation. In addition, the data were also acquired from interviewing three political activists and five political strategists with national and local experiences. In this case, political activists represent citizens' perspective since they came from citizens' element of eParticipation whereas political strategists represent politicians' perspective as they usually are hired by politicians. In total we interviewed 22 informants. We expected that the variety of perspective brought in by the informants provided a more complete picture about the topic under investigation. We also include secondary data from social media such as status updates, blogs, and comments related to eParticipation in our analysis to enrich our understanding of the phenomena.

3.3   Data Analysis

We used the concept of internal and external social media affordances obtained from our previous work [9] and the concept of eParticipation includes information, consultation, and active participation [16] to guide the data analysis. We revisited the identified internal and external affordances from the collected data. We coded the transcription in an iterative manner where we go back and forth to code the actualized affordances with the matched internal and external affordance concept. In addition to the coding process, partly we used NVivo to help us identifying important concepts and categories. We used hermeneutic circle as a sense-making strategy in which we moved back and forth between detail and sense of a whole, brought together two different realms, textual and social, in the process of interpretation [23].

After the identification of internal and external affordances, we looked for possible strategies. In this study, inspired by the work of Mintzberg [24], we define strategy as "plan, ploy, pattern, position, or perspective adopted by politicians in using social media to achieve specific goals". In short, a strategy may be developed in advance and with purpose (*plan*), serve as a means to win the competition (*ploy*), repetition of successful initiatives from the past (*pattern*), a means of locating actions in the environment (*position*), and actions influenced by a worldview (*perspective*).

4   Findings and Analysis

Our previous data analysis found a set of affordances offered by social media used by politicians [9]. When further analysing the findings, we revisited the data. Affordances emerge from the coupling between politicians and social media can be classified into two groups: internal and external affordances. The internal affordances of social media use among politicians include *idea storming, information storing, information sharing*, peer *entertaining*, and *sending event invitation*. The external affordance of social media when used in connecting politicians and their constituencies, include *value sharing, opinion gathering, political networking, personal branding, maintaining political existence*, and *promoting participation*. When re-analysing the data, we found additional external affordance of *mobilizing supporters,* which we did not reveal in the previous study. As can be seen in Table 1, while internal affordances are mutually exclusive among the identified strategies, perceived external affordances do not exclusively fall under one strategy category only (except for *nominal*).

Table 1. The identified strategies based on internal and external affordances

Strategy	Internal affordance	External affordance
Nominal	1. Information storing	None
Instrumental	None	1. Value sharing 2. Opinion gathering 3. Promoting participation
Manipulative	None	1. Value sharing 2. Opinion gathering 3. Political networking 4. Promoting participation 5. Personal branding 6. Mobilizing supporters
Genuine	1. Idea storming 2. Information sharing 3. Peer entertaining 4. Sending event invitation	1. Value sharing 2. Opinion gathering 3. Political networking 4. Promoting participation

4.1   Strategies of Social Media Use

After the identification of internal and external affordances, we looked for patterns. We grouped politicians reported a set of similar affordances or were being reported by their social media strategist about their social media. One politician may belong to more than one group. In this case, we grouped them into only one group that best represents strategy they adopted. This technique resulted in four categories of strategies: *nominal, instrumental, manipulative,* and *genuine* (see Table 1).

One member of national parliament from North Maluku who chose *nominal* strategy states, *"Internet exposure is uneven in my constituency, so the communication frequency via social media is very seldom to none but I (still) use my blogs for archiving my political activities"*. One national politician from West Java opted to use instrumental strategy told us, *"using social media is too time consuming and I can't fully concentrate on my work, thus I hire administrator even though the content is all from me"*. Whereas one social media strategist reveals *manipulative* strategy used by a politician during his campaign. He states, *"We were building a better image of politician to approach youth, so it's like rebranding"*. The strategist also identified that some politicians obviously adopted *genuine* strategy which are not many.

4.2   Understanding the Chosen Strategies

The question raises is then, how to understand why certain strategy is chosen by politicians? The relationship between the perceived affordances and the strategies are explained using other findings from the field, especially those related to constraints (see Table 2). Table 2 summarises constraints reported by politicians with various strategies selection.

Table 2. The identified strategies and reported constraints

Strategy	Constraint
Nominal	1. Poor Internet connection 2. Limited capabilities of politicians 3. Low ICT literacy among constituents
Instrumental	1. Security issues 2. Personal attack
Manipulative	1. Security issues 2. Personal attack 3. Unsupportive regulation 4. Fake accounts
Genuine	1. Security issues 2. Personal attack 3. Distraction of focus

Nominal. Politicians who cannot perceive any external affordances and only perceived internal affordance of information storing chose to have minimal presence on social media due to its impracticability for eParticipation where social media exposure is still low in the electoral base. Nominal strategy explains the minimalist approach of politicians' involvement in using social media for a two-way communication with the constituents. Politicians in this category may still perceive internal social media affordance as a tool for communication between fellow politicians. From politicians' point of view, they do not perceive the existence of external affordances of social media due to many contextual issues such as ICT infrastructure and cultural characteristic [5]. First constraint is poor Internet connection in the electoral base. This is particularly evident in the case of politicians who came from a fairly secluded electoral base such as North Maluku and Gunungkidul. In line with that, having observed two of national and district politician's web blogs, web traffic from North Maluku and from Gunungkidul is relatively low. Politicians use web blogs only to document activities for personal use such as making a personal report or preparation of plenary meeting regardless the unintended effects of doing such thing, which may induce the emergence of external affordance. In addition, politicians use WhatsApp for storing information such as political views and summary of pre-meeting discussion for effectiveness reason. Second, limited capabilities such as lack of time and lack of technical skills also hinder politicians from perceiving external affordances [9]. Third, low ICT literacy in the electoral base also gives rise to the non-use of social media for eParticipation. Evidently, all politicians at district parliament perceived that ICT literacy in the constituents is still an issue and therefore they chose conventional ways such as direct public hearing and direct meeting for opinion gathering.

Instrumental. The term describes politicians who use social media for eParticipation purpose with citizens, however due to some circumstances the politicians hire an administrator for their social media. Politicians in this stream are incapable perceiving internal affordances due to indirect relationship with social media; instead they perceive only external affordances of value sharing, opinion gathering, and promoting participation indirectly via the administrator. Lack of time is one of the reason politicians chose *instrumental* strategy. At first politicians handled social media accounts directly, however once they become busy and overwhelmed with the work, social media activities disrupted their workflows and therefore they decided to hire administrators. In addition, communication skill may also hinder politicians to handle social media directly, especially micro-blogging site like Twitter, which has character limitation for each posting. According to a national parliamentarian, *"He (the administrator) knows my mind-set, my perspective on politics, democracy, and economics, so we communicate then he will post according to my direction, the content is my responsibility but the language is all his (responsibility)"*. One key factor in *instrumental* strategy is that the content posted on social media is the extension of the attitude of the politicians. Despite all of the reasons above, politicians still want to keep strong presence on social media as there is a demand from the constituents, therefore hiring administrator is the solution.

Manipulative. Politicians have to be cautious of their social media post since open platforms could leave politicians vulnerable to criticism from within the ranks of their constituents [10]. According to our study, the main objective of social media strategist is to manage social media content include first, to make positive image of the politicians. Second, to make politicians look capable in their own field or according to what kind of self-presentation the politicians wanted to be. Lastly, strategist usually makes provocative issues merely to boost politicians rating on social media. Not uncommon strategists were demanded to issue unusual, unique, and sometimes misleading maneuver that the public would never thought of [9]. This is done to approach segmented target on social media for instance, by paying Internet buzzer, key opinion leader and celebrities to endorse politicians with fabricated comment made by the strategist. Hence, we label this maneuver as *manipulative* strategy. Politicians following this strategy usually have every moment scripted and always pay attention and know when to speak up on social media. Politician perceived the affordance of personal branding highly in this strategy. Arguably because social media affords politicians to tailor the content of social media and enable them to craft and re-crafting content before it goes public [7]. Besides personal branding, affordance of value sharing, opinion gathering, political networking, mobilizing supporters, and promoting participation are also perceived by politicians in this group indirectly.

Genuine. We label the strategy of managing social media directly to interact with fellow politicians and constituents without using intermediary (e.g. social media strategist, administrator) as *genuine*. The data reveal that politicians who personally managed social media account are likely to have more political connection with fellow politicians since associations are most often conceptualized by actor-initiated action [7]. Politicians following this stream perceived most of internal affordances such as idea storming, information sharing, peer entertaining and sending event invitation. For instance, politicians within the same party or commission created a WhatsApp group for information sharing and idea storming to keep the connection close. Supporting that, using social media for peer-entertaining by sharing funny content and jokes through WhatsApp group or Twitter may produce a more fluid relationship between politicians and between politicians and citizens [9]. To perceive internal affordances as mentioned requires direct hands on from politicians and it would not be accomplished if intermediaries were hired for this purpose. We found that politicians at the provincial and district level are either following the *nominal* strategy or *genuine*. There is no urgency to employ intermediary since social media penetration is low to none at the provincial and district level.

5 Discussion

Practically, from the eParticipation perspective, the chosen strategies will have impact on the level of citizen engagement. This at least can be approached from three levels of relationship quality between politicians and citizens: *information, consultation*, and *active participation* [16]. In the context of this study, *information* relationship is one-way where politicians produces and delivers information to citizens. Next, *consultation* happens through a two-way communication in which citizens are invited to give feedback to politicians, and *active participation* may manifest where citizens are actively engaged in defining the policy-making process although the final decision rests on the politicians.

Politicians who chose *nominal* strategy cannot optimally develop relationship with citizens through social media. Those in this group are neither incapable nor reluctant in using social media but rather because there is no demand from the constituents. In this case, politicians may or may not perceive internal affordances of information storing, idea storming, information sharing, peer-entertaining, and sending event invitation but when the citizens cannot afford all social media affordances then the *consultation* and *active participation* aspects would not be accomplished. The *information* aspect of eParticipation could still be delivered as a consequence of unintended effect of perceiving internal affordance. For instance, when politicians use social media to store information in their blogs, it creates affordance effect of value sharing to the public regardless the intention of social media use in the first place, whether to store information for personal use or to archive activities. Social media affordances at the district and provincial level is mainly perceived as internal affordance where affordance emerged from practice and perceived only between politicians, not to the external actors or constituents [9]. In the *nominal* category, citizen could not perceive social media affordances for two reasons; first, owing to the characteristic of citizens, local communities at the provincial level are still conventional even though Internet exposure is widespread. Following the customary, provincial level constituents chose to have a direct public hearing over communication via social media. Second, politicians at the district level do not perceive functional affordances due to low ICT literacy and low Internet exposure among citizens. Based on the data from the local government[2], Internet users are minority; with only 10% of the total population have access to the Internet. These perceived constraints serve as the reference for politicians to choose the appropriate strategy in certain context [19]. To develop a better relationship with citizens, politicians use other channels, such as face-to-face physical meetings.

Both politicians and citizens' side perceived internal and external affordances when both are capable affording all social media functional affordances. This is evident in *genuine* strategy for instance, all identified internal and external affordances in our research include idea storming, information sharing, information storing, peer-entertaining, invitation of events, value sharing, opinion gathering, political networking, personal branding, maintaining political existence, promoting participation and mobilizing supporters are related to association. Identified affordances contribute to the connection establishment between individuals and between individuals and content. The possibility to create social tie is high when politicians afford political networking via social media by connecting directly with fellow politicians and citizens as well. Other form of association is of individual with social media content that they created or recognized. For instance, information and value sharing on social media are affording relationship between the contributors of the post (e.g. politicians, citizens, social media strategist) and the audiences (social tie) plus between contributors and content. The use of *hashtag* and *mention* feature to show content reuse of the original contributors also encourage association of individuals and a piece of information as well as association between individuals [7]. Association afforded by social media is leading to participation due to the ability to forge new relationship of people whom they knew little. This stream is able to deliver the three aspects of eParticipation, *information, active participation,* and *consultation.*

Example from a social media strategist informed that a location-based social media developed exclusively to certain party may strengthen association between politicians within the same party since usually one party has widespread members across country. The location-based social media may help politicians and member of party to recognize colleague in the same area within the same party. The study also found that association in social media increased social connection for eParticipation actors by simplify easy interaction among actors. Association afforded by politicians at the national and provincial level is both social tie between politicians, politicians and citizens, and politicians and social media content. However, at the district level of parliament,

---

[2] http://www.gunungkidulkab.go.id/.

politicians only afford association of individuals to a piece of information not the social relationship. This is due to the nature of social media communication at the district level is one way, from politicians to citizens with minimum to none feedback.

Politicians in *instrumental* and *manipulative* strategies can't fully perceive all internal affordances due to the indirect engagement with social media. Instead they afford only external affordances indebted to a high demand from citizens. The characteristics of constituents in both strategies are ready in terms of ICT literacy, education, and Internet exposure. The demand is explained by the active participation of citizens to do a two-way *consultation* with politicians in many issues notably after the politicians shared *information* via social media. Politicians' perception of the editability of social media is exceptionally high particularly in the manipulative strategy. Editability gives opportunities for politicians to hire social media strategist to "make over" their online appearance [10]. Editability of social media allows users to strategically manipulate the ways that personal information is shared with others [7]. The interview unfold that a unified online presence of political campaign is important thus editability feature on social media is necessary. By doing this, campaign delivered the same messages the supporters wanted in the format they wanted it. The challenge towards content uniformity, however, is apparent. From the interviews, two political strategists are cautious that allowing politicians to interact directly with the constituents via social media may result in embarrassing missteps that can cost them the campaign [10].

The difference between *instrumental* and *manipulative* from the standpoint of politicians is assertive, content in *instrumental* is the extension of genuine idea and opinion of the politicians whilst in the *manipulative* usually is pre-designed and crafted by social media strategist. On top of that, as explained in instrumental strategy, lack of capability (time and skills) of the politicians is the main driver to hire administrator whereas politicians following manipulative stream sometimes are capable enough to use social media but want to stitch up the presence excellently according to their goals. Through citizens' point of view, there is no obvious difference however some active youth questioned the reliability of online content by politicians, some are even aware that social media content may be manipulated [9]. In both strategies, the deliverability of *information, active participation, and consultation* aspects of eParticipation is highly visible since both constituents and politicians are active on social media.

6   Conclusions

Building on our previous work, in this article we have identified social media strategies in eParticipation exemplified by several eParticipation actors include politicians, citizens, and social media strategists. By doing so, we have contributed to the area of eParticipation by unveiling strategies of social media use among politicians. Identified strategies are *nominal, instrumental, manipulative,* and *genuine.* As strategy may manifest in various forms (plan, ploy, pattern, position, or perspective [24]), it is then not easy to conclude whether the perceived internal and external affordances will lead to a certain selection of strategy or another way around. Several constraints are also identified during the data analysis and are influencing the choice of strategies. Identified constraints include poor Internet connection, limited capabilities, characteristic of citizens, low ICT literacy, and unreliable social media content. Each of the strategies is affected by different motivations and constraints of social media use.

Our study offered two main contributions. *Firstly*, practical contribution identifies strategies of social media use that may advise politicians in formulating eParticipation include nominal, instrumental, manipulative, and genuine. Secondly, conceptualization of internal and external affordances from the perspective of politicians and citizens projected by eParticipation concept of *information, consultation, and active participation* allows us to understand how social media affordances encourage politicians' choice of strategies to promote citizens participation. By so doing, we have contributed, albeit minor, to the theory of social media affordances by demonstrating that politicians who perceived affordances-for-practise are also motivated by their perception of functional affordances offered by social media. Hence, not only could social media functional affordances bring changes to the way that many processes are carried out in organizational context [7], but also it can bring changes to many processes carried out by individual.

We have argued that the presence of social media technology may help politicians in delivering information, encouraging active participation as well as providing a two-way consultation between politicians and constituents depending on the choice of strategies. First, *nominal* strategy explains the minimalist presence of politicians on social media due to several constraints such as low ICT literacy and poor Internet connection. Second, *instrumental* strategy describes politicians who hire social media administrator due to their lack of capabilities in using social media. Third, *manipulative* explains the strategy to employ strategist to make up social media appearance in accordance with certain goals by creating provocative political maneuver. Lastly, *genuine* strategy describes the way in which social media are managed and used by the politicians for eParticipation without any intermediaries. Moreover, herein, citizens played an important role in this scene; citizens' perception of social media affordance may encourage or discourage politicians in using social media.

We provide several future avenues, first, since our study does not discuss constraints in any depth, but only acknowledging constraints as factors that may prevent actors from perceiving affordances, further investigation may discuss how constraints can be overcome in order to better utilize social media in eParticipation. Second, our study has not examined further on the possibility of choosing more than one strategy for eParticipation by the politicians. Future study may investigate the choice of strategy and examine how and when certain strategy is better than others in a particular time such as before or after election.

References

1. Bertot, J.C., Jaeger, P.T., Grimes, J.M.: Using ICTs to create a culture of transparency: e-government and social media as openness and anti-corruption tools for societies. Gov. Inf. Q. **27**, 264–271 (2010)

2. Halpern, D., Gibbs, J.: Social media as a catalyst for online deliberation? Exploring the affordances of Facebook and YouTube for political expression. Comput. Hum. Behav. **29**, 1159–1168 (2013)
3. Shirky, C.: The political power of social media: technology, the public sphere, and political change. Foreign Aff. **90**, 28–41 (2011)
4. Macintosh, A.: E-democracy and e-participation research in Europe. In: Chen, H., Brandt, L., Gregg, V., Traunmüller, R., Dawes, S., Hovy, E., Macintosh, A., Larson, C.A. (eds.) Digital Government, pp. 85–102. Springer, New York (2008)
5. Dini, A.A., Sæbo, Ø.: The current state of social media research for eParticipation in developing countries: a literature review. In: Proceedings of the 49th Hawaii International Conference on System Sciences. IEEE (2016)
6. Medaglia, R.: eParticipation research: moving characterization forward (2006–2011). Gov. Inf. Q. **29**, 346–360 (2012)
7. Treem, J.W., Leonardi, P.M.: Social media use in organizations: exploring the affordances of visibility, editability, persistence, and association. Ann. Int. Commun. Assoc. **36**, 143–189 (2013)
8. Greeno, J.G.: Gibson's affordances. Psychol. Rev. **101**, 336–342 (1994)
9. Dini, A.A., Wahid, F., Sæbo, Ø.: Affordances and constraints of social media use in eParticipation: perspectives from Indonesian politicians. In: Proceedings of Pacific Asia Conference on Information Systems (PACIS), Chiayi, Taiwan (2016)
10. Smith, K.N.: Social media and political campaigns. Thesis Project (2011)
11. Zammuto, R.F., Griffith, T.L., Majchrzak, A., Dougherty, D.J., Faraj, S.: Information technology and the changing fabric of organization. Organ. Sci. **18**, 749–762 (2007)
12. Strong, D.M., Johnson, S.A., Tulu, B., Trudel, J., Volkoff, O., Pelletier, L.R., Bar-On, I., Garber, L.: A theory of organization-EHR affordance actualization. J. Assoc. Inf. Syst. **15**, 53–85 (2014)
13. Wahid, F., Sæbø, Ø.: Affordances and effects of promoting eParticipation through social media. In: Tambouris, E., Panagiotopoulos, P., Sæbø, Ø., Tarabanis, K., Wimmer, M.A., Milano, M., Pardo, T.A. (eds.) ePart 2015. LNCS, vol. 9249, pp. 3–14. Springer, Cham (2015). doi:10.1007/978-3-319-22500-5_1
14. Jensen, T.B., Dyrby, S.: Exploring affordances of Facebook as a social media platform in political campaigning. In: ECIS, p. 40 (2013)
15. Zheng, Y., Yu, A.: Affordances of social media in collective action: the case of Free Lunch for Children in China. Inf. Syst. J. **26**, 289–313 (2016)
16. Macintosh, A.: Characterizing e-participation in policy-making. In: Proceedings of the 37th Annual Hawaii International Conference on System Sciences. IEEE (2004)
17. Gibson, J.J.: The theory of affordances, pp. 67–82. Erlbaum, Hilldale (1977)
18. Pozzi, G., Pigni, F., Vitari, C.: Affordance theory in the IS discipline: a review and synthesis of the literature. In: Proceeding of the 20th Americas Conference on Information Systems (AMCIS), Savannah, USA (2014)
19. Flach, J.M., Smith, M.R.H.: Right strategy, wrong tactic. Ecol. Psychol. **12**, 43–51 (2000)
20. Fayard, A.-L., Weeks, J.: Affordances for practice. Inf. Organ. **24**, 236–249 (2014)
21. Bloomfield, B.P., Latham, Y., Vurdubakis, T.: Bodies, technologies and action possibilities when is an affordance? Sociology **44**, 415–433 (2010)
22. Walsham, G.: Interpreting Information Systems in Organizations. Wiley, New York (1993)
23. Boland, R.J., Newman, M., Pentland, B.T.: Hermeneutical exegesis in information systems design and use. Inf. Organ. **20**, 1–20 (2010)
24. Mintzberg, H.: The strategy concept I: five Ps for strategy. Calif. Manag. Rev. **30**, 11–24 (1987)

From Longhand Writing to Word Processing: A Phenomenological Study of the Technophobe Turned Novelist

Antonio Díaz Andrade(✉)

Auckland University of Technology, Auckland, New Zealand
antonio.diaz@aut.ac.nz

Abstract. Firmly grounded on the assumption that using digital technology is an intentional, conscious and subjective experience, this study adopts a transcendental phenomenological approach to reveal the meaning of the individual experience of using digital technology. This study reports the experience of a self-described technophobe, creative woman, who, after learning how to type on a computer keyboard, used word processor software on a donated computer to write and eventually publish a novel. As result of a reflective analysis, according to the tenets of transcendental phenomenology, the essence of the lifeworld phenomenon of using digital technology revealed three interdependent experiences: imaginative, epiphanic and symbiotic. This study explains how an individual uses digital technology to fulfil her needs and achieve her goals as well as demonstrates the potential of transcendental phenomenology in information systems research.

Keywords: Essence · Experience · Technophobe · Transcendental phenomenology

1 Introduction

The ability to use digital technology can have major repercussions on the pursuit of personal goals. Indeed, digital technology can serve as a vehicle to unravel talents that otherwise would remain unrealised and ultimately contribute to fulfilment of the individual.

Unlike previous information and communication technology for development studies that investigate the collective dimension – e.g., data standardisation in healthcare systems [1], technological platforms for poverty alleviation [2], integration of scientific and indigenous knowledge [3], institutional contexts in the implementation of information systems [4] – this paper emphasises the individual experience. In this study, I present the analysis of the journey experienced by an extraordinarily creative woman from outright refusal of using digital technology to embracing the use of word processor software. The fact that she still admits a high degree of fear when using digital technology, regardless of the benefits she derives from word processor software, characterises her as a technophobe.

© IFIP International Federation for Information Processing 2017
Published by Springer International Publishing AG 2017. All Rights Reserved
J. Choudrie et al. (Eds.): ICT4D 2017, IFIP AICT 504, pp. 693–706, 2017.
DOI: 10.1007/978-3-319-59111-7_56

The use of digital technology by a technophobe to achieve her goals and fulfil her needs constitutes an exceptional phenomenon. In order to understand the essence of her technophobic experience in relation to digital technology use, I give primacy to her lifeworld as experienced and described by her. Therefore, I adopt a transcendental phenomenological approach to address the following research question:

What is the experience of a technophobe when using digital technology?

This paper is organised as follows. The next section provides the theoretical background of lifeworld experience in relation to digital technology use. The third section explains the research methods. The fourth section introduces the research participant. The fifth section presents the synthesis of my research participant's experience in relation to digital technology use. The last section presents the conclusions of the paper.

2   The Experience of Using Digital Technology

In this section, I discuss conscious actions in relation to digital technology use and present an outline of previous research on technophobia.

2.1   Conscious Use of Digital Technology

Using digital technology is a conscious act. In their engagement with technology, individuals are not merely passive subjects with no sense of purpose. Labelling individuals who use technologies merely as 'users' is a misnomer. The term 'users' evokes an homogenising and rather inaccurate description of what in reality constitutes a collection of diverse individuals with unique interests in a particular context that characterises their encounter with technology. Digital technology is an inviting and interpretively flexible artefact that offers a dense and variable set of functionalities to individuals [5].

Individuals exercise judgment through critical consciousness in order to assess how and to what extent digital technology can help them address their needs and achieve their goals [6, 7]. Furthermore, the assessment of the usefulness of technology for attaining specific aims is influenced by their personal histories and circumstances [8]. Individuals use digital technology for multiple purposes: to access information, to produce content, to connect with others and to participate in social life. Consequently, what individuals make of a particular technology is a complex accomplishment involving human intentions, the properties of technology and the specific environment in which they are located [9]. Although recognising the malleable properties of digital technology allows a fine-grained analysis of the interlock between individual actions and technology performance [10], it does not reveal how emotions emerge in this interaction.

Understanding emotions when individuals engage in digital technology use in an everyday situation requires recognising the indivisibility of individuals' histories and their efforts to make sense of technology in their pursuit of goals and fulfilment of needs. Emotions can be intimate and somewhat unfathomable, but "they precede or, better, ground any mental representation of the situation and action strategy … they are not the direct consequence of our thinking, doing, and acting. Instead, they are the presupposition, the medium within which those activities take place" [11, pp. 32–33]. The mechanisms that explain how individuals use – or avoid using – digital technology are "are to be found in the intersubjective, intentional actions of human beings, not some mythological rational calculus that stands us as general law" [12, p. 198]. This is particularly true in the case of individuals who fear using digital technology.

2.2 Technophobic Feelings and Using Digital Technology

With the popularisation of personal computers in the early 1980s also came the fear of using them. The term computerphobia described the anxiety generated by using computers, the concerns about the societal implications of computer technology and/or "specific negative cognitions … during present computer interaction or when contemplating future computer interaction" [13, p. 362]. Grounded on the observation that individuals avoid engaging in activities that they believe they will not be able to cope with – cf. Bandura's [14] notion of self-efficacy, research corroborated that low perceptions of self-efficacy in computer use makes the individual believe not only that the outcome will be negative but also will reinforce their fear about computers [15].

The term computerphobia was abandoned in favour of a more comprehensive one, technophobia. A perverse circle between internally-generated anxiety about using technology and the reluctance of using it "maintains the technophobe's belief system as the technophobe never comfortably interacts with technology and thereby challenges or changes these beliefs" [16, p. 28]. The lack of experience in the first encounter with digital technology generates anxiety that persists in future encounters [17]. However, a distinction needs to be made between using digital technology and the task that it facilitates. Digital technology is the tool that mediates the accomplishment of a task. This distinction is illustrated in Brosnan's [18] study, who observes that the action of writing does not produce anxiety; the use of word processor software does. Unravelling the feelings of fear and anxiety that technophobes experience in their engagement with technology requires bringing to the foreground the messiness of the managing-in-the-now that characterises digital technology use. These fears and anxieties can only be understood and explained by the individual who experiences using digital technology.

3   Research Methods

Understanding the essence of the experience of what really is using technology for a technophobe requires privileging the standpoint of the person who lives the experience. By rejecting the dichotomous conceptualisations of subject/object, mind/body and cognition/action [19], phenomenology focusses on consciousness and subjectivity to derive knowledge about the intimate experience of using technology [12]. In general, phenomenology is a "method of scientific philosophy [that] tries to discover the essences of appearances which are anything which human beings can become conscious" [20, p. 53]. Rooted on how individuals construct meanings and values, phenomenology is a critical reflection on conscious experience designed to uncover the essential invariant features of that experience [21]. Therefore, the task of phenomenology is to understand "the way in which consciousness gives meaning" [22, p. 10].

Transcendental phenomenology is the thick description of "what one perceives, senses, and knows in one's immediate awareness and experience… [that] provides the impetus for experience and generating new knowledge" [23, p. 26]. Two key elements of Husserl's thinking are reflected as central tenets of transcendental phenomenology. The first one is the understanding that consciousness is intentional: it "is always 'consciousness' of something; it always 'intends' something, or is 'about' something" [24, p. 1236]. The second one is that objective reality only exists in mental representations; therefore, the former is nothing else than subjective reality [23].

3.1   Data Collection

I sought for individuals whose use of digital technology had a substantial repercussion in their lives. I directed my search to beneficiaries of the *Computers in Homes* programme, a New Zealand government-funded initiative that provides basic computer training to parents with school-aged children of low socio-economic background. Upon satisfactory completion of the computer-training course, participants receive a refurbished desktop computer with free broadband connection for one year. I was put in contact with Sarah,[1] a 56-year-old solo mother of a teenage daughter. As a self-confessed "technophobe" that learned how to use word processor software to write her novels, Sarah's experience is particularly interesting for this phenomenological study.

Data were collected through a series of three face-to-to-face, in-depth, unstructured interviews. In line with the tenets of phenomenological research, I refer to Sarah not as my research participant but as my co-researcher. Although I had developed a series of questions aimed at prompting Sarah to share with me her overall experience with digital technology, they were used as a guide only. In my interaction with her, I endeavoured to capture faithfully the essence of the phenomenon while suspending any pre-conceived judgement [22]. The interviews flowed as natural conversations; I actively listened to her experiences and followed her leads with probing questions whenever it was necessary. Her talkative character and well-articulated reflections about the phenomenon under study facilitated my access to her lived experiences.

The three interviews, conducted over a period of two weeks between June and July 2016, took place in a meeting room at the local library of Waitopu Island,[2] where Sarah lives. With her consent, we produced 3 h and 20 min of audio recordings, which were later uploaded into NVivo software package. However, our interaction went beyond the

---

[1] Sarah is a pseudonym.
[2] The name of this island is fictitious.

audio-recorded interviews. When I met Sarah for the first time, Sarah gave me a 10-min tour around the public library before we went into the meeting room for the 1-hour-and-10-minute audio-recorded interview. Following this conversation, we continued the talk for another hour at a local café and then strolled together for ten more minutes. The second audio-recorded interview took place one week later and lasted for over one and half hours; the third one went for 40 min. As in the first interview, for the subsequent ones we also had short conversations before and after the interviews. These conversations, which were not audio-recorded, contributed to establish a trusting atmosphere between Sarah and me. Overall, our face-to-face interaction extended for over five hours and we continue the communication via email.

3.2 Data Analysis

Given its focus on the phenomenon as lived by the individual [25], transcendental phenomenological analysis proceeds by describing the essence of a lived experience, which represents the true nature of the phenomenon being studied [26]. As such, the results of phenomenological enquiry should be a thick and direct description of the lived experience [27]. Adopting a transcendental phenomenology approach required making Sarah the focal actor in the analysis. Thus, in this study, I focussed my attention on her involvement with digital technology and its meaning for her.

Doing transcendental phenomenological research requires intuitive thinking to derive knowledge "from first-person reports of life experiences" [23, p. 84]. In doing so, when I analysed Sarah's inward experiences of her use of digital technology, I followed four analytical processes in order to discover the essence of the phenomenon: epoché, transcendental-phenomenological reduction, imaginative variation and synthesis.

Practicing the epoché involves bracketing and putting aside pre-conceived ideas to have a fresh look at the phenomenon under study [23]. Epoché started early in the research process, when I interacted with Sarah for the first time and before each subsequent interview. At this stage, I endeavoured to be receptive to what just Sarah was saying, making a conscious effort to avoid having my intuitive thinking clouded with my own preconceptions. I primed myself to observe and learn about the phenomenon as it appeared and nothing else. In my first encounter with the audio-recorded data, I practised the procedure of "horizonalising the data" [23, p. 118], by which every one of Sarah's statements relevant to the research question were granted equal value.

Transcendental-phenomenological reduction entails deriving a "textural description of the meanings and essences of the phenomenon, the constituents that comprise the experience in consciousness" [23, p. 34]. I was looking at the elements of Sarah's experience that appeared in front of me in order to produce a list of meaning units. I relied on NVivo for recording these meaning units through a taxonomy exercise that involved an iterative process of looking at the data to notice something and reflectively looking again to get an understanding of the phenomenon in its totality. The horizonalising process continued during the transcendental-phenomenological reduction since "a new horizon arises each time that one recedes" [23, p. 95].

Having already identified the meaning units, I embarked on the imaginative variation to produce a portrayal of the essences of the experience. Imaginative variation demands assuming that "existence no longer is central, anything whatever becomes possible. The thrust is away from facts and measurable entities and toward meanings and essences" [23, p. 98]. I implemented the imaginative variation by debating with myself, until I got a sense of conceptual closure, for alternative explanations of what invariant structures triggered Sarah's feelings and thoughts in her interaction with digital technology. Eventually, by clustering the meaning units I had previously identified under three essences that provide a structural description of the phenomenon.

Finally, for the synthesis, I integrated the meanings and essences. I am cognizant that the account I render of Sarah's lived experience in relation to digital technology reflects the thick description of the phenomenon, circumscribed by my reflective and intuitive analysis conducted at a particular time and space.

4 Introducing Sarah

Sarah loves the "sense of island community", although laments that Waitopu Island is no longer what used to be. She broadly describes the socioeconomic composition of the island as one of two extremes: "you have the extremely wealthy, multimillionaires … and then you have the rest of the population". She proudly declares that she belongs to the latter group. Waitopu Island was traditionally the home of retirees, beneficiaries and alternative people; not anymore. She remembers the days on which whenever a helicopter flew over the island, it was the police searching for weed plantations; nowadays, hovering helicopters are manned by the affluent locals or flying rich tourists.

Her three-month stay in Nowhere Island,[3] after completing her first year of university studies in the late 1970s, reinforced her liking for the sense of island community. Initially, Sarah was hesitant to take a waitressing role there because she was just 17 and "quite reserved" but eventually accepted the challenge. After this period, she returned to New Zealand to continue her university studies. Then, she decided to go back to Nowhere Island, but this time to work as a painter full-time and to do dishwashing on a part-time basis for one year. During this period, she painted intensely and learned to be an independent person. Once back in New Zealand, she completed her Bachelor of Arts in Art History in 1980. Upon graduation, she worked for two years "just drilling holes in circuit boards" only because she had a mortgage to pay for the house she bought in Waitopu Island in 1980. In 1984, she got a job as a receptionist in a physiotherapy clinic, where she worked for 12 years until the final stages of her pregnancy. In 1997, she suffered a serious accident when an elder driver blacked out: "he literally ran over top of me, I was caught up under the wheels and sprang out and somersaulted into the path of incoming traffic. It was really bad". After recovery, Sarah worked at a toy store for the next few years and, for the last six years, as a cleaner. She never enjoyed the jobs that she has done but conceded that they gave her time to do the

---

[3] The name of this island located in the South Pacific is fictitious too.

activities that she really was passionate about: painting, sculpting and, during the last few years, writing.

5   Findings

In the following sub-sections, I present the synthesis of Sarah's experiences in relation to digital technology use: imaginative, epiphanic and symbiotic experiences. These experiences are the result of my reflective and intuitive analysis that have been corroborated by Sarah. She received a copy of the text below and confirmed that these three experiences reflect well her overall involvement with digital technology.

5.1   Imaginative Experience

Sarah's appearance, attitude and utterance reveal a creative mind. This preliminary impression was soon substantiated by the description of her early beginnings in artistic expressions, just before leaving for Nowhere Island for the first time:

> I remember having this fantasy the night before I left. This fantasy was, I would be sitting at the bar in this, er, I visualised it, sitting at the bar in this hotel where I was working, and all these guests buying me drinks, which is really funny because I did not drink. But the main thing I would also be doing, they would be commissioning me to do paintings for them to take back from their holiday. And the thing was, it was such a vivid fantasy, I was in that job for only three months, but that is exactly what happened. I used to waitress during the day. I would be serving breakfast; then, I would go off and pencil in a sketch, then I would serve lunch. After lunch, I would pen it in and then the following day I would put in the wash, so I had this process and by the evening, I have sold it. I was selling these paintings [at] 50 [New Zealand] dollars. It was in 1977, 50 dollars, unframed, no mount or anything ... I was earning far more from my paintings than what I was from waitressing full time.

Many years later, when she worked as a receptionist at physiotherapy clinic, a well-known New Zealand painter went to her place to collect a lumbar roll needed for his treatment. The paintings he saw hanging on her walls overwhelmed him, "Oh, my God! Who did those?" Upon Sarah's reply that she was the author of those paintings, he candidly rebutted, "You? ... I have known you all these years and thought you were a frivolous, empty-headed receptionist". Sarah giggled while sharing this experience. In addition to painting, Sarah also did sculpting; however, writing defines her imaginative experience. While Sarah acknowledges that her university studies equipped her well with writing skills, she hastily explains that these are subordinated to her creative spirit:

> What I have always had was a really wonderful imagination, I have always been able to imagine things to the extent that I can feel and see and hear the characters in my head. I hear the dialogue ... In my mind it is almost like watching a film, and I hear the dialogues that I am writing down, what the characters are saying.

Sarah goes back in time and remembers her early writings of black comedy:

> There was a phase in about 1984 when I wrote short stories. Just a few ... And I remember very nervously showing them to [my daughter's] father ... [who] was a poet, a pub poet ... His opinion meant a lot to me and I remember very nervously reading out one of my short stories.

He sat there and went very quiet ... I said, 'Is it any good?' [laughs] Because I got the feeling that it was not any good, you know. He said, 'Well, actually it is good. In fact, it is very good ... I do not mind you painting, but I would rather you do not write anymore because I cannot handle competition'. That is what he said. Me being me I was a fool and I was mad in love with him I did not bother writing anymore. That is the only time I wrote short stories.

However, it was not only love that stopped her from continuing writing; it was the clumsiness of handwriting. Sarah wrote these short stories by longhand and reasoned that making changes on her handwritten drafts encompassed an arduous endeavour. She was not able to type, a limitation that she wanted to overcome when she enrolled in a computer-training course at Waitopu Community Education Centre in 2002. Her first encounter with digital technology was tremendously frustrating:

I enrolled in this course, and the woman said, 'Can you type?' I said, 'No'. She said, 'Oh! I will get you on this' ... And I swear! If I could have killed the woman at the end of the week, I would have done it, the woman on the computer screen. Because you get to, say, 99%, if you got one wrong, you go back to square one again. It just drove me nuts! And everybody else in the course was off doing interesting things and I was stuck because I was the only one who could not type ... 'Oh, I cannot be bothered with this', and just quit ... And in the end ... it reinforced my fear of technology really [laughs]. 'Oh, I would not be any good at that'. 'Oh, I am going to avoid it'. 'I can get by without it in my life'.

Sarah describes herself as a "technophobe": "[My daughter keeps telling me], 'You will never get it. Even if you spend a year, you still would not get it' … She must be right [laughs]." Her daughter customises the setting options according to Sarah's preferences. Sarah admits that she cannot do it: "As I said, I am technophobic".

5.2   Epiphanic Experience

After her first frustrating encounter, Sarah had to reconsider her averseness to digital technology as her daughter was growing up. She recalls her reflections of the consequences of not using technology: "There were teachers asking to email them assignments and I thought, 'Oh God, this is going to be a real problem for my daughter'". While this realisation urged Sarah to make a second attempt, it was a turn of fate – something that she qualifies as a "happy accident" – that eventually brought digital technology closer to her. Sarah vividly remembers the morning of 26 August 2010:

It was one of those days, you know, when you look back to a key day, when everything kind of changes. That was the day I was in this particular [that] I only bought ... to do it up because I wanted another house, which was my original house ... I decided I wanted it back when [my daughter] was getting a bit older. And in order to get it back, I bought this other property to do it up, so I could have enough money to buy it back ... so I was happily doing up this other property. Then, there was a huge, torrential, downpour of rain the previous night. And there was a stream running through at the back of the property and the next morning I went to the end of my garden to look at the stream and it was not there. There was basically this massive landslip, a huge mudslide. 'Oh my God!' ... I remember walking back into the house thinking 'Stay calm, make a cup of tea' [laughs]. That is my answer to everything. And I made a cup of tea and could not deal with everything ... 'Can I ever be able to sell this property? Will I able to get my house back, the one that I owned?' [I] ... just wanted to escape and I just kind of opened the Waitopu News and there was an article about the Computers in Homes scheme and it mentioned there were only a couple of places left. And I thought, 'Oh, right, I'd better ring up', because it said that you get a free, er, a computer for 50 [New Zealand] dollars, if you do the course. So, I said, 'OK, well, I only have to stick to the course' ... I rang up, er, the Computers [in Homes] to get on the scheme ... And then, basically, I did something I have done since I was a little kid, I made stories in my head and I escaped into them.

Sarah recalls, "[The instructor] went back to basics for us... Even turning the computer on for me was, you know. It had to be basic". What she enjoyed the most was the entirely different approach the instructor took, compared to the course she failed to complete eight years earlier, in 2002.

The beauty of the course was that we barely had to do any typing [laughs]. That is why I was able to stick the course out because I knew I could not type. Oh God! I forgot the tutor's name now, but he was a lovely man and he sort of said, 'Look, you will be at different stages of how fast you can type ... I do not want the whole course governed by your different stages'. So he said, '... You just copy and paste the bits on, so you do not have to type the whole stuff ... Then, I teach you how you can manipulate and move things around'. The text was already there ... I barely had to type much at all.

Twenty-six years after her false start in 1984, Sarah went back to writing her stories while doing the computer-training course in October 2010. However, she was still trying to write them by hand. Although she was not happy with the quality of her drafts, she had the determination to complete her writing:

I was to give up after the first chapter because it was, like, painful. It was an involved story, and I had already seen that I wanted to change things. But I was doing this course, I thought, 'Hey, if I type this on the computer, I could change this and switch paragraphs around so much easier'. So before the computer even arrived at home, I was already seeing the potential of the computer. Yeah, because I can remember the deputy principal of the high school coming round and saying, 'What do you think you will end up using your computer for?' I think I said, '[My daughter] will be doing school work and homework, but I have a book in my head that I want to get down'. I already knew then, while I was doing the course, that as soon as that computer arrived the first thing I would started doing was write the story down.

Eventually, Sarah learned how to type on a keyboard. She reasons, "Because I got the computer ... 'I'd better practice typing on it'. Because I was so slow, and thought, er, 'What should I write? I will write down the story that is in my head". Acquiring the ability to type only occurred after she discovered the editing functionalities of word processor software; the prospect of easily modifying text was an epiphany for Sarah:

Oh my God! This whole copy-and-paste thing, I realised that I could move things around so easily. When I had written those short stories [by hand because I was not able to type] in the early 80s, er, it is painful! I mean, if you wanted to change, move things around was a pain. It was like, er, I always painted and when you paint either it really goes well or starts going to custard and you try to retrieve the situation, usually it gets worse ... Whereas when I was writing on the computer, even if what I wrote was crap, I knew by the time I finished that day, by the time I changed things around and copied and pasted and deleted and everything and rewrote, it would be really good. So there will not be mistakes, in a sense. I could be totally relaxed and free to put anything I want down because I knew I could change it so easily with the click of a button. It gave me this freedom, I do not remember who said that, 'Creativity is allowing yourself to make mistakes; art is knowing which ones to keep'.

The discovery of using digital technology for writing the stories that Sarah always had in her head was a liberating experience. She confesses that the possibility of making mistakes has always caused anxiety on her:

So the computer gave me this means to be totally free to make mistakes, so I do. I always had this fear as a kid, I was always a nervous kid, I was terrified to make mistakes. My father used to come down on me so hard. I mean, I came home from school as a six years old and he would not allow me to go outside to play, unless I recited the tables and did it perfectly. And of course, I did not do it perfect ... So there is always that fear, the more nervous I got, the more anxious I got to do it right, the more is guaranteed I would do it wrong. Whereas with the computer, what I found is that it did not matter. I could do any mistakes I like because there is the delete button [laughs]. Nobody needs to know how many attempts I made to write something; they just see the end result, you know. And that is enormously liberating!

Sarah has nevertheless mixed feelings toward digital technology. She enjoys using a word processor, but her aversion to digital technology remains unchanged:

I find computers and technology, generally, very frustrating ... If I do not understand it and it does not do what I want it to do, I get really annoyed quite quickly. But with writing is the opposite; it makes life easier. It is not frustrating when I write; the computer tends to do what I want. It is funny because with other things, because I do not know anything about computers.

Sarah conveys a sense of uncertainty and despair when using digital technology:

I look at [my daughter] on the computer and she has no fear whatsoever. She is quite confident. If she loses something, she can get it back. There is definitely more anxiety with me ... I forgot to save just recently and suddenly the document disappeared, I do not know what I accidentally pressed. Then, I get anxious. 'Oh [expletive] that is my last hour's work! Where has it gone?' [My daughter] would come along and say 'Oh, it is alright. It is just here, yep. You just pressed this by accident'. Then, it comes, you know ... For me there is an element of anxiety because I do not understand it completely ... I would like to feel that I understand how it works, er ... It does not kind make a lot of sense [laughs]. The whole idea of different windows and all this, you know, how you can open so many up, it is like sci-fi to me.

Finally, the story that Sarah started handwriting in 2010 was completed using a word processor in late 2011. The original work was entirely rewritten; the main story was intertwined with other stories. The plot "changed dramatically" and one year later, the plot was modified again and put aside for two years. It was eventually published as a novel in June 2015. She praises digital technology for the flexibility it affords – e.g., "It was simply so much easier with the computer", "I can swap chapters around; it is so easy" – and sentences with a laugh, "I do not how people write novels by hand". In recognition of this achievement, she received a new laptop computer with the latest operating system in March 2016, which reminded her aversion to digital technology:

I hated the fact that when I got given the new laptop it was such a big adjustment as I had been used to working on the old [desktop computer] ... They gave me the laptop and I swear it sat there for about a month to six weeks ... I knew I had to get used to working with a different word [processor] programme. At one point, I was doing emails on the new laptop but still wrote on the old one because it is the one that I was used to. I do not like change.

In the end, Sarah "packed up the old desktop, put it on the shed and stuck the laptop there and then I had no choice. I had to get used to it. Thank God I did – it is so much faster!" Her laptop is now her default technology.

5.3   Symbiotic Experience

Sarah's creative mind and her ability to use a word processor constitute an inseparable unit in the writing endeavour. Sarah has a disciplined approach when it comes to writing. She does not like interruptions; she does not take phone calls and her daughter knows that she should not be around while Sarah is engrossed typing her stories. Even her fear of technology is temporarily suspended: "When I write I feel that the computer does what I want". She describes her state of immersion as a journey to another world: "I lose myself in [my writing]. Yeah. I lose myself in it. Even when I am buzzing, I am still wrapped up in the story. It takes me a while to get back to reality, I suppose".

Sarah sees the monotony of her job as a cleaner beneficial to her imaginative undertakings. The manual nature of the cleaning work she performs gives her the mental space to develop stories in her head. Furthermore, her imaginative mind manifested conspicuously during the long hours of conversations we had; they were interspersed with passages of these stories. However, these stories would never see the light of the day if it not were by digital technology. She grants it a prominent role in the materialisation of her imagination:

> For me, the stories I write are that inner world. With the computer, once again, it was finding the tool to express the inner world ... So it is like I am just putting in what I already see, but just to allow others to see it. So when I write a story, it is often like a movie I watch and then, it is just putting it down, so other people can watch the movie ... The story was in my head, but I want to share it. I do not think people would have seen it without my computer.

In expressing her inner world, Sarah takes advantage of some functionalities of word processor software. In her own account, she never "thought of writing [her stories] down" before discovering the editing functionalities available on a word processor. Moreover, she does not want to go back to hand writing anymore: "I find longhand writing so difficult now. I would say, I am so hooked into [digital technology] now". Sarah uses her latest work to exemplify her reliance on digital technology:

> The children's book I am working on is so short, there are so few words, I mean, you are looking at about 400 words. They are not an issue to writing down on longhand anyway, although I have done it on the computer ... If it breaks down, I would just replace it ... It is like going back ... It is just too painful ... I would not write novels without the computer.

Although Sarah admits that she does not utilise the advanced editing functionalities of word processor software (e.g., creation of sections, page numbering, track changes), she feels confident modifying text. She explains how seeing her stories written in front of her, as opposed to mental plots, helps her improve the structure and narrative:

> When I talked to the editor the other day, I told him, 'Chapter 19 is too short; chapter 20 is too long'. So I took the beginning of chapter 20 and put it in chapter 19 ... And it is so much easier on the computer. It was not a biggie. In just a few seconds I altered that, completely altered the length of the chapter. I did not write anymore ... I do not necessarily see where the end of the chapter is when I am writing. I have a sense of it, but maybe not exactly ... Certainly, when I start writing a book, but the time I finish it, the start will change two or three times ... I do play around still a lot. It is afterwards that you can look back, almost outside yourself and say, 'Ah, this could be better here or that better there'. It is like my built-in editor. And that probably is the part that I really enjoy of the benefits of the computer.

The materialisation of her mental stories does not indicate the culmination of the imaginative process though. Sarah experiences the contradiction between her tendency of incessantly producing stories in her inner world and the prospect of having her stories truncated in a final document ready to be published. She describes this dilemma between her desire to keep her story evolving and releasing it:

> The worst fear ... I certainly did not find it easy right at the end when the publishers or editors say, 'This is the final edit; this is it' ... I hated those emails because I still want to fiddle and change something ... Until it was actually in print, I wanted to keep it changing. Once it was in print, that was it. It is like it was done ... It is like giving birth and that is it. OK? Even if it is a deformity, you accept it. That is it ... Once it is in print, I have to let it go.

Interestingly, digital technology represents more than just a convenient labour-saving tool to Sarah. She engages in online research to portray an accurate depiction of the background in which her stories are set up. Sarah describes herself as a perfectionist and wants to reflect this in her writing. She wants to make sure that the terms, historical details, temporal and geographical references are correct. Her meticulous style can be appreciated in her first published novel, which contains many references to Roman history in the first century of the Christian era. Sarah describes with detail certain aspects of the scenery, such as sunrise and sunset times as well as tide levels. Online searches furnish her with all these details. Sarah summarises the symbiotic interaction between her creative mind and digital technology with the following statement: "It is where the computer works perfectly with my imagination ... it is a sort of collaboration".

6 Discussion and Conclusion

This phenomenological study reveals the lived experience of Sarah, a self-confessed technophobe, who has been able to write a novel using word processor software and get it published. Attributing her achievements as a writer solely to digital technology likens to assuming a technological deterministic position, which I reject. Her ability of using digital technology did not make Sarah a writer. However, digital technology – especially word processor software – became a catalyst that allowed Sarah to materialise her talent as a storyteller. She is a creative person that has established a disciplined routine for writing stories in which word processor software plays a crucial role. The essence of the phenomenon under study is constituted by three interdependent experiences. First, the imaginative experience, which reveals her creative character that is incessantly visualising fantastic stories. Second, the epiphanic experience as the moment of discovery, when Sarah realised that word processor software constitutes the platform for her imagination coming into being. Third, the symbiotic experience that represents how ingrained digital technology has become in her writing; not only to produce the text of her novels but also as a source of information for giving her stories factual accuracy. However, there is an element that still lies underneath these three experiences, the anxiety that using digital technology produces on her.

Although this phenomenological study relies on the experience of one participant only, it offers two contributions. The first one is a demonstration of the repercussions digital technology can have on people's lives. Sarah has reasons to believe now that she is in the path of leaving her job as a cleaner to become a novelist. Sarah intimates, "When I have another couple of books out there, I would probably think of myself as a writer". After a pause, she assertively reflects, "I would like to end up thinking of myself as a writer". At the time of writing this paper, Sarah's second novel had already been completed. In addition, Sarah is working simultaneously on a new novel and a children's book. In this sense, her experience is an instantiation of how individuals derive value from using digital technology as a sense of personal achievement that transcends purely monetary considerations – cf. Sen's capability approach [28]. Sarah shares her intention to continue writing after retirement simply "because it is fun". The second contribution of this study lies on the insights transcendental phenomenology reveals. By adopting transcendental phenomenology as a method of inquiry, I do not aim at making this study replicable; even less, making my findings predictable. What this study offers instead is a thick description that reveals the essence of the phenomenon of engaging with digital technology as lived by Sarah, a self-confessed technophobe. The analysis reveals Sarah's intentions and consciousness in her use of word processor software. Given that at its fundamental level, information systems research is about understanding the interplay between individuals and digital technology, phenomenology as a method affords scrutinising the process of how "data becomes information in the consciousness of a human subject" [12, p. 200]. Researchers interested in understanding how individuals exercise judgment and construct meaning in their engagement with digital technology can adopt a transcendental phenomenological approach.

The findings of this research signal a promising research direction. The discovery of the symbiotic experience opens opportunities for further studying contemporary phenomena characterised by the intimate relationship with digital technology in multiple spheres of personal life, such as health and sports, human interaction and entertainment.

Acknowledgement. *2020 Trust* made possible the fieldwork of this study.

References

1. Braa, J., Hanseth, O., Heywood, A., Mohammed, W., Shaw, V.: Developing health information systems in developing countries: the flexible standards strategy. MIS Q. **31**, 381–402 (2007)
2. Jha, S.K., Pinsonneault, A., Dubé, L.: The evolution of an ICT platform-enabled ecosystem for poverty alleviation: the case of eKutir. MIS Q. **40**, 431–445 (2016)
3. Puri, S.K.: Integrating scientific with indigenous knowledge: constructing knowledge alliances for land management in India. MIS Q. **31**, 355–379 (2007)
4. Silva, L.: Institutionalization does not occur by decree: institutional obstacles in implementing a land administration system in a developing country. Inf. Technol. Dev. **13**, 27–48 (2007)
5. Suchman, L.A.: Human-Machine Reconfigurations: Plans and Situated Actions, 2nd edn. Cambridge University Press, New York (2007)

6. Faraj, S., Azad, B.: The materiality of technology: an affordance perspective. In: Leonardi, P. M., Nardi, B.A., Kallinikos, J. (eds.) Materiality and Organizing: Social Interaction in a Technological World, pp. 237–258. Oxford University Press, Oxford (2012)

7. Robey, D., Raymond, B., Anderson, C.: Theorizing information technology as a material artifact in information systems research. In: Leonardi, P.M., Nardi, B.A., Kallinikos, J. (eds.) Materiality and Organizing: Social Interaction in a Technological World, pp. 217–236. Oxford University Press, Oxford (2012)

8. Introna, L.: Epilogue: performativity and the becoming of sociomaterial assemblages. In: de Vaujany, F.-X., Mitev, N. (eds.) Materiality and Space: Organizations, Artefacts and Practices. Palgrave Macmillan, Basingstoke (2013)

9. Orlikowski, W.J.: Using technology and constituting structures: a practice lens for studying technology in organizations. Organ. Sci. **11**, 404–428 (2000)

10. Kallinikos, J., Aaltonen, A., Marton, A.: The ambivalent ontology of digital artifacts. MIS Q. **37**, 357–370 (2013)

11. Ciborra, C.: Encountering information systems as a phenomenon. In: Avgerou, C., Ciborra, C., Land, F. (eds.) The Social Study of Information and Communication Technology: Innovation, Actors, and Contexts, pp. 17–37. Oxford University Press, Oxford (2004)

12. Boland Jr., R.J.: Phenomenology: a preferred approach to research in information systems. In: Mumford, E., Hirscheim, R.A., Fitzgerald, G., Wood-Harper, A.T. (eds.) Research Methods in Information Systems, pp. 193–201. North Holland Publishing Co., Netherlands (1985)

13. Weil, M.M., Rosen, L.D., Wugalter, S.E.: The etiology of computerphobia. Comput. Hum. Behav. **6**, 361–379 (1990)

14. Bandura, A.: Self-efficacy mechanism in human agency. Am. Psychol. **37**, 122–147 (1982)

15. Meier, S.T.: Computer aversion. Comput. Hum. Behav. **1**, 171–179 (1985)

16. Rosen, L.D., Weil, M.M.: Computer availability, computer experience and technophobia among public school teachers. Comput. Hum. Behav. **11**, 9–31 (1995)

17. Beckers, J.J., Schmidt, H.G.: Computer experience and computer anxiety. Comput. Hum. Behav. **19**, 785–797 (2003)

18. Brosnan, M.J.: Modeling technophobia: a case for word processing. Comput. Hum. Behav. **15**, 105–121 (1999)

19. Introna, L.D., Whittaker, L.: The phenomenology of information systems evaluation: overcoming the subject/object dualism. In: Wynn, E.H., Whitley, E.A., Myers, M.D., DeGross, J.I. (eds.) Global and Organizational Discourse about Information Technology. ITIFIP, vol. 110, pp. 155–175. Springer, New York (2003). doi:10.1007/978-0-387-35634-1_9

20. Küpers, W.M.: The status and relevance of phenomenology for integral research: or why phenomenology is more and different than an "Upper Left" or "Zone #1" affair. Integr. Rev. **5**, 51–95 (2009)

21. Jopling, D.A.: Sub-phenomenology. Hum. Stud. **19**, 153–173 (1996)

22. Küpers, W.M.: Phenomenology of the Embodied Organization: The Contribution of Merleau-Ponty for Organizational Studies and Practice. Palgrave Macmillan, Basingstoke (2015)

23. Moustakas, C.: Phenomenological Research Methods. Sage, Thousand Oaks (1994)

24. Jennings, J.L.: Husserl revisited: the forgotten distinction between distinction and phenomenology. Am. Psychol. **41**, 1231–1240 (1986)

25. Lopez, K.A., Willis, D.G.: Descriptive versus interpretive phenomenology: their contributions to nursing knowledge. Qual. Health Res. **14**, 726–735 (2004)

26. Creswell, J.W.: Research Design: Qualitative, Quantitative, and Mixed Methods Approaches, 3rd edn. Sage, Los Angeles (2009)

27. Merleau-Ponty, M.: Phenomenology of Perception (1974). Routledge, London (2014)

28. Sen, A.K.: Development as Freedom. Alfred A. Knopf, New York (1999)

A Preliminary Testing of the Strategic IT Decision Making Model

Sherah Kurnia[1(✉)], Dora Constantinidis[1], Alison Parkes[2],
Toomas Tamm[3], and Peter Seddon[1]

[1] University of Melbourne, Melbourne, Australia
{sherahk,dorac,p.seddon}@unimelb.edu.au
[2] La Trobe University, Melbourne, Australia
A.Parkes@latrobe.edu.au
[3] University of NSW, Sydney, Australia
Toomas.tamm@unsw.edu.au

Abstract. Strategic IT decisions are critical and can result in major impacts on an organization's ability to remain competitive. Improved management of influencing factors on such decisions can lead to a reduction of cost overruns and greater return on the investment of large-scale IT expenditures. However, limited IS research has investigated strategic IT decision making processes and their associated influencing factors. To address the current knowledge gap, Tamm et al. (2014) proposed a Strategic IT Decision Making Model (SITDMM) based on a comprehensive literature synthesis. However, the SITDMM had not been tested with empirical data. This research-in-progress paper conducted a preliminary testing of the SITDM model by using a qualitative approach. An initial interview was conducted with a senior executive who was involved in a strategic IT decision at an Australian pharmaceutical company.

The preliminary testing of the model demonstrates the usefulness of the SITDMM in capturing key influencing factors affecting the strategic decision making process in the case organization. This paper demonstrates that the Top Management Team played the most significant role in influencing the extent to which the SITDMM process was analytical, intuitive, and political. These factors influenced the final decision outcome. Future research will include the analysis of more strategic IT decision cases in order to further test the SITDMM and provide a framework which organizations can use to better assess and therefore manage factors influencing strategic IT decision making processes.

Keywords: Strategic decision making · Strategic IT decision · Strategic decision making process · Influence factors · SITDMM · ERP

1 Introduction

Organizations in both developed and developing countries have adopted and implemented various technological innovations over time to stay competitive. Some technological innovations within organizations are strategic in nature because they have a broad impact across the entire organization and have short and long-term implications to the overall competitiveness. Such technologies typically require significant expenditure and

J. Choudrie et al. (Eds.): ICT4D 2017, IFIP AICT 504, pp. 707–717, 2017.
DOI: 10.1007/978-3-319-59111-7_57

need to be implemented over an extended period of time affecting a large number of stakeholders. Enterprise System (ES) applications such as Enterprise Resource Planning (ERP) systems are an example of strategic IT applications.

Implementing strategic IT applications, however, is a risky undertaking due to the size and complexity involved and the high investment required. Many studies show that the failure rate of ES implementation is significantly high in both developed and developing countries [1]. Many projects experienced cost overruns and struggled to gain the expected benefits from the ES investment, while some projects were altogether abandoned after significant expenditure had been made [2–4]. Most existing studies have associated such failures with ineffective project management without exploring decision making related to the associated IT projects [5, 6].

The decisions made by senior executives regarding strategic IT implementations including what, when and how the systems are to be implemented are likely to impact the ensuing outcomes. If all aspects of the decision making process are systematically accounted for and better managed, this may lead to more successful outcomes. Nevertheless, there are many challenges surrounding the determination of costs, benefits, risks and long-term implications on the future state of technologies, processes and management of the organization [7]. Furthermore, strategic IT decisions made by senior executives are often constrained by previous decisions which may have been made by different management teams with different sets of goals and interests [8]. Additionally, within the decision making team, there are personal biases and preferences that each member brings to the table which further complicate the decision making process [9]. Organizations rarely effectively manage such a variety of factors that influence their strategic IT decision making processes and associated outcomes. Therefore, a better understanding of strategic IT decision making including the process and key influence factors would provide further insights and potentially help decision makers establish necessary measures to avoid future failures.

Despite the importance of strategic IT decision making processes and their significant consequences on organizations, there has been limited IS research investigating the major factors influencing such processes. In addressing this knowledge gap, [10] proposed the Strategic IT Decision Making Model (SITDMM) that captures key factors influencing the strategic IT decision making process. This model, however, has not been tested and hence the applicability and comprehensiveness of the factors captured are still questionable. To contribute to the existing research efforts in enhancing the current understanding of strategic IT decision making, our study aims to investigate a strategic IT decision made by a large Australian organization to test the SITDMM. The key research question addressed is: *To what extent does the SITDMM capture key factors affecting a strategic IT decision making process?* To address the research question, we conducted a qualitative research involving an interview with a senior executive from a large Australian organization and reviews of its relevant organizational documents. In this research-in-progress paper we include the findings of a preliminary testing of the SITDMM by examining the key factors that influenced a strategic IT decision process. This paper will focus on how this qualitative analysis was conducted for an Australian pharmaceutical company by providing examples of coded statements from the interview. The outline of this paper is as follows. In the next section, the SITDMM is presented with the 7 propositions. Then the research methodology and the context of the case organization are described. Findings are then presented and discussed. The paper concludes by summarizing key observations obtained from this study and explains the next step of the study.

2 The Strategic IT Decision Making Model

The SITDMM posits that strategic IT decision making processes are influenced by a number of key factors. [11] had previously delineated similar factors, by conducting a literature review, in relation to how these affected generic strategic decision-making. However, the factors identified by [11] had not been developed into an overarching model with propositions linked to the decision making process and final decision outcome. [10] extended the results of their own literature review to develop the SITDMM with propositions that could be more easily tested on interview datasets. The key factors that affect strategic-decision-making processes are presented by the model in Fig. 1 and are grouped as (1) the decision context; (2) individuals and teams involved; and (3) the source and characteristics of the available information. The SITDMM seeks to capture the extent to which the strategic IT decision making process is analytical, intuitive and political by addressing the key influence factors.

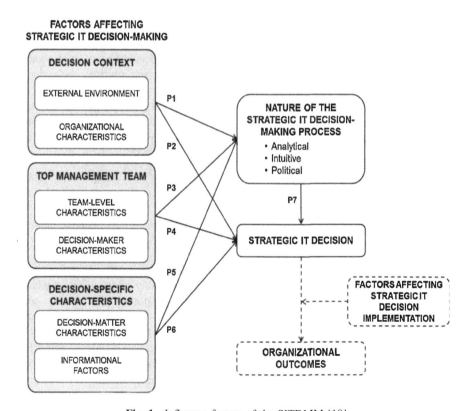

Fig. 1. Influence factors of the SITDMM [10].

Even though similar factors have been previously discussed to some extent in the IS literature, no model comparable to the SITDMM had been derived until that presented by [10]. The SITDMM in Fig. 1 presents factors that can impact the strategic IT decision process and subsequent decision. The influence of each factor can be positive or negative based on the context. The propositions make no claims about the outcomes of the influence of those factors shown in the SITDMM. The model only suggests that those factors are a relevant part of the decision process. Each module component of the factors and related propositions are briefly described below summarizing the previous literature research.

Decision Context refers to the nature of the environment in which the decision is made. The *external environment* includes national culture, legislation, economic climate, and environmental dynamism [7, 8]. The *organizational characteristics* include organizational culture, routines, processes, governance, and munificence [8, 9, 12]. It is posited that:

P1:   *The Decision Context influences the nature of the Strategic IT Decision-making processes in an organization especially the extent to which such processes are analytical, intuitive, and political*

P2:   *The Decision Context influences the actual strategic IT decision made*

Top Management Team is the group of senior managers and their advisors who make the final decision in terms of the strategic directions of the organization. The *team-level characteristics* refer to the collective characteristics of the decision team, such as team diversity (demographic, cognitive), size, team dynamics and routines, behavioural integration, and power distribution. The *decision-maker characteristics* refer to the individual characteristics of each decision team member that influence their perceptions of the decision problem, approaches to problem solving, and ability to influence others, e.g., cognitive style, personality, personal values, aspirations, incentives, and self-confidence [8, 9]. It is posited that:

P3:   *The Top Management Team influence the nature of the strategic IT decision-making processes in an organization, especially the extent to which such processes are analytical, intuitive, and political*

P4:   *The Top Management Team influence the actual strategic IT decision made*

Decision-Specific Characteristics refer to the characteristics of, and information relevant to, the specific strategic decision. The *decision-matter characteristics* include perceived decision importance, time pressure, motive (opportunity or threat), complexity, and politicality [8]. *Informational factors* refer to the information relevant to the strategic decision that is provided to or encountered by some or all of the decision team members and that affect their understanding of the decision problem and/or their preferred course of action. Sources of such information include internal analyst reports, opinions of peers, consultant advice, precedents and competitor actions, and press reports on technologies, their adoption, and economic outlook [10]. It is posited that:

P5:   *The Decision-specific Characteristics of a strategic proposal under consideration influence the nature of the Strategic IT Decision-making processes, especially the extent to which they are analytical, intuitive, and political*

P6:   *The Decision-specific Characteristics of a strategic proposal under consideration influence the actual strategic IT decision made*

Therefore, changes in the Decision-specific Characteristics of a strategic IT proposal under consideration may result in the Top Management Team making different strategic IT decisions.

Nature of the Strategic IT Decision-making Process refers to the characterisation of the decision process under three key dimensions [10]: (1) Analytical-Rational, the degree to which the process relies on detailed rational analysis of relevant factors, (2) Intuitive-Judgmental, the degree to which the decision team members rely on personal and/or collective intuition or "gut feel" in reaching their final decision [13], and (3) Political-Bargaining, the degree to which the process is characterized by political behaviour (e.g., coalitions, information tactics, use of external advisors) [7, 12]. Therefore it is posited that:

P7:   *The extent to which strategic IT decision-making processes in an organization are analytical, intuitive, and political, influences the strategic IT decisions that emerge from the process*

3   Research Methodology

In-depth qualitative research is considered appropriate to investigate strategic IT decision making which is complex in nature [14]. For our initial test of the key factors posited by the SITDMM an interview with a senior executive who was involved in a strategic IT decision at a large organization was conducted. For this research-in-progress paper, overall results for the initial analysis are presented as part of a preliminary testing of the SITDMM. The organization is a large pharmaceutical company. Current industry trends and other organizational documents (organizational chart, reports, etc.) were used to contextualize the comments provided by the interviewee [15]. Three coders with IS Academic backgrounds then coded statements from the interview transcript of the CFO who was interviewed for this research.

Since information in the interview was provided in a narrative format, we considered the narrative analysis methodology to help improve our coding. Narrative analysis can be applied to assist with interpretation of the social context of interviewees [16]. The strength of evidence for the model was derived by coding statements [17] in the interview transcript in relation to the seven SITDMM propositions. Each coder assigned a number (0, 1 or 2) to indicate the strength of evidence for each proposition. A score of 0 indicates no evidence found, 1 indicates there is evidence identified, and 2 indicates strong evidence found. All results were then correlated and cross-coded. Rigor is addressed by following the guidelines by [18, 14]. The research validity is further enhanced by conducting a thorough analysis of the relevant literature to ensure that we capture the valid factors and concepts, establishing chain of evidence through the use of case study repository, and a careful selection of the research participant. Reliability is ensured through the use of interview protocol and a pilot study with 2 senior executives to ensure the interview questions are appropriate.

4 Case Description

A major Australian pharmaceutical company, which for anonymity is referred to as PHARMA, is used to present an example of how the analysis was conducted in more detail. The increasing competition in the pharmaceutical industry has made modern ERP and Supply Chain Management (SCM) systems with demand forecasting capability critical to remaining competitive. With increasing changes to expectations of how the demand and supply of pharmaceuticals is managed, careful consideration of operating with an appropriate supply chain framework is needed by all pharmaceutical companies. Given PHARMA's large distribution network across Australia, appropriate access to information about supply and demand is essential. However the core module of the ERP was only just meeting their basic supply chain demands but could not provide demand forecasting and planning. The reliance on this core system meant that the company remained largely reactive rather than proactively delivering stock to the pharmacy outlets. PHARMA needed to increase their capability to forecast demand and create more predictive and proactive provisioning of supplies. PHARMA was confronted with two options: (1) implement a completely new ERP system or (2) upgrade. The final *decision to upgrade their existing ERP* was based on information provided by managers who were largely trusted by the decision making team.

The key decision making team comprised the Chief Executive Officer (CEO), the Chief Financial Officer (CFO), and the Chief Operations Officer (COO). The Chief Information Officer (CIO) reported to the CFO and was not directly involved in the decision making. Three other senior managers in sales, distribution and supply chain areas provided major input to the CIO. The supply chain manager in particular was new and produced a very convincing business case to upgrade the existing ERP based on a successful experience in a previous company. The executive committee placed a high level of trust and did not spend sufficient time to investigate the available options due to time pressure. As a result, the outcome was not considered optimal since they ended up spending a significant amount of financial resources for little improvements to the existing system and capability.

5 Preliminary Testing

The testing of the model so far indicates that key influence factors presented by the SITDMM are evident. An initial analysis was conducted for PHARMA. Table 1 summarizes the strength-of-evidence obtained for each proposition at PHARMA.

Table 1. The Strength-of-Evidence (SoE) for each proposition

Proposition	P1	P2	P3	P4	P5	P6	P7
Coder 1	1	1	2	2	2	2	1
Coder 2	2	1	2	2	2	1	1
Coder 3	2	1	2	1	1	2	1
Overall	**2**	**1**	**2**	**2**	**2**	**2**	**1**

Overall, the results indicate that the Top Management Team played the most significant role in influencing the extent to which the SITDMM process is analytical, intuitive, and political which has an implication on the decision outcome. Illustrative quotes from PHARMA provide examples of what was considered to be evidence for each of the propositions.

P1: *Decision context influences the decision process.* There is clear evidence that both the *external environment* such as markets and industry dynamics and *organizational characteristics* influenced the decision making process. For example, when explaining about the reason for deciding to upgrade the ERP system, the CFO asserts: *"...some of that's because of factors outside of our control ... the industry dynamics are changing...."* The success of other companies in upgrading a similar ERP system appeared to affect PHARMA's decision which shows the influence the *external environment*. The CFO indicates the influence of *organizational characteristic* by: *"... someone who's built up this power base around a core system"* and how *"someone's really pushed something into the business"*. This indicates a more political rather than analytical decision making process.

P2: *Decision context influences the decision.* There was no evidence for *external factors* in influencing the final decision at PHARMA. For *organizational characteristics,* the CFO described *"They [IT] were more sort of infrastructure focused and sort of run maintain focused."* This seems to have impacted the choice to upgrade the existing ERP.

P3: *The Top Management Team influences the decision process.* An example of the influence of *team-level characteristics* is where key decision makers at PHARMA placed a lot of trust in the information they were provided with: *"The board would pretty much be guided by what management tell them."* The influence of *decision-maker characteristics* is also evident. Who is part of the decision team and how persuasive they are can also impact strategic IT decision making processes: *"I think some of that is very much driven by the leader of the organization".*

P4: *Decision team influences the decision.* Indicative statements of how influential the *team-level characteristics* impact the final decision were identified. For example, *"...we did a lot of change so we brought in a whole new management team... and they'll often bring their biases from those organizations with them."* The supply chain manager apparently wanted the ERP system to be updated and upgraded: *"...he obviously came to the view pretty quickly actually that he wanted to both update and* *upgrade."* Furthermore, the final decision made at PHARMA was clearly influenced by the *decision-maker characteristics* of high levels of trust: *"...I think in hindsight myself and the CEO probably were guided by what the CIO was telling us."*

P5: *Decision-specific factors influence the decision process.* There is evidence of the influence of *decision-matter characteristics* since the supply chain manager deemed it was necessary to quickly take an action-based on minimal information- to address the issues caused by the previous ERP system: *"He put together a business case, he worked with the vendor of the SCM which is never a good thing quite frankly."* However due to the time pressure, thorough and objective assessments of the available options were not conducted. Moreover, the case confirms the influence of *informational factors* as the CFO explained the importance of gathering information from various sources during the decision making process. However, PHARMA did not address this factor very well: *"there wasn't enough work done."*

P6: *Decision-specific factors influence the decision.* The decision to upgrade the existing ERP system was significantly influenced by the urgency to improve the overall performance and competitiveness of PHARMA, which typifies the influence of *decision-matter characteristics*. As a result, the senior executives simply followed minimal information provided for the recommendation to upgrade: *"I kind of went off what they told me and I probably didn't dig below the surface."*

P7: *The decision process influences the decision.* The CFO believed that the decision making process was more intuitive which had led to a sub-optimal decision: *"In hindsight, I suppose it was more intuitive than political".*

6   Discussion and Conclusions

The SITDMM provides a fundamental set of key factors that can influence strategic IT decision making. Through this research-in-progress paper, some initial insights have been established about how inter-related key factors impacted a strategic IT decision making process and its subsequent outcome. The overall scores of the strength-of-evidence provided for the seven propositions suggest that all factors in the SITDMM warrant careful consideration in relation to any strategic IT decision making. This preliminary testing of the SITDMM demonstrates that strategic IT decisions are influenced by an intricate combination of contextual, team, and decision-specific factors. Of most significance is the top management team, whose views, previous experiences and biases influenced both their analysis of information and contextual circumstances leading to final decisions. Since Proposition 3 (*The Top Management Team influences the decision process*) ranked highest in terms of strength of evidence it is proposed that comprehensively managing factors related to the top management team may provide additional accountability and allow for a more reliable decision making platform. Reducing political clout, managing team biases from previous successes or failures of implementing IT in another context, and seeking more evidence based information may lead to improving such decisions.

Our study also highlights the fact that strategic IT decision making process often involves a considerable level of intuition, regardless of the effort to make the process analytical. Senior executives usually believe that they have been analytical in making specific strategic IT decisions, but they may later realize that intuition and politics have affected their decisions, as revealed by the CFO at PHARMA. Therefore, it is suggested that a thorough feasibility study is critical to avoid making rushed decisions based on insufficient information. As it is challenging to obtain accurate cost and benefit estimations of any large IT investments, the CFO recognized the importance of stage gating the process to help manage the overall strategic decision process and the related cost-estimation. This suggestion is in line with [19, 20].

Additional insights that arose from the analysis indicate that senior executives do not always sufficiently question the validity of the evidence provided. The level of trust and relationship senior executives have cultivated with their teams appeared to be important in decision making. It is hence critical for senior executives to stay objective when dealing with strategic IT decision making. Ensuring adequate time to explore possible options and gather unbiased information from various sources would be useful to enhance strategic IT decision making as identified by this case.

For PHARMA we conclude that there are 3 key issues that affected the sub-optimal decision outcome. Firstly, there was time pressure to make a decision to address the ERP system limitations and declining organizational performance. The final decision to upgrade the ERP was not based on adequate assessment of possible options. Secondly, restrictive organizational structure and culture in which the CIO was not involved in the executive committee might have affected the decision making process. Limitations associated with the CIO's level of strategic decision-making authority as demonstrated in the PHARMA case have been identified in [21]. Without the direct influence of the CIO on the executive committee, it is challenging to properly align IT's contribution to organizational performance. Thirdly, ineffective cost-benefit analysis hampered the senior executives to make an optimal decision. The cost-benefit estimates provided by the managers and vendor were not reliable leading to cost overruns and a poor outcome.

Through this preliminary assessment of the SITDM model, we offer a modest contribution in enhancing the current understanding of strategic IT decision making that potentially may help improve the success of strategic IT projects. A better understanding of influence factors that can impact the decision making process can equip organizations to devise appropriate mitigation strategies to improve their overall strategic IT decision making process. Even though analytical dimensions are by far the most explored in IS research, the intuitive and political dimensions are just as important as is evidenced in this paper. Results of this initial analysis have previously been presented as a case study designed to provide teaching insights for graduate students about Strategic IT decision making [22]. With increasing interest in strategic decision making in organizations [23] the next step of our study will be to analyze interviews from more case organizations. This should further refine our observations and testing of the influence of the key factors identified by the SITDMM. Ultimately a framework for Strategic IT decision making will be developed to assist organizations improve their decision making capabilities and outcomes.

Acknowledgement. This case study is derived from an interview data set that was conducted for a research project funded by an Australian Research Council Discovery grant DP130103535.

References

1. Huang, Z., Palvia, P.: ERP implementation issues in advanced and developing countries. Bus. Process Manage. J. **7**(3), 276–284 (2001)
2. Davenport, T.H.: Mission Critical – Realizing the Promise of Enterprise Systems. Harvard Business School Press, Boston (2000)
3. Finney, S., Corbett, M.: ERP implementation: a compilation and analysis of critical success factors. Bus. Process Manag. J. **13**(3), 329–347 (2007)
4. Schniederjans, D., Yadav, S.: Successful ERP implementation: an integrative model. Bus. Process Manag. J. **19**(2), 364–398 (2013)
5. Shang, S., Seddon, P.B.: Assessing and managing the benefits of enterprise systems: the business manager's perspective. Inf. Syst. J. **12**, 271–299 (2002)
6. Staehr, L., Shanks, G., Seddon, P.B.: An explanatory framework for achieving business benefits from ERP systems. J. Assoc. Inf. Syst. **13**(6), 424–465 (2012)
7. Elbanna, S.: Strategic decision-making: process perspectives. Int. J. Manage. Rev. **8**(1), 1–20 (2006)
8. Shepherd, N.G., Rudd, J.M.: The influence of context on the strategic decision-making process: a review of the literature. Int. J. Manage. Rev. **16**(3), 340–364 (2014)
9. Carpenter, M.A., Geletkanycz, M.A., Sanders, W.G.: Upper echelons research revisited: antecedents, elements, and consequences of top management team composition. J. Manage. **30**(6), 749–778 (2004)
10. Tamm, T., Seddon, P., Parkes, A., Kurnia, S.: A model of strategic IT decision-making processes. In: 25th Australasian Conference on Information Systems, 8th–10th Dec 2014, Auckland, New Zealand, pp. 1–11 (2014)
11. Nooraie, M.: Factors influencing strategic decision-making processes. Int. J. Acad. Res. Bus. Soc. Sci. **2**(7), 405–429 (2012)
12. Eisenhardt, K.M., Zbaracki, M.J.: Strategic decision-making. Strateg. Manage. J. **13**(S2), 17–37 (1992)
13. Akinci, C., Sadler-Smith, E.: Intuition in management research: a historical review. Int. J. Manage. Rev. **14**(1), 104–122 (2012)
14. Patton, M.Q.: Qualitative Research. Wiley, Chichester (2005)
15. Walsham, G.: Interpretive case studies in IS research: nature and method. Eur. J. Inf. Syst. **4**, 74–81 (1995)
16. Reissman, C.K.: Narrative Analysis. Qualitative Research Methods Series 30. Sage Publications, Newbury Park (1993)
17. Strauss, A., Corbin, J.: Basics of Qualitative Research: Techniques and Procedures for Developing Grounded Theory. Sage Publications, Thousand Oaks (1998)
18. Yin, R.K.: Case Study Research: Design and Methods. Sage publications, Thousand Oaks (2013)
19. Merrow, E.W.: Industrial Megaprojects: Concepts, Strategies, and Practices for Success. Wiley, Hoboken (2011)
20. Lawrence, G.R.: Stage gated approval processes–a practical way to develop and filter capital investment ideas. Int. Soc. Pharm. Eng. **28**(2), 1–9 (2008). Tampa, Florida: Pharmaceutical Engineering

21. Preston, D.S., Chen, D., Leidner, D.E.: Examining the antecedents and consequences of CIO strategic decision-making authority: an empirical study. Decis. Sci. **39**(4), 605–642 (2008)
22. Sherah, K., Constantinidis, D., Parkes, A.J., Seddon, P.B.: Is there a prescription for strategic IT decisions? J. Inf. Technol. Teach. Cases **11**, 1–9 (2016)
23. Al Jassism, W.H.: An investigation of the strategic decision making process in SME's. Brunel University Research Archive BURA (2014)

Cancer Patients on Facebook: A Theoretical Framework

Marva Mirabolghasemi[1] and Noorminshah A. Iahad[2(✉)]

[1] Lahijan Branch, Islamic Azad University, Lahijan, Iran
d.m.mirabolghasemi@gmail.com
[2] Universiti Teknologi Malaysia, Johor Bahru, Malaysia
minshah@utm.my

Abstract. The growing presence of the technology cause of an essential need to explore cancer patients' behavior in online communities. Social Network Sites (SNS) such as Facebook provide an interactive environment to deliver health information to cancer patients. Only a few studies have looked at the role of Facebook for cancer patients despite their potential deliver health messages to large audiences. Hence, there should be more rigorous research to explain the cancer patients' behavior in SNS. This study propose a theoretical framework to explore the cognitive, social and technological constructs that affect the performance of cancer patients in Facebook by using social cognitive theory (SCT). Based on purposive sampling, questionnaires were distributed to 178 breast cancer patients in cancer support groups in Peninsular Malaysia. Through this study, a basis for the investigation of Malaysian social network support in using SNSs is successfully established.

Keywords: Cancer · E-Patients · Health 2.0 · Social Cognitive Theory · Social Network Sites

1 Introduction

One of the main health dilemmas afflicting Malaysia is cancer [1]. The incidence of cancer is 30000 yearly and Breast Cancer (BC) is the most common cancer [1]. Nowadays, patients and their families often cite difficulties such as lack of information, insufficient psychosocial support, and uncoordinated care [2]. There are some studies that described improvements that Social Network Sites (SNS) could offer to health care such as openness, communication, greater transparency, improved patient support and knowledge translation [3]. It can serve as key health communication channels to provide a location for online dialogue and encourage communities and individuals to interact by providing information related to disease treatment, and survivorship [4].

SNS have attracted general population in middle-income and high-income countries. Hospitals and cancer support groups should embrace SNS that they may contribute to quality improvements in healthcare. Active use of SNS by healthcare institutions could also speed up information and communication provision to patients and their families, thus increasing quality even more [5, 6]. Applying theories are useful because they provide a framework to help identify the determinants of successful

© IFIP International Federation for Information Processing 2017
Published by Springer International Publishing AG 2017. All Rights Reserved
J. Choudrie et al. (Eds.): ICT4D 2017, IFIP AICT 504, pp. 718–727, 2017.
DOI: 10.1007/978-3-319-59111-7_58

intervention. Koskan et al. [7] have done a systematic literature review on SNS in cancer related research and the results show that the usage of theories is still lacking. However, Social Cognitive Theory (SCT) is the most comprehensive theory that could explain the effect of individual and environmental constructs on certain behavioral patterns in the context of Health Information Systems (HIS).

Since using SNS seems to be significant for individuals with cancer; there is a need for conducting more research to understand factors that can potentially affect cancer patients' performance in using SNS. Early research (1996–2007) was mainly descriptive studies of online discussion forums. Later, researchers began analyzing SNS; therefore, future research should determine how SNS can influence cancer patients' behavior [7]. Impact of SNS on users can be estimated through their performance [8]. There is still the lack of studies consider the impact of participating in BC Facebook groups [9]. Therefore, the main objective of this study is to determine the factors that affect the performance of cancer patients in SNS.

2 Literature Review

The research study's literature review is divided into two main sections. Firstly, a brief description of SNS in healthcare is provided. Secondly, the theoretical perspective is considered.

2.1 Social Network Sites in Healthcare

The increase in SNS membership has been followed by an increase in SNS user research [10]. Previous studies have identified improvements that social networks could offer to health care such as openness, communication, greater transparency, improved patient support and knowledge translation [3]. Hospitals and cancer support groups should embrace social network as they may contribute to quality improvements in health care. Active use of SNS in health care institutions could also speed up information and communication provision to patients and their families, thus increasing quality even more [5, 6].

There is very little literature is known about the advantages of support services for cancer patients. Loader et al., [11] distinguished that informational support can be provided in online communities by virtual relationships. These kinds of support can be received through online interactive services as the helpful real-world contact persons' support [12]. SNS provide the ability for patients to exchange information on subjects such as clinical diagnosis sources of medical evidence, treatment options, adverse treatment effects, the experience of bodily symptoms and experiences with health care providers [13].

2.2 Social Cognitive Theory

SCT is found to be the most comprehensive theory that could explain the performance of cancer patients in SNS because it considers the individual performance and identifies how people acquire and maintain certain behavioral patterns. In addition, SCT describes that there is a dynamic and continuous interaction among the behavior, individual and environment.

The behavioral factors can be the performance, use or adoption. It is important to note that, according to SCT, the environmental factors are twofold which are social support and situational factors [14]. The situational factors are system and task characteristics and the TTF theory can explain them properly [15]. Among individual factors, the literature revealed the important role of cognitive factors. Figure 1 shows there is not any Information Systems (IS) model which considers the effect of both environmental and individual factors on behavior and there is still the lack of comprehensive model which consider the effect of those factors on behavior.

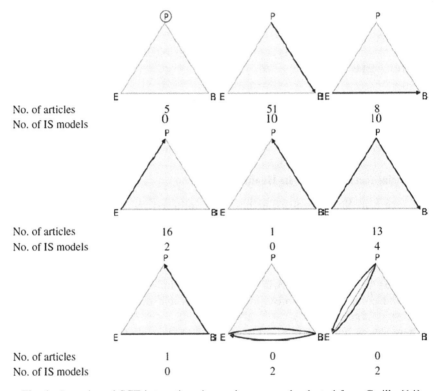

Fig. 1. Investigated SCT interactions in previous research adapted from Carillo [14]

The developed conceptual model must allow the testing and hypothesizing of certain relationships to consider whether or not the formulated theory is valid [16]. Our contention is that integrating both personal and environmental factors can enhance our understanding of individuals' performance in the context of Health Information Systems (HIS).

3   Methodology

This research applied a survey method. To increase the reliability and validity of the research instrument, three experts with HIS research experience in quantitative methods and scale development evaluated the survey's content validity. Based on purposive sampling, 178 breast cancer patients who had experience of using cancer support groups answered the questionnaire. Smart PLS 3 was used to conduct analysis in two main stages: (1) the assessment of the measurement model, including items reliability, convergent and discriminate validities, and (2) the assessment of the structural model.

Based on the research model and hypotheses, we included the following variables in this study: outcome expectation, self-efficacy, social support, task characteristics, technology characteristics, task technology fit, and performance. A 5-point Likert scale was adopted for the evaluation. Outcome expectation was taken from [17, 18] and self-efficacy was adopted from [19, 20]. Social support adopted from [21–25]. Task characteristics, technology characteristics, task technology fit and performance were based on the variables used by Mirabolghasemi and Iahad [4].

4   Results

4.1   The Demographic Information of Respondents

This study collected data from 178 respondents in cancer support groups in Peninsular Malaysia. Table 1 shows the demographic details of the respondents.

Out of 178 respondents 38% are aged 35 to 44, 24% are aged 45–54, 19% are aged 55 to 64, 18% are aged 25 to 34, and 1% is aged 18–24. The majority of respondents, 53% are Chinese, 33% are Malay, and 14% are Indian. The majority of respondents, or 87%, are in stages 2 or 3 of breast cancer, 5% are in stage 4, and only 8% are in the early stage of breast cancer. Only 15% of the respondents used SNS monthly, and while 48% used SNS daily, and remainder used SNS on a weekly.

4.2   Validity of Survey

The reliability of the survey was assessed through the use of Cronbach's Alpha and Composite reliability tests. Table 2 shows that the Cronbach's Alpha for this study ranges from 0.718 to 0.896, and the Composite Reliability ranges from 0.842 to 0.918. The above results consequently have the recommended value of 0.70, indicating that the items used represent the constructs are reliable. Convergent validity was then tested using Average Variance Extracted (AVE) that should be a value greater than 0.5 to be confirmed [26]. AVE is greater than 0.5 for all of the constructs so the value was considered to indicate good convergent validity. Therefore, sufficient reliability and convergent validity are demonstrated in Table 2.

Table 1. The demographic details of respondents

		Frequency (N = 178)	Percentage (%)
Age	18–24	2	1
	25–34	33	18
	35–44	67	38
	45–54	42	24
	55–64	34	19
Race	Malay	58	33
	Chinese	95	53
	Indian	25	14
Education	High school	55	31
	Diploma	40	22
	College certificate	45	25
	Bachelor's degree	33	19
	Master degree	5	3
Stage of cancer	Stage1	14	8
	Stage 2–3	155	87
	Stage 4	9	5
The times of using SNS	Daily	87	48
	Weekly	64	35
	Monthly	27	15

Table 2. Results of reliability and convergent validity tests

Constructs	Reliability		Convergent validity
	Cronbach's alpha	Composite reliability	AVE
Outcome expectation	0.718	0.842	0.640
Self-efficacy	0.863	0.902	0.648
Social support	0.881	0.913	0.678
Task characteristics	0.849	0.888	0.571
Technology characteristics	0.787	0.858	0.525
Task-technology fit	0.857	0.913	0.778
Performance as a behavior	0.844	0.906	0.763
Performance as an outcome	0.868	0.910	0.717
Performance	0.896	0.918	0.616

4.3   Discriminant Validity

The discriminate validity of these measures was also tested by evaluating AVE, and comparing the square root of its value to the latent variable's inter- correlations with other latent variables [27]. As presented in Table 3, the square root of AVE is greater than the latent variable inter-correlations with other latent variables. The HTMT value

Table 3. Results of Fornell-Larcker's criterion test

	OE	Performance	SE	SS	TAC	TTF	TEC
OE	**0.800**						
Performance	0.667	**0.784**					
SE	0.661	0.772	**0.805**				
SS	0.561	0.726	0.681	**0.823**			
TAC	0.449	0.619	0.674	0.617	**0.756**		
TTF	0.508	0.641	0.603	0.522	0.647	**0.882**	
TEC	0.400	0.497	0.517	0.363	0.546	0.716	**0.725**

*Note: OE = Outcome Expectation, PA = Positive Affect, SE = Self-Efficacy, SS = Social Support, TAC = Task Characteristics, TTF = Task-Technology Fit, TEC = Technology Characteristics

was also below 0.90. Therefore, discriminant validity was established between the reflective constructs.

4.4   Assessment of Structural Model

Once the construct measures are reliable and valid the structural model is assessed. This consists testing the relationships between the constructs and the model's predictive capabilities [27]. Structural model results are summarized in Table 4.

Table 4. Structural model results

Hypothesis	Path coefficient	t-value	Result
Outcome expectation -> Performance	0.182	2.373	Supported
Self-efficacy -> Performance	0.332	3.508	Supported
Social support -> Performance	0.297	3.772	Supported
Task characteristics -> Task-technology fit	0.365	5.985	Supported
Technology characteristics -> Task-technology fit	0.517	2.738	Supported
Task-technology fit -> Performance	0.198	3.972	Supported

As can be seen in Table 4, outcome expectation ($\beta = 0.182$, t value = 2.373), self-efficacy ($\beta = 0.332$, t value = 3.508), social support ($\beta = 0.297$, t value = 3.772), all showed a significant positive relationship with performance. On the other hand, task characteristics and technology characteristics should fit to have ($\beta = 0.198$, t value = 3.972) a significant positive relationship with performance.

The model as presented in Fig. 2, demonstrated 77% variance in cancer patients performance in using SNS. The results of the hypotheses testing showed that outcome expectation, self-efficacy, social support had a significant positive relationship with performance. Meanwhile, cancer patients' performance in using SNS was determined

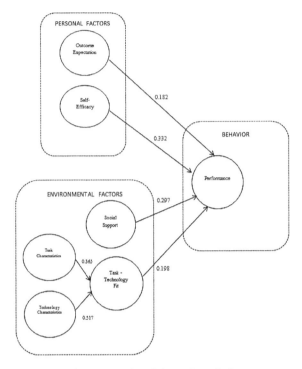

Fig. 2. Results of the PLS analysis

directly by the fit between task and technology characteristics. The last criterion for assessing the structural model is the evaluation of effect size f^2 in the structural model [27]. If $0.02 < f^2 \leq 0.15$ the effect is small, $0.15 < f^2 \leq 0.35$ the effect is medium, and if $f^2 > 0.35$ the effect is large. The results of this study showed that the independent constructs had small effect size on performance.

5   Discussion

SNS provide an interactive environment to deliver health information to cancer patients. Growing presence of the technology cause of an essential need to explore performance in the context of IS [28]. Most of the studies on SNS for cancer patients are more descriptive rather than theory building. Therefore, this study explores factors that can affect on the performance of cancer patients in using SNS.

The hypotheses of this study consider whether combinations of outcome expectation, self-efficacy, social support and task technology fit lead to increased performance in using SNS. Moreover, this study's findings provide evidence supporting hypotheses stating that task characteristics and technology characteristics have significant and positive impact on TTF, and that TTF has a significant and positive impact on cancer patients' performance in using SNS. The major contribution of this study is the formation of a theory-based model which integrates SCT and the theory of TTF.

The findings have resulted in practical and theoretical contributions, which may help online cancer support groups to obtain a more comprehensive perspective of the way SNS affect the performance of cancer patients when using SNS. In particular, researchers in the field of HIS would get an opportunity to explore how this integrated model helps to predict cancer patients' performance in using SNS.

6 Conclusion

SNS have attracted millions of users and many of them have integrated these sites into their daily practices. The factors that affect the performance of cancer patients in SNS is investigated using 178 respondents in two hospitals and four cancer support groups in peninsular Malaysia. The results show that outcome expectation, self-efficacy, social support had significant positive relationship with performance. Moreover, cancer patients' performance in using SNS was determined directly by fit between task and technology characteristics.

Finding factors that are related to performance of cancer patients in the SNS will enable health care providers to generate ideas on how an effective social network intervention for cancer patients can be conducted and it can help health care providers to design intervention more clearly. In addition, meeting patients' needs may result in cost savings, patient empowerment and activation and these are ways for achieving patient cantered care.

While contributing to both theoretical and practical contributions, the study had some limitations that should be dealt with future studies. First, gathering data from the whole population of cancer patients using Facebook were not possible and the data collection had done using 178 respondents. The reason was that some of the cancer patients were not keen to answer the questionnaire. Therefore, the broader sample size and the cross-cultural research in the broader geographical sample distribution may provide the new contributions in the future research. This study considered breast cancer patients' performance in using Facebook which is the most popular SNS among cancer support groups. Future research should validate and test the findings using other types of SNS.

Acknowledgement. A special thank you goes to Cancer Support Groups in Peninsular Malaysia who contributed to the survey and Universiti Teknologi Malaysia (UTM) for hosting the research.

References

1. National Cancer Registry. Malaysia Cancer Statistics – Data & Figure (2007)
2. Clauser, S.B., Wagner, E.H., Bowles, E.J.A., Tuzzio, L., Greene, S.M.: Improving modern cancer care through information technology. Am. J. Prev. Med. **40**(5), S198–S207 (2012)
3. Bacigalupe, G.: Is there a role for social technologies in collaborative healthcare? Fam. Syst. Health **29**(1), 1–14 (2011)

4. Mirabolghasemi, M., Iahad, N.A.: Malaysian breast cancer patients' performance in using social network sites: a task person technology fit model. Jurnal Teknologi **78**(8–2), 42–49 (2016)
5. Van De Belt, T.H., Engelen, L.J., Berben, S.A., Schoonhoven, L.: Definition of Health 2.0 and Medicine 2.0: a systematic review. J. Med. Internet Res. **12**(2), e18 (2010)
6. Van de Belt, T.H., Berben, S.A., Samsom, M., Engelen, L.J., Schoonhoven, L.: Use of social media by Western European hospitals: longitudinal study. J. Med. Internet Res. **14**(3), e61 (2012)
7. Koskan, A., Klasko, L., Davis, S.N., Gwede, C.K., Wells, K.J., Kumar, A., Meade, C.D.: Use and taxonomy of social media in cancer-related research: a systematic review. Am. J. Public Health **104**(7), e20–e37 (2014)
8. Cao, J., Basoglu, K.A., Sheng, H., Lowry, P.B.: A systematic review of social networks research in information systems: building a foundation for exciting future research. Commun. Assoc. Inf. Syst. **36**, 727–759 (2015)
9. Bender, J.L., Jimenez-Marroquin, M.C., Jadad, A.R.: Seeking support on Facebook: a content analysis of breast cancer groups. J. Med. Internet Res. **13**(1), e16 (2011)
10. Wells, T., Link, M.: Facebook user research using a probability-based sample and behavioral data. J. Comput. Mediat. Commun. **19**(4), 922–937 (2014)
11. Loader, B.D., Muncer, S., Burrows, R., Pleace, N., Nettleton, S.: Medicine on the line? Computer-mediated social support and advice for people with diabetes. Int. J. Soc. Welf. **11**(1), 53–65 (2002)
12. Turner, J.W., Grube, J.A., Meyers, J.: Developing an optimal match within online communities: an exploration of CMC support communities and traditional support. J. Commun. **51**(2), 231–251 (2001)
13. Griffiths, F., Cave, J., Boardman, F., Ren, J., Pawlikowska, T., Ball, R., Cohen, A.: Social networks–the future for health care delivery. Soc. Sci. Med. **75**(12), 2233–2241 (2012)
14. Carillo, Kévin D.: Social cognitive theory in is research – literature review, criticism, and research agenda. In: Prasad, Sushil K., Vin, Harrick M., Sahni, S., Jaiswal, Mahadeo P., Thipakorn, B. (eds.) ICISTM 2010. CCIS, vol. 54, pp. 20–31. Springer, Heidelberg (2010). doi:10.1007/978-3-642-12035-0_4
15. Mirabolghasemi, M., Iahad, N.A., Miskon, S.: Exploring factors that affect on cancer patients performance in social networks for informational support. Int. J. Bus. Inf. Syst. **20**, 348–361 (2015)
16. Sekaran, U., Bougie, R.: Research Methods for Business: A Skill Building Approach, 5th edn. Wiley, New York (2010)
17. Khalifa, M., Vanissa, L.: Determinants of satisfaction at different adoption stages of internet-based services. J. Assoc. Inf. Syst. **4**, 206–233 (2003)
18. Koo, C., Wati, Y., Park, K., Lim, M.K.: Website quality, expectation, confirmation, and end user satisfaction: the knowledge-intensive website of the Korean National Cancer Information Center. J. Med. Internet Res. **13**, e81 (2011)
19. Wu, S.Y., Wang, S.T., Liu, F., Hu, D.C., Hwang, W.Y.: The influences of social self-efficacy on social trust and social Capital-A case study of Facebook. Turk. Online J. Educ. Technol. TOJET **11**, 246–254 (2012)
20. Sherer, M., Maddux, J.E., Mercandante, B., Prentice-Dunn, S., Jacobs, B., Rogers, R.W.: The self-efficacy scale: construction and validation. Psychol. Rep. **51**, 663–671 (1982)
21. Gustafson, D.H., Hawkins, R., Pingree, S., McTavish, F., Arora, N.K., Mendenhall, J., Salner, A.: Effect of computer support on younger women with breast cancer. J. General Internal Med. **16**(7), 435–445 (2001)

22. Gustafson, D.H., McTavish, F.M., Stengle, W., Ballard, D., Hawkins, R., Shaw, B.R., Landucci, G.: Use and impact of eHealth system by low-income women with breast cancer. J. Health Commun. **10**(S1), 195–218 (2005)
23. Shaw, B.R., DuBenske, L.L., Han, J.Y., Cofta-Woerpel, L., Bush, N., Gustafson, D.H., McTavish, F.: Antecedent characteristics of online cancer information seeking among rural breast cancer patients: an application of the Cognitive-Social Health Information Processing (C-SHIP) model. J. Health Commun. **13**(4), 389–408 (2008)
24. Han, J.Y., Wise, M., Kim, E., Pingree, R., Hawkins, R.P., Pingree, S., Gustafson, D.H.: Factors associated with use of interactive cancer communication system: an application of the comprehensive model of information seeking. J. Comput. Mediat. Commun. **15**(3), 367–388 (2010)
25. Kim, S.C., Shah, D.V., Namkoong, K., McTavish, F.M., Gustafson, D.H.: Predictors of online health information seeking among women with breast cancer: the role of social support perception and emotional well-being. J. Comput. Mediat. Commun. **18**, 98–118 (2013)
26. Fornell, C., Larcker, D.F.: Evaluating structural equation models with unobservable and measurement error. J. Market. Res. **34**(2), 161–188 (1981)
27. Hair, J.F., Hult, G.T.M., Ringle, C.M., Sarstedt, M.: A Primer on Partial Least Squares Structural Equation Modeling (PLS-SEM). Sage, Thousand Oaks (2017)
28. Bravo, E.R., Santana, M., Rodon, J.: Information systems and performance: the role of technology, the task and the individual. Behav. Inf. Technol. **34**(3), 247–260 (2015)

Factors Affecting the Growth of the ICT Industry: The Case of Bhutan

Deepika Rai[1(✉)] and Sherah Kurnia[2]

[1] Department of IT and Telecom, Thimphu, Bhutan
deepikarais.ditt@gmail.com
[2] University of Melbourne, Melbourne, Australia
sherahk@unimelb.edu.au

Abstract. The ICT industry that consists of IT and IT- Enabled Services (ITES) components has been contributing significantly to the economy of many countries globally. Due to its importance, understanding factors affecting the growth of this industry is critical for developed and developing countries. Currently, there is still a limited understanding of relevant factors and their influence on the IT/ITES industry growth in developing countries. Bhutan, in particular, is a small developing country that is striving to build this industry to diversify its economy. This study is the first study that explores factors affecting the growth of the IT/ITES industry in Bhutan. Qualitative research involving different stakeholders is employed to gain an understanding on factors facilitating and inhibiting the growth. The study findings indicate that Human Resources, Policy, Infrastructure, Foreign Direct Investment (FDI) and Culture are particularly crucial for Bhutan's context. Due to the uniqueness of Bhutan, this study helps drive the development of the industry and enhance the current understanding in this area particularly in the context of developing countries.

Keywords: IT/ITES industry · ICT industry · Developing countries · Bhutan

1 Introduction

Information and Communication Technology (ICT) has revolutionized the global economy by enabling cross border businesses [1]. The ICT industry comprises of two components: Information Technology (IT) and Information Technology-Enabled Services (ITES). The IT component encompasses IT application and engineering while the ITES component includes services offered through electronic means [2]. The Gartner's forecast for 2016 IT spending is projected to be US$3.54 trillion, reflecting a huge market for the ICT industry [3]. This industry contributes significantly to a country's economy and creates valuable employment. A study by UNCTAD in 2008 shows that in developing countries, the service sector inclusive of IT/ITES accounted for 51% of gross domestic product (GDP) and 35% of employment [4]. Beside increasing employment and boosting GDP, the ICT industry has a ripple effect on the development of the country through the need for efficient ICT infrastructure, transport infrastructure, educational infrastructure and enabling policy reforms. To emphasize

© IFIP International Federation for Information Processing 2017
Published by Springer International Publishing AG 2017. All Rights Reserved
J. Choudrie et al. (Eds.): ICT4D 2017, IFIP AICT 504, pp. 728–739, 2017.
DOI: 10.1007/978-3-319-59111-7_59

the two important components of the ICT industry, the term IT/ITES industry is explicitly used in the remainder of the paper.

The existing literature identifies several factors affecting IT/ITES industry growth in both developed and developing countries. However, most of them are focused on developed countries such as Ireland, Israel or Singapore where the industry is well established or favorable factors exist in promoting the industry development. Although a few studies focus on developing countries (e.g. India, Philippines and Thailand) but those countries have different contextual factors. In addition, though most studies have adopted qualitative study, they differ in depth and data collection methods. The majority relied on secondary resources and only a handful of studies involved empirical data. Hence, considering the uniqueness of Bhutan as a country and the fact that the IT/ITES industry in Bhutan is still at the early stage of growth, it is necessary to understand the contextual condition of Bhutan and identify relevant key factors affecting the development of the industry. It would be impractical to assume that critical factors identified in other studies will also be applicable in Bhutan. The importance of considering contextual differences in understanding a particular phenomenon has been well recognized in the literature [5, 6].

Therefore, this research aims to explore factors affecting the growth of the IT/ITES industry from the perspective of key stakeholder groups. The following questions are addressed in this study:

What are the key factors affecting the growth of the IT/ITES industry in Bhutan?
How do these factors affect the growth of the IT/ITES industry in Bhutan?

A qualitative research involving interviews with major industry stakeholders is adopted as a research method to enable a detailed investigation of the industry from all perspectives. In addition, multiple secondary resources are also used to enrich the understanding obtained from the interviews. The study findings indicate that Human Resources, Policy, Infrastructure, FDI and Culture play a crucial role in the growth of Bhutan's IT/ITES industry. Currently, the first four factors in Bhutan are at a formative state and have impeded the growth of the industry. By contrast, Culture appears to be conducive for the growth of the IT/ITES industry in Bhutan. We identify a number of issues pertaining to Culture, but they appear to be relatively easy to address. Based on the findings, a number of recommendations are proposed to facilitate the growth of the IT/ITES industry in Bhutan.

The study contributes to both researchers and practitioners. For researchers, the study synthesizes useful factors affecting the growth of the IT/ITES industry. The study also enriches the existing studies by conducting an in depth qualitative study in a unique context. For practitioners, the study reflects the criticality of collaboration among stakeholders and strategic implementation and customization of each factor for successful growth of the industry. This paper is structured as follows. First, it presents the background, the opportunity of the global IT/ITES industry, the motivation for conducting this study, followed by a literature review. Then an overview of current state of the industry in Bhutan is presented. The research methodology is then briefly outlined, followed by the research findings and discussion. Finally, we conclude the paper by outlining implications, study limitations and future research work.

2   Literature Synthesis of Factors Affecting the IT/ITES Industry Growth

The IT/ITES industry has a tremendous potential to contribute to a country's GDP, employment generation and overall development. However, different countries face diverse challenges to grow the industry. There are also various factors that drive the development of this industry differently across countries [1, 7, 8]. To identify possible factors affecting the growth of the IT/ITES industry, existing studies related to development of IT/ITES industry were examined. We searched for studies using Google scholar and various online databases such as Computer and Applied Sciences Complete (EBSCO), Engineering Village and Web of Science (ISI). The keywords used for the searches include 'factors affecting IT/ITES industry development' and 'factors impacting ICT industry growth'.

There were plethora of papers related to IT/ITES industry but we only selected papers that were related to factors affecting the IT/ITES industry growth. Although the literature reviewed is not extensive, it is adequate to provide an overview of existing studies on this subject. The synthesis of factors affecting the growth of the IT/ITES industry identified from our literature analysis is presented below with brief explanations.

Human Resources. This industry is driven by human capital as a key component for production of knowledge or ideas [10, 11]. For example, previous studies indicate that the IT/ITES industry in India advanced rapidly because of the availability of a large, well educated, high quality, English speaking workforce [1, 9, 10]. Similarly, the study by Carayannis and Sagi [7] highlights that one of the key factors contributing to the success of the IT/ITES industry is the possession of a highly-skilled worked force. Furthermore, Philippine's strength is in the ITES segment which is enabled by the availability of a large pool of highly-educated English speakers [11, 12]. Previous studies also indicate important role played by government in offering incentives such as education and training grants [7, 11] to build the human resources for this industry.

Foreign Direct Investment (FDI). The presence of FDI in a country adds value to its IT/ITES industry growth [16] and offers a "demonstration effect" to the host countries [9, 13, 15]. FDI brings in superior technologies, expertise, money, and ideas which developing countries generally lack. Hence, this is believed to be the largest type of equity flow in developing countries [12, 17]. Thus, many developing countries depend on FDI to sustain their economic growth [17]. Another benefit of FDI is that it enables local businesses to compete or take part in the global market [17].

Infrastructure is broadly divided into ICT infrastructure and Technology Park infrastructure.

ICT infrastructure. An efficient ICT infrastructure is essential for facilitating and supporting IT/ITES industry growth [5, 12, 14]. For instance, Singapore's success in attracting multinational companies (MNC) is because of the high investment in creating efficient infrastructure [18]. Cost of ICT infrastructure including cost of internet access is another crucial element affecting the IT/ITES industry growth [7]. Higher cost impedes adoption of ICT in a country, while reliable ICT infrastructure attracts FDI [17]. India's low infrastructure cost is attractive and has also enabled the rapid growth of entrepreneurs [9]. Usually ICT infrastructure is either deregulated or privatized for maintaining service efficiency and low access cost as in the Philippines, Singapore and Ireland cases [14, 18, 19].

Technology Park. The technology park can promote knowledge transfer for developing and marketing high-technology products. It also facilitates promotion and commercialization of products [7, 8]. A study by Harbi et al. [8] indicates that such parks attract and defuse the need to have proximity/location attractiveness. India established special economic zones equivalent to technology parks to facilitate rapid growth of its IT/ITES industry, increase exports and counter the infrastructure issue [21]. Thailand established software parks to accelerate the development of its software industry [5, 9, 20]. Technology parks played a crucial role for the industry growth in the Philippines by attracting manpower, FDI and local investment [11, 12].

Policy. Policies such as fiscal incentives that includes tax advantage, subsidy and regulatory environment encourage the growth of the IT/ITES industry [5, 7, 11]. Policy can be used to attract FDI to establish subsidiary companies, increase FDI production and encourage collaborations with local firms [11]. Policy should also consider the local conditions such as protection and support for local firms' growth [7]. Countries such as the Philippines, Korea, Japan, Taiwan and India give preferential treatment to local firms' development while promoting FDI [7, 12]. Furthermore, policy should promote entrepreneurial culture and encourage local firms to internationalize [11, 19]. Finally, strong coordination among various stakeholders is required to ensure policy effectiveness [19].

Culture. Culture in this study refers to bureaucracy and work ethics. Culture plays a role in ensuring "what and how things get done" [20]. High level of bureaucracy affects the efficiency, flexibility and innovativeness for the industry growth as was the case of Thailand [5]. However, India has bureaucratic structure with a disciplined approach to work [9] but in addition India also possesses work culture that is similar to western culture where majority of the IT/ITES businesses emanates [1]. The study by Trauth [20] states that global investments introduce global culture such as high standard work ethics to the workplace that enhances the development of domestic industry in a country.

Geographic Location. Country location affects the direction of the trade [14] such as Poland and Ireland are strategically located near other regions with a rapid growth in ICT and have experienced significant business benefits [7]. However, the study by Heeks [11] argued that location relates to export only and do not impact industry growth focused on IT products and services [15]. Dedrick and Kraemer [17] also indicates that countries with favorable geographic location have an advantage for a successful hardware industry as in the case of Thailand's successful hardware industry. Furthermore, in the case of India, location did not affect the industry growth, but rather the difference in time and distance offered an advantage [1, 9]. This factor, however, is compensated with the advent of technology parks that facilitates access to markets and counter the infrastructure issues [21].

Domestic IT use. An increase in domestic IT use most likely increases investment in the IT/ITES industry and promotion of the local IT industry [15, 18]. However, in Thailand, domestic IT consumption was less yet the industry was booming [18]. Thus not a significant relation seems to be there between domestic IT use and the success of the industry [16, 18]. Therefore, this factor is not relevant if a country is focused on external market or if the local market is small [16–18]. For instance, despite low domestic IT use, India has a fast growing IT industry [14, 16] and it is the small market size and low profitability that forced entrepreneurs to focus on export activities [9].

Economic Development. A country's level of economic development determines the size of the local IT/ITES market and the quality of infrastructure [17]. The greater the economic development, the greater the quality of infrastructure in supporting the growth and use of IT [18]. The pace of economic development and technical capabilities contributes to the success of the IT/ITES industry [1]. However, the study by Dedrick and Kraemer [17] states that this factor is affected by the country's policies and is thus closely related to government policies.

Research and Development (R&D). A correlation may exist between industry attractiveness and R&D initiatives [7]. However, Harbi et al. [8] argue that R&D activities do not determine the success of the IT/ITES industry but it promotes innovation in the industry. However, the study by Bhattacharjee and Chakrabarti [10] noted that, recently there have been increasing investments in R&D in India that contribute to the growth of the IT/ITES industry.

Access to finance. Access to finance is important where the focus is on supporting startups, innovation, entrepreneurship and for maintaining growth of existing firms necessary for IT industry development [1, 8, 12, 15]. Further, this factor is linked with IT industry ranking [15] which contributes to branding of the industry in specific countries.

Political stability. In developing countries, politics influence transition to an information society [17]. A country's political stability influences private sector decisions, especially whether to invest in setting up IT/ITES businesses [5]. A study by Dedrick and Kraemer [17] considers the IT/ITES industry to be a high risk business and political stability represents trust to investors [13].

IT Export, Sale and Production. The success of the IT/ITES industry is measured by the ability to produce and export technology related products [18]. This factor also imposes limitations to countries which enforce protectionism, competition and lack of support for exporting products [17]. Furthermore, an export strategy is expensive and only viable for larger global companies [17].

3   Current State of the IT/ITES Industry in Bhutan

Bhutan is a small country positioned between China and India, with a population of 757,042. Bhutan connected to the global information and communication technology (ICT) only in 1999 and thereafter prioritized ICT. The prioritization of ICT is also to diversify and create a sustainable economic development which is currently dependent largely on hydropower and tourism. Furthermore, Bhutan's late entry is believed to give the advantage of being able to learn from other countries, and leapfrog to enter into global IT/ITES business within a short period of time. However, according to the study by Infocomm Development Authority (IDA), Bhutan's IT/ITES industry ecosystem is "loosely defined" with lack of clarity about what comprises this industry which has resulted in slow growth of this industry [22]. The industry is dominated with retail in computer products with minimal usage of domestic skills. Significant amounts of work are also outsourced to companies outside the country and local companies leverage overseas skills with very limited usage of local resources and competency [22].

Government implemented numerous initiatives that enabled the development of the IT/ITES industry. For example, ICT infrastructures specifically telecommunication and internet access were promptly established. As of 2015, the mobile penetration has reached 87% and 62% internet penetration [23]. E-government services were introduced and ICT literacy and adoption programs were conducted across the country to all level of the society. Further, to enhance the entrepreneurship culture, an incubation center was established in technology park [24] beside few other agencies providing support to entrepreneurs. Several policy reforms were also made to create an enabling environment for the IT/ITES industry. In 2008, Bhutan initiated a private sector development (PSD) project funded by the World Bank which focused on a holistic approach to development of the IT/ITES industry [24]. Through the project, a technology park was built, skills development initiatives were undertaken with international and local firms and financial environment reforms were also undertaken [24]. As of 2014, approximately three FDI firms have established business in the technology park and lately there has been an increase in the establishment of service focused small domestic IT/ITES firms.

4   Methodology

This study aims to explore key factors affecting the IT/ITES industry growth in Bhutan from the perspective of multiple stakeholder groups. Because of the exploratory nature of the study, qualitative research method is considered to be the most appropriate for this study since it enables in depth investigation of the phenomenon of interest [25]. The unit of analysis for the study is each key stakeholder group. The stakeholder groups comprises of Government, IT/ITES Consultants, Private Sector and Telecom Operators.

Data collection involved interviews as a primary source, along with multiple secondary sources including government reports, industry reports and news clippings. The main instrument was semi-structured open-ended questions. The interview questions were developed based on the research questions for the study. Interviews were non-directive allowing freedom and flexibility to respond. Each interview took approximately one hour. For data analysis, the transcribed interviews were analyzed using qualitative techniques as suggested by a number of qualitative research methodologists [25, 26]. Open coding was first conducted to identify the key themes relevant for answering the research questions, followed by axial coding to establish relationships between the themes identified. Selective coding was finally conducted for additional evidence to support the key themes.

Based on Yin [26] and Neuman [25], construct validity in this study is addressed through the use of multiple sources of evidence, a comprehensive review of relevant literature, and the use of case study repository to establish a chain of evidence. To maximize external and internal validity, a rigorous data collection procedure and systematic data analyses were performed. Reliability is ensured through the development of appropriate interview protocol and pilot test of the questions with relevant practitioners to assess the clarity of the questions and identify errors and possible biases [26].

5 Findings and Discussion

The analysis of the interview data indicates that Human Resources, Infrastructure, Policy, FDI and Culture are considered to be the most notable factors affecting the industry growth in Bhutan. Country's Accessibility and Cost of Operation were two additional factors identified to be important for Bhutan's IT/ITES Industry growth. The two additional factors identified are likely due to the geographical position of the country and higher dependency on import of raw materials. Therefore, as compared to the previous studies, there are added challenges for Bhutan which were not encountered by other countries studied in the past. All these factors were then further assessed to explore how they affect the IT/ITES industry growth in Bhutan. Based on the analysis, a number of recommendations are proposed to address those important factors to contribute to the industry growth. The new factors that have impeded the industry growth, however, are still challenging to address.

5.1 Culture

Focus on enhancement of work ethics
The finding related to Culture indicates that Culture is conducive for the industry growth. The reasons cited by stakeholders on their beliefs are Bhutan does not have a difficult bureaucratic system and work ethics is closely related with a reward system. Stakeholders also felt that in comparison with the international industry standards, Bhutan still needs to improve on the work ethics as people in Bhutan are laid back and non-competitive. They rationalized that this might be due to local business not having to follow strict corporate disciplines. All participants believe that work ethics is directly related to remuneration and motivation and that additional training and orientation within the corporate culture can address the issue of work culture. In addition, the private sector also plays a crucial role in attracting people to this industry and improving work ethics. The literature suggest, financial incentives, professional development and career progression can attract people to the industry and improve works ethics [10, 20].

5.2 Human Resources

Building skilled Human Resources
Based on the finding, Bhutan lacks skills in the IT segment which has impacted the industry growth. The main reason cited for skills shortage in IT segment was due to

mismatch in university curriculum and market needs. As a strategy by Singapore on building its talent pool, necessary IT curriculum were embedded within the school systems itself [19]. In countries like India, Ireland, Poland and the Philippines, government collaborated with private sector and universities to address the issue of mismatch in university curriculum and market needs as well as provided grants for skills development [1, 7, 12, 13, 20]. Therefore, Bhutan could take a similar path by introducing IT curriculum in the education system and establishing linkages among government, academia and industry to build skilled human resources that meet the industry demand.

Creating opportunities and platform for IT/ITES professionals
An interesting observation from the study is that there is lack of opportunities and platform for professionals in this area to develop their skills. One of the example cited was, generally the domestic firms subcontract their IT projects to firms outside Bhutan. This might be the result of uncertainty within the industry and inability of both government and the private sector to foresee business opportunities in this industry which may be dissuading stakeholders from creating opportunities and platform for this industry [22]. Therefore, firms consider quick gains utilizing cheaper resources from outside. Further, absence of opportunity was also referred to dearth of environment for innovation and entrepreneurship in the country. Although Bhutan has established incubation facilities as a platform to promote entrepreneurship [24], but there has been little uptake. This might be due to absence of financial support for entrepreneurs as access to capital is necessary to promote entrepreneurship, innovations and to maintain the growth of existing firms [8, 12, 16]. Hence, effort towards creating an enabling platform and opportunities for professionals in this industry is essential to build the skilled human resources.

5.3   FDI

Creating enabling environment for FDI
Majority of the stakeholder groups perceived that Bhutan lacks an enabling environment to attract FDI despite of having enabling polices supporting FDI. Study participants cited that it is lack of coordination in policy implementation which is impeding attractiveness. Further, consistent support and examination of FDI's health, to check if FDI is facing any issues, is missing in Bhutan. In addition, there has been limited association between FDI and local companies thereby creating an unhealthy environment. Therefore, as stated in the study by Mitra [13], strategic alliances between local and FDI companies are necessary to expand the IT/ITES industry. Furthermore, policies should be used as a tool for sharing the risk with FDI, for example fiscal incentives to make the cost of operation competitive for FDI companies. The government also has a crucial role in policy implementation to ensure the stated FDI benefits are delivered to maintain the attractive environment for FDI.

5.4   Infrastructure

Improving ICT infrastructure to meet the industry standards

Majority of stakeholder groups raised reliability, redundancy and cost of ICT infrastructure as the foremost issues that was also highlighted in several government reports [22, 24]. By contrast, Singapore's attractiveness stems from having an efficient ICT infrastructure [19]. Most of the literature considers the efficiency and cost of ICT infrastructure to be crucial for attractiveness [1, 5, 7, 18]. Study participants suggest that introduction of a third international gateway, coming via a completely different international route, will resolve the issue of reliability and redundancy. Alternatively, in order to provide uninterrupted services, Indian companies set up multiple business sites within and outside India [1]. So until the third gateway is installed, Bhutan could perhaps be positioned as business continuity planning (BCP) location for FDI or to address the redundancy issue within, the Bhutan's industry could consider other countries as a BCP for their business.

The prohibitive cost of bandwidth (internet) has been another challenge for Bhutan. Study participants proposed introducing a third telecom operator or subsidy from government to make access affordable. However, subsidy is not a sustainable strategy and as previous studies have reflected deregulation and privatization of the state-owned telecom operator as a successful strategy in reducing cost and improving the quality of service [1, 19, 20]. Thus, deregulating and privatizing Bhutan's stated-owned telecom operator might provide competition, increase quality and reduce cost.

Leveraging Technology Park to foster the industry growth

The technology park is increasingly valued in creating an overall ecosystem and replaces unreliable public infrastructure [2, 7, 8]. However, the study participant's contend that technology park in Bhutan has little to no impact on the industry growth as well as slow in creating a fully operational park. This is perhaps due to absence of collaboration between the FDI and domestic firms because the technology park is more focused towards attracting FDI. On the contrary, countries such as India, Singapore and Taiwan established technology parks with an export-oriented focus [21] irrespective of domestic or FDI firms. In both India and Thailand, technology parks were also established to promote rapid growth in the IT/ITES industry [1, 5]. Similarly, Bhutan could take a balance approach by encouraging both FDI and domestic firms to leverage the technology park. This can be possible through offering a tailored economically suitable package for domestic firms to locate at technology park.

5.5   Policy

Policies need to facilitate growth of domestic firms

The finding of this study indicates policies are more focused on attracting FDI and neglected the growth of local IT/ITES firms. This is in contrast with the literature, which suggests that any nations striving to build this industry had policies and strategies that always balanced the development of both local and FDI companies because local companies are considered a long term investment for sustainability [12, 17, 20]. For example, Japanese government ensured protection and support for the domestic market to compete globally and Korean government's policy gave preferential treatment to local companies [17]. Furthermore, literature claims that policy should be developed based on the country's environment [5, 17]. This is clearly lacking in Bhutan's case. Therefore, Bhutan needs to realign the policies to balance the growth of the industry through creation of enabling business environment for both FDI and domestic firms. The collaboration between private sector and government also needs to be strengthened. This can be achieved through strengthening the national IT association as identified in previous studies [1, 2, 22].

Encouraging stakeholder collaboration for effective policy implementation
The government has introduced various policies to enable the development of the IT/ITES industry. Such policies create attractiveness for the IT/ITES industry as supported by previous studies. Such policies can also address the cost of operation factor [1, 5, 7, 18]. However, despite creating such an enabling environment, the industry growth has still not been impressive as expected. This indicates the need for ensuring the successful implementation of such policies. The literature claims that the efficiency of government in administration and coordination of policy is one of the reasons for Singapore's success in growing its industry. Singapore has also established a special agency to overcome compartmentalization of government effort [19]. Similarly Bhutan needs to consider eliminating coordination issues through taking Singapore's path or through development of application systems to integrate all the stakeholders for policy implementation thus ensuring collaboration.

5.6   Accessibility to the Country

This has been identified as a factor that can impact the growth of the industry in Bhutan. It is a new factor that has not been mentioned in previous studies. The reason could likely be due to the geographical position of the country since Bhutan is a landlocked and mountainous country with limited accessibility. The national airlines are only allowed to fly in and out of the country, which are also limited in numbers and frequency. Bhutan has only one international airport providing air connectivity to five countries. The airport allows only the country's airline to operate and thus have two airline companies. By surface transport there is exit to India only. The challenge faced by this industry is travel time taken to and from Bhutan. The stakeholder group cited that for this industry, travelling to the business locations has to be easy with minimal turnaround time to reach the destination. This is by far a challenge that stakeholder groups felt is difficult to address and to an extent a factor that is deterring FDI investment into the country.

5.7   Cost of Operation

The participants cited cost of general operation to be a factor that can impact the growth of the industry. This factor again was not mentioned in previous studies likely due to the kind of countries that were studied. Bhutan is different with added challenges like the cost of operation which is high as compared to the region with similar or better facilities and service than Bhutan. Bhutan mostly imports raw materials and products for consumption therefore, the high cost can also be due to import of raw materials for all the facilities and services offered. The cost of operation excludes cost of internet access and cost of operation at the technology park. The cost of operation is related with cost of living, cost of hiring, cost of travel and real estate cost. Generally, the cost of operation in Bhutan is extremely high comparable with metropolitan cities in India and region but with less facilities and choices. Thus, the cost of operation was identified by stakeholder groups as a factor that is positioning Bhutan as an unattractive business location for this industry and is still challenging to address.

6 Conclusion and Implications

This study provides a useful synthesis of factors affecting the growth of the IT/ITES industry. It is also a first study conducted in the context of Bhutan, employing a qualitative approach. Two additional factors, Country's Accessibility and Cost of Operation have been identified for Bhutan's context, which are likely to be important factors for countries similar to Bhutan. As indicated in this study, all the factors identified as key influential factors, though have been consistent with previous studies, the state and effect of each factor differs slightly across contexts. For example, for Thailand, Policy did not have impact on the success of the IT industry [18], whereas for Bhutan, Policy seems to play a crucial role in the growth of the industry.

For researchers, the study synthesizes useful factors affecting the growth of the IT/ITES industry. The study also enriches the existing studies by conducting an in depth qualitative study in a unique context that was not explored in earlier studies. This study also reaffirms previous studies' recommendation that one size fit all is not possible for understanding factors affecting the development of IT/ITES industry in different countries [5, 17]. The applicability and influence of each factor varies from country to country. For practitioners, the study reflects the criticality of strategic implementation of each factor for successful growth of the industry. The study also presents the need for strategic collaboration and customization of the factors according to the environment of the country. This study is also an eye-opener in showcasing the need for strategic alliance among the government, private sector and academia.

However, there are limitations to this study due to time and resource constraints. This study is only a preliminary study with limitation in total number of participants and the number of stakeholder groups. For instance, the study could also include consumer stakeholder group. Nevertheless, the preliminary understanding obtained from this study is valuable to recognize the IT/ITES industry in Bhutan and its development. Further, the two new factors identified in this study have set context for further study to analyze if the identified factors are important for the industry growth as these factors has not been explicitly studied in detail for other countries. For Bhutan, this study has also laid a path for future in depth study in this area.

References

1. Joshi, K., Mudigonda, S.: An analysis of India's future attractiveness as an offshore destination for IT and IT-enabled services. J. Inf. Technol. **23**(1), 21–227 (2008)

2. Sudan, R., Ayers, S.: The Global Opportunity in IT-Based Services. ..., World Bank [Internet] (2010). https://observatorio.iti.upv.es/media/managed_files/2009/07/01/The_Global_Opportunity_in_IT-Based_Services.pdf. Accessed 9 Apr 2015
3. Gartner Says Worldwide IT Spending is Forecast to Grow 0.6 Percent in 2016 [Internet] (2016). http://www.gartner.com/newsroom/id/3186517. Accessed 3 Feb 2016
4. (United Nations). Globalization For Development : The International Trade Perspective, New York (2008)
5. Techatassanasoontorn, A.A., Huang, H., Trauth, E.M., Juntiwasarakij, S.: Analyzing ICT and development. J. Global Inf. Manage. 19(1), 1–29 (2011)
6. Kurnia, S., Karnali, R.J., Rahim, M.M.: A qualitative study of business-to-business electronic commerce adoption within the Indonesian grocery industry: a multi-theory perspective. Inf. Manage. 52(4), 518–536 (2015)
7. Carayannis, E.G., Sagi, J.: Exploiting opportunities of the new economy: developing nations in support of the ICT industry. Technovation 22(8), 517–524 (2002)
8. Harbi, S., Amamou, M., Anderson, A.R.: Establishing high-tech industry: The Tunisian ICT experience. Technovation 29(1), 465–480 (2009)
9. Heeks, R.: Using competitive advantage theory to analyze IT sectors in developing countries: a software industry case analysis. Inf. Technol. Int. Dev. 3(3), 5–34 (2006)
10. Bhattacharjee, S., Chakrabarti, D.: Investigating India's competitive edge in the IT-ITeS sector. IIMB Manage. Rev. 27(1), 19–34 (2015)
11. Chebolu, R.M.: A critical perspective of information technology (IT) industry growth in India. ANVESHAK Int. J. Manage. 3(1), 152–160 (2014)
12. Abara, A.C., Heo, Y.: Resilience and recovery: The Philippine IT-BPO industry during the global crisis. Int. Area Stud. Rev. 16(2), 160–183 (2013)
13. Mitra, R.M.: BPO Sector Growth and Inclusive Development in the Philippines, World Bank Group (2011). http://documents.worldbank.org/curated/en/715341468295535070/pdf/660930WP0P122100B0BPO0Sector0Growth.pdf. Accessed 10 March 2015
14. Heeks, R., Nicholson, B.: Software export success factors and strategies in "Follower" Nations. Compet. Change 8(3), 267–303 (2004)
15. Ein-dor, P., Myers, M.D., Raman, K.S.: Information technology in three small developed countries. J. Manage. Inf. Syst. 13(4), 61–89 (1997)
16. Ein-Dor, P., Myers, M.D., Raman, K.S.: IT industry development and the knowledge economy: a four country study. J. Global Inf. Manage. 12(4), 23–49 (2004)
17. Dedrick, J., Kraemer, K.L.: National technology policy and computer production in Asia pacific countries. Inf. Soc. 11(1), 29–58 (1995)
18. Tan, F.B., Leewongcharoen, K.: Factors contributing to IT industry success in developing countries: the case of Thailand. Inf. Technol. Dev. 11(2), 161–194 (2005)
19. Poh-Kam, W.: Leveraging the global information revolution for economic development: Singapore's evolving information industry strategy. Inf. Syst. Res. 9(4), 323–341 (1998)
20. Trauth, E.M.: The Culture of An Infromation Economy. Kluwer Academic Publishers, Dordrecht (2000)
21. Vaidyanathan, G.: Technology parks in a developing country: the case of India. J. Technol. Transf. 33(3), 285–299 (2008)
22. IDA International Pte Ltd. Recommendations for Bhutan ICT Industry Development (2012)
23. Bhutan Infocomm and Media Authority. Annual Report 2015 (2015)
24. World Bank. Implementation Completion and Results Report (2013)
25. Neuman, W.: Social Research Methods Qualitative and Quantitative Approaches. Allyn & Bacon, Boston (2011)
26. Yin, R.K.: Qualitative Research from Start to Finish. The Guildford Press, New York (2016)

The Impact of Facebook on the Quality of Life of Senior Citizens in Cape Town

Denaneer Rylands and Jean-Paul Van Belle[✉]

Department of Information Systems, University of Cape Town,
Rondebosch, South Africa
Dee.Rylands@gmail.com, Jean-Paul.VanBelle@uct.ac.za

Abstract. Social Networking Sites (SNSs), such as Facebook, can be used to maintain social connectedness especially with friends and family, irrespective of geographical distances or physical impairments. This is particularly beneficial for older people who are more prone to social exclusion. This paper investigates the impact that the use of Facebook has on the quality of life (QOL) of senior citizens living in Cape Town. The study use a positivist approach with a conceptual model comprised of parts of Kleine's Choice Framework and CASP-19 as the theoretical lens for evaluation of how Facebook impacts the QOL of senior citizens in Cape Town. Results of an anonymous survey confirmed that respondents were light users of Facebook, using only a limited number of features. The research also revealed that the respondents used Facebook primarily to stay socially engaged with their friends and family which adds happiness to their lives and ultimately translates to an improved QOL. The results reinforced a causal relationship between Facebook use and the QOL of senior citizens in Cape Town.

Keywords: Social networking sites · Facebook · Senior citizens · Quality of life

1 Introduction

Research concerning the benefits of information and communication technologies (ICTs) for improving productivity and efficiency is pervasive. However, in terms of how ICTs are able to improve the general quality of life (QOL) of marginalised demographics such as senior citizens is still lacking [1]. The Sustainable Development Goals, as agreed by 193 United Nations member countries, specifically include the directive to "leave no one behind", emphasizing the predicament of neglected population groups such as the lesser abled, the poor and – the focus of this research – the aged. The increase in life expectancy, faced by many countries globally, highlights the important issue of how to maintain social relationships, particularly with friends and family, which is regarded as a critical factor for ageing well [2].

Although the use of SNSs, such as Facebook, is pervasive amongst young people, use by senior citizens is still lagging behind the younger demographic [3]. Research has revealed that lack of social contact as a result of living alone or of having limited social networks, could lead to social isolation and ultimately impact negatively on the health

© IFIP International Federation for Information Processing 2017
Published by Springer International Publishing AG 2017. All Rights Reserved
J. Choudrie et al. (Eds.): ICT4D 2017, IFIP AICT 504, pp. 740–752, 2017.
DOI: 10.1007/978-3-319-59111-7_60

of senior citizens. However, through the use of Facebook, senior citizens are able to remain socially connected irrespective of geographical distances or most physical impairments brought about by old age [4]. It possesses the ability to change people's lives, specifically for marginalised groups such as senior citizens whose levels of social engagement and social connections decrease due to retirement and loss of friends or partners [4]. It stands to reason that, with a growing ageing population increasingly making use of SNSs, understanding how the use of SNSs by senior citizens can positively impact their quality of life is of great value to society at large. But there is a shortage of research on how SNSs are able to improve social connectedness and support for the elderly [4, 5]. The purpose of this study was, therefore, to address the gap in research in understanding how the use of SNSs, Facebook in particular, impacts the QOL of senior citizens in Cape Town.

The main aim of this study was to analyse and evaluate the impact of SNSs on the QOL of senior citizens in Cape Town. The two research questions being addressed in this research paper are: Q1 "How do senior citizens in Cape Town use Facebook?" and Q2 "Does the use of Facebook impact the QOL of senior citizens in Cape Town?" Question Q1 will be explored with descriptive statistics. Question Q2 was explored both with descriptive and inferential statistics; the null hypothesis for question Q2 is H_0: The use of Facebook does not impact the QOL of senior citizens in Cape Town.

This research contributes insights to the body of knowledge on how ICTs such as SNS can be used to increase the quality of life of marginalised members of society, i.e. our senior citizens. More specifically, it investigates which aspects of the QOL are perceived as being impacted the most.

2   Concepts and Literature Review

2.1   The Social Media Landscape Today

The use of social media has become pervasive. From a global perspective, approximately two billion users of the internet are currently using SNSs with Facebook as the market leader, with 1.59 billion active monthly users [6]. From a local perspective, a quarter of all South Africans, approximately thirteen million people, now use Facebook [7].

2.2   Senior Citizens

Defining age can be difficult and complex due to its multi-dimensionality. Ageing can be conceptualised within the context of a four-dimensional model based on biological (looks), cognitive (interests), social (actions) and psychological (feelings) functional areas of self [8]. The aged can be referred to as the elderly, third age or seniors [9]. The increase in lifespan due to advances in health and medicine has sparked a global ageing phenomenon that has resulted in an energetic older population compared to a few decades ago, thereby questioning traditional definitions and boundaries. But, typically, chronological age has been used to define the elderly, predominantly for research on ageing and communication, as it is easy to measure [10]. The retirement age from 2008 to 2015 for men in South Africa averaged 60.3 with a high of sixty-five in 2008 and a low of sixty in 2009. For women, the retirement age remained unchanged at sixty in 2015 from sixty in 2014 [9]. Senior citizens are therefore defined as age sixty and older for the purpose of this study.

2.3 Senior Citizens and Technology Use

The use of ICT has changed the way people live today. It has become an essential component for living in an age of information where technology has become pervasive across all aspects of life [11, 12]. It has the ability to change people's lives by improving their level of independence, specifically marginalised groups such as senior citizens [1]. Due to improvements in the health sector resulting in an increase in life expectancy, the world is currently experiencing an unprecedented shift in demographic profile of an increasing ageing population [13]. Although technology can play a vital role in improving the lives of senior citizens, it could also exacerbate the problem of a digital divide between younger and older demographics; studies have revealed that older people tend to lag behind younger people with regards to ICT adoption [14].

Despite the rapid uptake of social media over the last decade, a gap in academia exists in understanding the convergence of online social media and older people [15]. Maintaining social relationships with friends and family that are meaningful has been factored as a vital component for ageing well [2]. While usage is pervasive amongst the younger population, usage by senior citizens is still lagging by a huge margin [3, 4]. The majority of research has focused on younger age groups such as teenagers and university students. Despite the increase in adoption rates of SNS's by senior citizens, not much is known yet regarding reasons and motivations for adoption and use within this age category [16–18]. Previous research suggests issues such as perceived lack of usefulness, ease of use as well as privacy and security concerns as key factors contributing to the slower adoption rates by senior citizens [16, 18]. Senior citizens are influenced by their social peers and members of their family, particularly their children and grandchildren who play the role of change agents in creating awareness and ultimately the use of the technology [19].

2.4 Benefits of Social Networking Sites for Senior Citizens

The benefit of improved social connectedness and support for senior citizens through the use of SNSs has been well documented. Senior citizens are able to maintain social connectivity irrespective of geographical distances or loss of physical mobility as a result of ageing [19]. The ability to feel socially included without leaving the comfort of their homes, promotes feelings of safety and autonomy [3]. Improved social connectedness assists in lower levels of loneliness and depression amongst senior citizens [10, 19]. Another key benefit highlighted by research is the improvement in intergenerational communication [15]. Communication between senior citizens and their children or grandchildren is often not reciprocal with more effort being placed on the part of senior citizens. SNSs strengthen this notion and change the flow of communication from asymmetrical to symmetrical [20].

2.5   Challenges Faced by Senior Citizens Using Social Networking Sites

Despite the surge in use of SNSs by senior citizens, significant barriers exist that prevent many seniors from using SNSs. Lack of access to the service can be an issue as older people often don't have access to either a computer or a broadband connection [10]. Lack of training was also cited as a barrier; although senior citizens in some cases are willing and able to make use of SNSs, they often lack the knowledge and support to do so [17]. Sensory impairment such as loss of vision as a result of old age can hinder the use of SNSs by senior citizens [2]. Another common barrier featured in the literature is that of poor interface design [21]. Design features such as font size and colour as well as content layout often do not take into account the physical limitations of older people. Older users often find the use of SNSs complex and difficult to navigate [21]. Concerns around security and privacy remains a major concern for senior citizens [14, 15].

2.6   Defining Quality of Life

QOL is a complex and multi-dimensional phenomenon and therefore should be viewed holistically [22] It is influenced at a macro-level within society as well as at an individual level, and it encompasses both objective and subjective dimensions [23]. QOL has been defined as an "individuals' perception of their position in life in the context of the culture and value systems in which they live and in relation to their goals, expectations, standards and concerns" [22, p. 1405].

Based on Brocks' theory of a good life [24], QOL can be measured in three different ways: (1) normative (2) preference satisfaction (3) subjective evaluation. The normative approach refers to the standard or norms that define a good life and is influenced by the core belief system of an individual. This approach is not subjective by nature but rather is based on societal norms and traditions of what constitutes a good life or QOL. Preference satisfaction as an approach to QOL has an economic undercurrent. It is based on the availability of material goods and the satisfaction obtained in the ability to acquire these goods, thereby improving QOL. The final approach, subjective evaluation, refers to each individual's subjective experience of QOL and is associated with the more traditional sense of subjective well-being [9].

Two other QOL approaches are the subjective and objective approaches. The subjective approach of QOL refers to each individual's evaluation and feelings of how they personally view whether they are content and happy with their life [25].

2.7   Quality of Life Instruments and Frameworks

There is no definitive model or instrument used to measure QOL. The instruments available can measure QOL based on global measures (global QOL), as well as health measures or health related QOL (HRQOL). The WHOQOL group's instrument is a multi-dimensional, 28-item global measure which include the domains of physical, psychological, level of independence, social relationships, environment and personal beliefs or spirituality [22]. The CASP-19 QOL instrument is a more recent measure of QOL focussing on old age [9]. It is comprised of 19 Likert-scaled questions based on four domains: control, autonomy, self-realisation and pleasure [9].

Given that none of the above focus on how information technology can impact QOL, we also explored Kleine's Choice Framework. The Framework which is rooted conceptually in Amartya Sen's capabilities approach, seeks to operationalise the capabilities approach [26]. According to Sen's capabilities approach, development centres on an individual's freedom of choice. An individual's "functionings" refers to things which individuals value doing or being, and "capabilities" refer to the functionings that are possible or viable for an individual to achieve. The Choice framework explains how an individual is able to achieve the outcomes they wish to achieve as a result of choices, resources, and social structures available to them, but it foregrounds the role which the use of IT can play in this dynamic [26]. We focussed on the agency factors of the Choice framework i.e. the individual resources which are potentially influenced or affected by the use of information technology i and the moderating role of demographic attributes such as gender and age.

2.8   Research Model

A conceptual model constructed in a similar study [1] to assess the impact of mobile phones on the QOL of the elderly was utilised. The model builds on a number of existing models and frameworks, namely, (1) Foley's internet adoption framework [27], (2) the CASP-19 quality of life measurement [9], and (3) Kleine's Choice Framework [26]. "Use" was measured in two different ways: through the use of features which represented how people use Facebook, and through functionality which represented what people use Facebook for.

The QOL construct is measured through two different lenses to obtain a richer overall perspective on QOL. As the CASP-19 measure is specifically based on old age, it was deemed fit to be utilised for this study. Additionally, questions based on the agency factors of Kleine's Choice Framework were used to measure the outcomes of the Choice Framework. This shows how Facebook as a technology enables people to increase their choices and freedoms to live the life they want to live, leading to improved outcomes such as easier communication, increased knowledge, better or more social relationships, increased mobility and more time and autonomy, which ultimately impacts QOL.

3 Research Methodology

A positivist research philosophy was adhered to for this study as existing frameworks were used to objectively measure the impact of Facebook on the QOL of senior citizens in Cape Town. The primary goal of this research is to establish and explain the causal relationship between Facebook and the QOL of senior citizens in Cape Town. Since the use of Facebook is expected to make only a marginal contribution to the actual overall QOL, a crucial methodological decision was taken to *not* measure Facebook use separate from overall QOL and then attempt to explain the variation in the latter statistically by means of the independent variable. Instead, the seniors were asked *directly* whether their use of Facebook was seen to impact the various aspects of QOL. The quantitative data was collected through an anonymous questionnaire.

The target population for this study was senior citizens in Cape Town who are able to read and write, use the SNS Facebook and who are sixty years and older. Due to time constraints, the use of convenience-based, non-probability sampling was deployed. To obtain a somewhat representative population sample, a stratified sampling approach was also followed, including willing participants from various retirement villages who agreed to participate in the study. This approach enabled the inclusion of both people living in retirement villages or homes as well as in their own residences or with their families or friends. Retirement villages in affluent areas were approached as well as retirement homes and care facilities in less affluent areas to further ensure a more representative sample. A total of fifty-nine valid responses (n = 59) were received after removal of incomplete and invalid responses.

4 Analysis and Results

The following section is an explanatory analysis and evaluation of the quantitative data collected using the survey instrument discussed earlier.

4.1 Demographic Analysis

For the question regarding gender, respondents were given the options of selecting male, female, prefer not to answer and other. Of the fifty-nine valid survey responses collected, twenty-one (36%) were male and thirty-eight (64%) were female. A Mann-Whitney U test was performed on this data to determine if QOL differs between males and females. The results indicate no significant statistical difference at $p < 0.05$ between males and females in terms of QOL with the exception of the material and time resource variable of the Choice QOL construct.

The mean age of respondents was 65.9 with a minimum age of sixty and a maximum age of one hundred. The majority of respondents' age was between sixty and sixty-three. A Mann-Whitney U test to determine if QOL differs between respondents aged below and above 70, indicates a statistically significant difference (Z adjusted = 2.126, p = 0.033 < 0.05) only with regards to the health resource construct.

Forty-four percent of respondents (44%) were fully retired. However, 32% of respondents indicated full-time employment and a further 14% part-time employment. This is also an expected result as the majority of respondents are in early old age, slowly transitioning into third age [28]. The results of the Mann-Whitney U test to determine if QOL differs between respondents who were retired versus respondents who worked, reveal statistical significance at p < 0.05 for the Autonomy and Pleasure CASP-19 QOL constituent construct as well as the CASP-19 QOL construct as a whole. With regards to the Choice QOL construct, all the constituent constructs are significant with the exception of the material, social and informational resources. The Choice QOL construct as a whole, however, reveals a statistical significant difference.

4.2   Research Question Q1: How Facebook Is Used

Previous research conducted, identified children and family as an influential factor specifically in relation to senior citizens' adoption of ICT [12]. Respondents were therefore asked who introduced them to Facebook. The majority of respondents, thirty-four respondents (58%), indicated that family was the main factor influencing the adoption of Facebook which is aligned to the studies mentioned above.

Respondents were also asked how long they were using Facebook and, on average, how much time they spent on Facebook. Of the fifty-nine valid responses received, only fifty-seven respondents answered the question regarding how long they were using Facebook which resulted in a mean value of 4.9 years. In terms of time spent on Facebook, the majority of respondents (nineteen) spent thirty minutes to one hour a day on Facebook, followed by fifteen respondents who spent less than thirty minutes a day on Facebook. Twelve only checked once or a few times a week whereas eight respondents spent more than an hour each day. The results of the Mann-Whitney U test to determine if QOL differs between respondents who spent less than once a week on Facebook versus respondents who spent more than or equal to once a week on Facebook, reveal statistical significance at p < 0.05 for the Pleasure, Self-realisation and CASP-19 QOL constituent construct as well as the CASP-19 QOL as a whole. With regards to the Choice QOL construct, all the constituent constructs are significant with the exception of the cultural resources.

The proposed research model looks at Facebook use as an independent variable measured in two different ways, through the use of features which represents what people use on Facebook, and functionality which represents how people used Facebook. The results support previous research on social media use by the elderly, indicating that social media is used primarily to stay connected with friends and family and not to create new ties or relationships [4]. Thirty-one respondents indicated that they never use Facebook to meet new people; only two respondents indicated that they use Facebook to meet new people 'a lot of the time' (Fig. 1).

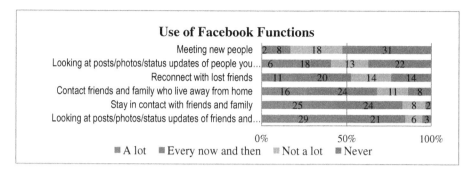

Fig. 1. Use of Facebook functions

In terms of features used on Facebook, the results indicate that the respondents used only a limited set of features such as the Like button, commenting on other Facebook users' activities, birthday notifications, messaging people, writing posts on a wall and uploading pictures. Features such as updating security and privacy settings, profile settings and clicking on advertisements were used in a very limited capacity. Further statistical tests including reliability and validity tests were performed on this construct which is discussed in a later section of the document (Fig. 2).

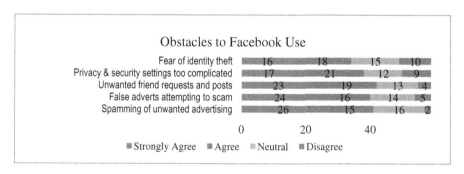

Fig. 2. Obstacles to using Facebook

Questions regarding ten possible obstacles to using Facebook were also asked. Only five were seen as significant. Surprisingly, the cost of using Facebook and design and layout was not seen as a major obstacle as noted in previous studies. The majority of respondents were in agreement that spamming, false advertising and complicated privacy and security settings were seen as obstacles to using Facebook which is aligned to previous studies (Fig. 2) [3, 16].

4.3   Research Question Q2: Descriptive Analysis of Quality of Life Impacts

Respondents were asked to answer nineteen questions based on the CASP-19 QOL instrument but these questions were modified by linking the (perceived) impact of each QOL item to their Facebook use (Fig. 3).

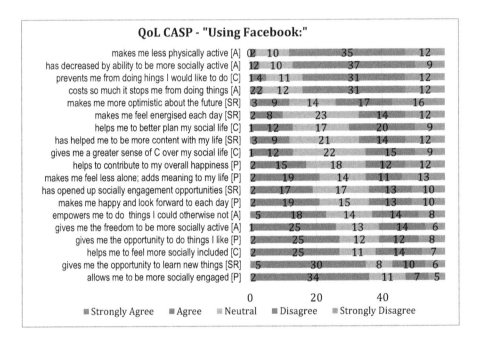

Fig. 3. Quality of Life measure – CASP-19

Twenty-one questions were based on the *relevant* agency factors of Kleine's Choice Framework but also phrased to measure how Facebook as a technology enabled the participants to increase their resources, choices and freedoms available to them in life thereby impacting their QOL (Fig. 4).

What is highly surprising is that only *two* CASP-19 measures were perceived to be positively influenced by the use of Facebook: allowing the seniors to be more socially engaged with friends and family, and giving them the opportunity of learning new things. All other measures had an average rating which was statistically not different from "Neutral" or fell into the "Disagree" range.

By sharp contrast, many of the findings relating to how the use of Facebook results in perceived increases in the choices and agency freedom are much more significant. The respondents perceived, on average, that Facebook allowed them to increase their educational resources, health resources (by finding out about health issues), social resources (connect better with existing friends and family; find new friends), saved time and allowed them to tap into the cultural and newsworthy happenings and events in

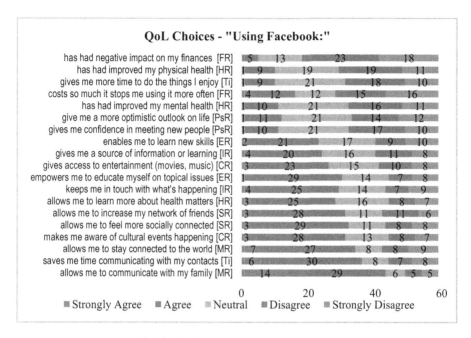

Fig. 4. Quality of Life measure – Choice

their local community as well as the global world. It did not appear to have an impact on their financial or psychological resources.

4.4 Research Question Q2: Reliability and Correlation Analysis

Reliability analysis was conducted on the dependent and independent constructs and all Cronbach alpha coefficients of the retained constructs were well above 0.70.

The distribution-free non-parametric Spearman Rank Order Correlation test was used to analyse the data. The Facebook features generally show a significant, negative but relatively small correlation with both the CASP-19 and Choice QOL variables. The Facebook functionality, however, shows a statistically positive moderate to strong correlation with both the CASP-19 and Choice QOL variables.

Multiple regression analysis was conducted to test the null hypothesis that the use of Facebook does not impact the QOL of senior citizens in Cape Town. Two models were run, first with the CASP-19 QOL construct as the dependent variable and then with the Choice QOL dependent variable. The results for the first model revealed that the independent variable Facebook functionality is statistically highly significant at predicting QOL because of the low p-value of 0.000079 (<0.001). The same is not true for the independent variable Facebook features with a p-value of 0.0629 (>0.05). The results for the second model revealed that both the independent variables Facebook functionality and features are significant at predicting QOL because of the low p-value's (<0.05). The results revealed a definite causal relationship between Facebook use and the QOL of senior citizens in Cape Town, thereby rejecting the null hypothesis.

5   Findings and Implications

Results of the data analysed confirms that a strong relationship exists between the use of Facebook and the QOL for senior citizens living in Cape Town. The researcher is therefore able to reject the null hypothesis that there is no relationship between Facebook use and the QOL of senior citizens in Cape Town. The objective of this research was to determine (1) how do senior citizens in Cape Town use Facebook, (2) what do senior citizens in Cape Town primarily use Facebook for, and (3) does the use of Facebook impact the QOL of senior citizens in Cape Town. The following section will provide a breakdown of the findings for these objectives.

5.1   The Use of Facebook

To address the question regarding what senior citizens in Cape Town use Facebook for, the results reveal that Facebook is primarily used to stay connected with friends and family and not to create new ties or relationships with new people. In terms of the features senior citizens in Cape Town use on Facebook, they tend to steer away from using administrative type of features such as updating security and privacy settings, profile settings and clicking on advertisements. Only a limited set of fun features to stay connected with friends and family on Facebook are used, such as the Like button, commenting on other Facebook users' activities, birthday notifications, messaging people, writing posts on a wall and uploading pictures. The majority of respondents agreed that spamming, false advertising and complicated privacy and security settings serve as obstacles to using Facebook. Although cost and complicated design and layout were seen as barriers to Facebook use in previous studies regarding the use of social media by the elderly, this was not the case for this research study.

5.2   Impact on Quality of Life and Agency

Perhaps the most surprising finding is that, even when measured perceptually, the use of Facebook does not appear to link significantly to any of the Quality of Life dimensions as measured through the CASP-19 instrument. However, Facebook *does* allow seniors to increase many of the resources identified in the Choice framework, thus affording them with more freedom and agency. The inability of information technology to make people happier whilst affording them more freedoms and agency is an important finding and should be pursued further in future studies.

6   Conclusion

Senior citizens in Cape Town have become regular users of Facebook. The majority of respondents mostly attributed their reason for using Facebook to the appreciation of the ability to remain socially connected with the lives of the friends, children and grand-children. The manner in which Facebook is used was also attributed to the fact that it afforded them the opportunity to view and comment on pictures and posts of friends and family. Overall, a strong perceived positive relationship between Facebook use and the social dimension of QOL was established, rooted in the notion that improved social connectedness between friends and family ultimately leads to a better QOL especially for senior citizens who are more prone to social exclusion due to a decreasing social network brought about by old age.

However, most other aspects of QOL as measured through the traditional CASP-19 instrument appears to be unaffected by Facebook use. By contrast, Facebook was experienced to significantly increase a number of resources allowing seniors with greater agency and freedom; particularly social, educational, psychological, financial, informational, cultural and time resources. The lack of a link between the ability of ICTs to allow more freedoms and agency, on the one hand, but not experiencing an increase in overall quality of life, is an interesting finding worthy of further pursuit.

A limitation of this study was the use of convenience-based, non-probability sampling, as well as the relatively small sample. A higher response rate, especially from respondents living in old age homes, might have been beneficial in providing insight from people more prone to social isolation due to limited participation in social activities. Future research could explore the use of other social media applications such as WhatsApp on influencing the overall well-being of the elderly. The reason for this is that many potential respondents were not able to participate in the study as they have migrated from using Facebook to using WhatsApp, confirming its status as the top active social platform in South Africa, just ahead of Facebook [6]. Also, differentiating between the early and late aged seniors might yield additional insights.

References

1. Mealor, B., Van Belle, J.P.: The impact of mobile phones on quality of life of the elderly. In: Proceedings of the 8th International Development Informatics Association Conference, Port Elizabeth, South Africa, pp. 223–240 (2014)
2. Leist, A.K.: Social media use of older adults: a mini-review. Gerontology **59**(4), 378–384 (2014)
3. Norval, C.: Understanding the incentives of older adults' participation on social networking sites. ACM Sigaccess Access. Comput. **102**, 25–29 (2012)
4. Bell, C., Fausset, C., Farmer, S., et al.: Examining social media use among older adults. In: Proceedings of the 24th ACM Conference on Hypertext & Social Media, Paris, France, pp. 158–163 (2013)
5. Yu, R.P., McCammon, R.J., Ellison, N.B., Langa, K.M.: The relationships that matter: social network site use and social wellbeing among older adults in the United States of America. Ageing Soc. **36**, 1–27 (2015)
6. Kemp, S.: Digital in 2016: We Are Social's Compendium of Global Digital, Social, and Mobile Data. http://wearesocial.com/uk/special-reports/digital-in-2016
7. Van Zyl, G.: SA social media by the numbers. http://www.fin24.com/Tech/Multimedia/SA-social-media-by-the-numbers-20150917
8. Barak, B., Mathur, A., Lee, K., Zhang, Y.: Perceptions of age–identity: a cross-cultural inner-age exploration. Psychol. Mark. **18**(10), 1003–1029 (2001)

9. Netuveli, G., Blane, D.: Quality of life in older ages. Br. Med. Bull. **85**(1), 113–126 (2008)

10. Nimrod, G.: Seniors' online communities: a quantitative content analysis. Gerontologist **50** (3), 149–158 (2010)

11. Mitzner, T.L., Boron, J.B., Fausset, C.B., Adams, A.E., et al.: Older adults talk technology: technology usage and attitudes. Comput. Hum. Behav. **26**(6), 1710–1721 (2010)

12. Selwyn, N.: The information aged: a qualitative study of older adults' use of information and communications technology. J. Aging Stud. **18**(4), 369–384 (2004)

13. He, W., Muenchrath, M.N., Kowal, P.R.: Shades of gray: a cross-country study of health and well-being of the older populations in SAGE countries, 2007–2010. US Department of Commerce, Economics and Statistics Administration, US Census Bureau (2012)

14. Ji, Y.G., Choi, J., Lee, J.Y., Han, K.H., Kim, J., Lee, I.K.: Older adults in an aging society and social computing: a research agenda. Int. J. Hum. Comput. Interact. **26**(11–12), 1122–1146 (2010)

15. Xie, B., Watkins, I., Golbeck, J., Huang, M.: Understanding and changing older adults' perceptions and learning of social media. Educ. Gerontol. **38**(4), 282–296 (2012)

16. Braun, M.T.: Obstacles to social networking website use among older adults. Comput. Hum. Behav. **29**(3), 673–680 (2013)

17. Lehtinen, V., Näsänen, J., Sarvas, R.: A little silly and empty-headed: older adults' understandings of social networking sites. In: Proceedings of the 23rd British HCI Group Annual Conference on People and Computers, Cambridge, UK, pp. 45–54 (2009)

18. Norval, C., Arnott, J.L., Hine, N.A., Hanson, V.L.: Purposeful social media as support platform: communication frameworks for older adults requiring care. In: Proceedings of the 5th International Conference on Pervasive Computing Technologies for Healthcare (PervasiveHealth), Dublin, Ireland, pp. 492–494 (2011)

19. Gibson, L., Moncur, W., Forbes, P., et al.: Designing social networking sites for older adults. In: Proceedings of the 24th BCS Interaction Specialist Group Conference, Dundee, UK, pp. 186–194 (2010)

20. Hope, A., Schwaba, T., Piper, A.M.: Understanding digital and material social communications for older adults. In: Proceedings SIGCHI Conference on Human Factors in Computing Systems, Toronto, Canada, pp. 3903–3912 (2014)

21. Nef, T., Ganea, R.L., Müri, R.M., Mosimann, U.P.: Social networking sites and older users–a systematic review. Int. Psychogeriatr. **25**(07), 1041–1053 (2013)

22. WHOQOL group: The World Health Organization quality of life assessment: position paper. Soc. Sci. Med. **41**(10), 1403–1409 (1995)

23. Bowling, A., Banister, D., Sutton, S., Evans, O., Windsor, J.: A multidimensional model of the quality of life in older age. Aging Ment. Health **6**(4), 355–371 (2002)

24. Brock, D.W.: Quality of life measures in health care and medical ethics (Working Paper WP66). World Institute for Development Economics Research of the UN University (1989)

25. Diener, E., Suh, E.: Measuring quality of life: economic, social, and subjective indicators. Soc. Indic. Res. **40**(1–2), 189–216 (1997)

26. Kleine, D.: ICT4WHAT? Using the choice framework to operationalise the capability approach to development. J. Int. Dev. **22**(5), 674–692 (2010)

27. Foley, P.: Does the Internet help to overcome social exclusion? Electr. J. E-gov. **2**(2), 139–146 (2004)

28. Higgs, P., Hyde, M., Wiggins, R., Blane, D.: Researching quality of life in early old age: the importance of the sociological dimension. Soc. Policy Adm. **37**(3), 239–252 (2003)

Mobile Phones as a Citizen-Controlled Anti-corruption Tool in East Africa - A Literature Review

Cecilia Strand[1](✉) and Mathias Hatakka[2]

[1] Department for Informatics and Media, Uppsala University, Uppsala, Sweden
cecilia.strand@im.uu.se
[2] Department of Informatics, Dalarna University, Borlänge, Sweden
mht@du.se

Abstract. Despite agreement amongst donors, business and political leaders concerning the negative effects of corruption, levels have not fallen in East Africa. The continued high levels of corruption, reassert the need for a better understanding if mobile phones, if prolific enough, can be an effective tool against corruption. Through a literature review of ten years M4D and ICT4D research on mobiles as a citizens-controlled tool for (a) accessing government information either directly or through citizens' crowd-sourcing of information and (b) mobilization to demand greater government transparency, as well as, (c) instantaneous reporting of corruption in East Africa; this study attempts to gauge the status of this research field. The review included the ten highest ranking open access ICT4D journals, and six journals from parent disciplines; information system and development studies, as well as conference proceedings from the M4D conferences, and the SIG Globdev Workshops. The review concludes that earlier optimism around mobiles' potential to support citizens' counter-corruption actions, has not resulted in a significant body of research. Nor does the literature provide any substantive clues as to why this urgent topic has not been explored more fully.

Keywords: Mobiles · Corruption · Transparency · Accountability · East Africa

1 Introduction

Corruption levels in East Africa, with the notable exception of Rwanda have not fallen despite significant donor attention, negative business community reviews, and repeated commitments across the political spectrum to forcefully address corruption [1]. Corruption can take on different forms, such as bribe-soliciting, where public officials demand payment in return for administrative advantages, or introducing unofficial fees for basic services that should be free [2]. It can take on more hidden forms, such as when officials skim a portion of development assistance or government funding. Corruption also exist in the shape of nepotism, i.e., favors to ethnic or clan co-patriots. Regardless of form, corruption threatens the very core of societies as it erodes citizens' trust in institutions and willingness to contribute to them, as well as defend the same institutions. Furthermore, corruption does not affect all citizens equally. The poorest

© IFIP International Federation for Information Processing 2017
Published by Springer International Publishing AG 2017. All Rights Reserved
J. Choudrie et al. (Eds.): ICT4D 2017, IFIP AICT 504, pp. 753–764, 2017.
DOI: 10.1007/978-3-319-59111-7_61

citizens, who cannot afford alternative service providers, and thus are the most dependent on basic services, are also the most likely to pay a bribe [3]. In a region with many of the Millennium Development Goals still unmet [4], and half of the population living below the poverty line, corruption thus hits hard.

Across the region, citizens convey frustrations with high and even increasing levels of corruption [5]. The 2015 East Africa Bribery Index analysis, covering five sectors (police, judiciary, registry and licensing services as well as tax services), from 2010 to 2014, found that the core institutions meant to uphold the rule of law (the police and court system) sadly were the most bribe prone institution across the region [5]. The 2015 East Africa Bribery Index, mirror outcomes from other surveys, such as the World Bank's Ease of Doing Business, the Mo Ibrahim Index on Africa Governance, and the Transparency International's Africa report [5].

All countries in the region are signatories to international and regional instruments to combat corruption such as UN Convention against Corruption and the African Union Convention on Preventing and Combatting Corruption. The 2015 East Africa Bribery Index report concluded that the existence of a legal framework and emergence of rudimentary anti-corruption institutions appear to have had little impact on corruption levels. This failure to deliver on past pledges to stamp out corruption and proceed with institutional reforms related to anti-corruption, with the exception of Rwanda, indicates a lack of genuine political will. Failures to deliver on past commitments and implement policies has also resulted in citizens losing faith in governments' interests in addressing corruption [5, 6].

The continued high levels of corruption across the region and government failures to respond, renews the need for a better understanding of mobiles as a citizen-controlled tool to push Governments to address corruption. In short, can mobile phones, or under what specific conditions, can they be an effective citizen-controlled anti-corruption tool? Through a literature review of the past ten years (2006–2016) of ICT4D and M4D research on mobiles as a citizen-controlled tool against corruption in East African; i.e. Burundi, Kenya, Rwanda, Tanzania, and Uganda; this study attempts to gauge the status of this research field. Furthermore, as corruption hits the poor the hardest, this study focuses on corruption in basic services, as opposed to corruption in connection with skimming in development assistance programs, or bribes in connection with international or domestic tender processes and business transactions.

2   Corruption Erodes Capabilities and Functionings

Curbing corruption is pivotal to development. Our theoretical understanding of development is rooted in the concept 'development as freedom' by Amartya Sen [7]. Sen argues that development entails individuals' having the freedom to choose the life that they have a reason to value [7]. This can either be achieved by making new freedoms available or by removing 'unfreedoms'. The main concepts in the approach is capabilities and functionings. Functionings are the doings and beings of individuals and the realized achievements of individuals' choices. Capabilities are a set of potential functionings that individuals can choose from and hence, represent the extent of individual's freedoms [8]. Sen lists five interlinked and interdependent instrumental freedoms that help advance the general capabilities of an individual: (i) political freedoms, (ii) economic facilities, (iii) social opportunities, (iv) transparency guarantees, and (v) protective security [7]. In relating the five instrumental freedoms to the concept of capabilities, functionings and development, Andrade and Urquhart [9] developed the framework presented in Fig. 1 below.

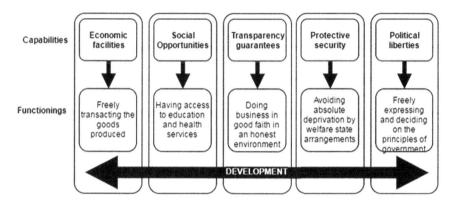

Fig. 1. The complementary nature of capabilities and functionings to attain development [9, p. 284].

Economic facilities which is the opportunity for individuals to freely sell the goods and/or services they produce. Taking part in economic activities is essential to enjoying a sustainable livelihood. Corruption create 'unfreedoms' in that the commercial activity becomes limited by the need to pay bribes to get access to the market, to get permits to conduct trade and so on. Market access and economic success, in the sense that seller makes a profit, is no longer correlated to quality and price factors.

Social opportunities can be effected by corruption in that individuals are excluded from public goods and welfare systems based on unjust premises. Services that should be available to all individuals can be 'hidden' behind illegal fee-systems. For example, fees will improve access and priority to health care, education opportunities, faster transaction times for services such as to get a permit.

Transparency guarantees are the most apparent example where corruption effects individuals. According to Andrade and Urquhart [9] transparency guarantees means that individuals can do business in good faith and in an honest environment, and "making transactions visible and represent a safeguard against corrupt practices and dishonest behavior, generally of government officials" (p. 285). Corrupt systems thus create 'unfreedoms' and inequalities if the business environments and arrangements depend on social relations and bribes.

The *protective security* is individuals' ability to avoid destitution by relying on arrangements made by the welfare state. This relates to the "state to look after their citizens when they face ominous situations as a consequence of, say, unemployment or natural disasters" [9, p. 285]. Corruption in relation to protective securities results in relief funds not reaching the poor and marginalized, or that they have to pay for aid that they are entitled to. Unreliable safety nets typically results in parallel kin-based systems that requires constant resource input.

Political liberties relate to individuals' ability to enjoy freedom of speech and assembly as well as partake in governance process by participating in various decision making processes or by periodical voting. Nepotism and cronyism, erodes government's institutions' ability to be responsive to all its citizens, and political liberties may become empty concepts.

As these instrumental freedoms are both interlinked and interdependent, government needs to deliver in all sectors to enhance citizen's capabilities. With a responsive government with a clear understanding of its status as an agent to the principle agent- the citizenry- citizens only intermittently evaluate government performance through elections. The next two sections explore how mobiles can assist citizens in performing oversight and both detect corruption and its threat to instrumental freedoms, as well as enhance citizens' ability to demand better performance and hold their government accountable.

2.1   A Citizen-Controlled (Anti-corruption) Tool in Each Pocket

As a result of governments' policies and active strategies of offering mobile network licenses to the highest-bidding private investors to establish a backbone infrastructure, East Africa has seen impressive growth in mobile phone access since 2000 and access rates range from 46% in Burundi to 80% in Kenya [10]. Even if the mobile phone market is controlled by commercial entities and operated on commercial grounds, relatively cheap smart phones have allowed for lower income groups to own mobile phones [11]. So despite access remaining unequally distributed for the foreseeable future, the proliferation of mobile technology even in lower income brackets shows the importance placed on mobile phone access and usage across income groups [11]. From an anti-corruption perspective, access rates indicate that also the citizens most adversely affected by corruption in East Africa, are increasing connected. In short, they have access to a tool that at least, in theory, could facilitate access to government information either from government directly or through citizens' crowd-sourcing of available information and opportunities to protest and report poor service delivery.

2.2   Enlisting Mobiles in the Expansion of Freedoms

The importance placed on transparency as a tool for improved accountability in development efforts, was clearly articulated through the 2008 launch of the International Aid Transparency Initiative, an online open access platform created by bilateral and multilateral development partners to ensure greater transparency around fiscal flows and supply development partners with the necessary information to hold governments and implementers accountable [12]. Access to government information was seen as a key component in improving receiving partners and ordinary citizens' ability to hold their government accountable.

Similarly, it was suggested that mobiles could play a key role. A Swedish Development Agency report argue that there "is big potential in using mobile phones for increased participation, holding governments' accountable and promoting transparency" [13, p. 53]. U4/Transparency International echoed similar sentiments, "Mobile technologies offer remarkable opportunities for promoting good governance, increasing accountability and fighting corruption allow rapid data collection and access to information and offer innovative avenues for social mobilisation and participation" [14, p. 1]. World Bank together with African Development Bank [15], highlight the many and diverse expectations placed on emerging platforms and applications, when they call on African governments to take advantage of "the power of social media and exploit it to their advantage, in particular to reinforce democratic processes, drive efficiency, foster innovation, empower public sector workers and expose corruption" [15, p. 17].

The basic rational behind the techno-optimistim was that mobiles would facilitate information flows and thus equip citizens with new opportunities to recognize corruption and mobilize around corruption, as well as provide opportunities to at a minimal cost instantaneously report absences of services or if the public officials requested an unlawful fee. The development industry's rhetoric resulted in significant investments into citizens' reporting though various free hotlines and text-based reporting platforms, such as World Bank's Integrity App [16], Ureport in Uganda, and Kenyan website "I paid a bribe", to mention a few [1].

Research on mobiles as a tool against corruption includes similar propositions arguing that one of mobiles' key contribution is its power to increase access and decentralizes information and thereby diminish the opportunities for public servants to engage in corruption secretly. With improved transparency citizens simply knows what type of services they are entitled to and to what cost. Increased transparency is seen as an effective anti-dote to corruption as it addresses the traditional information asymmetry between government and the citizenry [17, 18]. Mobiles can directly challenge government's traditional information monopoly and "corruption prefers the shadows and abhors transparency" [19, p. 337]. Gaskin [20] argues that access to Internet significantly impact corruption through increased transparency, but that the diffusion of mobiles have a, although statistically significant, weaker impact on transparency. Although mobiles have a weaker impact on transparency, the study found a connection between diffusion of mobiles and a reduction in corruption. Zanello and Maassen [21] argues that although ICTs have not yet reached its full potential in East Africa, based on the predicted growth of mobile phone access, information is more readily available than ever before to those who want it, and thus provide new opportunities for demanding accountability.

Mobiles as an anti-corruption tool, have also been connected to its ability to facilitate citizens taking action once they discovered corruption by providing new opportunities to report it. Bailard's [19] suggests a direct and significant correlation between higher mobile phone penetration and lower levels of corruption in Africa. The study showed, by examining 46 African countries, from 1999 to 2006, that there is validity to the claim that mobile phones have reduced corruption levels in Africa, or at least the perception of corruption. Bailard argues that corrupt officials weigh the benefits of the corrupt act against the potential cost, such as being detected and reported. Before the diffusion of mobile phones, there were very few tools in the hands of ordinary citizens that would allow them to report corruption anonymously and bring the information outside their community.

Improved opportunities to report corruption does however not automatically compel citizens to take action. A report from iHub [22] states that even if mobile applications may lessen the fear of reporting corruption, such citizen action is significantly hampered by governments' unresponsiveness and unwillingness to investigate and punish corrupt public servants. Transparency International [1] similarly finds that although almost a third of the respondents (28%) across East Africa, identified reporting corruption as the most effective action to take to tackle corruption, only 12% admitted having reported paying a bribe. Fear of the consequences, such as self - incrimination and that lack of visible outcome, i.e. government reaction and punishment of the culprit, made reporting less likely, even if modes of reporting was known and easy.

In summary, we argue that corruption creates unfreedoms for individuals in relation to all five instrumental freedoms and that mobiles *could* function as a tool to remove unfreedoms. We understand the causalities around mobile phones as a viable tool against corruption, as centered on their ability to (a) facilitate citizens' access to government-related information, either by direct access or through citizen horizontal crowd-sourcing information, (b) mobilize around poor service delivery once it has been recognized, and (c) facilitate reporting corruption if it occurs and thus function as a technology for accountability. Mobiles also function as a deterrent for corruption as it increases the risk of detection.

With this basic conceptual framework in place, the next question is; how has the ICT4D and M4D research field, explored and expanded the understanding of mobile phones as an effective anti-corruption tool?

3   Methodology

The objective with a literature review is to synthesize prior research and support the advancing of knowledge in a particular research domain [23]. This paper utilizes the leading journals-procedure and departs from Heek's [24] ranking of open source ICT4D journals. The list was slightly adjusted to better fit the geographical focus of this study and subsequently one journal covering Asia was replaced by the next journal on the list. The final list comprised ten journals (Table 1).

By applying the Boolean search phrase: corrupt* OR bribe AND Mobile* OR Cell phone* OR ICT AND Africa, each ICT4D journal were scanned for articles that contained items on mobiles as a tool for anti-corruption between 1st January 2006 to 30th June 2016, in Sub-Saharan Africa. After a manually scanning of 71 articles, none were found meet our inclusion criteria, i.e. mobile phones as a tool for anti-corruption in East Africa (preferably) or sub-Saharan Africa. A schematic analysis of the disqualified articles showed that most articles contained references to corruption as a general development challenge, but failed to connect it to mobile phone access, usages and practices in the focused region. As the initial literature review did not generate enough research articles, the scope of literature was expanded to cover journals which

Table 1. Heeks ranking of ICT4D journals

Name of journal	Boolean search	*Papers
Information Technologies and International Development	16	0
Electronic Journal of Information Systems in Developing Countries	0	0
Information Technology for Development	33	0
African Journal of Information and Communication	n/a	0
Int. Journal of Education and Development Using Information and Communication Technology	10	0
Journal of Health Informatics in Developing Countries	0	0
Information Development	5	0
International Journal on Advances in ICT for Emerging Regions	1	0
African Journal of Information & Communication Technology	1	0
South African Journal of Information Management	5	0

*Papers fulfilling search criteria of addressing mobiles and anti-corruption in Sub-Saharan Africa

are ICT4D's "parent disciplines," namely Development and Information Systems [24]. By using the SCImago ranking, the three top ranked development journals and information system journals covering international social science aspects of IS were added to the literature review (Tables 2 and 3). The same Boolean search was applied. Most articles in this second sample in the parent disciplines were multi-country studies, in particular in the parent discipline Development. However, several articles in Development journals turned out to be ineligible as they focused on mobile as mobility of people, goods and services, as opposed to the intended reference to mobile phones.

Table 2. Parent discipline: information systems

Journal name	Boolean search	Papers
MIS Quarterly	4	0
Information Systems Research	0	0
Journal of Service Research	1	Sub-Saharan Africa: [26]

Table 3. ICT parent discipline: development

Journals	Boolean search	Papers
Journal of Development Economics	6/3	0
World Development	57/44	Multi-country study: [25]
Economic Development and Cultural Change	4/0	0

Finally, to further expand the scope of the review, two peer-reviewed conference proceedings were included in the review: The M4D Conferences and the annual SIG Globdev Workshops. Both conferences, was instituted in 2008 and were thus able to provide a sufficient historical record of ICT4D and M4D research.

4 Results

Despite including ten years of research on mobile phones and corruption in the ten highest ranking open access ICT4D journals (Table 1) and expanding the review to include six journals from parent disciplines; development and information systems (Tables 2 and 3), result in terms of number of articles remained very small.

As indicated by the number of hits based on Boolean search in Tables 1, 2 and 3; corruption is frequently featured. But corruption is not related to mobiles or the ICT initiative that was many articles' main focus, but rather appears as a judiciously covered background factor. Furthermore, a third of the articles from the ICT4D journal sample make general statement around unspecified ICTs' potential to combat corruption by increasing citizens' access to information. But these statements are not elaborated on in the sense that the features of platform or service are divulged, or how information would support citizens' anti-corruption actions. None of the articles engage with the opportunities connected with the last five years rapid diffusion of mobiles or its potential as a citizen- controlled tool along previously explored causalities. The review of the ICT4D sample thus indicates that the topic is neglected, at least within the core ICT4D journals.

Surprisingly, it was the parent disciplines' six journals that generated some input with two articles (article in last column Tables 2 and 3). Even if the number is small, and unable to provide a substantively deeper understanding of mobile phones as a citizen- controlled anti-corruption tool; the two articles highlight a common theme, namely transparency as an anti-dote to corruption. Asongu and Nwachukwuy [25] argued that after analyzing 49 Sub-Saharan nations using World Bank data, that mobile phone penetration has a positive effect on good governance and that mobile phones help reduce information asymmetry and monopoly which traditionally provide elite actors with conducive conditions for bribe-soliciting and minimal risk of detection of mismanagement of public funds. In short, mobile phones removed important conditions for corruption: namely, secrecy and low risk of detection. Martin and Hill [26] echoing the issue of transparency in their study of the relationship between saving and well-being at the base of the pyramid, i.e., the 3 billion people who live on less than US $2.50 per day. They argue that digital financial services, often in the shape of m-banking for the poor, made financial flows visible and traceable and thus should result in "safer and speedier transactions and less corruption and theft" [26, p. 415]. Both studies thus appeared to argue that mobiles address information asymmetries and secrecy, which are key conditions for corruption.

Although the body of research did more than double with the inclusion of conference proceedings the academic output remained at low levels (Tables 4 and 5). Furthermore, The M4D Conference included one of the earliest contributions to the field [27]. The piece argues, "there is great potential for the use of mobile technology to deliver social protection, but that active partnerships between governments and private sector partners will be required" p. 1). In techno-optimistic manner it fails to analytically engage with exactly how mobiles can address the leakages' and corruption connected with middle-men administering 'cash in transit' in Lesotho.

Table 4. M4D Conferences: 2008, 2010, 2012, 2014 and 2016

Year	No. of conf. entries	Boolean search	Papers
2008	17	1	Sub-Saharan Africa: [27]
2010	21	0	0
2012	62	2	Sub-Saharan Africa: [28] Multi-country study: [29]
2014	28	0	0
2016	19	1	0

Table 5. SIG Globdev Workshop: 2008–2015

Year	No. of conf. entries	Boolean search	Papers
2008	23	0	0
2009	19	0	0
2010	18	0	0
2011	21	1	Sub-Saharan Africa: [30]
2012	18	0	0
2013	22	1	Sub-Saharan Africa: [31]
2014	8	0	0
2015	13	0	0

Thinyane and Coulson's [28] article describes how MobiSAM polling stations were intended to support citizens' involvement in municipality affairs and facilitate social auditing of service delivery, as well as encourage whistle-blowing and reporting of corruption. They however concluded that without political leadership at the municipal level and political will to genuinely include and engage with citizens; ICT4D and M4D interventions have little chance to deliver. The MobiSAM project was substantially revised due to structural and contextual constraints. Talukdar [29] raise similar hopes when arguing that mobiles, "can directly fight corruption through ensuring increased civic participation and promoting systematic transparency in governance and development process, and holding governments increasingly accountable" (p. 250). Talukdar thus appears to suggest that mobile phones could have a key role to play in supporting civic education to build better corruption awareness and civic overseeing systems.

The early years of SIG Globdev output wrongly gives the impression that the area of ICT and corruption is entirely missing. Although none of the WS papers 2008-2010 engage with the topic of mobiles as an anti-corruption tool in Sub-Saharan Africa; corruption itself is mentioned as a crippling barrier to development of ICT4D related interventions. Twinomurinzi and Ghartey-Tagoe [30] explores citizens from 11 sub-Saharan countries perception of their role and ability to fight against corruption. The study finds that although citizens recognize a duty to act, citizens are concerned about their personal security and question their ability to successfully challenge the powerful groups that control government. The article thus highlights an important caveat. Understanding the user's faith in the technology's ability to function as a power leverage against political and bureaucratic corruption is essential.

In 2013, A submission on the MobiSAM project [28] appears as a slightly reworked article. MobiSAM mobile platforms were planned to support citizens' oversight, which would lead to improved accountability of municipal employees as well as providing evidence that could be used for corrective action [31]. The project failed as local municipal employees had little interests in supporting the development of a system that ultimately removed their discretionary powers in local affairs. The article thus highlights the formidable resistance vested interest will produce when their interests are being challenged.

5 Discussion

Following our argument that corruption creates unfreedoms for individuals, and that mobile phones can be used to combat corruption; empirical evidence is essential to move our assumptions from the realm of what is theoretical possible to what can be verified. Sadly, our review of mobiles as a citizen-controlled tool for fighting corruption in East Africa, did not provide us with enough research to systematically verify or discard earlier claims or hopes connected with mobiles. The "result" is thus; not much is known about the real effects of mobile phones on corruption in the region.

Consequently, it could be argued that the lack of research is indicative of mobiles inability to deliver in this field. We, however argue that it is still too early to conclusively write off mobiles as an anti-corruption tool. The functions provided by a mobile phone can undoubtable be used for anti-corruption, but are not used for those purposes at any significant scale. Following Sen's reasoning that individuals are active agents of change [7], we suggest greater attention should be directed towards understanding users' interpretation of mobiles in relation to their contexts. All action for change, including using a phone for anti-corruption purposes takes place in a context which contains both constraints and opportunities defined by the existing institutional arrangements and distribution of political power. Individual and collective agency are thus confined the 'political opportunity structures' [32]. According to Kitschelt [32] social actors need to discern an opportunity to mobilize for social change. A crucial dimension of political opportunity structures are thus the perceived openness or closeness of state institutions to inputs from other actors, as well as the institutional capacity to advance change. Approaching mobiles' from this perspective would move us away from technical solutions and mobiles' technical potential, which undoubtedly are plentiful, into the situated user- perceived potentials. Some studies, highlight this dimension in particular, i.e., mobile's ability to counter corruption is intimately intertwined and dependent on the degree of government responsiveness and political will address corruption [1, 22, 31].

More research is needed to explore citizens' evaluative mapping and interpretations of their agency in relations to the perceived opportunities to understand under which contextual conditions a mobile with its portability, simplicity, and affordability is transformed into a viable tool to fight corruption. A mobile phone, just like a Swiss army knife can theoretically be used for many different things, but it may also never be used for any of these. This study reminds us all of the dangers in prematurely assuming that a technological potential in itself will produce a particular behavior.

References

1. Transparency International: People and corruption: Africa survey. Corruption barometer (2015). (Pring, C., Research coordinator, Global surveys). ISBN: 978-3-943497-93-9
2. LeVine, V.T.: Political corruption: the Ghana case. Hoover Institution Press, Stanford (1975)
3. Justesen, M., Bjørnskov, C.: Exploiting the poor: Bureaucratic corruption and poverty in Africa. Afrobarometer Working Paper No. 139, pp. 1–31 (2012). doi:10.2139/ssrn.2168119
4. Centre for Global Development: East Africa overall MDG achievement (2015). http://www.cgdev.org/page/mdg-progress-index-gauging-country-level-achievements
5. Transparency International Kenya: Eastern Africa bribery index 2010–2015 (2015). http://www.tikenya.org/index.php/the-east-african-bribery-index
6. Richmond, S., Alpin, C.: Governments falter in fight to curb corruption: the people give most a failing grade. Afrobarometer Policy Paper No. 4, pp. 1–34 (2013)
7. Sen, A.: Development as Freedom. Anchor Books, New York (1999)
8. Gasper, D.: Is Sen's capability approach an adequate basis for considering human development? Rev. Polit. Econ. **14**(4), 435–461 (2002). doi:10.1080/0953825022000009898
9. Andrade, A.D., Urquhart, C.: Unveiling the modernity bias: a critical examination of the politics of ICT4D. Inf. Technol. Dev. **18**(4), 281–292 (2012). doi:10.1080/02681102.2011.643204
10. International Telecommunication Union: Mobile-cellular subscriptions (2017). http://www.itu.int/en/ITU-D/Statistics/Pages/stat/default.aspx
11. Chabossou, A., Stork, C., Stork, M., Zahonogo, Z.: Mobile telephony access and usage in Africa. In: Proceedings of the 3rd International Conference on Information and Communication Technologies and Development, Doha, Qatar, pp. 392–405 (2009)
12. Davies, T.: Who is doing what when it comes to technology for transparency, accountability and anti-corruption Practical Participation. Global Information Society Watch (2011)
13. Hellström, J.: The innovative use of mobile applications in East Africa. Sida Review 2010:12 (2010). (Tröften, P.-E. (ed.) Sida, Stockholm, Sweden)
14. U4 Transparency International: Use of mobile phones to detect and deter corruption, author Marie Chêne. Transparency International, Number: 321 (2010). http://www.u4.no/publications/use-of-mobile-phones-to-detect-and-deter-corruption/
15. World Bank: The transformational use of information and communication technologies in Africa and the African Development Bank, with the support of the African Union (2011). (Yonazi, E., Kelly, T., Halewood, N., Blackman, C. (eds.) eTransform AFRICA. World Bank Report)
16. World Bank: World Bank introduces new integrity app at the international anti-corruption conference (2012). Press release: www.worldbank.org/integrity
17. Sturges, P.: Corruption, transparency and a role for ICT? Int. J. Inf. Ethics **2**(11), 1–9 (2004)
18. García-Murillo, M.: The effect of internet access on government corruption. Electron. Gov. Int. J. **7**(1), 22–40 (2010)
19. Bailard, S.C.: Mobile phone diffusion and corruption in Africa. Polit. Commun. **26**, 333–353 (2009)
20. Gaskins, L.E.: The effect of Information and Communications Technology (ICT) diffusion on corruption and transparency (a global study) (Doctoral dissertation, Texas A&M International University) (2013)
21. Zanello, G., Maassen, P.: Strengthening citizen agency through ICT: an extrapolation for Eastern Africa. Publ. Manage. Rev. **13**(3), 363–382 (2011)
22. iHub: ICT and governance in East Africa: A landscape analysis in Kenya, Uganda and Tanzania (2014). (Report by Sika, V., Sambuli, N., Orwa, A., Salim, A.)

23. Webster, J., Watson, R.: Analyzing the past to prepare for the future: writing a literature review. MIS Q. **26**(2), xiii–xxiii (2002)
24. Heeks, R.: Do information and communication technologies (ICTs) contribute to development? J. Int. Dev. **22**(5), 625–640 (2010). doi:10.1002/jid.1716
25. Asongu, S.A., Nwachukwu, J.: The mobile phone in the diffusion of knowledge for institutional quality in sub-Saharan Africa. World Dev. **86**, 133–147 (2016). doi:10.1016/j.worlddev.2016.05.012
26. Martin, K.D., Hill, R.P.: Saving and well-being at the base of the pyramid, implications for transformative financial services delivery. J. Serv. Res. **18**(3), 405–421 (2015). doi:10.1177/1094670514563496
27. Vincent, K., Freeland, N.: Upwardly mobile: the potential to deliver social protection by cellphone – Lessons from Lesotho. In: Proceedings of the International Conference on M4D Mobile Communication Technology for Development, Karlstad, Sweden, pp. 100–107 (2008)
28. Thinyane, H., Coulson, D.: MobiSAM: mobile social accountability monitoring in South Africa. In: Proceedings of the International Conference on M4D Mobile Communication Technology for Development, New Deli, India, pp. 170–181 (2012)
29. Talukdar MRI: Mobile communications and fighting corruption. In: Proceedings of the International Conference on M4D Mobile Communication Technology for Development, New Deli, India, pp. 244–259 (2012)
30. Twinomurinzi, H., Ghartey-Tagoe, K.B.: Corruption in African democratic developing countries and ICT: apathy, anxiety and patriotism. In: Proceedings of the 4th Annual SIG Globdev Workshop, Shanghai, China (2011)
31. Thinyane, H.: Stumbling at the start line: an analysis of factors affecting participation with local government in South Africa. In: Proceedings of the 6th Annual SIG Globdev Workshop, Milano, Italy (2013)
32. Kitschelt, H.P.: Political opportunity structures and political protest: Anti-nuclear movements in four democracies. Br. J. Polit. Sci. **16**(1), 57–85 (1986). doi:10.1017/S000712340000380X

Tensions in Information System Artefacts: Explaining Land Information Systems' Sub-optimal Impact in Indonesia

Fathul Wahid[1,2], Øystein Sæbø[2(✉)], and Bjørn Furuholt[2]

[1] Department of Informatics, Universitas Islam Indonesia,
Yogyakarta, Indonesia
fathul.wahid@uii.ac.id
[2] Department of Information Systems,
University of Agder, Kristiansand, Norway
{oystein.sabo,bjorn.furuholt}@uia.no

Abstract. Despite the advancement of more integrated land information systems (LIS), conflicts and disputes over land in Indonesia remain. Our study seeks to explain this situation. Using an interpretive case study conducted in Eastern Indonesia and framed within the concepts of information system (IS) artefacts, we find that tensions within and between information, technology, and social artefacts help to explain the sub-optimal LIS impacts. Inconsistent information, unsuitable technology, and conflicting social arrangements are examples of such tensions. Unless the tensions are properly resolved, LIS use cannot fulfil its potential for more appropriate management of land administration.

Keywords: eGovernment · Land information systems · Tension · Information system artefact · Indonesia · Developing country

1 Introduction

Information concerning land and land ownership is of critical importance for the development developing countries, facing severe challenges related to land management, including unclear responsibility distribution between the involved stakeholders [2], conflicting legal arrangements [3], and non-transparent systems [4]. Modern land information systems (LIS), consisting of a database containing spatially referenced data and procedures and techniques for the systematic collection, updating, processing and distribution of the data, are arguably a basic infrastructure for environmental management as well as economic and social development, particularly in developing countries [1]. Despite the advancements of more integrated LIS, conflicts over land [1], specifically uncontrolled land use and conversion [5], remain, with large areas of land remaining unregistered. While LIS play an important role within this field, research focusing on such issues has so far been rather incomplete [6].

We aim at contributing to this important field of interest by exploring LIS use in Indonesia. In 1997, Indonesia initiated the use of IS within their land management. However, the aforementioned problems remained unresolved [3, 5], and there have

J. Choudrie et al. (Eds.): ICT4D 2017, IFIP AICT 504, pp. 765–777, 2017.
DOI: 10.1007/978-3-319-59111-7_62

been a significant number of disputes reported over land. In 2007, for example, the National Land Agency (Badan Pertanahan Nasional [BPN]) recorded more than 7,000 cases of land conflicts covering almost 608,000 hectares of land [7]. By 2013, there were still more than 4,000 cases [8]. These conflicts occur for various reasons [9], such as illegal occupancy, border disputes, inheritance disputes, multiple sales, double certificates, false transaction letters, and overlapping borders. Until 2013, only around 45% of private ownership land parcels had been formally registered [8], which equals 5% of Indonesia's land area [10].

Given these considerations, it is clear that the effectiveness of LIS needs to be better understood. As will be further elaborated below, we found only sub-optimal use of LIS while conducting our fieldwork. Here, we aim to explore why by reflecting on the following research question: What can explain the sub-optimal impact of LIS use in Indonesia? To explore this, we conducted an interpretive case study in rural Eastern Indonesia (in the district of Nagekeo).

In order to fully understand the use and potential of introducing LIS, we need to understand technical, human [11], and contextual issues [12]. One way to do so is to introduce the concept of an ensemble artefact, which has been a core issue of concern within IS research [13]. We introduce the IS artefact concept, [13] which consists of three subsystems: the technology part, or the tools used to solve a problem, achieve a goal, or serve a purpose defined by humans; the information part, or the information instantiation occurring through a human act; and the social part, or the nature of the relationships or interactions between individuals (hence social) in attempts to solve problems, achieve goals, or serve one's purposes [14].

While Lee et al. [13] make an important theoretical contribution by clarifying the use of the term and emphasising IT artefacts' socio-technical elements, empirical work is still needed in order to further explore the IS artefact way of thinking. For instance, they argue that the 'whole IS artefact is greater than the sum of its subsystem' without really discussing how or why it is so. The framework talks about the three components as single entities, while in real-life examples there are several analysis units within each of these. Therefore, empirical work is still needed in order to better understand the connection between the three subsystems.

The IS artefact concept allows us to elaborate on the informational, technological, and social aspects of an ensemble artefact, but more emphasis is needed in order to understand potential conflicts between these subsystems, as well as how such conflicts could influence projects. We also introduce the concept of tensions to identify the challenges, internal or external, that must be managed so that the community can achieve the intended aims [15–17]. Tensions will lead to unstable conditions, oscillating between two different and competing states; this must be managed to ensure community survival over time [18]. Specific tensions should be carefully managed. As argued below, the identification of tension within the IS artefact subsystem allows us to further elaborate the understanding of why studied LIS achieved only a sub-optimal impact.

This work's main contribution is twofold. First, we contribute by developing a more detailed understanding of LIS introduction by identifying tensions between IS artefact subsystems and their influence on LIS success (or otherwise). Second, by identifying these tensions, we contribute theoretically by providing a better explanation of tension's role between IS-artefact subsystems, a perspective so far being unexplored.

The rest of the paper is organised as follows: first, we introduce the theoretical premises for our works; then, before introducing our results, we briefly present the research context and approach. We conclude by discussing our findings and providing avenues for practice and future research

2 Theoretical Premises

The IS artefact concept is introduced here to provide a more detailed understanding of the technological, informational, and social aspects of the introduced LIS. The notion of 'artefact' has been highly debated within IS research [13] ever since the desperate call for more information technology (IT) artefact knowledge was raised by Orlikowski and Iacono [11]. The ensemble artefact view has its roots within the interpretation of IS being a socio-technical construction that ensures equal consideration of technical and human factors in the design process [19]. The socio-technical design's objective, 'the joint optimisation of the social and technical systems' [19], guides the idea of the ensemble view of an artefact [11, 20], as well as the IS artefact [13].

Scholars have recently criticised the artefact concept for being too broad and therefore no longer of value for IS research [21], while others argue for the need for more detailed exploration of IT artefacts [13, 22, 23]. The latter argument resonates with our view and is introduced here in order to explore LIS use within Indonesia, which allows for understanding the sub-optimal usage of such systems. Introducing the IS artefact perspective allows for focusing on how the system is dynamically shaped by the contextual dependencies of its context of use, adoption, and implementation [14].

The technology subsystem, the human-made tool created to solve a problem, achieve a goal, or serve a purpose, has several characteristics [13]. The technological subsystem does not include only digital or electronic components, but can also include non-digital parts of the system, such as face-to-face meetings, books, or paper-based library systems. Moreover, it might not be about information but still contain the technology, like the computer or the mobile phone. A technological subsystem does not need to have a physical representation [13]. The information subsystem is an information instantiation that is based on a direct or indirect human act [13]. Information can include numbers, letters, or symbols, or even relationships between such information tokens. Information is processed or adapted by an actor in order to achieve (or otherwise) the intended outcome. The social subsystem focuses on the relationships and interactions between individuals [13]. By focusing on interactions and relationships, this subsystem necessarily involves more than one individual, focusing instead on the social aspect. The social artefacts can include stable and established social relationships or more dynamic and fluid interactions.

According to Lee et al. [13], the IS artefact represents the technological, informational, and social subsystems and is more than the sum of its part, since part of the artefact relates to the relationship between its sub-systems. The features of both the technology and information subsystems are mainly seen as necessary conditions that render possible the social features through which users are linked to other content creators [24]. The three subsystems are clearly assembled so that each component relates to the presence of the other. The three IS artefact subsystems, as well as how they are related, are summarised in Fig. 1.

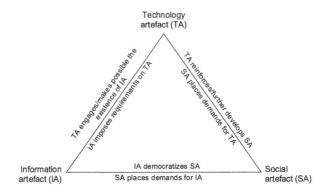

Fig. 1. The 'triangle' relationships among IS artefacts (based on [13])

While the IS artefact perspective is useful in analysing various IT artefact characteristics and the relationships between them, less emphasis is placed on how these subsystems can conflict with each other, or how such conflicts potentially influence the success or otherwise when introducing ICT. We explore this perspective by looking at tensions between these subsystems. Tensions need to be managed; the question is how to combine 'sub-artefact' elements (internally and externally) to address these tensions.

Tensions can be defined as a state of contrast between opposite forces, each one leading an entity to a different – opposite – condition or state, or as a relationship between ideas and qualities with conflicting demands or implications. Out of these conditions, one could be the desirable while the other the undesirable. This concept is used by the literature in order to identify difficulties, internal or external, that could lead to an unstable oscillating condition between two different and competing states, which needs to be managed [25]. Focusing on tensions reveals the participants' conflicting goals, purposes, and motivations. They are not hidden; rather, as a form of sense-making, participants regularly discuss their problems as tensions [26].

3   Research Context and Approach

Indonesia, comprised of approximately 17,000 islands, covers an area of 1.9 million square kilometres (km) supporting a population of more than 225 million people. During the 350-year period before its independence in 1945, Indonesia was constantly under some form of colonial rule. Land law was dualistic, representing Western-style systems – to meet the colonial governments' interests – and traditional unwritten laws based on customary rights to land, which exist in Indonesia's diverse cultural groups. This dualism in land law was expected to end in 1960 with the enactment of the Basic Agrarian Law (Undang-Undang Pokok Agraria). This national law recognises traditional concepts and institutions, while at the same time provides for the registration of individual land rights. Within this framework, Indonesia operates a complex land management system [27].

The legal issues are complex, as land administration is managed under two national government agencies, BPN and the Ministry of Forestry (MoF). These government agencies refer to different laws in determining land borders under their jurisdiction [28]. To some extent, this policy leads to conflicts and power struggles between land management officials and Indonesian administration [3, 28].

Our study site is the district of Nagekeo located in the province of East Nusa Tenggara (see Fig. 1). Approximately 110,000 people inhabit this area, which covers 1,417 km^2. This newly established district was part of the district of Ngada until 2007. A large proportion of this district's land is community land (tanah ulayat) without certificates. That often triggers land conflicts, either between tribal groups or between tribal groups and the local government [29, 30]. Nagekeo was selected in order to represent an area where conflicts concerning community land ownership are prevalent.

Nagekeo's local BPN office was officially founded in 2010. One year later the office introduced Larasita, a mobile land office (a modified van) that services remote areas and is equipped with laptops connected through a virtual private network to the national BPN office's main databases. They use a LIS called Geo-KKP, which is a web-based system that connects textual and spatial land data. Technically, a LIS is already in place, to some extent, in order to support certification and other related services.

One of the flagship programmes established by BPN and the national government intended to speed up asset legalisation (i.e. certification of lands). To this end, BPN launched the Prona scheme, which offered free block registration to certain disadvantaged communities. In Nagekeo, the local BPN office expects to issue 1,200–1,400 land certificates annually. Of these, 800 certificates were through the Prona scheme (where 75 certificates were allocated to fishermen). This number is considered low, since only 5% of Nagekeo land has been certified to date.

3.1   Research Approach

In this interpretative case study, data were collected primarily through interviews with actors from different backgrounds: farmers, fishermen, BPN service users, the heads of tribal groups, members of cooperatives, financial institutions (i.e. bank), and government officers from district, sub-district, and village levels. These informants represent the various stakeholders involved in land-related issues, representing both the people and the government. Stakeholders from the people's side include the head of tribal groups, (migrant/local) farmers, (migrant/local) fishermen, and local businessmen. On the government's side, there is BPN, a local planning agency, and various departments responsible for forestry, settlement, city planning, and the development of the fishery sector and small and medium-sized enterprises.

In total, we conducted 25 interviews with 31 informants, whereof 20 interviews were carried out in Nagekeo including 24 informants. In order to provide a broader national perspective, the rest of the interviews were done with Jakarta BPN officers at the Geospatial Information Agency (Badan Informasi Geospasial [BIG]) in Bogor and Jakarta's WWF Indonesia. All of the interviews were either recorded or extensively noted.

In analysing the data, we used the concepts depicting the artefact relationships (i.e. information, technology, and social) composing the IS artefact as the coding template. We identified all of the tensions that happened in all of the relationships and mapped them into specific relationships. When the tensions involve at least two different instantiations at the same artefact, we termed them as 'tensions within artefacts'. Otherwise, when more than one composing artefact is involved in the tensions, we named them 'tension between artefacts'.

4   Findings

Before presenting the main findings on the tensions within and between IS artefacts, it is necessary to identify examples of each composing artefact (i.e. information, technology, and social) in play within the LIS uptake context. Information artefact (IA) examples include land-related laws, information on procedures for land certification application, costs that may be incurred, the consequences of having certified land (e.g. paying annual land tax, securing land ownership), and the land certificate itself. The technology artefacts identified included all technologies that constitute the LIS, such as Internet, virtual private network (VPN), a modified van for Larasita, laptops, other network infrastructure, land measurement tools, and the information system applications (e.g. Geo-KKP). The social artefacts comprised of all possible relationships and interactions among the involved actors (e.g. citizens, BPN, local government agencies, head of tribal groups).

4.1   Tensions Within Artefacts

First, we present the findings indicating the tensions found within each composing artefact.

Within information artefact. This artefact manifest in various forms. Unclear or conflicting information on many aspects can create tension. For example, one village official says, '*Prona is prioritised for those with low economic status, and it's free of charge*'. But in the field, we found that some informants are expected to pay certain amounts of money. One BPN official says in defence, '*Well, the village might charge something. But that's their village's regulations. The thing is, BPN doesn't charge anything*'. One informant further asserts, '*The payment [for BPN employees in the field during the measurement process] is unclear which may result in corruption and manipulation. It is because of unclear payment for transport, food, and accommodation. This type of payment for land certification tends to be expensive. This discourages people to certify their land*'. Another tension within information artefact is illustrated by one national BPN office director, who asserts, '*There are 13 laws related to land which are not harmonised, either horizontally among the laws or vertically with their references, namely the constitution'.*

Within technology artefact. The modified Larasita van was originally designed to provide mobile land certification services directly to the citizens, especially those residing in remote areas. But, as one BPN official tells us, *'It's because we moved the office and there were problems with Internet network. We have no network at all. ... I think Larasita's van hasn't had it yet. The van is just an operational vehicle when we need to go to the field. ...We haven't been able to run Larasita properly'.*

Within social artefact. Land certification is not available for everyone, since many fishermen do not own their lands – a landlord (the tribal group) does. Potential land ownership conflicts can also hinder land certification. We found that many of the land certification applications sent to BPN were going nowhere, even after many years, because indigenous people are claiming back the land. In such cases, BPN never issues certificates over those lands. One informant illustrates, *'Well here, the problems related to lands are usually among the society, related to the tribal groups, within the tribal groups, among individuals, and the most frequently is related to the government'.* Another informant adds, *'The government wants to do something, but the society feels that the lands are their living sources so they refuse it. Conflicts happen then'.* Further, another informant asserts, *'Sometimes the government is not neutral, they are not strict. And related to the border problems, there hasn't been one solved so far'.*

Table 1 summarises examples of tensions between instantiations within a composing artefact.

Table 1. Tensions within artefact

No.	Artefact	Example of identified tension
1	IA × IA	Inconsistent information about the cost for certifying a land parcel
2	TA × TA	The national BPN office's designed technology does not fit the available local infrastructure
3	SA × SA	Disputes between tribal groups over land claims

4.2 Tensions Between Artefacts

Next, we present the identified tensions between instantiations from two different artefacts. These tensions happen when the involved artefact's relationship goes in an unexpected direction. Each of the identified tensions is presented below.

Between technology and information artefact. A technology artefact can engage, or make possible, the existence of an information artefact. As the main LIS application, Geo-KKP provides and connects textual and spatial land data. However, it only records the already certified private lands; it does not provide information about uncertified land borders. These lead to land disputes. One local BPN office official comments: *'For measurement, the common problem is any claims related to the land borders among* *the society. ... For the measurement workers, they should clear the problems right away. We look for win-win solution. We set the border both sides agree to it'.*

Between information and technology artefacts. An information artefact can impose requirements on a technology artefact. Even though the national government enacted a law in 2011 concerning geospatial information to provide legal support for the 'One Map Policy' initiative, Geo-KKP does not have an integrated map, which is managed by the Ministry of Forestry (MoF). Both BPN and MoF refer to different laws in determining land borders under their jurisdiction, which is substantiated by tales from the field. An official from the local government states, *'There should be a proposal from village people for land certification. With the proposal, BPN will investigate in the field for issuing the land certificate. However, BPN always coordinate with the Department of Forestry, especially to get recommendation that the lands for certification are not within the government forests'.*

Between technology and social artefacts. The use of technology can either further improve or hurt social artefacts. As one informant says, *'By having technology, there are many references that can be searched, so there will be plenty of sources that can be adopted. Moreover, there will be new insights. Therefore, if they know the technology better, they may be able to clear the facts'.* However, he later adds, *'It may create the problem ... if the people actually do not play an important role, but they know technology very well. Finally, they can manipulate the truth. And actually, the problems here are because the acknowledgement among the tribes does not get stronger'.* In a different fragment, another informant tells us, *'The previous BPN officials were not good and worked very slow. If people want to speed up their land certification process, they just give some money as greasing oil'.*

Between social and technology artefacts. The social artefact can place demand for the technology artefact. Moreover, lack of education restricts the use of technology. When asked about the conflict's nature, one informant asserts, *'So far, it is the personal conflict, because all people obey the head of tribal group, when it is customary conflict. The difficult part is the informal claim, such claiming certain lands, which belong to other people. This is basically related to the technology and educational level of the community. For example, people who are well educated, they sometimes even become the one who start the problem. The real owner can lose the case because they have lower education'.* In this case, social relation problems cannot always be resolved by the help of technology.

Between social and information artefacts. The social artefact can also place demand for an information artefact. However, this is not always the case in practice. When discussing land certification challenges, one informant clearly explains, *'There are two main challenges. The first one relates to administration where people could not provide with administrative proof of owning the lands. The second one is that different claims over the same land that is proposed for land certification. This disputed claims over lands use to occur in the customary lands'.* Here, the tribal group's social arrangement does not allow the group members to certify their lands.

Between information and social artefacts. An information artefact can democratise a social artefact, such as by providing accessible and symmetric information. In our case, however, this relation is disrupted. One migrant farmer states, *'The certificate for the land of this house has been issued. ... But the land of rice field [certificate] has not been issued yet. ... Although measurement had been conducted'*. When asked for the reason behind this, he says, *'I don't know, as it is the government's responsibility. We do not know because we are only stupid people'*. However, he should pay land taxes for both parcels of land. He further tells us, *'Fifty thousand for the yard [the house]. ... For the rice fields, it is 100 thousand per year'*. In fact, in 2014, the national BPN office launched a SMS service that enable the land certification applicants to obtain a variety of information, such as measurement cost, land rights transfer cost, and complaints. The informants that we interviewed did not use this service. The un-informed people have no choice other than doing what government officials should do. Table 2 summarises the composing artefact tensions.

Table 2. Tensions between artefacts

No.	Relationship	Example of identified tension
1	TA × IA	The existing LIS does not provide information on borders of uncertified lands
2	IA × TA	The requirement to have information on the border between private lands and government forestlands is not readily available in the existing LIS
3	TA × SA	The existent LIS does not always speed up the certification process
4	SA × TA	The problems in social relations that create land ownership disputes cannot be resolved by the technology in place
5	SA × IA	The tribal group's social arrangement does not allow the group members to certificate their lands
6	IA × SA	The un-informed people have no choice other than doing what government officials should do

5 Discussion

The findings presented above support our projection that tensions emerge when LIS' social and technical aspects interact. The concept of the IS artefact, with its composing artefacts that we used as an analytical lens, helps us in unveiling these tensions. We also found that each composing artefact is not a single uniform entity, but rather another smaller ensemble consisting of a variety of artefact instantiations from the same class. These instantiations do not always go hand in hand or interact without any problem. We found, for example, that information artefacts can manifest in various forms and versions. If these versions are not congruent, tensions can occur. Another example is within the social artefact, such as when different tribal groups fail to find agreement on certain land borders.

We also found tensions between composing artefacts. These happen when an artefact cannot play its role, or when the relationships do not develop as expected. For example, LIS as a technology artefact cannot provide information about uncertified lands (such as between forestlands and community lands), as the information is not readily available. This is beyond LIS capabilities because the social artefacts in question (such as between tribal groups and the department of forestry) have not yet agreed on the disputed land borders. This tension will hinder LIS in fulfilling its promises to speed up land certification. Figure 2 illustrates the identified tensions both within and between the three composing artefacts.

Fig. 2. Map of Nagekeo: the study site

The findings indicate that if tensions within and between artefacts are not properly resolved, they will limit the ability of an IS artefact (in this case, LIS) to be optimally harvested. In our study site, land-related problems are very prevalent or even escalating, which may trigger long lasting social conflicts [29, 30]. Theoretically, the IS artefact concept equips us with vocabularies for identifying the building blocks of LIS and their relationships, but this does not provide further possibilities for explaining possible problems when the relationships do go in the expected directions. Using just the IS artefact concept, we can only draw a foggy picture. By bringing in the concept of tensions, we sharpen the analytical lens and make the picture clearer (Fig. 3).

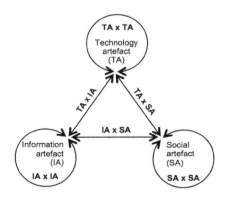

Fig. 3. Tensions within and between the composing IS artefacts

From a conceptual viewpoint, our study contributes to extending the IS artefact concept [13] by introducing the concept of tensions in order to explain unexpected results that occur when the composing artefacts interact. We can then explore how the relationship between instantiations within and between composing artefacts are dialectical and therefore not always moving in positive directions. By this improved analytical lens, we contribute practically to the field development of eGovernment within ICT4D research by providing a clear explanation for the emerging problems when a nationally designed initiative is implemented in various local contexts.

6 Conclusion

We have here discussed a case study that explore the LIS' sub-optimal impact in Indonesia. In so doing, we developed a sharper analytical lens by introducing the concept of tension in order to extend the IS artefact concept [13]. Our study found that tensions within and between the technology, information, and social artefacts (the composing artefacts) restrict the optimal impact LIS may have.

Our study offers two main contributions. First, it offers a more detailed understanding of LIS introduction within Indonesia by identifying tensions between the composing IS artefacts, as well as their influence on LIS success (or otherwise). Second, it proposes to incorporate the concept of tensions into the IS artefact concept to provide a better explanation of tension's role between the composing artefacts.

More work is needed to further elaborate on the findings introduced here, which is based on one single case study and therefore has only limited possibilities for provide all possible explanations. Future studies should go more into detail by unpacking each composing artefact and exploring other important composing artefacts. For example, the social artefact can be broken down into various artefacts, including political and legal artefacts, as already called for [31]. Scrutinising a phenomenon using more granulated artefacts could reveal a richer picture and more detailed practical insights, providing avenues for further research.

References

1. Arko-Adjei, A.: A conceptual approach for enhancing customary land management: case from Ghana. In: 5th FIG Regional Conference: Promoting Land Administration and Good Governance, Accra, Ghana (2006)
2. Bennett, R., Rajabifard, A., Williamson, I., Wallace, J.: On the need for national land administration infrastructures. Land Use Policy **29**, 208–219 (2012)
3. Bakker, L., Moniaga, S.: The space between: land claims and the law in Indonesia. Asian J. Soc. Sci. **38**, 187–203 (2010)
4. Chawla, R., Bhatnagar, S.: Online delivery of land titles to rural farmers in Karnataka, India. In: Scaling Up Poverty Reduction: A Global Learning Process and Conference. World Bank, Shanghai (2004)
5. Firman, T.: Major issues in Indonesia's urban land development. Land Use Policy **21**, 347–355 (2004)

6. Furuholt, B., Wahid, F., Sæbø, Ø.: Land information systems for development (LIS4D): a neglected area within ICT4D research? In: Proceedings of the 48th Hawaii International Conference on System Sciences (HICSS 2015), pp. 2158–2167. IEEE (2015)
7. Winoto, J.: Taking land policy and administration in Indonesia to the next stage and National Land Agency's strategic plan. In: Workshop in International Federation of Surveyors' Forum, Washington DC (2009)
8. Badan Pertanahan Nasional. http://www.bpn.go.id/Publikasi/Data-Pertanahan/Kasus-Pertanahan/Nasional
9. Badan Pertanahan Nasional. http://www.bpn.go.id/Program-Prioritas/Penanganan-Kasus-Pertanahan
10. Yusuf, H.: Land administration system in Indonesia. In: Pre-17th AVA Congress, Siem Reap, Cambodia (2011)
11. Orlikowski, W.J., Iacono, C.S.: Research commentary: desperately seeking the "IT" in IT research—a call to theorizing the IT artifact. Inf. Syst. Res. 12, 121–134 (2001)
12. Davison, R.M., Martinsons, M.G.: Context is king! Considering particularism in research design and reporting. J. Inf. Technol. 31, 241–249 (2016)
13. Lee, A.S., Thomas, M., Baskerville, R.L.: Going back to basics in design science: from the information technology artifact to the information systems artifact. Inf. Syst. J. 25, 5–21 (2015)
14. Spagnoletti, P., Resca, A., Sæbø, Ø.: Design for social media engagement: insights from elderly care assistance. J. Strateg. Inf. Syst. 24, 128–145 (2015)
15. Ågerfalk, P.J., Fitzgerald, B.: Outsourcing to an unknown workforce: exploring opensourcing as a global sourcing strategy. MIS Q. 32, 385–409 (2008)
16. Hutter, K., Hautz, J., Füller, J., Mueller, J., Matzler, K.: Communitition: the tension between competition and collaboration in community-based design contests. Creat. Innov. Manage. 20, 3–21 (2011)
17. Kozinets, R.V., De Valck, K., Wojnicki, A.C., Wilner, S.J.S.: Networked narratives: understanding word-of-mouth marketing in online communities. J. Mark. 74, 71–89 (2010)
18. Faraj, S., Jarvenpaa, S.L., Majchrzak, A.: Knowledge collaboration in online communities. Organ. Sci. 22, 1224–1239 (2011)
19. Mumford, E.: The story of socio-technical design: reflections on its successes, failures and potential. Inf. Syst. J. 16, 317–342 (2006)
20. Sein, M., Henfridsson, O., Purao, S., Rossi, M., Lindgren, R.: Action design research. MIS Q. 35, 37–56 (2011)
21. Alter, S.: The concept of 'IT artifact' has outlived its usefulness and should be retired now. Inf. Syst. J. 25, 47–60 (2015)
22. Goldkuhl, G.: The IT artefact: an ensemble of the social and the technical?–A rejoinder. Syst. Signs Actions 7, 90–99 (2013)
23. Silver, M.S., Markus, M.L.: Conceptualizing the SocioTechnical (ST) artifact. Syst. Signs Actions 7, 82–89 (2013)
24. Kaplan, A.M., Haenlein, M.: Users of the world, unite! The challenges and opportunities of social media. Bus. Horiz. 53, 59–68 (2010)
25. Salem, P.: The seven communication reasons organizations do not change. Corp. Commun. Int. J. 13, 333–348 (2008)
26. Ribes, D., Finholt, T.A.: The long now of technology infrastructure: articulating tensions in development. J. Assoc. Inf. Syst. 10, 375 (2009)
27. Heryani, E., Grant, C.: Land administration in Indonesia. In: 3rd FIG Regional Conference, Jakarta (2004)

28. Sekretariat Kabinet. http://www.setkab.go.id/berita-8452-redam-konflik-penguasaan-lahan-badan-informasi-geospasial-susun-satu-peta-dasar.html
29. Suara Pembaruan: Sengketa tanah ulayat di Nagekeo, NTT: Bupati diduga pakai polisi sebagai beking. Suara Pembaruan (2014)
30. Rahalaka, K.: Pendekatan budaya, solusi penyelesaian masalah tanah di Nagekeo. Floresbangkit.com (2014)
31. Winner, L.: Do artifacts have politics? Daedalus **109**, 121–136 (1980)

Assessing the E-Government Maturity for Public Sector Innovation in Developing Countries: Case of National Informatization Assessment Tool (NIAT)

Hanah Zoo[1], Heejin Lee[1(✉)], and Jeongwon Yoon[2]

[1] Graduate School of International Studies, Yonsei University, Seoul, Korea
heejinmelb@yonsei.ac.kr
[2] National Informatization Agency, Seoul, Korea

Abstract. This paper presents a new approach to assess the e-Government maturity with an aim to facilitate public sector innovation in developing countries. NIAT takes a rare approach to comprehensively assess the needs and capabilities by a participatory measure. It provides a standardized assessment process in order to ensure the quality of data. NIAT contributes to the service innovation by providing improved contents for e-Government services and identifying priorities of ICT strategy. It also stimulates organizational innovation in the public sector by building capacity of stakeholders across governmental silos and sectors. NIAT is a toolkit for quick deployment of ICT strategy and action plan grounded on actual experiences of e-Government developments in Korea. By offering a proven, pre-costed pool of projects readily applicable in practice, NIAT allows an accelerated prioritization of the relevant projects. In addition, the participatory process involving key actors in the government is a consensus building mechanism to generate political buy-ins for the project chosen.

Keywords: e-Government · Developing countries · Public service innovation · e-Government maturity · National informatization assessment tool

1 Introduction

Over the last decade, there has been a plethora of initiatives of e-Government implementation in developing countries [1]. Reflecting the movement, e-Government has been one of the most frequently researched topics in the field of studies that examine the role of information and communication technologies for socioeconomic development (ICT4D) [2–6]. In particular, with the launch of the Sustainable Development Goals (SDGs) as a new agenda for international development cooperation, e-Governance in developing countries receives a renewed attention as an instrument of public service innovation [7–9]. In general, innovation in the public sector refers to "significant improvements to public administration and/or services" [10]. E-Government is more than "government-as-usual" on top of the existence of ICT [11]. Once necessary infrastructure is in place, e-Government increases the efficiency of public service by saving time and cost required for the delivery, as well as broadening

© IFIP International Federation for Information Processing 2017
Published by Springer International Publishing AG 2017. All Rights Reserved
J. Choudrie et al. (Eds.): ICT4D 2017, IFIP AICT 504, pp. 778–789, 2017.
DOI: 10.1007/978-3-319-59111-7_63

the outreach, of service. Further, improved visibility and transparency of the public services put pressure for increased accountability on the government agencies, thereby help building citizen trust in the government. Particularly in developing countries, e-Government is expected to contribute to inclusive development by allowing equitable access to key public services for all citizens, while strengthening the institutional capacities of the government by providing opportunities for civil servants to learn about, and adopt, the standardized best practices.

With this shift of focus, the method to decide the priorities of development areas in e-Government, particularly in the context of resource-poor developing countries, also faces a call for change. There are a number of existing methodologies to assess the priorities of e-Government development [12–14]. While details may differ, they tend to emphasize in common the delivery aspect of e-Government. Considering that one of the most pressing challenges in e-Government implementation in developing countries arises from the inadequate level of ICT infrastructure, the accessibility to online pubic service occupies one of the top concerns in the decision-making related to e-Government. However, when applied from the perspective of public sector innovation, the decision of the priority areas in e-Government should also be made with a renewed set of criteria. As Windrum and Koch [15] note, public sector innovation encompasses improvements in a variety of areas, not only including the methods of delivery, but also the contents of the service as well as the institutional and organizational structures in which decisions are made. In this sense, a new approach to assess the levels of development and the priorities of e-Government is needed that considers beyond the expansion of delivery channels of existing public services.

With this background, this paper proposes a new method titled National Informatization Assessment Tool (NIAT) to assess the priorities of e-Government development for developing countries particularly under the context of international development cooperation projects. Based on e-Government development from the perspective of public service innovation, NIAT offers: (1) a set of proven, readily available options extracted from previous surveys to improve the contents and delivery of online-based public services, reflecting the supply side capabilities of the e-Government development, and; (2) opportunities for organizational innovation within the government agencies based on a participatory assessment process.

This paper is organized as follows. In the next section, we explore the literature and the context of e-Government development in developing countries, and review existing tools for the assessment of e-Government priorities in developing countries. In Sect. 3, we explain the background of the NIAT development. In the following Sects. 4 and 5, we discuss the NIAT model in detail in terms of its theoretical backgrounds and implementation stages. Finally, in Sect. 6, we discuss the contribution of NIAT in public sector innovation in developing countries and conclude with prospects for future works.

2 Review of Literature and Context

2.1 E-Government Development in Developing Countries

Much research exists that explores the challenges of e-Government implementation in developing countries. A stream of research explores the factors influencing the high failure rates of e-Government in developing countries [2, 3, 5]. The digital divide, both in terms of the technical infrastructure as well as the institutional and human capabilities to utilize ICT, poses a significant challenge to the widespread adoption of e-Government in developing countries. The income level of a country is a general indicator of economic capacity and progress, which thus influences its e-Government development particularly concerning the availability of technical infrastructure [16]. However, another stream of research suggests the importance of social and organizational changes for e-Government to be fully functional [17]. It requires much more than the technical capabilities to successfully implement and operate online public services; constraints are typically a combination of political, legal, financial, organizational, institutional and human capital factors [18, p. 4, 19].

Among these difficulties, one of the major challenges in the e-Government development is the problem of fragmentation. Fragmentation in ICT systems usually refers to a lack of coherency in the different applications composing a larger system. Fragmentation is more likely to happen and difficult to remedy in e-Government which is usually composed of systems in different subject areas under the supervision of different government agencies and departments. The sources of such fragmentation may vary. Sometimes the weak institutional capabilities result into unclear objectives and inadequately designed systems. Insufficient planning may cause cost overruns and even unfinished projects, which inevitably interrupt the continuity and coherency of e-Government initiatives. The same result can be caused by a simple lack of, or unpredictability of, funding arrangements from the government or donors. In addition, there is a general shortage of specialized human resources in developing countries, which leads to reliance on support from external expertise.

In sum, despite the already significant level of exposure to e-Government initiatives in developing countries, there is a high prevalence of failures which makes the governments in developing countries start to realize that ICT projects are not necessarily a silver bullet. A greater amount of political capital is needed in order for a project to go through. Additionally, although government officers have a general idea of what they want for ICT innovation, in many cases they lack the technical expertise to design and implement the e-Government projects. Combined together, they result in the problem of a fragmented and incoherent approach to national ICT development.

2.2   Assessment of E-Government Development

One method to alleviate this problem of fragmentation is to enhance the policy coherency of e-Government initiatives through the establishment of tailored national e-Government development plan. There are certain advantages a country can attain by establishing a sound blueprint. For example, it allows developing a long-term strategy, possibly linked with the national ICT master plan. Vertical and horizontal coordination within the national ICT master plan and across other key development areas is also possible. It also allows reflecting the priority areas of e-Government into the national plan much easier. Last but not least, a blueprint with specific goals helps establishing benchmark goals for evaluation, as well as facilitating resource mobilization.

There are several existing methodologies and global indicators that seek to measure the maturity level of a country's e-Government development and recommend areas of priority to establish a national blueprint that reflects the current status.

First, the United Nations e-Government survey is a well-known assessment tool [16]. The survey provides a systematic approach to measure the degree of e-Government development in three dimensions including telecommunication infrastructure, human capital, and online services and contents. While it offers a globally comparable snapshot of e-Government development of a country, the index in its nature is simply a policy research report. As such, its utility as a tool for development planning is limited. Therefore, it is not easy to readily apply the findings of the e-Government survey into actual project development and implementation in developing countries.

Second, ITU's e-Government Implementation Toolkit [13] takes a consulting-oriented approach and provides priority areas of action based on the level of ICT readiness and national development strategies in the country. Specifically targeted for decision-makers in developing countries, it aims to provide a hands-on tool for national initiatives for e-Government development. However, the degree of customization available in the toolkit is not sufficient to fully reflect the political and organizational concerns and priorities that are not necessarily captured in statistics on national income and ICT usage. And it currently lacks a detailed guideline on how to utilize this tool, from the assessment leading to the establishment of a customized e-Government development plan.

Apart from these two international initiatives, there are other public, private, and research-led approaches on e-Government assessment. Even though they offer unique strengths that make them worth referencing, they share similar limitations such as limited data availability outside the authoring organization, insufficient room for national contribution and customization, and lack of linkages to actual projects for easier implementation.

With this background, we propose a new methodology to respond to the following three objectives: (1) assessing the degree of e-Government development in a country, (2) providing a policy-oriented approach for easier establishment and implementation of a national e-Government development plan, and (3) providing a participatory approach for enhanced ownership and coherence.

3   Research Background

3.1   Background of NIAT Development

The National Informatization Assessment Tool aims to provide a quick solution to examine the current status of informatization including the level of e-Government maturity, and recommend priorities of initiatives and actions for e-Government projects through a consensus-based approach for easier application in the field. NIAT is a product of decades-long ICT and e-Government consultations carried out by the National Information Society Agency of Korea (NIA), a key wing for ICT4D in the Korean government's ODA (official development assistance). NIA is a statutory agency affiliated with the Ministry of Science, ICT and Future Planning and responsible for the overall implementation of and support for national informatization [20]. NIAT has been developed amid the increasing requests from developing countries to provide consultations on national ICT and e-Government strategy and action plan. These consultations naturally led to the use of templates and checklists to ensure the quality of the output. The quality of the consultations has been further developed through process standardization with support from specialists in diverse areas to streamline and improve the overall consultation processes.

3.2   Development History of NIAT

The development of NIAT entailed three simultaneous activities: accumulation of knowledge and know-hows by consultants, process standardization led by experts from both academic and practice, and streamlining of the process for the development of a software tool.

First, for the accumulation activities, data was collected by internal and external consultants who directly participated in the consultation for e-Government mater plan development in four countries, including Bulgaria, Columbia, Ecuador, and Uganda. The consultation was conducted under a public-private-academic partnership: NIA as a government agency, an information systems (IS) company, and university-based researchers. Consultation encompassed the areas of inter-governmental cooperation framework, policy consultations with high level officials and workshops, strategy planning including action plans and budgetary allocation, and feasibility studies for specific areas of application. These experiences were shared and accumulated in internal meetings and documents. Even though this knowledge existed in an unstructured form, piecemeal, incremental process revisions were made.

Second, the process standardization was carried out in two phases in 2014 and 2015. Reviews of existing research on e-Government maturity assessment were conducted to fine-tune the NIAT process. Based on the result of literature review, expert interviews and accumulated knowledge from previous applications, seven stages of the NIAT standard procedure were defined (see Sect. 5.2). Particularly for the stages 3 and 5 where weighted calculations are required to draw out stage outputs, a modified analytical hierarchical process (AHP) was applied to decide appropriate weights. AHP is a widely used method to derive priority scales based on pairwise comparisons conducted by experts [21]. A team of external experts from both academic and industry participated in the standardization process including the AHP.

Lastly for the streamlining, inputs were collected from the workshops among consultants in the field, as well as interviews from the national stakeholders who participated in the NIAT consultation process in their countries. The updated NIAT was then developed into a web-based tool.

4   Theoretical Framework of NIAT

NIAT is composed of three dimensions: (1) Macro analyses, (2) Improvement Themes, and (3) Maturity Evaluation. Combined together, they provide a comprehensive view over what development opportunities lie ahead in e-Government in the country under study.

First, the macro analyses are further divided into two parts: Country Positioning and PESTLE Analysis. Country Positioning draws on the country classification conducted by the ITU toolkit [13], and provides a general idea of project priorities according to the country's income level. The PESTLE (Political, Economic, Social, Technological, Legal, and Environmental) Analysis is an expansion of the original PEST analysis suggested by Aguilar [22], which assumes that external industry conditions have causal relationship with implications and consequences for the organization. These external conditions are also causally related with the areas of management attention in strategic management. The NIAT PESTLE analysis also looks at the country's informatization ecosystem to derive implications for priority areas of development. In particular, the following six questions are asked. What is the political situation of the country and how does it affect national informatization? What are the prevalent economic factors influencing national informatization? What are the prevalent social factors influencing national informatization? What technological trends and innovations are expected to affect national informatization? Are there any current legislations, or changes in the legislations that are relevant to national informatization? What are the current environmental concerns?

Second, the Improvement Themes refer to pre-defined strategic areas in which the country's national ICT development plan can focus on. They are categorized into four groups: Government, Citizen & Society, Business, and ICT Infrastructure. The four groups are made of a total of 17 Improvement Themes, and 17 Improvement Themes are further broken down into 64 maturity indicators. For each group, relevant Improvement Themes and maturity indicators have been identified by defining service needs that arise as national informatization progresses and by referring to Korea's benchmark cases.

Third, NIAT assesses the degree of national e-Government development using a 5-level maturity model, which is adapted from the UN e-Government Survey [12]. The model covers four areas including the processes, systems, services, and organization of e-Government, and classifies them into 5 levels. Level 1, Initial level, refers to a situation where e-Government process has not been stabilized yet. In Level 2, Developing level, a basic e-Government process as well as a computerized database (DB) is established for each unit of action. In terms of the organization and service, general guidelines and services are available but with limited information. Level 3 indicates a Defined level, where the processes are established for each entity composed multiple units. Systems and DB are also connected intra-entity level. From the service aspect, users may find information on the web, and download key information and forms. In Level 4, Managed level, processes are established across different entities, and the systems are connected at the inter-entity level. In terms of the services, online processing of administrative services is available. In Level 5, Integrated level, the processes and systems are integrated into a generalized process and a common operation system. e-Resources are also managed through a generalized management system. Users enjoy seamless one-stop service offerings across departments and entities.

5 Application of NIAT

5.1 A Participatory Workshop

In many ICT projects in developing countries, employees and managers of the institution concerned do not have the technical education, training, and means to develop a solution that will sustain the transformation process [1]. They usually do not participate in the development processes and such a lack of participation has been identified as a challenge to public sector innovation in developing countries.

NIAT primarily draws meaning from the insights of the national stakeholders, since they have the best understanding of what needs to be done. This in mind, NIAT is designed to be conducted in a one-day workshop; national stakeholders can participate in a simplified consulting process structured in 7 stages of standardized activities. It is important to involve a diverse group of stakeholders in the participatory workshop, including: government officers both executive and working levels, ICT and e-Government domain experts from national organizations, private sector, academia, and citizens represented by the NGOs and civic groups. Previous NIAT workshop experiences show that an appropriate size of the group ranges from 20 to 50 persons in one setting.

Such a workshop gives the stakeholders a general idea of what types of national e-Government projects should be implemented. By introducing Korea's e-Government and national informatization benchmark cases alongside the identification of priorities, quick win projects can be rapidly identified. In addition, the workshop focuses on reaching a consensus of stakeholders on the results of each of the stages, thereby enhancing their ownership over the project and offering a shared learning opportunity.

5.2 NIAT Process: A 7-Stage Model

This section explains the 7 stages of NIAT application. The first stage of NIAT, Country Positioning, begins with identifying the country's economic position according to its income level in terms of gross domestic product (GDP) per capita in USD. Based on the country's income level, different weights are automatically given to each Improvement Theme. In order to assign weight, NIAT draws on from the ITU e-Government Implementation Toolkit [13]. The ITU undertook a statistical analysis of countries with different income levels and found out that there is a statistical correlation between income levels and different priorities of projects. Following the ITU approach, countries are classified into four groups including: low-income, lower-middle-income, upper-middle-income, and high-income economies. For each income group, different weights are given to each Improvement Theme, reflecting the relevance and impact of the specific Theme under the income group.

Stage 2 is the PESTLE Analysis stage for analyzing the country's macro-environment in six areas including political, economic, social, technical, legal and environmental, in order to further prioritize the Improvement Themes. Various factors have been identified for each of the six areas, which are divided into a total of 64

PESTLE indicators. The actual analysis is carried out by rating the current status of 64 PESTLE indicators of the country using a five-point scale. In-depth interviews with key stakeholders in the country are necessary to adequately capture different factors that may affect the informatization level of a country. Combined with the result of the Country Positioning, the output from this exercise provides additional weighting values for calculating the final prioritization list.

Stage 3 is Selection of Improvement Themes where priority Improvement Themes are selected, which indicate the areas of the most pressing needs. The selection is automatically generated based on the input from the second stage, combined with a pre-defined, weighted mapping logic embedded in NIAT. As mentioned earlier, a group of experts conducted a modified AHP to map the PESTLE factors to the improvement themes. The panel of experts in AHP conducted the mapping process based on the two main criteria of relevance and impact.

Stage 4 is dedicated to reviewing the automatically selected list of Improvement Themes in the previous stage, reflecting any specific conditions or needs identified through the deliberation process among participating stakeholders. In particular, the selected Improvement Themes should be reviewed in comparison with the results of income-group categorization from Stage 1, reflecting the intuition and experiences of the stakeholders and the consultants.

Stage 5 is Maturity Evaluation. Maturity Evaluation is conducted for the 17 Improvement Themes. For each Improvement Theme, two to four maturity indicators are defined to measure different dimensions of achievement, adding up to a total of 48 indicators for all the 17 Improvement Themes. For each maturity indicator, the participating stakeholders evaluate three aspects: Current situation (As-Is), Future demand (To-Be), and Ease of implementation. To facilitate the evaluation process, a five-level maturity model has been adopted from the UN e-Government Development Survey [16]. The results of the maturity evaluation are used as additional weighting values to calculate a prioritized list of informatization projects in Stage 6.

Stage 6 is Prioritization where a list of priority maturity indicators is automatically identified based on the results of the previous stages. Three criteria, defined by the expert panel and tested in Korean informatization cases, are used to decide the priority of maturity indicators, including the impact, urgency and ease of implementation. Maturity indicators that have the highest values from each of the three criteria are selected as priorities, which should be the first concern when implementing a national e-Government development plan.

Stage 7, Recommendation, displays the final result of NIAT, that is, a list of recommend projects aligned with the prioritized maturity indicators from Stage 6. A repository of e-Government projects has been created from Korean ICT development history and other global good practices, which provides an access to readily available projects for implementation. The result can be used as a basis for a general roadmap of the national e-Government development plan. However, additional modifications may be needed depending on prerequisites that are different for each country.

6 Discussion and Conclusion

6.1 Improving the Contents of E-Government

While the focus of e-Government literature in general is expanding to cover a citizen-centric perspective on e-Government under the theme of e-Participation [23], the difficulties of capturing the demand side reality in developing countries still make it a challenge to produce meaningful findings for both academic and policy-oriented research. In fact, those attempts to measure the demand of e-Government in developing countries constitute necessary and legitimate efforts to respond to the societal requirement. However, given the situation of developing countries where information gathering from the citizen is constrained due to the lack of technical capabilities and paucity of resources, their merits in practice still remain a question. Incomplete and incorrect information on e-Government demand may mislead or sometimes even distort the allocation of already scarce resources in developing countries, defeating the goals of achieving efficient and innovative public service delivery. In this sense, particularly for the purpose of policy consultation in developing countries, a shift of focus towards the supply side requirements may yield more practical and useful results.

NIAT focuses on adequately addressing the supply side requirements on three fronts, first by comprehensively collecting the policy needs through a series of participatory analyses, second by providing a pool of proven, readily available policy options from the Korean and global good practices, and third by matching the policy options to meet the specific needs of the country through a refined approach. That said, NIAT assists to enrich the contents of public service innovation through e-Government, as it provides a set of proven, ready-to-implement e-Government projects based on the strategic needs of the country.

6.2 Enhancing Participatory Innovation Through E-Government

As Eggers and Singh [24] argue, the particular problem with innovation in public sector is not so much about the absence of innovation per se, but the ad hoc nature of the innovation which often fails to develop the very own capacity of the public sector to continuously innovate. Particularly in developing countries where e-Government implementation in many cases is associated with a large-scale donor support, it is the external experts from the outside of the country who usually drive the initiative. Given the circumstances, e-Government development tends to focus on giving the fish rather than teaching how to fish. The lack of involvement of national stakeholders in the process of e-Government development, in this sense, significantly impedes the potential of locally-driven, sustainable public sector innovation in developing countries.

NIAT, by offering a standardized procedure to conduct a participatory decision-making in the national e-Government development, contributes to growing this key capability of national stakeholders. Apart from the existing approaches where the focus of attention lies in the application of technological inventions in the public sector, NIAT emphasizes the important contributions of the social and political actors either in the e-Government and/or national ICT strategy development processes. In particular, NIAT invites a variety of stakeholders in a participatory workshop to make important development decisions in e-Government. This workshop provides a platform for collaborative interaction and learning among different stakeholders. In the workshop, stakeholders may share the objectives of the innovation, build a consensus on the areas and methods to respond to a call for innovation, and check whether the relevant stakeholders possess the necessary skills to make the innovation work [25]. Such a shared understanding of goals and methods of e-Government among stakeholders may reduce the problem of fragmentation, by facilitating collaboration across different departments in the government and different sectors of expertise. In addition, NIAT emphasizes the input from the government officials when prioritizing the areas of development. Such a focus enhances the ownership of the government officials as a key actor of the project, coordinating the innovation network and sometimes brokering an emergence of a new one as an entrepreneur in the public sector [15].

6.3 Ensuring the Quality of Innovation in a Standardized Process

NIAT offers a standardized process of e-Government assessment to enhance the quality of public service innovation in developing countries. As mentioned earlier, NIAT offers a set of structured activities in each stage to prioritize the areas of e-Government development. In particular, this process of standardization takes up an important part of the NIAT development. Generally speaking, a typical consultation process requires substantive efforts in preparation. It entails a variety of quantitative and qualitative measurements of the governance structure, policies, and economy as a prerequisite. Therefore, ensuring a consistent quality of the outcome remains a challenge. Sometimes the analyses may derive different outcomes depending on the institutional factors such as the degree of political will, availability of data, and human factors such as the capacity of the consultants and the quality and scope of participating stakeholders in the country. In this regard, the development of a standardized assessment method and a software tool for additional support, despite the significant amount of initial works required, offers advantages. For one thing, NIAT ensures the quality of the consulting outcome based on refined, proven experiences. In addition, by defining a set of common, objective standards, it helps reduce the cost of coordination and prevent redundancy of work.

6.4 Limitations and Future Work

In this paper, we presented a novel approach to assess the e-Government maturity with a particular aim to help facilitate public sector innovation in developing countries. From the research aspect, NIAT takes a rare approach to comprehensively assess the supply side needs and capabilities from a participatory measure. It also provides a standardized assessment process in order to ensure the quality of data for a more accurate and customized outcome. NIAT not only contributes to the service innovation by providing new contents for e-Government services, but also stimulates organizational innovation in the public sector by offering a learning opportunity among stakeholders across governmental silos and sectors. In the practice side, NIAT is a time-saving method for practical application grounded on actual experiences of e-Government development and national informatization in Korea. By offering a proven, pre-costed pool of projects readily applicable in practice, NIAT allows an accelerated prioritization of the relevant projects. In addition, the participatory process involving key actors in the government is a consensus building mechanism to generate political buy-ins for the project. Despite these contributions of NIAT, there are certain limitations. For one thing, more empirical data should be collected from actual consultations of e-Government development in developing countries, in order to verify the efficacy of NIAT as a policy-oriented tool for e-Government assessment. Additionally, even though the lack of attention to the demand side requirements in NIAT is intentional in the design, further efforts are needed to identify the needs of citizens in developing countries and assess their levels of engagement in e-Participation. Considering the particular context of e-Government in developing countries as a solution to improve the delivery and contents of public services to the disadvantaged, e-Participation should be approached not only to assess their degree of access but also the needs to improve their livelihoods.

References

1. Kettani, D., Moulin, B.: E-Government for Good Governance in Developing Countries: Empirical Evidence from the eFez Project. Anthem Press, London (2014)
2. Heeks, R.: iGovernment Working Paper Series Most e-Government-for-Development Projects Fail: How Can Risks be Reduced? (2003)
3. Stanforth, C.: Using actor-network theory to analyze E-government implementation in developing countries. Inf. Technol. Int. Dev. 3(3), 35–60 (2006)
4. Basu, S.: e-Government and developing countries: An overview. Int. Rev. Law Comput. Technol. 18(1), 109–132 (2004)
5. Danish, D.: The failure of e-Government in developing countries: A literature review. Electron. J. Inf. Syst. Dev. Ctries. 26(7), 1–10 (2006)
6. Madon, S.: IT-based government reform initiatives in the Indian state of Gujarat. J. Int. Dev. 18(6), 877–888 (2006)
7. United Nations: UN highlights role of public service in achieving SDGs. http://www.un.org/sustainabledevelopment/blog/2016/06/un-highlights-role-of-public-service-in-achieving-sdgs/
8. Griffin, D., Trevorrow, P., Halpin, E. (eds.): Developments in e-Government. IOS Press, Amsterdam (2007). NLD
9. OECD: e-Government for Better Government, Paris (2005)
10. Daglio, M., Gerson, D., Kitchen, H.: Building organisational capacity for public sector innovation. In: Background Paper prepared for the OECD Conference 'Innovating the Public Sector: From Ideas to Impact,' Paris (2015)
11. Bryant, A.: Government, e-Government and modernity. In: Griffin, D., Trevorrow, P., Halpin, E. (eds.) Developments in e-Government, pp. 3–15. IOS Press, Amsterdam (2007). NLD
12. United Nations: E-Government Survey 2014 (2014)

13. ITU: ITU e-Government Implementation Toolkit: A Framework for e-Government Readiness and Action Priorities. Geneva (2009)
14. UNESCO: E-government Toolkit for Developing Countries. Delhi (2005)
15. Windrum, P., Koch, P. (eds.): Innovation in Public Sector Services: Entrepreneurship, Creativity and Management. Edward Elga, Cheltenham (2008)
16. United Nations: UN E-Government Survey 2014: e-Government for the Future We Want. New York (2014)
17. Lee, J.: Search for stage theory in e-government development. In: Griffin, D., Trevorrow, P., Halpin, E. (eds.) Developments in e-Government. NLD, IOS Press, Amsterdam (2007)
18. ITU: Electronic Government for Developing Countries, Geneva (2008)
19. Ndou, V.(D.): E-goverment for developing countries opportunities and challenges. Electron. J. Inf. Syst. Dev. Countries 18(1), 1–24 (2004)
20. NIA: Introduction to NIA, National Information Society Agency. http://eng.nia.or.kr/english/Contents/01_about/introduction.asp?BoardID=201112231150126087&Order=103
21. Saaty, T.L.: Decision making with the analytic hierarchy process. Int. J. Serv. Sci. 1(1), 83 (2008)
22. Aguilar, F.J.: Scanning the Business Environment. Macmillan, New York (1967)
23. Reddick, C.G., Weerakkody, V.: Public Sector Transformation Through E-government: Experiences from Europe and North America. Routledge, New York (2013)
24. Eggers, W.D., Singh, S.K.: The Public Innovator's Playbook: Nurturing Bold Ideas in Government. Deloitte Research, Washington (2009)
25. Sorensen, E., Torfing, J.: Enhancing collaborative innovation in the public sector. Adm. Soc. 43(8), 842–868 (2011)

Notes

An Analysis of Accountability Concepts
for Open Development

Caitlin Bentley[(✉)]

Singapore Internet Research Centre, Nanyang Technological University,
Singapore, Singapore
cmbentley@ntu.edu.sg

Abstract. Open development is the public, networked sharing of communication and information resources towards a process of positive social transformation. Open development likewise imposes a challenge, because new actors,
practices and problems of inequality are introduced. Accountability at its core is
meant to redress issues of power and inequality [1], thus offering potential to
improve open development processes and initiatives. However, the distinct and
innovative characteristics of open processes render some concepts of accountability inadequate. This article compares three purposes and perspectives on
accountability for their relevance to open development. The purpose of which is
to suggest future areas of research and theoretical development in this field.

Keywords: Open development · Accountability · ICT4D

1 Introduction

This paper adopts two key ideas to frame open development which are drawn from
Smith and Seward [2] and Reilly and Smith [3]. Open development can be defined in
terms of *what it is for,* and *how it works.* In terms of how it works, Smith and Seward
[2] outline three processes that set open development apart from other forms of ICT
supported interaction: open consumption (e.g. using, remixing, and repurposing content), open distribution (e.g. sharing and republishing content) and open production
(e.g. peer production). These processes explain how and why particular arrangements
of people, technology and content offer distinct opportunities for development. Second,
open development can be defined in terms of *what it is for.* Reilly and Smith [3], in
accordance with Sen [4], argue that open development, like human development, is the
expansion of freedom. However, scholars also emphasise that institutional structures of
society play a significant role in shaping the freedom of groups and individuals [5, 6].

A debate has occurred amongst scholars in this field regarding whether or not what
open processes *are* lead to what open development *is for.* Some have argued that open
processes enable radical transformations away from bureaucratic modes of doing
development, towards freer, less exclusive arrangements [3, 7]. In contrast, other scholars

The original version of this chapter was revised: The erratum to this chapter is available at https://
doi.org/10.1007/978-3-319-59111-7_72

J. Choudrie et al. (Eds.): ICT4D 2017, IFIP AICT 504, pp. 793–802, 2017.
DOI: 10.1007/978-3-319-59111-7_64

argue that open processes replicate wider structures of power and inequality within society, which open processes do not influence in and of themselves [8, 9]. The middle ground is that due to the complexity and flexibility of open processes, a wide spectrum of outcomes occurs. Outcomes are therefore contingent on a variety of contextual factors. Thus, there is a need to differentiate how and why certain development actors, particularly the poorest and most marginalised, may be positively or negatively affected.

Accountability is a concept that can potentially be used to understand and influence whether open processes are having positive development effects. Accountability can be broadly seen as the tools and processes that protect and empower individuals' opportunity to experience freedom [1, 10, 11]. However, what accountability means, and how it operates has not been explored within open development in detail. Much of the discourse on accountability in open development has focused on making use of new technology to hold development actors, such as governments, to account. ICT tools created to collect feedback directly from citizens can change accountability relationships, such that new channels between development aid recipients and the institutions serving them have been created [12]. Governments making public data available for free, hope to deliver greater transparency and accountability towards citizens [13, 14]. However, the links between accountability and open development are far more pervasive.

Yet, accountability is a contested concept, and there is no set of accountability concepts that apply universally. This paper addresses a gap in the literature by outlining three purposes and three groups of concepts of accountability, through a review of the literature, which seem pertinent to explore further in the area of open development. I provide suggestions regarding the types of concepts and purposes as a means to begin discussions, and to develop a future research agenda in this area.

2   Comparing Accountability Concepts for Open Development

Accountability, like open development, has also been theorised as both processes and outcomes [15–17]. I begin by outlining three purposes of accountability, which aid in differentiating potential applications of accountability to open development. These draw out the justification for focusing the conceptual review of accountability according to three themes: relationship-based concepts, practice and actor-based concepts, and normative or tool-based concepts. The subsections go into more detail regarding these themes of accountability concepts, and analyse them for their suitability for open development.

A fundamental debate in accountability literature centres on the role of individuals in governing their own lives [18, 19]. When people are directly involved in governing aspects of their lives, they are more likely to make choices that suit their own needs [18]. However, Cooke and Kothari's [20] argue that instrumentalising participation has a detrimental effect. This is especially true when people have limited opportunity to make decisions about how and why they contribute and/or benefit. Ebrahim [15] therefore posited that higher levels of participation, where individuals have full decision-making power and control over their actions constitutes greater accountability. Likewise, when individuals have fewer options to choose how to participate, accountability is weakened.

There is a parallel between this proposition and the technical design of open processes, because there are usually no imposed restrictions on who or how people contribute. Thus, the assumption is that individuals have the opportunity to govern how they use and benefit from their participation in open processes. However, in practice, empirical research has demonstrated that poor and marginalised people face many structural barriers that inhibit their participation in open processes [21]. Hence, it is worthwhile to explore additional purposes of accountability for open development.

Alternatively, responsiveness is a form of accountability that considers the perspectives of individuals and groups in need first and foremost [22]. Politicians are presumably re-elected when they listen and respond to the needs of their constituents [23] (perhaps a false truth these days!). The same principle holds true for actors and roles across different kinds of institutions. Empirical research has focused on analysing how responsiveness is enacted in private, public and third sector institutions [24–26]. However, open processes can be enacted across institutions, having variable levels of consistency and structure. This characteristic poses a problem to use responsiveness as the primary basis of accountability within open development. For example, a high level of responsiveness might seem realistic for a teacher using or producing open educational resources for one classroom, but once those resources are released for public consumption the teacher might not have close relationships with external users of the content. Likewise, a teacher facilitating a Massive Open Online Course serving thousands of individuals is not likely going to be able to respond to all learners. In this case, it may be necessary to explore both tools and processes for responsiveness. For instance, a survey tool to collect and consolidate feedback could help her to respond to groups of needs. In general, the major concern with responsiveness development is that it fails to differentiate between active and passive actors. Active actors may not be ideally positioned to respond to passive actors. For example, open source software developers might not be in a position to understand the needs of passive users of their software. This implies a need to consider the role of actors and institutions who have obligations towards passive actors.

The last framing of accountability discussed is therefore obligation. Obligation refers to the normative and contractual terms of accountability and potential sanctions [1]. This includes legal and regulatory frameworks that outline clear institutional rules and expectations for open development. Obligation also refers to actors' duty, which is contingent on roles, formal and felt responsibilities, identities and relationships [27]. For instance, Handlykken [28] examined the impact of a government policy to adopt open source software, which has shown little effect in practice. There has also been a wealth of research on opening up government data, and instituting strategies to garner meaningful use of this data [29–31]. In particular, Gigler et al. [12] reported that new citizen feedback channels changed obligations of traditional development actors. Another example, Uber, a ride-sharing platform, came under fire in Pakistan for the corrupt practices of rental car agencies who use the platform to exploit cheap illiterate workers [32]. However, understanding, shaping and/or regulating the obligations of actors in certain circumstances within open processes is a nascent area. Moreover, in many instances, obligations may not need regulating or shaping, as most open processes may never grow to the scale of Uber or government. Yet, as Forte and Lampe [33] argued, open systems tend to have emergent social structures which shape obligations. This can also be problematic for open development when certain groups of people may tend to dominate and render the system highly unequal. This is why there is also a need to contemplate obligations in terms of individual responsibilities, and how people may come to develop obligations towards others and to their role within open processes.

In summary, the table below outlines key concerns according to three accountability purposes in open development. The questions in Table 1 are only meant to help to differentiate how accountability purposes and concerns might change across purposes and types of open processes. Whilst I do not attempt to answer each question specifically in the remainder of this paper due to length requirements and scope of this discussion, these questions framed my engagement with the three themes of accountability concepts in the remainder of the paper. I turn now to explore three groups of accountability concepts for their relevance to understand and influence the relationship between what open development *is* and what it *is for*.

Table 1. Key accountability concerns across purposes of accountability and open processes

	Participation	Responsiveness	Obligation
Open consumption • Using • Revising • Remixing	(1) Do people apply, not only access resources? (2) Can people choose how to participate?	(3) Do resources respond to needs? (4) Are the needs of actors both directly and indirectly involved considered?	(5) What are the conditions for access to, and facilitation, maintenance and replenishment of resources?
Open distribution • Sharing • Republishing	(1), (2) and (9) Are distribution platforms accessible and appropriate?	(3), (4) and (10) Does the distribution platform respond to user needs and usability requirements?	(6) What roles, identities and responsibilities do actors have and experience? (7) What social and political structures influence behaviours and actions? (8) What liabilities and sanctions will actors be subjected to if they do not uphold their duties?
Open production • Peer production • Crowdsourcing	(1), (2) and (11) Do people have the skills and opportunity to contribute in the ways they see fit?	(3), (4) and (12) Does the production process deliver the required resources at an acceptable quality standard and timeframe?	

2.1   Relationship-Based Concepts

Relationship-based theories of accountability tend to focus on what actors are owed by those responsible for fulfilling agreed upon commitments. Agency theory focuses on the principal-agent model such that a principal brokers a deal with an agent to deliver an artefact. Actors may have tangential interests than what the principal has asked for, and thus agents have an incentive to avoid accomplishing what was mutually agreed, and or to selectively share or hide information [34, 35]. Principals have an incentive to control known problems as a means to protect their brokered deal from known negative influences [34]. This accountability concept is highly transactional in nature because it emphasises conditions imposed on relationships to ensure that each actor is held to account, and that sanctions can be applied when actors do not fulfill their obligations.

This concept could be useful to understand how open development works because it assumes that actors are motivated by individual interest. Within open distribution and consumption processes, the underlying premise is that people are free to use resources in ways they see fit, which ignores the underlying interests of open distributors. Agency theory implies that open consumers (agents) have privileged information over their actions with these resources, whilst open distributors (principals) have authority over the provision of them. Principals may seek methods to control how resources are used to suit their own interests. Based on this notion, this theory might aid in researching all three accountability purposes as the interests of authoritative actors may skew participation, responsiveness, and their perceived obligations. A weakness of this theory is that relationships between actors, may be ambiguous, especially when there are many distributors involved. It is best used when there are well-established actors and relationships, as with Murillo's [13] application of this theory to open government initiatives in Latin American countries. Similarly, within open production processes, this theory may not be informative for highly decentralised open production processes and communities, especially when membership is in flux. A task-based scale may be the most appropriate application, as this theory might inform on why or why not actors may be motivated to contribute to a specific task.

In contrast, development scholars contextualised the principal-agent model to address the more realistic situation when actors have multiple accountabilities, not only between one principal and an agent [36, 37]. The idea is to identify multiple accountabilities across relationships in order to assess how actors prioritise certain accountability relationships over others. These relational concepts of accountability are more focused on determining power asymmetries between the actors, and how power influences the actors' choices to uphold their commitments. Whilst relational concepts of accountability are more realistic in development contexts and processes, as they can identify key pitfalls to watch out for, it is still problematic within cases where the actors are not well-known, or directly related, making it ambiguous to apply. Nevertheless, relational concepts draw attention to the need to recognise multiple relationships and how and why accountabilities are prioritised. These concepts seem to offer significant value for targeted analysis of specific relationships within open processes. However, identifying which relationships to study may be problematic. The next group offers insight into how relevant actors might be targeted.

2.2 Practice- or Actor-Based Concepts

The second group of concepts emphasises the contextual and situated nature of accountability. Theories within this group operate on the assumption that accountability is intertwined with its context, and are inseparable from other aspects of purposeful action [16, 38]. This means that theorists have focused on practices of accountability in certain settings, like organisations, public or educational institutions. Examining the practice perspective enables understanding how actors and organisations enact accountability, and the tools and procedures they make use of. Practice-based perspectives also shed light on the resultant structures and dynamics of accountability, thus dealing with complexity of relationships and multiple accountabilities. However, these concepts do not provide a means for comparing alternatives or understanding whether one way of doing is better than another [39]. Therefore, these concepts are advantageous for understanding how accountability functions in new, under-explored open processes and settings.

This perspective is particularly relevant for understanding accountability in new and innovative open processes. For instance, accountability in open production communities, many of which are self-organised and highly decentralised, is likely to be distinct from the institutional contexts mentioned above. Practice-based notions of accountability may also help organisations inform their understanding of how new open methods of working interact with existing practice. For example, many aid institutions have established funding programmes, institutional policies and procedures around the ethos of sharing their knowledge resources in open formats. This brought about new institutional contexts emphasising freedom and inclusion, but may also have knock-on effects in complementary aspects of its development work.

In a similar vein, researchers have also focused on the roles and identities of actors to frame accountability, and how these are constructed in context. Bovens [27] argued that actors experience five types of responsibilities which influence their contributions to accountability: (1) hierarchical responsibility (loyalty to superiors); (2) personal responsibility (relating to conscience and personal ethics); (3) social responsibility (relating to social norms and peers); (4) professional responsibility (profession and professional ethics); (5) civic (citizen and civic values). These dimensions seem particularly pertinent to organise an exploratory study of accountability in open processes because of the way that open processes involve multiple actors and contexts. For instance, the tendency to assume that open distribution models, like open government data initiatives, can be replicated and transported across contexts fails to acknowledge how people and institutions are shaped by different values, ethics and obligations. Actor-based concepts highlight the importance of understanding multiple perspectives within open processes. These concepts may also aid in exploring roles and responsibilities of new actors that have entered traditional development practice spheres. However, these concepts likewise have difficulty to establish normative aspects of what actors roles and responsibilities should be.

2.3   Normative or Tool-Based Concepts

Normative or tool-based concepts refer to objective standards and processes to oversee and entrench aspects of accountability. It is unlikely that an overarching accountability framework for open development is possible or desirable. Nevertheless, normative or tool-based concepts of accountability could be helpful under many sets of circumstances. To give an explanation of what types of norms or tools are possible, Bendell [40] outlines a list of tools such as legal and policy frameworks, elections, boards of officials, codes of conduct, certifications, ratings, summative reports, monitoring and evaluation, and dialogue and participation. At face value, some of these are more applicable to open development than others. First, elections, boards of officials, codes of conduct and certification imply a highly defined regulatory area because these accountability tools would likely emerge only after a substantial institutional base has been established. Therefore, governments, institutions, networks, communities and services that persist for long periods of time might be the most pertinent to consider for these types of accountability tools. However, as Handlykken's [28] discussion of open source policy implementation in South Africa mentioned above notes, policies do not always have the intended effects. Conceptualising accountability as a particular tool or normative framework, nevertheless, does enable greater cross-comparison. This indicates that research incorporating both practice-based and tool-based concepts might be valuable.

The remaining tools from the list, such as monitoring and evaluation, ratings, and dialogue are perhaps of wider significance at the present stage because these tools can be useful to a more heterogeneous group of actors and contexts. The benefit of accountability tools, such as monitoring and evaluation, is that the connections between what open development is and what it is for can be made explicit. For instance, Smith and Seward [2] state that open processes are socially-embedded, but they do not theorise the links between how open processes function and what they achieve. In contrast, Zheng and Stahl's [41] critical capability approach to open development enables the investigation of open processes in terms of explicit outcomes related to capabilities, human diversity, marginalisation and inclusion. The main issue with monitoring and evaluation is that this tool requires that an actor has the will or obligation to apply it. In contrast, many open production communities are instead quite decentralised and self-organising, implying that formative evaluations may never come to light. An interesting application to note is Sharp's [42] open source community heartbeat tool, which tracks and visualises statistics, showing how newcomers are integrated and contributing code. However, these sorts of tools have not been explored in depth, warranting further research on the matter.

3   Conclusion

Overall, accountability concepts are highly relevant for reducing ambiguities between what open development is, and what it is for. The problem is that there are still ambiguities relating to what accountability is and how and why it can be applied to open development. This conceptual review of three purposes of accountability and three groups of accountability concepts has attempted to clarify matters. In general, there is value in pursuing all three purposes and perspectives of accountability mentioned above for open development in four key ways. First, at this juncture, empirical study is warranted to understand accountability practices across open processes and contexts. Second, exploratory studies may also be used to test specific assumptions regarding the purposes of accountability. Third, deeper understandings of accountability practices may also enable researchers to engage more thoroughly with excluded and neglected populations of open development. Fourth, there is a lack of ideas and evidence relating to accountability tools and norms specific to open development.

Acknowledgements. This research was conducted as part of the Singapore Internet Research Centre's SIRCA III programme and is funded by the International Development Research Centre (IDRC) of Canada.

References

1. Schedler, A.: Conceptualising accountability. In: Schedler, A., Diamond, L., Plattner, M.F. (eds.) The Self-Restraining State: Power and Accountability in New Democracies, pp. 13–27. Lynne Rienner Publishers Inc., London (1999)
2. Smith, M.L., Seward, R.K.: Openness as social praxis. Unpublished manuscript, Ottawa (2016)
3. Reilly, K.M.A., Smith, M.L.: The emergence of open development in a network society. In: Smith, M.L., Reilly, K.M.A. (eds.) Open Development: Networked Innovations in International Development, pp. 15–50. The MIT Press and International Development Research Centre, Ottawa (2013)
4. Sen, A.: Development as Freedom. Oxford University Press, Oxford (2001)
5. Zheng, Y., Stahl, B.C.: Technology, capabilities and critical perspectives: what can critical theory contribute to Sen's capability approach? Ethics Inf. Technol. **13**, 69–80 (2011). doi:10.1007/s10676-011-9264-8
6. Buskens, I.: Open development is a freedom song: revealing intent and freeing power. In: Smith, M.L., Reilly, K.M.A. (eds.) Open Development: Networked Innovations in International Development, pp. 327–352. The MIT Press and International Development Research Centre, Ottawa (2013)
7. Smith, M.L., Smith, M., Elder, L.: Open ICT ecosystems transforming the developing world. Inf. Technol. Int. Dev. **6**, 65–71 (2010)
8. Singh, P.J., Gurumurthy, A.: Establishing public-ness in the network: new moorings for development—a critique of the concepts of openness and open development. In: Smith, M.L., Reilly, K.M.A. (eds.) Open Development: Networked Innovations in International Development, pp. 173–196. The MIT Press and International Development Research Centre, Ottawa (2013)
9. Gurstein, M.: Open data: empowering the empowered or effective data use for everyone? In: Gurstein's Community Informatics (2010). http://gurstein.wordpress.com/2010/09/02/open-data-empowering-the-empowered-or-effective-data-use-for-everyone/. Accessed 28 Feb 2017
10. Grant, R.W., Keohane, R.O.: Accountability and abuses of power in world politics. Am. Polit. Sci. Rev. **99**, 29–43 (2005)
11. Tetlock, P.E.: Accountability: the neglected social context of judgment and choice. Res. Organ. Behav. (1985)
12. Gigler, B.-S., Custer, S., Bailur, S., et al.: Closing the feedback loop: can technology amplify citizen voices?. World Bank, Washington DC (2014)
13. Murillo, M.J.: Evaluating the role of online data availability: the case of economic and institutional transparency in sixteen Latin American nations. Int. Polit. Sci. Rev. **36**, 42–59 (2015). doi:10.1177/0192512114541163
14. Aryan, P.R., Ekaputra, F.J., Sunindyo, W.D., Akbar, S.: Fostering government transparency and public participation through linked open government data: case study: Indonesian public information service. In: 2014 International Conference on Data and Software Engineering (ICODSE), Bandung, pp. 1–6. IEEE (2014)

15. Ebrahim, A.: Accountability in practice: mechanisms for NGOs. World Dev. **31**, 813–829 (2003). doi:10.1016/S0305-750X(03)00014-7
16. Frink, D.D., Klimoski, R.J.: Toward a theory of accountability in organizations and human resource management. Res. Pers. Hum. Resour. Manage. **16**, 1–51 (1998)
17. Brees, J., Martinko, M.J.: Judgments of responsibility versus accountability. J. Leadersh. Organ. Stud. **22**, 443–453 (2015). doi:10.1177/1548051815603127
18. Chambers, R.: Whose Reality Counts?: Putting the First Last, 2nd edn. ITDG Publishing, London (1997)
19. Gaventa, J.: Towards a participatory governance: assessing the transformative possibilities. In: Hickey, S., Mohan, G. (eds.) Participation–From Tyranny to Transformation?: Exploring New Approaches to Participation in Development, pp. 25–39. Zed Books, London (2005)
20. Cooke, B., Kothari, U.: Participation: The New Tyranny? Zed Books, London (2001)
21. Kuriyan, R., Bailur, S., Gigler, B.-S., Park, K.R.: Technologies for transparency and accountability, pp. 1–67 (2011)
22. Leat, D.: Voluntary Organisations and Accountability. Policy Analysis Unit/Billing & Sons, London (1988)
23. Oliver, D.: Government in the United Kingdom. Open University, Milton Keynes (1991)
24. Hupe, P., Hill, M.: Street-level bureaucracy and public accountability. Public Adm. **85**, 279–299 (2007). doi:10.1111/j.1467-9299.2007.00650.x
25. Ebrahim, A., Weisband, E.: Global Accountabilities. Cambridge University Press, Cambridge (2007)
26. Peruzzotti, E.: Civil society, representation and accountability: restating current debates on the representativeness and accountability of civic associations. In: Jordan, L., van Tuijl, P. (eds.) NGO Accountability, pp. 43–58. Earthscan Publications Ltd., London (2006)
27. Bovens, M.: The Quest for Responsibility: Accountability and Citizenship in Complex Organisations (Theories of Institutional Design). Cambridge University Press, Cambridge (1998)
28. Handlykken, A.K.: Exploring the politics of Free/Libre/Open Source Software (FLOSS) in the context of contemporary South Africa; how are open policies implemented in practice? J. Community Inform. (2012)
29. Canares, M.P.: Opening the local: full disclosure policy and its impact on local governments in the Philippines. In: ICEGOV 2014, Guimaraes, pp. 89–98. ACM Press (2014)
30. Davies, T., Perini, F.: Researching the emerging impacts of open data: revisiting the ODDC conceptual framework. J. Commun. Inform. (2016)
31. Ohemeng, F.L.K., Ofosu-Adarkwa, K.: One way traffic: the open data initiative project and the need for an effective demand side initiative in Ghana. GovUK **32**, 1–10 (2015). doi:10.1016/j.giq.2015.07.005
32. Daily Pakistan Global: Corruption drives into Uber in Pakistan (2016). https://en.dailypakistan.com.pk/technology/corruption-drives-into-uber-in-pakistan/. Accessed 28 Feb 2016
33. Forte, A., Lampe, C.: Defining, understanding, and supporting open collaboration: lessons from the literature. Am. Behav. Sci. **57**, 535–547 (2013). doi:10.1177/0002764212469362
34. Jensen, M.C., Meckling, W.H.: Theory of the firm: managerial behaviour, agency costs, and ownership structure. J. Financ. Econ. **3**, 305–360 (1976). doi:10.1002/9780470752135.ch17
35. Shapiro, S.P.: Agency theory. Ann. Rev. Sociol. **31**, 263–284 (2005). doi:10.1146/annurev.soc.31.041304.122159
36. Koppell, J.G.: Pathologies of accountability: ICANN and the challenge of "multiple accountabilities disorder". Public Adm. Rev. **65**, 94–108 (2005)
37. Ebrahim, A.: Towards a reflective accountability in NGOs. In: Ebrahim, A., Weisband, E. (eds.) Global Accountabilities, pp. 193–223. Cambridge University Press, Cambridge (2007)

38. Roberts, J.: The possibilities of accountability. Acc. Organ. Soc. **16**, 355–368 (1991). doi:10. 1016/0361-3682(91)90027-C
39. Weisband, E.: Conclusion: prolegomena to a post-modern public ethics: images of accountability in global frames (2009). doi:10.1017/CBO9780511490903
40. Bendell, J.: Debating NGO Accountability. United Nations Publications, New York and Geneva (2006)
41. Zheng, Y., Stahl, B.C.: A critical capability approach to open development. Strengthening Information Society Research Capacity Alliance (SIRCA), Singapore (2016). http://www.sirca.org.sg/wp-content/uploads/2015/08/Zheng_WhitePaper.pdf. Accessed 28 Feb 2017
42. Sharp, S.: FOSS Heartbeat. In: sarahsharp.github.io. https://sarahsharp.github.io/foss-heartbeat/. Accessed 28 Feb 2017

Information Ecology as a Framework for South-South Cooperation: Case Studies of Rwanda and Bangladesh ICT-Based Health Applications

Suzana Brown$^{(\boxtimes)}$ⓘ and Faheem Hussainⓘ

Department of Technology and Society, SUNY Korea,
119 Songdo, Incheon 21985, Korea
suzana.brown@sunykorea.ac.kr,
faheem.hussain@stonybrook.edu

Abstract. Information Ecology represents a system of people, values, and technologies in a specific local environment. What makes Information Ecology different is that the spotlight is not on the technology but on human activities that are served by technology. As such it could be a powerful lens for understanding, evaluating, and eventually guiding South-South cooperation. We use Information Ecology to critically analyze two ICT-infused community health services, one in Bangladesh and one in Rwanda; and propose improvements for each case. Based on that analysis we believe that this framework can facilitate theoretical basis for guiding South-South cooperation, transferring knowledge and technology, and implementing policy recommendations.

Keywords: South-South · Cooperation · Framework · Community health

1 Introduction

In this note, we argue that Information Ecology is a powerful lens for understanding, evaluating, and guiding South-South cooperation. Information Ecology borrows its concept from biology with its complex dynamic interactions, diverse species and coevolution of the system. Information Ecology's main contribution is that the role of technology should not be isolated but interpreted as a part of the system [1].

South-South cooperation is led by the developing countries with positive signs of development. Countries like India, Brazil, and China are the leaders in disseminating their expertise and building new types of relationship with the other emerging countries, the relationship of exchange and economic cooperation. We analyze Rwanda and Bangladesh because of their prominent place in the emerging economies of Africa and South Asia. In addition, both countries have identified ICT as an enabler for coming out of poverty, so we critically analyze two specific ICT-infused community health services, using Information Ecology. Valuable field research experience in the above countries is allowing us firsthand knowledge about local and regional conditions.

© IFIP International Federation for Information Processing 2017
Published by Springer International Publishing AG 2017. All Rights Reserved
J. Choudrie et al. (Eds.): ICT4D 2017, IFIP AICT 504, pp. 803–808, 2017.
DOI: 10.1007/978-3-319-59111-7_65

2   Related Work

South-South collaboration is a new area of research, with studies on scientific and technical collaborations [2], as well as economic and social collaboration [3]. However, with no studies on collaboration and sharing in community healthcare design. In addition, comparing lessons from development projects from multiple countries, has always been a struggle mostly because there is no common framework. In attempt to bridge that gap, we turn to Information Ecology. Information Ecology is a new concept in ICT for development but already used as a theoretical framework to explore technology-focused initiatives that attempt to narrow the digital divide in education [4], and disaster management [5]. To our knowledge, Information Ecology had not been applied to the knowledge transfer in the health field.

Rwanda bases its health system on Community Health Workers (CHWs) who connect population to a scarce medical personal. CHWs, frequently the backbone of preventative and curative care [6], often work as volunteers. A review of literature [7] on CHWs and mobile technology finds that CHWs have used mobile tools for maternal and child health, HIV/AIDS, and reproductive health. CHWs often use mobile technology to collect field based health data, receive alerts and reminders, and facilitate health education sessions.

In Bangladesh, there is a multitude of electronic health applications [8] but we focus on Info Ladies because of their unique position as entrepreneurs who connect population to electronic health and other information. Despite the rapid popularity of mobile phone, researchers identified the need for a human interface alongside the last mile of ICT solutions for information access in Bangladesh. A local NGO, D.Net, explored this synergy between mobile telephony and local women, and establish the Info Lady network [9].

3   Information Ecology as a Framework

Information Ecology represents a complex ecosystem of parts and relationships [1]. It is a system of people, values, and technologies in a specific local environment. What makes information ecology different is that the spotlight is not on technology itself but on human activities that are served by technology [1]. The ecosystem exhibits diversity and continual evolution. Different parts of ecology coevolve, changing together their relationships in the system. Several keystone species are necessary for the survival of the ecosystem. Finally, information ecologies have a sense of locality. Next, we apply Information Ecology lens to analyze two community health case studies.

4   Bangladesh Case Description

Bangladesh has come a long way from its struggling past, the country's economy is growing fast, predicted to be among the 25 largest economies by 2050. In addition, Bangladesh has performed well in education, women empowerment, and other social development benchmarks [8]. Within Bangladesh, community-based health programs play a major role in the national health sector [10]. We have chosen the "Info Lady" program of D.Net for our analysis. The primary reason behind this selection is its significant positive impact in rural Bangladesh. Info Lady program is a synergy between mobile telephony and local women for providing information services. Info Ladies primarily provide services in Health and Agriculture [11]. Currently, there are 50 Info Ladies, providing their services in 300 villages of Bangladesh. On average, an Info Lady earns around $100, a significant amount for working women in Bangladesh. The initial setup cost of an Info Lady is around $600, which includes a laptop and a bicycle. Women interested in becoming Info Ladies can buy the necessary equipment from the D.Net supply stores [11].

Information Ecology Analysis

System. The government initiative "Digital Bangladesh" was critical for the system creation in Bangladesh. It allowed D.Net to roll out the Info Lady program to reach the underserved communities with health and other information services. The other major element of Bangladesh's ecosystem in community-based health service are the info-mediaries or Info Ladies, who have multiple roles, as a source of critical health information and an interface between the government/NGOs and the general population in participatory design.

Diversity. As a community-based organization, D.Net offers support service on agriculture and women health care. Info Ladies focus on support for pregnant women, livelihood information for farmers, information services for youth, health checkups for rural people, and ICT-enabled life skills.

Coevolution. Infomediaries introduced ICT-enabled services in communities where there was a scarcity of useful information. Such introductions resulted in more access to ICTs and more communication with the rest of world. Cheaper and more convenient information access meant new needs, thus pushing the Info Lady initiative to new terrains professional development.

Keystone species. Info Ladies, as infomediaries, are the most critical group of keystone species. Their customers have been satisfied with the effective use communication technologies to address their problems. Another important species is the supporting organization, D.Net. This organization's focus on the underserved communities in Bangladesh helped immensely in designing and managing the Info Lady initiative [11].

Locality. The Info Lady project by design is a hybrid solution, where the socially acceptable human factor is providing the information to women using ICTs. The physical access challenge is being addressed with the use of bicycles (by infomediaries) and digital proximity of expert consultants from D.Net. Such localization of service meant better acceptability of Info Lady project within the communities it's serving, ensuring further collaboration.

5 Rwanda Case Description

Since its genocide in 1994 Rwandan economic growth has been impressive 8% per year [12]. Strong economic growth was accompanied by substantial drop in child mortality [12]. In the health sector, Rwanda has been leveraging ICT technology to improve access to healthcare. However, the country still faces the most severe shortages of human resources for health on the continent. In response to these health burdens, Rwanda introduced CHWs as major participants in the Rwandan health system. Rwanda implemented one e-health initiative based on open source software, RapidSMS, which allows CHWs to follow mother-infant pair [13]. However, it is used only for emergency cases. We have chosen a different case study which requires a system in which CHWs are infomediaries. The study tested a hypothesis that Rwandan CHWs could use smartphones for health data collection to monitor children's growth. This study demonstrated that using electronic tools for health data collection allows better tracking of health indicators [14].

Information Ecology Analysis System. Rwandan MoH is the leader of community health system with little involvement of NGOs. CHWs only visit population and collect information. The following groups are part of the ecosystem: mobile service operators provide connectivity; software engineers design and maintain EHR system.

Diversity. Rwanda is missing many actors of community health system. CHWs do not give feedbacks about the issues regarding implementation, and NGOs are on the fringes of the system collecting their own health data.

Coevolution. Coevolution involves generating new ideas, tools, or activities. In Rwanda, it requires a transformation on two levels: (1) from aggregate paper tracking to individual tracking of health indicators; and (2) from emergency case responses to a long term electronic health data collection.

Keystone species. CHWs are mediators, common for a keystone species. MoH is not compensating CHWs for their service. Instead, it contributes to their cooperatives, and it encourages them to start a small business. However, there is no synergy in such approach. MoH should find a better motivation tool to ensure the survival of CHWs as a keystone species.

Locality. One Rwandan challenge is inadequate ICT literacy. Ministry of Youth and ICT reports only 3.3% of the population has adequate ICT literacy. Opportunities in Rwanda are: high penetration of cellular network and the extensive network of CHWs already trained to collect basic health indicators.

6 Discussion

Information Ecology framework allows us to analyze the two cases using same parameters. Based on this comparative analysis, we found out that major changes are needed in the domains of Diversify, Coevolution, and Keystone Species. Comparing systems between Rwandan and Bangladesh we observe several key differences.

Bangladesh has a better diversity of services in comparison to Rwanda where CHWs are limiting their role to data collection. In addition, Rwandan system does not include CHWs in the system design, which hampers coevolution of the ecosystem. Bangladesh has a better community participation, with the role of different systems well defined.

Keystone species are clear in both cases. However, one main difference is that Info Ladies are entrepreneurs who provide information services. As volunteers Rwandan CHWs are less motived to ensure system survival, finding a proper motivation for their survival should be a priority for Rwanda. Local obstacles also differ, the main local problem in Rwanda is ICT literacy. In Bangladesh, the proliferation of mobile devices and cheap network connections has enabled population to have access to basic information, so Info Ladies must evolve and be innovative about their services.

7 Conclusions

Comparative research using Information Ecology framework allow us to propose the following recommendations for improving ICT-based health services in Rwanda and Bangladesh: improve support for keystone species to improve their engagement and motivation, and ensure the survival of the system; increase diversity in the ecosystem by offering a variety of services and involving diverse providers; invite community participation in the system design to improve coevolution. Enabling experience transfer and guiding South-South cooperation the research community requires a common framework. We believe this framework can facilitate strong theoretical basis for guiding South-South cooperation and transferring knowledge.

Acknowledgment. This research was supported by the MSIP (Ministry of Science, ICT and Future Planning), Korea, under the "ICT Consilience Creative Program" (IITP-2015-R0346-15-1007) supervised by the IITP (Institute for Information & communications Technology Promotion).

References

1. Nardi, B., O'Day, V.: Information ecologies. Ref. User Serv. Q. **38**(1), 49–58 (1998)
2. Centellas, K.: Cameroon is just like Bolivia: Southern expertise and the construction of equivalency in South-South scientific collaborations. Inf. Cult. **49**(2) (2014). University of Texas Press. doi:10.7560/IC49203
3. Izuchukw, O., Ofori, D.: Why South-South FDI is booming: case study of China FDI in Nigeria. J. Asian Econ. Financ. Rev. **4**(3), 361–376 (2014)
4. Thapa, D., Sein, M.: Information ecology as a holistic lens to understand ICTD initiatives: a case study of OLPC deployment in Nepal. In: Proceedings of ICTD 2016, Ann Arbor, MI, USA, 03–06 June 2016. doi:10.1145/2909609.2909610
5. Sakurai, M., Thapa, D.: Exploring effective ecosystems in disaster management: case studies of Japan and Nepal. In: Hawaii International Conference on System Sciences, 4–7 January 2017

6. Hermann, K., et al.: Community health workers for ART in sub-Saharan Africa: learning from experience – capitalizing on new opportunities. Hum. Resour. Health **7**(31), 1–11 (2009). doi:10.1186/1478-4491-7-31

7. Braun, R., Catalani, C., Wimbush, J., Israelski, D.: Community health workers and mobile technology: a systematic review of the literature. PLoS ONE **8**(6), e65772 (2013). doi:10.1371/journal.pone.0065772

8. Arifeen, S., Christou, A., Reichenbach, L., Osman, F.A., Azad, K., Islam, K., Ahmed, F., Perry, H.B., Peters, D.H.: Community-based approaches and partnerships: innovations in health-service delivery in Bangladesh. Lancet **382**, 2012–2026 (2013)

9. Dnet web site. http://dnet.org.bd/page/Gneric/0/61/145/85#sthash.qleLVYOK.dpuf

10. Raihan, A.: Public Access ICT in Bangladesh. In: Libraries, Telecentres, Cybercafes and Public Access to ICT: International Comparisons, p. 249 (2011). doi:10.4018/978-1-60960-771-5.ch019

11. Philanthropy Age: Bangladeshi traveling Infoladies: a rural revolution, January 2015. http://www.philanthropyage.org/2015/01/25/bangladeshs-travelling-infoladies-rural-revolution/

12. Rwanda Economic Outlook. In: African Development Bank Group web page. https://www.afdb.org/en/countries/east-africa/rwanda/rwanda-economic-outlook/. Accessed January 15, 2017

13. Ngabo, F., Nguimfack, J., Nwaigwe, F.: Designing and implementing an innovative SMS-based alert system (RapidSMS-MCH) to monitor pregnancy and reduce maternal and child deaths in Rwanda. Pan Afr. Med. J. (BMJ Open) **13**, 31 (2012)

14. Brown, S., McSharry, P.: Improving accuracy and usability of growth charts: case study of Rwanda. Br. Med. J. (BMJ Open) **6**(1), e009046 (2016). doi:10.1136/bmjopen-2015-009046

Actor-Networks and "Practices" of Development: Impact of a Weather Information System in West Bengal

Bidisha Chaudhuri[1], Purnabha Dasgupta[2], Onkar Hoysala[1],
Linus Kendall[3(✉)], and Janaki Srinivasan[1]

[1] International Institute of Information Technology Bangalore, Bangalore, India
{bidisha, janaki.srinivasan}@iiitb.ac.in,
onkar.hoysala@iiitb.org
[2] Development Research Communication and Services Center, Kolkata, India
purnabha.irdm@gmail.com
[3] Sheffield Hallam University, Sheffield, UK
linus.e.kendall@student.shu.ac.uk

Abstract. In this paper, we leverage an actor-network theory approach to examine an information system that produces and disseminates weather forecasts and associated agricultural recommendations to small-scale and marginal farmers in two districts in West Bengal in India. We find an actor-network important in understanding technology-related social practices. The emphasis ANT places on the negotiations and contestations in the context of a technological initiative allows us to understand the mechanisms (rather than merely the outcomes) of such developmental interventions.

Keywords: Actor network theory · ICT4D · Capability approach · Practice theories

1 Introduction

Practice theories have become increasingly prominent in fields such as Human Computer Interaction (HCI), Information Systems (IS) and ICT for development (ICT4D) [1–3]. By centering the analysis on what people do, practice provides a useful lens to "open the black box" of processes of change that involve technology [4]. That is why practice theories are being adopted for research which recognizes and allows for deconstruction of complex sociotechnical relationships involved in IS.

Actor Network Theory (ANT), in particular, is a practice theory that has been gaining popularity in IS and ICT4D research [3–5]. ANT has the aim of resolving the social determinism/technological determinism dichotomy and help bridge the duality between the technological artefact and the agent [6–8]. ANT sees society as made of a network of human and non-human actors, or actants [9–11]. It features a strong theorisation of the artefact, placing it in a symmetrical position with that of humans [12], providing for technologies to exercise agency – though not intentionality [10] – by becoming "delegates who stand in and speak for particular viewpoints" [8, 13]. It inverts

J. Choudrie et al. (Eds.): ICT4D 2017, IFIP AICT 504, pp. 809–815, 2017.
DOI: 10.1007/978-3-319-59111-7_66

the traditional use of descriptions of social structure as a means to explain processes, focusing instead on description of processes to explain resulting structures [4]. Furthermore, an ANT approach sees the social world as inherently unstable and capable of falling apart but for negotiations between actors [9, 10]. Actor-networks are heterogeneous networks of aligned interests which can include people, technologies, standards, and organisations. Actors, through a process of translating their interests, enrol and align themselves with the network

We apply ANT to the case of an information system to produce and disseminate weather forecasts and associated agricultural recommendations to small-scale and marginal farmers in West Bengal in India. The system was initiated as part of the UN Adaptation Fund and implemented by a non-profit organisation called DRCSC. The intended impact of the system was to enable farmers to better understand changing weather patterns and respond with changes to their agricultural practices. The objective of our analysis is to understand developmental impact of the IS. In conceptualising what constitutes development, we align ourselves with the capabilities approach [14–16]. We draw on existing research on capabilities and ICTD [17–19] to position our findings from the ANT framework within the broader discourse of development.

2 Methodology

We adopt a case study approach [20] to examine the weather information system. A case study oriented approach entailed using multiple methods, collecting data through participant observation, semi-structured interviews, informal conversations, focused group discussions, taking pictures at various sites as well as collection of work materials and project documentation. We have limited the scale of our case and analysis to a single village and have based our descriptions and interpretations on observations of and interviews with actors such as the NGO field workers responsible for the system, local village volunteers, village heads and local self-help group (SHG) members from both men's and women's groups. Field visits spanned a few days up to a week at a time, and were conducted monthly between June and December 2016.

The methodological approach to the field study as well as the analytical approach taken in this paper is based on the "moments of translation" framework within the ANT tradition [9]. The starting point of the study was the central actor – the implementing organisation, DRCSC – and we then followed the way they sought to involve other actors in the project [4]. Interviews with head office staff were followed by an introduction to the field offices. From there, the actor-network was traced through the work of the field office and in the villages. We use the four "moments" of the ANT translation framework (as defined in [9]) – problematisation, interessement, enrolment and mobilisation to examine the working of the information system. While we have by necessity included references to parts of the actor-network that extend beyond the village, our attempt has been to delineate our discussion by the geographical area of the village. We have sought to describe the case in detail while also providing our interpretations and explanations of the context [5]. This follows from our intention to illustrate how ANT can elucidate processes of capability enhancement.

3   Applying an Actor Network Lens: Moments of Translation

Problematisation: While initial participatory vulnerability assessment exercises revealed a long list of problems and challenges, including lack of jobs, nutrition, lack of government linkages, and poor access to credit, the "summary of problems" to be addressed by the project (as written in the funding proposal) were defined by the central actor's focus on agriculture: "water availability", "drought", "long rain break", "depleting natural resources" and "uncertain climactic pattern". The proposal suggested that *"crop-weather advisories will help to reduce the risks and damages caused by climate change. It will capacitate the farmers to take more effective decisions regarding farm management"*. The initial project proposal highlighted how experts need to be engaged to prepare meteorological forecasts and appropriate agricultural advisories which should *"minimize the loss of farmers and also optimize input and thereby its costs in the form of irrigation, seed, fertilizer or pesticides"*. While the range of issues that emerged from the appraisal was wide, what was eventually proposed by the organization were based on the areas in which the organization had capabilities. The "obligatory passage point" [9], thus, became the local, related issues of water availability, drought, reduced rainfall and depleting natural resources; which were also in alignment with the external interests – that of the UN Adaptation Fund. The problematisation in the actor-network was how the organization made itself indispensable by bringing in its capabilities to negotiate the obligatory passage point.

Interessement: Here, the organisation set forth several processes to lock-in other actors into its network. It conducted a Participatory Rural Assessment (PRA) exercise to raise awareness of the programme and introduce villagers to the weather data, recruit interested parties and highlight challenges which the project might address. Further, the organisation sought permission from the village head or *majhi*, to run the programme in the village. However, as one of the NGO staff members expressed, there was initially some resistance to using the data, as the villagers were not aware that creating such predictions was even possible at all. The organisation also installed a blackboard on the main road leading through the village, and collected phone numbers from some of the villagers, with the intention of sending them weather updates via SMS. The organisation sent two sets of messages, after which it became clear that messages using Bengali script were not readable on the villagers' phones.

Enrolment: The organisation sought to work through the existing network of power in the village by asking the village *majhi* to be a volunteer for the project. They also installed a manual rain gauge on his property for him to use in collecting weather data for the village – this data was intended to be used by the meteorologist to improve forecasts. The *majhi* related that he saw little benefit in undertaking the work involved and thus passed the responsibility to one of his male relatives. The male relative in turn, feeling that he did not have time to conduct this work, handed the responsibility to his 18-year-old daughter. These events initially caused the network to be unstable, with long periods of data not updated on the blackboard. However, once the daughter got involved, the regularity of management of the blackboard picked up. Being literate, and studying in class 12, made it possible for her to undertake the activities of the project.

She expressed how she felt happy to have the responsibility as there were no other jobs for her in the village. The organisation recruited a young woman who had undertaken college education, as a field officer in charge of the village. The establishment of this village-level infrastructure by the organisation – volunteer & field officer – provided some organisation to the network. It was not only the enrolment of human actors that the organisation was involved in. Noticing that weather data dissemination over SMS was not functioning as expected, the organisation adopted paper print-outs of forecasts and recommendations which were provided to the field worker and the volunteer. They, in turn, shared them with the villagers in group meetings.

Mobilisation: Taking the case of the blackboard on the central street, the now regular updates on the it provided a visual reminder of the existence of the weather forecasts. It also provided a performance of the village volunteer's (the *majhi's* relative's daughter) role in the network. Her role furthermore included regularly collecting the rainfall measurements from the rain gauge installed on the *majhi's* plot. Along with the other female village worker, she began introducing the weather recommendations to the women's groups of the village. As women in the village do not regularly spend their time in the public spaces of the village main street, only a few members of these groups were even aware that the blackboard with weather data existed. As the volunteer introduced them to the weather forecasts, they began to apply the knowledge of predicted temperatures to decide whether to allow their livestock to graze or children to go to school. Thus, we see that while the project's stated focus was to provide recommendations for issues such as pest management and irrigation, the inclusion of temperature measurements allowed the print-outs to act on behalf of the network to engage the women's groups in it. Having a public role in the village, along with interactions with the *majhi* and the responsibility to speak on behalf of the project, provided the village volunteer with a new position in the actor-network of the village. As she related in answer to the question: *"Do you think you get better treatment from the village after becoming the [volunteer]?"*

"Yes, I think my friends become jealous of me and aged people seek solution regarding the weather information from me."

Through these four stages we have illustrated the initial establishment of the actor-network in the village over two years. They highlight how the network has passed through several moments of negotiation and potential instabilities – for example the general lack of interest from the *majhi* and his male relative or the inaccessibility – and therefore lack of use – of the weather data by the women. We trace the establishment and endurance of the network in the face of these challenges to the ANT concept of "substantial, material and procedural devices", the interplay of which establishes the network [5]. The substantial device is the weather data, forecasts and agricultural recommendations. The maintenance of the actor-network depended on the existence of multiple parallel material and procedural devices. SMSes proved to be an unsuitable material device to the local conditions, whereas paper print-outs worked better. The material device of the blackboard served to interest men in the project, but the inability of movement between the network of women and the network of the public space acted as an initial barrier to women's participation. The pre-existing village SHG meetings were a procedural device that not only suited existing information exchange patterns, but also enabled the discovery of productive uses of the information for the women of the village. The procedural device of writing on the blackboard served to mobilise the village volunteer through her public performances, publicly associating her with the knowledge she thus shared. Throughout, we found that the introduction of a new technology was about the processes of constant negotiation that lead up to short-term stability in the social world, rather than a final, stable outcome. Examining how the effort of actors together holds changes tells us a lot about the process of development and social change. Specifically, it tells us about the capabilities that actors have developed and could leverage.

Following a capabilities approach to development, ICTs are a means by which an individual's capability set can be increased [17]. In this view, ICTs do not themselves contribute to development but are resources which, when combined with personal, social and environmental "conversion factors"[1] can result in capability enhancement [17, 18]. We strive to understand *the process* by which this is achieved through two foci: the role of human actors, and the role of technological actors.

One of the examples of capability enhancement could be seen in the village volunteer. Through participating in the actor-network, she became an actor—within the village—who had a direct relationship to the village *majhi*. The ANT analysis highlights the role that specific resources—pre-existing social relations, education and material devices—played in enabling the capability enhancement of the volunteer. In terms of the technologies, we see that the format of the print-outs and the resulting negotiation of women's participation in the actor-network enabled capability enhancement outside of the problematisation by the leading actor. For example, even though livestock is recognised as an important aspect of women's lives in the district, the initial proposal to the UN Adaptation Fund considered only the management of "water scarcity" and financing. The provision of temperature data in the print-outs, however, enabled women to maintain the health of their children and livestock by keeping them home on the hottest of days. While this was not considered in the proposal, it resulted from the interplay of devices and negotiations taking place in the actor-network.

4   Conclusion

We used an ANT lens to illustrate the working of an IS. The lens allowed us to treat the agency of the human and the technological actors symmetrically and to appreciate how a process of technological adoption and social change involves constant negotiation. Through the limited examples elaborated above, we propose that understanding capability enhancement through the interplays and negotiations of an actor-network provides a valuable perspective to highlight some of the complexities and locally situated practices which can enable or hinder development. While we focus on demonstrating the actual practices around a development initiative, our broader aim

---

[1] Conversion factors are those that allow an individual freedom to achieve certain capabilities, using all the commodities at the individual's disposal (the means to achieve). For a detailed explanation, see Zheng [19].

will be to understand how social processes of negotiation help people enhance their freedom and capability to make choices.

References

1. Kuutti, K., Bannon, L.: The turn to practice in HCI: towards a research agenda. In: Proceedings of the 32nd Annual ACM Conference on Human Factors in Computing Systems, pp. 3543–3552 (2014)
2. Schmidt, K.: The concept of 'practice': what's the point? In: Rossitto, C., Ciolfi, L., Martin, D., Conein, B. (eds.) COOP 2014 - Proceedings of the 11th International Conference on the Design of Cooperative Systems, 27-30 May 2014, Nice (France), pp. 427–444. Springer, Cham (2014). doi:10.1007/978-3-319-06498-7_26
3. Walsham, G.: Actor-network theory and is research: current status and future prospects. In: Lee, A.S., Liebenau, J., DeGross, Janice I. (eds.) Information Systems and Qualitative Research. ITIFIP, pp. 466–480. Springer, Boston, MA (1997). doi:10.1007/978-0-387-35309-8_23
4. Heeks, R., Stanforth, C.: Technological change in developing countries: opening the black box of process using actor–network theory. Dev. Stud. Res. 2, 33–50 (2015)
5. Urquhart, C.: The affordances of actor network theory in ICT for development research. Inf. Technol. People 23, 352–374 (2010)
6. Østerlund, C., Carlile, P.: Relations in practice: Sorting through practice theories on knowledge sharing in complex organizations. Inf. Soc. 21, 91–107 (2005)
7. Latour, B.: Where are the missing masses? The sociology of a few mundane artefacts. In: Wiebe, E., Bijker, J.L. (eds.) Shaping Technology, Building Society: Studies in Sociotechnical Change. MIT Press, Cambridge (1992)
8. Callon, M., Latour, B.: Don't throw the baby out with the bath school! a reply to Collins and Yearley. In: Science as Practice and Culture, p. 368. University of Chicago Press, Chicago (1992)
9. Callon, M.: Some elements of a sociology of translation: domestication of the scallops and the fishermen of St. Brieuc Bay. In: Law, J. (ed.) Power, Action, and Belief: A New Sociology of Knowledge? Routledge and Kegan Paul, London (1986)
10. Latour, B.: Reassembling the Social: An Introduction to Actor-Network-Theory. Oxford University Press, New York (2005)
11. Law, J.: Notes on the theory of the actor-network: ordering, strategy, and heterogeneity. Syst. Pract. 5, 379–393 (1992)
12. Williams, R., Edge, D.: The social shaping of technology. Res. Policy 25, 865–899 (1996)
13. Walsham, G., Sahay, S.: GIS for district-level administration in India: problems and opportunities. MIS Q. 23(1), 39–65 (1999)
14. Sen, A.: Capability and well-being. In: Nussbaum, M.C., Sen, A.K. (eds.) The Quality of Life, p. 30. Oxford University Press, New York (1993)
15. Alkire, S.: Why the capability approach? J. Hum. Dev. 6, 115–135 (2005)
16. Robeyns, I.: The capability approach: a theoretical survey. J. Hum. Dev. 6, 93–117 (2005)
17. Thapa, D., Sæbø, Ø.: Exploring the link between ICT and development in the context of developing countries: a literature review. Electron. J. Inf. Syst. Dev. Countries 64, 1–15 (2014)

18. Kleine, D.: ICT4WHAT?—Using the choice framework to operationalise the capability approach to development. J. Int. Dev. **22**, 592–674 (2010)
19. Zheng, Y.: Different spaces for e-development: What can we learn from the capability approach? Inf. Technol. Dev. **15**, 66–82 (2009)
20. Ridder, H.-G., Yin, R.K.: Case Study Research. Design and Methods, 4th edn. Sage Publications, Thousand Oaks (2012)

Understanding the Dilemma of the Municipal Solid Waste Management System in Alexandria, Egypt: Could ICT Improve the System?

Rasha F. Elgazzar[1]([⊠]), Rania F. El-Gazzar[2],
and Mohamed A. El-Gohary[3]

[1] Department of Architectural Engineering and Environmental Design,
College of Engineering, Arab Academy for Science,
Technology and Maritime Transport, Alexandria, Egypt
arch.rashafahim@gmail.com
[2] Department of Economics, Marketing and Law, School of Business,
University College of Southeast Norway, Hønefoss, Norway
Rania.El-gazzar@usn.no
[3] Faculty of Engineering, Department of Mechanical Engineering,
Alexandria University, Alexandria, Egypt
melgohary@alexu.edu.eg

Abstract. Waste management is one of the significant activities for preserving the environment from pollution that has impact on society mirrored on people's health. This study approaches the topic of waste management using interpretive qualitative case study method to understand problems in the Municipal Solid Waste Management (MSWM) system in Alexandria city, the second largest city in Egypt. Alexandria has been facing a problematic situation with regard to MSWM, which is worth paying attention to. Furthermore, we explore opportunities for benefiting from Information and Communication Technology (ICT) to improve the MSWM system in Alexandria.

Keywords: Municipal solid waste management · ICT · Environment · Sustainable development · Developing countries · Alexandria city · Waste management problems

1 Research Problem

The density of population in developing countries has undesirable implications on many aspects, particularly the environmental sustainable development [1]. One of the key operations to drive the wheel of environmental sustainable development is the Municipal Solid Waste Management (MSWM) [2]. MSWM in developing countries is lacking availability of the data in an integrated and timely manner to capture the MSWM system's problems or informal activities and make better decisions [3]. MSWM in developing countries is unsatisfactory [4]; up to 60% of all the urban solid waste in developing countries is uncollected, less than 50% of the population is served,

© IFIP International Federation for Information Processing 2017
Published by Springer International Publishing AG 2017. All Rights Reserved
J. Choudrie et al. (Eds.): ICT4D 2017, IFIP AICT 504, pp. 816–822, 2017.
DOI: 10.1007/978-3-319-59111-7_67

and most developing countries use the least preferred waste management methods, such as open dumping and open burning [5]. Developing countries generate organic waste far more than the developed countries, which can be turned into 'gold' only if effective waste management programs exist [3].

In Egypt, MSWM has been and will be a constant challenge. The recent estimate of population in Egypt is 91.854.596 according to the Central Agency for Public Mobilization and Statistics (CAPMAS) [6]. Egypt generates 21 million tons of Municipal Solid Waste (MSW) yearly [7], of which 46% is uncollected and 43% is covered by formal collection, while 11% is covered by informal collection [8]. The uncollected MSW is dumped into the river, canals, and streets posing a major threat to the environment (i.e., pollution) and public health (i.e., spread of diseases) [9]. The MSWM system in Egypt is inefficient; one side of this dilemma relates to the improper handling of the MSW and other legal, institutional, financial, and cultural factors. The other side of the dilemma is that there is no adequate data to support the assessment of MSWM sector and inform decision-making regarding the improvement of the MSWM system [10]. The same dilemma applies to Alexandria city, the second largest city in Egypt.

Alexandria city was voted the cleanest city of the Arab world in 2003, a winner of a prize in the environment category in 2005, and awarded the Habitat Scroll of Honour from the United Nations (UN) in 2006. However, several factors (i.e., social, urban, technical, and cultural) and institutional actors (i.e., public, private, and informal sector) contributed to the previously flourished MSWM era and the currently problematic MSW situation. We commenced the study with the following Research Questions (RQs) to understand the MSW problems in Alexandria and the constituents of such problems, and explore opportunities for Information and Communication Technology (ICT) to improve the MSWM system in Alexandria: "RQ1: What are the problems in the MSWM system in Alexandria?" and "RQ2: How can ICT help improving those problems?"

We attempt to define the research problem in relation to the literature and the social context. Literature on MSWM in Egypt mainly focused on exploring techniques for treating organic MSW [11], suggesting a sustainable strategy for MSWM based on successful international models, which is not actualized yet [12], assessing MSWM in Egypt and the role of Public-Private Partnership (PPP) in that process [13], proposing a MSWM quality assurance program that unfortunately lacks in Egypt [14], highlighting the importance of raising the environmental awareness of SWM in the Egyptian education System [15], and proposing standard codes of practice for MSWM in Egypt [16]. However, the power of ICT in improving MSWM system in the Egyptian context has not been explicitly appreciated yet. Very few studies contributed to identifying problems and suggesting solutions for MSWM in three Egyptian governorates, namely, Cairo [17], Port Said [18], and El-Beheira [19]. However, MSWM problems in Alexandria city have not been explored and addressed properly yet given the city is equally important in size and location, and it has been through ups and downs in the process of MSWM that ended in a worse MSW situation.

The approximate population of Alexandria governorate is five million [6], and eight million in the summer due to the massive summer visitors [20]. The MSW generation in Alexandria governorate is 4200 tons per day and 1.53 million tons per year according to a recent report on the state of environment in Egypt 2014 [21]. Alexandria had an experience of unsustainable MSWM system throughout the time. We describe three key periods, each period witnessed differences in processes, actors, and issues in the MSWM system in particular and unsustainable MSW situation in Alexandria city in general.

The first period of "manual labor" covers the years before 2000 and witnessed poor MSWM operations that involved manual labor, namely, informal sector (i.e., Zabbaleen who are individual garbage collecting people). It should be noted that the General Authority for Cleanness & Beautification, that was part of Alexandria governorate, was and is still responsible for the MSWM, but has no active role to mention in Alexandria City. Furthermore, each district had a cleanness unit with its own equipment that still operates until now, but does not have the proper capacity to cover all MSWM responsibilities solely. In addition, waste collection and sweeping activities were not regular causing being scattered by stray animals, which results in a disastrous scene in Alexandria city's streets. Furthermore, waste disposal and treatment activities were unorganized.

The second period of "Veolia/Onyx Company" covers 2001–2011 witnessed a flourished era of cleanliness for the city, labor training, and appropriate management of MSW using modern equipment and techniques according to international standards. Veolia is specialized in environmental services including water, waste management, energy, and transportation. Veolia has signed a contract with the governorate of Alexandria in 2000 to commence operations of the waste management system in Alexandria city for the period of 15 years (2001–2015). The contract was the first Public-Private Partnership (PPP) in waste management sector in Egypt, and it included operations of waste collection and transfer, street cleaning, treatment of waste, and rehabilitation of two old dump sites. However, the contract was terminated in 2011 earlier than the agreed termination year in the contract 2015. Several problems caused early termination of the contract, such as the instability after the Egyptian uprising posed a threat for the company as an investor, delayed financial dues by the governorate for paying wages of the company's labor, and people used to steal garbage cans for storage purposes, which did cost the company buying new garbage cans.

The third period of "Egypt renaissance or Nahdet Misr Company" covers 2011–2016, the company is established by "Arab Contractors or El-Mokawloon El-Arab Company" that is a public-sector construction and contracting company. Nahdet Misr started officially its waste management duties in December 2011 in collaboration with "Falcon Group Company" specialized in security services, after Veolia's early contract termination in October 2011. Nahdet Misr took over the waste management operations in a critical time at the year of Egyptian uprising in 2011; hence, the company faced major problems. The company did not have enough experience in MSWM, thus, the company hired subcontractor (scavengers) to collect the waste from particular.

2 Methodological Approach

In this study, we conducted an interpretive case study method, that is suitable for studying a phenomenon within its social context [22], to investigate the problems that surfaced in the current MSWM system (see Table 1).

Table 1. Overview on methodology

Data collection/analysis	Description
Primary data sources	• Seven interviews with duration of 15 min to three hours and 30 min with citizens, labors in Nahdet Misr, Alexandria governate consultants and service directors • One of the authors is a consultant for Alexandria governorate projects and has hands on experience regarding MSWM problems and solutions • Observations by the researchers in different areas of the Alexandria city • Recorded videos by the researchers • Captured photos by the researchers
Secondary data sources	Online news articles, posts on online communities (e.g., Facebook), statistical reports by CAPMAS, status reports by the Ministry of environment and Egyptian Environmental Affairs Agency, documents published by Veolia Environment Service Company, and reports by other external agencies (i.e., SWEEP-Net)
Data analysis	Data analysis involved applying open coding of the themes that emerged from the data. Through the framework for MSWM in developing countries [4], we looked in the data at the political, institutional, social, financial, economic, and technical problems caused by various actors and led to degrade MSWM processes at present

3 Findings and Discussion

Our key contributions from this study are: (1) the pressing problems in the current MSWM system at the time of Nahdet Misr company have been identified (See Table 2), and (2) the current ICT initiatives have been identified along with their limitations.

There is a number of scattered initiatives of using ICT in the current MSWM system in Alexandria by different actors. The use of ICT is limited to WhatsApp, Facebook, and Web portal, which had some implications, yet, not actualized impacts on addressing the problems of MSWM in Alexandria: (1) Spreading awareness: this manifested in the effort by Alexandria governorate to use Facebook to launch awareness campaigns through light comics targeting households to separate recyclable waste from the organic waste. (2) Coordinating and monitoring waste collection activities: in Nahdet Misr, the use of WhatsApp is intended to keep communication between the company and the subcontractors and workers who collect the waste from the streets and send them to locations where more labor is needed to collect the waste. In addition, the waste collectors are asked to take photos for the spots they collected the waste from and send the photos via WhatsApp to confirm that they have cleaned up the spot. However, there are still more opportunities for ICT to solve governance problems concerning the phenomenon of scavengers who scavenge the waste after collecting it and before reaching the intermediate stations. (3) Reporting waste-related problems: on the Web portal of Alexandria governorate, there is a section dedicated for the environmental

Table 2. MSWM problems in Alexandria

Problems	Description
Political	Regulations are neither strict nor clearly defined
Institutional	– Quantity of waste exceeded the agreed quantity in the contract – Waste management responsibilities are beyond the capacity of the company – Delayed financial dues by the governorate to the company for paying the wages of its labor
Social	– The workers of Nahdet Misr used to strike for not having their wages paid regularly, which caused mountains of waste to appear in the streets – Shortage of labor to be engaged in waste collection and transfer activities – People do not adhere to MWM-related laws and waste collection times – People do random burning of waste causing air pollution – People used to steal garbage bins for storage purposes, which did cost the company buying new garbage cans – Random behavior of scavengers causes garbage being scattered in the streets and makes it difficult for the company to collect the waste – The increased population density as a result of the illegal high rise residential buildings caused an increase in the amount of generated waste than before
Financial	– Bearing extra costs of buying new garbage bins instead of the stolen ones – The company lacked financial resources to buy extra equipment and collaborated with subcontractors to collect the waste – The company had financial dues to those subcontractors – Penalties on the company from the environmental monitoring authority (which is part of Alexandria governorate) for the delay in lifting the waste and random disposal methods
Economic	– The random behavior of scavengers caused the company not benefiting from the economic value of the recyclable waste – Increased maintenance and labor costs
Technical	– The company used rudimentary equipment (i.e., loaders and open top vehicles and tipper trucks) and did not have enough waste collection trucks – The company had few compactor vehicles – The company had trucks and equipment that needed maintenance – The company uses open dumps and random open burning, which are the least preferred methods – No ICT applications mentioned to organize and track the MSWM system's activities, only using WhatsApp groups to communicate with waste collectors
Environmental[a]	– Problems in the urban infrastructure, such as the narrow streets in the majority of the city's districts, which are difficult to reach by regular waste collection trucks

[a]Environmental category is not among the strategic issues listed in the MSWM framework [4], but emerged from the findings.

monitoring authority to receive waste related complaints from citizens either through phone numbers or a Web form enabling citizens to upload files/photos about waste-related problems; thus, leveraging citizen involvement.

The use of ICT as is in the current MSWM system in Alexandria is lacking integration of MSWM activities and involved actors. ICT proved to (1) improve route planning and scheduling of waste collection and transportation using GIS applications [23] incorporated with Big Data analytics [24], which can reduce costs of such tedious activities, as they heavily depend on various behavioral patterns of people, (2) automate waste segregation using scanning spectroscopy technology [25], and (3) have the most relevant and direct effect on MSWM through enabling intelligent recycling systems [26]. Advanced ICT solutions (i.e., Big Data, GPS, and GIS database) could improve the current MSWM system in Alexandria and help the Nahdet Misr manage its limited resources efficiently. This study has reported on MSWM problems in Alexandria, and it is part of an ongoing research effort that seeks to propose an integrated solution for some of the identified problems, taking into account social mechanisms of the problems and opportunities for exploiting ICT.

References

1. UN: Towards sustainable cities: world economic and social survey 2013 (2013)
2. Bithas, K.P., Christofakis, M.: Environmentally sustainable cities. critical review and operational conditions. Sustain. Dev. **14**, 177–189 (2006)
3. UNEP: Municipal solid waste: is it garbage or gold? (2013). http://www.unep.org/pdf/ UNEP_GEAS_oct_2013.pdf
4. Schübeler, P., Wehrle, K., Christen, J.: Conceptual Framework for Municipal Solid Waste Management in Low-Income Countries, vol. 9. SKAT (Swiss Center for Development Cooperation), St. Gallen (1996)
5. Wilson, D.C., Velis, C.A., Rodic, L.: Integrated sustainable waste management in developing countries. In: Proceedings of the Institution of Civil Engineers: Waste and Resource Management, pp. 52–68 (2013)
6. CAPMAS: Statistical yearbook (2016)
7. Zaki, T., Khial, A.: Country report on the solid waste management in Egypt (2014)
8. Mehlhart, G., Merz, C.: greenhouse gas emissions from MSW management in Egypt (2014). http://nswmp.net/wp-content/uploads/2016/02/2014-SWM-Forum_GEORG-MEHLHART_ Climate-Change_EN-1.pdf
9. Al-Akkad, F.: Egypt's garbage problem. http://weekly.ahram.org.eg/News/14892/32/ Egypt's-garbage-problem.aspx
10. Zaki, T., Kafafi, A.G., Mina, M.B., El-Halim, A., Saber, M.: Annual report for solid waste management in Egypt (2013)
11. Elfeki, M., Tkadlec, E.: Treatment of municipal organic solid waste in Egypt. Environ. Sci. **6**, 756–764 (2015)
12. Ibrahim, M.I.M., Mohamed, N.A.E.M.: Towards sustainable management of solid waste in Egypt. Procedia Environ. Sci. **34**, 336–347 (2016)
13. Milik, S.M.: Assessment of solid waste management in Egypt during the last decade in light of the partnership between the Egyptian government and the private sector (2011)
14. Rahman, R.A., El-Kamash, A.: Planning for a solid waste management quality assurance program in Egypt. Qual. Assur. J. **11**, 53–59 (2007)

15. Kandil, S.H., Abou Bakr, H., Mortensen, L.: Incorporating environmental awareness of solid waste management within the education system: (a case from Egypt). Polym.-Plast. Technol. Eng. **43**, 1795–1803 (2004)
16. Ghosh, S.K., El Sheltawy, S.T., El Sherbiny, S.A., Fouad, M.M.K.: codes for solid waste management for developing countries: India and Egypt. J. Solid Waste Technol. Manag. **42**, 467–485 (2016)
17. World Bank: Project information document (concept stage) - cairo municipal solid waste management project - P152961 (2014). http://documents.worldbank.org/curated/en/245761468024247659/pdf/PID-Print-P152961-01-05-2015-1420469398757.pdf
18. Badran, M., El-Haggar, S.: Optimization of municipal solid waste management in Port Said–Egypt. Waste Manage. **26**(5), 534–545 (2006)
19. El-Salam, M.: Municipal solid waste management in El-Beheira governorate, Egypt: a case study in Damanhour city. J. Environ. Occup. Sci. **2**(3), 131–140 (2013)
20. Crawford, G.: Public private partnership in the European union (2013)
21. EEAA: Egypt state of the environment report. http://www.eeaa.gov.eg/en-us/mediacenter/reports/soereports.aspx
22. Walsham, G.: Interpretive case studies in IS research: nature and method. Eur. J. Inf. Syst. **4**, 74–81 (1995)
23. Rada, E., Ragazzi, M., Fedrizzi, P.: Web-GIS oriented systems viability for municipal solid waste selective collection optimization in developed and transient economies. Waste Manage. **33**(4), 785–792 (2013)
24. Shahrokni, H., van der Heijde, B., Lazarevic, D., Brandt, N.: Big data GIS analytics towards efficient waste management in Stockholm. In: The 2nd International Conference on ICT for Sustainability (ICT4S 2014) (2014)
25. Durgekar, V.: Towards sustainable waste management through technological innovations, effective policy, supply chain integration & participation. Procedia Environ. Sci. **35**, 140–149 (2016)
26. Hilty, L., Arnfalk, P., Erdmann, L., Goodman, J.: The relevance of information and communication technologies for environmental sustainability–a prospective simulation study. Environ. Model Softw. **21**(11), 1618–1629 (2006)

A Reflection on IT Implementation Challenges in State Institution: A Case Study on Development Projects at Indonesian Judiciary

Haemiwan Z. Fathony[(⊠)] and Bobby A.A. Nazief

Faculty of Computer Science, University of Indonesia, Depok, Indonesia
haemiwan.z@ui.ac.id, nazief@cs.ui.ac.id

Abstract. There are two major challenges in implementing technological solutions as part of institutional reform in development project: the alignment issues with bigger – nationwide – agenda and addressing the resistance in – usually – corrupt environment. This paper aim to provide some reflections on the implementation of information technology to reform the Indonesian judiciaries. Lessons learned from past experiences are provided, as well as a proposal to modify the classic IT-business alignment model and the use of agent based approach to determine the information technology implementation roadmap.

Keywords: IT alignment · Strategic alignment · Resistance · Corruption · Rational choice · Judiciary reform

1 Introduction

The Indonesian judiciary has been implementing various development projects with some information technology related components in the last 10 years. Some notable foreign aid projects that has IT elements are the USAID funded Indonesia Anti-Corruption and Commercial Court Enhancement Project, The Indonesia Threshold Program from the Millennium Challenge Corporation, The Indonesia Australia Legal Development Facility and the Australia Indonesia Partnerships for Justice from the Australian AID, The Change for Justice from USAID, EU-funded Support for Reform of the Justice Sector in Indonesia – managed by the UNDP, and the new USAID funded CEGAH Project.

Despite all of those initiatives and millions of dollars that has been invested in technology modernisation, the improvement on the quality and integrity of public services are still low or marginally improving. However there are some notable

---

H.Z. Fathony—Former Deputy Coordinator at the Judicial Reform Team Office, Supreme Court Republic of Indonesia, that is responsible to oversee various reform initiatives including technology modernisation and process reengineering at the Indonesian judiciaries. This paper is a reflection of the experience during his tenure (2010–2014).

© IFIP International Federation for Information Processing 2017
Published by Springer International Publishing AG 2017. All Rights Reserved
J. Choudrie et al. (Eds.): ICT4D 2017, IFIP AICT 504, pp. 823–828, 2017.
DOI: 10.1007/978-3-319-59111-7_68

improvements in terms of accessibility to court information and better transparency in the court processes and the resulting court decisions as well [2, 23].

This paper aim to provide a reflective view on various issues and challenges during the implementation of several information technology solutions to support the institutional reform at the Indonesian Judiciaries. The methodology is interpretive in nature, adopting the reflective writing approach as described by Jasper [27], by modifying it in the context of reflective writing for information systems domain. The discussion will be started with quick elaboration taken from reflections of the previous experience, followed by a higher level view in term of strategy to implement the technology. It will be followed by some initial ideas to improve the level of success on the information technology implementation at state institutions, especially to the initiatives that are supported by development projects. The ideas will be refined with some relevant literature reviews, followed by more detailed analysis and elaborations to conclude some possible approaches.

2 Reflections and Findings

Some of the identified challenges in regards to information technology implementation at Indonesian judiciaries are the IT literacy problems, resistance for change, funding availability as well as lack of the internal technical skill sets [2, 3, 9]. Looking at the lessons learned from failed implementations in the past, the tactical approach to address the challenges is to start simple and then gradually move into more complex implementation approach [2].

To address the resistance and the complexity to use the system, the Court deliberately request the user to input the main data only, like case registration number, common case identities (e.g. name of the parties), important processing dates (registration dates, decision dates, etc.), and the judgment itself. Those are kind of data have been used to manage the case administration. Hence it met their need as well as eliminating the issues of having no data to enter. It is also considered as common data that should be available, yet considered as the most traded information [8, 9].

The goal is to establish the habit to use the electronic data among the users. The dependencies to use the electronic data will create a point of no return to use the manual process. This approach is aligned with the key principles in the rational choice theory [4]. Providing the tool with minimum data provision efforts is the sweetener that become the most rational options for the users. Gradually the Court increased the threshold to input more data. Currently all important data are required to be entered in the case management system. All court decisions are also need to be uploaded in the central repository, resulting a vast knowledge based for further operational and judicial knowledge development [8, 10].

The information technology literacy issues is creating resistance (due to the difficulty to use the technology) and alienated feeling among the users. It was threatening for staffs that currently do the manual works. Technology also push and enforce the transparency and accountability of court processes that in the end will make it difficult to conduct the corruptive and manipulative behaviour on the case handling at the courts [21]. This also became another threat for those who tend to get the benefits from it. Those interests are uniting in the resistance of change on the technology at work in the court. This also supported by the fact during information technology implementations, organisations sometime also fail to recognise that employee as the shareholder like to see the return of their personal investment [16]. Recognising the key actor's interest and providing them with the most rational choice to move forward is the key in the successful IT implementation at the Indonesian judiciary.

The resistance also got coincidence support with the fact that there was lack of the technical personnel. Some implementation failures and the inability of the courts to manage their own information technology facilities became the common reasons to resist. This also commemorates with the fact that the personnel recruitment is mostly focusing on the judicial staffs and general administration positions. Hence this also create the issue of the sustainability of various foreign assistance related with the technological solutions at the state institutions. The situation is not helped with the fact that the foreign assistance projects often not in-sync with the annual state budgeting process as well as some misalignment between the institutions' strategic plan, the government-wide mid-term development plan, and is not reflected in the annual budget plan.

Those two teething issues: addressing the misalignment and handling resistance are – in author's view – the two most strategic issues to be addressed in implementing technological solutions at state institutions.

3 Addressing the Misalignment Issue

To address the misalignment issue, the author proposed a revisit to the classic information technology and business alignment approach as elaborated by Henderson and Venkatraman [12, 13]. However the approach needs to be taken into broader context by taking into account the structure of the mid-term planning that provide the underlying strategy for the annual state budget. The adaption could follow the idea on IT-business alignment in multi-business environment [26]. The proposed approach is using an "anchored alignment" of "stacked" alignment as multi-business alignment model [26].

In the context of Indonesia, the strategic alignment has been guided and described in the Nation-wide Mid Term Development Plan. The Mid Term Plan act as the anchor point to align the strategic fit and functional integrations between relevant state institutions. The adaptation of the approach is depicted in the Fig. 1. The initial model consists of four main elements: business strategy, business infrastructure and processes, information technology strategy and information technology infrastructure and processes. The proposed alignment model is to add the nation-wide strategy into the alignment model. The rationale is that it will not only provide the necessary context for the institutional scope and mandate, but also providing clarity related to the resources and budget allocations as well as distribution of responsibilities among state institutions. The use of alignment measurement approach such as proposed by Luftman [17] could also be used to monitor and evaluate the implementation.

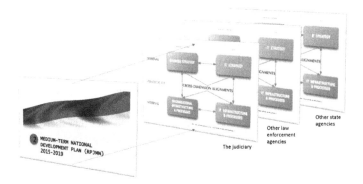

Fig. 1. Proposed IT – business alignment for state institutions; adapted from the model as proposed by Henderson and Venkatraman [12, 13]

4 Addressing the Resistance Issue

The second proposal is related with addressing the resistance issue, especially in corrupt environment. There is a strong believe that information technology will improve the organisational performance and address the corruptive behaviour, hence the resistance is expected [3, 14, 15, 20, 21, 25]. However, the question will be how to conduct the information technology implementation in the corrupt environment?

To address that issue, the author propose the use of agent-based approach to select the most viable implementation path for the given information technology projects. The proposal based on the previously mentioned experience to use the rational choice theory [4]. The agent based model could be used to address the issue of information asymmetry in the market of lemon [1]. The goal is to drive the implementation toward sets of equilibrium condition as defined the Nash's equilibrium theory [18]. It is also related with the use of game theory to determine the rational economics behaviour [19].

The corrupt actors are basically working due to the information asymmetry. The use of agent-based model will help to address the dynamics and changes of the information and interests. The use of agent-based approach to address the corruption issues itself has been elaborated in various papers [5–7, 11, 22, 24].

The illustrative implementation of the agent based approach could be depicted in simple four-by-four Nash Equilibrium matrix. There are four options: win-win, win-lose, lose-win, and lose-lose. The rational choice theory and previous agent-based simulations suggest that any (corrupt) agent will seek a condition where at least there is a win. The determination of the win situation is largely determined by the information received by those agent. By playing with the asymmetry of information and multiple matrices, we could develop a viable implementation roadmap for corrupt environment.

5 Concluding Remarks and Way Forward

The adoption of strategic alignment model [12, 13] may provide the framework to address the alignment issues in public sector IT implementation, especially those funded by donor projects that has limited constraints and time frame to support. It is also possible to use the game theory approach to determine the most viable path for information technology implementation roadmap. It may help to address the resistance issues, since technology has its potential to address the corrupt behaviour.

One further potential research isabout IT-business alignment not only within the organisation of the Indonesian judiciary but also within the framework of national strategy in reforming the law enforcement agencies. The high-level alignment is already established at the strategic level as elaborated in the Medium Term Development Plan. However it needs further elaboration related with the implementation of the technology itself. The theoretical framework could modify the IT-business alignment issues in multi-business organisations [26], since the organisation of the government and state institutions itself is a "multi-business" in nature.

The second potential research is developing or simulating the agent based behaviour based on sets of possible game and equilibrium situations. The agents are the actors involved and have interests in the technology implementation. It is not only the users or the organisations, but also the funding institutions or donor projects as mentioned in the beginning of the articles. International development projects have limited time frame and relatively tight constraints to implement the reform. Fostering the change by engineering the possible rational choice in corrupt and resistance environment has deliver the successful results in the past [2]. The establishment of certain agent-based interaction models will help further projects to learn and establish the environment to achieve successful IT implementations.

Further researches on those two topics and reflection reports on various challenges in implementing technological solutions in corrupt state institutions will enrich the discussion and may trigger the development of practical framework on information technology implementation in misaligned and corrupt environment.

References

1. Akerlof, G.A.: The market for 'Lemons': quality uncertainty and the market mechanism. Q. J. Econ. **84**(3), 488–500 (1970). The MIT Press
2. Alkostar, A., Fathony, H.Z., Mulyana, F.: Start simple: using technology to improve governance, transparency and accountability - an Indonesian court experience. In: Paper and Presentation for the 4th Asia Pacific Judicial Reform Forum, Beijing (2010)
3. Ayuba, B., Aliyu, I.A.: The role of information communication technology (ICT) in combating corrupt business activities in Nigeria. IOSR J. Bus. Manage. **16**(7), 7–14 (2014)
4. Becker, G.S.: The Economic Approach to Human Behavior. University of Chicago Press, Chicago (1976)
5. Bockova, K.H., Slavikova, G., Gabrhel, J.: Game theory as tool of project management. In: Proceeding at 20th International Scientific Conference Economics and Management, (ICEM-2015) (2015)

6. Dzutsati, V.: An Agent-Based Model of Corruption: Micro Approach The ODD Protocol of a Replication of Ross Hammond's Corruption Model, Open Agent Based Model (2015)
7. Epstein, B.: Agent-based modeling and the fallacies of individualism. In: Humphreys, P., Imbert, C. (eds.) Models, Simulations, and Representations, pp. 115–144. Routledge, New York (2011)
8. Fathony, H.Z.: Assessing corruption risks in the judiciary: what role for the community? In: Presentation for the 16th International Anti-Corruption Conference, Putrajaya, Malaysia (2015)
9. Fathony, H.Z.: Developing relevant judicial capabilities: efforts to regain the confidence – the Indonesia experience. In: Presentation for the 5th Asia Pacific Judical Reform Forum, Singapore (2013)
10. Fathony, H.Z.: Knowledge management for legal education: expanding the use of supreme court judgement directory. In: Presentation for the International Conference Southeast Asia Legal Education: Preparing Lawyers for Tomorrow's Society and Profession, A Joint Conference Between University of Washington Law School and Faculty of Law Universitas Airlangga, Surabaya, Indonesia (2013)
11. Hammond, R.: Endogenous transition dynamics in corruption: an agent-based computer model, Center on Social and Economic Dynamics Working Paper No. 19 (2000)
12. Henderson, J.C., Venkatraman, N.: Strategic Alignment-A Model for Organizational Transformation Through Information Technology, pp. 97–117. Oxford University Press, New York (1992)
13. Henderson, J.C., Venkatraman, N.: Strategic alignment—leveraging information technology for transforming organizations. IBM Syst. J. **32**(1), 4–16 (1993)
14. Grönlund A., Heacock, R., Sasaki, D., Hellström, J., Al-Saqaf, W.: Increasing transparency and fighting corruption through ICT empowering people and communities, SPIDER ICT4D Series No. 3 (2010)
15. Ionescu, L.: The role of technology in combating corruption. Econ. Manage. Finan. Markets **8**(3), 101–106 (2013)
16. Luftman, J.N.: Managing the Information Technology Resource: Leadership in the Information Age. Prentice Hall, Upper Saddle River (2004)
17. Luftman, J., Kempaiah, R.: An update on business-IT alignment: a line has been drawn. MIS Q. Executive **6**(3), 165–177 (2007)
18. Nash, J.: Non-cooperative games. Ann. Math. **54**(2), 286–295 (1951)
19. Neumann, J.V., Morgenstern, O.: Theory of Games and Economic Behavior. Princeton University Press, Princeton (1953)
20. Prasad, A., Shivarajan, S.: Understanding the role of technology in reducing corruption: a transaction cost approach. J. Public Aff. **15**(1), 22–39 (2015)
21. Reiling, D.: Technology for Justice. Leiden University Press, Leiden (2010)
22. Situngkir, H., Khanafiah, D.: Theorizing corruption through agent-based modeling. In: Advances in Intelligent Systems Research (2006)
23. Suyudi, A., Fathony, H.Z., Putra, H.A., Eisenhart, D., dan Rodja, S.M.: Pemetaan Implementasi Teknologi Informasi di Mahkamah Agung Republik Indonesia, Pusat Studi Hukum dan Kebijakan (2010)
24. Voinea, C.F.: Briberyscape: an artificial society-based simulation model of corruption's emergence and growth. Eur. Q. Polit. Attitudes Mentalities **2**(1), 27–54 (2013)
25. Wickberg, S.: Technological innovations to identify and reduce corruption. U4 and Transparency International, March 2013
26. Reynolds, P., Yetton, P.: Aligning business and IT strategies in multi-business organizations. J. Inf. Technol. **30**(2), 101–118 (2015)
27. Jasper, M.A.: Using reflective writing within research. J. Res. Nurs. **10**(3), 247–260 (2016)

Analysis of Impact Sourcing by Infusing Social Innovation in Outsourcing for Nepal

Sojen Pradhan[✉]

Faculty of Engineering and IT, School of Systems, Management and Leadership,
University of Technology Sydney, Sydney, Australia
Sojendra.Pradhan@uts.edu.au

Abstract. Outsourcing is a popular term in the business world for last several decades. Information Technology Outsourcing (ITO) and Business Process Outsourcing (BPO) have been dominating the outsourcing jobs to developing countries. Recently, a new shift of outsourcing to impact sourcing have emerged through which digitally-enabled jobs are given to marginalized individuals so that their conditions would be improved. However, only limited studies have been done to explore the recruiting process of marginalized communities and the impacts to the workers and their families.

Cloud Factory, as one of the pioneer impact sourcing service providers in Nepal, is targeted to conduct further research. Initial investigation has shown that flexibility to work from any place such as their own home or internet cafes on flexible hours have attracted college students to this impact sourcing model in Nepal. In the future, further analysis on improvement on employees' lives by impact sourcing will be conducted.

Keywords: Business processes outsourcing (BPO) · Impact sourcing · Social enterprise · Social innovation

1   Introduction

The philosophy of 'social enterprise' and 'corporate social responsibility (CSR)' of organizations have been promoted in outsourcing and referred as 'impact sourcing'. This concept introduced a significant positive impact to the marginalized individuals of communities by providing them with gainful employments so that their living standard would be improved [1]. To promote this concept with an objective to improve the lives of the poor and vulnerable worldwide [2], Rockefeller Foundation, one of the biggest private charitable foundations, endorsed and supported 'impact sourcing' as they have similar goals in their initiatives like Poverty Reduction through Information and Digital Employment (PRIDE). Possible outcomes from impact sourcing have inspired this foundation and have committed to support by providing funding to some African projects [3], such as $100 million to Digital Jobs Africa Initiatives. Since impact sourcing is relatively new concept, not much research has been done, except few researchers [1, 4–7] who mainly focused on the providers of impact sourcing. In this study, however, Cloud Factory in Nepal, is taken as a case study to examine the effect of impact sourcing. Our research goal is to analyze socio-economical profile of employees

© IFIP International Federation for Information Processing 2017
Published by Springer International Publishing AG 2017. All Rights Reserved
J. Choudrie et al. (Eds.): ICT4D 2017, IFIP AICT 504, pp. 829–834, 2017.
DOI: 10.1007/978-3-319-59111-7_69

and the changes that impact sourcing model has made in their lives. Initially, we have analyzed the publicly available information. The current employment situation of the country is analyzed, where majority of youth strive to go foreign countries.

This paper continues by describing how the emergence of impact sourcing concept developed by exploring types of social value it creates and types of values it proposes to outsourcing clients. It is followed by critiques around impact sourcing and classified ISSPs as per their business goals, capital investment provider, and targeted marginalized communities. Conclusion is drawn with future research directions to evaluate the impacts in the communities.

2 Emergence of Impact Sourcing

Information Technology outsourcing (ITOs) and Business Processes Outsourcing (BPOs) are main two categories of outsourcing work. ITOs are focused on work related to information systems such as systems administration, database administration, mainframe, help desk, network management, website development, content development, data conversion etc. and BPOs are usually non-IT related work such as call centers, data entry, transcribing, HR administration, finance, accounting and so on [8]. Due to the greater advancement in technology and robust IT enabled services (ITES), BPOs have been one of the fastest growing sectors and has now spread to more countries in the world [9].

Impact sourcing distributes services offered by traditional BPOs plus social value creation to disadvantaged communities in developing countries by providing work and necessary training to marginalized individuals. However, massive growth of BPO to the country like India, has instigated some human resource challenges [10]. Most common challenges are: managing new generation of employees (college graduates), supply of skilled labor, retaining employees, job hopping etc. Alternative solution to this rising problem, in conjunction with possible social impacts to poor and vulnerable, the outsourcing moved to rural area of the country in some cases. Thus, a company called Ruralshores began in 2008, which expanded the concept of impact sourcing to rural, vulnerable and marginalized communities. It has been noticed that people in rural areas are more reliable [1] and do not necessarily face the same human resource challenges as urban areas. Level of skills is the main issue but when simple tasks are considered, people in rural area outperformed. Thus, impact sourcing claims to provide 'win-win strategy for both clients and communities [11].

The concept of impact sourcing has been gradually gaining popularity due to its practice of employing socioeconomically disadvantaged people, and thus creating social value in those communities [4, 6]. The concept and practice evolved as several social enterprises got involved in ITOs and BPOs to reduce poverty by engaging, training and creating jobs for disadvantaged people [12]. Within the paradigm of impact sourcing, Sandeep and Ravishankar [4] investigated individual and organizational level social entrepreneurship and advocated that social innovation in outsourcing has emerged. The positive impacts to people in developing countries from ITOs and BPOs are re-iterated. For example, one of the impact sourcing service providers, Digital Divide Data (DDD) is operating from countries such as Cambodia, Laos and Kenya and provided work experience to several hundreds of disadvantaged young people from poor families in those countries. The company not only provides necessary training and education to make them ready to work in BPO, but also offers scholarship to enroll in university for upskilling in the process of reducing poverty in the region [12].

2.1 Critique of Impact Sourcing

Generally, one of the primary goals of for-profit organizations is to increase profit and decrease cost of operating the business. Outsourcing has been an effective strategy to save cost by contracting out services and activities [13–15] and to remain competitive in the market [16]. Malik et al. [11] reiterated that relationship between business and society is only economic and criticized the concept of impact sourcing as it emerged to save cost and reduce employee turnover symptom outsourcing company faced, rather than impacting marginalized individuals and communities. Some other researchers also criticized that CSR is used as marketing tool for public relations and as corporate mask to legitimate business activities [11]. It is further intensified by viewing the impact sourcing as 'exploitation' of people in marginalized communities of developing countries rather than creating social value. However, these critics ignore the challenges faced by organizations to take work to those communities such as lack of infrastructure, information security, data confidentiality and lower technical and other desired skills in those communities in rural areas.

3 Research Method

A literature review of related articles in impact sourcing is conducted to show how it emerged from traditional outsourcing domain. Criticism of impact sourcing has also been scrutinized. A case study of the company 'Cloud Factory' in Nepal has been initiated to examine the impacts to the impact workers. At this stage, publicly available information about the company is presented in this paper. In the future, however, thorough analysis of this company is planned by interviewing several employees, different managerial levels, including the founder. This study is planned to conduct a longitudinal study outlining the effect to impact workers' families and eventually to the societies.

4 Impact Sourcing Service Providers (ISSPs)

Based on structures and intentions of ISSPs, Malik et al. [11] grouped and described the impact sourcing service providers into the four categories. They have also divided the 4 groups of ISSPs into 2 categories broadly first as shown in Table 1 below.

- *Non-profit social outsourcing organizations* have primary objective to create social value and community development. They are funded by donations from both commercial and charity organizations. Profit and revenue generation are not the aim of these organizations but they pride themselves by giving opportunities and creating employment to disadvantaged individuals. DDD and Samasource are examples.

Table 1. Groups of ISSPs with targeted individuals and locations (source: [7, 11])

	Groups	ISSPs	Targeted individuals	Location/Country
Social IT outsourcing	Non-profit	Digital Divide Data (DDD)	Unemployed high school graduates	Cambodia, Laos, Kenya
		Samasource	Poor and disadvantaged	India, Kenya, Uganda, Ghana
		KGVK	Poor youth	India (Jharkhand)
	For-profit	Kudumbasree	Poor rural women	India (Kerala)
		Cloud Factory*	Poor and unemployed people	Nepal and Kenya
Socio-commercial IT outsourcing	Socially responsible	Tata Rural	Poor and disadvantaged rural	India (Maharashtra)
		Wipro Rural	Poor and disadvantaged rural	India (Tamil Nadu)
	Dual-value	Ruralshores	Disadvantaged and disabled	India
		Harva	Rural women	India
		eGramIT	Rural youth	India (Andhra Pradesh)

- *For-profit social outsourcing organizations* are driven by market opportunities to create social value but their focus is also to run as commercial companies. State government in Kerala, India supported an initiative, Kudumbasree which helps poor rural women to establish social ICT enterprises. *Cloud Factory is another company which is privately founded to help people in Nepal and Kenya.
- *Socially responsible outsourcing organizations* - are founded with the CSR view in mind by commercial outsourcing service providers. Although the motive is in social development in communities, they would also account for profit.
- *Dual value outsourcing organizations* - focus at setting up outsourcing centers in rural areas to stay competitive in the market, thus they have dual goals to create business and social value. Initial investment for these organizations are provided usually by individual investor and hence needs to generate profit to sustain in the market. Ruralshores opened several rural BPO centers in remote villages in India to reduce the migration of rural people to urban areas. They trained and employed poor and disabled people in those areas, thus contributing to the local economy in villages by empowering local people through ICT trainings.

5 Impact Sourcing in Nepal – Cloud Factory

Nepal is sandwiched in between two top countries, India and China, in terms of attracting the highest number of BPO services to. Although it is a small country, there is a big potential impact sourcing to change socio-economic status of rural communities and sustain local economic development. A significant number of Nepalese youth (2,226,152 between 2008/09 and 2013/14) goes to foreign countries such as Middle Eastern countries, Israel, Malaysia, Korea etc. for basic employment [17]. They are departing for foreign jobs because there is no employment available in the local areas for them.

Cloud Factory has been operating as a successful ISSP since 2012. This company is founded by Mark Sears as he was impressed by skills of local people in Nepal. Core focus of this company is not to make profit only but to grow the company and make social impact by giving more opportunities to talented people who will otherwise not have opportunities. Cloud Factory has so far employed 6,738 members of community in developing countries like Kenya and Nepal. Types of jobs carried on by Cloud Factory are; transcribing bills, restaurant menus, categorize images, tag images, face detection, virtual assistant training, ChaBot training etc. [18]. It has published that 59% of the employees are currently enrolled in college and working part time. 47% of its employees gained new management skills and 30% leadership skills. It has clearly demonstrated that majority of earnings (62%) is spent for their personal expenses and 22% were used to support their families. The most important figure is happy index. 92% of the employees agreed that they are happier because what they learnt there. The company is operating from the capital of the country, Kathmandu.

6   Conclusion and Future Direction

The new trend of impact sourcing in the space of outsourcing has been gradually evolving and creating social values to the disadvantaged communities. With the increased awareness of social responsibilities and inclusive business attitudes, businesses are more likely to use the service provided by impact sourcing service provider than traditional outsourcers. In the context of Nepal where growing youth departing the country to find basic employment in foreign countries, expanding impact sourcing to reach rural parts of the country is pragmatic. In the future, this study will be expanded to analyze and compare the 'before and after' condition of the employees. Lack of infrastructure and higher illiteracy rate are main challenges to implement impact sourcing in rural areas, but these issues can be reduced by partnering with NGOs, microfinances and government bodies. We strongly believe and recommend that the concept of impact sourcing will be more effective in rural areas of Nepal to utilize skills of local rural youth and establishing impact sourcing organizations successfully.

References

1. Burgess, A., Ravishankar, M. N., Oshri, I.: Getting impact sourcing right. Professional Outsourcing, (21) Summer, pp. 26–35 (2015)
2. Accenture.: Exploring the value proposition for impact sourcing. In: Bulloch, G., Long, J. (eds.) The Buyer's Perspectives (2012). https://www.rockefellerfoundation.org/app/uploads/Exploring-the-Value-Proposition-for-Impact-for-Impact-Sourcing.pdf

3. Troup, S.: The financial and social value of impact sourcing. Rockefeller Foundation (2014). https://www.rockefellerfoundation.org/blog/the-financial-and-social-value-of-impact-sourcing/

4. Sandeep, M.S., Ravishankar, M.N.: Social innovations in outsourcing: an empirical investigation of impact sourcing companies in India. J. Strateg. Inf. Syst. 24(4), 270–288 (2015)

5. Carmel, E., Lacity, Mary C., Doty, A.: The impact of impact sourcing: framing a research agenda. In: Hirschheim, R., Heinzl, A., Dibbern, J. (eds.) Information Systems Outsourcing. PI, pp. 397–429. Springer, Heidelberg (2014). doi:10.1007/978-3-662-43820-6_16

6. Heeks, R.: Emerging markets, information technology impact sourcing. Commun. ACM 56 (12), 22–25 (2013). doi:10.1145/2535913

7. Lacity, M.C., Willcocks, L.P., Solomon, S.: Robust practices from two decades of ITO and BPO research. In: Advanced Outsourcing Practice. Palgrave Macmillan, Basingstoke (2012)

8. Sen, R., Islam, M.S.: Southeast Asia in the global wave of outsourcing: Trends, opportunities, and challenges, Regional Outlook, p. 75 (2005)

9. Ocra, B., Ntim, B.A.: The BPO country competency model (CCM). Int. J. Comput. Sci. Eng. IT Res (IJCSEITR) 3(4), 113–120 (2013). ISSN 2249-6831, © TJPRC Pvt. Ltd.

10. Kuruvilla, S., Ranganathan, A.: Globalisation and outsourcing: confronting new human resource challenges in India's business process outsourcing industry. Ind. Relat. J. 41(2), 136–153 (2010)

11. Malik, F., Nicholson, B., Morgan, S.: Assessing the social development potential of impact sourcing. In: Proceedings of 6th Annual SIG GlobDev Pre ICIS Workshop on ICT in Global Development, vol. 14, Milan, Italy (2013)

12. Madon, S., Sharanappa, S.: Social IT outsourcing and development: theorising the linkage. Inf. Syst. J. 23(5), 381–399 (2013)

13. Hendry, J.: Culture, community and networks: the hidden cost of outsourcing. Eur. Manage. J. 13(2), 193–200 (1995)

14. Görg, H., Hanley, A.: Does outsourcing increase profitability? Econ. Soc. Rev. 35(3), 267–288 (2004)

15. Lacity, M.C., Khan, S., Yan, A., Willcocks, L.P.: A review of the IT outsourcing empirical literature and future research directions. J. Inf. Technol. 25(4), 395–433 (2010)

16. Antonucci, Y.L., Lordi, F.C., Tucker III, J.J.: The pros and cons of IT outsourcing. J. Accountancy 185(6), 26 (1998)

17. Government of Nepal.: Labour Migration for Employment (2015). https://asiafoundation.org/resources/pdfs/MigrationReportbyGovernmentofNepal.pdf

18. Cloudfactory (n.d.), Cloud Factory. https://www.cloudfactory.com/

Exploring Personal Computing Devices Ownership Among University Students in Indonesia

Ahmad R. Pratama[1,2(✉)]

[1] Department of Technology and Society, Stony Brook University,
Stony Brook, NY 11794, USA
ahmad.pratama@stonybrook.edu
[2] Department of Informatics, Universitas Islam Indonesia,
Sleman, DIY, Indonesia 55584
ahmad.rafie@uii.ac.id

Abstract. This study investigated ownership of desktops, laptops, smartphones, and tablets using survey information on Indonesian university students. The data show that 98% of students own at least two of these personal computing devices. Laptop & smartphone are the most common bundle to have, owned by 41% while 15% own all four of them. Applying logistic regression method to the dataset shows that student socioeconomic status has no effect on laptop and smartphone ownership but it is strongly associated with desktop and tablet ownership. Gender preference is also indicated in tablet ownership where females are more likely to own than males. Furthermore, the same logistic regression method applied to device bundle ownership shows that students with high socioeconomic status are way more likely to own all four devices while the opposite is true for laptop & smartphone bundle ownership. The findings in this research can serve as a foundation for further research in quest of optimizing technology use to improve educational attainment, especially among Indonesian students.

Keywords: Indonesia · Higher education · Smartphone · Tablet · Laptop · Desktop

1 Introduction

Personal computer has been around for home use since the 1970s, followed by portable computer or laptop in the 1980s. By 1990s, people started using the Internet at home and by 2000s smartphone gained its popularity, all the more so with the release of Apple iPhone and Google Android OS in 2007 and 2008 respectively. With the launch of iPad and multiple variants of Android counterpart in the 2010s, tablets were the latest addition to the lineup. The trend shows it is becoming more and more mobile oriented. It is also worth to note that many studies confirmed the assertion that device ownership is growing rapidly among university students all over the world [4, 13, 14].

Meanwhile in Indonesia, the fourth most populous country in the world, the statistics of ICT adoption are promising. Internet penetration went up significantly from 15% [9] to 51% within the past three years [12]. Indonesia has the highest growth in internet

© IFIP International Federation for Information Processing 2017
Published by Springer International Publishing AG 2017. All Rights Reserved
J. Choudrie et al. (Eds.): ICT4D 2017, IFIP AICT 504, pp. 835–841, 2017.
DOI: 10.1007/978-3-319-59111-7_70

user (51%), more than five times of the global average between 2016 to 2017 [12]. In 2014, mobile connections in Indonesia was already outnumbered the total population itself (112%) placing Indonesia ahead of some developed countries like the US, France, Australia, Japan, or South Korea [9]. In terms of the time spent on the Internet, Indonesian people consistently ranked way above the average every year. Only Thailand, The Philippines, and Brazil ranked better within the past three years. [9–12]. While these statistics do not necessarily represent quality of technology use, it is clear that Indonesia thrives in terms of technology adoption, particularly in mobile frontline.

2 Literature Review

Despite the increasing access to personal computing devices over time at both global and nationals level, there is one big inequality problem in access to, attitude towards, and the use of these devices, also known as digital divide, a term that was first coined in late 20th century and has been well researched topic ever since [16, 19, 20]. Some studies confirmed the existence of digital divide between race, age, and gender [3, 7] while some other argue that income or socioeconomic status (SES) is the most important factor of digital divide [1, 2]. In terms of university students, major is also considered important factor where students from engineering and technical courses use considerably more technology than students in social sciences majors [14].

On many occasions, several researchers have tried to investigate the relationship between device ownership or use and educational attainment. Some studies suggest the use of mobile device can help improve the quality of education [6, 15]. On the other hand, some other studies also suggest problematic relationship between two of them. In many cases, problematic use of mobile device is mostly about addiction [5, 8, 17]. Either way, the relationship between ICT and education are two-folds, higher participation rate in education, especially in secondary and higher education increases technology utilization, which in turn helps promote better outcomes of education [18].

Finally, while many studies in this topic were done in different parts of the world, there is nothing much learned yet from Indonesian settings. While results from those studies can definitely give a good insight of what might happen in any other places, including Indonesia, there are still some differences, particularly in culture and any other characteristics that may lead to different outcomes. This is why before we can proceed with some sort of conclusion or alternative solutions on how to optimize the use of technology for educational purposes in Indonesia, it will be much better to explore what is actually happening in there in the first place.

3 Methodology

An online survey was conducted in a private university in Indonesia within the first quarter of 2016. A total of 189 undergraduate students (81 females, 43% and 108 males, 57%) participated in the study. They came from 7 different majors and ranged from 19 to 27 years of age ($M = 21.44, SD = 1.59$). Participants were also categorized based on year in college (26 1st year, 13.76%, 35 2nd year, 18.52%, 60 3rd year,

31.75%, 39 4th year, 20.63%, and 29 other in their 5th year or above, 15.34%), place of origin (121 Java, 64% and 68 outside Java, 36%), self-perceived ICT adoption level representing attitude towards ICT (39 early adopters, 21%, 129 majorities, 68%, and 21 laggards, 11%), and socioeconomic status (SES) measured by the purchase price of their devices (36 high SES, 19% and 153 middle to low SES, 81%). Data analysis includes both descriptive and inferential statistics in form of chi-square test and logistic regression models, the latter is used due to the nature of the dependent variables that are in binary form. Due to multicollinearity with year in college, age is omitted in all analyses.

4 Results and Discussion

Table 1 provides information on device ownership among these students, categorized by gender, major, place of origin, SES, attitude towards ICT, and year in college. Laptop and smartphone have the highest ownership rate, close to 100% in all groups. Males have higher ownership rate on desktop and smartphone as opposed to females on laptop and tablet. However, the difference is only significant for laptop ($Pr < .05$) and tablet ($Pr < .1$). Students in the high-SES group consistently have higher

Table 1. Descriptive statistics on device ownership

	Desktop		Laptop		Smartphone		Tablet	
	Freq	(%)	Freq	(%)	Freq	(%)	Freq	(%)
Gender: Male	53	49.07	102	94.44	105	97.22	22	20.37
Female	36	44.44	81	100.00	75	92.59	26	32.10
Major: STEMM	52	45.61	109	95.31	108	94.74	28	24.56
Social Sciences	37	49.33	74	98.67	72	96.00	20	26.67
Place of Origin: Java	58	47.93	119	98.35	115	95.04	31	25.62
Non-Java	31	45.59	64	94.12	65	95.59	17	25.00
Socioeconomic status: High	26	72.22	36	100.00	36	100.00	19	52.78
Middle to Low	63	41.18	147	96.08	144	94.12	29	18.95
Attitude towards ICT: Early adopter	20	51.28	36	92.31	38	97.44	14	35.90
Majority	64	49.61	126	97.67	123	95.35	30	23.26
Laggard	5	23.81	21	100.00	19	90.48	4	19.05
Year in college: 1st year	12	46.15	25	96.15	26	100.00	9	34.62
2nd year	18	51.43	34	97.14	34	97.14	9	25.71
3rd year	28	46.67	59	98.33	54	90.00	17	28.33
4th year	15	38.46	38	97.44	38	97.44	8	20.51
≥ 5th year	16	55.17	27	93.10	28	96.55	5	17.24
All Samples	89	47.09	183	96.83	180	95.24	48	25.40

Table 2. Descriptive statistics on device bundle ownership

	All four devices		Desktop, Laptop & Smartphone		Laptop, Smartphone & Tablet		Laptop & Smartphone		Either one only		Other bundles	
	Freq	(%)	Freq	(%)	Freq	(%)	Freq	(%)	Freq	(%)	Freq	(%)
Gender: Male	12	11.11	35	32.41	9	8.33	43	39.81	3	2.78	6	5.56
Female	16	19.75	19	23.46	5	6.17	35	43.21	1	1.23	5	6.18
Major: STEMM	13	11.40	33	28.95	10	8.77	47	41.23	2	1.75	9	7.90
Social Sciences	15	20.00	21	28.00	4	5.33	31	41.33	2	2.67	2	2.67
Place of Origin: Java	19	15.70	37	30.58	9	7.44	48	39.67	4	3.31	4	3.31
Non-Java	9	13.24	17	25.00	5	7.35	30	44.12	0	0.00	7	10.29
SES: High	14	38.89	12	33.33	5	13.89	5	13.89	0	0.00	0	0.00
Middle to Low	14	9.15	42	27.45	9	5.88	73	47.71	4	2.61	11	7.20
Attitude: Early adopter	9	23.08	8	20.51	4	10.26	14	35.90	1	2.56	3	7.69
Majority	18	13.95	42	32.56	7	5.43	53	41.09	1	0.78	8	6.19
Laggard	1	4.76	4	19.05	3	14.29	11	52.38	2	9.52	0	0.00
Year in college: 1st year	5	19.23	6	23.08	4	15.38	10	38.46	0	0.00	1	3.85
2nd year	7	20.00	11	31.43	1	2.86	14	40.00	1	2.86	1	2.86
3rd year	8	13.33	18	30.00	5	8.33	22	36.67	2	3.33	5	8.35
4th year	5	12.82	9	23.08	3	7.69	20	51.28	1	2.56	1	2.56
≥ 5th year	3	10.34	10	34.48	1	3.45	12	41.38	0	0.00	3	10.35
All samples	28	**14.81**	54	**28.57**	14	**7.41**	78	**41.27**	4	**2.12**	11	**5.82**

ownership rate for all four devices, albeit significant only for desktop (Pr = .001) and tablet (Pr < .001). Attitude towards ICT has linear relationship with ownership except for laptop that is inverse linear instead. However, the difference is only significant for desktop (Pr < .1). No difference is found in major, place of origin, and year in college.

The fact that 98% of these students own at least two devices suggests the need for same analysis with device bundle ownership. Out of 16 possible bundle types, only four major bundles are identified. In decreasing order, they are (1) laptop & smartphone, (2) desktop, laptop, & smartphone, (3) all four devices, and (4) laptop, smartphone, & tablet. Table 2 provides information on these four bundles in addition to those who own only either one of four devices and those who own other types of bundle, each combined as one category. One interesting finding here is that in three major bundles with at least three devices, students with high-SES have higher rate of ownership while the opposite is true for laptop & smartphone bundle, which is also the most common bundle, owned by 41% of the students. The difference is highly significant (Pr < .001) in both the bundle with most devices and the bundle with most owners. Another interesting finding is at the attitude towards ICT where it has different relationship (i.e. linear, inverse linear, u-shaped nonlinear, and inverted u-shaped nonlinear) with the ownership of each one of the four major bundles. This indicates each bundle represents different state of technology adoption level. The most common bundle is associated with the laggards while the bundle with most devices is associated with the early adopters.

Table 3. Logistic regression estimates of device & device bundle ownership

	Device ownership		Device bundle ownership	
	Desktop	Tablet	All four devices	Laptop & Smartphone
Gender	1.307	**.476***	.513	.828
(Male)	(.444)	**(.190)**	(.254)	(.284)
Attitude towards ICT	.700	.621	**.440***	1.175
	(.201)	(.213)	**(.196)**	(.341)
Socioeconomic status	3.737***	4.299***	5.332***	**.171***
(High income)	(1.569)	(1.760)	(2.476)	**(.089)**
Year in college	1.114	.898	.985	1.005
	(.121)	(.120)	(.161)	(.110)
Major	.752	1.351	.615	.946
(STEMM)	(.260)	(.546)	(.302)	(.332)
Place of origin	1.152	1.223	1.506	.782
(Java)	(.371)	(.463)	(.720)	(.255)
Constant	.912	.894	.699	.893
	(.674)	(.785)	(.781)	(.673)
Model x^2	15.32**	21.64***	23.63***	17.07***
Pseudo R^2 (McFadden)	.059	.101	.149	.067
Df	6	6	6	6
Observation	189	189	189	189

Note: Number reported is the odds ratio with the standard error between parentheses;
$*p < .1$. $**p < .05$ $***p < .01$

In the last analysis, several models were developed to see the effect of all variables of interest to the ownership of both devices and bundles at a multivariate level. The models were significant in the ownership of two devices (i.e. desktop and tablet) and two device bundles (i.e. all four device bundle and laptop & smartphone bundle) only. Table 3 provides information on these four models. Again, socioeconomic status is proven to be the most important predictor of all. Students with high SES are more likely to own either desktop, tablet, or all four device bundle than students with middle to low SES while the opposite is true for laptop & smartphone bundle. Gender preference is also confirmed in tablet ownership where females are more likely to own it than males. Finally, attitude towards ICT is also confirmed to be significant predictor of the ownership. Early adopters are more likely to be the owner of this bundle than those in the majorities group while the laggards are the least likely to be the owner of all. The effect of all other independent variables (i.e. year in college, major, and place of origin) is not significant in any model, contrary to what previous studies in other countries suggested.

5 Conclusion and Future Works

In this paper, differences in device ownership are identified where students with high-SES are about four times more likely to own either desktop or tablet than those with middle to low SES while females are about twice more likely to own tablet than males.

Contrary to previous studies in other countries, the difference in major was not found in this study, STEMM students are not more likely to own devices or bundles than social sciences students. The same is true for location where students from both Java and outside Java Island, each representing more and less developed area, don't differ in the likelihood of ownership. There is also no significant difference found in terms of age or year in college, presumably due to the fact that all of these students are basically the same millennial generation born in 1990s. The age factor would have had stronger role if the comparison was made with older (e.g. postgraduate) students born in 1980s and later or with younger (e.g. secondary school) students born in 2000s and later. Despite its merit in identifying differences and important factor of device ownership, this study is still in preliminary phase. The long-term goal is to investigate the relationship between device ownership/use and educational attainment, especially with the fact that same online survey used in this study contains more data related to students' activities with mobile device, their online & mobile learning activities and their attitude toward them.

References

1. Calvert, S.L., Rideout, V.J., Woolard, J.L., Barr, R.F., Strouse, G.A.: Age, ethnicity, and socioeconomic patterns in early computer use a national survey. Am. Behav. Sci. **48**(5), 590–607 (2005)
2. Chinn, M.D., Fairlie, R.W.: The determinants of the global digital divide: a cross-country analysis of computer and internet penetration. Oxf. Econ. Pap. **59**, 16–44 (2006)
3. Colley, A., Comber, C.: Age and gender differences in computer use and attitudes among secondary school students: what has changed? Educ. Res. **45**(2), 155–165 (2003)
4. Goerke, V., Oliver, B.: Australian undergraduates' use and ownership of emerging technologies: Implications and opportunities for creating engaging learning experiences for the net generation. Australas. J. Educ. Technol. **23**(2), 171 (2007)
5. Hong, F.Y., Chiu, S.I., Huang, D.H.: A model of the relationship between psychological characteristics, mobile phone addiction and use of mobile phones by Taiwanese university female students. Comput. Hum. Behav. **28**(6), 2152–2159 (2012)
6. Hwang, G.J., Wu, P.H., Ke, H.R.: An interactive concept map approach to supporting mobile learning activities for natural science courses. Comput. Educ. **57**(4), 2272–2280 (2011)
7. Jackson, L.A., Zhao, Y., Kolenic III, A., Fitzgerald, H.E., Harold, R., Von Eye, A.: Race, gender, and information technology use: the new digital divide. CyberPsychol. Behav. **11**(4), 437–442 (2008)
8. Kamibeppu, K., Sugiura, H.: Impact of the mobile phone on junior high-school students' friendships in the Tokyo metropolitan area. Cyberpsychol. Behav. **8**(2), 121–130 (2005)
9. Kemp, S.: Social, digital and mobile worldwide in 2014 (2014). http://wearesocial.com/uk/special-reports/social-digital-mobile-worldwide-2014. Accessed 7 Dec 2015
10. Kemp, S.: Social, digital and mobile worldwide in 2015 (2015). http://wearesocial.com/uk/special-reports/social-digital-mobile-worldwide-2015. Accessed 7 Dec 2015
11. Kemp, S.: Digital in 2016 (2016). http://wearesocial.com/uk/special-reports/digital-in-2016. Accessed 9 Feb 2017
12. Kemp, S.: Digital in 2017: global review. (2017). http://wearesocial.com/blog/2017/01/digital-in-2017-global-overview. Accessed 9 Feb 2017

13. Kobus, M.B., Rietveld, P., Van Ommeren, J.N.: Ownership versus on-campus use of mobile IT devices by university students. Comput. Educ. **68**, 29–41 (2013)
14. Margaryan, A., Littlejohn, A., Vojt, G.: Are digital natives a myth or reality? university students' use of digital technologies. Comput. Educ. **56**(2), 429–440 (2011)
15. Martin, F., Ertzberger, J.: Here and now mobile learning: an experimental study on the use of mobile technology. Comput. Educ. **68**, 76–85 (2013)
16. Norris, P.: Digital Divide: Civic Engagement, Information Poverty, and the Internet Worldwide. Cambridge University Press, New York (2001)
17. Ozkan, M., Solmaz, B.: Mobile addiction of generation Z and its effects on their social lifes: (an application among university students in the 18–23 age group). Procedia-Soc. Behav. Sci. **205**, 92–98 (2015)
18. Pratama, A.R.: Cross-country analysis of ICT and education indicators: an exploratory study. In: IOP Conference Series: Materials Science and Engineering, vol. 185, no. 1. IOP Publishing (2017)
19. Pratama, A.R., Al-Shaikh, M.: Relation and growth of internet penetration rate with human development level from 2000 to 2010. Commun. IBIMA **2012**, 1–8 (2012)
20. Sidorenko, A., Findlay, C.: The digital divide in East Asia. Asian Pac. Econ. Lit. **15**(2), 18–30 (2001)

A Conceptual Framework of ICT4D Champion Origins

Jaco Renken$^{(\boxtimes)}$ and Richard Heeks

Centre for Development Informatics, University of Manchester, Manchester, UK
jaco.renken@manchester.ac.uk

Abstract. Where do ICT4D champions come from? The paper explores this question because, as is demonstrated from literature, knowledge and understanding about the origins of champions are insufficient, yet these individuals are known for their decisive contributions to ICT4D initiatives. An empirical exploration of the origins of three ICT4D champions is reported. Following an inductive methodology, the paper proposes an ICT4D Champion Origin Conceptual Framework; it demonstrates that this model both synthesises and extends existing understanding about champion origins thereby contributing to the identified knowledge gap. The model is significant because it lays the foundation for future ICT4D champion research and suggests to practitioners that champions can be identified, developed and deployed in ICT4D initiatives thereby harnessing the potential positive contributions these individuals can make to digital development.

Keywords: ICT4D champions · Champion origin · Champion genesis · Champion identification · Champion development · Champion deployment · ICT4D Champion Origin Conceptual Framework

1 Introduction

ICT4D champions are *"individuals who make decisive contributions to ICT4D initiatives by actively and enthusiastically promoting their progress through critical stages in order to mobilise resources and/or active support and cooperation from all stakeholders"* [12: 1]. Such individuals can be found in ICT4D initiatives of various kinds and across diverse geographical and cultural contexts. Yet we do not know where they come from; what factors have led to them becoming champions? Did their upbringing play a part, or did circumstances and opportunities shape them into becoming ICT4D champions? A better understanding of their origins holds the potential to help practitioners better identify these individuals and potentially involve them in ICT4D initiatives, because their contributions are mostly associated with positive outcomes [5]. Furthermore, a better understanding of their origins might suggest interventions, such as relevant skills training, which could lead to the development of more people into ICT4D champions. It is for these reasons that this paper seeks to contribute towards this knowledge gap about ICT4D champion origins.

The paper starts with a brief analysis of the literature aiming to demonstrate the insufficiency of knowledge about champion origins. Next will follow a brief outline of

© IFIP International Federation for Information Processing 2017
Published by Springer International Publishing AG 2017. All Rights Reserved
J. Choudrie et al. (Eds.): ICT4D 2017, IFIP AICT 504, pp. 842–847, 2017.
DOI: 10.1007/978-3-319-59111-7_71

the inductive methodology that was followed to explore the research question: where do ICT4D champions come from? A conceptual framework of ICT4D champion origins will be introduced in the findings section, before concluding with a discussion of the key implications of this new framework.

2 Literature

Very little research is available on ICT4D champions to date and within the small pool of literature almost no explicit attention is given to their origins. Even within cognate disciplines – Information Systems and Innovation Studies – where champion research is better established, few studies explicitly address this. As such, this theme still represents an important gap in conceptualisation of champions that future work needs to address [13]. This paper seeks to address this gap, firstly, by offering a synthesis of literature on the origin of champions.

From the reviewed literature it became evident that authors characterise champions' origins in different ways and that there is little agreement on this matter. One perspective proposes that some individuals are predisposed to champion behaviour on the basis of their personality traits (e.g. [7, 8]). As such, champions are seen to be born with the inclination to adopt a particular cause or initiative and actively promote it; they would argue that these predisposed individuals would emerge as champions when exposed to favourable contextual factors and influences. Beath [1] largely agrees with this notion, however, studies are not in agreement about how context shapes champion emergence: the earlier studies by Howell and Higgins [8] and Beath [1] pointed to organisations with many barriers to innovation as a favourable context, while Mullins et al. [9] found that the need to overcome organisational resistance is less important in champion emergence than was previously thought. Slightly more light is shed on this by Howell and Boies [6] who found that the emergence of champions can be linked to early involvement during the idea generation stage of a new initiative.

Others see the origin of champions less in individuals and more within particular organisational roles. Esteves and Pastor [4] and Negoita et al. [11], for example, see champions deriving internally and mainly from senior-level project sponsor roles. Thus, unlike the personality-based argument, champions are seen to emerge from positions of authority. Others construe variants of this – Dong et al. [3] see champions emerging from a wider variety of managerial roles; Van Laere and Aggestam [14] offer an interactive perspective forwarding the view that championing is catalysed within the informal but intensive collaboration between people working on the same initiative; and Kamal [10] also sees IT champions as being appointed rather than originating from a more organic route, but in this case arguing those appointments are best made on the basis of a mix of domain knowledge and expertise as well as personality-based factors.

In sum, champion origins are conceptualised in diverse ways; notions about champions being born or made, or that they spontaneously emerge or are appointed can be distilled from the literature, but little evidence of progressive building of knowledge or convergence of ideas can be found. It is for this purpose that an inductive exploration of the origins of champions – specifically in ICT4D initiatives – was deemed necessary and important.

3 Methodology

Nine candidate cases – ICT4D champions – were identified in South Africa (SA) using a multiple peer nomination and verification protocol. Based on alignment with the definition above [12] three (anonymised) champions were selected for inclusion in the study:

1. Mandisa: She is in her early thirties and pursued the opportunity to become involved with a Broadband Access Initiative (BAI) in The Village where she grew up. Her involvement in BAI brought together a passion to see the social ills in the community alleviated together with her enthusiasm for ICTs, and in the end led her to become the ICT4D champion that she is today.
2. Kagiso: He is in his early thirties and persisted for more than ten years in a quest to narrow the digital divide by trying to find ways to reduce the cost of telecommunications and extend access to previously disadvantaged and under-serviced sectors of the community. His breakthrough finally came when he built a relationship with someone that could assist him with the needed resources that led to the establishment of the Wireless Connectivity Initiative (WCI) in The Township.
3. Sarah: She is in her late fifties; her transitioning from being an ordinary maths teacher to become a champion of ICTs for education was enabled by the rise of social media. The technology-enabled means to disseminate resources and interact with the SA teaching community was the final link that connected her passion to improve the education system and her enthusiasm for ICTs. It was for this reason that she was invited to become involved in the Tablet Teaching Initiative (TTI) in The District and made a decisive contribution to the success thereof.

In-depth interviews with the three champions themselves, as well as semi-structured interviews with a total of 29 initiative stakeholders, formed the pool of qualitative data. Interviews were recorded and verbatim transcribed – these were subsequently analysed following the six phased approach to thematic analysis outlined by Braun and Clark [2]. NVivo 9, a computer assisted qualitative data analysis software tool, was used to manage the data and facilitate the thematic analysis.

4 Findings

Analysis of the case data showed that ICT4D champion origins can be linked to all four of the notions synthesised from literature – being born or made, or that they spontaneously emerge or are appointed. None of these perspectives on their own accurately or adequately represents the origin of champions; at best the four notions can be seen as mutually constitutive as a means of describing their origins. Moreover, multiple factors, beyond those portrayed in literature, were found to influence champion genesis (see empirical examples in Table 1). It also became clear that it is inadequate to conceive champion genesis as an *event*, which is how literature mostly portrays it, as opposed to a *process* that unfolds over time. Drawing on the empirical case evidence, Fig. 1 proposes a framework to characterise and analyse ICT4D champion genesis.

Table 1. Empirical examples of ESPOSE factors influencing champion genesis

Environmental Factors

The social motives of all three champions – to bridge the digital divide (Mandisa & Kagiso) or to improve the education system (Sarah) – can be linked to the influence of the Apartheid era in South Africa (*Political*). New *technology* also played a key role in these champions' genesis

Social Networks

The influence and importance of key enabling relationships, such as meeting an investment partner (Kagiso – *acquaintances*) or encouragement and support from *family* members (Mandisa), were instrumental in developing these individuals into the champions they are today

Personal Characteristics

The champions differ somewhat from one individual to the next, but the three individuals studied can be characterised as highly *agreeable* – amiable and cooperative in nature (team players). They are also creative, intellectually stimulating and innovative

Organisational Factors

The *organisational culture* in BAI (Mandisa) and TTI (Sarah) were conducive to enthusiastic contributions from champion-type individuals; the lack of steep hierarchies, bureaucratic red tape, or strict control over individuals provided them the freedom to become champions

Skills and Education

Formal tertiary education played a key enabling role in the genesis of Mandisa (graduate certificate in management) and Kagiso (ICT and business customer relationship management studies at degree level). Sarah did a technical certification (A+ webmaster) after being a teacher for 20 years – this equipped her to effectively use social media in her championing endeavours

Experience

Kagiso *personally experienced* consequences of Apartheid – discrimination, unequal opportunities and poverty. His championing is motivated to bring correction to some of these

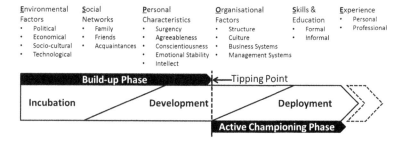

Fig. 1. ICT4D Champion Origin Conceptual Framework

Three aspects are captured in the Fig. 1 framework. Firstly, a spread of factors has been identified from the case data that could potentially characterise or influence ICT4D champion origins; these are captured in the acronym ESPOSE. Lists of sample qualifiers are included with each of the factors in Fig. 1, but it is quite conceivable that different qualifiers can be used to analyse a particular factor. The same factors did not underpin the genesis of all three ICT4D champions in this research, but a more accurate description of their origins can be constructed by identifying and analysing different combinations from this collection.

Secondly, ICT4D champion genesis can be considered in three sequential stages: an initial, passive, incubation stage – the personal characteristics, competencies and motivations of ICT4D champions are shaped by various ESPOSE factors; a developmental stage – formal studies or informal acquisition of skills and knowledge needed for championing; and an active deployment stage – a specific cause, innovation or ICT4D initiative is adopted and actively promoted. The stages overlap as indicated in Fig. 1. This implies, for example, that while the champion is shaped by environmental factors (e.g. the influences of a political regime such as Apartheid) in the early incubation stage, they can already gain valuable personal and professional experience. They can also continue developing, through formal and informal education and training, as well as being influenced by other work and personal experiences, while already actively championing an ICT4D innovation. Combining the three stages and the ESPOSE factors in an analytic framework therefore enables a longitudinal, *process-based* analysis of ICT4D champion genesis.

Thirdly, the process of becoming a champion can be considered in two phases: an initial phase that builds up to a tipping point, followed by the active championing phase. These tipping points – *events* or changes in their environment, social networks, or organisational settings that trigger the individual into championing action – have been observed in all three of the empirical cases. It is proposed that a combination of the ESPOSE factors, a three stage process view, and the notion of tipping points, offer a richer and more accurate descriptive and analytic framework to characterise and analyse ICT4D champion genesis.

5   Discussion and Conclusions

By proposing the ICT4D Champion Origin Conceptual Framework, the paper seeks to make three contributions. Firstly, it seeks to demonstrate the inadequacy of current literature about the origin of champions and offer empirically-based findings as a step towards filling this knowledge gap. The key notion is that ICT4D champion genesis is a *process* shaped by environmental factors as well as key *events*; this finding thereby both synthesises and extends earlier knowledge about champion origins. Secondly, it proposes the inductively developed framework as a theoretical contribution that aims to anchor current understanding and future research on ICT4D champion genesis. Important next steps would be to test the framework in other empirical settings and to improve/enhance it. Finally, the framework suggests important implications for ICT4D practice. To start with, it holds the potential to assist with the identification of champion-type individuals. On the organisational level it suggests the potential for a champion development programme to be established whereby key individuals can be empowered to become champions. It is hoped that the results reported here will lead to further research and practical impact.

References

1. Beath, C.M.: Supporting the information technology champion. MIS Q. **15**(3), 355–372 (1991)
2. Braun, V., Clarke, V.: Using thematic analysis in psychology. Qual. Res. Psychol. **3**(2), 77–101 (2006)
3. Dong, L., Sun, H., Fang, Y.: Do perceived leadership behaviors affect user technology beliefs? Commun. AIS **19**, 655–664 (2007)
4. Esteves, J., Pastor, J.A.: Understanding the ERP project champion role and its criticality. In: European Conference on Information Systems, Gdańsk, Poland (2002)
5. Howell, J.M.: The right stuff: identifying and developing effective champions of innovation. Acad. Manag. Exec. **19**(2), 108–119 (2005)
6. Howell, J.M., Boies, K.: Champions of technological innovation: the influence of contextual knowledge, role orientation, idea generation, and idea promotion on champion emergence. Leadersh. Quart. **15**(1), 123–143 (2004)
7. Howell, J.M., Higgins, C.A.: Champions of technological innovation. Adm. Sci. Q. **35**(2), 317–341 (1990)
8. Howell, J.M., Higgins, C.A.: Leadership behaviors, influence tactics, and career experiences of champions of technological innovation. Leadersh. Quart. **1**(4), 249–264 (1990)
9. Mullins, M.E., Kozlowski, S.W.J., Schmitt, N., Howell, A.W.: The role of the idea champion in innovation: the case of the internet in the mid-1990s. Comput. Hum. Behav. **24** (2), 451–467 (2008)
10. Kamal, M.: Investigating the role of project champions in e-government integration initiatives in local government domain. In: Americas Conference on Information Systems (AMCIS) (2010)
11. Negoita, B., Rahrovani, Y., Lapointe, L., Pinsonneault, A., Mirza, M.: IT champions as agents of change. In: ICIS 2012 Proceedings, pp. 1–12 (2012)
12. Renken, J.C., Heeks, R.B.: Conceptualising ICT4D project champions. In: The Sixth International ICTD Conference, Cape Town, South Africa, pp. 1–4 (2013)
13. Renken, J.C., Heeks, R.B.: Champions of information system innovations: thematic analysis and future research agenda. In: UK Academy for Information Systems (UKAIS) International Conference, Oxford, UK, pp. 1–27 (2014)
14. Van Laere, J., Aggestam, L.: Understanding champion behaviour in a health-care information system development project. Eur. J. Inf. Syst., 1–17 (2015)

Erratum to: An Analysis of Accountability Concepts for Open Development

Caitlin Bentley

Erratum to:
Chapter "An Analysis of Accountability Concepts for Open Development" in: J. Choudrie et al. (Eds.):
Information and Communication Technologies for Development, **IFIP AICT 504,**
https://doi.org/10.1007/978-3-319-59111-7_64

The updated online version of this chapter can be found at
https://doi.org/10.1007/978-3-319-59111-7_64

© Springer International Publishing AG 2018
J. Choudrie et al. (Eds.): ICT4D 2017, IFIP AICT 504, p. E1, 2018.
https://doi.org/10.1007/978-3-319-59111-7_72

Author Index

Printed in the United States
By Bookmasters